The German Law of Torts
A Comparative Treatise

Fourth Edition
Entirely Revised and Updated

Basil S. Markesinis

and

Hannes Unberath

With a Foreword by
Professor Dr. Walter Odersky
Emeritus President of the BGH
and
The Rt. Hon. Lord Justice Sedley

HART PUBLISHING
OXFORD AND PORTLAND, OREGON
2002

Hart Publishing
Oxford and Portland, Oregon

Published in North America (US and Canada) by
Hart Publishing
c/o International Specialized Book Services
5804 NE Hassalo Street
Portland, Oregon
97213-3644
USA

Distributed in Netherlands, Belgium and Luxembourg by
Intersentia, Churchillaan 108
B2900 Schoten
Antwerpen
Belgium

First Edition 1986
Second Edition 1990
Third Edition 1994
Third Edition reprinted with amendments and additions 1997.

Hart Publishing is a specialist legal publisher based in Oxford, England. To order further copies of this book or to
request a list of other publications please write to:

Hart Publishing, Salters Boatyard, Folly Bridge, Abingdon Rd, Oxford, OX1 4LB
Telephone: +44 (0)1865 245533 Fax: +44 (0) 1865 794882
email: mail@hartpub.co.uk
WEBSITE: http//:www.hartpub.co.uk

British Library Cataloguing in Publication Data
Data Available

ISBN 1-84113-297-7 (hardback)
1-84113-298-5 (paperback)

Typeset by SNP Best-set Typesetter Ltd., Hong Kong
Printed and bound in Great Britain by
Biddles Ltd, Guildford and Kings Lynn

92056

THE GERMAN LAW OF TORTS

A COMPARATIVE TREATISE

To Tom,
in friendship and admiration

14 June 2002   Basil

To the memory of my father,
who like all Greeks loved Bavaria
and the memory of my mother,
who transmitted to me her enduring love for England

BSM

Preface to the Fourth Edition

THIS IS the fourth edition—fifth if one counts as a new edition the corrected and with some additions reprint of 1997—of *The German Law of Torts* and it takes place sixteen years after this work first saw the light of day. This must be a record of sorts for a book, which is substantial in size, not cheap in price, and specialised in nature. The initial proposal to the OUP to publish the book succeeded only because of the unflinching support of my former Oxford colleague and friend Tony Honoré and the tenacity and imagination of Richard Hart who had to fight hard to create an interest in foreign and comparative law. It is thus fitting that the book should now appear in the lists of Hart Publishing; and it does so in a substantially revised, up-dated, and enlarged form. Though the book still bears my own brand of comparative methodology, and I have done much work myself to up-date both its German and Common law parts, the new edition also owes a great deal to my (and Professor Francis Reynolds') former Oxford student Dr Hannes Unberath. For his brilliant D.Phil. dissertation—*Recovery of Third Parties' Losses in Contractual Actions—a Comparative Study of English and German Law*—prepared him well for the task of comparing systems. Indeed, as readers will soon discover when it sees the light of day, it has provided a new benchmark for anyone who wishes to undertake as Dr Unberath did a perceptive, measured, and comparative examination of a foreign legal system. The result of our combined efforts is that very few parts of the book have escaped a substantial re-writing or, at the very least, an updating revision. The number of decisions reproduced in translated form has also increased dramatically from 86 in the first edition to 151 in the present. More will follow in the years to come in the website I have set up at the Institute of Global Law of University College London making the richness of German legal culture more widely available to Common lawyers.

The commercial success of this book has been surpassed only by the critical acclaim that it has received from numerous comparatists. They include such luminaries as (in alphabetical order) Professors Christian von Bar, Hein Kötz and Werner Lorenz from Germany and John Fleming, Kurt Lipstein, Barry Nicholas, Bernard Rudden and, of course, Tony Honoré from our own legal world. In one sense even more important is the judicial approbation that the book has also received from such eminent judges as Lord Bingham, Lord Goff and now Professor Dr Walter Odersky, emeritus President of the Supreme German Federal Court whose case law this book discusses in some detail and who is therefore more qualified than most to judge its contents. His Foreword shows that he has done this carefully; and both of us are deeply in his debt for his generous suggestions and kind endorsement. My own debt to him in fact goes back quite a few years since with his encouragement I repeatedly drew on his immense learning and experience. My German friends have never let me down; nor I them. Of a different nature but equally profound is my debt to Sir Stephen Sedley. For not only did he generously accepted the onerous task of reading the entire manuscript and contributing an "endorsing" Foreword to the book. In his professional life he has also managed to combine the role of judge and jurist, thus doubly (as well as significantly) influencing legal thought in this country.

But how can one explain the success of this book? It would be nice for the author(s) to claim the major part of the credit but I suspect the reasons are wider and thus much more noteworthy.

I suppose the first and foremost reason is that the study of foreign law and the quest of ways of presenting it to British lawyers is growing as we are increasingly coming within the gravitational force of Europe. If a section of the political world refuses to accept this, the City and the legal profession have taken stock of this change. A few years ago, I looked at this phenomenon in my inaugural lecture as Corresponding Fellow of the Royal Netherlands Academy of Arts and Sciences focusing, of course, on the growing impact that the case law of Luxembourg and Strasbourg are having on our own law. But the last decade and a half have also seen our courts (as well as those of Canada, Australia, New Zealand, and South Africa) slowly but steadily entering into the realms of foreign—especially German—law, private as well as public. The citations to this book suggest that its ideas and the material made available by it have facilitated this trend. Certainly, the subsequent appearance of other books or case-books dealing with tort law in a comparative context also shows that the topic this book dealt with first has now almost acquired a niche of its own in the legal curricula of many European Universities.

My own belief is that the "more the merrier". Yet I have still to convince most writers in this field that our prime target should be judges and practitioners and not academics. For judges, including our own, are increasingly thirsting for new ideas when confronted with problems that do not have obvious or satisfactory answers in the national law. If it becomes known that the judges have an interest in foreign law, as I think they do, practitioners will oblige. Indeed, they are already obliging; and if they go on obliging, the subject will come out of the "ghetto", as one academic once put it, and acquire a student following that it has not hitherto enjoyed. In the years to come, the growing numbers of law students spending study time abroad will, I am sure, strengthen this trend. It will also increasingly make mature English lawyers aware of the fact that in both the areas of private as well as constitutional law they have a choice to make from different alternatives. For the days when one looked for inspiration to the law of the USA only are, I think, decreasing and the shrewd and intellectually agile lawyer will want to consider not only the American model for, say, federalism or speech rights but also the Canadian, the Australian, and the German. If this book assists this trend it will not only have helped create a new way at making foreign law more user friendly to national lawyers; it will have also helped broaden legal minds. For someone who started and is ending his life as a teacher that can be no mean achievement.

Bentham's College   B. S. MARKESINIS
London

26 October 2001

Acknowledgements

A WORK of this size is not written without substantial intellectual debts being incurred towards a host of colleagues and friends who have assisted in its preparation. Thus, first and foremost, I wish to thank my colleagues at the Law Faculty of the Ludwigs-Maximilians University of Munich in Bavaria. For they hosted my stay with them for five consecutive summers, first as a holder of a Senior Prize awarded by the Deutsche Forschungs Gemeinschaft and then as a Visiting Professor at the famous Law Faculty. It was during this time that this substantial revision took place in the excellent library of the Institute of Comparative Law run so competently by Herr Rols Riss. To the Director of the Institute, Professor Dr Dagmar Coester-Waltjen as well as her predecessor—for many years my mentor in matters of German and comparative law—Professor Dr Dr hc Werner Lorenz I extend my warmest and most profound thanks.

The Munich Law Faculty has always been a hothouse of ideas and, naturally, I benefited greatly from many conversations I have had with some of my colleagues there. It is the nature of such discussions that they do not produce precise debts. Still, I wish to record my thanks to (in alphabetical order) Professors Michael Coester, Dagmar Coester-Waltjen, Claus-Wilhelm Canaris, Andreas Heldrich, Stephan Lorenz, Gerhard Ries, and Peter Schlosser while hastening to add the usual disclaimer that they bear no responsibility for what is contained in this book. Dr Unberath would like to express his gratitude to Professor Joachim Hruschka of the University of Erlangen-Nürnberg to whose chair he was attached while working on this book. Thanks are also due to Professor Reinhard Greger for guidance and advice on the Road Traffic Act regime.

Dr Unberath and I, likewise, benefited greatly from the fact that almost the entirety of our text was carefully read by Professor Dr Wulf-Hennig Roth of the Law Faculty of the University of Bonn. In my experience German scholars excel in the thoroughness with which they scrutinise texts submitted for their comments. Professor Roth did even more. For he corrected with elegance and style and even willingly accepted the possibility that on some matters views could legitimately diverge. He, as well as Dr Jörg Fedtke, formerly of the University of Hamburg and now DAAD/Clifford Chance lecturer in German Law at University College London saved us both of many errors and contributed many helpful additions for which we are both most grateful. We are likewise grateful to Ms Maria Schuster for preparing with exemplary diligence the list of cases that appear at the beginning of this book.

The writing of this book, which started in Germany, was completed in the marvellous Jamail Research Centre of the School of Law of the University of Texas at Austin where its Director Professor Roy Mersky and his helpful staff, notably Jon Pratter and Keith Ann Stiverson, do not know the sentence "this book does not exist"! My debt to Joe Jamail is, however, also a personal one since the Chair I hold at Texas (thanks to the exertions of two Deans—Michael Sharlot and Bill Powers—and my good friend, the late Charlie Wright) is yet another tangible sign of Joe's uniquely generous spirit. Joe has made for himself a great name as a formidable tort litigator. I hope this book does justice to the subject he has made his own during a lifetime in court.

The second major debt is towards the colleagues and friends who helped with the translations contained in this book. In fact just under half of this book is taken up by translations of German decisions that come from the pens of Kurt Lipsten, Tony Weir, Raymond Youngs, Josephine Shaw, Irene Snook, and the late Harry Lawson (with some help from his late wife Elspeth and myself). The list that follows provides a detailed attribution; but to all these colleagues I wish—yet again—to express my sincere thanks for the professional work they did and the cheerful way they put up with my (occasional) interferences! Harry Lawson, Kurt Lipstein and Tony Weir, of course, deserve additonal thanks since for over thirty years now not only have they helped with translations but also instructed, inspired, intellectually provoked, and even "ticked me off."

List of Cases Reproduced in This Book and Their Translators

Case 1	BGHZ 56, 163	Translated by J A Weir
Case 2	BGH NJW 1989, 2317	Translated by J Shaw
Case 3	RGZ 133, 270	Translated by Kurt Lipstein
Case 4	BGHZ 58, 48	Translated by Kurt Lipstein
Case 5	BGHZ 8, 243	Translated by Kurt Lipstein
Case 6	BGHZ 86, 240	Translated by Kurt Lipstein
Case 7	BVerfGE 88, 203	Translated by I Snook
Case 8	BGHZ 124, 128	Translated by I Snook
Case 9	BVerfGE 96, 375	Translated by R Youngs
Case 10	BGHZ 129, 178	Translated by R Youngs
Case 11	BGHZ 29, 65	Translated by F H Lawson & B S Markesinis
Case 12	BGHZ 66, 388	Translated by F H Lawson & B S Markesinis
Case 13	BGH NJW 1977, 2208	Translated by J A Weir
Case 14	BGHZ 55, 153	Translated by F H Lawson & B S Markesinis
Case 15	BGH NJW 1977, 2264	Translated by Kurt Lipstein
Case 16	BGH NJW 1984, 2569	Translated by J A Weir
Case 17	BGH NJW 1981, 1779	Translated by Kurt Lipstein
Case 18	BGHZ 137, 89	Translated by R Youngs
Case 19	BGH WM 1979, 548	Translated by F H Lawson & B S Markesinis
Case 20	BGHZ 69, 82	Translated by Kurt Lipstein
Case 21	BGH NJW 1982, 2431	Translated by Kurt Lipstein
Case 22	BGH NJW 1984, 355	Translated by Kurt Lipstein
Case 23	BGHZ 127, 378	Translated by I Snook
Case 24	BGHZ 138, 257	Translated by R Youngs
Case 25	BGH NJW 1985, 2411	Translated by H Unberath
Case 26	BGH VersR 1972, 274	Translated by H Unberath
Case 27	BGH NJW 1977, 2073	Translated by J A Weir
Case 28	BGHZ 23, 215	Translated by Kurt Lipstein
Case 29	BGHZ 26, 217	Translated by Kurt Lipstein
Case 30	BGH JZ 1973, 668	Translated by R Youngs
Case 31	BGH NJW 1990, 706	Translated by J A Weir
Case 32	RGZ 58, 24	Translated by F H Lawson & B S Markesinis
Case 33	RGZ 94, 248	Translated by F H Lawson & B S Markesinis
Case 34	BGHZ 3, 270	Translated by F H Lawson & B S Markesinis
Case 35	BGH NJW 1999, 279	Translated by R Youngs
Case 36	BVerfGE 7, 198	Translated by J A Weir
Case 37	BVerfGE 30, 173	Translated by J A Weir
Case 38	BVerfGE 34, 269	Translated by H Baade
Case 39	BGHZ 13, 334	Translated by F H Lawson & B S Markesinis
Case 40	BGHZ 26, 349	Translated by F H Lawson & B S Markesinis

Case 41	BGHZ 35, 363	Translated by F H Lawson & B S Markesinis
Case 42	BVerfGE 35, 202	Translated by F H Lawson & B S Markesinis
Case 43	OLG Cologne NJW 1987, 2682	Translated by Josephine Shaw
Case 44	OLG Hamburg NJW-RR 1988, 737	Translated by Kurt Lipstein
Case 45	BGHZ 73, 120	Translated by R Youngs
Case 46	BGHZ 131, 332	Translated by I Snook
Case 47	BVerfGE 101, 361	Translated by R Youngs
Case 48	BVerGE 97, 391	Translated by R Youngs
Case 49	BGH NJW 1999, 2893	Translated by R Youngs
Case 50	RGZ 119, 397	Translated by Kurt Lipstein
Case 51	BGH JZ 1968, 103	Translated by Kurt Lipstein
Case 52	BGHZ 90, 96	Translated by None given
Case 53	BGHZ 29, 46	Translated by Kurt Lipstein
Case 54	NJW 1996, 776	Translated by R Youngs
Case 55	BGHZ 144, 1	Translated by R Youngs
Case 56	BGH NJW 1975, 1161	Translated by Kurt Lipstein
Case 57	BGH JZ 1962, 570	Translated by R Youngs
Case 58	BGH NJW 1991, 2340	Translated by J A Weir
Case 59	BGH NJW-RR 1990, 726	Translated by J Shaw
Case 60	BGH NJW 1991, 562	Translated by J Shaw
Case 61	BGHZ 51, 91	Translated by F H Lawson & B S Markesinis
Case 62	BGHZ 59, 172	Translated by Kurt Lipstein
Case 63	BGHZ 75, 75	Translated by J A Weir
Case 64	BGHZ 104, 323	Translated by J Shaw
Case 65	BGHZ 116, 104	Translated by J A Weir
Case 66	BGHZ 129, 353	Translated by J A Weir
Case 67	BGH NJW 2001, 964	Translated by R Youngs
Case 68	BGHZ 67, 359	Translated by F H Lawson & B S Markesinis
Case 69	BGH NJW 1978, 1051	Translated by J Shaw
Case 70	BGH NJW 1978, 2241	Translated by F H Lawson & B S Markesinis
Case 71	BGHZ 86, 256	Translated by J A Weir
Case 72	BGH NJW 1985, 2420	Translated by J A Weir
Case 73	BGH NJW 1992, 1678	Translated by J Shaw
Case 74	BGHZ 39, 358	Translated by J A Weir
Case 75	BGHZ 39, 366	Translated by J A Weir
Case 76	RGZ 105, 264	Translated by F H Lawson & B S Markesinis
Case 77	RGZ 133, 126	Translated by F H Lawson & B S Markesinis
Case 78	RGZ 155, 37	Translated by F H Lawson & B S Markesinis
Case 79	RGZ 169, 117	Translated by F H Lawson & B S Markesinis
Case 80	BGHZ 3, 261	Translated by F H Lawson & B S Markesinis
Case 81	BGHZ 132, 164	Translated by R Youngs
Case 82	BGH NJW 1952, 1010	Translated by F H Lawson & B S Markesinis
Case 83	BGHZ 7, 198	Translated by F H Lawson & B S Markesinis
Case 84	BGHZ 18, 286	Translated by F H Lawson & B S Markesinis
Case 85	BGHZ 27, 137	Translated by F H Lawson & B S Markesinis
Case 86	BGHZ 58, 162	Translated by F H Lawson & B S Markesinis
Case 87	OLG Stuttgart NJW 1965, 112	Translated by F H Lawson & B S Markesinis
Case 88	BGHZ 101, 215	Translated by Kurt Lipstein
Case 89	BGHZ 20, 137	Translated by Kurt Lipstein
Case 90	BGHZ 137, 142	Translated by R Youngs
Case 91	BGH NJW 1969, 789	Translated by J A Weir
Case 92	RGZ 83, 15	Translated by J A Weir
Case 93	BGHZ 34, 355	Translated by J A Weir
Case 94	BGH NJW 1991, 3275	Translated by J Shaw
Case 95	BGH JZ 1975, 733	Translated by Kurt Lipstein
Case 96	BGHZ 49, 19	Translated by Kurt Lipstein
Case 97	BGH NJW 1971, 31	Translated by Kurt Lipstein

Case 98	BGHZ 12, 94	Translated by Kurt Lipstein
Case 99	BGH NJW 1956, 1106	Translated by Kurt Lipstein
Case 100	BGH NJW 1971, 1313	Translated by Kurt Lipstein
Case 101	BGH NJW 1965, 391	Translated by Kurt Lipstein
Case 102	BGH NJW 1957, 499	Translated by Kurt Lipstein
Case 103	BGHZ 5, 321	Translated by J A Weir
Case 104	BGHZ 45, 311	Translated by Von Mehren and Gordley
Case 105	BGH VersR 1969, 518	Translated by Von Mehren and Gordley
Case 106	BGH VersR 1966, 364	Translated by Von Mehren and Gordley
Case 107	BGHZ 4, 1	Translated by Von Mehren and Gordley
Case 108	BGH MDR 1957, 214	Translated by Von Mehren and Gordley
Case 109	BGHZ 24, 21	Translated by F H Lawson & B S Markesinis
Case 110	BAGE 70, 337	Translated by R Youngs
Case 111	RGZ 78, 239	Translated by F H Lawson & B S Markesinis
Case 112	BGHZ 66, 51	Translated by F H Lawson & B S Markesinis
Case 113	BGHZ 2, 94	Translated by J A Weir
Case 114	OLG Düsseldorf NJW 1975, 596	Translated by J A Weir
Case 115	BGHZ 33, 247	Translated by F H Lawson & B S Markesinis
Case 116	RGZ 127, 218	Translated by F H Lawson & B S Markesinis
Case 117	RGZ 102, 232	Translated by J A Weir
Case 118	RGZ 87, 64	Translated by J A Weir
Case 119	RGZ 91, 21	Translated by J A Weir
Case 120	BGHZ 1, 383	Translated by J A Weir
Case 121	RGZ 112, 290	Translated by F H Lawson & B S Markesinis
Case 122	BGHZ 29, 163	Translated by F H Lawson & B S Markesinis
Case 123	BGHZ 19, 114	Translated by Kurt Lipstein
Case 124	BGH NJW 1975, 1886	Translated by Kurt Lipstein
Case 125	BGHZ 107, 359	Translated by J Shaw
Case 126	BGHZ 20, 259	Translated by J A Weir
Case 127	BGHZ 30, 203	Translated by J A Weir
Case 128	RGZ 78, 171	Translated by F H Lawson & B S Markesinis
Case 129	BGHZ 26, 42	Translated by Kurt Lipstein
Case 130	BGHZ 15, 315	Translated by Kurt Lipstein
Case 131	BGHZ 29, 100	Translated by Kurt Lipstein
Case 132	BGH LM 839 [Fg] BGB no. 5	Translated by R Youngs
Case 133	BGH NJW 1980, 2194	Translated by R Youngs
Case 134	BGH NJW 1996, 2372	Translated by R Youngs
Case 135	BGH NJW 1998, 751	Translated by R Youngs
Case 136	OLG Oldenburg VersR 1991, 306	Translated by R Youngs
Case 137	OLG Hamm FamRZ 1993,	Translated by R Youngs
Case 138	OLG Hamm ZfJ 1997, 433 704	Translated by R Youngs
Case 139	OLG Hamm Az: 11 U 108/89	Translated by R Youngs
Case 140	BGHZ 18, 149	Translated by Kurt Lipstein
Case 141	BGHZ 86, 212	Translated by Kurt Lipstein
Case 142	BGHZ 97, 14	Translated by R Youngs
Case 143	BGHZ 120, 1	Translated by R Youngs
Case 144	NJW 1995, 452	Translated by R Youngs
Case 145	BGH NJW 1971, 698	Translated by Kurt Lipstein
Case 146	BVerfG NJW 2000, 2187	Translated by R Youngs
Case 147	BGH NJW 1986, 2037	Translated by J A Weir
Case 148	BGHZ 98, 212	Translated by J A Weir
Case 149	BGHZ 115, 364	Translated by R Youngs
Case 150	BGH NJW 1993, 3381	Translated by R Youngs
Case 151	BGH JZ 1996, 1076	Translated by R Youngs

Contents

Table of Cases
(Common law jurisdictions)

(German)

Abbreviations

ABGB	Austrian General Civil Code
AC	Law Reports, Appeal Cases (Decisions of the House of Lords and the Privy Council from 1891)
AcP	*Archiv für die civilistische Praxis*
AfP	*Archiv für Privatrecht*
A. J. Comp. L.	*American Journal of Comparative Law*
ALJR	*Australian Law Journal Reports*
All ER	All England Law Reports
Am. Rep.	American Reports
AOK	*Allgemeine Ortskrankenkasse* (National Health Insurance Scheme)
App. Cas.	Law Reports, Appeal Cases (1875–90)
ATF	Recueil officiel d'arrêts du Tribunal fédéral suisse (can also be referred to as BGE-Entscheidungen des schweizerischen Bundesgerichtes)
AuR	*Arbeit und Recht*
B.	*Beklagter* (defendant)
BayObLG	Bayerisches Oberstes Landesgericht
BB	*Der Betriebsberater*
DB	*Der Betrieb*
BGB	Bürgerliches Gesetzbuch (German Civil Code)
BGBl	Bundesgesetzblatt (Government Gazette)
BGE	Entscheidungen des schweizerischen Bundesgerichtes (can also be referred to as ATF-Recueil officiel d'arrêts du Tribunal fédéral suisse)
BGH	Bundesgerichtshof (Germany's Federal (Supreme) Court)
BGHZ	Entscheidungen des Bundesgerichtshofs in Zivilsachen (Decisions of the German Supreme Court in civil matters)
Buffalo L. Rev.	*Buffalo Law Review*
BVerfG	Bundesverfassungsgericht
BVerfGE	Entscheidungen des Bundesverfassungsgerichts (Decisions of the Federal Constitutional Court)
BVerfGG	Bundesverfassungsgerichtsgesetz (Statute of the Constitutional Court of the FRG)
B. Y. B. I. L.	*British Year Book of International Law*
CA	Decisions of the English Court of Appeal
Cal. L. Rev.	*California Law Review*
Cal. Rptr. 2d	California Reporter, 2nd series (American law reports)
Cal. Rptr. 3d	California Reporter, 3rd series (American law reports)
Campbell L. Rev.	*Campbell Law Review*
Can. Bar Rev.	*The Canadian Bar Review*

Cass.	Cour de cassation
CC	*Code Civil*
CCLT	Canadian Cases on the Law of Torts
Ch.	Law Reports, Chancery Division (from 1891)
Ch. Civ.	Cour de cassation, Chambre Civile
Ch. Civ. 2e	Cour de cassation (French Court of Cassation, 2nd civil chamber)
Ch. Comm.	Cour de cassation, Chambre Commerciale
Ch. Crim.	Cour de cassation, Chambre Criminelle
Ch. D.	Law Reports, Chancery Division (1875–90)
Ch. Mixte	Cour de cassation, Chambre Mixte
Ch. Req.	Cour de cassation, Chambre des Requêtes
Ch. Réun.	Cour de cassation, Chambres Réunies
Cincinnati L. Rev.	*Cincinnati Law Review*
C. L.	*Current Law*
CLJ	*Cambridge Law Journal*
Colum. L. Rev.	*Columbia Law Review*
Connecticut L. Rev.	*Connecticut Law Review*
Cornell L. Rev.	*Cornell Law Review*
Cumb. L. Rev.	*Cumberland Law Review*
D.	Recueil Dalloz (1945–64)
DB	*Der Betrieb*
DC	Dalloz, recueil critique de jurisprudence et de législation (1941–44)
Depaul L. Rev.	*Depaul Law Review*
Dickinson L. Rev.	*Dickinson Law Review*
DLR	Dominion Law Reports
Duke LJ	*Duke Law Journal*
DS	Recueil Dalloz et Sirey (1965–)
D. StR.	Deutsches Steuerrecht
Duq. L. Rev.	*Duquesne Law Review*
EG BGB	Einführungsgesetz zum BGB (introductory law to the BGB)
Encyclopedia	*International Encyclopedia of Comparative Law*, vol. xi (Chief ed. A. Tunc, 1975)
EuGRZ	*Europäische Grundrechtezeitung*
Ex. D.	Law Reports, Exchequer Division (1875–80)
FamRZ	*Zeitschrift für das gesamte Familienrecht*
F. Supp.	Federal Supplement (American law reports)
F. 2d	Federal Reporter, 2nd series (American law reports)
Fordham L. Journ.	*Fordham Urban Law Journal*
Fordham L. Rev.	*Fordham Law Review*
Ga. L. Rev.	*Georgia Law Review*
GG	Grundgesetz (the Constitution of Western Germany)
Harv. L. Rev.	*Harvard Law Review*
Hastings LJ	*Hastings Law Journal*
Haw.	Hawaii Supreme Court Reports
ICLQ	*International and Comparative Law Quarterly*

IDHL	*International Digest of Health Law*
Indiana L. Rev.	*Indiana Law Review*
Indiana LJ	*Indiana Law Journal*
JA	*Juristische Arbeitsblätter*
JCP	*Juris-Classeur Périodique* (also referred to as *SJ* (*La Semaine juridique*))
J. Leg. Stud.	*Journal of Legal Studies*
J. of Law, Econ. and Org.	*Journal of Law, Economics and Organics*
JSPTL	*Journal of the Society of Public Teachers of Law*
JuS	*Juristische Schulung*
JW	*Juristische Wochenschrift* (from 1872 to 1939)
JZ	*Juristenzeitung*
KB	Law Reports, King's Bench (1901–52)
Kentucky LJ	*Kentucky Law Journal*
KG	Kammergericht (Court of Appeal of Berlin)
KUG	Gesetz betreffend das Urheberrecht an Werken der bildenden Künste und der Photographie (translated and abbreviated as the Law on Artistic Creations)
La. L. Rev.	*Louisiana Law Review*
LMCLQ	*Lloyds Maritime and Commercial Law Quarterly*
LQR	*Law Quarterly Review*
LR Ch. App.	Law Reports, Chancery Appeal Cases (1865–75)
LRCP	Law Reports, Common Pleas Cases (1865–75)
LR Ex.	Law Reports, Exchequer Cases (1965–75)
LRHL	Law Reports, English and Irish Appeals (1866–75)
LRQB	Law Reports, Queen's Bench (1865–75)
LT	Law Times Reports (1859–1947)
Maryland L. Rev.	*Maryland Law Review*
Mass.	Massachusetts
Med. R	*Medizin und Recht*
MDR	*Monatsschrift für Deutsches Recht*
Miss. LJ	*Mississippi Law Journal*
Mercer L. Rev.	*Mercer Law Review*
MLR	*Modern Law Review*
N. Carolina L. Rev.	*North Carolina Law Review*
NE	North Eastern Reporter (American law reports)
NJ	*Neue Justiz*
NJSA	New Jersey Statutes Annotated
NJW	*Neue Juristische Wochenschrift*
NW	North Western Reporter (American law reports)
NYU L. R.	*New York University Law Review*
NZLJ	*New Zealand Law Journal*
NZLR	New Zealand Law Reports
OblG	Oberstes Landesgericht
OGH	Oberster Gerichtshof (Austrian Supreme Court)
OLG	Oberlandesgericht (German Court of Appeal)
OR	Swiss Code of Obligations
Ore. L. Rev.	*Oregon Law Review*

Oxford J. L. Studies	*Oxford Journal of Legal Studies*
P.	Law Reports, Probate Division (1891–)
P. 2d	Pacific Reporter, 2nd series (American law reports)
QB	Law Reports, Queen's Bench (1891–1900; 1952–)
QBD	Law Reports, Queen's Bench Division (1875–90)
RabelsZ	*Rabels Zeitschrift für ausländisches und internationales Recht*
Rev. int. dr. comp.	*Revue international de droit comparé*
Rev. trim. dr. civ.	*Revue trimestrielle de droit civil*
RG	Reichsgericht
RGBl.	Reichsgesetzblatt (Government Gazette)
RGSt	Amtliche Sammlung der Entscheidungen des Reichsgerichts in Strafsachen
RGZ	Entscheidungen des Reichsgerichts in Zivilsachen (Decisions of the German Imperial Court in civil matters)
Rutgers L. Rev.	*Rutgers Law Review*
RVO	Reichsversicherungsordnung (Imperial Insurance Act)
S.	Recueil Sirey
St John's L. Rev.	*St John's Law Review*
San D. L. Rev.	*San Diego Law Review*
S. Ct.	Supreme Court
S. C. R.	Supreme Court Reports
Seton Hall L. Rev.	*Seton Hall Law Review*
SJ	*La Semaine juridique* (also referred to as *JCP* (*Juris-Classeur Périodique*))
So.	Southern Reporter (American law reports)
So. 2d	Southern Reporter, 2nd series (American law reports)
So. Cal. L. Rev.	*Southern California Law Review*
Stan. L. Rev.	*Stanford Law Review*
StGB	Strafgesetzbuch (German Criminal Code)
StVG	Strassenverkehrsgesetz (Road Traffic Act)
Suffolk Univ. L. Rev.	*Suffolk University Law Review*
SW	South Western Reporter (American law reports)
Sydney L. Rev.	*Sydney Law Review*
Temple L. Rev.	*Temple Law Review*
Texas Tech. L. Rev.	*Texas Technical Law Review*
Trib. Civ.	Tribunal Civil
Tulane L. Rev.	*Tulane Law Review*
Tul. L. Rev.	*Tuluna Law Review*
UBC L. Rev.	*University of British Columbia Law Review*
U. Ch. L. Rev.	*University of Chicago Law Review*
UCLA L. Rev.	*University of California Los Angeles Law Review*
U. Fla. L. Rev.	*University of Florida Law Review*
U. Haw. L. Rev.	*University of Hawaii Law Review*
Univ. of Cincinnati L. Rev.	*University of Cincinnati Law Review*
UP L. Rev.	*University of Pennsylvania Law Review*
UTLJ	*University of Toronto Law Journal*

Va. L. Rev.	*Virginia Law Review*
Vand. L. Rev.	*Vanderbilt Law Review*
VersR	*Versicherungsrecht*
Villanova L. Rev.	*Villanova Law Review*
Washburn LJ	*Washburn Law Journal*
Wash. and Lee L. Rev.	*Washington and Lee Law Review*
Wash. L. Rev.	*Washington Law Review*
WHG	Wasserhaushaltsgesetz (German Act on the Use of Water)
Wis.	Wisconsin
WLR	Weekly Law Reports
WM	*Wertpapier-Mitteilungen*
ZfRV	*Zeitschrift für Rechtsvergleichung, Internationales Privatrecht und Europarecht*
ZIP	*Zeitschrift für Wirtschaftsrecht und Insolvenzpraxis*
ZRP	*Zeitschrift für Rechtspolitik*

Books Cited Only by Names of Their Authors

IN GERMAN

Deutsch = E. Deutsch *Allgemeines Haftungsrecht* (2nd edn., 1996).

Esser/Schmidt = J. Esser and E. Schmidt, *Schuldrecht* I (General part, first volume, 8th edn., 1995, second volume, 8th edn., 2000).

Esser/Weyers = J. Esser and H. L. Weyers, Schuldrecht II (Special part, first volume, 8th edn. 1998, second volume, 8th edn., 2000).

Fikentscher = W. Fikentscher, *Schuldrecht* (9th edn., 1997).

Kötz / Wagner = H. Kötz, G. Wagner *Deliktsrecht* (9th edn., 2001).

Larenz I = K. Larenz, *Lehrbuch des Schuldrechts* I (General part, 14th edn., 1987).

Larenz II = K. Larenz, *Lehrbuch des Schuldrechts* II 1 (Special part, first vol., 13th edn., 1986).

Larenz / Canaris = *Lehrbuch des Schuldrechts* II 2 (Special part, second vol., 14th edn., 1994).

Medicus = D. Medicus, *Bürgerliches Recht* (18th edn., 1999).

Palandt = O. Palandt, *Bürgerliches Gesetzbuch* (60th edn., 2001).

IN ENGLISH

Clerk and Lindsell = Clerk and Lindsell, *On Torts* (Gen. 18th edn. 2000 with supplements).

Dobbs = Dan B. Dobbs, *The Law of Torts*, (2000).

Fleming = J. G. Fleming, *The Law of Torts* (9th edn., 1998).

Franklin = M. A. Franklin and R. L. Rabin, *Tort Law and Alternatives* (7th edn., 2001).

Epstein = R. A. Epstein, *Cases and Materials on Torts* (5th edn., 1990).

Harper, James, and Gray = F. V. Harper, Fleming James, Jr., and O. S. Gray, *The Law of Torts* (2nd edn., 1986).

Henderson, Pearson and Siciliano = J. A. Henderson, R. N. Pearson and J. A. Siciliano, *The Torts Process* (5th edn., 1999).

Lawson and Markesinis = F. H. Lawson and B. S. Markesinis, *Tortious Liability for Unintentional Harm in the Common Law and the Civil Law*, 2 vols. (1982).

Markesinis and Deakin = B. S. Markesinis and S. F. Deakin, *Tort Law*, (4th ed. 1999)

Posner = R. A. Posner, *Tort Law-Cases and Economic Analysis* (1982).

Prosser, Wade, and Schwartz = John Wade, Victor Schwartz, Kathryn Kelly and David Partlett, *Cases and Materials on Torts* (10th edn., 2000).

Prosser and Keeton = W. L. Prosser, W. Page Keeton, D. B. Dobbs, R. E. Keeton, and D. G. Owen, *Law of Torts* (5th edn., 1984).

Robertson, Powers, Anderson and Wellborn = D. W. Robertson, W. Powers Jr., D. A. Anderson and O. G. Wellborn III, *Cases and Materials on TORTS*, (2nd ed. 1998).

Zweigert, K., and Kötz, H. = *An Introduction to Comparative Law* (3rd edn., 1998) (Eng. trans. By Tony Weir).

Foreword to the Fourth Edition

This is the fourth edition of *The German Law of Torts* by Professor Basil S. Markesinis and with Dr Hannes Unberath appearing for the first time as a co-author. The three previous editions of the book, despite being modestly subtitled *A Comparative Introduction*, already presented a comprehensive and excellent comparative account of the German law of torts. That is why from the very outset this work proved such a remarkable success among jurists the world over. This success has been confirmed by the fact that the work has seen four editions in the space of about sixteen years. It was thus a great honour for me to be invited to write the foreword to its latest edition. The writers of the earlier forewords included two Senior Law Lords, Lord Goff of Chieveley and Lord Bingham of Cornhill, colleagues for whom I have the highest esteem and to whom I feel bound by ties of true friendship.

The high regard I have always had for the previous editions of this work also extends to the companion volume entitled *The German Law of Contracts and Restitution*, which Professor Markesinis wrote together with two other German colleagues. Taken together the two volumes present a full and complete account of the German law of obligations. Now I have read through the latest edition of *The German Law of Torts* I note that a large number of its passages have been changed, some substantially expanded, and all entirely updated. For the first time the book also includes more than 150 fully translated decisions of German courts, most of them being accompanied by highly stimulating and informative notes.

The material in this book is throughout presented in an elegant and most instructive way. For the authors display their thorough learning with a lightness of touch and, even humour—a feature of English writing which we Germans so often admire.

This work has been written primarily for the English-speaking jurist in mind: the student and, as Lord Goff convincingly argued in his earlier and learned foreword, the practitioner as well. Nonetheless, I would like to add that it is also a most inspiring book for someone who has been educated in German law and practises law in Germany. This is not only because the subject matter has been handled in such an intellectually stimulating manner. One can also benefit directly from seeing how problems encountered in one's own system (and the methods developed to solve them) have been handled from the Common law perspective. It was thus with great pleasure that I read the passages in the Introduction under the title "Style, form, and content of the judgments of the BGH". For it was rewarding to see one's own experience reflected through the eyes of a foreign colleague and one, whom I might add, is willing to look at my system in a benevolent and perceptive manner. The exercise was invaluable in broadening and complementing my own perception of my experience in this matter.

It seems logical to the German reader that each section contains a self-contained dogmatic part followed by cases most of which are followed by highly instructive and informative notes. The latter undoubtedly reflect the case-law approach of the Anglo-American systems. I would like to stress however that the importance of precedents has increased significantly in Germany as well over the last few decades. For though in German law there is formally no doctrine of *stare decisis*, as a matter of fact past decisions determine the entire legal reality—in and outside the courtroom. This is particularly true of the decisions of the Bundesgerichtshof. A distinguished comparative lawyer, Professor Andreas Heldrich, currently Rector of the Ludwig-Maximilians University of Munich (where Professor Markesinis did so much of his work on this book), examined this important question in his lecture celebrating 50 years since the founding of the Bundesgerichtshof on 1 October 2000. ("50 Jahre Rechtsprechung des BGH—auf dem Weg zum Präjudizienrecht?" ZRP 2000, 497). There he concluded that despite differences in emphasis, judge-made law and statutory law were in equal ways the cornerstones of the Anglo-American and German systems.

We live in an age of ever-increasing co-operation between the European nations and we can consider ourselves privileged to be witnesses of this process. Its future success will crucially depend on finding the right balance between convergence on a broader scale and conserving the particular characteristics and traditions of the individual legal systems. The same can be said about the harmonisation brought about by the European Institutions. However, the desire to preserve one's own tradition should not prevent one from studying the weaknesses and the strengths of the legal system of one's neighbours. On the contrary, doing so will be extremely rewarding and will contribute to one's own strength. Where the native legal system encounters difficulties or novel situations, it is particularly desirable to rely on arguments derived from comparative law while searching for the appropriate answer to such difficulties elsewhere. This book greatly assists this process.

In a letter which he once wrote to me Basil Markesinis mentioned that *The German Law of Torts* "has been the work of my life for over twenty years". This remark, uttered in the most modest and endearing of ways, deeply impressed me. The author, having completed the fourth edition of his book (together with Hannes Unberath), has truly taken his vision of generating greater understanding between Anglo-American and German jurists to new heights. I am thus confident that I speak on behalf of all my colleagues at the Bundesgerichtshof when I say we wish this remarkable book the continuing success it so richly deserves.

Emeritus President of the Bundesgerichtshof   PROF. DR. WALTER ODERSKY

December 2001

Foreword to the Fourth Edition

I KNOW that I shall be forgiven if, in a foreword to the fourth edition in only sixteen years of this path-breaking book, I do not traverse the high ground covered with such distinction by my predecessors Professor Lorenz, Lord Goff and Lord Bingham. There is nothing in this new edition which does not justify their praise, and much—not least the judgments in translation—which gives fresh grounds for it.

Instead let me reflect briefly on the significance of the point of time at which the book appears. It is a moment when the United Kingdom, by now accustomed to the supremacy of the law of the European Union, has newly patriated the European Convention on Human Rights and is learning to live with its occasionally demanding norms. It has in consequence found its own law of torts under unexpected pressure as the Strasbourg court has found unacceptable the sometimes high thresholds being set by the common law for access to justice against state entities. Such decisions provoke regular journalistic and political assaults on an undifferentiated place called "Europe" where foreign judges ordain how the United Kingdom should be run.

Germany (and its juridical predecessor, the Federal Republic) has travelled this road for much longer than we have, but without quite the same sense of imposition. Its postwar Grundgesetz has been the primary source of those civil rights for which we look first to the common law and then to the European Convention. Its civil code, like other codes, is not a comprehensive set of answers but a framework for finding them, and in that respect not very different from the common law. So it is unsurprising to find a strong emergent parallelism not only between the problems each jurisdiction has had to deal with but between the modes of reasoning by which they are resolved. One sees it in the tentative movement of the United Kingdom's courts towards the kind of indirect horizontal application of rights with which German theory and practice are already familiar. When, as has begun to happen, the United Kingdom's courts have to decide how far they are called upon to protect the privacy of individuals from unwanted intrusion, they will have the reasoning and experience of the German courts—the French courts too—to call upon. It is reasoning and experience which extends into areas that are familiar but still extremely troublesome to our courts, such as state liability and economic loss, and into others which we are still coming to grips with, such as wrongful procreation.

On these and some of the many other topics which it covers, *The German Law of Torts* has already been cited in the judgments of anglophone courts from Australia to Canada to South Africa, as well as those of England and Wales. This is its great and growing value. It no longer represents, as comparative law used to represent, an absorbing academic pursuit. It represents a body of working jurisprudence developed by able lawyers to cope with problems common to both our jurisdictions, and doing so on a largely shared foundation of basic rights and norms. To an increasing extent judges as well as practitioners will turn to books like this (in the too-rare instances where they exist) for workable ways of developing law for the new millennium in the United Kingdom and elsewhere. Whether convergence or divergence follows, it will be time and effort well spent.

Once again, by making educated inquiry possible and furnishing a wealth of otherwise inaccessible information about the German law of torts, Professor Markesinis, with his new co-author Dr Unberath, has earned the gratitude of more people than he will ever know.

Royal Courts of Justice   THE RT. HON. SIR STEPHEN SEDLEY
London

December 2001

Foreword to the Third Edition

THE *German Law of Torts* has, within a remarkably short period, become a classic of European legal literature. Three editions in under eight years: the record speaks for itself. For the monoglot English-speaking reader, Professor Markesinis' book has no peer and no rival.

The reasons for the book's outstanding success are not hard to divine. First is the intrinsic interest and importance of the subject. Only a small part of the German Civil Code is devoted to the law of torts, but it is an important, perhaps increasingly important, part. And the Code itself, described by Maitland as "the most carefully considered statement of a nation's law that the world has ever seen", is a work well worthy of serious study. That is a truth which our fathers perhaps overlooked, but of which our grandfathers were fully aware.

A distinguished scholarly survey of the tort paragraphs in the German Code would be achievement enough. But it would scarcely earn the widespread acclaim with which successive editions of the book have been greeted. That is the product of the book's second great virtue: its treatment of German tort law not as a series of abstract principles or general theories but as a code of legal rules worked out and refined by practical application in the courts to actual human beings in real situations. So the law comes to life in a way readily understood by the common lawyer, and congenial to him, not as the dream of a legal philosopher but as a source of solutions to practical problems, a system deeply rooted in the untidy earth of ordinary life. This is as much a casebook as a treatise on jurisprudence.

It is, however, the book's third great virtue which assures it a place in the library of the well-armed practitioner (and even judge). That virtue, proclaimed in the full title to the book, lies in the expert and skilful comparisons persistently drawn between the solutions achieved by German judges applying the Code and judges in the United Kingdom and other common law jurisdictions applying rules derived from statute and authority. Problems which have exercised, and often baffled, common law judges—responsibility for economic loss, the scope of duties of care, liability for psychiatric damage, the protection of privacy, environmental liability—are here set in a comparative context which yields fresh insights, suggests new possibilities and stimulates the jaded imagination.

Professor Markesinis has chosen his moment well. As the countries of Western Europe draw closer together, as frontiers disappear and barriers fall, opportunities to learn from the experience of others become more plentiful and the need to take advantage of those opportunities more obvious. This important book may fairly be seen as contributing to that increase in mutual understanding upon which international harmony and co-operation so closely depend.

Royal Courts of Justice   T. H. BINGHAM MR

25 March 1994

Foreword to the Second Edition

I AM honoured to be invited to contribute a Foreword to the Second Edition of this remarkable and, certainly to me, most valuable book.

The theoretical case for the study of comparative law has long been made out. The problem now is not *whether* comparative law should be taught in our universities, and studied by our law students. The problem is rather *how* it should be presented, not merely as an aspect of legal culture, but as a subject which is capable of influencing our work, whether as scholars or as practising lawyers in the development, exposition and application of legal principles, in the context of our own domestic legal system.

It must never be forgotten, by those who teach and write about law, that, for those who study it and those who practise it, our own domestic law bristles with difficulties which are hard to master, and problems which are difficult to solve. In working through a heavy university curriculum, and in the helter-skelter of professional life (whether in practice or on the bench), it is not at all easy to accommodate the introduction of material from other legal systems, and especially from civil law systems with which we are unfamiliar. Even in appellate tribunals, it is hard enough to master and to reconcile existing English material—statutes, cases and academic writings. Moreover, in the great majority of cases, the point is a relatively narrow one which is subjected to intensive examination; and it is the practical implications of any particular solution which exercise, perhaps, the greatest influence.

It is only by grasping the practicalities of university study, of professional lawyers' practices, and of work in the courts, that it is possible to conceive an appropriate vehicle for bringing comparative law to bear, as a useful tool, and as an effective influence. For these purposes, books on comparative law which are general in nature, however admirable in themselves, however educational in a cultural sense, are of little direct use. To be influential in a more practical way, comparative law material has to be far more closely focused; and, not only that, it has to be readily comprehensible, practically orientated, and thoroughly reliable, by which I mean both accurate and up to date.

It stands to Professor Markesinis' great credit that he has fully grasped the realities of the situation in which the comparative lawyer finds himself. He understands how necessary it is that work on comparative law should be closely focused, for it to be of practical benefit to English lawyers. He understands how necessary it is that such work should be thoroughly reliable, demonstrating the author's deep and genuine understanding of this subject, set in the practical and theoretical context of its own legal system. He understands how necessary it is that it should be readily comprehensible; for example, despite his own mastery of languages, he recognises the need to present the primary sources in copious and felicitous translation for the English lawyer. He understands, too, the need for it to be practically useful, by travelling far beyond the provisions of codes to the real cases which trouble the courts and by including reported judgments from those cases, set in their theoretical context as seen by indigenous lawyers.

It is perhaps even more to Professor Markesinis' credit that he is not only capable of mastering fully a substantial topic from a foreign system of law demonstrating his expertise to the satisfaction of leading lawyers from that legal system; he also has the courage to embark upon so exacting a task as the critical exposition of such a topic, and the determination and industry to carry that task through to its fulfilment.

I speak, of course, of the present book, his *Comparative Introduction to the German Law of Torts*. It came as no surprise to me that the first edition of the book was so successful and was so warmly received. I know of no more directly useful book on comparative law than this. It is a book which can not only be usefully consulted by creative lawyers in this country; it is one which is capable of influencing directly the solution of problems with which we have to grapple in our own domestic law. Too often, German law is presented to us as over-theoretical and ridden with concepts. Here, however, we can see German judges at work, tackling the same problems as we have to tackle, coming up with solutions sometimes the same as ours, sometimes different—and, when they are different, sometimes (it may be thought) better than those which we have chosen. It has truly been said that the most beneficent effect of the study of other systems of law is that we learn more about our own. In this book, Professor Markesinis has taught us all how comparative law is best presented to achieve that admirable objective.

I gladly commend this new edition. As with all new editions of successful law books, it has grown in size. But, as the reader will soon discover, this is no mere update; it has involved substantial rewriting, as well as the incorporation of much new and valuable material, from Anglo-American law as well as from German law. In the result, it will be even more useful to us than its predecessor; and I am bold enough to predict that it will be even more successful.

House of Lords ROBERT GOFF

Foreword to the First Edition

WHEN I was invited to write a few words of introduction to this book I accepted immediately and without any hesitation, even though at that time I had not yet read the manuscript. Lawyers usually are cautious people, but in this case there was no risk involved. Since I knew the author's previous publications dealing with the law of tort on a comparative basis, I had no doubt that his project of a *Comparative Introduction to the German Law of Tort* would be a great success. There were two further reasons why I gladly accepted this invitation. For many years the author co-operated most fruitfully with the late Professor Lawson, who some decades ago was my tutor in Oxford. Both Dr Markesinis and I owe this great comparatist very much, for he had the rare gift of illuminating difficult problems by quick and penetrating observations. The other reason is the author's connection with Cornell Law School, which encouraged and supported this book. This brings back to my memory the wonderful time I spent there working in Rudi Schlesinger's team exploring the common core of legal systems in the area of formation of contracts—a project of comparative law conducted under the auspices of the Cornell Law School which has been favourably received by scholars all over the world.

The present book, I am sure, will not merely serve its immediate purpose of introducing the reader to the German law of tort; no doubt it will also open many new perspectives for the general understanding of this legal system belonging to the civil law. Apart from family law, which has undergone rapid changes in most countries since 1945, the law of liability is an area where many important developments have taken place. Even a superficial look at the index of any of the ninety volumes of the official collection of civil cases decided by the Federal Supreme Court will suffice to confirm this impression: the number of reported cases on problems of civil liability is remarkable. Many of them have given rise to vivid discussion in German legal literature, thus confronting the courts with new ideas. This had led to a fruitful exchange of ideas between bench and scholars unknown in most of the other legal systems. The care with which the Federal Supreme Court considers critical views put forward against its opinions is sufficient evidence of this.

The importance of the law of liability and its special value for academic teaching in the Federal Republic of Germany is further stressed by the somewhat complicated interaction of contract and tort which has reached the point where the boundaries between these two areas of the law have become blurred. The different approaches taken by the German Civil Code in regard to vicarious liability in contractual relations on the one hand, and in the law of tort on the other, have certainly contributed much to the tendency to enlarge the field of contractual liability, thus filling gaps found to exist in the law of tort. However, the much disputed § 831 of the Civil Code dealing with the responsibility of employers for tortious acts committed by their employees in the course of employment which used to be a stumbling-block for plaintiffs in former times has lost much of its significance in actual legal practice, because increasingly the courts have shifted the emphasis on the basic rule contained in § 823 I Civil Code. This means that they will look into the relevant business organisation rather than try to establish the employer's fault in the selection or supervision of an individual, thereby depriving the employer of the chance to exculpate himself. The burning problem nowadays is whether purely economic loss must be made good in ordinary negligence cases, where the parties have not been in contractual relations *stricto sensu*. Liability for negligent misstatements is but one group of cases in which this problem has arisen. Here as elsewhere in this book Dr Markesinis has succeeded completely in selecting those cases which are most instructive. Therefore the reader obtains all the information he needs in order to find out how the law stands in such important fields as, for instance, products liability, medical malpractice, and traffic accidents. However, it is the thorough, comparative discussion accompanying each group of cases that makes reading this book a great pleasure even for one already familiar with the material. Although this book was written for students belonging to the Anglo-American legal family I would, therefore, like to recommend it to students of other legal backgrounds as well, because the problems dealt with are of a universal nature in the sense that each developed legal system has to deal with them.

University of Munich   WERNER LORENZ

Faculty of Law

"What is striking and mysterious in comparing two legal systems is the ways they are similar and the ways they are different. Much of what follows will be of immediate use to [Common] lawyers only in so far as the contrasts between German and [Common] law make them more sharply aware of the fundamental character of their own legal system. By seeing how another . . . advanced culture can make entirely different arrangements for things they have always supposed to be matters of course—things that obviously must be this way and not the other—they also may gain a critical outlook and an expanded capacity for adapting their own system's traditional institutions to the practical needs of real life as they evolve. On the other hand, much in this book addresses problems that are virtually identical in both systems. Recognising and solving a problem becomes remarkably easier when it shows up wearing a peculiar foreign costume."*

* Karl N. Llewellyn, *The Case Law System in America*, English edition by P. Gewirtz and M. Ausaldi (1989), 1. (In Llewellyn's original the word used in the first bracket is "German" and in the second is "American".)

1

Introduction

1. A BIRD'S-EYE VIEW OF THE ORGANISATION OF
THE GERMAN COURTS IN CIVIL MATTERS

THE idea of a German Supreme Court can be traced back to at least the end of the fifteenth century and the creation in 1495 of the Reichskammergericht of the Holy Roman
Empire, which originally sat in Frankfurt. The prevailing political fragmentation,
however, prevented it from exercising any effective influence, especially in the area of the
unification of the law, and even the Emperor himself held his own court in Vienna which
often competed with the Reichskammergericht. A truly central Supreme Court had thus
to await the unification of Germany which was eventually realised under Bismarck's
strong hand in 1871. This occurred when the Second German Reich came into being,
embracing Prussia (which retained a special status and dominated the new federal state),
the kingdoms of Bavaria, Saxony, and Wurttemberg. Also incorporated were eighteen
"lesser" states, the three "free" cities of Hamburg, Bremen, and Lübeck, and the so-called
Reichsland (imperial territory) of Alsace-Lorraine which was ceded to the Empire by the
Treaty of Frankfurt of 10 May 1871 but which for some time thereafter retained a special
status (indeed was until 1879 administered directly from Bismarck's office). This was a
complicated constitutional arrangement, as were many that had preceded it. But before
a British lawyer hurriedly condemns it as "typically" German, he should pause for a
moment and reflect on the difficulties faced by his Continental counterparts trying to
comprehend the equally complex constitutional arrangements between England and
Wales, Scotland, and Northern Ireland, not to mention the special status of the Channel
Islands. Here then, again, history provides, if not a convincing justification, at least an
explanation for the existing complications.

We need not reflect here on the extent to which this unification can, just over one
hundred and thirty years later, be judged as satisfactory or, even, complete. Certainly,
those who know Germany well will be quick to mention both substantial differences in
the language (there are over one hundred dialects) and lingering mutual suspicions
between the various States that form the Federation. Yet again, however, the English
lawyer (who has also assumed the role of speaking for the Welshman while ignoring the
historically more cosmopolitan Scot or his counterpart from Northern Ireland) can easily
overstate the cohesiveness (especially since the reunification of the two Germanies on
3 October 1990) or understate it if he is—subconsciously perhaps—concerned about the
size and power of the new state. The Germans, themselves, seem to share this ambiva-
lence, so it is fortunate that the tort lawyer need not explore these fascinating questions
any further. For present purposes it will suffice merely to say that the political union,
which was forged in the 1870s made inevitable the legal union, that followed. Indeed,
if a common reason often invoked for codification is the need for "simplification, clarification and unification", the German Civil Code of 1900 satisfied all three. (On the
other hand, as Van Gerven and others have been quick to point out, "the codification

FEO ERAL LEVEL

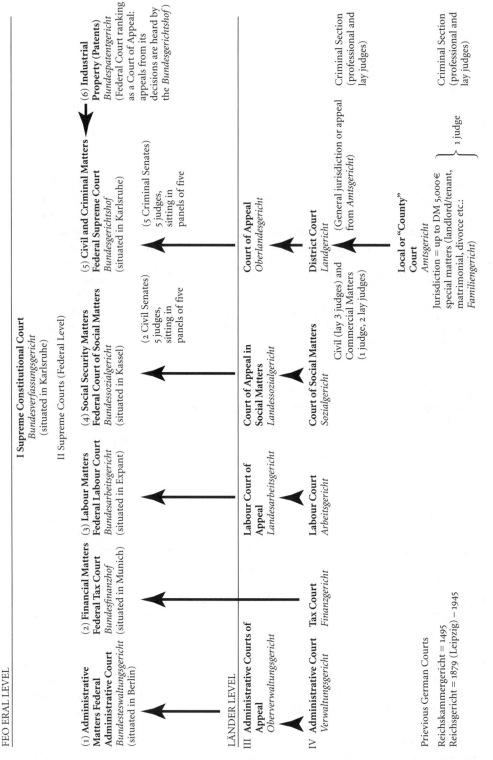

I Supreme Constitutional Court
Bundesverfassungsgericht
(situated in Karlsruhe)

II Supreme Courts (Federal Level)

| (1) Administrative Matters Federal Administrative Court *Bundesverwaltungsgericht* (situated in Berlin) | (2) Financial Matters Federal Tax Court *Bundesfinanzhof* (situated in Munich) | (3) Labour Matters Federal Labour Court *Bundesarbeitsgericht* (situated in Expant) | (4) Social Security Matters Federal Court of Social Matters *Bundessozialgericht* (situated in Kassel) | (5) Civil and Criminal Matters Federal Supreme Court *Bundesgerichtshof* (situated in Karlsruhe) | (6) Industrial Property (Patents) *Bundespatentgericht* (Federal Court ranking as a Court of Appeal: appeals from its decisions are heard by the *Bundesgerichtshof*) |

(2 Civil Senates)
5 judges, sitting in
panels of five

(2 Civil Senates)
5 judges, sitting in
panels of five

(5 Criminal Senates)
5 judges,
sitting in
panels of five

LÄNDER LEVEL

| III Administrative Courts of Appeal *Oberverwaltungsgericht* | | Labour Court of Appeal *Landesarbeitsgericht* | Court of Appeal in Social Matters *Landessozialgericht* | Court of Appeal *Oberlandesgericht* |

| IV Administrative Court *Verwaltungsgericht* | Tax Court *Finanzgericht* | Labour Court *Arbeitsgericht* | Court of Social Matters *Sozialgericht* | District Court *Landgericht* |

Civil (lay 3 judges) and
Commercial Matters
(1 judge, 2 lay judges)

(General jurisdiction or appeal
from *Amtsgericht*)

Criminal Section
(professional and
lay judges)

Local or "County" Court
Amtsgericht

Jurisdiction = up to DM 5,000 €
special matters (landlord/tenant,
matrimonial, divorce etc.:
Familiengericht)

Criminal Section
(professional and
lay judges)

} 1 judge

Prievious German Courts

Reichskammergericht = 1495
Reichsgericht = 1879 (Leipzig) – 1945

Fig: 1

movement on the European Continent has done a lot to undo the *ius commune* which previously existed". *Cases, Materials and Text on National, Supranational and International Tort Law* 2nd ed. (2000), 9.)

Even then it was some years before the Reichsgericht came into being on 1 October 1879, this time, however, sitting in Leipzig. This was truly the first Supreme Court for the whole of Germany, and though other high federal courts subsequently saw the light of day, jurisdiction at the highest level was never divided. Indeed, the personal that staffed these administrative and financial courts was not, until the coming into force of the Constitution of 24 May 1949, given the rank and tenure of "ordinary" judges. (Wolf, Gerichtsverfassungsrecht aller Verfahrenszweige, 6th ed. (1987), 91.) The Reichsgericht thus survived until the end of the Second World War (1945). During the next few years, while Germany lay in ruins and under foreign occupation, there was no federal Supreme Court, and as a result there followed an immediate and disturbing fragmentation of the law administered in the different parts of the country. The first attempts to re-establish some semblance of unity were made in 1947 in the British-occupied zone when a special Court of Justice was entrusted with this task. However, it was not until 1 October 1950, a year after the enactment of the Constitution of Bonn (known as the Grundgestez and abbreviated as GG), that the Bundesgerichtshof was established, this time in Karlsruhe. The scene was thus set for a "judicial recovery" from the traumatic years of the Nazi period and the post-war chaos—a recovery which, in some respects, is as admirable as the more publicised "economic miracle" of the 1950s which so symbolises the tenacity and determination of the German people.

Though in most respects modelled on the Reichsgericht, the Bundesgerichtshof was no longer accepted as the unique, supreme federal court. The desire for increased specialisation, which is an important characteristic of the contemporary German judicial structure, meant that along with the Bundesgerichtshof, which became the Supreme Court for civil and criminal matters, four other Supreme Courts also came into being. Each was placed at the head of a separate set of courts with its own organisation and personnel and dealt with, respectively, administrative law, financial matters, labour matters, and social legislation (Art. 95 GG). Alongside these, the Federal Constitutional Court (Bundesverfassungsgericht) was entrusted with the task of ensuring the preservation of the new Constitution and the control of the constitutionality of legislation (Arts. 93, 94 GG). These six courts, and the Federal Patent Court (Bundespatentgericht) (which, however, acts and ranks as a Court of Appeal) are federal courts; *all* other courts are State courts (i.e. equipped and maintained by the now (since reunification) sixteen States (Länder)). Two differences thus spring to mind with the United States where a federal structure has been adopted by the Constitution. First, in Germany unlike the USA, the Federal Government maintains no federal courts at the first and second level (the Patent Court, mentioned above, being the only exception). Secondly, however, in Germany and unlike America, each State has its own Constitutional Court, which is meant to ensure that the *State* constitution is observed. The patterns of federalism are thus truly almost endless (See Fig. 1.), and if we ever have to tow with the notion ourselves we must not commit the error of having the USA alone before our eyes.

This proliferation of supreme courts in Germany has brought with it the possibility of jurisdictional conflicts, positive or negative in nature (e.g. two or more courts asserting or denying jurisdiction over the same dispute, now largely regulated by the Gerichtsverfassungsgesetz as amended in 1960). There is, as well, the likelihood of a diverging case law on matters of substance. To resolve this latter conflict, and in order to ensure the unity of the federal law, Art. 95 of the Constitution of Bonn provided for the creation of a highest federal court (Oberstes Bundesgericht). This, however, never came into being, and a constitutional amendment, effected by means of a special statute on 18 June 1968 (BGBl. 1968.I., 657) provided, instead, for a "Common Senate" (Gemeinsamer Senat) composed of judges from the other five Supreme Courts. The task of this court is to rule whenever one of the Supreme Courts "consciously" departs (or proposes to depart) from the case law of another Supreme Court or a holding of the Common Senate. This body, which meets on average twice a year, does not seem to see its task as being one to force a compromise but come up with the most appropriate solution so, often it has sided with one rivalling court or the other. (Thus, see, Common Senate 24 October 1973, BGHZ 60, 392. On this court see, inter alia, Miebach, "Der Gemeinsame Senat der obersten Gerichtshöfe des Bundes" Schriften zum Prozeßrecht, vol. 25, p. 129.) Since in this work our emphasis will be on the civil law, the remaining observations will be devoted to the organisation of the civil courts and the civil side of the Bundesgerichtshof. In Germany this is known as the "ordinary jurisdiction" (ordentiche Gerichtsbarkeit) so as to be distinguished from the jurisdiction of the other courts (labour, administrative, financial etc.)

The lowest court on civil matters is the Amtsgericht of which there are a large number (693 in the reunited Germany receiving over 1.2–1.4 million applications/writs per year—a figure which excludes the family side of their business). They sit as single judge courts and have limited and specifically ascribed jurisdiction which included disputes up to the value of DM 10,000. As of 1 January 2002 the threshold is 5,000 € (§ 23 Nr. 1 Gerichtsverfassungsgesetz as amended by the Zivilprozeßreformgesetz of 27 July 2001).* In addition they deal with such varied matters as disputes between landlords and tenants; claims for financial support arising from marital or extramarital relationships; the supervision of guardians, executors, and trustees in bankruptcy; and the handling of various registers including the all-important land register. Since 1977 all family matters, especially those associated with divorce proceedings, matrimonial property, alimony, etc., are heard by a special division of the court, the Familiengericht, and from there an appeal lies directly to the appropriate Oberlandesgericht. Appeals from all other decisions of an Amtsgericht can be filed with the appropriate Landgericht (Berufung). (Provided the amount in dispute exceeds DM 1,200; § 511a ZPO. As of 1 January 2002 the amount in dispute must exceed 600 €; in other cases an appeal may be allowed if the case concerns questions of fundamental importance: § 511 ZPO as amended by the Zivilprozeßreformgesetz of 27 July 2001). Though hierarchically inferior courts (and, in some respects, analogous to our County Court), the Amtsgerichte are courts of singular importance to the average citizen who in his lifetime is usually spared the agony and the cost of the more prolonged or difficult type of litigation. These are also courts where legal representation is not obligatory (though in about in the vast majority of cases one party at least is represented by a lawyer). They are also courts which seem to dispatch their work expeditiously, the average time of a case before them being, depending on its complexity, between four and five months.

It is in the Landgericht (cited as LG), however, that one finds the equivalent of the English High Court, and their large number (116) brings out clearly the second important characteristic of the German judicial organisation, namely the considerable decentralisation in the administration of justice. The Landgericht is a court of general

---

* As of 1 January 2002 the Euro is official currency. However, the decisions and most statutory provisions reproduced and annotated in this book refer to amounts in DM. The fixed conversion rate is € 1 = DM 1.95583.

jurisdiction and sits as either a trial court or a court of review from any Amtsgericht of its district—legal representation by a lawyer (*Rechtsanwalt*) being, in this case, obligatory. The Landgericht is usually divided into sections (or chambers) each of which includes a presiding judge and two associates (all three being professional and academically trained judges.) Lay representation exists in the Kammer für Handelssachen (the commercial division) which is composed of one professional judge (acting as president) and two lay-men, experienced in commercial matters. Since the 1993 reforms (Gesetz zur Entlastung der Rechtspflege, BGBl. I. 1993 p. 50 on which Markwardt, "Das Rechtspflege-Entlas-tungsgesetz bei den Zivilgerichten", *MDR* 1993, 189), the bulk of this court's work is heard before a singly judge. The recent reform brought about by the *Zivilprozeßreformgesetz* of 27 July 2001 strengthens this trend and in most instances introduces a "single judge" (§§ 348, 348a ZPO). Henceforth, a three-judge panel will sit only if the legal issues involved are highly complex or of fundamental importance. The Landgerichte process 325,000–360,000 writs they receive (on average) per annum. (To this figure one must add the approximately 80,000 appeals from the Amtsgerichte). The higher complexity of the civil procedure, however, means a growing backlog of work which, in Germany as elsewhere, is the subject of periodic complaints and talk of reform.

From these courts an appeal (*Berufung*) lies to one of the twenty-four Courts of Appeal which is called the Oberlandesgericht (cited as OLG) except for the one that sits in Berlin, which has always been known as the Kammergericht. (Again, the amount in dispute must exceed 600 €; in other cases an appeal may be allowed if it concerns questions of funda-mental importance: § 511 ZPO as amended). Some Länder (namely Bremen, Hamburg, Hessen, Saarland, and Schleswig-Holstein) have only one Court of Appeal; others (e.g. Bavaria) have more. (Bavaria, in fact, also has an *Oberstes Landesgericht* (ObLG) which handles applications for revision related to State law.) Quite exceptionally, a Court of Appeal can be bypassed and an appeal against a decision of the Landgericht can be lodged directly with the Bundesgerichtshof provided that leave to appeal is granted. This, however, is likely to occur only where the facts of the case are not in dispute and both parties, desirous of an early solution to their dispute, are willing to utilize this leap-frogging procedure (*Sprungrevision*) (§ 566a ZPO; as of 1 January 2002: § 566 ZPO).

Before we turn to the *Revision* (appeal on questions of law) and the Bundesgerichtshof a few words must be said about the recent reform of the *Berufung* (appeal on questions of fact) brought about by the *Zivilprozeßreformgesetz* of 27 July 2001. Until 1 January 2002 the right to *Berufung* meant, in theory as well as in practice, that the litigants could effec-tively have a second trial. The reform seeks to change this and transform the nature of the *Berufungsverhandlung* by enhancing the importance of the decision of the first instance (be it a decision of an Amtsgericht or a Landgericht) and limiting the scope of review of the *Berufungsgericht*. Henceforth, the parties must present all available evidence on time, namely before the court of first instance. If they do not, they will normally be precluded from arguing points of fact on appeal (§ 531 ZPO as amended). This means also that the appeal court (*Berufungsgericht*) will, to a great extent, be bound by the find-ings of the court of first instance (§ 529 ZPO as amended). Only exceptionally, where the findings are inconsistent or give rise to doubts, or new evidence can be admitted in accor-dance with § 531 ZPO, will the appeal court be able to make its own findings. The details of this—controversial—reform have yet to be worked out by the courts.

The Bundesgerichtshof (henceforth BGH in short) stands, as already stated, at the apex of the judicial hierarchy in civil and criminal matters, now hearing cases from all courts of the re-united Germany. (Cases from the "new" Länder can be found reported from vol. 117 of the BGHZ; Z stands for Reports of Civil cases). It is divided into twelve Civil Senates (or Divisions) and five Criminal Senates (of which one always sits in Leipzig). Each Senate specialises in different matters. The Sixth Civil Senate, for example, deals with problems of delictual liability; the Seventh Civil Senate with various types of contract and cases of unjust enrichment; the Eighth Civil Senate handles disputes related to sales of goods, leases, etc. When deciding a case each Senate is composed of one presiding judge and four other Supreme Court judges, and the entire Bundesgerichtshof is now staffed by over one hundred and ten Supreme Court judges who are aided by specialist staff. (Supreme Court justices are nominated by a special committee (Richterwahlausschuß), composed of the Ministers of Justice of the Lander and an equal number of members of the Lower House. This committee is convened by the Federal Minister of Justice, who does not have the right to vote, but whose consent is necessary before a nomination, decided by a majority of this committee, can be passed on to the Federal President to make the appointment.)

The large number of sections makes it once again necessary to provide for a mechanism, which will solve potential conflicts between them and ensure the unity of the case law at the highest level. This task is entrusted to the Great Senate (Grosser Senat für Zivilsachen) and there is also a Great Senate for criminal matters, which performs a similar function for the five Criminal Senates. The Great Senate is composed of the President of the entire court and eight other judges and is seized of a dispute whenever one of the Civil Senates wishes to depart from the case-law of another Civil Senate or the case-law of the Great Civil Senate itself. Before this happens, however, the Senate about to embark on a different course will enquire of the other Senate whether the latter wishes to abide by its jurisprudence. If it does not, then there is no reason to convene the Great Senate; but if the second Senate does not wish to alter its case-law, then the Great Civil Senate becomes seized of the dispute. The Great Civil Senate may also become involved in a case even where there is no dispute in a narrow sense between various Senates of the court, but one of them is anxious that the Great Civil Senate pronounce its opinion on a matter of particular significance. Conflicts between one of the Civil Senates and one of the Criminal Senates (or between one of them and the Supreme Civil Senate of the other branch) are resolved by the Combined Great Senate (Vereinigte Grosse Senate) which includes judges from both civil and criminal sections of the court.

The decision to take a case to the Bundesgerichtshof can be taken by both litigants. However if both of them are content with or acquiesce in the result reached by the Court of Appeal the case can never reach the Supreme Court (even where a gross and obvious error of law has been made at the lower level). But though the parties decide whether they will take their case to a higher level the decision whether their appeal will be admissible does not rest with them. There is a right of appeal (or, more technically, of a revision) only if the case was for technical reasons deemed inadmissible by the Court of Appeal. The reason for this exception is to ensure that all parties have at least two chances of having their case heard by a court of law. Review is also available as of right where the Court of Appeal has departed from a decision of the Bundesgerichtshof or of the Common Senate of the highest courts. Otherwise, a distinction used to be made between pecuniary and non-pecuniary disputes.

The former, included cases which refer to a dispute estimable in money terms (e.g. disputes over contracts, delicts, etc.); the latter related to cases such as marriage or filiation proceedings, etc. In non-pecuniary cases and in pecuniary cases, which did not exceed DM 60,000, the admissibility of the review depended on permission being granted by the Court of Appeal. This would be granted where the legal issues involved were of fundamental importance (*grundsätzliche Bedeutung*, § 546 ZPO), but not otherwise, the idea being to shield the Supreme Court from overwork. In pecuniary matters exceeding DM 60,000, the lodging of an appeal did not depend on the permission of the lower court. The Supreme Court itself could refuse by a two-thirds majority to consider the case if the matter of law was not of fundamental importance (§ 554b ZPO).

This exception has now become the general rule. As of 1 January 2002 an appeal on questions of law (*Revision*) to the Bundesgerichtshof can only be lodged if leave to appeal has been granted by the appeal court (*Berufungsgericht*); § 543 ZPO as amended by the *Zivilprozeßreformgesetz* of 27 July 2001. Leave to appeal must be granted if the legal issues involved are of fundamental importance or the appeal is necessary to ensure the conformity and consistency of the case law. The decision denying leave to appeal can itself be appealed (§ 544 ZPO). If the appeal is of fundamental importance, the review will take place, and a motivated judgment will be delivered either rejecting the appeal, or accepting it and remitting the case to the lower court for retrial or, finally, substituting the court's own judgment in the place of the decision that is quashed.

What is an important or fundamental matter has never been authoritatively defined. In one of its early decisions—BGH 5 July 1951, BGHZ 2, 397—the Supreme court talked in terms of the matter being of general not particular importance (Allgemeine Bedeutung des Rechtsstreits, Nicht bloß den Einzelfall berührend). In a later decision—BGH 26 September 1978, NJW 1979, 219—it clarified, that the (potential) appellant's own interest was never, on its own, sufficient to give the appeal this characteristic however great it may be. On the whole, therefore, the vagueness of the terms has enabled the Courts of Appeal to act out efficiently their roles as gatekeepers. (On the whole matter, Prütting, *Die Zulassung der Revision* (1977) suggesting at pp. 164 ff. that permission is granted with restraint.)

One should conclude this section by stating that the doctrine of binding precedent is, in principle, not known to German law. We shall again refer briefly to this point in the next section when discussing how this may affect the style and form of a judgment. But it must be mentioned here, as well, since a "right" to take a case before the Supreme Court may arise if one of the exceptional rules of binding precedent has been violated. For present purposes, the most important instances where decisions can be binding on other courts are the following three. First, binding is a decision of the Federal Constitutional Court on the constitutional organs of the Federal and State government. Secondly, a decision of one Senate of the Federal Supreme Court departing from an earlier ruling of another Senate of the same court, if it has obtained a special ruling by the Great Senate (on civil or criminal matters, as the case may be). Thirdly, if, after an appeal on a point of law (*Revision*), the Bundesgerichtshof has reversed a decision of a Court of Appeal or District Court and sent the case for retrial before a lower court. This latter court is then bound by the ruling of the Bundesgerichtshof on the matter of law, which was before it.

Further reading

For a more detailed discussion, see Kern, *Gerichtsverfassungsrecht* (6th edn., 1987); Vogel, "Die Revision in Zivilsachen", *NJW* 1975, 1297; Schneider, "Das neue Revisionsrecht aus der Sicht des Anwalts", *NJW* 1975, 1537; Kissel, *Gerichtsverfassungsgesetz. Kommentar* (3rd edn., 2001); Wolf, *Gerichtsverfassungsrecht aller Verfahrenszweige* (6th edn., 1987), and for statistical information H. Salger (and others) "La cour fédérale de justice de la république fédérale d'Allemagne" *Rev. int. dr. comp.* (1978) 811. See, also, Fikentscher, "Etat de la doctrine de la force obligatoire des précédents en droit privé allemand", 4èmes Journées Franco-Allemandes, 13–17 juin 1984 in *Rev. intern. dr.*

comp. no. spécial, vol. 6, p. 189 (1984). Many of the points made in this section are also discussed in greater detail in the standard textbooks on the law of civil procedure (*Zivilprozeßordnung*). For a more general discussion of the legal aspects of re-unification see Hailbronner, "Legal Aspects of the Unification of the Two German States" 1991 *European Journal of International Law* no. 2, pp. 18 *et seq.* The recent reform is discussed in e.g. Däubler-Gmelin, "Reform des Zivilprozesses", *ZRP* 2000, 33; Greger, "Justizreform? Ja, aber . . .", *JZ* 2000, 842; Münchbach, "Justizreform—Reform oder gut verkaufter Abbau des Rechtsschutzsystems?", *ZRP* 1999, 374; Musielak, "Reform des Zivil-prozesses, Zum Entwurf eines Gesetzes zur Reform des Zivilprozesses (Zivilprozeßreformgesetz—ZPO-RG)", *NJW* 2000, 2769; Renk, "Rechtsmittelreform—so nicht!, Die Stellungnahme des DRB zum Referentenentwurf eines Gesetzes zur Reform des Zivilprozesses", *DRiZ* 2000, 171.

2. STYLE, FORM, AND CONTENT OF ARGUMENT IN THE JUDGMENTS OF THE BGH

A judgment of the German Supreme Court presents some marked differences both in style and form from the judgments of, say, the House of Lords or the French *Cour de cassation*. In terms of length, the contrast is greater with the French decisions (especially of the Cour de cassation), which are unparalleled in terseness and peculiarity of grammatical style. For example, a typical German judgment dealing with a contractual or delictual matter will run to about 2,000–2,500 words—in a minority of cases reaching the 5,000–word range. (Judgments of the Federal Constitutional Court tend to be much longer, some like the abortion cases, reaching truly gigantic proportions!) In length they thus tend to be closer to the average American decision than to the longer judgments of the House of Lords. One also acquires the impression—though to our knowledge no empirical study has been conducted on this matter—that the average decision of the Reichsgericht was shorter during the nineteenth century and the earlier part of this century than it has been since the end of the Second World War. If that is true, there is a parallel here with modern English practice which is also producing longer judgments than it did in the past. The trend, if a trend it is, is understandable, not least if one takes into account the growing volume of authority that the courts have to take into account. Whether it is all commendable is another matter.

Like the French decisions, but unlike the Anglo-American equivalents, the decisions of the German Supreme Court are unanimous decisions of the entire court. Clearly this does not mean that there are never any disagreements between the judges trying a particular case; but it does mean that in the published decision there are no open dissents. The court decides by simple majority (judges voting in inverted order of seniority, the presiding judge voting last). Thus, on occasion, the phrasing of the judgment requires very careful drafting in order to express the compromise formula agreed upon by the members of the court. By contrast, dissenting judgments are allowed in the Federal Constitutional Court and the judges there make frequent use of this right.

Typically the report of a judgment will commence with a couple of paragraphs (*Leitsätze*) containing in abstract form the propositions of the law supported by the decision. This section of the report forms no part of the decision and in the translations reproduced in this book it has, consequently, been omitted. These paragraphs will be followed by references to the Articles of the Civil or Criminal Code (or other enactments) that had to be construed and applied in the case. The section of the court that had to decide the case will then be given and this will be followed by the date on which the trial was concluded. The initials of the parties to the action will also be given but never their names, famous cases thus becoming known through some other attribution e.g. "the chicken pest case", "the gentleman rider case". (Exceptions to this rule are found more often in the case law of the Constitutional court and in unfair competition and intellectual property cases decided by the Supreme Court. Thus, for instance, the "Lüth" case, "the Soraya" case, "the Lebach," the "Strauss Placard" case.) The above is the form adopted in the semi-official reports quoted as BGHZ and followed by the number of the volume and the page on which the decision is reproduced. Other reports—the *NJW*, or the *JZ* for example—follow a slightly different order of presentation. An important case, reported in various journals, will usually be cited by giving all its references. But the text in the official report will usually be given first. (Thus, for instance, BGHZ 2, 397 = NJW 1951, 762 = ZZP 64, 474.)

The facts of the case will then follow—usually—an abbreviated form of the judgment of the Court of Appeal. Quite frequently, sections of the legal reasoning of the Court of Appeal will also be reproduced and the court will then indicate whether it agrees or disagrees with the reasoning and/or the result. It will then proceed to consider the grounds for appeal advanced by the appellant and give its own reasons for its conclusions.

The extent to which the facts will be given in detail will vary from case to case. Sometimes the court merely states them, as found by the lower court. It then gives its opinion on the question of law and finally, refers the case back to the lower courts to discover the relevant facts in the light of the law as stated by the court. But the statement of facts is rarely as detailed as it is in English (or American) judgments and never as colourfully presented. For the German courts are not obliged to attempt the detailed consideration of material which is necessary in the Common law whose courts must decide whether the case under consideration is covered by earlier authority or whether, on the contrary, it is materially different and thus distinguishable from earlier precedents.

The legal arguments that follow are presented in an abstract manner, which is not always easy for a Common lawyer to follow or even to translate accurately. For first of all, the tone of the argument can be highly conceptual, even metaphysical. Sections of the judgments dealing with the protection of human personality (see below, cases 36–49) are just that, and they will, in turn, generate academic literature which can reach heights of abstraction un-thought of in the Common law. The discussion of the notion of "unlawfulness" in the decision of the Great Senate (below, case 109) provides yet another example of this phenomenon (though this controversial judgment is now, for all practical intents and purposes, obsolete). Clearly, on its face, the decision is incomprehensible (even to a young German lawyer) and some explanation of the problem and the disputes it has generated must precede any study of the problem with which it is concerned.

Another difference—especially from English decisions—is the detailed consideration of the views of contemporary (and past) academic writers dealing with the subject before the court. In particular, what is usually referred to as the "dominant opinion" (*herrschende Meinung*), which is the opinion on a certain matter as reflected in the majority of writings and decisions, will enjoy strong persuasive authority. Sometimes judgments contain more than a mere reference to academic literature. When this happens, one may end up with an admirably lucid summary of the views of the academic world. On some occasions, the court may, however, add—one suspects with a tinge of despair—that the solution to the problem should, in the end, depend on common sense and not theoretical constructions, however admirable they may be. One of the leading judgments on legal cause (case 80)—a subject that has greatly attracted the German legal mind—offers an excellent illustration, and should act as a caution for those who over-stress the Germanic tendency towards conceptualism and abstraction. The "chicken-pest" case (below, case 61) furnishes yet another example of the court's willingness to take into account the views of academic writers, if only to reject them at the end and then offer its own solution. This judgment is, in fact, a teacher's dream in so far as it offers an excellent springboard from which to consider the various theories behind modern products liability law. Moreover, the interesting thing about this dialogue between court and academics is that it helps perpetuate this interaction from which, apparently, both branches of the profession stand to gain. For writers will respond to such judicial criticism and often come up with new theories or modifications of existing theories, which may later be accepted by the court. The overall impression that one gets is one of mutual respect and reciprocal influence and it is not uncommon to find the court expressly adopting the views of a certain writer on a particular problem. Thus, to give but one example, the whole doctrine of contract with protective effects towards third parties (as a variant of the classical contract in favour of third parties regulated by the BGB in §§ 328 ff.) was largely taken over by the courts from the teachings of the late Professor Karl Larenz. Another example of this close co-operation between academic writers and the courts can be found in the judicial development of § 242 BGB (good faith) which is discussed in greater detail in the first volume of this work.

The previous case-law—especially of the Supreme Court itself—is also considered and quoted in the judgments but again in a manner quite different from that adopted by the Anglo-American courts. Rarely will a quote be given in order to distinguish one case before the court from the previous one. More often, it will be given to show what the established practice of the court is on a particular matter and to reinforce the present argument. Many of the differences with Anglo-American law are obviously due to the doctrine of *stare decisis* which, subject to the rather few special occasions already alluded to in the previous section, is not known to German law. This is not to say, of course, that an inferior court will easily depart from the line taken by the BGH—especially if there is a series of decisions (*ständige Rechtsprechung*) substantially to the same effect. Also, the BGH has repeatedly stressed that it will overrule a long-lasting and steady adjudication concerning a certain legal issue only if overpowering reasons compel it to do so. (See e.g. BGHZ 85, 64. For an overview: Bydlinski, "Richterrecht über Richterrecht" in *50 Jahre Bundesgerichtshof* Vol. 1 (2000) 1)

Statute and custom are, therefore, technically the only true sources of law (though unlike England (until recent times) *published* preparatory works have always been used in order to discover the intention of the legislator). On the other hand, it is not unknown for the various State Courts of Appeal to "rebel" against a particular decision of the Supreme Court. Sometimes—as in the case of the recognition of the general right to one's personality—the rebellion will be short-lived and within a relatively short period of time the Supreme Court will manage to assert its will. In other instances, however, the reaction of the Courts of Appeal may be stronger and more persistent, which can then force the BGH to reconsider its own decision on this matter. As we shall see (below, case 11), this is what happened in the context of the "cable" cases and the reparation of purely economic loss through § 823 II BGB. In the wrongful life/birth cases we face yet another "peculiarity" of German law: the Constitutional court saying one thing and then inviting the ordinary courts to take its views into account. This, they courteously do, but if the opinion of the Constitutional court does not refer to the constitutionality of a particular decision, the ordinary courts may and do abide by their own case law. To a Common lawyer, the resulting "conflict" is troublesome; and it becomes positively irritating when the two parts of the Constitutional court, itself, are unable to agree on a common position. (We shall encounter further down one or two instances of this phenomenon e.g. in the case of claims for wrongful birth.) The history of the German Constitutional court accounts for this peculiarity; but to foreign eyes at least it is hardly justified.

German judges (and lawyers generally) could be accused of leaving nothing to the imagination. Certainly the elegance, humour, and high literary style achieved by some English and American judges are often sacrificed at the altar of accuracy and thoroughness (and the strongly felt need to keep humour out of official business.) For example, the Lord Denning type of presentation of facts, with the judge in the middle of the human drama rather than in the role of an impersonal adjudicator, is quite unknown in Germany. Equally, the desire to express in accurate and impersonal terminology a particular problem can deprive the judgment of elegance, even of life. An excellent illustration of this can be found by comparing two rescue cases—one German and one American (below, case 87 compared with *Wagner* v. *International Ry Co.*, 232 NY 176, 133 NE 437 (1921)). The problem and the solution proposed are identical. This should cause no surprise, since the policy reasons behind the similar results are the same. But Cardozo J's memorable words: "Danger invites rescue. The cry of distress is the summons of relief . . ." are replaced by dry, causative language of the type which helps create the popularly conceived image of German law and its lawyers.

Like all generalisations, however, the above observations must be treated with some caution. For the contact with "reality" and the true forces that shape the law can often be found in the short but clear references to various policy factors that the judges are increasingly making. The fear of "innumerable claims", if negligently inflicted economic loss were to become compensatable, is clearly voiced in some of the "cable" cases (11 and 12). If this is read in conjunction with the writings of modern commentators on this subject, one realises that this policy factor (and others, such as insurance) lie behind the refusal to compensate cases of negligently inflicted economic loss. All of a sudden, the impressive conceptual armoury used by the courts to deny the plaintiff's claim becomes a façade; the concepts are nothing but devices that formulate the conclusions of the judges but do not really explain them. (For the importance that insurance may have on the outcome of a dispute see case 144.) A wise Munich colleague, much learned in our law, thus always warned me that all German judgments contain two reasons for their results: the published ones and the real ones. The realisation that the true reasons for a decision may lie elsewhere is an important one for it will accustom the comparatist to take his research beyond the text of a judgment to other sources such as preparatory works and, of course, academic commentaries. Only when this task has been performed fully and properly will the real similarities between the different legal systems begin to be understood.

The "contact" with the real world and its sufferings is also seen in many contract cases. The revalorisation cases of the early and middle twenties, discussed in volume one in connection with § 242 BGB, reveal the German judges at their boldest and most human (and for some the most controversial). Incidentally, this is not only one of the most remarkable areas of judge-made law in a country of codes. It also offers the interested student excellent material for an excursus into sociology, politics, and economics and an opportunity to see how law is shaped by the changing demands of social life. In one of these leading cases the Reichsgericht thus stressed that: "The first and noblest task of the judge is . . . to satisfy in his decisions the imperative demands of life and to allow himself in this respect to be guided by the experience of life" (see RGZ 100, 129). (For more details, see chapter eight of the first volume of this work.)

Finally, a few words must be added about the form the arguments take and the reasons behind them. This is particularly important given the recent tendency of contemporary British judges to give elaborate, often sophisticated, accounts of the policy reasons, which have dictated their conclusions. This is rarely *obvious* in the judgments of the BGH.

A judgment of the *Bundesgerichtshof* reveals much about German legal history, the kind of education German judges receive at University, the impact that a largely written/codified system has on the way German judges perceive their job, and much else besides. Let us look briefly at these points under three different headings: history, legal education, and the existence of a codal text.

(i) History. The original versions of the German judgments reproduced in this book show that reference to earlier decisional law is smaller than is the case with Anglo-American judgments. In Germany the frequency with which a court will make use of earlier judicial work is, in fact, even less significant than these figures suggest. This becomes obvious when, through careful reading of the judgments, one realises that the earlier case law is either quoted as an illustration of a particular view or as an example of an established practice. Rarely if ever, though, is this case law *scrutinised* in the way an English court would consider its earlier decisional law. There is thus little or no evidence of the previous cases having been used as building blocks for the new decision. The reason for this different treatment is, of course, to be found on the combined impact that the three factors—history, legal education and codal background—have had on the nature of German judicial work. Equally important is the fact that for the German judge the primary building block is the Code that has to be applied, followed only by the academic exegesis to which this enactment has been subjected. Incidentally, we refer to the Code as the primary building block for two reasons. The first, and better known to English lawyers, is the fact that the judge's reasoning process starts by reference to a particular provision or provisions in the Code and proceeds deductively to the facts before him. But the second, less noticed yet crucial for present purposes, reason, is the fact that the codal text often spares the German judge the trouble of having to do and formulate some of the basic thinking that his English colleague has to do for himself. The arguments, for example, that militate (or seem to militate) against the recognition of a tort action to recover pure economic loss need not be mentioned by the judge since they were considered when the Code was being drafted and the basic decision not to "recognise" pure economic loss was taken by the legislator. Likewise, if we move to another topic, the tortious liability of statutory bodies, the decisions of principle—should the government be liable; should the negligent official, himself, be liable—were discussed by the drafting committee of the code and their decisions on these topics are reflected in their § 839 BGB.

(ii) Legal education. The education received at law school is also different and, thus, both the result and the cause of the above-mentioned difference in the finished product. For at law school, especially the so-called academic phase of his training which will culminate with the first State exam, the aspiring German judge will be taught how to use the codes, learn how to inter-link their various parts (and then combine the Codes with one another) and—to begin at least—to apply the texts he has been taught deductively. In all this, he will be expected to make as logical and as consistent a use as he can of the many concepts that will be drummed into his head during a period of at least seven—if one includes the preparation for the second state exam—years of training. Though references to cases figure increasingly in lectures—and appear even more frequently in the so-called privately financed *repetitoria* which are attended by most German students—the constant

refining and re-defining of earlier case law, with the frequent use of the untested hypothesis, is absent from the legal training which is otherwise both long and very thorough. Thus, once again, the German judgment reflects this difference which merges very much with that mentioned under the previous sub-heading. For the same two reasons German judgments, as a rule, also make greater use of academic literature than their English counterparts. (For figures and an interesting discussion see Kötz, "Scholarship and the Courts: A Comparative Survey" in *Essays in Honour of Henry Merryman on his Seventieth Birthday* (1990) pp. 190 ff.)

(iii) The Codal background. As stated under (i), the Code—and we are here concerned with the Civil Code—*and its preparatory works* has, in most cases at least, provided for the German judge some of the decisions of principle. Paragraph 823 I BGB has thus told him that pure economic loss is not included among the list of protected interests. As stated, the German judge thus does not have to search for wider—we could call them policy—reasons "of principle" that will lead him, as they lead his English counterpart, to the conclusion to "strike out a claim" for pure economic loss. The wider issues concerning floodgates, insurability, and the like will thus not be invoked (or even hinted at) in the German judgment whereas they will play a major part in the Common law counterpart. It is only when the German judge feels that circumstances require a deviation from the basic codal text that he will feel the need to start being inventive. Sticking with the same subject—pure economic loss—we thus see this where recovery has, despite the general rule, been allowed. This has necessitated either the creation of a new protected interest—e.g. the right to an established and operating business—or an ingenious (or ingenuous) use of some other concept in order to cover the perceived legal gap. (Such as that of *Weiterfresserschaden, Vertrag mit Schutzwirkung für Dritte* or *Drittschadensliquidation* which are discussed in the section on pure economic loss.) It should be noted, however, that *Drittschadensliquidation* is one of the rare instances where the legislator left it to, or even encouraged, the courts to fill the gap, see Mugdan, *Materialien zum BGB*, vol. 2, (1899) reprinted 1979, 517–18. Incidentally, the Law Commission in its Law Com. No. 242 (1996) arrived at a similar conclusion in respect of the promisee's remedy to recover damages on behalf of a third party. That is what *Drittschadensliquidation* is all about, and the relevant passage of the Law Commission paper reads almost as a word for word translation of the *Materialien*: "Our recommendation is that this is a matter at present better left to the evolving common law. Certainly we would not wish to forestall further judicial development of this area of the law of damages." (para. 5.15). In the end, therefore, devices such as these have allowed "deviations" from the original position of the Code. Characteristically, however, these innovations have not come about painlessly but, on the contrary, have caused much discussion and dispute in German academic and judicial circles. (See, for instance, the reaction that followed BGH of 24. 11. 1976, BGHZ 67, 359. Thus, Hager, "Zum Schutzbereich der Produzentenhaftung", AcP 184 (1984), 413. But *cf.* Steffen, "Die Bedeutung der 'Stoffgleichheit' mit dem 'Mangelunwert' für die Herstellerhaftung aus Weiterfresserschäden", VersR 1988, 977.)

Likewise, background differences—such as different history and different constitutional texts—largely explain the differences that exist between German and American law when it comes to the clash of free speech and reputation and privacy. In Germany, the statutory regime—Constitution and Code—have here encouraged the judge to seek an *ad hoc* reconciliation of the competing values and only occasionally has it given textually a hint as to which value should prevail. By contrast, the American Constitution has, in its First Amendment, made up the mind for all subsequent judges by giving a pre-dominant, some would say, exaggerated preference to the value of free speech and, effectively, deprived them of the opportunity even to attempt any balancing of values. (Thus in *Konigsberg* v. *State Bar* 366 US 36, 61 (1961) Mr Justice Black said: "I believe that the First Amendment's unequivocal command that there shall be no abridgement of the rights of free speech and assembly shows that the men who drafted our Bill of Rights *did all the 'balancing' that was to be done* in this field . . ." Italics added.) Finally, to return to one last illustration, the same is true in the German cases that deal with the liability of statutory bodies (discussed towards the end of this book: cases 132–139.). Much of the discussion about the desirability of the courts second-guessing other parts of the Administration or weighing the economic consequences of a liability rule, which appears in the comparable English (and American judgments), in Germany was done by the legislator when the Code was drafted. (For instance, *Protokolle*, vol. II, at p. 662, about the value of the "economic-consequences argument" as a reason for not imposing lia-bility or, more recently, when its revision was planned. (Thus, see, *Zur Reform des Staatshaftungsrechts* (1976), p. 5, 71.) The result of all this is that much of what appears in the English judicial opinion will not figure (and does not have to figure) in the comparable German judgment. But, as we have already suggested, this does not mean that the issues that have occupied the English judges have escaped the attention of their German legal establishment. What it does mean is that considera-tion of some of those issues has almost certainly taken place in a different forum and must be searched for in different texts. For those involved in the comparative exam-ination of legal systems, this undoubtedly adds both an intellectual challenge and considerable complexity to their work. The scholar who studies a foreign legal system, though advised to start his research in a narrow and focused manner, is thus eventually forced to cast his research net more widely than he originally thought was necessary if he is to obtain a decent understanding of the foreign system. How he does that is some-thing that is acquired through reading and experience and no easy short cuts can be recommended.

3. THE DELICT PROVISIONS OF THE BGB

§ 823. A person who wilfully or negligently injures the life, body, health, freedom, prop-erty, or other right of another contrary to law is bound to compensate him for any damage arising therefrom.

The same obligation attaches to a person who infringes a statutory provision intended for the protection of others. If according to the purview of the statute infringement is possible even without fault, the duty to make compensation arises only if some fault can be imputed to the wrongdoer.

§ 824. A person who maintains or publishes, contrary to the truth, a statement calcu-lated to endanger the credit of another, or to injure his earnings or prospects in any other manner, must compensate the other for any damage arising therefrom, even if he does not know of its untruth, provided he ought to know.

A communication the untruth of which is unknown to the person making it does not thereby render him liable to make compensation, if he or the recipient of the communi-cation has a justifiable interest in it.

§ 825. A person who by fraud or threats, or by an abuse of the relation of dependence, induces a woman to permit illicit cohabitation is bound to compensate her for damage arising therefrom.

§ 826. A person who wilfully causes damage to another in a manner *contra bonos mores* is bound to compensate the other for the damage.

§ 827. A person who does damage to another in a condition of unconsciousness, or in a condition of morbid disturbance of the mental activity, incompatible with a free determination of the will, is not responsible for the damage. If he had brought himself into a temporary condition of this kind by spirituous liquors or similar means, he is responsible for any damage which he unlawfully causes in this condition in the same manner as if negligence were imputable to him; the responsibility does not arise if he has been brought into this condition without fault.

§ 828. A person who has not completed his seventh year of age is not responsible for any damage which he does to another.

A person who has completed his seventh year but not his eighteenth year of age is not responsible for any damage which he does to another, if at the time of committing the damaging act he did not have the understanding necessary to realize his responsibility. The same rule applies to a deaf mute.

§ 829. A person who in any one of the cases specified in §§ 823–6 is by virtue of §§ 827, 828 not responsible for any damage caused by him, must, nevertheless, to the extent that compensation cannot be obtained from a third party charged with the duty of supervision, make compensation for the damage in so far as according to the circumstances —in particular according to the relative positions of the parties—equity requires indemnification, and he is not deprived of the means which he needs for his own maintenance according to his station in life and for the fulfilment of his statutory duties to furnish maintenance to others.

§ 830. If several persons have caused damage by an unlawful act committed in common, each is responsible for the damage. The same rule applies if it cannot be discovered which of several participants has actually caused the damage.

Instigators and accomplices are in the same position as joint-doers.

§ 831. A person who employs another to do any work is bound to compensate for damage which the other unlawfully causes to a third party in the performance of his work. The duty to compensate does not arise if the employer has exercised ordinary care in the choice of the employee, and, where he has to supply appliances or implements or to superintend the work, has also exercised ordinary care as regards such supply or superintendence, or if the damage would have arisen, notwithstanding the exercise of such care.

The same responsibility attaches to a person who takes over the charge of any of the affairs specified in para. 1, sentence 2, by contract with the employer.

§ 832. A person who is bound by law to exercise supervision over a person on account of minority, or of his mental or physical condition, is bound to make compensation for any damage which the latter unlawfully does to a third party. The duty to compensate does not arise if he fulfils his duty of supervision, or if the damage would have occurred notwithstanding the proper exercise of supervision.

The same responsibility attaches to a person who takes over by contract the exercise of supervision.

§ 833. If a person is killed or injured, or the health of a person is affected, or a thing is damaged by an animal, the person who keeps the animal is bound to compensate the injured party for any damage arising therefrom. The duty to make compensation does not arise if the damage is caused by a domestic animal which is intended to serve the profession, the business activities, or the support of the keeper of the animal and if the keeper of the animal has either exercised the requisite care in supervising the animal or if the damage would have occurred notwithstanding the exercise of such care.

§ 834. A person who undertakes to supervise an animal under a contract with the keeper of the animal is responsible for any damage which the animal causes to a third party in the manner specified in § 833. The responsibility does not arise if he has exercised the requisite care in the supervision of the animal, or if the damage would have occurred notwithstanding the exercise of such care.

§ 835. [Repealed.]

§ 836. (1) If, by the collapse of a building or other structure attached to a piece of land, or by the detachment of parts of the building or structure, a person is killed or injured, or the health of a person is affected, or a thing is damaged, and if the collapse or the detachment was caused by defective construction or inadequate maintenance, the possessor of the land is bound to compensate the injured party for any damage arising therefrom. The duty to make compensation does not arise if the possessor has exercised the requisite care for the purpose of averting danger.

(2) A former possessor of the land is responsible for the damage if the collapse or the detachment occurs within one year after the termination of his possession, unless during his possession he exercised the requisite care, or unless a subsequent possessor could have averted the danger by the exercise of such care.

(3) The possessor within the meaning of these provisions is the proprietary possessor.

§ 837. If a person in the exercise of a right possesses a building or other structure on the land of another, the responsibility specified in § 836 attaches to him instead of the possessor of the land.

§ 838. A person who undertakes for the possessor the maintenance of a building or a structure attached to land, or who has to maintain the building or the structure by virtue of a right of use belonging to him, is responsible in the same manner as the possessor for any damage caused by the collapse or the detachment of parts.

§ 839. (1) If an official wilfully or negligently commits a breach of official duty incumbent upon him towards a third party, he shall compensate the third party for any damage arising therefrom. If only negligence is imputable to the official, he may be held liable only if the injured party is unable to obtain compensation otherwise.

(2) If an official commits a breach of his official duty in giving judgment in an action, he is not responsible for any damage arising therefrom, unless the breach of duty is subject to a public penalty to be enforced by criminal proceedings. This provision does not apply to a breach of duty consisting of refusal or delay in the exercise of the office.

(3) The duty to make compensation does not arise if the injured party has wilfully or negligently omitted to avert the injury by making use of a legal remedy.

§ 840. If several persons are together responsible for damage arising from an unlawful act, they are liable, subject to the provisions of § 835, section 3, as joint debtors.

If, in addition to the person liable under §§ 831, 832 to make compensation for the damage caused by another, that other person is also liable, as between themselves only the latter is liable, or in the case provided for by § 829, only the person who has the duty of supervision.

If, in addition to the person liable under §§ 833–8 to make compensation for any damage, a third party is also liable for the damage, as between themselves only such third party is liable.

§ 841. If an official whose public duty requires him to appoint another person for the purpose of acting for a third party or to supervise such an activity or to co-operate in this activity by giving his consent to legal transactions is responsible with the other person for the damage caused by him through neglect of his duties to that other party, between the two of them, is solely liable.

§ 842. The obligation to make compensation for damage on account of an unlawful act directed against the person of another extends to the detriment which the act occasions to his earnings or prospects.

§ 843. If, in consequence of an injury to body or health, the earning capacity of the injured party is destroyed or diminished or an increase of his necessities arises, compensation must be made to the injured party by the payment of a money annuity.

The provisions of § 760 apply to the annuity. Whether, in what manner, and to what amount, the person bound to make compensation has to give security is determined according to the circumstances. Instead of an annuity the victim may demand a lump sum settlement, if a serious reason exists for it.

The claim is not excluded by the fact that another person has to furnish maintenance to the injured party.

§ 844. In the case of causing death the person bound to make compensation must make good the funeral expenses to the person on whom the obligation of bearing such expenses lies.

If the deceased at the time of the injury stood in a relation to a third party by virtue of which he was or might become bound by law to furnish maintenance to him, and if in consequence of the death such third party is deprived of the right to claim maintenance, the person bound to make compensation must compensate the third party by the payment of a money annuity, in so far as the deceased would have been bound to furnish maintenance during the presumable duration of his life; the provisions of § 843, sections 2–3, apply *mutatis mutandis*. The obligation to make compensation arises even if at the time of the injury the third party was only *en ventre sa mère*.

§ 845. In the case of causing death, or of causing injury to body or health, or in the case of deprivation of liberty, if the injured party was bound by law to perform services in favour of a third party in his household or industry, the person bound to make compensation must compensate the third party for the loss of services by the payment of a money annuity. The provisions of § 843, sections 2–4, apply *mutatis mutandis*.

§ 846. If, in the cases provided for by §§ 844, 845, some fault of the injured party has contributed to cause the damage which the third party has sustained, the provisions of § 254 apply to the claim of the third party.

§ 847. In the case of injury to body or health, or in the case of deprivation of liberty, the injured party may also demand an equitable compensation in money for the damage which is not a pecuniary loss.

A like claim belongs to a woman against whom a crime or offence against morality is committed, or who is induced by fraud, or by threats, or by an abuse of a relation of dependence to permit illicit cohabitation.

§ 848. A person liable to restore an object of which he deprived another unlawfully is also liable if it perished accidentally, if its return has become impossible accidentally for any other reason, or if it deteriorated accidentally, unless the destruction, the impossibility to return it for other reasons, or its deterioration, would also have occurred if it had not been taken.

§ 849. If a party can claim damages because he was deprived of an object or because it had been damaged and has suffered in value, he can claim interest on the sum representing damages from the time which serves to determine its taking.

§ 850. Where the person liable to restore an object unlawfully withheld has incurred outlays in respect of that object, he is entitled, as against the injured party, to claim the same rights as the possessor of an object has against the owner for outlays incurred.

§ 851. If a person bound to make compensation for any damage on account of taking or damaging of a moveable compensates the person in whose possession the thing was at the time of the taking or damage, he is discharged by so doing even if a third party was owner of the thing, or had some other right in the thing, unless the right of the third party is known to him or remains unknown in consequence of gross negligence.

§ 852. (1) The claims for compensation for any damage arising from a delict is barred by prescription in three years from the time at which the injured party obtained knowledge of the injury and of the identity of the person liable to make compensation, and without regard to such knowledge in thirty years from doing the act.

(2) If negotiations are pending between the party liable and the party entitled to compensation with regard to the compensation, the running of the period of prescription is interrupted until one of the parties continues the negotiations.

(3) If the person liable has acquired anything by the delict at the expense of the injured party, he is, even after the running of the period of prescription, bound to return it under the provisions relating to the return of unjust enrichment.

§ 853. If by an illegal act a person acquires a contractual claim, the injured party may refuse to perform even if the time has passed for hearing the contractual claim.

4. OTHER RELEVANT PROVISIONS OF THE BGB

§ 31 The association is liable for any damage which the board, a member of the board, or other duly appointed representative may, in carrying out his duty, cause a third party, if the act obliges the making of compensation.

§ 226. The exercise of a right is inadmissible if it can only have the purpose of causing damage to another.

§ 227. An act required by self-defence is not unlawful.

Self-defence is that defence which is necessary in order to ward off from oneself or another an actual unlawful attack.

§ 228. Anyone who damages or destroys a thing belonging to another in order to ward off from himself or another a danger threatened by it, does not act unlawfully, if the damage or destruction is necessary to ward off the danger and the damage is not out of proportion to the danger. If the person acting is to blame for the danger, he is bound to make good the damage.

§ 229. Anyone who for purposes of self-help takes away, destroys, or damages a thing or for purposes of self-help apprehends an obligor suspected of intending flight or overcomes the resistance of the obligor to an act which the latter is bound to suffer, does not act unlawfully if the help of the authorities cannot be obtained in good time and there is danger that unless he acts at once the realisation of the claim will be frustrated or appreciably impeded.

§ 230. Self-help must not go further than is necessary to ward off the danger.

In case of the seizure of things, in so far as compulsory execution is not effected, leave to distrain must be applied for.

In case of the apprehension of the obligor, in so far as he is not set free again, leave for the precautionary detention of his person must be applied for to the District Court in whose district the apprehension has taken place; the obligor must be brought before the Court without delay.

If the application is delayed or rejected, the restitution of the things seized and the liberation of the person apprehended must follow without delay.

§ 231. Anyone who does one of the acts specified in § 229 under the mistaken assumption that the necessary presuppositions for the exclusion of illegality are in existence, is bound to compensate the other party, even if the mistake is not due to negligence.

§ 249. The person who is bound to make compensation must restore the situation which would exist if the circumstance making him liable to compensate had not occurred. If compensation is to be made for injury to a person or damage to a thing the creditor may demand, instead of restitution in kind, the sum of money necessary to effect such restitution.

§ 250. The creditor may by notice to the person liable to compensate, fix a reasonable period for the restitution in kind with a declaration that he will not accept restitution after the expiration of the period. After the expiration of the period, the creditor may demand the compensation in money if the restitution is not effected in due time; the claim for restitution is barred.

§ 251. If performance in kind is impossible or insufficient to compensate the creditor, the party obliged to provide reparation must do so in money.

The party obliged to provide reparation may do so by paying money only if performance in kind requires disproportionate expenditure. Expenditure incurred in healing an injured animal is not disproportionate for the reason alone that it exceeds its value considerably.

§ 252. The damage to be made good includes also lost profits. Profit is deemed to have been lost which would have been expected with probability according to the ordinary course of things, or according to the particular circumstances, in particular, according to the preparation and provisions made.

§ 253. For an injury which is not an injury to property compensation in money may be demanded only in the cases specified by law.

§ 254. If any fault of the injured party has contributed to the occurrence of the damage, the duty to compensate and the extent of the compensation to be made depend upon the circumstances, especially upon how far the injury has been caused predominantly by the one or the other party.

This applies also if the fault of the injured party was limited to omission to call the attention of the debtor to the danger of unusual serious damage, of which the debtor neither knew nor ought to have known, or to an omission to avert or mitigate the damage. The provision of § 278 applies *mutatis mutandis*.

§ 255. The person who is to make compensation for the loss of a thing or of a right is bound to make compensation only upon an assignment to him of the claims which belong to the person entitled to compensation by virtue of his ownership of the thing or by virtue of his right against third parties.

§ 276. The debtor is responsible, unless otherwise provided, for recklessness and negligence. A person who does not exercise the care expected in daily affairs acts negligently. The provisions of §§ 827 and 828 apply.

The debtor may not be released beforehand from responsibility for recklessness.

§ 277. The person who is answerable only for such care as he is accustomed to exercise in his own affairs is not relieved from liability for gross negligence.

§ 278. A debtor is responsible for the fault of his statutory agent, and of persons whom he employs in fulfilling his obligation, to the same extent as for his own fault. The provision of § 276 II does not apply.

Promise of performance for the benefit of a third party

§ 328. (1) A contract may stipulate for performance to a third party, so that the third party acquires a right to demand performance.

(2) In the absence of express stipulation it is to be deduced from the circumstances, especially from the object of the contract, whether the right of the third party shall arise forthwith or only under certain conditions, and whether any right shall be reserved to the contracting parties to take away or modify the right of the third party without his consent.

§ 329. If in a contract one party binds himself to satisfy a creditor of the other party without assuming the debt, it is not to be presumed, in case of doubt, that the creditor shall acquire a direct right to demand satisfaction from him.

§ 330. If, in a contract for life insurance or an annuity, payment of the insurance or annuity to a third party is stipulated for, it is to be presumed, in case of doubt, that the third party shall directly acquire the right to demand the performance. The same rule applies, if in a gratuitous transfer of property the duty to perform the act to a third party is imposed upon the recipient, or if a person, on taking over the whole of another person's property or goods, promises an act of performance to a third party for the purpose of settling the latter's debts.

§ 331. (1) If the performance to the third party is to be made after the death of the person to whom it was promised, in case of doubt the third party acquires the right to the performance upon the death of the promisee.

(2) If the promisee dies before the birth of the third party, the promise to perform to the third party can be revoked or altered only if the right to do so has been reserved.

§ 676. A person who gives advice or a recommendation to another is not bound to compensate for any damage arising from following the advice or the recommendation, without prejudice to his responsibility resulting from a contract or delict.

§ 803. The owner of a thing may deal with it in his discretion and exclude others from any interference, subject to the laws or to the rights of third parties.

§ 904. [Emergency] The owner of a thing is not entitled to prohibit the interference of another with the thing, if the interference is necessary for the avoidance of a present danger and the damage threatened is disproportionately great compared to the damage caused to the owner by the interference. The owner may demand compensation for the loss suffered by him.

§ 906. [Interference from adjacent land]

(1) The owner of a piece of land is not entitled to prohibit the intrusion of gases, vapours, smells, smoke, soot, heat, noises, shocks and similar interferences emanating from another piece of land to the extent that the interference does not or only immaterially prejudices the use of his piece of land.

(2) The same applies in so far as a substantial prejudice is caused by the use of another piece of land in conformity with local custom and it cannot be prevented by measures, the financing of which can be reasonably expected of users of this kind. If by virtue of this, the owner must tolerate an interference, he may demand from the user of the other piece of land an appropriate settlement in money, if by the interference in conformity with local custom the use of, or income from, his piece of land is prejudiced over and above the expected degree.

(3) The causing of intrusion through a special conduit is not permissible.

§ 907. [Works threatening prejudice]

(1) The owner of a piece of land may demand that on adjacent land no works be installed or maintained as to which it is to be foreseen with certainty, that their existence or use will result in an inadmissible interference with his piece of land. If a plant satisfies the provisions of the State law, which prescribe a certain distance from the boundary or other protective measures, the removal of the plant may not be demanded until the inadmissible interference actually results.

(2) Trees and bushes do not belong to works within the meaning of these provisions.

§ 1004. [Claims for removal and for injunction]

(1) If the ownership is interfered with otherwise than by dispossession or withholding of possession, the owner may demand from the disturber the removal of the interference. If further interference is to be apprehended, the owner may sue for an injunction.

(2) The claim is excluded, if the owner is obliged to tolerate the interference.

5. REFORM PROPOSALS CONCERNING SOME OF THE BGB PROVISIONS REPRODUCED ABOVE DATED 24 SEPTEMBER 2001

§ 249 (2) sentence 2 added

When an object is damaged, the necessary sum of money in accordance with sentence 1 only includes VAT if and in so far as it is actually incurred.

§ 253 (2) added

If compensation is to be made because of injury to the body, health, freedom or sexual self-determination, fair compensation in money can also be demanded for harm which is not economic if

1. the injury was caused intentionally or
2. the harm is not insubstantial having regard to its type and duration.

§ 825 amended

A person who induces another by deceit, threat or abuse of a relationship of dependence to undertake or suffer sexual acts is obliged to compensate him for the harm arising out of this.

§ 828 amended

(2) A person who has completed his seventh but not his tenth year is not responsible for the harm which he has inflicted on another in an accident with a motor vehicle, a railway or a suspension railway. This does not apply if he has caused the injury intentionally.

(3) A person who has not completed his eighteenth year is, in so far as his responsibility is not excluded under paragraphs 1 or 2, not responsible for the harm which he inflicts on another, if, on commission of the act causing the harm, he does not have the understanding necessary for recognition of responsibility.

New § 839a introduced (Liability of a forensic expert)

(1) If an expert nominated by the court submits an incorrect report intentionally or with gross negligence, he is under a duty to compensate for the harm which arises for a party to the proceedings through a court decision which is based on this report.

(2) § 839 para 3 is to be applied accordingly.

§ 847 BGB repealed (but see § 253 (2) as amended)

6. THE BGB-REFORM IN FORCE AS OF 1 JANUARY 2002[*]

§ 195. The regular period of limitation is three years.

§ 199. (1) The regular period of limitation starts from the end of the year in which
1. the claim arises and
2. the creditor obtains knowledge or but for his gross negligence ought to have obtained knowledge of the circumstances that found his claim as well as of the debtor's identity.

(2) The claims for damages arising from injury to life, body, health, or violation of freedom are time-barred irrespective of when the claim arises and the victim obtains, or with gross negligence fails to obtain, knowledge after thirty years from the time at which the wrongful conduct occurred, the duty was breached, or the other event occurred that caused the damage.

(3) Other claims for damages are time-barred
1. irrespective of whether the victim obtains, or with gross negligence fails to obtain, knowledge within ten years from the time at which the claim arises
2. irrespective of when the claim arises and the victim obtains, or with gross negligence fails to obtain, knowledge within thirty years from the time at which the wrongful conduct occurred, the duty was breached or the other event occurred that caused the damage. Whichever of these limitation periods is shorter, prevails. . . .

§ 241. (1) The effect of an obligation is that the creditor is entitled to claim performance from the debtor. The performance may consist of refraining from acting.

(2) Each party to the obligation may according to the content of the obligation be required to apply proper care as to the rights and interests of the other party.

§ 276. (1) The debtor is responsible for recklessness and negligence, unless a stricter or less strict liability is otherwise provided or is to be inferred from the content of the obligation, especially if the debtor guaranteed performance or undertook the risk of supply. The provisions of §§ 827 and 828 apply.

(2) A person who does not exercise the care expected in daily affairs acts negligently.

(3) The debtor may not be released beforehand from responsibility for recklessness.

§ 280. (1) If the debtor violates an obligation he is liable to the creditor for the damages arising therefrom. This does not apply, when the debtor did not act wilfully or negligently. . . .

§ 311. . . . (2) An obligation involving duties according to § 241 (2) may also arise by
1. entering into contractual negotiations,
2. establishing contacts with a potential contract partner which allow this partner to affect the rights or interests of the other party, or
3. similar business contacts.

(3) An obligation involving duties according to § 241 (2) may also arise with regard to persons who are not meant to become a party to the contract. Such duties arise especially where a third party claims special trustworthiness for itself and thereby considerably influences the contract negotiations or the conclusion of the contract.

§ 852. If the person liable has acquired anything by the delict at the expense of the injured party, he is, even after the expiry of the limitation period, bound to return it under the provisions relating to the return of unjust enrichment. This claim is time-barred in

---

[*] A selection of provisions form the BGB affecting some of the material discussed in this book as amended by the *Gesetz zur Modernisierung des Schuldrechts* of 26 November 2001, BGB1 I, 3138.

ten years from the time it arose, or irrespective of the time at which the claim arises in thirty years from the time at which the wrongful conduct occurred or the other event occurred that caused the damage.

7. SOME PRELIMINARY OBSERVATIONS ON THE BGB IN GENERAL AND THE DELICT PROVISIONS IN PARTICULAR

A. The German Parliament passed the German Civil Code (BGB) on 1 July 1896, and it was promulgated by the Emperor on 18 August of the same year. Its coming into force on 1 January 1900 not only marked the end of the long codification process which had commenced with the appointment of the first Commission on 2 July 1874, but more importantly it also completed the unification of the modern German State. This "unification process" was tortuous and convoluted. But the landmark dates are three. First, is 1843, when the German Customs Union abolished the "internal" customs regulations between the various German States while, at the same time, erecting a common tariff wall to protect the "internal" economy from foreign competition. Then comes 1871, when the German Empire was founded under the strong hand of Bismarck. The last stage (as far as the civil law is concerned) is 1900, the year when the BGB came into force ending the fragmentation of the legal system that existed until that date.

The extent to which German law was fragmented prior to the codification is rarely fully appreciated. A glance at contemporary maps of Germany would give one an approximate idea of the different systems applicable in Germany on the eve of codification. In reality, however, even this picture would be misleading for two reasons. First because it would convey the impression that there were five legal "systems" vying for superiority whereas, in fact, alongside these there were—according to a memorandum submitted to the Reichstag—a multitude of other "systems", mostly hybrids of sorts. Secondly, maps showing the component parts of the German Empire might convey the impression that each "system" was limited to a particular "State" or locality, which was not the case. For example, the Prussian Code (*Allgemeines Landrecht für die Preussischen Staaten*)—enacted in 1794—applied to only seven of the eleven provinces of Prussia, but it also was in force in some parts of Bavaria and other localities of Germany linked with the Kingdom of Prussia. In fact in 1896, out of an estimated population of forty-two million, eighteen million lived under the Prussian Code. A further fourteen million were subject to the Common (mainly Roman) German law. Seven and a half million inhabitants were subjected to the Napoleonic Code, which was adopted in the Prussian Rhine Province, the Rhenish part of the Grand Duchy of Hesse, and the Bavarian Palatinate. Two and a half million lived under a Code enacted by the State of Saxony in 1863, and, finally, half a million more were subject to Scandinavian law. Voltaire's quip, that in his time in France one changed one's law as often as, when travelling, a man changed his horses, thus applied to Germany as well. The enactment of the Civil Code thus put an end to a confusing diversity of local law (Landesrecht e.g. the Bavarian and Prussian Codes), municipal law (Stadtrecht, e.g. Lübeck), customary law (Gewohnheitsrecht), French *Code civil* (applicable to the territories lying on the west side of the Rhine and Bade), and gemeines Recht which was the Roman law in those areas that had "received" it.

The picture of diversity was partly mitigated by the enactment, prior to codification, of a number of statutes, which applied to all the States. The Bill of Exchange Act (Allgemeine Deutsche Wechselordnung = ADWO) was the first such Act enacted by various States between 1848 and 1850 (following the Customs' Union of 1848). Others, dealing with such matters as criminal law, (Strafprozeßordnung), bankruptcy law, and commercial law (Allgemeines Deutsches Handelsgesetzbuch of 1861, replaced in 1900 by the Handelsgesetzbuch, many times updated and adapted since) followed and were later re-enacted as Imperial laws of the Reich.

Further reading

An account of German legal history and of the emergence of the West German State lies clearly outside the scope of this work. German legal history is usually taught either as part of constitutional history—usually called *Deutsche Rechtsgeschichte*—or focuses more on the institutions of private law and is called *Deutsches Privatrecht*. Fehr and Schwerin–Thieme have written treatises using the first title and their popularity and rich references have ensured successive editions. (Fehr's work is now in its 6th edn. (1962).) Mitteis–Lieberich have written on *Deutsche Rechtsgeschichte*, a work which is currently in its 19th edn. (1992). Hübner's *Grundzüge des deutschen Privatrechts* (1982) (reprint of 1930 edn.) was also translated into English in 1918 and appeared in the Continental Legal History Series under the title *A History of Germanic Private Law*. Other works on the subject have been written by: Coing, *Epochen der Rechtsgeschichte in Deutschland* (4th edn., 1981); Koebler, *Rechtsgeschichte* (4th edn., 1990); Kroeschell, *Deutsche Rechtsgeschichte* (I, 8th edn., 1987; II, 7th edn., 1989; III, 1st edn., 1989); Laufs, *Rechtsentwicklungen in Deutschland* (5th edn., 1996); Schlosser, *Grundzüge der neueren Privatrechtsgeschichte* (8th edn., 1996); Wesenberg–Wesener, *Neuere deutsche Rechtsgeschichte im Rahmen der europäischen Rechtsentwicklung* (4th edn., 1985) and last but by no means least the excellent work by Wieacker, *Privatrechtsgeschichte der Neuzeit unter besonderer Berücksichtigung der deutschen Entwicklung* (2nd edn., 1967). A more than adequate and very readable account in English of the development of modern European law can be found in von Mehren and Gordley, *The Civil Law System* (2nd edn., 1977) 3–96. For a more detailed account see: J P Dawson's classic *The Oracles of the Law* (1967). English accounts of the history of the codification can also be found in Schuster, "The German Civil Code" 12 *LQR* 17 (1896), Freund, "The New German Code", 13 *Harv. L. Rev.* 627 (1899–1900), Michael John's excellent *Politics and the Law in Late Nineteenth-Century Germany* (1989). This last work, however, may prove heavy going for those students who know little about 19th century German history. Mary Fulbrook's *A Concise History of Germany* (1990) offers to all "beginners" a most readable and informed introduction. For further references see also Zweigert and Kötz, *An Introduction to Comparative Law* (1998), para. 10, p. 132.

B. The BGB consists of 2,385 articles or, as they are more usually referred to, paragraphs. The BGB devotes thirty paragraphs (not including § 835 BGB which was repealed) to the law of torts—and they form the twenty-fifth title of the second book dealing with obligations. The term *unerlaubte Handlungen* is often used to cover the domain that Anglo-American lawyers would ascribe to "torts" but the term used precisely is best understood to cover faulty conduct (*Verschuldenshaftung*). The wider term *Deliktsrecht* probably covers better liability that is both based on fault (proved or presumed) and is strict. Contractual obligations, on the other hand, are covered by some 570 paragraphs (§§ 241–811 BGB) of which the first 191 (§§ 241–432 BGB) refer to problems common to all obligations. The remainder deal with specific contracts. They include sale and exchange (§§ 433–515 BGB), gift (§§ 516–34 BGB which, in the civil law systems, is regarded as a contract), lease (§§ 535–97 BGB), basic rules of labour law (§§ 611–30 BGB) and contract of labour and services (§§ 631 *et seq.*, BGB) and others. The law of *negotiorum gestio* (*Geschäftsführung ohne Auftrag*) follows in §§ 677 BGB while unjustified enrichment (*ungerechtfertigte Bereicherung*) is regulated by §§ 812 ff BGB.

The thirty paragraphs devoted to the law of tort represent a marked difference from the five articles devoted to this matter by the French Civil Code (Articles 1382–6 CC). This more systematic treatment of a subject is symptomatic of the more exhaustive approach taken by German lawyers. It also reflects the fact that between 1804—the year of the enactment of the French Code—and 1900—the year when the BGB came into force—legal science had made great forward strides and had considered in detail problems which were non-existent or relatively unimportant during the early part of the nineteenth century. The treatment offered by the two Codes on other matters, besides torts, supports the accuracy of this observation. Unjustified enrichment, for example, receives no particular treatment in the French Code, but, as stated, has eleven articles dedicated to it by the BGB (§§ 812–22 BGB). Similarly, the problems of offer and acceptance have, in France, been worked out by the courts without any legislative guidance beyond the requirement that there be consent. The BGB by contrast devotes (cross-references not included) thirteen articles to this subject (§§ 145–57 BGB) though, naturally, the case law has added considerable flesh to these bones.

The fairly detailed regulation of tort law, however, also represents a compromise to a dispute, which divided the members of the codifying Commission. For the authors of the first draft had reached the conclusion that widely drafted provisions were necessary in order to achieve full protection against tortious conduct. The first draft of the BGB thus contained in its § 704 (1) a general clause, which in substance if not in its number of words came very close to the general provision of § 1382 of the *Code civil*. (This Article still differed from its French predecessor insofar as it made use of the notion of "unlawfulness" which German law had inherited from the Roman law notion of *iniuria*. More, below (**at p. 79**). Indeed, both the Prussian and Austrian Codes contained such general clauses so the technique was far from unknown to the German jurists. On the other hand, the more casuistic approach to tort law—well known to Common lawyers—was also the method adopted by Roman law and this, it must be recalled, formed part of the legal heritage of most of Germany. In addition, many felt that a general clause type of regulation of the matter would only transfer the burden from the shoulders of the legislator to those of the judges. This was disliked. But even more suspect was the open-ended case law that could be found in France and which was treated with great scepticism by the Germans. In the end, therefore, the Code finally opted for a compromise, adopting three general provisions—§§ 823 I, 823 II, and 826 BGB—and some specific provisions, which dealt with a number of rather narrowly defined tortious situations. Thus § 824 BGB deals with cases where untrue statements damage one's credit. § 825 BGB imposes an obligation to pay compensation on anyone who has indecently induced a female person to have sexual intercourse with him. § 834 BGB deals with the liability of animal supervision; and § 836 BGB deals with liability to ruinous buildings, § 839 with the liability of public officials, etc. Such a mixture of the general with the particular was thus deemed the best compromise between the manifesto provisions of the French Civil Code and the pigeon hole approach derived from the English writ system.

A different and, perhaps, more meaningful way of dividing these tort provisions of the Code is as follows. One should first mention the provisions, which impose liability for fault. §§ 823 I and II, 824–6, 830, and 839 BGB come under this category and it should be stated immediately that (subject to the minor reservations given below) the Code system of liability is a system of fault-based liability. Then one should mention the provisions of the Code, which make liability depend on a rebuttable presumption of fault. §§ 831, 832, 833 (second sentence), 834, 836–8 BGB belong here. Thirdly, one should mention liability for created risks, independent of fault. A number of independent statutes deal with these situations, the most important being certain sections of the Strict Liability Act and the Road Traffic Act extracted below (chapter 3, section B. 3). Finally, in some cases one person

is liable strictly but for some other person's fault. In the Common law of vicarious liability we find the best example. As we shall see, German law does not take this view; but
various proposals for reform, if enacted, would place vicarious liability in this group.
Certain provisions of strict liability statutes (e.g. § 3 of the Strict Liability Act) also fall
into this category.

Three further preliminary points must also be made at this stage.

First, it must be stressed that the BGB is a typical product of the Pandectist scholarship, abstract, conceptual, and meticulous in the extreme. (For a more detailed sketch,
see chapter one of volume one of this series.) It is a Code which addresses itself to
lawyers—if not university professors—and thus lacks the vivacity and style of the French
or Swiss Codes, though it is certainly superior to its French competitor when it comes to
fullness, accuracy and consistency in the use of terms. Its influence has thus been felt in
countries as far apart as Greece and Japan (to mention just two countries). This impact
was largely because of the Code's intellectual power (which once led Maitland to describe
it as "the best code the world has yet seen") rather than to its immediate appeal to the
people whose lives it is meant to regulate. But there were other reasons, as well. In Greece,
for instance, the Roman law origins of the law were common to other countries; and it
was reinforced since the Bavarian Royal family provided in the nineteenth century the
first Kings of Greece.

The BGB's abstract conceptualism is immediately obvious in the first delict provision—
§ 823 I BGB—where the cardinal notion of unlawfulness (*Rechtswidrigkeit*) has provoked
rivers of ink to flow in an attempt to give it a precise meaning (see below, chapter 2, section
A. 3). In fairness, however, one must equally state that the Common law notion of "duty
of care" and the French notion of *faute* have given rise to similar difficulties in their
respective countries. Later on, we shall thus stress that for the purposes of comparison
these concepts should be down-played, where possible, and the lawyer should, instead,
look for the functions they wish to fulfil.

Second, §§ 823 ff. BGB are not independent and self-sufficient provisions of the Code
but must often be read in conjunction with other parts of it, particularly the general part
of the law of obligations. Numerous such cross-references will be encountered in the
pages that follow, but four important illustrations may be given at this stage.

The question of contributory negligence of the victim, which was the subject of
considerable controversy in French law during the 1970s and 1980s (in particular the
faute de la victime in the context of Article 1384 CC) is, essentially, regulated by § 254
I BGB. This makes the obligation to compensate the negligent plaintiff depend on
how far the injury has been *caused* predominantly by the one or the other party (plain-
tiff/defendant).

Another illustration of this trend can be found in the interpretation of the troublesome concept of unlawfulness. This, according to one school of thought (see below,
chapter 2, section A. 3), is satisfied whenever one of the interests enumerated by § 823 I
BGB has been infringed *in the absence of a legally recognised defence* (*Rechtfertigungsgrund*). But to determine this one must, *inter alia*, look at §§ 227–31, 904 BGB and their
interpretation by the case law.

A third illustration can be found in § 847 BGB, which allows monetary compensation
for injuries to body or health or for the deprivation of liberty. The full significance of this
paragraph can only be appreciated when it is realised that it forms an exception to the

general rule enunciated in § 253 BGB which prohibits monetary compensation for harm which is not damage to pecuniary interests *unless* otherwise provided by the Code. As will be explained later on one of the difficulties to which these provisions give rise is whether § 847 BGB can be extended analogically to cover instances other than the ones which it expressly provides for in the light of the categorical phrasing of § 253. This, incidentally, can raise the acutely controversial problem as to whether judges can also make law and not merely interpret the Code. It will be discussed briefly in section 6 of this chapter and also in the section dealing with the judicially created right of privacy (see below, cases 39–49). Finally, to complete this brief list of illustrations, mention should be made of § 278 BGB which has been closely linked with many attempts to circumvent the unfortunate provision of § 831 (discussed in detail in chapter 3, below).

The final preliminary point is really a warning to the Common lawyer not to expect to find in the law of tort all the material included in his own tort courses. Defamation, for example, is primarily a crime, though it may also have tort consequences if used in conjunction with § 823 II BGB (see also the rather limited provision in § 824 BGB). Liability for failure to act to save another person who is in danger appears primarily in the law of crimes (§ 323c StGB but serves more of an "educational function" than any real need in every day life). More importantly, perhaps, trespass to land and nuisance are not normally included in the German law of tort, but in the German law of property—though they may also attract the operation of the law of tort.

History can explain this difference. Roman law—from which most of the Western European systems derive—was, as is well known, a system based on a set of actions and conveyances. But with the progress of time—certainly by the middle of the third century AD—the emphasis shifted steadily from the form of action to the cause of action and from there to the right which the plaintiff was wishing to enforce. As actions became subservient to the rights they were designed to enforce, they inevitably started to move away from the law of actions into the law of property or obligations. The law relating to the formation and extinction of contracts and the law of delict easily slid into the law of obligations. The actions that helped assert proprietary rights caused more difficulties. Yet there was no doubt that in the end these actions, having shed their substantive content and, as a law of mere procedure, being thrust outside the Civil Code, would go with property rather than obligations. Thus, when the civilians, and above all the natural lawyers, began to tackle the work of classifying the law, many parts of it went into quite different pigeonholes from those which are familiar to Common lawyers with their forms of action abolished only the day before yesterday. Common lawyers must thus be prepared to find much of their law of torts in the civil law of property; the same is also true of the extensions (by analogy) of the proprietary actions dealing with matters which a Common lawyer would expect to find in his law of tort. The tort of nuisance is one such example.

Rei vindicatio was the Roman form of action that helped to establish property rights. That its progenies in modern German (and French) law would be regarded as incidental to ownership and thus be dealt with in the property sections of the codes (the third book of the BGB) is easy to comprehend. The same is true of the *actio confessoria* which helped protect rights less than ownership such as easements and life interests, and the *actio negatoria* which was given to an owner who wished to assert the freedom of his land from an easement. But then came the extension in the medieval and modern law. For suppose your neighbour does not walk across your land under a claim to an easement, but merely sends fumes across your land or makes life unbearable by noise. Can he not then be said to be really claiming something in the nature of an easement to these things even though no such easement would be recognised by the law? On that fictitious reasoning you can claim the freedom of your land from his encroachment as if it had been an easement, and your action will be an *actio quasi-negatoria*, which will sound in property and not in delict. From the substantive point of view, what will be in issue will be the ambit of ownership, not the personal duty of your neighbour not to commit a delict of encroachment. Incidentally, this attitude of mind led German law and some of its derivatives to restrict the remedy, if no fault were proved in the neighbour, to a declaration or injunction. French and Swiss law, on the other hand, which do not take their classifications so seriously, have found it possible to award damages as well. But to Common lawyers this is the tort of nuisance and hence a tort, for we think instinctively, even now that we have got rid of the forms of actions, of the wrong rather than the right. To the Common lawyer, therefore, the civilian classification is not always easy to understand and one of his first tasks will be to learn how to jump over the barriers of classification, which his own system has adopted.

Further reading

For further details see Lawson and Markesinis, *Tortious Liability for Unintentional Harm in the Common Law and the Civil Law* (1982) I, 36–41 and above all, Lawson, *A Common Lawyer Looks at the Civil Law* (1955).

8. THE CONSTITUTIONALISATION OF PRIVATE LAW

Traditional comparatists have, on the whole, underplayed the importance of public law compared to private law. For at least half of this century this may have been understandable as far as the English comparatists are concerned. For they, like the rest of the English lawyers, were under the pervading influence of Dicey who, through his misunderstanding of the French scene, had stunted all interest in administrative law during the first half of the twentieth century. Yet, paradoxically, even the French comparatists were (and still are) primarily *privatistes* and one explanation for this must surely be found in the dominant belief of the day that the study of the *civil codes* lay at the core of the legal formation.

   In recent times, however, interest in comparative public law has grown; and the impact that the constitutional law background has had on the development of private law is also attracting increased attention. The phenomenon is not limited to Germany. For example, students of American law are aware of the fact that in *New York Times Co.* v. *Sullivan* (376 US 254, 84 S. Ct. 710) the American common law of defamation yielded much ground to the constitutional requirement that free speech be safeguarded. (Attempts to extend these ideas to the area of products liability, e.g. defectively written manuals, have so far failed; but they are nonetheless indicative of the American tendency to constitutionalise much of the private law. On this see: Note, "Products Liability and the First Amendment" 59 *Indiana LJ* 503 (1984).) Similarly, *Roe* v. *Wade* (410 US 113, 93 S. Ct. 705 (1973)), by accepting that women had a constitutional right to choose to terminate their pregnancy, had an impact in other areas of tort law e.g., actions for wrongful birth. (*Berman* v. *Allan* 404 A. 2d 8; *Procanik* v. *Cillo* 97 NJ 339, 478 A. 2d 755, 1984.) For a doctor's negligent failure to warn a pregnant woman of the fact that, say, she was infected by rubella during the critical months of pregnancy, deprived her of her right to abort. In turn, this justified the award of damages (initially for emotional suffering only) in an action for wrongful birth.

The constitutionalisation of the civil law has, if anything, been even more dramatic and influential in Germany—though not in this area of the law, pro-bably because the Constitutional Court, itself, is divided on the issue. (See notes to cases 6–9.) But the growing impact of the Constitution on the private law of the land is a fact, so it is necessary to mention it, albeit briefly, even in a book devoted to the law of torts.

A principal aim of the Constitution of Bonn of 1949 (Basic Law—*Grundgesetz*) was to establish unequivocally the liberal, social, democratic order of the new state based on the principle of legality (*Rechtsstaat*). The memory of the national-socialist background, with its many attempts to discover and revive traditional Germanic values, had affected the law in almost all its aspects and was still alive well into the middle of the last century. So the framers of the Constitution, departing from the Weimar model, deliberately placed at the *head* of the constitutional text nineteen articles dealing with fundamental human rights (*Grundrechte*). (For the Nazi period see: Laufs, *Rechtsentwicklungen in Deutschland*; Weinkauf and Wagner, *Die deutsche Justiz und der National-Sozialismus* (1968). Articles 1–19 are reproduced in the next sub-section, below.) These rights primarily protect the citizen in his various dealings with the state. To what extent do they also regulate the relations between individuals? This is the so-called problem of *Drittwirkung der Grundrechte* and some authors (including some courts, e.g. the *Bundesarbeitsgericht*) have favoured the *direct* application of these constitutionally proclaimed rights in the area of private law. See, for example BAGE 4, 240 (employees have constitutionally protected rights of free speech against employers). Likewise, BAGE 1, 258 (labour agreements providing for lower wages for women may be invalidated), and BAGE 4, 274, (agreement which gives the employer the right to terminate contract on marriage of his employee may be invalidated. For a more recent example see: BAGE 46, 98.) The Federal Labour Court has in many cases maintained this stance despite the *Lüth* decision of the Constitutional Court which, as is explained in the text, refused to follow the "direct applicability" theory primarily expounded by the author and judge Hans Carl Nipperdey. The prevailing view, however, espoused by the *Bundesverfassungsgericht* (its important *Lüth* decision is reproduced below as case 36) has opted for a theory of *indirect* influence first strongly advocated by the distinguished constitutional lawyer Günter Dürig in "Grundrechte und Zivilrecht-sprechung", *Festschrift zum 75. Geburtstag von Hans Nawiasky* (1956) 158 ff. According to this the basic rights form an "objective system of values" (*objektive Wertordnung*). This, via the medium of the general clauses of the BGB (e.g. §§ 134, 138, 242, 826, etc., (used and abused by the Nazis: Hedemann, *Die Flucht in die Generalklauseln* (1933); Adami, "Das Programm der NSDAP und die Rechtsprechung", *Deutsches Recht*, 1939, 486), influences the private law. Thus, an injured party may, irrespective of nationality, by means of a constitutional appeal (*Verfassungsbeschwerde wegen Grundrechts verletzungen*; Article 93 I, no. 4a, GG), complain of any direct and actual (*unmittelbar und gegenwärtig*) violation of his rights. Such a complaint will be received by the Constitutional Court only after all other remedies have been exhausted; and, if successful, it will lead to the annulment of the offending law, decree, or judgment. (During the first thirty years of the court's life over 50,000 "requests" have been considered, the vast majority complaining about violations of fundamental rights.) Where, then, did this constitutionalisation of private law first manifest itself?

The answer must surely be first in the area of family law and then in a narrow but no less spectacular way in the creation of a general right of privacy. The latter creation will be considered in more detail in later sections of this book, so at this stage a few general observations will suffice.

What brought about the court revolution of the 1950s in the area of family law was the neglect of Article 117 of the Constitution of Bonn of 1949. This proclaimed that all legal norms (including those in the Civil Code) that were incompatible with the newly pro-claimed equality of sexes (Article 3, II, GG) would have to be abolished by 31 March 1953. (On this see: Nipperdey, "Gleicher Lohn der Frau für gleiche Leistung. Ein Beitrag zur Auslegung der Grundrechte" in *Recht der Arbeit,* 1950, 121 *et seq.*) This, however, did not happen since—in Professor Rheinstein's words—"the politically dominant group [in the ruling Christian-Democratic party included] both Catholic and Protestant [believers] who tend[ed] to identify the Christian pattern of family and society with the ancient pattern of the patriarchal family and general male dominance. [And] they were not overly zealous to implement a command that happened to find expression in the Constitution". ("The Law of Family and Succession" in A. Yiannopoulos (ed.), *Civil Law in the Modern World* (1965) 25–57, reprinted in his *Gesammelte Schriften* (ed.), H. G. Leser) (1972) 212, 219–20.) The combined action of the Constitutional Court (BVerfG NJW 1954, 65; BVerfGE 3, 225) and the Federal Court (in its earlier advisory opinion of 6 September 1953, BGHZ 11, 34) were the catalysts to this change. For these courts declared §§ 1354 BGB (the final word on all matters concerning marriage, including residence and domicile, belongs to the husband except where he is abusing this right) to be incompatible with the idea of equality between sexes. They took the same view with regard to § 1387 BGB (husband bears certain litigation costs during marriage). Having "tasted blood" the courts went further and, in a manner which is unique in the modern civil law systems, they pushed the entire law of marriage into a state of legislative vacuum in which, one by one, they fashioned the rules that they deemed compatible with the Constitution. This first phase did not come to an end until the *Gleichberechtigungsgesetz* of 18 June 1957, BGBl. 1, 609 (Act Concerning Legal Equality of Men and Women in Matters of Private Law) came into force.

Yet old attitudes die slowly and even though the new Act improved, among other things, the property rights of women after divorce by introducing the system of "community of acquired benefits" (*Zugewinngemeinschaft*), it left untouched other aspects of male pre-dominance. For instance, the father's pre-eminent powers in the context of parental authority (old § 1627 BGB) still remained alive. But the Constitutional Court having won the first round of battles with the Bundestag, again forced a change in the law, this time through its decision of 29 July 1959 (BVerfGE 10, 59). This process of rejuvenation of German family law was, in a sense, completed by the decision of 29 January 1969 (BVerfGE 25, 157; FamRZ 1969, 196) where the complete equality of legitimate and illegitimate chil-dren was established. If anything, this was an even more remarkable result than the pre-vious ones since in this case there was no time limit imposed by the Constitution on legislative reform, as there had been by Article 117 in the case of equality of the sexes. The intervention was, however, constitutionally inspired, based on Article 6 V, which required that legislation be passed to that effect.

A sketch of great judicial developments even as brief and as inadequate as the above, is bound to be crass. Yet it suffices to support the following statements. First, it shows that accounts (both by English and continental European lawyers) concerning case law in continental Europe and its significance in the development of the law hardly do justice to the subject. At best, they convey to a Common law reader a diminished picture of the role of the courts in the civil law system and confirm—tacitly at least—his misconcep-tion of civil law judges as law bureaucrats mechanically applying the Codes. Bureaucrats (in the sense of civil servants) they may be; automata deprived of will and vision they are not. Indeed, Article 132 of the Law Concerning Judicial Organisation expressly confers upon German judges a substantial power of judicial development of the law (*richterliche Rechtsfortbildung*) which is not (openly) matched in France and has hitherto received insufficient attention in the Common law world.

Secondly, the study of the case law itself gives the lie to the statement that the courts are not a creative source of law. Of course, this does not mean that the judge can create law by giving effect to his own personal views or considerations of expediency. Things, however, are different where the constitutional legislator has established a general and enforceable guiding principle (i.e. that of equality) as it did in Article 3 II of the Constitution. (Contrast with this, Article 109 of the Weimar Constitution.) In this case the legislator has, in effect, "transferred part of the law to be regulated by judicial decision" (BGHZ 11, 34). This is perfectly possible according to the Constitution which, though it gives the legislature a *dominant* position in the making of laws, it does not treat it as an *exclusive* one. According to the same decision "the doctrine of separation of powers which is constitutionally guaranteed is not violated whenever the judge is left to find the law within the parameters of a general norm" (such as that contained in Article 3 II). Indeed, the decision goes on, Article 117 I assumes that "as of 1 April 1953 the judge, through the gradual development of judge-formulated and accepted customary law, will progressively transform the general norms about equality into a more precise and generally binding set of rules". And the court concludes this part of the judgment by openly admitting that the combined effect of the aforementioned articles of the Constitution is to "entrust it with the task of bringing about the [constitutionally desired] equality of sexes by means of a judge-made law in the Anglo-Saxon fashion".

These are bold words and the court, itself, has on different occasions tried to disguise somewhat its creative role. But the disguise is thin at best, as the following statement of the Constitutional Court (taken from the development of the right of privacy) itself shows:

Occasionally, the law can be found outside the positive legal rules erected by the state; this is law which emanates from the entire constitutional order and which has as its purpose the "correction" of written law. It is for the judge to "discover" this law and through his opinions give it concrete effect. The Constitution does not restrict judges to apply statutes in their literary sense when deciding cases put before them. Such an approach assumes a basic completeness of statutory rules which is not attainable in practice . . . The insight of the judge may bring to light certain values of society . . . which are implicitly accepted by the constitutional order but which have received an insufficient expression in statutory texts. The judge's decision can help realise such ideas and give effect to such values (BVerfGE 34, 269).

Thirdly, the product of these judicial interventions was original. In fact it was more than that. For many of the ideas are transplantable and, in some cases, have expressly been followed by legislative attempts to reform other systems which, like the English, have shown themselves to have been more conservative (backward some might say) in matters of family law. In English, good accounts of the constitutional background can be found in Koch's *A Constitutional History of Germany* (1984) and Kommers' *The Constitutional Jurisprudence of the Federal Republic of Germany* 2nd ed. (1996) and Currie, *The German Constitution* (1997). A basic introduction (in English) to the *Drittwirkung* doctrine can be found in Markesinis, "Privacy, Freedom of Speech and the Horizontality of the Human Rights Bill" *1998 Wilberforce Lecture*, 115 (1999) *LQR* 47–88. See, also, Markesinis and Enchelmaier, "The Applicability of Human Rights as Between Individuals under German

Constitutional Law" in *Protecting Privacy*, (1998) (ed. Basil Markesinis). (The English literature on *Drittwirkung* is growing with the passion which one finds in newly discovered pleasures. Yet, though impressively good at analysing the wording of the Human Rights Act of 1998 (on which any attempts to introduce the idea in English law will have to depend) this literature seems to be text-oriented and doctrinally poor when compared with the German. What, in particular, is missing from the contemporary English discussions is any theoretical consideration of the need to abandon the traditional conception of human rights as binding only on the State and extending human rights to regulate the activity of "others" who wield excessive power such as trade unions, multinational corporations, and the Press. Also lacking all discussions is consideration of the dangers which the abandonment of the traditional doctrine about human rights could have for other basic principles of the law such as freedom of contract. But if this discussion has been poor in England, this is not the case in other "common law/mixed systems" such as that of the modern State of Israel where the Germanic ideas and even language have made great inroads largely as a result of the fertile mind of Chief Justice Barak.)

But family law was not the only area of private law that succumbed to constitutional dictates. The law of defamation and the development of the protection for human privacy offer further evidence of the encroaching cohabitation. We need do no more than mention them here for two reasons. The first and most important is because these topics will receive detailed attention later on in this book. (**See below, p. 74**) But there is a second reason why the subject need not detain us further at this stage and that is easy to state. For though reputation and privacy are protected in private law against offending or invading speech, they both form part of the wider notion of human dignity; and dignity like speech belong primarily to the constitutional sphere. Seen in this light, the invasion of constitutional ideas into the sphere of private law seems less brutal. But, later in the next chapter we shall encounter a new right—the right of an established and operating business—which the German courts created from the early part of the twentieth century in order to offer greater protection to the proper and efficient functioning of commercial enterprises. Or more capitalist and private law concern there thus could not be. And when later, the German courts discovered that protecting the economic life of the enterprise could mean curtailing the expression rights of those who criticised it, they opted, as is their style, for a balancing exercise of competing interests that was in strict adherence to the purest dictates of the proportionality principle. (See the *Konstanz* decision of the BGH of 26 October 1951, BGHZ 3, 270, reproduced in translated form, case 34). Yet this approach changed and the constitutional idea of free speech began to gain momentum from the time the "Hellfire" decision of the BGH was handed down in 1966. (BGH 21 June 1966, BGHZ 45, 296.) Longer translated extracts of the case are reproduced in van Gerven, *op. cit.*, at pp. 230–2. Here suffice to state one statement only where the Court tersely stated that ". . . the protection of personal legal interests must sometimes give way in order to secure the free discussion of important social issues." The Court was thus taking a stand here, in the area of commercial interests, as it was later to take the same stand in the area of personality rights. (See the *Greenpeace* decision of the BGH of 12 October 1993, NJW 1994, 124.) And the position of principle was simply. "There was a presumption that speech prevailed if it represented a contribution to the free discussion of important social issues." Many of the cases reproduced below in the privacy section of this book are thus replete with such statements giving the lie to those who argue that because Germany has an effective law of privacy it has down plaid speech rights. The result is a happy one; and we owe it to the cohabitation of private and public law.

9. THE HUMAN RIGHTS PROVISIONS OF THE CONSTITUTION
OF THE FEDERAL REPUBLIC OF GERMANY OF 8 MAY 1949 (AS
SUBSEQUENTLY AMENDED)

1. Basic Rights

Article 1 (Protection of human dignity)

(1) The dignity of man shall be inviolable. To respect and protect it shall be the duty of all state authority.

(2) The German people therefore acknowledge inviolable and inalienable human rights as the basis of every community, of peace and of justice in the world.

(3) The following basic rights shall bind the legislature, the executive, and the judiciary as directly enforceable law.

Article 2 (Rights of liberty)

(1) Everyone shall have the right to the free development of his personality in so far as he does not violate the rights of others or offend against the constitutional order or the moral code.

(2) Everyone shall have the right to life and to inviolability of his person. The liberty of the individual shall be inviolable. These rights may only be encroached upon pursuant to a law.

Article 3 (Equality before the law)

(1) All persons shall be equal before the law.

(2) Men and women shall have equal rights. The state shall promote the actual implementation of equal rights for women and men and take steps to eliminate disadvantages that now exist.

(3) No person shall be favoured or disfavoured because of sex, parentage, race, language, homeland and origin, faith, or religious or political opinions. No person shall be disfavoured because of disability.

Article 4 (Freedom of faith and creed)

(1) Freedom of faith, of conscience, and freedom to profess a religious or philosophical creed, shall be inviolable.

(2) The undisturbed practice of religion is guaranteed.

(3) No one may be compelled against his conscience to render military service involving the use of arms. Details shall be regulated by a federal law.

Article 5 (Freedom of expression)

(1) Everyone shall have the right freely to express and disseminate his opinion by speech, writing, and pictures and freely to inform himself from generally accessible sources. Freedom of the press and freedom of reporting by means of broadcasts and films shall be guaranteed. There shall be no censorship.

(2) These rights are limited by the provisions of the general laws, the provisions of law for the protection of youth, and by the right to inviolability of personal honour.

(3) Art and scholarship, research and teaching, shall be free. Freedom of teaching shall not absolve anyone from loyalty to the Constitution.

Article 6 (Marriage, Family, Illegitimate children)

(1) Marriage and family shall enjoy the special protection of the state.

(2) The care and upbringing of children are a natural right of, and a duty primarily incumbent on, the parents. The state shall watch over their endeavours in this respect.

(3) Children may not be separated from their families against the will of the persons entitled to bring them up, except pursuant to a law, if those so entitled fail or the children are otherwise threatened with neglect.

(4) Every mother shall be entitled to the protection and care of the community.

(5) Illegitimate children shall be provided by legislation with the same opportunities for their physical and spiritual development and their place in society as are enjoyed by legitimate children.

Article 7 (Education)

(1) The entire educational system shall be under the supervision of the state.

(2) The persons entitled to bring up a child shall have the right to decide whether it shall receive religious instruction.

(3) Religious instruction shall form part of the ordinary curriculum in state and municipal schools, except in secular (*bekenntnisfrei*) schools. Without prejudice to the state's right of supervision, religious instruction shall be given in accordance with the tenets of the religious communities. No teacher may be obliged against his will to give religious instruction.

(4) The right to establish private schools is guaranteed. Private schools, as a substitute for state or municipal schools, shall require the approval of the state and shall be subject to the laws of the *Land*. Such approval must be given if private schools are not inferior to the state or municipal schools in their educational aims, their facilities, and the professional training of their teaching staff, and if segregation of pupils according to the means of the parents is not promoted thereby. Approval must be withheld if the economic and legal position of the teaching staff is not sufficiently assured.

(5) A private elementary school shall be permitted only if the education authority finds that it serves a special pedagogic interest, or if, on the application of persons entitled to bring up children, it is to be established as an inter-denominational or denominational or ideological school and a state or municipal elementary school of this type does not exist in the commun[ity] (*Gemeinde*).

(6) Preparatory schools (*Vorschulen*) shall remain abolished.

Article 8 (Freedom of assembly)

(1) All Germans shall have the right to assemble peaceably and unarmed without prior notification or permission.

(2) With regard to open-air meetings the right may be restricted by or pursuant to a law.

Article 9 (Freedom of association)

(1) All Germans shall have the right to form associations and societies.

(2) Associations, the purposes or activities of which conflict with criminal laws or which are directed against the constitutional order or the concept of international understanding, are prohibited.

(3) The right to form associations to safeguard and improve working and economic conditions is guaranteed to everyone and to all trades, occupations, and professions. Agreements which restrict or seek to impair this right shall be null and void; measures directed to this end shall be illegal. Measures taken pursuant to Article 12a, to paragraphs (2) and (3) of Article 35, to paragraph (4) of Article 87a, or to Article 91, may not be directed against any industrial conflicts engaged in by associations within the meaning of the first sentence of this paragraph in order to safeguard and improve working and economic conditions.

Article 10 (Privacy of posts and telecommunications)

(1) Privacy of posts and telecommunications shall be inviolable.

(2) This right may be restricted only pursuant to a law. Such law may lay down that the person affected shall not be informed of any such restriction if it serves to protect the free democratic basic order or the existence or security of the Federation or a *Land*, and that recourse to the courts shall be replaced by a review of the case by bodies and auxiliary bodies appointed by Parliament.

Article 11 (Freedom of movement)

(1) All Germans shall enjoy freedom of movement throughout the federal territory.

(2) This right may be restricted only by or pursuant to a law and only in cases in which an adequate basis of existence is lacking and special burdens would arise to the community as a result thereof, or in which such restriction is necessary to avert an imminent danger to the existence or the free democratic basic order of the Federation or a *Land*, to combat the danger of epidemics, to deal with natural disasters or particularly grave accidents, to protect young people from neglect or to prevent crime.

Article 12 (Right to choose trade, occupation, or profession)

(1) All Germans shall have the right freely to choose their trade, occupation, or profession, their place of work and their place of training. The practice of trades, occupations, and professions may be regulated by or pursuant to a law.

(2) No specific occupation may be imposed on any person except within the framework of a traditional compulsory public service that applies generally and equally to all.

(3) Forced labour may be imposed only on persons deprived of their liberty by court sentence.

Article 12a (Liability to military and other service)

Article 13 (Inviolability of the home)

(1) The home shall be inviolable.

(2) Searches may be ordered only by a judge or, in the event of danger in delay, by other organs as provided by law and may be carried out only in the form prescribed by law.

(3) If particular facts justify the suspicion that any person has committed an especially serious crime specifically defined by a law, technical means of acoustical surveillance of any

home in which the suspect is supposedly staying may be employed pursuant to judicial order for the purposes of prosecution the offence, provided that alternative methods of investigating the matter would be disproportionately difficult or unproductive. The authorization shall be for a limited time. The order shall be issued by a panel composed of three judges. When time is of the essence, it may also be issued by a single judge.

(4) To avert acute dangers to public safety, especially dangers to life or to the public, technical means of surveillance of the home may be employed only pursuant to judicial order. When time is of the essence, such measures may also be ordered by other authorities designated by a law. A judicial decision shall subsequently be obtained without delay.

(5) If technical means are contemplated solely for the protection of persons officially deployed in a home, the measure may be ordered by an authority designated by a law. The information thereby obtained may be otherwise used only for purposes of criminal prosecution or to avert danger and only if the legality of the measure has been previously determined by a judge; when time is of the essence, a judicial decision shall subsequently be obtained without delay.

(6) The Federal Government shall report to the Bundestag annually as to the employment of technical means pursuant to paragraph (3) and, within the jurisdiction of the federation, pursuant to paragraph (4) and, insofar as judicial approval is required, pursuant to paragraph (5) of this Article. A panel elected by the Bundestag shall exercise parliamentary control on the basis of this report. A comparable parliamentary control shall be afforded by the Länder.

(7) Interferences and restrictions shall otherwise only be permissible to avert a danger to the public or to the life of an individual, or, pursuant to a law, to confront an acute danger to public safety and order, in particular to relieve a housing shortage, to combat the danger of an epidemic, or to protect young persons at risk.

Article 14 (Property, Right of inheritance, Expropriation)

(1) Property and the right of inheritance are guaranteed. Their content and limits shall be determined by the laws.

(2) Property imposes duties. Its use should also serve the public weal.

(3) Expropriation shall be permitted only in the public weal. It may be effected only by or pursuant to a law which shall provide for the nature and extent of the compensation. Such compensation shall be determined by establishing an equitable balance between the public interest and the interests of those affected. In case of dispute regarding the amount of compensation, recourse may be had to the ordinary courts.

Article 15 (Socialisation)

Land, natural resources, and means of production may for the purpose of socialisation be transferred to public ownership or other forms of publicly controlled economy by a law which shall provide for the nature and extent of compensation; the third and fourth sentences of paragraph (3) of Article 14 shall apply *mutatis mutandis.*

Article 16 (Deprivation of citizenship, Extradition)

(1) No one may be deprived of his German citizenship. Loss of citizenship may arise only pursuant to a law, and against the will of the person affected only if such person does not thereby become stateless.

(2) No German may be extradited to a foreign country.

Article 16a (Right of Asylum)

Article 17 (Right of petition)

Everyone shall have the right individually or jointly with others to address written requests or complaints to the appropriate agencies and to parliamentary bodies.

Article 17a (Restriction of basic rights for members of the Armed Forces etc.)

(1) Laws concerning military service and substitute service may, by provisions applying to members of the Armed Forces and of substitute services during their period of military or substitute service, restrict the basic right freely to express and to disseminate opinions by speech, writing, and pictures (first half-sentence of paragraph (1) of Article 5), the basic right of assembly (Article 8), and the right of petition (Article 17) in so far as this right permits the submission of requests or complaints jointly with others.

(2) Laws for defence purposes including the protection of the civilian population may provide for the restriction of the basic rights of freedom of movement (Article 11) and inviolability of the home (Article 13).

Article 18 (Forfeiture of basic rights)

Whoever abuses freedom of expression of opinion, in particular freedom of the press [paragraph (1) of Article 5], freedom of teaching [paragraph (3) of Article 5], freedom of assembly [Article 8], freedom of association [Article 9], privacy of posts and telecommunications [Article 10], property [Article 14], or the right of asylum [paragraph (2) of Article 16] in order to attack the free democratic basic order, shall forfeit these basic rights. Such forfeiture and the extent thereof shall be pronounced by the Federal Constitutional Court.

Article 19 (Restriction of basic rights)

(1) In so far as a basic right may, under this Basic Law, be restricted by or pursuant to a law, such law must apply generally and not solely to an individual case. Furthermore, such law must name the basic right, indicating the Article concerned.

(2) In no case may the essential content of a basic right be encroached upon.

(3) The basic rights shall apply also to domestic juristic persons to the extent that the nature of such rights permits.

(4) Should any person's right be violated by public authority, recourse to the court shall be open to him. If jurisdiction is not specified, recourse shall be to the ordinary courts. The second sentence of paragraph (2) of Article 10 shall not be affected by the provisions of this paragraph.

10. AMENDING THE CODE

Legal systems which adopt Codes, especially codifications of private law, treat them with great respect. Hierarchically, a Code stands below the country's constitution but no higher than any other piece of ordinary legislation. But in the national psyche it occupies a special place; and can even be seen as one of the country's symbols. There are many reasons for this. First, a code is the product of wide consultation and, invariably, a long—

or very long as is the case with the BGB—period of gestation. It is thus not seen as an embodiment of the party political will of the government that enacted it. Secondly, it attempts to provide a comprehensive regulation of the area of the law that it is codifying and, usually, this demands much effort to achieve consistency among its various parts. This was certainly true in the case of the German Civil Code and, in turn, made it difficult to tamper with one part of it without affecting others. In this book we shall thus encounter many situations where the tort answers are inter-related with positions adopted in other parts of the Code such as its General Part or its Family or Property law. Thirdly, through its language the code should be able to perceive and address problems in a broad way, thus making judicial development and adaptation of its text possible. Again, we shall encounter in the chapters that follow many examples of this even though at times the interpretation of a text borders upon a complete rejection of what the draftsmen had in mind. Fourthly, the German Code also facilitated its organic growth through its general clauses—such as the famous §§ 242 or 826 BGB—which gave judges even more room for creative work than the bulk of its provisions normally allow. All these attributes have enabled the German Code to withstand fairly successfully the enormous social, political, and economic challenges that confronted it throughout the twentieth century. This, however, does not mean that legislative amendments to its text did not also take place.

This is no place to discuss the precise form that they took. Thus, in some cases, individual provisions of the Code were either removed, amended, or new ones put in their place. (E.g. §§ 13, 14, 355-359 BGB, concerning consumer protection). In other cases, lengthier amendments/innovations were made and introduced into the Code (e.g. 651a–651l BGB, travel contract) while in yet others a new regime was created, governing a particular legal problem, but took the form of a statute that stood alongside the Code. An important example of proceeding in this way is found in the Law of General Conditions of Business. This enactment, which largely codified existing judge-made law, was probably kept outside the main framework of the Code because the legislature was anxious to enact it quickly and felt it unwise to wait for the longer process that would be involved if it tried to tamper with the text of the Code, itself. However, recently this enactment was incorporated into the code (§§ 305–310 BGB). For our purposes, a more relevant example can be found in the many strict liability statutes which are discussed below in chapter four. Here, however, one reason why this "new" material was kept outside the Code was because the view prevailed that the codal regime should remain consistent with the notion of fault-based liability. Yet in another group of cases, the Courts struck the first blow invalidating large parts of the 1900 Code as being incompatible to the new and hierarchically superior Constitution of 1949. This, as we noted earlier on, was the case with large parts of the family book of the Code until the legislator himself re-drafted it in the mid 1970s. As this book is about to go to print, we are experiencing changes in the law of obligations. The main impetus for reform is the Council Directive 1999/44 on Certain Aspects of the Sale of Consumer Goods and Associated Guarantees. However, the implementation of this directive forms part of a more comprehensive reform of the German law of obligations (Gesetz zur Modernisicrung des schuedrechts, extracts are reproduced above, 6). The reform affects tort law only marginally. The reader should note, however, the following three points. *First*, the limitation period for tort claims remains three years (§ 195 BGB), though its starting point is slightly altered (compare the old § 852 with § 199 I). § 199 II and III BGB now contain objective *maximum* periods of limitation. *Secondly*, § 280 BGB introduces a *common* remedy of damages for irregularities of performance; the burden of proof as to the debtor'a fault is placed on him. *Thirdly*, a number of concepts developed by case-law have now been included in the Code. For instance, § 311 II BGB incorporates the idea of *culpa in contrahendo* into the code, while § 311 III deals with obligations arising in relattion to strangers to the contract. Noteworthy is sentence 2 of § 311 III which mentions the factor of reliance. This may acquire particular relevance in "negligent misstatements" cases. (For a fuller discussion see pp. 59 ff., and notes to cases 19–24.) Yet, in assessing the impact of the reform one should bear in mind that the new texts show signs of the doctrinal disputes that must have taken place between the various members of the drafting committee. With respect, however, they also leave a fair number of points open to further discussion—a bait which the German academic world will, no doubt, be quick to take. Our prediction thus is that it will take years before the full meaning of the reformed provisions becomes clear by court decisions. (For a fuller discussion in English of this part of the law, imminently to be reformed, see Markesinis et al, *The German Law of Contract and Restitution*, (1997) chapter 6. From the abundant material on the highly controversial reform see for instance: Honsell, "Die EU-Richtlinie über den Verbrauchsgüterkauf und ihre Umsetzung in deutsches Recht", *JZ* 2001, 278; Heldrich, "Ein zeitgemäßes Gesicht für unser Schuldrecht" *NJW* 2001, 2521; and the papers of Professors W.-H. Roth, Ulmer, Canaris, Westermann, H. Roth, and Leenen in issue no. 10 of the *Juristenzeitung* 2001; all with further references).

From the perspective of tort law it suffices here to mention briefly one possible consequence of the reform. In chapter 2 section B.16 (cases 68–72) we will give examples from the jurisprudence of the BGH, in which damage to the product itself was regarded as physical damage to property within the meaning of § 823 I BGB (so called: *Weiterfresserschaden*). The advantage of tort in this area is the relatively long limitation period contained in § 852 I BGB, now § 195 BGB (three years). The specific criteria developed in order to decide when a buyer could rely on § 823 I BGB and avoid the short limitation period of § 477 I BGB (six month) have given rise to intricate and prolonged debates among academics as well as practitioners. (See notes to cases 68–75.) The reform entails a convergence of the limitation periods (contracts of sale: now two years compared to six month under the old § 477 BGB) and thus reduces the practical relevance of this issue. At least this is what the drafters hope to achieve. (Contrast Dr. Geiger's account in *JZ* 2001, 474 with the more sceptical views of Professor Zimmermann *et al* in *JZ* 2001, 684, 692). In England the parallel "complex structure theory" emerged in the context of interferences with buildings, not chattels, and was finally abandoned in *Murphy* v. *Brentwood DC* [1991] 1 AC 398. Recently, the BGH, 12 December 2000, *NJW* 2001, 1346, took a step in the opposite direction. It confirmed that the concept of *Weiterfresserschaden* stemming from the area of product liability could in principle also apply to buildings and their components. This is not to say, however, that problems of distinguishing damage to "components" of products from damage to "other property" than the product itself do not arise in English law in the area of product liability. (See Tettenborn, "Components and Product Liability: Damage to 'Other Property'", [2000] *LMCLQ* 338.)

Other proposed reforms will affect areas of the law of tort more directly and these we shall mention in the appropriate section of this book. But these tort-related reforms have not thus far received the same degree of attention as the ones previously mentioned. On the contrary, at the time of writing they are still at the stage of Regienurgsenting entous. (See, above, 5, and p. 820, below.) The account that will thus be given in the appropriate parts of the text must not be assumed to describe the new law but only give an indication of the re-orientation which is currently thought to be desirable.

11. BIBLIOGRAPHICAL SURVEY

The literature of the German law of torts is vast and growing faster than ever. For present purposes we can ignore references to classic works such as Enneccerus and Lehmann, *Recht der Schuldverhältnisse* (1958). However, for the sake of relative completeness three standard treatises must be mentioned: Staudinger's multi-volume *Kommentar zum Bürgerlichen Gesetzbuch—Recht der Schuldverhältnisse* II, §§ 823–825 (13th edn., 1999); §§ 826–829 (13th edn., 1998); §§ 830–838 (13th edn., 1997); §§ 839–853 (12th edn., 1986); Palandt's *Bürgerliches Gesetzbuch* (60th edn., 2001), and the newer but highly regarded *Münchener Kommentar zum Bürgerlichen Gesetzbuch—Schuldrecht* (Special part) 5, §§ 705–853 (3rd edn., 1997). All these are, essentially, reference works which, because of their frequent citations of the case-law, present a particular appeal to practitioners.

More academically oriented, but by no means less authoritative, are five excellent works: Larenz, *Lehrbuch des Schuldrechts* I (General part, 14th edn., 1987), II (Special part, first vol., 13th edn., 1986; second volume containing the law of torts, continued by Canaris, is in its 14th edn., 1994); Esser/Schmidt *Schuldrecht* (General part, first volume, 8th edn., 1995, second volume, 8th edn., 2000); Esser/Weyers, *Schuldrecht* (Special part, first volume, 8th edn. 1998, second volume containing the law of torts, 8th edn., 2000); Deutsch, *Allgemeines Haftungsrecht* (2nd edn., 1996); Fikentscher, *Schuldrecht* (9th edn., 1997).

Larenz's book is the classic post-war work on the subject, and its author, whose *Methodenlehre der Rechtswissenschaft* (6th edn. 1991) can also be usefully consulted, has justly enjoyed a great reputation in Germany. Esser/Weyer's work is no less erudite than Larenz's and often gives a different approach to problems of tortious liability; but, to foreign readers at any rate, it may appear more difficult to follow. Deutsch's book is a comparative newcomer in this class of books, but has had considerable impact on both the academic and judicial world. It contains in particular excellent accounts of such topics as "unlawfulness" and "culpability" on which the author had earlier written a notable *Habilitation* (*Fahrlässigkeit und erforderliche Sorgfalt*, 1963). The same author has entered the short textbook market also with his informative *Unerlaubte Handlungen, Schadensersatz und Schmerzensgeld* (4th edn., 2000). Other valuable works in this category include: Schlechtriem *Schuldrecht* II (Special part, 5th edn. 1998), Brüggemeier *Deliktsrecht* (1986).

Because of their smaller size Medicus's *Schuldrecht* II (Special part, 9th edn., 1999) (but see also his *Bürgerliches Recht* (18th edn., 1999)), and Kötz's *Deliktsrecht* (9th edn., 2001; together with Wagner) would probably be described by an American readership as "small-horn" books. Their size, however, should in no way detract from their great value; nor does it hide the indisputable scholarship of their authors. Medicus's work is a master-work of conciseness which, despite its size, does not eschew difficult or controversial points and often gives the author's own trenchant criticisms of the law. *Multum in parvo* aptly describes this work. Kötz's book is equally informative, and for a foreign reader even more readable than that of Medicus. Moreover, its author often uses his considerable comparative expertise to criticise in a stimulating and policy-orientated manner the positive law. The present work has been greatly influenced both in content and arrangement of material by these two excellent short books. Finally, from the growing literature that adopts the economic analysis of law, see Adams, *Ökonomische Analyse der Gefährdungs- und Verschuldenshaftung* (1985).

The periodic literature on the subject is enormous and references to it as well as to leading monographs will appear at the head of various sections of this book as well as in its footnotes. However, one work in particular must be singled out: it is von Caemmerer's

"Wandlungen des Deliktsrechts" in *Hundert Jahre deutsches Rechtsleben, Festschrift zum hundertjährigen Bestehen des Deutschen Juristentages, 1860–1960* (1960), reprinted in his *Gesammelte Schriften* (Collected Works) (1968) 452 ff. A long Article rather than a book, this masterly account of the changes in the law of delict brought about by the courts gives a general view of the whole law of civil responsibility. Von Caemmerer's influence on German delict law is probably unparalleled in our times and, in a sense, it is all the more remarkable since it has been exercised through learned articles rather than a fully fledged treatise—a form of writing so appreciated by the German legal mind.

The English literature on the subject is, on the whole, very poor. The most updated translation of the text of the Code (BGB) is by Forrester, Goren, and Ilgen entitled *The German Civil Code* (1975) (with an up-to-date supplement published in 1981), while certain portions of the BGB have also been included in translated form in Lawson and Markesinis, *Tortious Liability for Unintentional Harm in the Common Law and the Civil Law*, 2 vols. (1982) and von Mehren and Gordley, *The Civil Law System* (2nd edn., 1977).

Until recently English-speaking readers had to content themselves with two books: Rayan's *An Introduction to the Civil Law* (1962) (dealing with French and German law) and Cohn's *Manual of German Law*, 2 vols. (1968, 1971). Though the latter was in many respects the more satisfactory of the two, they were both elementary, their aim being to give the general reader some knowledge of the German legal system as a whole rather than to provide him with a detailed knowledge of a single branch of German law or supply him with further aids for research. They also make little or no use of the rich case-law. More recently, another introductory book has appeared written by Professors Horn, Kötz, and Leser. It is entitled *German Private and Commercial Law: An Introduction* (1982) and despite some shortcomings (see this author's review in [1982] *Cambridge Law Journal* 360) it is in many respects a useful book which will, no doubt, be greatly appreciated by the complete beginner. But its delict section (chapter 9) is largely based on §§ 17–20 of Zweigert and Kötz's *An Introduction to Comparative Law* and if the reader has a choice of reading either of these books, he is advised to use the latter rather than the former work. Nigel Foster's recent *German Law and Legal System* (1993) is the latest book about German law written in English which, in a mere 336 pages provides a brief but good introduction to the entire legal system.

At a more sophisticated level mention should be made of six works. First and foremost is vol. XI of the *International Encyclopaedia of Comparative Law* edited by Professor A Tunc. Some of the leading authorities on the subject have collaborated to produce a book, which, though its parts are uneven in some respects, represents a work of great erudition and a veritable mine of information, though it is rapidly becoming out of date.

The second work that must be singled out here is Zweigert and Kötz, *An Introduction to Comparative Law* (3rd end., 1998). Superbly translated into English by Tony Weir, it achieves a closely-knit exposition of the American, English, French, and German law of contract and tort and is indisputably one of the masterpieces of comparative law literature.

Von Mehren and Gordley, *The Civil Law System* (2nd edn., 1977) is the third significant work in this field. A selection of translated cases, accompanied by other supporting material and the authors' own pertinent commentary, has for many years made this work the ideal book for the comparative study of the law—especially for American law schools which are accustomed to operate through case-books.

Lawson and Markesinis, *Tortious Liability for Unintentional Harm in the Common Law and Civil Law*, 2 vols. (1982) should, perhaps, also be added to this section of the bibliography. Though by no means a textbook in the usual format taken by this species of legal works, it is a work essentially for law students. Its main aim is to attempt a "thematic" exposition of certain problems of the law of torts in America, England, France, and Germany and to single out the similarities rather than the differences that exist between these four legal systems. Each chapter of vol. I contains extensive bibliographical references and vol. II provides a selection of materials (mainly French and German cases). It can be used either on its own or as a "companion volume" to vol. I.

Walter van Gerven's *Tort Law* (full title: *Cases, Materials and Text on National, Supranational and International Tort Law*) 2nd edn. published in 2000 must also be mentioned here. As the title suggests, this is a casebook, accompanied by lengthy and often perceptive annotations. The unusual feature of this book is that it does not limit its scope to German law but includes approximately equal number of references to French law and a somewhat small number of extracts to other European systems.

Finally, we must mention Professor Christian von Bar's massive *Common European Law of Tort*, 2 vols (English text, 1999 and 2000). This remarkable work, the fruit of a collective research effort under the guidance and leadership of Professor von Bar, is likely to be of more use as a reference work than a classroom tool.

More specialised literature in English on German law is referred to in various sections of this book. A full list can be found in the impressive work that Professor Szladits has for many years now been conducting for the Parker School in New York. It is published periodically under the title *A Bibliography of Foreign and Comparative Law*. Finally, references to Anglo-American law can be found in the introductory sections of each chapter but especially in the notes that accompany the translated German judgments.

2
Liability under § 823 I BGB

SECTION A. COMMENTARY

1. INTRODUCTORY REMARKS

AMONG the three general provisions of the BGB—§§ 823 I, 823 II, and 826—§ 823 I has, traditionally, been accorded a special pre-eminence even though we shall see that § 823 II BGB is nowadays considered as a close rival, and for some writers, has an even wider potential ambit. Compared with § 826 BGB, § 823 I BGB is both wider and narrower. It is "objectively" narrower, in so far as it can be invoked only if one of the enumerated interests (discussed below) has been violated, whereas there is no such limitation with § 826 BGB. In practical terms, the "kind of harm" which is *not* protected by § 823 I BGB is economic loss (unless it results out of the violation of the interests and rights protected by § 823 I BGB; i.e. unless it is consequential upon physical damage or it follows from the violation of intellectual property rights, the right to free movement etc.), whereas claims for economic loss are the most usual claims brought under § 826 BGB. § 823 I BGB is, however, "subjectively" wider than § 826 BGB in so far as it covers intention as well as negligence, whereas § 826 BGB is limited to intentional activities which, in addition, must be *contra bonos mores*. On the other hand, the ambit of § 823 II BGB is made to depend on the notion of "protective law" (*Schutzgesetz*). Its effect is to give rise to civil liability in the event of a violation of some statute or other enactment—usually of a criminal nature—if this enactment is a "protective law" in the sense that will be explained below. The only additional requirement introduced by this section is that if the protective law in question imposes liability irrespective of fault, additional civil liability will not be engendered unless the defendant was also guilty of fault. (See chapter 4, below.)

For an action to be based on § 823 I BGB the following requirements must be satisfied. First there must be a violation through human conduct of one of the enumerated rights (*Rechte*) or interests (*Rechtsgüter*), namely, life, body, health, freedom, property, or any "other right" (*sonstiges Recht*). The use of these concepts allows German law to restrict liability from the very outset in a clear and manageable manner. In essence, therefore, this approach does for German law what the notion of duty of care does for the Common law though it is done in a pre-determined (and thus arguably clearer) manner. Secondly, this interference must be unlawful (*Rechtswidrigkeit*). Thirdly, it must be culpable (intentional or negligent). Finally, there must be a causal link between the defendant's conduct (which can be an act or an omission) and the plaintiff's harm as defined by this paragraph. We shall examine these four elements in turn.

2. THE RIGHTS AND INTERESTS PROTECTED BY § 823 I BGB

Select bibliography

Von Bar, *Gutachten und Vorschläge zur Überarbeitung des Schuldrechts—Deliktsrecht*, herausgegeben vom Bundesminister der Justiz (1980); *idem*, "Probleme der Haftpflicht für deliktsrechtliche Eigentumsverletzungen" no. 55 *Mannheimer Vorträge zur Versicherungswissenschaft* (1992); Brüggemeier, "Gesellschaftliche Schadensverteilung und Deliktsrecht", *AcP* 1982 (1982) 385; von Caemmerer, "Wandlungen des Deliktsrechts", *op. cit.* (select bibliography, above, p. 41); *idem*, "Die absoluten Rechte in § 823 I BGB", reprinted in *Gesammelte Schriften* I, 554; *idem*, "Das Verschuldensprinzip in rechtsvergleichender Sicht", *RabelsZ* (1978), 1; Canaris, "Schutzgesetze—Verkehrspflichten—Schutzpflichten", *Festschrift für Larenz* (1983) 27; Deutsch, "Entwicklung und Entwicklungsfunktion der Deliktstatbestände", *JZ* 1963, 385; *idem*, "Freiheit und Freiheitsverletzung im Haftungsrecht" *Festschrift Hauss* (1978) 43; *idem*, "Entwicklungstendenzen des Schadensrechts in Rechtsprechung und Wissenschaft", *JuS* 1967, 152; *idem*, "System und Aufbau der Schadenshaftung im Deliktsrecht" in *Festschrift F. Weber* (1975) 125; idem, "Die neuere Entwicklung der Rechtsprechung zum Haftungsrecht", *JZ* 1984, 308; *JZ* 1990, 733; Fabricius, "Zur Dogmatik des "sonstigen Rechts" gemäss § 823 I BGB", *AcP* 160 (1961) 273; Fraenkel, *Tatbestand und Zurechnung bei § 823 I BGB* (1979); Honig, "Die neuere Entwicklung der Rechtsprechung zum Haftungsrecht", *JZ* 1984, 308; Hübner, "Zur Reform von Deliktsrecht und Gefährdungshaftung", *NJW* 1982, 2041; Kupisch-Krüger, "Grundfälle zum Recht der unerlaubten Handlungen", *JuS* 1980, 270, 422, 574, 727; *JuS* 1981, 30, 347, 584, 737; idem, *Deliktsrecht* (1983); Lang, *Normzweck und Duty of Care* (1983); Leser, "Zu den Instrumenten des Rechtsgüterschutzes im Delikts- und Gefährdungshaftungsrecht", *AcP* 183 (1983) 568; Lorenz, "Verkehrspflichten zum Schutze fremden Vermögens", 25 *Jahre Kalrsruher Forum* 48 (1983); Löwisch, *Der Deliktsschutz relativer Rechte* (1970); Mertens, "Deliktsrecht und Sonderprivatrecht. Zur Rechtsfortbildung des deliktischen Schutzes von Vermögensinteressen", *AcP* 178 (1978) 227; Reinhardt, "Das Subjektive Recht in § 823 I BGB", *JZ* 1961, 713; Schildt, "Der deliktische Schutz des Rechts am Gewerbebetrieb", *WM* 1996, 2261; Schulz, "Überlegungen zur ökonomischen Analyse des Haftungsrechts", *VersR* 1984, 608; Stoll, *Richterliche Fortbildung und gesetzliche Überarbeitung des Deliktsrechts* (1984); Taupitz, "Der deliktsrechtliche Schutz des menschlichen Körpers und seiner Teile", *NJW* 1995, 745; *idem*, "Ökonomische Analyse und Haftungsrecht—Eine Zwischenbilanz", *AcP* 196 (1996), 114; Wussow, *Unfallhaftpflichtrecht* (14th edn. by Dressler, 1996); Zeuner, "Historische Linien in der Entwicklung des Rechts am Gewerbebetrieb, des allgemeinen Persönlichkeitsrechts und der Verkehrssicherungspflichten", *VersR* 1983, 196. *In English*: Opoku, "Delictual Liability in German Law" 21 *Int. Comp. L. Quart.* (1972) 230; Zweigert and Kötz, p. 598.

(a) Life

Interference with "life" here means killing a person, in which case the claim for compensation rests with third parties, their claim being based on §§ 844–6 BGB (see below). This, of course, is principally the action which an English Common lawyer would describe as the fatal accident action and American lawyers would consider under their Wrongful Death Statutes. It is, in other words, the *new* action given by *statute* both in Anglo-American law (since it was never recognised by the Common law) and the German Code (§ 844 BGB) to the "dependants" of the deceased (primary) victim for their loss of dependency. (Reimbursement of funeral expenses (*Beerdigungskosten*) by whomsoever has legally incurred them is also available.) The question of the deceased's own action—to be brought by his estate—is, of course, another matter and one which—in the civil law systems in general—is related to the part of the law which deals with succession or the administration of the estates. However, the delict section of the Code does contain one provision, which is relevant to this matter. It is § 847 I BGB, which, principally deals with monetary compensation for pain and suffering for living plaintiffs (and thus forms a clear legislative exception to the restrictive § 253 BGB). But it also allows such a claim to be brought by the plaintiff's estate for the deceased's pain and suffering, suffered between accident and death. But, unlike other systems (e.g. French law, the USA under the headings of loss of consortium etc.), German law gives no damages for *solatium*, bereavement, or other forms of pain and suffering to the deceased's dependants.

§§ 844–6 BGB deal, as stated, with the *new* action given to the victim's "dependants". They are discussed in greater detail in chapter 4, below. The reader is urged to read (if not study) this material at an early stage so that the (relevant) points made in this section are fleshed out in a more satisfactory way. For present purposes, it will suffice to note that § 844 II BGB specifies the "dependants" by reference to those persons whom the deceased would have been "obliged to support by law" (*kraft Gesetzes unterhaltspflichtig*). Who these people are can be found in the family law section of the BGB. They, obviously, include spouses and minor children (§§ 1360, 1602 BGB), all ascendants in the direct line (§ 1601 BGB) and (in certain circumstances) even separated (§ 1361 BGB) and divorced spouses (§§ 1569 ff. BGB), subject always to the detailed provisions contained in the family law book of the BGB. In his meticulousness, the German legislator has also provided at the end of § 844 II BGB that a child conceived but unborn at the time of the injury is not excluded as a potential claimant.

(b) Body and health

These headings cover any adverse interference with the person without consent (which is discussed below at pp. 536 ff.). Terminological precision has, again, dictated the use of two words—the first signifying any interference with the body of the plaintiff, such as severing his finger, breaking his leg, or external abrasions of the kind typically found in car accident cases. Interference with the plaintiff's health, on the other hand, refers to externally provoked malfunctions of his inner body. Internal infections, gastro-enteritis, bacterial infection, inhalation of poisonous fumes, etc. would come in this category as, might in appropriate circumstances, loss of sleep. (On this possibility see: BGH 25 September 1970, MDR 1971, 37: noise from neighbouring land preventing plaintiff from sleeping.) Psychological disturbances that we would classify under the heading of psychiatric injures would also be brought under this heading though not, of course, mere pain, grief and suffering. Under this heading, the BGH has also held that the transmission of the aids virus constitutes an injury to health even when it has not yet developed into AIDS. Rendering the plaintiff HIV positive is thus actionable under the heading of interference with health even though the infection has "not apparently affected the plaintiff's physical condition". "For the contamination of blood with HIV is known to have devastating consequences for the person affected and those who come in close contact with him . . . ". (BGH 30 April 1991, NJW 1991, 1948). In all these instances, the interference must emanate from a source *external* to the plaintiff. Nevertheless, even when this requirement is satisfied, the full extent of the plaintiff's hurt may be partly attributable to the external factors and partly linked with his own constitution or predisposition as, for example, some kind of dormant cancer. Whether this result, as well, can be attributed to the defendant's conduct is a question of legal cause and will be discussed in § 5, below.

In German law (as in other systems) physical injury is widely compensated. In *The Hua Lien* ([1991] 1 *Lloyd's Rep.* 309, 328–9) Lord Brandon maintained that "in most claims in respect of physical damage to property [and, one might add, personal injury] the question of the existence of a duty of care does not give rise to any problem, because it is self-evident that such a duty exists and the contrary view is unarguable." This "duty" language may not be entirely appropriate to German law, but the general idea expressed by the statement is as true of German law as it is of English and American law. In this spirit of generosity, the BGH has since 1993 also treated the accidental destruction of frozen sperm deposited in a "sperm bank" as amounting to physical harm. It thus awarded to the donor who had deposited the sperm in the bank in the light of his impending sterility damages worth DM 25,000 for pain and suffering (BGH 9 November 1993, NJW 1994, 127 = JZ 1994, 464.) The judgment held that parts of a human body, once detached from it, can be treated for the purposes of tort law as "things". But if they are destined to be "re-introduced into the body" or perform a function typically ascribed to the human body, then interference with them should be treated as interference with the human body for the purposes of § 823 I BGB. Understandably, the decision, reversing a contrary decision of the Court of Appeal, has not passed without comment. (See: Laufs, "Schmerzensgeld wegen schuldhafter Vernichtung deponierten Spermas?", NJW 1994, 775.) Nonetheless, it is a remarkable proof of judicial inventiveness when faced with the problems that result from new medical technology. (The case is translated in van Gerven, pp. 147–9.)

To the above possibilities for compensation arising from the "ordinary" regime one must now also add specific statutory regimes such as the AIDS Act of 24 July 1995 (Gesetz über die humanitäre Hilfe für durch Blutprodukte HIV-infizierte Personen. The earlier French statute—Loi 91—1406 of 31 December 1991—dealing with this problem is briefly discussed in English by van Gerven, Cases, Materials and Texts, op cit., pp. 629 ff. Though the reason behind these enactments is the same in both countries, the way they have handled the problem is different so the comparison of the two regimes offers an interesting comparative exercise. In both systems, the question of the inter-relationship of these new, special regimes and the ordinary, tort rules can raise delicate questions. The same points can, incidentally, be raised of the traffic accident regimes of both of these countries. The relevant German Act is discussed below at p. 728). To deal with this problem, the German statute has set up a Foundation, endowed with a substantial capital provided by the Federal Government, the Länder, major pharmaceutical companies, and the blood bank of the German Red Cross. Independent persons who must perform their duties in absolute secrecy administer this fund. Persons proving to have received a blood transfusion in Germany prior to 1 January 1988 and producing a medical certificate stating that they are now HIV positive (or suffering from AIDS), will be presumed to have suffered the illness from the transfusion. Without more, they are then entitled to receive DM 1,500 per month in the first instance or DM 3,000 in the second. Special provisions in the statute also extend these rights to a number of other persons such as the spouses, fiancés, or cohabitees of the recipients of the infected blood. Decisions taken by the Administration Council of the Foundation (Stiftungsrat) can be appealed before the normal administrative courts.

Notwithstanding the above general generosity that the legal system adopts towards physical injury, there do exist (in German as well in Anglo-American law) three "types" of physical injury which have given rise to considerable difficulties. These situations involve nervous shock, pre-natal injuries (including pre-conception injuries) and claims for "wrongful birth and wrongful life." To these last claims, one must also add an interesting variant—the so-called wrongful conception (and failed sterilisation) cases.

Nervous shock, or as it is nowadays more accurately called "psychiatric illness", is one kind of interference with a person's health which has given rise to many difficulties in German law, as well as English and American law. It should be noted at the outset that in Germany private or social insurance schemes, to be discussed in chapter 4, will often take care of the matter. Shock may be the result of fear generated for one's own safety and personal integrity or it may be the result of witnessing some gruesome accident. Should recovery here be limited only to nervous shock suffered by close relatives of the victim or to persons who only saw or heard the accident with their own unaided senses (but not to those who some time after the accident became aware of its consequences, perhaps through hearsay)? And should well-intended rescuers, who come to the accident scene to offer their services and are subject to horrifying sights, be all allowed to claim damages for their shock? Three cases dealing with these matters are reproduced below (cases 1–3) and should be read in conjunction with their annotations in order to obtain a fuller picture of German law. (In chapter 4 at p. 922 the reader can find an overview of current awards for non-pecuniary harm in cases of nervous shock.) Here suffice it to say that psychiatric injury is, clearly, injury to health in the sense of § 823 I BGB, so long as it entails medically recognisable physical or psychological consequences which would not have been suffered by the ordinary, not over-sensitive, citizen.

The decision of the BGH of 11 May 1971 (BGHZ 56, 163 = Case 1, below), though not without its critics, is still good law. It illustrates, especially when read in conjunction with other similar decisions, the strong emphasis that German courts put on the seriousness and extraordinary nature of the shock before they treat it as compensatable (for a more recent confirmation see: BGH NJW 1989, 2317 = Case 2, below). The expression often used is that the shock must be an "appropriate" and "understandable" (*verständliche*) consequence of witnessing *or being told* of the accident. The italicised words suggest an area of difference with Anglo-American law; otherwise, however, the terms used imply flexible standards which, more often than not, do not seem to work in favour of plaintiffs. Thus, shock suffered as a result of being told that one's car was damaged has not been allowed. (LG Hildesheim, VersR 1970, 720). Likewise, no compensation was given for shock suffered by the plaintiff when he was told that the police were investigating a close relative. (LG Hamburg NJW 1969, 615.) Further, though a close family relationship with the primary victim will, typically, make it easier for the plaintiff to obtain damages for his nervous shock, it is by no means obvious that this is seen as a rigid, additional condition for recovery. The issue has not been decided by the BGH. However, in OLG Stuttgart VersR 1988, 1187 the court restricted the scope of claims based on distant shock to relatives.

Thus, non-relatives of the prime victim have often been denied recovery (LG Tübingen NJW 1968, 1187; LG Stuttgart VersR 1973, 648). But an accompanying *fiancée* has succeeded; and, in similar circumstances, so might a partner in a "serious love relationship" (LG Frankfurt NJW 1969, 2286). If the shock leads to a premature birth, the *nasciturus* may also be entitled to sue for any damages that he may have suffered (BGH NJW 1985, 1391). (For further details see: *Münchener Kommentar*-Grunsky, Vor § 249 BGB, nos. 54 and 54a)

Can one draw any preliminary conclusions from such a brief sketch? Three, perhaps, can be put forward here, though somewhat tentatively since cases such as those cited above technically have no value as precedents and can only serve as indications of how a court might decide a case.

First, German law is more generous than the Common law in cases of distant shock; this *may* be due in part to the absence of juries and a smaller and more closely-monitored medical profession which reduces the chances of "faked" medical evidence. It is also potentially more open-minded towards claims brought by non-relatives. Secondly, in other contexts the greater "generosity" of German law may be more apparent than real. This seems reasonable enough to infer from the fact that (*a*) many claims which would be unacceptable to the Common law are also rejected by the German courts and (*b*) that damages awarded under this heading to successful claimants seem to be modest. Finally, and from a purely conceptual point of view, it may be worth noting that German courts tend to approach problems of nervous shock in terms of causation (rather than duty). Increasingly, however, German writers are recognising that the demarcation line really depends on policy considerations and that causative language merely provides the technical device to draw these lines rather than explaining why some plaintiffs fall on their wrong side. To these writers, therefore, the main attraction of the German approach may, lie in the fact that it makes the seriousness of the harm the determinative factor rather than basing recovery on such fortuitous elements as the plaintiff's proximity to the scene of the accident or his familial relationship with the primary victim.

Pre-natal injuries is the second kind of "physical" injury that has given rise to considerable difficulties both in German law and the Common law systems. There are a number of reasons why this is so. First, the *nasciturus*—as the child still in the womb is often called in the civil law systems—though a "living entity" is not a person. If it is to be accorded legal rights, these may be in conflict with those of the mother (e.g. right to live and to abort). Secondly, it may be thought proper to vest some of these rights immediately (e.g. after a certain period, usually the twenty-fourth week of pregnancy, you may not kill the embryo) while others will mature upon live birth. The right to inherit belongs to this category (§ 1923 II BGB). As we shall observe in the notes to cases 4 and 5 (reproduced below), German and English law adopt the same position with regard to the right to sue for injuries sustained while *in utero*: the rights of the nasciturus vest only upon live birth. On the other hand, some (but not all) American courts do not require "live birth" and are willing to grant tort actions to persons who were merely "viable" at the time of the injury (even if there was subsequently no live birth). This solution can accentuate the third difficulty that these cases create namely, difficulties with causation and proof.

The protection afforded by German law goes beyond this point as the decision in BGHZ 8, 243 (reproduced below as case 5) clearly shows. In chronological terms this is a pioneering decision, allowing an action to a child born with impairments as a result of a tortious act which took place prior to conception. In the main, the Common law solutions in this context are similar to the German.

The third and last category of "physical" injury cases which have given trouble to the courts (both in Common law and Civil law jurisdictions) involve three kinds of actions. These include the so-called "wrongful life" and "wrongful birth" cases (involving the birth of impaired children) and the "wrongful conception" cases (involving birth of healthy (but sometimes also impaired) children following a failed sterilisation operation). All these are claims more modern in origin and raise profound philosophical questions as well as difficult questions of evaluation of damages. This time, developments in this field started in the USA and later spread to European systems. BGHZ 86, 240 (reproduced as case 6) and the decision of the Supreme Court of New Jersey in *Procanik* v. *Cillo* (reproduced as an appendix to the German decision) bring out very clearly most of the relevant points. For further details the reader is thus referred to the notes that accompany these two leading cases. (See, below, pp. 178–186) Here suffice it to say that German law has produced a rich and not always easily reconcilable case law. The German picture is further confused by the existence of two important decisions of the Constitutional Court, which have given diametrically different opinions on this issue. In fact, the first of these (BVerfGE 88, 203, reproduced as case 7) left the BGH singularly unimpressed. (BGH *NJW* 1994, 788, Case 8). On the other hand, the second decision of the Constitutional Court generally sided with the traditional liberal view that allowed such claims. (See, BVerfGE 96, 375, Case 9).

Further reading

For nervous shock in German law see, *inter alia*, Berg note to LG Frankfurt of 23 March 1969 in *NJW* 1970, 515; Deutsch/Schramm, "Schockschaden und frustrierte Aufwendungen", *VersR* 1990, 715; von Hippel, "Haftung für Schockschäden Dritter" *NJW* 1965, 1890; Karczewski, *Die Haftung für Schockschäden* (1992); Krüger, "Schadensersatzprobleme bei sogenannten Schockschäden", *JuS* 1986, 214; Park, *Grund und Umfang der Haftung für Schockschäden nach § 823 I BGB* (1997); E. Schmidt, "Schockschäden Dritter und adäquate Kausalität", *MDR* 1971, 538; *Münchener Kommentar*, Vor § 249 BGB, nos. 53–56; § 823 no. 57. English: Fleming, "Distant Shock in Germany and Elsewhere" 20 *A. J. Comp. L.* 485 (1972).

For "wrongful life" etc claims, especially in the light of the clash between constitutional and ordinary courts, see: Engelhardt, "Kind als Schaden", *VersR* 1988, 540 See, also, Franzki, "Neue Dimensionen in der Arzthaftung: Schäden bei der Gebursthilfe und *Wrongful Life* als Exponenten einer Entwicklung?", *VersR* 1990, 1181; Deutsch, "Neues Verfassungszivilrecht: Rechtswidriger Abtreibensvertrag Gültig—Unterhaltspflicht aber kein Schaden", *NJW* 1993, 2361; *idem*, "Schadensrecht und Verfassungsrecht: Akt II", *NJW* 1994, 776; Giesen, "Schadenbegriff und Menschenwürde", *JZ* 1994, 286; Picker "Schadensersatz für das unerwünschte Kind ("Wrongful birth")", *AcP* 195 (1995), 483—see also Zimmermann's reply in *JZ* 1997, 131; Roth, "Kindesunterhalt als Schaden", *NJW* 1995, 2399. For a comparative study of American and German law see Deutchler, *Die Haftung des Arztes für die unerwünschte Geburt eines Kindes* ("*wrongful birth*") (1984). For a comparative (American, German, and French law) examination of some of these cases see: Markesinis, "Reading Through a Foreign Judgment", *The Law of Obligations, Essays in Celebration of John Fleming* ((eds.), P. Cane and Jane Stapleton) (1998), pp. 261–283.

(c) Freedom

Any interference with the person's liberty and freedom of *movement* (*körperliche Fortbewegungsfreiheit*) will (if the other elements of § 823 I BGB are satisfied) give rise to a civil claim and, often, a criminal action as well. Torts like that of false imprisonment (*Einsperrung*) and even threats with menaces are covered by this heading as are instances of false information given to the police in order to have the plaintiff arrested. However, freedom of religion or speech are not covered by this term nor, more generally, freedom to act (Fikentscher, *Schuldrecht* (9th edn., 1997) § 103, I, 3; *Staudinger*-Hager, § 823, no. B53 ff. etc. *contra* Leinemann, *Der Begriff Freiheit nach § 823 I BGB* (1969).) Overall, therefore, the notion of freedom in § 823 I BGB is, as a leading textbook suggests, interpreted "restrictively" (Larenz/Canaris, § 76 II 2, p. 385.) and its field of application seems analogous to that of Article 5 of the European Convention of Human Rights.

(d) Property

(i) Ownership

Ownership, the cardinal property right regulated by §§ 903 ff. BGB is, of course, completely protected by § 823 I BGB against culpable interferences. The interference with the substance of a thing (whether moveable or immovable), of the type that one would encounter in, say, a traffic accident case, would thus form the typical kind of interference under this heading. Likewise, preventing an owner from using his property will amount to an actionable interference, certainly if the deprivation of use is total. (BGH 21 June 1977, NJW 1977, 2264.) Likewise, the contamination of animal foods by pharmaceutical products which then makes the herd that eat them impossible to sell, will also be actionable under this heading. (BGH 8 November 1988, MDR 1989, 244.) Removing the property from where its owner wished it to be may also be actionable under this heading, as would any defacement or denigration of it, for instance, by means of graffiti. Even the *use* of a thing without the permission of its owner, would be actionable as an interference with property, although it did not entail its destruction or damage. Dropping the plaintiff's engagement ring in the river, or grazing one's animals on the plaintiff's land without his permission, would thus be covered by this provision. The reverse, i.e. deprivation of use by the owner, may also be actionable under this heading, even though such interference is not with the substance of the property and really leads to pure economic loss being the only harm suffered by the owner. It would seem, however that the German courts allow such actions under this heading only if the deprivation of use is total (BGH 21 December 1970, BGHZ 55, 153) and prolonged (BGH 21 June 1977, NJW 1977, 2264). One test that has been considered is whether the property, as a consequence of the interference with its use, is less worth. In BGHZ 55, 153 the value of the ship that was trapped in the harbour certainly declined for the time being, while a ship outside the harbour kept its value. But if such actions can succeed, the theoretical explanation is disputed in academic literature. (*Cf.* Larenz/Canaris, pp. 388–90). They are also treated as "exceptional" in the sense that they have never been extended to cover economic losses suffered by car owners trapped in traffic jams. (Thus, Kötz/Wagner, no. 60.) Also actionable under the heading of property is damage caused to a car by dust emanating from a neighbouring factory, though here the German courts are careful to merge the provisions of tort law and property law and not to impose liability if the substantive requirements of § 906 (2) BGB are not met. (BGH 18 September 1984, NJW 1985, 47, translated in van Gerven, pp. 192–5.) All of the above, varied instances involve some kind of physical interference with the property. But physical interference is not always necessary. Legal interference with the right of ownership will also be actionable under the same rules. (BGH 7 December 1993, MDR 1994, 254: borrower selling loaned item.) Incidentally, this right for compensation could arise only if the other elements of § 823 I BGB (and particularly the requirement of fault) were satisfied. (Though *cf.* BGH NJW 1985, 47.) In the absence of fault, the owner would have to rely on the remedies given him in the third book of the Code dealing with the law of property. Thus, § 985 BGB gives him a real action for dispossession; or § 1004 BGB which provides a remedy for interferences which do not amount to dispossession (right to demand a cessation of the interference and/or an injunction for the future); or the remedy given by § 906 BGB which is analogous to the Common law injunctions in nuisance cases. Ownership is also protected by the Constitution, which contains special provisions concerning expropriation for the "public good"; but this topic lies outside the ambit of this book.

The illustrations given above demonstrate that a wide—by Common law standards almost excessive interpretation—given to the term "ownership" may in part be prompted by the desire to escape the rigidly-phrased rule that pure economic loss is not actionable under § 823 I BGB. This thought prompts another and related one. The judicial creation of the *Recht am Gewerbebetrieb* (discussed below) may also have been prompted by this desire; and these two developments taken together may illustrate the difficulties that flow from any written attempts to exclude the compensation of pure economic loss through tort actions. By contrast, the Common law's supple way of achieving this result through the notion of duty of care has avoided such "debatable" extensions though done so at the cost of the uncertainty that accompanies the notion of duty of care. In the end, therefore, all one can say is that there are different ways in which one may pursue the same policy, each with its own merits and drawbacks.

(ii) Possession

Difficulties have arisen with regard to the concept of possession, which the Code treats more as a physical relation to a thing than a right. § 854 BGB thus states that "possession of a thing is acquired by obtaining *actual* power of control over the thing".

Possession is thus, clearly, not "ownership"; but could it be regarded as sufficiently akin to this latter notion to receive protection under the words "or *other* rights" (*sonstiges Recht*) of § 823 I BGB?

The paragraphs that follow § 854 BGB make clear that possession is given special protection by the law regardless of the possessor's title and this, partly because the law wishes to discourage—within certain limits (see § 859 BGB)—self-redress, but also because possession is often in practice the outward manifestation of ownership. But does a possessor, whose physical relationship with a thing has been disturbed, also have the right to claim monetary compensation under § 823 I BGB?

Professor Medicus gives the following illustration using, incidentally, the statutory notion of "indirect possession". This is defined by § 868 BGB and deals with a person exercising factual control over a thing but in pursuance to a contract with another person (the mediate or indirect possessor). The typical example is a lease. Now suppose that a lessee fails to vacate an apartment that has been leased from the lessor who has given him legal notice to terminate the contract. If the lessor forcibly ejects the lessee, the latter's remedies—set out in §§ 859, I, III and 861 BGB—include a limited right of self-help as well as the right to demand the return of possession. But can he also demand damages— for example to cover his expenses for staying in a hotel—under § 823 I BGB? As stated, the position of possessors is, in this respect, not entirely clear, but according to Professor Medicus (no. 607; see also Esser/Weyers, *Schuldrecht* II, 2, § 55 2*b*, p. 163) the answer should depend upon whether the possessor is in a position similar to that of an owner, i.e. he has the "negative" advantage usually associated with ownership (e.g. right to stop others from interfering), but also the "positive" advantages, namely the right to use and exploit the thing (§ 903 BGB). This would include all lawful possessors but also a *bona fide* possessor during pending litigation. The solution to the hypothetical example, therefore, should be that the lessee could obtain damages for his loss sustained for the period during which—in accordance with the rules of civil procedure (§§ 721, 765a ZPO)—he might have obtained a reprieve from the eviction. (For rich references to case-law on this and related matters see Deutsch in *JZ* 1984, 308; *JZ* 1990, 733.)

Similarly, other limited property rights like servitudes (§§ 1018 ff. BGB) and usufruct (§§ 1030 ff. BGB) should also receive protection by being included under the heading "other [absolute] rights" of § 823 I BGB.

Further reading on § 823 I and ownership

Von Bar, *Probleme der Haftpflicht für deliktsrechtliche Eigentumsverletzung* (1992); Derlder-Meyer, "Deliktshaftung für Werkmängel", *AcP* 1994 (1995), 137; Deutsch, "Das Eigentum als absolutes Recht und als Schutzgegenstand der Haftung", *MDR* 1988, 441; *Staudinger*-Hager, § 823 BGB, nos. B58 ff.; Plum, "Zur Abgrenzung des Eigentums—und Vermögensschadens", *AcP* 181 (1981), 68.

(iii) Economic loss

It will have been noticed that the protection of wealth (*Vermögen*) as such is not included in the list of enumerated interests of § 823 I BGB. This does not mean that economic losses will never be compensated. A person who is injured and incurs medical expenses will receive monetary compensation both for his pain and suffering (in accordance with § 847 BGB) as well as for his economic loss (e.g. medical expenses, lost earnings, etc.). Equally, a person whose car has been damaged in a traffic accident will be able to claim compensation for it, which may also include the cost of hiring a substitute. Finally, to give one last illustration, if the defendant's negligent activities lead to the severing of an electricity cable, thereby causing a power cut which affects the plaintiff's electrically operated egg-hatching machines, the plaintiff will be able to claim both the value of the eggs and the profit he would have made on those eggs which would have statistically hatched into chickens and then been sold (BGHZ 41, 123 = BGH NJW 1964, 720 but see Hager's criticisms in *JZ* 1979, 53 ff.). In all these cases we are talking of economic loss *immediately consequential* to injury to the person or property and the only problem that the court will have to face will be one of remoteness: how much of the plaintiff's loss to allocate to the defendant's conduct. By contrast, when we move to pure economic loss (*reiner Vermögensschaden*) the difficulties experienced by German law are multiplied; in addition, they are experienced in areas which are well known to Common lawyers. Indeed, it could be argued that in no other area of its law of torts does German law demonstrate such an ideological affinity with the Common law as in its refusal to compensate pure economic loss through the medium of tort rules. Yet, as we shall note below, in both systems this basic premise has, in recent times, come under constant and ingenious attacks with practitioners (and judges) showing in many instances a willingness to probe for weak points in the wall of the citadel. Such an attitude, inevitably, gives rise to the question why should this be so. The question becomes more pressing (and, to some extent has defied a conclusive answer) whenever the problem is examined against the background of French law (and its derivatives). For these systems have adopted the exact opposite solution, equated for all intents and purposes economic loss with physical injury, and have not incurred the dire consequences that Common lawyers and German lawyers so fear.

Stripped to its essentials, the first argument is that economic loss (like nervous shock), tends to give rise to difficulties of an administrative nature such as, for example, a potentially *indeterminate* number of claims (and, it should be stressed, it is the indeterminacy that matters rather than the number of claims itself), unreliable evidence, and collusive actions. These fears were succinctly voiced as early as 1861 by the great German jurist Rudolf von Jhering who wrote:

> What would it lead to if one could be sued in non-contractual relations generally for gross negligence as well as intent! A careless utterance, carrying a tale, giving false information and bad advice, uttering a thoughtless judgment, recommending an undeserving housemaid one used to employ, answering a traveller's question about the way or the time, and so on, in a word, everything and anything, if grossly negligent, would make one liable for the harm it caused in spite of all *bona fides*; and in the course of such an extension the *actio de dolo* would become the veritable scourge of commercial and social intercourse, free conversation would be greatly inhibited, the most innocent word would become a snare! (R. Jhering, "Culpa in Contrahendo", *Jahrbücher für die Dogmatik des heutigen römischen und deutschen Privatrechts* 4 (1861) 1, 12.).

This clearly echoes what was to become one of the best-known aphorisms of Cardozo J in his famous judgment in *Ultramares Corp.* v. *Touche* 255 NY 170, 174; NE 441, 444 (1931). Similar concerns have been voiced in England. In a free market economy financial harm of some kind to some persons is to be expected: "Competition involves traders being entitled to damage their rivals interest by promoting their own.": *Home Office* v. *Dorset Yacht Co. Ltd.* [1970] AC 1004, 1027 per Lord Reid. Or, as Robert Goff LJ (as he then was) put it in his Court of Appeal judgment in *The Aliakmon* [1985] QB 350, 393: "The philosophy of the market place presumes that it is lawful to gain profit by causing others economic loss, and that recognised wrongs involving interference with others contracts are limited to specific intentional wrongs such as inducing a breach of contract or conspiracy." The same justification for the exclusion of economic loss is given in German law. The most audible exponent of this view is probably Professor Canaris (Larenz/Canaris, p. 357) who concludes that the rule against recoverability of pure economic loss serves the purpose of guaranteeing individual freedom. However, this does not necessarily exclude the desirability (in Germany *de lege ferenda*) of well-defined exceptions in specific circumstances. The main concern is to keep these exceptions under control in the light of the individual's right to self determination in a market economy (see also Lord Goff's comments in Markesinis (ed.), *The Gradual Convergence* (1994) p. 130 and Picker "Gutachterhaftung" in Beuthien and others (eds.), *Festschrift für Dieter Medicus* (1999) 397, 433). In any case, the methodological differences between English and German law in the field of negligent misstatements, where such exceptions have been mainly discussed, may be less significant than one might expect, see notes to cases 19–26.

Another argument is that "insurance considerations" often favour the non-liability rule. It is useful to put this argument in such a stark manner since lawyers in Europe, especially Continental Europe, are less accustomed to analysing tort cases in an overtly economic manner. The German decisions bear witness to the validity of this assertion, though it is no longer entirely true of academic literature. (But see, case 144, below.) Yet the assumption that the "insurance factor" *always* favours the non-liability rule is simply not correct. The decision of the Canadian Supreme Court in *Canadian National Railway Co.* v. *Norsk Pacific Steamship Co. Ltd.* [1992] 1 S.C.R. 1021 (reproduced below, p. 243) contains one of the interesting (if long) judicial discussions of the subject. (But it has not pleased all academics. Thus, see, Stapleton, "Tort, Insurance and Ideology" (1995) 58 *MLR*, 820 ff.)

In the early 1980s there were signs that English law was slowly relaxing the attitude towards economic loss even though no one was predicting that it would reach the very liberal position of French, Belgian, or Dutch law where tort compensation for pure economic loss is, quite simply, a non-problem. (See Fokkema and Markesinis, "All or Nothing? The Compensation of Pure Economic Loss in English and Dutch Law" in *Ex Iure* (a collection of essays published in 1987 by Gouda Quint) 63; Herbots, "Le 'Duty of Care' et le dommage purement financier en droit comparé" ((1985) *Revue de droit internationale et de droit comparé* 52.) In England the move expressing a dissatisfaction with the status quo received its first major boost in some wide propositions about the tort of negligence in *Anns* v. *Merton London Borough Council* [1978] AC 728, and it peaked with the decision in *Junior Books Ltd.* v. *Veitchi Co. Ltd.* [1983] 1 AC 520. The result reached in this last case is arguably fair and right *on its facts*. Yet some unnecessarily wide and inadequately thought out dicta precipitated a spectacular demise, first by means of clumsy attempts to show that *Junior Books* was not really a case of economic loss at all (*Tate & Lyle Industries.* v. *GLC* [1983] 2 AC 509) and then by more sustained attacks (e.g. in

Governors of the Peabody Donation Fund v. *Sir Lindsay Parkinson & Co. Ltd.* [1985] AC 210; *Leigh and Sillivan* v. *Aliakmon Shipping Co. Ltd.* [1986] AC 785; *Yuen Kun Yeu* v. *A. G. of Hong Kong* [1988] AC 175) leading to the ignominious statement by a Court of Appeal judge in *Simaan General Contracting Co.* v. *Pilkington Glass Ltd.* (*No. 2*) [1988] 2 WLR 761 at p. 778, that even citing the case served no "useful purpose". This process of disman-tling *Anns* was completed by the House of Lords in *Murphy* v. *Brentwood DC* [1991] 1 AC 398, a decision, however, which may have created its own considerable difficulties and which has not, on the whole, met with a warm reception from all British academics. (See: Markesinis and Deakin, "The Random Element of Their Lordships" Infallible Judgment: An Economic and Comparative Analysis of the Tort of Negligence from *Anns* to *Murphy*", (1992) 55 *MLR* 619 and further references to academic literature on page 621, n. 15.) Yet even if the discrediting of *Anns* turns out to be short lived, the potential "abandonment" of *Murphy* is unlikely to be followed by a move towards the "French position". Rather, it may signal a move towards a more flexible attitude, which will make recovery easier but dependant on factual circumstances grouped under characteristic headings. This approach has already been advocated by a number of academics (e.g. Professor Feldthusen in Canada: *Economic Negligence: The Recovery of Pure Economic Loss*, 2nd edn. (1989); *idem*, "Economic Loss in the Supreme Court of Canada: Yesterday and Tomorrow" 17 *Can. Bus. L.J.* 356 (1990–91)); and it can also find some (influential) judicial support in the Common law world. (E.g. in the majority in *Norsk, op. cit.*, above). It is also largely adopted in this book since it makes the comparative presentation of the rich and varied material more digestible. Overall, however, there is no denying the fact that English law on this topic is confused and often contradictory. In *Murphy* v. *Brentwood DC* [1991] 1 AC 398 the House of Lords significantly reduced recourse to the law of tort to provide efficient remedies for deficient work in the area of construction law. Interestingly enough, one can observe in recent cases a trend towards contract law whereas previously claimants would resort to the "*Anns* type of remedy". Thus far, the new Contracts (Rights of Third Parties) Act 1999 has not played much of a role; and the construction industry appears to be keen to exclude its application for the future. It must also be noted that the expan-sion of contract has come about incrementally through the activity of the courts. (Thus, see, *Linden Gardens Trust Ltd.* v. *Lenesta Sludge Disposals Ltd.* [1994] 1 AC 85. See, also, *Darlington BC* v. *Wiltshier Northern Ltd.* [1995] 1 WLR 68 (Court of Appeal), containing a highly influential attack by Steyn LJ (as he then was) on the traditional doctrine of privity, though now only of historic interest.) This trend reached its provisional peak in *Alfred McAlpine Construction Ltd.* v. *Panatown Ltd.* (No 1) [2001] 1 AC 518 (extracts of which are reproduced below, p. 320) and stems from a newly discovered flexibility of con-tractual reasoning in cases where the performance of a contract also affects a third party. The details of this new approach are controversial; and have yet to be worked out by the courts. However, it can be safely stated that in effect these cases allow a building employer to recover substantial damages even though a third party to the building contract suffers the financial loss caused by the defective performance. These cases remind one of the German concept of *Drittschadensliquidation*, though if one scrutinises the reasoning of the minority in *Panatown* other parallels to German contract principles surface. For a more detailed discussion of the interplay between contract and tort in the area of economic loss see also notes to cases 19–26 below.

In the USA one finds a similar attempt to confine recovery of pure economic loss by decisions like *State of Louisiana ex rel. Guste* v. *M/V Testbank* (752 F. 2d 1019 (1985), repro-duced in part in the 2nd edn. of this book, pp. 184–203 and 3rd edn. pp. 211–216). For in

this case the majority tried (and to a large extent succeeded) in halting the more liberalising rules found in such important, earlier decisions as *Petitions of Kinsman Transit Co.*
(388 F. 2d 821) and *Union Oil Co. v. Oppen* (501 F. 2d 558). This attempt to adopt "bright
line" rules (e.g. economic loss is compensatable *only* if connected to physical injury or
property damage) seems to have succeeded, though one also finds some important decisions in the opposite direction. Thus see: *People Express Airlines, Inc. v. Consolidated Rail
Corp.* 100 NJ 246, 495 A. 2d 107 (1985); *J'Aire Corp. v. Gregory* 598 P. 2d 60 (1979). Selecting cases for inclusion in works such as this is not easy; and, to some extent, it must reflect
personal ideas and preconceptions. Nevertheless, the selection has been made on the basis
of methodological criteria as well as for the intrinsic merit of the judgments reproduced.
In the case of economic loss two leading cases have been selected for special treatment.
The first—*Norsk*—comes from Canada and adopts a "liberal" approach; the second, delivered by the US Supreme Court—*East River S.S. Corp. v. Transamerica Deleval Inc. 476 US
858 (1986)*—is more traditional but no less impressive for that. The two decisions may
not be as irreconcilable as they appear at first sight if one adopts the more nuanced view
that recovery for economic loss may be desirable in some factual situations but not in
others.

In Germany, too, the rigid anti-compensation rule has been doubted by some academics and severely eroded *in some situations* by the courts, themselves, despite strong
academic criticism. But, overall, the challenge has, again, been unsuccessful since the non-
liability rule was clearly incorporated in the Code in accordance with the demands of
both the socio-economic environment of the nineteenth century and Roman legal tradition. For the socio-economic environment clearly ranked tactile forms of property above
pure economic interests, and what is more, expressed a clear preference for land over
moveables. And legal tradition was also hostile towards pure economic loss, since the *lex
Aquilia* and classical Roman law formed part of the German Common law and this system
of compensation was devised for damage to physical objects.

Many consequences follow from this basic attitude of German law. Here we can only
outline a few fundamental points; and further details will be given in the annotations to
the translated decisions.

First one must note that as a result of the rigidity of tort law, German contract law has
been expanded (many academics would argue excessively), to meet new situations calling
for a pro-plaintiff solution. More about this (and recent similar trends in England) in the
notes on the cases dealing with liability for negligent statements and the liability of attorneys towards non-clients.

Secondly, the expansion has often been the result of bold judicial creativity. This
creativity has not, as already alluded, been met with "enthusiasm" by the academic side
of the profession. In this context, therefore, the harmonious collaboration between the
two sides of the legal profession, so much the hallmark of German law (and so different
from English law), has been ruptured.

Thirdly, despite the above, there exist large areas of tort law where no recovery is
allowed for pure economic loss and, in this sense, German law is very close to English law
in result if not in methodology. The "cable cases" provide an obvious example; but many
others exist. Thus, for example, if the defendant injures the plaintiff's employee, or debtor,
an English plaintiff has no longer (i.e. since 1982) an action in tort for his economic loss
(though some Common law systems—Australian, New Zealand, Canadian—may, in
limited instances, allow such claims.) According to the prevailing view, interferences with
contractual or quasi-contractual relations are not actionable under § 823 I BGB. (See,

however, Koziol, *Die Beeinträchtigung fremder Forderungsrechte* (1967); Löwisch, *Der Deliktsschutz relativer Rechte* (1970); Mincke, "Forderungsrechte als 'sonstige Rechte' im Sinne des § 823 Abs. I BGB", *JZ* 1984, 862). Thus, the famous French decision (Colmar, 20 avril 1955, *D.* 1956, 723), which allowed a football club to claim the economic loss it suffered as a result of the injury of one of its leading players, would be decided differently in Germany. And so would be a number of other such cases which have received more generous treatment at the hands of French courts (though see Professor Durry's remarks in 1976 *Rev. trim. dr. civ.*, 134).

Fourthly, demarcation lines cannot always be drawn easily, especially in cases involving pure economic loss. The distinction between damage to "property" and economic loss has thus caused many difficulties. For example, A damages B's cable and C's factory comes to a halt. Molten material in his electrically operated machines solidifies and has to be discarded. This, clearly, is physical damage, actionable under § 823 I BGB. But what if the solidified material can be re-melted—no doubt at an extra cost—and re-used? In trying to answer this question, German courts have come up with some rather abstract analyses. (See, for example, OLG Hamm NJW 1973, 760 and notes by Isenbeck in *NJW* 1973, 1755; Möschel, *JuS* 1977, 5.)

Fifthly, the different methodology—dictated by the Code, German legal history, or legal education should not deter the reader from using "constructively" the German ideas which may yet be transplantable into the Common law. At the very least, these ideas should provide the Common lawyer with food for thought. This point will be amplified in the sections that follow, and in the notes to the legal malpractice and negligent misstatement cases. Decisions such as that of the House of Lords in *Henderson* v. *Merrett Syndicates Ltd* [1995] 2 AC 145 (reproduced in part at p. 348), where comparative law was put to practical use, will surely encourage jurists to engage in such exercises in the future, in this field and elsewhere. In his leading speech, Lord Goff of Chieveley, after having carefully reviewed the available solutions in French and German law, opted for a concurrence of contractual and tortious actions. The German model, and the way it had worked in practice without any problems, clearly aided the learned Law Lord to reach his own conclusion as to what English law should be.

Finally, for the reasons already given, the economic loss cases will be grouped under different headings and discussed separately, the assumption being that different factual situations call for different legal (and economic) analyses and, therefore, different solutions.

Cable cases. The first three cases (BGHZ 29, 65; BGH NJW 1976, 1740; BGH NJW 1977, 2208, cases 11–13) deal with a problem that has also exercised the English courts. Their annotations will bring out particular points and provide the reader with further bibliographical references. Three points, however, should also be made at this stage. The first is the fact that English and German law essentially reach the same result in this factual situation. It is by no means clear what is the right answer to this problem. If—and we need not give a conclusive answer at this point—the law ought to be changed, the question then arises as to *how* this should be done, given the rigid phrasing of § 823 I BGB. Of course, it should be noted that German attorneys have not been short of ideas in their attempt to circumvent the leading tort provision. But the Supreme Court, apart from a brief period of hesitation, has been as quick to reject them as the practising lawyers have been to invent them.

Secondly, the cases are also noteworthy in their relatively open allusion to policy and, in this respect, they can easily be compared with some of the more recent English decisions. The awareness that policy will decide the outcome is also increasingly shared by the academics who have commented on these decisions. Once again, the *Norsk* decision contains a good discussion of the issues.

Finally, both the English and German cases reveal how various legal devices have been used interchangeably in order to produce the desired result. This equivocation between the various elements of liability must be clearly stressed, for it will accustom the Common lawyer to the fact that he must often seek to find in the German theory of legal cause the answers which he tends to produce through the notion of duty. For comparative studies on this subject see: Hilgenfeldt, *Der Ersatz von Vermögensschäden bei der Unterbrechung von Versorgungsleitungen* (1981); Schulze, "Die Beschädigung von Erdkabeln und sonstigen Erdleitungen der Energieversorgungsunternehmen durch unerlaubte Handlungen Dritter, insbesondere durch Tiefbauunternehmen", *VersR* 1998, 12; Taupitz, *Haftung für Energieleiterstörungen durch Dritte* (1981).

Loss of use. Two cases (BGHZ 55, 153 and BGH NJW 1977, 2264) dealing with this issue are reproduced below (cases 14 and 15). The annotations to them will make it clear that the results achieved by the courts have been seriously questioned by many academics. These cases also show how difficult it is to draw a line between what constitutes an interference with property, actionable under § 823 I BGB, and what should be called pure economic loss.

Damage caused to the product. This is an economic loss which, arguably, should be left to contract rather than tort. Nevertheless, in Germany, tort law is increasingly expanding to cover this type of economic loss, mainly to circumvent some shorter limitation periods in contract. A number of cases reproduced in section B. 16 of this chapter deal with this problem and their annotations will make it obvious to the Anglo-American reader that the problem is not unknown to the Common law world. Perhaps they will also make clear that—to quote Professor Kötz's words (*Deliktsrecht*, nos. 65–6)—letting the [tort] bull into the [contract] china shop can create serious demarcation problems and entail unbearable economic consequences. This judicial trend seems well entrenched; but the literature is divided. Broadly supportive is Hager, "Zum Schutzbereich der Produzentenhaftung", *AcP* (184) 1984, 413. The judges who have created this case law have also defended it extra-judicially. See: Steffen in *VersR* 1988, 977 and Kullmann in *NJW* 1991, 675. For criticism and further references, see: Kötz/Wagner, *Deliktsrecht*, pp. 27 *et seq.* *Staudinger*-Hager, § 823 BGB nos. B105 ff. *Cf.* also the views of the US Supreme Court in *East River Steamship Corp.* v. *Transamerica Delaval, Inc.* Note also that German law seems to have applied different rules to defective chattels (which damage themselves: case 68) and to immovables (case 74).

Economic loss as a result of negligent misstatements. Here, too, we are dealing with economic loss which in the Common law systems will, if at all, be actionable in tort. The development of the *tort* action in England and the United States was largely brought about by the doctrine of consideration which (especially in England) made the expansion of the notion of contract impossible. (See Lord Devlin's judgment in *Hedley Byrne & Co. Ltd.* v. *Heller & Partners Ltd.* [1964] AC 465, 529.) In Germany the pressure was the reverse. A tort action under § 823 I BGB was and is impossible; and an action under § 826 BGB tends to be limited to the most opprobrious forms of misconduct. Though § 826 BGB has, in recent times, received an expansive interpretation, it is still unable to deal with the most common situations. The expansion of contractual or quasi-contractual remedies was the only answer German law could produce. (Note, however, that in both systems great use is made of the notion of reliance, which can transcend the classical distinction between contract and tort and in cases like negligent misstatements make it almost meaningless.) A number of translated German decisions deal with this problem which, in recent years, has also occupied the House of Lords in such cases as *Smith* v. *Eric Bush*; *Harris* v. *Wyre Forest DC* [1990] 1 AC 831 and *Caparo Industries plc* v. *Dickman* [1990] 2 AC 605. Though the results reached by the German courts are often identical to those accepted by the English courts *Caparo*, for example, could have been decided in the same way under German law. However, one must also note that recently the BGH extended liability in this field. (See the controversial decision reproduced as case 24.) Notwithstanding the possible convergence in solutions, the reasoning used by these two national courts remains different. This may be largely due to the fact that in these disputes the sources of the law are multiple and highly complex. More about the contractually "flavoured" methodology will be said in the next sub-section; and the complexity of the sources that must be used by German judges to solve these cases will be discussed in the notes to the translated decisions.

The case that follows (27) deals with a related topic. A notary, solicitor, or attorney is negligent in the drafting of the will of the testator and, as a result, a potential legatee is deprived of the benefit he would have otherwise derived from the will. The lawyer's contractual and/or delictual liability towards his client is not, of course, in doubt. But can he be made liable to the "third" party/potential legatee? German law (as indeed English and American law) has given a positive answer, but has again justified it in contractual, not delictual terms. Common lawyers have opted for a different justification of the same result, but the comparison of the various cases shows that the problem—the limit of the potential liability—is the same. Incidentally, in these cases liability can often be said to result from what the lawyer *says* (i.e. negligent statement); but it can also result from what the lawyer *does*. In the annotation in this case we shall examine the English and American approaches to the problem. The advantages of contract over tort are set out in section B, the notes to case 27, below.

Economic loss at the borderline of contract and tort. The divide between contract and tort, not always easy to draw, becomes very vague when the tortious conduct produces pure economic loss instead of the more typical physical injury or property damage. This division, explicable by reference to history, is more rigidly maintained by the Common law where some of its jurists have even produced eloquently pithy but, it is submitted, not always persuasive reasons for its maintenance. (See, for example, Weir, *International Encyclopaedia of Comparative Law* (1975), XI, ch. 12, "Complex Liabilities", 5 and, more sceptically, Markesinis, "An Expanding Tort Law—the Price of a Rigid Contract Law" *LQR* 103 (1987) 354, 384 ff.). This is not so in the modern civil law in general and the German law of torts in particular. For there, contract and tort are seen as species of the wider notion of obligation. In this system, codal provisions or other reasons have forced lawyers, while not abandoning the search for doctrinal clarity, to cross often the boundaries of contract, law, and *negotiorum gestio* in an attempt to find a solution (not necessarily the best one) to a problem. We shall note later on (in the section on products liability and liability for harm caused to third parties) how this has worked out in specific instances of potential liability. Here suffice it to sketch two of the main contractual solutions devised to overcome shortcomings of the German law of tort. They are contracts with protective effects *vis-à-vis* third parties (*Verträge mit Schutzwirkung zugunsten Dritter*) and the (untranslatable) concept of *Drittschadensliquidation*; and their treatment in Germany is usually found in books dealing with the law of contract or the "general part" of the law of obligations.

(i) Contracts in favour of third parties

Contracts in favour of third parties (*Verträge zugunsten Dritter*) giving, under certain circumstances, a third party the right to demand that a promisor in a contract perform his primary obligation to him (and not to the co-contractor/promisee) are regulated by §§ 328–35 BGB. They are similarly recognized by section 302 *Restatement* (*Second*) *Contracts*, Article 4 of the 1982 Contracts (Privity) Act of New Zealand and, indeed, by other legal systems (e.g. Israel). Not so, however, by the English Common law which, until recently, remained rigidly faithful to all the facts of its doctrine of consideration. (For a recent thoughtful and critical discussion of the English Common law, see: Law Commission "Privity of Contract: Contracts for the Benefit of Third Parties", Law Com. No. 242 (1996). See, also, Beatson, "Reforming the Law of Contracts for the Benefit of Third Parties. A Second Bite at the Cherry" (1992) *Current Law* 1, where one also finds some interesting insights about the Law Commission's research into foreign (including German) law. Finally, however, the Contracts (Rights of Third Parties) Act 1999 (reproduced in part at p. 319) did make considerable inroads into the doctrine of privity and introduced the concept of a contract for the benefit of a third party into English law. (The 1999 Act is annotated in the notes to cases 19–26, see p. 301). But this is not the contractual device that concerns us here. What is of interest here is the judicially created variant of contract with protective effects *vis-à-vis* third parties which brings strangers to a contract under its protective umbrella and allows them to entertain an action for damages for breach of one of the contract's *secondary* obligations. The situations in which this concept has provided a solution originally involved physical injury; and this contractual device enabled the German courts to overcome the restrictive provision of liability for harm caused by third parties found in § 831 BGB (discussed below in chapter 3). The German equivalent of cases like *Cavalier* v. *Pope* ([1906] AC 428 *cf.* RGZ 102, 231; see, also, RGZ 127, 218, reprinted below as case 116) show the difference with the more traditional concept of contract in favour of third parties (§§ 328 ff. BGB). For the problem in *Cavalier* v. *Pope* (and the German equivalents) is not whether the plaintiff (wife of the lessee of premises) can sue the lessor for delivery of the leased premises (the *primary* obligation of the contract). The disputed point is whether she is entitled to claim damages if she is injured as a result of a breach of one of the *secondary* obligations imposed on the lessor by law or the contract (e.g. the duty to keep the premises in good repair). (see, now, § 311 III 1 BGB.) In German law, in this and other similar cases, the defendant often benefits from the immunity given to him by the narrow rule or, to be more precise, the absence of true "vicarious liability". For in § 831 the BGB stipulates that the defendant is liable for his own negligence in selecting or supervising his servant but does not impute the servant's negligence to him. (This can be achieved only by relying on § 278 BGB which, in turn, applies only in a contractual context. For more details on this see chapter 3, below.). So the German courts (as is explained below in chapter 3. 2) have been forced to resort to various contractual devices (including that of contracts with protective effects *vis-à-vis* third parties) in order to provide greater protection for plaintiffs. Clearly, such a convoluted technique was never necessary for the Common law (and, indeed, for those systems (e.g. French) that opt for the true vicarious liability rule). The German "refinement" of the traditional contract in favour of third parties has thus, understandably, escaped the attention of most Common lawyers. Yet, German law may, in this context as well, hold out some interesting ideas for discerning Common lawyers dealing with the *Ross* v. *Caunters* [1980] Ch. 297 type of situation. (Attorney's liability towards a non-client/third party which has suffered pure economic loss as a result of the attorney's negligence.) The same may be true in cases where a sub-contractor causes, through his negligence economic loss not just to his co-contractor (the general contractor) but also the owner of the building. (E.g., *Junior Books* v. *Veitchi* [1983] 1 AC 520 (England); *J'Aire Corp.* v. *Gregory* 24 Cal. 3rd 799, 598 P. 2d 60 (1979) (USA).) For, it will be argued (in the notes to the relevant German cases), that in almost all of these situations (for an exception see case 23) the defendant (attorney or sub-contractor, as the case may be), must not be made more extensively liable towards the third party than he would be if sued by his co-contractor. For this to be achieved, however, the cause of action against such defendants will have to be contractual. If, for whatever reasons, tort terminology is chosen, it will have to be made clear that the scope and extent of any tortious duty will have to be determined by the underlying contract between attorney/client or owner/contractor. (See: Lorenz and Markesinis, "Solicitors' Liability Towards Third Parties; Back into the Troubled Waters of the Contract/Tort Divide" (1993) 56 *MLR* 558, replying to Beatson, *op. cit.* (1992) *Current Law*, 1.)

At this juncture a clarification is necessary. For it is important to note that German courts have deployed the concept of a contract with protective effects in *two quite different groups of cases*. In the first category the function of the *Vertrag mit Schutzwirkung* is to frame certain protective duties of care as collateral obligations under the contract (or in pre-contractual situations as *culpa in contrahendo*) in order to avoid the weak vicarious liability rule contained in § 831 BGB. The well-known decision in *Cavalier* v. *Pope* provides an excellent English illustration of the problem that has to be solved. These cases involve physical damage to property or to the person and, clearly, this aspect of the concept is of less interest to English lawyers. The second type of situation in which the notion of *Vertrag mit Schutzwirkung* has been used is, however, much more interesting and it concerns the so-called "liability of experts". Here the absence (in Germany) of a tortious exception to the rule that pure economic loss is not recoverable in tort (such as the *Hedley Byrne* principle) has prompted German courts to extend contractual reasoning. It is thus in this context that the German case law deserves attention and provides useful insights into the scope and nature of liability for the negligent performance of services by professionals. For this category of liability causes great conceptual difficulties in both systems. (For a more detailed account see notes to cases 19–24 and case 27. The need to differentiate between these two groups of cases is highlighted by Kötz, "The Doctrine of Privity of Contract" (1990) 10 *Tel Aviv Univer. Studies in Law*, 195 and Martiny, "Pflichtenorientierter Drittschutz beim Vertrag mit Schutzwirkung für Dritte", *JZ* 1996, 19.)

Yet the option of framing the action in contract has also crossed the minds of some lawyers. In *Cavalier* v. *Pope*, mentioned earlier on, the possibility was considered but rejected on the grounds that the plaintiff's wife was not a party to the contract of lease. In *J'Aire* the case was initially also pleaded in contract on the ground that the plaintiff could be regarded as an intended beneficiary of the contract between the owner of the premises and the defendants. This argument, however, was later abandoned by the plaintiff's attorney, probably in the belief that the court would not have accepted it. Nevertheless, a Californian commentator has come out in favour of the contractual approach arguing that it would have been less drastic to discover a contract in favour of the plaintiff than to grant the plaintiff's claim by extending tort to cover negligently inflicted economic loss. (Schwartz, "Economic Loss in American Tort Law: The Examples of *J'Aire* and of Products Liability" 23 *San D. L. Rev.*, 40 ff. Contrast Rubin's view in "Tort Recovery for Negligently Inflicted Economic Loss: A Reassessment" 37 *Stan. L. Rev.* 1513 (1985). Also, *Junior Books* v. *Veitchi* has also been seen by an English tort expert as supportable "in a legal system which admits that [a third party] beneficiary of a contract can sue" (Weir, *A Casebook on Tort*, 5th edn. (1983) 34).) However, the Law Commission was at pains to emphasise that the 1999 Act does not cover situations such as *White* v. *Jones* or *Junior Books* and expressly clarified that its reform proposal did not make allowance for the German concept of a contract with protective effects towards third parties. Whether this has been sufficiently expressed in the wording of the Act is controversial and gives rise to considerable uncertainty. (*Cf.* Bridge [1996] *JBL* 602, 604; Macaulay (2000) 16 *Constr LJ* 265, 268.) But the German experience suggests that it is possible to apply the distinction between a classic contract for the benefit of a third party entitling to primary performance and other situations in which a third party seeks to enforce only isolated secondary obligations in practice. Hence, tort techniques will continue to dominate the reasoning in such cases outside the scope of the 1999 Act with one notable exception: the availability of an exclusion clause in the main contract to third parties who are employed in the exercise of the main contractor's duties.

It would appear that German law has found a better practical way round this problem—at least in the context of building contracts of the type envisaged in both *Junior Books* and *J'Aire*. (If so, this might well be a point that the Royal Institute of British Architects might wish to study carefully. For it is, we understand, common practice in Germany for contractors, using the general conditions of trade, to assign in advance all claims they may have against their sub-contractors arising from breach of warranties. This means that one does not have to structure the relationship of the parties in such a way as to make it difficult (if not impossible) to make the sub-contractor liable to the employer for the bad quality of the work. But a building owner accepting such an assignment (of the contractor's claims against the sub-contractor) does not thereby lose his possible claims against the main contractor. (For details see: BGHZ 62, 351; 67, 101; 74, 258. See, also, § 11 no. 10(a) of the AGB-Gesetz of 1976 which is the German equivalent of our Unfair Contract Terms Act 1977. See, now, § 309 no. 8 b) aa) BGB.) Indeed, so common this practice appears to be, the *Junior Books* type of case apparently has not been litigated in the courts. Well-known academic writers, however, have speculated that, if no assignment had taken place and/or the main contractor was not worth suing, a result similar to that reached by the House of Lords would be achieved by German courts through the medium of contract with protective effects *vis-à-vis* third parties. (Schlechtriem, "Deliktshaftung des Subunternehmers gegenüber dem Bauherrn wegen Minderwerts seines Werks—Eine neue Entscheidung des House of Lords", *Versicherungsrecht*, 25 *Jahre Karlsruher Forum* (1983), 64, 65, especially in view of BGH NJW 1965, 1955 and BGH NJW 1982, 2431. Neither case, however, deals with building contracts. Lorenz in *Essays in Memory of Professor F. H. Lawson* (1986) 86, 97, seems to agree. On the other hand, BGH NJW 1981, 1779, case 17 below, in what appears to be an *obiter dictum*, denies a direct action against the subcontractor.) As stated, the advantages of this contractually flavoured action will be considered more carefully below. Here suffice it to state that the contract with protective effects *vis-à-vis* third parties makes contractual protection possible while avoiding all the consequences of a fully-fledged contract in favour of third parties.

Clearly, then, the above technique goes some way towards solving the kind of problem faced by Anglo-American courts in cases like *J'Aire* and *Junior Books* v. *Veitchi*. However, it also challenges the doctrine of contractual privity, which is accepted by German law as it is by the Common law systems. Some kind of workable compromise is thus needed if a right balance is to be preserved between the traditional doctrine and the judicially fashioned deviation. It follows that if the ambit of contract is to be enlarged—as it is by constructions such as the contract with protective effects *vis-à-vis* third parties—special care must be taken so that the expansion is kept under control. For if it is not, the dividing line between contractual and tortious liability may be blurred or, even, abolished. The way German lawyers have grappled with these, at times, incompatible aims is instructive for a number of reasons.

Noteworthy is first of all the fact that we are here faced with a judge-made doctrine. True, courts and academics have tried—as is customary in German law—to pin their views on some article of the Code. Thus, sometimes the expansion of the contract has been based on § 157 BGB. (Broad interpretation of the contract; implied intentions of the parties; end-aim of the transaction. RGZ 87, 292; 98, 213; 106, 126; 127, 218 (an interesting decision); 152, 177. The BGH continued this practice. Thus see: BGHZ 1, 383, 386; 5, 378, 384; BGH NJW 1956, 1193.) In others the even more amorphous § 242 BGB (good faith) has been invoked to render respectability to what is a clear example of judicial activism. (Larenz, *Schuldrecht* I (1st edn. 1953), 16. III; *idem*, NJW 1956, 1193; NJW 1960, 79. Larenz's work changed not only the theoretical foundation of the new concept. Indeed, it also helped distinguish it from the traditional contract in favour of third parties regulated by §§ 328 ff. BGB creating a new notion for German private law.) This problem has greatly exercised academics but the courts, in what I have elsewhere called fits of "pragmatism" ("Conceptualism, pragmatism and courage: a common lawyer looks at some judgments of the German Federal Court", 34 *A. J. Comp. L.* 349 (1986)) have refused to resolve this "theoretical" issue, preferring to focus on the narrow aspects of each action before them. (Thus in BGHZ 56, 269, 273 the theoretical basis of the concept was deliberately left undecided; and in BGH NJW 1977, 2073, 2074 it was regarded as irrelevant!)

A second interesting feature is, as we shall see, the emphasis on the relationship between contractual creditor and plaintiff/third party (which is *known* to the defendant/debtor) rather than on the foreseeability of the plaintiff/third party by the contractual debtor/defendant. The weakness of the latter (tort) approach is the potential open-endedness of the liability; an open-endedness which could, given the vagueness of the foreseeability test, lead to the blurring of contractual and tortious liability. Nevertheless, we can notice over the years a gradual weakening, or as some might say, erosion of the requirement of an interest of the creditor in including the third party into the protective scope of the contract (in one sense the most important element). As the concept of *Vertrag mit Schutzwirkung* was first applied to situations such as *Cavalier* v. *Pope* involving physical damage to a third party, it was natural to demand that the creditor was responsible for the well being (*Wohl und Wehe*, "for better or worse") of the third party. Any injury to the latter could be analysed as an injury to the creditor himself which in turn explained the third party's inclusion in the contract (BGHZ 51, 91, 96). However, the extension of the *Vertrag mit Schutzwirkung* into the realm of pure economic loss in the context of misstatements or other services by professionals prompted also a shift of the emphasis from the relationship creditor/third party to that between third party/defendant. Here in this category of cases, of what has been called above "expert liability" (*Expertenhaftung*), the criterion of the creditor's interest in the third party's well being is much less appropriate and as a consequence was soon abandoned (see Medicus, *Schuldrecht AT* (11th edn. 1999) p. 374). This last point is particularly obvious from recent decisions (taken from what one might describe broadly as the banking/financial area, as well as the provision of expert opinions and legal service). Cases 19–24 illustrate this trend, which many (even in Germany) regard as dangerously expansive. The widening of the protective ambit of the contract is obvious not only in the fact that the courts no longer insist that the protected third party may be specifically identified in advance. More importantly, it is evident from the fact that the third party no longer needs to be in a close, personal, relationship with the creditor. Instead, the paramount question is "in what circumstances the *objective interests involved* [sic] permit the inference that the parties [debtor/creditor] have [even] implicitly stipulated a duty of care towards third parties" (BGH NJW 1984, 355, 356). While the BGH still founds the concept on implied terms reasoning and thus derives the rights of the third party from the contract between creditor and defendant, the third party's (reasonable) *reliance on the accuracy of the statement and the special skill* of the defendant attains special weight in the individual case. (See, now, § 311 III 2 BGB, which stresses the importance of reliance.) It comes as little surprise therefore to see that more recent decisions apply the concept also to situations where there is a potential or actual conflict of interest between the contractual creditor and the third party (BGHZ 127, 378; for details see note to case 23). This move away from the requirement of the creditor's interest points towards a gradual convergence with the approach established in *Hedley Byrne*. But the reader should be aware that in this area of the law it is difficult to generalise from individual cases. For instance, in a recent decision the tenth senate of the BGH reasserted the contractual foundations of the concept. (See, BGH NJW 2001, 514.) The Court of Appeal Frankfurt had argued that certain heads of damages were not included in the scope of the duty owed by the surveyor. This was confined to the creditor's (or for that matter the third party's) reliance on the correctness of the commissioned report concerning the presence of toxic substances in the soil of the development site. The BGH rejected this line of reasoning as being too restrictive. In this context the court stressed that once the third party was included in the contract and had a relation with the promisee, reliance was not the main element in determining the extent of the surveyor's liability.

Let us then turn to the conditions required for what we shall call "the opening of the contractual umbrella". We note that they are—in theory—three. (Rich references to the case-law illustrating these requirements are given by Sonnenschein, "Der Vertrag mit Schutzwirkung für Dritte—und immer neue Fragen", *JA* 1979, 225, and Beyer, "Vertraglicher Drittschutz", *JuS* 1996, 473.) First, the third party must come into contact with the performance of the contractual debtor and be endangered (or otherwise affected) by any misperformance in (roughly) the same way as the contractual creditor. This is commonly known as the requirement of proximity of performance (*Leistungsnähe*). Secondly, according to what is probably the better view and subject to the qualifications already made, the contractual creditor must have some interest in protecting the third party, and thirdly, the above two elements must be known to the debtor/defendant at the time of conclusion of the contract (or the commencement of the contractual negotiations).

This, as stated, is a subject rich in case-law where most generalisations are dangerous; not all decisions are clearly reconcilable with one another (as German lawyers readily admit); and where the only discernible trend is for the courts—despite academic doubts—to move towards an expansion of the contractual umbrella.

(ii) Drittschadensliquidation

The advantages, if any, that the contractual approach offers over the tort reasoning will be considered in the note to cases 25 and 26, below. Here, let us look briefly at the other concept devised by German lawyers to solve cases of pure economic loss in cases like (arguably) *Ross v. Caunters* [1980] Ch. 297 and *Leigh and Sillavan v. Aliakmon Shipping Co. Ltd. (The Aliakmon)* [1986] AC 785.

Drittschadensliquidation is a judge-made doctrine which allows a creditor (the promisee) to a contract to claim (in contract) for loss resulting from the non-execution or bad execution of the contract, which falls not upon him (the creditor) but upon a third party *provided that* the third party has suffered a loss instead of the promisee. (For a similar approach see Lord Clyde's speech in *Alfred McAlpine Construction Ltd. v. Panatown Ltd.* (No. 1) [2001] 1 AC 518, 529). It is of first importance to note that the third party is entitled to have the right assigned. The principle involves an exception to the so-called doctrine of the creditor's interest according to which as a general rule a claimant can recover for his own loss only. Unlike the concept of the *Vertrag mit Schutzwirkung* it does not affect the notion of relativity of contract for it does not enable the third party to sue directly.

Sometimes, however, a contract action may not be available, for instance where a third party to a contract of carriage damages goods in transit in an accident. If the buyer is on risk the seller will not suffer a financial loss as he remains entitled to claim from the buyer the price of the goods (see § 447 BGB). Yet, if the seller is the owner of the goods at the time of the accident, only he is entitled to bring an action under § 823 I BGB. BGHZ 49, 356 allowed the action of the seller and applied the concept of *Drittschadensliquidation*. From this perspective the concept appears as a general question of the law of damages. Still if the contract route is available the action will most likely be in contract due to the absence of true vicarious liability in tort, which will be examined more closely in chapter 3.

The main rational of the doctrine of *Drittschadensliquidation* is to ensure that the defaulting party in the contract (or the tortfeasor) does not benefit from the fact that in these cases the loss has been shifted (*Gefahrenlastung, zufällige Schadensverlagerung*) from the creditor to the third party. If this exception to the doctrine of the creditor's interest had not been accepted, the defaulting party would not be liable to his creditor (since the latter has suffered no loss). Nor would the guilty party been liable (in contract) to the third party in the absence of any contractual link between the two of them. Like all judge-made rights, however, this right is kept under close scrutiny lest it get out of control and expose the contractual debtor to an unlimited number of claims. Thus, the third party will be allowed to rely on the doctrine and seek assignment of the creditor's rights against the promisor or the tortfeasor only where special relations between him and the creditor to the contract cause the interest (and the loss) to be shifted on to him. *Drittschadensliquidation* applies only in certain traditionally recognised situations. These are mainly three: certain agency situations, given that German law does not accept undisclosed agency; trust and bailment cases; and, finally, in relation to carriage of goods. Indeed, the courts are reluctant to extend its scope except in an incremental manner. Thus, the BGH dismissed *Drittschadensliquidation* as an inappropriate way of solving the problem of product liability (see case 61); and denied its application to the factual context of the cable cases (see case 13). These two cases contain very useful comments on the scope and rationale of the doctrine.

The *fons et origo* of this development seems to be a decision of the Court of Appeal in Lübeck (*Seufferts Archiv* II (1857), 36 at p. 47), where an agent was allowed to claim damages suffered by his "undisclosed" principal. The need for a concept such as *Drittschadensliquidation* becomes obvious if one takes into account that German law does not accept undisclosed agency. (See Zweigert and Kötz pp. 436 ff.) This is so even though many situations occur which involve factually analogous situations; see in particular §§ 383 ff. HGB (contract of commission) and §§ 453 ff. HGB (forwarding agents). Thus, on the one hand the agent does not sustain loss because he is acting on account of the "principal" who reimburses him, but on the other hand the "principal" cannot sue directly on the contract. Hence, the agent is allowed to sue on behalf of the "principal". (E.g. RGZ 75, 169; 115, 419; BGH NJW 1989, 3099.) An equally important example of the application of the theory can be found in cases where the risk (but not the property) in goods has passed from the seller to the buyer (e.g. §§ 446 and 447 BGB). In this type of situation German law has for a long time now (see e.g. RGZ 62, 331, 335; BGH VersR 1972, 1138; VersR 1976, 168) accepted that the seller can recover damages from the wrongdoer in order to hand them over to the buyer or assign this claim to the buyer. (Indeed, because of § 281 BGB he is obliged, if requested, to do so.) One should add, however, that in cases involving carriage of goods by land the contract of carriage is normally treated as a contract for the benefit of the consignee which is a source of additional rights. (On this see the recently reformed § 421 HGB and Herber, *NJW* 1999, 3297, 3302). *Drittschadensliquidation* has also been applied to cases of carriage of goods by sea where, as in English law, the rights under the bill of lading are transferred upon indorsement. (See: BGHZ 25, 250.)

Simplifying the facts of *The Aliakmon*, one notes that there the buyer, who had the risk but not the property in the purchased goods and who was not the carrier's contracting party, failed in his action against the ship owner whose negligent storage had damaged the goods resulting in the plaintiff's economic loss. BGH VersR 1972, 1138 was a decision involving land transport. The seller was the contracting party as also the owner of the goods, while the buyer was on risk. The BGH, following established case-law (starting with RGZ 62, 331), had no difficulty in resorting to the theory of *Drittschadensliquidation*. This meant that the seller, was entitled to recover damages in respect of the buyer's loss, and since this right had been assigned to the plaintiff buyer, the latter was allowed to recover damages for his own loss from the defendant carrier. In German law the plaintiff buyer in *The Aliakmon* would have been entitled to require the promisee, the seller, to assign his remedy against the carrier (by relying on § 281 I BGB). In practical terms, this addresses Lord Goff's main objection against a contractually-founded theory of transferred loss. See, *The Aliakmon* ([1985] 1 QB 350, 390); *White v. Jones* [1995] 2 AC 207, 257; and most recently in *Panatown* [2001] 1 AC 518, 544–545: "The shortcomings of this rule must, I imagine, have been that it left the initiative with the seller, rather than with the consignee who was the person who had suffered the loss of or damage to the goods". Thus, the doctrine of *Drittschadensliquidation* also provides a solution in those cases where the promisee might not have an incentive to enforce the right on behalf of the third party. (Whether or not such a solution would be available in English law is a matter for speculation. Thus, contrast Lord Diplock's (unfavourable) dicta in *The Albazero* [1977] AC 774, 845 (a case involving associated companies) with Professor Goode's forceful criticism in (1987) 103 *LQR* 433, 457.)

The appropriateness of this approach to solve the kind of problem that faced the English courts in *The Aliakmon* or *The Albazero* and also to address some of the difficulties that occurred in cases such as *Panatown* is obvious to a comparative lawyer. This belief is reinforced by Lord Justice Robert Goff's judgment in the Court of Appeal ([1985] QB 350) where the learned judge, in effect, invented his "parallel" theory of "transferred loss" without being aware of the German counterpart (see his comments in Markesinis (ed.), *The Gradual Convergence* (1994) p. 129). However, his theory of "transferred loss" differs in so far as it aimed at creating a *direct* right of action in tort of the third party, i.e. the plaintiff *buyer*. Although in some instances the German concept may also serve to found a—concurrent—action in tort, it is a prerequisite of such an action that the plaintiff has a proprietary interest in the goods. So for instance if the goods are carried at the buyer's risk but property passes late, *the seller* may recover the buyer's loss in tort. Unlike the principle of "transferred loss" suggested by Goff LJ in *The Aliakmon*, the German concept does not establish a direct third party right but merely entitles the buyer to have the seller's remedy assigned.

Ironically, in the House of Lords, Lord Brandon of Oakbrook rejected the principle of "transferred loss" as a principle of tort law by arguing that contract law provided sufficient and adequate protection in the field of carriage of goods. But the doctrine he relied upon in this context, *The Albazero* principle ([1977] AC 774), is a contractual device that is a functional equivalent of *Drittschadensliquidation* and was later (following the House of Lords' retreat from *Anns* in *Murphy*) to be extended to cover construction cases. Thus, once again, we can notice here how closely interrelated are the two areas of pure economic loss and contract law. The trend in English law now seems to be to apply reasoning similar to *Drittschadensliquidation* instead of extending recoverability of pure economic loss in tort. It will be interesting to see how those Common law jurisdictions which have not followed *Murphy* will react to *Panatown*. (E.g. Canada: *Winnipeg Condominium Corp.* v. *Bird Construction Co. Ltd* (1995) 121 DLR (4th) 193; Australia: *Bryan* v. *Maloney* (1995) 182 CLR 609; New Zealand: *Invercargill City Council* v. *Hamlin* [1994] 3 NZLR 513; [1996] AC 624 (PC, NZ)). Nowadays, the situation in *The Aliakmon* is covered by the Carriage of Goods by Sea Act 1992 which simplifies the transfer of the rights under the contract of carriage contained in the bill of lading. This Act was introduced in Parliament by Lord Goff, himself, as a private peer's Bill. (For a fuller examination see notes to cases 25–26.)

What unites the large miscellany of cases which the Germans have systematically brought under the heading of *Drittschadensliquidation* are two common elements. (Tägert's *Die Geltendmachung des Drittschadens* (1938) was groundbreaking in identifying these common features.) First is the fact that in these cases the invocation of the floodgates argument—the "shop soiled" argument of the timorous as Professor Fleming calls it in his *Introduction to the Law of Torts* (2nd edn. 1985, p. 3)—is inappropriate since one person only suffers loss. This feature, incidentally, also serves to distinguish the concept from the wider *Vertrag mit Schutzwirkung für Dritte*. Secondly, the co-contractor of the defaulting party—in our two examples the testator or the seller of the goods—will have no incentive to sue (or may simply no longer be around to sue!). As German lawyers argue, in these cases the person who has suffered the loss has no remedy while the person who has the remedy has suffered no loss. If such a situation is left unchallenged, the defaulting party may never face the consequences of his negligent conduct; his insurer may receive an unexpected (and undeserved) windfall; and the person on whom the loss has fallen may be left without any redress; a meritorious claim would go down a "legal black hole" to use the more vivid English term. The question to our mind is not whether the plaintiffs should be allowed to recover—we believe the answer must be in the affirmative. The real question is whether the defaulting defendants should run the risk of incurring greater liability towards these plaintiffs than they would have incurred had they been sued by their co-contractor. The German reply is negative; and their contractually flavoured solutions offer a neater explanation of this result than the tentative English attempts to harness tort for an answer.

Further reading

von Caemmerer, "Das Problem des Drittschadensersatzes", *ZHR* 127 (1965), 241; Lange, *Schadensersatz, Handbuch des Schuldrechts* i (2nd edn. 1990) pp. 447–479; Ries, "Grundprobleme der Drittschadensliquidation und des Vertrags mit Schutzwirkung für Dritte", *JA* 1982, 453; Schiemann in *Staudingers Kommentar zum BGB*, Buch 2, *Recht der Schuldverhältnisse*, Erster Abschnitt, §§ 249–254 (13th ed. 1998) Vorbem. zu §§ 249 ff. Rn. 49–78; von Schroeter, "Die Haftung für Drittschäden", *Jura* 1997, 343; Traugott *Das Verhältnis von Drittschadensliquidation und vertraglichem Drittschutz* (1997); and for more sceptical views see: e.g. Büdenbender, "Wechselwirkungen zwischen Vorteilsausgleichung und Drittschadensliquidation", *JZ* 1995, 920; Hagen, *Drittschadensliquidation im Wandel der Rechtsdogmatik* (1971); Peters, "Zum Problem der Drittschadensliquidation", *AcP* 180 (1980) 329; Selb, "Kritik formaler Drittschadensthesen", NJW 1964, 1765 (however, these writers, who very often reach the same result by more elaborate alternative means, have not persuaded the BGH to depart from its line of reasoning).

(iii) Some preliminary reactions to the German concepts and techniques

The comparatist must first describe a foreign system to his readership and then see what conclusions can be drawn from it to benefit his national law. The picture of German law given thus far is, inevitably, a simplified one. The reality is infinitely more complex, if not inscrutable to the foreign observer who treads on perilous ground when expressing a critical view of this system. But even the potentially distorted appreciation of foreign law by the comparatist may be of use to the national lawyer. Four points should, thus, be made at this stage.

First, the test that will determine who is to be included within the protective umbrella of the contract is crucial if the concept of contract with protective effects *vis-à-vis* third parties is to be employed. Most German lawyers agree that the list of such persons must be limited; but they differ greatly as to the criteria that must be employed to achieve this aim and, as a result, as to who precisely enjoys such protection. The traditional emphasis on the creditor's interest to protect the third party/plaintiff seems to me to be the most precise test without being excessively restrictive. In any event in our opinion it is probably more workable to place the emphasis on the relationship between creditor and third party/plaintiff (which is *known* to the debtor/defendant) than to operate, as the Common law does, on the basis of the amorphous foreseeability test applied to the plaintiff/defendant relationship. However, as recent developments show, this approach might reach its limit where there is a potential conflict of interest between creditor and third party. This demonstrates that recourse must also be had to the reliance placed on the special skill of the professional in addition to the purpose and scope of the defendant's undertaking to the contractual creditor.

Secondly, one might venture the thought that the more recent attempts to enlarge the circle of contractually protected persons threatens to undermine the security and (relative) predictability provided by the older tests. If the current trend remains limited, however, to the banking/financial services, it is understandable if not necessarily justifiable. For in these cases the German courts are essentially faced with variations of the *Hedley Byrne & Co. Ltd* v. *Heller & Partners Ltd* ([1964] AC 465) problem which they cannot solve through tort law because of the restrictive provision of § 823 I BGB. The way they expand contract is thus, essentially, as arbitrary as our own attempts to limit tort duties in similar factual situations. Though the pressures are exerted in different directions in the two systems, the problem is the same: discovering the proper bounds of liability which modern insurance practices tend to expand outwards.

Thirdly, the concept of contract with protective effects *vis-à-vis* third parties and the theory of transferred loss originally had a different area of application. The first was used in cases of physical injury and property damage (mainly in order to avoid the problems created by § 831 BGB); the latter applied to cases of pure economic loss, which had not always received full and adequate regulation by the positive law. In this original context the two notions presented one further difference. In the former, the risk of the contractual debtor was *widened* by the inclusion of a third party within the contractual umbrella. For example, in the *Cavalier* v. *Pope* type of situation, the landlord's liability was *extended* to cover injury suffered by the tenant's family as well as by the tenant himself. On the other hand, in the "transferred loss" type of case, all that happens is a "fortuitous" *shift* of liability as the loss is transferred from the contractual creditor to the third party. As stated, however, the concept of contract with protective effects *vis-à-vis* third parties was extended in 1965 by the legal malpractice case (concerning the defective will) to cover pure economic loss. Therefore, one now has two essentially contractual devices for dealing with these cases of economic loss.

Fourthly, and most important, I am inclined to think that German law, once stripped of its many technicalities and competing theories, is characterised essentially by one central idea that could be useful to both English and American Common lawyers. This is that these actions are contractual not tortious in nature. No matter that this approach grew out of the necessity to avoid defective or narrow tort provisions. No matter which device is used to accomplish the end aim (contract with protective effects *vis-à-vis* third parties or "transferred loss"). In the end, what matters is that the result achieved through the medium of *contract* ensures that the plaintiff succeeds in these cases but that the defendant's liability remains similar to that which he had agreed with his co-contractor. This is not the right approach for all instances of pure economic loss; but it seems to be eminently suitable for those cases that straddle the traditional contract/tort divide. (This is, certainly, the position *de lege lata, de lege ferenda*, however, some German lawyers (e.g. von Bar, *Gutachten und Vorschläge zur Überarbeitung des Schuldrechts—herausgegeben vom Bundesminister der Justiz*) who have studied the Anglo-American scene believe that the answer may lie in expanding tort law. As already stated, this is perfectly acceptable provided one then makes it clear that, generally speaking, the "tort" duty is shaped, both in its scope and extent, by the underlying contract. If, however, this is accepted, the discussion about contract/tort becomes entirely academic.)

Further reading

The following is only a selection of the literature on the subject of negligent misstatements and more generally the *Vertrag mit Schutzwirkung für Dritte*: von Bar, "Unentgeltliche Investitionsempfehlungen im Wandel der Wirtschaftsverfassungen Deutschlands und Englands", *RabelsZ* 44

(1980) 455; Beatson, "Reforming the Law of Contracts for the Benefit of Third Parties" 1992 *Current Law* 1; von Caemmerer in *Gesammelte Schriften* I, 597 ff.; Canaris, "Die Reichweite der Experten-haftung gegenüber Dritten", *ZHR* 163 (1999) 206; idem, "Schutzwirkungen zugunsten Dritter bei 'Gegenläufigkeit' der Interessen", *JZ* 1995, 441; Kötz, "The Doctrine of Privity of Contract", (1990) 10 *Tel Aviv Univ. Studies of Law*, 1; Lammel, "Zur Auskunftshaftung", *AcP* (179) 1979, 337; Larenz I, *op. cit.*, § 17. II; Lorenz, "Die Einbeziehung Dritter in vertragliche Schuldverhältnisse", *JZ* 1960, 108 ff.; idem, "Das Problem der Haftung für primäre Vermögensschäden bei der Erteilung einer unrichtigen Auskunft" *Festschrift Larenz* (1973) 575; Markesinis, "Doctrinal Clarity in Tort Litigation: A Comparative Lawyer's Viewpoint", (1991) *The International Lawyer*, 953; Musielak, *Haftung für Rat, Auskunft und Gutachten* (1974); Scheerer, "Probleme der Haftung der Kreditinsti-tute für die Erteilung von Auskünften in Deutschland und Frankreich unter besonderer Berück-sichtigung der Haftungsfreizeichnungsklauseln", *Festschrift Bärmann* (1975) 801; Schlechtriem, "Schutzpflichten und geschützte Personen", *Festschrift für Dieter Medicus* (1999) 529; Strauch, "Verträge mit Drittschutzwirkung", *JuS* 1982, 823; Schwerdtner, "Verträge mit Schutzwirkung für Dritte", *Jura* 1980, 493; Picker, "Gutachterhaftung", *Festschrift für Dieter Medicus* (1999) 397. For further references see notes to cases 19–24. For an interesting illustration see BGH NJW 1984, 355 (and in abbreviated form in JZ 1984, 246), related to the Lorenz–von Bar "dispute". For another solution see Grünewald, "Zur Haftung von Fachleuten im Zivilrechtsverkehr", *JZ* 1982, 627. During the 1980s, the flow of literature showed no sign of abating, as demonstrated by the following titles: Assmann, *Prospekthaftung* (1985); idem, "Prospekthaftung als unerlaubter Handlungsdurchgriff?" in Doehring (ed.), *Richterliche Rechtsfortbildung, Festschrift der Juristischen Fakultät zur 600-Jahr-Feier der Ruprechts-Karls-Universität Heidelberg* (1986) 300 ff.; Ebke, *Wirtschaftsprüfer und Drit-thaftung* (1983); Grünewald, "Die Haftung des Experten für seine Expertise gegenüber Dritten", *AcP* 187 (1987) 285; Hopt, "Dritthaftung für Testate", *NJW* 1987, 1745; idem, "Die Haftung des Wirtschaft-sprüfers. Rechtsprobleme zu § 323 HGB (§ 168AktG a. F.) und zur Auskunfts- und Prospekthaf-tung", *Festschrift für Pleyer* (1986) 341. For a discussion of Anglo-Australian law see: Nicholson, "Third Party Reliance on Negligent Advice" (1991) 40 *ICLQ*, 551.

(e) Other rights (sonstige Rechte)

(i) Generally

The term "other rights" sounds and is open-ended giving judges a relatively free hand in the determination of its scope and that is why some German authors (Medicus, for instance, *Schuldrecht II* (9th edn., 1999) no. 744) refer to it as a mini-general clause (*kleine Generalklausel*). But this judicial freedom is relative in the sense that it has always been understood that the rights and interests protected by this formulation must be *absolute* rights, i.e. rights which can be interfered with by everyone and which can be asserted against everyone. We have thus seen how possession can—in certain circumstances—be covered by § 823 I BGB (and, incidentally, asserted even against the rightful owner) (BGH 13 July 1976, VersR 1976, 943; BGH 18 November 1980, VersR 1981, 161.); and the same goes for other "real" rights (*dingliche Rechte*) such as servitudes (*Dientsbarkeit*), pledges (*Sachpfandrecht*) and mortgages (*Hypothek*). (BGH 6 November 1990, NJW 1991, 695.) Other *absolute* rights are patents (see § 47 of the Patent Law), copyrights, trademarks, and also the name of a physical or legal (commercial) person (§§ 12 BGB and 37 of the HBG). The right to one's image (or picture) (*Recht am eigenen Bilde* = §§ 22 ff. of the Act on Artistic Creations) is also included under this heading. But not every attempt to create new entitlements will succeed under this heading. The Bundesarbeitsgericht, for instance, in its judgment of 4 June 1998 (NJW 1999, 164) refused to hold that there was a "right to one's employment" that could be brought under this rubric. More importantly, *relative* rights, such as rights arising under a contract and owed by one contractor to the other,

are not included in this article. The breach of an obligation, which arises only from a contract (e.g. failure to repay a debt) and does not also amount to the commission of a tort
(e.g. dentist negligently removing the wrong tooth), will not be actionable in tort. But if
the same set of facts amounts to a breach of contract and a tort, the plaintiff is free to
choose the type of action, which is more favourable to him. For German law—unlike
French law—ignores the rule against cumulation of actions (RGZ 88, 433, 434–5; BGHZ
55, 392, 395). Equally, as already stated, if one person induces another person to break his
contractual obligations towards a third party, he will not be liable under § 823 I BGB
towards this third party for his economic loss. He may, however, be liable to him under
§ 826 BGB if the other conditions of liability in this paragraph are satisfied.

Three types of situation have given rise to considerable literature and case-law and they
must now be examined. The first is related to the possible use of § 823 I BGB within the
context of family relations; the second deals with the right of an established and operating business; and the third with the general right to one's personality and privacy. The
last two "rights" are very important judicial creations and *seventeen* decisions dealing with
them are reproduced below (cases 32–49).

(ii) Delictual protection of family relationships

It is by no means clear to what extent a person's family status and his legal rights there-
under are protected by § 823 I BGB. In some cases, the answer seems clearer than in others.
"Parental power" is, generally, regarded as an "other" right. Thus, if in the course of his
divorce proceedings, a father has lost the right to exercise those powers and refuses to
hand the child over to the mother, he may be held liable under § 823 I BGB (see RGZ 141,
319). But do spouses have an *absolute* right *erga omnes* to demand the respect of their
marital bond? Though in some cases the BGH has given a positive answer to the above
question (see, for example, BGHZ 6, 630 where a wife was given redress (maintenance)
against an unfaithful husband), the attitude of the Supreme Court is, on the whole, quite
negative. Thus the "marital intruder" (*Ehestörer*) will not be liable to the husband in tort
for enticing his wife away and then causing the husband the cost of instituting adultery
and divorce proceedings (BGHZ 23, 279). Neither will the wife be liable to the husband
on this ground (BGHZ 23, 215 and, more recently, BGH NJW 1990, 706).

Though this solution has not passed without criticism, it does appear to be correct. As
the Supreme Court itself remarked in the above decisions, *vis-à-vis* the parties in the marriage there is no reason for the law of delict to operate, their relationship being the exclusive concern of the provisions of the family law section of the Code. Equally, the third
party should not be held liable for causing the breach of the marriage, since marital
fidelity is something that concerns the spouses and them alone. This approach, that marriage as an institution is subject to its own rules and lies outside the protective ambit of
the rules of the law of tort, has also been adopted by even more recent decisions of the
Supreme Court (e.g. BGH JZ 1973, 668). However, not all lawyers are convinced by this
kind of reasoning so the debate cannot be regarded as being closed. Nevertheless, it should
be made clear that those academics who argue against the established view are only
arguing for a limited extension of § 823 I BGB so as to allow certain claims. What, more
precisely, they have in mind are the costs of divorce, delivery of a child born of an adulterous relationship, litigation for illegitimisation proceedings (BGHZ 57, 229), and maintenance of the child (before 1998 there was a special maintenance provision in § 1615 b II

BGB for illegitimate children; since then they are covered by the *general* maintenance provision of § 1601 BGB).

Further reading

Lüderitz, *Familienrecht* (27th edn. 1999), § 12 III; Boehmer, "Zur Ehestörungsklage", *AcP* 155 (1956) 181; Engel, *Der Rückgriff des Scheinvaters wegen Unterhaltsleistungen* (1974); Gernhuber and Coester-Waltjen, *Lehrbuch des Familienrechts* (4th edn., 1994) § 17 II; von Hippel, "Schadensersatz bei Ehestörung", *NJW* 1965, 664; Jayme, *Die Familie im Recht der unerlaubten Handlungen* (1971); Schwab, *Familienrecht* (9th edn., 1999) § 22; Rieger, "Grenzen des Schutzes des räumlichgegenständlichen Bereichs der Ehe", *NJW* 1989, 2798; Smid, *Zur Dogmatik der Klage auf Schutz des "räumlich-gegenständlichen Bereiches" der Ehe* (1983).

(iii) The right of an established and operating business

This is a judge-made right (BGH 21 June 1966, BGHZ 45, 307) which, came into existence soon after the Code came into effect and gradually developed its present contours. Like the next right (on human personality), it has developed into a kind of general clause intended to protect commercial enterprises against the infliction of certain types of rather vaguely defined interferences with their economic interests. These include such varied topics as area of operations, customers, commercial rights not already covered by patent or copyright law, boycotts etc. Its emergence may be due to certain gaps that were found to exist in the delictual provisions of the Code and the system of private law as a whole. Nonetheless, it is remarkable not only as a judicial creation but also because in a freeenterprise economy, where free competition is both the justification and the result of the system, the protection afforded to business entities cannot be as extensive as that given to property. This is why the contours of the right are rather vague and have to be determined with caution by the courts.

As stated, the development of this right began only four years after the BGB had come into force when the courts realised that the protection given by the Code in cases of pure economic loss was very limited. § 826 BGB, for example, only caught intentional activities which were contrary to "public policy"; and § 824 BGB caught only *untrue* statements damaging the *credit* of another person. Nor was § 823 I BGB of any help in many instances.

The first cases were mainly concerned with one type of conduct, which hindered the business activities of a competing enterprise. The noxious activity typically took the form of the defendant claiming unjustifiably that the plaintiff had no right to use a particular industrial property right (patent, registered design) held by him (the defendant). If the plaintiff ceased his activities, thereby suffering economic loss, but subsequently discovered that the defendant's claim was groundless and also was made in a careless manner, then he should be and was allowed to claim his loss. From the very beginning, therefore, it was made clear, and was subsequently repeatedly confirmed, that this kind of protection could only avail business or commercial enterprises and not, for example, a legal partnership or a trade union or a club. This distinction, which has not passed without criticism, was perhaps explained by the desire of the courts to keep within reasonable bounds the newly created right which, however, was destined to develop even further.

Four decisions are reproduced below (32–35) to illustrate the development of this new right and the accompanying annotations show that the literature to which it has given rise is considerable. (To these four cases one should add two of the cable cases (11 and 12) which also contain clear evidence of the desire of the courts not to extend unduly the ambit of the new right. This is obvious also from: BGH JZ 1983, 857.)

The doubts expressed about this right are understandable, not only in view of the fact that court-made rights are typically followed by an expression of concern by the judges that the new right (or tort) be kept within reasonable bounds. (*Cf.* the debates, especially among academics, after the decision of the House of Lords in *Anns* v. *Merton London Borough Council* [1978] AC 728.) These doubts are also explicable by the fact that the new right was soon expanded to cover cases where issues (like freedom of expression) were involved alongside the right of a business enterprise to safeguard its financial interests. This was the case with the extension of the right in order to protect entrepreneurs against criticisms that adversely affected their business but which were not caught by either §§ 824 or 826 BGB. For example, organising boycotts of the plaintiff's business or making factually true statements about it which the defendant culpably knew would severely affect the plaintiff but which he had no legitimate interest to make (see a call for a boycott in a commercial setting, case 35, BGH NJW 1999, 279). As stated, the danger of inhibiting free speech in these cases is considerable; and the need to "balance" the competing interests before giving judgment is also very great. (This balancing is, incidentally, a feature of the rights that are brought under the heading of *sonstige Rechte*. For interference with them does not, automatically, satisfy the requirement of unlawfulness (as it does with, say, interference with body or property); it must be weighed against competing rights before the element of unlawfulness is satisfied.)

Not every call for an economic boycott will be censured. The famous *Lüth* decision (BVerfGE 7, 212 of 15 January 1958; a translation of the key parts of this important decision is reproduced as case 36) shows that the motives of the boycott caller (defendant in that ensuing action) may save him from censure and give protection to his speech. But the *Blinkfüer* case (26 February 1969, BVerfGE 25, 256) also demonstrates the limits of this immunity. The litigation was born of the cold war, which was intensified when the Berlin wall was erected in 1961. An important publishing group—the Axel Springer group—instructed its dealers and distributors not to handle journals, which contained information about television programmes made in what used to be Eastern Germany. Dealers who refused to comply with this instruction would, in future, be barred from selling Springer newspapers. The letter was mainly directed against *Blinkfüer*, a *small*, left wing publication. It immediately sued Springer, relying on § 823 I BGB and claiming that the call for a boycott was "unlawful" under that paragraph of the Civil Code which protects its rights as an established and operating business and was causing it a 10 per cent reduction in its trade. Springer's defence, that the call for the boycott was that, notwithstanding the provision of the Civil Code, it was constitutionally protected along the lines of *Lüth*. But the argument was turned down since Springer's call for a boycott was different from *Lüth*'s in so far as the latter "was simply an appeal to the moral and political responsibility of his audience". (BVerfGE 25, at 267. The translation is taken from Professor Kommers', *The Constitutional Jurisprudence of the Federal Republic of Germany*, 2nd edn. (1997), 374.) Moreover, Lüth's call for a boycott [in the earlier litigation] "was incapable of directly and effectively restricting the human and artistic freedom of . . . Harlan [the plaintiff in that earlier action who complained of the call to boycott his work] for Lüth [unlike Axel Springer, the defendant in the second action] had no means of coercion at his disposal . . .". In the end, therefore, Springer's economic might, its "financial grip" over its distributors, and the threatening tone in which the letter calling for a boycott was written, all weighed against them. The court thus treated the call for boycott as a self-seeking speech worthy of no protection in law. But the Constitutional Court, true to its self-appointed task of weighing each case separately, refused to go as far as saying that all calls for economic boycott were worthy of constitutional protection. "The Constitution", reasoned the Court in some interesting *obiter dicta,* "does not bar the economically more powerful from engaging in the intellectual struggle of opinion . . . provided that the means employed by the person who calls for a boycott [are] constitutionally acceptable". This would have been the case, for instance, had Springer called for a "reader" boycott rather than tried to exploit the economic dependence of the subjects of the boycott. Once again, the reasoning is nuanced and the result not that different from that reached in the USA where, for instance, courts have held that picketing aimed at encouraging consumers to boycott a secondary business does not enjoy First Amendment protection. (*Cf. NLRB v. Retail Store Employees Union Local 1001* 447 US 607 (1980).) In this context one should also look at case 18 (BGH NJW 1998, 377) in which the German court came to a very similar conclusion. In that case, a blockade by protesters (who sought to exercise their rights under Articles 5 and 8 GG) was, somewhat unusually, not dealt with under the heading of the right of an established and operating business (as in BGHZ 59, 30; BGHZ 63, 124; BGHZ 89, 383). The balancing of interests thus took place in respect of the right to possession of the equipment which the contractors brought on to the proposed industrial park.

One should also note that the desire of the courts to keep this new right within manageable bounds has also been expressed in the form of an imperative that the interference with the established and operating business is "direct" before it can become actionable under this heading. The notion of directness, however, as Common lawyers know only too well from their experience with the "remoteness" cases, is an invitation to the judge to hide his own value judgment behind an apparently unimpeachable concept. Not surprisingly, perhaps, it also gave rise to numerous other attempts to discover the right test. Perhaps, the most often quoted test is in fact one given by the BGH itself. Thus, for the Supreme Court the conduct of the defendant will constitute an invasion of the plaintiff's right if it is "business-connected". According to this court, this means that it must be "in some way directed against the business as such . . . and must not simply affect rights and interests which are separable from the business as a functioning unit". This formula, as many academics have admitted quite bluntly, is nothing but an empty shell of words, and perhaps the courts should attempt more openly to weigh the reciprocal interests rather than to indulge in the creation of opaque formulae.

Finally, since the element of "unlawfulness" (on which see below 3(*a*)) has to be positively established in each single case, the result is that the new general clause has to receive its precise content by continuous judicial activity. This, in fact, has been happening, as Deutsch points out most clearly in *JZ* 1984, 308. The right of an operating and established business is further restricted by the subsidiary nature of the right (*Subsidiarität*) which means that the right can only be invoked in the absence of any other relevant provision (on which, for example, see BGH 5 November 1962, BGHZ 38, 204.)

Further reading

The literature on the subject is enormous; what follows is only a selection. Buchner, *Die Bedeutung des Rechts am eingerichteten und ausgeübten Gewerbebetrieb für den deliktsrechtlichen Unternehmensschutz* (1971); idem, "Konsolidierung des deliktsrechtlichen Unternehmensschutzes",

DB 1979, 1069 f.; Canaris, "Grundrechte und Privatrecht", *AcP* 184 (1984) 201; Fikentscher, "Das Recht am Gewerbebetrieb (Unternehmen) als "sonstiges Recht" im Sinne des § 823 Abs. 1", *Festgabe für Kronstein* (1967) 261 ff.; Larenz/Canaris, § 81 II-IV; Neumann-Duesberg, "Zum Recht am eingerichteten und ausgeübten Gewerbebetrieb", *NJW* 1972, 133 ff.; Raiser, *Das Unternehmen als Organisation* (1969); Schippel, *Das Recht am eingerichteten und ausgeübten Gewerbebetrieb* (1956); Schnug, "Das Recht am Gewerbebetrieb—ein Fremdkörper im deliktischen Haftungssystem?", *JA* 1985, 440; Schwabe/Canaris, "Grundrechte und Privatrecht", *AcP* 185 (1985) 1, 9; Schwitanski, *Deliktsrecht, Unternehmensschutz und Arbeitskampfrecht* (1986) 21 ff., 59 ff.; *Staudinger*-Hagen, § 823, section D; Suppes, *Die Rechtsprechung des BGH zum Recht am eingerichteten und ausgeübten Gewerbebetrieb* (1965); Wiethölter, "Zur politischen Funktion des Rechts am eingerichteten und ausgeübten Gewerbebetrieb", *Kritische Justiz* 1970, 121; Wolf, "Das Recht am eingerichteten und ausgeübten Gewerbebetrieb", *Festschrift von Hippel* (1967) 665 ff.

(iv) The general right to one's personality

In the united Germany, as indeed in the United States, the first attempts to recognise a general right of privacy (and, more generally, a wider protection of the human personality) were made by distinguished academics towards the end of the nineteenth century. (Thus, Kohler "Das Recht an Briefen", *Archiv für bürgerliches Recht* VII, 94 ff.; Gierke, *Deutsches Privatrecht* I, 707; III, 887) On a more regional basis, however, one must note the Civil Code of Saxony of 1863—greatly admired at the time—gave judges the *discretion* to award damages in cases involving the "dissemination of *untrue* statements about a person's life, personal abilities, conduct of office, established business, or other relations." Of course, the emphasis on *untrue* statements brings this provision closer to defamation than privacy. This caveat, however, does not really affect the pioneering nature of the Code given the feeling, widely accepted at that time, that interferences with honour, reputation, and other such personal interests should not be vindicated through an action for damages. (See, for example, various *obiter* in RGZ 7, 295, which reflects the view taken by most German courts.) This sceptical attitude towards a general right was, however, also adopted by the Committee, which was entrusted with the task of drafting the BGB. Indeed, in its Report, it expressed its doubts in uncompromising (and socially divisive) terms when it stated that "it [would be] repugnant to the dominant opinion among the population to place non-material values on the same level as property interests and to make good with money interferences with non-material interests. The Code [which was being drafted at the time]" continued the Report, "should not ignore this view, *especially prevalent among the better circles of society* [*sic*]. Only the *worst elements* [of society] would try to take advantage [of such a provision]. Pursuit of profit, selfishness, and covetousness would be promoted and wrongful proceedings, started from ulterior motives, would be encouraged." (*Protokolle der Kommission für die Zweite Lesung des Entwurfs des Bügerlichen Gesetzbuchs*, vol. I (1897), pp. 622–3).

Clearly, the times were not yet ripe for the recognition of any wide-ranging rights of personality; and the "toughness" of living conditions at that time made the average citizen quite indifferent towards such "lesser" interferences with his daily life. Inevitably, therefore, German law opted for a more gradual extension of the protection of the various aspects of the human personality. It was not until the Nazi holocaust demonstrated its utter disregard for human beings, their life, and their dignity, that the need for a greater legal protection began to be felt. And even then it was strongly resisted by sections of the Press which managed to scupper two legislative attempts to deal with this problem. The next move was thus facilitated by the post-war climate, the newly sanctioned Bill of Rights (contained in the first twenty articles of the Constitution of Bonn of 1949), and the growing willingness to entertain the possibility that human rights provisions could be applied not only vertically (to control the State) but also horizontally affecting (but not directly regulating) the relations of private citizens. What happened next is explained in the translated cases and their annotations—more than usually detailed since many comparatists would take the view that the German law of privacy holds some interesting lessons for the English Common law. Here, therefore, only four general observations will be made.

First, the judicially created general right of personality covers invasions of privacy of human beings and (less convincingly) legal entities (Palandt, *BGB* (60th edn. 2001) § 823 BGB, nos 181 *et seq.*); but it also goes well beyond what we, in the Common law, understand as privacy rights. Thus, in German law, damages—calculated on a compensatory or restitutionary basis—or injunctions (*Unterlassungsanspruch*), have been granted for varied violations of personality rights. They include the following. "Appropriation of likeness" (BGH February 14, 1958, BGHZ 26, 349). Unlawful release of an insured person's medical record (BGH April 2, 1957, BGHZ 24, 72.). "Neighbour snooping" (OLG Köln 13 October 1988, NJW 1989, 720; DM 7,000 were awarded to the successful plaintiff). Unnecessary publicity about an impending divorce of a member of the aristocracy (OLG Hamburg 26 March 1970, *NJW* 1970, 1325. Since the case involved a member of the Hohenzollern family the court carefully considered (and, in this case rejected as inapplicable) the possible (statutory) exception which applies to "persons of contemporary history". An injunction against publication was thus granted to the plaintiff. If the "private" information is already in the public domain, the courts will be reluctant to accord privacy protection. Yet even in such cases the courts will investigate whether a full identification of the complainant is necessary or, in effect, is part of a gold-digging operation on the part of the defendant/publisher. Thus, see, BGH 26 January 1965, JZ 1965, 411; BGH 24 November 1987, NJW 1988, 1984. But *cf.* BGH 15 April 1980, NJW 1980, 1790). The removal of organs from a dead body without permission. (LG Bonn, 25 February 1970, JZ 1971, 56.) The right to one's sexual identity, which includes the right of a transsexual to obtain a correction of his/her birth certificate recording the change of sex. (1st Division of the Constitutional Court of 16 March 1982, BVerfGE 60, 123.) The publication (by *Der Stern* magazine) of an unlawfully recorded telephone conversation (made by persons unknown) between two leading politicians. (BGH 19 December 1978, BGHZ 73, 120. The court decision is noteworthy for the detailed balancing of privacy rights versus speech rights. The conversation was between Helmut Kohl (at the time of writing, former Federal Chancellor) and Kurt Biedenkopf (former Prime Minister of the State of Saxony). Incidentally, this is a rare example of a suit brought by Mr. Kohl who, unlike the former Prime Minister of Bavaria Josef Strauss, avoided recourse to the courts.) The false signing of a painting with the name of a famous, contemporary German painter. (BGH 8 June 1989, BGHZ 107, 384.) The false and thereby damaging attribution of a statement to an important contemporary personality. (BVerfGE 3 June 1980, NJW 1980, 2070.) The unauthorised opening of sealed mail (BGH 20 February 1990, VersR 1990, 531. The opening of the sealed letter violates the personality rights of both sender and receiver.) The unauthorised imitation of the voice (of a recently deceased actor) for the sake of advertising a product (OLG Hamburg 8 May 1989, NJW 1990, 1995) and, most recently, photographing a public figure in a public place (BGH 19 Dec. 1995, BGHZ 131, 332 = NJW 1996, 1128 (third *Caroline* case, case 46). In a fourth and contemporaneous decision, known as the *Caroline Son* case—BGH 12. 12. 1995, BGH NJW 1996, 985—the court placed great emphasis on the defendant's obvious commercial motives in the taking of the prince's photographs.) That these results were achieved through an often bold re-appraisal of codal provisions of the Civil Code which, in the event were found to be outdated, can only be seen as a sign of open-mindedness on the part of the German judiciary.

Secondly, one must stress that the absence (until the *Schacht* decision of 1954) of a general right of personality did not mean that the protection afforded by German law (at any rate while the democratic order was respected) was inadequate, let alone non-existent. Nonetheless, the way the courts managed to afford protection was, at times, achieved in a somewhat crude legal manner and, in some respects, the current casuistic method of the English courts. When, for example, in 1899 the defendants broke into Bismarck's death chamber and photographed his corpse, public resentment was such that the court that had to hear the case against the photographers *had* to discover a way to deny the offenders the financial advantages of their conduct. In the event, the defendants were forced to hand over to the plaintiffs the negatives of the photographs. The actual decision, however, is more complicated than this summary suggests, since it had to be decided according to the old *Gemeines Recht*—i.e. the *usus modernus Pandectarum*—and was related to a bankruptcy question (since the defendants were insolvent): were the negatives part of their estate? (RGZ 45, 170). By 1907 this rather primitive protection was further extended by the Act on Artistic Creations (*Kunsturhebergesetz*) which, in §§ 22 *et seq.*, prohibited the publication of a person's picture without his consent unless he was a "public figure" (though see KG JW 1928, 363). The unauthorised publication of private letters was also increasingly restricted, though in the beginning the protection afforded to the "author" (or, more typically, his heirs wishing to prevent publication of letters that were in their possession) depended upon whether the letters in question could be considered as "literary works". This move started with RGZ 69, 401 where the Imperial Court demonstrated great ingenuity when Nietzsche's sole heiress sought to prevent the publication of letters written by the philosopher, which the heirs of the addressee wished to publish. In the absence of a general right of personality, the court reasoned that the ownership in the letters had passed to the addressee (and to his heirs). But if the letters could be regarded as "artistic creations", they could then be given copyright protection. Thus, to start with, the publication of private facts, lying outside the range of fiduciary relations, received little or no publicity. Fifty years later, however, the Federal Court in the *second* Wagner case (BGHZ 15, 249), which involved the private diaries of Cosima Wagner written during her marriage to the great composer, held that the publication of private notes or records could be enjoined on privacy grounds. This was so, even if they fell short of the standards of "literary merit" that would ensure them protection under copyright laws. Other aspects of the human personality received more clearly defined protection by the Civil Code or other enactments. Thus, § 12 of the BGB protects the human name and § 826 BGB can also, on occasion, be of use. § 824 BGB can give an action against a person who publishes wrong facts which endanger the credit of the plaintiff and which he knows or ought to know are false. Finally, the crime of insult or slander (§ 185 of the Criminal Code) can be used in conjunction with § 823 II BGB to give rise to a civil action.

Thirdly, one should note that the new *right* created in 1954 and added to the list of other rights ought to have been modelled on the *interests* of life, body, health, and freedom. If the Code were ever to be redrafted, the protection of personality should be added to the list of those *interests* with which it is more related, rather than be treated as another *right* analogous, perhaps, to that of ownership. One must add, however, that such redrafting of the Code seems unlikely; at any rate, it has failed up to now to materialise since the protection of one person's personality and privacy can mean that another person's freedom of speech can be curtailed. The issues raised by this new right are highly sensitive. One must thus never forget that the right to be protected against an often irresponsible Press must be counterbalanced by the equally important need to preserve the freedom of the Press guaranteed by Article 5 of the Constitution (see also § 193 of the Criminal Code). Where the line will be drawn will thus depend on the circumstances of each case and the rich case law will, at best, provide useful guidelines but not binding rules. The famous "Lebach decision" (BVerfGE 35, 202), case 42, illustrates how difficult it can be to balance on the one hand the right to publish information and, on the other, "the right to anonymity". (The anonymity of criminals and, more, generally persons prosecuted for offences, has been discussed in a number of cases. Interesting dicta can be found, *inter alia*, in: OLG Düsseldorf NJW 1980, 599; OLG Hamburg NJW 1980, 842; OLG Hamm NJW 1982, 458; OLG Köln NJW 1987, 2682—the last one linking German domestic law with the European Convention on Human Rights.) It would appear, however, that the more active a person becomes in the "public domain" the less he will be able to argue successfully that criticisms of his conduct amount to actionable invasions of his privacy. (Thus, see BGHZ 36, 77, 80; BGH NJW 1964, 1471 and many others.) In the light of the above, the German courts have adopted a much-nuanced approach. On an ad hoc, basis they thus tend to take into account the following criteria, the rationality of which must be compared with the English tendency to stretch or adapt the parameters of old torts. Thus, in cases where speech clashes with privacy we find German courts weighing such factors: (a) the motives of the publisher. (Contrast BVerfGE 7, 198 (*Lüth*) with BVerfGE 25, 256 (*Blinkfüer*).) In the context of privacy protection, this has been taken to mean that if the invasion was motivated by a wish to make money at the expense of the plaintiff, damages should be assessed in a way that would deprive the tortfeasor of his ill-gotten gains. (See, for instance, BGH 19 September 1961, BGHZ 35, 363, 369 ff and, more recently and in a more elaborated manner, BGH 15 November 1994, BGHZ 128, 14–16. This introduction of "punitive" damages into German law has generated much (and not always favourable) comment from academic commentators. See, for instance, Stoll, *Haftungsfolgen im bürgerlichen Recht* (1993), 57–67; 79–82; 210 ff.; Rosengarten, "Der Präventionsgedanke im Zivilrecht", *NJW* 1996, 1935–1938.) (b) the importance of the speech e.g. does it advance knowledge and public debate or merely benefit the speaker financially. (BVerfGE 7, 198, 219 (*Lüth*). For more interesting pronouncements on this sensitive point see: BGH 12 October 1993, NJW 1994, 124, translated in van Gerven, pp. 179–182.) (c) The way in which the information about the plaintiff was obtained: illegal means, (BVerfGE 66, 116 (1984) (*Bild-Wallraff*).) telephoto lens (indicating to the "intruder" that the plaintiff wished to be left alone: BGH 19 Dec. 1995, BGHZ 131, 332. The overall damages for Princess Caroline's harassment were fixed at 180,000 DM: OLG Hamburg, 25 July 1996, NJW 1996, 2870.) (d) The extent of the dissemination of the information is also a factor. (BVerfGE 35, 202 (*Lebach*); OLG Saarbrücken NJW 1997, 1376, 1379.) (e) The accuracy of the statement or whether it was fabricated by a news medium. (See: BVerfGE 34 269 (1973) (*Soraya*), case 38; BVerfGE 54, 208 (1980) (*Böll*); BGHZ 128, 1 (first *Caroline* Case). (f) The breadth of the restriction which the plaintiff wishes to place on the defendant's speech rights must also be reviewed; unnecessary restrictions will be denied or cut down to size. (BVerfGE 42, 143 (1976).) (g) Other, wider societal objectives which may be involved in the dispute BVerfGE 35, 202 (1973) (*Lebach*); BGH 12 October 1993, NJW 1994, 124 (*Greenpeace*).) and so on. (BGH 5 May 1964, NJW 1964, 1471 offers a good example of the position taken by German courts that not everything that interests the public can be published in the public interest. In that case, the defendant magazine, wrote an article about a criminal prosecution brought against the plaintiff. In it, it also referred to his repeatedly adulterous life. The court stressed that, normally, such revelations will be treated as amounting to actionable instances of violated privacy. In this case, however, the revelation was left un-punished since the plaintiff had, in the past, held himself out as a moralist.) The courts also take the view that a severe attack may justify an otherwise excessive counter-attack. (The *Gegenschlag* theory of speech: BVerfGE 12, 113 (1961) (*Schmid-Spiegel*), re-confirmed by BVerfGE 54, 129 (1980) (*Art critic*).) Despite the above-mentioned and, it is submitted supportable wide protection of different aspects of the human personality the German courts—ordinary and constitutional—have stressed from the early days of this jurisprudence that the balancing process must be undertaken with care and that, if in doubt, there is a kind of presumption in favour of the right of freedom of expression and opinion. (See, for instance, BGH 2 April 1957, BGHZ 24, 72; BGH 9 November 1993, NJW 1994, 127 and our discussion accompanying the translated extracts of cases given below in sections B. 11, 12.)

Finally, as has been already noted, the development of the new right was prompted by the Constitution's protection of the human personality (Articles 1 and 2). That this constitutional provision should be given material effect on the civil law plane was desirable and necessary. Less straightforward, however, was the method of widening the remedies available to the aggrieved plaintiff in order to make this protection more complete. Thus, in the first decision that recognised the new right—the *Schacht* case (case 39)—the court decreed, and the plaintiff was content to demand, reparation *in specie* (correction of statement published in a newspaper). In the second important judgment—the *Herrenreiter* case (case 40)—the court argued in favour of the analogical extension of § 847 BGB while in case 41 the court finally decided to base the award of monetary compensation on § 253 BGB in conjunction with Article 1 of the Constitution. If natural restitution is insufficient under § 253 BGB—reasoned the court—then that paragraph should be interpreted to allow even monetary compensation. The constitutional text, in its express desire to protect human dignity and personality, makes *this* extension of *this civil* remedy (damages) both desirable and necessary. This last part of the reasoning may be doubtful (see Medicus, no. 615). But given the legislative inactivity in the field, the Federal Supreme Court has repeatedly upheld it; indeed, the Constitutional Court itself held in a long and interesting judgment (BVerfGE 34, 269) that this "extension" in no way violated the constitutional order.

Further reading

On the right of judges to make law see BGHZ 11, 34; BVerfGE 34, 269; BAG NJW 1988, 2816 and NJW 1993, 1732 (case 110); and the following works: Canaris, *Die Feststellung von Lücken im Gesetz— Eine methodologische Studie über Voraussetzungen und Grenzen der richterlichen Rechtsfortbildung praeter legem* (2nd edn., 1983); Doehring (ed.), *Richterliche Rechtsfortbildung, Festschrift der Juristischen Fakultät zur 600-Jahr-Feier der Ruprechts-Karls-Universität Heidelberg* (1986); Esser, "Richterrecht, Gerichtsgebrauch und Gewohnheitsrecht", *Festschrift von Hippel* (1967) 95; idem, "In welchem Ausmaß bilden Rechtsprechung und Lehre Rechtsquellen", 75 *Zeitschrift für vergleichende Rechtswissenschaft* (1975) 67; Flume, "Richter und Recht", *Verhandlungen des sechsundvierzigsten deutschen Juristentages* (1966) K5 (1967); Heussner, "Die Rechtsprechung des Bundesverfassungsgerichts zum Richterrecht", *Festschrift für Hilger/Stumpf* (1983) 317; Larenz, *Methodenlehre der Rechtswissenschaft* (6th edn., 1991) (the relevant pages (341–412) of the 2nd edn. of 1969 can be found translated in *The Role of Judicial Decisions and Doctrine in Civil Law and in Mixed Jurisdictions* (ed. J. Dainow, 1975)).

On the right of privacy and personality see Baston-Vogt, *Der sachliche Schutzbereich des zivilrechtlichen allgemeinen Persönlichkeitsrechts* (1997); Brandner, "Das allgemeine Persönlichkeitsrecht in der Entwicklung durch die Rechtsprechung", *JZ* 1983, 689; von Caemmerer, "Der privatrechtliche Persönlichkeitsschutz nach deutschem Recht", *Festschrift von Hippel* (1967) 27; Canaris, "Grundrechte und Privatrecht", *AcP* 184 (1984) 201; *idem, Grundrechte und Privatrecht* (1996); Freund, "Der persönlichkeitsrechtliche Schutz des Werbeadressaten", *BB* 1986, 409; von Gamm, "Persönlichkeitsschutz und Massenmedien", *NJW* 1979, 513; Grimm, "Die Meinungsfreiheit in der Rechtsprechung des Bundesverfassungsgerichts", *NJW* 1995, 1697; Hager, "Der Schutz der Ehre im Zivilrecht", *AcP* 196 (1996), 168; Hubmann, *Das Persönlichkeitsrecht* (1967); Larenz, "Das 'allgemeine Persönlichkeitsrecht' im Recht der unerlaubten Handlungen", *NJW* 1955, 521; Löffler/Ricker, *Handbuch des Presserechts* (3rd edn. 1994); Max-Planck-Institut für ausländisches und internationales Privatrecht (ed.), *Der zivilrechtliche Persönlichkeits- und Ehrenschutz in Frankreich, der Schweiz, England und den USA* (1970); Mertens, "Persönlichkeitsrecht und Schadenersatz", *JuS* 1962, 261; Schwerdtner, *Das Persönlichkeitsrecht in der deutschen Zivilrechtsordnung* (1977); idem, "Der zivilrechtliche Persönlichkeitsschutz", *JuS* 1978, 289; Solyom, *Die Persönlichkeitsrechte. Eine vergleichend-historische Studie über ihre Grundlagen* (1984); Stark, *Ehrenschutz in Deutschland* (1996); Stein, "Der Schutz von Ansehen und Geheimsphäre Verstorbener", *FamRZ* 1986, 7; *Staudinger*-Hager, § 823 BGB, section C; Tettinger, "Der Schutz der persönlichen Ehre im freien Meinungskampf", *JZ* 1983, 317. For a comparative discussion in German see Dworkin, Fleming, Hubrecht, Strömholm, Finzgar and Kübler, *Die Haftung der Massenmedien, insbesondere der Presse, bei Eingriffen in persönliche oder gewerbliche Rechtspositionen* (Arbeiten zur Rechtsvergleichung, 1972); Wagner, "Geldersatz für Persönlichkeitsverletzungen", *ZEuP* 2000, 200; in English: Zweigert and Kötz, para. 43, p. 685; Handford, "Moral Damage in Germany" 27 *ICLQ* 849 (1978); Humphries, *Media and Media Policy in West Germany. The Press and Broadcasting since 1945* (1990); Krause, "The Right of Privacy—Pointers for American Legislation?" [1965] *Duke L. J.* 481; Lorenz, "Privacy and the Press—A German Experience", *Butterworths Lectures 1989–90,* 79–119 (1990); Markesinis, "The Right to be Let Alone Versus Freedom of Speech", 1986 *Public Law* 67; UNESCO Report: "The Legal Protection of Privacy: A Comparative Survey of Ten Countries", *UNESCO International Social Science J.* 1972, 417. A topic not discussed in this book is employee protection against violations of their privacy by their employers which has increased in recent times as computers enable employers to gather and store much personal information about their workers. German law is ahead of the law in both England and the United States; and it is discussed by Schwarz, "Privacy in German Employment Law" 15 *Hastings International and Comparative Law Rev.* 135 (1992)—an article with rich references to the relevant German literature.

3. UNLAWFULNESS AND FAULT

(a) Unlawfulness

Unlike French law, German law has kept the element of fault (*Verschulden*) separate from that of objective unlawfulness (*Rechtswidrigkeit*). The first is understood as an attitude (the attitude of a person who intentionally or negligently causes damage to another) while the second simply indicates the violation of a legal norm in the absence of a legally recognised excuse. How far these two concepts can actually be kept apart is a matter of considerable controversy and what follows is a bird's-eye view of one of the most hotly debated—but essentially—theoretical areas of the German law of torts.

The traditional school of thought on the matter, which still enjoys much support with the courts, takes the view that the element of unlawfulness is automatically satisfied whenever one of the names rights or interests in § 823 I BGB has been violated. (Matters are, as we have seen, slightly more nuanced when one is talking of some of the new interests that have been brought under the term "other rights".) For example, running over the plaintiff or damaging his property is an act, which brings about a consequence, which deserves the disapproval of the legal order. Unlawfulness, in other words, depends on the harmful result (*Erfolgsunrecht*). The only thing that can remove the "unlawfulness" is the presence of a legally recognized defence (*Rechtfertigungsgrund*). Action taken in order to repel an actual unlawful act upon oneself or another person is, according to § 227 BGB, such a defence (*Notwehr*). Equally, the destruction of a thing belonging to another person will, according to § 228 BGB, also be a lawful defence, so long as it does not represent a disproportionate reaction to the threatened danger (*Notstand*). Various forms of self-help can, within limits, remove the element of unlawfulness in the defendant's conduct. (§ 228 BGB, for example, allows one to destroy the object from which the danger emanates; § 904 allows one—in certain circumstances—to destroy an object *other* than the one, which is the source of the danger). §§ 561, 859 and 1029 BGB contain specific applications of the same general rule in the context of possession and ownership. Another legally recognised defence is found in § 34 StGB (necessity).

Consent (*Einwilligung des Geschädigten*) can also have a bearing on the issue under consideration if it is lawfully given with full knowledge of all the facts and prior to the accomplishment of the activity complained of. How this works in the field of medical operations (where it is most relevant) is a matter of some dispute. For some academics, (e.g. Laufs, NJW 1969, 529) a properly performed medical operation forms part of the process of healing the plaintiff, it is an act done in his interest and, therefore, the element of unlawfulness is not satisfied. Case law takes the opposite view and regards every medical intervention as tantamount to an interference with a person's corporal integrity. (Constant case law since BGH 16 January 1959, BGHZ 29, 179.) The patient's consent will, however, remove the "unlawfulness" of the interference but only if it was "informed" i.e. given after all the information necessary to him to decide has been provided by the doctor. The need to obtain consent in advance of the medical intervention is taken very seriously in Germany and so is the need that it be "informed". Thus, if the risk of an impending operation is summarily or inaccurately described in the form signed by the patient, the paucity of the information on the form will not be compensated by the fact that the doctor gave the patient ample opportunity to question him about the risks. (BGH 2 November 1993, NJW 1994, 793.) On the whole, if doubts are raised about the amount of information given to the patient, it is for the doctor to prove that he satisfied the appropriate standard. It goes without saying that in practice many difficulties can arise. This is especially true in cases of minors (who can give their own consent provided they are possessed of the required capacity of discernment). The same great care is taken in cases concerning the degree of information that the doctor has to supply to the patient (concerning the gravity of his illness) in order to obtain his consent (case 52–55, in section B deal with this problem). Clearly, other factors may come into play and the solution may, for instance, be affected by the likelihood of causing a neurotic plaintiff even greater injuries by revealing to him the full extent of his illness. All that can be said here is that these difficulties are in no way restricted to German law. (On problems of medical malpractice see, notes to cases 50–56, below, pp. 535 ff and also: Kern, "Fremdbestimmung bei der Einwilligung in ärztliche Eingriffe", *NJW* 1994, 753; for more recent developments see the articles by A. Laufs in *NJW* 1994, 1562; *NJW* 1995, 1590; *NJW* 1997, 1609; *NJW* 1998, 1750; *NJW* 1999, 1758; and *NJW* 2000, 1757.)

If the defendant produces no justification, and a protective interest or right has been shown to have been violated, the element of unlawfulness is satisfied. The plaintiff must then go on to prove the defendant's fault, at least in those cases where the liability is not strict or based on presumed fault. The question whether the defendant acted intentionally or negligently becomes then the second phase of the inquiry and more about this will be said in sub-section (b) of this section.

This approach was challenged in the late 1950s and 60s by a host of distinguished academics like Nipperdey, von Caemmerer, Esser, and others. According to these authors, unlawfulness should be determined by looking not at the result of the conduct but at the conduct itself (*Handlungsunrecht*). The mere violation of one of the enumerated interests of § 823 I BGB, if done unintentionally, does not necessarily satisfy the element of unlawfulness. According to this school of thought, something more is required to do this and the missing element can be supplied by proof that the defendant's conduct has failed to measure up to the standard of conduct imposed by a particular imperative rule applicable to the occasion in question (*Verhaltensnorm*). Alternatively, it could be shown that the defendant's conduct violated the general duty imposed upon all human beings to take care not to inflict injury on others. The need for such a duty is obvious in every civilised society. And the scope and content of this general duty of care (*allgemeine Sorgfaltspflicht*), should be deduced from § 276 BGB, which imposes upon human beings the obligation to exercise in their ordinary daily affairs (*im Verkehr*) the care that the occasion demands. So the objective approach will determine what the defendant's behaviour should have been. Moreover, in determining this standard, the social utility of the activity in question will have to be taken into account (*Sozialadäquanz*). Indeed, influential authors who favour this type of approach have openly stated that policy considerations should ultimately determine the existence as well as the limits of such duties. When we discuss the "duties of care" in the next section, ample illustrations will be provided of how all this has worked in practice.

It was inevitable that a system like the German, which flourishes on legal theories, would respond to this approach with a stream of legal literature accepting, condemning, or varying the new theory. For present purposes these variations on the new theme are irrelevant. In any event, all authors agree that the new theory has no application to intentional acts. The intentional interference with any of the enumerated interests cannot and will not be condoned by the legal order. But for unintentional interferences, the kind of inquiry described in the previous paragraph will have to be conducted before the defendant's conduct can be treated as unlawful.

What is the difference between these two approaches? Theoretically, the answer is obvious. The first approach (the wrongful consequence approach) treats unlawfulness and fault separately; the latter will only be considered if the former has been satisfied. The wrongful conduct theory, on the other hand, is prepared to regard lack of reasonable care as being part of the concept of unlawfulness and to understand fault (*Verschulden*) more in the sense of imputability (*Vorwerfbarkeit*). In practical terms, however, these two theories will, in the vast majority of cases, produce the same result, for it makes little *practical* difference if one's liability under § 823 I BGB is excluded for lack of fault or unlawfulness. As Professor Kötz has remarked (*Deliktsrecht*, no. 99) "one can scarcely imagine a case which the proponents of the old and new theories would solve in a different manner". In view of this remark some attempt must be made to explain briefly the reasons for the (apparently) greater popularity of the new approach which, incidentally, has also received the approval of the Supreme Court (see case 109).

Thus, first of all, this more *subtle* approach in determining the unlawfulness by the defendant's activity seems more appropriate for the two new rights—the right of the established and operating business and the right to one's privacy. Both are vague, and as indicated, require this careful balancing of interests before their violation can be established. (See, for example, Deutsch in *JZ* 1984, 308 at 309.) In these instances, it makes little sense to attempt this weighing of conflicting interests at the later stage of the inquiry when the defendant's fault is being considered, for without such weighing of interests the interference cannot be branded as unlawful in the first place. The traditional theory about unlawfulness may be suitable for the clearly defined and delineated rights and interests of § 823 I BGB; but it is less satisfactory in the case of the *new* rights created by the Federal Supreme Court.

Secondly, the new theory may even be appropriate in the case of the enumerated rights and interests of § 823 I BGB. For example, if the manufacture of certain goods is statistically bound to lead to the death or injury of people and/or damage to their property. Is such an activity to be branded as unlawful without more ado? In Germany some 7,000 people are killed on the roads every year. It would be theoretically possible for every car manufacturer to calculate, by reference to his share of the car market, the number of deaths or injuries related to his cars. Since we are talking of positive acts (the manufacturing of the cars), leading to an interference with one of the protected rights or interests, the element of unlawfulness is fulfilled and the answer to our question must be positive: the activity is unlawful. This qualification is absurd; and in order to avoid going a step further and imposing liability on the manufacturer one is forced to deny fault or, even more artificially, deny "adequate causation". This latter way of denying liability is clearly very artificial, for the result (death or injury) is neither an atypical nor an improbable consequence of the activity (the manufacturing of cars), so adequate causation must be there. What may render the manufacturer liable for the harmful consequence is not whether it is (or is not) adequately linked to his activity, but his violation (if that be the case) of one of the duties which the law imposes upon persons in comparable situations. Only if one of those duties has been violated should the manufacturer be held liable to the plaintiff. This idea can be generalised. The duty-based approach is the more appropriate approach in all cases involving a so-called indirect interference (*mittelbare Schädigungshandlungen*) with the interests protected in § 823 I BGB, while in cases of a direct interference with these interests, the unlawfulness of the conduct may be presumed. (E.g. Larenz/Canaris, § 75 II, p. 366). To use a well-known example of a *direct* interference (which was envisaged by the fathers of the BGB as the paradigmatic case): a nurse injects a lethal dose of poison into the victim's arm. The courts and most academics have meanwhile, accepted this distinction between direct and indirect interference. Naturally, it can be criticised for some measure of artificiality. But it is certainly a step in the right direction. The presumption of unlawfulness in § 823 I BGB does not only cease to be an adequate response to modern areas of tort law; it is also contrasts unfavourably with the English more flexible duty of care concept. The theory of indirect interference requires the violation of a specific duty of care to establish unlawfulness. Moreover, in cases of presumed unlawfulness, a German lawyer will have to inquire whether there was a duty of care at the stage of determining negligence in the meaning of § 276 II BGB, for to establish fault *a priori* entails stating that a duty of care was breached. The nature of the inquiry is surely somewhat cumbersome. But if one looks at the substance rather than the form, the duty of care is just as much a central concept to German tort law as it is to the Common law. The importance of the duty concept can be also seen from the significance given by German courts to the scope and purpose of the duty owed which for a long time now has replaced the criterion of *adequate* causation as the main controlling factor of causation. (For further details, see the section in causation below). So the common lawyer should not be deterred by the apparent differences between § 823 I BGB and the table of content of any English textbook on tort.

Common lawyers, accustomed to dealing interchangeably with the same problems under different rubrics (duty, duty owed to the plaintiff, carelessness, or foreseeability), should not be surprised at this equivocation between the various concepts, nor dismayed by the fact that the same issues emerge for consideration under separate headings. If there is some advantage in considering some of these points under the heading of unlawfulness (or duty) instead of adequate causation (remoteness/foreseeability) it is, in Dean Prosser's words, that it can "serve to direct attention to these policy issues which determine the extent of the original obligation and of its continuance, rather than to the mechanical sequence of events which goes to make up causation in fact" (*Law of Torts* (4th edn., 1971) 244).

Thirdly, the new theory *may* in some limited instances lead to a different way of looking at problems and producing a different result. When the element of unlawfulness in the context of § 831 BGB is considered this statement will be made clearer (see below, chapter 3, § A1(*d*)).

Finally, one should, perhaps, add that this new approach, and the increased willingness to think in terms of duties of care, has had a considerable impact on the law relating to liability for omissions as will become clear from the discussion in the next section.

Notwithstanding all these points one must, however, repeat that one is going into these matters not because of their true significance in practice but because one wishes to give Common lawyers a taste of a German academic debate!

Further reading

Von Caemmerer, "Wandlungen des Deliktsrechts", reprinted in *Gesammelte Schriften* (see Select Bibliography); idem, "Die absoluten Rechte in § 823 I BGB", reprinted in *Gesammelte Schriften* I, 554–72; Deutsch, *Fahrlässigkeit und erforderliche Sorgfalt* (1963); Esser/Schmidt, *Schuldrecht* I (General part) §§ 25 IV.I.3.2 and 25.V; Hager, "Zum Begriff der Rechtswidrigkeit im Zivilrecht", *Festschrift für E. Wolf* (1985) 133; Larenz, "Rechtswidrigkeit und Handlungsbegriff im Zivilrecht: Vom deutschen zum europäischen Recht", *Festschrift H. Dölle* (1965) 119; idem, *Schuldrecht* II, 607 ff.; Münzberg, *Verhalten und Erfolg als Grundlagen der Rechtswidrigkeit und Haftung* (1966); Nipperdey, "Rechtswidrigkeit, Sozialadäquanz, Fahrlässigkeit und Schuld im Zivilrecht", *NJW* 1957, 1977; Rother, "Die Begriffe Kausalität, Rechtswidrigkeit und Verschulden in ihrer Beziehung zueinander", *Festschrift für Larenz* (1983), 583; Stoll, "Zum Rechtfertigungsgrund des verkehrsrichtigen Verhaltens" *JZ* 1958, 137; Wiethölter, *Der Rechtfertigungsgrund des verkehrsrichtigen Verhaltens* (1960).

(b) Fault

A number of decisions are given below as illustrations. Generally speaking, however, and subject to one point only, the treatment which this topic receives in German law greatly resembles that found in common law textbooks.

The difference which sets German law apart can be found in its tendency to analyse the problems of fault in a highly abstract manner and to categorise the various types of fault under five, arguably six, different headings. Thus, a distinction is drawn between: (*a*) dolus directus (*direkter Vorsatz*); (*b*) dolus eventualis (*bedingter Vorsatz*); (*c*) gross negligence (*grobe Fahrlässigkeit*); (*d*) ordinary negligence (*mittlere Fahrlässigkeit*) and (*e*) light negligence (*leichte Fahrlässigkeit*). These categories can best be illustrated by means of specific examples. (Ordinary negligence is defined in § 276 BGB and we shall return to it further down. In addition to the above headings, recklessness may form a separate heading of fault).

(*a*) *Dolus directus.* It can come in two forms, e.g. I aim at a child standing behind a house window and I kill it. *Alternatively,* I set fire to a house in order to burn it *knowing* that a young child is inside and knowing (and accepting) that the inevitable result of my burning the house will be the death of the child.

(*b*) *Dolus eventualis.* For instance, I hit a man on the head with the intention of injuring him; but I also realise that he *may* die as a result of the blow. Despite this knowledge, I persist with my action.

(*c*) Negligence. The differences between the three types mentioned above is one of degree. In most *tort* cases the distinction between the various types of negligence (particularly light and average or normal negligence) is of little significance (though see case 110 as to liability regimes in labour law, discussed below in chapter 3); but it is of some importance for contract law.

A further distinction is made and it seems of particular importance to criminal law. This is between advertent negligence (*luxuria*) and inadvertent negligence (*negligentia*). Sometimes these terms are rendered into English as conscious and unconscious negligence. Adverted negligence comes close to intention (*dolus eventualis*) in the sense that the actor (personally) foresaw the criminal consequences as likely to materialise. The difference, however, is that in the case of *dolus* the actor accepts the result whereas in the case of *luxuria* he does not. (Indeed, he goes ahead with his action in the belief that the criminal event will not materialise). Inadvertent negligence, on the other hand, approximates the notion of *casus*. The difference is that *negligentia* (unlike *casus*) is a form of culpability since the actor could, had he applied himself, foreseen and avoided the consequences of his act.

At the beginning of this section, the state of recklessness (*Leichtfertigkeit*) is suggested as an independent heading of fault. This is because many lawyers would find it difficult to say how it differs in *practice* from gross negligence. The theoretical answer often given is that recklessness is a slightly worse form of conduct than gross negligence, involving a higher degree of deviation from the accepted norm. In practice, however, non-German observers are likely to take the view that their German colleagues are, in this instance, splitting hairs. Additionally, one has the impression that recklessness is a term reserved more for the criminal law while gross negligence is used in the context of civil law—contract and tort (e.g. § 826 BGB which requires *dolus*; the BGH, however, is content with recklessness: e.g. BGH NJW 2001, 3115, 3118).

§ 276 II BGB contains the definition of negligence. The person who fails to observe the ordinary care, which is required in everyday life, is guilty of negligence. This means doing what the reasonable man (or woman) would not have done or not doing what they would have done. As in English and American law, the standard of care is objective and the test— the *bonus pater familias*, as the man on the Clapham omnibus is sometimes called—is wide enough to allow plenty of room for judicial creativity. If the defendant belongs to a particular group or profession he will be judged against the standard expected to be attained by members of that profession. So a general medical practitioner will have to demonstrate the standard of care expected of general medical practitioners and not the standard of the specialised consultant. In our example, however, he will be negligent if he realizes (or ought to realise) that a specialised second opinion on the state of the health of his patient ought to have been obtained but was in fact never obtained.

Personal shortcomings of the defendant will not normally be taken into account and German writers often quote as an illustration of this the learner-driver who commits the kind of error of judgment which his experienced colleagues would have avoided. The reasoning is similar to that given by Lord Denning MR in *Nettleship* v. *Weston* ([1971] 2 QB 691) and it is clear that negligence in these cases does not necessarily involve any moral blameworthiness. One is also tempted to speculate that, as in *Nettleship* v. *Weston*, compulsory motor car insurance may account for this very high (if not unattainable) standard of care. Certainly, one case reproduced below (case 36), which has French and English equivalents, suggests that negligent liability often is strict liability in everything but name. Having stressed the objective standard of the test, one must add that there is also room for certain subjective elements to enter into the equation. Thus, the defendant's conduct will be measured against the conduct of the hypothetical reasonable man who was in the same *external* circumstances as was the defendant.

As stated, the reasonable man is nothing more than the anthropomorphic conception of justice. German judges, like their English, French, and American counterparts, will thus formulate their value judgment in the light of such factors as the probability of harm, the cost of avoidance, and the magnitude of danger if it is realized. German case law is very rich on this point and it really serves no purpose to provide further details since the examples and reasoning are very similar to those found in other systems. It is noteworthy, however, that mathematical formulae, which attempt to work out negligence on the basis of a yield–cost analysis, and which are so favoured by many American judges and academics, can also be found in German legal writings. It is unclear, however, whether this suggests that the German legal literature is ready for a more economic analysis of legal problems such as is found in American academic literature.

One should, perhaps, conclude this section by stating that the "*objectivization*" of negligence represents one of the inroads into the fault principle. The theoretical distinction between fault and risk-based liability is often very blurred in practice, especially where it is aided by a statutory (e.g. §§ 836 and 833(2) BGB) or case-law-created (e.g. § 823 II BGB) reversal of the onus of proof. The same is true whenever the notion of prima-facie proof, which is analogous to our doctrine of *res ipsa loquitur*, can be invoked. This change has involved a transformation or even perversion of traditional doctrines and notions and may be largely due to the impact that the insurance factor has had on the modern law of torts.

Further reading

On this issue see Brüggemeier, *Prinzipien des Haftungsrechts* (1999), pp. 55–88; Deutsch, "Der Begriff der Fahrlässigkeit im Zivilrecht", *Jura* 1987, 505; Esser, "Die Zweispurigkeit unseres Haftpflichtrechts", *JZ* 1953, 129; for France see Viney, *Le déclin de la responsabilité civile* (1965) and for some comparative observations see Markesinis, "La perversion des notions de responsabilité civile délictuelle par la pratique de l'assurance" [1983] *Rev. int. dr. comp.* 301 ff.

4. THE DUTIES OF CARE

(a) Generally

It has already been noted how the duty concept has been introduced into the notion of unlawfulness. *Acts*, according to this view, which indirectly infringe one of the protected interests, are not automatically unlawful unless it can be shown that the defendant has failed to satisfy the standard of care demanded by society. This duty-oriented approach becomes even more obviously necessary in the case of liability for omissions. From Roman times to today, it has been well known that liability for an omission could be imposed if a previous duty to act could be discovered. In early times, statute and contract were the main progenitors for duties of affirmative action. Later, the area of liability for omissions was widened, even though technical administrative difficulties, as well as ideological objections (especially in the Common law), strongly militated against such an extension. In German law, one of the most fertile sources of the development of liability for omissions and, indeed, of the whole law of tort, was the development of the idea that a preceding dangerous (or potentially dangerous) activity or state of affairs should give rise to a duty of care. From this idea, the courts slowly but steadily developed the famous *Verkehrssicherungspflichten*. The term *Verkehrssicherungspflicht* is not easy to translate. But its meaning could be summarised by saying that whoever by his activity or through his property establishes in everyday life a source of potential danger which is likely to affect the interests and rights of others, is obliged to ensure their protection against the risks thus created by him.

It has been a matter of some dispute *where* these duties of care should be considered. Should they be examined under the heading of conduct or unlawfulness or even remoteness? For present purposes it is not necessary to enter into these disputes, not least because once again the final *practical* result is not so very different. However, the purpose of these duties of care must be made clear. They are there to delineate the range of relationships which will be protected by careless interference; they are also there to limit (more effectively than the theory of adequate cause can do) the range of persons who could be held liable for a particular harmful result. To put it differently, does the relationship between the parties put one of them under a duty to take care *vis-à-vis* the other? Whether this is so, as well as the precise content of the duty, is a matter of judicial policy. This will be largely determined *inter alia* by the kind of factors we have already considered in the previous section, namely gravity of harm, probability of occurrence, cost of prevention and so on. As one would expect, the case law is extremely rich. And once one excludes theoretical disputes, the factual situations considered and the solutions given to the problems they raise are very similar in American, English, and German law.

The way the rich case law can be classified may vary. Situations giving rise to risks (and hence, duties) can be and are often classed alphabetically. Alternatively, the duties may be said to derive from family or business relationships, or where no relationship (in the usual sense of the word) exists, this last heading, for example, including a discussion of the problem of products liability. In this section one important group of cases dealing with safety on highways and premises will be examined, and the next section will discuss certain problems related to the law of product liability.

(b) Traffic safety on highways and places open to the public including dangerous premises

Historically, this is the area where the duties of care made their first appearance and they cover a large number of different factual situations which have exact equivalents in both English and American law. Thus, plaintiffs injured on public highways (or, indeed, smaller roads of all types), business premises, factories, shops, or homes may have a right of action against those who opened these facilities to the public or are in some way responsible for their upkeep. As the Imperial Court put it in its seminal judgment of 23 February 1903

(RGZ 54, 53) ". . . a person who makes his land available for use by the public is obliged to do so in a manner which accords with public safety." (Longer extracts can be found in van Gerven, *op. cit.*, p. 288, from where the above quotation is taken.) The following are illustrations from the recent case law; and they are noticeable for the fact that they have also figured in Common law litigation.

Thus, the President of a sports club who instructed a 14-year-old boy to mow the playing field with a self-propelled mower which, according to safety regulations should not be operated by anyone under 16 years of age, owes a duty of care to children injured nearby. (BGH NJW-RR 1991, 668). Likewise, the organiser of a hockey match owes a duty of care to his spectators who are hit by the ball because he failed to protect them by inter-jecting between them and the playing field a sheet of protective plexi-glass. (BGH 29 November 1983, NJW 1984, 801.) The proprietor of a restaurant should foresee that some of his customers may have difficulty with walking and should thus take appropriate meas-ures to protect them against the dangers of a very slippery floor (BGH NJW 1991, 921). Organisers of a mass spectacle are under a duty to ensure that the public is given safe ways to enter and exit the area where the event is being organised (BGH NJW 1990, 905). The owner of a building is prima facie liable if one of its visitors is injured on its escala-tors. (BGH 14 December 1993, NJW 1994, 945. Onus of proof reversed in favour of plain-tiff.) Examples such as these abound in the books; and, of course, it need not be repeated in detail here that all these are cases of fault-based liabilities.

Such duties are owed towards all people and, therefore, are classified under the law of delict. But additional contractual liability is not excluded. As English Common lawyers say when discussing their Occupiers Liability Act 1957, occupation of premises is a ground of liability not a reason for excluding other rules of liability. This can be the case, for example, where a customer is injured in a shop after he has concluded his purchases. Contractual and tortious duties may, in this case, coexist; but they do not overlap in the sense that each is subject to its own rules about limitation, measure of damages, proof, and responsibility for the unlawful conduct of other persons. Indeed, the tort reme-dies may, in this respect, be distinctly inferior to contractual remedies. This is why, as we shall see below (chapter 3, section A.2), the German courts have expanded the contractual remedies to cover the time *before* the contract is concluded (in our case before the customer has agreed to buy the goods). Indeed, the expansion has gone further and included even third parties accompanying the potential purchaser (see below, case 112).

The duty to take reasonable care to protect (lawful) entrants to premises (and their property) is primarily imposed on the owner of the premises but it may also be imposed upon a hirer or lessee, depending on their degree of control. The problems here and the solutions they receive by German courts are, essentially, no different from the ones encountered in Anglo-American law. Thus, for example, a contractual agreement between a landlord and his tenant, that only the latter will be responsible for the maintenance and safety of the premises and be liable to third parties, will have only limited effect *vis-à-vis* the injured third party. (But it may well be valid with regard to the *internal relationship* between owner–lessee: see RGZ 95, 61). Where the owner has delegated the performance of his duties to a third party, he remains answerable for his own fault in selecting and supervising the third party. Sometimes express statutory law permits such delegation and grants immunity to the delegating person for the bad performance. This is often the case with local communities who, for example, are allowed to subcontract to private com-panies their duty to clear snow from roads and spread salt in order to make them safer.

In such cases their responsibility will, normally, be limited to careful selection and supervision.

So far the discussion has been limited to the owner's general liability towards persons injured while on his premises. In principle, German law has not made the sharp distinction that the Common law made between lawful visitors and trespassers, and even less has it opted for the irrational distinctions adopted by the old Common law between different types of lawful visitors. These duties are owed towards all persons, the underlying idea being is that the "occupier" of the land is, usually, in a better position to know the risk and prevent it from materialising, and also to insure against its occurrence. Thus, the "occupier's" liability towards a trespassing child will, invariably, be upheld, a result, which is increasingly accepted as fair in the Common law jurisdictions as well. But liability towards the more obnoxious type of intruders (such as burglars) can and will be limited in various ways. Thus the court may not protect such persons either on the ground that their presence was not foreseeable (causative grounds); or because they may be found guilty of contributory fault (contributory negligence or *volenti* in the Common law). Alternatively, protection may be denied because the requisite standard of care has been satisfied by the defendant/occupier (*cf.* the humanitarian duty in *British Railways Board v. Herrington* [1972] AC 877). Equally, "no trespass" signs, if clearly phrased, may afford some (or full) protection to the occupier, though other factors (including statutes prohibiting such clauses) may also have to be taken into account. (Note, also, the parents' obligation to look after their children.) The extensive case law is reviewed by Marburger in *Jura* 1971, 481 and Stoll, *Das Handeln auf eigene Gefahr, eine rechtsvergleichende Untersuchung* (1961) and, on the whole, its comparison with the Common law is both easy and fruitful.

The liability of an occupier of premises may be engaged otherwise than by means of one of the duties of care. §§ 836–8 BGB are, in this respect, particularly noteworthy for two reasons. First, because they can be regarded as particular statutory expressions of the general principle discussed in this section. Quite simply, this is that anyone who exercises a sufficient degree of control over a particular thing (moveable or immovable) which is likely to cause danger is under a duty to take reasonable care to ensure that this danger does not materialise. Secondly, and more importantly, because they contain rules of presumed fault. In such circumstances it is, therefore, for the defendant to exculpate himself and not—as is normal—for the plaintiff to prove the formers fault.

The overlap between these two sets of rules (§§ 836–8 BGB and the duties of care) is not complete. § 836 BGB—more or less like the analogous rules contained in Article 1386 of the French Civil Code—deals with collapsing buildings or other structures attached to land. Collapsing walls or scaffolding, falling tiles, windowpanes that become detached from their frames, are all included under this heading. But snow falling off rooftops, tree branches being broken off, or even a falling gravestone which injures a passer-by would be covered not by the aforementioned paragraph of the Code, but by the duties of care. As stated, the precise content of those duties would vary from case to case. The measures necessary to prevent a "roof avalanche" would depend on a variety of local factors, such as frequency and volume of the snowfalls, the slope of the roof, the frequency of such accidents, and so on (*cf.* BGH NJW 1955, 300; OLG München, MDR 1965, 905). Damage from collapsing trees or branches might entail liability if proper checks on the state of the health of the trees were not carried out at the correct intervals (BGH NJW 1965, 815). Irregularly maintained gravestones could render liable not only the owners of the burial plots so long as they have control over them (BGH NJW 1971, 2308), but also the cemetery authorities who open this area to the general public (BGHZ 34, 206). Other instances from the very rich case law, which can in every way be matched by Anglo-American cases, include the following. A self-service store may be liable to a customer (or potential customer) who slips on a vegetable leaf or other slippery substance (BGH NJW 1976, 712; *cf. Ward* v. *Tesco Stores Ltd* [1976] 1 *WLR* 810). The same may be true of organisers of a motor-car race who fail to take the necessary precautions in order to prevent spectators being injured (BGH NJW 1975, 533; *cf. White* v. *Blackmore* [1972] 2 QB 651). A house-owner has been held liable to his visitor who is injured by defective banisters (BGHZ 5, 378; *cf. Wheat* v. *E. Lacon & Co. Ltd* [1966] 1 QB 355). Landowners can be liable to a plaintiff whose car was damaged by a train passing through an unfenced crossing on the defendant's land (BGHZ 11, 175; *cf. Commissioner for Rly.* v. *McDermott* [1967] 1 AC 169). House owners are liable to persons injured because the steps leading to their home have not been swept of ice and snow (RG 23 February 1903, RGZ 54, 53) or pavements not gritted. (BGH 27 January 1987, NJW 1987, 2671; BGH 15 December 1992, NJW 1993, 655; BGH 1 July 1993, MDR 1994, 256.) (A local authority will be liable if it fails to trim a hedge, which obstructs the view of users of a highway and leads to a car accident. (BGH 10 July 1980, BGH NJW 1980, 2192; contrast *Stovin* v. *Wise and Norfolk County Council* [1996] 3 *WLR* 388. The case is reproduced below as case 133.) One can practically match every case that exists in English tort books with a German equivalent.

With regard to accidents happening on highways or Federal roads, the actions will be directed against the authorities entrusted with their upkeep and maintenance. In the case of Federal roads, this body is one of the States (Article 90 of the Constitution). Local towns or districts are responsible for the smaller roads.

Less clear are the legal grounds of liability. Theoretically, this can be justified either by reference to § 823 I or § 839 BGB. The latter, in conjunction with Article 34 of the Constitution, makes the State (or other public authority) liable for breaches of official duties. From the State's point of view, this second method is preferable since § 839 I 2 BGB provides that in cases of negligence the official (and the State) will only be liable if the injured party is unable to obtain compensation from elsewhere. But liability under § 839 is not avoided if the victim is entitled to any insurance funds and this irrespective of whether their source is a private or a public insurance. (See *Münchener Kommentar*, § 839 BGB, no. 264; BGHZ 79, 26; BGH NJW 1983, 2181.) In this respect, matters are simplified whenever statute expressly designates such duties imposed on the state as *public law* duties, for in such cases the State is liable under Article 34 of the Constitution in conjunction with § 839 BGB. By contrast, the situation can become more obscure whenever the nature of the duties has not been expressly designated. (For further details see *Münchener Kommentar* § 839 BGB, no. 156. See, also, BGHZ 68, 217 and the discussion below, p. 893)

Further reading

For further literature on the "duties of care" see von Bar, *Verkehrspflichten* (1980) (the leading modern monograph); Canaris, "Schutzgesetze–Verkehrspflichten–Schutzpflichten" in *Festschrift Larenz zum 80 Geburtstag* (1983) 27; Deckert, "Die Verkehrspflichten", *Jura* 1996, 348; Deutsch, "Die neuere Entwicklung der Rechtsprechung zum Haftungsrecht", *JZ* 1984, 308, 309–11; Esser, *Grundlagen und Entwicklung der Gefährdungshaftung* (1969); Marburger, "Die Verkehrssicherungspflicht gegenüber Unbefugten", *Jura* 1971, 481; Mertens, "Verkehrspflichten und Deliktsrecht",

VersR 1980, 397; *Staudinger*-Hager, § 823 BGB, section E; Steffen, "Verkehrspflichten im Spannungs-feld von Bestandsschutz und Handlungsfreiheit", *VersR* 1980, 409; Stoll, *Das Handeln auf eigene Gefahr, eine rechtsvergleichende Untersuchung* (1961); *idem, Richterliche Fortbildung und gesetzliche Überarbeitung des Deliktsrechts* (1984); Westen, "Zur Frage einer Garantie- und Risikohaftung für sog. "Verkehrspflichtverletzungen"" in *Festschrift von Hippel* (1967) 591.

(c) Good Samaritans

Nowhere is the difference between the individualistic English Common law and the more socially impregnated Civil law seen more clearly than in the area of potential liability for failure to come to the rescue of another human being. Nineteenth century English philo-sophical thinking ensued that the medieval reasons for not punishing people for not being good but only making them pay damages when they were bad ensured the non-liability rule in England. For a time America followed suit and thus the Common law contrasted sharply with the Civil law systems which, through varying formulations, adopted the Good Samaritan precept and obliged persons to come to the aid of endangered strangers if they could so without danger to themselves. In ethical terms, the civilian solution was so obviously placed on high ground that, eventually, it even found support in some American Sates. (The states that passed so-called Good Samaritan statutes are: Florida (Fla. Stat. Ann. § 794.027), Hawaii (Rev. Stat. § 663-1.6 (a) 1985), Massachusetts (Ann. Laws ch 268 § 40), Minnesota (Minn. Stat. Ann. § 604.01 (1) (Supp. 1999), Navada (N.R.S. 202.882 (1999)), Ohio (Rev. Code Ann. § 2921. 22 (A), (I)), Rhode Island (Gen. Laws § 11-56-1 (1994)), Vermont (Vt. Stat. Ann. tit. 12 § 519 (1973)), Washington (Wash. Rev. Code Ann. § 9.69.100 (4) and Wisconsin (Wis. Stat. Ann. § 940.34.) Yet in pragmatic terms, the rule poses serious problems and has proved difficult to invoke in practice. Thus a study of what the systems do rather than proclaim reveals them to be much closer than the mere study of their books would suggest. This is true of English and American law. (The Vermont statute—the oldest of the batch, in force since 1968—has produced two cases: *State* v. *Joyce* 433 A. 2d 271 (Vt. 1981) and *Sabia* v. *State* 669 A. 2d 1187 (Vt. 1995). Hawaii's 1984 statute, produced a case in 1991: *State* v. *Cabral* 810 P. 2d 672 (1991). Likewise, Minnesota' statute seems to have been applied only once in *Johnson* v. *Thompson Motors of Wykoff Inc.* 2000 WL 136076 (Minn. App. 2000). Further references are unnecessary for this paper.) And it is also true of English and German law, which has confined its § 323c StGB to a state of an attractive ornament that rarely occupies its courts. (Thus, during the decade of 1990–2000, only nine cases were found dealing with 323 StGB. The six that bear some (faint) proximity to our topic are: OLG Düsseldorf, NJW 1991, 2979 and NJW 1995, 799 respectively. Two more cases, heard by the BGH, were remanded back to Court of Appeal for more findings: BGH NJW 1993, 1871 and NStJ 1997 127. In the last two, the accused were acquitted: OLG Köln, NJW 1991, 764 and BGH, MDR 1993, 721.) These actions, of course, are criminal actions; and on the rare occasion where they succeed, they result in modest fines (approximately US$1,500) but not in civil damages. In the light of the above, one is entitled to enquire whether the insertion of such rules in the statute book achieves anything than a programmatic statement? For detailed accounts of the case law see the *Strafgesetzbuch* commentaries on § 323c StGB: Schönke/ Schröder/ Lenckner, *Strafgesetzbuch*, (25th edn. 2001); Tröndle/ Fischer, *Strafge-setzbuch*, (50 edn. 2001); see, also: Maurach/ Schröder/ Maiwald, *Strafrecht, Besonderer Teil 2*, (8th edn. 1999), p. 45; Wessels/ Hettinger, *Strafrecht, Besonderer Teil*, (23rd edn. 1999), p. 266.

(d) Problems related to the liability of manufacturers of defective goods

Select bibliography

Despite its youthful age, this subject has generated an enormous legal literature. The following is a selection.

For mainly German law: Brüggemeier, "Produzentenhaftung", *WM* 1982, 1294; Buchner, "Neuorientierung des Produkthaftungrechts'. Auswirkungen der EG-Richtlinie auf das deutsche Recht", *DB* (1988) 32; von Caemmerer, "Products liability" in *Ius Privatum Gentium, Festschrift Max Rheinstein* (1966) 659 ff.; *idem*, "Das Problem des Drittschadensersatzes", repr. in *Gesammelte Schriften* I (1969) 597 ff.; Canaris, "Die Produzentenhaftpflicht in dogmatischer und rechtspolitischer Sicht", *JZ* 1968, 494 ff.; Deutsch, "Produkthaftung: Der besteuerte und mit Gewinnanteilen belastete Griff des Kunden in die eigene Tasche", *BB* 1979, 1325; *idem*, "Der Zurechnungsgrund der Produzentenhaftung", *VersR* 1988, 1197; *idem*, "Fallgruppen der Produkthaftung: gelöste und ungelöste Probleme", *VersR* 1992, 521; Diederichsen, *Die Haftung des Warenherstellers* (1967); *idem*, "Die Entwicklung der Produzentenhaftung", *VersR* 1984, 797; Ficker, "Grundprobleme der Produzentenhaftung", in *Festschrift Duden* (1977) 93; Gernhuber, "Drittwirkungen im Schuldverhältnis kraft Leistungsnähe", *Festschrift Nikisch* (1958) 249 ff.; Giesen, "Die Haftung des Warenherstellers", *NJW* 1969, 582; Hager, "Zum Schutzbereich der Produzentenhaftung", *AcP* 1984, 413–38 (dealing mainly with problems of economic loss); von Hippel, "Produkthaftung und Verbraucherschutz", *BB* 1978, 721; Honsell, "Produkthaftungsgesetz und allgemeine Deliktshaftung", *JuS* 1995, 211; Kullmann, "Die Rechtsprechung des BGH zum Produkthaftpflichtrecht", *NJW* 1996, 16, *NJW* 1997, 1764; *NJW* 1999, 96, and *NJW* 2000, 1912; *idem*, "Die Rechtsprechung des BGH zur deliktischen Haftung des Herstellers für Schäden an der von ihm hergestellten Sache", *BB* 1985, 409; Larenz, "Culpa in contrahendo, Verkehrssicherungspflicht und 'Sozialer Kontakt'", *MDR* 1954, 515 ff.; Lorenz, "Rechtsvergleichendes zur Haftung des Warenherstellers und Lieferanten gegenüber Dritten", *Festschrift Nottarp* (1961) 59 ff.; *idem*, "Warenabsatz und Vertrauensschutz", *Karlsruher Forum* (1963) 8 ff.; Lukes, "Produzentenhaftung und Maschinenschutz", *JuS* 1968, 345 ff.; *idem, Reform der Produkthaftung* (1979); Mankiewicz, "Products Liability—Judicial Breakthrough in West Germany", 19 *ICLQ* (1970) 99 ff.; Schmidt-Salzer, *Produkthaftung*: vol. I, 2nd edn., 1988; vol. II, 2nd edn., 1985; vol. III/1, 2nd edn., 1990; vol. IV/2, 2nd edn., 1990; Simitis, "Produzentenhaftung: Von der strikten Haftung zur Schadensprävention" in *Festschrift Duden* (1977) 605; idem, "Soll die Haftung des Produzenten gegenüber dem Verbraucher durch Gesetz, kann sie durch richterliche Fortbildung des Rechts geordnet werden? In welchem Sinne?" *Gutachten für den 47. Deutschen Juristentag* (1968); idem, *Grundfragen der Produzentenhaftung* (1965); *Staudinger*-Hager, § 823 BGB, section F; *Staudinger*-Oechsler, Produkthaftungsgesetz; Steffen, Posch and Schilcher (eds.), *Rechtsentwicklung in der Produkthaftung* (1981); Weitnauer, "Die Haftung des Warenherstellers", *NJW* 1968, 1593; idem, "Beweisfragen in der Produkthaftung", *Festschrift Larenz* (1973) 905; von Westphalen (ed.), *Produkthaftungshandbuch* Vol. 1 (2nd edn. 1997). For comparative works see Tebbens, *International Product Liability: A study of comparative and international legal aspects of product liability* (1979); Shapo, "Comparing Products Liability: Concepts in European and American Law", 26 *Cornell International Law Journal*, 279 (1993); Stucki and Altenburger, *Product Liability: A manual of practice in selected nations*, 2 vols. (1980); Faculté de droit d'Aix en Provence, *La responsabilité du fabricant dans les états membres du Marché commun* (1974); Schmidt-Salzer, *Produkthaftung im französischen, belgischen, deutschen, schweizerischen, englischen, kanadischen und US-amerikanischen Recht sowie in rechtspolitischer Sicht* (1975); C. Szladits, "Comparative Aspects of Products Liability" 16 *Buffalo L. Rev.* 229 (1966–7). On the European Directive on product liability and its relation to German law note: Brüggemeier/Reich, "Die EG-Produkthaftungsrichtlinie 1985 und ihr Verhältnis zur Produzentenhaftung nach § 823 Abs. 1 BGB", *WM* 1986, 149; Dielman, "The New German Product Liability Act", 13 *Hastings Intern. and Comp. L. Rev.* 425 (1990); Hollmann, "Zum Stand der Umsetzung der EG-Produkthaftungsrichtlinie", 34 *Recht der Internationalen Wirtschaft* 1988, 81; Lorenz, "Europäische Rechtsangleichung auf dem Gebiet der Produzentenhaftung", *Zeitschrift für das Gesamte Handels- und Wirtschaftsrecht* (1987) 151; Opfermann, "Der neue Produkthaftungsentwurf", *Zeitschrift für Wirtschaftsrecht* 1988, 462; Pfeifer, *Produktfehler oder Fehlverhalten des Produzenten. Das neue Produkthaftungsrecht in Deutschland, den USA und nach der EG-Richtlinie* (1987); Schlechtriem, "Die EG-Richtlinie zur Produkthaftung", *VersR* 1986, 1033; Schmidt-Salzer, "Entscheidungssammlung Produkthaftung und die EG-Richtlinie Produkt-thaftung", *BB* 1986, 1103; Schmidt-Salzer/Hollmann, *Kommentar EG-Richtlinie Produkthaftung* (1986); von Westphalen (ed.), *Produkthaftungshandbuch* Vol. 2 (2nd edn. 1999). For a brief commentary on the British Act and further references see: Markesinis and Deakin *Tort Law* 4th edn. (1999) pp. 558 ff.

(i) Introduction

The law of product liability—and German lawyers have adopted this American term— was one of the most hotly debated issues during the 1960s and 1970s, the voluminous literature and case-law constantly proving the theoretical and practical interest in the subject. American lawyers will not be surprised at this since they, too, have managed to turn this subject into a prime area of tort law, often used as an ideal course for advanced tort classes. What will, however, come as a surprise is how "new" this area of the law is to the Germans. That is not to imply, of course, that product liability cases cannot be found before the sixties. But it does mean that until about the late fifties important instances of product liability would not only remain uncompensated; they would also pass almost unnoticed by the law reports and the academic literature. In 1956, for example, the Federal Supreme Court had to deal with a claim brought by a plaintiff whose bicycle suddenly collapsed and injured him. The accident was not due to a defect in design but in the production of the particular bicycle. But the court had little sympathy with the plaintiff's complaint and dismissed it in a cavalier manner with the statement that "common experience suggests . . . that such technical defects cannot be prevented". In the court's view, the accident should have been treated as one of those unfortunate things that happen in life and must remain uncompensated. That the case was only reported in a specialised legal journal also indicates that it was not treated as one of general interest. With two interesting exceptions of dissertations written in the 1930s under the direction of the famous Ernst Rabel, the academic literature showed equal lack of enthusiasm for a topic, which nowadays is, if anything, overworked.

The change came in the early 1960s when Professor Werner Lorenz published an article, which for the first time made the majority of German lawyers aware of development in this field in the United States. The article, making excellent use of the comparative method—Lorenz had studied in Oxford with the late Professor Lawson and later worked at Cornell with Professor Schlesinger—appeared at the right time even though in the beginning legal practitioners vehemently opposed the introduction of American ideas. However, the 1960s and 1970s were decades that witnessed a number of spectacular products liability accidents, which triggered off public interest in this problem. In 1967, for example, nearly 800,000 owners of Ford cars were informed of design defects in a particular model and were advised to take certain precautionary steps. A year later, Volkswagen in Germany had to recall some 160,000 defective cars; and then the thalidomide scandal broke out leading to the birth of thousands of seriously incapacitated children and to worldwide litigation. These events, coupled with a general increase in consumer-orientated legislation, resulted in the development of the law; that the protection afforded now, some forty years later, might be seen by some to have gone too far is another matter. These problems are too complicated to receive a summary answer here.

(ii) Damage to the product

Before we proceed to examine the further development of the law we should try to delineate the province of product liability. It has traditionally been assumed that this topic refers to personal injury or damage to *other* things caused *by* the defective product. Damage *to* the thing rather than damage caused *by* the thing is not included under this heading. The distinction is conceptually convincing and economically sound, but it is not always easy to draw. For, in between the black and white areas lies contested ground, which has given rise to many problems. One of them is when the defective product causes further damage to itself, or, which is a variant, when a defective component of the product "spreads" the defect to the whole product and thus reduces its efficiency and/or value. Once again, we are here talking of the troublesome distinction between property damage and economic loss.

We have already touched upon this subject and stated that this type of loss cannot be brought under the heading of damage to property under § 823 I BGB. Two cases reproduced below (74 and 75), dealing with negligent inspections of buildings under construction which lead to the reduction of their value (economic loss) but not to injuries or damage to *other* property, show how clearly the German judges have understood the problem in question. As the Supreme Court said (BGHZ 39, 366) "To make someone the owner of a defective building is not to invade an already existing ownership". Incidentally, the annotation to this case will also show how superior the German reasoning (arguably) is compared to the less satisfactory analysis adopted in the late 1970s in similar cases in England. Some ten years later, however, English law moved slowly closer to the position expressed in cases 74 and 75, while, in the meantime the German case law has shifted towards the position previously adopted in England, though many uncertainties still remain.

There is more than a desire for conceptual clarity, however, that dictates (or should dictate) a denial of a *tort* remedy in such a situation. To allow tort to demolish contract in such circumstances can have important and not necessarily welcome consequences. For contract law can produce a more complete and subtle distribution of risks. Moreover, burdening the manufacturer with claims of this kind might have insupportable economic and insurance consequences.

Despite these objections against extending delictual remedies to cases of damage *to* the product, German courts, presumably under the prevailing climate of consumer protection, have not applied the above-mentioned sound rule to defective *movables*. Thus, cases 68–73 show how tort actions have succeeded in such instances; but their solutions have attracted considerable criticism from academics and the demarcation problems to which they can give rise have not yet been fully worked out. This becomes quite obvious when one studies the shifting views of the Supreme Court on this subject. (See notes to these cases and p. 39, above.) It is little comfort to tell German lawyers that the Americans have faced similar difficulties. However, the decision of the US Supreme Court in *East River S.S. Corp.* v. *Transamerica Delaval Inc.* (476 US 858, 106 S. Ct. 2295, reproduced below as addendum 2 to B. 14) has done much to clarify matters and will repay careful reading.

Further reading

For relevant discussions see Brüggermeier in *VersR* 1983, 501; Rengier note in *JZ* 1977, 346; Schubert note in *JR* 1977, 458; Schmidt-Salzer in *BB* 1979, 1 and, again, in *BB* 1983, 534. For a

comparative discussion with references to English and American case-law see the annotations to
these decisions and Hager, in *AcP* 1984, 413. See, also, notes to cases 68–75.

(iii) Contractual or quasi-contractual solutions to the problem

To return to our main topic, we should now discuss briefly how the modern law came to
be developed although it should be noted from the outset that contractual solutions to
the problem of product liability are only of historic interest. Broadly speaking, one can
divide this development into two phases. The first, which culminates with the seminal
judgment of the Supreme Court in 1968 (BGHZ 51, 91), is basically preoccupied with
finding a legal basis for this essentially new heading of liability. The second was one of
consolidation, elaboration, and even expansion of the delictual action firmly established
since 1968. The latest phase, not significantly different from the previous one, will be
dominated by the adjustments made by the Product Liability Act of 1989 giving effect to
the European Community's Directive of 25 July 1985. (Both documents are reproduced
in section B. 15 below, along with the English equivalent enactment.)

The leading judgment of 1968 clearly reflects the preoccupations of academics to find
a legal basis for products liability in so far as it devotes much space to the detailed consideration of the various contractual or quasi-contractual theories developed in the 1960s
to meet the new situation. If a Common lawyer were to express surprise that this search
for a juristic basis would be conducted in the area of contract law rather than tort law he
should then consider the following two points.

First, one must repeat what was said earlier on, namely that the law of contracts has
proved more pliable and able to expand on the civil law systems than it has in the
Common law. The doctrine of consideration is the main reason why the Common law
was forced to develop its law of torts. But wherever consideration has been taken somewhat less seriously—e.g. in the United States—the concurrent growth of contractual and
delictual remedies has been a notable feature. The UCC doctrine of "warranty without
privity" is one of these developments and, incidentally, brings American law quite close
to French law, which has developed its strict law of products' liability through the law of
sales but has also accepted strict or semi-strict tortious liability.

Further reading

For details on this see J. Ghestin, *Conformité et garanties dans la vente (produits mobiliers)* (1983);
La responsabilité des fabricants et distributeurs (1975) (collection of essays, ed. by Professor Gavalda);
La responsabilité civile du fabricant dans les états membres du Marché Commun (1974) with inter-
esting essays by Professors Bigot (213), Ghestin (17), and Malinvaud (131).

Secondly, one should note the considerable advantages that a plaintiff could obtain if his
action was dubbed by German law contractual or quasi-contractual. Two of them should
be mentioned here. The first is related to the burden of proof. Though in the civil law
systems (unlike the Common law) fault is an element of an action for breach of contract
as well as tort, the burden of proof may be different in these two actions. Thus, § 282
BGB, which was applied, by analogy, to other contractual remedies, provided that, "If it
is disputed whether the impossibility of performance is the result of a circumstance for
which the debtor is responsible, the burden of proof falls on the debtor", i.e. if contested,
the defendant has to disprove his fault. (This result follows now from § 280 2 BGB.) On
the other hand, according to the general rules of tort law, in a product liability case the

plaintiff had to show that the product left the defendant's enterprise in a faulty condition and that the defendant, or his legally appointed representative, had not organised his business in such a way as to enable the defect to be detected. The second, and not entirely unrelated, reason that made contractual actions preferable to those founded in tort could be found in § 831 BGB. This deals with the problems of vicarious liability and will be discussed in greater detail below (chapter 3, A. 1 and 2). Here suffice it to say that it does not establish a true rule of vicarious liability but makes employers liable for the unlawful acts of their employees only where they are themselves guilty of negligent selection or supervision of the employees. In contrast debtors are, according to § 278 BGB, fully liable for the faults of the persons whom they employ in the execution of their *contractual* obligations. Finally, one should also bear in mind the relatively short period of limitation applicable to tort claims (§ 195 BGB) (though, admittedly, in some instances the period of limitation may be shorter in contract than it is in tort and this has caused a flight into tort. Thus, see the cases discussed in section 16, and p. 93).

Having stated the reasons, which prompted German lawyers to turn to the law of contract rather than the law of tort initially, one should look briefly at the various contractual or quasi-contractual methods advanced by academic writers. The brief comments that follow should be read in conjunction with the relevant passages of the leading case (No. 61) which is reproduced below (chapter 2, section B. 15).

One way of making the manufacturer liable to the ultimate consumer is by discovering an express or implied guarantee, which is directed to the ultimate consumer and on which he relies to his detriment. The difficulties with this approach are the same that eventually forced American lawyers to abandon a similar kind of reasoning—widely prevalent in the United States during the 1950s—but which proved to be inadequate in practice.

A second contractual method can be found in the various attempts to discover a contract in favour of a third party or a contract with protective effects *vis-à-vis* third parties. The first type of contract (*Vertrag zugunsten Dritter*) is regulated by §§ 328 ff. BGB and is not unknown to American lawyers who, since *Lawrence* v. *Fox*, 20 NY 268 (1859), have broken away from the English tradition on this matter. As already explained, this type of contract allows a third party (the ultimate consumer) to require performance of the contract concluded between the creditor and the debtor (for example, the manufacturer and the wholesaler). On reflection, however, this is a rather awkward notion. For what the third party/consumer needs is not the right to enforce the *prime* contractual obligation (delivery of the thing in exchange for payment of the price). Rather, his need is to be included under the protective umbrella of the *subsidiary* contractual obligations (in our case to deliver the thing in good order and with clear instruction, etc.). This way of reasoning led German courts to develop, under the influence of Professor Larenz, a variant to the contract in favour of third parties which can be called a contract with protective effects *vis-à-vis* third parties (*Vertrag mit Schutzwirkung für Dritte*). In this way, third parties can be given the protection afforded to the main creditor which emanates from a cluster of subsidiary obligations which would be included in every such contract in accordance with § 242 BGB (contracts to be performed according to good faith).

However, we have already noted the need to keep this expansion of the contractual umbrella under control lest it undermine completely the relativity of the contractual bond. To put it differently, *who* will be treated as a third party and receive such protection? Though as already stated the requirement of "proximity to the performance" (*Leistungsnähe*), a close relationship (*personenrechtliches Fürsorgeverhältnis*) between the contractual creditor and the third party has been relaxed by some recent decisions, this has not occurred in the context of products liability. Indeed, it is noteworthy that even those authors who have argued in favour of expanding the circle of "protected" third parties have refused to apply their theories to this area of the law. (See, for example, Canaris, "Die Produzentenhaftpflicht in dogmatischer und rechtspolitischer Sicht", *JZ* 1968, 494, 499 ff.)

The theory of "transferred loss" (or, to give its German name, *Drittschadensliquidation*) has also been considered but rejected. In the chicken pest case the Supreme Court, disagreeing with the Court of Appeal, would not allow the veterinarian to demand from the pharmaceutical company (which had sold him the defective vaccine) the loss *suffered by the owner* of the chickens which died as a result of the inoculation. (If such a claim had been recognised it could have been transferred by the veterinarian to the plaintiff and pursued by the latter.)

For further reading concerning the concepts of *Drittschadensliquidation* and contracts for the benefit of a third party see the references given in section 2 (d)(iii), above pp. 59 ff.

In addition to the above contractual theories, the court also dealt with a number of others, which share some common elements including the desire to justify a strict or semi-strict type of liability. Two of them deserve a brief look since they are expressly referred to (and rejected) by the court.

The first, advanced by a leading expert in the field (Diederichsen, *Die Haftung des Warenherstellers* (1967) 297 ff., 327 ff., 345 ff.) can, in a rather crass manner but for simplicity's sake, be reduced to two basic propositions. First, the basic relationship in these cases is that between manufacturer and ultimate consumer. This is one of "reliance", irrespective of any awareness of any advertisements by the manufacturer so long as the defective goods were purchased from a sales network set up by the manufacturer and were already defective at the time they left his factory. Secondly, that this relation is *sui generis*, not regulated by the written law and must thus be shaped in its details by the judge. A corollary to this is that the liability is strict.

The court's dislike of any theory, which cannot be pegged on a clear provision of the Code, is obvious from the way this theory is dismissed. Equally obvious—and in tune with the court's long-established practice—is its refusal to discover new headings of strict liability in the absence of legislative intervention (see below, chapter 3, section A. 5). A third objection, not mentioned by the court but stressed by academics, is the following. If the manufacturer of goods is to be strictly liable, why should this liability be limited to cases where his goods were sold bearing his name (or through a sales network set up by him) and excluded whenever the same goods were sold unidentified in a department store or, even, bearing the latter's commercial brand?

Lorenz's theory ("Warenabsatz und Vertrauensschutz" *Karlsruher Forum* (1963) 8, especially 14 ff.) shares a number of common points with some other theories also considered and rejected by the court (see the work of Canaris in the Select Bibliography, above p. 91). He, too, for example, puts the emphasis on the relationship between producer and ultimate consumer and he, also, is prepared to attach considerable significance to the reliance that one person (the consumer) places on the conduct of another (the manufacturer). Like other writers, Lorenz also accepts that we are here faced with a *lacuna* in the written law which must be filled in a way that will ensure that the plaintiff is given a protection equal to (if not greater than) that enjoyed by contracting parties (moving towards strict liability). Unlike other authors, however, Lorenz makes a clear attempt to base his solution on a specific provision of the Code and this, in his opinion, is § 122 BGB.

This provides that if a declaration of an intention is void, either because it was made in error or because it was not seriously intended, the person who made the declaration must compensate the other party for the damages he has sustained as a result of relying upon the validity of the declaration. (Incidentally, the damages in this case cover only the reliance interest and not the expectation loss). This provision, according to Lorenz, can be analogically extended to cover the present problem, since the manufacturer, through the advertising of his products, leads the ultimate consumer to expect that his products will be free of all defects. In its judgment the Supreme Court directs its criticism mainly towards Lorenz's point about the significance of modern advertising techniques and the effect they can be taken to have on the ultimate purchaser. It is submitted, however, that Lorenz's view has two further weaknesses: first, it is by no means clear (to a non-German lawyer at least) that § 122 BGB, which envisages an entirely different situation, is capable of such an extension. It would appear more likely that Lorenz is trying to make in a very ingenious way the best of a bad situation, i.e. to use the Code to solve a problem which could not have really been envisaged by its draftsmen. Secondly, even if § 122 BGB could be so extended, it would lead to the imposition of *strict* liability on the manufacturer towards the ultimate consumer (with whom the manufacturer has no contract), but to liability based on fault (in accordance with the contract of sale) towards his (the manufacturer's) *immediate* purchaser—a solution which seems neither very reasonable nor attractive. (Lorenz himself accepted in a later article the limitations of § 122 BGB: see "Die Haftung des Warenherstellers" *Band 28 der Arbeiten zur Rechtsvergleichung* (1966) 51–2.)

(iv) The decision of 1968 and the move from contract to delict

The contractual or semi-contractual theories considered and rejected by the Supreme Court in its 1968 decision suffered from one further defect which was shared by all of them. For they all aimed at protecting the person who was in some way involved in the sales-chain and somehow could justify a "relationship" with the manufacturer by means of reliance or a guarantee or some other manifestation on his part concerning his goods. True, some theories went further by trying to include within the protective circle other persons such as the family of the ultimate consumer or others living or working in his household. But if the policy reasons for imposing liability on the manufacturer are correct—and these include his greater ability to detect and correct a defect, to insure against the risk, and to shift the cost of accident when it is realised—then the same type of protection should be afforded even to third parties, such as the proverbial bystander who is injured by the exploding ginger-beer bottle. Basing liability on tort, and in particular § 823 I BGB, provided the necessary breakthrough. The court realised that contract law had exhausted its limits and the time had come to utilise the law of tort. When studying the judgment (case 61) the reader should, among other points, also note the following.

It is first worth noting that the court could and did base liability on § 823 II BGB since the defendant (vaccine manufacturer) was in breach of a special statute which was correctly deemed to be a protective statute in the sense of § 823 II BGB. This is important since the manufacturer's duties of care will, in most cases, be judge-made; but they can also emanate from the breach of duties laid down by specific statutes. The Machinery Protection Act (*Maschinenschutzgesetz*) of 24 June 1968, for example, renders manufacturers (and distributors) of a whole range of machinery, tools etc. liable for personal injury or death (but not property damage or economic loss) suffered by all users. Many instances of accidents resulting from defective equipment will thus easily lead to the imposition of liability. The Pharmaceuticals Act (to be discussed below) and the food and drug legislation should also be included in this category and can easily dispose of the manufacturer's liability in the kind of situations which provided the first opportunities to American courts to deal with products liability problems. But the significance of the decision lies in the fact that it did not stop at § 823 II BGB but, instead, proceeded to state that § 823 I BGB should also apply.

As stated, the difficulty with § 823 I BGB is its requirement that the plaintiff prove the defendant/manufacturer's fault. One way round this problem would be for the court to invoke the prima-facie rule (not dissimilar to the Common law doctrine of *res ipsa loquitur*); indeed, this had been done successfully in several cases involving § 831 BGB. However, the court considered this to be an inadequate measure since

all too often the owner of a business can show that the defect in the product might have been caused in a way that does not point to his fault—evidence which generally relies on activities in his business and which is difficult for the injured party to disprove. Consequently, when damage has arisen within the range of the manufacturer's business risks, he cannot be regarded as exonerated *merely* because he points out that the defect in the product might have arisen without any organisation fault of his. On the contrary, he must supply positive and complete evidence that the defect in the product is not due to his fault.

The courts had already (as we shall note below, chapter 4, section A. 1) reversed the onus of proving fault in the context of § 823 II BGB. They now saw no good reason why the same should not also be done with § 823 I BGB, given the special features of product liability and in particular the victim's *de facto* inability to know what was happening in the manufacturer's enterprise. The development of a separate category of liability under the heading of the so-called *Produzentenhaftung* brought about a further significant departure from orthodox reasoning, namely §§ 831 and 31 BGB. § 831 BGB which—originally—was confined to negligent selection or supervision of employees was re-interpreted and widened to encompass also the very organisation of the company. It also served to found an obligation to put schemes of production in place that would ensure that the product is free from dangerous defects. The appropriateness of § 31 BGB, which imputes the negligence of members of the management to the company, also seems doubtful. Both these provisions do not fit easily into the problem of product liability. In this category we are not in fact dealing with issues of vicarious liability. For the duties of care are primarily addressed *to the manufacturer*, who has to avoid putting into circulation dangerous products. (This can be seen clearly from the Directive and the relevant national statutes.) Thus, the company and not its employees or executives is the direct addressee of these duties of care to structure the manufacturing process in an adequate way. The difficulties to which this slight discrepancy between the written law and law in action has given rise to, come to light more fully in the cases regarding the liability of employees or executives themselves under the heading of product liability (cases 65 and 67).

As expected, the decision resulted in the insurance market promptly producing a new form of products liability insurance for industrial enterprises. It also gave rise to a rich case law which German scholars discuss under four different headings: (I) defects in manufacture; (II) defects in design; (III) defects in instructions, and (IV) development risks. These distinctions are likely to remain in use even though, following the European

Community's Directive, there now exists a parallel regime of liability governed by the 1989 Product Liability Act.

(v) The various forms of product liability

(a) *The producer's liability for defects in manufacture* (*Fabrikationsfehler*). Here one is talking of an *individually* defective product, the defect usually being due to some kind of negligence or inattention in the manufacturing process. The leading case was precisely one of those cases so, strictly speaking, its ruling as to the burden of proof was directed only to this type of products liability situation. It will be noted, however, that subsequent cases have extended the application of the rule to include categories (b) and (c) discussed below.

In these instances the plaintiff's task is usually limited to proving that his hurt emanated from the area of the producer's organisation and the risks attendant on it, and that it resulted from an objective defect of the product which made it unsuitable to be put into circulation. (BGHZ 51, 91, 105; BGH NJW 1973, 1602). This burden is easily discharged save in those cases where the evidence may suggest that the defect arose *after* it had left the manufacturer's zone of influence. (See on this Lorenz's observations in "Beweisprobleme bei der Produzentenhaftung", *AcP* 170 (1970) 366, 381 ff., where, once again, he makes extensive use of the American case-law).

Once the plaintiff has established the above, the onus shifts to the defendant (manufacturer). He must then show that he, himself, was not in breach of one of his duties of care (imposed by statute or the case-law) and that all persons in his employment were equally innocent of such a breach. In theory, therefore, a manufacturer of an isolated defective product—sometimes referred to as a "runaway" (*Ausreisser*)—can escape liability. Nevertheless, this exculpatory proof under § 831 BGB requires the manufacturer—at any rate whenever the manufacturing process is not fully automated—to name *every* individual involved in the manufacturing process and prove his "innocence" (BGH NJW 1973, 1602, 1603). This is clearly a burden of proof which makes this in name only fault-based liability but, in effect, greatly approximates the strict tort liability that is imposed by American courts. Once again, this misuse of terms has not passed without criticism, not least because the fault-based system can increase the time and cost of litigation and impede settlements out of court. This tendency to extend the area of quasi-strict liability was also underscored by a decision of the Supreme Court in 1975 (BGH NJW 1975, 1827) which held that the above-mentioned liability would be imposed not only on the manufacturer but also on his "high-ranking" employees. This result, however, appears to be very dubious to say the least; and it has not been adopted by the EEC-inspired legislation. (For criticisms see Lieb, note to BGH 3 June 1975 in *JZ* 1976, 526; Stoll, "Haftungsverlagerung durch beweisrechtliche Mittel" in *AcP* 176 (1976) 145, 170; *contra*, Schmidt-Salzer *BB* 1975, 1031.) However, the possibility of avoiding liability for "runaways" has been removed, strict liability having been openly introduced in this context.

(b) *The producer's liability for defective design* (*Konstruktionsfehler*). It has been noted that the leading case dealt with an individually defective product. But the case law did not stop there. It extended the new rule to apply also to cases of defective design (see BGHZ 67, 359, 362) and in these instances, since many products may be involved, the defendant may be held liable to extensive damages. On the other hand, the plaintiff's

position in this case *may* be more difficult than in the previous one, since he will not only have to prove that the product was defective (in the sense that the defective design was avoidable given existing scientific and technical knowledge). He will also have to persuade the court that its design was defective in a way that it created an unreasonably great risk of danger for him and/or third parties. Whether this is so, will depend on the court's appreciation of all the circumstances in accordance with the formula already given. Factors to be taken into account include the normal or extraordinary conditions of use, the type of average user, and the kind of dangers that may be specific to this type of product. Product liability may also extend to risks which arise from improper use of a product where the manufacturer should foresee that, in the light of the conditions under which the product was used, it would not always be used with the utmost care. (OLG Köln NJW-RR 1991, 285.) The court may also weigh carefully whether an alternative design would be economically feasible and to what extent it would reduce the risk of such damage occurring. (See, Kötz, *Deliktsrecht*, nos. 445–450. For interesting illustrations raised by the problem of defective design see: BGH VersR 1960, 1095; VersR 1967, 498; VersR 1972, 559; NJW 1990, 906.) If such a defect in design is proved, then the manufacturer's breach of the required standard of care will also be established.

Nowadays, many administrative regulations determine the standards that must be met by particular products. For example, the *Gerätesicherheitsgesetz* (GSG), (Act on the Safety of Technical Equipment, of 24 June 1968, BGBl. I. 717 as amended on 18 February 1986, BGBl. I. 265 (1986)) requires that "technical equipment"—a term widely construed to include factory and sports equipment, household appliances, safety devices (such as belts and masks), and even toys—meets certain standards when sold in Germany. § 3 I of the Act talks in particular of "generally recognised technical principles and rules" (*allgemein anerkannte Regeln der Technik*)—an important catch-all term which has no official legal definition. In many cases the rules and standards are set by officially recognized legal institutions (e.g. the Deutsches Institut für Normung (DIN), the Technischer Überwachungs-Verein (TÜV), etc.) and conformity with these rules will, invariably, improve the manufacturer's/defendant's position in a lawsuit involving one of his products. Compliance with mandatory regulations may now even afford a manufacturer with a complete defence in accordance with Article 7(d) of the Council Directive (para. 1 (2) no. 4 of the 1989 Act). Some commentators, however, feel that compliance with minimum standards may not, necessarily, exonerate the manufacturer.

The picture described above could become more complicated where the ultimate damage could be attributed to a defective component. The permutations here are innumerable. The defective component—provided by a supplier—might have been incorporated in the final product by the main manufacturer. Should his liability depend on whether he checked or ought to have checked the component before incorporating it in his product? Should the answer be different if the component was manufactured to his specifications? And what if the defect is not due to the component but is due to the way the components were put together?

The rich case-law made a general answer impossible (see BGH NJW 1968, 247; BGH NJW 1975, 1827; BGH BB 1977, 1117); but Professor Kötz summarised the guiding principle of the law (as it then stood) as follows:

In all these cases the strict rules of the law of products liability are applicable only in so far as their policy aims make them suitable for the occasion. This will be the case whenever the defendant is under an obligation to take the necessary measures within the organisation and area of his responsibility in order to prevent or remove the kind of defects which have led to the harm in suit (*Deliktsrecht*, 2nd edn. 204).

This, for example, was the result whenever components were incorporated in a product which was finally marketed and sold under the manufacturer's own name (e.g. BGH NJW 1985, 2420). Liability was also, invariably, imposed where components were not carefully selected, tested, or constructed in accordance with the manufacturer's specifications. (See, for example, BGHZ 86, 256; BGH NJW 1985, 2420; OLG Köln NJW RR 1990, 414.) As a result of the 1989 Act, however, the new products liability law will apply alike to manu-facturers of finished products and component parts. (The manufacturer of the *compo-nent* is not liable if the deficiency is due to instructions given by the manufacturer of the *finished* product or is attributable to the defectiveness of the finished product.) Similarly, dealers and importers who were *generally* not liable under the old regime (BGH NJW 1980, 121 and BGH NJW 1987, 1009 respectively), may now be saddled with liability in accordance with the 1989 Act.

(c) *The producer's liability for defective instructions* (*Instruktionsfehler*). Once again the scope and extent of these duties of care are in principle fixed by the rich case law (e.g. BGHZ 64, 46; BGH NJW 1972, 2217; NJW 1981, 2514; NJW 1986, 1863). The duty to provide instructions arises at the time when the product is put into circulation though the manufacturer is under a duty to monitor new developments and, if necessary, alter the instructions that originally accompanied his product. The law on this subject was reviewed by the BGH in the "apple-scab" case (BGHZ 80, 186; NJW 1981, 1603). Where apple producers suffered serious production losses after having used a spray which was meant to prevent apple scab but which became useless after repeated use. Laboratory experiments (already published at that time of the accident) had mentioned this possi-bility, but the manufacturers of the spray had failed to bring this information to the atten-tion of the apple producers. Had the knowledge that the spray was ineffective emanated from the manufacturers' own sphere of control, then the usual reversal of the onus of proof would have operated in favour of the plaintiffs; but since it was generally available at the time of the incident, their claim was rejected. (*Cf.* Kötz/Wagner, *Deliktsrecht*, no. 457.) In another contemporaneous judgment the BGH held that the duty to provide infor-mation is linked to the intended use of the product. Thus, a manufacturer is under no duty to provide warnings against dangers, which will arise if the product is put to a use other than that for which it was intended (BGH NJW 1981, 2514). The degree of danger posed by the product and the interests likely to be affected (life, property, etc.) will, however, ultimately influence the scope and standard of duty of the manufacturer. Thus, warning labels must clearly specify the kind of dangers, which may arise from the use of a particular product. If considerable injury to body or health may result from the product's misuse, the consumer must be able to discern from the warning label why the product may be dangerous (BGH NJW 1992, 560). And if infants develop cavities from constant sucking of sweetened children's tea drunk out of plastic bottles, the manufac-turer of the tea is liable if he failed to place a clear warning on the product (BGHZ 116, 60 (Kindertee I); BGH NJW 1994, 932 (Kindertee II); BGH NJW 1995, 1286 (Kindertee III). Thus, adequate warnings must always be given in the case of pharmaceutical prod-ucts likely to be misused—especially those likely to be misused by children. There is no special heading for instruction defects in the European Directive; but the issue is dealt with under the general heading of product defects (Article 6).

(*d*) *The producer's liability for development risks (Entwicklungsfehler).* The problems here are, essentially, different from those discussed in the earlier sections and thus make the return to the fault principle easy to recommend. Typically, in these cases the product will have been manufactured in accordance with the technological knowledge of the time, but subsequently acquired information reveals its potentially harmful effects. Many believe that to make manufacturers carry such a risk could hinder technological progress. To make them strictly liable for such development risks would also run counter to the rationale of imposing such a strict liability in the first place. For, it will be remembered, one of the justifications of imposing strict liability on the manufacturer is his ability to detect and avoid the defect. In the present instance, however, by definition this is not possible and the manufacturer's duties are limited to an obligation to warn consumers or even withdraw their products once they become aware (or ought to become aware) of the defect or of their potential harmful consequences. The rules of the leading case have thus not been extended to this category. Article 15(8) of the European Directive gives Member States the option of deleting the defence of state of art contained in Article 7(e) but the Federal Republic has not exercised this right so the defence has been retained. (Note, however, that the defence is not available under the Pharmaceutical Act; and the relationship between this enactment and the 1989 Act has not been clarified.) The retention of the state of art defence will not, however, absolve the manufacturer from continuously observing his products and warning users of (and if necessary recalling) products that are subsequently revealed as defective. (BGH NJW 1987, 1009 = WM 1987, 126, is an interesting case since it extends the manufacturer's post-marketing duties concerning his own product to the performance of component parts.)

The Act on Pharmaceutical Products of 1976, in force since 1 January 1978, is the leading exception in this respect. This enactment imposes strict liability on pharmaceutical concerns which introduce into the market drugs for human use or consumption which produce harmful results that go beyond those which current medical opinion regards as acceptable. The risk-based liability is incurred irrespective of whether the damage is the result of bad development, production, or labelling. But like most German laws of strict liability, the Pharmaceutical Products Act lays down certain maxima for monetary compensation. (Lump sums of up to DM 500,000 or annuities of up to DM 30,000 where one person is killed or injured or, in cases of defects in mass production killing or injuring more than one person, 200 million or 12 million DM respectively per incident). And payment of these sums is ensured by obliging the pharmaceutical concerns to create special "cover funds" (*Deckungsvorsorge*) which, in practice, means taking out liability insurance. Victims who wish to attempt to recover further compensation are, of course, free to make use of the normal fault-based provisions of the Code.

Further reading

For further discussion of the new Act see Deutsch, "Das Arzneimittelrecht im Haftungssystem", *VersR* 1979, 685; *idem*, "Arzneimittelschaden: Gefährdungshaftung, Verschuldenshaftung, Staatshaftung" in *Festschrift Larenz* (1983) 111 (with further references); idem, *Arztrecht und Arzneimittelrecht. Eine zusammenfassende Darstellung mit Fallbeispielen und Texten* (2nd edn. 1991); idem, *Medizinrecht* (4th edn. 1999); Kullmann, "Die Haftungsregelung des § 84 AMG" *PharmaR* 81, 112; Wolter, "Die Haftungsregelung des neuen AMG", *DB* 1976, 2001. For a comparative discussion in English see: Fleming, "Drug Injury Compensation Plans", 30 *A. J. Comp. Law* 297 (1982).

(*vi*) *The Product Liability Act 1989*

(For the text of the Act and a brief discussion of its provisions, see pp. 868 ff. below.)

5. CAUSATION

French lawyers, paraphrasing Voltaire's dictum about the existence of God, have often teased the Germans by saying that if causation did not exist as a subject it would have to be invented so that German lawyers would have something to exercise their minds. There is a great deal of truth in this statement though it could also convey a misleading picture in at least two respects. For, if one is thinking in terms of the volume of the legal literature, the Germans are not alone in having devoted a great deal of effort to this topic. The Americans, for instance, have rivalled this literature in size and, probably, in ingenuity. Secondly, the theoretical preoccupation of German scholars with this subject has not prevented their courts from stating more than once that the solution should, in the end, be one dictated by common sense and equity (see, for example, BGHZ 3, 261, 267; BGHZ 30, 154, 157, etc.).

(a) Conditions and causes

The Germans (like the Americans and the English but more clearly so than the French) adopt a bifurcated approach to problems of causation. This they do by insisting that the defendant's conduct (or the event for which he is to be held responsible) cannot claim to be a legal "cause" of the plaintiff's hurt, unless it is previously established that it is at least a "condition" (*Bedingung*) of that harm. This leads to a two-phased inquiry, the first being preoccupied with the question whether the defendant's conduct played some role in bringing about the plaintiff's hurt, while the second seeks to discover which of the many conditions of the harm will also be treated as its legal cause. This first phase of the inquiry is strongly causative rather than normative in nature and hence American scholars often refer to it with some justification as the cause-in-fact stage of the inquiry. This labelling of this phase as factual or causative is correct, especially if it is compared with the second phase of the inquiry, which is more normative and policy-orientated. This does not mean, however, that it cannot involve issues of valuation and therefore acquire strong normative overtones as well. This becomes clear in those cases where the "standard" test (to be discussed in the next paragraph) cannot be operated without serious injustice.

The test used to determine whether a particular piece of conduct is a condition of the plaintiff's hurt is that of the *conditio sine qua non*, better known to Common lawyers as the "but-for" test (also referred to as the *Äquivalenztheorie*). Would the plaintiff's harm have occurred but for the defendant's conduct? If it would, then the defendant's conduct is not a cause of the harm. A doctor who negligently examines (or treats) a patient who dies from another ailment will not be causally linked with (and hence will not be responsible for) that death. Equally, a chemist who negligently renews a prescription without previously consulting the patient's doctor will not be liable once it is shown that the doctor, had he been asked, would certainly have continued the treatment with the same drug (RGSt 15 (1886) 151; RGSt 63 (1929) 211). The point need not be laboured, since it raises no issues, which are not already known to a Common law audience. Where the German thoroughness emerges quite clearly is in the effort to determine how the defendant's conduct (or the event complained of) will be deemed to be or not to be a *conditio sine qua non* of the plaintiff's harm. One of the first to attempt an answer to this problem was the Austrian criminal lawyer Glaser who in 1858 (*Abhandlungen aus dem österreichischen Strafrechte* I, 298; translated by Hart and Honoré *Causation in the Law* 2nd edn. (1985), 443) wrote:

If one attempts wholly to eliminate in thought the alleged author (of the act) from the sum of events in question and it then appears that nevertheless the sequence of intermediate causes remains the same, it is clear that the act and its consequences cannot be referred to him . . . but if it appears that, once the person in question is eliminated in thought from the scene, the consequences cannot come about, or that they can come about only in a completely different way, then one is fully justified in attributing the consequences to him and explaining it as the effect of his activity.

This has been termed the method of elimination (*Hinwegdenken*) since it assumes the notional elimination of the propositus from the scene, the other conditions remaining exactly the same. It should be contrasted with a different method—that of substitution—which, far from eliminating the propositus from the scene, assumes, on the contrary, that he was there and acted lawfully, the other conditions remaining the same except in so far as they would have been altered by the lawful conduct of the person in question.

The elimination theory seems more acceptable when the alleged cause is a positive act. What we have to do is to reconstruct the sequence of events, omitting the tortfeasor's conduct. If, despite this, the sequence of events remains unaltered, then the conduct has no causal relation to subsequent events. If, on the other hand, the final result is changed as a consequence of the theoretical suppression of the tortfeasor's act, then that act must have played an active and necessary part in producing the plaintiff's harm. Thus, if A shoots B and A's shot is eliminated, then B's death goes also. In the case of omissions, however, the situation is more complex, for if the "procedure of elimination without substitution is adopted no omission can ever be treated as a *conditio sine qua non* of an event" (Hart and Honoré, *Causation in the Law* (1959) 403). What is necessary here is the substitution of the act that the defendant omitted. Would the harmful result nevertheless have occurred? If it would, then the defendant's omission is not the cause of the result. Let us look at an example often given by German textbooks to illustrate how the above works in practice.

Suppose that a passenger ship is not properly equipped with lifebuoys and one of its passengers falls into the sea. If the shipowner's wrongful omission is eliminated and the correct conduct is substituted, we must assume that adequate lifebuoys would have been provided. That, in itself, however, provides no solution to the question whether the drowning was connected with the absence of lifebuoys. A partial substitution of the wrongful conduct by lawful conduct is not enough. What we must further do, in addition to eliminating the wrongful omission is to assume that the ship's crew could and would have used the lifebuoys promptly and that the passenger would have seized one in time. The answer to our question, therefore, can be provided only if we substitute the right for the wrong conduct and then enquire what further changes would have taken place in that event. In the case of omissions, therefore, *total substitution* (as the above process is sometimes referred to) is, in principle, necessary in order to produce a reasonable result (BGHZ 12, 94). Only if all the conditions mentioned above are satisfied, can the drowning be attributed to the absence of lifebuoys.

A further difficulty occurs if the victim, himself, intervenes in the chain of causation. Normally one would assume that the application of the *conditio sine qua non* formula is at least problematic in such a case. "The general principle of the traditional doctrine is that *the free deliberate and informed act or omission of a human being, intended to exploit the situation created by the defendant, negatives causal connection.*" (Hart and Honoré *Causation in the Law* (2nd edn. 1985) p. 136). The BGH was *inter alia* confronted with the problem in a series of cases concerning police pursuits (see case 81). The court, apparently, did not deny the causal nexus between the defendant's flight and the injury of the policemen in the course of his pursuit (the but for test is, on its face, fulfilled). However, liability is not imposed *per se*, but depends on whether the victim's conduct was provoked by the defendant's behaviour. The BGH prefers the somewhat open-textured principle of "objective attribution", probably in order to maintain a more flexible and policy-orientated approach. (See, also, next section on legal cause.) However, the rationale of the decision clearly reflects that the but for test does not provide—even prima facie—the solution to these cases in which the victim, himself, inflicts the injury.

The above represents little more than a crass abridgement of the difficulties and diverging views that one can find on this subject. Perhaps, one could thus say that the choice between the elimination and the substitution theories is, in the end, one of policy. The former can lead to more extensive liability (especially in cases of hypothetical causes) and was, apparently, preferred by the Reichsgericht (RGZ 141, 365); the latter can reduce liability within narrow limits and has received the support of the Bundesgerichtshof (BGHZ 10, 6). (For a more detailed analysis consult Honoré, *International Encyclopaedia of Comparative Law* XI, ch. 7, 74–6, 79 ff.)

In the examples given up to this point the *conditio sine qua non* rule has been able to produce acceptable results. But there are many instances where the test breaks down completely. This, for example, is the case whenever it can be shown that the event complained of could have been brought about in more than one way. Suppose, for example, that two motorcyclists simultaneously pass the plaintiff's horse in a way that makes it bolt and it is subsequently proved that either of them alone could have caused the fright of the horse. Or imagine two chemical factories releasing independently of each other toxic liquids into a nearby river and thus affecting the riparian owner's fishing-rights. Or, finally, suppose that a garage sells a car which has defective brakes to the plaintiff who, at the critical moment, makes no attempt to apply them. Would the horse have bolted in our first example but for the conduct of the first motorcyclist? The answer is yes, because of the way the other motorcyclist rode quickly past it. The same reasoning can be applied to our other examples. It is thus clear that a strict application of the *conditio sine qua non* test would hold that neither of the motor-cyclists in the first example, nor the polluting factories in the second, nor the garage in the third, would be held liable since each of these acts was a sufficient cause of the plaintiff's hurt. But, however impeccable the logic of this approach may be, the solution is patently unjust, and unless we hold liable each of the persons who has done enough to bring about the harmful result, the victim will remain uncompensated. The word "enough" supplies the clue for one possible solution. This is found in the adoption of the "substantial factor" formula which was first applied by the Minnesota court (*Anderson v. Minneapolis, St. P. and S.MRY Co.* 146 Minn. 430, 179 NW 45 (1920)) some eighty years ago and has more recently been sanctioned by the American *Restatement Second, Torts* § 432.2. According to this theory, the defendant's conduct is a cause of the plaintiff's harm if it was a material element and a substantial factor in bringing it about. There is nothing to stop a German judge from following a similar reasoning and eliminating the insubstantial factors at this stage of the enquiry. On the whole, however, one is left with the impression that this "evaluation process" will be attempted later and at this cause-in-fact stage of the process all activities will be retained as "conditions" of the plaintiff's harm.

In the last three examples we have been faced with what have been termed "multiple sufficient causes" in the sense that each is normally "sufficient" to produce the harmful result. In the first two examples they have both operated simultaneously and have been positive in nature; in the third example, the second cause was negative in nature (i.e. failure to apply the brakes). But the most fiercely debated of "multiple sufficient causes" are the so-called "overtaking causes" (see von Caemmerer, "Das Problem der überholenden Kausalität" in *Gesammelte Schriften* I, 411). Examples include the case of the medical practitioner who blinds the patient who would, in any event, have subsequently become blind. Another is the case of a house which is damaged by a negligently caused explosion of gas but which would, in any event, have been destroyed by a subsequent bombing attack. In these cases the second cause, i.e. blindness, bomb attack (commonly referred to as the "overtaking" cause but, in actual fact, the cause "overtaken" by the "operative" cause for which the tortfeasor is responsible), is sufficient by itself to produce the harmful result in question. In actual fact, however, it does not do so since the causal process initiated by the tortfeasor prevents, or has already prevented, this from happening. In such cases, can the propositus rely on the second sufficient cause and argue that he did not occasion the whole or part of the harm, or that if he did so, he ought for some other reason (causal or equitable) to be relieved from at least part of the liability? One can envisage a host of possible answers ranging between two extremes, namely, that of completely disregarding the overtaking cause (RGZ 169, 117, 120), and that according to which damages must always be assessed by taking into account events subsequent to the appearance of the cause of action but before trial (BGHZ 10, 6). Larenz's solution occupies the middle ground. (See his *Schuldrecht I*, § 30 I, pp. 481 ff.) He distinguishes between the damage caused to the protected interest as such (i.e. a chattel) (so called *Objektschaden*) and consequential loss. As far as the *Objektschaden* is concerned the right of action accrues instantly and therefore the hypothetical cause cannot be taken into account, while in respect of consequential loss the hypothetical cause is relevant. All these are issues, which are hotly debated in Germany and cannot be discussed in a book of this kind which has, as its primary aim, to introduce foreign readers to the mysteries of German law. But we shall glance briefly, at the end of this section, at one of these overtaking causes, namely the victim's predispositions.

(b) Legal cause

The simplicity (or apparent simplicity) of the *conditio sine qua non* theory led some authors to consider extending its application to the domain of legal cause. Indeed, this is still the case in the area of criminal law since in that branch of the law the element of fault (invariably intention though there do exist criminal offences where negligence will suffice, e.g. §§ 222, 229 StGB) provides a good corrective device against the risk of extensive liability. But in the context of private law, where liability often does not depend on fault, this theory met with little success—German authors opting instead for one of the variants of the adequate causation theory. (German authors make a distinction between causation giving rise to the violation of a protected interest (*haftungsbegründende Kausalität*) and what we would call remoteness of damage (*haftungsausfüllende Kausalität*). See Deutsch, 141; Larenz I, § 27, III, 435; Esser/Schmidt I, § 33, II; Traeger, *Kausalbegriff*, 219.)

This theory was first expounded by the German physiologist von Kries (*Die Prinzipien der Wahrscheinlichkeitsrechnung; über den Begriff der objektiven Möglichkeit*) and its central idea was simple enough. The defendant's conduct (or specified event for which he is responsible), which must be a condition of the plaintiff's hurt, will further qualify as an adequate cause of that harm if it is such that it significantly increases the risk of the type of harm which actually occurs. Theoretically, this approach tends to achieve a compromise between the extension of liability which the theory of direct consequences (known to Common lawyers from the *Re Polemis* litigation) is *capable* of producing, and the greater restriction of liability which *could* result from the use of the foreseeability theory. For, it could be argued, the adequacy theory can set realistic limits of liability by relying on common sense notions of causal connection. Put differently, a "significantly increased probability" is a test less vague than the notion of foreseeability. So, at least, runs the traditional argument for it was eventually realised that the real problem behind these notions is, essentially, one of responsibility and not of causality. A value judgment, foreign to the notion of causation, could and should in the end determine the difficult cases that reached the courts. This became obvious the moment one had to determine *how* the increased probability of the harm would have to be assessed. Academic writers were quick to offer their views. For von Kries—the originator of the theory—the valuation should be undertaken on the basis of all the circumstances which were known, or ought to have been known, to the originator of the condition at the time of its entry (*ex ante*) and also taking into account *general practical knowledge* (*ex post*) based on experience. Rümelin, on the other hand, advanced the theory of "objective hindsight". For him consideration should be given to the whole empirical knowledge of mankind and all the circumstances anywhere to hand at the time the condition occurred, whether they were recognisable by the most *superior* discernment *or* had first become recognisable *ex post* from events following the condition in question.

Von Kries's "individual foresight" approach proved too narrow for private law cases of objective (no fault) liability and contractual liability; Rümelin's "objective hindsight" theory was, on the other hand, too wide to exclude with certainty the inequitable results of the condition theory. *The Wagon Mound* I ([1961] AC 388) litigation, for example, would have been decided differently if the objective hindsight test was applied. For it will be remembered, that by the time of the second *Wagon Mound II* ([1967] 1 AC 617) trial, scientific opinion had changed with regard to the crucial factor which had led to the fire damage in that case (i.e. possibility of oil igniting in water). So a compromise solution was proposed by yet another author—Traeger (*Kausalbegriff im Zivil- und Strafrecht* (1904), para. 159)—and this came to be adopted by the courts. According to this view, an event is an adequate condition of a consequence if it has in a general and appreciable way enhanced the objective possibility of a consequence of the kind coming about. In deciding this, account is to be taken of (i) all the circumstances recognisable by an "optimal" observer *at the time the event occurred* and, (ii) the additional circumstances known to the originator of the condition. The factual situation so established must be examined in the light of the whole human experience available at the time the decision is made, to see whether it appreciably favoured the occurrence of the damage-producing event.

A number of cases are reproduced below (see case 80) which show that the case law is not clear and the problems of applying these tests in practice are not solved. In particular, how much knowledge should be credited to the "optimal" observer? Professor Larenz takes the example of a plaintiff who is slightly injured by the defendant but who dies as a result of a heart condition from which he is already suffering and continues:

Is the observer to be credited with knowledge of the heart condition if it was then unknown but could have been discovered by a competent physician? Or need the observer know only that the possibility of such a condition was not completely remote? In that event, the fatal outcome was not wholly unlikely and should have been taken into consideration as well. Or should the observer be taken to know that a pillar struck by a truck had been so weakened that ordinary strains would cause it and the entry of the building to collapse, when this knowledge would have been possessed by an expert in building construction but not by an ordinary worker? The more one credits the observer with knowledge of circumstances which produced the event in question but which could be known only with difficulty, the more one expands the area in which consequences are to be adjudged "adequate". For the "optimal" observer described by the Bundesgerichtshof, almost nothing is secret; he is practically omniscient. For the omniscient, the actual course of events is always foreseeable, however abnormal it may have been. If one takes the Bundesgerichtshof's standard of the optimal observer seriously, then the criterion of adequacy loses most of its ability to limit the area of responsibility of the person liable (*Lehrbuch des Schuldrechts* (11th edn., 1976) 354 ff. trans. by von Mehren, in von Mehren and Gordley, *The Civil Law System* (2nd edn., 1977) 586; in the 1st edn. the text can be found on pp. 436–7).

In view of the above, it is not surprising that more recent court decisions have shown a marked inclination to state that the problem they have to solve is not "exactly one of causality but rather the discovery of a corrective device which can limit the purely logical consequences in the interests of equity". (See BGHZ 30, 154, 157 and also BGHZ 3, 261, 267). Seen in this light, the adequacy theory has proved an inefficient controlling device. Von Caemmerer has thus argued that an exhaustive examination of the case-law of the Reichsgericht shows that only in a handful of cases the court was able (or willing) to deny the existence of a causal link on the basis of this theory. (*Das Problem des Kausalzusammenhangs*, in *Gesammelte Schriften* I, 395, 403 ff.) An effort to combine the adequate cause theory with a more normative theory of causation was thus inevitable; the development of the "scope of the rule" theory was its result.

This theory, first elaborated by Rabel (*Das Recht des Warenkaufs* (1936) 495 ff.) in relation to breaches of *contractual* duties, and more recently, also adopted by tort lawyers, postulates that there should be no recovery if the harm in suit is not within the scope of the rule violated. This may be because the harm is not within the protective purpose of the rule in question (*Schutzzweck der Norm*) (i.e. it is not the mischief the statute was designed to prevent) or, according to a variant, because it has not come about in an unlawful manner (*Rechtswidrigkeitszusammenhang*). Interestingly enough, Lord Hoffmann appears to have attempted to establish a similar approach in English law which is—like its German counter-part—founded on the purpose and scope of the duty owed. (This is primarily in the field of tort law but it seems, as the German jurisprudence also demonstrates, that the test can be applied to both areas of the law of obligation.) (For Lord Hoffmann's views see his speech in *South Australia Asset Management Corp. v. York Montague Ltd.* [1997] AC 191.) However, it has not yet been worked out how this new approach fits in with the other traditional requirements of remoteness in English law, so it will be interesting to observe its further development. Two leading German cases applying this theory are reproduced below (cases 64 and 65); and for a more recent illustration see BGH NJW 1985, 791; BGH NJW 1991, 3275. Here one could add two English examples, which can illustrate the above propositions. In *Gorris v. Scott* ((1874) LR 9 Ex. 125) a statute provided that sheep carried as deck cargo should be enclosed in proper pens. They were not, and during rough weather they were washed overboard. The plaintiff's claim for damages was dismissed on the ground that the purpose of the requirement of the fencing was to prevent the spreading of contagious disease among the animals and not to safeguard them against the perils of the sea. In other words, the mischief that occurred was not the one the statute wanted to prevent. Two more cases (reproduced below, cases 74 and 75), dealing with the duties of local authorities to inspect the foundations of buildings, also provide an illustration of how this normative theory of causation can be used to exclude compensation.

In other instances the plaintiff may not belong to the class of people the statute intended to protect or, alternatively, the statute may have meant to protect only the general interest and not individual interests. This point is illustrated in the cable case reproduced below (case 11). Finally, the harm may have been inflicted in a manner not envisaged by the statute. In *Close v. Steel Co. of Wales Ltd.* ([1962] AC 367), for example, the House of Lords was concerned with the proper construction of a section of the English Factories Act which provided for the "fencing in" of dangerous machinery. The plaintiff was injured by material which "flew out" of the machinery. The House of Lords took the view that he could not avail himself of this provision since it was designed to protect workmen from coming into contact with moving parts of the machinery and not to protect them from injury inflicted through fragments flying out of the machine itself. Examples such as these abound in German textbooks. (For more details see Larenz, *Schuldrecht* I, 508 ff.)

It would be futile to add that the new theory has not solved all problems or that it has led to the formulation of a number of variations. But one of its limitations must be stressed. Though the new theory can work well whenever it is easy to assign a particular purpose to a particular rule, it breaks down almost completely when it is difficult or impossible to define with precision the scope of the rule in question. Thus, it works rather well in cases of tortious liability resulting from breach of statutes or subsidiary regulations, and also in the case of some "nominate torts". But it becomes almost unworkable in the cases of widely conceived tortious conduct (e.g. liability *contra bonos mores* under § 826 BGB or even § 823 I BGB, on which see Professor Kötz's comments in his *Deliktsrecht*, pp. 75–81). Of course, it can be and has been argued that even in these cases the purpose of the rule that is violated can be discovered. For "all rules of conduct, irrespective of whether they are the product of a legislative act or are a part of the fabric of the court-made law of negligence, exist for a purpose. They are designed to protect *some* persons under *some* circumstances against *some* risks" (Malone, 9 *Stan. L. Rev.* 50, 73 (1956–7)). Yet, as stated, where wrongful conduct is only vaguely defined or definable, it is well-nigh impossible to ascribe a specific purpose to the rule in question, and to invite a judge to do so is to invite him to fix the limits of recovery for himself. This may be desirable whenever reasons of expediency or of policy militate for or against the imposition of liability. In these cases, the "scope of the rule" theory has the clear advantage of making the judge aware of his quasi-legislative functions in deciding the kind of damage which shall be compensated. But this solution is more doubtful when the harm in suit is one, which is clearly recognized but the manner of its infliction is dubious or unusual. Here recourse to the probability or explanatory theories may supply better guidance.

(c) Some special problem areas

It has been noted that causation theories do not really solve all problems. In particular, there are some factual situations which have given rise to considerable difficulties and, incidentally, shown that these theories offer only a conceptual framework within which the judges express their value judgments. Three of these factual situations will be briefly examined in the remaining part of this chapter. The first deals with the fault of the injured party, the second with rescue cases, and the last with the predispositions of the victim/plaintiff.

(i) Fault of the injured party

It will be noticed that we are using here the continental term "fault of the injured party" rather than the approximately equivalent Common law term "contributory negligence". This is because in the modern civil law fault of the injured party is wider than contributory negligence in so far as it includes intentional activities on behalf of the victim. More importantly, fault of the injured party is often taken to include not only his fault in the production of his hurt but also his failure to minimise its consequences *after* the harmful result has occurred. The German Civil Code makes this distinction most clearly and regulates the fault of the injured party to mitigate his damage in § 254 II BGB. The distinction, however, is more the result of the wish to establish conceptual clarity rather than the desire to dictate a different treatment. Thus in both cases the victim's responsibility will be taken into account to reduce his damages. It will be noticed that the legislator leaves considerable freedom to the judge to determine how to work out the reduction of damages. Everything will depend on the circumstances of each case, though the Code does mention one particular factor, which must be carefully weighed by the judge: "How far the injury has been *caused* predominantly by the one or the other party." The causative potency of the victim's conduct in producing his hurt will thus be vital but not the unique factor to be taken into account. For example, the victim's failure to obtain medical treatment after his injury (RGZ 139, 131, 136), to submit to a medical operation (RGZ 129, 398), or to accept a retraining job because he can no longer pursue his original calling (RGZ 160, 119), will all have to be assessed from a point of view of fault. Only if the *tortfeasor* can show that the victim's failure to pursue one of these courses and mitigate his loss was unreasonable, will the victim's failure to minimise his loss be held against him. (Likewise in English law: *Steele* v. *Robert George & Co.* [1942] AC 497; *Richardson* v. *Redpath, Brown & Co.* [1944] AC 62. Contra *Selvanayagam* v. *University of the West Indies* [1983] 1 All ER 824.) Incidentally, German law requires the tortfeasor to meet the reasonable costs of a retraining programme in order to give the victim the chance to minimise his loss of earnings (BGHZ 10, 18). Beyond stating these general rules, it is difficult to say how far the courts lean over backwards in order not to "discover" contributory fault and thus give the victim his full compensation. It could be argued that they appear to be more eager to discover fault in defendants—especially where insurance is obligatory or prevalent—than they are to find it in plaintiffs. If this "impressionistic" reaction is correct, and there is some authority in England to support this (see, for example, *Gough* v. *Thorne* [1966] 1 WLR 1387 and *Daly* v. *Liverpool Corp.* [1939] 1 KB 394), it would certainly be in tune with the more modern trend to disregard the victim's own fault unless it is particularly flagrant or obnoxious, and to let him recover full compensation. This view has been officially adopted by the 1964 Soviet Civil Code and sanctioned by the French Cour de Cassation in the context of traffic accident actions based on Article 1384 CC. (On this last point see Cass 2ème civ. 21 juillet 1982, 1982 D. 449 and *Gazette du Palais*, 18–19 mars 1983, with rich references to the case-law and literature, and see, now, the Law of 5 July 1985, Article 3 reproduced below.)

(ii) Rescue cases

If the victim is injured while attempting to avert or minimize harm to another he could be said to have brought about (caused) his own hurt or to be at fault. The problem of his compensation can thus be approached in terms of causation, fault or, for the Common law system, duty of care: does the tortfeasor owe a duty not only to the immediate victim but also to the rescuer? How one approaches the problem is a matter of technique and legal tradition and, for present purposes, is less important. The case reproduced below (87) shows that German lawyers prefer the causative approach. The practical answer, however, is not in doubt: reasonable attempts to avert or minimise harm will not be treated as faults; or (which is another way of putting it) they will not interrupt the original chain of causation and hence the rescuer will be entitled to claim compensation. This can be justified slightly differently depending on which of the many causal theories one wishes to adopt—but the end result is not in doubt: unless entirely foolhardy, the rescue will not render the victim's harm too remote. The fact that in § 323c of the Criminal Code the German legal system imposes a limited duty to come to the aid of others, only helps accentuate this greater willingness to be lenient towards rescuers, even where they are acting beyond the requirements of § 323c.

(iii) Predispositions

We spoke at the beginning of the section of overtaking causes which were described as additional causes capable of bringing about the harm in question which the tortfeasor's conduct has actually produced. Some of them can be referred to as *external* overtaking causes. For example, A damages B's car in a way that makes respraying necessary. Subsequently, C damages the car so that there would have to be a respraying even if there had been no previous collision. C, if sued, can argue that he caused no *new* damage and A, if sued, could rely on the but-for test and argue that he is not the cause of B's damage for it would have occurred even if he (A) had not committed the tort. Other overtaking causes can be described as *internal* and here one includes the plaintiff's predispositions. We must, of course, hasten to add that here we are *not* talking of the state of the plaintiff's health which is due to his *own* fault. The fact that he is an alcoholic, for example, may in some way increase the harm he has suffered. This, if at all relevant, will be discussed under the heading of contributory fault. But what if the injured party suffers from a hereditary abnormality (e.g. he is a haemophiliac) which increases the extent of the injury inflicted by the defendant? Whether the susceptibility or defect of the injured party is latent, quiescent, or whatever, the general principle of German law (and, indeed, other systems as well, including the Common law) is that the defendant must take his victim as he finds him. (See BGHZ 20, 137. For more recent examples see BGH NJW 1982, 168—man bitten by a dog in the stomach; war wound had resulted in an unusually thin abdominal wall which resulted in the bite having more serious consequences than otherwise would have been the case; court found for plaintiff and refused to hold him contributorily negligent for not wearing a protective belt or corset—and BGH VersR 1986, 812.) This has been extended to include not only physical but also psychological weaknesses (RGZ 133, 270, 272; BGH NJW 1958, 1579) and, indeed, any further weaknesses caused by the accident. (For a more recent case see OLG Frankfurt JZ 1982, 201 with a disapproving note by Stoll which shows, for example, how a defendant who injured the plaintiff was held responsible for the latter's death caused by influenza contracted in the hospital where the victim was taken for treatment for the original injury.) Needless to say, various causal explanations have been advanced to support this conclusion but, clearly, they are all strained in the extreme and the explanation must be sought in the realm of policy—namely the growing desire to afford the maximum possible protection to human health and life. An even more extreme application of this kind of reasoning can be found in case 58. There the tortfeasor was held liable not only for the amputation of the plaintiff's leg caused by the tortfeasor's act, but also for the injury suffered by the victim twenty years later and due to the fact that he had never become accustomed to the artificial leg fitted after the first injury. These results are so obviously incompatible with all probability theories of causation that they put in question the whole policy decision to protect the victim. One wonders in other words whether, in some cases at least, it would not be sounder policy to oblige a person with a given weakness or predisposition to take greater care for himself rather than make the tortfeasor face the bill of even the remotest consequences of his conduct (see Stoll's criticism in *Kausalzusammenhang und Normzweck im Deliktsrecht* (1968) 43). This willingness to "take the tortfeasor's side" and deny the victim all his demands is clearly visible in certain types of neurotic reactions which can follow an accident. Thus, the victim may suffer a neurotic fear, which may impede his return to work (accident neurosis). Or he may demonstrate a neurotic refusal to return to work, prompted by the desire to continue receiving periodical payments or damages (compensation neurosis). Or he may display similar symptoms, prompted by the anxiety caused by litigation (litigation neurosis). All these instances could easily be attributed to a pre-existing weak or even defective psychological state and could thus impose unacceptably far-reaching liability on the tortfeasor, besides giving a premium to the victim's lack of personal effort to overcome these emotional reactions and return to work. Whenever this is particular evident, the German courts will ignore causation theories and openly deny compensation. In these cases one can even find an open allusion to policy which militates in favour of a denial of compensation in order to facilitate the victim's "return" to social life (see BGHZ 20, 137, 142).

What is true of the physical condition of the victim is to a great extent also true of his economic position. If the tortfeasor injures a man who happens to look like a tramp but is actually a skilled neuro-surgeon he will have to pay more (though this is, strictly speaking, a rule of compensation and not a rule of remoteness of damage) since it is concerned with unexpected costs of expected consequences). This may, at first sight, sound unfair and it is, undoubtedly, a relic of a highly individualistic age. And it is ill at ease with social security systems, which limit disability benefits to "average" earnings and, in the end, it may even be abandoned. But for the time being this is, with few exceptions, the position taken by most systems. The greater the economic strength of the victim, the greater the size of the compensation. But if the victim's great economic robustness affects the quantum of his damages should not his weakness also be taken into account? The problem has arisen in cases, which have to decide whether the victim should be allowed to claim a sum of money to buy a substitute for the property destroyed by the tortfeasor. Logically, the solution should be the same; the German courts have in fact allowed victims the cost of acquiring substitute property.

(d) Comparative conclusions

The Common law reader of the preceding pages should have had no difficulty in following the exposition of the German law. True, some different solutions to specific problems can be found here and there; and the English Common lawyer (but not the American) may find the German theoretical approach to be in stark contrast to his own pragmatic appraisal of the problems of causation. But, as already observed, even this difference can be overstated; and the similarities can be just as striking. Striking if not at times uncanny when, for example, one considers how, within a short space of time, Rabel in Berlin and Green in Texas could come up with more or less the same theory. Thus, this comparative excursus need not be too long. (For details see Honoré's excellent contribution on this subject in the *International Encyclopaedia of Comparative Law* XI, ch. 7 and for a more brief comparative discussion Lawson and Markesinis, *Tortious Liability for Unintentional Harm in the Common Law and the Civil Law* (1982) I, 106–41 both providing extensive bibliographical references.)

The first thing to note is that the adequate causation theory has come to mean slightly different things to different people. But in its less expansive form (to be found, for example, in France) it tends to produce results very similar to those achieved by the foreseeability theory, which is favoured by the Common law system. Indeed, one of France's leading contemporary jurists—Professor Carbonnier—has described the adequate cause theory as a variant of the foreseeability approach (*Droit Civil* IV, 323). Nevertheless, the foreseeability test is primarily a test for remoteness of damage for the tort of negligence and—since the *Wagon Mound II* litigation—also for the tort of nuisance. The adequate cause theory, on the other hand, is applied to all forms of tort liability and is not limited to cases of liability based on fault. However, its practical value is limited since it does not effectively exclude problematic cases and imposes a very low threshold. As a result, yet another theory had to be created, based on protective purpose of the duty in question (*Schutzzwecklehre*). This approach is flexible, as it can react to the peculiarities of each case. More importantly, it very often makes it easy to import policy arguments while maintaining a legalistic tone (this will be noted in greater detail when we discuss the examples of its application, e.g. wrongful life, state liability). Secondly, the Common law systems also possess an additional doctrine—that of the unforeseeable plaintiff. To put it differently, there is often a tendency to rephrase certain problems of legal or "proximate" cause in terms of legal duty. Given that the same test (foreseeability) determines both the "remote plaintiff" (illustrated by the leading cases of *Palsgraf* v. *Long Island Ry Co.* (248 NY 339, 162 NE 99, (1928) and *Hay* (*Bourhill*) v. *Young* ([1943] AC 92)) and the "remote damage", one wonders whether anything is gained by this "dichotomy" of what is essentially one subject: the subject of remoteness. This, however, is essentially a problem of classification or, as Dean Prosser once observed (*Law of Torts* (4th edn., 1971) 244), to opt for "duty" rather than "proximate cause" only restates the problem but does not solve it. The only conceivable advantage of opting for the "duty" approach is that it can help—in Prosser's words again—"direct attention to the policy issues which determine the extent of the original obligation and of its continuance, rather than to the mechanical sequence of events which goes to make up causation in fact".

Noting this difference is more important than trying to defend the Common or civil law approach. For, as has been stated in the preceding pages, many problems such as nervous shock and rescue cases will in one system be treated in the causation section of some books and in the duty section of others. The comparatist will have to learn to jump over these artificial hurdles of classification and, in so doing, reflect once again on how policy and not concepts or theories determine the ultimate result.

Further reading

On causation see Brehm, "Zur Haftung bei alternativer Kausalität", *JZ* 1980, 586; Bydlinski, *Probleme der Schadensverursachung nach deutschem und österreichischem Recht* (1964); von Caemmerer, "Das Problem des Kausalzusammenhanges im Privatrecht" (1956) reproduced in his *Gesammelte Schriften* I (1968) 395; idem, "Das Problem der überholenden Kausalität im Schadensersatzrecht" (1962) reproduced in *Gesammelte Schriften* I (1968) 411; Deutsch, "Die dem Geschädigten nachteilige Adäquanz", *NJW* 1981, 2731; Deutsch and von Bar, "Schutzbereich und wesentliche Bedingung im Versicherungs- und Haftungsrecht", *MDR* 1979, 536; Frank-Löffler, "Grundfragen der überholenden Kausalität", *JuS* 1985, 689; Huber, "Normzwecktheorie und Adäquanztheorie", *JZ* 1969, 677; idem, "Verschulden, Gefährdung und Adäquanz", *Festschrift Wahl* (1973) 301; von Kries, *Die Prinzipien der Wahrscheinlichkeitsrechnung* (1886); Lang, *Normzweck und Duty of Care* (1983); Larenz, "Zum heutigen Stand der Lehre von der objektiven Zurechnung", *Festschrift Honig* (1970) 79; *Münchener Kommentar*-Grunsky, Vor § 249 BGB, nos. 36–112; Stoll, *Kausalzusammenhang und Normzweck im Deliktsrecht* (1968); Sourlas, *Adäquanztheorie und Normzwecktheorie bei der Begründung der Haftung nach § 823 I BGB* (1974); Träger, *Der Kausalbegriff im Straf- und Zivilrecht* (1904); Weitnauer, "Zur Lehre vom adäquaten Kausalzusammenhang", *Festschrift Oftinger* (1969) 321. For further references see Larenz, *Schuldrecht* I, 390. Finally, special reference must be made to the classic work of Hart and Honoré, *Causation in the Law* (2nd edn., 1985).

SECTION B. CASES

1. NERVOUS SHOCK

Case 1

BUNDESGERICHTSHOF (SIXTH CIVIL SENATE) 11 MAY 1971
BGHZ 56, 163 = NJW 1971, 1883 = VERSR 1971, 905, 1140

On 6 March 1965, when he was sixty-four years old, the plaintiff's husband was fatally injured in a collision with the defendant's motor vehicle. The plaintiff was fifty years old at the time. In this suit she claims damages for the injury to her health which she suffered through the death of her husband.

The Landgericht allowed the claim in full, the Oberlandesgericht in part. The defendant appealed with permission, and his appeal was allowed. The judgments below were vacated, and the case remanded to the Court of Appeal.

Reasons

A ...
2 (*a*) ...
(*b*) The Court of Appeal was wrong to find that the plaintiff suffered any real injury to her health as a result of hearing of the accident (see BGH VersR 1966, 283, 285 ff.; OLG Freiburg, JZ 1953, 705, 709).

Apart from a few special instances not here in point, our law consciously rejects any claim for harm due to psychical pain unless it results from injury to the plaintiff's own body or health. This is a policy decision of the legislator. It does not, however, prevent our granting an independent claim to the exceptional person who is "traumatised" by being involved in an accident, or hearing of one, and who in consequence suffers real damage to body or mind. Nor, if we leave aside the cases of "purposive neuroses" and supervening causes, for which special rules have been developed, is it an objection to granting such a claim that the only reason the victim's reaction was so severe was that he had a pre-existing organic or psychical weakness which was triggered by the accident. The opposite view is taken by Stoll in his paper for the 45th German Juristentag 1964, 20, but we cannot agree with it, if only because such an unusual reaction normally lies outside the victim's control as well as the defendant's.

On the other hand it is a matter of common knowledge that the pain, grief, and fright arising from a very negative experience can have a very marked effect on one's physiological system and one's ability to cope. Yet to treat such disturbances as invasions of health in the sense of § 823 I BGB would be inconsistent with the binding decision of the legislator (Stoll, idem, 19 ff.). Except in cases where the injury was intended by the actor, liability for harm psychically occasioned, even though it may be adequately caused according to the traditional formula, must be limited to cases where the man in the street, and not only a medical practitioner, would describe it as injury to body and health [reference omitted]. Under certain circumstances, therefore, injuries which are medically ascertainable but do not amount to a "shock" to the system will go uncompensated. Accordingly, no claim can be made in the normal case of deeply felt grief, which, as everybody knows, may have quite serious effects on a person's general well being.

(*c*) In the light of these principles, the opinion of the Court of Appeal cannot stand.

The Court of Appeal laid weight on the expert's finding that "the plaintiff naturally suffered severe psychic shock on first hearing of the death of her husband". But the court read too much into this. The court had formally asked the expert to report on whether the plaintiff had suffered "a severe psychic shock which altered her personality and made her depressed, unduly excitable, sleepless, tearful, and apt to shiver on the slightest occasion", taking these terms from the written evidence of Dr C, the plaintiff's general practitioner, evidence of which the expert was somewhat critical. In his reply the expert simply confirmed in general terms that there had been a "severe psychical shock", though it is doubtful, in view of what he said immediately thereafter, whether he intended this to constitute a medical finding. As to the other symptoms about which he was asked, he made no positive finding, but rather indicated that he himself had not observed them. It would require stronger evidence than this before the Court of Appeal could properly hold that the plaintiff had suffered an injury to health sufficient to ground a claim.

In everyday speech the phrase "severe psychical shock" denotes a violent temperamental reaction which may have nothing in common with an illness of any kind. Medical men do not use the notion of shock to describe a psychopathological condition. Used to describe a pathological condition (apart from the special case of shock therapy) "shock" denotes simply an acute disturbance of the circulation [reference omitted] which can result from experiencing an accident or, more rarely, hearing of one. This is naturally of a transitory nature, though it can lead to lasting organic damage. It is by no means clear that the expert believed this to have occurred. A person who experiences an accident, and less often a person who hears of one, may also suffer psychopathological effects. Doctors call this "neurosis" (not necessarily a purposive neurosis of the kind for which no compensation may be given) or in serious cases even "psychosis" [reference omitted]. The expert's affidavit does not suggest that he was testifying to any illness of this kind. It is not enough that he did not say there was none: a positive finding is necessary or the plaintiff will fail to meet her burden of proof.

IV. To the extent, therefore, that it grants the plaintiff a claim for damages on her own account, the judgment under appeal cannot be sustained.

When the Court of Appeal re-examines the matter it will need to be convinced, before it can allow the plaintiff's claim even in part, that on hearing of the accident she not only experienced the normal reactions of pain, grief, and depression, but also directly suffered a "traumatic" injury to her physical and psychical health. Further expert evidence may be required, and if the expert testifies to such a condition, it will be necessary to ask to what extent he is relying on the evidence of the general practitioner, which is inadmissible in its present form.

B. I. If, after further investigation, the Court of Appeal holds that the claim should be admitted, the question of the deceased husband's contributory fault will arise. This must be dealt with in a different manner.

1. The Court of Appeal held that in cases like the present one cannot apply § 846 BGB by analogy, and in so holding it was consciously deviating from a view laid down by the Reichsgericht (RGZ 157, 11; RG DR 1940, 163) and supported by some scholars [reference omitted]. We agree with the Court of Appeal on this point: the opinion of the Reichsgericht is unacceptable in the form in which it was expressed. It was certainly right to emphasize that the basic rule of law is that only the direct victim of a tort may sue, a rule to which exceptions are made by §§ 844 and 845 BGB in favour of surviving dependants and persons entitled to services. But it was in error to treat the claim by a third party who suffers injury to his own health when someone else is injured or killed as if this were another case of "indirect injury to a third party" and to apply § 846 BGB to it by analogy. The difference between this case and those in §§ 844, 845 BGB is essentially that here the third party is affected in one of the legal interests specified in § 823 I BGB and that he is therefore a direct victim with an independent claim of his own under that section. Claims by the indirect victim under §§ 844, 845 BGB presuppose that the primary victim's harm resulted from a tort done to him (BGH VersR 1961, 846, 847) and that is why § 846 BGB provides that any fault on the part of the primary victim which contributed to the harm suffered by the third party must be taken into account in any claim the third party may bring under §§ 844, 845 BGB. This provision is perfectly sensible in relation to claims brought under §§ 844, 845 BGB, but it cannot apply to an independent claim brought under § 823 I BGB, for it must be irrelevant to a claim for harm done directly to the third party that it occurred by means of an injury to someone else. Indeed, the third party's rights may arise regardless of whether the primary victim of the accident had or has any claim for damages at all [OLG Munich NJW 1959, 819d; other reference omitted].

2. Yet we must agree with the result reached by the Reichsgericht, at least in cases of the kind before us, that in considering the personal claim of the indirectly injured widow one must take account of any contributory fault of the deceased husband. This, however, results from an analogical application of § 254 BGB, itself a specific application of the more general principle of law contained in § 242 BGB (BGHZ 4, 355).

(*a*) This is quite clear in relation to a claim for damages for *pain and suffering* (*Schmerzensgeld*; § 847 BGB), to which equitable principles apply. The Bundesgerichtshof has held (VersR 1962, 93) that a claim for damages for pain and suffering, unlike a claim for material damage, may be reduced because the victim was especially vulnerable to harm by reason of his bodily or psychical constitution, and that the *personal* contributory fault of the victim, which does not arise in this case, is only one of the factors to be taken into account in estimating the damages which are equitable in the circumstances (BGHZ 18, 149, 157). The same must be true of other factors in the victim's area of responsibility which contribute to the harm, such as a close personal relationship to the primary accident victim, as in this case.

(*b*) But even in cases of *material harm* the result reached by the Reichsgericht is correct. Where, as here, injury to health is caused at a distance, so to speak, the contributory fault of the damaged must be laid to the plaintiff's account. For here the accident to her husband was only able to cause the harm supposedly suffered by the plaintiff because as a result of their close personal relationship his tragedy became hers. One cannot imagine a person suffering in this manner on hearing of a fatal accident to a total stranger; indeed, if it happened, it would be so unusual that one would decline to impute it to the defendant on the ground that it was unforeseeable. But if the critical reason for the plaintiff's suffering this injury to her health was her close personal relationship to her husband, it is only fair that her claim should be affected by his fault in contributing to the accident. We must apply by analogy the basic idea of § 254 BGB, that a person's claim for damages must be reduced to the extent that the occurrence of the harm was due to a contributory factor from the plaintiff's sphere of responsibility. In this connection we must make a further observation. If the husband's death had been *solely* attributable to his failure to take care of himself, the plaintiff would have had no claim whatever for compensation for the consequent injury to herself. A person is under no legal duty, whatever the moral position may be, to look after his own life and limb simply in order to save his dependants from the likely psychical effects on them if he is killed or maimed: to impose such a legal duty, except in very peculiar cases, for instance, wherever a person commits suicide in a deliberately shocking manner, would be to restrict a person's self-determination in a manner inconsistent with our legal system.

It will be seen from this that unsatisfactory results follow from the view adopted by the Court of Appeal and some writers, which is that the primary victim's contributory fault is not to be taken into account when shock damage is caused at a distance. We have seen that, contrary to the view expressed by the Reichsgericht (RGZ 157, 11, 14) and by some of the writers, a tortfeasor cannot claim contribution under §§ 840, 254 BGB from the heirs of the primary victim, since the primary victim is not liable to the shock victim at all, much less as a common debtor. It follows that unless our present view is adopted, the tortfeasor would owe the shocked widow a full indemnity for her lost earnings even if the husband was so much more to blame for his own death than the tortfeasor that in a suit by the husband the tortfeasor would be wholly exonerated under § 254 BGB. This would be quite unacceptable.

Now it is true that in principle when a tortfeasor is sued he bears the risk of there being no solvent joint tortfeasor from whom he can claim contribution. But there are exceptions. For example, the courts have held that if, by reason of personal relationship with him, the victim releases one tortfeasor from liability in advance, the other tortfeasor should be protected (BGHZ 12, 213). In our case the third party has not been exonerated by release or by capricious conduct on the part of the creditor, but it is none the less true that the primary victim has, though involuntarily, had an adverse effect on the health of the shock victim in respect of which he is not liable. Once again, in these peculiar cases, the harm is caused only because of the very close personal relationship between the plaintiff and the primary victim, thanks to which the plaintiff adopts as her own the harm done to another, and the loss of his life becomes a loss, a serious loss, to her. In such a case, where it would be wrong to require the primary victim or his heirs to make contribution to the tortfeasor, it is only fair that the primary victim's causal contribution to the accident should be borne not by the stranger who triggered the harm but by the dependant who was hurt only because of her personal relationship with the primary victim and her identification with him. It was equitable considerations such as these that led the legislator to enact § 846 BGB though, as we have said, it covers a different case. In relation to that paragraph the *Protokolle* (vol. 2, II, 638 ff.) explain that to treat the third party's claim against the tortfeasor as entirely independent is too theoretical and logically extreme, and that to apply that view strictly would lead to unjust and inequitable results; the claims of a dead man's survivors result from his death, and if his careless conduct conduced to or accelerated his death, it is only right, in view of their relations with him, that the survivors should have to bear the consequences.

The claim for shock damage which arises in this distinctive manner is a judge-made claim, and though the Court of Appeal would like to extend it beyond the limits set by the Reichsgericht, we are not persuaded by any of the objections which its position on this question has elicited. It only remains to say that, contrary to what is stated in a number of the books, the Reichsgericht was always perfectly clear (see RGZ 162, 321) that cases of shock damage are cases of direct injury to a legal interest protected by § 823 I BGB and not simply instances of indirect harm of the kind covered by §§ 844, 845 BGB.

(c) The present case does not raise the issue of how the decision would be if the occurrence of the harm were wholly or partly independent of any personal relationship, or indeed how far a tortfeasor might be liable at all if the persons suffering the damaging reaction were third parties in no way related to the primary victim.

Case 2

BUNDESGERICHTSHOF (SIXTH CIVIL SENATE) 4 APRIL 1989
NJW 1989, 2317

Facts

The plaintiff and her husband had booked a cruise in the eastern Mediterranean scheduled to start on April 26, 1984 and paid the organisers the full price of DM 10,130. On April 21, 1984 the plaintiff's son C, then aged 22, was killed in a road accident. It is not contested by the parties that the defendant is liable in full for the damage resulting from the accident. On account of the pressures placed upon them, the plaintiff and her husband were unable to take the cruise which began one day after the funeral. They were not able to claim reimbursement of the DM 10,130 from the organisers. The plaintiff claimed for the loss of potential support under § 845 BGB arising from her rights as the mother of the victim of the accident and from her husband's corresponding rights which were assigned to her. In addition she claimed compensation for the expenditure on the lost holiday.

Although the LG rejected the claim based on § 845 BGB, it awarded her DM 10,130 as compensation for the holiday expenses. The OLG dismissed the appeals of both parties, but the defendant's appeal to the BGH was successful in respect of the lost holiday expenditure. The plaintiff's cross-appeal for the loss of support was denied.

For the following reasons:

I. The OLG accepted the claim brought by the plaintiff for the recovery of money spent on the holiday booked but not taken and made the following findings of law:

As a result of their son's death, the plaintiff and her husband were harmed in respect of their "right of health" protected by § 823 I BGB. The general view is that damages for pain and suffering are only available in respect of loss in the form of nervous shock which has the degree of severity of an illness. This does not necessarily mean that psychological impairment can only represent an infringement of a right protected by § 823 I BGB when it has the degree of severity of an illness. On the contrary, any form of invasion of the plaintiff's general bodily condition such as the infliction of worry and discomfort is sufficient for there to be damage to the plaintiff's health. Furthermore, the court believed the plaintiff's assertion that she and her husband were psychologically incapable of going on holiday as a result of the death of their son. The principles developed by the case law on the "*Vorhaltekosten*" [costs of maintaining a replacement vehicle whenever the plaintiff's own vehicle is out of circulation as a result of an accident] must be applied in this case and, as a result, the expenditure on the holiday must be treated as a recoverable form of damage.

II. The appeal judgment cannot be upheld in law.

1. On the basis of the facts as established, the OLG sees the plaintiff and her husband as having suffered an injury to their right of health protected under § 823 I BGB as a direct consequence of the accident suffered by their son. As a result, it held that the defendant was under a duty to make good the lost expenditure on the holiday as a consequence of the injury.

(a) This approach is not correct as a matter of law. True, the case law has long recognised [references omitted] that the concept of injury to the health within the meaning of § 823 I BGB not only covers physical impairment of the body, but also impairment of a psychological form. However, the law at present denies recovery for mental pain in so far as this is not a consequence of the effects of the injury to the (plaintiff's own) body or the (plaintiff's own) health. Feelings such as sorrow and pain, which are generated by the negative experience itself, are always linked in serious cases with disturbances in the plaintiff's physiological make-up and can, therefore, be directly relevant in a medical sense to the plaintiff's bodily state. To recognise these matters in law as injuries to the plaintiff's health within the meaning of § 823 I BGB . . . would contradict the intention of the legislator to limit tortious liability in § 823 I BGB to clearly defined sets of circumstances by restricting the range of protected interests and the prohibited forms of conduct. In particular, the BGB [never intended] to give a remedy, except where §§ 844 and 845 BGB apply, in cases where the interference with the protected interests of a person has an effect on third parties, unless the latter have suffered an injury in their own right. Thus, precisely in cases such as the present one, the close relatives will normally experience an effect upon their psychological and mental condition on hearing of the victim's death in an accident and as a consequence will suffer not only non-pecuniary, but also pecuniary loss. Nevertheless, the law has restricted recovery for pecuniary loss in the case of the person "indirectly" injured by a death to the more precisely defined types of loss set out in §§ 844 and 845 BGB. This legislative determination in favour of a basic limitation of tortious liability to recovery by the person "directly" injured, would be undermined if those types of psychological and mental effects resulting from the experience of the death of a close relative amounted to recoverable injury to health under § 823 I BGB simply because they are recognised by medical science. Consequently, this court has, since its decision in BGHZ 56, 163 [references omitted], only recognised a right to compensation in these types of cases for those types of psychologically inflicted impairments which have psychopathological effects lasting for some time, which exceed by some degree the already not inconsiderable detriment caused by a painful trauma for a person's general state of health, and which can therefore "be regarded in accordance with the general view as injuries to the body or to the health of the victim" [references omitted]. For this reason it is wrong for the OLG to take the view, in cases such as the present one where the loss is in the nature of psychological pressure upon the relatives as a result of the death, that even in the context of psychological injuries any invasion of the plaintiff's general bodily condition, or any infliction of worry and discomfort would suffice even if it did not display the severity of an illness. This point of view is not even supported by the references cited by the OLG itself such as Thomas in Palandt in *BGB Kommentar*, 48th Edition, § 823 note

3b. In that commentary upon the law relating to injuries to mental and bodily health through psychological effects [reference omitted] it is stated that "in accordance with the protective purpose of § 823 I BGB a claim for compensation should exist only where the injury to health exceeds, in the type and degree, that which close relatives must expect to suffer by way of impairment in these kinds of cases." In making this statement, Thomas also cited the judgment of this court of May 11 1971 (NJW 1971, 1883 [other references omitted]). The court confirms the approach taken there according to which the only psychological impairments which will amount to injuries to health under § 823 I BGB are those which display the characteristics of an obvious pathology and which will, therefore, be seen by the general public as injuries to the body or the health of the victim [references omitted]. Findings of fact to this effect were not discussed by the OLG and were not advanced by the plaintiff.

(b) If an injury to the health of the plaintiff or her husband within the meaning of § 823 I BGB as a consequence of the fatal accident involving their son cannot be established, then it may be left open whether, if such psychological impairments did in the particular circumstances of this case lead to a genuine injury to the plaintiff's health in the sense defined above, lost expenditure on a holiday which was booked but not taken could be brought within the scope and purpose of the legal norm which has been violated [references omitted]. There is also no need to decide whether, for example, recovery for such a form of detriment is excluded as a form of recoverable compensation for injury to health because experience would indicate that regardless of whether the psychological and physical impairments which they might have suffered as a result of the traumatic event had the degree of severity of an illness as required by § 823 I BGB, parents would not, normally, go on holiday one day after the funeral of their child.

2. The appeal judgment is further unsustainable on other legal grounds. Consideration should be given in this context to § 844 I BGB. Even if with respect to this claim for damages (which here accrues to a third party due to his duty to bear the funeral costs) one could give the term "funeral" expenses a wide meaning to include all expenditures associated with an appropriate and dignified burial, the presence of proximate cause (*Zurechnungszusammenhang*) would be questionable. This is because the plaintiff, according to her own pleadings, failed to take the holiday because of the psychological pressures she was experiencing as a result of the accident and not because of the timing of the funeral.

However, even if the focus were solely upon the funeral, it must be held that expenditure upon a holiday which is booked but not taken falls outside the protective scope of § 844 I BGB. For as exceptions to the general principle of the law of tort, that only persons who are directly injured by an accident will normally have a claim for compensation, §§ 844 and 845 BGB are to be narrowly interpreted. This means that in the context of § 844 I BGB it is the duty of the victim's heirs to bear the costs of the funeral which must form the focus of attention; but the concept of funeral expenses cannot be extended to cover expenditure which has been wasted because the third party (plaintiff) had to attend the funeral. Even if, exceptionally, § 844 I BGB can be construed as encompassing also the recovery of the travelling expenses of close relatives to attend the victim's funeral [references omitted], compensation for the above types of expenditure would go beyond the scope of liability set by the legislator. This court finds itself precluded from giving a wider interpretation of § 844 I BGB both by the terms of the law, itself, and the place of § 844 I BGB within the [wider] systematic framework of the law of tort.

Notes to Cases 1–2

1. The previous two and the next one case deal with the compensation of what used to be known in English law as nervous shock but nowadays goes by under the name of psychiatric injury. In the United States the term used is emotional harm and this is wider than the English term for two reasons. First, because, as we shall note below, in some jurisdictions this is seen to include distress, anxiety, and diminished enjoyment of life, types of harm which are seen with greater distrust both by English and German law. Secondly, American lawyers award compensation for emotional harm in factual instances such as discrimination (sexual or racial), violation of religious freedom, sexual harassment, and other such instances in which English and Continental European courts (and the legislature) have yet to make comparable inroads. In these notes we shall thus focus on the factual situations covered by the three German cases, all of which involve psychiatric injury inflicted as a result of experiencing unusually distressing scenes. Seen in this context, the first two cases raise four important points.

2. The first is connected with the problem of distant shock. Endorsing the view of earlier courts—of which RGZ 133, 270 is reproduced below as case 3—the court took the view that recovery should not be confined to eye-witnessing relatives but should also be allowed where the injurious effect was distant (*Fernwirkung*). This point, though never seriously contested, has been reaffirmed in more recent times by the Federal Court. (BGH 5 February 1985, BGHZ 93, 351 = NJW 1985, 1390 with note by Deubner at p. 1392). In that case the plaintiff was *en ventre sa mère* when the latter was told of her husband's serious injuries in a traffic accident. As a result, the mother suffered severe physiological and psychological reactions, which affected the birth process and led to the plaintiff being born seriously impaired. The child's claim for a declaratory judgment that she was entitled to damages was accepted, the court rejecting the defendant's argument that there was no causal nexus between the mother's shock and the plaintiff's injury. This is one of the crucial issues in nervous shock cases and is discussed more fully in the notes to the next case. For a summary of German law see chap. 2, A. 2, (*c*), above.

3. The second point decided by the Federal Court was that recovery should be limited to cases of psychiatric injury. See: *Attia* v. *British Gas Plc*, [1988] QB 304, 317, 320, per Bingham LJ. *Cf. Toms* v. *McConnell*, 45 Mich. App. 647, 207 NW 2d 140 (1973). See, also, *De Franceschi* v. *Storrier* (1989) 85 ACTR 1. This includes cases where there is a recognisable medical illness entailing such consequences as sleeping disorders, headaches, vomiting, speech disturbances, inability to concentrate, loss of libido and, in the most serious types of cases, even suicidal mania. (A fuller list can be found in *Alcock* v. *Chief Constable of South Yorkshire* [1992] 1 AC 310, 317.) Attempts by German lawyers to enlarge the definition of compensatable harm to include life's general risks—*allgemeines Lebensrisiko*—such as pain, grief, and other expenses connected with the "inconvenience" suffered as a result of the death of a close relative, have been rebuffed by the courts. (See BGH NJW 1989, 2317, reproduced above as case 2. Point re-confirmed in BGH 9 April 1991, NJW 1991, 2347. Likewise in English law—Lord Lloyd in *Page* v. *Smith* [1996] 1 AC 155—and in most but not all the jurisdictions of the United States.) However, the dividing line between, on the one hand psychiatric injury with *recognised* medical symptoms, and on the other hand "ordinary" pain and grief is sometimes more easy to state than to apply. An able lawyer and a sympathetic court can also manipulate it in favour of the plaintiff—if operating under a jury system. Case 2 shows how, with the help of a wider, teleological interpretation of all the relevant provisions of the Code, the temptation has been avoided in Germany. In this context, therefore, German law greatly resembles the English approach, though the juxtaposition of the German and English decisions (e.g. *Hinz* v. *Berry* [1970] 2 QB 40, 42) reveals some interesting differences at the level of writing style. (*Cf.* in this respect, the comments of Professor Kötz in *La Sentenza in Europa: Metodo Tecnica e Stile* (1988),

Einführungsvortrag, 129.) On the other hand, in German law, ". . . it is not a precondition of the tortfeasor's liability that the psychological effects had a physical cause. It is sufficient if it is clear enough that the psychological impairment would not have occurred but for the accident." (BGH 9 April 1991 NJW 1991, 2347; trans. by Weir taken from van Gerven, *op. cit.*, p. 92.)

4. The diversity of American solutions makes comparisons with the law in the USA more difficult, especially with the legal scene of the last thirty years ago. For here one finds diametrically different trends and a continuing and bewildering state of flux. The comments in this note must thus be read in conjunction with what is said in the notes to the next case and with the important caveat that in the United States one can find decisional law that can support almost every conceivable proposition. Such uncertainty and flux are unlikely to make American law a model for exportation, though landmark decisions such as *Dillon* v. *Legg*, 68 Cal. 2d 728, 69 Cal. Rptr. 72, 441 P. 2d 912 (1968), have had an important impact on other systems, including the English, and still repay careful reading.

In the United States, the first (and liberalising) trend manifested itself in the late seventies and early 1980s and was mostly to be found in the Western States of America. Those courts, which adopted it, inclined towards a wide (but erratic) interpretation of *Dillon*, undermining the calm authority of the case. They thus seemed willing to consider sympathetically claims for "emotional distress" *un*accompanied by obvious physical manifestations. See *Molien* v. *Kaiser Foundation Hospitals*, 27 Cal. 3d 916, 616 P. 2d 813 (1980); *Whitmore* v. *Euroways Express Coaches Ltd*, *The Times*, 4 May 1984. In the *Molien* case the main controlling device introduced by the court was the requirement that the emotional harm suffered by the plaintiff be "serious". This was defined in *Rodrigues* v. *State*, 52 Haw. 156, 472 P. 2d 509 (1970) (and approved by *Molien*) as "*serious mental distress . . . found where a reasonable man, normally constituted, would be unable to adequately cope with the mental stress engendered by the circumstances of the case*". If the italicised words are properly utilised they could be sufficient: but the Hawaiian courts have certainly not taken it seriously: see the bizarre case of *Campbell* v. *Animal Quarantine Station* 63 Haw. 557, 632 P. 2d 1066 (1981). There, five plaintiffs recovered a total of $1,000 for the anguish they suffered when they were told over the phone that their ageing dog had died the previous day after it had been forgotten in an unventilated van for over an hour exposed to the Hawaiian sun! (Some of these decisions, which are not without parallels in other systems such as the French, are discussed by Wise, "Recovery of Common Law damages for Emotional Distress, Loss of Society, and Loss of Companionship for the Wrongful death of a Companion Animal", 4 *Animal Law* 33 (1998).) But this shift towards plaintiffs courted a reaction which came with a vengeance as the changed of political climate in the 1980s put more conservatively inclined judges on the Bench. The decision of the Supreme Court of California in *Elden* v. *Sheldon* 250 Cal., 254 (1988), is an excellent example. *Thing* v. *La Chusa*, 48 Cal. 3rd 644, 257 Cal. Rptr. 865, 771 P. 2d 814 (1989), another "leading" case, confirmed this swing; and it presents a particular interest to English lawyers in so far as it involved facts very similar to those of the English case of *McLoughlin* v. *O'Brian* [1983] 1 AC 410. But in the California case, the mother who rushed to the scene of the accident after it had occurred to find her son bloody and apparently dead, failed to recover for her own emotional distress whereas in the England the opposite result was reached. This antithesis of the late 1980s to the thesis of the previous ten years thus marks a return to a more traditional understanding of the meaning of emotional distress. It also radically restricts the range of claimants under the *Dillon* v. *Legg* rule. This will be discussed briefly in the notes that accompany the translation of the third German decision on nervous shock.

5. But the battle between liberal and conservative judges is not over. *Molien*, allowing recovery for mental anguish even in the absence of physical injury, now seems to be accepted by some ten states with the Texas Supreme Court joining this move in its majority decision in *Moore* v. *Lillebo* 722 SW 2d 683 (1986). As is explained in greater detail in the note 4 to the next German decision, Tennessee and Montana are also showing signs of being content to rely on foreseeability as the main if not sole controlling device. Even California has in one sense swung back to a more liberal stance in its decision in *Burgess* (discussed in the next note). It remains to be seen whether this

emerging "independent" cause of action for pure emotional distress will displace the *Dillon* v. *Legg* rule. On this see the notes to the next German case and, *inter alia*, Nola and Ursin, "Negligent Infliction of Emotional Distress: Coherence Emerging from Chaos" 33 *Hastings LJ* 583 (1982). See, also, Hughes, "Recovering Damages for Mental Anguish in Wrongful Death Suits: The Elimination of the Physical Injury/Physical Manifestation Requirement" 18 *Texas Tech. L. Rev.* 893 (1987). An interesting compromise is proposed by Miller, "The Scope of Liability for Negligent Infliction of Emotional Distress: Making 'the Punishment Fit the Crime'" *U. Haw. L. Rev.* 1 (1979). Cases such as these prompt many questions. Here are some:

(*i*) How does one define mental anguish that merits compensation? Some Texas courts have understood the term to imply "a relatively high degree of mental pain and distress. It is more than mere disappointment, anger, resentment, or embarrassment, although it may include all of these . . .", *Trevino* v. *Southwestern Bell Tel. Co.*, 582 SW 2d 582, 584 (Tex. Civ. App. 1979). But *Rodrigues* (cited above) shows that it is easier to formulate a test than to apply it.

(*ii*) What is the legal position of absent members of a community hit by a natural disaster? See Labin, "Dealing with Disasters: Some Thoughts on the Adequacy of the Legal System" 30 *Stan. L. Rev.* 281 (1978).

(*iii*) What if the victim suffers mental anguish because physical harm *may* follow the negligently caused event, e.g. in the case of a man who had a homosexual relationship with another man who, unbeknown to him, was infected by AIDS? Courts have allowed damages for fear of future cancer—cancerphobia—as a result of exposure to toxic substances, e.g. *Jackson* v. *Johns-Manville Sales Corp.*, 781 F. 2d 394 5th Cir. (1986); *Herber* v. *Johns-Manville Corp.*, 785 F. 2d 79 (1986); *Eagle-Pitcher Indus. Inc.* v. *Cox*, 481 So. 2d 517 (1987), rev. denied, 492 So. 2d 1331 (1986). On this see: Gale and Goyer, "Recovery for Cancerphobia and Increased Risk of Cancer" 15 *Cumb. L. Rev.* 723 (1985); Dworkin, "Fear of Disease and Delayed Manifestation Injuries: A Solution or a Pandora's Box?" 53 *Fordham L. Rev.* 527 (1984); Note, "Tort Liability for the Transmission of AIDS Virus: Damages for Fear of AIDS and Prospective AIDS" 45 *Wash. and Lee L. Rev.* 185 (1988); "Emotional Distress Damages for fear of Contracting AIDS: Should Plaintiff have to show exposure to HIV?" 99 *Dick L. Rev.* 779 (1995). Some courts have made recovery depend on "actual exposure"; and have understood this notion restrictively. Thus in *K.A.C.* v. *Benson*, 527 NW 2d 553 (Minn. 1995) a woman who was subjected to gynaecological examinations by a doctor who had lesions in his hands and forearms and had tested HIV positive, was refused recovery. Others, however, have taken the view that subjecting the plaintiff to reasonable fear of exposure to AIDS infection is sufficient and in similar circumstances such as the one just given have allowed recovery. See: *Faya* v. *Almaraz*, 329 Md. 435, 620 A. 2d 327 (1993); *Williamson* v. *Waldman*, 150 NJ 232, 696 A. 2d 14 (1997); *Hartwig* v. *Oregon Trail Eye Clinic*, 254 Neb. 777, 580 NW 2d 86 (1998). The recovery however tends to be limited for the period until testing can assuage the fears.

(*iv*) How does one reconcile the law's general reluctance to allow recovery for pure emotional harm if the plaintiff has not suffered recognisable physical or psychological effects with the statutes and decisions in some States which allow damages for mere grief in wrongful death settings? This heading, which goes beyond the more widely recognisable claim for "loss of companionship", (discussed below in chapter 4) has emerged as a result of legislative intervention (e.g. Kan. Stat. Ann. § 60–1904) as well as judicial creativity. (See, *St. Louis Southwestern Ry.* v. *Pennington*, 261 Ark 650, 553 SW 2d 436 (1977).)

6. The problem of contributory negligence examined in the leading German case is a difficult one; and in England it recently surfaced in an interesting judgment by Cazalet J reproduced as an addendum, below. The German case concerned the deceased's (primary victim's) own contributory fault and whether this should be taken into account when calculating the plaintiff's damages. (The plaintiff was the primary victim's wife who claimed for the psychiatric injury that resulted from her being told of her spouse's death.) The German court's decision was affirmative; but its reasoning has to be studied carefully before it is fully understood. Two points thus need to be separated from the outset.

First, it is clear that any claim brought by the plaintiff as a *dependant* under the English Fatal Accidents Acts (or the German equivalent) will be affected by the contributory negligence of the deceased; in both cases the relevant statutory material says so. (§ 846 BGB.) The more difficult question is the second one namely, whether the same apportionment should take place in the case of any *personal* claims which the plaintiff/secondary victim might have for his or her nervous shock. Now in German law such a plaintiff's nervous shock claim will be an *independent* claim based on § 823 I BGB and not a *derivative* one based on §§ 843–4 BGB (wrongful death). Put in this way, it is prima facie difficult to see how the primary victim's own contributory fault could be imputed to his wife/plaintiff. The German court by-passed this difficulty by basing its decision on the pervading notion of good faith (embodied in § 242 BGB). The *Kammergericht Berlin* has subsequently followed this approach, in its decision of 10 November 1997, VersR 1999, 504, though this solution has not been without its critics. (Thus see the strong doubts expressed about the first decision by the late John Fleming in 20 *A. J. Comp. Law* 485, 488–9 (1972).) (The rationale behind imputing the "primary" victim's negligence is further examined in note 7, below.)

Prior to *Greatorex* v. *Greatorex* [2000] 1 WLR 1970=[2000] 4 All ER 769 (reproduced as an addendum, below), common law courts do not appear to have faced this problem squarely *in the context of nervous shock*—at any rate in England—though in his judgment Cazalet J alluded to some inconclusive Commonwealth authority. The picture in the USA may not be much clearer, though *Dillon* v. *Legg* (441 P. 2d 912 (1968)) contains some (seemingly) confused views on the subject. (In *Dillon* the majority, at p. 916, asked the question whether the contributory negligence of the victim *and* the plaintiffs should affect their claims whereas the minority, at p. 928, asked the very different question whether the deceased child's negligence can affect the living plaintiffs' claims.) However, the same point (about contributory negligence) may also arise in "rescue" cases and in those States (in the United States) which still recognise actions for "loss of consortium" or loss of "parental or children's companionship". In the first instance, and *perhaps* also in the second, the current tendency is to treat the claims as "*independent*", but to reduce them to take into account the contributory negligence of the physically injured spouse. (For a review of the case law, see *Blagg* v. *Illinois F.W.D. Truck and Equipment Company* 572 NE 2d, 920 (with references at p. 925.) See, also, *Mallett* v. *Dunn* [1949] 2 KB 180 (England); *Feltch* v. *General Rental Co.*, 383 Mass. 603, 421 NE 2d 67 (1981), reviewing the contradictory American case law and *Handeland* v. *Brown*, 216 NW 2d 574 (Iowa, 1974) where the conflicting views of the majority and the dissent repay careful reading and reveal that many of the problems in US law may be linked to the differing views adopted towards contributory and comparative negligence. Imputed contributory negligence is discussed in detail in Gregory, Kalven, and Epstein, 716 ff., especially 730 ff. and Harper, Fleming James Jr and Gray, vol. II, chap. 8.8 and 8.9. In Germany, as far as the rescue situation is concerned, it has been argued that, since there is a duty to rescue under § 323c StGB, a person wishing to commit suicide has a duty to carry it out in a way which does not "provoke" any rescue by third parties; otherwise he *may* be liable for any damage suffered during the rescue. (See Medicus *Schuldrecht BT* (9th edn.) (1999) p. 302.) The point, however, does not appear to have been settled by the courts.

7. *Greatorex* v. *Greatorex* raised the question whether a "primary victim" owed a duty of care to a "secondary victim" not to harm himself. The (first) defendant was injured in an accident caused by his grossly negligent driving. The plaintiff, his father, a professional fire officer, suffered nervous shock as a result of attending his son at the scene of the accident. As stated, Cazalet J acknowledged that there was no binding authority on this issue. Interestingly enough, his conclusion was, to a large extent, influenced by BGHZ 56, 163 (case 1) which was cited to him by counsel. The question the judge asked himself was whether a person owes a duty of care to other persons not to harm himself. It will be recalled that the BGH had suggested that the imposition of such a duty would unduly restrict the person's right of self-determination. We also noted that an exception might have to be considered where the suicide was committed in a "deliberately shocking manner". (Similarly, in BGH ZIP 1990, 1485, the court held that as a general rule a lessor did not owe a contractual duty to the lessee not to commit suicide and as a result the estate was not answerable for

the termination of the lease. To impose such a duty would have amounted to an unjustifiable intrusion of the right of self-determination of the lessor.) Cazalet J expressly followed the reasoning of the BGH and regarded the argument derived from the right of self-determination in case 1 as "powerful". (See also the Law Commission's report on Liability for Psychiatric Illness Law Com. No. 249 (1998) para. 5.34–5.44.) Matters might be different where, by harming himself, the "primary victim" causes damage other than nervous shock to another. (See A v. B's Trustees (1906) 13 SLT 830.) The ethical duty not to harm oneself becomes a legal duty as soon as the self-harming activity also causes physical harm to another person. From this perspective the "primary victim's" immunity from liability for nervous shock (suffered by others) constitutes an exception. In other words, the "primary victim's" right of self-determination prevails only if we regard this injury as special. Cazalet's J constant reference to "policy" lends credence to this view and illustrates, once again, the difficulty the legal system has coping with the ramifications of nervous shock and emotional injuries.

In case 1, above, the issue was whether the contributory negligence by the primary victim could be imputed to the secondary victim and his claim for damages against a third party accordingly reduced. At this stage, it is useful to reconsider the argument in favour of imputing the primary victim's contributory negligence to the secondary victim in the light of Cazalet's J analysis of the "primary victim's" (limited or non-existent) liability to others for causing harm to himself. For the two issues are interrelated.

The rationale seems to be this. If, generally speaking, a person ("primary victim") does not owe a duty of care to others ("secondary victims") not to harm himself, then "it is only fair" that if a third person causes physical injury to the primary victim, the secondary victim should bear the primary victim's causal contribution to the accident. This problem has occurred also in other contexts of adjustment among multiple "debtors" and the BGH has (not always consistently) applied similar considerations. (Thus, e.g. BGH, JR 1989, 60, but see BGHZ 12, 213.) Because of special circumstances, characteristic of the relationship between primary and secondary victim, the secondary victim does not have a cause of action against the primary victim (all other conditions of liability for nervous shock being fulfilled). This is because such a cause of action would be contrary to the primary victim's right of self-determination; but one could easily replace this with an exclusion clause. So the secondary victim sues the third party (case 1). If the third party could subsequently claim contribution from the primary victim, then *in the end* the primary victim would be held liable for his causal contribution to the accident. (*Albeit* the risk of insolvency of the primary victim would be transferred from the secondary victim to the third party.) But this result of holding the primary victim liable is regarded as undesirable (because of his right of self-determination). Therefore, the third party cannot claim contribution from the primary victim even if the latter was primarily responsible for the accident. (*Cf. Alcock* v. *Chief Constable of South Yorkshire Police* [1992] 1 AC 310, 418 per Lord Oliver.) This result may not be satisfactory. It would not seem fair in such circumstances, the BGH stressed, to impose full liability on the third party, especially if his contribution to the harm was in causative terms very low and that of the primary victim very high. Why should the third party (rather than the secondary victim) bear the primary victim's causal contribution to the accident? After all, it is because of special circumstances arising out of the relationship between primary and secondary victim, that the primary victim cannot be made liable for causing nervous shock. It is therefore plausible to apply the rationale of § 846 BGB also to claims of secondary victims in respect of nervous shock and to reduce the secondary victim's claim accordingly. This implies that where the primary victim is solely answerable for the accident, the secondary victim cannot recover. We are thus back to our point of departure.

8. There is a final issue that needs to be considered and it concerns the level of damages that are recoverable. Pecuniary losses caused by the psychiatric illness induced by the accident are, of course, recoverable. (For instance lost earnings, case 1). But an English lawyer will also need to know the level of damages that can be recovered for "pain and suffering" under § 847 BGB. Are they/should they be high or low? And should they be influenced by the level of awards found in other cases? These questions are examined in detail in chapter 4 section A.3(c).

Addendum

Extracts from *Greatorex* v. *Greatorex* [2000] 1 WLR 1970

Facts and proceedings

On 11 April 1996 the first defendant had been drinking with a friend, who is the defendant in the proceedings made pursuant to Part 20 of the Civil Procedure Rules. The first defendant was driving a car belonging to the Part 20 defendant, who had given him permission to drive the car and was a passenger in it. Whilst overtaking on a blind brow the first defendant negligently drove over on to the wrong side of the road and was hit by an oncoming vehicle. The Part 20 defendant was uninjured. The defendant's head was injured and he was unconscious for about an hour. Initially he was trapped inside the car. The police, ambulance and fire services attended the scene of the accident. Among the fire officers who attended the scene was the plaintiff. He is the defendant's father. At the time of the accident he was employed as a leading fire officer. He was nowhere near the scene of the accident when it happened. He went there in the course of his employment. Having been informed that his son had been injured, he attended to him. The plaintiff was later diagnosed as suffering from long-term, severe, post-traumatic stress disorder as a result of the accident. The first defendant was subsequently convicted of driving a motor vehicle without due care and attention, driving without insurance and failing to provide a specimen. The plaintiff brought proceedings claiming damages against the first defendant, his son. Since the first defendant was uninsured at the time of the accident, the Motor Insurers' Bureau has been joined as the second defendant. The second defendant has in turn brought proceedings under Part 20 of the Civil Procedure Rules against the Part 20 defendant seeking an indemnity from him on the basis that he allowed the first defendant to drive his car without insurance against third party risks in breach of the Road Traffic Act 1988. On the basis of these facts the court had to determine the following three preliminary questions of law:

"1. Does a primary victim (i.e. the first defendant) owe a duty of care to a third party in circumstances where his self-inflicted injuries caused that third party psychiatric injury? 2. On the agreed facts, did the first defendant owe the plaintiff a duty of care not to harm himself? 3. On the agreed facts, did the first defendant owe the plaintiff a duty of care not to cause him psychiatric injury as a result of exposing him to the sight of the defendant's self-inflicted injuries?"

CAZALET J.

The role of policy considerations

It is not in dispute that the onus is on the plaintiff to show that a duty of care exits, either on the basis of existing authority or by the application of established principle. It is well settled that whilst foreseeability is a necessary condition for the existence of such a duty it is not of itself a sufficient condition. It must, in addition, be fair, just and reasonable for a duty of care to be imposed in a particular situation. The law was encapsulated by Lord Bridge of Harwich in *Caparo Industries Plc* v. *Dickman* [1990] 2 AC 605, 617–618 in the following well known passage:

"in addition to the foreseeability of damage, necessary ingredients in any situation giving rise to a duty of care are that there should exist between the party owing the duty and the party to whom it is owed a relationship characterised by the law as one of "proximity" or "neighbourhood" and that the situation should be one in which the court considers it fair, just and reasonable that the law should impose a duty of a given scope upon the one party for the benefit of the other ... the concepts of proximity and fairness embodied in these additional ingredients are not susceptible of any precise definition as would be necessary to give them utility as practical tests, but amount in effect to little more than convenient labels to attach to the features of different specific situations which, on a detailed examination of all the circumstances, the law recognises pragmatically as giving rise to a duty of care of a given scope."

These observations apply with particular force in the field of negligently inflicted psychiatric injury, where policy considerations loom large. This is evident from each of the quartet of decisions in which the House of Lords has reviewed this area of the law in the last two decades,

[Then follow references to *McLoughlin* v. *O'Brian* [1983] 1 AC 410, 420 per Lord Wilberforce; *Alcock* v. *Chief Constable of South Yorkshire Police* [1992] 1 AC 310, 411 (the first of two House of Lords decisions arising out of the Hillsborough football stadium disaster) per Lord Oliver of Aylmerton; *Page* v. *Smith* [1996] AC 155, 197E per Lord Lloyd of Berwick; and *Frost* v. *Chief Constable of South Yorkshire Police* [1999] 2 AC 455, 493A (the second of the Hillsborough disaster cases) per Lord Steyn].

The control mechanisms

The control mechanisms which restrict the scope of the duty of care where damages for psychiatric injury arising out of an accident are claimed by claimants who were not directly threatened by the accident but learned of it through seeing it or hearing of it were defined in *Alcock* v. *Chief Constable of South Yorkshire Police* [1992] 1 AC 310. In *Frost* v. *Chief Constable of South Yorkshire Police* [1999] 2 AC 455, 502 Lord Hoffmann conveniently stated them in summary form:

"(1) The plaintiff must have close ties of love and affection with the victim. Such ties may be presumed in some cases (e.g. spouses, parent and child) but must otherwise be established by evidence. (2) The plaintiff must have been present at the accident or its immediate aftermath. (3) The psychiatric injury must have been caused by direct perception of the accident or its immediate aftermath and not upon hearing about it from someone else."

Primary and secondary victims

In *Page* v. *Smith* [1996] AC 155, 197 Lord Lloyd, with whose speech Lord Ackner and Lord Browne-Wilkinson agreed, placed emphasis upon the distinction in nervous shock cases between the position of a primary victim of an accident, who is directly involved as a participant and is within the range of foreseeable physical injury, and that of a secondary victim, whose psychiatric injury is caused by witnessing or participating in the aftermath of an accident which causes or threatens death or injury to others. Among the principal consequences of this distinction are that the primary victim, unlike the secondary victim, can recover damages for his psychiatric injury even if such injury was unforeseeable, and that he can do so even if he suffered the psychiatric harm because he lacked normal fortitude or "ordinary phlegm."

I turn to the competing arguments which have been urged upon me as to whether a duty of care situation arose on the facts of this case.

The plaintiff as a rescuer

Mr Mason, for the plaintiff, first submits that the first defendant owed the plaintiff a duty of care in his capacity as a rescuer, separate and apart from, for the purpose of this submission, the fact that he was also a close relative of the first defendant.

It seems reasonably clear that prior to the decision of the House of Lords in *Frost* rescuers were treated as coming within a special category. Lord Oliver in *Alcock* v. *Chief Constable of South Yorkshire Police* [1992] 1 AC 310, 408 summarised the position of the rescuer as it was then seen to be as follows:

"Into the same category, as it seems to me, fall the so called 'rescue cases.' It is well established that the defendant owes a duty of care not only to those who are directly threatened or injured by his careless acts but also to those who, as a result, are induced to go to their rescue and stiffer injury in so doing. The fact that the injury suffered is psychiatric and is caused by the impact on the mind of becoming involved in personal danger or in scenes of horror and destruction makes no difference. 'Danger invites rescue. The cry of distress is the summons to relief . . . the act, whether impulsive or deliberate, is the child of the occasion: "*Wagner v. International Railway Co* (1921) 232 NY 176, 180–181, per Cardozo J." . . . However, in *Frost v. Chief Constable of South Yorkshire Police* [1999] 2 AC 455 the House of Lords concluded by a majority of three to two that for policy reasons rescuers should no longer be regarded as coming within a special category. Lord Steyn and Lord Hoffmann, with both of whose speeches Lord Browne-Wilkinson agreed, concurred in dismissing claims by police officers who had suffered psychiatric injury as a result of their experiences at the Hillsborough disaster. The effect of the majority decision is that in order to recover compensation for pure psychiatric injury suffered as a rescuer the plaintiff has at least to satisfy the threshold requirement that he objectively exposed himself to danger or reasonably believed that he was doing so, although it is not necessary for him to establish that his psychiatric condition was caused by the perception of personal danger. Where this element of personal danger is lacking his position is no different from that of other secondary victims who are subject to the control mechanisms to which I have referred above: see the *Frost* case, at pp. 497, 499, per Lord Steyn: at pp. 509–511, per Lord Hoffmann.

The speeches of Lord Steyn and Lord Hoffmann are to be compared with the no less powerful dissenting speeches of Lord Griffiths and Lord Goff of Chieveley, both of whom were of the opinion that rescuers should remain in the special category in which they had previously appeared to be placed. Both Lord Griffiths and Lord Goff accepted, however, that it should only be in exceptional cases that rescuers who were not in any physical danger should be permitted to recover for their psychiatric injury. Lord Griffiths said, at p. 465:

"If the rescuer is in no physical danger it will only be in exceptional cases that personal injury in the form of psychiatric injury will be foreseeable for the law must take us to be sufficiently robust to give help at accidents that are a daily occurrence without suffering a psychiatric breakdown. But where the accident is of a particularly horrifying kind and the rescuer is involved with the victims in the immediate aftermath it may be reasonably foreseeable that the rescuer will suffer psychiatric injury . . ."

Lord Goff having described the circumstances in which the rescuer found himself in *Chadwick v. British Railways Board* [1967] 1 WLR 912 (the Lewisham train disaster case) as "wholly exceptional," stated, at p. 484: "It must be very rare that a person bringing aid and comfort to a victim or victims will be held to have suffered foreseeable psychiatric injury as a result." Both Lord Griffiths and Lord Goff regarded the circumstances of the Hillsborough disaster as falling within that exceptional category.

Mr Mason urges me not to follow the majority opinion in the House of Lords on the ground that it constituted an unwarranted departure from previous authority, which, he submitted, had firmly established the rescuer claiming damages for psychiatric injury as being within a special category. He submits that the minority views of Lord Griffiths and Lord Goff should be followed. He argues that in the case of a particularly horrific accident in which the rescuer finds himself in exceptional circumstances justice may cry out for compensation for the psychiatric harm he suffers in consequence, even if he is not exposed to any physical danger and does not reasonably apprehend such danger.

It seems to me that this submission is nothing less than an attempt to reopen the argument which was rejected by the majority opinion in *Frost v. Chief Constable of South Yorkshire Police* [1999] 2 AC 455. The majority decision in that case has made it clear that the rescuer seeking to recover damages for purely psychiatric injury is to be regarded as a secondary victim having no special status. It is clearly not open to me to decline to follow that decision. The consequence is that on the agreed facts of the present case, it being accepted on all sides that the plaintiff was never in any physical danger nor in fear of such danger, his claim qua rescuer must fail.

I would add, for the sake of completeness, that even had I been persuaded by Mr Mason to discard our doctrine of precedent and follow the minority views of Lord Griffiths and Lord Goff in the Frost case, my conclusion on the agreed facts would not have been any different. Although the accident involved a potentially serious injury to the first defendant, the circumstances in which the rescuers involved in the aftermath of that accident found themselves in no way approached the horror of the circumstances in which the rescuers found themselves in the Lewisham train disaster or in the Hillsborough football stadium disaster. Even on the minority view in the Frost case, a rescuer who suffered psychiatric injury in consequence of his experiences after arriving at the scene of this accident would not on the facts of this case be entitled, as a rescuer, to recover damages for his injury.

Accordingly the plaintiff cannot succeed in this case on the sole ground that he was a rescuer.

The plaintiff as father

Mr Mason next submits that the plaintiff, as the first defendant's father, meets the requirements of each of the control mechanisms applicable to claims by secondary victims, to which I have referred above. Mr Eklund, for the second defendant, the Motor Insurers' Bureau, concedes that on the agreed facts both the first requirement, that there must be close ties of love and affection between the primary and the secondary victims, and the third requirement, that the psychiatric injury must have been caused by direct perception as opposed to hearing about the accident from someone else, appear to be satisfied. He contends, however, that the plaintiff does not satisfy the second requirement, that he must have been present at the accident or its immediate aftermath.

In *McLoughlin* v. *O'Brian* [1983] 1 AC 410 the plaintiff was held by the House of Lords to have been present at the immediate aftermath of the accident when she attended hospital to see her injured family somewhat over an hour after the accident. In contrast, in *Alcock* v. *Chief Constable of South Yorkshire Police* [1992] 1 AC 310 Lord Ackner, at p. 405, and Lord Jauncey of Tullichettle, at p. 424, were both of the opinion that a visit to the mortuary some eight or nine hours after the disaster could not qualify as being within its immediate aftermath. In the present case the plaintiff was at the scene of the accident very shortly after its occurrence, at a time when the first defendant was still trapped in the wreckage and in urgent need of help from the emergency services. The facts of the present case are much stronger than the facts of *McLoughlin* v. *O'Brian*, both as regards timing and as regards location. I therefore reject Mr Eklund's submission.

I find that the plaintiff meets the requirements of each of the control mechanisms, which govern a claim for psychiatric injury suffered by a secondary victim of an accident.

The plaintiff as rescuer and father

. . . On analysis, what is said to be the unique feature of the present case is the fact that the plaintiff happens to be a professional rescuer. That feature of the case, adds nothing to the strength of his claim. Lord Hoffmann's observation in the *Frost* case, at p. 510, seems in point:

". . . I have no doubt that most people would regard it as wrong to award compensation for psychiatric injury to the professionals and deny compensation for similar injury to the relatives." . . .

Duty owed by victim of self-inflicted injuries: the authorities

There is no reported English decision on the question whether a victim of self-inflicted injuries owes a duty of care to a third party not to cause him psychiatric injury. Lord Ackner referred to the issue in *Alcock* v. *Chief Constable of South Yorkshire Police* [1992] 1 AC 310, 401:

"As yet there is no authority establishing that there is liability on the part of the inured person, his or her estate, for mere psychiatric injury which was sustained by another by reason of shock, as a result of a self-inflicted death, injury or peril of the negligent person, in circumstances where the risk of such psychiatric injury was reasonably foreseeable. On the basis that there must be a limit at some reasonable point to the extent of the duty of care owed to third parties which rests upon everyone in all his actions, Lord Robertson, the Lord Ordinary, in his judgment in the *Bourhill* case, 1941 SC 395, 399, did not view with favour the suggestion that a negligent window-cleaner who loses his grip and falls from a height, impaling himself on spiked railings, would be liable for the shock-induced psychiatric illness occasioned to a pregnant woman looking out of the window of a house situated on the opposite side of the street."

Lord Oliver also considered the question and said, at p. 418:

"Whilst not dissenting from the case-by-case approach advocated by Lord Bridge in *McLaughlin's* case, the ultimate boundaries within which claims for damages in such cases can be entertained must I think depend in the end upon considerations of policy. For example, in his illuminating judgment in *Jaensch* v. *Coffey* (1984) 155 CLR 549, Deane J expressed the view that no claim could be entertained as a matter of law in a case where the primary victim is the negligent defendant himself and the shock to the plaintiff arises from witnessing the victim's self-inflicted injury. The question does not, fortunately, fall to be determined in the instant case, but I suspect that an English court would be likely to take a similar view. But if that be so, the limitation must be based upon policy rather than upon logic for the suffering and shock of a wife or mother at witnessing the death of her husband or son is just as immediate, just as great and just as foreseeable whether the accident be due to the victim's own or to another's negligence and if the claim is based, as it must be, on the combination of proximity and foreseeability, there is certainly no logical reason why a remedy should be denied in such a case. Indeed, Mr Hytner, for the plaintiffs, has boldly claimed that it should not be. Take, for instance, the case of a mother who suffers shock and psychiatric injury through witnessing the death of her son when he negligently walks in front of an oncoming motor car. If liability is to be denied in such a case such a denial can only be because the policy of the law forbids such a claim, for it is difficult to visualise a greater proximity or a greater degree of foreseeability. Moreover, I can visualise great difficulty arising, if this be the law, where the accident, though not solely caused by the primary victim has been materially contributed to by his negligence. If, for instance, the primary victim is himself 75 per cent responsible for the accident, it would be a curious and wholly unfair situation if the plaintiff were enabled to recover damages for his or her traumatic injury from the person responsible only in a minor degree whilst he in turn remained unable to recover any contribution from the person primarily responsible since the latter's negligence vis-a-vis the plaintiff would not even have been tortious."

Jaensch v. *Coffey* (1984) 155 CLR 549, referred to by Lord Oliver, was a decision of the High Court of Australia. It has been considered in other decisions in that jurisdiction. It is right that I should take into account further Commonwealth authorities bearing upon the issue which I have to decide. I can do no better than refer to the words of Lord Goff in *Frost* v. *Chief Constable of South Yorkshire Police* [1999] 2 AC 455, 471–472:

"In this, as in other areas of tortious liability in which the law is in a state of development, the courts proceed cautiously from one category of case to another. We should be wise to heed the words of Windeyer J spoken nearly 30 years ago in *Mount Isa Mines Ltd* v. *Pusey* (1970) 125 CLR 383, 396: 'The field is one in which the common law is still in course of development. Courts must therefore act in company and not alone. Analogies in other courts, and persuasive precedents as well as authoritative pronouncements, must be regarded.'"

In *Jaensch* v. *Coffey*, 155 CLR 549 a motor cyclist suffered severe injuries in a collision with a vehicle which was driven negligently. The motor cyclists wife, who was not at the scene of the accident but who saw him in hospital and was told that he was "pretty bad," suffered nervous shock as a result of what she had seen and been told. The wife succeeded in her claim for damages on the basis of her relationship with her husband and the fact that the events which had caused the nervous shock to her were part of the aftermath of the accident resulting from the defendant's negligence.

Deane J, at p. 604, in referring to the duty of care to avoid psychiatric injury unassociated with physical injury, said:

"such a duty of care will not exist unless the reasonably foreseeable psychiatric injury was sustained as a result of the death, injury or peril of someone other than a person whose carelessness is alleged to have caused the injury . . ."

Dawson J appears to have inclined towards the same view. He said, at p. 612:

"On the other hand, there appear to be strictures upon liability for the infliction of nervous shock which are not readily explicable in terms of foreseeability and which may be seen to be the result of the application of policy considerations. For example, if no action will lie in negligence against a defendant who carelessly injures himself and thereby inflicts nervous shock upon the plaintiff, there would seem to be a limit imposed which is outside the test of foreseeability."

These observations were not necessary for the decision in the case and thus were plainly obiter.

Mr Eklund has referred me to a number of other Australian authorities in which the issue in question has received consideration. [*Harrison* v. *State Government Insurance Office* [1985] Aust Torts Rep 80–723, a decision of the Supreme Court of Queensland, was considered] . . .

Mr Eklund further pointed out that the same conclusion was reached in a decision of the Supreme Court of British Columbia, *Cady* v. *Anderson* [1993] BCWLD 200. In that case the plaintiff was prevented from recovering for psychiatric injury caused by witnessing the death of her fiancé in a car accident caused by his negligence. One of the two grounds given for this decision was the fact that the fiancé was the tortfeasor.

The weight of the Commonwealth authorities to which I have been referred clearly tends to support Mr Eklund's submission that there is no duty of care in the situation presently under consideration.

Whilst acknowledging that the authorities to which I have made reference were not helpful to his case, Mr Mason submitted that the decision of the Scottish Outer House in *A* v. *B's Trustees* (1906) 13 SLT 830, a decision much closer to home than the Commonwealth cases, provided authority for the sustainability of the plaintiff's claim for nervous shock, notwithstanding that the first defendant's injuries were self-inflicted. The action was brought at the instance of a lady and her daughter, landladies of a furnished apartment in Glasgow, against the trustees and executors of a man to whom the apartment had been let, seeking damages in respect of nervous shock suffered by them as a result of his having committed suicide in the bathroom of that apartment. The action succeeded. Mr Mason submitted that the ratio decidendi of the decision was that a tortfeasor is liable for psychiatric illness caused by his self-inflicted injuries. On analysis of the judgment of the Lord Ordinary, Lord Johnston, I do not consider the case to have been decided on that basis. The following passage from the judgment of Lord Johnston, at p. 831, shows that he based liability on contract:

"Is it one of the purposes of renting lodgings that they should be taken for the purpose of committing suicide? I think that it is not, and that in so using the lodgings in turning the bathroom into a slaughter house, this man was performing a wrongful act, an act in breach of the contract under which he received possession of the premises."

In *Bourhill* v. *Young* [1943] AC 92, 120 Lord Porter stated that the decision in *A* v. *B's Trustees*, 13 SLT 830 may be explained as "founded on contract or on the fact that the material damage might have been anticipated." Leaving aside any question of breach of contract, in my view such a claim, if made in tort, would now fail for want of the close ties of love and affection.

Accordingly I do not consider that the decision in *A* v. *B's Trustees* is of assistance to the plaintiff's case.

Mr Mason went on to submit that Deane J's approach in *Jaensch* v. *Coffey*, 155 CLR 549 that as a matter of law no claim can be entertained where the primary victim is the negligent defendant himself and the shock to the plaintiff arises from witnessing the victims self-inflicted injury, is not only unworkable but also unjust in that, for example, it would preclude claims such as those of train drivers who suffer nervous shock when a person throws himself in front of their train in order to commit suicide. Although I shall be referring to potentially relevant policy considerations later in this judgment, it seems convenient to deal with this submission at this stage, because Mr Mason relies upon authority in support of it. . . .

It is clear, however, that the case of the train driver falls into a particular category of cases, including *Dooley* v. *Cammell Laird & Co Ltd* [1951] 1 Lloyds Rep 271, in which a duty of care has been held to exist, and which was described by Lord Oliver in *Alcock* v. *Chief Constable of South Yorkshire Police* [1992] 1 AC 310, 408 in these terms:

"where the negligent act of the defendant has put the plaintiff in the position of being, or of thinking that he is about to be or has been, the involuntary cause of another's death or injury and the illness complained of stems from the shock to the plaintiff of the consciousness of this supposed fact." . . .

Whether claimants in this category are to be treated as primary victims, as Lord Oliver treated them, or as secondary victims, its Lord Hoffmann [in *Frost* at pp. 507–508] appears to have viewed them, does not seem to me to be a matter of critical importance. There is room for the law to make provision for them on either basis.

My conclusion on this issue is that cases which fall into this particular category raise materially different considerations from those which arise in the instant case, and that the authorities would not necessarily preclude such cases from receiving separate treatment were I to rule against the plaintiff on the preliminary issue which I have to decide. I therefore do not find myself assisted by the submission based on the case of Watkins LJ's engine driver.

Duty owed by victim of self-inflicted injuries: policy considerations

Although it appears from the body of authority referred to above that the preponderance of opinion is unfavourable to the concept of a victim of self-inflicted injuries owing a duty of care to a third party not to cause him psychiatric harm in consequence of his injuries, there is no decision on the point which is binding upon this court. Accordingly the court, in the light of such guidance as has been given, including such assistance as may be gleaned from the Commonwealth decisions, must reach its own conclusion. It is at this stage that policy considerations come into play.

I observe, first, that since a claim for psychiatric illness suffered by a secondary victim in consequence of injury to a primary victim is not admitted by our law unless the three elements of the control mechanism are present, it follows that it will normally only be in cases where close family ties exist between the primary and secondary victim that the particular issue with which this case is concerned will arise. For reasons which will shortly appear, I regard that as a matter of significance.

In the second place, the issue which I have to resolve raises, as it seems to me, a question which impinges upon a person's right of self-determination. Mr Eklund has drawn my attention to a decision of the German Bundesgerichtshof (Sixth Civil Division) (11 May 1971), where this problem was identified. A translation of an extract from that judgment (translated by Mr Tony Weir) which appears in Markesinis *The German Law of Torts*, 3rd edn (1994), p. 109 was produced to the court [case 1 above]. That case concerned a wife's claim for damages for psychiatric injury suffered by her as a secondary victim of an accident in which her husband had died and which had been partly caused by his own negligence. I shall describe in a moment how the court dealt with the question of contribution between joint tortfeasors in that case. The immediately relevant passage in the judgment of the German court relates to the court's observation that if the death of the primary victim had been exclusively caused by his own negligence, the plaintiff could not have recovered anything in respect of her injuries. The court reasoned, at p. 113 of that translation:

"A person is under no legal duty, whatever the moral position may be, to look after his own life and limb simply in order to save his dependants from the likely psychical effects on them if he is killed or maimed: to impose such a legal duty, except in very peculiar cases, for instance, wherever a person commits suicide in a deliberately shocking manner, would be to restrict a person's self-determination in a manner inconsistent with our legal system."

Both counsel maintain that self-harming, whether by negligence or deliberately, would not be expected to give rise to any criminal liability. Mr Eklund, relying upon the opinion of the

Bundesgerichtshof, argues that to impose the proposed liability for psychiatric harm caused to another through such acts would be to curtail the right of self-determination and the liberty of the individual. There is, of course, a duty not to cause foreseeable physical injury to another in such circumstances, but in my judgment to extend that duty so as to bring within its compass purely psychiatric injury would indeed be to create a significant further limitation upon an individual's freedom of action. That seems to me to be a powerful objection to the imposition of such a duty. Mr Eklund maintains that there are strong policy reasons for holding that the victim of self-inflicted injury, whether caused negligently or deliberately, should not owe a duty of care to someone who suffers psychiatric injury as a result of seeing him in an injured state. He postulates certain examples, in each of which A causes himself harm and B, who fulfils all the preconditions for classification as a secondary victim, suffers psychiatric injury as a result of seeing A in his injured state: (1) A commits suicide and the body is found by B, his son; (2) A negligently wounds himself with a kitchen knife in front of B, his wife; (3) A suffers extensive loss of blood as a result of a fall caused by his own negligence and is found by B, his mother. In all these circumstances, he submits, public policy ought to prevent B from suing A or A's estate if he or she suffers psychiatric injury in consequence of what he or she has seen.

His argument is as follows. The first *Alcock* control mechanism means that such claims must of necessity be between close relatives. Regrettably, the suffering of close relatives for self-induced or natural reasons is an inherent part of family life. It is only when someone else inflicts the injuries that the incident is taken out of the category of everyday family life and into the law of tort. There seems to me to be force in this argument. Tragedy and misfortune may befall any family. Where the cause arises within the family there would, in my view, have to be good reason for further extending the law to provide a remedy in such a case.

That takes me to a related point, which in my view is of some importance. Home life may involve many instances of a family member causing himself injury through his own fault. Should the law allow one family member, B, to sue another family member, A, or his estate in respect of psychiatric illness suffered as a result of B either having been present when the injury was sustained or having come upon A in his injured state? Mr Mason argues that such claims will be rare, because such events will not normally cause psychiatric illness, and because the courts may be expected strictly to enforce the requirement that a secondary victim must show that the circumstances were such that a person of normal fortitude might foreseeably suffer psychiatric harm. That may be so, but experience shows that it is not only successful claimants who sue. To allow a cause of action in this type of situation is to open up the possibility of a particularly undesirable type of litigation within the family, involving questions of relative fault as between its members. Issues of contributory negligence might be raised, not only where the self-inflicted harm is caused negligently, but also where it is caused intentionally. To take an example, A, while drunk, seriously injures himself. B, his wife, suffers nervous shock. What if A raises by way of defence the fact that he had drunk too much because B had unjustifiably threatened to leave him for another man or had fabricated an allegation of child sexual abuse against him? Should the law of tort concern itself with this kind of issue? In a case where A's self-harm is deliberate, the possibility that B's claim may be met by a defence of contributory negligence, alleging that B's behaviour caused A to harm himself, is an alarming one. And that is without allowing for the further impact of possible Part 20 claims being brought against other members of the family.

I appreciate, of course, that one member of the family may already sue another family member in respect of physical injury caused by that other, so that in cases of physical injury there is already the potential for personal injury litigation within the family; but the fact that family members have the same right as others to make a claim for physical injury does not necessarily mean that they should have the right to make a claim for a different kind of harm in respect of which, because of the first *Alcock* control mechanism, others have no such right. Further, where a family member suffers psychiatric harm as a result of the self-inflicted injuries of another family member, the psychiatric illness in itself may well have an adverse effect upon family relationships which the law should be astute not to exacerbate by allowing litigation between those family members. In my judgment, to permit a cause of action for purely psychiatric injury in these circumstances would be potentially productive of acute family strife.

Mr Mason's best point in answer to these policy considerations, as it seems to me, derives from the passage in Lord Oliver's speech in *Alcock* v. *Chief Constable of South Yorkshire Police* [1992] 1 AC 310, 418 to which I have already referred, where Lord Oliver referred to the anomaly that might arise where an accident, though not solely caused by the primary victim, has been materially contributed to by his negligence. Lord Oliver pointed to the unfair situation which would arise if a claimant were to recover damages in full for his or her traumatic injuries from a person who had in fact been responsible in only a minor degree whilst he in turn remained unable to recover any contribution from the person primarily responsible, since the latter's negligence vis-a-vis the plaintiff would not even have been tortious.

I fully recognise the force of this objection to a denial of a duty of care in the type of situation under consideration in this judgment, but it does not seem to me to outweigh the policy considerations to which I have referred above. There is no easy answer to the point, save to observe that, as has often been pointed out, the area of law relating to so-called nervous shock cases is bedevilled by inconsistencies. The particular anomaly identified by Lord Oliver, which springs from the wording of section 1(1) of the Civil Liability (Contribution) Act 1978 providing that a tortfeasor may recover contribution "from any other person liable in respect of the same damage," is perhaps more easily capable of remedy by Parliament than some of the other problems created by the existing limitations on liability for negligently caused psychiatric harm. One possibility is suggested by the judgment of the Bundesgerichtshof (Sixth Civil Division) to which I have already referred. In that case the court held that the secondary victim's damages ought to be reduced to the extent of the primary victim's contributory negligence. The court pointed out (The German Law of Torts, p. 112):

"if the critical reason for the plaintiff's suffering this injury to her health was her close personal relationship to her husband, it is only fair that her claim should be affected by his fault in contributing to the accident."

I note that this is not a suggestion which has found favour in the Law Commission Report on Liability for Psychiatric Illness (1998) (Law Com No 249), which states, at paragraph 5.39:

"It would be contrary to the underlying principle that the defendant owes a separate duty of care directly to the plaintiff, and would mean that the plaintiff was unable to obtain full compensation for his or her psychiatric illness."

That is of course true, but the competing policy considerations in this area of the law are such that I suspect that any statutory reform is likely to have its own drawbacks and imperfections.

Mr Eklund submits that any decision that there should be civil liability to a secondary victim who suffers psychiatric harm in consequence of a primary victim's self-inflicted injuries is better left to Parliament than taken by the courts. It seems to me that there is substance in this submission. There is ample support in the authorities to which I have referred for the argument that Parliament is the best arbiter of what the public interest requires in this difficult field of the law. Indeed, in *Alcock* v. *Chief Constable of South Yorkshire Police* [1992] 1 AC 310, 419, Lord Oliver, in a passage immediately after the passage to which I have referred above, said:

"Policy considerations such as this could, I cannot help feeling, be much better accommodated if the rights of persons injured in this way were to be enshrined in and limited by legislation as they have been in the Australian statute law . . ."

In this context, it is interesting to note that in *Jaensch* v. *Coffey*, 155 CLR 549, 601–602 Deane J drew attention to the fact that three states in Australia had introduced legislation to deal with this area of the law and that in none of them did the legislation extend to cover liability in respect of nervous shock sustained as a consequence of the death, injury or peril of the person whose negligence caused the accident.

The Law Commissions report on Liability for Psychiatric Illness, at paragraphs 5.34–5.44, considered the very question which is before me as a preliminary issue. The report gives weight to the argument that to create a duty of care in the situation under consideration would place an undesirably restrictive burden on a person's self-determination, but it appears not to take account of the potentially destructive impact upon family relationships of the introduction of such a duty. It recommends that legislation should provide for such a duty to exist where the defendant has negligently harmed himself, but for the courts to have scope to decide not to impose the duty where the defendant has chosen to harm himself. The purpose of the latter provision would be to allow room for respect to be accorded to the defendant's right of self-determination. At common law, a claimant who has a cause of action where he is injured by the defendant's negligent act has a stronger claim if the defendant acted intentionally. If the Law Commission's proposal commends itself to Parliament, a somewhat paradoxical situation will arise, in which it will be in the defendant's interest to argue that the act by means of which he caused the harm was deliberate, while the plaintiff will be seeking to persuade the court that it was inadvertent.

Conclusion

I have come to the conclusion that the policy considerations against there being a duty of care in the situation under consideration in this judgment clearly outweigh the arguments in favour of there being such a duty. Reinforced in my conclusion by the authorities to which I have referred, I find that there is no duty of care owed by a primary victim of self-inflicted injuries towards a secondary party who suffers psychiatric illness as a result of those injuries.

I therefore answer the three questions of law as follows. 1. A primary victim does not owe a duty of care to a third party in circumstances where his self-inflicted injuries caused that third party psychiatric injury. 2. On the agreed facts the first defendant did not owe the plaintiff a duty of care not to harm himself. 3. On the agreed facts the first defendant did not owe the plaintiff a duty of care not to cause him psychiatric injury as a result of exposing him to the sight of the first defendant's self-inflicted injuries.

Case 3

REICHSGERICHT (SIXTH CIVIL SENATE) 21 SEPTEMBER 1931
RGZ 133, 270 = JZ 1929, 914 (with a note by Bezold and Plum)

On 5 October 1929 the second defendant, driving the car belonging to his father, the first defendant, mounted the pavement and killed the plaintiffs' seven-year-old son. In criminal proceedings he was sentenced to nine months' imprisonment. The plaintiffs now sued both defendants as joint and several debtors for liquidated damages in respect of the cost of medical attempts to save the child's life, burial, and loss of business profits, and asked for a declaration of liability in respect of loss of future maintenance and services by the plaintiffs' son as well as for damages arising from the nervous breakdown of the plaintiff wife. The defendants paid RM 850 and alleged to have discharged their liability thereby.

The District Court of Cologne held the defendants jointly and severally liable to make periodic payments to the plaintiffs to the extent that the deceased would have been obliged during his estimated life-span to provide them with maintenance and services; in other respects it dismissed the claim. On appeal the Court of Appeal of Cologne allowed the claim for RM 1,200 in respect of loss of business profits due to the reduced earning capacity of the plaintiff wife and held that the costs of attempted medical care and of the burial had been discharged; in addition it held the defendants liable as joint and several debtors to compensate the plaintiffs in respect of the loss suffered by them as a result of the past or future injury to the health of the plaintiff mother arising from the accident, including the present or future loss of services, until she reached the age of sixty-five. The appeal by the defendants was successful in part for the following

Reasons

... in this appeal the question is only whether the defendants are also liable for the effects of the plaintiff wife's nervous breakdown which she suffered upon receiving the news of the accident, but which she did not witness herself ... the Court of Appeal found that the emotional excitement on hearing of her child's death caused the plaintiff wife's nervous breakdown, which had affected her earning capacity and was likely to continue to do so in the future.

The Court of Appeal has held correctly that the damage in question is not indirect in the sense that it is only covered by the duty to compensate under § 823 BGB in the exceptional circumstances of §§ 844, 845 BGB. Indirect damage is that damage suffered by a person who is not himself a victim of a tort but is only affected by its reflex effect upon his assets. In the present case, however, the plaintiff wife herself has been injured in her health by the tort, and the plaintiffs sue in respect of this injury to health. It has never been stated in the practice of the Reichsgericht that the legal interests or rights enumerated in § 823 I BGB must be violated directly and that an indirect violation does not suffice [reference]; the view to the contrary, put forward by the appellants, is unfounded. However, two questions must be examined in such cases; firstly, whether the causal nexus can still be regarded as adequate and, if this question should be answered in the affirmative; secondly, whether the indirect violation could be foreseen. The Court of Appeal has examined both questions and has answered them in the affirmative.

It is normally to be expected that a fatal accident of her child will greatly excite the mother emotionally, and it is not unusual if a grave emotional excitement of this kind results in a nervous breakdown which affects the capacity to work. Thus adequate causality exists [reference]. One can go even further and add ... that this result could be foreseen. The contention of the appellants that the second defendant could not even have known whether the seven-year-old boy had any parents cannot be accepted. The question is not whether the defendant could know but whether he ought to have considered the shock of the parents and the possible effects of the shock. In answering these questions in the affirmative the Court of Appeal has not broadened the concept of negligence excessively.

These statements only apply to liability according to the general rules of tort. In the case of the second defendant, his liability under § 823 BGB has been sufficiently justified by the judgment of the Court of Appeal. For, having regard to findings of fact of the accident, it cannot be doubted that the second defendant caused it negligently ... On the other hand, the Court of Appeal has not given sufficient grounds for holding the first defendant liable, as it does on the basis of § 831 BGB. The appellants point out rightly that it has not been established at all whether and now the first defendant had appointed the second defendant to carry out this 'task'. ... The fact that the first defendant denied the claim to a limited extent only does not permit the conclusion that he appointed his son to carry out the task. In so far as the claim is based on the injury to her health suffered by the plaintiff wife, the defendants have denied its substance throughout. The Court of Appeal will therefore have to examine again whether the first defendant has incurred liability, which it had held to be the case without restricting it to the provisions of the Act on Motor Vehicles.

If the defendant should only be liable under § 7 of the Act on Motor Vehicles, in addition to the conditions set out above in which liability to compensate the plaintiff wife in respect of injury to her health would exist, the problem would arise whether this injury to her health had occurred "in the course of operating" the motor vehicle. The courts below have held that it did. From their point of view this finding was superfluous, since judgment against the defendants was based on §§ 823, 831 BGB. However, the affirmative answer to this problem cannot be approved. The Court of Appeal itself refers to the decision of the Reichsgericht [reference] where that court refused to regard as an injury to health "in the course of operating" a railway, a mental illness suffered by a father as a result of the shock occasioned by a railway accident involving his daughter. This decision is in keeping with the constant practice of the Reichsgericht in applying the Act on the Tortious Liability of the Reich. The onset of the mental illness was not directly connected with the operational process or with a specific installation of the operation; nor could it be traced to a danger peculiar to the operation of railways [reference], but it could have happened as a result of any accident or fright. The Court of Appeal believes however . . . that the words in § 7 of the Law on Motor Vehicles bear a different meaning from the corresponding words in § 1 of the Law on the Tortious Liability of the Reich. The . . . [reference] legislative history of § 7 shows clearly, however, that in this respect the Law on the Tortious Liability of the Reich was copied deliberately by the Law on Motor Vehicles in order to make use of the extensive practice and literature on the law on liability. . . . Nevertheless it is conceivable that in individual cases the determination may differ as to whether an accident is to be regarded as having occurred "in the course of operating", given the technical differences between operating railways and motor vehicles. It is difficult to perceive, however, how a difference can be established in the present case. In both situations the question is whether the effect of a shock suffered by a relative on the occasion of an operational accident is still to be regarded itself as an injury to health in the "course of operating". The difference in the types of operations is irrelevant for this purpose . . . Accordingly the first defendant can be held liable under § 831 BGB for the nervous breakdown of the plaintiff wife if the conditions for its application should have been fulfilled but not under the Law on Motor Vehicles. It is a different question, not in issue here, whether the determination must be different, if the plaintiff wife had been present where the accident occurred and whether in such a case the opinion expressed in [reference] can be maintained [reference].

It follows that the judgment against the first defendant must be quashed and the case referred back. On the other hand the appeal of the second defendant must be rejected.

Notes to Case 3

For a number of reasons this is a very important case.

1. First of all it shows the tendency of German law (and modern civil law in general) to use normative concepts of causation in cases where Common lawyers would more evidently have recourse to the notion of duty of care. Note, however, that this was not always so: *Victorian Railways Commissioners* v. *Coultas* (1888) LR 13 App. Cas. 222, 226 (the earliest English case on nervous shock, decided before the concept of duty had started its meteoric rise). This equivocation between "duty" and "remoteness" will figure in other cases as well (e.g. economic loss, rescue etc.) and is discussed,

inter alia, by Fleming, "Remoteness and Duty: the Control Devices in Liability for Negligence" 31 *Can. Bar. Rev.* 471 (1953) (a seminal article) and Lawson and Markesinis I, ch. 2. See also Prosser's remarks at 244–5.

2. Secondly, the German decision addresses itself to the key issue of distant nervous shock and opts for the more liberal view according to which compensation is not limited to persons suffering shock as a result of witnessing the accident. Bystanders or "secondary" victims, may also, under certain circumstances, be compensated. However, it seems that strangers who are not closely related to a primary victim of an accident will have difficulties to prove their case. So we note that in none of the cases 1–3 was the claimant a stranger to the victim. However, as in English law so in German law, this restriction does not apply to primary victims: BGH NJW 1986, 777. In that case the claimant was severely injured in an accident that was negligently caused by another person who had crossed the motorway on foot and who was killed in the accident. The claimant also suffered "nervous shock" and it was this part of his claim that was the subject matter of the dispute. He was allowed to recover damages for pecuniary losses and for pain and suffering from the deceased's estate. The court argued that it was immaterial that the claimant did not have any "ties of love and affection" to the deceased who had, through his own conduct, caused the accident because the claimant was directly involved in the accident and suffered physical injury as a result. It was left to a subsequent court to decide whether additional requirements would be necessary as far as "secondary victims" (the court called them "indirect victims") were concerned.

3. This approach, which has been followed many times since the principal case was decided in 1931, arguably places German law in a more pioneering position when compared with the English and American law. (See, also, RGZ 157, 11; BGH NJW 1971, 1883, BGHZ 93, 351 = NJW 1985, 1390, and further references and commentary by von Hippel, in "Haftung für Schockschäden Dritter", *NJW* 1965, 1890) But even if one does not like the German approach one must, at least, credit the system with the fact that, in its essentials, it has remained constant. The same cannot be said of the House of Lords, which in fifty years, has revisited the topic five times and—some would say—made it more confusing than ever. Their Lordships tergiversations can be seen when the following cases are read in their chronological sequence. *Bourhill* v. *Young* [1943] AC 92 (restrictive view); *McLoughlin* v. *O'Brian* [1983] 1 AC 410 (liberal adaptation to new conditions); *Alcock* v. *Chief Constable of South Yorkshire* [1992] 1 AC 310 (the beginnings of a retreat to a more cautious approach); *Page* v. *Smith* [1996] AC 155 (confusion resulting from a well-intended attempt to make use of a sensible distinction); *White* v. *Chief Constable of South Yorkshire* [1999] 2 AC 455 (back to a conservative position justified by an open appeal to policy). Ironically, these multi-judgment decisions have provided a steady stream of dicta, which practising lawyers can use ad infinitum to "argue" minor embellishments. They are thus defeating the current judicial preference for a bright line rule in favour of restricted liability. The latest decision—again from the House of Lords and sixth in number if we added to the above list—that leaves many questions unanswered is *W* v. *Essex County Council* [2000] 2 WLR 601. The following position of bystanders or "secondary" victims is thus attempted with some trepidation.

Traditionally, the view was that the plaintiff should have heard or seen the accident with his own unaided senses. In the early 1980s, however, the House of Lords awarded damages to a mother and wife who rushed to the hospital to see her injured family a few hours *after* the accident had occurred and then suffered shock (*McLoughlin* v. *O'Brian* [1983] 1 AC 410). The decision though criticised, is remarkable for the frankness of the judicial turnabout *vis-à-vis* the value of the "floodgates" argument, which up to that point had received an almost exaggerated respect. (In part this result must be credited to the pioneering remarks of Tobriner, J in *Dillon* v. *Legg* 68 Cal. 2d 728, 441 P. 2d 912 (1968) which was cited by Lord Wilberforce.) However, the liberating effect of *McLoughlin* was neither immediate nor radical nor long lasting. To be sure, in the early 1990s it led to two interesting decisions at first instance, which through interesting pronouncements effected a further extension in the law. Thus, in *Hevican* v. *Ruane* [1991] 3 All ER 65 compensation was granted to a father who suffered nervous shock as a result of being told of his son's death and subsequently seeing his body in the mortuary. And in *Ravenscroft* v. *Rederi AB Transatlantic* [1991] 3 All ER 73 the same result was reached in the case of a mother who, however, never saw the body of the killed son. But these decisions were soon to be discredited by pronouncements in *Alcock* v. *Chief Constable of South Yorkshire* [1992] 1 AC 310 where the House of Lords sounded a cautious retreat from its earlier position. The facts of the case that gave rise to this retrenchment were, admittedly, difficult. They involved claims by relatives and friends of the victims of the Hillsborough Stadium disaster, some of whom saw on live television the spectators crushed to death against the stadium railings that were meant to prevent the crowds from getting onto the football pitch. The reason for this horrifying accident was the decision taken by the police locally to allow extra people to enter a restricted area without foreseeing the sudden surge of the crowd, which caused the disaster. A carefully argued decision of the Court of First Instance in favour of *some* of the claimants (in the first, test action) was overturned both by the Court of Appeal and the House of Lords relying largely on the usual grounds advanced against psychiatric injury. However, unlike some recent American pronouncements, the House of Lords did not limit (potential) recovery to close relatives. The key sections of Lord Keith's leading speech deserves to be quoted in full since it provides a sensible test for solving this aspect of the problem and one which, incidentally, could have produced results approximating those of German law. He said (at p. 397):

"As regards the class of persons to whom a duty may be owed . . . I think it sufficient that reasonable foreseeability should be the guide. I would not seek to limit the class by reference to particular relationships such as husband and wife or parent and child. The kinds of relationship which may involve close ties of love and affection are numerous . . . They may be present in family relationships or those of close friendship, and may be stronger in the case of engaged couples than in that of persons who have been married to each other for many years. It is common knowledge that such ties exist, and reasonably foreseeable that those bound by them may in certain circumstances be at real risk of psychiatric illness if the loved one is injured or put in peril. The closeness of the tie would, however, require to be proved by a plaintiff, though no doubt being capable of being presumed in appropriate cases. Psychiatric damage to [a bystander] would not ordinarily be within the range of reasonable foreseeability, but could not perhaps be entirely excluded from it if the circumstances of a catastrophe occurring very close to him were particularly horrific."

Alcock is an interesting decision, which will repay careful reading. Here, for lack of space, two further points will be mentioned. *First*, Lord Keith departed from Lord Wilberforce's dicta and denied that liability could arise if the shock had been induced from witnessing the scenes on television. Broadcasting rules prohibit the showing of the suffering of recognisable individuals; and warnings usually advert viewers to the imminent showing of distressing pictures. If by some peradventure, pictures of identifiable victims were shown, Lord Keith thought this might amount to a *novus actus interveniens* and interrupt the causation between negligence and hurt. But what then of the possible liability of the news medium itself? Neither the decision (nor its commentators) seems to have considered the possibility of a media defendant being held liable for showing a distressing scene on air. Would, for example, liability depend on whether "identifiable" victims were shown on the screen (not the case here)? What effect would "warning notices" have? More importantly, would such (potential) liability have a "chilling effect" on news reporting and thus amount to a restriction on free speech? In the USA such an argument would, probably, have a crucial effect on the issue of liability, but in England it might prove less decisive. *Secondly*, the overruling of some of the earlier, more liberal decisions (e.g. *Hevican, Ravenscroft*) will, inevitably, cast doubts over some interesting dicta, which they contained. In *Ravenscroft*, for example, Mr. (now Lord) Justice Ward stressed that the need to prove "psychiatric illness" and "causation" were hurdles that "not many [litigants] will jump" and this would, inevitably, allay "fears of the floodgates opening too wide" ([1991] 3 All ER 73, 76). It is submitted that there is much to be said for the view that psychiatric injury can, nowadays, be treated as a form of injury in its own right, that the plaintiff need not be seen as a "secondary victim" of the accident, and that the seriousness of the injury, coupled with rigid causal proof can be workable controlling devices, sufficiently countering the fear of numerous suits. (See Markesinis and Deakin ch. 2). This was clearly rejected as an option by

White—the most recent, major pronouncement of the House of Lords. But discussion of this case makes sense only after we have said a few words about *Page*, the decision of the House of Lords that came immediately before it.

Page, by a majority, drew a clear distinction between *primary* and *secondary* victims. The first category included those who suffered psychiatric injury either because they were themselves physically injured or put in fear of injury. For persons in this category one question only had to be asked: was it foreseeable that they suffered injury—physical or psychiatric? If physical injury were foreseeable, recovery would be allowed even if psychiatric injury, which was not foreseeable, resulted. Matters, however, were different where "secondary" victims were involved. These were persons who were neither injured physically nor threatened by such injury. In such cases, foreseeability of psychiatric injury was a necessary but not sufficient condition for liability. Additional, arbitrary, factors had to be satisfied. These included the need to prove that the shock was the result of the accident. (So, one who suffers psychiatric injury as a result of caring for a loved one seriously injury in an accident will not be compensated under this heading. *Jaensch* v. *Coffey* (1984) 155 CLR 549, 569 (per Brennan J), cited with approval by Lord Ackner in *Alcock*, [1992] 1 AC 310, 403.) It was also necessary to show that the victim had witnessed the shock-producing event either directly or upon coming upon its immediate aftermath. Finally, it was necessary to show that the relationship with the accident victim was sufficiently proximate in the sense defined by the cases.

White—by a majority—took the process of non-assimilation of physical and psychiatric harm a step further while admitting its open attachment to policy as well as the fact that this did not result in neatness and consistency in the law. (Contrast Lord Goff's powerful dissent.) The claims of the policemen, who attended the Hillsborough incident, were also rejected, the House of Lords considering it unfair to treat their claims differently from the claims of the ordinary by-standers, which had been dismissed by *Alcock*. Thus, recovery will now be allowed only if the following conditions are satisfied. The plaintiff was (a) not abnormally susceptible to psychiatric illness; (b) his psychiatric harm occurred through shock; (c) he was in physical proximity to the accident or its aftermath, and (d) he had a close personal or familial relationship with the accident victim. One casualty of this restricted approach was "rescuers", traditionally favoured by English law. (*Chadwick* v. *British Railways Board* [1967] 1 WLR 912.) But the plaintiff in that case was disingenuously treated as a "primary" victim (which he was not) so the case ceased being of any relevance to the policemen/plaintiffs in this case since, clearly, they were in no physical danger when helping in the Stadium. Rescuers can thus nowadays recover only if they can show that because of their physical proximity to the scene of the accident, they had been in fear of physical injury.

4. Comparative lawyers accustomed to the fact that ideas these days tend to move from West to East (and no longer the other way round) will be surprised to see how cautious American courts are in this area of the law. True, the original impact rule, which insisted on contemporaneous personal injury before nervous shock was compensated, was increasingly found to be too rigid and nowadays it has gone out of fashion. (*Woodman* v. *Dever*, 367 So. 2d 1061 (Fla. App. 1979) shows its unfairness; and *Payton* v. *Abbott Labs*, 386 Mass. 540, 437 NE 2d 171, 176 (1982), discusses judicial dissatisfaction with the rule. Florida, however, still retains this rule: *Champion* v. *Gray*, 478 So. 2d 17 (1985).) Most jurisdictions, in conformity with s. 313 of the *Restatement* (*Second*) *of Torts*, still require the plaintiff to be in the danger zone before he can recover. (Henderson and Pearson, 363; Prosser, Schwartz, and Wade, 458 ff.; see also *Rickey* v. *Chicago Transit Authority*, 98 Ill. 2d 546, 457 NE 2d 1 (1983); *Stadler* v. *Cross*, 295 NW 2d 552 (Minn., 1980) and the courts of some twenty jurisdictions). The pioneering decision of *Dillon* v. *Legg* (above) is thus still the subject of mixed feelings: see, for example, Pearson, in 34 *U. Fla. L. Rev.* 477 (1982).

Dillon, which nevertheless contains one of the best discussions on the subject, extended recovery to bystanders (outside the immediate danger zone). This could happen only if (1) the "plaintiff was located near the scene of the accident . . . (2) the shock resulted from a direct emotional impact upon plaintiff from the sensory and contemporaneous observance of the accident, as contrasted with learning of the accident from others after its occurrence, [and] (3) . . . plaintiff and the victim were closely related . . ." (441 P. 2d 912 at 920). The requirements of "physical proximity", "temporal proximity" and "relational proximity" have been the subject of much discussion, both inside and outside the courtroom. Nowadays, there is a tendency to give this last requirement—relational proximity—a very narrow interpretation. It is certainly narrower than that adopted, in theory at least, by German law. This has occurred wherever (in the USA) the decisions of the California Supreme Court in *Elden* v. *Sheldon* 758 P. 2d 582 (1988) and *Thing* v. *La Chusa* 771 P. 2d 814 (1989) are used as models. For the first denied the plaintiff recovery for his shock upon seeing his injured girl friend on the grounds that he was not married to her while the second reached the same result in the case of a mother who suffered shock in circumstances not dissimilar to those in *McLoughlin*. *Elden* reminds one of the old French debates about "concubinage" though the (at times) sanctimonious tone of the American judgment exceeds the moral revulsion which French Catholics claimed to have felt whenever a single woman claimed compensation for the loss of support resulting from the tortious killing of her lover.

A similar, narrowing tendency *may* be developing for the other two kinds of "proximity" (spatial and temporal) stressed by *Dillon*. (See Prosser *On the Law of Torts*, 5th edn. (1984), 366 and supplements.) These requirements of "nearness, hearness, and dearness" have certainly proved difficult to define as, indeed, the dissent in *Dillon* had predicted (p. 926). Californian courts have thus much vacillated and the confusing case-law—reviewed in *Justus* v. *Atchison*, 19 Cal. 3d 564, 565 P. 2d 122 (1977), and by Quai-Smith, "The Negligent Infliction of Emotional Distress" 19 *Indiana L. Rev.* 809, 818 ff. (1986)—has not been unravelled (as it could have been) by the decision of the Supreme Court of California in *Ochoa* v. *Superior Court* 39 Cal. 3d 159, 703 P. 2d 1 (1985). Thus cases like *Justus* suggest that only plaintiffs who have observed the accident will be allowed to recover. See also *Parsons* v. *Superior Court*, 81 Cal. App. 3d 506, 146 Cal. Rptr. 495 (1978) and contrast this with the *McLoughlin* judgment. On the other hand, in *General Motors Corp.* v. *Grizzle* 642 SW 2d 837 (Tex. App. 1982) a mother, who arrived at the scene shortly after the accident and saw her injured daughter, succeeded in her action for damages. All one can say, therefore, is that spatial and temporal proximity will remain crucial factors even though they are likely to be understood differently by different courts. See, for example, *Cohen* v. *McDonnell Douglas Corp.*, 389 Mass. 327, 450 2d NE 581 (1983). However, these problems, too, must now be approached bearing in mind the restrictive philosophy of decisions like *Thing* v. *La Chusa* 771 P. 2d 814 (1989) though beyond that it is dangerous to attempt any specific predictions.

5. Yet even the above do not complete the summary of the differing American trends. That is because for every thesis, an antithesis soon appears; and the mixed reception it receives from other American jurisdictions, only goes to prove that in the United States the richness of the case law. Thus the following three variations to the theme of non- recovery described above must also be born in mind.

First, one must note cases as *Sanchez* v. *Schindler*, 651 SW 2d 249 (1983) which suggest yet a different approach to this problem. It relies on a wider interpretation of the Wrongful Death Statute (in that case, the Texas version) and allows parents the right to recover damages for mental distress resulting from the death of their child. This solution—praised by some Texan commentators (e.g. Mendel in 26 *South Texas Law Journal*, 305 (1985))—is, however, dubious. For not only is it contrary to the intentions of Lord Campbell's Act (on which the Texas Wrongful Death Statute is, apparently, based); but, more importantly, it produces the strange result of making the parents' right of recovery depend on their child's death.

More importantly, one must note the innovation introduced by the California decision of *Burgess* v. *Superior Court* 2 Cal. 4th 1064, 831 P. 2d 1197, 9 Cal. Rptr. 2d 615 (1992). In that case the defendant doctor treated the plaintiff during her pregnancy. When the day of birth arrived, problems were detected and for reasons which are unclear from the judgment a caesarean delivery was delayed for nearly an hour with the result that the child was born deprived of oxygen and suffering from severe brain damage. It sued and so did its mother. The claim could have been excluded on the grounds that the mother may not have experienced a contemporaneous observance of her child's condition. (Again, the facts are not clearly stated.) Nevertheless the mother's claim succeeded on the grounds that the physician's duty to the mother was independent from whatever duty he may have owed to the child. Professor Dobbs neatly summarises the new theory of recovery thus (*op. cit.*, 849):

"When the defendant owes an independent duty of care to the plaintiff, there is no risk of unlimited liability to an unlimited number of people. Liability turns solely on relationships accepted by the defendant, usually under a contractual arrangement. Consequently, the duty extends only to those for whom the contract was made. When the defendant contracts to provide services for childbirth, he is on notice that negligent acts will likely cause emotional harm. For these two reasons, the zone of danger and contemporaneous awareness rules are not needed to limit liability to an appropriate sphere. An assumed duty or a special relationship with a duty imposed by law might arguably eliminate other restrictive rules, for example, those requiring a physical manifestation or symptom of harm and those requiring a sudden event . . ."

Finally, whether the assumed or independent duty approach alluded to above prevails or not, the fact is that other courts have also manifested a tendency to abolish restrictive rules and rely solely on foreseeability and other such devices. The Montana and Tennessee courts seem to be veering in that direction with their decisions in *Sacco* v. *High Country Indep. Press, Inc,* 271 Mont. 209, 220, 896 P. 2d 411 (1995) and *Camper* v. *Minor*, 915 SW 2d 437 (Tenn. 1996). The guess can thus be made that American courts may be about to go around the same circle again, vacillating between conservative and liberal views. It would be unwise to try and predict whether in the end they will adopt the current conservative model that one finds in England or they will ever opt for the (theoretically) more open German model which treats psychiatric injury as a species of physical harm.

6. Finally, students should note how articulate the Anglo-American decisions are about the policy issues, which have justified first the strict and then more relaxed treatment of claims for nervous shock. The best discussions in America can be found in *Amaya* v. *Home Ice, Fuel & Supply Co.* 59 Cal. 2d 295, 29 Cal. Rptr. 33 (1963); *Dillon* v. *Legg* (above), and in England, *McLoughlin* v. *O'Brian* (above) including the judgments in the Court of Appeal: (1981) QB 599. By contrast the German decisions give little away about policy. There is no doubt, however, that the same policy reasons are at work in this system as well, and contemporary writers are prepared to admit that the problem is not one of causation but one of policy. (See von Hippel in *NJW* 1965, 1890 at 1891. Huber in *Festschrift E. Wahl*, 301 ff. agrees.) Thus, increasing reliance can be found on more normative theories of causation (like the *Normzweck* approach); and even the contractual concept of *Vertrag mit Schutzwirkung für Dritte* has been mentioned as a possible source of inspiration. See Berg in *NJW* 1970, 515.

7. Though articulated in different ways the policy reasons are mainly three. First is the fear of fraudulent or vexatious claims. Tobriner J's answer (in *Dillon* v. *Legg*, above) that ". . . the possibility that fraudulent assertions may prompt recovery in isolated cases does not justify a wholesale rejection of the entire class of claims in which that potentiality arises" seems to be winning the day. Secondly is the "floodgates" argument which has prompted the development of numerous rules of thumb (impact theory, danger zone theory; relatives only can recover etc.). Though not without some merit, this objection, too, is falling into disfavour as an increasing number of dicta in English decisions (dealing with economic loss as well as nervous shock) clearly suggest, though the California cases of *Elden* and *La Chusa* show that it still finds favour with cautiously-inclined judges. Finally, one might argue with Professor Atiyah (*Accidents, Compensation and the Law* (3rd edn., 1980) 80) that ". . . the claims of such a person [i.e. one who suffers distress and/or shock as a result of witnessing an accident] must have a low priority when it is remembered that thousands of victims with physical injury go uncompensated every year because they are injured in accidents not caused by negligence". Further policy reasons are discussed by Professor Dobbs, *op. cit.*, at pp.821–4.

8. In this note the approach of three systems was compared briefly. Is there any other factor (not mentioned above) that has to be borne in mind when explaining the differences between them? Could the absence of civil juries in England and the European continent explain why these systems can afford to disregard the floodgates argument more easily than, perhaps, American courts can?

To what extent can this ebb and flow of the law be linked to changing attitudes in society? Could the decisions of the Supreme Court of California in *Elden* v. *Sheldon* 758 P. 2d 582, denying damages for nervous shock to the plaintiff who actually *witnessed* the death of his girl friend (with whom he had a "stable and significant relationship") be linked to policy factors such as the State's need (real or perceived) to discourage extra-matrimonial cohabitation? Would not this argument appeal more to the wave of "conservative" judges who were appointed (or elected) from about the mid-eighties onwards? Incidentally, this "conservative" approach found favour with some French judges in the 1940s, 50s, and 60s (in the slightly different context of wrongful death actions), but was abandoned in the early 70s as being legally unconvincing and morally sanctimonious. For further details on this see: Lawson and Markesinis, *Tortious Liability for Unintentional Harm in the Common Law and the Civil Law* I, (1982), chap. 2. The importance of such background factors in the development of American tort law is fully explored in Professor Fleming's *The American Tort Process* (1988), his observations being particularly useful to European lawyers trying to understand tort law in America.

9. For further discussion see, Prosser, Wade, and Schwartz, 446 ff. Further references to cases and periodical literature can be found in the following articles. Chesley, "The Increasingly Disparate Standards of Recovery for Negligently Inflicted Emotional Injuries" 52 *Cincinnati L. Rev.* 1017 (1983); Dupuy, "Negligent Infliction of Emotional Distress", 53 *Louisiana L. Rev.* 555 (1992); Hughes, "Recovering Damages for Mental Anguish in Wrongful Death Suits: The Elimination of the Physical Injury/Physical Manifestation Requirement" 18 *Texas Tech. L. Rev.* 893 (1987); Rose, "Negligent Infliction of Emotional Distress: Formulating the Psycho-Legal Inquiry" 18 *Suffolk Univ. L. Rev.* 401 (1984); Quai-Smith, "The Negligent Infliction of Emotional Distress: A Critical Analysis of Various Approaches to the Tort in Light of *Ochoa* v. *Superior Court*" 19 *Indiana L. Rev.* 809 (1986); Comment, "Negligent Infliction of Mental Distress: A Jurisdictional Survey of Existing Limitation Devices and Proposals Based on an Analysis of Objective Versus Subjective Indices of Distress" 33 *Villanova Law Rev.* 781 (1988); Sitzman, "*Marlene F.* v. *Affiliated Psychiatric Medical Clinic Inc.*: Negligent Infliction of Emotional Distress Bounces Out of Bounds", 22 *Pacific Law Journal* 189 (1990); Leesfield "Negligent Infliction of Emotional Distress; Where are we Now?" 71 Feb. *Fla. B.J.* 42 (1997); "Recovery for negligent Infliction of Emotional Distress requires Witnessing of Accident" 29 *Suffolk U.L. Rev* 647 (1995); Davies, "Direct Actions for Emotional harm: Is Compromise Possible?", 67 *Wash. L. Rev.* 1 (1992). For a discussion of English and Commonwealth cases see: Trindade, "The Principles Governing the Recovery of Damages for Negligently Caused Nervous Shock" [1986] *CLJ* 476.

2. PRE-NATAL INJURIES AND PRE-CONCEPTION INJURIES

Case 4

BUNDESGERICHTSHOF (SIXTH CIVIL SENATE) 11 JANUARY 1972
BGHZ 58, 48 = NJW 1972, 1126 = JZ 1972, 363
(with an approving note by H Stoll = VERSR 1972, 372)

On 7 June 1964, the plaintiffs, husband and wife, were severely injured in a collision between their motor car and that of the defendant, who was solely to blame. At the time of the accident, the plaintiff wife was six months pregnant. On 16 September 1964 she gave birth to a child, the third plaintiff, who was a spastic because he suffered from brain damage. The parties disputed as to whether this was caused by the injury to the mother. Both instances below allowed the claim. A second appeal by the defendant was unsuccessful for the following

Reasons

A. . . .

B. *The action by the third plaintiff for a declaration*

I. The Court of Appeal has assumed without discussion that the plaintiff could demand damages under § 823 I BGB for injury to his health, although he was not yet born at the time when the defendants committed the tort. Clearly the Court of Appeal relied on the decision of the Bundesgericht of 20 December 1952 [reference] which had no hesitation in applying § 823 I BGB, even if a child which was born with a defect was not even conceived when the tort was committed against the mother.

This approach, which was adopted by the judgment appealed against, must be applied. In the present case, too, the plaintiff must be treated as "another person" in the meaning of § 823 BGB, whose health was injured by the defendant; for the purpose of this provision establishing liability the plaintiff is a "human being" even if he was injured before birth *en ventre sa mère* [references]. Similarly § 25 of the Nuclear Energy Act of 23 December 1959 refers to injury to a human being, but includes in this term also those who have suffered injuries to their health before birth and even before their conception [references]. The fact that the plaintiff suffered the injury to her health before birth cannot be determining if these preceding processes provided by nature and by creation are considered in their own setting.

The objections against applying § 823 BGB, which are mainly conceptual, must and can be overcome; true, in cases of this kind it does not assist that the liability of a tortfeasor does not presuppose the existence at the time of his action of the object, the violation of which leads to liability (distance tort). In the cases now under consideration the (illegal) act injures the foetus directly; the only "distance" consists in that between this injury and the moment in which the injuries to health become apparent when the child is born, that is to say moment in which the object of the liability first reaches its existence. In particular, difficulties arise in applying § 823 BGB if it is considered that at the time of the injury the foetus was not yet a human being and cannot therefore be regarded as "another person" [references].

Nevertheless, no objections exist against applying § 823 BGB, a view shared in the literature, albeit for a number of different reasons [references].

1. The provision of § 823 BGB protects the right of a human being, once born, to the integrity of his body and his health; nobody is allowed to injure the health of a human being. It is unnecessary in the present case to consider the question as to whether in the case of an injury to the foetus the protected interest is the health and corporeal integrity of a person alive (later on) or whether a right of a foetus to integrity and health is to be recognised [references]. In the present case the issue is not one of compensation for damage which the foetus has suffered—if it were to be granted limited legal personality (see § 844 II BGB, second sentence)—but the injury to health which the child has suffered, being born alive but sick [reference]. In these circumstances it is only necessary to take into account in favour of the tortfeasor that this claim for damages does not arise, if no live birth occurs [references], or if the injury to the foetus has disappeared by the time of the child's birth and has therefore not affected the health of the newly born. It is also clear that the claim for damages only comes into being with the birth, irrespective

of the conceptual ground on which it is based (see reference). Apart from this, the fact that the injury was suffered by the foetus before a human being came into being and before legal personality was acquired does not preclude the application of § 823 BGB. This cannot be doubted, not only if, for instance, the tortfeasor injures a pregnant woman intentionally or if the injury is caused by a professional mistake of a gynaecologist who examines her or of the midwife or the doctor etc., in the course of the birth, but also before its conception. The foetus is destined to enter life as a human being; it is identical with the child born subsequently, a fact of nature which the law concerning liability must take into account. Therefore an injury to the foetus becomes an injury to the health of a human being, at least upon birth, for which the tortfeasor must pay damages under § 823 BGB.

2. Nor do any doubts against the applications of § 823 BGB arise in the light of the legal system as a whole. In this connection it need not be considered that by the prohibition of abortion, i.e. of its destruction, criminal law provides a certain protection for the foetus. The fact that a mere injury to the foetus, which is in issue here, is not punishable does not exclude the view that a human being is protected in private law at least as far as a claim for damages is concerned, if an injury to his health is derived from preceding damage inflicted during his embryonic state. Even at that stage of his development he is exposed to dangers and to biological damage which result later on in injuries to his health in the meaning of § 823 BGB; he therefore requires protection. Private law protects developing human beings by numerous special provisions. It accords therefore with its spirit if for the purposes of the law relating to liability in tort developing life is also capable of being injured, with the result that the human being who is born subsequently has the same rights to damages as the person who is injured only at the moment after he has seen the light of day.

II. . . .

1 . . .

2 (a) . . .

(aa) . . . If the Court of Appeal should have assumed that the damage alleged by the child was only a "reflected damage" resulting from the injuries which the defendant has inflicted upon the mother, it would have been wrong in law. The claim for damages in issue in this case is a claim of the child and not part of the mother's claim for damages [references]. As regards legal liability, two injured parties stand side by side, with the result that each claim must be examined separately [references]. . . .

(b) . . .

III. On the basis that the paralysis of the plaintiff child was caused by the accident, the consequences must also be attributed to the defendant.

It cannot be doubted that these consequences are connected by a link of adequate causation with the accident for which the defendant is to blame. It is impossible equally to fault the view of the Court of Appeal that the defendant's negligence extended not only to the injuries suffered by the mother but also to those of the embryo and therefore of the child. This does not follow simply because the defendant is to blame for having injured the mother and is therefore liable for all consequential damage suffered by her. However, the child need not prove that the defendant could foresee the possibility of injuring a pregnant woman or an embryo as such. It need not be considered here whether this means that mother and child constitute a "unit of life" [references]. It suffices to render the person liable who inflicted the injury if he should have realised the possibility of a damaging result in general; it need not be foreseeable what form the damage would take in detail and what damage might occur [references].

Case 5

BUNDESGERICHTSHOF (SECOND CIVIL SENATE) 20 DECEMBER 1952
BGHZ 8, 243 = NJW 1953, 417 = JZ 1953, 307
(with an approving note by R Schmidt)

On the occasion of the birth of a previous child, the plaintiff's mother was a patient in the defendant hospital from 29 August until 9 September 1946. On that day she received a blood transfusion which was administered by Dr A who was an employee of the hospital where the donor had first offered himself for this purpose. Dr A had called for a blood test which did not disclose any syphilitic infection, but had not conducted any further examination of the donor. When the donor was again examined in January 1948, the Wassermann test was positive. The defendant hospital, on learning this, recalled all those patients who had been recipients of the donor's blood. It appeared after a further examination that as a result of the transfusion the plaintiff's mother had been infected with syphilis and that, in consequence the plaintiff, who was born on 13 October 1947, was suffering from congenital syphilis.

The plaintiff applied for a declaration that the defendant hospital was liable to pay damages in respect of all damage caused to her now or which might arise in the future as a result of the infection of her mother with syphilis on the occasion of the blood transfusion on 9 September 1946, and for the payment of damages for pain and suffering. The judgments by the courts below allowing the claim were upheld for the following

Reasons

The Court of Appeal has found that the mother of the plaintiff was infected with syphilis because the medical officer at the defendant hospital, when carrying out the blood transfusion on 9 September 1946, did not follow the measures prescribed by the order and the guide-lines of the Reichsminister of the Interior dated 5 March 1940 concerning the examination of donors of blood. According to the Court of Appeal the omission to take these measures was due to the fact that the medical staff of the hospital had not been informed of the guide-lines published by the Minister of the Interior. It is undisputed that the Chief Medical Officer, Dr X, who was a member of the defendant's board in 1940, failed to give notice to the departments of surgery and gynaecology of the hospital of the order and the guide-lines of the Reichsminister of the Interior. This Division has had occasion to state before in the judgment of 27 February 1952 [reference], which had rejected a second appeal by the defendant in an action by the mother of the plaintiff, that this situation involves not only contractual negligence towards the plaintiff's mother who had been received by the hospital as a patient under the medical insurance scheme but also a tort by the defendant hospital committed by Dr X, a member of the board, for whom the defendant is responsible according to § 31 BGB. In the present case liability for the damage suffered by the plaintiff can only arise in tort. Such a claim is well founded in the present case.

1. The act of the defendant hospital is to be found in the failure to take the necessary precautions on the occasion of the blood transfusion administered to the mother of the child at a time before the child was conceived. Thereby the defendant has violated a legal duty incumbent upon it. Even if at first this act affected directly the health of the mother alone, the same act had nevertheless caused subsequently an injury to the health of the plaintiff as well, who was born on 13 October 1947. The appellant defendant is wrong in arguing that the injury is indirect with the result that it cannot render the defendant liable. For a claim for damages to arise it suffices if the act causing the damage violates directly or indirectly one of the protected interests or absolute rights set out in § 823 I BGB, provided only that a causal nexus exists in the meaning of the theory of adequate causation between the act creating the damage and the resulting violation of a protected interest [reference]. This can be assumed to exist in the present case, for it is common experience that an infection of a married woman with syphilis is likely to transmit this illness later on to a child conceived by her.

2. The appellant objects above all that in the present case the application of § 823 I BGB is logically excluded because at the time when the act causing damage occurred the plaintiff was not in an intact state which could have been violated by an act causing damage. The appellant argues that § 823 I presupposes logically that damage can only be claimed by those who were intact at one time. If such a state never existed, however, because the egg or the foetus was already sick from the moment of conception as a result of the mother's illness, no interference had ever occurred with the state of health of a child born subsequently. The same view had been expressed in a decision of the Third Civil Division of this court [reference]. Upon enquiry, however, the Third Division has replied that it no longer maintains this view, and therefore this Division is not bound by the above-mentioned decision. The arguments of the appellant cannot be accepted. They are based on a purely concrete manner of thinking which proceeds on the whole from the individual rights, ownership, and the other absolute rights enumerated in § 823 I BGB but does not pay sufficient attention to the special character of the values of life to which § 823 I BGB refers above all. The difference between these values of life and individual rights on the other hand was stressed by the Reichsgericht as early as 1902, following the observations of Planck [reference]. These values of life themselves are clearly not individual rights, instead it is only possible to state that every individual is entitled to have them granted to him, just as the Constitution of Bonn speaks of the right of every person to life and physical integrity [reference].

Absolute rights are clearly determined by law. Accordingly it is logically impossible, e.g. to damage property before any property has come into being. However, it is fundamentally wrong in law to apply to interference with the values of life protected by § 823 I BGB the principles concerning the distinction between injurious acts affecting absolute rights and injurious acts causing damage to other resources. Therefore one must also reject the observations of Rudolf Smend [reference], according to whom, in the case of injury to health the circumstances in which that tort can be committed must be interpreted in the same distinctive manner as in the case of a violation of individual absolute right, as distinct from that of damage to other resources.

The view rejected here is met by the decisive argument that it pays insufficient attention to the special character of the values of life protected by § 823 I BGB. These values precede the legal system. They express the individuality of human beings as part of nature and of creation. They represent life itself, the essence of all that is alive and derive their substance from it. Every human being has a right to these values of life and is therefore entitled to expect that organic growth will not be disturbed or curtailed by human hand. Every deprivation or disturbance by human beings which hinders or curtails natural growth and natural development constitutes a violation of these protected interests. Thus injury to health has been described accurately as "causing a disturbance of the internal processes of life" [reference]. Common parlance too adopts this attitude in describing a child, such as the plaintiff, whose health was severely impaired at birth, as being a sick child, that is to say as a child whose internal processes of life are disturbed and who has not been endowed with that degree of health with which creation and nature has predisposed the living organism of a human being. In this respect the legal order must follow the phenomenon of nature; it cannot and must not disregard the facts of nature. What is an injury or a curtailment of health cannot therefore be determined by the logical concepts of legal techniques, but is, like the gift of health itself, predetermined by creation and nature which must be recognised as natural reality by the legal system, if it is to derive therefrom any legal conclusions in law.

Following these considerations it is not possible to apply to the health of human beings, which is protected by § 823 I BGB the legal principles based on formal legal technique which governs the violation of individual rights.

It is not possible, either, to agree with the appellant who argues that § 823 I presupposes the existence of a physical person and that it cannot therefore be applied to injuries affecting those who were not yet conceived when the tort was committed, since in such a case "another person" in the meaning of § 823 I BGB does not exist . . . the plaintiff was conceived in the body of the mother who suffered from syphilis and developed in it as a human being affected by syphilis by absorbing the illness. This would not have happened without the tortious act or omission of the defendant; in short without it she would not have become a person suffering from syphilis.

The object of the argument is thus not damage to a foetus or to an unborn child, but the damage which the plaintiff has suffered by the fact that she was born a sick person affected by syphilis. As stated before, her damage is connected by a link of adequate causation with the infection with syphilis of her mother by the defendant. This damage was suffered by the plaintiff when she was born and constituted an injury to her health. Thus the conditions of § 823 I BGB exist for allowing the claim.

Notes to Cases 4 and 5

1. Prenatal injuries typically involved an impact on a pregnant woman that also harmed the later-born child. Could it recover for its injuries (if born alive); and could a wrongful death action be brought if it died? The latter cases, have been the more difficult of the two; and the original problems confronting the law have now become greater as foetal toxic harm has multiplied the difficulties of causation. We shall return to this aspect of the problem under 6, below.

2. For evidentiary and conceptual reasons Common law courts originally displayed a marked reluctance to sanction damages for pre-natal injuries. The evidentiary obstacles were primarily connected with the difficulties of establishing a causal link between accident and foetal injury. (Note the grotesque results in *Montreal Tramways* v. *Léveillé* [1933] 4 DLR 337 (Quebec) where club-feet, a congenital defect, were treated as the result of a traffic accident! For a more troublesome (and recent) example see: *Mulcahy* v. *Eli Lilly & Co.* 386 NW 2d 67 (1986).) The conceptual difficulties were connected with the foreseeability of the victim (in this case the foetus) and, more importantly, to the question whether a foetus could be treated as a "person". This controversy in turn raised many conceptual, religious, medical, and philosophical issues—in the US highlighted further

by *Roe* v. *Wade* 410 US 113, 93 S. Ct. 705 (1973)—as to the rights of a foetus and its mother. The question, does a foetus enjoy the same rights as a person has received a varied response. Thus, for the purposes of property, and particularly inheritance, the foetus has traditionally been treated as a person: *In Re Trattner's Estate* 394 Pa. 133, 145 A. 2d 678 (1958). On the other hand, in criminal law the killing of a foetus has not been treated as homicide: *People* v. *Greer*, 79 Ill. 2d 103, 402 NE 2d 203 (1980) but has been handled under some, lesser, criminal offence. The question how the foetus' rights can be dove-tailed with its mother's have raised an even greater controversy; and the aspect that is most relevant to our subject, will be discussed briefly below.

3. The traditional hostile view of the courts can be found clearly expressed in *Dietrich* v. *Inhabitants of Northampton*, 138 Mass. 14 (1884). Neither its causative nor conceptual objections to recognising a cause of action are convincing. (See, Dobbs, 781); but it took American courts over sixty years to abandon a position that had enjoyed the support of the great Holmes. One of the earliest decisions to make a break with this approach was *Bonbrest* v. *Kötz* 65 F. Supp. 138 (DDC 1946) which, interestingly enough, also referred to Justinian's *Digest* and Blackstone's *Commentaries* (*ibid.* 140). The change in other Common law jurisdictions came somewhat later. For Australia see *Watt* v. *Rama* [1972] VR 353; for Canada see *Duval* v. *Seguin* [1973] 40 DLR 3d 666; and for England see *Congenital Disabilities (Civil Liability) Act* 1976. In chronological terms, therefore, German law gave an early lead.

4. *Todd* v. *Sandidge Construction Co.*, 341 F. 2d 75 (4th Cir.1964) can, in some respects, be treated as an equivalent to case 4; *Renslow* v. *Mennonite Hospital*, 67 Ill. 2d 348, 367 NE 2d 1250 (1977) as an analogue to case 5. But see comments in paragraph 5, below. (Contrast, however, *Albala* v. *City of New York*, 54 NY 2d 269, 429 NE 2d 786 (1981).) Note also that whereas *Todd* permits token recovery even where the foetus is born dead (so long as it was viable at the time of the accident), the German decision and the English Act (reproduced below) require that the child be born alive. Which of these variants is preferable and why? Opinions differ; and so do their consequences. On the "born alive" requirement the American courts seem divided. Most take the view that live birth is not necessary for a wrongful death action. Thus *Volk* v. *Baldazo*, 103 Idaho 570, 651 P. 2d 11 (1982); *Dunn* v. *Rose Way, Inc.*, 333 NW 2d 830 (Iowa 1983); *Summerfield* v. *Superior Court*, 144 Ariz. 467, 698 P. 2d 712 (1985); *Moen* v. *Hanson*, 85 Wash. 2d 597, 537 P. 2d 266 (1975). Others, probably under the influence of *Roe* v. *Wade*, 410 US 113, 93 S. Ct. 705 (1973), have held that live birth is a prerequisite of recovery. Thus, see, *State ex rel. Hardin* v. *Sanders*, 538 SW 2d 336 (Mo. 1976); *Justus* v. *Atchison*, 19 Cal. 3d 564, 565 P. 2d 122 (1977); *Chatelain* v. *Kelley*, 322 Ark. 517, 910 SW 2d 215 (1995). A number of recent decisions have adopted this position, often reaching this result on the ground that a stillborn foetus is not a "person" under applicable wrongful death legislation. Thus: *Witty* v. *American Gen. Capital Distrib. Inc.*, 727 SW 2d 503 (Tex. 1987); *Milton* v. *Carey Medical Center*, 538 A. 2d 252 (Me. 1988); *Giardina* v. *Bennett*, 545 A. 2d 139 (NJ 1988)—criticised in 21 *Rutgers L. Journ.*, 227 (1989). A final variation to this kaleidoscope of differing solutions can be found in cases that refuse wrongful death actions where foetus' are born dead, but allow the mother to recover for her mental anguish. Thus, see, *Tanner* v. *Hartog* 696 So. 2d 705 (Fla. 1997); *Giardina* v. *Bennett*, 545 A. 2d 139 (1988); *Krishnan* v. *Sepulveda*, 916 SW 2d 478 (Tex. 1995). Though these last cases do not come anywhere near representing the majority of jurisdictions, they seem to have much to commend them since, at least, they seem to have grasped the nettle. Simply put, this is that compensating parents under wrongful statute clauses seems inappropriate given that these enactments were always intended to compensate the loss of a provable pecuniary advantage i.e. the lost dependency. In our cases, however, such pecuniary advantage is extremely speculative; and if it could somehow be divined, tort law rules would require that they be reduced to take into account the "savings" made by the parents (who did not have to bear the cost of upbringing these children). So, in these cases, all one is really trying to achieve is to compensate the parents lost dependency but give the mother some money for her emotional harm (on top of course to that which she may, herself, be able to claim for her own injury). The drawback of the proposed solution—and drawback it will be to all those who tend to favour plaintiffs indiscriminately—is that the father of the killed foetus cannot claim anything (unless he witnessed the commission of the wrong and

suffered personal, psychiatric injury). So whatever, the equity reasons in favour of a remedy to the mother for the death of her child, it is difficult to justify given the intention and the wording of the original statutes.

In America, the legalistic (but not substantive) objections to such an extended interpretation of the Wrongful Death Statutes have been addressed by those States which have amended the wording of their statutes to allow overtly "loss of companionship" claims. For these claims are not meant to make up for loss of future support but are intended to compensate spouses for the interference with their right to "affection, solace, comfort, companionship, society, assistance, and sexual relations necessary to a successful marriage." (*Wal-Mart Stores, Inc.* v. *Alexander*, 868 SW 2d 322, 328 (Tex. 1993). These "companionship" claims are also widely (but not uniformly) recognised in the kind of situations discussed here where the death of a young child is involved; and since they 1980s have even been extended to the reverse situation allowing children to claim for the loss of parental consortium. (See, *Giuliani* v. *Guiler*, 951 SW 2d 318 (Ky 1997). Though not up-to-date, the most informative Article on this point is by Love, "Tortious Interference with the Parent-Child Relationship: Loss of an Injured Person's Society and Companionship" 51 *Ind. L.J.* 591 (1976). Even more sporadic seems to be the making of companionship awards for severely *injured* children (*Masaki* v. *General Motors Corp.*, 780 P. 2d 566 (1989)), or parents (*Robert C. Theama and others* v. *City of Kenosha*, 344 NW 2d 513 (Wisc. 1984); contra, *Joe Bennight* v. *Western Auto Supply Company*, 670 SW 2d 373.).

5. When comparing the American and German cases the reader should note that the issues of "viability" and "live birth" are often discussed in the context of who can sue. Putting the emphasis on "live birth" means that the *child* that was injured while a foetus or because of an injurious act to its mother prior to conception can sue for its injuries; and this is the point made in case no. 4. But if one accepts that viability at the time of the injury will be sufficient to give rise to a cause of action (and no live birth is required) then two questions may arise. The first is that the *estate* of the unborn child might have a right to claim pecuniary compensation relying on a survival action. The second is that its survivors might wish to sue invoking the appropriate Wrongful Death Statutes and claim their lost dependency. To a non-American lawyer the first possibility appears little short of monstrous. (*Cf. Scott* v. *Kopp*, 494 Pa. 487, 491, 431 A. 2d 959, 961 (1981).) But the second, where it is allowed, is no less unorthodox since it represents a marked departure from English law which, through the medium of Lord Campbell's Act of 1846, originally inspired the USA. (But see discussion about more recent developments in American law in previous paragraph.) The solution ceases to be unorthodox and becomes bizarre in those American jurisdictions which allow punitive damages to be claimed under Wrongful Death Statutes. (See: Moeller, "Punitive Damages in Wrongful Death Actions", 39 *The Univ. of Kansas L. Rev.*, 199 (1990).) A further point that is sometimes forgotten is that such awards to the survivors of the still-born foetus are often cumulated with the personal claims that the survivors may have themselves (for example for shock or loss of companionship) and where this occurs, double compensation is a real danger. (See the points raised at the end of the previous paragraph.) Most American courts and academics (see, for instance, Dobbs, 783) however, do not seem to be unduly concerned by these considerations.

6. It was noted that prenatal injuries were originally inflicted through impact upon the mother. Nowadays, however, the bulk of these injuries are brought about as a result of the (licit or illicit) use of drugs, alcohol, environmental toxins and workplace exposures to harmful substances. The problem with this manner of infliction of the harm is that it is slow and surreptitious and thus likely to raise considerable difficulties with causation. One way around these difficulties is to relax the rules of causation: see, for instance, Berger, "Eliminating General Causation: Notes Towards a New Theory of Justice and Toxic Torts", *Colum. L. Rev.* 2117 (1997). But such calls have been counteracted by others who are anxious to protect possible defendants and who have thus argued for more demanding standards. Thus, see, Boston, "A Mass-exposure Model of Toxic Causation: the Content of Scientific Proof and the Regulatory Experience", 18 *Colum. J. Environ. L.* 181 (1993). The important thing to note, however, is that the scientific literature that explains how these substances can affect a foetus is growing in numbers and sophistication. Thus, see Gideon Koren (ed.) *Maternal-Fetal Toxicology:*

A Clinician's Guide, 2nd edn., (1994). An interesting slant to these problems can also be found in cases which have attempted to address the dangers of mass exposure—including foetal exposure—to toxic substances through the use of injunctions. Thus, see, *Williamsburg Around the Bridge Block Association* v. *Giuliani*, 223 A.D. 2d 64, 644 N.Y.S. 2d 252 (1996), where a New York court prohibited the sandblasting of a bridge in order to remove lead paint on the ground that the resulting dust could have serious consequences on the children of pregnant women in the area. (On the effect of lead on a developing foetus see: Dietrich and others, "Low-Level Lead Exposure Effect on Neurobehavioral Development in early Infancy", 80 *Pediatrics* 721 (1987).)

7. The legal problems can be compounded where the toxic substance has been in the workplace. The question that then has to be addressed is whether the workers' compensation regimes, which exclude tort remedies, also operate against claims brought by children affected in utero by their mother's exposure to the hazardous materials. The limited case law that exists suggests that these restrictions do not affect the claiming children. See: *Hitachi Chemical Electro-Products, Inc.* v. *Gurley*, 219 Ga. App. 675, 466 SE 2d 867 (1995); *Snyder* v. *Michael's Stores, Inc.*, 16 Cal. 4th 991, 945 P. 2d 781, 68 Cal. Rptr. 2d 476 (1997).

8. There is not much case law that deals with the parents' duties to the foetus; but there is little doubt that the use of licit or illicit substances during pregnancy can cause harm to it. The question then is, can it sue its parents? The answer has often been linked to the wider issue of parental immunities and their varied fate over the years in the different states. One claim, brought by children against their parents which has consistently failed is that of causing their birth outside wedlock: *Slawek* v. *Stroh*, 62 Wis. 2d 295, 215 NW 2d 9 (1974). A child's action against its mother for negligent driving while pregnant has also failed: *Stallman* v. *Youngquist*, 125 Ill. 2d 267, 531 NE 2d 355 (1988). Neither case was a toxic substance case but the reasoning used in the second of these clearly alluded to the mother's autonomy, privacy, and control of her body etc all of which would suggest that the mother's rights would prevail over those of the unborn foetus and thus deprive it of a tort action. A subsequent decision from Texas, dealing with a cocaine inhalation by a pregnant mother, supports this conclusion. See: *Chenault* v. *Huie*, 989 SW 2d 474 (Tex. App. 1999). There is no German decision raising these points directly. However, in case 7 (below) the BVerfG stated that, as a matter of constitutional law, the mother, generally speaking, was under a duty to give life to the unborn child. If that is the case it may be argued that tort law imposes some duty of care on the parents towards the unborn child.

9. No student of American law will be surprised to be told that on the pre-conception front American courts have, once again, divided. Adamantly opposed to any duty being owed to the unconceived child are the New York courts. See *Albala* v. *City of New York* 54 N.Y 2d 269, 445 N. Y. S. 2d 108, 429 NE 2d 786 (1981); *Park* v. *Chessin*, 46 N. Y. 2d 401, 413 N.Y.S. 2d 895, 386 NE 2d 807 (1978). The reasons for such a rejection are two. The first is metaphysical: the plaintiff was not a person in existence at the time of the defendant's negligence. This point has been well addressed by the German court. The BGH has thus forcefully argued that unlike the concept of "subjective rights" (namely property), which is determined by law, the value of life and the gift of good health must be recognised by the legal system as natural phenomena and thereby be seen logically to precede the application of legal techniques. Thus, every deprivation of the choices of actions of a future human being that curtails its natural development constitutes a violation of the interests of that (future) human being with respect to these values of life. The second stems from the fear that such a duty might place health carers—who are the typical defendants in these cases—in a possible position of conflict; for what might be advisable for the mother might entail dangers for the as yet not conceived child. The latter argument is, prima facie, more noteworthy than the former. Yet interestingly enough, no case thus far litigated has indicated anything other than that both interests have been coterminous. (In the event that they were not, no doubt the conflict could be solved by giving the mother the information needed to make an informed choice.) For these reasons but, also because the arguments have not been fully aired by counsel before any courts, the New York position seems to be an isolated one, though one or two other jurisdictions have produced inconclusive pronouncements that seem to lean in the same direction. Thus, *Loerch* v.

Eli Lilly & Co., 445 NW 2d 560 (Minn. 1989). At the other end of the spectrum stand a dozen or so courts, with the Illinois case of *Renslow* cited above as a leader, which have gone the other way and found a duty in favour of the not conceived child. Finally, a small minority has taken a different view and limited such duty to care professionals who are treating the mother. On this approach, a drug manufacturer has been held not to be expected to foresee the harm that one of his drugs administered to the mother may one day cause to her grandchild: *Grover* v. *Eli Lilly & Company*, 63 Ohio St. 3d 756, 591 NE 2d 696 (1992). For further details see: Greenberg, "Reconceptualizing Preconception Torts" 64 *Tenn. L. Rev.* 315, 349 ff. (1997).

10. For further references to these points see Harper, Fleming James Jr., and Gray, *The Law of Torts* 2nd edn. (1986) iii. 677–80. See also: Kodilinye, "Tortious Liability for 'In Utero' Injuries", 3 *Caribbean L. Rev.* 122 (1993); McCavitt, "The 'Born Alive' Rule: A Proposed Change to the New York Law Based on Modern Medical Technology", 4 *New York Law School Law Rev.* 609 (1991); Note, "Negligent Infliction of Prenatal Death: New York's Unrecompensed Injury after *Tebbut* v. *Vizostak*" 19 *Connecticut L. Rev.* 365 (1987); Robertson, "Toward Rational Boundaries of Tort Liability for Injury to the Unborn: Prenatal Injuries, Preconception Injuries and Wrongful Life" *Duke LJ* 1401 (1978); Note, "Wrongful Death of a Fetus: Does a Cause of Action Arise When There is No Live Birth?" 31 *Villanova L. Rev.* 669 (1986); Batchelor, "The Expansion of the Viable Fetus Wrongful Death Action" 11 *Campbell L. Rev.* 91 (1988); Wilhelm, "Protection of Prenatal Life through Wrongful Death Statutes", 15 *Univ. of Dayton L. Rev.*, 157 (1989); Hartsoe, "Person or Thing. In Search of the Legal Status of a Fetus: A Survey of North Carolina Law", 17 *Campbell L. Rev.* 169 (1995); Parsi, "Metaphorical Imagination: The Moral and Legal Status of Fetuses and Embryos", 4 *De Paul J. of Health Care Law*, 703 (1999).

11. In the USA, the law concerning survival actions and Wrongful Death Statutes is complicated. To an outside observer, the topic also appears to be inadequately covered in the law curriculum. The following summary may thus be of some use to lawyers who wish to compare the German cases here reproduced with their American analogues but find themselves confused by the somewhat sloppy use of terms by many State courts.

(i) When someone dies, his estate can claim the damages he could have claimed for the period he remained alive after the accident. In the USA this is commonly referred to as the "survival action" and in England as the Law Reform Action. If the victim dies instantly, only funeral costs can be claimed. In the USA the claim for such expenses may depend on whether the estate was legally obliged to incur them.

(ii) If the injured person is compensated while alive and later dies, his dependants will not be able to bring a claim under the Wrongful Death Statutes. The same is true if the injured person allows his claim to become statute-barred or, otherwise, settles his claim with the defendant. In a very narrow area of American maritime law the position may be different. See: *Miles* v. *Apex Marine Corp.*, 498 U. S. 19, 111 S.Ct. 317 (1990); *Sea-Land Services Inc.* v. *Gaudet*, 414 US 573, 94 S. Ct. 806 (1974). *Gaudet* (allowing dependants of deceased longshoreman to recover damages for loss of companionship) nowadays applies only to *widows* of *longshoremen* who died in *territorial waters* i.e. within a marine league from the shore. The distinction between such cases and all other maritime death cases is so bizarre that it must indicate a good chance that the Supreme Court will overrule *Gaudet* when it next has the chance to do so.

(iii) If the deceased dies without having been compensated through his personal action, certain dependant relatives may have a cause of action under the Wrongful Death Statutes. This will depend primarily on the wording of the relevant (State) statute, whether it lists the claimants as proper dependants, whether it has mutually exclusive classes of beneficiaries, and so forth.

(iv) In England, compensation for wrongful death is governed by the Fatal Accidents Act of 1846 as repeatedly amended. Many American statutes, passed from about the 1860s onwards, are modelled on the English Act. With significant exceptions (see, for example, *Moragne* v. *State Marine Lines Inc.*, 398 US 375, 90 S. Ct. 1772 (1970); *Gaudette* v. *Webb* 362 Mass. 60, 284 NE 2d 222 (1972)), American courts take the view that there is no Common law (i.e. non-statutory) right to recover for a fatal accident.

(v) In wrongful death cases, English courts have always allowed only claims for monetary losses. No compensation has been given for *dommage morale*, loss of companionship, solatium etc., though, since 1982 there is the possibility to claim a small, fixed amount for bereavement.

(vi) In some USA jurisdictions, the wording of the statute has been interpreted to allow bereavement claims. But since this is a question of statutory interpretation, this extension, though "novel" to English eyes, cannot be regarded as wrong.

(vii) Some US statutes also allow punitive damages. The award of punitive damages to the dependants, even when authorised by statute, is, *de lege ferenda* very dubious.

Addendum: The Congenital Disabilities (Civil Liability) Act 1976

1 (1) If a child is born disabled as the result of such an occurrence before its birth as is mentioned in subsection (2) below, and a person (other than the child's own mother) is under this section answerable to the child in respect of the occurrence, the child's disabilities are to be regarded as damage resulting from the wrongful act of that person and actionable accordingly at the suit of the child.

(2) An occurrence to which this section applies is one which:
  (a) Affected either parent of the child in his or her ability to have a normal, healthy child, or
  (b) affected the mother during her pregnancy, or affected her or the child in the course of its birth, so that the child is born with disabilities which would not otherwise have been present.

(3) Subject to the following subsections, a person (here referred to as "the defendant") is answerable to the child if he was liable in tort to the parent or would, if sued in due time, have been so; and it is no answer that there could not have been such liability because the parent suffered no actionable injury, if there was a breach of duty which, accompanied by injury, would have given rise to the liability.

(4) In the case of an occurrence preceding the time of conception, the defendant is not answerable to the child if at that time either or both of the parents knew the risk of their child being born disabled (that is to say, the particular risk created by the occurrence); but should it be the child's father who is the defendant, this subsection does not apply if he knew of the risk and the mother did not.

(5) The defendant is not answerable to the child, for anything he did or omitted to do when responsible in a professional capacity for treating or advising the parent, if he took reasonable care having due regard to then received professional opinion applicable to the particular class of case; but this does not mean that he is answerable only because he departed from received opinion.

(6) Liability to the child under this section may be treated as having been excluded or limited by contract made with the parent affected, to the same extent and subject to the same restrictions as liability in the parent's own case; and a contract term which could have been set up by the defendant in an action by the parent, so as to exclude or limit his liability to him or her, operates in the defendant's favour to the same, but no greater, extent in an action under this section by the child.

(7) If in the child's action under this section it is shown that the parent affected shared the responsibility for the child being born disabled, the damages are to be reduced to such extent as the court thinks just and equitable having regard to the extent of the parent's responsibility.

2. A woman driving a motor vehicle when she knows (or ought reasonably to know) herself to be pregnant is to be regarded as being under the same duty to take care for the safety of her unborn child as the law imposes on her with respect to the safety of other people; and if in consequence of her breach of that duty her child is born with disabilities which would not otherwise have been

present, those disabilities are to be regarded as damage resulting from her wrongful act and actionable accordingly at the suit of the child.

3 (1) Section 1 of this Act does not affect the operation of the Nuclear Installations Act 1965 as to liability for, and compensation in respect of, injury or damage caused by occurrences involving nuclear matter or the emission of ionising radiations.

(2) For the avoidance of doubt anything which:
    (*a*) affects a man in his ability to have a normal, healthy child; or
    (*b*) affects a woman in that ability, or so affects her when she is pregnant that her child is born with disabilities which would not otherwise have been present
is an injury for the purposes of that Act.

(3) If a child is born disabled as the result of an injury to either of its parents caused in breach of a duty imposed by any of ss. 7 to 11 of the Act (nuclear site licensees and others to secure that nuclear incidents do not cause injury to persons, etc.), the child's disabilities are to be regarded under the subsequent provisions of that Act (compensation and other matters) as injuries caused on the same occasion, and by the same breach of duty, as was the injury to the parent.

(4) As respects compensation to the child, s. 13(6) of the Act (contributory fault of person injured by radiation) is to be applied as if the reference there to fault were to the fault of the parent.

(5) Compensation is not payable in the child's case if the injury to the parent preceded the time of the child's conception and at that time either or both of the parents knew the risk of their child being born disabled (that is to say, the particular risk created by the injury).

4 (1) References in this Act to a child being born disabled or with disabilities are to its being born with any deformity, disease or abnormality, including predisposition (whether or not susceptible of immediate prognosis) to physical or mental defects in the future.

(2) In this Act:
    (*a*) "born" means born alive (the moment of a child's birth being when it first has a life separate from its mother), and "birth" has a corresponding meaning; and
    (*b*) "motor vehicle" means a mechanically propelled vehicle intended or adapted for use on roads.

(3) Liability to a child under s. 1 or 2 of this Act is to be regarded:
    (*a*) as respects all its accidents and any matters arising or to arise out of it; and
    (*b*) subject to any contrary context or intention, for the purpose of construing references in enactments and documents to personal or bodily injuries and cognate matters.
as liability for personal injuries sustained by the child immediately after its birth.

(4) No damages shall be recoverable under either of those sections in respect of any loss of expectation of life, nor shall any such loss be taken into account in the compensations payable in respect of a child under the Nuclear Installations Act 1965 as extended by s. 3, unless (in either case) the child lives for at least forty-eight hours.

(5) This Act applies in respect of births after (but not before) its passing, and in respect of any such birth it replaces any law in force before its passing, whereby a person could be liable to a child in respect of disabilities with which it might be born; but in s. 1(3) of this Act the expression "liable in tort" does not include any reference to liability by virtue of this Act or to liability by virtue of any such law.

(6) . . .

5 . . .

6(1) . . .

7 [This Act applies to England, Wales, Northern Ireland, but *not* Scotland.]

3. "WRONGFUL LIFE" AND "WRONGFUL BIRTH"

Case 6

BUNDESGERICHTSHOF (SIXTH CIVIL SENATE) 18 JANUARY 1983
BGHZ 86, 240, JZ 1983, 447 with note by Deutsch at 651

The first plaintiff, born on 24 February 1977, is the legitimate daughter of the second and third plaintiffs (henceforth called the plaintiffs). The first plaintiff suffered severe damage to her health because the second plaintiff, her mother, had caught German measles (rubella) during the first weeks of her pregnancy. The plaintiffs charge the defendant gynaecologist with having failed to diagnose the mother's illness with the result that the pregnancy—which had been desired in principle—had not been terminated.

The child and her parents ask for a declaration that—subject to a statutory assignment—the defendant is liable "to pay compensation in respect of all the damage which they have suffered or will suffer in the future as a result of the second plaintiff's infection with German measles during her pregnancy".

The District Court dismissed the first plaintiff's claim but granted the parents the declaration which they had sought. The Court of Appeal of Munich rejected the first plaintiff's appeal and, upon the defendant's appeal, rejected the parents' claim as well [reference].

Upon a second appeal by the three plaintiffs the decision of the Court of Appeal was quashed in so far as the claims of the parents were concerned for the following.

Reasons

A

The Court of Appeal has held that the claims of all the plaintiffs are unsubstantiated. In particular it has held:

I. Even if an error had occurred in the treatment of the patient, the defendant had not injured a protected interest or a right of the first plaintiff. It was true that according to a constant practice an act could result in damages if the party whose health had been adversely affected had not been born or not been conceived at the relevant time. In the present case, however, the defendant had not caused the injury to the first plaintiff; instead he was responsible for the fact that the first plaintiff was alive and enjoyed legal capacity. The foetus had no right to its abortion if only for the reason that, in so far as the abortion was legally admissible, the decision was that of the mother alone. Furthermore, the alternative between existence and no existence could not be expressed in legal terms of damage. Finally, by impeding an abortion the defendant had not violated a law for the protection of the plaintiff.

Admittedly the contract for treatment concluded between the defendant and the second plaintiff also exercised a protective effect in favour of the first plaintiff. However, the defendant's duty to explain to the second plaintiff the risks in the pregnancy itself and the possible injury to the foetus was only incumbent upon him in the interest of the second plaintiff.

II. In the opinion of the Court of Appeal the claims of the parents amount to a claim for a declaration by the second plaintiff in respect of non-pecuniary damages (owing to the difficult birth requiring a Caesarean delivery) while the claim of the first plaintiff was for pecuniary damages. It rejected both claims.

(a) *Claims of the second plaintiff*

(aa) The Court of Appeal held that it was not called upon to decide whether the burden of economic maintenance (increased in the present case) could be regarded as damage. In any event, the principles developed by this Division in the two decisions of 18 March 1980 [references] did not apply in the present case. An error in treatment on the part of the defendant . . . would of course have adequately caused the second plaintiff's burden of maintenance. However, abortion, as distinct from sterilization was an act of killing [references] and according to some was only not punishable, but remained unjustified. Apart from this, unlike in the case of a request for sterilization, the defendant was not obliged in the present case also to take into account the financial interests of the second plaintiff. The defendant was only obliged to explain the medical and eugenic aspects of a pregnancy in so far as the life and health of the second plaintiff was endangered. In the present case the only concern had been to spare the first plaintiff a life under the severest conditions. In addition, financial considerations may have played a role, but these alone would not have justified a termination of the pregnancy. An *excessive* financial burden, which was also considered by some as a justification had not been proved. Consequently, the contractual duties of the defendant did not include the protection of those financial interests which had been pleaded. To this intent, too, the claim for damages was not justified.

(bb) *Claims of the third plaintiff*

Any contractual claims, alone in issue in the case of this plaintiff, were ruled out for the reasons set out when dealing with those of the second plaintiff, although the third plaintiff was included in the sphere of protection created by the contract between the second plaintiff and the defendant [reference].

B

These conclusions are valid in so far as the first plaintiff's (the child's) appeal is directed against them, but do not as a whole stand up against the appeal by the parents:

I. 1. In the light of the undisputed facts it cannot be doubted that the defendant, in his capacity as a medical practitioner, received and accepted the mandate of investigating the danger of serious injury to the first plaintiff (the child) as a result of the infection of the mother (the second plaintiff) with German measles during the first weeks of her pregnancy. The District Court has found that he carried out this mandate negligently.

The facts as found leave no doubt, moreover, that the second plaintiff, who had some medical knowledge, was particularly concerned, in consulting the defendant, to prevent any likely serious danger of permanent damage to the infant which had just been conceived, by terminating the pregnancy. It is also to be presumed in this second appeal that if the defendant had acted in accordance with his mandate he would have confirmed this fear and would thus have made a timely termination of the pregnancy possible as the sole remedy. Consequently, in these circumstances the defendant has caused by his negligent breach of the contract to treat the plaintiff the damage complained of by the latter.

2. It could be doubted whether the defendant had broken his contract, if it were assumed that a termination of a pregnancy, which is only regulated in criminal law (§ 218 ff. of the Criminal Code), is merely exempt from penalties, but remains illegal as a crime of killing. This view is supported generally by *Sax* [references]. However, as *Sax* himself observes expressly [references], it seems contrary not only to the view of the legislature but also to generally accepted opinion, as the Court of Appeal realized also. This Division sees no reason for going into this dogmatic dispute. It holds, in accordance with the generally accepted view, that an abortion which is exempt from penalties according to § 218 ff. of the Criminal Code is certainly not illegal. This view is borne out not only by the Prepara- tory Materials accompanying the present statutory provisions but also by the position taken by the Federal Constitutional Court [reference] which [reference] supports a clear distinction between lawfulness and illegality.

Consequently an abortion which is exempt from penalties according to § 218 of the Criminal Code can form the object of a valid contract with a medical practitioner . . .

The Court of Appeal does not question *that* an infection with German measles during the particularly vulnerable period of early pregnancy may justify the mother in deciding to terminate it. Such an infection involves the risk, which is not overwhelming but at least highly likely, that the child will be born with severe or even extremely severe injuries [references]; the evidence in the present case is to the same effect. In these circumstances the future mother must have the right and the possibility, having regard to the present law, to call for an abortion. It is irrelevant in the present circumstances that the medical adviser is not under a direct duty to collaborate. The defendant has not alleged that he would have refused the plaintiff mother's request, had the danger been diagnosed.

No different conclusions can be derived from the fact that the statute does not concentrate on the prognosis for the welfare of the child but on whether the mother can be required to bear the burden. This does not mean that the test is only restricted to considerations of the danger facing the mother of a severe financial and work-load, as well as of the mental anguish through sharing the fate of a severely handicapped child. In addition, the ethical interest of the mother who is the sole person, according to what seems to be the general opinion, entitled to take this decision, must be taken into account. It is not to be held against her and she must not reproach herself for having failed, by a decision placed in her hands, to have spared the child a life which may be often painful and makes integration into society difficult.

Consequently it is generally believed, and held on the facts in practice, that an infec- tion with German measles at a period when it may have dangerous repercussions is a ground which entitles the mother to demand an abortion.

II. In the opinion of this Division the negligent breach of contract by the defendant which constitutes at the same time an injury to the second plaintiff (the mother) may certainly lead to claims by the plaintiff parents, though not to a separate claim by the child.

1. *Claims of the parents*

In recent literature the predominant view appears to be that, in principle, claims of the parents may arise in the circumstances [references]. However, the decision forming the present appeal is mentioned several times with approval. The possibility of such claims is denied, in particular, by those who hold, for various reasons, that abortion is merely not visited with penalties, but illegal [reference]. This Division, as stated before, shares the former opinion.

(a) *Claims of the mother*

(aa) One starts from the fact that with the birth of the child the danger has materialised which the mother had decided to prevent by having an abortion. The total damage suffered by the child . . . is so grave that a mother who was prepared to undergo an abortion, if necessary, would have decided not to give birth to the child, had she been cognisant of the damage in advance. The damage suffered by the mother as a result was caused by the defendant's breach of contract and, generally speaking, he is therefore liable to repair it. The damage, being pecuniary damage due according to the law of contract, can consist in the additional expenses, financial and material (labour) which the mother will have to assume *in toto* or in part, possibly for her whole life. Plaintiff's counsel has stated expressly that their claim is limited to the additional expenses and is not concerned with the amount of maintenance which a healthy child would have required; therefore this Division can limit the decision to *that* claim in the case before it. The fact that this additional expense, too, arises from a duty of support imposed by family law, does not prevent its characterisation as pecuniary damage, in so far as a third-party liability is concerned [reference].

It follows that—as in the case of a child born owing to a failure of preventive measures—also in the case of a child which the mother did not wish to be born in a condition as the present, i.e. handicapped, at least the additional expenses caused by the handicap can be claimed as damage to be made good (a point still left open [reference]). Of course, this is true only if and to the extent that the danger to be avoided has in fact occurred, so as to show that the severity of the actual damage—if it could have been foreseen—would have made it unreasonable to let the child be born. This must be assumed in the present appeal.

This is the only means of providing reparation for the defendant's negligence which imposed upon the mother a burden not required by law to be borne by her and which she was entitled to evade.

(bb) In addition this Division holds that, having regard to need for a Caesarean operation, the question must be considered whether the mother is entitled to damages for pain and suffering.

As distinct from the other cases referred to above decided by the Federal Supreme Court (Civil Division), the pregnancy, as such, was not due to the medical adviser's negligence, but was freely chosen or at least accepted by the mother (the second plaintiff). Thus, the defendant did not interfere directly with the personal health of the second plaintiff by involving her in an unwanted birth (as distinct from [reference]). Therefore this Division holds that only that infliction of pain and suffering can justify a claim according to § 847 BGB which, as an aspect of damage, exceeds the inflictions which accompany a birth without complications. This may happen if—once again the evidence is not available— the Caesarean operation only became necessary because the child was injured, as the plaintiffs maintain. In *assessing damages*, it would have to be considered, on the other hand, that thereby the mother was spared an abortion which—as the defendant contends—would not have been without complications, and which she would have suffered if the defendant had fulfilled his obligation.

No additional claims of the mother arise by applying § 847 literally or by way of analogy. Nor did the Court of Appeal discern such a claim in the plaintiff's pleadings, a conclusion which remains unchallenged in the present appeal. For this reason it may be observed in passing only that such a claim based on the mental burden, not amounting exceptionally to an illness, resulting from being burdened with a severely handicapped child would be alien to German law (contrary to several foreign legal systems, as evidenced, e.g., by *Howard* v. *Lecher*, decided by the Court of Appeals of New York, 366 NE (2d) 64 (1977)—"mental and emotional suffering"). The practice of the Federal Supreme Court, which grants damages similar to those for pain and suffering within a strictly defined area in respect of the right to one's personality [reference], cannot be extended to the present issue. In particular, no pecuniary damages can be awarded, contrary to principle underlying the statutory provisions, in respect of a violation of the "right to plan a family" as an emanation of the general right to one's personality [references] if a decision involving the personality of the party affected was only frustrated *in fact*—as was the case here.

(b) Claims of the plaintiff husband

The husband is entitled to expenses in money and kind to the same extent as the wife. To this extent he was included in the sphere of protection resulting from the contract for medical treatment; as far as the liability to pay damages of the responsible medical practitioner is concerned it is irrelevant to what extent the burden created by him is distributed between the spouses. The principle laid down by this Division [reference] apply here as well. The present case shows clearly that normally no other conclusion can be reached for at least according to the allegations of the plaintiff parents—the father, acting as a "houseman", has now assumed the time-consuming care of the handicapped child, in order to enable the mother to continue her professional career and thus to provide the financial means for maintaining the family.

No claims of the third plaintiff for damages other than financial are in issue.

2. Claims of the child

In the present case the highest German Court is confronted for the first time with the problem which has been described in Anglo-Saxon parlance as "wrongful life". As stated above, the defendant did not cause the child's deplorable condition; nor is it contended that by taking special measures he could have prevented it. However, in breach of his obligation towards the mother to treat her, he failed to prevent by means of an abortion the birth of a child, the health of which was severely endangered and in whose person this danger materialised in a severe form. To this extent this Division agrees with the Court of Appeal that the *child* cannot raise any claims based on these facts.

As stated above, little German practice has come to light. Apart from the decision under appeal here, an appeal against a judgment of the Court of Appeal of Hamm of 25 January 1982 [reference] is pending before this Division in which, however, claims by the child itself were not considered for procedural reasons. Foreign judgments, which for the reason alone that they are based on different laws are only of limited relevance for German law, appear to have been rendered in England and the United States. In England a claim by the child has recently been rejected (Court of Appeal, 19 February 1982, *McKay* v. *Essex Health Authority and Another* [1982] 2 *WLR* 890). In the meantime, legislation has excluded a claim by the child altogether. In the United States, too, this opinion has been generally accepted for some time (Court of Appeal, California, *Curlender* v. *Bio-Science* (1980) 165 Cal. 477).

Writers on the law of the Federal German Republic relating to this topic are divided, but the majority denies a claim to the child. Such a claim is, however, advocated by Deutsch [reference] and probably also by Plum [references]. On the other hand, claims by the child itself are denied not only by all those who do not accept failure to facilitate an abortion as a ground for liability, but also by those writers who would allow claims by the parents in these circumstances [references]. In rejecting a claim by the child based on "wrongful life" or "wrongful birth" this Division is guided by the following considerations:

(*a*) A direct *duty*, enforceable by an *action in tort*, to prevent the birth of a child on the ground that in all probability it will be affected by an infirmity which makes its life appear "valueless" in the eyes of society or in its own presumed opinion (for which naturally no evidence can be produced) would be alien to the duties sanctioned by the law of tort which are normally centred on the protection of personal integrity. No such duty exists. This applies even in cases—different from the present—where there exists not only a danger of damage, but, e.g. where a fairly reliable prognosis of a serious genetic defect is possible, e.g. by means of amniocentesis—as in the case of mongolism. This principle holds good, although according to what is probably the dominant opinion as well as the actual legal practice the birth of such children should be prevented. Human life, which at the conclusion of implantation includes also the foetus, is a legally protected interest of the highest order deserving absolute protection. No third party may determine its value. For this reason it is recognised that the duty to save the life of a sick person or one who is seriously injured must not be made to depend upon a judgment as to the value of the life to be saved. Only when the question is whether isolated single human functions are to be sustained by artificial means without any hope of improvement, this principle may have to yield [references].

Such is not the case here. Quite generally, having regard to the experience under the national socialist regime of lawlessness, the practice of the courts in the Federal Republic does not permit, with good reason, any legally relevant judgment about the value of the lives of others [reference].

(*b*) Therefore any breach of duty which might render the defendant liable in damages could only be derived from the contract to treat the mother.

(*aa*) On the one hand, it is possible that contractual duties, including those towards third parties, may constitute duties to be accounted for in tort [reference]. In this respect reference may be made to what has been stated before. Neither the fact of bringing life into being nor of failing to prevent it (as distinct from affecting the quality of life by an act of omission) violates the legal interest protected by § 823 BGB. This is not merely a dogmatic consideration. It is also supported by the fact that the ethical evaluation by public opinion of permissible abortions is not uniform (it is true that the defendant has never relied on ethical scruples; if so, he would have had to refuse to advise and to treat the mother).

Above all, seeing that no interest of personal integrity is involved, it is impossible to determine with binding effect whether a life affected by serious handicaps as an alternative to absence of existence can be regarded at all in law as damage, or whether it is a better condition that the latter [Stephenson LJ [1982] 2 *WLR* 890: "Man, who knows nothing of death or nothingness, cannot possibly know whether that is so"].

(*bb*) Thus it remains only to examine whether the defendant is bound by a direct contractual obligation which obliged the latter to protect the child as a result of the protective effect of an agreement (possibly implied only) in favour of the unborn child. Once again this Division is unable to give an affirmative answer, although such a contract for medical treatment may well have protective effects in favour of the child in *other respects*, as the Court of Appeal has also recognised.

It would not be an obstacle that at the time when the defendant committed the act resulting in his liability the plaintiff child did not yet enjoy legal personality (§ 1 BGB). In the law of tort, too (see above) it is recognised that an act causing liability may be committed before the injured party was born [reference] and even before he was conceived [reference]. The same applies to a claim for damages which is based on a contractual duty in favour of the unborn child.

This Division is, however, unable to find that such a protective effect was stipulated since the law in force at present expressly authorises the mother in her own interest alone to demand an abortion. This attitude of the law may not be convincing in its reasons; also, as far as can be ascertained, it does not exist in other countries, where the law does not reject abortion in principle. Nevertheless, the attitude taken by German law must be respected within the confines of the Federal Republic, if only for reasons of constitutional law [reference]. Consequently it precludes not only a broad interpretation of the contract to treat the mother so as to benefit the child, the birth of which was to be prevented, but also as already stated, any direct guarantee actionable in tort of the medical adviser towards the child arising from the assumption of the mandate to treat the mother.

(*cc*) Leaving aside the special features of the German rules on abortion, this Division regards the denial of claims by the child itself as imperative in such cases. Such claims are only admissible if the child's interest in personal integrity has been violated culpably by human activity which, as stated before, may have occurred even before the child was conceived. For the rest, the question is not so much one of arguments based on formal logic, also relied upon by the Court of Appeal, as for instance to the effect that those having legal personality cannot conceivably derive claims from acts which gave rise to the claimant's existence and legal personality [reference]. Instead, this Division believes that in cases such as the present the limits within which claims can be adjudicated according to law have been reached altogether and even exceeded. As a matter of principle a human being has to accept his life as nature has endowed him and has no claim against others to be born or to be eliminated. If a mother—and she alone—is nevertheless accorded such a choice by the law, this does not mean either that the child is granted a *right* as against her not to exist. It is irrelevant that the mother's decision may legitimately have been influenced by compassion for the severely injured life [reference].

If a decision to the contrary were to be reached against the medical adviser, it would follow that liability would also have to be admitted in other cases; for example that of parents who, although suffering from severe genetic defects, gave life to a child, and whose liability consists at present, as the case may be, in an increased duty of maintenance; or that of persons who are responsible for those genetic defects, even if these defects were known to the parents, who are primarily liable, when they produced the child (as distinct from the case [reference] where the issue was the infection of the mother with lues as a result of a blood transfusion . . .). Thus liability to pay damages could arise for several generations, a possibility which has already led to suggestions to restrict liability to the first generation [references].

These considerations show in the opinion of this Division, as stated before, that an area has been touched on in which the legal regulation of liability for far-reaching fateful and natural developments is neither reasonable nor acceptable.

(*dd*) This Division is not oblivious of the fact that as a result seriously handicapped children remain without financial protection, once the duty of the parents to maintain them comes to an end—as for instance when they die. This must be accepted, just as when the mother could not make up her mind to call for an abortion or if the period set by law for having an abortion has been allowed to pass, for no matter what reason.

In all these cases a fateful development takes place the interruption of which cannot be demanded by the child and the effects of which must be made good by the community within the bounds of the possible.

Case 7

BUNDESVERFASSUNGSGERICHT (SECOND DIVISION) 28 MAY 1993
BVERFGE 88, 203 = NJW 1993, 1751

Reasons

D V 6. The duty of the State to protect the nasciturus does not require that contracts are classed as non-binding which were concluded with doctors and hospitals for abortions which are not punishable under the (new) counselling programme. The programme rather requires that the mutual tie of obligations between doctor and patient take the form of a legal relationship so that all obligations are fulfilled for valid legal reasons. Irrespective of any specific contractual consequences, §§ 134, 138 BGB are inapplicable. Doctors and hospitals only take part in abortions on the basis of a valid contract which safeguards their claim for payment and outlines their duties. It is in particular the doctor's duty towards the unborn child and the patient's health which needs contractual safeguards. As a consequence, faulty performance of the duties to provide counselling and treatment must in principle be able to trigger contractual and tortious sanctions.

However, in the light of the Constitution this result needs to be differentiated. A civil law sanction for faulty performance of the contract or for tortious infringement of the patient's physical integrity is basically necessary; this entails not only the duty to pay back any wasted fees, but also the duty to compensate for damage under the provisions of §§ 823, 847 BGB, including compensation for pain and suffering resulting from a failed abortion or from the birth of a handicapped child. But as a result of Article 1 I GG, the child's existence cannot legally be classified as damage. The duty of all public bodies to respect every human being for its own sake, prohibits maintenance for a child to be classified as damage. In the light of this fact, the case law of the civil courts on liability for medical mistakes in counselling or in performing failed abortions needs to be reconsidered (see for abortion BGHZ 86, 240 *et seq.*; 89, 95 *et seq.*; BGH NJW 1985, 671 *et seq.*; VersR 1985, 1068 *et seq.*; VersR 1986, 869 *et seq.*; VersR 1988, 155 *et seq.*; NJW 1992, 1556 *et seq.*; for

sterilisations see BGHZ 76, 249 *et seq.*; 76, 259 *et seq.*; BGH NJW 1984, 2625 *et seq.*).
However, the doctor's duty to pay damages to the child for damage caused in the course
of an unskilfully attempted and thus failed abortion remains unaffected (see BGHZ 58,
48 [49 *et seq.*]; BGH NJW 1989, 1538 [1539]).

Case 8

BUNDESGERICHTSHOF (SIXTH CIVIL SENATE) 16 NOVEMBER 1993
BGHZ 124, 128 = NJW 1994, 788

Facts

The first and second plaintiffs are the parents of a girl born in 1982 with a mental and
physical handicap. Suspecting that they might have an abnormal genetic disposition, they
were, in August 1983, referred by their GP to the Department of Clinical Genetics (run
by the first defendant) of the Institute of Anthropology and Human Genetics of the
University (third defendant), because they wished to be advised, prior to deciding on a
second pregnancy, of the possibility of an adverse hereditary disposition. The second
defendant, a doctor at the Institute's clinic, made tests and on 27 October 1983 and wrote
a report, which was signed by himself and the first defendant. Copies of this report,
informing the two plaintiffs that an inherited adverse disposition was very unlikely and
that the couple should not be dissuaded from further pregnancies, were also sent to their
GP. On 6 March 1985, the third plaintiff was born with the same mental and physical
handicaps as the first child. The plaintiffs, believing that the genetic consultation and
advice had been faulty, claimed damages from the defendants. The first and second defendants requested the court to clarify whether they were liable to make compensation for
any current and future material losses stemming from the third plaintiff's brain damage,
as far as these claims have not been transferred to the social security bodies. The second
and third plaintiffs also demanded damages for pain and suffering.

The Landgericht rejected the claim. On appeal by the first and second plaintiff, the
Oberlandesgericht declared that the first defendant must compensate the (first and
second) plaintiffs for all current and future losses originating from the birth of the third
plaintiff, including the entire costs of living. The Court also decided that the first and
second defendant are liable as joint and several debtors to pay the second plaintiff
damages for pain and suffering for the birth of the third plaintiff. The Court rejected all
other claims. By this further appeal, the first and second defendants requested that the
Landgericht decision be restored; the first and second plaintiff (hereinafter: "the plaintiffs") claimed that the third defendant should be included in the decision on liability.
The third plaintiff's further appeal was withdrawn. This Division only accepted the first
defendant's further appeal in so far as it concerned the claim for financial losses. The
further appeal was unsuccessful.

Reasons

I. The Appeal Court held that the first defendant was liable for his breach of the consultation contract, including his liability for the breach committed by the second defendant
as employee performing his obligation (§ 278 BGB). . . .

II. The further appeal fails to challenge the Appeal Court's reasoning.

1. In respect of the contract of genetic consultation, the further appeal unsuccessfully challenges the first defendant's status as the mainly liable contractual partner. . . .

According to the findings of the Court of Appeal, the plaintiffs were referred for genetic counselling by their GP to the department run by the first defendant of the institute run by the third defendant. The Appeal Court also correctly ascertained that the first defendant was authorised by the National Health Service to provide this kind of service. . . .

In view of this situation, the Appeal Court followed the principle repeatedly expressed by this Division (BGHZ 100, 363 [367 et seq.]; BGHZ 105, 189 [194]; BGHZ 120, 376 [382 et seq.]) that the first and second plaintiffs only entered into a contract with the first defendant, since the out-patient treatment of National Health patients is not first and foremost the duty of the body running the hospital, but is rather that of the approved National Health doctor or the chief consultant appointed for National Health patients. As a result, a National Health patient only enters into a contract with the chief consultant running the out-patient National Health department, and not with the hospital even where the GP's referral names the hospital (BGHZ 105, 189 [194]). . . .

A genetic consultation is not an alternative to out-patient and in-house treatment but is rather a form of out-patient treatment . . . The first defendant, not the Institute itself, was the person authorised by the National Health organisation to provide such counselling, . . . Internal arrangements as to payment between the doctor and the Institute cannot alter the fact that as regards the consultancy contract, the duly appointed chief consultant was the plaintiffs' contractual partner.

2. The further appeal unsuccessfully challenges the opinion of the Court of Appeal that the counselling by the second defendant (for which the first defendant is responsible) was wrong . . .

(a) . . . According to the undisputed findings of the Court of Appeal, the question whether the first-born child suffered from genetic or prenatal damage was at the time of consultation left unanswered. The Appeal Court, therefore, held that the letter written on 27 October 1983 by the first and second defendants, stating that (a) an adverse inherited disposition was extremely unlikely and an as yet unknown prenatal damage was the most likely cause of the disabilities; (b) a repetition was not to be expected; and (c) a further pregnancy should not be dissuaded, misrepresented this uncertainty. In view of the open-ended medical results, the advice which the parents derived from this letter was not sound enough. The genetic counselling should have made this point clear.

The further appeal submits that the letter had been sent to the GP, and the plaintiffs had only been sent a copy of it . . . In view of the clear statements contained in the defendants' letter, the further appeal fails to show how the GP could have advised his patients as to possible risks along any other lines . . . For its opinion that the risks had been assessed too optimistically and that the recommendations had been insufficiently safe, the Appeal Court could unreservedly rely on expert advice. . . .

The Court of Further Appeal does not doubt that the lower court's findings show a connection between the tortious act (the wrongful consultation) and the resulting damage; had the consultation been complete and correct, the plaintiffs would not have had another child. The Appeal Court correctly held that the damage claimed resulted from a breach of duty which the first defendant had under the consultancy contract, since the genetic consultation was intended to prevent the birth of a genetically damaged child by allowing the parents to make a reasoned decision. The Appeal Court held that there existed a sufficient with the protective purpose of the consultancy contract if any kind of genetic damage to the third plaintiff was at least a factor contributing to any mental or physical handicap. In view of the facts of the case this could be easily ascertained: both children had the same symptoms of damage, suggesting a combination of genetic and exogenic damage. As regards the third plaintiff, mere prenatal damage could, for all intents and purposes, be ruled out . . . The fact that the exact nature of the third claimant's established genetic damage could not be exactly ascertained, prevents neither the finding of a causal connection between the wrongful advice and the birth of a genetically damaged child, nor the inclusion of the damage to health under the scope of protection of the consultancy contract since by this contract all possible genetic damage was to be excluded . . .

3. The further appeal fails in so far as it opposes the finding that the plaintiffs' claim for damages comprises the total costs of living necessary for the third plaintiff. . . .

(b) In view of the findings of the Court of Appeal that the plaintiffs would have refrained from having another child if they had fully and correctly been advised on the genetic implications, the opinion of the Court of Appeal is in line with the case law of this Division, according to which the costs of maintenance resulting from the birth of the further child can be claimed from the wrongly advising doctor as damages for breach of the consultancy contract. This Division has decided this point on a number of occasions for comparable groups of cases, i.e. for cases of (a) wrong advice on the prevention of the birth of a severely prenatally damaged child (BGHZ 86, 240 et seq.; BGHZ, 89, 95 et seq.; NJW 1987, 2923), (b) failed sterilisation (BGHZ 76, 249 et seq.; BGHZ 76, 259 et seq.; VersR 1980, 719; NJW 1981, 630; NJW 1981, 2002; NJW 1984, 2625; NJW 1992, 2961), and (c) failed (permissible) abortions (BGHZ 95, 199; NJW 1985, 2752; NJW 1985, 671; NJW 1985, 2749; VersR 1986, 869; NJW 1992, 1556). The facts of this case provide no reasons why the principles developed for those cases cannot be applied to a case where the parents of a handicapped child, before procreation of another child, undergo genetic counselling in order to prevent the risk of giving birth to a second handicapped child.

(c) The Second Division of the Bundesverfassungsgericht (Federal Constitutional Court) in its decision of 28 May 1993 (NJW 1993, 1751 et seq.), headnote no. 14, and in its reasons under D V 6, expressed its doubts as regards the decisions of this Division. Although the remarks of the Bundesverfassungsgericht are not binding on this Court, and this Division has already repeatedly and critically reviewed its own previous findings (see BGHZ 76, 249 [252] and NJW 1984, 2625), a further detailed analysis of the legal position is called for.

The Bundesverfassungsgericht decided that the legal possibility that a child's existence may be a source for damages is constitutionally barred under Article 1 I GG. The duty of all organs of the state to honour every human being in its existence, (and here reference is made to Part I 1 a of the decision) prohibits, in itself, the view that maintenance of a child can be seen as financial loss. The case law of the civil courts on liability for medical errors in counselling on failed abortions should therefore be reviewed.

This Division fails to find this remark of the BVerfG a reason why in the case here under investigation expenses for maintenance cannot be seen as financial loss.

(aa) The legal classification of expenses for maintenance proceeds from the contractual liability of the doctor to full all medical requirements in order that the treatment or consultancy undertaken by him be successful. Such legal liability can, however, only be used as a starting point for contracts whose legality is not in question. As regards abortions without legal justification which, as a result of the Constitutional decision of 1993 must now be regarded as illegal (for instance because the previously applied justifications are no longer accepted as valid . . .), this Division can here leave undecided, whether in such cases the need to prevent economic loss arising from a child's existence is at all relevant for the contractual relationship and, even where such need existed, if it could be the starting point for a claim for damages.

On the other hand, (a) consultancy contracts intended to prevent, as here, the procreation or, in other cases, the birth of a genetically damaged child; or (b) sterilisation contracts aimed at preventing the birth of any, or any further, children or (c) contracts for the legally permitted abortion of a pregnancy, (for instance in cases where such termination is undertaken for criminological or embryopathic reasons), are all contracts intended to reach a legally permissible objective. If there are no qualms about the legal validity of a contract for sterilisation (see this Division BGHZ 67, 48 [51 et seq.] and NJW 1984, 2625), there should, a fortiori, be none in cases like the present. The plaintiffs' intended to have a second, but not as handicapped child as their first, and in order to prevent the damage feared as a result of the first child's handicap, they wished to make procreation dependant on the outcome of a consultation. Such intentions cannot meet with moral qualms. Such behaviour is due to a high degree of parental responsibility.

Where a contract is geared to reaching a legally permitted aim, i.e. the birth of a child (in this case potentially genetically impaired), the doctor is responsible for obtaining the contractually agreed aim by fulfilling his accepted duties. The Division cannot see any constitutional doubts. In the cited decision, the BVerfG in its reasons expressly points out that faulty performance of medical duties in respect of treatment or advice can in principle lead to civil liability. The constitutional and general legality of contracts such as the ones described above is reflected in the contents of these contracts in so far as they are geared to prevent economic burdens incurred from the birth of children. Where this was properly contractually agreed, such economic protection is part of the duties which the doctor accepted and the legal order condones. Thus, this Division adheres to its previously reasoned opinion that the doctor's liability includes liability for the prevention of this economic consequence where, as part of the specific aims of the contract for treatment and consultation, he had also accepted that of the prevention of such losses. This Division has affirmed this result for cases of sterilisation for reasons of family planning (BGHZ 76, 249 [256]; 76, 259 [263 et seq.]; NJW 1981, 630; NJW 1981, 2002 and NJW 1984, 2625). In a case similar to this one, where during pregnancy a consultation took place aimed at preventing the birth of a severely disabled child, this Division (BGHZ 89, 95 [104 et seq.] held that even in such cases the prevention of economic burdens is part of the protection envisaged by the consultancy contract, even where this is not its paramount reason, as in cases of sterilisation for economic reasons.

Where in the course of such contracts the doctor commits a medical error leading to the birth of a child, his liability includes his duty to reimburse the contractual partner for all economic losses which the contract was intended to prevent. Accepting a medical duty aimed at attaining a permitted contractual purpose makes the doctor legally responsible and has consequences for his liability. In the last instance the protection afforded to the contractual partner, which stems from the doctor's liability, is a consequence of medical progress which, within the boundaries of the law, opened up the possibility of preventing the birth of a child.

(bb) Given these facts, it would be a grave incursion into the parties' contractual interests if the doctor were free from consequential liability in cases of culpable breach of contractual duties. Even when considering the BVerfG's opinion, this Division cannot detect any constitutionally-based reason why such a grave incursion into contractual liability is needed. Here, protection of a nasciturus from abortion is not at issue. This point of view is also obviously not the starting point of the BVerfG's criticisms, which are directed, without differentiation, at this Division's jurisdictional principles. Nor can an opposing constitutional reason be derived from the view that the economic burden which must be borne by the doctor as a result of his breach of contract actually consists of the costs of living of a child.

(i) This Division shares the views underlying the reasoning of the BVerfG in its decision of 28 May 1993 (NJW 1993, 1751 *et seq.*) that it is constitutionally prohibited (Article 1 GG) to classify the very existence of a child as damage, even within the laws of contract and tort. This Division has repeatedly expressed this view (BGHZ 76, 249 [253 *et seq.*]; NJW 1984, 2625).

But in its leading decision (BGHZ 76, 249) this Division has already pointed out that to use the slogan "child as damage" is an inappropriate and legally useless way of looking at the problem. Instead, the Court in this and later decisions, especially in its decision of 19 June 1984 (NJW 1984, 2625) declared that the damage consists of the costs of maintenance incurred by the unplanned birth of the child. The Court held that in this respect the distinction between the child's existence and its undoubted value as a person on the one hand, and the parents' maintenance burden on the other, does not represent an artificial disintegration or a "dissection of the child's personal integrity" (see for instance Lankers in *FamRZ* 1969, 384), but is rather a logical consequence of looking at the problem from the point of view of the law of damages. In order to reach the consequences of the law of damages here under discussion, neither the legal provisions of the law of damages nor those of family law, nor an unrestrained contemplation of the entire facts, require that the very existence of the child is seen as the damaging event. It is only the ensuing financial burden to the parents, i.e. the cost of maintaining the child, which represents the damaging economic loss. The provisions on liability do not exonerate the parents from their own duty to provide maintenance for their child. Their own duty to the child and their costs in maintaining the child are only partially met by the doctor's liability.

(ii) According to the opinion of this Division, considerations of liability and damage are not precluded by the fact that the economic burden takes the form of maintenance for a child. The legally necessary comparison of the economic situation with and without the damaging event does not mean that the child's existence and its non-existence are compared in the sense that the child's non-existence is regarded as a positive and its actual existence as a negative economic factor. This point of view would certainly meet with constitutional objections under Article 1 GG. But such a comparison would also be wrong under the law of damages. When the considerations of liability and damage are solely restricted to the economic side of the complex facts which the birth of a child involves, the conclusion is reached that for the person liable to provide maintenance, the comparison of the two economic situations needed to determine the actual loss merely comprises the economic situation with and without the duty to provide such maintenance.

In this respect, the Division is aware that the economic burden is only brought about by the child's existence. But this is merely a causal link provided by natural science, which in itself is free from value judgments. Even in the case of a "longed-for child", the parents' duty to provide maintenance is expressed as a burden on their finances without any negative consequence for the relationship between the parents and the child. Moreover, even in cases where the BVerfG has expressly acknowledged the duty to compensate for losses incurred in connection with the birth of a child, the birth must be seen as the "source of loss" intended by the BVerfG, if this expression has any relevance at all to the law of damages (for the different view held by Deutsch, see *NJW*, 1993, 2361 [2362]). This Division has also contemplated whether in consultancy cases such as this one or in cases of failed family planning, it could, for constitutional reasons, be necessary to acknowledge a claim to fair monetary compensation for immaterial damages on the basis of breach of the parents' personal rights, as has been considered in academic literature (see Diederichsen, *VersR*, 1981, 693 [696]; Stürner *VersR* 1984, 305 and *FamRZ* 1985, 753 [760 *et seq.*]; H. Lange, *Schadensersatz*, 2. edn., section 6 IX 7h). However, this point of view does not dispense with a comparison with the situation had the child not been born. A classification as immaterial damage to its parents would have a more direct and graver effect on the child as a person than the ascertainment of the parents' economic burden for which the doctor must (partially) relieve them. Moreover, as regards questions of liability, such a stance seems rather dubious, since the economic burden arising from the birth of the child would indirectly affect the calculation of compensation, since under this legal concept (damages for pain and suffering) compensation for economic losses is not possible. The differences between economic and immaterial losses would be blurred.

(*c*) In cases where the burden of the costs of living was meant to be prevented through a contract with a doctor, an economic approach in assessing the burden does not negatively affect the views of the value of the child's person and existence. According to the compensatory nature of the law of liability and damages, the doctor's share of the economic burden is reduced to a mere financial obligation which neither taints the child nor questions its right to live. Neither the law nor the practice on damage and compensation links the term "damage" to such negative value judgements; if this were the case it would necessarily be prohibited to classify the birth of a child as damage. The classification of maintenance costs as losses in the relationship between parents and doctor means, however, neither that a value judgment is made in respect of the child nor that its personality is degraded by connection with the term "damage". According to the opinion of this Division, the term " damage" does not include such connotations which, in the light of the Constitution, would in any case be objectionable. When the BGB was enacted, the legislator deliberately refrained from clearly defining the terms "financial and economic losses" and instead left their interpretation to jurisprudence and the courts. From the very beginning the courts interpreted economic losses as the diminution of assets and the increase of debts, calculated by way of a mathematical comparison between the economic situation brought about by the damaging event and the situation which would have existed had the event never occurred (*Großer Senat für Zivilsachen* BGHZ 98, 212 [217 *et seq.*]). This method of calculating the difference through a neutral mathematical operation cannot, however, dispense with an assessment of the various mathematical positions to be employed when calculating the difference; these need to be evaluated according to the protective purpose of all liability and the compensatory function of damages (BGHZ *98*, 212 [217 *et seq.*]) But where a contract with a doctor was intended to prevent the parents being burdened with maintenance costs, and this burden is incurred as a direct result of a breach of contract, the protective purpose of the contract and the purpose of damages as equalisation of burdens demand that it be seen as economic loss. The fact that this balancing of losses cannot result in a "negative value judgement" of the child as a person follows from the above-outlined restriction of the assessment of losses to the economic aspect of the facts of the case. Nor does this comparison under the law of

damages between the two economic situations reduce the human existence in a degrading manner to a mere item of accounting and balancing. The comparison is merely the
basically value-free method of calculating economic consequences on which the law of
damages always relies and whose classification as a mere tool for establishing facts affects
the meaning of term "loss". This is the ultimate purpose of the law of damages; to compare
economic situations and to provide economically expressed differences for the purposes
of the law of liability which then establishes who is responsible for the creation of the
burden and to whom it must accordingly be attributed. This function of the law of
damages does not involve a negative value judgement of the economic difference as "loss".
If compensation is nowadays understood as a just allocation of burdens according to the
various criteria of liability, and not as a sanction for damaging behaviour, this Division
sees no reason why the classification of maintenance costs as "loss" should be detrimental to the honour of the child.

This Division is rather of the opinion that, especially in cases such as this, granting
compensation not only has no detrimental effect on the child, but can rather be beneficial to it, since it improves its financial situation and possibly even its standing within the
family. The shifting of the maintenance burden to the attending doctor appears especially
satisfactory where, due to his faulty consultation, he is co-responsible for the economic
burden which, if a severely handicapped child is in constant need of care, can even
threaten the family's existence. As this Division has previously stated (BGHZ 76, 259 [266
et seq.]), even in cases where the doctor is fully liable for all extra expenditure calculated
by means of an economic comparison, the parents are still burdened with the total
personal care of the child and also with a certain amount of financial losses and sacrifices which they cannot transfer to the person who created the damage. The Court fails
to detect any constitutionally objectionable attack on the honour of the child from this
partial economic alleviation of the parents' burden. Should the parents in fact treat the
child badly because they blame it for the additional maintenance costs, such behaviour
would not be improved by the legal order refusing to shift some of the burden to the
person who, by his breach of contract, created it. . . .

4. As regards consultancy contracts of the kind here under investigation, the compensatory purpose of damages prohibits a restriction of the claim for damages to the amount
of extra expenditure incurred by reason the child's congenital handicap . . .

(b) As this Division has previously stated, a doctor who culpably breaches his duty to
provide a proper consultation, and who is therefore liable for maintenance costs, must,
within the limits set out by this Division, pay compensation for the entire maintenance
costs of the child and not only for the additional expenditure caused by the handicap.
After a further review, the Court has decided to uphold its previous opinion even for cases
such as the present. As far as liability is concerned, there are no grave differences between
the two cases of consultancy. In both instances the parents required medical advice in
order not to give birth to a congenitally damaged child. If, in view of the risk of having
a second handicapped child, they intended to forego a second pregnancy if the doctor
advised them in that direction, it is clear that they would not have given birth to the child
had they been correctly advised. According to the parties' intentions, the scope of protection afforded by a consultancy contract always includes those losses arising from financial expenditure on severely handicapped children which the parents intended to prevent,
for themselves and the child, by consulting a doctor. As this Division stated in its decision (BGHZ 89, 95 [105]), these maintenance costs cannot be split into those which are
legally expected to be incurred by parents of a (hypothetically healthy) child and the

additional costs which stem from the child's handicap. The necessary expenditure for safeguarding the existence of a severely handicapped child is indivisible. Moreover, this Division is of the opinion that it is irreconcilable with the respect for the child's person in the sense of Article 1 I GG to measure its existence and the various corresponding needs by using the yardstick of a "normal" child. Compensating the parents for the entire costs of maintenance is thus no disregard of the child's honour but rather an appropriate means of protecting it from losses, and of guaranteeing such protection.

Case 9

BUNDESVEFASSUNGSGERICHT (FIRST SENATE) 12 NOVEMER 1997
BVERFGE 96, 375 = NJW 1998, 519 = JZ 1998, 352

The constitutional complaints are dismissed.

Reasons

A.

The constitutional complaints, joined together for a joint decision, concern the case law of the civil courts, according to which the duty to maintain a child in the case of unsuccessful sterilisation or defective genetic advice can constitute a loss which has to be compensated.

I.

Case 1 BvR 479/92

1. The complainant is a practising urologist. He advised the husband of the claimant in the original proceedings on questions of family planning and carried out on him a medical operation for the purpose of sterilisation. The sterilisation was unsuccessful and the patient was not told of this. His wife gave birth in May 1984 to their fourth son. The complainant and his liability insurer refused claims for compensation for loss.

2. a) In the original proceedings the wife asked for compensation for maintenance expenditure for the child as well as compensation for pain and suffering because of the unwanted pregnancy and the birth of the child.

The Landgericht ordered the complainant to provide the basic maintenance which would be payable for illegitimate children and to pay a supplement of 70 percent of that basic maintenance for expenditure on care. As the mother had sued alone, only half of the total maintenance expenditure to be paid was awarded to her, in accordance with the legal concept expressed in § 1360 sentence 2 and § 1606 (3) sentence 2 of the BGB. Besides this, the Landgericht held compensation for pain and suffering in the sum of DM 6000 to be appropriate.

II.

Case 1 BvR 307/94

1. The first and second claimants in the original proceedings are the parents of a daughter who was born in 1982 and was mentally and physically handicapped from birth onwards. Because they feared a genetic disposition to the procreation of handicapped children, in August 1983 they visited the department for clinical genetics of a university

institute, which was at that time headed by the complainant, to have the risk of heredi-tary diseases clarified before deciding to have a further child. The complainant signed a doctor's letter a copy of which was shown to the two claimants. According to this, a hered-itary disorder was extremely unlikely; the couple need not be advised against a further pregnancy. In March 1985, a second daughter was born with the same mental and physi-cal handicaps as her sister.

2. (a) The Landgericht dismissed the claim to compensation for maintenance (by the parents) as well as the claim to damages for pain and suffering (by the mother and the handicapped daughter) on the basis that the claimants had not succeeded in proving that the advice given was in breach of duty.

(b) The Oberlandesgericht awarded the parents on their appeal compensation for the material harm which had arisen and would arise for them in the future from the total expenditure on maintenance for the handicapped child. It granted to the mother damages for pain and suffering in addition to this. It refused claims by the child herself.

(c) The child withdrew the appeal in law which had originally been submitted. The appeal in law by the complainant was only accepted and referred back by the Bundesgerichtshof in relation to the contractual liability for compensation for harm (reference omitted).

In the grounds, it states as follows. The Senate adheres to its case law that a doctor's contractual liability can include expenditure on maintenance of a child. This case law was applicable to the case of defective genetic advice before the conception of a child. It was true that the Second Senate of the Federal Constitutional Court in its judgment of the 28 May 1993 in the 14th paragraph of the summary, as well as under D V 6 of the reasons, (reference omitted) raised doubts about this point. Even if no binding effect is to be attrib-uted to these statements and although the Senate has subjected its case law to critical examination on several occasions, they do however make a further detailed scrutiny of the legal situation necessary. The Senate cannot however infer from this reference by the Federal Constitutional Court any reasoning which would prevent adjudging maintenance expenses to be loss in the present case.

III.

The Second Senate of the Federal Constitutional Court has expressed itself in the form of a decision of the 22 October 1997 on the present case. The majority was of the opinion that the legal view expressed in [reference omitted] to the effect that it was not permis-sible on constitutional grounds (Article 1 para. 1 of the Basic Law) to see the duty to main-tain a child as loss was a legal view fundamental to the decision of the Senate. Further, the majority took the view that the deciding of the preliminary question of whether a legal view was of fundamental importance ought to be by a plenary session of the Court if the Senate which expressed the legal view stated that it was of fundamental importance, whilst the other Senate held it not to be fundamental.

An inquiry under § 48 (2) of the Standing Orders of the Federal Constitutional Court by the First Senate has not taken place.

B.

The constitutional complaints are unfounded. The decisions under challenge do not exceed the boundaries which are set constitutionally for the development of the law by judicial decisions (I). They also do not in their material content violate the basic rights (II).

I.

The decisions under challenge by which the complainants have been ordered to pay compensation for harm and for pain and suffering adhere to the principle that the judge is bound by statute and law, so a violation of the basic rights from this point of view is eliminated.

1. The provisions of the civil law of contract and tort which form the basis of the judgment (in particular §§ 611, 276 and 249 as well as §§ 823 (1) and 847 of the BGB) do not meet with any doubts in constitutional law. They have always served the judge as a sufficiently definite basis for deciding questions of liability.

2. The interpretation of these provisions by the civil courts does not overstep the boundaries of the judges' authority to make decisions, which arises from Article 20 paras. 2 and 3 of the Basic Law.

a) The interpretation of simple statute law (inclusive of the choice of the method to be used in this connection) is a matter for the specialist courts and not to be investigated by the Federal Constitutional Court as to its correctness. The Federal Constitutional Court only has to ensure that the requirements of the Basic Law are observed in this respect.

Article 20 para. 2 of the Basic Law gives expression to the principle of separation of powers. Even if this principle was not formulated in the Basic Law in the sense of strict division of functions and monopoly of each power by a single organ (references omitted), it in any case excludes the courts from claiming powers which have been conferred unambiguously on the legislator by the Constitution (references omitted). Article 20 para. 3 of the Basic Law binds the judiciary to statute and law. It would be incompatible with this if the courts progressed from the role of applying of norms to that of setting norms and thus, from an objective point of view escaped from being bound by law and statute (references omitted).

These constitutional principles admittedly do not prohibit the judge from developing the law. On the contrary, in the face of accelerated change in social relations and the limited possibilities of reaction by the legislator, as well as the open formulation of numerous norms, the adoption of applicable law to changed circumstances is part of the tasks of the third power [ie the judiciary]. That applies especially as the distance in time between the statutory command and the judicial decision in the individual case increases. The Federal Constitutional Court has made this point with regard to the Bürgerliches Gesetzbuch (reference omitted).

The judge certainly cannot escape here from the meaning and purpose of the statute laid down by the legislator. His task is limited to bringing it into effect in the most reliable way under changed conditions. If, in the changed conditions, new possibilities of action or influence are created by scientific and technical progress, finding the law will as a rule consist of widening of the field of application of an interpretation which is already current. The legislator's prerogative of setting the purpose is not generally affected by this.

As the development of the law affects the ordinary law, answering the question of whether and to what extent changed circumstances require new legal answers is likewise incumbent on the specialist courts. The Federal Constitutional Court is not therefore in principle allowed to replace their assessment by its own. Its control is limited from the point of view of Article 20 of the Basic Law to whether the specialist court, in developing the law, has respected the basic statutory decision and has followed the recognised methods of statutory interpretation.

b) The decisions under challenge satisfy this standard in relation to contractual liability for the maintenance of children as well as with reference to compensation for pain and suffering because of a pregnancy and birth which have occurred contrary to the woman's intention.

In relation to contractual liability the decisions under challenge are based on the conventional understanding of financial harm, according to which, in principle, duties to maintain can be seen as harm in the sense of § 249 of the BGB. The decisions are also based on the ascertaining of harm according to the "difference" method. The Bundesgerichtshof measures contractual liability by contractual purpose—avoidance of conception and birth of a legitimate child on economic grounds as well—and limits the area of protection of the contract to the marriage partner. The decisions rest on the principles on general contractual liability which have been developed over a long period, and which have been extended to new cases of medical professional activity. Whether a development of the case law on compensation for harm would have been possible in another direction needs no discussion here, as the Federal Constitutional Court does not in principle have to test questions of civil law doctrine in the ordinary law sphere. It corresponds in any case to the consequence of medical liability law as developed over a long period that, in cases of the present kind, the civil law has sought to give appropriate answers to new possibilities of influence and direction in reproductive medicine. It cannot be raised as an objection to this that the Bundesgerichtshof has, in laying down the scope of the duty to compensate for harm, held that limitations on the development of the law are necessary. The Bundesgerichtshof has, in its case law, restricted the liability of doctors in the light of value decisions at the point where problems of compensation law and family law meet. That does not call in question the route to ascertainment of harm.

The boundaries of judicial discovery of law are also not exceeded by the decisions giving to women who did not want to be pregnant damages for pain and suffering for the pain associated with pregnancy and delivery. The objection that this is an impermissible widening of § 253 of the BGB does not sufficiently take into consideration the fact that § 847 of the BGB expressly permits monetary compensation for non-material harm. The Bundesgerichtshof is keeping within the framework of conventional civil law doctrine when as it assesses an undesired pregnancy as a substantial unauthorised invasion of physical integrity and therefore as physical injury.

II.

The decisions, which are made by permissible judicial interpretation and development of the law, are also reconcilable with the Basic Law in their material content.

The subject matter of the examination here is the interpretation of norms which are not open to objection in constitutional law and the outcome and basis of the discovery of law by civil court decisions. The complainants object to the fact that they should have to be liable for the maintenance of a child when they have not fulfilled their contractual duties in relation to sterilisation and a child comes into the world as a result; or when, as a consequence of defective genetic advice, parents refrain from a form of contraception which they would otherwise have chosen and a disabled child is conceived and born.

According to their view, for constitutional reasons, neither the duty of the parents to maintain ought to be understood as harm in the sense of contract law, nor the pains associated with pregnancy and birth as harm in the sense of tort law.

1 . . .

2. The decisions to be examined are likewise not to be measured against the basic right of freedom of vocation under Article 12 para. 1 of the Basic Law. The civil law consequences of defective performance of contracts and liability for harm which arises from tort arise independently of whether the prerequisites for liability in the exercise of the profession are fulfilled or not. Neither the underlying norms of civil law nor their application in the original proceedings concern sanctions specific to a profession. The duty to provide compensation for harm can in any event have indirect effects on the exercise of professional activity as it emphatically underlines the expectation of careful fulfilment of the contract whilst observing professional standards; and it also has an effect on the scope of the required liability insurance. Contract law and tort law are not however norms which only concern in marginal areas those who not acting professionally and which therefore have a close relationship with the exercise of a profession. Objectively they have no tendency to regulate professions (references omitted).

3. There accordingly remains, as a standard for testing the imposition of requirements to pay money, the general freedom of action which is protected in Article 2 para. 1 of the Basic Law. The basic right is admittedly only guaranteed within the framework of the constitutional order. All the legal norms which are formally and materially compatible with the Basic Law are included in this. Article 2 para. 1 of the Basic Law is violated if, in the interpretation and application of such norms, objective constitutional law is contravened. In this connection, it can remain undecided here how far Article 2 para. 1 of the Basic Law, in its character as guarantee of the general freedom of action, enables a complainant to rely on the violation of objective constitutional law where the protective purpose of the concrete basic right norm cannot be attached to him unambiguously (references omitted); this purpose is rather intended to protect the legal position of the successful opponent in the original proceedings. This is because the complainants complain of a violation of Article 1 para. 1 of the Basic Law and therefore of a fundamental principle of the Constitution and the chief basic value of the free democratic basic order (references omitted). Whether the complainants could complain of a violation of Article 6 paras. 1 or 2 of the Basic Law needs no final examination because these provision have no independent weight here as against Article 1 para. 1 of the Basic Law.

(a) The answer to questions of value in civil law is influenced by the objective decisions of principle which are expressed in the catalogue of basic rights in the Constitution. The specialist courts are accordingly under a duty on constitutional grounds to have regard to the basic rights as "guidelines" in the interpretation and application of civil law provisions. Just as with the interpretation of general clauses, special consideration must be taken of the constitutional law basic decisions in development of the law. If the courts overlook or misjudge their radiation effect in a decision in an actual case, they as exercisers of public power violate the basic rights of the party thereby affected (references omitted). A power of control (limited, though, to questions of constitutional law) arises from this for the Federal Constitutional Court. It only concerns mistakes in interpretation which reveal a fundamentally incorrect view of the meaning of a basic right, especially of the extent of its area of protection, and are also of some weight in their material scope (references omitted).

In this constitutional control of civil court judgments, it ought also to be borne in mind here that the protective content of the basic rights can also be required to be put into the balancing process on the side of the person who benefits from the decisions under challenge. In this case it is a question of the point where medical responsibility and the family sphere meet. When the further development of medicine facilitates medical assistance in the extremely private sphere of conception, for which the sexual partners are independently responsible, the tortious and contractual liability law of the Bürgerliches Gesetzbuch acquires in particular the function of safeguarding the personality rights of parent and child thereby endangered, the physical integrity of the wife and the personal right of self-determination of the parents. The detailed balancing of conflicting interests here is left to the judiciary, insofar as existing liability law is open to such a development. It ought to be borne in mind here that the married couple would unilaterally carry the risk of a medical mistake if culpable medical treatment remained to a large extent without sanction in this area.

(b) The Bundesgerichtshof has taken sufficient account of the radiation effect of Article 1 para. 1 of the Basic Law in the shaping of the conditions for liability.

(1) A human being's social value and claim to respect, which prevents him or her being made a mere pawn of the state or exposed to treatment which in principle puts his or her quality in question, is connected with human dignity as the highest value in the Basic Law and a fundamental constitution principle (references omitted). It is inherent in each human being without regard to his or her qualities, achievements and social status. The worth and claim to respect which arises from it is capable of being violated (reference omitted). What respect for human dignity requires in detail cannot be completely detached from the social circumstances of the time (reference omitted). A violation of the claim to respect can exist not only in humiliating, denouncing, persecuting or ostracising people (reference omitted) but also in commercialising human existence.

(2) The decisions under challenge do not contain any mistake which is relevant here.

That applies first of all to the assumption that sterilisation and genetic advice before the conception of a child are to be approved by the legal order and are legitimate. Further, the assumption that a doctor who undertakes such tasks under a contract must take responsibility for culpable mistakes is not open to doubt. The case law of the Bundesgerichtshof that the duty to maintain a child on the facts to be assessed here is to be seen as loss does not represent commercialisation which robs the child of its personal worth. The liability structure of civil law does not in principle affect human dignity, even where a claim to compensation for harm is directly linked to the existence of a human being. Human beings are not thereby reduced to objects i.e. replaceable quantities within the framework of contractual or tortious relationships. The civil law provisions and their interpretation by case law are planned on a just division of burdens. They do not result in fundamental areas of personality being commercialised. The application of the law of compensation for harm to personal relationships does not turn the human being as a person or his inalienable rights into a commodity. No more does the—partial—transfer of the burden of maintenance to third parties contain a negative value judgement against the particular person entitled to maintenance.

The personal recognition of a child does not rest on the acceptance of duties of maintenance by the parents. Even according to civil law, the existence of a child is only one of the defining conditions for the burden of maintenance arising under §§ 1601ff. of the BGB. Not every child needs maintenance (§ 1602 (2) of the BGB). The duty of maintenance and parenthood can separate (references omitted). A full duty to maintain does not follow the adoption of children who have only lost one parent (§ 1755 (1) sentence 2 of the BGB in combination with § 48 (6) of the Social Code VI). Even the Reichsgericht differentiated between the existence of a child, which was not seen as loss, and the duty to maintain applying to the father which was classified as financial loss for him (reference omitted). The Bürgerliches Gesetzbuch forms the basis of relationships in compensation law between the members of a family under a duty to maintain and a person causing harm, without any debasing or objectification of the person entitled to maintenance being expressed thereby (§ 844 (2) in combination with § 843 (4) of the BGB). The same concept of compensation is taken up in numerous modern statutes on product, environmental and traffic liability (reference omitted). The inclusion of the foetus in accident insurance also presupposes that the dignity of the child is not violated by the persons under a duty to maintain it receiving a partial release (reference omitted).

No decision has to be made on what form of compensation for harm would be better to bring it into harmony with civil law doctrine. The Bundesgerichtshof has chosen the route of contractual liability for material harm, and not that of compensation for non-material harm, which it also considered. It has taken into account here that determination of harm by the "difference" method, as well as fair indemnification in money for the harm which arose though the unwanted conception, do not relieve the court from comparing the situations in life of parents with or without a child. It is only of importance in constitutional law that the division of burdens which the Bundesgerichtshof seeks to achieve, having regard to the statutory duties of maintenance accruing to the parents, does not violate Article 1 para. 1 of the Basic Law.

It is also not the task of the Federal Constitutional Court to examine the arguments of the Bundesgerichtshof in all their details. They are not inconsistent with Article 1 para. 1 of the Basic Law. The doctors ordered to pay compensation have freely undertaken contractual duties which are not disapproved of by the legal order. Medical assistance in family planning through sterilisation or advice about genetic risks before the conception of a child do not affect Article 1 para. 1 of the Basic Law. If such advice conflicts with the personal ethical convictions of a doctor, he can refrain from concluding a contract; defective performance of a contractual duty willingly undertaken can find no justification here.

Insofar as doctors are active in this area, their specialist medical competence is in the service of responsible parents, if the parents do not want to have further children because they wish to protect economically children already born or because they are concerned about being overtaxed (here, by the birth of a second severely disabled child). Civil law liability for defective performance can, in cases of this kind, increase the parents' acceptance of the children who are nevertheless born and accepted into the family, as the Bundesgerichtshof has plausibly explained.

The arguments presented by the constitutional complaints that the case law of the Bundesgerichtshof contradicts the system of maintenance in family law, or that the child could be threatened with psychological harm if it heard that its conception should have been avoided, do not affect the basic concepts of Article 1 para. 1 of the Basic Law. In this respect it is claimed that financial relief for the parents does not prevent different losses in view of the complexity of family relationships. That concerns questions of civil law appraisal which the Bundesgerichtshof has tackled in detail.

In the original proceedings it was a question of children to whom the parents have committed themselves after conception. Thwarted family planning, which has been used here by the Bundesgerichtshof as a basis of liability, can become known to children in many ways. Whether harm is produced by this does not depend on economic relief for the parents but on the parent-child relationship after birth. The claim for compensation for harm which has been allowed does not assume any alienation from the child (references omitted). There is also no fear that the judgments under challenge could give rise to or reinforce a negative attitude of the parties against the unplanned life which has been conceived. It cannot be assumed that doctors will advise abortion contrary to their ethical conceptions only because of the threatened liability or its effect on their professional liability insurance. It is even less likely that parents, because of the economic burdens from a further or a disabled child, would decide against the child, if relief is granted to them in this respect. The Bundesgerichtshof excludes any duty to reduce harm by means of an abortion. From the point of view of the parents, the case law under challenge here gives effect instead to the necessary protection against risks which are threatened for the parents' rights of personality and self-determination within the framework of planned parenthood as a result of medical involvement in sterilisation or genetic advice.

C.

The above judgment does not, in view of the decision of the Second Senate of the 28 May 1993 (reference omitted), require the calling of a plenary session of the Federal Constitutional Court. The prerequisites of § 16 of the Federal Constitutional Court Act and of § 48 para. 1 of the Standing Orders of the Federal Constitutional Court are not present. (However, see the decision of the Second Senate of the Federal Constitutional Court of the 22 October 1997.)

D.

The decision is made as to section B by 6 votes to 2 and as to section C by 5 votes to 3.

Notes to Cases 6–9

1. Case 6 is an important decision both for the purposes of teaching and applying the comparative law method and for the substantive issues it raises. As far as the first is concerned two things must be noted. First is the German, indeed civil law, tendency to turn to contract rather than tort when trying to solve a new problem. Thus, almost half of the judgment deals with claims based on contract rather than tort—something, which clearly does not happen in the Anglo-American equivalents. The approach adopted by the BGH is to ask whether there was a contractual duty to protect the mother against the economic burden resulting from the maintenance of the child. (See, for a more recent illustration, BGH NJW 2000, 1782). Secondly this, as far as one can tell, is one of a handful of decisions of the German Supreme Court which have made an open allusion to a foreign system. (The other decisions are reproduced in English as nos. 88 and 130, below.) Unlike decision 130, however, which looked at the much more "similar" Swiss law, the present decision, as well as decision 88, refer to the more "different" Common law. In the present context this means *Curlender* v. *Bio-Science Laboratories*, 106 Cal. App. 3d 811, 165 Cal. Rptr. 477 (1980) and *McKay* v. *Essex Health Authority and Another* [1982] 2 *WLR* 890. The "suspicion" of the German court towards the Common law is evidenced by its cursory statement that the foreign judgments are "of limited relevance [since] they are based on different laws". This is a surprising statement, not only because the German court admits that the problem of "wrongful life" is novel to German law and, therefore, one would have thought that inspiration from foreign system should have, at least, been

permissible. It is also odd given that the German reasoning in the tort section of the judgment reveals similarities with the philosophical opinions expressed by the Anglo-American decisions which we must assume were known to the German judges. One should, perhaps, add that in such cases, it is primarily for counsel to notify national courts of foreign decisions and to press the analogies where such exist and can be of use to the development of national law. (On the impact of foreign and comparative law on German case-law see Drobnig, *RabelsZ* 50 (1986) 610 ff. and nn. 48–9 on p. 621 and, more recently, Kötz, "*Der Bundesgerichtshof und die Rechtsvergleichung*" 50 *Jahre Bundesgerichtshof* (2000).)

2. The issue of substance raised by the German decision has proved controversial in that country as it has in the USA. The decision of the Second Division of the Constitutional Court (BVerfGE 88, 203 = NJW 1993, 1751 "second abortion" case)—known for its conservative tendencies—thus echoes the doubts expressed in the USA by those who sympathise with the pro-life position. Some (lower) courts immediately heeded the advice of the Constitutional Court to reconsider the question of civil damages and took a similar, conservative stance on the issue. (Thus, LG Düsseldorf 2 December 1993, NJW 1994, 805, refusing to follow the BGH decision of 16 November 1993, NJW 1994, 788, decided only a fortnight earlier. Likewise, OLG Zweibrücken, 18 February 1997, NJW—RR 1997, 666). In some instances, they were able to do this on the technical argument that the case before them involved a maintenance claims for a *healthy* child (whereas the BGH decision of 16 November had been concerned with the claims of the parents of an *impaired* child). But other courts refused to accept this as a valid distinction and abided by the more liberal position that awarded full maintenance costs to the parents. (OLG Düsseldorf, 15 December 1994, NJW 1995, 788.) In this steadfastness, these courts found an ally in the BGH. For this court not only had by-passed skilfully the Constitutional Court by drawing a distinction between the "existence of the child" and "the obligation to maintain it" (BGH 16 November 1993, NJW 1994, 788, case 8); it had also been quick to reaffirm its views in a quick succession of judgments. (For instance, BGH 23 March 1995, NJW 1995, 1609, case 10.) The subsequent and most recent decision of the First Division of the Constitutional Court (BVerfG, 12 November 1997, BVerfGE 96, 375 = NJW 1998, 519, case 9)—which, unlike the Second Division, is known for its liberal tendencies—has broadly followed the line of the BGH. And the decision *not* to refer to the Plenum of the Court the dispute between its two rivalling Divisions (BVerfG, 22 November 1997, NJW 1998, 523) suggests that the *status quo* is unlikely to be disturbed in the near future. The position in private law thus seems to have settled in the following way. (i) Both parents have a contractual claim for wrongful birth and pregnancy cases; (ii) this entitles them to full maintenance costs (whether the child is healthy or not; if it is not the measure of damages may be greater to cover the extraordinary medical expenses); (iii) the mother may additionally claim pain and suffering in cases of wrongful birth that result from a complicated birth. In all these actions, the child, itself, had no claims.

Before leaving this point one must note the unsatisfactory result of the same issue being decided by two different senates of the Court each of which is effectively an independent court, each with its own philosophical orientation and traditions. This unsatisfactory result is due to the fact that, for historical reasons, constitutional complaints (*Verfassungsbeschwerde*) are usually heard by the First Chamber whereas the so-called *Normenkontrolle*, reserved for the review of legislation, is mainly carried out by the Second Chamber.

3. The position in the USA is well discussed in all the American textbooks. See, for instance, Franklin and Rabin, 257 ff. Prosser, Wade and Schwartz, 472–5. for England see Mason and McCall, *Law and Medical Ethics* 4th edn. (1994); Markesinis and Deakin, *Tort Law*, 273 ff. Here then a few general points will suffice.

First, a point of terminology. "Wrongful birth" and "wrongful life", as terms go, are unfortunate. As an American court noted: "Any 'wrongfulness' lies not in the life, the birth, the conception, or the pregnancy, but in the negligence of the physician. The harm, if any, is not the birth itself but the effect of the defendant's negligence on the [parents] resulting from the denial to the parents of their right . . . to decide whether to bear a child or whether to bear a child with a genetic or other defect" (*Viccaro* v. *Milunsky*, 406 Mass. 777; 551 NE 2d 10 n. 3.) The various terms are also not used consistently in the American periodical literature and this can lead to confusion. It is too late to alter existing terminological practice, however unfortunate it may be; but in order to minimise confusion we have, at the end of this section, provided a glossary of how we think the terms should be understood. The German term "ungewolte Schwangerschaft"—unwanted pregnancy—suffers from no similar defects. However, in its neutrality it could be said to be too opaque in so far as it gives no hint whether the pregnancy was always not wanted or subsequently became so. Related to these question, is another namely, does it involve a healthy or unhealthy child—a point once taken by some courts but nowadays one that may have lost its significance. It is a weakness shared by most German textbooks that they leave these points (mostly) open and that the brevity of the treatment given to this subject leaves the student unaware how the contradictory German cases can be made to dovetail with one another. (Professor Peter Schlechtriem, who has one of the more jurisprudentially oriented accounts, devotes in his learned textbook a mere twenty-five lines. (*Schuldrecht, Besonderer Teil,* 5th edn. 1998, no 747. Another famous student textbook—Medicus, *Bürgerliches Recht,* 18th edn. 1999—ignores the subject altogether.)

Secondly, we must note that here the movement of ideas is from America to Europe and not the other way round. (See the judgments in *McKay,* above, and *Udale* v. *Bloomsbury Area Health Authority* [1983] 1 WLR 1098.) Though the imitation in Europe is obvious (and likely to increase as more European lawyers follow graduate law courses in the USA) it is not slavish. Thus, when noting the differences that exist between American and German law, one must also be ready to seek explanations for them in the *wider* context of each system. Thus, the *Procanik* decision (reprinted below) to grant the plaintiff boy "special" damages *appears* to be more generous than the German which denies them to *him.* Yet the difference is more apparent than real if one remembers that in German law the parental maintenance does not cease (as it does in most American jurisdictions) upon the child attaining majority. But if the different German law of maintenance helps minimise the differences between Case no. 6 and *Procanik,* it does not completely eliminate them. We get a clue of this towards the end of the German judgment where the court, itself, accepts that its solution to grant the parents special damages may not be enough "once the duty to maintain [the child] comes to an end, *as for instance, when they die".* Here, as stated, the American solution appears if not preferable certainly more generous to the child; that is until one notes the way the German court completes the above-mentioned thought. "In all these cases" says the court "a fateful development takes place . . . and the effects of which must be made good by the community within the bounds of the possible." An admission here, that the social security net (effectively absent in the USA) will thus take over, but also a very important explanation for the fact that American tort law is so often more generous than its European counterparts. For social security will provide only a limited relief—"within the bounds of the possible"—and will thus be less generous than the tort/damages system of compensation. So the verdict at then end of this complicated journey into the recesses of German family and social security law is that the German solution is roughly as good as the American and vice versa!

Thirdly, it is clear that the vast majority of courts—both in the USA and in Germany—have little or no difficulty in allowing parents to recover at least some elements of damage in "wrongful *birth"* actions. (Though in the United States, a few courts have, on a variety of policy grounds, denied altogether wrongful birth claims. See: *Wilson* v. *Kuenzi,* 751 SW 2d 741 (Mo. 1988); *Azzolino* v. *Dingfelder,* 315 N.C. 103, 337 SE 2d 528 (1985).) Note, however, that (most) American courts award mothers damages for emotional distress as well, which German courts do not. (Awarding such damages: *Berman* v. *Allan,* 80 NJ 421, 404 A. 2d 8 (1979); *Keel* v. *Banach,* 624 So. 2d 1022 (Ala. 1993); *Greco* v. *United States,* 111 Nev. 405, 893 P. 2d 345 (1995). Denying recovery for emotional harm: *Siemieniec* v. *Lutheran General Hosp.,* 117 Ill. 2d 230, 512 NE 2d 691 (1987); *Smith* v. *Cote,* 128 N.H. 231, 513 A. 2d 341 (1986).) On the other hand the claim of children for what the Common law calls "general damages" in "wrongful *life"* actions have failed in all three systems—English, German and American—the decision of the California Court of Appeal in *Curlender,* above, being the boldest on this point. The issue finally came before the California Supreme Court in *Turpin* v. *Sortini,* 31 Cal. Rptr. 3d 220, 643 P. 2d 954 (1982) which disagreed with *Curlender* that damages for pain and suffering should be awarded to the child for being born. The Supreme Court, however, was prepared to grant the child—for the reasons given in the previous paragraph—*special* damages for costs connected with its handicap. (As *Procanik* explains clearly, these will not overlap with the damages given to the parents for the child's maintenance.) Such a "limited recognition of a wrongful life" claim can also be found in New Jersey (*Procanik* v. *Cillo* 478 A 2d 755 (1984) and Washington (*Harbeson* v. *Parke-Davis, Inc.* 656 P. 2d 483 (1983). Otherwise, however, it remains the exception. The significance of these three Supreme Court decisions is dubious for they could be seen as a step both forwards and backwards. Forwards in so far as they represented a move closer towards accepting in principle claims for wrongful life; backwards in that they stopped short of considering the full consequences of such a move. This ambiguity, plus a certain tendency to inflate where possible the parents' claims, may suggest that the move towards recognising claims for wrongful life, proper, has lost most of its urgency. In the USA, this "braking trend" may have also been reinforced by the dislike of the pro-life lobbies of abortion and, by extension, the claims discussed in this section.

4. The arguments put forward against the recognition of claims for "wrongful life" are as follows. (*cf. Viccaro* v. *Milunsky* 406 Mass.777, 551 NE 2d 8 (1990). The issues here are also discussed in a note in 71 *Calif. L. Rev.* 1278 (1983) and in the literature given in number 8, below.)

(i) In *Gleitman* v. *Cosgrove*, 49 NJ 22, 227 A. 2d 689 (1967) the court refused to recognise claims for wrongful life on the ground that damages would be impossible to assess. One American court thus put the dilemma in the following way: "Determining damage from the birth of a child [is] an 'exercise in prophecy'. Such a weighing process might be applied at the end of a life but not at the beginning". (*Emerson* v. *Magendantz*, 689 A 2d 409, 413 (R.I. 1997).) This point was also taken in the *McKay* case, above. However, can it really be considered as decisive? Have not English courts for many years awarded damages for "loss of expectation of life" (now abolished by the Administration of Justice Act 1982)? Kaus J in *Turpin* v. *Sortini* thought otherwise when he said that ". . . there is a profound *qualitative* difference between the difficulties faced by a jury in assessing general damages in a normal personal injury . . . and the task before a jury in assessing general damages in a wrongful life case"? (Italics supplied.)

(ii) A second reason that is often given is that the child/plaintiff has not suffered a "legally cognisable injury". This is often presented in philosophical terms, namely that "impaired life" is preferable to "non life". A host of constitutional arguments, especially after *Roe* v. *Wade*, above, can be used to strengthen this point (see *Berman* v. *Allan*, 80 NJ 421, 404 A. 2d 8 (1979). However, as *Procanik* v. *Cillo* admits, decisions such as *Roe* v. *Wade* can also improve the mother's right to claim for wrongful birth; see also Stephenson LJ in *McKay*, 902). But how convincing are such arguments? In any event, why should the court decide this question and not someone else, e.g. the parents, or the plaintiff himself if and when this is possible?

(iii) *McKay* also tried to justify its result in terms of "duty". True, in one sense it may be grotesque to say that a doctor owes the foetus a duty to kill it; but if such a duty can, under circumstances, be owed to the mother, why can it not be owed to the foetus? In any event, is it not true to suggest that recourse to the language of "duty of care" really conceals an unwillingness on the part of the judge to decide the real policy issues?

(iv) Alternatively, in cases with facts like those of *McKay* (foetus *already* infected by rubella; doctor negligently fails to discover it and give the mother the chance to abort) one could argue that there is "no damage". (In this sense Weir in a critical note of the *McKay* decision in 41 *CLJ* 225, 227 (1982).) For damage is to make something worse, not to make *simpliciter*; and the fact is that in this case if the doctor had done his duty the child would not have been better, but she would not have been at all. Weir's comparison of *McKay* with the defective premises case of *Dutton* v. *Bognor Regis Urban DC* [1972] 1 QB 373 is, in conceptual terms, interesting. But the analogy totally underestimates the human and philosophical aspects of the *McKay* type of case. Disapproval for the Weir "analogy" can be found in German works of authority as well. See Larenz/Canaris, p. 385; and it was, in any event, rejected by the BGH in Case no 4, above.

Overall, therefore, how do these arguments fare? It is difficult to deny that they have some strength. Equally it is impossible to accept them as conclusive. If that is so, could it be that at present the courts (and public opinion) are not (yet?) ready to cope with this problem and are merely grasping at any argument or concept that is available?

5. In part 2 of its judgment the court in Case 6 states that in this case [it] "is confronted for the *first time* [italics supplied] with the problem of . . . 'wrongful life'". This is not so, however, with claims brought by the parents—the so-called "wrongful birth" actions, which had occupied the courts before 1983 and several times since. (See, for example, BGH NJW 1984, 2625; NJW 1984, 688; NJW 1985, 2749; NJW 1985, 671 with note by Deutsch.). In fact the first such claim (brought by a distraught father against a *pharmacist* who negligently sold him enzymes instead of the requested contraceptives) was upheld by the Court of First Instance of Itzehoe (LG Itzehoe, FamRZ 1969, 90; VersR 69, 265. In actual fact there exists a strange case which can, probably, claim to be the first to raise the question of the cost of maintaining an unwanted child. Thus, in 1924 the Reichsgericht imposed on a mental institution the cost of maintaining an unwanted child conceived by one of its nurses who had sexual intercourse with a mentally retarded patient (RGZ 108, 87.).

6. In the US the picture is quite complicated. Generally speaking it would appear that many courts are prepared to grant parents the expenses involved in raising the child. See Annotation, 83 ALR 3d 15 (1978). Others, however, have denied recovery on the (*not always convincing*) ground that the benefit of having a child exceeds the cost of raising it. See *Cockrum* v. *Baumgartner*, 95 Ill. 2d 193, 447 NE 2d 385 (1983). In *Hartke* v. *McKelway*, 526 F. Supp. 97 (DDC 1981) the court held that claims for raising a *healthy* child born after an unsuccessful sterilisation operation would be rejected where the purpose of the sterilisation was for therapeutic and not economic reasons. On this see Einheuser in 61 *University of Detroit Journal of Urban Law*, 651 (1984). See also Franklin and Rabin, pp. 257–268. The questions raised by unsuccessful abortions are discussed in case 10, and its notes. This follows addendum 2 below. There, we shall also deal with the cognate problem of measure of damages given in the event of failed sterilisations. (Wrongful conception or pregnancy claims.)

American cases have, in this context, considered one further point: should the parents of a healthy child born after an unsuccessful sterilisation operation be under some kind of duty to mitigate their loss? Under the avoidance of consequences doctrine envisaged by s. 918 of the Restatement (Second) of Torts, some courts have considered the mother's duty to abort or the parents' duty to place the child for adoption. A few courts have taken the view (mainly in *obiter*) that, as a matter of law, reasonable mitigation includes abortion when pregnancy is discovered during the first trimester. See *Ziemba* v. *Sternberg*, 357 NYS 2d 265 (1974); *Sorkin* v. *Lee* 434 NYS 2d 300 (1980). Most courts, however, have taken a different view, tending to leave the issue to the jury. See *Univ. of Arizona Health Sciences Center* v. *Superior Court*, 667 P. 2d 1294, 1301 (1983). The option to place the child for adoption seems to have encountered less opposition, though in *Marciniak* v. *Lundborg*, 153 Wis. 2d 59, 450 NW 2d 243, 247 (1990) the court rejected as unreasonable "the argument that parents must select either abortion or adoption as a method of mitigation . . .". This view has much to commend it, even though the relinquishing of the child for adoption may well produce a sound economic result. For, as Professor Dobbs has rightly pointed out, " . . . the tort [in these cases] is not exclusively an economic tort. The defendant, having deprived the mother of one choice, has no right to force upon her another choice she does not want to make." (Dobbs, 801.) The relevant case law that has considered these unattractive and legalistic options that encourage litigation has been collected in Note, "Wrongful Birth: The Avoidance of Consequences Doctrine in Mitigation of Damages", 53 *Fordham L. Rev.* 1107 (1985). The same point about mitigation could, in theory, be raised in order to reduce damages in a claim for wrongful birth brought by the parents of an impaired child.

7. When considering the points raised in this section the reader, especially the non-American reader, should bear in mind that the usually inactive (in tort matters) American legislator has, in this context, been mobilised into action by the pro-life movement. The result has been either statutes prohibiting wrongful life actions against parents (e.g. see West's Ann. Cal. Civ. Code para.

43.6) or prohibiting wrongful life *and* wrongful birth actions, though (arguably in some cases) allowing wrongful pregnancy actions. (See Minn. Stat. Ann. para. 145.424.) In a book such as this, precise details need not be given so suffice it to say that during the 1980's nine States—Idaho, Minnesota, Missouri, Montana, North Carolina, Pennsylvania and Utah—passed statutes barring wrongful birth and wrongful life claims. Indiana and North Dakota barred only wrongful life actions; and South Dakota barred wrongful pregnancy suits as well. One State—Maine—passed a statute, which explicitly details which damages are recoverable for each of the prenatal tort actions. (24 Maine Rev. Stat. Ann. S 2931 (1985). The attempt to curtail these actions has met with some opposition. See: Note, "Wrongful Birth Actions: The Case Against Legislative Curtailment", 100 *Harv. L. Rev.* 2017 (1987); Kowitz, "Note, Not Your Garden Variety Tort Reform: Statutes Barring Claims for Wrongful Life and Wrongful Birth are Unconstitutional", 61 *Brook. L. Rev.* 235 (1995); Gold, "An Equitable Approach to Wrongful Birth Statutes", 65 *Fordham L. Rev.* 1005 (1996); Gantz, "State Statutory Preclusion of Wrongful Birth Relief: a Troubling Re-Writing of a Woman's Right to Choose and the Doctor-Patient Relationship", 4 *Va. J. Soc. Policy and L.* 795 (1997).

Three general points, though, ought to be made and, perhaps, attract some discussion in the classroom.

First, the reason for shielding doctors from such actions appears less compelling than the reason for granting immunity to (one or both) parents. Note, in this respect, the immunity granted by the (English) Congenital Disabilities (Civil Liability) Act 1976 to the *mother* (in the slightly different context of foetal injuries). Note, also, that even that immunity is lifted where the mother is covered by obligatory insurance (s. 2, dealing with the case where the pregnant mother injures the child while driving a car—third party liability insurance being obligatory in England and other European states). Doctors, too, are (and should be) insured—in Europe, in many cases by the state. Why, then, should they not pay for their negligent diagnoses? What reason, other than pressure from the medical/insurance lobby can you invoke in favour of conferring immunity upon doctors?

Secondly, the majority of States allow a cause of action for wrongful birth, though the level of damages awarded differs depending whether the child born is healthy or impaired. Illinois (*Siemieniec v. Lutheran General Hosp.*, 512 NE 2d 691 (1987), Colorado (*Lininger v. Eisenbaum*, 764 P. 2d 1202, 1988—a treasure source, at p. 1208, n. 9, of similar case law), Maryland (*Reed v. Campagnolo*, 630 A 2d 1145 (1993), and New Jersey (*Procanik v. Cillo*, 478 A. 2d 755 (1984), are in this category. Even more States—approximately thirty five—have recognised wrongful conception (or pregnancy) cases i.e. claims arising our of failed sterilisation operations. (*Emerson v. Magendantz*, 689 A 2d 409, 411 (R.I. 1997). A few, including New York, seem to have taken a very restrictive view, even for failed sterilisation claims. (*Abbariao v. Blumenthal*, 483 NYS 2d 296 (N.Y. App. Div. 1985.)

Thirdly, in the USA these tort actions were, as is made clear in *Procanik*, greatly facilitated by *Roe* v. *Wade*. In the late 1980s *Roe* was progressively eroded by the prevailing "conservative" climate of the day; and this, undoubtedly, assisted the passing of the statutes mentioned in the previous paragraphs. Matters, however, may again be about to change, though few can tell how such changes will affect this part of tort law. This, incidentally, is a (wider) aspect of American law which European lawyers (teachers and practitioners) tend to underestimate, often to their detriment. For changing views on, for example, such (*apparently* non-political) topics as *forum non conveniens*, can have important consequences for transnational litigation.

8. The position in English law was, for some time, unclear, especially in the light of dicta in the *McKay* case which suggested that no action for wrongful birth (or life) could lie under the Congenital Disabilities Act 1976. Academic position was divided but the point was not tested in the courts. The discussion was re-opened when attempts were made to impose liability on *Hedley Byrne* principles and the question then arose whether the House of Lords dicta in *McFarlane* v. *Tayside* [2000] 2 AC 59 (a case of a failed sterilisation leading to the birth of a healthy child, excerpted in the addendum to case 10, below) would prevent the award of damages on the ground that the birth of a child should really be regarded as a "gift". The guiding rules, as they stand now and until the matter receives more authoritative formulation by a higher court, can be found in *Hardman* v.

Amin [2000] Lloyd's Rep. Med. 498 and *Lee* v. *Taunton and Somerset NHS Trust* [2001] 1 FLR 419. All have opted for generous awards for the parents of the impaired children (though some uncertainty still remains as to the compensatable headings of damage).

Just as important is the fact that all of these courts rejected in strong terms the view that such claims would offend public policy for treating life as a kind of harm or damage. The judicial reasoning on this point was reinforced by the text of the Abortion Act 1967 (S 1 (1) (d)) which permits abortions for eugenic reasons when there is a danger of the child being affected by a serious impairment. This can certainly be seen as implicitly accepting the view that not every life, however, impaired, is to be seen as gift. Mr Justice Toulson was, arguably, the most explicit, when he thus said in his judgment in *Lee* (at p. 430; italics supplied) that:

"I do not believe that it would be right for the law to deem the birth of a disabled child to be a blessing, *in all circumstances and regardless of the extent of the child's disabilities*; or to regard the responsibility for the care of such a child as so enriching . . . that it would be unjust for a parent to recover the cost from the negligent doctor on whose skill that parent had properly relied to prevent the situation."

The two decisions dealing with the wrongful birth claims are also noteworthy for the relatively large amounts awarded to the claimants by these courts. The *Lee* case, for instance, is an interim judgment; but it makes an interim award of £100,000 which, if added to an interim payment of £120,000 already paid to the plaintiffs, makes a total of £220,000 paid *thus far*. The total award could thus be much larger. Additionally, one must note that fairly large amounts have also been given to the parents for their distress in discovering either that a new child was on its way despite their attempts to achieve sterility or their shock, and pain for the birth of an impaired child. These sums have also been fairly generous. Thus, in one of the earliest of the "recent" cases—*Rand* v. *East Dorset Health Authority* [2000] Lloyd's Rep. Med. 377—the court awarded the parents £50,000 despite the attempts of Counsel for the defendants to reduce this heading of the award to about one tenth of its actual size. Continental European lawyers should be slow to ascribe this trend of the English courts to an "assumed" greater generosity of English law compared to that of France or Germany. For such evidence as exists, especially coming from the area of medical malpractice and personal injury cases suggests that the overall difference in the size of awards in the two systems is less pronounced than many assume it to be. In fact, in both French and English law, the overall level of awards seems to be only slightly *lower* than the highest awards obtained in Germany.

Who gets the money in such cases is the last question which must be answered. This is essential if wider conclusions are to be drawn about wrongful birth and wrongful life actions in the three systems compared in this work: American, English, and German.

The tradition of giving the money to the parents is maintained in all of these English cases. This technique ensures that justice is done without getting embroiled in the philosophical problems which the wrongful life claims raise more acutely. Yet arguably what the English courts are doing is moving towards the more honest (but controversial) position adopted by the French *Cour de cassation* in an important judgment handed down by the Assemblée Plénière on 17 November 2000. (JCP 13 déc. 2000, no. 50, p. 2293; arrêt Perruche). This view is arguable for three reasons.

First, though the money was in the English cases given to the parents, the judges repeatedly stated that it was meant to compensate the child's needs. It is implicit in some of these cases (E.g. in *Hardman* at p. 507) that the life expectancy that is taken into account in fixing these damages is that of the child not the parents (though in some cases, and given the nature of the handicap, these children may not live a full life). But implicit is not as good as explicit!

This linking of the award to the *child's needs* can also be seen by the fact that the courts do not take into account what the parents could have spent to help the child but calculate the award by reference to its needs and not its parents means. Finally, the sheer size of the awards suggests that the courts are conscious of the need to provide proper compensation for the impaired child.

Yet the method of granting all this money to the parents rather than giving the child, itself, the awarded amounts remains unsatisfactory. For what if the parents obtain the award and then put the child in care? Have *they* not then been enriched and *it* denied the chance of a better living? And if the money is given to the parents (and calculated to last for as long as their obligation to maintain the child lasts i.e. until it reaches the age of eighteen), is not the child, once again, worse off than it would be had it received the money, itself? To these arguments one must add a third. In English law damages are awarded as lump sums at the end of the trial and not as annuities. Annuities stop when those entitled to them die. If the mother dies and the impaired child is still alive, it gets nothing for the remainder of its life. Thus, from that moment onwards, the state takes over; and we all know, as Frederick the Great of Prussia used to say, that the protective cloak of the state is warm but it is also small. Would it thus not be more honest to do what some American courts—*Turpin* v. *Sortini*, 31 Cal.3d 220, 643 P. 2d 954 (1982); *Procanik* v. *Cillo*, 478 A 2d 755 (1984); *Harbeson* v. *Parke-Davis, Inc.*, 656 P. 2d 483 (1983)—have done and give the child the money it needs to look after itself once the parental obligation has come to an end?

The correct inference from the size of awards of the recent English decisions is crucial. For if the arguments put forward above are correct, then part of the award made to the parents under their wrongful birth actions is, in effect, a claim for special damages by the child along the lines followed by the four American jurisdictions mentioned above. But by being disguised it may not be achieving the aim of the judges or, at any rate, of justice itself.

9. The periodic literature in the USA is growing (though some articles are worth consulting mainly for the references they provide and little more). For England see: Grubb, "Conceiving: A New Cause of Action?" Current Legal Problems, Special Issue (1988) 121 ff. In the USA, Capron's "Tort Liability and Genetic Counselling" 79 *Colum. L. Rev.* 619 (1979) is an oft-cited piece. See also Bopp, Bostrom and McKinney, "The 'Rights' and 'Wrongs' of Wrongful Birth and Wrongful Life: A Jurisprudential Analysis of Birth Related Torts", 27 *Duq. L. Rev.* 461 (1989); Collins, "An Overview and Analysis: Prenatal Torts, Preconception Torts, Wrongful Life, Wrongful Death and Wrongful Birth: Time for a New Framework" 22 *Journal of Family Law* 677 (1983/4); Note, "Wrongful Birth Actions: The Case Against Legislative Curtailment" 100 *Harv. L. Rev.* 2017 (1987); Note, "A Preference for Non-existence: Wrongful Life and a Proposed Tort of Genetic Malpractice" 55 *So. Cal. Law Rev.* 477 (1982); Note, "Legislative Prohibition of Wrongful Birth Actions" 44 *Wash. and Lee L. Rev.* 1331 (1987); Comment, "Meeting the 'Needs of the Living': A Child's Right to Bring a 'Wrongful Life' Action for Medical Malpractice in New Jersey: *Procanik* v. *Cillo*" 38 *Rutgers L. Rev.* 557 (1986); Hom, "Wrongful Conception: North Carolina's Newest Prenatal Tort Claim: *Jackson* v. *Bumgardner*" 65 *N. Carolina L. Rev.* 1077 (1987); Furrow, "Diminished Lives and Malpractice: Courts Stalled in Transition" [1982] *Law Med. Health Care* 100; Gallagher, "Wrongful Life: Should the Action be Allowed?" 47 *Louisiana L. Rev.* 1314 (1987); idem, "Tort Law: Wrongful Birth and Wrongful Life Actions: *Siemieniec* v. *Lutheran General Hospital*" 11 *Harv. J. of Law and Public Policy* 859 (1988); Jankowski, "Wrongful Birth and Wrongful Life Actions Arising from Negligent Genetic Counselling: The Need for Legislation Supporting Reproductive Choice", 17 *Fordham L. Journ.* 27 (1988–9); Kelly, "The Rightful Position in 'Wrongful Life' Actions", 42 *Hastings L J* 505 (1991); Rogers, "Wrongful Life and Wrongful Birth: Medical Malpractice in Genetic Counseling and Prenatal Testing", 33 *S. Carolina L. Rev.* 713 (1982); Annotation, "Recoverability of Compensatory Damages for Mental Anguish or Emotional Distress for Tortiously Causing Another's Birth", 74 ALR 4th 798 (1989); Strasser, "Misconceptions and Wrongful Births: A Call for a Principled Jurisprudence", 31 *Ariz. St. L. J.* 161 (1999); Strasser, "Wrongful Life, Wrongful Birth, Wrongful Death, and the Right to Treatment", 64 *Mo. L. Rev.* 29 (1999); Finally, a comparative examination of some English, French, and German decisions (and what they reveal about a "foreign system") can be found in Markesinis, "Reading Through a Foreign Judgment", *The Law of Obligations, Essays in Celebration of John Fleming* (eds. P. Cane and Jane Stapleton) (1998), pp. 261–283; Harrer, "Aspects of Failed Family Planning in the United States of America and Germany", 15 *J. Legal Med.* 89 (1994); Jackson, "Action for Wrongful Life, Wrongful Pregnancy, and Wrongful Birth in the United States and England", 17 *Loy. L.A. Int'l & Comp. L.J.* 535 (1995). *Procanik* v. *Cillo*, reproduced below as addendum 2, offers the best introduction to the subject.

Addendum 1

The terminology used by the courts is not always clear; indeed some courts have condemned the use of the word "wrongful" and have attempted to avoid labels altogether. See: *Burke* v. *Rivo* 406 Mass. 764, 551 NE 2d 1 (1990); *Viccaro* v. *Milunsky* 406 Mass. 777, 551 NE 2d 8 (1990). The (inexperienced) reader may also not realise that often many *different* claims are involved. The following may thus be of use:

1. *Wrongful life claim.* Action brought by the handicapped child; it includes among other things, a claim for pain and suffering and for extraordinary medical expenses. The first has failed everywhere; the second has succeeded in three States in the USA.

2. *Wrongful birth claim.* Brought by the parents in the above-mentioned situation and includes claims for emotional harm and medical expenses. The cost of bringing up the child tends to be the major item of such claims.

3. *Wrongful conception (or pregnancy) claim.* Brought by parents for the birth of a (usually) healthy but unplanned child.

4. *Wrongful death claims* (known in English law as the Fatal Accident Acts claims). Brought, in England, by the dependants of a deceased person—in most cases the breadwinner. In the USA claims for *speculative* dependency are allowed, though sometimes the award is made to compensate the loss of "future companionship".

5. *Parents' personal claims.* Often the parents of an injured person (typically a child) have their own claims, for example for shock for witnessing (or more controversially) of being told of the accident. So-called "loss of consortium" claims may be included in this category.

6. *Foetal injuries claims.* Typically to be made by a foetus once born alive. Jurisdictions which do not require "live birth", but content themselves with "viability" at the time of the injury, may allow these claims to be brought by the estate.

7. *Pre-conception claims.* Claims made by a child for an injurious act (e.g. defective blood transfusion) to the mother prior to conception.

Though awards made under these headings may often be low (by US standards at any rate), the *total* amount for all or most of these headings may soon mount up. Litigants (and some courts) are not always aware of the danger of double compensation. Thus, despite frequent references to appealing ideas and attractive ideals, gold-digging actions are possible if not, indeed, frequent.

Addendum 2

Procanik by Procanik v. *Cillo* 97 NJ 339, 478 A. 2d 755 (1984)

I. . . . the complaint contains three counts. In the first count, Peter, through his guardian *ad litem*, seeks damages for birth defects and impaired childhood; in the second count, his parents seek damages for emotional distress and extraordinary medical expenses attributable to Peter's defects; and in the third count, his parents assert a claim for malpractice against their former attorneys.

The defendant doctors, Joseph Cillo, Herbert Langer, and Ernest P Greenberg, are board-certified obstetricians and gynaecologists who apparently conduct a group practice. On 9 June 1977, during the first trimester of her pregnancy with Peter, Mrs Procanik consulted the defendant doctors and informed Dr Cillo "that she had recently been diagnosed as having measles but did not know if it was German measles". Dr Cillo examined Mrs Procanik and ordered "tests for German Measles, known as Rubella Titer Test". The results "were 'indicative of past infection of Rubella'". Instead of ordering further tests, Dr Cillo negligently interpreted the results and told Mrs Procanik that she "had nothing to worry about because she had become immune to German Measles as a child". In fact, the "past infection" disclosed by the tests was the German measles that had prompted Mrs Procanik to consult the defendant doctors.

Ignorant of what an accurate diagnosis would have disclosed, Mrs Procanik allowed her pregnancy to continue, and Peter was born on 26 December 1977. Shortly thereafter, on 16 January 1978, he was diagnosed as suffering from congenital rubella syndrome. As a result of the doctors' negligence, Mr and Mrs Procanik were deprived of the choice of terminating the pregnancy, and Peter was "born with multiple birth defects", including eye lesions, heart disease, and auditory defects. The infant plaintiff states further that "he has suffered because of his parents' impaired capacity to cope with his problems", and seeks damages for his pain and suffering and for his "impaired childhood".

In April 1983, while this matter was pending in the Appellate Division, Peter moved to amend the first count to assert a claim to recover, as special damages, the expenses he will incur as an adult for medical, nursing, and related health care services. In its opinion, the Appellate Division denied without prejudice leave to amend. Although this claim was not raised before the trial court and not considered by the Appellate Division, fairness, justice, and judicial efficiency persuade us to consider the claim for special damages.

The complaint, which was filed on 8 April 1981, contains two other counts. In the second count, Peter's parents seek damages for their emotional distress and for the extraordinary medical expenses attributable to Peter's birth defects. Before the trial court they stipulated, however, that they knew they had a potential cause of action by January 1978, nearly three years before instituting suit. The trial court ruled, therefore, that the parents' claim was barred by the two-year statute of limitations . . . Before us, however, the parents contend that their claim is derived from Peter's claim and that [the statute], which tolls the statute of limitations during infancy, protects their claim. Hence, the parents ask us to recognise their claim.

In the third count, the parents assert a claim for malpractice against their former attorneys, alleging that they consulted defendant attorney Harold A Sherman, who undertook to advise them of their legal rights. Mr Sherman consulted with defendant attorneys Greenstone, Greenstone & Naishuler, a professional corporation specialising in medical malpractice claims. After conferring with Mr Goldsmith of that firm, Mr Sherman advised the parents on 2 May 1979 that they did not have a cause of action, and he never informed them that this Court had granted certification in *Berman* v. *Allan* on 5 September 1978.

In *Berman*, 80 NJ 421, 404 A. 2d 8, which was decided on 26 June 1979, we recognised that parents may recover for emotional distress for the "wrongful birth" of a child born with birth defects. The defendant attorneys, however, never advised Mr and Mrs Procanik that they had a cause of action, and the two-year statute of limitations ran on their claim on 16 January 1980. The trial court did not rule on the attorney malpractice claim, and that issue is not before us.

II. In this case we survey again the changing landscape of family torts. See *Schroeder* v. *Perkel*, 87 NJ 53, 71, 432 A. 2d 834 (1981). Originally that landscape presented a bleak prospect both to children born with birth defects and to their parents. If a doctor negligently diagnosed or treated a pregnant woman who was suffering from a condition that might cause her to give birth to a defective child, neither the parents nor the child could maintain a cause of action against the negligent doctor. *Gleitman* v. *Cosgrove*, 49 NJ 22, 227 A. 2d 689 (1967).

Like the present case, *Gleitman* involved a doctor who negligently treated a pregnant woman who had contracted German measles in the first trimester of her pregnancy. Reasoning from the premise that the doctor did not cause the infant plaintiff's birth defects, the *Gleitman* Court found it impossible to compare the infant's condition if the defendant doctor had not been negligent with the infant's impaired condition as a result of the negligence. Measurement of "the value of life with impairments against the nonexistence of life itself" was, the Court declared, a logical impossibility. Id. at 28, 227, A. 2d 689. Consequently, the Court rejected the infant's claim.

The Court denied the parents' claim for emotional distress and the costs of caring for the infant, because of the impossibility of weighing the intangible benefits of parenthood against the emotional and monetary injuries sustained by them. Prevailing policy considerations, which included a reluctance to acknowledge the availability of abortions and the mother's right to choose to terminate her pregnancy, prevented the Court from awarding damages to a woman for not having an abortion. Another consideration was the Court's belief that "[i]t is basic to the human condition to seek life and hold on to it however heavily burdened". 49 NJ at 30, 227 A. 2d 689.

In *Berman*, the parents sought to recover for their emotional distress and for the expenses of raising a child born with Down's Syndrome. Relying on *Roe* v. *Wade*, above, 410 US 113, 93 S. Ct. 705, 35 L. Ed. 2d 147, the Court found that public policy now supports the right of a woman to choose to terminate a pregnancy. *Berman* v. *Allan*, above, 80 NJ at 431–2, 404 A. 2d 8. That finding eliminated one of the supports for the *Gleitman* decision—i.e. that public policy prohibited an award for depriving a woman of the right to choose whether to have an abortion. Finding that a trier of fact could place a dollar value on the parents' emotional suffering, the *Berman* Court concluded "that the monetary equivalent of this distress is an appropriate measure of the harm suffered by the parents". 80 NJ at 433, 404 A. 2d 8.

Nonetheless, the Court rejected the parents' claim for "medical and other expenses that will be incurred in order to properly raise, educate, and supervise the child". Id. at 432, 404 A. 2d 8. The Court reasoned that the parents wanted to retain "all the benefits inhering in the birth of the child—i.e. the love and joy they will experience as parents—while saddling defendants with enormous expenses attendant upon her rearing". Id. Such an award would be disproportionate to the negligence of the defendants and constitute a windfall to the parents. Id.

The *Berman* Court also declined to recognize a cause of action in an infant born with birth defects. Writing for the Court, Justice Pashman reasoned that even a life with serious defects is more valuable than non-existence, the alternative for the infant plaintiff if his mother chose to have an abortion. Id. at 429, 404 A. 2d 8.

More recently we advanced the parents' right to compensation by permitting recovery of the extraordinary expenses of raising a child born with cystic fibrosis, including medical, hospital, and pharmaceutical expenses. *Schroeder* v. *Perkel*, above, 87 NJ at 68–9, 432 A. 2d 834. No claim on behalf of the infant was raised in that case, id. at 61, 432 A. 2d 834, and we elected to defer consideration of such a claim until another day. Id. at 66, 432 A. 2d 834. That day is now upon us, and we must reconsider the right of an infant in a "wrongful life" claim to recover general damages for diminished childhood and pain and suffering, as well as special damages for medical care and the like.

III. [1, 2] The terms "wrongful birth" and "wrongful life" are but shorthand phrases that describe the causes of action of parents and children when negligent medical treatment deprives parents of the option to terminate a pregnancy to avoid the birth of a defective child. See *Schroeder* v. *Perkel*, above, 87 NJ at 75–6, 432 A. 2d 834 (Handler J concurring and dissenting). In the present context, "wrongful life" refers to a cause of action brought by or on behalf of a defective child who claims that but for the defendant doctor's negligent advice to or treatment of its parents, the child would not have been born. "Wrongful birth" applies to the cause of action of parents who claim that the negligent advice or treatment deprived them of the choice of avoiding conception or, as here, of terminating the pregnancy. See Comment, "'Wrongful Life': The Right Not To Be Born' 54 *Tul. L. Rev.* 480, 484–5 (1980); A Capron, "Tort Liability in Genetic Counseling" 79 *Colum. L. Rev.* 618, 630–57 (1979).

[3] Both causes of action are distinguishable from the situation where negligent injury to a foetus causes an otherwise normal child to be born in an impaired condition. See e.g. *Smith* v. *Brennan*, 31 NJ 353, 157 A. 2d 497 (1960); W Prosser, *Law of Torts* § 55 at 335–8 (4th edn., 1971). In the present case, the plaintiffs do not allege that the negligence of the defendant doctors caused the congenital rubella syndrome from which the infant plaintiff suffers. Neither do plaintiffs claim that the infant ever had a chance to be a normal child. The essence of the infant's claim is that the defendant doctors wrongfully deprived his mother of information that would have prevented his birth.

Analysis of the infant's cause of action begins with the determination whether the defendant doctors owed a duty to him. The defendant doctors do not deny they owed a duty to the infant plaintiff, and we find such a duty exists. See *Berman* v. *Allan*, above, 80 NJ at 444, 404 A. 2d 8 (Handler J concurring and dissenting); *Gleitman* v. *Cosgrove*, above, 49 NJ at 50, 227 A. 2d 689 (Jacobs J. dissenting). In evaluating the infant's cause of action, we assume, furthermore, that the defendant doctors were negligent in treating the mother. Moreover, we assume that their negligence deprived the parents of the choice of terminating the pregnancy and of preventing the birth of the infant plaintiff.

Notwithstanding recognition of the existence of a duty and its breach, policy considerations have led this Court in the past to decline to recognise any cause of action in an infant for his wrongful life. The threshold problem has been the assertion by infant plaintiffs not that they should not have been born without defects, but that they should not have been born at all. *Gleitman v. Cosgrove*, above, 49 NJ at 28, 227 A. 2d 689. The essence of the infant's cause of action is that its very life is wrongful. *Berman v. Allen*, above, 80 NJ at 427, 404 A. 2d 8. Resting on the belief that life, no matter how burdened, is preferable to non-existence, the *Berman* Court stated that the infant "has not suffered any damage cognisable at law by being brought into existence". Id. at 429, 404 A. 2d 8. Although the premise for this part of the *Berman* decision was the absence of cognisable damages, the Court continued to be troubled, as it was in *Gleitman*, by the problem of ascertaining the measure of damages. Id. at 428, 404 A. 2d 8.

The courts of other jurisdictions have also struggled with the issues of injury and damages when faced with suits for wrongful life. . . .

Even when this Court declined to recognise a cause of action for wrongful life in *Gleitman* and *Berman*, dissenting members urged recognition of that claim. . . . Extending through these opinions is an awareness that damages would be appropriate if they were measurable by acceptable standards.

Recently we recognised that extraordinary medical expenses incurred by parents on behalf of a birth-defective child were predictable, certain, and recoverable. *Schroeder v. Perkel*, above, 87 NJ at 68–9, 432 A. 2d 834. In reaching that conclusion, we discussed the interdependence of the interests of parents and children in a family tort:

The foreseeability of injury to members of a family other than one immediately injured by the wrongdoing of another must be viewed in light of the legal relationships among family members. A family is woven of the fibres of life; if one strand is damaged, the whole structure may suffer. The filaments of family life, although individually spun, create a web of interconnected legal interests. This Court has recognised that a wrongdoer who causes a direct injury to one member of the family may indirectly damage another. [Id. at 63–4, 432 A. 2d 834.]

When a child requires extraordinary medical care, the financial impact is felt not just by the parents, but also by the injured child. As a practical matter, the impact may extend beyond the injured child to his brothers or sisters. Money that is spent for the health care of one child is not available for the clothes, food, or college education of another child.

Recovery of the cost of extraordinary medical expenses by either the parents or the infant, but not both, is consistent with the principle that the doctor's negligence vitally affects the entire family. . . .

[4] Law is more than an exercise in logic, and logical analysis, although essential to a system of ordered justice, should not become an instrument of injustice. Whatever logic inheres in permitting parents to recover for the cost of extraordinary medical care incurred by a birth-defective child, but in denying the child's own right to recover those expenses, must yield to the injustice of that result. The right to recover the often crushing burden of extraordinary expenses visited by an act of medical malpractice should not depend on the "wholly fortuitous circumstance of whether the parents are available to sue". *Turpin v. Sortini*, above, 31 Cal. 3d at 328, 643 P. 2d at 965, 182 Cal. Rptr. at 348.

[5] The present case proves the point. Here, the parents' claim is barred by the statute of limitations. Does this mean that Peter must forgo medical treatment for his blindness, deafness, and retardation? We think not. His claim for the medical expenses attributable to his birth defects is reasonably certain, readily calculable, and of a kind daily determined by judges and juries. We hold that a child or his parents may recover special damages for extraordinary

medical expenses incurred during infancy, and that the infant may recover those expenses during his majority.

Our decision is consistent with recent decisions of the Supreme Courts of California and Washington. The Supreme Court of California has held that special damages related to the infant's birth defects may be recovered in a wrongful life suit. *Turpin* v. *Sortini*, above, 31 Cal. 3d at 238, 643 P. 2d at 965, 182 Cal. Rptr. at 348. Following *Turpin*, the Supreme Court of Washington has held that either the parents or the child may recover special damages for medical and other extraordinary expenses incurred during the infant's minority, and that the child may recover for those costs to be incurred during majority. *Harbeson* v. *Parke-Davis*, 98 Wash. 2d 460, 656 P. 2d 483 (1983).

In restricting the infant's claim to one for special damages, we recognise that our colleagues, Justice Schreiber and Justice Handler, disagree with us and with each other. From the premise that "man does not know whether non-life would have been preferable to an impaired life", at 369, Justice Schreiber concludes that a child does not have a cause of action for wrongful life and, therefore, that it is "unfair and unjust to charge the doctors with the infant's medical expenses". At 370 Justice Handler reaches a diametrically opposite conclusion. He would allow the infant to recover not only his medical expenses, but also general damages for his pain and suffering and for his impaired childhood.

We find, however, that the infant's claim for pain and suffering and for a diminished childhood presents insurmountable problems. The philosophical problem of finding that such a defective life is worth less than no life at all has perplexed not only Justice Schreiber, but such other distinguished members of this Court as Chief Justice Weintraub, *Gleitman*, above, 49 NJ at 63, 227 A. 2d 689 (Weintraub CJ dissenting in part), Justice Proctor, *Gleitman*, above, 49 NJ at 30, 227 A. 2d 689, and Justice Pashman, *Berman* v. *Allan*, above, 80 NJ at 429, 404 A. 2d 8. We need not become preoccupied, however, with these metaphysical considerations. Our decision to allow the recovery of extraordinary medical expenses is not premised on the concept that non-life is preferable to an impaired life, but is predicated on the needs of the living. We seek only to respond to the call of the living for help in bearing the burden of their affliction.

[6] Sound reasons exist not to recognize a claim for general damages. Our analysis begins with the unfortunate fact that the infant plaintiff never had a chance of being born as a normal, healthy child. Tragically, his only choice was a life burdened with his handicaps or no life at all. The congenital rubella syndrome that plagues him was not caused by the negligence of the defendant doctors; the only proximate result of their negligence was the child's birth.

The crux of the problem is that there is no rational way to measure non-existence or to compare non-existence with the pain and suffering of his impaired existence. Whatever theoretical appeal one might find in recognising a claim for pain and suffering is outweighed by the essentially irrational and unpredictable nature of that claim. Although damages in a personal injury action need not be calculated with mathematical precision, they require at their base some modicum of rationality.

Underlying our conclusion is an evaluation of the capability of the judicial system, often proceeding in these cases through trial by jury, to appraise such a claim. Also at work is an appraisal of the role of tort law in compensating injured parties, involving as that role does, not only reason, but also fairness, predictability, and even deterrence of future wrongful acts. In brief, the ultimate decision is a policy choice summoning the most sensitive and careful judgment.

From that perspective it is simply too speculative to permit an infant plaintiff to recover for emotional distress attendant on birth defects when that plaintiff claims he would be better off if he had not been born. Such a claim would stir the passions of jurors about the nature and value of life, the fear of non-existence, and about abortion. That mix is more than the judicial system can digest. We believe that the interests of fairness and justice are better served through more predictably measured damages—the cost of the extraordinary medical expenses necessitated by the infant plaintiff's handicaps. Damages so measured are not subject to the same wild swings as a claim for pain and suffering and will carry a sufficient sting to deter future acts of medical malpractice.

As speculative and uncertain as is a comparison of the value of an impaired life with non-existence, even more problematic is the evaluation of a claim for diminished childhood. The essential proof in such a claim is that the doctor's negligence deprives the parents of the knowledge of the condition of the foetus. The deprivation of that information precludes the choice of terminating the pregnancy by abortion and leaves the parents unprepared for the birth of a defective child, a birth that causes them emotional harm. The argument proceeds that the parents are less able to love and care for the child, who thereby suffers an impaired childhood. *Schroeder* v. *Perkel*, above, 87 NJ at 72, 432 A. 2d 834 (Handler J concurring and dissenting) *Berman* v. *Allan*, above, 80 NJ at 434, 404 A. 2d 8 (Handler J concurring and dissenting).

[7, 8] Several considerations lead us to decline to recognise a cause of action for impaired childhood. At the outset, we note the flaw in such a claim in those instances in which the parents assert not that the information would have prepared them for the birth of the defective child, but that they would have used the information to prevent that birth. Furthermore, even its advocates recognise that a claim for "the kind of injury suffered by the child in this context may not be readily divisible from that suffered by her wronged parents". *Berman* v. *Allan*, above, 80 NJ at 445, 404 A. 2d 8 (Handler J concurring and dissenting). We believe the award of the cost of the extraordinary medical care to the child or the parents, when combined with the right of the parents to assert a claim for their own emotional distress, comes closer to filling the dual objectives of a tort system: the compensation of injured parties and the deterrence of future wrongful conduct.

The final issue is whether the time-barred claim of Mr and Mrs Procanik may be revived as a claim that derives from the infant's timely action. At one time Mr and Mrs Procanik had independent claims for their emotional distress, *Berman* v. *Allan*, above, 80 NJ 421, 404 A. 2d 8, and for the extraordinary medical expenses arising from Peter's multiple birth defects. *Schroeder* v. *Perkel*, above, 87 NJ 53, 432 A. 2d 834.

[9, 10] The trial court ruled that the parents' claims were barred by the two-year period of limitations contained in NJSA 2A: 14–2. Although the parents recognise that their claim, if viewed as independent, is time-barred, they contend that the claim should be viewed as derivative from the infant's claim and, therefore, that it should not have been dismissed. In making that contention, they rely on NJSA 2A: 14–2.1, which pertains to a parent who "has a claim for damages suffered by him because of an injury to a minor child caused by the wrongful act, neglect or default of any person . . .". A parent in such a case may commence an action "within the same period of time as provided" for the commencement of the minor's action. Just three years ago, however, in *Schroeder* v. *Perkel*, above, 87 NJ 53, 432 A. 2d 834, we declared that the parents' claim was independent from that of the child's. The defect in the parents' argument in the present case is that their right to recover is not "because of injury" to their child, but because of direct injury to their own independent rights. Consequently, the parents' right to recover is not derivative from the claim of the child and is, therefore, barred by NJSA 2A: 14–2.

Our decision today recognises Peter's right to recover the extraordinary expenses necessitated by his birth defects and also recognizes that the parents, even if they had instituted a timely action, could not recover a second time for those expenses. Finally, Peter's right to recover the costs of his health care is separate from his parents' claim for their own pain and suffering, and recognition of Peter's right to recover does not resuscitate the expired independent claim of the parents.

HANDLER J. concurring in part and dissenting in part.

[An interesting dissent which is not reproduced here because of lack of space but one which merits careful reading.]

4. UNWANTED PREGNANCIES FOLLOWING FAILED STERILISATIONS OR FAILED ABORTIONS

Case 10

BUNDESGERICHTSHOF (SIXTH CIVIL SENAT) 28 MARCH 1995
BGHZ 129, 178 = NJW 1995, 1609

Facts

The claimants claim compensation for a failed abortion in September 1979 in connection with the birth of their child E on the 5 April 1980. The operation was carried out by the defendant gynaecologist on emergency grounds (§ 218a (2) no. 3 of the Criminal Code in the version of the 15th Criminal Amendment Act of the 18 May 1976 (hereafter called § 218a of the Criminal Code, old version)). The claimants say the defendant made mistakes in treatment and seek, amongst other things, compensation for maintenance expenditure on E. The appeal court dismissed the claim on the 26 February 1985. The Senate quashed this judgment on the 15 April 1986 and referred the case back to the appeal court for another hearing and decision. After further elucidation of the matter, the appeal court on the 16 January 1991 amongst other things ordered the defendant to pay DM 188 a month from June to December 1988 as maintenance compensation, but rejected the rest of the claim. The Senate on the 25 February 1992 referred the case back to the appeal court, as claims to compensation for further material harm had been disallowed. The parties agreed to settle the main issue by payment of DM 4936 with 4 precent interest from the 5 February 1991, but the claimants applied for interest on this sum at 4 per cent from the 15 March 1982 to the 4 February 1991 and for payment for E of maintenance increasing incrementally to the end of E's eighteenth year. They also asked for a declaration that the defendant was obliged from then on to make periodic payments in accordance with the then current Standard Subsistence Order, so as to relieve the claimants from their duty of maintenance if E could not work or received long term academic or vocational education, and to compensate them for all additional financial burdens in connection with the birth of E, insofar as third parties had no duty to provide an indemnity for these. The first claimant's claim is limited to a sum equal to the monthly interest on the owner-occupied flat and expenses exceeding the normal duty of maintenance.

The appeal court awarded the interest claimed and otherwise rejected the claimants' appeal. The claimants' appeal in law was unsuccessful.

Reasons

I. The appeal court states that, having regard to the judgment of the Federal Constitutional Court of the 28 May 1993 (reference omitted), doubts existed about following the case law of the *BGH* so far on failed abortion in respect of the claims made in the present proceedings. It was in fact to be deduced from this judgment that expenditure on maintenance for an undesired healthy child could not in any case be the basis of a claim to compensation, for constitutional reasons (Article 1 of the Basic Law). Therefore the material claim to compensation on defective performance of the doctor's contract in cases of this kind was limited to the payment back of the remuneration given and to compensation for the woman for the failed abortion. Nor could any different view be derived from the judgment of the deciding Senate of the 16 November 1993 (references omitted) which instead left open whether contracts about abortions could still be the basis of a claim for compensation within the framework of the earlier abortion time limit or in cases of so-called emergency grounds . . .

II. These statements withstand the challenges in the appeal in law in the end result.

1. (a) The deciding Senate admittedly does not agree with the appeal court in its view, referring to the judgment of the Federal Constitutional Court of the 28 May 1993, that Article 1 para. 1 of the Basic Law prevented the claimants in the present case from asking for compensation for their burden of maintaining their son E from the defendant doctor, because it violated the basic right of the child to respect for his human dignity to conceive of the duty of the parents to provide maintenance for him as harm. Certainly Article 1 of the Basic Law prevents the existence of a child being assessed as harm. However, in cases in which the doctor has bound himself by contract to avoid the burden of maintenance resulting from a child, the classification of this burden as harm to the other party to the contract for which he must provide compensation does not lead to such an assessment. The deciding Senate has given more precise reasons for this in its judgment of the 16 November 1993. It also explains that the statements of the Federal Constitutional Court in the judgment of the 28 May 1993 do not acquire any binding force on this point. The Senate makes reference to this.

(b) Nevertheless the judgment on appeal still stands in the end result. The basis of the case law of the deciding Senate so far on such claims was the view that a contract for the undertaking of an abortion where one of the grounds described in § 218a of the Criminal Code, old version, here the so-called emergency ground under paragraph 2 no. 3, was present, could be effective in law and in the case of defective performance could be the starting point for a claim for compensation in civil law (references omitted) . . .

In the light of this interpretation of the Constitution, by which the deciding Senate considers itself to be bound, the initial question of whether and to what extent the contract about the abortion gave rise to legal consequences, which has so far been given a positive answer by the Senate in the present case, needs fresh examination.

(aa) Until the decision of the Federal Constitutional Court of the 28 May 1993, and therefore also in the present case, the Senate proceeded on the basis that abortion in order to prevent the danger of an emergency for the pregnant woman was not only unpunishable but also legal if it fulfilled the material prerequisites of § 218 (2) no. 3, (3) of the Criminal Code, old version, the pregnant woman had taken advice in accordance with § 218b of the Criminal Code, old version, and the emergency had been established by a second doctor in accordance with § 219 (1) of the Criminal Code, old version, as well as by the doctor entrusted with the abortion itself. In this connection the Senate has attached central importance to the findings of the doctors concerned for affirming the presence of such a ground . . .

(bb) These findings do not suffice to allow the intended abortion to appear as legal according to the interpretation of the Basic Law by the Federal Constitutional Court in its judgment of the 28 May 1993, which binds the courts. It is true that according to this (reference omitted) an abortion on the basis of a social or personal psychological emergency in respect of the pregnant woman can exceptionally be declared by the legislator not only to be unpunishable but also to be legal. However the prerequisite for this is the imposition of a burden on the pregnant woman which requires such a degree of sacrifice of her own basic human values that the duty to carry a child to full term cannot be required of her. As the Federal Constitutional Court has further stated, this only applies for emergencies of the kind under consideration here if the severity of the social or personal psychological conflict is so clearly recognisable that—looked at from the viewpoint of unreasonableness—congruity is preserved with the other grounds, namely medical and criminological grounds, and even (assuming it is sufficiently precisely defined) the ground of abnormality of the embryo. Such an exceptional state of affairs could additionally, so the Federal Constitutional Court states, only provide justification if its prerequisites have been assessed and established, having regard to the claim to protection of the unborn human life, by the courts or by third parties whom the state can trust by virtue of their special position of duty and whose decisions are not beyond any review by the state (reference omitted).

(cc) On this basis an emergency ground justifying the abortion cannot be assumed on the ground of the stress syndrome claimed by the second claimant. Admittedly the deciding Senate in the present case, as on other occasions, proceeded on the basis that for the emergency ground, as an exceptional state of affairs justifying the abortion, requirements were to be placed on the situation of conflict for the pregnant woman which were comparable to those for the medical ground or the ground of abnormality of the embryo. The Senate has particularly emphasised this by the reference to the judgment of the Federal Constitutional Court of the 25 February 1975 (reference omitted). However the Federal Constitutional Court has in the judgment of the 28 May 1993 asked for special requirements in respect of the guarantee for these prerequisites being really fulfilled in the actual case. These requirements do not permit such an emergency ground to be assumed simply from the carrying out of counselling and medical examination procedures until proof of the contrary by the defendant doctor. Instead, concrete findings of an exceptional situation, which is clearly demonstrated as such for the benefit of the courts as well, are necessary here. The appeal court has however not been able to make such findings even after repeated examination of the claimants' arguments. It is not evident that it had made any requirements in this connection which were legally incorrect.

(dd) Therefore it must be assumed that the abortion to which the defendant committed himself was not justified by an emergency ground, even on fulfilment of the prerequisites for freedom from punishment. Whether in the present case the contract is therefore to be regarded as void under §§ 134 or 138 of the BGB or whether it fulfills the prerequisites under which, according to the judgment of the Federal Constitutional Court of the 28 May 1993 (reference omitted), these provisions, in the case of defective performance, may not on constitutional grounds in principle stand in the way of more precisely described contract law sanctions, can remain open. In any case, the contract cannot be the basis for a contractual claim for compensation, at least at the economic level, to restore the result which the parties intended by the contract, which was avoidance by the claimants of the social and economic burdens of another child, which is disapproved by the legal order under the given circumstances. Therefore the basis is removed from the claimants' request for compensation for their maintenance expenses . . .

Notes to Case 10

1. In the (former) West Germany abortion was regulated since 1976 by §§ 218–219d of the German Criminal Code and is legal—broadly speaking—if: (*a*) the continuation of the pregnancy poses serious danger to the life or physical or mental health of the woman which cannot be averted

in any other reasonable way; (*b*) the child is likely to be born with severe defects which would make it unreasonable for the woman to continue with the pregnancy; (*c*) the pregnancy was the result of an illegal act on the woman and (*d*) the pregnancy results in serious hardship that cannot be otherwise avoided. For a translation of the relevant texts see 27 IDHL 562 (1976); and for an excellent discussion of some of the issues see Mary Ann Glendon's *Abortion and Divorce in Western Law* (1987). On the other hand, in what used to be East Germany, a much more liberal regime prevailed until recently with the consequence that in practice the State met all such expenses. When in 1990 Germany was re-united, the regime in the East was expressly retained in force by the re-unification treaties until such time as a new law was passed by the German Parliament. Such an Act was, indeed, passed in 1992, but the (mainly) Catholic Government of the State of Bavaria and 249 deputies of the ruling Christian Democratic Party immediately challenged its constitutionality. On 28 May 1993 the Constitutional Court ruled that abortion was in principle illegal, though it allowed it to remain unpunishable if carried out during the first three months of the pregnancy and provided certain carefully laid down guidelines had been observed. Among these is the obligation to seek "counseling" before the operation can be carried out, the purposes of such counseling being to try and dissuade the woman from proceeding with her plan to abort. The decision has sparked off a debate similar to that found in the USA (though, probably, not of the same intensity). It has also fuelled the fear that its main effect will be to deny State funds to clinics carrying out abortions for the poor thus making them available only to those who can afford the $250–$700 that are usually required for the operation. The decision, of 28 May 1993, long and fairly legalistic in tone, has been reported in BVerfGE 88, 203 = NJW 1993, 1751 = EuGRZ 1993, 229. It has spawned critical articles (e.g. Hermes and Walther, "Schwangerschaftsabbruch—zwischen Recht und Unrecht" *NJW* 1993, 2337—2347) as well as the passing of a further law attempting a complex political compromise (*Schwangeren-und Familienhilfeänderungsgesetz* of 21 August 1995, BGBl 1995. I. 1050), which, happily, falls to be discussed by specialist works, see Schönke/Schröder *Strafgesetzbuch Kommentar* (26th edn. 2001) Vorbem. §§ 218 ff. nos. 1–54 for details and references.

2. The principal case (case 10) shows that even after the reform of abortion law and the more conservative approach adopted by the BVerfG in its second abortion decision of 28 May 1993 (abortion is as a general rule illegal but tolerated for most purposes) the cost of maintenance of the child can be claimed if the (failed) abortion would have been legal. This is only exceptionally the case, as for instance if the abortion is necessary to save the mother, on eugenic grounds, or in other cases of necessity which have the same quality as the two aforementioned: BGHZ 129, 178 (confirmed in BGH NJW 2000, 1782). In all other cases, no compensation can be obtained since the purpose of the contract of abortion is not recognised by the law. The mother's pain and suffering may also be compensated—a point which many academics find grotesque. (Thus, Larenz/ Canaris, *op. cit.*, p. 383. Contrast, however, how this element of damage was the first to be recognised in the USA.) The case on failed abortion which was reproduced in the 3rd edn. on p. 166 (BGH NJW 1985, 671) must be read with caution in the light of the more restrictive approach advocated in case 10. Yet, at a basic level, the approach has remained the same. Liability for the economic consequences of the unsuccessful abortion arises in principle, provided that the abortion is "permitted" or, to be more precise, is "legally recognised". What has changed therefore is that there are now fewer instances of legally recognised abortions, a fact highlighted by case 10. The court's stance should however be contrasted with the even more restrictive second abortion decision of the BVerfG (case 7) which denied compensation altogether. BGH NJW 1985, 671 also considers the difficult point of whether—time permitting—the mother may be under an obligation to submit herself to a second abortion. The academic literature on all these points is divided. See, for example, Deutsch, *NJW* 1985, 674; Stürner, *FamRZ*, 753; Waibl, *NJW* 1987, 1513.

3. In BGH NJW 1985, 2749 (wrongful conception) the mother/plaintiff, who had had four previous complicated pregnancies, decided to interrupt her fifth pregnancy when she discovered it in the eighth week. The abortion was unsuccessful but by the time this was discovered it was too late to have a second abortion. The pregnancy was uneventful and resulted in a healthy child being born. The mother's claim for pain and suffering was successful but her attempt to obtain

maintenance failed on the ground that the purpose of the contract (to carry out an abortion) was to prevent injury to the mother and the child and no such injury had, in fact, resulted. (The same solution would have been reached if the purpose of the abortion was an eugenic one but the child that had been born was healthy.) A similar point arose in BGH NJW 2000, 1782. The mother was examined in order to determine whether she was pregnant because—and this was crucial—she had to undergo an operation which could have had harmful effects to the child. Her pregnancy was not noticed, but no injury to the child occurred in the course of the operation that did ensue. The parents claimed that had they known about the pregnancy they would have decided to have an abortion on eugenic grounds. Their claim for maintenance costs failed. The BGH argued that under the circumstances, the cost of maintenance was not a head of damage that was included in the protective scope of the specific duty owed to the mother. The object of the examination was to eliminate health risks resulting out of the operation. As a matter of fact these risks did not materialize since the child was born healthy. We can see here how the *Schutzzwecklehre* (focusing on the scope of the duty owed) can be successfully used to exclude heads of damages that are too remote, see chapter 2 section A5(b).

4. Another instance of "wrongful conception" is found in "failed sterilization" cases resulting in unwanted pregnancies. However, while since 1993 a more restrictive approach is applied in failed abortion cases, depending on whether the abortion could be legally recognised, failed sterilisation cases have not been affected by the second abortion decision of the Constitutional Court (BVerfGE 88, 203, case 7). The first decision where the BGH refused to follow the dicta of the BVerfG in case 7 was BGHZ 124, 128 (case 8). It concerned a wrongful birth claim (the mother became pregnant after the defendant had failed to diagnose a specific genetic disposition). The parents were in principle allowed to recover full maintenance costs. However, the court also stressed that the case would have been decided in the same way had the pregnancy resulted out of a failed sterilisation. The scope of the duty owed to the parents was the same, namely to prevent the economic burden of raising a child. The sterilisation aims at reducing the family's living costs and therefore the costs of maintaining the child are recoverable. These remarks were obiter but, more recently, the Federal Court (BGH 27 June 1995, NJW 1995, 2407) expressly allowed damages. Thus, once again the BGH has refused to be budged on this issue by the views of the Second Senate of the Constitutional Court. Prior to that case, the BGH had repeatedly allowed recovery by parents of expenses connected with the upbringing of a healthy child born after a sterilisation attempt. (See the two leading decisions of 18 March 1980, BGHZ 76, 249 and 259; confirmed in e.g. BGH NJW 1981, 630; NJW 1981, 2002; NJW 1984, 2625; NJW 1992, 2961.) Finally, the issue of failed sterilisation came before the First Senate of the Constitutional Court in case 9: BVerfGE 96, 375. One of the two constitutional complaints (namely 1 BvR 479/92) concerned a failed sterilisation the purpose of which was family planning. The First Senate of the BVerfG held that awarding the full cost of maintenance to the parents in cases of failed sterilizations did not violate the dignity of the child. It expressly approved of the jurisprudence of the BGH. It should be noted that all these cases concerned failed sterilisations leading to the birth of a *healthy* child. The result and reasoning of these German decisions could not be more different from Lord Steyn's approach in the *Tayside* case reproduced as *Addendum*, below. Yet, this topic is so inherently difficult, that the sketch attempted in this section, cannot be completed without mentioning the fact that divisions exist even within the Germanic world. Thus in a judgment handed down in 1999, the Austrian Supreme Court, while following German law in cases where the child born is impaired, chose to strike out in a different direction and refuse the parents maintenance costs in the case of a healthy but "unwanted" child. (OGH, 25 May 1999, JBl 1999, 593; and for a (comparative) commentary Bernat, "Unerwünschte Geburt und Arzthaftung; der österreichische 'case of first impression' vor dem Hintergrund der anglo-amerikanischen Rechtsentwicklung", *Festschrift Heinz Krejci zum 60. Geburtstag*, (2001), 1041–1077.)

5. American courts have also uniformly awarded damages for failed sterilisations. *Emerson* v. *Magendantz*, 689 A 2d 409 (R.I. 1997), contains a fairly exhaustive review of the case law of most of the States. But it also reveals that American courts have considered three models when it comes

to fixing the level of damages. The vast majority of States opt for a "limited" recovery which means that they limit compensation to the medical expenses of the failed sterilisation, hospital expenses for the pregnancy, costs of subsequent sterilisation (where this occurs), lost wages during the above periods and, occasionally, emotional distress. Three States—Arizona (*Univ. of Arizona Health Sciences Center. v. Superior Cour*, 667 P. 2d 1294 (1983), Connecticut (*Ochs v. Borrelli*, 445 A 2d 883 (1982), and Massachusetts (*Burke v. Rivo*, 551 NE 2d 1 (1990)—allow full recovery. This includes the cost of rearing the child but these States also expect the courts to balance these costs (and reduce the damages) to take into account the benefits—emotional and financial—of having the child. (Severely criticised by the House of Lords in *McFarlane v. Tayside Health Board* [2000] 2 AC 59. On the other hand, the Dutch Supreme Court recently took the view that a mother/claimant in a failed contraception case could claim maintenance costs (as well as damages for an loss of personal income resulting from her reasonably giving up her job in order to look after her child). But money thus obtained from the defendant was not subject to a reduction because of the pleasures associated with having the child. Hoge Raad, 21 February 1997, NJ 1999, 145. A translation of the key passages can be found in van Gerven, *Tort Law*, 2nd edn., pp. 134–5.) Finally, two States—Wisconsin (*Marciniak v. Lundborg*, 450 NW 2d 243 (1990) and New Mexico (*Lovelace Medical Ctr. v. Mendez*, 805 P. 2d. 603 (1991)—have gone even further and have allowed full recovery of foreseeable costs *without* demanding a "balancing" exercise (to take into account the said benefits.) (On all this see 83 A.L.R. 3rd 15, 3a 2000).

6. English law, as well, has experienced difficulties with this topic. In *Scuriaga v. Powell* (1979) 123 SJ 406, a negligently performed abortion failed to terminate the plaintiff's pregnancy and, as a result, she gave birth to a healthy child. The court took the view that she was entitled to damages for loss of earnings, for pain and suffering, and for diminution of her marriage prospects. In *Udale v. Bloomsbury Area Health Authority* [1983] 1 WLR 1098, which had analogous facts, the mother was allowed damages for pain and suffering and discomfort but was denied damages for the cost of rearing the child until it was 16. The main reason for this was the metaphysical argument that it was impossible to value the life of the child in order to set it off against the considerable financial disadvantages that its unwanted birth brought to its family. On the other hand, a more recent English case—*Thake v. Maurice* [1985] 2 All ER 513—granted to the parents of a healthy child, born after an unsuccessful vasectomy operation, the cost of its upkeep. Adopting a reasoning which is very similar to that of the majority in *Sherlock v. Stillwater Clinic*, 260 NW 2d 169, 174–5 (Minn.1977), Peter Pain J held that the birth of a healthy child was not always "a blessing" (p. 526). Other cases followed and mirrored the difficulties experienced by other systems. The uncertainty was finally resolved in 1999 when the House of Lords in *McFarlane v. Tayside Health Board* [2000] 2 AC 59, reproduced in part as *Addendum* opted for the view that currently prevails in the USA (and denied to the plaintiffs the costs of rearing their child.) The judgments are noted for their use of the comparative method, which Lord Steyn was quick to praise as "providing the inestimable value of sharpening our focus on the weight of competing considerations." On this and related matters see: Grubb, "Conceiving: A New Cause of Action?", Current Legal Problems, Special Issue, (1988) 121 ff.; Reichman, "Damages in Tort for Wrongful Conception: Who Bears the Cost of Raising the Child?" 3 *Sydney L. Rev.* 568 (1985).

In *McFarlane v. Tayside Health Board* [2000] 2 AC 59, the House of Lords had to deal with a case of a negligently performed sterilisation which led to the birth of a *healthy* child. The parents' attempt to claim its maintenance costs failed. Irreconcilable dicta from five law lords—some of wider philosophical import—have re-opened the debate about failed sterilisations. The point fell to be decided by the Court of Appeal in *P v. St. James and Seacroft University Hospital NHS Trust* ([2001] 3 All ER 97). The view there taken was that Lord Steyn's dicta applied only to healthy children and not impaired ones, whose parents were thus entitled to claim substantial damages. However, the award of compensation was limited to the special upbringing costs associated with rearing a child with a serious disability. (Likewise, the issues are also relevant in wrongful birth actions on which see note 8 to cases 6 to 9, above. Presumably, the same principles would apply to failed abortions—where *impaired* children are concerned.)

It seems questionable whether such a distinction can or should be made. In the end it rests on the fact that in *Tayside* Lord Steyn held on principles of "distributive justice" that "ordinary people" would not regard awarding compensation for bringing up a healthy child as necessary, while the court in *Seacroft* held that on such principles "ordinary people" would consider it to be "fair" for the law to make an award (e.g. *Seacroft* para. no. 50). So far there seems to be no decision of the BGH which, like the *Seacroft* case, concerned a failed sterilisation leading to a seriously disabled child. The cases referred to above (note no. 4) dealt with the birth of a healthy child. However, it can be stated with some confidence that a German court would have also awarded damages in a case like *Seacroft*. Dicta in case 8, BGHZ 124, 128, suggest that it is irrelevant whether the child is born healthy or whether the failed sterilisation leads to an impaired child. The decisive issue is whether the economic burden is included in the ambit of the duty owed to the parents. For, as the court put it, "If under such contracts the doctor makes a mistake, which leads to the birth of the child, his liability includes the contractual partner's release from economic burdens that the contract with the doctor was aiming to avoid. But the measure of damages remains the same whether or not the purpose of the sterilisation or the abortion was to prevent the birth of a disabled child. For according to the intention of contracting parties, the area of protection covered by the consulting contract regularly also includes the financial burden for a heavily disabled child, which the parents are anxious to avoid for themselves as well as for the child. As the Senate explained in its opinion in BGHZ 89, 95, 105, these maintenance costs cannot be split into one part that covers the parents obligations under family law to a hypothetically healthy child and another that depends on the child's disability. The necessary costs for the livelihood of a heavily disabled child cannot be separated into two parts."

Addendum

McFarlane v. *Tayside Health Board* House of Lords (Scotland) [2000] 2 AC 59

LORD STEYN.

My Lords, a surgeon wrongly and negligently advised a husband and wife that a vasectomy had rendered the husband infertile. Acting on his advice they ceased to take contraceptive precautions. The wife became pregnant and gave birth to a healthy child. The question is what damages, if any, the parents are in principle entitled to recover.

It may be helpful to state at the outset the nature and shape of the case before the House. First, a distinction must be made between two types of claims which can arise from the failure of a sterilisation procedure, resulting in the birth of a child. There is the action (if permitted) for "wrongful life" brought by a disadvantaged or disabled child for damage to himself arising from the fact of his birth. The present case does not fall within this category. It is what in the literature is called an action for "wrongful birth." It is an action by parents of an unwanted child for damage resulting to them from the birth of the child. Secondly, the claim before the House is framed in delict [i.e. in tort]. Counsel cited observations to the effect that it is immaterial whether such an action is brought in contract or in delict. The correctness of this assumption may depend on the nature of the term of the contract alleged to have been breached. Usually, since a contract of services is involved, it may be an obligation to take reasonable care. On the other hand, the term may be expressed more stringently and may amount to a warranty of an outcome. It is unnecessary in the present case to consider whether different considerations may arise in such cases. My views are confined to claims in delict. Thirdly, the claim is brought under the extended *Hedley Byrne* principle (*Hedley Byrne & Co Ltd* v. *Heller & Partners Ltd* [1964] AC 465) as explained in *Henderson* v. *Merrett Syndicates Ltd* [1995] 2 AC 145 and *Williams* v. *Natural Life Health Foods Ltd* [1998] 1 WLR 830 that is, it is based on an assumption of responsibility by the doctor who gave the negligent advice.

The unwanted child

In 1989 Mr and Mrs McFarlane already had four children. They decided to move to a bigger house. They needed a larger mortgage. In order to meet the increased financial commitments Mrs McFarlane returned to work. They further decided not to have any more children and that Mr McFarlane would undergo a vasectomy operation. On 16 October 1989 a consultant surgeon performed the operation on Mr McFarlane at a hospital for which Tayside Health Board is responsible. The operation was carried out without complication. One of the risks of a vasectomy operation is spontaneous recanalisation of the divided vas. For this reason Mr and Mrs McFarlane were advised to adopt contraceptive precautions until sperm samples had been analysed. In January and February 1990 that was done. On 23 March 1990 the consultant surgeon wrote to Mr McFarlane saying "your sperm counts are now negative and you may dispense with contraceptive precautions." Mr and Mrs McFarlane acted on this advice. Nevertheless in September 1991 Mrs McFarlane became pregnant. On 6 May 1992 Mrs McFarlane gave birth to a healthy daughter, Catherine. Mr and Mrs McFarlane love their daughter and care for her as an integral part of the family.

The legal proceedings in Scotland

The parents sued the Tayside Health Board in delict. The claim is divided into two parts. First, Mrs McFarlane claimed a sum of £10,000 in respect of pain, suffering and distress resulting from the unwanted pregnancy. Secondly, Mr and Mrs McFarlane claimed a sum of £100,000 in respect of the financial cost of bringing up Catherine.

The issues

The statement of facts and issues summarised the questions to be considered as follows. (i) Are the pursuers entitled to damages? (ii) Is the second pursuer entitled to claim solarium? (iii) Are the pursuers entitled to claim for the financial consequences of pregnancy and the birth of the child? (iv) Is a claim for the financial consequences of the pregnancy and birth excluded as being for pure economic loss? (v) Does public policy exclude the pursuers' claims for damages in whole or in part? (vi) Does the fact that the pursuers now have, as a result of the alleged negligence, a live healthy child, disentitle them to damages in whole or in part? These issues overlap. Different considerations apply to the two heads of claim and it will be necessary to consider them separately. It will be convenient first to consider the claim of the parents for the total cost of bringing up Catherine and then to consider the smaller claim of Mrs McFarlane for a solatium for pain, suffering and distress resulting from her pregnancy. It is common ground that in regard to the sustainability in law of the two heads of claim there are no material differences between the law of Scotland and the law of England.

The cost of bringing up Catherine

It will be convenient to examine first the line of English cases on which the Inner House founded its decision that the cost of bringing up Catherine is a sustainable claim. In *Udale* v. *Bloomsbury Health Authority* [1983] 1 WLR 1098 Jupp J rejected a claim for the cost of bringing up an unwanted child. The judge observed, at p. 1109, that the birth of a child is "a blessing and an occasion for rejoicing." In *Thake* v. *Maurice* [1986] QB 644 Peter Pain J refused to follow *Udale*'s case and allowed such a claim. He observed, at p. 666G, that social policy, which permitted abortion and sterilisation, implied that it was generally recognised that the birth of a healthy child was not always a blessing. In *Emeh* v. *Kensington and Chelsea and Westminster Area Health Authority* [1985] QB 1012 the Court of Appeal had to consider divergent approaches in the cases of *Udale* and *Thake*. But the unwanted child in *Emeh*'s case had been born with congenital disabilities. The defendants' contention was that the cost of upbringing should be limited to the extra costs attributable to the child's disabilities. Full costs were allowed but in a modest sum of the order of £6,000. Angus Stewart QC in "Damages for the Birth of a Child," (1995) 40 JLSS 298, 300 pointed out:

"The issue [in *Emeh*] possibly presented as one of deceptive simplicity given that the claim was by the mother alone: it was held that the compensable loss extended to any reasonably foreseeable financial loss directly caused by the unexpected pregnancy. The formulation equates pregnancy with personal injury giving rise to consequential (as opposed to pure) economic loss which includes upbringing costs."

That I regard as a perceptive explanation of the context of the judgment. In unreserved judgments the Court of Appeal chose to follow the judgment of Peter Pain J rather than the judgment of Jupp J. This decision has been considered binding on lower courts and on the Court of Appeal in regard to claims by parents for wrongful birth of a healthy child. It is the critical decision in the line of authority in England. It is unnecessary to discuss the subsequent English decisions which followed *Emeh*'s case but I list them in chronological order: see *Thake* v. *Maurice* [1986] QB 644; *Gold* v. *Haringey Health Authority* [1988] QB 481; *Benarr* v. *Kettering Health Authority* [1988] NLJR 179; *Allen* v. *Bloomsbury Health Authority* [1993] 1 All ER 651; *Salih* v. *Enfield Health Authority* [1991] 3 All ER 400; *Robinson* v. *Salford Health Authority* [1992] 3 Med LR 270; *Fish* v. *Wilcox* [1994] 5 Med LR 230; *Watkin* v. *South Manchester Health Authority* [1995] 1 WLR 1543; *Goodwill* v. *British Pregnancy Advisory Service* [1996] 1 WLR 1397. It is only necessary to mention one specific matter about those decisions. In *Benarr*'s case the court held that health authorities were liable to pay for private education of the unwanted child.

It is right to point out that the Court of Appeal decision in *Emeh*'s case predates the full retreat from *Anns* v. *Merton London Borough Council* [1978] AC 728 which was announced by the decision of the House in *Murphy* v. *Brentwood District Council* [1991] 1 AC 398. Since then a judicial scepticism has prevailed about an overarching principle for the recovery of new categories of economic loss. Here the father's part of the claim for the cost of bringing up the unwanted child is undoubtedly a claim for pure economic loss. Realistically, despite the pregnancy and child birth, the mother's part of the claim is also for pure economic loss. In any event, in respect of the claim for the costs of bringing up the unwanted child, it would be absurd to distinguish between the claims of the father and the mother. This feature of the claim is important. The common law has a great capacity for growth but the development of a new ground of liability, or a new head of such liability, for the recovery of economic loss must be justified by cogent reasons. Even before *Murphy*'s case there was unease among judges about the decision in *Emeh*'s case. This was memorably articulated in *Jones* v. *Berkshire Area Health Authority* (unreported), 2 July 1986, another unwanted pregnancy case. Ognall J said:

"I pause only to observe that, speaking purely personally, it remains a matter of surprise to me that the law acknowledges an entitlement in a mother to claim damages for the blessing of a healthy child. Certain it is that those who are afflicted with a handicapped child or who long desperately to have a child at all and are denied that good fortune, would regard an award for this sort of contingency with a measure of astonishment. But there it is: that is the law."

In *Gold* v. *Haringey Health Authority* [1988] QB 481, 484F Lloyd J (with the agreement of the other members of the court) cited this observation and said that "many would no doubt agree with this observation."

In the present case your Lordships have had the advantage of considering this issue in the light of far more analytical and comprehensive arguments from both counsel than were put before the Court of Appeal in *Emeh*'s case. Counsel took your Lordships on a valuable tour d'horizon of comparative jurisprudence. Claims by parents for the cost of bringing up an unwanted but healthy child as opposed to more limited claims by the mother in respect of pain, suffering and distress associated with the pregnancy have proved controversial in foreign jurisdictions: compare the valuable comparative article by Angus Stewart QC, 40 JLSS 298, 300. In the United States the overwhelming majority of state courts do not allow recovery of the costs of bringing up a healthy child:

see the review in *Johnson* v. *University Hospitals of Cleveland*, 540 NE 2d 1370; Annotation, 89 ALR 4th 632 (May 1998), passim. In Canada the trend is against such claims: see *Kealey* v. *Berezowski* (1996) 136 DLR (4th) 708, 724–730, which contains a review. By a majority the New South Wales Court of Appeal in *C.E.S.* v. *Superclinics (Australia) Pty Ltd*, 38 NSWLR 47 held that the plaintiff had, through the negligence of the defendants, lost the opportunity to have an abortion which would not necessarily have been unlawful. The court ordered a retrial on the issue as to whether an abortion would have been unlawful. Kirby P considered that damages could be awarded for the cost of bringing up the child. Priestly JA was prepared to allow a limited recovery for "wrongful birth" but not for child-rearing expenses. Meagher JA agreed with Priestly JA on this point, though in a dissenting opinion he concluded that public policy was an absolute bar to the award of damages in "wrongful birth" cases. In New Zealand there is a no-fault compensation scheme. It is, however, instructive to note that the Accident and Compensation Authority held that there was no causal connection between the medical error and the cost of raising the child: *In re Z* [1982] 3 NZAR 161 and *XY* v. *Accident Compensation Corporation* [1984] 4 NZAR 219. In Germany the Constitutional Court has ruled that such a claim is unconstitutional inasmuch as it is subversive of the dignity of the child. But the Bundesgerichtshof has rejected this view and permits recovery of the costs of bringing up the child. The Federal Court observed that compensation not only has no detrimental effect on the child, but can be beneficial to it: see BS Markesinis, *The German Law of Obligations*, vol. II: *Torts*, 3rd edn. (1997), pp. 155–156. In France the Cour de Cassation has ruled that

"whereas the existence of the child she has conceived cannot in itself constitute for the mother a loss legally justifying compensation, even if the birth occurred after an unsuccessful intervention intended to terminate the pregnancy:" see Mlle. Xc. Picard (Cour de Cass. Civ. 1 re 25 June 1991 D. 1991, 566).

Such claims are not allowed. From this comparative survey I deduce that claims by parents for full compensation for the financial consequences of the birth of a healthy child have sometimes been allowed. It may be that the major theme in such cases is that one is simply dealing with an ordinary tort case in which there are no factors negativing liability in delict. Considerations of corrective justice as between the negligent surgeon and the parents were dominant in such decisions. In an overview one would have to say that more often such claims are not allowed. The grounds for decision are diverse. Sometimes it is said that there was no personal injury, a lack of foreseeability of the costs of bringing up the child, no causative link between the breach of duty and the birth of a healthy child, or no loss since the joys of having a healthy child always outweigh the financial losses. Sometimes the idea that the couple could have avoided the financial cost of bringing up the unwanted child by abortion or adoption has influenced decisions. Policy considerations undoubtedly played a role in decisions denying a remedy for the cost of bringing up an unwanted child. My Lords, the discipline of comparative law does not aim at a poll of the solutions adopted in different countries. It has the different and inestimable value of sharpening our focus on the weight of competing considerations. And it reminds us that the law is part of the world of competing ideas markedly influenced by cultural differences. Thus Fleming has demonstrated that it may be of relevance, depending on the context, to know whether the particular state has an effective social security safety net: see Fleming, *The American Tort Process* (1988), pp. 26–27.

I will now eliminate the grounds upon which I would not decide against the parents' claim for compensation for financial loss arising from the child's birth. Counsel for the health board rightly did not argue that it is a factor against the claim that the parents should have resorted to abortion or adoption. I cannot conceive of any circumstances in which the autonomous decision of the parents not to resort to even a lawful abortion could be questioned. For similar reasons the parents' decision not to have the child adopted was plainly natural and commendable. It is difficult to envisage any circumstances in which it would be right to challenge such a decision of the parents. The starting point is the right of parents to make decisions on family planning and, if those plans fail, their right to care for an initially unwanted child. The law does and must respect these decisions of parents which are so closely tied to their basic freedoms and rights of personal autonomy.

Counsel for the health authority argued as his primary submission that the whole claim should fail because the natural processes of conception and childbirth cannot in law amount to personal injury. This is a view taken in some jurisdictions. On the other hand, it is inconsistent with many other decisions, notably where limited recovery of compensation for pain, suffering and distress is allowed. I would not follow this path.

After all, the hypothesis is that the negligence of the surgeon caused the physical consequences of pain and suffering associated with pregnancy and childbirth. And every pregnancy involves substantial discomfort and pain. I would therefore reject the argument of the health authority on this point. In the alternative counsel argued that, if money spent on Catherine is regarded as a detriment to her parents, it is outweighed by the many and undisputed benefits which they have derived and will derive from Catherine. While this factor is relevant in an assessment of the justice of the parents' claim I do not regard such a "set-off" as the correct legal analysis of the position.

It is possible to view the case simply from the perspective of corrective justice. It requires somebody who has harmed another without justification to indemnify the other. On this approach the parents' claim for the cost of bringing up Catherine must succeed. But one may also approach the case from the vantage point of distributive justice. It requires a focus on the just distribution of burdens and losses among members of a society. If the matter is approached in this way, it may become relevant to ask of the commuters on the Underground the following question: "Should the parents of an unwanted but healthy child be able to sue the doctor or hospital for compensation equivalent to the cost of bringing up the child for the years of his or her minority, i.e. until about 18 years?" My Lords, I have not consulted my fellow travellers on the London Underground but I am firmly of the view that an overwhelming number of ordinary men and women would answer the question with an emphatic "No." And the reason for such a response would be an inarticulate premise as to what is morally acceptable and what is not. Like Ognall J in *Jones* v. *Berkshire Area Health Authority*, 2 July 1986, they will have in mind that many couples cannot have children and others have the sorrow and burden of looking after a disabled child. The realisation that compensation for financial loss in respect of the upbringing of a child would necessarily have to discriminate between rich and poor would, surely appear unseemly to them. It would also worry them that parents may be put in a position of arguing in court that the unwanted child, which they accepted and care for, is more trouble than it is worth. Instinctively, the traveller on the Underground would consider that the law of tort has no business to provide legal remedies consequent upon the birth of a healthy child, which all of us regard as a valuable and good thing.

My Lords, to explain decisions denying a remedy for the cost of bringing up an unwanted child by saying that there is no loss, no foreseeable loss, no causative link or no ground for reasonable restitution is to resort to unrealistic and formalistic propositions which mask the real reasons for the decisions. And judges ought to strive to give the real reasons for their decision. It is my firm conviction that where courts of law have denied a remedy for the cost of bringing up an unwanted child the real reasons have been grounds of distributive justice. That is of course, a moral theory. It may be objected that the House must act like a court of law and not like a court of morals. That would only be partly right. The court must apply positive law. But judges' sense of the moral answer to a question, or the justice of the case, has been one of the great shaping forces of the common law. What may count in a situation of difficulty and uncertainty is not the subjective view of the judge but what he reasonably believes that the ordinary citizen would regard as right.

In my view it is legitimate in the present case to take into account considerations of distributive justice. That does not mean that I would decide the case on grounds of public policy. On the contrary, I would avoid those quicksands. Relying on principles of distributive justice I am persuaded that our tort law does not permit parents of a healthy unwanted child to claim the costs of bringing up the child from a health authority or a doctor. If it were necessary to do so, I would say that the claim does not satisfy the requirement of being fair, just and reasonable.

This conclusion is reinforced by an argument of coherence. There is no support in Scotland and England for a claim by a disadvantaged child for damage to him arising from his birth: see *McKay*

v. *Essex Area Health Authority* [1982] QB 1166. Given this position, which also prevails in Australia, Trindade and Cane, *The Law of Torts in Australia*, 3rd edn. (1999), p. 434, observe:

"it might seem inconsistent to allow a claim by the parents while that of the child, whether healthy or disabled, is rejected. Surely the parents' claim is equally repugnant to ideas of the sanctity and value of human life and rests, like that of the child, on a comparison between a situation where a human being exists and one where it does not."

In my view this reasoning is sound. Coherence and rationality demand that the claim by the parents should also be rejected.

Two supplementary points remain to be mentioned. First, I have taken into account that the claim in the present case is based on an assumption of responsibility by the doctor who gave negligent advice. But in regard to the sustainability of a claim for the cost of bringing up the child it ought not to make any difference whether the claim is based on negligence simpliciter or on the extended *Hedley Byrne* principle. After all, the latter is simply the rationalisation adopted by the common law to provide a remedy for the recovery of economic low for a species of negligently performed services: see *Williams* v. *Natural Life Health Foods Ltd* [1998] 1 WLR 830, 834G. Secondly, counsel for the health board was inclined to concede that in the case of an unwanted child who was born seriously disabled the rule may have to be different. There may be force in this concession but it does not arise in the present appeal and it ought to await decision where the focus is on such cases.

I would hold that the Inner House erred in ruling that Mr and Mrs McFarlane are entitled in principle to recover the costs of bringing up Catherine.

The claim for a solatium simply alleges that Mrs McFarlane became pregnant and had to undergo a pregnancy and confinement and the pain and distress of giving birth to the child. It will be recalled that I have already rejected the argument that Mrs McFarlane suffered no personal injury. The considerations of distributive justice which militated against the claim for the cost of bringing up Catherine do not apply to the claim for a solatium. The constituent elements of a claim in delict are present. There is nothing objectionable to allowing such a claim. And such limited recovery is supported by a great deal of authority worldwide. I would uphold it. The pleadings also allege that the wife gave up work during the later stages of her pregnancy. Counsel for the health authority concedes that if a claim for limited recovery is allowed such an ancillary claim would also be sustainable. This consequential relief is within the spirit of the limited recovery principle and I would endorse it.

For the reasons I have given I would uphold the decision of the Inner House on this part of the claim.

The disposal of the appeal

I would allow the appeal on the cost of bringing up Catherine and dismiss the appeal on the claim for a solatium by Mrs McFarlane.

5. ECONOMIC LOSS ("CABLE CASES")

Case 11

BUNDESGERICHTSHOF (SIXTH CIVIL SENATE) 9 DECEMBER 1958
BGHZ 29, 65 = NJW 1959, 479
(with an approving note by H Lehman in NJW 1959, 670)

The plaintiff was the owner of a factory. In September 1955 an employee of the defendant, a civil engineer, operating an excavator on the premises of M, an enterprise engaged in graphic work, damaged a subterranean power cable belonging to the electricity works in E, which led from M's works to the plaintiff's factory. At approximately 9.40 am on 18 June 1956, another employee of the defendant excavating a pit intended for an oil-tank cut the cable once again at a distance of about 60 metres behind the previous break. As a result production in the plaintiff's factory was interrupted until 6.30 am on 19 June.

The plaintiff contended that the power cable, which from the place of the break onwards served only the graphic enterprise and his factory, was part of his enterprise from an economic point of view. The defendant, in cutting the cable had interfered illegally and culpably with his enterprise and was liable for the damages caused by the interruption of production. Alternatively, he contended that the defendant had failed to observe the necessary care for the safety of others. The defendant argued that the plaintiff's enterprise had only been indirectly affected by the cutting of the cable and that only direct interference would have rendered him liable. He also contended that he had exercised the necessary care in selecting and supervising his employees.

The Landgericht in Bielefeld and the Court of Appeal of Hanover allowed the claim. Upon a further appeal the claim was dismissed for the following

Reasons

1. The courts below both held the defendant liable in damages on the ground that by cutting the power cable leading to the plaintiff's factory with the result that the supply of power was interrupted, the defendant had illegally and culpably interfered with the plaintiff's established and active commercial or industrial enterprise. The Court of Appeal held the defendant liable on the basis of § 823 I BGB in conjunction with § 831 BGB in as much as the defendant had failed to produce sufficient evidence to exculpate himself. It also held him liable on the basis of § 823 I BGB alone for having failed to observe the required care for the safety of others (*Verkehrssicherungspflicht*).

The appellant objects against the treatment of the cutting of the power cable as an interference with an established and active commercial or industrial enterprise.

The appeal must be successful in the result

(*a*) The Reichsgericht has acknowledged in the constant practice that the right in an existing commercial or industrial enterprise is "another right" in the meaning of § 823 I BGB.

As early as its decision RGZ 58, 29 it has regarded the right in an established and active commercial or industrial enterprise as an individual right which can be violated directly; any direct disturbance or interference with the commercial or industrial enterprise is, therefore, a violation of a right protected by § 823 I BGB. During the ensuing period the Reichsgericht at first accorded the protection of § 823 I BGB to an established and active commercial or industrial enterprise only if interference involved the *existence* of the commercial or industrial enterprise; that is to say if an enterprise was in fact obstructed, if it was alleged to be illegal, or if its restriction or closure was demanded; sometimes the Reichsgericht has expressed it in the terms that the bases of the commercial or industrial enterprise must be directly affected [references]. According to this practice, which was developed in dealing with problems of competition and boycott, acts which damaged the commercial or industrial enterprise indirectly only were not regarded as illegal acts in the meaning of § 823 I BGB. Examples are: if the person carrying on a commercial or industrial enterprise is only deprived of economic profit [references], or if the relationship with suppliers is affected detrimentally [reference] or that with the range of customers [reference], or, finally, if only the prospect of gain is diminished or endangered [references]. The protection of § 823 I BGB was granted in those cases especially where the termination of the commercial or industrial activity of another was demanded on the ground that the activity violated an industrial or commercial right protected by law of the person seeking the termination (design, patents), and it appeared later on that no such right existed, the allegation to this effect having been made falsely due to the objector's negligence at least [references]; further, e.g. if in the course of a boycott, clients had been prevented from entering an eating-house by picketing and by force [references].

The strict requirements for protecting the right in an established and active commercial or industrial enterprise were relaxed by the subsequent practice of the Second Civil Division of the Reichsgericht, the final indication appeared already in the decision of 7 June 1929 [reference] where an order of the local Sickness Insurance Office that no payments would be made for certain branded medicines was treated as an act endangering deliberately the commercial or industrial enterprise engaged in the production of the branded medicines, seeing that the full effect of the order of the local Sickness Insurance Office was to force the producer to curtail production. In its decision of 9 October 1934 [reference] the Second Division abandoned clearly the principle that *only* the existence of the enterprise was being protected and expressed the view that it sufficed to render § 823 I BGB applicable in making the law concerning trademarks and competition if a claim for damages was based on a culpable interference with the commercial or industrial activity of another. This was confirmed by the same division in its decision of 19 December 1938 [references]; the court stated there that in so holding it took into consideration that every owner of an enterprise could demand to be protected against illegal disturbances which prevented his enterprise from devoting its full potential based on the totality of its components and means employed, even if the disturbance did not threaten the existence of the enterprise as such [references]. The Second Division considered further [references] whether the same principle did not apply also outside the sphere of the law of competition and designs. In its decision of 3 October 1936 [reference] the First Division of the Reichsgericht expressly approved the view of the Second Division that for the purpose of applying § 823 I BGB a direct attack on the existence of the enterprise was not required where the commercial or industrial activity of another had been interfered with culpably (but see to the contrary the Fifth Division of the Reichsgericht [reference]).

According to the practice of the Bundesgerichtshof, the protection of § 823 I BGB is granted in respect of any interference with the right of an established and active commercial or industrial enterprise, if it constitutes a direct interference with the commercial or industrial activity, even if it does not involve competition and industrial property rights [references]. In the decision cited here [reference] it is stated that the right in an existing commercial or industrial enterprise—like ownership—must be protected by § 823 I BGB against direct interference not only in its substantive existence but also in its various manifestations, which include the entire sphere of commercial and industrial activity. This practice must be followed.

(b) In consequence of the practice of the court to range the right in an existing or commercial industrial enterprise among the number of "other rights" mentioned in § 823 I BGB this right is placed on an equal footing for the purpose of protection with the other protected legal interest and rights enumerated there, i.e. life, health, liberty, and property. Therefore it must also be examined in the case of a violation of a right in an existing commercial or industrial enterprise whether its consequences, for which damages are claimed, are covered by the protection of the law (the decision of this division [references]).

Admittedly in so far as the protection of an established and active commercial or industrial enterprise is concerned, the question is not unlike the above-mentioned fundamental judgment of this division regarding the limits of liability, as to whether damage complained of resulted from the violation of a protected interest, the safeguarding of which is the purpose of the law. The reason is that when § 823 I BGB was formulated, the legislature had not yet envisaged the protection of established and active commercial or industrial enterprises. In the present case, the question as to the limits of liability is therefore to be considered and decided mainly from the angle as to what is the object of protection accorded by the practice of this court to established and active commercial or industrial enterprises.

The notion of a commercial or industrial enterprise includes everything which in its totality enables the enterprise to develop and to operate in the economy. Thus it includes not only the premises and the land used by it, machinery and tools, furniture and stock but also business connections, the circle of clients, and debtors. The protection accorded and gradually extended by the practice of the courts to established and active commercial or industrial enterprises is intended to safeguard the enterprise against legal interference with its economic activity and functioning. Even if the Bundesgerichtshof in a previous decision [reference] regarded the individual situation in which the commercial or industrial activity is carried out as determining the extent of the area of commercial or industrial activity, nevertheless all the cases in which the Bundesgerichtshof had held that a right in an established and active commercial or industrial enterprise had been violated involved the protection of those characteristics of a commercial or industrial enterprise which are specifically its own. The objects of protection are the substance and the emanations of the commercial or industrial enterprise to the extent that they constitute its natural and characteristic features of economic and technical activities.

(*c*) Then as now, as the Court of Appeal has observed correctly, the interference with the sphere of the commercial or industrial enterprise must be direct if § 823 I BGB is to apply [references]. The plaintiff is wrong when he refers to the decision of the Reichsgericht [references] in support of a view to the contrary; it was held there only that to restrict the right in an established and active commercial or industrial enterprise to the protection of its substance was too narrow and that every culpable interference with the commercial or industrial activity of another was sufficient to render § 823 I BGB applicable; the requirement that the interference must be direct was not affected thereby. It is true, of course, as the Court of Appeal has stated, that the notion of "direct interference" has not been defined by the practice of the courts. Baumbach and Hefermehl [references] point out correctly that the difficulties in drawing the line between direct and indirect interference are particularly great in the case of such a complex legal term as enterprise. Contrary to the view of the appellant the purely linguistic distinction between "indirect" and "direct" cannot yield the criteria for the necessary delimitation of these notions. The question as to when interference with the right in an established and active commercial or industrial enterprise is direct cannot be answered either by reference to the doctrine of causality alone, and the absence of so-called intermediate causes is also not decisive, as the Court of Appeal has pointed out in agreement with the practice of the Bundesgerichtshof [references; *contra* RGZ 163, 21, 32 where the court relied on directness of the causal nexus; similarly the Court of Appeal of Munich, 21 March 1956, NJW 1956, 1769]. The suggestion of Larenz [reference] in his note to the aforementioned decision of the Court of Appeal of Munich—upon which both parties rely in support of their legal position—does not lead to a sufficiently clear limitation of direct and indirect interference. Larenz argues that whether an interference is direct must be determined teleologically, i.e. in the sense that the act of interference must have the purpose of restricting the commercial or industrial activity, and that, consequently, the purpose must disclose the direction towards inflicting damage upon the commercial or industrial enterprise. Inasmuch as Larenz wishes to treat as "direct" every interference with a commercial or industrial enterprise the purpose of which is, or at least could have been, to reduce or to affect detrimentally the difficulties become obvious immediately when the interference was due to negligence. Nevertheless it is not possible to agree with Baumbach and Hefermehl [references] that in view of the existing difficulties of delimitation the requirement that the interference must be direct should be abandoned and that instead the effect of the interference upon the sphere of activity should be decisive in favour of the retention of the requirement of directness [references].

The Court of Appeal, relying on the decision of this Division dated 14 April 1954 [reference] is of the opinion that the notion of directness was characterised by its objective. From this it concluded that a workable delimitation could be established in the case of intentional acts; if they were committed negligently it was sufficient if in the circumstances the act might have been intended to affect the commercial or industrial enterprise adversely and the person so acting had been aware of this consequence of his act, but had hoped that the consequence would not materialise. The Court of Appeal held that in the present case a negligent interference causing liability to pay damages had in fact taken place. This Division in the decision cited above has held that an act to constitute a violation of the right in a commercial or industrial enterprise must somehow be directed against the enterprise as such. For this reason this Division did not regard as illegal interference in a commercial or industrial enterprise the fact alone that one unfounded claim for the restitution of a parcel of land attached to the enterprise had been raised by a claimant seeking restitution under the Military Government no. 52, resulting in the administration of the land by trustees. The reason was that the attack was directed against the owner of the enterprise, but not against the enterprise itself, even if thereby it may have caused damages to the commercial or industrial enterprise indirectly. Similarly it is not an interference with commercial or industrial activities if as a result of injuries to persons an enterprise is deprived of the personnel which is indispensable for its operation [reference]. These decisions which require that in order to be covered by § 823 I BGB an attack must be directed against the industrial or commercial enterprise itself indicate the general approach of the predominant practice. It is to avoid an excessive extension of the right in an established and active commercial or industrial enterprise which would run counter to the casuistic enumeration in the German legal system of situations constituting torts. Voices have been raised by courts and in legal literature which advocate a return to the older practice of the Reichsgericht according to which only an interference with an industrial or commercial enterprise which affects its substance is to be regarded as an attack against an absolute right [references]. These opinions are clearly inspired by the view that, in the words of Lehman [reference], the recognition of an excessively broad general protection of commercial or industrial enterprise might easily lead to a surreptitious creation of rules.

Certainly the protection which was originally accorded only to the existence of a commercial or industrial enterprise was extended when subsequently the Reichsgericht and then the Bundesgerichtshof in a constant practice have held that every illegal direct interference with commercial or industrial activity constitutes a violation of an established and active commercial or industrial enterprise which is protected by § 823 I BGB even if the attack is directed not against its existence but against any one of its emanations. This does not mean that by the circuitous route of protecting commercial or industrial enterprises protection is being granted to contractual rights which, in contrast to absolute rights, only bind certain persons and are therefore not "other rights" in the meaning of § 823 I BGB [references] or that economic aspects as a whole are being protected, although these are only given protection by the law of tort in special circumstances, e.g. by § 826 BGB; to protect either of these would be alien to the present legal system. In addition the need to enquire carefully in connection with the question of illegality whether, having regard to the principle of balancing the respective interests and duties, the defendant can perhaps rely on special grounds of justification [reference] has a restrictive effect. In fact the extent and the limits within which the right in an established and active commercial or industrial enterprise is to be protected must be determined precisely by an appropriate amplification of the notion that the interference must be "direct".

Direct interference with the right in an existing commercial or industrial enterprise against which § 823 I BGB provides a remedy is only that which is somehow directed against the enterprise as such, i.e. which is aimed at the enterprise and does not affect rights or legal interests which can be detached from the enterprise without difficulty. All the cases in which the Bundesgerichtshof acknowledged that a right in an established and active commercial or industrial enterprise had been violated involved interferences of this kind which were aimed at the enterprise. Just as an injury to an employer or the destruction of or damage to a lorry belonging to an enterprise is not specifically connected with the enterprise, the cutting of the cable by the defendant or his employee operating the tractor is not so connected either; the defendant's enterprise operating the excavator had damaged a power cable which apart from supplying power to the graphic working of M, almost by chance serves in addition the plaintiff's enterprise only, although it could equally well have been intended to supply electric current to other customers. Furthermore the supply of electric current by a cable and the right to receive it does not constitute a natural characteristic of an established and active commercial or industrial enterprise, but represents a relationship based on the duty to supply current incumbent upon the public supply undertaking, identical with that which connects, e.g. household and members of the professions with the electricity works. Consequently the fact that a cable has been damaged on land not belonging to the enterprise concerned resulting in a cut in the electricity supply cannot, in the absence of special circumstances which do not exist here, be regarded as an interference aimed at the area of operation of the enterprise concerned. It is true that when the defendant's excavator cut the power cable leading to the plaintiff's factory, the material and technical bases were already affected whereby the plaintiff could and did receive electric power from the electricity works in accordance with the contract existing between them. However this does not constitute interference with an established and active commercial or individual enterprise; to do so would exceed the range of protection accorded to commercial or industrial enterprises by the practice of the courts; instead the issue involves a violation of property in the cable belonging to the electricity works and of the right of the plaintiff against the electricity works for the supply of electric power, limited by the latter's general conditions of trade.

If, therefore, the plaintiff's claim cannot be based on a violation of his right to an established and active commercial or individual enterprise, it cannot be supported either, contrary to the view of the Court of Appeal, on the ground that the defendant had violated the required care of the safety of others [*Verkehrssicherungspflicht*].

Case 12

BUNDESGERICHTSHOF (SIXTH CIVIL SENATE) 8 JUNE 1976
BGHZ 66, 388 = NJW 1976, 1740 = VersR 1976, 1043

The defendant company, which ran a building enterprise, was on 23 November 1973 carrying out excavations on private property in the Württemberg town W. An electric cable was negligently damaged. This led to a 27-minute interruption of the current used in the plaintiff's manufacturing business. The plaintiff estimated that the interruption led, through a failure of production, to a loss of DM 1157. The plaintiff claims that amount as damages from the defendant.

Both lower instances rejected the claim. The plaintiff is granted leave to apply for review, but is unsuccessful for the following reasons:

I. 1. The appellate court is of opinion that:

(*a*) The claim can find no support in § 823 I BGB; for not property of the plaintiff's was damaged or destroyed by the electricity failure. Moreover, no legal injury was done to the plaintiff's right of an established and active business, since there was no direct interference with it.

(*b*) Moreover, the appellate court rejects a claim for compensation under § 823 II BGB; for the defendant's contravention of § 18 III of the Baden-Württemberg Building Regulations (LBauO) did not constitute a breach of an enactment designed for the plaintiff's protection. The provision says:

"Public spaces, supply, run-off and warning apparatuses and also hydrants, survey marks, and boundary marks must be protected during the process of building and, where necessary, be kept accessible subject to the necessary precautions."

In essentials the appellate court says: The language of this provision contemplates damage only to things, not persons. Moreover, the Regulations as a whole belong to the law of *public* security and order. § 18 III cannot be assumed to afford to electricity users a claim to compensation not otherwise provided for, all the more since it would lead to a great and intolerable extension of liability. It would also be consistent with the fact that § 1 II no. 1 of the Regulations affords no private law right to compensation where a similar accident occurs in the course of building in places open to public traffic. This reasoning is in open conflict with the BGH decision of 12 March 1968 about the corresponding regulations of Land Nordrhein-Westfalen.

It is against this reasoning (i.e., of BGH NJW 1968, 1279) that this appeal is lodged. In support of the appeal a question is raised whether, contrary to the principles laid down by BGHZ 29, 65 (74) = NJW 1959, 479, an interruption of electricity supply is not to be regarded as an invasion of the right of an established and active business, in the sense of § 823 I BGB.

II. The appeal is unsuccessful.

1. The Senate deciding the case agrees with the appellate court in holding that the plaintiff cannot invoke § 18 III 1 of the Regulations as a protective enactment for the purposes of § 823 II BGB. In so far as this runs counter to the principles of the aforementioned

decision of the BGH of 12 March 1968, the Court rejects them. The decision of 12 March 1968 is not followed.

(*a*) [Earlier decisions elsewhere are in agreement.]

(*b*) There are convincing reasons for approving the appellate decision. That certain provisions of the Regulations, especially those for the protection of neighbours, can be treated as protective enactments for the purposes of § 823 II BGB does not stand in the way. For no such purpose can be detected in favour of electricity users.

(*aa*) The provision of the Regulations here in question is not an enactment for the protection of the plaintiff. Although admittedly most rules of a public law character operate in a general way to protect and further the interest of individual citizens, it does not follow that that *general* operation also specifies the cases where a protective enactment in question affords *him* an *individual protection*. That is not difficult to establish if the protective function of a rule can be detected in the statement of its purpose; but if, as often happens with recent enactments, the *travaux préparatoires* give only an imperfect indication or none at all, it is of no use to consider legislative purpose in the abstract: nor has this been done so far by the Federal High Court, despite some ambiguous formulations. In the last resort the question must be attacked directly, whether the creation of an individual claim for compensation appears meaningful, sensible, and tolerable in the light of the whole system of liability. Only by doing so can a development, rightly feared by the appellate court, be avoided, namely that the increasing tendency to base claims on § 823 II BGB might undermine Parliament's ruling *against* a general liability for purely economic loss. In this connection it may be useful to ask whether in such cases an individual claim for an injunction would be sensible and tolerable.

(*c*) There is no need to go further into these aspects of the decision; for it appears from what has been said that the appellate court properly decided that the Regulations afforded no individual protection to users of electricity against possible economic damage.

(*aa*) According to the basic principle of liability laid down by federal law there is, as a rule, no liability for indirect damage (economic damage that a third party suffers by mere reflex operation through injury to another's property); and this includes damage to an electricity user resulting from damage to a cable owned by an electricity supplier. That the failure to afford compensation is not felt to be intolerable is shown *inter alia* by the fact that the responsibility of electricity suppliers even for vital failures is excluded by regular nation-wide conditions of supply. Although the possibility cannot be absolutely excluded that this principle may be set aside by protective *Land* legislation, nevertheless, such legislation should be interpreted to extend protection only if the need for it arises from a state of affairs in the law of the *Land* which could not have been anticipated on a federal level. Since that is obviously not the case here, the constitutional distribution of powers makes it unlikely that the *Land* legislator wantonly intended to extent protection by action repugnant to the federal rule.

(*bb*) But even apart from this constitutional aspect, based on the concept of constitutional demarcation of authority, the appellate decision must be approved. There is nothing to be said for the view that the Regulations, when regulating building, intended to afford to electricity users an abnormal individual protection when a cable is damaged. The appellate court rightly points to the lack of any corresponding provision in § 1 II of the LBauO (*Landesbauordnung*), where danger to cables is especially to be anticipated, that is to say, where works are conducted in places open to public traffic. In other fields also electricity users have no individual protection, for instance where cables are endangered in traffic, mining, or agricultural accidents. The possibility that a building regulation intends to afford a protection so much out of line in this particular field is very remote. The official statement of motives leading to the Regulations here in question lends no assistance. Moreover, it is noticeable that the basic duty of care already existed in the general law and was not originally created by the Regulations as part of *Land* law. Its inclusion in § 18 III only serves to sum up precautions required to be taken in works regulated by statute, and to form a basis for prosecution. There is nothing to show that an arbitrary individual protection was aimed at, alien to federal law and as part of a generally inappropriate set of regulations.

2. The appellate court also appropriately rejects any liability to compensate for an interference with the plaintiff's business. It finds itself in agreement with the Senate decision of 1959 which dealt with a case on all fours with this one. The Senate, on reconsideration, holds fast in principle to its decision in spite of some loudly expressed academic criticism. The need to relate to a trade, as established by the 1959 judgment, which is denied in cases such as the present one, is essential if the protection provided by case-law in the event of a violation of the right of an established and active business is not to be enlarged into a general delictual rule for the protection of traders. The highest court has always taken this point into account although the boundaries of this "residual right" affording special protection to traders have never been fully defined and much could be said in favour of a restrictive application of this delictual rule. In any event, matters cannot be otherwise in the case of a power cut of this nature which affects everyone and which is liable to cause widespread financial loss to persons who do not exercise any trade and to whom the general law of delict affords no claim for damages.

The above cannot be countered with the argument that where damage is caused by an electricity failure a distinction between physical and economic damage makes little sense. In fact the Senate has so far awarded damages for physical damage in business according to § 823 I BGB. This, it must be admitted, somewhat surprising limitation—von Caemmerer calls it "crude"—rests on a binding general decision of the delictual law in force. It is impossible to recognize any reason for departing from it in favour of businesses. In any event, might not the danger of less foreseeable and perhaps much greater physical damage involved in such accidents justify a partial exemption of the tortfeasor from a risk that the electricity supplier frees himself from with state approval? But the present case affords no occasion for such an examination, since physical damage is neither manifest nor even doubtful.

Case 13

BUNDESGERICHTSHOF (SIXTH CIVIL SENATE) 12 JULY 1977
NJW 1977, 2208 = JZ 1977, 721 = VERSR 1977, 1006

The defendant was carrying out earth removal operations required in the construction of an aqueduct and reservoir for the city B and the local water authority. In the course of the works a mechanical digger operated by one of the defendant's men damaged an electric cable which supplied several concerns. As a result current to the plaintiff's business was interrupted for 32 minutes, and the work of its 1385 employees brought to a halt.

The Landgericht and the Oberlandesgericht dismissed the claim for damages. The plaintiff's appeal was also dismissed.

Reasons

I. 1. The Court of Appeal held that the plaintiff had no tort claim under § 823 I BGB, since no legal interest protected by this rule had been invaded: in having to pay wages when no work could be done owing to the lack of current the plaintiff suffered a purely economic loss. The court also held that there had been no invasion of an established and operative business. Furthermore, no claim arose under § 823 II BGB, for although there was a provincial regulation regarding the safeguarding of electric cables during building operations (§ 18 III Provincial Building Ordinance of Baden-Württemberg—BadWürttBauO), it did not have the character of a protective law (*Schutzgesetz*) in favour of customers supplied from the national electricity grid.

2. This is perfectly in line with the decision of this court.

(*a*) This court has frequently stated the preconditions which must be met before damages are payable for affecting a business (BGHZ 29, 65; 41, 123; 66, 388, 393). Those principles involve the conclusion that the damage done by the defendant's mechanical digger to the electric cable was not an invasion of the plaintiff's business as such, since there is lacking the requirement of intimate connection with the business (*Betriebsbezogenheit*). In a similar case (BGHZ 29, 65, 74) the court said that the breaking of an electric cable supplying a factory is no more intimately connected with the business than injury to its employees or damage to its vehicles: it is not an essential characteristic feature of an established and operative business that it have an uninterrupted supply of electricity, especially as all the other customers connected to the same cable have the same legal relationship with the utility that supplies the current. We need not dwell on this point since even the appellant does not contest it.

(*b*) Although it had previously held otherwise (see, for example, NJW 1968, 1279), this court in its decision of 8 June 1976 (BGHZ 66, 388) stated that § 18 III BadWürttBauO (and the similar provisions of the building ordinances of other Länder) are not protective laws in favour of subscribers who suffer economic loss through a lack of current due to damage to a cable. Accordingly there are no legal objections to the view of the Court of Appeal, which evidently was unaware of that decision. Nor, indeed, does the appellant himself contest this part of the judgment.

II. The plaintiff also puts forward a contractual claim both in his own right and by assignment. The Court of Appeal rejected this. The underlying facts are that representatives of the parties had a meeting on site with representatives of the water authority and the city, that the plaintiff's business manager and the city representative drew attention to the presence of the main electric cable where the earthworks were about to begin and stressed how vital it was for the plaintiff's business, and that the defendant's clerk of works was then told that any digging in the neighbourhood of the cable must be done by hand rather than by machine. The Court of Appeal analysed these facts correctly, and its holding that the plaintiff was not drawn into the protective ambit of the contract of services between the water authority and the defendant cannot be faulted.

1. Case-law recognises that persons not immediately involved in a contract may yet be drawn within its protective ambit, with the result that although they cannot bring a claim for performance, as would be the case if it were a true contract for the benefit of third parties under § 328 I BGB, they may nevertheless have a contractual claim for damages if they suffer harm owing to faulty conduct by the debtor in breach of contract (on this see BGHZ 49, 350; NJW 1975, 344; NJW 1954, 874; BGH VersR 1955, 750; NJW 1956, 1193; NJW 1959, 1676; BGHZ 51, 91, 96).

The cases agree that whether third parties are to be included in the protective area of a contract when they were not involved in its formation and have not been expressly covered by the parties, depends on the meaning and purpose of the contract and its construction in accordance with the principle of good faith (§ 157 BGB) (see BGHZ 56, 269, 273); in the long run what is critical is not so much the relationship between the contractors themselves as the special relationship between the creditor and the third party whose inclusion is in question (see especially BGHZ 51, 91, 96). In order to avoid an intolerable extension of contractual duties of care beyond what the principle of good faith can demand of the debtor of the contractual performance, the court has frequently observed that the duties of care and protection can only be extended beyond the actual parties to the contract if the principal creditor (here the water authority) has some responsibility for the well-being of the third party, as owing him protection and care (see especially BGHZ 51, 91, 96; NJW 1974, 1189). This requirement, which is needed so as to avoid blurring the line between contractual and tortious liability in an insupportable manner and contrary to the will of the legislature, is normally present only when there is a legal relationship of a personal nature between the contractual creditor and the third party, such as commonly arises in family relationships, in employment, and in landlord and tenant cases (see BGHZ 51, 91, 96).

2. Contrary to the appellant's contention, the Court of Appeal acted consistently with these principles in holding that the requirements for including the plaintiff in the protective area of the contract for work between the defendant and the water authority were not satisfied in this case.

(*a*) In particular the water authority here was in no way responsible for the well-being of the plaintiff. For the contractual creditor, the plaintiff was only one of a large number of subscribers that might be affected by damage to the cable. As this court said in its judgment of 3 November 1961 (VersR 1962, 86, 88), contractual duties must not be extended in cases where faulty work or failure to take security measures could cause harm to people of all kinds—houseowners, tenants, entrepreneurs, and so on—for then the class of people protected by the contract would be unlimited and unenforceable. The mere fact that the plaintiff's business was apt to suffer a considerable economic loss through interruption of the electricity supply does not justify holding that the water authority which could itself suffer if the plaintiff was damaged, must look out for its well-being. Even if it be true that the contractual creditor had a certain interest in the safety of the cable, this interest was only a general one, and not one solely or predominantly related to the needs of the plaintiff for which the plaintiff could claim protection from the creditor.

(*b*) Nor can it be said that the meeting on site modified the contract of works between the defendant and the water authority. The water authority was bound to give such instructions before the work started in order to enable the defendant to take the necessary steps to protect the utility cables (including telephone cables—§ 317 StGB), and the special reference to the harm the plaintiff might suffer if the current were interrupted was insufficient to bring it within the protective area of the contract contrary to the principles already stated. It is important that at the time he concludes the contract, the contractual debtor should be able to see what risk he is undertaking, and this would be impossible if the creditor could later determine what third parties were to be included in its protective area by making a unilateral declaration to the debtor or to some unauthorised employee.

3. The Court of Appeal was also right to hold that the plaintiff had no assigned claim for damages from the water authority. The requirements of *Drittschadensliquidation* are not met (BGHZ 51, 91, 93 ff.). There is no special legal relationship between the plaintiff and the water authority, the defendant's contractual creditor, such as would justify holding that in law it was not the creditor but the plaintiff who suffered the harm. Only if, at the time of the wrong, the creditor's interest is vested in, or has passed to, the third party, does the party liable have to make good to the creditor what is lost by reason of the creditor's legal and economic relations with the third party. Apart from a few exceptional cases (e.g. BGHZ 40, 91, 100) this only applies when the creditor has contracted on the third party's account (e.g. BGHZ 25, 250, 258) or when the object which the debtor was to safeguard belonged not to the creditor but to the third party (as in BGHZ 15, 224). No such fact situation is present here (see also NJW 1959, 479). We need not now enquire what the case would be if the defendant contractor had undertaken by contract a specific duty of care towards the third party since, as has been stated, no such agreement is shown to have been made.

Notes to Cases 11–13

1. These cases represent one facet of the wider problem of compensability of purely economic loss which remains, both in German and Anglo-American law, a central topic of the law of torts: (i) because it impinges (as cases 19 and 27 also show) on the uneasy relationship between contract and tort and (ii) because the decisions on this topic show how judicial fashions change *vis-à-vis* the concepts used to limit liability for negligence. We shall return to these more general points later; here suffice it to make a few general remarks about these "cable cases".

2. The factual situation is, typically, the following: A damages B's property and as a result C, (and, perhaps, others) suffer economic loss. Cases 8, 9, and 10 fall into this pattern and find an excellent English equivalent in *Spartan Steel* v. *Martin and Co.* [1973] 1 QB 27 and an American parallel in *Beck* v. *FMC Corporation*, 385 NYS 2d 956; aff'd, 369 NE 2d 10 (1977). A factual variant, raising analogous problems, is the following: A, a water company usually under a contractual obligation with a local authority B to provide water and maintain proper water pressures, fails to do so. As a result of this, firemen are unable to extinguish a fire that breaks out and consumes C's house. In all but four American jurisdictions C's claims against A are turned down, *H. R. Moch Co.* v. *Rensselaer Water Co.*, 247 NY 160, 159 NE 896 (1928) being, perhaps, the *locus classicus*. These negative results of Anglo-American and German law call for a comment, not least because they are in stark contrast with the attitude taken by other systems (e.g. the French).

3. It is interesting to compare case 12 with *Spartan Steel*, above, and discover the true reasons that lie behind these judgments. Which of these judgments do you find most convincing? How many of the reasons given by Lord Denning MR, whose judgment is extracted below, can also be found in the German decision? Zweigert and Kötz, § 5, maintain that "style" is one of the most important distinguishing features between Common law and modern civil law (though they do not specifically discuss judicial styles). How different do you find the style of: (i) the American and German judgments; (ii) the American and English judgments?

4. A policy factor which gets short shrift in these judgments is the insurance factor. The American water cases display an amazing ingenuity in utilising every legal concept under the sun to turn down these claims while at the same time avoiding talking openly about insurance considerations. In these cases two types of insurance can be envisaged: loss insurance (which would justify the status quo) and liability insurance (which would argue in favour of a change in the law). Which of the two is cheaper and more efficient and why? A good discussion of the insurance factor can be found in 51 *Cornell Law Rev.* 142 (1965) and, most recently, in the decision of the Canadian Supreme Court in *Norsk Pacific Steamship Co. Ltd.* v. *Canadian National Railway Co.* [1992] 1 S.C.R. 1021 (extracts of which are reproduced below, pp. 243 ff.). The insurance aspect of the case is also increasingly considered by the German legal literature which seems divided as to whether a change in the law is desirable. For further details see Hager, "Haftung bei Störung der Energiezufuhr", *JZ* 1979, 53 and Bürge, "Die Kabelbruchfälle . . .", *Juristische Blätter* 1981, 57. The two most thorough monographs on the subject are by Hermann, *Zum Nachteil des Vermögens* (1979) and Taupitz, *Haftung für Energieleiterstörungen durch Dritte* (1981).

5. In England the attitude of the courts towards economic loss has vacillated in the late 1970s, the 1980 and the early 1990s. Though these doubts can also be found in other Common law jurisdictions such as Australia, Canada, and New Zealand the trend has, if anything, been towards a renunciation of the categorical exclusion rule. This is certainly the case in the last two of the aforementioned countries whereas the first seems to have opted for a nuanced approach. (For Canada see: *Kamloops* v. *Nielsen* [1984] 2 SCR 2; *Norsk Pacific Steamship Co.* v. *CNR* [1992] 1 SCR 1021; *Winnipeg Condominium Corp. No. 36* v. *Bird Construction Co. Ltd.* [1995] 1 SCR 85 = (1995) 121 DLR (4th) 193. For New Zealand see *Invercargill CC* v. *Hamlin* [1994] 3 NZLR 513—a decision which forced the Privy Council—[1996] 2 WLR 367 P.C.—to accept that Commonwealth jurisdictions could agree to differ among themselves! For Australia see *Bryan* v. *Maloney* (1995) 182 CLR 609 but, also, *Hill* v. *Van Erp* (1997) 188 CLR 159. The different Commonwealth authorities are discussed by Mullany *Torts in the Nineties* (1997), chapter 1. The cable cases, however, in England (and elsewhere) have remained unaffected so one is forced to cope with some fine distinctions they have provoked and which can also be found in America.

One situation where recovery is allowed is where the plaintiff can prove that his economic loss is immediately consequential upon damage to property. Cf. *Newlin* v. *New England Tel and Tel Co.*, 316 Mass. 234, 54 NE 2d 929 (1944) (USA); *SCM (UK) Ltd.* v. *W J Whittal and Son Ltd* [1971] 1 QB 337 (England); and BGHZ 41, 123 and, more recently, BGH VersR 85, 1147 (Germany). This distinction helps to keep litigation under control, but it is crude and it has not passed uncriticised. (See the powerful dissenting judgment of Edmund Davies LJ in the *Spartan Steel* case.) The comparison of two American cases, *Beck* (above) and *Dunlop Tire and Rubber Corp.* v. *FM Corp.*, 53 App. Div. 2d 150, 385 NYS 2d 971 (1976), offers a good illustration of the problem.

In *Beck* an explosion in factory A (FMC) damaged an electric power plant B (Niagara Mohawk) which supplied electricity to C (a Chevrolet plant). During the power cut, C laid off its hourly-paid work-force, and refused to pay it. D, one of the workers, sued B for breach of warranty and negligence, and A for negligence. The contract-based action was dismissed on the convincing ground that D was only an *incidental* beneficiary of the contract between B and C. The tortious actions against A and B were dismissed on the ground that no duty was owed by either of them to D. The reasoning begs the question, but the court let the cat out of the bag when it said that any ". . . contrary determination would unduly extend the liability of this defendant to an indefinite number of potential beneficiaries".

Dunlop's facts were slightly different, though the action arose out of the same incident at FMC's factory. In *Dunlop* the explosion in A, besides damaging the power company B, also caused stones and debris to fall on C's (Dunlop's) plant. (Dunlop was about a mile closer to the centre of the explosion that Chevrolet was in the *Beck* case.) C (Dunlop) sustained lost profits of $170,000 due to the power cut and a further $16,445 due to the power cut as well as the prejudicial effect that the explosion had on its machinery. With regard to the latter, the court felt that *Beck*'s case did not apply since C's claim was not "vicarious or derivative" (by which the court must have meant ricochet). But is C's tortious action in *Dunlop* really different from that of D in *Beck*? Was *Beck* adequately distinguished, or was the real reason for granting the claim in *Dunlop* connected with the fact that it was closely linked with material damage? This crucial point is only raised as a secondary point by the court.

Dunlop's first and main claim for their purely economic loss was rejected. This time, however, causative language was used.

"Logically [said the court] if damage from the loss of power was foreseeable, then the interruption of production was also foreseeable and the lost profits resulting from the interruption should be compensatable, if proved and if, indeed, lost profits are recoverable at all in a tort action. However, while there is some limited authority that lost profits may be recovered [citations] such damages are subject to the general rule of certainty which requires that the plaintiff prove the extent of the damage and the causal relationship between the defendant's negligence and the damage."

And the court concluded: "A stoppage in production . . . does not necessarily result in lost profits and the damage which a manufacturer may sustain for a 24-hour shut-down of electrical power may well be too remote and speculative to be compensated." Can this reasoning be squared with that in *Beck*? The reasoning of the *Dunlop* court suggests that the floodgates of litigation can be controlled through the medium of foreseeability and remoteness. If that is so why use (as *Beck* did) the duty concept and frustrate recovery in *all* cases?

6. If distinctions are to be made what about the following situations?

(*a*) A damages B's cable which has been installed to service *only* C's factory. Can C recover? The point does not appear to have been decided in either England or Germany but an Australian case has given an affirmative answer. *Caltex Oil (Australia) pty* v. *The Dredge "Willemstad"* (1976) 11 ALR 227. Here the floodgates argument cannot be invoked. Could this case be solved by applying Lord Goff's theory of "transferred loss" or the Germanic equivalent of *Drittschadensliquidation*? (See discussion above, p. 214.) In the *Caltex* case the Australian High Court distanced itself from the broad exclusionary rule so favoured by England courts. But the rich variety of views found in the multi-judgment decision makes it difficult to extract a common ratio decidendi and for this reason its precedental value in subsequent "leading" cases—such as *Norsk*—seems to have been limited.

(*b*) If A damages B's cable and C's molten material solidifies during the power cut *and* has *to be thrown away*, C has suffered material damage and can therefore recover damages for it (and for consequential loss of profits). But what if the solidified material can be remelted and used after the restoration of the power? A German court (OLG Hamm NJW 1973, 760) held that this was not interference with *property* since there was no permanent interference with its *substance*. The reasoning appears too abstract and conceptual, and perhaps it would be more convincing to accept that there is material damage. That the damage was only temporary should thus only influence the quantum of damages rather than the characterization of the loss as material or economic. On these points see Möschel, "Der Schutzbereich des Eigentums nach § 823 I BGB", *JuS* 1977, 1, 5; Isenbeck, note on OLG Hamm in NJW 1973, 1755.

7. Case 9 also considers whether a claim can be based on § 823 II BGB (see discussion in text, chapter 4). In the late 1960s the Supreme Court held that it could: BGH NJW 1968, 1279. The State Court of Appeals refused, however, to follow suit (see, for example, BayObLG NJW 1972, 1085; OLG Hamm NJW 1973, 760; OLG Saarbrücken VersR 1976, 176) and in the end forced the Supreme Court to recant. The answer, however, once again depends on unexpressed policy views about the issues. How else can one explain the fact that identically phrased statutory provisions have received different characterisations in Germany, Austria, and Switzerland? On this see the exhaustive treatment of Bürge in *Juristische Blätter* 1981, 57.

Addendum

Extracts from Lord Denning MR's judgment in *Spartan Steel* v. *Martin and Co.* [1973] 1 QB 27, 36.

At bottom I think the question of recovering economic loss is one of policy. Whenever the courts draw a line to mark out the bounds of duty, they do it as matter of policy so as to limit the responsibility of the defendant. Whenever the courts set bounds to the damages recoverable—saying that they are, or are not, too remote—they do it as matter of policy so as to limit the liability of the defendant.

In many of the cases where economic loss has been held not to be recoverable, it has been put on the ground that the defendant was under no duty to the plaintiff. Thus where a person is injured in a road accident by the negligence of another, the negligent driver owes a duty to the injured man himself, but he owes no duty to the servant of the injured man—see *Best* v. *Samuel Fox and Co. Ltd* [1952] AC 716, 731; nor to the master of the injured man—*Inland Revenue Commissioners* v. *Hambrook* [1956] QB 641, 660; nor to anyone else who suffers loss because he had a contract with the injured man—see *Simpson and Co.* v. *Thomson* (1877) 3 App. Cas. 279, 289; nor indeed to anyone who only suffers economic loss on account of the accident—see *Kirkham* v. *Boughey* [1958] 2 QB 338, 341. Likewise, when property is damaged by the negligence of another, the negligent tortfeasor owes a duty to the owner or possessor of the chattel, but not to one who suffers loss only because he had a contract entitling him to use the chattel or giving him a right to receive it at some later date—see *Elliott Steam Tug Co. Ltd.* v. *Shipping Controller* [1922] 1 KB 127, 139 and *Margarine Union GMBH* v. *Cambay Prince Steamship Co. Ltd* [1969] 1 QB 219, 251–2.

In other cases, however, the defendant seems clearly to have been under a duty to the plaintiff, but the economic loss has not been recovered because it is *too* remote. Take the illustration given by Blackburn J. in *Cattle* v. *Stockton Waterworks Co.* (1875) LR 10 QB 453, 457, when water escapes from a reservoir and floods a coal mine where many men are working. Those who had their tools or clothes destroyed could recover, but those who only lost their wages could not. Similarly, when the defendants' ship negligently sank a ship which was being towed by a tug, the owner of the tug lost his remuneration, but he could not recover it from the negligent ship, though the same duty (of navigation with reasonable care) was owed to both tug and tow—see *Société Anonyme de Remorquage à Hélice* v. *Bennetts* [1911] 1 KB 243, 248. In such cases if the plaintiff or his property had been physically injured, he would have recovered: but, as he only suffered economic loss, he is held not entitled to recover. This is, I should think, because the loss is regarded by the law as too remote—see *King* v. *Phillips* [1953] 1 QB 429, 439–40.

On the other hand, in the cases where economic loss by itself has been held to be recoverable, it is plain that there was a duty to the plaintiff and the loss was not too remote. Such as when one ship negligently runs down another ship, and damages it, with the result that the cargo has to be discharged and reloaded. The negligent ship was already under a duty to the owners of the cargo, and they can recover the cost of discharging and reloading it, as it is not too remote—see *Morrison Steamship Co. Ltd* v. *Greystoke Castle (Cargo Owners)* [1947] AC 265. Likewise, when a banker negligently gives a reference to one who acts on it, the duty is plain and the damage is not too remote—see *Hedley Byrne and Co. Ltd* v. *Heller and Partners Ltd* [1964] AC 465.

The more I think about these cases, the more difficult I find it to put each into its proper pigeon-hole. Sometimes I say: "There was no duty." In others I say: "The damage was too remote." So much so that I think that the time has come to discard those tests which have proved so elusive. It seems to me better to consider the particular relationship in hand, and see whether or not, as a matter of policy, economic loss should be recoverable, or not. Thus in *Weller and Co.* v. *Foot and Mouth Disease Research Institute* [1966] 1 QB 569 it was plain that the loss suffered by the auctioneers was not recoverable, no matter whether it is put on the ground that there was no duty or that the damage was too remote. Again in *Electrochrome Ltd* v. *Welsh Plastics Ltd* [1968] 2 All ER 205, it is plain that the economic loss suffered by the plaintiffs' factory (due to the damage to the fire hydrant) was not recoverable, whether because there was no duty or that it was too remote.

So I turn to the relationship in the present case. It is of common occurrence. The parties concerned are: the electricity board who are under a statutory duty to maintain supplies of electricity in their district; the inhabitants of the district, including this factory, who are entitled by statute to a continuous supply of electricity for their use; and the contractors who dig up the road. Similar relationships occur with other statutory bodies, such as gas and water undertakings. The cable may be damaged by the negligence of the statutory undertaker, or by the negligence of the contractor, or by accident without any negligence by anyone, and the power may have to be cut off whilst the cable is repaired. Or the power may be cut off owing to a short circuit in the power house and so forth. If the cutting-off of the supply causes economic loss to the consumers, should it as matter of policy be recoverable? And against whom?

The first consideration is the position of the statutory undertakers. If the board do not keep up the voltage or pressure of electricity, gas, or water—or, likewise, if they shut it off for repairs—and thereby cause economic loss to their consumers, they are not liable in damages, not even if the cause of it is due to their own negligence. The only remedy (which is hardly ever pursued) is to prosecute the board before the magistrates. Such is the result of many cases, starting with a water board—*Atkinson v. Newcastle and Gateshead Waterworks Co.* (1877) 2 Ex. D. 441; going on to a gas board—*Clegg, Parkinson and Co. v. Earby Gas Co.* [1896] 1 QB 592; and then on to an electricity company—*Stevens v. Aldershot Gas, Water and District Lighting Co. Ltd* best reported in (1932) 31 LGR 68; also in 102 LJKB 12. In those cases the courts, looking at the legislative enactments, held that Parliament did not intend to expose the board to liability for damages to the inhabitants *en masse*: see what Lord Cairns LC said in *Atkinson v. Newcastle and Gateshead Waterworks Co.* 2 Ex. D. 441, 445 and Wills J in *Clegg, Parkinson and Co. v. Earby Gas Co.* [1896] 1 QB 592, 595. In those cases there was indirect damage to the plaintiffs but it was not recoverable. There is another group of cases which go to show that, if the board, by their negligence in the conduct of their supply cause direct physical damage or injury to person or property, they are liable: see *Milnes v. Huddersfield Corporation* (1886) 11 App. Cas. 511, 530 by Lord Blackburn; *Midwood and Co. Ltd v. Manchester Corporation* [1905] 2 KB 597; *Heard v. Brymbo Steel Co. Ltd* [1947] KB 692 and *Hartley v. Mayoh and Co.* [1954] 1 QB 383. But one thing is clear: the statutory undertakers have never been held liable for economic loss only. If such be the policy of the legislature in regard to electricity boards, it would seem right for the Common law to adopt a similar policy in regard to contractors. If the electricity boards are not liable for economic loss due to negligence which results in cutting off the supply, nor should a contractor be liable.

The second consideration is the nature of the hazard, namely cutting off the supply of electricity. This is a hazard which we all run. It may be due to a short circuit, to a flash of lightning, to a tree falling in the wires, to an accidental cutting of the cable, or even to the negligence of someone or other. And when it does happen, it affects a multitude of persons: not as a rule by way of physical damage to them or their property, but by putting them to inconvenience, and sometimes to economic loss. The supply is usually restored in a few hours, so the economic loss is not very large. Such a hazard is regarded by most people as a thing they must put up with—without seeking compensation from anyone. Some there are who install a stand-by system. Others seek refuge by taking out an insurance policy against breakdown in the supply. But most people are content to take the risk on themselves. When the supply is cut off, they do not go running round to their solicitor. They do not try to find out whether it was anyone's fault. They just put up with it. They try to make up the economic loss by doing more work next day. This is a healthy attitude which the law should encourage.

The third consideration is this: if claims for economic loss were permitted for this particular hazard, there would be no end of claims. Some might be genuine, but many might be inflated, or even false. A machine might not have been in use anyway, but it would be easy to put it down to the cut in supply. It would be well nigh impossible to check the claims. If there was economic loss on one day, did the claimant do his best to mitigate it by working harder next day? And so forth. Rather than expose claimants to such temptation and defendants to such hard labour—on comparatively small claims—it is better to disallow economic loss altogether, at any rate when it stands alone, independent of any physical damage.

The fourth consideration is that, in such a hazard as this, the risk of economic loss should be suffered by the whole community who suffer the losses—usually many but comparatively small losses—rather than on the one pair of shoulders, that is, on the contractor on whom the total of them, all added together, might be very heavy.

The fifth consideration is that the law provides for deserving cases. If the defendant is guilty of negligence which cuts off the electricity supply and causes actual physical damage to person or property, that physical damage can be recovered: see *Baker* v. *Crow Carrying Co. Ltd.* (unreported) 1 February 1960; Bar Library Transcript No. 45, referred to by Buckley LJ in *SCM (UK) Ltd.* v. *W J Whittall and Son Ltd.* [1971] 1 QB 337, 356; and also any economic loss truly consequential on the material damage; see *British Celanese Ltd.* v. *A H Hunt (Capacitors) Ltd.* [1969] 1 WLR 959 and *SCM (UK) Ltd.* v. *W J Whittall and Son Ltd.* [1971] 1 QB 337. Such cases will be comparatively few. They will be readily capable of proof and will be easily checked. They should be and are admitted.

These considerations lead me to the conclusion that the plaintiffs should recover for the physical damage to the one melt (£368), and the loss of profit on that melt consequent thereon (£400): but not for the loss of profit on the four melts (£1,767), because that was economic loss independent of the physical damage.

6. ECONOMIC LOSS (LOSS OF USE; OTHER POSSIBLE HEADINGS)

Case 14

BUNDESGERICHTSHOF (SECOND CIVIL SENATE) 21 DECEMBER 1970
BGHZ 55, 153 = NJW 1971, 886 = VERSR 1971, 418

The defendant Federal Republic of Germany was the owner of a navigable channel which connected a mill with the port of B. During the night of 21 October 1965 part of the wall forming the bank collapsed bringing down part of the external wall of a dwelling house based on it. In order to prevent a further collapse of the house, its owner, acting in accordance with an order of the competent authority, the City of B inserted beams as support. Two of these were inserted between the two banks of the channel immediately upon its surface. Thus the channel was effectively closed until the bank of the channel was provisionally restored during the middle of 1966. As a result the plaintiff's motor vessel *Christel* was immobilised at the mill; nor could the plaintiff approach the mill with his other vessels, as he was contractually bound to do, in order to carry goods to and from the mill. He claimed damages amounting to DM 31,061 for loss of earnings.

The Landgericht Stade and the Court of Appeal of Celle allowed the claim. Upon a second appeal, the claim was rejected in part for the following.

Reasons

I. . . .

II. . . .

1. The Court of Appeal is correct in holding that the case of a culpable violation of the duty incumbent upon the defendant by its constitutionally appointed organs to maintain the channel, § 823 I, §§ 89, 31 BGB must be considered as forming the basis of the claim, and not, as the appellant contends § 839 BGB in conjunction with Article 34 of the Federal Constitution (GG) . . .

Prior to and at the time of the collapse of the wall forming the bank the duty to maintain it was vested (by State) in a particular authority. The culpable violation of this duty gives rise to claims under § 823 I BGB [references] . . .

2. . . . it follows from the existing duties of the defendant [references] to keep the channel open to navigation that it is also obliged to prevent the threatening collapse of the wall of the channel by suitable safety measures which the owner must tolerate . . .

In the special circumstances the duty of the defendant to secure the navigability of the channel included not only the duty to restore it when obstructed or rendered impassable, but also the duty to remedy by suitable measures any immediate danger which endangered the navigability of the channel owing to the state of the walls or the banks.

3. As the Court of Appeal has held with justification, the authority constitutionally appointed by the defendant has culpably violated this duty . . .

The appellant is wrong in contending that the culpable violation of this duty was the adequate causation for the closure of the channel and therefore for the losses of the plaintiff resulting therefrom. It is true that the immediate cause for closure of the channel was the order of the city of B of 22 October 1965 and the propping-up of the house, street no. 10 in the execution of this order. Both were only the adequate consequence of the preceding violation of the duty incumbent upon the authority constitutionally appointed by the defendant. For it is not outside common experience that the failure to secure a defective wall of a bank which supports an external wall of a building, can lead to consequences of this kind.

4. The Court of Appeal denies that the provisions concerning the duty to maintain a waterway constitute a protective law in the meaning of § 823 II BGB. This is correct in law [references]. Nevertheless it holds the defendant liable in damages for the loss incurred by the plaintiff through the closure of the channel because the conduct of its constitutionally appointed organ in violation of its duty is to be regarded as an inadmissible interference with an established and active commercial or industrial enterprise. This reasoning, and partly also the result, are open to legal doubts.

(a) Liability based on interference with the right to an established and active commercial or industrial enterprise is subsidiary in character and is incurred only if no other remedy exists, and if the rules in force governing a certain topic viewed as a whole disclose the existence of a gap, which must be closed with the help of § 823 I BGB [reference]. An examination of the case from this angle leads to the following conclusions.

As regards the plaintiff's motor vessel *Christel*, any claim for damages on the ground of interference with a right to an established and active commercial or industrial enterprise is ruled out to the extent that damage to property has occurred which leads to loss. For property is damaged not only if the substance of an object is adversely affected but also by any other actual interference with the right of an owner [references]. In the present case property of the plaintiff in the motor vessel *Christel* has been damaged inasmuch as the vessel was forced to remain at the loading stage of the mill because the channel was closed. It was consequently unable to move beyond that area of the channel between the loading-stage and the beams which formed a bar. It was therefore practically eliminated as a means of transport and was incapable of normal use. The "imprisonment" of the vessel therefore constituted a factual interference with this vessel which affected the rights of the plaintiff as an owner. In denying an interference with property in a similar case the Reichsgericht [reference], contrary to the present Division, clearly proceeded from the assumption that an interference with property in the meaning of § 823 I BGB can exist only in an interference with the substance of an object, but not in any other kind of interference [reference]. Such a narrow interpretation of § 823 I BGB does not, however, accord with the purpose of this provision. This is to protect the rights enumerated therein against any culpable illegal violation. The defendant, who is responsible for the conduct of its constitutionally appointed representative (§§ 89, 31 BGB), who, in violating its duty caused damage, is therefore liable to pay compensation to the plaintiff for the damage arising from the "imprisonment" of the motor vessel *Christel*: § 823 I BGB. To this extent any liability of the defendant is excluded on the ground of illegal culpable interference with the rights of the plaintiff in an established and active commercial or industrial enterprise. Moreover it must remain undecided as to whether any such interference has taken place at all.

As regards the claim for damages in respect of the river boats which could not use the channel the answer must be different. To this extent the defendant has not interfered with the property of the plaintiff for the reason that the river-boats were not affected in their capacity of means of transport by the closure of the channel and were thus not diverted from their natural use. This conclusion is not altered by the fact that the plaintiff was unable to dispatch the river-boats to the loading-stage of the mill while the channel was closed. This cannot be regarded as an interference with property, but is a restriction of the plaintiff in the enjoyment of the common use of the channel together with all others who engage in shipping. Such common use is not, however, "another right" in the meaning of § 823 I BGB [reference].

(*b*) Therefore the question as to whether the violation of their duty by the constitutionally appointed authority is to be regarded as an inadmissible interference with an established and active commercial or industrial enterprise is only relevant in respect of the plaintiff's claim for damages arising out of the closure of the channel. This court disagrees with the Court of Appeal which answered the question in the affirmative. The appellant is, however, wrong in arguing that in the present no right of the plaintiff in an established and active commercial or industrial enterprise has been violated if only for the reason that such a violation cannot be committed by an omission. The rights and legal interest which are protected by § 823 I BGB can also be violated through an omission [reference]. The appellant is right, however, in contending that the observations of the Court of Appeal as to whether in the present case the defendant has directly interfered with the plaintiff's established and active commercial or industrial enterprise is not open to legal objections, at least in so far as they concern the amount of damages in issue.

It is recognised by the practice of the courts that not every illegal and culpable interference with the business activity of another gives rise to claims for damages in accordance with § 823 I BGB. Instead, this is only the case if the interference touches directly the sphere of the commercial or industrial enterprise, therefore centred on the enterprise and does not affect rights or protected interests which can be separated without difficulty from the commercial or industrial enterprise [references]. In the present case no such interference aimed at the plaintiff's enterprise has taken place. The navigability of a waterway does not fall within the ambit of the commercial enterprise of a person engaged in shipping. A temporary closure of a waterway which also concerns others engaged in shipping does not therefore interfere with the plaintiff's commercial enterprise. The Court of Appeal wishes to come to a different conclusion in the present case on the ground that the plaintiff's vessels had used the channel, before its closure, more than others engaged in shipping—at times almost exclusively—and that the closure has temporarily prevented the plaintiff from complying with his contractual obligations towards the mill; but this reasoning cannot be accepted. The existence of such obligations does not mean that the navigability of a waterway, which a person engaged in shipping has to use within the framework of his contractual obligations, is to be regarded as falling within the sphere of that person's commercial enterprises. The contrary opinion of the Court of Appeal cannot be supported either by the consideration that at the time when the river-wall collapsed the journeys of the plaintiff's vessel on behalf of the mill represented an important part of the plaintiff's commercial activities. The question as to what falls within the commercial enterprise of a person engaged in shipping cannot be determined by the fact that one or several of his vessels are principally employed on certain river routes, seeing that this depends on the offers to load them made by third parties. The Court of Appeal is therefore wrong in holding that in the present case the defendant is liable to pay damages for having interfered with the plaintiff's established and active commercial enterprise also in so far as he could not for a time use the channel for his vessels. If this opinion were accepted it would mean that common users would be protected under the heading of "any other rights" of § 823 I BGB, if only by the circuitous route of a right in an established and active commercial or industrial enterprise.

It follows that the judgment appealed against is only to be upheld to the extent that it declares the plaintiff's claim arising out of the "imprisonment" of the motor vessel *Christel* to be justified (DM 24,086). The additional claim (DM 6965) must be dismissed.

Case 15

BUNDESGERICHTSHOF (SIXTH CIVIL SENATE) 21 JUNE 1977
NJW 1977, 2264 = VERSR 1977, 965

The defendant was the liquidator in the bankruptcy of a limited partnership and of its deceased partner D who was personally liable. The partnership had conducted the business of a major petrol depot. In May 1972, a motorised petrol tanker belonging to a third party attended the depot in order to take on petrol. Owing to the negligence of the tanker's driver, a fire broke out, but the partnership as owners of the premises and the deceased partner were also to be blamed for having failed to prevent the negligent handling of the loading process by the driver of the tanker. Fearing that the fire might spread to the depot as a whole, the police ordered the temporary closure of the plaintiff's business premises for two hours and blocked for another three hours the access roads in order to keep them clear for the fire brigade. The plaintiff, on whose premises work had stopped for five hours, claimed damages representing wages paid and general expenses incurred in respect of the period of closure. He sued the defendant, the owner of the tanker and his employee.

The Court of First Instance and the Court of Appeal of Bamberg gave judgment for the plaintiff. Upon a second appeal by the defendant the judgment of the Court was quashed and the case was referred back to the Court of First Instance for the following.

Reasons

I. The Court of Appeal is of the opinion that the bankrupt is liable to pay damages because he has negligently damaged the established and active commercial enterprise of the plaintiff ("another right" in the meaning of § 823 I BGB). It held that in view of the existing danger to life the police could not allow the persons necessary to run the plaintiff's business to remain; thus the head office of the enterprise had ceased to function between 8.30 am and 10.30 am. Thus the fire had directly affected the running of the plaintiff's enterprise. Therefore the non-productive expenditure of wages and other running costs covering the five hours during which business was interrupted, as alleged by the plaintiff, constituted a direct damage to be compensated in accordance with § 823 I BGB. In this respect it held that the claim for damages was well founded. The Court of Appeal refrained therefore from determining whether the claim could also be maintained on the ground that the plaintiff's property in the business premises had been violated or on the basis of § 823 II BGB in conjunction with the Decree concerning Inflammable Liquids of 5 June 1970 (henceforth called the Decree) [reference].

II. The arguments cannot be supported in law for several reasons. It must be objected in the first place that the Court of Appeal has wrongly simplified the account of the facts referred to in the plaintiff's pleadings seeking to establish liability. A distinction must be drawn between the first period of two hours during which the business premises of the plaintiff were in immediate danger and were evacuated upon the order of the police and the ensuing period when, because of the fire in the tank depot, vehicles of the police and the fire brigade only blocked the (public) access road to the plaintiff's business premises, as a result of which, as the plaintiff alleges, no vehicles could leave the premises, thus making it impossible to supply the building lots for which he was responsible.

These two situations must be considered separately from the legal point of view. During the first period the plaintiff's premises and his power to dispose of them were directly curtailed. Subsequently however, the plaintiff was only prevented from enjoying the common use of a public highway, although he may have been particularly affected, since his premises border on to it, particularly as it provided the only access. The facts as found by the Court of First Instance do not disclose whether this interruption of traffic was damage resulting from the dangerous situation which threatened the plaintiff's premises or was the result of the measures to remove the danger.

1. Damage resulting from the closure of the business premises during the final two hours

(a) In this respect it is altogether questionable why the Court of Appeal was able to affirm that an interference with an established and active commercial enterprise had occurred. It is noted in the judgment and admitted that the Bundesgerichtshof regards it as imperative that the interference must be aimed at the enterprise [references] and that the Bundesgerichtshof is concerned above all to counter any excess, contrary to the legal system, of this special remedy in tort [reference]. The requirement that the interference must be aimed at the enterprise, to be meaningful, can only be understood in the sense that he who interfered must have violated those duties of conduct incumbent upon him in view of the particular needs of protection of a commercial or industrial enterprise. Nothing else can be deduced either from the dogmatic considerations contained in the aforementioned decision of this Division [reference], contrary to the Court of Appeal. It is necessary, however, to enlarge on this aspect. Precisely for the reason that the special remedy in tort created by the practice of this court is only intended to fulfil a need peculiar to commercial or industrial enterprise, it only concerns a situation not covered otherwise [references] which must give way to other legal grounds [references]. For this reason alone it was therefore wrong for the Court of Appeal, without considering other grounds for the claim, to proceed immediately to an examination as to whether a right in an established and active commercial or industrial enterprise had been violated.

(*b*) In fact, to the extent that it is based on the temporary evacuation on the order of the police and the acute danger of a fire and an explosion which was the reason for it, the plaintiff's claim for damages is justified under § 823 I BGB because his ownership and possession were infringed.

It is true that the substance of the premises and of the installations of the enterprise were not touched; this, however, is not essential [references]. As this Division has already stated in its decision of 14 February 1967 [references], the deprivation of an object, even if unaccompanied by damage or destruction, may constitute a violation of ownership in the meaning of § 823 I BGB [references]; the same applies to interference with an object which renders its use impossible [references]. On the other hand the mere fact that an object was endangered physically was not always treated as a violation of property [references]. This Division cannot share that view in a case such as the present where the existence of an acute danger obviously precluded any use, at least for a while. Moreover the right of ownership of the plaintiff (§ 903 BGB) was seriously restricted by the order of the police to evacuate the premises, even if only temporarily. For both these reasons those responsible for the fire in the petrol depot are liable for the violation of another's protected legal interest.

Thus the claim, to the extent considered at this stage, is justified as a violation of property (§ 823 I BGB). It need not be decided here whether the same result could be reached by applying § 823 II BGB in conjunction with the Decree or with § 309 of the Criminal Code.

2. *Damage resulting from the blocking of the public access road*

According to the plaintiff's pleadings . . . after the evacuation of his premises at the orders of the police had come to an end, he was prevented from dispatching his vehicles loaded with materials because the feeder road providing access to the business premises of the plaintiff continued to be blocked by vehicles of the police and of the fire brigade. Their presence, it would appear, no longer served the direct purpose of protecting the plaintiff's premises but in order to secure and to guard the place of the fire itself (see above, Introduction to II). It would seem that in the opinion of the Court of Appeal, the plaintiff's claim in respect of the ensuing loss was justified. This Division cannot accept this conclusion even in principle—unlike in the situation dealt with in (1), above.

(*a*) As stated previously, there are no indications that the damage is connected with the temporary danger to and evacuation of the premises of the plaintiff's enterprise. Consequently the damage cannot, to this extent, be the result of the violation of property examined in (1), above. It would also be wrong to regard the short-time interruption of public traffic on the access roads to the plaintiff's premises as an interference with the ownership of business premises. The difference from the case decided by the Bundesgerichtshof in [reference] (an inland waterways vessel being detained for months in a channel of a river) is obvious. The plaintiff has not put forward this view either; further, it is unnecessary to take into account that the Court of First Instance—the Court of Appeal left the question open—rightly requested the negligent conduct of the bankrupt owners of the petrol depot as involving several violations of provisions of the Decree. The reason is that there are no indications that these provisions of § 309 of the Criminal Code are intended to provide protection individually for traffic users [reference] whose freedom of movement is restricted temporarily as a result of the closure of a road for the purpose of extinguishing a fire and for safety measures. It is insufficient that the plaintiff, as the owner of neighbouring premises, was particularly affected by the closure.

The special remedy intended to cover a situation not provided for otherwise, namely for interference with a facility and an active or commercial or industrial enterprise cannot assist either. It is not the purpose of this special remedy to provide businessmen with a claim for damages in respect of losses which others would have to bear in similar circumstances without being able to make any claim. This applies at all events where the common user of a public highway is obstructed temporarily. For it is recognized that a common user is not "another right" protected by § 823 I BGB [reference]. This principle must not be evaded by granting protection to an established and active commercial or industrial enterprise. For the same reason any such interference must not be regarded as aimed at an enterprise [reference]. In the absence of evidence to the contrary it cannot be so aimed if every other interested person is exposed to the same impediment and must bear his own losses having regard to the substantive principles which attribute liability in damages. Such is the case where the common user of a public highway is interrupted temporarily. As regards the provisions of the Decree and of § 309 of the Criminal Code this conclusion was reached before. The same applies to infringements of the law which typically leads to a temporary standstill of traffic, in particular if provisions of the Road Traffic Regulations are contravened. In such cases the practice of the courts has attributed to the guilty party accidents suffered by others which resulted from a continuing situation creating a danger [reference]. On the other hand, it would seem that claims for damages by such users of a public highway have never been allowed under § 823 II BGB in conjunction with the traffic regulations which had been violated, if the claimants suffered pecuniary losses as a result of a hold-up of traffic following an accident. Here the argument applies once again that the purpose of traffic regulations cannot be to provide protection to that extent, seeing that such adverse consequences must be accepted without compensation by every person using public highways as a matter of chance.

(b) If this is so, no special right can exist either viewed from the perspective of a right in an established and active commercial or industrial enterprise. Instead those carrying on a commercial or an industrial enterprise can be expected to bear without compensation such losses as does everyone else living under the same law who suffers severe pecuniary damage through loss of time. This applies certainly to such restrictions in the common user of a public highway which, while they may be particularly serious for a commercial or industrial enterprise, remain on the whole within those limits which other road users must also tolerate without compensation. This applies in the present case. In view of the facts the question must not be decided here possibly in the light of the law relating to expropriation or of sacrifice for the public good as to whether a tort by a private person may so affect a common user adversely as to require that person to pay damages, at least when the interference is of long or even indeterminate duration [reference]. In such a case the commercial or industrial enterprise would be seriously prejudiced while any interference which may even last for several weeks would have to be tolerated without compensation [reference], and it would then have to be considered whether a tort had been committed by interference with an established and active commercial or industrial enterprise.

III. 1. . . .

The Court of First Instance, to which the issue will be referred back to determine the amount of damages will have to take into account in particular that the plaintiff cannot, as he has done hitherto, specify his damages in the abstract in accordance with the extent of his expenses which have turned out to be useless. No legal rule requires that all expenses which have become useless as a result of the damaging event must be compensated, [reference] . . . Instead the Court of First Instance will have to examine on its own to what extent the plaintiff has been lastingly deprived of profits as a result of those incidents of interference with his business which give rise to a claim for damages.

Case 16

BUNDESGERICHTSHOF (SECOND CIVIL SENATE) 9 APRIL 1984
NJW 1984, 2569 = VERSR 1984, 584

Facts

In the summer of 1980 the plaintiff started to construct an inner harbour wall about 230 metres long out of steel shuttering. The employer and owner of the harbour was the city. On 16 March 1981 while building operations were still in train, the barge TS on entering the harbour collided with and damaged the part of the wall, which had been constructed. The plaintiff repaired the wall and sued the defendant as owner of the barge for its expense in so doing, claiming both in its own right and as assignee of the city.

The Rhine Navigation Court held the claim admissible, but the Rhine Navigation Court of Appeal dismissed it. The Bundesgerichtshof reversed and remanded.

Reasons

1. The owner of a ship is answerable for damage done to a third party by the fault of any of the crew in the execution of his functions (§ 3 (1) BinnSchG). Not only must causative fault on the part of a crew member be shown but that person must actually be liable to the third party [references]. The relevant basis of liability here is § 823 I BGB.

2. The Court of Appeal did not decide whether any of the crew were at fault in the collision with the coffer-dam, nor whether the navigational signs at the harbour entrance had been correctly positioned by the city, as the plaintiff alleged. For the purposes of this appeal both assumptions must be made in favour of the plaintiff.

3. According to the Court of Appeal the plaintiff cannot complain of damage to property because the plaintiff did not own the part of the wall which was damaged: it belonged to the city.

The piles driven into the harbour bed were firmly attached to it and formed an essential component of the harbour itself, which was vested in the city. The piles were not there as a merely temporary measure: they were to remain there for the duration of the works. It is irrelevant that at the time of the accident the city had not yet accepted the half-built wall. Important as acceptance is for the contractual relations between the plaintiff and the city (see §§ 640 ff. BGB) it is irrelevant to the question of the ownership of the constructed part of the wall. That falls to be determined by §§ 94, 946 BGB, as the court below correctly stated. This turns on objective factors (permanent fixture to the soil) and not on the attitudes of the contractor and owner of the land. To the extent that these have a role to play under § 95 BGB, the appellant is bound by the finding that the piles were driven into the ground for the duration and not for subsequent removal, so that there can be no question of this being "a purely temporary measure" [references].

4. The Court of Appeal further held that the plaintiff could not base a claim on interference with possession. It held:

At the time of the accident the plaintiff was certainly still in possession of the standing portion of the wall; for the purpose of executing its building operations, it had direct physical control of the building site, the piles already installed, and the wall, on which they were still working. But possession is protected by § 823 I BGB only in so far as it confers a right to possession, use, or enjoyment. The claim under § 823 I BGB is geared in principle to the replacement of the injury to possession, not to injury to the thing itself; but the plaintiff's claim is addressed to injury to the thing itself so that it does not lie under the heading of interference with possession.

Contrary to the view of the Court of Appeal the plaintiff's possession of the cofferdam is a sufficient basis for its claim, on the factual assumptions made for the purposes of this appeal (2. above). The plaintiff was still bound to complete the work after it had been damaged (see §§ 631, 644 BGB). Until the city accepted it, the plaintiff bore the risk of having to repair at its own expense any damage to the wall caused by third parties, and until that was done the city was bound neither to accept the work nor pay the agreed fee. Thus the plaintiff's possession of the wall was associated with responsibility for its condition. This is enough to support a claim for the cost of the repairs. The case is akin to those where a tenant or lessee is contractually liable to the landlord or lessor for damage done to the thing by a third party. The tenant and lessee have been granted a claim for damages against the third party based on their possession [references]. Those are admittedly cases of "liability-harm" [reference], whereas here it is by reason of his duty of performance *vis-à-vis* the site owner that the possessor suffers. Nevertheless, this is equally a consequential loss attributable to invasion of a legally protected interest, and it is irrelevant that it is purely economic in nature [reference]. The Court of Appeal was in error to suppose that in NJW 1970, 38 ff. the Sixth Civil Senate had held that a building contractor had no claim based on possession against another contractor for damaging work done by the first contractor and not yet accepted. On the contrary, the judgment expressly left this question open, the first contractor in that case being no longer in possession of the work. . . .

Case 17

BUNDESGERICHTSHOF (SEVENTH CIVIL SENATE) 23 APRIL 1981
NJW 1981, 1779 = WM 1981, 773

In 1973 as the general building contractor for the District of M the plaintiff built a centre for the disabled. The plaintiff delegated to the defendant the tiling operation of the proposed structure. For this purpose they agreed that the standard contract VOB\B (1952) should apply, but they made special provision concerning delivery and conditions and warranties in respect of legal or physical defects. According to the list of work to be done, the surrounds of the swimming pool of the Special School were to be covered with tiles made of artificial stone which were to be "non-slip as a cover of the bottom". The architect K, who was appointed by the District of M, selected the tiles from samples submitted by the defendant.

When the swimming pool was opened, it appeared that the tiles submitted by the defendant did not prevent slipping. At first the District asked the plaintiff to remedy the defect free of cost. The plaintiff refused and referred the District to its remedy against the architect.

Thereupon the District instructed the plaintiff by an additional contract and against further payment to replace the unsuitable tiles by others which prevented slipping. The plaintiff once again employed the defendant for the fixed price of DM 7992 and received in return DM 9000 from the District. To the latter extent the District claimed damages from the architect on the ground that he made a mistake in selecting the tiles. The latter's Insurance Company paid this sum in full and in subsequent proceedings sued the plaintiff for the payment of two-thirds of this amount. The District Court of Essen, by a decision of 5 November 1976 condemned the plaintiff to pay one half of the amount (i.e. DM 4500). The plaintiff accepted this and, in turn, claimed compensation from the defendant.

The District Court rejected the claim. The Court of Appeal of Düsseldorf gave judgment in favour of the plaintiff for DM 1500. Upon leave to lodge a second appeal the judgment of the District Court was restored.

Reasons

The Court of Appeal allowed the plaintiff's claim to the extent of one half of the sum paid to the Insurance Company of the architect on the ground that the defendant's performance was fundamentally defective in the meaning of § 13 nos. 1 and 7 of the standard contract. It held that in selecting the tiles both the defendant as well as the clerk of the works had failed, in violation of their duty according to § 4 no. 3 of the standard contract, to make an examination and to give advice; as a result the work had been defective.

The liability of the defendant in respect of defects was not ruled out by the fact that the plaintiff had not asked the defendant to remedy the defect. It was true that, had the owner of the building sued the plaintiff as the principal contractor for damages in respect of defects, the plaintiff would have been obliged to give the defendant in his capacity of sub-contractor the opportunity to make good the defect. However, instead of asking for the defects to be remedied the District M had instructed the plaintiff to replace the defective tiles by non-slip tiles and had demanded with justification that the architect should pay for the expenses in remedying the defects. In the opinion of the Court of Appeal the plaintiff had been under an obligation to compensate in part the architect's insurance company and had been unable to rely in relation to the latter, upon its right to ask for the defect to be removed—even if the claims of limitations or if liability had been restricted by agreement. As between the principal building contractor and the sub-contractor it would be inequitable if the latter, who was the real cause of the damage, could effectively plead that he had not been asked to remedy the defect, while the principal contractor was precluded from relying on this defence. If the latter was liable to pay, he should also be entitled to hold the sub-contractor liable for the consequence of the defect.

The conclusions of the Court of Appeal cannot be accepted. They are contrary to the particular legal nature of sub-contracting.

1. Since no question arises as to claims sounding in tort, the plaintiff's claims against the defendant can only result from the instructions given on 4 April 1973. The contract of the general or principal building contractor with the sub-contractor is an independent contract to perform building operations; it creates mutual rights and duties which are independent of those which may exist between the owner of the building or others connected with the building operation and the principal building contractor and of the extent to which they rely on them [references].

The liability of the principal building contractor does not as such have any repercussions upon his contractual relationship with the sub-contractor. Neither the letter appointing the sub-contractor nor the documents accompanying the contract provide, in addition to liability for defects, for liability of the sub-contractor by way of recourse in the sense that he must assume liability for pecuniary obligations of the principal contractor, if the sub-contractor is liable in the last resort for the basis of this obligation. Such a right of recourse cannot be derived either from a general liability for a breach of contract by a positive act. If the breach of contractual duties to examine and to advise does not result in more than a defective performance, any liability of the sub-contractor—as the Court of Appeal does not fail to recognise—can only be based on the responsibility for defective performance (see §§ 4 no. 3 and 13 no. 3 of the standard contract); it cannot be based in addition on the failure to observe the general duty to protect the other party to the contract against loss [references].

2. Since the defendant fitted tiles on the surround of the swimming pool which were not anti-slip and thus were contrary to the contract and unsuitable, without having drawn the attention of the plaintiff that the tiles selected by the architect in the presence of the clerk of the works were unsuitable, the plaintiff has a claim to have the tiles replaced or— if the defendant should refuse to do so—for damages in remedying the defect. However, the plaintiff has forfeited this claim not only because he failed to invite the defendant to remedy the defect, as required by § 13 no. 7 of the standard contract [reference], but also because he gave additional instructions, accompanied by the promise of payment, to exchange the tiles for others [reference]. Thereby any claim for damages according to § 13 no. 7 of the standard contract was lost [reference].

3. It is true that the principal contractor is liable for the culpable acts of the sub-contractor as his aid in performing the contract; however they are not co-debtors of the owner of the building and of others connected therewith as regards their liability for defects. The sub-contractor owes his duty to the main contractor, not to the owner of the building, and thus § 421 BGB does not apply. A claim by the architect of the building owner against the main contractor for partial compensation cannot therefore be brought against the sub-contractor at the same time. The plaintiff, too, did not acquire a claim for partial compensation against the defendant by repaying to the architect and his insurance company half of the expenses in remedying the defects.

4. The plaintiff cannot either base his claim on considerations of equity.

(a) It is true that according to § 242 BGB reasons of equity may result in the reduction or even in the rejection of claims. On the other hand, reasons of equity cannot create claims which do not exist in law or in contract [reference].

(b) The rejection of the claim by the District Court is also not inequitable.

When the plaintiff received, on 20 June 1974, the additional order, he was not prevented from requesting the defendant to replace the tiles on the ground of liability for defects, seeing that they were clearly defective [references]. If the plaintiff should have regarded this as inequitable, having regard to the additional order received from the owner of the building, he could at least have reserved his right of recourse, in case the architect who was involved in the wrong selection should be sued by the owner of the building in respect of the defects in the building which were partly caused by the architect, but by the architect, who would ask for partial compensation, if sued by the owner of the building. A main or general contractor can provide adequately for such a risk in his contracts with the sub-contractors. If he fails to do so, he cannot shift the legal consequences to the subcontractor on the ground that they are inequitable.

The plaintiff as the main contractor has received a higher remuneration than the subcontractor in respect of the same performance. The fact that as the main contractor he received a higher remuneration is justified, in particular, by the higher risk run by the main contractor as a co-debtor side by side with the architect and other specialists.

Case 18

BUNDESGERICHTSHOF (SIXTH CIVIL SENATE) 4 NOVEMBER 1997
BGHZ 137, 89 = NJW 1998, 377

Facts

In this case a commune in Saxony is claiming damages in respect of the harm caused by unlawful interference with development on its land. Shortly after the reunification of Germany the plaintiff decided, against the wishes of a number of citizens, to construct an industrial park. It entered into a development contract with H., an architect, who entrusted the work to two named building contractors. The plans having been approved by Ministry for Economy and Employment in Saxony and the appropriate government committee, work was due to start on the morning of 22 April 1991. On that day, however—and, according to the plaintiff, the following day as well—demonstrators from the civic movement made it impossible for any work to be done. The plaintiff charges the defendants with taking part in the demonstration and collaborating in a plan to disrupt the work, thereby causing damage to the contractors which they put at DM 62,909.66. This sum the plaintiff paid to them and now, having prudently taken an assignment of the contractors' claim, seeks to recover it from the defendants.

Reasons

I. The court below was of opinion that the first, second, third and fifth defendants were liable to the plaintiff either in tort or in unjustified enrichment, regardless of whether the plaintiff had actually paid the sum in issue to the contractors: if it had paid, it could bring a *condictio* against the defendants under § 267(1) BGB as a third party who has paid off a debt due from the defendants; if they had not, they could sue in tort on the basis of the contractors' claim for damages duly assigned to it.

The court held that the defendants were at fault and had unlawfully infringed an interest of the contractors which was protected under § 823 I BGB, namely their lawful possession of the construction machinery, interference with its use being a relevant infringement. The members of the civic movement who foregathered on the morning of 24 April did so with the intention of disrupting the construction work. The disruption continued until the afternoon of the following day and only came to an end when, pursuant to a conversation with the mayor's office, the citizens were shown the documents authorising the works. During those two days the demonstrators positioned themselves so close to the machines that the work could not proceed in safety: they were effectively blockaded. This blockade was unlawful, and not protected as the exercise of fundamental rights under Article 5(1) and 8 of the constitution. The defendants were liable as collaborators and assistants for the harm resulting from this infringement of the contractors' protected interests, for they had all been present at least for part of the demonstration and had endorsed and helped in the blockade: the third defendant had acted as spokesperson for the demonstrators, the first defendant had furthered its purposes in an administrative capacity by making telephone calls to the authorities and so on, and the second defendant had posed in the shovel of a mechanical digger for a spectacular press photograph.

Further details were required of the loss of use of machinery and vehicles suffered by the contractors, but the claim for VAT on their losses could be dismissed right away. There was no question of contributory fault on the part of the contractors or of the present plaintiff.

Some of the appellants' criticisms of the decision below are justified: the judgment is not fully supported by findings of fact, some of which are procedurally flawed. [1, 2. Procedural points; 3. Discussion of the claim in unjust enrichment, and the validity of the assignment.]

The court below was right to start out from the position that the two-day blockade of the machines allocated to the construction work was an unlawful infringement, by persons at fault, of one of the contractor's protected interests. This in principle gave the contractors a claim under § 823 I BGB even under the conditions prevailing in the newly incorporated provinces so shortly after reunification.

(a) We may leave aside the question where and under what circumstances conduct such as is here alleged constitutes an unlawful infringement of an established and operative business (on which see BGHZ 59, 30, 34 = NJW 1972, 1366). For the court below did not err when it held that the contractors' lawful possession of the machinery was a legally protected interest which the blockade infringed.

(aa) It is established by case law that if an owner is prevented from using his property as intended, this may constitute an infringement of his ownership (BGHZ 55, 153, 159 = NJW 1971, 886).

(bb) The same must be true of the right of lawful possession: if the thing possessed is to be used in a particular way and such use is unlawfully inhibited, this is an infringement of a legally protected interest under § 823 I. The equipment which the contractors brought on to the proposed industrial park on the morning of 22 April 1991 was to be used for the work of construction they had undertaken. Conduct of the kind found by the court below which resulted in a total blockade of the machines so that they could not be used for two full working days—no negligible or fleeting disturbance (NJW 1977, 2264, 2265)—can amount to a tortious infringement of the contractors' lawful possession. In the circumstances we need not ask if the contractors actually owned the machines, since the appellants do not deny that the machines were in the contractors' lawful possession.

(b) On the basis that it was right to charge the defendants with the two-day blockade and consequently with an infringement, objectively speaking, of the contractors' possession under § 823 I BGB, the court below cannot be criticised, contrary to the view of the appellants, for holding that it was unlawful.

(aa) The appellants are right, however, to argue that the blockade cannot count as the "violence" required by § 240(1) Criminal Code for the crime of oppressive coercion (*Nötigung*). For demonstrators to place themselves in the immediate vicinity of vehicles, machinery and so on and thereby stymie the operations by bringing moral rather than physical pressure on the contractors' personnel does not amount to the violence required by that provision (for details see BVerfGE 92, 1 = NJW 1995, 1141). But this does not mean that such conduct cannot count as an unlawful infringement of a protected interest under the private law of tort.

(bb) But even conduct which objectively infringes an interest protected by § 823 I BGB is not unlawful if it is legitimated as the exercise of a constitutionally protected right. The relevant right here is the right of assembly under Article 8 GG, but it does not cover a blockade of the kind and extent found by the court below. A defendant who deliberately uses direct pressure against a particular protected interest of another cannot normally invoke the constitutional right of assembly (BGHZ 59, 30, 35 f. = NJW 1972, 1366), for this right, like that of freedom of expression of opinion, is designed to safeguard the right of a group to publicise their views by intelligible means when there is a conflict of opinions such as is inherent in a democratic society (BGHZ 59, 30, 36 = NJW 1972, 1366).

(cc) Even if contained within constitutional limits, the exercise of the basic right under Article 8 GG may well infringe the rights of others. If so, this must just be accepted. This may be the case when demonstrations have results which, though inevitable, are unintended (such as interference with traffic movements or access to the streets, squares and other places where the demonstration is being held), or when the intentional interferences are inconsiderable and of very short duration, as when, in this case, demonstrators climbed on to the machines for a media photo-call. But when, instead of exchanging views, presenting the other side of a dispute or making a protest as such, one actively puts pressure on third parties to prevent them from exercising their rights, one leaves the area protected by the freedom of assembly. The right of assembly protects attempts to convert opponents to one's own opinion, not measures designed to force others to submit against their will. The latter is the case here if, as the court below held, the demonstrators positioned themselves right beside the construction machinery and thereby, as intended, prevented the execution of the work for two full days.

(dd) Although these events took place in one of the newly incorporated provinces only a few months after reunification this does not, contrary to the view of the appellants, affect the decision that this conduct was unlawful. The special conditions facing the citizens in the new provinces at this period of abrupt change on all fronts may indeed be taken into account in the balancing and weighting of the parties' interests which is necessary in every case. Nevertheless the appellants cannot usefully invoke the "confrontational culture" which existed in the DDR when, in order to bring about changes in the one-party regime, citizens made frequent and intensive use of the right of demonstration. At the time of the events now in question the rule of law was already established in the new provinces, and it would be inconsistent with it to make the lawfulness of conduct depend on standards appropriate to conflict with the previous regime. Under the constitution, which was fully in force there at the time, the lawfulness of the exercise of a fundamental right and the unlawfulness of an infringement of the legally protected interests of third parties cannot be affected by considerations of what would have been licit or desirable during the events which triggered change in the DDR.

(c) There is no evidence that the defendants' experiences with the previous regime in the DDR actually led them to think that their actions were lawful, but in any case this would be relevant only to the question of whether they were at fault (see BGHZ 59, 30, 39 f. = NJW 1972, 1366). The judgment below hints that the failure of the police to intervene may have led the demonstrators to think that their actions were justified, but, as the court held, only if such a mistake of law were unavoidable could failure to realise the unlawfulness of their actions in the given circumstances prevent a finding of fault (BGHZ 118, 201, 208 = NJW 1992, 2014). If the defendants here supposed, without making any inquiries, that the conduct charged against them was lawful, they are guilty of negligence at least.

5. The appellants are right, however, to criticise the findings of the court below as to the extent and effect of the conduct of the several defendants against whom it entered judgment. The court based its holding that the contractors had a good claim for tortious infringement of their lawful possession on the view that the assemblies which hindered the construction works lasted for the whole of 22 and 23 April and that, as was intended, the use of the machines for their proper purpose was wholly prevented during that period. The findings underlying this conclusion are procedurally flawed.

(a) We cannot on review uphold the appellants' objection to the finding that, as the demonstrators intended, the blockade of the machines lasted for the whole of 22 April. This finding was open to the judge of fact, though it was based on very slender evidence. Nor, contrary to the view of the appellants, was it a fault of procedure that the judges whose decision was based on the evidence of M did not actually hear him give that evidence: that would be relevant only if it had had important aspects which did not figure in the written report.

(b) By contrast the finding that the demonstrators blockaded the construction machinery for the whole of the following day is flawed.

6. The court below held that the defendants' participation in the blockading measures rendered them liable in tort. The appellants are right to object to this: the findings of fact do not satisfy the requirements of § 830 I (1) and II BGB as to the liability of joint tortfeasors and accessories.

(a) The court below started out correctly by noting that the question whether a person who participates in conduct involving delictual liability falls within these provisions as a joint tortfeasor or accessory depends on principles developed in criminal law (BGHZ 63, 124, 126 = NJW 1975, 49; BGHZ 89, 383, 389 = NJW 1984, 1226). The participation must therefore be with knowledge of the facts and at least some degree of intention on the part of the individual to commit the act in conjunction with others or to facilitate the act of another; objectively there must in addition be some actual participation in the execution of the act which in some way advances its commission and is material to it. Thus a person who participates in a demonstration will be liable if he knows it is intended to create a blockade which infringes rights and causes harm (BGHZ 59, 30, 42 = NJW 1972, 1366).

There is no need to distinguish between co-authors and accessories since in tort law both are treated alike under § 830 II BGB. The assistance lent by an accessory need not be physical in nature—moral support may be sufficient (BGHZ 63, 124, 130 = NJW 1975, 49)—but it must be established, consistently with the requirements of the criminal law relevant to § 830 I (1) and II BGB, that each individual was guilty of conduct which supported the unlawful infringement of the rights of another and was associated with knowledge of the facts and the intention to commit such an infringement.

(b) In the light of these principles the third defendant is the only one for whose liability for participating in the blockade the court below has laid a proper foundation. The third defendant acted as spokesperson for the demonstrators so the court could rightly hold that she not only had a significant influence on the actual course of the demonstration but also, subjectively, intended that the harmful conduct should take place. To this extent the role and functions adopted by her in the demonstration may elucidate her inner intentions (BGHZ 63, 124, 128 = NJW 1975, 49); the court below could well base its judgment on the third defendant's leading role in the way the demonstration developed.

(c) However, the liability of the other defendants is not supported by the findings made thus far.

(aa) This is clearest in the case of the fifth defendant. On the wholly conclusory evidence of S, the court held that the fifth defendant participated in the demonstration on 22 April but it made no finding as to the nature, extent or duration of such participation. But temporary presence at the place of the demonstration and unspecified participation in the assembly are not enough in themselves to imply co-authorship or accessoryship as regards the infringements of rights here in issue. Mere "participation in an assembly" may be a permissible way of evincing in public one's opinion on the matter in issue, and thus be constitutionally protected by Article 5(1) and 8(1) of the constitution (see BGHZ 89, 383, 395 = NJW 1984, 1226). This is true not only of presence at mass demonstrations but also of participation in smaller and less unwieldy gatherings, provided that such participation does not go beyond what is permitted by the exercise of the rights mentioned, that the individual has no part in a project to invade rights, does not subjectively endorse the harmful conduct of the others and does not join the demonstration in knowledge of its intention to create a blockade (see BGHZ 63, 124, 128 = NJW 1975, 49). At present there is no sufficient finding that the fifth defendant in fact contributed even morally to the infringement of the contractors' rights in any legally relevant manner, much less any findings about his mental attitude.

(bb) Nor has any sufficient foundation been laid for the liability of the first defendant.

The court below relied essentially on the evidence of S, who testified that "he had spoken with her in the street and that she had said she was one of the demonstrators"; it was error in law for the court to hold that this was evidence of intentional support for the blockade and of sufficient practical assistance.

The finding actually amounts to no more than that the first defendant attended the demonstration for a short time (indeed not even on the construction site but "in the street", very close to where she lived), and it is not explained how such conduct, in so far as it might exceed what is permitted in the exercise of fundamental rights under Article 5(1) and 8(1) of the constitution, could be construed as intentional support for the unlawful measures of the blockade. Nor is it enough that the first defendant spoke on the telephone to senior members of the commune and province, for the court did not inquire whether these calls were made in aid of the blockade or in an attempt to broker a "peaceful" solution. In view of the first defendant's constitutional rights it was wrong to conclude without more that she was guilty of tortious interference with the rights of others.

(cc) Finally the facts found are insufficient to render the second defendant liable for relevant participation in the infringement of the contractors' rights. The court below founded particularly on R's evidence that at 1630 hours on 22 April he saw the second defendant taking part in the demonstration. Here again there is no legal justification for inferring from his brief presence at the demonstration in the late afternoon that he approved of, adopted and furthered the unlawful blockading. Nor does it follow from the fact that he briefly climbed into the shovel of a digger in response to a photo-call; such conduct, as has already been stated above, may well be covered by Article 8(1) of the constitution and need not constitute a relevant unlawful infringement of the rights of the contractors.

7. Finally the court has not found with the clarity required of a final judgment what harm, if any, was suffered by the contractors.

III. The decision below must therefore be vacated and the matter remanded, with leave to the defendants to raise again by way of appeal their objections to the prior findings of that court.

Notes to Cases 14–18

1. Purely economic loss can result from an infinite variety of factual situations—the cable cases, discussed above, offering but one example. Many other instances can be given. Unfair competition is one example, indeed the only instance of economic loss, which has troubled some systems (e.g. the French). Financial loss can also result from the death of a key employee. French law is, in theory, more generous than English and German law which deny such claims (see also chapter 4, section A). Economic loss can also be occasioned to the ultimate purchaser of a defective product who, though not actually injured by it, is forced to spend money to put the defect right. The point is discussed in cases 68–73. The same can happen where a local authority fails to exercise a statutory right to inspect the foundations of buildings under construction with the result that cracks appear on the ceilings causing loss of heat (and, hence, higher electricity bills) or requiring redecoration. This type of economic loss is discussed in cases 74 and 75, where one will find a spectacular U-turn by the English courts which has brought them closer to German solutions. Cases 14 and 15 deal with the situation where no property is damaged, but its owner is deprived of its use. Technically the loss is again purely financial but the decisions reproduced above rightly adopted a more subtle approach.

2. The canal case, like the cable cases, explores various ways of allowing the claim. One is the judge-made right of an established and operating business (discussed above), but its subsidiary nature prevents it from being invoked if there is another applicable rule. The plaintiff's argument that he was entitled to expect the proper maintenance of the canal did not fare better, the court refusing to hold that the statutory obligation to maintain the canal was a protective norm and therefore actionable under § 823 II BGB (see below, chapter 4). This is a debatable interpretation; and in Germany it has not pleased everyone. (See: Medicus, *op. cit.*, but *cf.* Möschel *JuS* 1977, 1, 3.) The crux of the decision lies clearly in its teleological interpretation of § 823 I BGB. Interference with property, reasoned the court, must be taken to include not only interference with its substance but also with the rights and the authority of the owner. This is sensible enough, but demarcation

lines must also be drawn. For the court the dividing line was between the vessel trapped for an indefinite time and the vessel which, though unable to perform its contract, has retained its freedom of movement. The distinction is repeated and refined in the next case 15, the crucial factor here being the duration of the interference. Both judgments raise as many problems as they solve and that, perhaps, explains why they have remained, if one can borrow the French expression, *arrêts d'espèce*. Must the interference be complete or prolonged, or both, before it is actionable? What if the vessel could return to its starting-point but by means of a circuitous and very expensive route? Why is an obstruction of someone else's waterway that hinders the use of my vessel actionable, while the interference with someone else's cable that stops me from using my machinery is not? Casuistry appears to have kept alive for so long the rule prohibiting the compensation of purely economic loss. It also explains why there are so many exceptions to the rule and why the law has become so difficult to present in a simple way. (See also BGH JZ 1983, 857; BGH NJW 1983, 812, and Deutsch, JZ 1984, 308–9.) Finally, the reader must be reminded of a point made earlier. Perhaps these cases—which turn on a wide interpretation of ownership (*Eigentum*)—are really reactions to the categorical exclusion of pure economic loss from the list of protected interests of § 823 I BGB. The acceptance of this explanation would ensure that little effort was spent on the kind of theoretical debates which one finds in the German literature and which—to foreign eyes—border on the abstract and legalistic for ignoring the realities of the situation. (Thus, see, the Larenz/Canaris, pp. 388–9, distinctions between a "locked in" (Einsperrung) and "locked-out" (*Aussperrung*) vessel (in the context of the "trapped ship" case and the search for the purpose of protection and the damage (*Schutzzweckzusammenhang*) leading to distinctions between an interference with the substance of the property (*Substanzschaden*) and the ability to use it (*Gebrauchsschaden*). Larenz/Canaris, pp. 390–1. Contrast Mertnes in Münchener Kommentar, § 823 at 1477–8, who brings into play yet another notion "the market value" (*Marktwert*). Thus, the nicest thing one can say about these debates is that they are too Germanic to be exportable. See, also, Ch. 2 2(d)(i).)

Case 16 raises similarly intricate points. The property inflicted was vested in the harbour authority. The construction firm had lawful possession of the wall. However, the infliction caused damage to the substance of the wall; the loss did not result out of loss of use of the wall. Therefore, one might object that the harbour authority as owner and not the actual plaintiff (possessor) was entitled to claim damages for the damage to the wall. The construction firm sued because in the end the loss fell on it: it could not charge the employer, the harbour authority, with the increased cost of building the wall under the risk provision of § 644 BGB. But then was this not a case of *Drittschadensliquidation*, of "transferred loss", allowing the owner to sue on behalf of the construction firm? Yet, the court did not consider this route.

3. It has been impossible to find an *exact* factual equivalent in English and American law. English law has, in some instances, used the tort of public nuisance. In *Rose* v. *Miles* (1815) 4 M and S 101, 103; 105 ER 773, a barge-owner navigating a creek obstructed by the defendant's barges was allowed to claim his extra costs for unloading the cargo from his barges and transporting it by land to its ultimate destination, since in Lord Ellenborough's view he had suffered greater damage than other members of the public who might have been contemplating using the creek. The decision, incidentally, has impeccable origins that can be traced back to *Iveson* v. *Moore* (1699) 1 Ld. Raym. 486 (another case allowing recovery for purely economic loss resulting from highway obstructions).

Analogous cases in the USA have taken a similar stand. See *In re China Union Lines Ltd*, 285 F. Supp. 426 (1967) and *In Re Lyra Shipping Co. Ltd*, 360 F. Supp. 1188 (1973). Both these decisions, however, were overruled by the Court of Appeals for the 5th Circuit in its decision *Louisiana* v. *M/V Testbank* of 11 Feb. 1985: 752 F. 2d 1019. Extracts were reproduced in the third edition of this book at pp. 211–216. In July 1980 two vessels collided in the Mississippi River Gulf Outlet. A large quantity of toxic chemicals was lost overboard one of the ships and, fearing greater contamination, the authorities closed the outlet to navigation for about twenty days. Fishing, shrimping, and other "related" activities were also suspended for a short while in a surrounding area of about four hundred square miles. Forty-one lawsuits were filed and were eventually consolidated. The plaintiffs came under various (fairly) distinct categories namely: commercial fishermen; recreational fishermen; operators of marinas; bait and tackle shops; cargo terminal operators; restaurants etc. (Presumably, these were "test" cases for, otherwise, the number of claims is very small.) The Court of First Instance dismissed all the claims save those brought by the commercial fishermen. A panel of the Court of Appeal affirmed, but since a minority felt that the problem of the compensability of pure economic loss was ripe for re-examination, the case was heard by the full Court of Appeals of the Fifth Circuit sitting *en banc*. The majority judgment, affirming the decisions below, was delivered by Judge Higginbotham. Six judges dissented and their dissent was delivered by Judge Wisdom. The majority argued that the bright line rule of damage to a proprietary interest had "the virtue of predictability with the vice of creating results in cases at its edge that are said to be 'unjust' or 'unfair.' Plaintiffs point to seemingly perverse results, where claims the rule allows and those it disallows are juxtaposed—such as vessels striking a dock, causing minor but recoverable damage, then lurching athwart a channel causing great but unrecoverable economic loss. The answer is that when lines are drawn sufficiently sharply in their definitional edges to be reasonable and predictable, such differing results are the inevitable result—indeed, decisions are the desired product." The rule, by making results more predictable, operated as a rule of law and allowed a court to adjudicate rather than "manage". In the case of a disaster inflicting large and reverberating injuries through the economy first party or loss insurance was preferable to a liability system of third party insurance in terms of costs of administration (see p. 1029). The emphasis placed by the majority on the impact of insurance practice on modern tort law is most welcome. But is its apparently unqualified preference for first party insurance always preferable? (See Professor Atiyah's comment in (1985) 3 *Oxford J. L. Studies* 485, 489: ". . . it is really high time (in both England and America) that lawyers informed themselves about such fundamental matters of insurability in new tort cases and saw to it that the courts were also informed." See also Rizzo in 11 *J. Leg. Stud.* (1982) where the author's economic analysis suggests that the majority's preference for first party insurance is wrong in situations like *Testbank*.) The case also raises the question whether one should try to solve the *Testbank* type of disaster by means of statute or international treaties imposing strict liability on the carriers of the polluting substances subject to certain monetary limits. On this see: Gaskell, "The Amoco Cadiz" 3 Journal of Energy and Natural Resources Law, 169 (1985).

One can hazard a guess, however, that the German solution would appeal to those jurisdictions which are moving towards recognising claims for economic loss. The following casuistry may support this statement.

(i) Negligent interference with existing contracts with resulting economic loss has not been traditionally actionable in the USA. *Robins Dry Dock and Repair Co.* v. *Flint*, 275 US 303, 48 S. Ct. 134 (1927) is the *locus classicus* for the proposition. *Petitions of Kinsman Transit Co.*, 388 F. 2d 821 (1968) marked a strong move towards the other direction, even though in that case the plaintiff's claim was rejected on causative grounds. (See, generally, Note, "Negligent Interference with Contract: Knowledge on a Standard for Recovery" 63 *Va. L. Rev.* 813 (1977).) See also the interesting Canadian case of *Seaway Hotels* v. *Canada Craggs and Consumers Gas Co.*, (1959) 17 DLR 2d 292.

(ii) Even in the absence of contract the parties may negligently be deprived of a prospective economic benefit. Their plight has not been dealt with consistently by the courts. Frustrated beneficiaries who lose their legacies due to the negligence of a lawyer advising the testator can usually recover (see case 19 and its notes); but in other cases the courts have not been so generous. In *Weller and Co.* v. *Foot and Mouth Disease Research Institute* [1966] 1 QB 569, a live virus escaped from the defendant's laboratory due to their admitted negligence and caused a cattle disease. As a result, cattle auctions were prohibited for a period of time and the plaintiffs, cattle auctioneers, tried to claim their lost profits from the defendants. Their action failed. In *Rickards* v. *Sun Oil Co.*, 23 NJ Misc. 89, 41 A. 2d 267 (Sup. Ct. 1945) a ship crashed into and destroyed a bridge which provided the only access to a small island town. The island businessmen claimed their lost profits for the period when outsiders could not visit their town but the action was turned down on the grounds that the damage was not foreseeable. (Do you agree with this or would it have been better to deny the claims on the grounds that the type of loss incurred (purely economic loss) was not recognized by the law?)

(iii) Loss of a chattel is not treated as economic loss. A bailee, for example, who has negligently lost the bailed chattel will be responsible to the bailor for its value. Bailment, however, is very "close" to contract so the theoretical difficulties concerning compensation are in this case minimised.

(iv) Where the tort of negligence fails the plaintiff, the older tort of nuisance may come to his aid. Obstructions on the highway—including access to the highway—may thus be actionable in nuisance, and here recovery of purely economic loss has traditionally been allowed. This could provide a remedy in the kind of factual situation envisaged in case 12; though the duration of the obstruction would again be crucial. *Rose* v. *Miles* (1815) 4 M and S 101 is also interesting. There the plaintiff's barges were prevented from navigating on a public navigable creek. The court allowed him to claim the extra cost he incurred by having to convey his goods overland. Cf. *In Re Lyra Shipping Co. Ltd.*, 360 F. Supp. 1188 (1973).

4. Only in exceptional cases does German tort law provide compensation for negligently caused pure economic harm. Case 18 illustrates the difficulties that must be surmounted by the court before compensation can be decreed and is yet another example of the constitutionalisation of private law. In this case construction equipment was immobilised for a short period. Normally damages can be claimed in tort only if a particular right or legal interest, listed exhaustively in § 823 I BGB, has been infringed. This rule has, however, proved to be unduly restrictive, so the German courts have evolved various ways of granting compensation for pure economic harm. Thus the courts "discovered" the "right of an established and operative business"—actually invoked by the plaintiff in this case (see II 4 a)—and included it as an "other right" under § 823 I BGB, and it was under this heading that blockades had been discussed in the past, see chapter 2, section A. 2 (e) (iii). Again the courts gave a very wide interpretation to "infringement of ownership" and held that physical damage was not required: prevention of use is now sufficient, as the present case confirms. Finally the courts further enlarged the scope of § 823 I BGB by holding that lawful possession is an "other right": damage to a thing or loss of its use may now be compensated without having to ask whether the claimant was actually owner. This can be seen in the instant case: the court could deal with the interference with the use of the construction equipment in the possession of the contractors without having to decide whether they owned it or not. It is noteworthy that two days of being unable to use the equipment already sufficed to amount to an interference with the lawful possession of it (contrast case 14 where the vessel was immobilised for as long as eight month). Thus, future litigants might decide to base their claim on possession rather than the right of an established and operating business governed by the somewhat ambiguous "directness" requirement; (the directness requirement is normally fulfilled only if the interference was intentional; with regard to possession as a right, negligence will suffice; see Ch. 2, section A. 2 (e) (iii).) Moreover, if the non-usability of the machines for two days constitutes an infringement under § 823 I BGB this decision is extremely difficult to reconcile with the cable cases (11 *et seq.*). From this perspective the case should have arguably been solved on the basis of the right of an established and operating business. Once again the difficulties in keeping § 823 I BGB in bounds and at the same time allow for the compensation for loss of use become apparent. Having dealt with this problem the court then had to surmount another: how to accommodate the protection of the contractors' interests (ownership or possession or, on a better view, the right of an established and operating business) with the exercise by the defendants of their right of assembly.

The court drew the line between demonstrations which simply seek to persuade people and influence opinion on a contested matter and those which are designed deliberately to bring pressure on others to prevent them using their rights as they wish. The court stressed that in the present instance the interference was not a mere side-effect of a demonstration but it was the very object of the protest to prevent access to the site. From a dogmatic point of view this required an elaborate balancing of interests before the unlawfulness of the demonstration could be positively established (see also Kullmann *LM* BGB § 823 (Ae) Nr. 6). The third relevant point of the decision concerns the liability of associates and assistants. In general tort liability requires a causal contribution to the infringement and the damage. In the case of group action the requisite contribution may take the form of moral support by the defendant for those whose acts directly cause the harm. But it is often difficult for the victim to establish the causal effect of any such moral support, so § 830 I(1) and II BGB lay down that associates and assistants are fully liable as joint tortfeasors even if the victim cannot establish their actual causal contribution. Such contribution is, however, presumed only of those whose association or assistance was voluntary and who with knowledge of the facts intended to act along with those who directly caused the harm. This may not be at all clear in the case of mass manifestations that get out of control so that infringements occur which some of the participants never intended. This was critical for the defendants here, as some of them were eager to persuade others to their point of view but were not ready to infringe their rights, such as those of the building contractors.

5. Older cases dealing with particular problems of economic loss must nowadays be constantly reviewed against the background of recent, wide pronouncements on the subject, e.g., *Union Oil Co. v. Oppen* 501 F. 2d 558 (1974); *J'Aire Corp. v. Gregory* 24 Cal. 3d 799, 598 P. 2d 60; *Junior Books v. Veitchi Co. Ltd* [1983] 1 AC 520. Other relevant "economic loss" cases are reviewed by Markesinis, "An Expanding Tort Law: The Price of a Rigid Contract Law" 103 [1987] *LQR* 354; Robertson, "Recovery in Louisiana Tort Law for Intangible Economic Loss: Negligence Actions and the Tort of Intentional Interference with Contractual Relations" 46 *Louisiana L. Rev.* 737 (1986); Goldberg, "Recovery for Pure Economic Loss in Tort: Another Look at *Robins Dry Dock v. Flint*" 20 *The Journal of Legal Studies* 249 (1991); Gonynor, "The *Robins Dry Dock* Rule: Is the "Bright Line" Fading?" 4 *University of San Francisco Maritime Law Journal* 85 (1992); Jutras, "Civil Law and Pure Economic Loss: What are we Missing?" 12 *The Canadian Business Law Journal* 295 (1986–7); Tetley, "Damages and Economic Loss in Marine Collision: Controlling the Floodgates" 22 *Journal of Maritime Law and Commerce* 539 (1991).

6. For a discussion of the issues raised by cases 16 and 17 see the text in ch. A2(e)(iii), and *cf.* the decisions of *Junior Books v. Veitchi* [1983] 1 AC 520 and the *J'Aire* decision reproduced in the first addendum.

Addendum 1

J'Aire Corp. v. Gregory, 24 Cal. 3d 799, 598 P. 2d 60, 157 Cal. Rptr. 407 (1979).

BIRD CJ

Appellant, a lessee, sued respondent, a general contractor, for damages resulting from the delay in completion of a construction project at the premises where appellant operated a restaurant. Respondent demurred successfully and the complaint was dismissed. This court must decide whether a contractor who undertakes construction work pursuant to a contract with the owner of premises may be held liable in tort for business losses suffered by a lessee when the contractor negligently fails to complete the project with due diligence.

The facts as pleaded are as follows. Appellant, J'Aire Corporation, operates a restaurant at the Sonoma County Airport in premises leased from the county of Sonoma. Under the terms of the lease the county was to provide heat and air conditioning. In 1975 the county entered into a contract with respondent for improvements to the restaurant premises, including renovation of the heating and air-conditioning systems and installation of insulation.

As the contract did not specify any date for completion of the work, appellant alleged the work was to have been completed within a reasonable time as defined by custom and usage (Civ. Code, § 1657). Despite requests that respondent complete the construction promptly, the work was not completed within a reasonable time. Because the restaurant could not operate during part of the construction and was without heat and air-conditioning for a longer period, appellant suffered loss of business and resulting loss of profits.

Appellant alleged two causes of action in its third amended complaint. The first cause of action was based upon the theory that it was a third-party beneficiary of the contract between the county and respondent. The second cause of action sounded in tort and was based upon negligence in completing the work within a reasonable time. Damages of £50,000 were claimed.

Respondent demurred on the ground that the complaint did not state facts sufficient to constitute a cause of action. The trial court sustained the demurrer without leave to amend and the complaint was dismissed. On appeal only the sustaining of the demurrer to the second cause of action is challenged.

. . . The only question before this court is whether a cause of action for negligent loss of expected economic advantage may be maintained under these facts.

Liability for negligent conduct may only be imposed where there is a duty of care owed by the defendant to the plaintiff or to a class of which the plaintiff is a member (*Richards* v. *Stanley* (1954) 43 Cal. 2d 60, 63, 271 P. 2d 23). A duty of care may arise through statute or by contract. Alternatively, a duty may be premised upon the general character of the activity in which the defendant engaged, the relationship between the parties, or even the interdependent nature of human society. Whether a duty is owed is simply a shorthand way of phrasing what is "the essential question— whether the plaintiff's interests are entitled to legal protection against the defendant's conduct" (*Dillon* v. *Legg* (1968) 69 Cal. Rptr. 72, P. 2d 912).

This court has held that a plaintiff's interest in prospective economic advantage may be protected against injury occasioned by negligent as well as intentional conduct. [Reference omitted.] For example, economic losses such as lost earnings or profits are recoverable as part of general damages in a suit for personal injury based on negligence. Where negligent conduct causes injury to real or personal property, the plaintiff may recover damages for profits lost during the time necessary to repair or replace the property. [Reference omitted.]

Even when only injury to prospective economic advantage is claimed, recovery is not foreclosed. Where a special relationship exists between the parties, a plaintiff may recover for loss of expected economic advantage through the negligent performance of a contract although the parties were not in contractual privity. [*Biakanja*, *Lucas*, and *Heyer*] held that intended beneficiaries of wills could sue to recover legacies lost through the negligent preparation of the will. [Reference omitted.]

In each of the above cases, the court determined that defendants owed plaintiffs a duty of care by applying criteria set forth in *Biakanja* v. *Irving*. [Reference omitted.] Those criteria are (1) the extent to which the transaction was intended to affect the plaintiff, (2) the foreseeability of harm to the plaintiff, (3) the degree of certainty that the plaintiff suffered injury, (4) the closeness of the connection between the defendant's conduct and the injury suffered, (5) the moral blame attached to the defendant's conduct, and (6) the policy of preventing future harm. [Reference omitted.]

Applying these criteria to the facts as pleaded, it is evident that a duty was owed by respondent to appellant in the present case. (1) The contract entered into between respondent and the county was for the renovation of the premises in which appellant maintained its business. The contract could not have been performed without impinging on that business. Thus respondent's performance was intended to, and did, directly affect appellant. (2) Accordingly, it was clearly foreseeable that any significant delay in completing the construction would adversely affect appellant's business beyond the normal disruption associated with such construction. Appellant alleges this fact was repeatedly drawn to respondent's attention. (3) Further, appellant's complaint leaves no doubt that appellant suffered harm since it was unable to operate its business for one month and suffered additional loss of business while the premises were without heat and air-conditioning. (4) Appellant has also alleged that delays occasioned by the respondent's conduct were closely connected to, indeed directly caused its injury. (5) In addition, respondent's lack of diligence in the present case was particularly blameworthy since it continued after the probability of damage was drawn directly to respondent's attention. (6) Finally, public policy supports finding a duty of care in the present case. The wilful failure or refusal of a contractor to prosecute a construction project with diligence, where another is injured as a result, has been made grounds for disciplining a licensed contractor (Bus. 6 Prof. Code, § 7119). Although this section does not provide a basis for imposing liability where the delay in completing construction is due merely to negligence, it does indicate the seriousness with which the Legislature views unnecessary delays in the completion of construction.

In the light of these factors, this court finds that respondent had a duty to complete construction in a manner that would have avoided unnecessary injury to appellant's business, even though the construction contract was with the owner of a building rather than with appellant, the tenant. It is settled that a contractor owes a duty to avoid injury to the person or property of third parties. As appellant points out, injury to a tenant's business can often result in greater hardship than damage to a tenant's person or property. Where the risk of harm is foreseeable, as it was in the present case, an injury to the plaintiff's economic interests should not go uncompensated merely because it was unaccompanied by any injury to his person or property.

To hold under these facts that a cause of action has been stated for negligent interference with prospective economic advantage is consistent with the recent trend in tort cases. This court has repeatedly eschewed overly rigid Common law formulations of duty in favour of allowing compensation for foreseeable injuries caused by a defendant's want of ordinary care. See, e.g., *Dillon v. Legg* [reference omitted]; *Rowland v. Christian* [reference omitted]; *cf. Brown v. Merlo* [reference omitted] (liability of automobile driver for injury to non-paying passenger); *Rodriguez v. Bethlehem Steel Corp.* [reference omitted] (liability for loss of consortium). Rather than traditional notions of duty, this court has focused on foreseeability as the key component necessary to establish liability: "While the question whether one owes a duty to another must be decided on a case-by-case basis, every case is governed by the rule of general application that all persons are required to use ordinary care to prevent others from being injured as the result of their conduct . . . Foreseeability of the risk is a primary consideration in establishing the element of duty" (*Weirum v. RKO General, Inc.* [reference omitted]). Similarly, respondent is liable if his lack of ordinary care caused foreseeable injury to the economic interests of appellant.

In addition, this holding is consistent with the legislature's declaration of the basic principle of tort liability, embodied in Civil Code, § 1714, that every person is responsible for injuries caused by his or her lack of ordinary care. (See *Rowland v. Christian* [reference omitted].) That section does not distinguish among injuries to one's person, one's property, or one's financial interests. Damages for loss of profits or earnings are recoverable where they result from an injury to one's person or property caused by another's negligence. Recovery for injury to one's economic interests, where it is the foreseeable result of another's want of ordinary care, should not be foreclosed simply because it is the only injury that occurs.

Respondent cites *Fifield Manor v. Finston* [reference omitted] for the proposition that recovery may not be had to negligent loss of prospective economic advantage. *Fifield* concerned the parallel tort of interference with contractual relations. There a non-profit retirement home that had contracted with Ross to provide him with lifetime medical care sued a driver who negligently struck and killed Ross. The plaintiff argued it had become liable under the contract for Ross's medical bills and sought recovery from the driver, on both a theory of direct liability and one of subrogation. Recovery was denied.

The critical factor of foreseeability distinguishes *Fifield* from the present case. Although it was reasonably foreseeable that defendant's negligence might cause injury to Ross, it was less foreseeable that it would injure the retirement home's economic interest. Defendant had not entered into any relationship or undertaken any activity where negligence on his part was reasonably likely to affect plaintiff adversely. Thus, the nexus between the defendant's conduct and the risk of the injury that occurred to the plaintiff was too tenuous to support the imposition of a duty owing to the retirement home. In contrast, the nexus in the present case between the injury that occurred and respondent's conduct is extremely close. *Fifield* does not entirely foreclose recovery for negligent interference with prospective economic advantage.

Respondent also relies on *Adams v. Southern Pac. Transportation Co.* [reference omitted]. In *Adams* plaintiff employees were held unable to sue the railroad whose cargo of bombs exploded, destroying the factory where they worked. It should be noted that the Court of Appeal in *Adams* clearly believed that plaintiffs should be permitted to maintain an action for negligent interference with prospective economic interests. It reluctantly held they could not only under the belief that *Fifield* precluded such recovery. Adhering to the *Fifield* rule, the Court of Appeal in *Adams* did not determine whether the railroad owed plaintiffs a duty of care. In the present case, plaintiff's injury stemmed directly from conduct intended to affect plaintiff and was more readily foreseeable than the damage to the employer's property in *Adams*. To the extent that *Adams* holds that there can be no recovery for negligent interference with prospective economic advantage, it is disapproved.

The chief dangers which have been cited in allowing recovery for negligent interference with prospective economic advantage are the possibility of excessive liability, the creation of an undue burden on freedom of action, the possibility of fraudulent or collusive claims, and the often speculative nature of damages . . . Central to these fears is the possibility that liability will be imposed for remote consequences, out of proportion to the magnitude of the defendant's wrongful conduct.

However, the factors enumerated in *Biakanja* and applied in subsequent cases place a limit on recovery by focusing judicial attention on the foreseeability of the injury and the nexus between the defendant's conduct and the plaintiff's injury. These factors and ordinary principles of tort law such as proximate cause are fully adequate to limit recovery without the drastic consequence of an absolute rule which bars recovery in all such cases. Following these principles, recovery for negligent interference with prospective economic advantage will be limited to instances where the risk of harm is foreseeable and is closely connected with the defendant's conduct, where damages are not wholly speculative and the injury is not part of the plaintiff's ordinary business risk.

Accordingly, this court holds that a contractor owes a duty of care to the tenant of a building undergoing construction work to prosecute that work in a manner which does not cause undue injury to the tenant's business, where such injury is reasonably foreseeable. The demurrer to appellant's second cause of action should not have been sustained. The judgment of dismissal is reversed.

Notes to J'Aire

1. For some time now, California has supplanted New Jersey in its role as trend-setter in the USA. The decisions of its Supreme Court attract particular attention. *J'Aire* is no exception and it is, therefore, regrettable that it has not been thought out fully; indeed, it is a shame that so many of its legal protagonists gave evidence of sloppiness which in the classroom would have earned them low marks.

2. Take, first, counsel for the plaintiffs. The case was originally argued in contract (first cause of action) and tort (second cause of action). Under laboratory conditions, one would have been inclined to argue that, given the nature of the plaintiff's loss (pure economic loss), the first cause of action was more likely to produce a pro-plaintiff decision. Yet in the judgment we are laconically told that "on appeal only the sustaining of the demurrer [by the trial court] to the second cause of action [was] challenged." Many a teacher may have spent much time speculating what strategic reasons may have led to this decision. Yet the answer is much more mundane; and we owe it to Professor Schwartz who had the brilliant idea of asking the attorney in question why he did this, only to be told that "contracts were never my strong point at [law] school." (Schwartz, "Economic Loss in American Tort Law: the Examples of J'Aire and of Products Liability", 23 *San Diego L. Rev.* 37, 43 (1986)). If one is willing to treat this as an answer containing an element of the truth, it can give rise to much comparative discussion about the "compartmentalised" way law is taught in American law schools.

3. So let us turn to the judgment of the Chief Justice. Early in her judgment, she tells us that "This court has held that a plaintiff's economic advantage may be protected against injury occasioned by negligent . . . conduct." Two illustrations are given to support this proposition, one of economic loss flowing from personal injury, the other from property damage. Neither is appropriate, for in both these cases economic loss causes no difficulties, the limits of recovery being set by the rules of factual and legal cause. The problem we are discussing here, and which confronted the court in *J'Aire*, is the (different) problem of *pure* economic loss. (How right those Germans are with their desire to be precise with the terms = _reine_ Vermögensschäden.) If this were a tutorial essay, one would be inclined to scribble in the margin "not relevant".

4. The Chief Justice continues in similar vein, placing great reliance on the decisions in *Biakanja*, *Lucas*, and *Heyer*. These, however, are cases of legal malpractice; they involve different types of relationships, different kinds of insurance arguments, and do not raise the spectre of unlimited liability which (indirectly) plays such a determinative role in pure economic loss cases. The decision thus compares unfavourably with the more subtle and carefully researched judgment of La Forest in *Norsk*, extracts of which are reproduced below.

5. The actual result in *J'Aire* may be supportable; indeed it may be reasonable, provided it is produced through contract (or, at least, a tort action, shaped in its scope and consequences by the underlying contract). This point is discussed in greater detail in the notes to the legal malpractice cases; and is made even more obvious when considered against the background of German law (also discussed briefly in these notes).

6. One final (minor) point—interesting from the point of view of comparative methodology. German lawyers studying the Common law always have some difficulty with the notion of duty of care. Conversely, Common lawyers cannot find this key concept in the codal provision which, instead, talks of "protected interests". The following sentence from Chief Justice Bird's judgment is, therefore, particularly interesting: "Liability for negligent conduct may only be imposed where there is a duty of care . . . whether a duty is owed is simply a short hand way of phrasing what is the essential question—whether the plaintiff's *interests* are entitled to legal protection . . .". Comparatists should rejoice at such sentences and treat them as the literary equivalents of musical cadenzas. For they offer a chance to escape the strictures imposed by textbooks, and an excellent opportunity to attempt one's own excursus into legal history, drafting techniques, and the merits and demerits of comparing systems via their concepts or through the functions which their concepts are meant to perform.

Addendum 2

Norsk Pacific Steamship Co. v. Canadian National Railway, [1992] 1 S.C.R. 1021

Summary of the facts

The New Westminster Railways Bridge, which spans the Fraser River near Vancouver and carries a *single* track, is owned by the Department of Public Works of Canada (PWC). A barge, towed by a tug owned by the defendants (Norsk), and negligently navigated by its captain, damaged the bridge, necessitating its closure for several weeks while it was being repaired. As a result of this closure, the Canadian National Railway (CNR), who were the plaintiffs in this action, had to re-route traffic over another bridge, incurring considerable additional expense. CNR, who accounted for 86 per cent of the use of the bridge, had a licence contract with PWC which, *inter alia*, obliged them to provide PWC with inspection, consulting, maintenance, and repair services for the bridge as and when requested by PWC and at PWC's expense. Since the marine traffic using the Fraser river was, at the site of the bridge, heavy and had, in the past, occasioned structural damage to the bridge leading to its closure, the licence agreement between CNR and PWC provided that the former could not claim damages from the latter in the event of closure of the bridge in an emergency. Finally, one should, perhaps, note that CNR owned the land (and tracks) on *either side* of the bridge (but not the rails on the damaged bridge). CNR's tort action for its economic losses was accepted at First Instance, by the Court of Appeal, and by four judges out of seven in the Supreme Court.

[Three long judgments were delivered in this case by McLachlin, Stevenson, and La Forest JJs. For reasons of space, only extracts from one of them are reproduced here. They are taken from the "dissent" since it, arguably, provides one of the most thorough judicial discussions of the problem of pure economic loss; but the case will be best understood if read in its entirety.]

La Forest J. (dissenting)—This case concerns recovery in tort for economic loss. Though some of the arguments are framed as if the case turned on the broad question whether such damages are generally recoverable, the specific issue is much narrower. It is whether a person (A) who contracts for the use of property belonging to another (B) can sue a person who damages that property for losses resulting from A's inability to use the property during the period of repair. (I call this "contractual relational economic loss", a convenient if somewhat barbarous phrase.)

The issue arises in a context where a barge collided with a bridge while being pulled by the defendants' tug, thereby preventing the plaintiff (CN) from making use of it. Ordinarily, a person whose operations are disrupted by damage to a bridge belonging to another cannot at common law pursue the person who caused the damage. But the plaintiff claims that it may do so by reason of its particular relationship with the owner of the bridge and with the tortfeasor. As in the case of three other railways, it has a contractual right to use the bridge for railway purposes, but the plaintiff relies on additional facts to establish its special relationship. It is by far the major user of the bridge, which is a central link in its operations, so much so that many of those who operated on the river, including the master of the defendants' tug, thought it belonged to the plaintiff. As well, CN's contract requires it to repair and maintain the bridge when necessary at the request of the owner; CN also owns land close to the bridge.

The courts below and my colleagues, Justices McLachlin and Stevenson, are all of the view that CN's claim should be upheld. But this unanimity is more apparent than real, for they do so for different reasons and, indeed, there is significant disagreement on the determining issues. I take the opposite view. For sound policy reasons, the courts have established a clear rule (the "bright line" rule) that persons cannot sue a tortfeasor for suffering losses to their contractual rights with the owner of property by reason of damages caused to that property by the tortfeasor. That rule, I have no doubt, may be subject to exceptions for clear and overriding policy reasons, but as I will indicate, I have been unable to determine any reason for excluding CN from the general rule in the present case.

[A detailed statement of the facts follows at this stage taking up 7 full columns of the SC Reports.]

The Issues

. . . .

Analysis

Part I: The Need to Recentre the Analysis on Contractual Relational Economic Loss

To phrase the key issue in this case as a simple one of "is pure economic loss recoverable in tort?" is misleading. I do not doubt that pure economic loss is recoverable in some cases. It does not follow, however, that all economic loss cases are susceptible to the same analysis, or that cases of one type are necessarily relevant to cases of another. Nor does it follow that the constellation of policy concerns that have grown up around the issue of economic loss can be ignored. The fact is that different types of factual situations may invite different approaches to economic loss, and it seems to me to be at best unwise to lump them all together for purposes of analysis. Professor Feldthusen distinguishes five different categories of economic loss cases which involve different policy considerations: see Feldthusen, "Economic Loss in the Supreme Court of Canada: Yesterday and Tomorrow" (1990–91), 17 *Can. Bus. L.J.* 356, at pp. 357–8. They are as follows:
1. The Independent Liability of Statutory Public Authorities;
2. Negligent Misrepresentation;
3. Negligent Performance of a Service;
4. Negligent Supply of Shoddy Goods or Structures;
5. Relational Economic Loss.

The present case fits into his fifth category. In my view, both policy and precedent justify narrowing the focus in the present case to loss cases of the kind described in that category.

. . . .

Policy

Cases of contractual relational loss have a number of specific characteristics that differentiate them from other economic loss cases, and certainly from other non-relational loss cases. The first is that in such cases, the right of action of the property owner already puts pressure on the defendants to act with care. The deterrent effect of tort law, to the extent that it survives the advent of widespread insurance, is already present. In this case PWC collected substantial damages. Consequently, Norsk was already under a substantial incentive to take care with respect to the bridge since its liability to the bridge owner would and did require the payment of substantial damages. In most cases of this type, imposing further liability cannot reasonably be justified on the grounds of deterrence (unless a policy of full internalisation of all losses resulting from accidents to the party who could have avoided the accident is to be pursued at all costs).

This is a critical difference with respect to the other types of economic loss cases. Professor Feldthusen underlines the importance of this first key aspect of contractual relational economic loss cases, in the following passage dealing with relational loss generally ((1990–91), 17 *Can. Bus. L.J.* 356, at p. 377):

. . . in each of [the first four] categories [identified above], the issue is whether the law of negligence *applies at all* to sanction the defendant's careless conduct. Relational loss cases are different because the defendant *will be held liable* to the victim of physical damage. The issue is whether *additional* liability to third parties is warranted. The better analogy is not to how the claim in *Hedley Byrne* or *Rivtow Marine* was resolved, but to how an *additional claim brought by the best customer of the plaintiffs in each of those cases* would have fared. [Emphasis added.]

I come now to a second distinction. A firm exclusionary rule in this area does not have the effect of necessarily excluding compensation to the plaintiff for his or her loss. Rather, it simply channels to the property owner both potential liability to the plaintiff and the right of recovery against the tortfeasor. The property owner is both entitled to recover from the tortfeasor and potentially liable under contract to the plaintiff. Here, the licence agreement explicitly rejected any liability, so the plaintiff cannot recover under it against PWC. In contracts between sophisticated parties such as those in the case at bar, who are well advised by counsel, such exclusions of liability often result from determinations regarding who is in the best position to insure the risk at the lowest cost.

A third distinction is that perfect compensation of all contractual relational economic loss is almost always impossible because of the ripple effects which are of the very essence of contractual relational economic loss. This aspect has been recognized as critical from the very beginning. It is in this sense that the solution to cases of this type is necessarily pragmatic and involves drawing a line that will exclude at least some people who have been undeniably injured owing to the tortfeasor's admitted failure to meet the requisite standard of care.

In other types of economic loss cases, ripple effects may not be of concern. Thus cases like the present are significantly different from the situation in *Rivtow Marine Ltd.* v. *Washington Iron Works*, [1974] S.C.R. 1189, in which Rivtow was the sole victim of the type of damage for which it claimed. Full compensation of all those to whom a private law duty is owed is also realistically possible in the situation dealt with in *Kamloops (City of)* v. *Nielsen*, [1984] 2 S.C.R. 2. In cases like the present, claims that the denial of recovery in the type of case here would be "unjust" must take into account that other "just" claims are inevitably denied in this type of case.

Finally, contractual relational economic loss cases typically involve accidents. This distinguishes them from both products liability economic loss cases like *Rivtow*, in which by definition there is no accident, and negligent misrepresentation cases like *Hedley Byrne & Co.* v. *Heller & Partners Ltd.*, [1964] AC 465. This aspect is of fundamental importance with respect to tests of liability founded on the foreseeability of an individual plaintiff or an ascertained class of plaintiffs, which I shall discuss in Part III.

In light of these substantial differences between contractual relational economic loss cases and other pure economic loss cases, I agree with Professor Feldthusen, that "it assists little, if at all, to generalise on the basis of proximity from other types of economic loss cases to the relational loss cases" ((1990–91), 17 *Can. Bus. L.J.* 356, at p. 376). For the purposes of the present case, it is not necessary to proceed to an exhaustive categorisation of economic loss cases. There is, in my view, at the very least a clear difference between economic loss in three types of cases.

In the first type, which involves what has been termed consequential economic loss, the plaintiff claims for economic loss in addition to his claims for property damage or personal injury. Focusing on the issue of remoteness of damage, the courts have established guidelines regarding the availability of damages for economic loss in these cases.

In the second type, which can be termed non-relational economic loss, the plaintiff claims for pure economic loss unrelated to any personal injury or property damage suffered by either the plaintiff or any third party. The law in this area is developing. In view of my analysis of the issues in this case, it is not necessary for me to say much about these cases. I doubt, however, that this group can be analyzed in terms of a single rule. The extract from Professor Feldthusen above contends that this group can be further broken down into four distinct categories. It is sufficient to say that I fully support this Court's rejection of the broad bar on recovery of pure economic loss in *Rivtow* and *Kamloops*. I would stress again the need to take into account the specific characteristics of each case. I agree with McLachlin J that *Murphy* v. *Brentwood District Council*, [1991] 1 AC 398, does not represent the law in Canada.

The present case, however, is of a third type. It involves a claim for contractual relational economic loss by the plaintiff as a result of damage caused to someone else's property.

Precedent

The English Background . . .

[There follows a brief review of Canadian and US law before La Forest turns his attention to the civil law systems.] . . . .

Civil Law Systems

Since my colleagues have also supported their conclusions by forays into comparative law, and notably their understanding of the civil law experience, I find it necessary to enter into some discussion of that experience. I say at the outset that it does not seem to me to provide as much comfort for my colleagues' views as they seem to derive from it.

It is undeniable that not all legal systems have isolated cases like the present as presenting specific problems. Some civil law systems do not apply any particular rules either to pure economic loss cases or to contractual relational economic loss cases. The opinions of my colleagues in this case particularly rely on the law of France and Quebec. The argument from French and Quebec law is really about the floodgates argument. Since those systems allow recovery for pure economic loss without breaking down, the argument goes, we should not be deterred by floodgates arguments: see Jutras, "Civil Law and Pure Economic Loss: What Are We Missing?" (1986–87), 12 *Can. Bus. L.J.* 295, at p. 310. In my opinion the relevant comparative reference is to contractual relational economic loss, not to the broad question of pure economic loss. To consider comparative law at the level of generality of "economic loss" is not, in my view, helpful. I have already explained why I think the cases grouped under the rubric of economic loss deserve a more refined analysis. The same narrowing of the question should be employed in the recourse to comparative law. The legal system of every society faces essentially the same problems and solves these problems by quite different means, though often with similar results: see Zweigert and Kötz, *Introduction to Comparative Law, Volume I—The Framework* (2nd edn. 1987), at p. 31. While some of these systems have not retained the concept of "economic loss" as a limiting factor, they have generally not recognized claims of the type put forward here.

Second, the French and Quebec approach involves applying the same criteria to a case of this type as to any other tort claim. Although some scholars argue that the Common law should change its focus entirely to a concern with causation as the limiting factor (see Tetley, "Damages and

Economic Loss in Marine Collision: Controlling the Floodgates" (1991), 22 *J. Mar. Law & Com.* 539, at p. 584), this does not appear to me to be an advisable option. Our current causality test of foreseeability is clearly insufficient to control liability. The directness criterion was rejected in *Overseas Tankship (UK) Ltd.* v. *Morts Dock & Engineering Co. (The Wagon Mound)*, [1961] AC 388, for determinations as to remoteness and does not seem to me to provide much predictive value: see *SCM (United Kingdom) Ltd.* v. *W J Whittall and Son Ltd.*, *supra*, at p. 343.

A close examination of French law in this area reveals that the floodgates problem is resolved by the use of a number of control devices such that liability is very rare. French delict doctrine treats the question of *dommage par ricochet* in relation first to the requirement that the injury suffered must have a "personal character"; see Viney, "Les obligations: La responsabilité: conditions" (1982), in Ghestin, *Traité de droit civil*, nos. 288 *et seq.* Undoubtedly, in general terms, French law allows generous recovery for *dommage par ricochet*: see Viney, at no. 309. However, with respect to persons who were contractually linked to the initial victim, Viney writes as follows, at no. 312:

> [Translation] The courts have from time to time had before them claims made by some customer, supplier or creditor, or by a partner, employee or employer, of the initial victim when the latter's death endangers their interests. *In general, the courts have so far been very hesitant to allow such claims, especially those made by a creditor, employer or partner; but at the same time a more liberal solution may well be envisaged in the case of employees who are thrown out of work by the employer's death.*
>
> The position in French law is no more harsh in this respect than that of foreign systems of law, which generally refuse to take into consideration this type of repercussive damage. . . . [Emphasis added.]

The distinction of the case of the employee is not specifically justified, but the most obvious rationale for distinguishing that particular case is surely that the employee is least able to protect himself or herself from the consequences of the accident. As for mere *créanciers* of the primary victim like CN, recovery is generally denied. The 1975 Cour de cassation case which left open the issue of recovery for a creditor whose debtor died as result of the defendant's fault, Cass. civ. 2ᵉ, June 25, 1975, Bull. II no. 195, eventually returned to that court in 1979: see Cass. civ. 2ᵉ, February 21, 1979, Bougues-Montès, J.C.P. 1979, IV, 145. The finding that the damages were indirect and hence unrecoverable was, as noted by Durry, partly justified by the fact that the lender should have protected himself by contract by requiring his debtor to contract life insurance; see "Obligations et contrats spéciaux" (1979), 77 *Rev. trim. dr. civ.* 610. Larroumet speaks of recovery in such cases (other than in cases of contracts concluded *intuitus personae*) as an [translation] "academic hypothesis" and notes that [translation] "it is rarely found in the cases": see Bordeaux, May 17, 1977, D.1978, I.R. 34, note Larroumet.

Cases in which contractual relational economic loss have been awarded as a result of property damage to a third party are even more rare. These cases are admittedly also subject to the same basic framework of analysis. However, the Cour de Cassation exercises its control over the lower courts' determinations of causality; see Starck, *Droit civil: Obligations: I. Responsabilité délictuelle* (3rd edn. 1988), by Roland and Boyer, at no. 851. Recovery is rarely allowed. Durry describes the state of the law in this area as follows, "Obligations et contrats spéciaux" (1976), 74 *Rev. trim. dr. civ.* 132, at p. 134:

> [Translation] Physical repercussive damage to one who is neither parent, relative, fiancé or mistress of the immediate victim responds to a well-known dialectic: though in principle compensation may be obtained it in fact rarely is.

Markesinis' comparative examination of English and French law in this area (Markesinis, "La politique jurisprudentielle et la réparation du préjudice économique en Angleterre: une approche comparative", [1983] *Rev. int. dr. comp.* 31, at pp. 44–5), also points out the remarkable similarity of result despite the different analytical approaches:

> [Translation] The first point to note is that French judges are fully aware of these dangers. Some fifty years ago the Tribunal civil of Bordeaux indicated it had no doubts on the matter when it said "that extending entitlement to damages to everyone who might in some way suffer tangible or intangible

injury from a quasi-delict *would amount to creating a kind of social disorder which can never be the purpose of the law*" ... Accordingly, what is special about this judgment is that it *openly* expresses the philosophy of many judgments which have followed and which, though in theory they admit the possibility of compensation, have in many if not all cases proceeded to a denial of the right of action in practice. Consequently, what is interesting in these cases is to examine the method used to arrive at the result which English law obtains in a generally and rigidly applicable manner.

A variety of "causal" dispositions, which sometimes seemed to involve duplication, have been skilfully (and at times arbitrarily) used to attain this result. In some cases, it is said that the victim assumed the risk; in other cases, that the injury suffered is only indirect; and in still others, that it is only hypothetical and not certain; but in all cases, the possibility of compensation is recognized in theory. [Emphasis added.]

Recovery has been allowed in a few contractual relational economic loss cases. The first is where the contract that is disturbed is *intuitus personae*, i.e., a personal service contract where the particular individual cannot be replaced. In one case, a soccer club recovered for damages incurred as a result of the death of a star player: see Cour d'appel de Colmar (chapter détachée à Metz), 20 April 1955, D.1956.723 (*Football Club de Metz c. Wiroth*). Even here, however, the law is not certain: recovery was denied to an opera director for the loss caused by an injury to the leading tenor: see Cass. civ. 2ᵉ, 14 November 1958, G.P. 1959.1.31 (*Demeyer c. Camerlo*). In a preliminary procedure at first instance, recovery was allowed to employees whose unemployment was caused by the tortfeasor who damaged their hair salon: see Trib. gr. inst. Nanterre, 22 October 1975, G.P. 1976.1.392 (*Brunet c. Rico et Caisse mutuelle d'assurance et de prévoyance*).

Marcailloux v. *R.A.T.V.M.*, Cass. civ. 2ᵉ, April 28, 1965, D.S. 1965.777, cited by McLachlin J, involved a traffic accident that led to a traffic jam. The person who caused the accident was held liable for damages of 39 francs to the local transport authority for the loss of receipts caused by the resulting delay to the circulation of its vehicles. It is unclear what distinguishes this claim from other potential traffic jam claims. The note by Professor Esmein in the *Marcailloux* case observes that the characterisation of a particular damage as direct or indirect, far from being a factual inquiry, is simply the statement of a conclusion as to recovery; in this regard, it plays a similar function to the concept of proximity in our law. See Note under Cass. civ. 2ᵉ, 28 April 1965, D.S. 1965.777.

In Quebec, the expansive interpretation of "another" in Article 1053 of the Civil Code of Lower Canada referred to by McLachlin J has served to shift the analysis to the terrain of causality: see Baudouin, *La responsabilité civile délictuelle* (3rd edn., 1990), at no. 177. Baudouin recognizes the difficulty of generalizing with respect to determinations of directness but he considers that a trend toward an exclusion of liability is discernible, *supra*, at no. 354:

[Translation] The problem of determining what is "direct" damage is complex and here again any attempt at generalisation would be presumptuous. However, one trend seems to be clear. The courts will not recognise loss the immediate source of which is not the fault itself but some other injury already caused by the fault. In other words, damage resulting from damage, repercussive damage, "second degree" damage, is indirect.

However, as the author recognises, this is at most a trend. He further notes that Quebec courts have tended to consider causality as a question of fact: *supra*, at no. 349. This would constitute a significant difference with the French regime. However, the author notes that the decision of this Court in *Morin* v. *Blais*, [1977] 1 S.C.R. 570, considered the question of causality to constitute a question of law. Recovery of contractual relational economic loss has been allowed in a few cases in Quebec. Employers have been allowed to recover for the loss of the services of their employees.

In my view, the French and Quebec experience remains inconclusive. Although the cases are theoretically not subject to any special requirements for recovery, cases of recovery of contractual relational economic loss are few. The rarity of the cases has resulted in little doctrinal discussion of the issues raised and the brevity of the reasons makes the grounds for determination difficult to analyse. While French law does not establish an absolute bar, it is very close to establishing a *de facto* bar through the use of the dual requirements of directness and proof of causality. The number of cases in which recovery has been allowed is very few when one considers that relational losses occur as a result of practically every accident causing property damage in the commercial area.

Furthermore, one is at pains to establish the grounds for distinguishing successful claims from other relational claims. What little doctrinal discussion there is appears to be both keenly aware of the potential for open-ended liability and conscious that recovery is generally denied. Such analysis also points to factors entering into the directness and causality analysis that would exclude CN's claim, factors such as the *intuitus personae* nature of the contractual relationship and the inability of the plaintiff to protect itself through contract or otherwise. I shall have occasion to consider such factors later.

In addition, civil law scholars have remarked on the lack of emphasis in French and Quebec law on the problems raised by the nature of particular protected interests; see Jutras, *supra*, at pp. 295–6 and 310–11. In civil law systems such as the German system which, unlike the French system, have focused significant attention on the problems posed by the nature of different protected interests (see Limpens, Kruithof and Meinertzhagen-Limpens, 'Liability for One's Own Act', in *International Encyclopedia of Comparative Law*, vol. XI, *Torts*, chapter 2, IV.), recovery is denied for contractual relational claims based on the type of damage; see Markesinis, *A Comparative Introduction to the German Law of Torts* (2nd edn. 1990), at pp. 39 *et seq*. Other civil law systems have strict exclusionary rules. Switzerland apparently excludes *le dommage par ricochet*, allowing only recovery for wrongful death; see Herbots, "Le 'duty of care' et le dommage purement financier en droit comparé" [1985], *Rev. dr. int. et dr. comp.* 7, at p. 32.

What conclusions can be drawn from the civil law? First, I think there is general agreement that economic loss cases cannot simply be subjected to the same analysis as cases involving other types of damage: see Atiyah, *supra*, at p. 270. No one is suggesting, after all, that we modify the rules adopted in *Hedley Byrne* for an undifferentiated *Donoghue* test in economic loss cases.

There remains the argument that French and Quebec experience puts the lie to the floodgates problem in this area. In my view, this is simply not borne out. First of all, as Markesinis points out, French judges are acutely aware of the potential for unlimited liability. They use different analytical tools to reach much the same result.

One can of course attempt to meet the floodgates argument by contending that recovery for contractual relational economic loss will remain exceptional even if the exclusionary rule is relaxed. This is perhaps the most that can be drawn from the civil law experience: the replacement of an exclusionary rule with what amounts to very close to a *de facto* bar will not lead to many cases being brought forward. Unlike the civil law rules in these areas, however, the traditional control devices in our tort law have been elaborated to deal with damages that are generally by their nature limited.

I am principally concerned about the relative advisability of attempting to draw a line within the group of contractual claimants as opposed to distinguishing based on the nature of the interest at stake. Specifically, I am concerned about the nature and the workability of the criteria used to distinguish valid claims. In my view, any incursions into the exclusionary rule should be carefully justified on policy grounds. With respect to this question, I do not find any theory put forward in either France or Quebec that would aid in making distinctions amongst contractual claimants on valid policy grounds; see the discussion by Mayrand JA of the difficulties in making the directness determination with respect to "victims by ricochet" in *JE Construction Inc. v. General Motors du Canada Ltée*, [1985] CA 275, at pp. 278–9.

To the extent that recovery has been allowed, the inability of doctrine to elucidate the characteristics leading to recovery or to a finding of directness gives the lie to the idea that allowing recovery in a few cases of this nature will provide material for an *ex post* rationalisation that the court is incapable of formulating beforehand. I do not share McLachlin J's confidence that turning this issue over to the Common law to decide cases on the basis of proximity will lead to the gradual formation of categories of recovery that make sense in policy terms, and nothing in the civil law experience with findings of directness leads me to greater confidence in this regard: see Herbots, *supra*, at p. 21.

The narrow exclusionary rule distinguishes between property claims and contract claims and excludes the latter in cases of property damage. This bright line test has been in the past extended to the wider field of pure economic loss; in this wider field, it is in retreat in a number of areas. In my view, this case presents the court with the following problem: should the court eliminate the bright line test in the narrow area of contractual relational economic loss in favour of a test that will discriminate differently, this time amongst the class of contractual claimants, those who merit recovery and those who do not? If yes, what criteria should govern recovery?

Before dealing further with the question of contractual relational economic loss, however, it is necessary to consider a different set of arguments advanced by the respondent.

Part II: Alternative Interest Theories

Introductory Remarks

CN argues that its case does not rest on a mere contractual interest. It seeks to avoid the application of the narrow exclusionary rule by arguing that it has alternative interests at stake that differentiate it from the ordinary contractual claimant. It does not seek to place itself under a long-standing exception to the exclusionary rule enunciated in *Simpson & Co.* v. *Thomson, supra*, at p. 290, which involves cases allowing recovery to a plaintiff with a proprietary or possessory interest. If CN could argue that its interest in the bridge was analogous to the interest of a demise charterer in the chartered ship, it would be able to recover since it would be, *vis-à-vis* third parties, the temporary owner of the bridge; see *Scrutton on Charterparties and Bills of Lading* (19th edn. 1984), at pp. 47–52; *Baumwoll Manufactur von Carl Scheibler* v. *Furness*, [1893] AC 8 (HL); *The "Father Thames"*, [1979] 2 Lloyd's Rep. 364. A demise charterer's interest typically entirely supplants the interest of the owner of the ship, even in the repair of physical damage: see *Candlewood, supra*, at p. 18. For example, in *Rivtow*, the plaintiff was a demise charterer. No argument was directed to contesting Rivtow's interest.

CN's licence agreement gives it no proprietary or possessory interest. This state of affairs was surely not entirely fortuitous in light of the fact that the existence of such an interest was a central consideration in the *Gypsum Carrier* case. CN's contract with PWC establishes no proprietary or possessory interest in the bridge, and it did not attempt to argue that its contract resembled that of a demise charterer.

Unable to contend for the existence of a possessory right to the bridge, CN, we saw, put forward essentially two arguments to the effect that its interest is more than that of a mere contractor. First, it says, it suffered from a transferred loss of use. Secondly, it maintains, it is involved in a common adventure with PWC. These arguments are centred on the relationship between the plaintiff and the property owner, i.e., between CN and PWC.

Transferred Loss Theories

CN frames its argument with respect to transferred loss in two different ways. First, it submits that "P.W.C. initially suffered the physical loss for the damage to the bridge, but pursuant to their contracts with the railways all costs are ultimately borne by the railways, substantially by the C.N.R.". Along a similar line, it contends that PWC "acted like a trustee" in providing the bridge to the railways and particularly CN. The second manner in which it frames its argument on transferred loss involves arguing that granting judgment to CN in this case would not impose additional liability on the defendants over and above what they would normally be incurred by the owner of commercial property. I will deal with these in turn.

The respondent's first argument, as I understand it, is that the contract provides for a particularly mechanical passing through of the costs of the accident to the eventual users. CN's claim is thus different from the typical contractual relational claim.

I find this unconvincing. The rates are not set after all the costs are established. Canada unilaterally sets the rate for each three-year period of the licence after the initial three-year period, in light of the principle set out in the preamble of "total recovery to Canada of all the costs of operating and maintaining the Bridge" (see Recital E of the Preamble of the License Agreement). After each renewal of the contract the railway has a guaranteed unit rate for three years. CN is less exposed to costs incurred by the property owner than the typical consumer, for whom the costs incurred today are often passed through almost immediately. Before any such costs are passed through to CN, the current unit rate must expire and CN must decide that it wishes to renew the contract for another three-year period.

Second, it must be noted that PWC recovered damages as property owner in this case. Since PWC was fully compensated, none of the costs of property damage in this case will be passed through, even in the future. The only transferred loss in this case concerned a loss of use.

Third, the real reason all the loss of use costs appear to be passed through in this case has nothing to do with any special characteristics of CN or of the licence agreement. Rather, it results from the fact that PWC runs the bridge on a non-profit basis. PWC did suffer a loss of use of its fee-earning capacity; its pricing policy is such that the economic value of its loss of use is zero. In most cases, the owner of a profit-making chattel damaged by the tortfeasor will suffer a loss of use in the form of reduced payments by users. Here, the loss of use appears to be transferred *in toto* only because PWC does not use the bridge to earn a profit so it incurs no financial loss owing to interruption of transit fees. PWC's pricing policy, which happens to be particularly advantageous to CN and the other users at the expense of the taxpayers of Canada, does not mean that any more transferred loss of use occurred in this case than in the typical case.

Fourth, the toll structure does not support the "unique relationship" theory since all railways were equally situated with respect to this factor. The loss of use in this case was initially spread over the four railways. A wide range of people and companies were undoubtedly affected by the unavailability of the bridge. People who contracted for carriage of their goods by the railways, for example, may well have had shipment of the goods delayed in transit. The eventual bearer of this loss would be determined by the terms of the contract of carriage.

As the appellants rightly suggest, the contract CN had for the shared use of the bridge puts it in no better position to recover its loss than a time charterer who contracts for the sole use of a vessel. Recovery has been regularly denied in the time charterer cases: see *Konstantinidis* v. *World Tankers Corp.* (*The World Harmony*), [1967] P. 341, at p. 362.

The unique features of the toll structure are not such as to found an alternative legally protected interest over and above the contractual interest of the plaintiff. *A fortiori*, they also are not such as to justify a characterisation of PWC as a trustee.

The second manner in which the respondent frames its loss of use argument involves arguing that granting judgment to CN in this case would not be extending the liability of the defendants over and above what they would normally incur to the owner of commercial property. Here, the respondent essentially argues that the defendants' liability should not be reduced merely because it was fortunate enough to strike a bridge being used by railways. Had PWC, i.e., the owner, been using the bridge, it could have recovered loss of use profits as consequential economic loss.

. . . .

I am uncertain whether it is advisable to so extend recovery to a type of damages that would normally be recovered by an owner. I am certain, however, that to extend recovery to everything that could be recovered by an owner would be impractical.

To accept wide recovery for transferred loss as proposed by the plaintiff here would have the effect of entitling the plaintiff to compensation in all cases dealing with contracts for the use of another's property. If loss of use is extended to include the costs of finding alternate sources for the same benefits, it goes considerably beyond what is normally payable to the owner in commercial cases, although admittedly it *could* be payable to the owner.

True transferred loss cases involve a claim which is in essence a claim for *property damage* which the owner himself would have recovered, had the loss not fallen on the plaintiff because of their contract. A true transferred loss case requires that the risk of *property damage* have passed, as in the case of goods damaged in transit after the risk (but not the property) has passed to the buyer. In such a case, unless the buyer is given a right of action, the carrier will be liable to neither party: not to the seller because he has suffered no loss, nor to the buyer who has no protected interest; see Fleming, *The Law of Torts* (7th edn. 1987), at pp. 164–5.

Even in that type of case, recovery was denied in the recent House of Lords decision in *Leigh and Sillavan Ltd.* v. *Aliakmon Shipping Co.*, *supra*, essentially on the ground that contract law provided a sufficient protection in the circumstances of that case. It was only the particular variation of the contract to which the buyers agreed that deprived them of their usual right of action.

The present is not a true transferred loss case. PWC has collected for the property damage it has sustained. The transferred loss claimed in this case is thus not with respect to the property damage claim. Rather, it is a claim for the transferred *loss of use, or transferred economic loss.*

In these circumstances, I fail to see how the respondent suffered a transferred loss such as to create an alternative protected interest to its contractual interest.

Common Adventure or Joint Venture

. . .

Part III: The Proposed Tests

CN argues that even if we reject its "alternative interests" argument and find its interest merely contractual, the existence of other factors is sufficient to constitute a special relationship with the tortfeasor and to ground recovery for its contractual claims in this case. In particular, it points to the high degree of subjective and objective foreseeability in this case as sufficient to constitute a special relationship between Norsk and CN, but other factors are invoked as well. The respondent does not deny the existence of the rule in *Cattle*. It contends, however, that the rationale for *Cattle* is simply that the *mere* disruption of contractual rights without more is insufficient to ground recovery. These arguments represent an attempt to *qualify* the application of the contractual relational economic loss exclusionary rule.

My colleague McLachlin J has set forth guideposts for the search for the answer to the issue in the case at bar. In brief, she underlines the need for limits to liability, the need for the limits to be reasonably clear and the need for the rule to respond to considerations of policy and fairness. She also recognises that a single rule for all economic loss cases is probably unattainable. I am in substantial agreement with her on these points but I consider that a number of additional aspects are relevant to the choice of a rule in this area.

First, with respect to the need for limits to liability, it is important to underline that perfect justice is not possible in this area; it is impossible to compensate everybody who suffers loss owing to their contractual relationships with the property owner. Some losses, which were undoubtedly incurred as a result of a defendant's negligence, are going to remain uncompensated. The challenge, then, is to come up with a rule that divides the winners and the losers in the best possible manner.

A good test should distinguish on a rational basis between potential plaintiffs, all of whom were injured by the defendants' negligence. The plaintiff's proposed rule should offer a convincing and practical rationale for distinguishing its claim from those other claims, contractual or otherwise, which are to be rejected. Victims whose claims are to be denied must perceive a minimum of justice in the result. In my view, none of the theories that involve the acceptance of CN's claim but which would lead to the rejection of the claims of the other railways can be accepted as just from this perspective.

A test for recovery in cases of economic loss to contractual entitlements caused by property damage to another party should reflect the characteristics of this type of litigation, described in Feldthusen, *Economic Negligence*, *supra*, at pp. 207–8:

The defendants in this type of case are not typically heinous wrongdoers, but rather individuals and enterprises engaged in common and useful social activity. The same is true of the plaintiffs who are inadvertently harmed by some unfortunate and often inevitable consequence of modern life. Few important moral, social or symbolic issues are involved. Here, if anywhere, the economists' suggestion that the law should devise rules which permit the occasionally incompatible activities of plaintiffs and defendants to continue at the lowest possible total social cost should be taken seriously. This includes rules which encourage *both parties* to take cost-efficient accident prevention measures. And in respect of the unavoidable accidents which remain, it suggests that the loss should be borne by the party who can insure against it at the lowest cost. [Emphasis in original.]

This description is pertinent in the present case. A good rule should thus place some incentive on both parties to act in an economically rational manner to reduce total accident costs.

The rule must, of course, also confront the problem of indeterminacy. It is often suggested that this is the <u>only</u> problem the rule must confront. This was perhaps natural in light of the importance of potential indeterminate liability in negligent misrepresentation cases and the fact that the breakthrough in allowing recovery for economic loss came in *Hedley Byrne*. However, this confusion between the two issues tended to obscure the variety of issues raised in different kinds of economic loss cases. If the principal reason lying behind the broad exclusionary rule for pure economic loss is the concern over indeterminate liability, then the exclusionary rule can be easily discarded in favour of a more direct test of whether liability would be indeterminate. The plaintiff's case here is essentially built on this proposition and they offer this Court a wide variety of factual distinctions which they contend respond to the concern about indeterminate liability. As the above discussion indicates, I do not agree with that approach; a rule in this area should serve to do more than simply exclude indeterminate liability. However, in contractual economic loss cases, the proposed rule must certainly confront this issue.

What then does it mean for a particular liability to be determinate? The first critical question is whether the liability needs to be determinate before or after the accident. It is important to underline that since most claims of this nature occur in the commercial area, the requisite certainty should exist <u>before</u> the accident occurs. A company like CN should be able to consult legal counsel and receive reasonably clear advice with respect to potential recovery in the case of an accident that it as common as a ship hitting a bridge. So should a company like Burlington Northern Railway. Even more importantly, when the shoe is on the other foot, CN should also be able to get some reasonably clear guidance from counsel with respect to its potential liabilities in a case where a train derails and damages a factory. Estimating such liability is, of course, a key aspect to the pricing of insurance for potential tortfeasors. Under the exclusionary rule, liability is determinate *before* the accident; unless the contract is such as to create a joint venture or a possessory interest, all parties are aware that no recovery will lie for damage to those contractual interests.

The second important point is that the objection is not simply to a large number of claims since an accident may injure a large number of people or cause extensive property damage. But in physical damage cases, the number of potential first-victim claims is usually foreseeable even when large. Even more importantly, it is rare for multiple physical damage claims to ripple down a chain; physical injury to one person rarely gives rise to physical injury to others down a chain: see Stapleton, *supra*, at p. 255. Such ripple effects are on the contrary the very essence of contractual relational economic loss. The concern is that the volume of claims is indeterminate and therefore difficult and expensive to insure against.

A third important consideration is *the indeterminacy of each claim*. Recovery for contractual expectancies requires analysis of who bore the loss. What would happen if CN effectively passed on any increased costs incurred owing to the unavailability of the bridge to its customers? Refusing to address this question could result in a very expensive tort case leading to compensation for a party who suffered no loss. In a multi-stage chain of contracts, it becomes very difficult to analyse the economic effects of an accident on a particular link in the chain. A related concern is with false or inflated claims: see *Spartan Steel, supra*.

The problem with this case from the perspective of indeterminacy is that it involves a *type of accident* that will very likely lead to a great number of claims. It so happens that on the facts of this case, the number of injured parties is small. The fact that Norsk was fortunate enough to hit a bridge with few users does not make its potential liability for contractual relational economic loss any less indeterminate. Its liability after the accident is, of course, determinate; but beforehand, when potential tortfeasors are looking for insurance, they and their insurance company do not know which bridge will be hit. It seems odd to establish one set of rules for negligent tortfeasors who hit busy bridges—liability for economic loss is excused because of indeterminacy—and a different set for those who hit bridges used by few users.

. . . .

Foreseeability of the individual plaintiff or of an ascertained class of plaintiffs

CN heavily stressed the defendants' undoubtedly high level of subjective and objective knowledge that CN as a particular company would suffer loss. My colleague Stevenson J relies on this factor as his principal ground for finding liability in this case. There is no question that Norsk knew and ought to have known that CN would suffer loss. Indeed, the facts reveal that the tug captain thought CN would suffer even more than it did, since he erroneously thought the bridge belonged to it. I am unable to see the importance of this "excess of foresight" in policy terms, however.

First, the subjective view of the defendants with respect to the ownership of the bridge is obviously not sufficient to ground a claim. Such an error does not, of course, negate the defendants' duty with respect to the actual owner of the property. Why should it have the effect of creating new duties in the absence of a protected interest? It remains true, however, that Norsk could reasonably foresee that a specific plaintiff, CN, would suffer loss as a *contractual* claimant. Should this factor distinguish CN from other contractual claimants?

Two judges in *Caltex* suggested versions of an individual plaintiff test, at least one that would allow recovery in this case. At the level of a general test for all cases of pure economic loss, Mason J. adopted what can be termed the specific individual test. "A defendant", he held at p. 274, "will then be liable for economic damage due to his negligent conduct when he can reasonably foresee that a specific individual, as distinct from a general class of persons, will suffer financial loss as a consequence of his conduct". Gibbs J also incorporated the known plaintiff test into his analysis as a necessary but not sufficient condition for liability (at p. 245). As he saw it, the existence of a common adventure or physical propinquity may have supporting roles, but are neither necessary nor sufficient. The ascertained class test would allow recovery where the defendant knows or has the means of knowing that the persons likely to be affected by his or her negligence consist of a definite number of persons.

In *Candlewood, supra*, at p. 24, the House of Lords rejected the individual plaintiff test and the ascertained class of plaintiffs test in the following terms:

> Their Lordships have carefully considered these reasons for the decision in the *Caltex* case, 136 C.L.R. 529. With regard to the reasons given by Gibbs and Mason JJ, their Lordships have difficulty in seeing how to distinguish between a plaintiff as an individual and a plaintiff as a member of an unascertained class. The test can hardly be whether the plaintiff is known by name to the wrongdoer. Nor does it seem logical for the test to depend upon the plaintiff being a single individual. Further, why should there be a distinction for this purpose between a case where the wrongdoer knows (or has the means of knowing) that the persons likely to be affected by his negligence consist of a definite number of persons whom he can identify either by name or in some other way (for example as being the owners of particular factories or hotels) and who may therefore be regarded as an ascertained class, and a case where the wrongdoer knows only that there are several persons, the exact number being to him unknown, and some or all of whom he could not identify by name or otherwise, and who may therefore be regarded as an unascertained class? Moreover much of the argument in favour of an ascertained class seems to depend upon the view that the class would normally consist of only a few individuals. But would it be different if the class, though ascertained, was large? Suppose for

instance that the class consisted of all the pupils in a particular school. If it was a kindergarten school with only six pupils they might be regarded as constituting an ascertained class, even if their names were unknown to the wrongdoer. If the school was a large one with over a thousand pupils it might be suggested that they were not an ascertained class. But it is not easy to see a distinction in principle merely because the number of possible claimants is larger in one case than in the other. Apart from cases of negligent misstatement, with which their Lordships are not here concerned, they do not consider that it is practicable by reference to an ascertained class to find a satisfactory control mechanism which could be applied in such a way as to give reasonable certainty in its results.

In *Kamloops, supra,* Wilson J also questioned the advisability of the individual plaintiff test. At pages 30–1, she stated:

It is quite apparent that Gibbs and Jacobs JJ, and possibly Stephen J also, were seeking some means of permitting recovery for pure economic loss while avoiding the undesirable consequences of applying the reasonable foreseeability rule, namely indeterminate liability to an indeterminate class. They saw the solution in limiting foreseeability to specific individuals rather than members of a class. I am not sure, however, that their exception solves the problem. It may make the class determinate but it gives no guarantee that it will be small.

Both Lord Fraser of Tullybelton's unanimous opinion and Wilson J's majority opinion stressed the practical difficulties in applying such a test. I agree that the practical difficulties of applying such a test are considerable to say the least.

In my view, problems also exist at the level of principle. In the absence of any malicious intent on the part of the defendant, of what significance is the fact that the defendant knew that the individual plaintiff would suffer? In my view, its only role is to limit liability. The individual plaintiff or class of plaintiff or special relationship test serves a very different and more focused policy function in the context of the negligent misrepresentation cases where it has been employed: see *Hedley Byrne, supra*; *Candler* v. *Crane, Christmas & Co.*, [1951] 2 KB 164. Professor Feldthusen remarks as follows on its function in those cases ((1990–91), 17 *Can. Bus. L.J.* 356, at pp. 376–7):

. . . the duty of care is derived from a business relationship between the parties which antedates, and is independent from, the negligent act. The assumption of responsibility or special relationship duty tests and the known limited class remoteness test were developed to deal with transaction-specific negligence. The defendant makes *a reflective transactional undertaking* to a third party which affects (and is probably intended to affect) the plaintiff. The defendant is actually contemplating advice or service and its consequences in the transaction. It makes some sense to speak of parties known to be at risk from the contemplated transaction. The entire thrust of misrepresentation and services law is to limit liability to contemplated transaction-specific situations. One may describe this in proximity language, but it is a different use of the proximity principle than in a relational case. [Emphasis added.]

Those cases involve the defendant's making a representation *voluntarily*. It makes sense to impose upon the defendant a requirement that he or she put his or her mind to the question of who might be affected, since the defendant has the opportunity to reflect on this issue before making the representation: see *Haig* v. *Bamford, supra*.

Here we are dealing with an *accident*. There is no intention to affect the plaintiff; rather the effect on the plaintiff is merely a result of the accident. Norsk cannot be said to contemplate a particular act of negligence, a particular plaintiff or a particular loss in the same sense as a bank manager who provides financial information. Knowledge of the individual plaintiff serves solely to eliminate "indeterminate liability": it operates arbitrarily both in terms of singling out defendants and in terms of singling out plaintiffs.

In the context of an accident, this criteria has thus no link with fault or with a lack of care; surely no one is suggesting tort law should strive to protect bridges with high profile users more than bridges used by anonymous users, or that defendants who damage bridges with high profile users are more guilty than others. Its sole function is to distinguish one plaintiff from another and thus "solve" the indeterminacy problem, a function that could be as effectively performed by a rule based on the colour of CN's trains.

Allowing CN's claim to be distinct from the other contractual victims by virtue of its particular foreseeability as an individual victim would in my view give rise to an unjust rule owing to its sheer arbitrariness. It serves neither to distinguish particularly meritorious victims, nor to single out particularly careless tortfeasors. Its sole function is to reduce the class of claimants to a small group, a function that could be equally well performed by any other factual distinction. Further, the test would have the effect of singling out the wrong parties for relief. It would offer a premium to notoriety, a premium for which I can find no legal or social justification, particularly since such persons are most likely to advert to the matter and to contract out or insure against the harm.

The defendant's foresight with respect to the specific nature of the loss incurred by the plaintiff

The second factor put forward as founding proximity is that Norsk foresaw the specific nature of the loss incurred by CN. The argument based on the foreseeability of the specific nature of the loss would presumably found recovery for all three railroads, so it sits rather awkwardly with CN's unique relationship claim. It is also clearly insufficient to function on its own as a limit on indeterminate damages, since even if there were thousands of users of the bridge, the specific nature of the losses incurred would be foreseeable for all users. In practically all cases of this type, the defendant will be aware that the "specific nature of the loss" will be the loss of use of the property he or she has damaged.

Additionally, the tortfeasor does not actually know the specific nature of the loss, since the allocation of the loss will depend primarily on the terms of the contract between the plaintiff and the property owner as well as on other contracts between the plaintiff and the other parties. It is certain that Norsk knew that CN's *use of the bridge* would be interrupted. What is less clear and in fact quite doubtful is whether Norsk knew about the *allocation of risk of bridge failure* in the contract between CN and PWC.

It is thus incorrect to say that, because Norsk knew that CN's use of the bridge would be interrupted, it knew the "precise nature of the loss" CN would incur. The precise nature of the loss, and in fact whether any loss is incurred at all, would be a result of the contractual allocation of risk, of which Norsk would normally be unaware. In many cases of contractual relational loss, the variety of contractual entitlements will be much greater and more complex.

Physical propinquity

The third factor that is said to found proximity is the physical proximity of CN's property to the accident. CN's property is closely joined to the bridge on both sides of the river and the bridge forms an integral part of its railway network. CN relies here primarily on the judgment of Jacobs J in *Caltex*. Jacobs J there recognised that where the plaintiff's loss arises solely from a contractual relationship with a third party, recovery will be denied (at p. 279). However, he held, at p. 279, that if the damage arose owing to "physical effect on the person or property of the plaintiff, it will not be irrecoverable simply because it is economic loss". The judge, at p. 278, defined physical effect short of physical injury as an act or omission that prevents physical movement of a person or physical movement or operation of property. In that case, the physical effect was the immobilisation of the flow of crude oil through the pipeline.

CN does not, in my view, meet this physical effect test, even if such a test were adopted. Its trains have certainly not been immobilised. Its land has not been damaged and it makes no sense to speak of its being immobilized. In the absence of such a "physical effect", physical propinquity of property cannot constitute an alternative potential interest. As the appellants rightly point out, the other railways suffered identical damages despite not owning any property in physical propinquity to the accident.

The application of this test would also lead to minimal damages even if it were met. Jacobs J describes the damages that flow from his test as being limited to those resulting from the physical effect. In the *Caltex* case, the quantification of the damage was conceded. No inquiry was required as to whether all the crude oil for which alternative arrangement had to be made was "at the time of the incident already in physical propinquity to the place of the incident". In the case at bar, however, damages under this test would presumably be recoverable only as regards those trains that were in "physical propinquity" to the bridge when the barge hit the bridge. How close they would have to be is a matter for speculation.

My colleague McLachlin J has adopted a geographic proximity factor as one element of her proximity analysis. With respect, I am unable to discern any policy significance in the fact that a particular plaintiff owns property in proximity to an accident.

Proximity

The fourth approach taken by the respondent is more general and involves deciding economic loss cases on the basis of proximity. To this end it puts forward not only the three above-mentioned factors regarding its relationship with Norsk but also the aspects of its relationship with PWC which I examined, i.e., the alleged common adventure and the transferred loss. In fact, it provides the Court with a lengthy list of factors which, it alleges, create the necessary proximity in this case.

Stephen J in *Caltex* adopted this approach. My colleague McLachlin J also relies on this approach. I agree with Stevenson J that the concept of proximity is incapable of providing a principled basis for drawing the line on the issue of liability for the reasons expressed by him (at p. 1178). As he notes, it expresses a result, rather than a principle.

The argument from morality

. . .

CN's argument

CN, of course, concedes that a line must be drawn and that not all losses can be compensated. It suggests, however, that the line be situated somewhere on the other side of its recovery. It suggests that although its own and at least some other contractually based claims should be allowed, the Court should re-erect a bright line barrier excluding all plaintiffs who are not contractually linked with the property owner victim. In particular, co-contractors of CN, whatever the circumstances with respect to foreseeability and other traditional tort doctrines, "clearly cannot recover" owing to the lack of a direct contractual relationship with PWC. It is unclear to me why drawing a new bright line around potential claimants in this manner is a significantly better solution.

Part IV: A Refined Proximity Analysis in Contractual Relational Economic Loss Cases

The crucial problem with the various formulations of the proximity test examined so far is that they look at the problem strictly from the perspective of the defendant. The defendant's negligence places it in a position of liability *vis-à-vis* the entire world. However, if it can show that its liability would be indeterminate, it can be excused. In my opinion, given the eminently pragmatic and policy basis of decisions about liability in this area, the situation of both the defendant *and the plaintiff* needs to be examined in cases of this kind. In particular, the plaintiff's ability to foresee and provide for the particular damage in question is a key factor in the proximity analysis.

The legitimacy of this type of consideration

In my view, it is legitimate to consider which party is the better loss bearer in this type of case. This term requires definition. Determining which party is best able to <u>bear</u> the loss essentially involves asking which party is in a better position to predict the frequency and severity of CN's economic loss when bridges are damaged, and to plan accordingly. Analysis of loss bearing ability emphasizes how the parties deal with accidents that tort law has not succeeded in preventing, rather than with preventing accidents.

The question of which party is best able to bear the loss should be distinguished from the question of which party is best able to avoid the accident's occurring. Analysis of the issues pertaining to deterrence, or accident avoidance, involves the question of the relative ability of parties to act in a way that will reduce the risk of occurrence of the type of accident in question and is widely recognized as relevant in tort law. In my view, analysis of loss *bearing* ability is particularly relevant in determining whether proximity exists in the context of contractual relational economic loss cases.

Tort law has not generally given much consideration to analysis of loss bearing ability. This type of approach is obviously ill-suited to personal injury cases. In property damage cases involving the primary liability of the tortfeasor, the courts have often rightly been more concerned to ensure deterrence by placing liability on the party best able to avoid the accident's occurring. Under modern conditions, deterrence may, of course, be difficult to effect through tort law; nonetheless, placing liability on the injurer serves to internalise the costs of accidents legitimately to the accident-causing activity. In many cases, loss shifting to the better loss bearer runs squarely into the powerful objection that it is not also the better risk avoider. When the case involves the question whether that party will be held liable at all, the concern for deterrence overrides the concern about loss-bearing ability. Thus, in cases involving primary liability for accidents, tort law has given priority to preventing accidents by requiring those who cause accidents to pay for their damage or more likely to pay for insurance.

Consideration of loss bearing ability is by no means entirely absent from the cases, however, and it has been increasingly recognized in recent cases. In *Leigh and Sillavan Ltd.* v. *Aliakmon Shipping Co., supra*, at p. 819, Lord Brandon relied on the fact that the plaintiff had open to it an adequate avenue of protection in contract in refusing liability. A recent article by Stapleton, *supra*, at pp. 270–1, has suggested a formulation that seems to me to encapsulate this aspect of that case and may well be of more general application, as the author suggests, in cases of economic loss. She writes:

> The power of this neglected argument [that the plaintiff had available to it an adequate avenue of protection] is that it does not depend on a circular proposition about where "principle"or precedent has in the past drawn the tort boundary. It is an argument explaining where that boundary should, on clear and stated principle, be placed. In our agenda of considerations, then, about where a tort duty in respect of economic loss should be recognised, we could place alongside the necessary (but not sufficient) condition of the absence or controllability of floodgates problems, a second requirement: the necessary but not sufficient condition that the plaintiff did not have, nor could reasonably be expected to have acquired, protection against the risk of economic loss.

In *Smith* v. *Bush*, [1990] 1 AC 831 (HL), the House of Lords, in allowing recovery in a case where a purchaser acquired defective property in reliance on the competence of a professional adviser, considered whether the plaintiff could have protected herself by contract. Prompted by the *Unfair Contract Terms Act 1977*, 1977 (UK), c. 50, the House expressly acknowledged the difficulty purchasers of small houses have in affording a second survey. The issue of indeterminacy became by the same token of lesser concern, since the ambit of liability was confined to a relevant vulnerable sub-set of property acquirers—those buying modest dwellings: see Stapleton, *supra*, at pp. 278–79. Moreover, as I noted in reference to comparative law, in those systems that in theory allow recovery for relational economic loss, recovery has apparently been denied in some cases where the plaintiff had adequate means of protecting itself.

Increasingly, our courts have openly addressed the issue of insurance as one of these policy concerns. In *Lamb* v. *Camden London Borough Council*, [1981] QB 625 (CA), at pp. 637–38, Lord Denning MR wrote as follows:

> On broader grounds of policy, I would add this: the criminal acts here—malicious damage and theft— are usually covered by insurance. By this means the risk of loss is spread throughout the community.

It does not fall too heavily on one pair of shoulders alone. The insurers take the premium to cover just this sort of risk and should not be allowed, by subrogation, to pass it on to others. . . . It is commonplace nowadays for the courts, when considering policy, to take insurance into account. It played a prominent part in *Photo Production Ltd. v. Securicor Transport Ltd.* [1980] AC 827. The House of Lords clearly thought that the risk of fire should be borne by the fire insurers who had received the full premium for fire risk—and not by Securicor's insurers, who had only received a tiny premium. That, too, was a policy decision. . . .

So here, it seems to me that if Mrs Lamb was insured against damage to the house and theft, the insurers should pay the loss. If she was not insured, that is her misfortune.

See also Fleming, *supra*, at p. 202 and p. 224.

The judges in *Caltex* implicitly or explicitly deny the importance of insurance considerations in resolving the pragmatic question of where to draw the line in this type of case. Four of the five judgments did not consider insurance issues at all. Stephen J explicitly denies the court any role in this regard. In his view, the task of the courts remains that of fixing loss rather than spreading loss, and if this is to be altered it is a matter for direct legislative action rather than for the courts (at p. 265).

With respect, I do not agree with Stephen J that the consideration of insurance changes the task of the courts from loss fixing to loss spreading. Insurance considerations are merely one element in an analysis of where it is appropriate to fix the loss, in a case where a solution is necessarily pragmatic. Many of the extensions of tort liability that have occurred over the last 50 years would have been inconceivable in the absence of insurance. Many cases have referred to insurance considerations to justify extending liability: see, for example, Laskin J. in *Rivtow, supra*, at p. 1221. To reject, as does Stephen J, the open consideration of insurance as "covert judicial action" is paradoxical, since what is proposed is to bring insurance considerations into the open rather than merely expressing conclusions in terms of proximity. Fleming notes that Stephen J's concern that the new policy dimension may appear more germane to the legislative than to the judicial function, but responds, in my view accurately, that "the change in perspective is dictated by inescapable external developments, to ignore which would be deliberately short-sighted and self-defeating": see Fleming, *supra*, at p. 11. I agree with my colleagues McLachlin J and Stevenson J that insurance deserves to be considered in cases of this kind; however, I disagree with them as to its relevance.

In the context of contractual relational economic loss, policy concerns with respect to which party can best bear the loss are particularly important for three reasons. First, policy concerns with respect to deterrence and cost internalisation are generally at least substantially met by the tortfeasor's primary liability to the property owner. In cases where the property damage is inconsequential, it might make sense to impose additional liability on deterrence grounds; that is not the case here, however, and I expressly reserve that question.

Second, they can be raised since current law denies recovery; rather than pose the risk of a revolutionary result, the approach merely articulates another policy lying behind a well-established rule. In some areas of the law, an examination of relative loss bearing ability might lead to arguments for fundamental changes in the law, changes best left to Parliament. Here, however, such considerations simply serve to establish a new rationale, or perhaps more accurately, to articulate explicitly an underlying rationale for a long-standing rule in an area of the law where the importance of policy considerations is now clearly recognised. As the law of torts has evolved, the courts have not been averse to modifying their mode of analysis of cases and have not waited for the legislature to do so. One imagines with difficulty a statute henceforth requiring the courts to take such considerations into account.

Finally, in this field the crucial problem remains that of limiting liability. All recognise that recovery of this type of claim must remain exceptional, if only because the potential number of claims of this type is practically unlimited. In these circumstances, a significantly higher threshold for recovery is, in my view, entirely justified. In other areas of tort law, where the trend has been towards extending liability, placing an onus on the plaintiff is inconceivable. In this area, however, there is an overriding need for strict controls on potential liability.

In my view, it is legitimate for these reasons to consider explicitly the ability of the plaintiff to bear the risk of loss in this type of case.

Turning then to an application of these criteria to this case, a determination of which party is the better loss bearer is relatively straightforward. CN is undoubtedly in a better position to bear the loss than Norsk. First, in light of the significant information available regarding bridge failure and CN's long use of the bridge, CN was probably at least equally competent in terms of *estimating the potential risks* of bridge failure. This aspect seems to me to be clear in light of the facts.

Second, CN would clearly be in a better position than PWC to *estimate the potential costs of bridge failure to CN's operations.* CN knows exactly how much use it gets out of the various bridges crossed by its trains. It also knows what the alternatives are in cases of bridge failure. Norsk, of course, is very poorly placed to estimate the value of the use that various people and companies get out of the bridges that cross the rivers its tugs sail on. It is also poorly placed to estimate the potential costs to those users of an interruption in bridge service. Unlike the first factor, which depends to a large degree on the facts of each case, this factor tends to weigh heavily in favour of the defendant in almost every case of this type.

Third, CN was better placed to *protect itself from the consequences of those losses.* This point requires further discussion. It is hard to imagine a more sophisticated group of plaintiffs than the users of railway bridges. These parties have access to the full range of protective options: first party commercial insurance or self-insurance, contracts both with the bridge owner and with the railway's customers.

Insurance

My colleague McLachlin J rejects the idea that insurance considerations justify a denial of liability and relies on an article by Bishop: see Bishop, "Economic Loss in Tort" (1982), 2 *Oxf. J. Legal Studies* 1. Bishop argues that the insurance argument must overcome two difficulties in the context of economic loss. First, he states that to eliminate recovery for economic loss would reduce the incentive to take care. With respect, I do not find this argument persuasive in the context of relational economic loss cases, since the primary liability of the tortfeasor to the owner of the bridge is largely sufficient to create incentives to take care. This, as I noted earlier, is one of the key distinguishing features that justifies separate treatment of relational economic loss cases.

Bishop's second argument is that insurance is unavailable at reasonable cost. He argues in particular that insurance for *loss of profits* is not available. Insurance companies understandably refuse to insure profitability. However, that is not the issue here. CN is not claiming for loss of profit, but rather for the costs occasioned by the *interruption of its access to the bridge.* That risk is analogous to a business interruption. Many businesses have interruption insurance covering interruption caused by factors other than breach of contract: see Waddams, *The Law of Damages* (2nd edn. 1991), at § 14.330. Even if insurance is not available in the commercial market, CN is ideally situated to self-insure.

Undoubtedly in certain cases, an affected business will not have purchased insurance. However, as James has noted, if the business community accepts a rule of non-liability for indirect economic losses without securing insurance protection against them by a relatively inexpensive method, then this fact at least suggests that these losses do not present a social problem serious enough to justify the cost to society in providing for their compensation by the most expensive method in its arsenal—liability based on fault: see James, *supra*, at p. 114. In other words, if the business community is insured, then there is no point in shifting the loss from one insurance company to another at high cost. If the business community is not insured, then that reveals that other ways of defraying such losses are perceived as superior to insurance and the problem is not that serious.

Conclusions about the insurance market are of course somewhat tentative and it would behoove lawyers, as Atiyah notes, to inform themselves about fundamental matters of insurability in new tort cases and to see to it that courts are also informed: see Atiyah, "Note: Economic Loss in the United States" (1985), 5 *Oxf. J. Legal Studies* 485. However, the weight of opinion is certainly to the effect that first-party insurance is a cheaper and more effective method of protecting against loss than liability insurance, particularly where the liability is of uncertain amount; see *Photo Production Ltd. v. Securicor Transport Ltd.*, [1980] AC 827, at p. 851; Smillie, "Negligence and Economic Loss" (1982), 32 *UTJ* 231, at pp. 240–2; James, *supra*, at pp. 113–16. In my opinion, the burden of showing otherwise must rest on those who would have the court overturn a long-standing rule excluding recovery.

Contract

I agree with McLachlin J that in many cases the contractual allocation of risk does not supply a rationale for refusing recovery. Inequality of bargaining power is in fact only one of a number of reasons why contract may not be a real alternative in a given case. In many cases, protecting oneself from economic losses through contract is not possible. In the cases involving interruptions in services provided by utilities, the service is often supplied by a monopoly supplier on standard form contracts. Any shifting of the risk from consumer to utility company may even be statutorily excluded. Such cases involve contracts in name only. Or again, the risk which materializes may be so unusual that the parties never contemplated it. Though there may be other reasons for denying liability, in all of these cases the argument from the contractual allocation of risk is not convincing.

In this case, however, it is. The facts in this case establish that all parties were well aware of the risk of bridge failure. CN knew what it was doing. The very bridge at issue here had been damaged on a number of previous occasions, and various studies of the problem had been carried out. CN participated actively in at least one of these studies. CN was even aware of the traditional legal rule; as I noted, it brought a very similar claim for bridge failure in similar circumstances in 1973 for which recovery was denied.

. . . .

In my view, a denial of recovery in this case is justified in light of CN's overwhelmingly superior risk bearing capacity on the facts of this case.

Before leaving the issue of CN's ability to protect itself, it should be noted that the rule proposed by my colleagues will *still* require parties such as CN to protect themselves since they will never know before the particular accident whether they will be part of the determinate class. It is to say the least difficult to predict whether a particular railway bridge will be knocked out by someone who knows you by name. Alternatively, it is difficult to know whether of the many possible bridges that will be damaged, the one that will be damaged is the one next to which you own property. As a result, the only solution for the prudent railway will be to purchase insurance. Presumably, the cost of this insurance will reflect the value the insurance company places on the possibility of its recovering from the tortfeasor.

The critical effect of allowing recovery is that it would ALSO require defendants in Norsk's position to insure for potential contractual relational economic loss as well, since they will obviously never know beforehand whether the bridges damaged by its tugs will be used by plaintiffs whose name it knows or who have property nearby. The principal beneficiaries of the rule proposed by my colleagues would be insurance companies, who would benefit from the existence of a new and highly uncertain risk against which companies likely to inflict property damage would need to insure.

The rules suggested by my colleagues thus will require that *both* parties insure at considerable additional social cost. The only gain will be a slight reduction in the plaintiff's first party insurance costs to take into account the possibility that the insurance company will recover from a tortfeasor under the new doctrine.

A further practical difficulty should be noted. In cases where the tortfeasor is either not insured or insufficiently insured with respect to the initial property damage or personal injury claim or the relational claim or both, serious problems will arise with respect to the primacy of one type of claim over another. For example, if the tortfeasor is liable for both a $500,000 personal injury claim and $500,000 in relational claims but his total assets and insurance only cover half of that amount, the actual compensation of the personal injury claim will presumably be halved in order to allow recovery for a relational claim which as noted will often involve recovery for a subrogated insurance company: see Feldthusen, *Economic Negligence, supra*, at p. 207.

Conclusion

It is unclear to me why the current state of the law on contractual relational economic loss, which channels claims to the property owner, is unsatisfactory at least in the commercial area involving sophisticated parties. It is also unclear whether significant amounts of court time should be expended in distinguishing between contractual relational economic loss sufferers—those who are proximate to the tortfeasor and those who are not.

There is no question that the outcome of cases of this nature under the exclusionary rule depends upon the terms of the contract. This operates in two ways: the contract may create a possessory interest or a joint venture or it may provide for an indemnity from the property owner. The question to be resolved is whether allowing the contract to determine whether the plaintiff has the requisite interest and where the loss falls is more arbitrary, unfair or unworkable than the various tests referred to above.

The arguments against recovery in this case can be summed up as follows. First, the arguments for recovery are weak. It is not necessary to impose liability to ensure that tortfeasors like Norsk are dissuaded from damaging bridges. The increase in deterrence that would result from imposing the additional liability called for in this case would not likely have much impact on the behaviour of potential tortfeasors. The only purpose served by recovery in this case to which the judgment of McLachlin J refers, at pp. 1162–63, is "the purpose of permitting a plaintiff whose position for practical purposes, *vis-à-vis* the tortfeasor, is indistinguishable from that of the owner of the damaged property, to recover what the actual owner could have recovered". In my view, the argument that CN is indistinguishable from the owner founders on the fact that CN does not qualify under the well-established cases in which the law provides for recovery by the contracting party where it in fact has a proprietary or possessory interest. CN's *interest* is merely contractual.

CN argues that restricting recovery to the owner or person in possession is based on pragmatism not logic, and therefore to require logical support for an exception to a pragmatic rule which in a particular case results in an injustice, is in itself illogical. In my view, cases such as *Rivtow* and *Kamloops* which have allowed recovery for pure economic loss have established criteria that do provide logical support for an exception to a pragmatic rule.

The argument that Norsk was at fault and CN was innocent and that fault should justify recovery is also unconvincing here. Fault alone cannot justify recovery in this area since some admittedly injured claimants will have their claims denied. Since the whole exercise in this kind of situation involves drawing a line *amongst those who are undeniably injured by the tortfeasor who was undeniably at fault*, appeals to fault beg the question. The defendants were equally at fault with respect to other claims that will be denied. CN is unable to show any special damage different in kind from that suffered by the other potential contractual claimants. None of the factual distinctions the company puts forward has any relevance with respect to the defendants' fault.

The second group of reasons focus on the weaknesses of the proposed rules that would allow recovery. The tests that would allow recovery do not meet the criteria that a rule should have in this area. The concept of a "special relationship" is not applicable to cases involving accidents. None of the facts put forward by CN as indicative of its special relationship has any other policy significance than to attempt to meet, after the fact, the problem of indeterminate liability. The individual plaintiff test would presumably preclude recovery by the other railways that suffered losses identical in nature to those suffered by CN. If the test were extended to cover a foreseeable class of plaintiffs such as users of the railway bridge, it would simply restate the general requirement that the plaintiff be foreseeable and recovery would be allowed whether the users of the bridge were four or four thousand. The proximity test has practically no predictive value; it remains impossible to say whether that test would lead to recovery for the other railways in this case, let alone its application in other cases.

Finally, there are the reasons supporting the exclusionary rule. These are, of course, essentially pragmatic, as has been recognised in cases of this type from the very beginning. First, denial of recovery places incentives on all parties to act in ways that will minimise overall losses, a legitimate and desirable goal for tort law in this area. Second, denial of recovery allows for only one party carrying insurance rather than both parties. Third, it will result in a great saving of judicial resources for cases in which more pressing concerns are put forward. The difficult job of drawing the line is at least done quickly without a great deal of factual investigation into the various factors that found proximity. The right to recover can be most often determined from the face of the contract. Fourth, it also eliminates difficult problems of sharing an impecunious defendant's limited resources between relational claims and direct claims. Fifth, the traditional rule is certain, and although like any pragmatic solution, borderline cases may cause problems, the exceptions to the rule in cases of joint ventures, general average contributions, and possessory and proprietorial interests are reasonably well defined and circumscribed. This case, in my view, does not even constitute a borderline case in this respect, since CN has no property interest of any kind. The consequence of that certainty is that contracting parties can be certain of where the loss with respect to the unavailability of property will lie in the absence of any contractual arrangement.

I add one final consideration. This case is one of maritime law, which in large measure encompasses a global system. The bright line exclusionary rule against recovery has for nearly a century been in effect in that system, and continues to be followed by the major trading nations, in particular Great Britain and the United States. In making arrangements for allocating risks in essentially maritime matters, those engaged in navigating and shipping should, as much as possible, be governed by a uniform rule, so that they can plan their affairs ahead of time, whether by contract or insurance against possible contingencies.

In my view, to justify recovery in cases of this nature, the plaintiff would, at the very least, have to respond effectively not only to the concern about indeterminacy but also show that no adequate alternative means of protection was available. Other concerns may also need to be met. At the very least, the requirement that the plaintiff not have had any commercially reasonable method of protecting itself is an important addition to what remains a conceptually difficult *ex post facto* inquiry into the "determinate nature" of the particular victim and damage from the perspective of the defendant.

The question of whether recovery should be allowed in the residual cases in which these two barriers are overcome does not require an answer in the context of this case. Individuals and small businesses may be incapable of effectively protecting themselves in any meaningful fashion. In some cases, of course, contractual relational economic loss may occur in a different form such as loss of salary and the failure to protect against it by first-party insurance cannot be said to lead to an inference of social unimportance. In such cases, however, the indeterminacy problem is often very acute. If the number of potential individual plaintiffs is great, recovery will be denied on the grounds of "indeterminacy", even though the plaintiffs may not have had any real ability to protect themselves. Where the plaintiff passes the indeterminacy tests, it will often be sophisticated. The argument that recovery should be denied to those who could have protected themselves does not support a bright line in and of itself. Rather, it complements the indeterminacy analysis. It suggests that those who are most likely to emerge from the indeterminacy analysis are those with the ability to protect themselves and questions the advisability of a rule with the effect of allowing recovery to only that group of contractual claimants, rather than denying recovery to all.

The exclusionary rule is not in itself attractive. It excludes recovery by people who have undeniably suffered losses as a result of an accident. It also leads to some arbitrary but generally predictable results in cases at the margin. The results with respect to time charters may be "capricious", but time charterers know their rights and obligations from the start and can act accordingly. The rule only becomes defensible when it is realised that full recovery is impossible, that recovery is in fact going to be refused in the vast majority of such claims regardless of the rule we adopt, and when the exclusionary rule is compared to the alternatives. In my view, it should not be disturbed on the facts of this case.

I should add a few words about McLachlin J's suggestion that the essential difference between her approach and mine lies in the flexibility allowed by her approach. She characterises my approach as providing for recovery depending exclusively on the terms of the formal contract between the plaintiff and the property owner. She considers an approach based on the terms of the contract involves a "rigid categorisation which denies the possibility of recovery in new cases which may not meet the categorical test" (at p. 1164), a problem that is avoided under the proximity test she sets forth.

I do not see the essential difference between our two approaches as that between certainty and flexibility. In my view, the key difference is between a principled flexibility, which adheres to a general rule in the absence of policy reasons for excluding its application, and arbitrariness. Among the policy factors considered in the course of this opinion that might justify relaxing the rule are the ability of the plaintiff to protect itself and the quantum of property damage caused by the tort-feasor with its attendant impact on the issue of deterrence. I have not found it necessary to consider the precise role of these factors in this case since CN was clearly able to protect itself and the property damage sustained was sufficient to afford deterrence. Whether such factors would in fact provide workable criteria sufficient to provide for recovery despite the strong arguments in favour of the long-standing exclusionary rule, based on certainty and other factors, is an open question. What I have decided is that in the absence of all of these factors, there is no reason to disturb the rule.

Thus I do not say that the right to recovery in all cases of contractual relational economic loss depends exclusively on the terms of the contract. Rather, I note that such is the tenor of the exclusionary rule and that departures from that rule should be justified on defensible policy grounds. The Court should do more than simply establish a rule that allows judges to resolve cases as they see fit. That, as I see it, is the effect of the approach proposed by my colleague.

Disposition

I would allow the appeal and dismiss the claim for damages.

Notes to Norsk

1. One must again warn the reader that the extracts reproduced above only convey part of the picture and that the strengths and weaknesses of this decision will only become fully apparent when all *three* of its judgments are carefully read.

2. Omitted from the extracts are the sections on the current state of Canadian law; but they, too, should be read by anyone who wishes to see how Canadian law has departed from the English "model" and adopted a less hostile view towards pure economic loss. The divergences between major Common law jurisdictions (Australia, Canada, New Zealand and, of course, the United States) must also be noted. Also noteworthy is the fact that English, Canadian, Australian and New Zealand courts refer to each others decisions *and* to American decisions. Nowadays, however, it is rare to find American courts referring to English or Commonwealth decisions. Is this due to overwork? Too much "local" material? Growing "local" confidence (or arrogance) which encourages the belief that they have "nothing to learn" from other (closely related) systems? All three? Is this "divergence" a healthy phenomenon? Or are there areas of the law where it should be avoided?

4. The "swing" judgment in this case was delivered by Stevenson J yet, strangely, it is the least effective of them all. For, first, his decision is, essentially, a variation of the views of Gibbs and Mason JJ in *Caltex Oil (Aust.) Pty* v. *The Dredge Willemstad* (1976) 136 C.L.R. 529. (The plaintiff should recover because the defendant knew or ought to have known that a "specific individual . . . as opposed to a general or unascertained class of the public" was likely in this instance to suffer the foreseeable kind of loss.) This approach has never met with much approval; and it seems to

place too great a premium on "notoriety". (For more criticisms see: pp. 1107–1112.) The second draw-back of Stevenson J's judgment is that it weakened the overall result of the case by expressly dis-approving of McLachlin J's proximity test (p. 1178). Thus, the most disturbing aspect of the case as a whole is that it has not left us with a clear *ratio decidendi*. For the proximity test advocated by the majority is espoused only by three justices out of seven; and if one looks at the case *purely from a Common law point of view* (and thus removed from the majority camp the Quebec judge), one is left with only two justices out of six advocating proximity as the appropriate controlling device. Those who like "bright line rules" will, no doubt, stress this point as *Norsk's* major defect.

5. Notwithstanding the force of the above-mentioned objection one must also stress the many areas where majority and minority found common ground. Thus both agreed that the "more flexible approach set out in *Anns*" was preferable to the *Murphy* reasoning, which was expressly stated as not representing the law in Canada (pp. 1054, 1163). In the words of La Forest J, who deliv-ered the minority judgment; "I fully support this court's rejection of the broad bar on recovery of pure economic loss . . ." (p. 1054). The dispute thus centred around what was termed "relational economic loss", i.e. economic loss suffered by the plaintiff as a result of property damage caused to a third party. Secondly, all agreed that "the law of tort does not permit recovery for *all* economic loss" (p. 1163). Thirdly, there was full agreement that cases like *Norsk* required a discussion of the underlying economic and wider policy considerations. Fourthly, all three judgments accepted Stevenson J's view that "the case at bar is a good example of how useful comparative law can be" (p. 1174). Finally, both majority and minority came within a whisker of bringing the case within the ambit of the rule in *Morrison Steamship Co. Ltd* v. *Greystoke Castle (Cargo Owners)* [1947] AC 265, long recognised as one of the allowable "exceptions" to the non-liability rule. Where they disagreed was in "the test for determining joint venture."

6. The case is a shining example of comparative law "in practice" since the judgments quote 32 academic writers (covering seven countries) and 62 decisions (from five different, international, jurisdictions). La Forest J's use of the rich material led him to conclude that (*a*) even the most liberal foreign systems (i.e. the Romanistic group) are "acutely aware of the potential for unlim-ited liability"; (*b*) they avoid it by establishing "a *de facto* [if not *de iure*] bar" to recovery; (*c*) they do this through a rich variety of "causal" devices, and (*d*) that the civilian experience could be taken to support the view (promoted by the majority) that "recovery for contractual relational economic loss [could] remain exceptional even if the exclusionary rule [were] relaxed" (p. 1985). *This is an important concession since it shows that the "floodgates" argument, currently in vogue with the House of Lords, is not empirically substantiated.*

7. For a number of commentators *Norsk* scores heavily (both in methodology and content) over its British contemporary "leading" judgment—*Murphy*. On this see, Fleming, "Economic Loss in Canada" (1993) *Tort L. Rev.* 68–74; Markesinis, "Compensation for Negligently Inflicted Pure Economic Loss: Some Canadian Views" (1993) 109 *LQR* 5–12, and decide which of the two judg-ments—the English or the Canadian: (*a*) provides you with a better introduction to the problem of economic loss; (*b*) comes up with the most satisfactory answer. Consider also the potential impact that research assistants (Clerks) may have in the style and thoroughness of a judgment.

7. ECONOMIC LOSS (NEGLIGENT STATEMENTS)

Case 19

BUNDESGERICHTSHOF (SIXTH CIVIL SENATE) 12 FEBRUARY 1979
WM 1979, 548 = NJW 1979, 1595

The plaintiff claims damages from the defendants, an international bank, for loss suffered as a result of inaccurate information supplied to her by their German branch (and con-cerning the creditworthiness of a third party).

Towards the end of 1970 the plaintiff was looking for a profitable way to invest some DM 130,000 and a finance broker, L, recommended the hotel P, built by U and opened to the public a few months earlier. U had financed his hotel by a number of loans including one for 2.5 million DM raised from the defendants and secured by a land charge. U, requiring a further 3.5 million DM, decided to raise this from private individuals with the help of advertisements and brokers offering 12 per cent interest on all loans as well as a land charge for security. More precisely, he registered a land charge for 3.5 million DM in favour of the defendants which was divided into smaller parts each securing sums of DM 10,000 and DM 25,000. The defendants, in consideration for the usual fee, were willing to assign these "part land charges" to lenders and place the funds in a blocked account for U until the completion of all formalities. On 3 February L, the broker, gave the plaintiff the following information which was written on the defendants' paper but gave neither date nor address: "Hotel P, George U. This is a newly built luxury hotel, with some 440 beds and conforming with international standards, was officially opened in June 1970 in the presence of many dignitaries. So far as we know it has already entered into long-term arrangements with a number of international travel agencies. It is owned by U, whom we know as a client and as a competent business man. U also owns a hotel in Tenerife and two sanatoria run by reputable persons. Owing to a great increase in building costs, U needs a further 3.5 million DM which is to be found on the open market. Any money advanced for this purpose will be credited to a blocked account with our bank, and after the notary has confirmed that the terms of the contract have been complied with, it will be credited to the hotel's current account. We ourselves have in the past made substantial payments to U against security but, due to an increase in building costs, U's liquidity is, at present, tight."

On 17 February, 1971 the plaintiff paid DM 130,000 which the defendants immediately credited to U's account. Three days earlier the defendants had asked U to repay their loans by 23 February and on 16 March they extended the repayment date to the end of May 1971. Meanwhile U was getting deeper and deeper into financial difficulties and on 23 December he applied for a composition with his creditors. Four months later bankruptcy proceedings followed. Both plaintiff and defendant withdrew from the auction of the hotel and the plaintiff will receive nothing from the bankrupt's estate.

The plaintiff brought an action claiming DM 65,000 since legal aid was granted to her only for this amount due to her contributory negligence. She argues that her loss is due to the defendant's letter which gave information which they knew to be false. The defendants deny that the information was wrong and also deny liability on the grounds that they had not entered into any contract to supply her with information.

The Court of First Instance awarded the plaintiff DM 32,500, and ruled that she should bear the rest of the loss herself because of her contributory negligence. The defendants' appeal was rejected and their further appeal on points of law is also dismissed.

Reasons

I. The Court of Appeal accepted that the defendant is liable according to the law of contract. Their appeal on points of law fails.

1. The Court of Appeal found that the defendants knowingly and deliberately composed the notice (quoted above) and put it into circulation with the view to its being shown to potential private lenders to U.

(*a*) The Court of Appeal (also) found that the information it contained was both in form and content intended to reach a circle of private potential investors. Stripped to its essential the notice gives information which is intended to appeal to private individuals. This is true both of the description of U and of his other businesses. For instance, the reference to the official opening of the hotel in the presence of local dignitaries could only have aimed at making his business appear reliable in the eyes of private persons. Much of this material would clearly have been written in a different way if the document had been intended to be used solely for internal banking purposes. Its contents make sense only if they are seen as aiming from the outset to attract private prospective investors. And this is corroborated by the statement in the notice that the money lent would be transferred from the blocked account with the defendants to the hotel's account only after a notary had confirmed that the terms of the contract had been complied with. This method of concluding a contract is less important to a bank than the encumbrances which are not mentioned in the notice. But it is calculated to dispel doubts that may arise in the mind of an individual, inexperienced in money matters, reading the preceding passages which explain why the extra sums are required. The outward appearance of the notice also speaks in favour of this interpretation. Thus, it bears the business name and the description of the defendant but gives no indication of the person addressed, or the date or any other details that usually accompany letter writing.

This interpretation is not only possible, but, indeed, necessary, the more so when one realises that the defendants, who were asked to handle the loan, were aware that only private individuals would be considered as lenders. The appeal is thus not able to reveal any error of law committed by the Court of Appeal when characterising the sense and purpose of the notice.

The argument that the Court of Appeal failed to take into account the fact that the defendants gave this kind of information in response to enquiries made by banks is also unsuccessful for if this is taken to imply that the defendants supplied information to banks only, it runs clearly counter to the defendants' submissions before the lower court. There the defendants maintained that information concerning U was given only to individuals making specific enquiries . . . On the appellate level, therefore, one must assume that the defendants gave information not *only* but *also* to banks. This does not necessarily run counter to the Court of Appeal's interpretation. Since only private individuals would be considered as lenders, the banks must have enquired on their behalf and thus the information so acquired must have been destined only for their clients and not for themselves.

(*b*) Once it is accepted, as it must be, that the information supplied by the defendants was meant for potential investors, one must then also accept the further finding of the Court of Appeal, namely that the defendants circulated this information so that it would be presented to a group of prospective investors. The assumption that the defendants intended to give the information to individual enquirers only, and had not agreed to its being passed on to other interested parties, is inconsistent with the purpose of preparing the information, namely to appeal to a group of individuals who might be interested in becoming lenders. Given that the defendants were themselves substantial creditors of U, and were anxious to relieve him of his financial difficulties, their intention was to bring the information to the notice of as many prospective lenders as possible. The assertion that the defendant supplied information concerning U only to individual enquirers does not rule out the possibility that the bank, in conformity with its purpose, approved of the information being passed on to other lenders. In any event, the defendants have failed to adduce any evidence to show that their notice had been brought to the attention of only a small group of individuals. The Court of Appeal was thus free to look at the objective contents of the notice.

2. The Court of Appeal was also not in error in finding that the defendants were fully aware that their information would be of great importance to the recipients and would be used as a basis of important investments. Since its prime purpose was to help attract finance for the hotel P, it is obvious that it was intended to help prospective investors to decide whether to lend money to U to the extent of at least DM 10,000 and was designed with that purpose in mind . . .

3. The Court of Appeal considered the information given to have been false in so far as it concealed facts which ought to have been disclosed. Thus, the reference to U's other properties created the impression that they also were available as additional security even though in actual fact they were already encumbered up to the hilt. The reference to the defendants' own substantial secured loans to U was also false since they had already called for their repayment at the time when the information (in the notice) reached the plaintiff . . . The inaccuracy of the notice is evident from a number of other undisputed facts such as, for example, the concealment of the various charges on the sanatoria properties. To a lender such information is particularly important when making up his mind as to whether to make a loan or not . . . Contrary to the view advanced in this appeal, it must be said that it is customary to mention all substantial charges when information is given about land by a bank. According to the findings of the Court of Appeal, when the information was issued by the defendants, the entire hotel facilities as well as the sanatoria had not been paid for and U was no longer in a position to honour any bills drawn for them. These circumstances, which would normally point towards an extremely delicate economic situation, should have been made clear by the defendants at the time of issuing of their notice since they would have had great bearing on the decision of the lenders. The defendants did not argue that they were unaware of the above, indeed this would have been unlikely for a bank like theirs, whose function it is to grant credit to borrowers. Nor did the defendants fulfil their duties by stating in their notice that U was faced with liquidity problems since this would not normally indicate to a private individual that bills had already been protested. All these findings are sufficient to characterise the information as false.

II. All the factual elements necessary to impose contractual liability for negligent advice are thus satisfied. According to the cases where information is supplied by a bank a contractual or quasi-contractual relationship already exists between the bank and the enquiring party whenever the information supplied by the bank is of manifest significance to the inquiring party and it is clear that the latter will be relying on it in making substantial capital allocations (cf. decision of the Senate of 6 July 1970, *WM* 1970, 1021 . . .). The situation in this present case is just that. In this case the bank addresses itself to a quite clearly defined group of prospective lenders who are interested in advancing money for a specific project. The information is aimed at this group, which the defendants wish to attract, and which they know will use this information to make vital economic decisions. This being clearly the purpose of the information it can make little difference in law whether the seeker (of the information) directs himself to the bank or the bank to him. Given the purposes to be achieved by the information, the bank must realise that the persons likely to rely on it must understand it in the sense of a legally binding declaration (the distributor of the notice is a mere messenger). That is why in this case good faith causes a contractual relation to arise when a potential addressee has relied on it in making his decision. The appellant's argument, unsubstantiated by the facts of this case, that the information was only intended for banks, is immaterial since this does not preclude the fact that banks were then allowed to pass it on. The Court of Appeal is indeed wrong in treating this as a case of "information to whom it may concern". The Supreme Court has repeatedly insisted that it is, in principle, not possible to assume that a bank when giving information is willing to put itself under an obligation to an indeterminate and incalculable number of persons . . . However, this is not the case here for, though the information is directed to persons still unknown to the bank, those persons can be determined by virtue of their interest and form part of a calculable group of persons.

III.

1. Given that a contract to supply information was thus concluded by the parties, it became incumbent upon the defendants to supply objectively correct information. This the defendants negligently failed to do (§§ 276, and 278 BGB) since as bankers they knew, or ought to have known, that the facts they failed to mention in their notice were important for the lenders in order to reach their decision.

2. The appeal before this court also claims unsuccessfully that the Court of Appeal erred on the aspect of causation . . . Practical experience however shows that the plaintiff would not have made U a loan if the defendants had given her adverse information by disclosing to her U's actual financial status.

IV. The argument raised in this appeal, that the defendant's negligence is overshadowed by the plaintiff's contributory fault in so far as she accepted the advice of the finance broker L against the advice of her bank and her tax accountant, cannot affect the judgment currently under appeal. For the Court of Appeal, in its exercise of its judicial functions, concluded all legal and factual aspects of the case, and the appellants can point to no legal error prejudicial to them. Their argument that these facts should, from a point of view of law, be now differently appraised cannot thus be accepted.

Case 20

BUNDESGERICHTSHOF (SECOND CIVIL SENATE) 28 FEBRUARY 1977
BGHZ 69, 82 = NJW 1977, 1916

The plaintiff, in the course of current business transactions delivered limestone to the building firm GmbH, until the latter was declared bankrupt on 7 August 1973. GmbH had agreed in 1972 that the claims of the plaintiff arising from its sales should be settled by directly debiting its account, and had on 13 September 1972 given a revocable instruction to the defendant *Volksbank*, where it kept an account, to pay the creditor upon the receipt of its invoices and to debit its account with the defendant. It is disputed whether GmbH authorised the plaintiff in addition to collect its claims. During the period in issue here the plaintiff, who had no business relations with the defendant, lodged with the *Bank für Gemeinwirtschaft*, where it had a giro account, the following invoices to be collected by directly debiting the account of GmbH with the defendant: on 30 May 1973 for deliveries on 29 May amounting to DM 13,100.25; on 6 June for deliveries on 31 May amounting to

DM 15,672.83; on 14 June for deliveries on 13 June amounting to DM 15,672.83; on 14 June for deliveries on 13 June amounting to DM 6016.88; on 20 June for deliveries on 19 June amounting to DM 12,835.18; and on 27 June for deliveries on 26 June amounting to DM 17,468.75. All these invoices carried the imprint: "The recipient of the payments holds an authorisation from the debtor to collect the amounts outstanding." When the invoices were received by the defendant the account of GmbH was overdrawn. Therefore the defendant did not credit the plaintiff. For reasons which form the object of a dispute between the parties, the invoices remained for the time being with the defendant and were only returned on 29 June 1973 to the *Bank für Gemeinwirtschaft* which had submitted them. According to the plaintiff he only got to know on 4 July 1973 that the invoices had not been paid, because on this day his account with the *Bank für Gemeinwirtschaft* had been debited again to the amount of the invoices previously credited to his account.

In the present proceedings the plaintiff claims damages in respect of losses suffered by him in that he continued to supply goods to GmbH on 13, 19, and 26 June 1973, to the value of DM 36,321.81 which remained unpaid. The plaintiff contends that if the defendant had returned the invoices immediately on 30 May 1973, the plaintiff would have known of the failure to pay by 8 June 1973 at the latest. He would then only have made the subsequent deliveries against pre-payment.

The Court of First Instance at Osnabrück and the Court of Appeal at Oldenburg rejected the claim. Upon a second appeal by the plaintiff the judgment below was quashed and the case referred back for the following.

Reasons

The plaintiff in setting out the facts has shown conclusively that he has suffered damage because the defendant bank kept the invoices submitted to it for direct debit until the end of the month without taking action. If, instead, it had returned the invoices immediately, the plaintiff would have known on 8 June 1973 at the latest that no further payments could be expected. The plaintiff would then not have made the deliveries which remained unpaid for. . . . The plaintiff in asking the defendant to compensate him for this loss is also established conclusively, contrary to the views expressed by the courts below; its basis is contractual.

1. The Court of Appeal has held correctly that the plaintiff was not entitled to claim any performance by the defendant which may lead to claims for damages. No direct contractual relations are created between the creditor and the debtor's bank as a result of direct debiting. Thus the situation is similar to that of giro proceedings. In the latter situation the fact that the transferor and the recipient of the transfer maintain giro accounts with different banks did not create a direct contractual relationship between the recipient and the bank of the transferor nor do the legal relationships between the transferor and his bank or between the individual banks constitute contracts in favour of the recipient of the transfer as a third party. The situation is no different in direct debit proceedings; they are a kind of "transfer in reverse". The recipient (creditor) is only contracting with his own bank. The debtor bank, which receives the invoices for payment, only acts upon instructions which the creditor bank (or another bank interposed by it) gives in its own name within the framework of giro activities between the banks concerned (again not in favour of the creditor). The debtor, on his part, either instructs his bank in writing to credit directly invoices submitted by a particular creditor (procedure

of direct crediting); as in the case of instructions to transfer money it constitutes an instruction (general in these circumstances) in the meaning of §§ 665, 675 BGB within the contract of giro between himself and his bank, with which the creditor is not concerned. Alternatively the debtor authorizes the creditor in writing to collect the payments which are due by way of debiting his account with the debtor bank ("Procedure authorising Collection"). Thereby, too, the creditor does not obtain a claim against the debtor bank. The procedure of direct debiting serves mainly the interest of the creditor in settling his affairs and involves additional risks for the debtor; in the light of the interests involved no reason exists for assuming that the debtor wishes to grant to the creditor more rights than he would enjoy if the payments were made by bank transfer. Finally, the Agreement between the Principal Organisations of Credit Institutions concerning the Principle of Direct Debiting [references] only creates rights and duties between the credit institutions involved. Contractual claims by clients of banks for performance by the banks concerned are not to be derived from this Agreement according to Part IV no. 1 of the Agreement itself. Contrary to some other legal problems arising from the procedure of direct debiting this represents essentially the general opinion [references].

2. The plaintiff's claim for damages is, however, presented conclusively from the point of view that a protective duty has been violated. It is to be derived in favour of the creditor of the direct debit from the legal relationship arising between the banks involved in carrying out the procedure of direct debit.

Claims for damages arising from a violation of a protective duty can arise in general if a legal relationship between two parties is not sufficient to fulfil the requirements of § 328 BGB, but where the inclusion of certain third parties in its protective sphere is indicated according to good faith by the purpose of the contract and in view of the apparent effect upon them of the contractual performance. In order to avoid a flood of claims of this kind to an incalculable extent and to establish limits beyond which the protection of third parties is restricted to the law of tort, the practice of the courts has stated repeatedly that such an inclusion of third parties can normally be considered only if the internal relationship between the creditor and the debtor discloses aspects of a personal law character and shows that the creditor acts on behalf of a third party for whom he shares responsibility and to whom he owes a duty of care. In so far as characteristics of a personal law nature are thus required, the principles developed in the light of individual agreements as to what should apply according to good faith, are unnecessarily narrow where—as in the present case—bulk transactions of a certain type are in issue which follow a uniformly practised procedure provided on a general scale for legal transactions based upon the confidence that they will be settled properly and with due regard for the interests involved. In these circumstances the inclusion of third parties in the protective sphere of the contractual relations in issue may be possible and indicated according to good faith, if the mechanism entails for the third party who employs it certain risks inherent in it and if the participants charged with handling the mechanism can be called upon without further discussion to keep these risks down. Such is the case in so far as in direct debit proceedings the debtor bank must return invoices because the payments cannot be made in the absence of funds. According to the Agreement of the Banks concerning direct debits, invoices exceeding DM 1,000 not met by payment must be returned together with a notice of dishonour either on the same day to the first payor (the creditor's bank) or latest on the second working day by the reverse process of claiming payment from the first payor, accompanied by a notification by telegram, telephone, or telex (Part II no. 1

para. 2). This solution may have been adopted primarily in the interest of the creditor bank concerned. When the invoices are submitted to it, it credits the creditor's account with the amount to be debited (subject to a proviso) and normally allows the creditor to dispose of it. Therefore it runs the risk of losing that sum when the invoices are not honoured if the customer has disposed of the amount in the meantime and is no longer able to repay it. Consequently the creditor bank has an interest that the "critical" interval between crediting the amount and a possible failure to honour the invoices is kept short; the debtor bank should therefore immediately provide the necessary information by returning the dishonoured invoices or in some other way, on the strength of which the creditor can be debited again. The interest of the creditor is, however, involved to an even greater extent since he issued the instruction to collect the debt. Firstly, he will be interested quite generally, having regard to his business arrangements, not to be surprised by a re-debiting; instead he wishes to be informed in good time that the amount credited to him provisionally on the strength of the invoices is not at his disposal in reality. Secondly, if he employs the procedure of direct debiting for the purpose of collecting outstanding monies, he will normally be engaged in current business relations with the debtor. If these relations extend over a longer period he has a considerable interest which goes beyond collecting whatever amount may have fallen due, to receive early notice of any difficulties in the operation of these relations. The fact that invoices are not honoured is often an alarm signal that the debtor is in payment difficulties. If the creditor is not notified in time but remains ignorant because the invoices are not dealt with, he will continue the business relationship in good faith and will be prevented, to his detriment, from discontinuing them or from continuing them subject to the usual measures of security. While not sharing an identical interest, the creditor bank and the creditor nevertheless share what is at least an equal interest, based on a similarity of risks, in the immediate return of unpaid invoices after having received and examined them, or in immediate notification. Every bank if interposed as the creditor's bank, must protect this interest of the creditor as if it were its own in relation to all other participating banks, having regard to the contractual fiduciary relationship with its own customer, since every bank acts from case to case either as the creditor or the debtor bank in the many proceedings of direct debiting; all other banks are aware of this and treat it as a matter of course. For these special reasons and because legal relationships rely upon the observance of the practice of the banks confirmed by the Agreement on Direct Debits, the duty to return dishonoured invoices constitutes not only a contractual obligation of the debtor bank towards the creditor bank which was created between the banks themselves in virtue of the Agreement, but also a protective obligation of the debtor bank, based on good faith, in favour of the particular creditor claiming a direct debit. In individual cases where the creditor bank sends invoices to the debtor bank direct this protective duty is based on the legal relationship between the two banks which is created in respect of the individual direct debit on the basis of the giro contract. If, however, additional banks are interposed in carrying out direct debiting procedures between the creditor bank and the debtor bank, this protective duty is based upon the legal relationship between the bank which is the last to be interposed and the debtor bank. The reason is that interposed banks, too, are bound, having regard to the chain of contractual relations which leads back to the creditor bank, to follow through to the debtor bank the obligation of the creditor bank to protect the interests of the creditor. From this follows naturally that the duty of protection incumbent upon the debtor bank for the benefit of the creditor of the direct debit is not excluded by Part IV no. 1 of the Agreement on Direct Debits, contrary to the contention of the defendant, although the Agreement is intended to create "only rights and duties between the participating credit institutions". The protective duty is not based upon the Agreement but on the legal relationships described above, their contractual purpose and the principle of good faith, and moreover this duty would also have to be recognised if the agreement between the banks did not exist. For the same reason the claims for damages of the creditor of the direct debit against the debtor bank are not affected by the internal special arrangement of Part IV no. 2 of the Agreement, if the protective duty has been violated.

In the present case the defendant bank, by failing to handle the invoices for a long time, has therefore violated the protective duty incumbent upon it and must compensate the plaintiff for the loss resulting therefrom, unless the defendant . . . had retained the invoices with the express consent of the plaintiff's manager . . .

Case 21

BUNDESGERICHTSHOF (FOURTH CIVIL SENATE) 28 AUGUST 1982
NJW 1982, 2431 = WM 1982, 762

The plaintiff, a Danish private bank, claims damages against the defendant because it was induced by an expert valuation made by the defendant and by information supplied by him to the Danish Consul in Munich to grant a credit which could not be recovered later on. The firm of P was the owner of a considerable area of building land. It intended to develop it by building an extensive holiday village. The project had been approved in principle in planning proceedings. No detailed building plans had, however, been drawn up. Only a draft existed which had been prepared by a private architect appointed by the firm of P in agreement with the local commune. At the request of the firm of P the defendant submitted on 10 August 1974 an expert opinion in which he concluded that the area of building land as a whole had a commercial value of DM 200,000,000. On 19 December 1974 the Danish Consul telephoned the defendant and informed him that the Consulate had received an enquiry as to whether the defendant was in fact an officially appointed and sworn expert. Upon receiving an affirmative reply, the Consul asked whether the expert valuation of the area of the holiday village, which the defendant had supplied, was still valid; in so doing he referred to the growing fall of prices in the market of immovables. The defendant replied that he had not heard anything since in this matter. However, in the meantime the proceedings for the approval of the plans should have been advanced. If so, the increased readiness of building operations was a positive factor which balanced the negative development on the market for immovable property. In particular the fact had to be taken into account that according to the practice of planning consent prevailing now, other projects of this kind would no longer receive approval. At the Consul's request the defendant wrote a letter to the Danish Consulate in which he stated: "In supplementation of my detailed expert opinion of 10 August 1974 I confirm that the value of the object mentioned above has remained unchanged to the present time. The negative effects of the general development on the market of immovable properties are balanced by the fact that the land is ready to be built upon. Moreover, no consent for further comparable projects in the German region of the Alps can be expected either at present or in the future." On 6 June 1975 the plaintiff entered into a contract for a loan of DM 15,000,000 with the firm of P. The two managers of the firm and the Danish firm of N became independently liable sureties; the Danish Export Council on its part became a surety for the last mentioned firm. In addition the loan was secured by a charge amounting to DM 18,000,000 on the immovable property of the firm of P. On 14 March (August) 1975 the net loan amounting to DM 14,305,000 was paid over. Subsequently the project of the holiday village was not pursued and the interest which had fallen due was not paid. Consequently the loan agreement was rescinded. Based on its charge over the land the plaintiff levied execution against it by way of a sale by auction and bought it on offering DM 1,900,000. The plaintiff contends that the firm of P had sought contacts with sources of money in order to obtain a loan of at least DM 15,000,000 for its planned holiday village. In this connection the firm had entered into negotiations with the Danish firm of N. It had held out the possibility of an order for the delivery of 600 prefabricated houses, if N would assist P in obtaining a credit of DM 15,000,000. In a letter of 28 September 1974 P had not set out its financial situation and the state of the project; in this connection P had referred to the annexed expert valuation by the defendant. N had approached the Danish Ministry of Commerce in order to obtain a guarantee by the State; for this purpose it had submitted the expert valuation by the defendant. The Ministry of Commerce had interposed the plaintiff as a bank, which was to be secured by way of reinsurance by a guarantee of the Danish State. In order to ascertain whether the conditions existed for granting the loan the Danish Export Credit Council had instructed the Danish Consul in Munich to obtain details from the defendant; it had been agreed between the Export Council and the plaintiff that the Consul had told the defendant expressly that a Danish enterprise intended to participate in the project by way of a guarantee or by granting a credit.

The plaintiff's claim was rejected by the courts, below. Upon a second appeal the judgment was quashed and the case referred back for the following.

Reasons

1. The Court of Appeal holds that the plaintiff is not entitled to damages in its own right. In making his enquiry the Consul had not made it clear that he acted as the plaintiff's agent. The information was not information "for those whom it may concern" which might have the consequence that the defendant was liable in contract "to any third party".

From the point of view taken by the Court of Appeal, it should also have been examined whether the plaintiff was included in the protection sphere of the contract. The practice of the courts—and to a great extent also the literature—acknowledges the admissibility of contracts with protective effects for the benefit of third parties [references]. The articles by Ziegler [reference] and Sonnenschein [reference] to which the defendant refers do not cause this Senate to deviate from this well established legal rule. Since the Consul obviously lacked any personal interest in examining the creditworthiness of the firm of P, it could be assumed, at least if it was denied that the Consul acted in the name of another, that future suppliers of credit were to be included in the protection sphere of the contract. The Court of Appeal should have examined the claim from this point of view as well.

In this connection the Court of Appeal adds: the expert valuation had clearly anticipated and assumed an expected development—namely the award of the necessary consent, division, and sale—although in law the possibility of developing the land had not yet been assured. The estimate of a value which was only expected to materialise could not as such have been of interest to third parties, especially credit institutions. However, on p. 2 of the expert valuation, the defendant stated expressly that he had been instructed to ascertain the "commercial value at the relevant time". It is true that in carrying out the instruction to supply an expert valuation the defendant had to take the future development into consideration. According to the customs of trade the (present) commercial value of an immovable is determined not only by the factual circumstances at the time when the valuation is made, but also by the expectation of future events (e.g. that it will be capable of development as building land). It is obvious that a credit institution which intends to secure a future loan by a mortgage of charge will be interested in the commercial value of the land to be encumbered. As the Court of Appeal has found, the Consul made it clear to the defendant that the information given by him was required for the purpose of deciding whether the loan was to be granted. The Consul was not content with the information given over the telephone, but asked for a written confirmation; thereby he demonstrated to the defendant that his expert opinion was to serve as the basis of a far-reaching decision. The question as to whether the defendant made it sufficiently clear in his expert opinion that the planning permits necessary for the development of the area in issue may be important in assessing the blameworthiness of the defendant and any possible contributory negligence on the part of the plaintiff, but it is irrelevant for determining whether the plaintiff can make any claims at all because the contract for the supply of information has been violated.

2. The Court of Appeal regards it as possible that in concluding the contract for the supply of information the Consul asked as a representative of the Danish State. If this point of view is adopted the question arises as to whether the Danish State can claim damages from the defendant because the contract to supply information has been violated. According to the plaintiff's pleadings, the Danish Export Council—apparently as representing the Danish State—became a surety for the credit to be granted. The plaintiff contends that the Export Credit Council had assigned to the plaintiff any possible claims for damages by the Danish State against the defendant; by way of a subsidiary argument the plaintiff relies also on this claim for damages. By the reference back the plaintiff is enabled to amplify its pleadings in this respect and especially to set out to what extent the Danish State has suffered damage. It will be useful if in this connection the plaintiff provides some information concerning the legal position of the Export Credit Council, and in particular whether it is an organ of the State which became a surety in the name of the Danish State and also whether on the latter's behalf it has assigned the claim to the plaintiff.

Case 22

BUNDESGERICHTSHOF (FOURTH CIVIL SENATE) 2 NOVEMBER 1983
NJW 1984, 355 = WM 1984, 34

The defendant is an officially appointed sworn expert for building construction and for valuing land and buildings. On 5 September 1977 he was asked by S, a merchant, to supply an expert opinion concerning the market value of and the estimated income from premises in N. The meeting, in the course of which the defendant received the order, was attended by S, who was accompanied by the plaintiff and by L, a banker. In his written opinion dated 19 September 1977 the defendant intimated that the apartment house erected in 1953 would bring in a gross annual income of DM 91,990 and a net annual income of DM 68,918. He assessed the market value of the premises at DM 1,447,715. The opinion failed to take into account that the premises are subject to restrictions connected with social housing. On 15 November 1977, the plaintiff bought the house on his own account for DM 540,000; S did not participate in the purchase. The premises were conveyed, but the transfer of title was not entered in the land register. The plaintiff financed the purchase by arranging for a loan of DM 500,000 from the City Savings Bank in N, which was secured by a charge on the newly acquired premises. By a contract dated 27 June 1978 the sale agreement of 15 November 1977 was rescinded *in toto* with effect from 1 July 1978. On 28 May 1978, the defendant wrote a letter to B, who was then interested in acquiring the premises, which contained, *inter alia*, the following passage: "Mr S instructed me on 5 September 1977 to value the premises. He indicated clearly in the presence of witnesses that he or the connections behind him intended to acquire the premises with a view to converting them into ownership flats. I do not know whether the premises were put up by private finance or whether they represent social housing. It is not the task of a sworn expert to consider this question. I took great care in ascertaining the rental values in the neighbourhood and, having consulted the City administration in N, I came to conclusion that the value of DM 7.50 per square metre is entirely appropriate . . ." The plaintiff alleges that the defendant knew that he and the witness S intended to acquire the premises together. He had bought the premises relying on the accuracy of the defendant's opinion. When the first rents had come in he had found out that the gross value of the income amounted only to DM 25,729.08, which meant that the income was substantially less than the annual payments of interest. For this reason, he had been compelled to rescind the contract of sale. If the defendant had assessed the annual income from the premises incorrectly, the plaintiff would not have bought the premises. As a result he would not have been liable to pay the agent's fee of DM 17,982; local charges of DM 3,973.09; interest on the loan amounting to DM 25,479.76 and notary's fees of DM 6,170.93 totalling DM 53,605.78. He claims this sum.

The District Court rejected the claim. An appeal to the Court of Appeal of Nuremberg was unsuccessful. Upon a second appeal the judgment below was quashed and the case referred back for the following

Reasons

The Court of Appeal denies that the instruction given to the defendant by the witness S to supply an expert opinion constitutes a contract in favour of third parties. No serious objections can be raised against this view. The circumstances indicate that the defendant only intended to assume a duty to perform an act—namely the duty to supply an expert opinion—in favour of the witness S; at least no legal reasons exist for criticising the court below which found the facts in having interpreted the agreement to this effect.

These considerations alone do not exclude the *locus standi* of the plaintiff to prosecute his claim for damages. It is necessary, in addition, to examine whether the plaintiff is included in the area protected by the contract. It is recognised today, both in the literature and by the practice of the courts, that a contractual obligation may create duties of care towards third parties who themselves are not entitled to seek performance of the principal obligation. As this Senate has stated [reference] this consideration applies also to contracts with officially appointed and sworn experts. The circumstances of the present case indicate the need to examine the facts from this point of view.

It is undisputed that the witness S, accompanied by the plaintiff, called upon the defendant. According to the plaintiff the defendant knew that the premises were to be purchased jointly by S and the plaintiff. The Court of Appeal, it is true, was not convinced that this allegation was correct; consequently it cannot be taken into account by this court. However, the defendant does not deny to have known that a consortium behind the witness S was contemplating the purchase of the premises. He said so clearly in his letter of 28 May 1978. He has also adhered to this account of the facts in the present dispute; he merely claims that he was not aware who belonged to this group. However, this fact is not decisive. Duties of care can also be created in favour of those persons who are not mentioned by name to the other contracting party. Nor is it necessary that the contracting party should know the correct number of persons to whom a duty of care is owed. The practice of the Federal Supreme Court has recognised in several cases that a contract includes a duty of care towards third parties even if the party owing the duty of care was ignorant of the number and the names of the persons to whom the duty was owed [references]. It is essential, however, that the group to whom the duty of care is owed should be capable of being determined objectively . . .

The District Court was of the opinion that the present contract did not include a duty of care towards third persons for the reason that the witness S did not himself owe a duty of care and protection towards the plaintiff. This consideration, too, does not exclude the *locus standi* of the plaintiff. In principle the parties are free to fashion a contract; they are only restricted in their freedom of choice by the binding rules of law and by the moral requirements to be observed in accordance with § 138 BGB. The parties are therefore at liberty to determine which persons are to be included in the duty of care owed by the contract; they can even extend this duty of care to persons who are not in the charge of either "for better or for worse" [reference]. This cannot be doubted in so far as the parties have inserted express provisions. Where the extent of the duty of care is to be implied from the unequivocal conduct of the parties, the conclusion must be the same; for in the absence of rules requiring the observance of particular formalities an implied declaration of intention is equivalent to one which is express. It is true that in several instances the Federal Supreme Court, in deciding whether a certain person is owed a duty of care by virtue of a contract, has examined whether the other contracting party, to whom the duty of care was owed, was in charge of that person for better or for worse [references]. These decisions must not, however, be interpreted in the sense that the Federal Supreme Court affirmed the legality of this type of contract only in these circumstances. Instead they only concern the question in what circumstances the objective interests involved permit the conclusion that the parties have implicitly stipulated a duty of care towards third parties—i.e. where neither any express statements by the parties nor their conduct otherwise offer any concrete evidence. Even within this approach which relies on typical situations the practice of the Federal Supreme Court [references] requires only that normally, but not always, a contracting party should have been in charge for better or for worse of the person to whom the duty of care is owed. It is another question, however, whether an extension of the duty of care arising from a contract beyond the contracting parties must be presumed having regard to the special circumstances of the particular case. It often happens when an expert is being engaged that the opinion to be supplied is to serve as a basis for a decision by persons who are not linked to the expert by contract [references]. In such a case the court ascertaining the facts must examine in accordance with the general principles of interpretation in the light of the circumstances whether the contracting parties intended to create a duty of care in favour of that person. In this connection, too, it may be relevant whether the instructing party was charged with the care of the third party in question; it is not, however, a necessary prerequisite for holding that such a duty of care exists. In the present case it will have to be considered that an interested party who asks for an expert opinion to form the basis of a decision by a certain group, will normally seek to protect not only his personal interests but also those of the other members of the group; consequently it will not normally be his intention, in entering into the contract, to limit the duty to pay compensation to damage which he suffers personally. In this connection the interests of the expert must also be taken into account; he must not be burdened unreasonably with the duty to pay compensation to third parties; it cannot be expected according to good faith (para. 157 BGB) that the other contracting party will assume such an obligation. In this respect it will have to be considered that the damage which may be suffered by a group of buyers in acquiring a house, if the expert opinion was wrong in estimating its value, are not normally higher than those which would be suffered in similar circumstances by an individual buyer.

Whether in an individual case the duty of care arising under the contract extends to third parties is a matter of interpreting the contract.

2. The Court of Appeal has examined the question whether in his expert opinion the defendant indicated expressly or by implication that he intended to be liable "to whom it concerns" for the accuracy of his report; it found that he did not. No legal reasons exist for contesting this view; in fact no indications exist that the defendant intended to assume liability towards persons who did not belong to the group of buyers behind the witness S.

3. No legal objections can be raised either against the rejection by the Court of Appeal of near-contractual liability of the expert. Those who commission an opinion frequently use the expert opinion of an officially appointed and sworn expert by referring to this opinion in their negotiations with third parties, e.g. in order to justify as vendors the amount of the purchase price demanded or in order to demonstrate that a certain object is credit-worthy. If an expert must assume that his expert opinion will be used for such purposes and is intended to serve as a basis for important financial transactions by third parties, he may be liable to these third parties for the accuracy of the expert opinion (see for this aspect the decision of the Federal Supreme Court [reference] concerning a bank reference and a certificate by a chartered accountant). No such use was, however, envisaged in the present case nor has it occurred in fact. The expert opinion was merely intended to inform the witness S and the group of buyers behind him; it was not meant to support statements in negotiations with third parties.

II. By way of a subsidiary argument the Court of Appeal states that the claim would have to be rejected, even if the plaintiff had a *locus standi*. In calculating the annual income he was not obliged to examine whether the house contained apartments which had been financed privately or by social housing aid. Since his instructions did not provide any relevant information, he was entitled to assume that the apartments had been financed privately; consequently he was only bound to rely on "the rental obtainable on the free housing market for the apartments of the premises". These statements cannot be supported in law. An expert opinion must be based on facts and not on guesses or assumptions. Therefore the defendant could only proceed on the assumption that the apartments had been financed privately, if he had reached the conclusion that this assumption was correct. If the expert is ignorant of the relevant circumstances for coming to a conclusion, he must enquire of those instructing him and must, if necessary, also make other investigations (as, for instance, by making enquiries with the authorities). If these attempts remain fruitless he may base his expert opinion on assumptions, but he must indicate this clearly in his opinion. Every expert valuer of premises must know that in assessing the rental of an apartment and, as a result of the income of an apartment house, the legal status of the apartments according to the Rent Control legislation is determining. The fact that the defendant has failed to take this into account may support the charge of negligence. The defendant argues in defence that even if the apartments had been financed privately the rents stated by him would not have been recoverable without further action; it would have been necessary to initiate proceedings for an increase in rents in accordance with § 2 of the Act regulating the Amount of Rent; in many cases this would have involved litigation. This pertinent argument only serves to increase the charge of negligence against the defendant. Precisely for the reason that the owner of the premises cannot enforce automatically the payment of rents which are objectively appropriate, the defendant was negligent to base his calculation of the annual income of the premises on purely theoretical considerations without taking into account the actual situation according to the Rent Control legislation. It is not alleged that, contrary to the usual practice, the defendant had been instructed to determine the hypothetical value of the house irrespective of any restrictions under the Rent Control legislation.

III. The Court of Appeal is of the opinion that the plaintiff is guilty of contributory negligence. It criticises him for not having asked the owner of the premises for his annual accounts and for having failed to call for details about the size of the rents. Such a risky undertaking required the greatest caution, diligence, and scrutiny on the part of the plaintiff. He could not argue successfully that as a layman and a student he was totally ignorant of the fundamentals of valuing. This argument only applied to the individual valuation by the expert but not to the actual rental income, which the plaintiff could have ascertained simply by making enquiries with the other contracting parties or through his agent. If he had received these details, he could have asked the defendant whether as a result his expert opinion had to be modified.

These statements, too, cannot be supported in law. S and the plaintiff realised clearly that they lacked the necessary technical knowledge in order to assess correctly the risk connected with the purchase. For this reason they called upon the expert assistance of the defendant. In his expert opinion the defendant has estimated the net annual income to be DM 68,918; it is not indicated anywhere that this valuation is purely theoretical, that the actual income might be considerably lower, that everything depended upon what rent had been paid hitherto and that, for this reason, it was desirable to make inquiries. The witness S and the plaintiff could assume that the annual income mentioned by the defendant could be obtained without difficulties, even in the case that the rents paid hitherto had been lower than those estimated by the defendant. In this case, however, the rental income in the past would have been irrelevant for the purpose of estimating the income in the future.

The plaintiff cannot be reproached either for not having considered that according to general experience the attempt to increase rents meets with difficulties and thus for having failed to entertain doubts about the accuracy of the expert opinion. Every contract for the supply of advice for a consideration (including in a broad sense also instructions to prepare an expert opinion) is based on the assumption that he who gives the advice possesses more knowledge and insight than he who receives it. The professional training and experience of the adviser is to supplement the deficient expertise of the other contracting party. Consequently it is obvious that the expert adviser is required to possess a greater degree of insight than the party instructing him. If the latter does not detect the mistakes made by the adviser or expert, this cannot normally be regarded as contributory negligence; in the present case it might possibly be found, *inter alia* in the fact that the plaintiff was not struck by the considerable difference between the valuation made by the defendant and the actual price demanded by the seller . . . In no circumstances can the plaintiff's contributory negligence, if it should be found to exist, be regarded as so serious as to exclude the liability of the adviser or expert altogether [references].

IV. The plaintiff can only claim damages if the faulty estimate of the net annual income by the defendant determined the plaintiff's decision to purchase the premises . . . If the view of the Court of Appeal should be correct that the group of buyers behind the witness S intended to convert the premises to be purchased into apartments to be sold to the occupiers, it is difficult to understand why the amount of income to be obtained through *letting* should have influenced the decision of the plaintiff at all. It must be admitted that, if this should be the case, it is equally difficult to understand why the defendant should have included in his expert opinion any details about the prospective rental income; in those circumstances it would have been more appropriate to state in the expert opinion what price could be obtained if the apartments to be constructed were to be placed on the property market.

Case 23

BUNDESGERICHTSHOF (THIRD CIVIL SENATE) 10 NOVEMBER 1994
BGHZ 127, 378 = NJW 1995, 392

Facts

[The case concerns the question of the protective scope of a report prepared by an architect / building expert submitted to the owner of the building pursuant to a contract concluded between the expert's employer and the owner of the building. The report concerned the value and state of repair of the said building. It was used as the basis for a purchase contract concluded between the plaintiff / purchaser and the owner of the building. After the transaction was completed, grave defects were detected in the building. Since the vendor had excluded his liability for visible or hidden defects, the purchaser sued the expert for damages. The Appeal Court dismissed the claim but the Federal Supreme Court quashed the judgment below and referred the case back for the following reasons.]

Reasons

1. The Appeal Court failed to discuss whether the plaintiffs had a claim for damages as a result of a direct contractual relationship in the form of a tacitly concluded contract to supply information (*Auskunftsvertrag*). (References omitted).

This cannot be challenged for legal reasons since prior to the conclusion of the purchase contract the parties had no direct contacts.

2. The Appeal Court interprets the contract to provide an expert report to the effect (§§ 133, 157 BGB) that, out of that contract with the owner, protective duties arose that

the expert owed towards the plaintiffs. For the court, the crucial point came when the son of the owner, who concluded the contract on his behalf, stated that the property valuation report was needed for the purposes of selling the property. The inclusion of the plaintiffs within the protective scope of the contract for a report on the state and value of the property is legally sound.

(a) In particular, and in this instance, the existence of a contract with protective effect for third persons cannot be denied with reference to the fact that the interests of the plaintiffs and the person who commissioned the report were contradictory. Where an expert report is requested from a person possessed of particular knowledge—which is certified or attested by official documents—for the purpose of using the report in contractual negotiations with a third person, the person commissioning the report normally has an interest in it as means of evidence. This can only be guaranteed if the report was prepared objectively, conscientiously, and in full knowledge of all facts and where its author accepts responsibility for its contents as towards third persons. Accordingly, the Federal Supreme Court has previously decided that in such a case the juxtaposition of interests of the person commissioning the report and the third person does not rule out the latter's inclusion in the protective scope of the contract authorising the preparation of the report (references). It is irrelevant that the defendant, when compiling his report, was unaware that his assessment was to be submitted to that particular plaintiff. Acknowledging his duty of care does not presuppose that the person so duty-bound knows the number or names of the persons to be protected. It suffices that the defendant knew that his valuation was intended for a (potential) buyer. (References omitted.)

[There follow passages dealing with the particular personal qualifications of the defendant, whose professional standing, duties in respect of the expert report submitted, and the inclusion of the plaintiff in the protective scope of the contract to provide the report, were likened to those of a publicly-appointed expert.]

(b) Contrary to the doubts raised in the defendant's reply to the further appeal, the existence of a contract with protective effects for third persons can arise even where, during inspections of the premises, the owner's representative deliberately concealed the defects of the property. This fact may be an indication that he was not interested in an objectively correct expert opinion on the value of the property that would take into account the interests of the buyer. But this hidden and unrevealed reservation has no bearing on the question as to what was objectively declared when an order was made for a valuation, i.e. in respect of the purpose of the report and a possible inclusion of third persons in the protective scope of the contract.

3. [There follow statements as to the specific duties to inspect fully the object to be valued, possible breaches of these duties by the expert, and their effects. The court also deals with the vicarious liability of the architect's/builder's employer.]

On the basis of the undisputed facts it must be assumed that the defendant, who under § 278 BGB is responsible for the acts of the expert, has performed his contractual duties badly and that this breach led to the submission of a report whose contents were incorrect. The Court of Appeal was convinced that an accurate expert opinion would have discouraged the buyer from concluding the purchase contract, i.e. that the defendant's wrongful act caused the damage.

4. The Court of Appeal held that—as towards the plaintiff—the defendant is not liable for damages according to the principles of "positive breach of contract" (*positive Forderungsverletzung*). [The lower court's reasoning follows].

The reasoning of the lower court is legally unsound.

(a) The Court of Appeal rightly assumed that a person commissioning a report, who deliberately intends it to reflect wrongly the actual state of repair of the object of the report, has no claim for damages against the author of the report.

Contracts for the provision of expert reports, like the one before the court, must be qualified as contracts for the production of work (§ 631 BGB). This means that in cases of an intentionally wrong assessment of real property, the person commissioning the report has either a claim for damages under § 635 BGB or a claim for positive breach of contract if the damage arose as a consequence of the first defect (*Mangelfolgeschaden*): in this case the original faulty report (reference). Such a claim for damages would not be affected by the knowledge of the commissioning person that the expert's report is flawed, since it is only in respect of claims listed in §§ 633, 634 BGB that § 640(2) BGB requires the commissioning person, at the point of acceptance, to reserve his rights. This provision does not apply to claims for damages (reference). But the person who commissions the report and who deliberately brings about a misleading expert report, exposes himself to the defence of abuse of right if he later bases his claims for damages on this defect (references). This defence of malice will be upheld even where the charge of "contradictory behaviour" (*venire contra factum proprium*) is based on the actions of a representative (§ 166 1 BGB) (reference).

(b) The starting point of the Appeal Court's reasoning is also in line with the Supreme Court's case law according to which the protected third person, who derives his rights from the contractual relationship between the initial contractual partners, has basically no wider rights than the tortfeasor's direct contractual partner. The courts deduced from this fact that the third person, deliberately damaged by the person liable to protect him will, under § 254 BGB, face the tortfeasor's defence that the contractual partner was co-responsible for the damage, unless this partner was a legal representative of the third person or employed by him to fulfil his own obligations (§ 278 BGB) (references). The same result applies for a contractually agreed exemption from liability (reference). This limitation of the third person's protection is based on the legal maxim expressed in § 334 BGB and the principle of good faith (§ 242 BGB).

Both arguments show that we are dealing here with merely a legal rule (reference) and not with an unshakeable principle. As far as the maxim of good faith is concerned, this fact is self-evident. Nothing different can be derived from the legal argument behind § 334 BGB or—as the Appeal Court held—from an analogous application of § 334 BGB.

The provisions of § 334 BGB which deal with the true contract for the benefit of a third person are of an optional nature. According to those provisions, the promisor can use contractual defences even against the third person. Their application can, even tacitly, be excluded as can be seen, in particular, from the nature of the covering (or underlying) relationship (*Deckungsverhältnis*) (reference). There is no apparent reason for applying more stringent rules in cases like the present where, when interpreting the contract in order to establish how and to what extent a third person was protected, these legal provisions are to be applied either directly or according to their underlying maxim. The lower court misjudged this point.

When interpreting the expert report, the Appeal Court should have considered that the "nature of this particular contract" resulted in an exception to the rule according to which the liability of a person who owes protection to a third person does not exceed his liability towards his direct contractual partner.

The defendant knew that the expert valuation had been commissioned for sales purposes. Accordingly, not only could he expect that his report would be submitted to interested buyers. He should further assume that, given the special trust which prospective buyers normally place in the reliability and expertise of an approved expert, the statements made in his report would probably be given a greater weight than the information provided by the seller. The maker of report should have thus assumed that his report was apt to disperse possible doubts of prospective buyers in the veracity of the seller's information. Herein lies the obvious and particular value that the report has for the vendor, i.e. its ability to promote the chances of a sale. Above all, it matches the obvious interests of a prospective buyer in legal protection for his trust in the veracity of the report, especially in cases where the seller dishonestly tries to conceal the true condition of the sales object. Where, therefore, a contract for the production of an expert report must be taken to include prospective buyers within its protective ambit, it must be assumed that the third person's trust in the expert's statements must be protected even where the incorrectness [of the report] was (also) instigated by the principal. This result does not depend on the effects which this inducement has on the liability of the supplier as against the principal (references).

Such contractual interpretation will not burden the expert with an unreasonable risk of liability. More precisely, it will, certainly, render him liable for the dishonesty of the person who commissioned the report from him. True, when providing his report, the expert can use information provided by his principal—and he will often be forced to do so—wherever he cannot himself verify the facts. But he must then make this clear in his report (reference). Normally, he will thereby indicate that he excludes his liability for the truth of these statements.

5. The reasoning of the Appeal Court, in denying the defendant's liability as towards the third person included in the protective scope of the contract, is thus legally flawed and its decision must, therefore, be quashed.

[There follow instructions as to the re-interpretation of the contract and the court's opinion that the plaintiffs cannot be held to have been co-responsible for the damage merely because they have not personally found any defects when inspecting the premises.]

Case 24

BUNDESGERICHTSHOF (THIRD CIVIL SENATE) 2 APRIL 1998
BGHZ 138, 257 = NJW 1998, 1948 = JZ 1998, 1013

Facts

The plaintiff is the receiver of the assets of the G AG. Its predecessor (G GmbH & Co.) acquired from H, the sole member of the S GmbH (hereafter called STN) all the shares in the business by a notarised contract dated the 12 October 1992. This was immediately after H had brought in to this company the real property company which owned the business premises and the buildings on them which were let to STN in accordance with § 20 of the Conversion Tax Act. The purchase price was 2.5 million DM, payable immediately.

The plaintiff demands from the defendant auditors compensation for incorrect information. The defendants had been commissioned by H to carry out a compulsory audit in accordance with §§ 316 ff HGB. They had been occupied since July 1992 with the audit of the annual accounts of STN for the year 1991, drawn up by the accountant R. Their complaints led to the annual accounts being altered by R and showing a balance of DM 21,891,249.03 and an annual surplus of DM 2,666,467.37 higher than that in the earlier accounts.

The defendants by a letter of 8 October 1992 to STN for the attention of H (and a further Telefax letter of 9 October 1992 to the B GmbH for the attention of the accountant St who had been consulted by the G GmbH & Co) stated that the now current annual accounts would not be changed by them and could be confirmed by them.

Later irregularities in STN's accounting came to light. H had at the end of 1991 incorrectly credited nine sums for a total of almost 25 million DM. The final annual accounts, for which the defendants issued a limited note of confirmation on the 30th March 1993 in accordance with § 322 HGB, showed a deficit of DM 11,049,361.15 instead of a surplus of DM 2,666,467.37.

The claim was in the end for 2.5 million DM. In it the plaintiff alleged that the G GmbH & Co would not have acquired the shares in the business in the knowledge of the actual business yield in 1991 (or would only have done so at a symbolic purchase price of DM 1). It was unsuccessful at first instance. The plaintiff lodges an appeal in law against this decision.

Reasons

The appeal in law leads to a quashing of the appeal judgment and a reference of the matter back to the appeal court.

I.

1. The appeal court, whose judgment is printed in [reference omitted], accepts that liability on the part of the defendants would come into consideration, because the subsequent insolvent has been included in the protected area of the audit contract between STN and the defendants. The appeal in law accepts this assessment as favourable to it. On the other hand, the reply to the appeal in law considers that the instructions for the compulsory audit, the communication about the status of the audit and the foreseeable outcome of it could not result in any protective effect in favour of third parties.

(a) According to § 323 para. 1 sentence 1 of the HGB the auditor of the accounts is under a duty to carry out a conscientious and unbiased examination and a duty of secrecy. If he breaches his duties intentionally or negligently, he is under a duty to compensate the company (and, if a connected undertaking has been harmed, this as well) for the harm arising from this (§ 323 para. 1 sentence 3 of the HGB). In the academic literature, it is deduced from this that according to § 323 para. 1 sentence 3 of the HGB ie for the area of the compulsory audit, where there is a violation of the duties of the auditor third parties are not entitled to any claims against him [references omitted].

Insofar as the duty to compensate for harm is extended to connected undertakings, this would rest—as a correlative—on this undertaking's duty of presentation and provision of information to the auditor of the accounts for the group in accordance with § 320 para. 2 sentence 2 of the HGB [references omitted]; the connected undertaking's entitlement to compensation presupposes that the auditor is violating a duty incumbent on him and owed to the connected undertaking [references omitted]. An extension of the duty to compensate to further third parties for harm by way of interpretation or analogy would therefore be forbidden [references omitted].

Besides this, an extension of the liability to shareholders/members or creditors of the company would run counter to the goal of—in cases of negligent breach of duty—limiting the risk of liability of the auditor (§ 323 para. 2 of the HGB). It would give rise to concern that the company would have to share its claims, which are in any case limited, with third parties [reference omitted].

(b) The Senate endorses this in principle. Liability of the defendants to the purchaser, who does not belong to the group of persons mentioned in § 323 of the HGB as entitled to compensation, does not therefore come into consideration from this point of view. The breach of duty of which the defendants are accused certainly belongs technically to the area which is covered by the regime of § 323 of the HGB. It is therefore here a matter of the more extensive question of whether and under what conditions an auditor who is entrusted with a compulsory audit can also be made liable for appraisals, certificates or other statements which are connected with the object of audit, to persons who are not contractual parties to the audit contract and are also not included in the associated undertakings addressed in § 323 of the HGB.

(aa) The appeal court takes into consideration (correctly here) the principles according to which protective duties can arise from a contract for the benefit of a third party, who himself has no claim to the main obligation under the contract. The case law has in particular accepted such protective effects for contracts by which the client commissions a report or an expert's opinion from a person who has at his disposal a particular specialist knowledge recognised by the state (eg publicly appointed expert, auditor, tax adviser) in order to make use of it as against a third party [references omitted].

As the purpose of the report is to induce trust in and possess evidential value for the third party, a conflict of the interests of the client and the third party is not an obstacle to the latter's incorporation into the protective area of the contract [reference omitted].

There are no difficulties about also applying these principles in cases in which an auditor of accounts is entrusted with the compulsory audit of a company provided that it appears sufficiently clear to him that on this audit a particular work product is wanted from him which is to be used as against a third party who trusts in his expert knowledge. If § 323 para. 1 sentence 3 of the HGB (only) regulates a statutory liability to the company and the associated undertaking, this does not mean that contractual liability of the auditor to third parties according to the principles developed by the case law on the third party liability of experts would thereby be excluded from the outset.

Such exclusion of the possibility of creating conditions of liability (which are justified by the interests involved and take account of the principle of private autonomy) cannot be inferred from this provision in this sort of generality. A third party liability which is essentially based on the fact that it is for the contracting parties to determine against whom a duty of protection is to be established [reference omitted] is not affected by the area of direct application of § 323 para. 1 of the HGB. It also does not signify, as Ebke/Scheel [reference omitted] think, a disregard of a basic decision of the legislator in favour of a limited liability of auditors expressed in this provision. This provision, according to paragraph 4 of which the duty to compensate may neither be excluded nor limited, does not pursue such an extensive purpose.

(bb) Nor does § 323 of the HGB create a material exclusionary effect against liability of the auditor in the run up to the issue of the certificate. The provision does not for instance connect the liability to the issue of the certificate as such; it presupposes instead a fault-based breach of duty in the carrying out of the audit in accordance with para. 1 sentences 1 and 2. Whether—in the relationship of the auditor to the company—mistakes in the context of the notification of a certificate are included as well, can be left undecided. There is in any case no ground for leaving the trust (which is worthy of protection) of a third party, who has been included within the protected area of the audit contract, that such a publication is correct simply without any sanction in liability law.

(cc) Certainly, the legislative intention which is expressed in § 323 of the HGB to limit appropriately the risk of the auditor's liability needs to be considered within the framework of the auditor's contractual liability to third parties. Incorporating an unknown number of creditors, members or acquirers of shares within the protective area of the audit task would militate against this. It cannot be assumed as a rule that the auditor will be ready to take on such an extensive risk of liability.

It is different however if the parties to the contract on the commissioning of the work (or possibly even at a later point in time) proceed on the agreed basis that audit is to be carried out in the interest of a certain third party as well and the outcome is to assist this third party as the basis for a decision. In any case, in such cases the undertaking of the task includes a conclusive declaration of the auditor that he intends to carry out the audit conscientiously and without bias in the interest of the third party as well. There is no ground in a case of this kind for denying to a third party claims against an auditor who breaches his duty in the audit [references omitted].

(c) The appeal court infers from the way the letter of the 9 October 1992 was addressed that it was recognisably intended for the use of a third party; it also considers that the defendants could have reckoned on their information being of importance for decisions by recipients with a business background. These findings are accepted by the appeal in law as favourable to it. They are unsuccessfully disputed by the reply to the appeal in law which claims on the contrary that the defendants did not have to reckon with a third party basing a purchase decision on a communication regarding the expected outcome of an audit, because in the legal world if need be an intermediate status report could be a basis for a decision of that kind.

The significance to be attributed to the letter of the 9 October 1992 is a question of interpretation which the judge of fact has to undertake, taking into consideration all the decisive circumstances, which can include the discussions preceding the letter. The appeal court will in the further proceedings have an opportunity to look at the objection raised by the reply to the appeal in law insofar as the letter of the 9 October 1992 contains no certificate corresponding to § 322 of the HGB and therefore also cannot form a basis for trust which is worthy of protection.

(d) The defendants also have an opportunity in the further proceedings to give a more precise basis to their objections, raised in the appeal in law, to the assumption by the appeal court that they had breached their audit duties and given an incorrect confirmation just because they had failed to obtain confirmation of the balances.

2. (a) The appeal court denies that the defendants are liable even though it bases its decision on a breach of duty. This was because the plaintiff has not proved that the insolvent would not have acquired the shares in the business of STN if the deficit for the year 1991 had been known to it. The appeal in law objects (correctly here) that its case was to the effect that the shares in the business would not have been acquired on the conditions of the contract of the 12 October 1992 if the deficit for the year 1991 had been known.

Besides this the appeal court considers the statements of the witnesses called by the defendants, in particular in relation to the calculation of the purchase price in the purchase contract, to be contrary to logic and experience and does not consider the plaintiff's argument on this issue. The circumstance that no special point of reference was established for the value of STN in the calculation of the purchase price and the piece of land included was the decisive valuation factor for the calculation of the purchase price does not justify the conclusion expressed by the appeal court that it was a matter of indifference to the purchaser whether STN had a value at all.

Even if the managing director of the subsequent insolvent should have declared in the purchase contract negotiations that the firm was no longer worth anything anyway and he did not want to pay anything for it, it does not follow from this that the purchaser would have been prepared to put its money into an undertaking which was heavily in debt by more than 10 million DM a good nine months previously. In this connection it may remain open in proceedings in the appeal in law exactly how the purchase price clause in § 4b of the purchase contract is to be understood. The decisive factor is that the annual account for the year 1991 addressed by the defendants in the letter of the 9 October 1992 revealed an annual surplus of about 2.6 million DM whilst the annual account which was later provided with a note of confirmation by the defendants documented a deficit of more than 11 million DM. It cannot be inferred from the statements of the witnesses who have been examined that such a difference did not influence the calculation of the purchase price.

In § 10 of the purchase contract the seller warrants that the principles of proper accounting had been observed and to his knowledge no liabilities of the business existed which were not evident from the accounts. The appeal in law correctly points out that this provision argues against the appeal court's assumption that the operative value of STN was without any significance for the purchase price. In the face of this provision and the fact that STN's inadequate financial cover existing at the end of 1991 could only be balanced by the bringing in of the business premises, it cannot be denied that the breach of duty by the defendants (which was accepted by the appeal court) caused the purchase decision on the basis which it gave. In fact, there is a prima facie case in favour of it.

(b) Also, if the appeal court had doubts about whether the breach of duty caused the purchase decision, it should not have disregarded the evidence of the witness Dr B who was called on this issue. Even if the negotiations about the purchase of the shares in the business were concluded on the 8 October 1992, the parties to the purchase contract were only finally bound by the documentation of the 12 October 1992. Therefore events between these two points in time could still be of importance. This applies for instance to the bringing in of the real property company by the seller on the day of the documentation of the purchase contract. Further, the appeal court itself—in spite of the conclusion of the negotiations on the 8 October 1992—proceeds decisively on the basis that the defendants' letter of the 9 October 1992 was a ground of liability.

But then prima facie evidence which refers to the causality of this letter is also important. The prima facie evidence ought not to be left out of consideration, as the reply to the appeal in law thinks it should be, just because the plaintiff has not explained why the witness should have had such an insight into the events relating to the decision. This is because there was a letter of the 7 October 1992 written by this witness, who represented the purchaser, which the appeal court mentioned in its version of the facts of the case and from which important circumstances for the calculation of the purchase price arise.

3. The appeal in law also correctly objects to the fact that the appeal court has denied damage. The deliberations of the appeal court are based in this respect on the legally incorrect idea that the shares in the business of STN were, insofar as they concerned the operative value of the company, without significance for the calculation of the purchase price, and it was only a matter of the value of the business premises which had been included. Whether damage has resulted to the purchaser, which has asserted that if it had been correctly informed about the circumstances of STN at the end of 1991 it would not have acquired the shares in the business or would only have acquired them for a symbolic purchase price of DM 1, can only be established by inclusion of the value of the undertaking as a whole. It cannot be ascertained solely by the purchase price which has been paid—as the claim of the plaintiff seems to suggest—nor solely by the value of the business premises which has been brought in.

II.

The Senate cannot make a decision in the case itself, because further findings by the judge of fact are necessary on the questions addressed under I. The appeal court will also have to investigate the argument of the defendants that the purchaser had been informed about the business circumstances of STN and it was in any case attributable to it as contributory fault that it had had no intermediate status report prepared. It will further have the opportunity within the framework of its new assessment to go into the question again of whether a claim by the plaintiff can be based on an information contract or on tort. Where liability which is merely based on the protective effect of the audit contract is being considered, the limitation of liability in § 323 para. 2 of the HGB is to be taken into account. This is because the provisions of § 323 of the HGB—in this respect also—take precedence as a special regime over the contract law provisions of civil law [references omitted].

Case 25

BUNDESGERICHTSHOF (FIRST CIVIL DIVISION) 10 MAY 1984
NJW 1985, 2411 = WM 1984, 1233

Facts

The first plaintiff had a continuous business relationship with the defendant, a forward-ing agent, since November 1976. In accordance with an agreement from 26 January 1978 the first plaintiff stored goods in one of the defendant's storehouses. The second plain-tiff owned the goods. The first plaintiff is the parent company of the second plaintiff. On 19 December 1979 the first plaintiff discovered that some of the goods had been stolen. The plaintiffs seek to obtain declaratory judgments to the effect that the defendant is liable in damages for the loss of the goods . . . The Court of First Instance and the Court of Appeal have rejected the claim. The appeal against these decisions was allowed.

Reasons

. . .

II. 2. The Court of Appeal denied the first plaintiff's entitlement to a contractual action on the following ground. The second plaintiff had direct rights of action founded on a contract for the benefit of a third party and on delict. In the view of the Court of Appeal it followed that the promisee could not recover damages in respect of the third party's loss (*Drittschadensliquidation*). The reasoning of the Court of Appeal is flawed.

(a) Only the contracting party to that contract, i.e. the first plaintiff as promisee, can enforce the contractual right of action derived from the agreement from 26 January 1978. The fact that the second plaintiff suffered the loss and not the first plaintiff is not a bar to that right of action. In cases like the present, where a bailor enters into a contract with a bailee whereunder the bailee undertakes to store and guard the goods the promisee or bailor is entitled to recover damages in respect of the loss suffered by the third party owner of the goods [references omitted].

(b) The second plaintiff could have enforced the rights under the agreement from 26 January 1978 instead of the first plaintiff only if the first plaintiff had assigned his con-tractual rights against the defendant to the second plaintiff or if the contract between the first plaintiff and the defendant from 26 January 1978 had been one for the benefit of the second plaintiff or at least with protective effects towards the second plaintiff. However, this is not the case here. . . .

(c) Therefore the second plaintiff's claim is exclusively founded on the law of delict. This direct right of action of the second plaintiff does not prevent the first plaintiff from pursuing his contractual claim founded on *Drittschadensliquidation* against the defend-ant. The first plaintiff may sue in addition to the action brought by the second plaintiff. The fact that the first plaintiff's claim flows from the same acts or omissions of the defen-dant as that of the second plaintiff does not indicate otherwise. The claims pursued by the plaintiffs in contract and tort respectively are independent from each other in that each right of action follows its own rules, they are also equally valuable each in its own right [reference omitted]. It follows that the contractual claims can be brought in addi-tion to and independently from an action in delict. The fact that the plaintiff is exposed to both claims does not amount to a double recovery prohibited for reasons of the law of civil procedure. . . .

To allow the first plaintiff to sue on the basis of third party loss compensation does not prejudice the defendant debtor in any interest that needs protection. The promisor does not lose the right to invoke limitations of liability, contributory negligence, limitation periods or other defences. This is true also for an extinction of the obligation by performance. If the promisor fulfils his obligations towards one of the creditors his obligations towards the other creditor cease to exist as well (see § 428 BGB; RGZ 170, 246, 250). . . .

Case 26

BUNDESGERICHTSHOF (SEVENTH CIVIL DIVISION) 25 NOVEMBER 1971
VERSR 1972, 274 = MDR 1972, 316

Facts

The plaintiff is the owner of a castle X. where he runs a hostel for the needy. The building has a mineral oil heating system. The oil is stored in two tanks. A mixer tap connects the two tanks. In May 1965 a company B. employed the first defendant, a mineral oil wholesale firm, to supply and install two devices the function of which is to detect leaks in the tanks. It is disputed whether the first defendant also undertook to remove the mixer tap. The plaintiff is economically linked with the company B. B. contracted in its own name but on the account of the plaintiff. The first defendant employed the subcontractor R who in turn instructed the second defendant to actually carry out the construction works.

Oil leaked from one of the tanks into the estate's soil and subsequently into the estate's lake by the end of August 1965. The leakage was caused by a defective weld. An employee of the second defendant had welded the respective airing pipe. However, the oil in the tank would not have spilled over had the mixer taps not been wrongly adjusted.

In the action before the Court the plaintiff seeks compensation from the defendants as joint and several liable debtors for the loss caused by the leaked oil. The loss has been provisionally estimated to amount to DM 171,589.88. The Court of First Instance (Landgericht) and the Court of Appeal (Berufungsgericht) allowed the claim. The appeal is rejected.

Reasons

I. 1. The Court of Appeal held that the plaintiff is entitled to a contractual remedy against the first defendant in respect of the loss although he is not a privy to the contract between the company B. and the first defendant. The company B. contracted in its own name but on the account of the plaintiff. Therefore, B. acted as indirect agent on behalf of the plaintiff. In view of these findings, the Court of Appeal applied the concept of recovery of damages in respect of a third party's loss (*Schadensliquidation im Drittinteresse*). According to this principle the promisee may authorise the third party to sue the defendant in its own name and claim compensation for the loss that falls on the third party. This line of the reasoning of the Court of Appeal is supported by a series of decisions substantially to the same effect (BGHZ 51, 91, 93 = VersR 69, 155, 156; BGHZ 40, 91, 100 = VersR 63, 1172, 1173; BGHZ 25, 250, 258 = VersR 57, 705, 706 with further references). This part of the judgment is not put into question by the defendant's submissions. . . .

4. According to the Court of Appeal the first defendant's breach of contract (*positive Vertragsverletzung*) for which he is liable lies in the fact that the airing pipe was not properly welded. The first defendant is legally answerable for this defect; the defect is at least a contributory cause for the loss. The fact that the mixer tap was not adjusted properly is contrary to the opinion of the defendant irrelevant because the leakage would have been avoided if the airing pipe had been sealed off properly. In that case the leakage would have been noticed on time. This suffices to meet the requirement of causality.

5. The Court of Appeal further assumes correctly that the first defendant is responsible for the fault of the employees of the second defendant according to § 278 BGB and that these employees have acted negligently; they have not taken sufficient care when welding the airing pipe. The first defendant could not convince this Court of the contrary.

II. 1. In the view of the Court of Appeal the liability of the second defendant is founded exclusively on the law of delict (§ 831 BGB). . . .

2. A pre-condition for § 831 BGB is physical damage to property, just as it is for § 823 I BGB. However, the second defendant's contention that the Court of Appeal did not positively establish that he has caused physical damage to property is not correct. Such physical damage was caused by the second defendant. . . .

3. In the view of the Court of Appeal the second defendant did not successfully proof that he had carefully selected and supervised his employees; according to § 831 BGB he bears the burden of proof. This finding is not questioned by the second defendant and the reasoning of the Court appears to be correct.

III. The Court of Appeal found that the plaintiff was not contributory negligent. . . .

Notes to Cases 19–26

1. Cases 19–24 deal with economic loss caused by negligent statements—typically taking the form of some certification. The law on this subject is complicated for two reasons. First because the potential liability flows from words and it is generally believed that people utter words with less care than they usually put in their actions. Words also "travel" far and thus, it is said, can cause more widespread harm. Neither argument is entirely convincing. In these days of worldwide class actions the asbestos, silicon breast implants, Dalcon Shield or defective heart valves disputes have put paid to this assertion. Nor is the distinction between words and actions always as easy or as obvious as those who advocate them believe. Thus, are negligent certifications words or documents based on negligent investigations i.e. acts or omissions? More likely, therefore, that the real problem here is, once again, the systems' dislike for pure economic loss, aggravated on occasion by the above-mentioned characteristics assigned to words. Whatever, the true reason, and often it is an accumulation of reasons that dictates an "attitude", the three legal systems examined in this book can boast an extremely rich case law which is not free from contradictions. This complexity is further increased if one bears in mind that the problems here discussed find their solutions sometimes in judge-made law and sometimes in statutes (which in Germany also show the signs of EC influences). For a legal rule that can claim its existence to a multiplicity of sources invariably courts interpretative difficulties.

German law can claim two additional interesting features. First, the "statutory" law, perhaps because it was drafted under the influence of powerful pressure groups, shows marked signs of being more "protective" of accountants and auditors. There are no such signs of leniency in the case law which, in its boldness, is provoking academics and testing the codal philosophy to its limits. For the academic lawyer in general, the comparatist in particular, this may well be one of the most striking features of the German position. For, as a Common lawyer with unique insights into German law once observed, it underscores ". . . the German willingness, indeed eagerness, to extend tort protection . . . [despite] the Civil Code's categorical exclusion of tort damages for pure economic loss and the great weight reputedly given by German law to theoretical orthodoxy over pragmatism." (Fleming (1989) 105 *LQR*, 508.) In this trend (rather than in the details of German law) may also lie the greatest lesson for the Common lawyer who, additionally, would not have to go to the same pains to justify similar results if (or when) he decided to adopt a more flexible attitude towards pure economic loss. Finally, many of the ideas, notions, and trends discussed in this section are also evident in two other areas of economic loss. The first is concerned with the consequences of mistakes made by lawyers (and is discussed in the next section); the other deals with damage caused *to* products (and is considered by the cases reproduced in section 15 and the notes that accompany them).

In the light of these introductory remarks, it is self-evident that an account such as the one that follows is bound to be somewhat crass—certainly to the extent that it attempts to summarise such an enormous volume of decisional law. Here more than elsewhere the reader should thus look at what follows more in search for signposts for further study of the law than as a source of detailed answers. If the material assembled here and the notes that accompany it also succeed to make the reader "think" that can only be regarded as a welcome bonus.

2. At first sight, German law is cautious and conservative. § 676 BGB provides that "A person who gives advice or a recommendation to another is not bound to compensate for any damage arising from following the advice or recommendation, without prejudice to his responsibility arising from contract or delict." Since the main tort provision (§ 823 I BGB) excludes, as we have seen, pure economic loss from its list of protected interests, liability in *tort* can only be based on § 824 BGB, § 826 BGB *or § 823 II BGB*. The first has minimal importance, while the second also has a limited application. This is despite the fact that in recent times the courts have widened the meaning of intention (in § 826 BGB) to include not only *dolus directus* but also *dolus eventualis* (a notion somewhat akin to our concept of reckless behaviour). Thus, in one decision (BGH NJW 1987, 1758–9) the court eased the fault requirement stating that (for the purposes of liability under § 826 BGB) it would suffice to show that the auditor expected his report to be used in connection with credit negotiations and that (if it were incorrect) it would cause harm to the relying creditor. Professor von Bar has, in fact, gone further by arguing that "a person who gives information off the cuff must . . . recognise that it could be false; and the very fact that he still goes ahead and gives that information demonstrates that he has reckoned with the possibility of damage to others and has accepted it." ("Liability for Information and Opinions Causing Pure Economic Loss to Third Parties" in *The Growing Convergence* (ed. B S Markesinis) OUP (1994). See, also, Palandt-Thomas, § 826 nos. 25–28.)

3. Because of the above strictures of the tort provisions of the Code the courts have had recourse to the notion of contract with protective effects *vis-à-vis* third parties with the result that the liability of auditors has been taken significantly further than the wording of § 826 could ever possibly justify. The absence in the German law of tort of any liability for negligently inflicted pure economic loss has resulted in a number of substitute legal constructions. One such device is the so-called contract with protective effects for third parties, a judicially-created variant of the better-known notion of contract in favour of third parties (see chap. 2 section A (d)(iii) and now § 311 III BGB). This construction makes it possible to treat pure economic losses of third persons, resulting from a faulty performance of contractual (or non-contractual) duties, as actionable harm resulting from a breach of a contractual duty. This contractually-based liability towards third parties for their pure economic loss, though now well acknowledged in principle, remains controversial; and the controversy rages as much over detail as it does over the dogmatic basis of the solution.

In German law (and often but not invariably in the Common law), liability, essentially, depends upon reliance on the report; and whether this was reasonable or not depends on the contract (commissioning the audit report) as well as all other relevant circumstances. (BGH NJW 2001, 534 now casts doubt on the relevance of reliance to determining the extent of the loss that can be recovered; the court regarded the scope of the duty owed as the decisive factor; see, also, above, Ch. 2A(d)(iii), p. 63. That case is noteworthy also in a different respect; the surveyor although a professional did not have a formally acknowledged expertise.) Thus, third parties may be able to sue for damages under contracts to which they are not signatories (BGH JZ 1986, 1111); or where their protection under the contract commissioning the report arises not from its wording but from necessary implication (BGH NJW 1987, 1758, 9). In order to adapt and apply the concept of a contract with protective effects towards third parties to the negligent misstatement situation—the so called "expert liability" category of cases—the Federal Court has held that for the protective effects to arise, it is no longer necessary for the requirement of "*Wohl und Wehe*" (for better or for worse) to be fulfilled. Until roughly 1984, this requirement had served as one of the main control factors of the concept since it limited its scope to situations where the promisee was responsible for the "well being" of the third party. This, for instance, was easily satisfied in the context of family relationships but also in employment settings where the employer's duties of care towards his employees were involved. But it was not adequate to cover relationships of commercial nature, so it was dropped. (See BGHZ 69, 82, 86; BGH NJW 1984, 355, 356; BGH NJW 1998, 1059.) A further bold step towards increasing the range of persons included under the "protective umbrella" of the contract was taken when the BGH abandoned the view that third party protection should be denied when there was a real or potential conflict of interests between the commissioning principal of the report and the third party. (BGH NJW 1987, 1758–9). This trend is continued in case 23. The decision deals with the problem whether and to what extent the co-responsibility of the contractual partner of the surveyor should be taken into account in an action by the third party/purchaser of the land. In this instance the site owner, who intended to sell the property, commissioned a report from a surveyor to estimate the value of the house. The surveyor over-valued the house. This was because he negligently relied on the misleading information given to him by the site owner. The third party/purchaser relied on the surveyor's report and bought the house at an unrealistic price. The court allowed the action of the third party. The actual result of the decision surely appears reasonable (in that sense, Medicus, JZ 1995, 309). In the final analysis, however, the BGH took another step in the direction of an extra-contractual/ tortious liability for certain cases of economic loss. But the court was not willing to adopt the language of a tortious "duty of care" towards certain third persons. Instead, it sought to derive this result from the intention of the parties to the contract of employment of the surveyor which was given protective effect towards the third party/purchaser. The BGH resorted to two fictions to achieve the "desired" result on the basis of contract.

The first was that the site-owner had a real interest in including the buyer in the protective scope of the contract. In fact he had not, since he and the purchaser were on opposite sides of the bargain and, as a result, the survey gave rise to a conflict of interests. (While the site-owner is clearly interested in a favourable valuation, the purchaser/plaintiff is interested in a valuation at the lower end of the scale). It is, therefore, difficult to argue that the site-owner wished to benefit the third party/plaintiff. Such an intention could only be "discovered" if one could show that had the parties openly discussed the issue they would have agreed that good faith required that the site-owner also contract for the benefit of the purchaser. Such a construction, however, is so unconvincing that, in reality, it shows that it is the law that is imposing upon the surveyor such a duty towards the purchaser and not the will of the parties.

The second fiction is even more striking. It is inherent in the derivative nature of the third party's cause of action that the promisor/ surveyor can avail himself towards the third party of any defences available to him against the promisee (§ 334 BGB, which corresponds to Contracts (Rights of Third Parties, Act 1999 s. 3(2)). In an action by the site owner the surveyor could have objected that the site owner who commissioned the report, had acted contrary to good faith in concealing a crucial defect of the property. The BGH held that the promisor could not avail himself of this defence as against the third party/purchaser. The court relied on a device—which is not always available—to solve this problem, namely implied term reasoning. Thus, it assumed that in the contract that created the "duty of care" towards certain third parties, the surveyor tacitly waived his right to avail himself of any defence against the plaintiff/potential purchaser which he, the contractual debtor, had against his contractual partner (the person commissioning the report). This waiver, the BGH stated, was justified by the fact that the expert knew that his performance was intended to form the basis of the financial calculations of the purchaser of the land (who, one might add will—reasonably—rely on the report). It goes without saying that these considerations might also justify imposing liability under the *Hedley Byrne* principle of reasonable reliance and assumption of responsibility. However, it is more difficult to see how this result, imposing liability, can be derived from applying the concept of a contract in favour of the third party. For not only is this result incompatible with the traditional model of a contract in favour of third parties; it is also doubtful that the surveyor would have accepted such a waiver had it been discussed before entering into the contract. Once again, such analysis indicates that the duty is imposed by law and does not flow from the will of the contracting parties. It also casts new doubt on the whole construction of a contract with protective effects towards the purchaser. (See Ebke *JZ* 1998, 991, 993 ff. who suggests that "implied term" reasoning is in such cases used to make up for the exclusion of pure economic loss from the list of protected interests in § 823 I BGB).

In the light of the above, it comes as no surprise to discover that some academic commentators have argued in favour of abandoning the contract with protective effects as theoretical basis of the decisions of the court—at least in cases such as the present one. But the BGH remains to be convinced and has yet to give any signs that it is about to change its present stance (see ch. 2 A(d)(iii)). See e.g. Canaris "Die Reichweite der Expertenhaftung gegenüber Dritten", *ZHR* 163 (1999) 206 and "Schutzwirkungen zugunsten Dritter bei 'Gegenläufigkeit' der Interessen", *JZ* 1995, 441. Professor Canaris submits that at least in situations like the present the theoretical basis of the liability of the "expert" for negligent misstatements in German law ought to be *culpa in contrahendo* (see now § 311 II BGB and § 311 III 2 BGB which refers to reliance). Such an analysis would entail a number of advantages such as a better explanation of the independence of the action from the contract between the person who commissioned the statement and the expert. It would also cater for the need to limit liability in relation to third parties by disclaimers etc. One is reminded here of the reasoning in *Smith* v. *Eric S Bush* [1990] 1 AC 831 (recently applied by the Court of Appeal in *Merrett* v. *Babb* [2001] 3 WLR 1). Professor Picker on the other hand (e.g. "Gutachterhaftung" in *Festschrift für Dieter Medicus* (1999) p. 397) rejects the reliance-based *culpa in contrahendo* model. Instead, he favours a limited and overt exception to the rule that pure economic loss is not recoverable in the law of delict (which would cover this and other similar cases of negligent miss-statements.) Whether this is *de lege lata* possible in German law is not for us to decide. But the discussion prompted by case 23 certainly indicates that the contractual approach currently prevailing in Germany may also have its shortcomings.

4. Cases 19–24 also highlight one of the main structural differences between German tort law and English law. German law has not developed a general exception to the general rule that pure economic loss cannot be recovered in the law of delict outside the framework of §§ 823 II, 826 BGB and apart from the "creation" of the protected interest under § 823 I BGB of an established and operating business. As a result, it has, once again, been forced into contractual thinking. As the cases reproduced above show, its contract law has proved flexible enough to accommodate the desire to hold liable those who give advice (or perform other services such as auditing or surveying) even if in a strict sense there is no privity of contract between the parties. This, for instance, could happen when third parties rely on statements by professionals given in the course of their employment by a different person. From a comparative perspective this confirms the insight formulated many years ago by Zweigert and Kötz and which still cannot be bettered. For, in their *Introduction to Comparative Law* (3rd edn. 1998) p. 44, the authors remarked that: ". . . when the process of comparison begins, each of the solutions must be freed from the context of its own system." And they continued: "Here, too, we must follow the principle of functionality: the

solutions we find in the different jurisdictions must be cut loose from their contextual context and stripped of their national doctrinal overtones so that they may be seen purely in the light of their function, as an attempt to satisfy a particular need."

The problem of negligent misstatements has caused major conceptual difficulties in both systems. The preferred option of English courts is, as we have seen, to extend liability in negligence to cover pure economic loss—a type of harm traditionally belonging to the realm of contract law. By contrast, the German predilection for contract appears at first sight to have an axiomatic advantage. On closer re-examination, however, it raises serious doubts whether liability really flows from the intention of the parties (essential if one is to remain faithful to contract theory) or whether it is more accurately imposed by the law. (For instance the contract route encounters difficulties if the contract is void; the issue has not been decided but the better view seems to be that liability to third parties should not cease in such a case.) The realisation that the theoretical basis might not, after all, lie in the intention of the parties has finally come to full light, especially in recent cases such as BGHZ 127, 378 (case 23). We must conclude therefore that in this area, if any, a functional approach is capable of providing insights of general interest. As Professor Schlechtriem remarked recently it is not so much the theoretical basis that counts. What really matters is that the specific criteria for imposing liability receive attention and are developed rationally on a case by case basis. (See his "Schutzpflichten und geschützte Personen" in Beuthien and others (eds.) *Festschrift für Dieter Medicus* (1999) p. 529.) More specifically his view is that the main emphasis should be laid upon the scope and purpose of the duty owed in the individual case. In his opinion, the relevant test is to be found in Lord Hoffmann's speech in *South Australian Asset Management Corp.* v. *York Montague Ltd.* [1997] AC 191, 211 where the learned Law Lord argued that the claimant has to show "that the duty was owed to him and that it was a duty in respect of the kind of loss which he has suffered". Against this background, the comparative study of each other's systems can provide useful insights to both of them and make the lawyer—student or practitioner—understand better what he is trying to achieve. Another and perhaps more important lesson that can be drawn from comparing liability for negligent misstatements is that in this field of "professional negligence" the traditional compartmentalisation of obligations into contractual and tortious lacks explanatory power. (*Cf.* Cartwright (1997) 13 *Constr LJ* 157). These observations will be best understood if read in conjunction with the text in chap. 2 section 2(d)(iii), above, and the notes to cases *11–13*. (For further details about the topics discussed above see in addition to those already referred to: Bamm, "Entwicklungstendenzen der Expertenhaftung", *JZ* 1991, 373; Ebke, "Die Haftung des Wirtschaftsprüfers für fahrlässig verursachte Vermögensschäden Dritter", *WM* 1991, 398; Hopt "Nichtvertragliche Haftung außerhalb von Schadens- und Bereicherungsausgleich", *AcP* 183 (1983) 608; Lang, "Die Rechtsprechung des Bundesgerichtshofes zur Dritthaftung der Wirtschaftsprüfer und anderer Sachverständiger", *WM* 1988, 1001; Müller, "Wirtschaftsprüfer und vereidigte Buchprüfer als Sachverständige und Gutachter", *WPK-Mitt* 1991, 3; Schneider "Die Reichweite der Expertenhaftung gegenüber Dritten", *ZHR* 163 (1999) 246 and Bosch ibid. at p. 274 with further references.)

5. The (German) case law regime just described is, as indicated at the beginning of this section, modified wherever the statutory regime takes precedence. This is the situation in the *Caparo* type of case where the result reached by the House of Lords is acceptable also to German law. (*Cf.* von Bar's comprehensive review of the *Caparo* case from a comparative perspective "Liability for Information and Opinions Causing Pure Economic Loss to Third Parties" in *The Growing Convergence*, ed. Markesinis, (1994) 98, 125). Contrast now case 24 on statutory audit under § 323 HGB. *Caparo*, it will be recalled, dealt with a "statutory" audit, prepared for the company but relied upon (to their detriment) by (*a*) existing and (*b*) potential shareholders of the said company. The Court of Appeal allowed the first (but not the second) to recover their losses, but the House of Lords overturned the decision denying both categories of plaintiff all redress against the negligent accountants. The same solution as in *Caparo* would still follow in German law *if* the result were to be determined solely by the wording of § 323 of the Commercial Code (HGB) which specifically regulates the legal position of auditors in the case of "mandatory audits" (*Pflichtprüfungen* viz., the formation audit,

the annual audits, and "special" reports) and which limits the auditor's liability for negligent breach of his duties to the company only. (For an English version of the text see: *Business Transactions in Germany*, Gen. Ed. Ruester, N.Y., Matthew Bender (1990). For a more detailed account in German see: Ebke, *Wirtschaftsprüfer und Dritthaftung* (1983), esp. pp. 38–43; 56–60.) Shareholders and potential shareholders are, thus, excluded for the purview of this paragraph. (This has been confirmed in case 24 though see, below, comments on the wider effect of this case which introduced a significant extension of this type of liability for statutory audit and, to that extent, may have caused the two systems to part company). And they are also denied an action under § 823 II BGB because § 323 HGB is not regarded as a protective norm (*Schutzgesetz*). (This has been well established for some time. See: *Aktiengesetz Kommentar*, 13th edn. by Baumbach, Hueck and Schulze (1968) § 168, no. 7; *Aktiengesetz Kommentar* by Gessler, Hefermehl, Eckhardt and Kropff, vol. III (1973) § 168, no. 31; *Kölner Kommentar zum Aktiengesetz* by Zoellner, vol. II (1971), § 168, no. 16. These are commentaries on § 168 of the *Aktiengesetz* which is now to be found as § 323 of the Commercial Code, quoted in the text above. See now Hopt *Handelsgesetzbuch Kommentar* (30th edn., 2000) § 323 HGB no. 8.) This restrictive interpretation is reinforced by § 340b (5) of the *Aktiengesetz* which deals with the potential liability of auditors in the event of mergers. For in this second instance, liability is expressly extended towards "the companies participating in the merger and their shareholders".

As already indicated in the previous paragraph, § 323 I HGB provides that if the auditor negligently fails to comply with his duties he is liable only to the company in question (and if an associated company sustains loss also to this company). Until this seminal judgment was published this was understood as implying that any other third party was prevented from suing the auditor. It thus came as a surprise that the BGH, in case 24, did not endorse fully this widely held view. While the court there acknowledged that the "legislative intention" which was expressed in this provision was "to limit appropriately the risk of the auditor's liability", it also stressed that this provision did not have an "exclusionary" effect. The consequence of such an approach is that the auditor could in principle owe a duty also to persons not expressly mentioned in § 323 HGB. This was the case where the auditor (contractually) undertook to perform his service without prejudicing the interests of a third party, in the instant case a purchaser of the company. It is not entirely clear whether this requires that the auditor issues a statement in addition to the actual audit before his liability widens to include third parties. In the somewhat unusual facts of the case in question, the auditor had confirmed to a second auditor employed by the purchaser that he would stand by the views expressed in the annual report. (The better view would seem to be that this extended liability is engaged only if such an additional statement is made. On this, see Canaris ZHR 163 (1999) 206, 208.) A consequence of this restrictive reading would be that in respect of the statutory audit, itself, no liability would arise in relation to third parties. But that does not affect the striking feature of the decision which is that such an undertaking was said to flow from the intentions of the parties and that it had been conclusively declared. Once again, therefore, one must express serious doubts as to whether the auditor was actually willing to accept liability beyond that which normally flows from § 323 HGB, especially in the light of the pre-existing and restrictive understanding of that provision. (See Ebke, "Abschlußprüfer, Bestätigungsvermerk und Drittschutz", JZ 1998, 991, 993.) The inescapable impression thus is that the duty is imposed by law with consequences which may not have yet been fully fathomed by the (German) courts. For, as Professor Ebke remarked: "If the intention of the parties as expressed in the contract no longer determines the existence and extent of liability and this is allowed to turn on 'objective interests' and the third party's reliance, then the choice of the [contracting] parties and their right to determine the extent of their obligations will take second place. A result-orientated risk allocation that does not flow from the will of the parties will then become predominant." This in turn is difficult to reconcile with those decisions in which it was held that § 323 HGB was not a provision which acquires protective effects towards third parties within the framework of § 823 II BGB already referred to, not to mention traditional contract dogma.

6. In this context, of particular interest is a decision of the BGH in 1985 where one reason given for the enlargement of the auditor's liability was the existence of mandatory liability insurance according to § 54 of the Accountants' Regulations (*Wirtschaftsprüferordnung, WPO*). (See, BGH WM 1985, 450, nos. 6 and 8). Also relevant may be the fact that under the WPO the auditors are allowed to make use of the General Commissioning Terms for Chartered Accountants (*Allgemeine Auftragsbedingungen für Wirtschaftsprüfer*) which restrict or (in certain circumstances) eliminate their liability. Statutes such as the General Conditions of Business of 1977, now contained in §§ 305–310 BGB, may also help define the ambit of liability and thus, *de facto*, limit litigation by reference to the amount of insurance coverage. (See: BGH NJW 1987, 1758, 1760.) One should add that if third parties are entitled to sue auditors, now subject however to the uncertain implications of the decision in case 23 above, they can be opposed by all the defences that may be available to auditors as a result of their contracts with the commissioning company. The contractual nature of this action makes this point obvious, whereas it would be more problematic if the action were tortious in nature.

7. Negligent statement relied upon by third persons have proved as troublesome in the USA as in other systems and, if anything, the case law here is both enormous in its volume and not possible to reconcile. The reasons for the difficulties inherent in this subject are many. First is the belief—not always factually correct—that words travel more than acts and can thus raise the spectrum of truly "indeterminate liability" in terms of time and persons. Second is the fact that the audited client retains a good deal of control over the records upon which the auditor bases his report. Thirdly, and not entirely unrelated to the previous point, is the fact that auditors will rarely be in a position to estimate anywhere near as accurately as will be necessary, the extent of their potential liability. This "informational asymmetry" has been examined more in the USA than in England by academic literature. (See, for instance, Siliciano, "Negligent Accounting and the Limits of Instrumental Tort Reform", 86 *Michigan L. Rev.* 1929 (1988). Finally, a few courts in the USA have also argued that its in most cases open to the plaintiff/lender to arrange to become a client of the auditor if he really wishes to be able to rely on his report. (See, *Bily* v. *Arthur Young & Co.*, 834 P. 2d 745 (1992). Situations of negligent misrepresentations can take an infinite variety of factual forms. These have been systematically analysed by Lorenz, "Das Problem der Haftung für primäre Vermögensschäden bei der Erteilung einer unrichtigen Auskunft", *Festschrift K. Larenz* (1973) 575. Here suffice it to divide them into two groups.

In the first, the defendant makes a statement (usually a report) to the person who asked for it (and, invariably, paid for it) but knows that it will be relied upon by a specified third person. OLG München BB 1956, 866 is such a case and it is discussed along with other similar cases in Lawson and Markesinis, I, 83 ff. In the USA this situation is usually described as being covered by the "privity or near privity rule". It finds an excellent illustration in *Glanzer* v. *Shepard*, 233 NY 236, 135 NE 275 (1922). That German law based its solution on contract whereas the American law opted for tort is mostly a matter of "emphasis", as Cardozo J put it, adding that if necessary he, too, could have based his decision on contract. (For further German decisions see, *inter alia*, BGH WM 1965, 287; BGH WM 1963, 913.)

Real difficulties appear in the second type of situation where A commissions the (negligently prepared) report from B and then shows it to others who rely on it to their detriment. Case 19 (WM 1979, 548) is such a case and it is here that the problem of "indeterminate liability", so well identified by Cardozo J in *Ultramares Marine Corp.* v. *Touche*, 255 NY 170, 174 NE 441 (1931), rears its ugly head. The courts, if they abandon strict adherence to the privity requirement (as they are nowadays inclined to do), are, in such cases, forced to seek a balance between two opposing positions. The first is liability resting on pure foresight (or some equivalent concept). The second is liability based only on a form of direct nexus between the representor and the representee of the kind found in the aforementioned decision of the Court of Appeal of Munich or in the *Glanzer* decision. (Yet a third option, available to some plaintiffs, is to rely on statutory enactments such as ss. 11 and 12 of the (American) Securities Act of 1932 or s. 18 of the Securities Exchange Act of 1934. But such actions have been of limited use to ordinary investors or creditors besides suffering from the drawback of a short—one year—limitation period. For the protection currently afforded by federal securities law see Kraakman, "Gatekeepers: The Anatomy of a Third-Party Enforcement Strategy?" 2 *J. of Law, Econ. and Org.* 53 (1986).)

The USA provides, as one would expect, the greatest variety of court-devised techniques to avoid the strictures of the *Ultramares* rule. Thus some courts, while not overruling *Ultramares*, appear to be extending the rationale of the *Glanzer* decision (third party can recover only if he is "the end and aim of the transaction"). See, for example, *White* v. *Guarente* 43 NY 2d 356, 372 NE 2d 315 (NY 1977); *Credit Alliance Corp.* v. *Arthur Andersen and Co.*, 476 NYS 2d 539 (1984); rev'd in 483 NE 2d 110, 493 NYS 2d 435 (1985); amended 489 NE 2d 249 (1985). According to this approach, if A prepares a report for B for a particular purpose knowing that C will, in furtherance of that purpose, rely upon the said report, then he will be liable to C if there is evidence of some conduct linking A to C and evincing A's understanding of C's reliance on his report. Though these conditions may represent a modification of the *Ultramares* tough stance, the court in *Credit Alliance* was eager to stress its willingness to adhere to the policy objectives set out in *Ultramares*. So, in the absence of some *actual and meaningful* contact between A and C—for instance a mere telephone exchange between A and C will not suffice. (*Security Pacific Business Credit, Inc.* v. *Peat Marwick Main & Co.*, 597 NE 2d 1080.)—there will be no liability. A New Jersey statute (New Jersey Stat. Ann. 2A: 53A-25) adopts a similar position and spares the accountant of all liability unless he knew the specific plaintiff and the specific transaction for which his report was intended; and four further States— Arkansas (Ark Code Ann § 16–114–302, (1995)), Illinois (Ill Ann Stat chap. 225 (1993)), Kansas (Kan Stat Ann § 1–402 (1991)), Utah (Utah Code Ann § 58–26–12 (1996)) and Wyoming (Wyo Stat § 33–3–201 (1995)) have passed analogous but differently phrased limiting legislation.

A more middling or flexible approach is that advocated by the *Restatement* (*Second*) *of Torts*, para. 552 (1977) which rejects the private requirement and renders accountants liable not only to those persons whom they intended to influence but also towards the persons whom the accountants know that their *clients* intended to influence. *Rusch Factors, Inc.* v. *Levin*, 284 F. Supp. 85 (DRI 1968) offers an early illustration, the court in that case being influenced by a tentative draft of the Restatement. (Note that the *Rusch* decision (at p. 93) talks of an "*actually* foreseen and *limited* class of persons" [italics supplied]. Whereas the German decision, while agreeing with the idea that the identity of the relying person need not be known to the representor, insists that he must be "part of a calculable group of persons".) Ohio (*Haddon View Investment Co.* v. *Coopers and Lybrand*, 436 NE 2d 212, 70 Ohio St. 2d 154 (1982)) and New Hampshire (*Spherex, Inc.* v. *Alexander Grant and Co.*, 122 N.H. 898, 451 A. 2d 1308 (1982)) were among the early converts to this rule. For other important decisions see: *Raritan River Steel Co.* v. *Cherry, Bekaert & Holland*, 367 SE 2d 609 (1988); *Bily* v. *Arthur Young & Co.*, 834 P. 2d 745 (1992) (indisputably a leading case); *Boykin* v. *Arthur Andersen & Co.*, 639 So. 2d 504 (1994); *Nycal Corp.* v. *KPMG Peat Marwick LLP*, 426 Mass. 491, 688 N.E 2d 1368 (1998). But the interpretative "refinements" attempted by some courts may have also made possible for "daring" practitioners or judges to go beyond the (undoubtedly) ambiguous wording of the Restatement (which, itself, has not escaped criticism). Thus in *Marcus Bros. Textiles, Inc.* v. *Price Waterhouse, LLP*, 350 NC 214 (1999) the Supreme Court of North Carolina "clarified" its aforementioned judgment in *Raritan* and held that actual knowledge by the accountant of those persons who might rely on the accountant's opinion is not necessary under Restatement 552, general business practices from which such reliance can be inferred being sufficient. And *NYCAL Corp.* v. *KPMG Peat Marwick LLP*, 426 Mass 491 (1998) the Supreme Court of Massachusetts, while following the Restatement rule, emphasized that its test would be construed in a way as to require the accountant to have actual knowledge of the limited—*though unnamed*—group of potential [third parties]" (Emphasis added.).

Finally, a number of minority decisions have moved towards the adoption of the most liberal test namely that of pure foreseeability. Thus see: *H. Rosenblum, Inc.* v. *Adler*, 93 NJ 324, 461 A. 2d 138 (1983) (now rejected by the legislator: see statute mentioned above). See, also *Citizens State Bank* v. *Timm, Schmidt and Co.* 335 NW 2d 361 (1983); *International Mortgage Co.* v. *John P Butler Accountancy Corp.* 223 Cal. Rptr. 218 (1986); *Touche Ross* v. *Commercial Union Ins.*, 514 So. 2d 315 (1987) (Mississippi). Yet even in these States, a variety of limitations help keep matters under control.

Wisconsin, for instance, the Supreme Court in its aforementioned decision in Citizens *State Bank* was eager to stress that liability would not be imposed where the harm was found to be too remote, disproportionate, or financially crushing. This approach may evince some awareness of the realities that troubled Cardozo; but it also suggests judicial reliance been placed more on causative notions rather than on the duty of care (with all the drawbacks that this approach may entail, especially in a jury dependant system.) Additionally, all States insist that "justifiable reliance" is a sine qua non. Thus a North Carolina court held that reliance on the audit, not directly but through a summary of it produced in a Dun & Bradstreet report, was not sufficient. (*Raritan*, above.)

The literature on the subject is enormous. An excellent review can be found in Guerci, "Liability of Independent Accountant to Investors or Shareholders", 48 *ALR* 5th 389 (1997). From the more recent literature see: Sinason, "Gaining a New Balance in Accountants' Liability to Nonclients for Negligence: Recent Developments and Emerging Trends", 103 *Com. L.J.* 15 (1998); Young et al., "Financial Reporting and the Accounting Profession: The Whirlwind Continues", 1151 *PLI/ Corp* 95 (1999).

8. English law, too, has vacillated on this topic in a manner which has been as confusing as it is difficult to summarise with any pretence to accuracy. The modern law starts with *Candler* v. *Crane Christmas and Co.* [1951] 2 KB 164 which, though denying recovery to the plaintiff, opened the door for future developments through the prophetic dissent of Denning LJ (as he then was). Some fifteen years later heresy was transformed into orthodoxy by the seminal judgment of the House of Lords in *Hedley Byrne and Co. Ltd.* v. *Heller and Partners Ltd.* [1964] AC 465. The rule was then settled that there would be liability for careless statements causing pure economic loss provided there was a "special relationship" between the plaintiff and the defendant *and* there was no disclosure of liability. "Special relationship" has obviously been a key phrase; and it has been subsequently interpreted to include a friend giving advice seriously though *not* in a professional context (*Chaudry* v. *Prabhaker* [1989] 1 *WLR* 29). Earlier attempts to narrow the *Hedley Byrne* rule only to cases where the party making the statement professed to give that kind of advice or held himself out as possessing special skills also proved unsuccessful. See: *Mutual Life and Citizens' Assurance Co. Ltd.* v. *Evatt* [1971] AC 793; *Esso Petroleum Co. Ltd.* v. *Mardon* [1976] QB 801.

The 1960s and 1970s found the English courts in an imaginative and expansionist mode. This can be seen in English administrative law, but it is also obvious in the decisions dealing with liability for negligent misstatement. Thus, in *Ministry of Housing and Local Government* v. *Sharp* [1970] 2 QB 223 two further extensions were made to the *Hedley Byrne* principle. (In *Hedley Byrne* A made a false statement to B who relied on it to his detriment; in *Sharp* A made the statement to B (who never repeated it to C) but it was C who suffered the loss and was allowed to recover. Secondly, in *Hedley Byrne* the plaintiff's loss was actual expenditure whereas in *Sharp* the harm suffered was failure to recover a sum that had become due). And a potentially more far-reaching extension came in *JEB Fasteners Ltd.* v. *Marks, Bloom and Co.* [1981] 3 All ER 289. For there liability was not based on the *Hedley Byrne* rule (which requires the establishment of a "special relationship") but on the more amorphous neighbourhood rule of *Donoghue* v. *Stevenson* [1932] AC 562 (which also provided the justification for the legal malpractice rule of *Ross* v. *Caunters* [1980] Chap. 297. In the latter case, however, it will be recalled that the economic loss was not caused by a false statement but by a negligent attestation of a will.

More recently, however, this expansionist mood has been checked. And in some cases this was accompanied by severely restricting dicta found in a long series of decisions expressing disapproval of the liberal tendencies which peaked with the decision of the House of Lords in *Junior Books* v. *Veitchi* [1938] 1 AC 520. (The case also involving pure economic loss though caused by negligent deeds, not words). In the context of negligent misstatements, the leading judgment can be found in *Caparo* v. *Dickman* [1990] 2 AC 605 where the House of Lords overruled an interesting and well thought-out judgment of the Court of Appeal. For in that case the House of Lords refused to hold that the auditors of a company owed a duty of care towards the shareholders of the company who suffered losses by purchasing shares in that company by relying on that report. The judgments of at least two Law Lords—Lords Bridge and Jauncey—suggest that liability can only arise if the statement was both intended to be relied upon for a particular purpose and was, in fact, relied upon. This, in the opinion of their Lordships, was not satisfied in this case. See, also, *Al Saudi Banque* v. *Clarke Pixley* [1990] Chap. 313 (company auditors not liable to a bank who lent to the company on the strength of their report); *The Morning Watch* [1990] 1 Lloyd's Rep. 547 (Lloyds Register, reporting on the condition of a vessel at the request of the owner, not liable to potential purchaser who relies on their report). As always, the plethora of dicta, often with relatively minor verbal variations, may one day enable a shift to more liberal positions, analogous to those one finds in some leading German judgments. For the time being, however, the following statements may provide a general indication of the current state of English law. Thus, in *Smith* v. *Eric S Bush; Harris* v. *Wyre Forest District Council* [1990] 1 AC 831, 865, Lord Griffiths stressed "that in cases where the advice has not been given for the specific purpose of the recipient acting upon it, it should only be in cases when the adviser knows that there is a high degree of probability that some other iden-tifiable person will act upon the advice that a duty of care should be imposed." Likewise, in *Caparo Industries Plc* v. *Dickman* [1990] 2 AC 605, 621 Lord Bridge argued that in these cases it is essential to prove

> "that the defendant knew that his statement would be communicated to the plaintiff, either as an individual or as a member of an identifiable class, specifically in connection with a particular trans-action or transactions of a particular kind (e.g. in a prospectus inviting investment) and that the plain-tiff would be very likely to rely on it for the purpose of deciding whether or not to enter upon that transaction or upon a transaction of that kind."

See, also, Lord Oliver's remarks at p. 652.

9. As a postscript one might add that inadequate consideration has been given to a point raised by Lord Justice Bingham in the *Caparo* case ([1989] QB 653, 689 *et seq.*) namely that the finding of a duty situation in such cases will by no means always lead to liability. For most claims would very likely fail (or would be settled at a very early state in the proceedings) on the grounds that no negligence can be proved or that the causation link between negligent misstatement and the loss has not been established. *Banque Financière de la Cité SA* v. *Westgate Insurance Co. Ltd.* [1991] 2 AC 249 supports this assertion though, given the paucity of case law on this point, this view in the text is only advanced as a tentative one.

Further reading

For further readings on the Common law see Franklin, (3rd edn.) 248 ff. (4th edn.) 347 ff.; Henderson and Pearson, 1129–37; Prosser, Wade, and Schwartz, 1035 ff.; Prosser in 19 *Vand. L. Rev.* 231 (1966); Craig in 92 *LQR* 213 (1976). For German law see Haller "Haftung für Rat und Auskunft", *Jura* 1997, 234; Honsell "Die Haftung für Gutachten und Auskunft unter besonderer Berücksichti-gung von Drittinteressen" in Beuthien and others (edd.) *Festschrift für Dieter Medicus* (1999) p. 211; Lammel, "Zur Auskunftshaftung", *AcP* 1979, 337; Martiny, "Pflichtenorientierter Drittschutz beim Vertrag mit Schutzwirkung für Dritte", *JZ* 1996, 19; Musielak, *Haftung für Rat, Auskunft und Gutachten* (1974); Scheerer, "Probleme der Haftung der Kreditinstitute für die Erteilung von Auskünften in Deutschland und Frankreich unter besonderer Berücksichtigung der Haftungsfreizeichnungsklauseln", *Festschrift Bärmann* (1975); Strauch "Rechtsgrundlagen der Haftung für Rat, Auskunft und Gutachten", *JuS* 1992, 897. Rich references to recent American deci-sions and the policies that lie behind them can be found in Bilek, "Accountants' Liability to the Third Party and Public Policy: A Calabresi Approach", 39 *Southwestern Law Journal* 689 (1985). See also: Achampong, "Common Law Liability of Accountants for Negligence to Non-Contractual Parties: Recent Developments" 91 *Dickinson L. Rev.* 677 (1987); Blaney, "The Citadel Falls? Liability for Accountants in Negligence to Third Parties Absent Privity: *Credit Alliance Corp.* v. *Arthur Ander-sen and Co.*" 59 *St John's L. Rev.* 348 (1985); Casazza, "*Rosenblum Inc.* v. *Adler*: CPA's Liability at Common Law to Certain Reasonably Foreseeable Third Parties Who Detrimentally Rely on Negligently Audited Financial Statements" 70 *Cornell L. Rev.* 335 (1985); Davies, "The Liability of

Auditors to Third Parties in Negligence" 14 *University of N.S. Wales Law Journal* 171 (1991); Chapman, "Limited Auditors' Liability: Economic Analysis and the Theory of Tort Law" 20 *Canadian Business Law Journal* 180 (1992); Nicholson, "Third Party Reliance on Negligent Advice" (1991) 40 *ICLQ,* 551; Gormley, "The Foreseen, the Foreseeable, and Beyond: Accountants' Liability to Non-clients" 14 *Seton Hall L. Rev.* 528 (1984); Pace, "Negligent Misrepresentation and the Certified Public Accountant: An Overview of Common Law Liability to Third Parties" 18 *Suffolk Univ. L. Rev.* 431 (1984); Causey, "Accountants' Liability in an Indeterminate Amount for an Indeterminate Time to an Indeterminate Class" 57 *Miss. LJ* 379 (1987); see, also, Whittaker, "Privity of Contract and the Tort of Negligence", 16 *OJLS* 191 (1996).

10. As has been suggested in Chap. 2 A (d) (iii), the different points of departure of German and English law are linked to the understanding of the doctrine of consideration in England (but not the USA). This has led to a "rigid" contract law which, in turn, has encouraged the expansion of tort law in order to meet new legal challenges, less known in the nineteenth century, such as product liability, liability for negligent statements and the like. In Germany the legal pressures were in the reverse. Strict if not rigidly conceived tort provisions (e.g. § 823 I BGB, § 831 etc) have meant that the pressure to meet the very same challenges had to be applied to the inherently more pliable law of contract since German tort law could not meet them. (On this see Markesinis (1987) 103 *LQR* 354; as late as 1993 Fleming arrived at a similar conclusion, (1993) 5 *Canterbury L Rev* 269, 279.) More recent developments require that the above picture be now modified, at any rate as far as English law is concerned. For, despite the fact that as we have seen some academic commentators would favour an extra-contractual approach to the problem of professional negligence, the BGH does not seem to be inclined to abandon the contractual analyses. But in recent years, English law has seen two remarkable developments that have a considerable potential to boost contract law and open new routes of recovery which might diminish the need to resort to the tort of negligence in the field of economic loss.

The first check on the expansion of tort law has come about with the adoption of the Contracts (Rights of Third Parties) Act 1999 (extracts of which are reproduced as *Addendum 2*) which implemented the long-standing proposals of the Law Commission. (See, Law Com No. 242 (1996).) With the new Act, much of the criticised rigidity of the English law of contract has disappeared. This, of course, does not mean that the recognition of contracts for the benefit of a third party will bring about the abolition of the rule that a third party cannot, generally speaking, derive rights from the contract. German law, which has known this institution for a long time now, proves as much. But it does mean that the 1999 Act adds another and wide-ranging exception to the privity doctrine even if it does not replace it with a different general rule. (See Treitel *Law of Contract* (10th edn. 1999) p. 600.) The doctrine of privity or, to use the German term "relativity of contract", will thus continue to apply "to prevent strangers from enforcing a contract." (Flannigan (1987) 103 *LQR* 564.) But the effect of importing the concept of a contract for the benefit of a third party into English law will be to allow a third party whom the original parties *intended* to benefit from their agreement to enforce such an agreement. The question, therefore, arises whether the Act will enable the range of claimants who previously resorted to tort remedies to base henceforth their claims on the new Act rather than to try and dress them up in tort clothing.

Under the Act the third party has a *direct* remedy in contract against the promisor. At this point, comparative analysis leads one to include a word of caution. Although in Germany contracts for the benefit of a third party have long been recognised, German jurists have been compelled to develop additional techniques and devices to deal with those problems which are also the most difficult ones to slot into the "correct" category. Cases involving negligent misstatements are an example. The central provision of the English Act is its test of enforceability contained in s. 1(1). According to this section a contract is for the benefit of a third party if it purports to confer a benefit on an expressly identified (including identifiable by class) third party, s. 1(3). Under the first limb of the test, s. 1(1)(a), the parties expressly declare the contract to be one in favour of a third party. The more difficult to apply is, obviously, the second limb, s. 1(1)(b). It is interesting to note that the English Act opted for a presumption in favour of such a contract if the contract confers a benefit on a third party, a solution which was rejected by the fathers of the BGB as being too sweeping (see § 328 BGB). (See, Kötz "Rights of Third Parties" in *International Encyclopaedia of Comparative Law* Vol. VII chap. 13 (1992), p. 22.) One might be tempted therefore to conclude that the scope of application of the Act is extremely wide. However, on closer analysis one can see that this will not be the case. For the presumption is founded on a specific preconception of a classic contract for the benefit of a third party which is very similar to that presupposed by § 328 BGB. The wording is meant to convey this even if the restriction envisaged by the Commission is not an easy one. The distinction relevant to the second limb is that between "to confer" a benefit and merely being (incidentally) "of" benefit. The first situation triggers the presumption and corresponds to the classic contract for a benefit of a third party. The special feature of it is that the third party is meant to be able to enforce the contract as a whole, s. 1(5), including for instance the right to rescind a contract or, where available, to seek specific performance. In the case of negligent misstatements these considerations do not apply. In these cases the promisee is entitled to the remedies under the contract and is meant to be the only party who can do so. It is only where the service is performed negligently and causes damage to a third party that the third party might acquire a right to hold the promisor liable in damages. But this isolated interest in the performance of the contract is not sufficient to bring the negligent misstatement cases under the principles flowing from the classic contract for the benefit of a third party. This insight lies at the heart of the contract with protective effects towards third parties. The BGH, following the teachings of Professor Larenz, (*NJW* 1959, 1976) did not regard the situations in the cases reproduced above to justify the application of § 328 BGB. These provisions apply only by analogy; and as case 23 shows the analogy does not always point to the right direction either (regarding § 334 BGB which corresponds to s. 3(3)). The Commission expressly sought to exclude *White* v. *Jones* (reproduced in part as *Addendum* to case 27 below and which will be discussed in more detail in the next section, No. 7) from the application of the Act, where primary performance was not owed to the third party but where the third party was, nonetheless, affected by a defective performance of the contract (Law Com. No. 242 (1996) para. 7.17–7.52). This analysis applies mutatis mutandis to most of the negligent misstatement cases. Another indication that the Commission regarded the second limb as confined to cases where the parties intended to grant the third party "primary enforcement" is contained in para. 7.25, note 22. The commissioners stressed that the intention test did not embrace the wider German concept of a contract with protective effects towards third parties (reference to Markesinis (1987) 103 *LQR* 354). Ironically enough, as a result of these refinements of the presumption contained in s. 1(1)(b), the 1999 Act is limited in a very similar way as the German (classic) contract for the benefit of a third party. However, unlike German law, these provisions cannot be applied analogically to those situations traditionally falling under the contract with protective effects towards third parties. So the tort of negligence, as explained in cases such as *White* v. *Jones* and *Henderson* v. *Merrett* (extracts of which are reproduced below as *Addendum* to case 27), will continue to play a crucial role in establishing liability. If the second limb of the enforceability test will be constructed in the way the Commission suggests, comparative law could thus provide invaluable assistance in deciding in which circumstances a contract "confers a benefit" in a third party, i.e. the presumption is raised. (See for "typical fact situations" in which § 328 BGB applies: Kötz *International Encyclopaedia of Comparative Law* Vol. VII chap. 13 (1992) pp. 27 ff.; Lorenz "Contracts and Third-Party Rights in German and English Law" in Markesinis (ed.) *The Growing Convergence* (1994) pp. 65 ff. and Markesinis et al. *The German Law of Obligations* vol. I, pp. 261 ff.) Finally, it should be noted also that there is one clear exception from the principle that the third party is entitled to "primary performance" of the contract. The 1999 Act applies where an exclusion clause is meant to benefit a third party, then the third party can enforce this (and only this) isolated provision of the contract. The fact that this is an exception is also confirmed by the realisation that the parallel situation in German law is regarded as an instance not of the classic contract for the benefit of a third party but as one of the contract with protective effects towards third parties. (See case 57 and also notes to case 27, below.)

Further reading

Adams, Beyleveld and Brownsword, "Privity of Contract", (1997) 60 *MLR* 238; Burrows, "Reforming Privity of Contract", [1996] *LMCQL* 467; *idem*, "The Contracts (Rights of Third Parties) Act 1999 and its Implications for Commercial Contracts", [2000] *LMCQL* 540; Dean, "Removing a Blot on the Landscape", [2000] *JBL* 143; Macaulay, "Warranting Third Party Rights", [2000] *Constr LJ* 265; Roe, "Contractual Intention under s. 1(1)(b) and 1(2) of the Contracts (Rights of Third Parties) Act 1999", (2000) 63 *MLR* 887; Tettenborn, "Third Party Contracts", [1996] *JBL* 602.

11. At this juncture, a brief excursus into a related area is desirable. It deals with the reform in the area of carriage of goods by sea introduced by the Carriage of Goods by Sea Act 1992. (Within its scope of application the 1999 Act does not apply (according to s. 6(5)) to these cases, except that a third party may in reliance on s. 1 avail himself of an exclusion or limitation of liability in such a contract). One of the problems that the Act tried to address was that in some cases loss and remedy part company. Thus, while one party may have had the interest in the goods (or carried the mercantile risk), the rights under the bill of lading might lie in the hands of another. In *The Albazero* [1977] AC 774 the House of Lords favoured a contractual solution to the problem allowing, in principle, recovery of damages in a contractual action on behalf of a third party. However, the perceived drawback of this solution was that the third party could not compel the promisee to bring such an action. In the Court of Appeal in *The Aliakmon* ([1985] QB 350) Robert Goff LJ was thus persuaded to attempt to create a tort remedy based on the "principle of transferred loss". This would have enabled the third party to sue the carrier directly even though he did not have a proprietary interest in the goods or possession of them at any material time. In the House of Lords ([1986] AC 785, 817–818), Lord Brandon of Oakbrook refused to follow this line of reasoning mainly because he did not accept that there was, in this respect, a lacuna of English law. The learned judge was also suspicious of the new remedy on doctrinal grounds since, in his eyes, it amounted to a derivative action, which was contrary to its tortious nature. For the special feature of the transferred loss principle was that the liability of the carrier was "contractually flavoured" in so far as the duty owed to the third party was shaped by the underlying duty to the goods owner. This, in turn, was determined by the exclusion and limitation clauses contained in the contract of carriage as contained in or evinced by the bill of lading. In 1992 the problem was remedied by statute, Carriage of Goods by Sea Act 1992. (The main impetus for the Act, however was not the decision in *The Aliakmon* but difficulties arising from modern forms of carriage, in particular the carriage of goods in bulk. (On this see Reynolds [1986] *LMCLQ* 97). The transfer of the rights under the bill of lading was no longer dependant upon a transfer of ownership in the goods but turned on the claimant's capacity as lawful holder of the bill of lading. Thus, Lord Goff's concerns were addressed and his ingenious theory did not have to be pursued any further. Not for the time being at least.

12. The second and perhaps more significant extension of contract occurred in the context of the promisee's remedies in respect of a third party's loss. In *St. Martins Property Corporation Ltd. v. Sir Robert McAlpine Ltd.* [1994] 1 AC 85 the principle in *The Albazero* was transferred to construction law. The essence of this development is an increasingly liberal attitude towards contractual claims by which a promisee is not suing for loss sustained by himself but is seeking to recover damages on behalf of a third party. (This area of the law has, in both systems, expressly been left to the courts; see chap. 2 A 1.). The key decisions are *St. Martins, Darlington BC* v. *Wiltshier Northern Ltd.* [1995] 1 WLR 68 and, most recently, *Alfred McAlpine Construction Ltd.* v. *Panatown Ltd.* (extracts of which are reproduced as *Addendum 3*). In these cases contractual remedies were extended to cover situations where a building employer is not the owner of the development site at the time of the breach of the building contract and, as a result, (arguably) suffers no financial loss. The builder/defendant in these cases based his defence on the "no loss argument". However, the courts allowed recovery in contract of substantial damages in respect of the site owner's loss. To hold otherwise, they stressed, would mean allowing a meritorious claim to disappear into a

"legal black hole". The need for a contractual solution, or, more crucially, the very danger of the "black hole", can be traced to the change of heart by the House of Lords in *Murphy* towards the builder's liability in tort. For, prior to that case, third parties to a building contract (for instance third party purchasers) could often avail themselves of the *Anns* type of remedy and recover pure economic loss in tort. In the seminal case of *Panatown* this re-orientation towards and rediscovery of contract principles reached a new peak. For not only was the contract route to recovery reinforced; but by a majority their lordships laid the foundation for an even more flexible approach to contractual actions where the performance of a service benefits as a matter of fact a third party. This new approach lays emphasis on the fact that a building employer is entitled to substantial damages because he does not get what he bargained for, whether or not he suffered a financial loss as a result of the breach. (See Lord Griffiths' speech in *St. Martins*, Beale (1995) 9 *Journal of Contract Law* 104 and Coote [1997] CLJ 537) It also brings English contract law closer to the typical features of German contract law. In the present context it is, of course, impossible to appreciate fully the impact of this remarkable decision. (For details of this development see Cartwright (1996) 10 *Journal of Contract Law* 244; Coote (2001) 117 *LQR* 81; Treitel (1998) 114 *LQR* 527 and Wallace (1999) 115 *LQR* 394). A few remarks, however, may help bring out more clearly our comparative observations and explore some future developments.

There is little doubt that the *Panatown* line of cases re-opens contractual avenues in the area of construction law. For they enable promisees to recover substantial damages even though they were not the owners of the development site at any material time and, arguably, did not suffer a financial loss as a result of the breach. Whether this remedy is more satisfactorily analysed as a remedy whereby one recovers a third party's loss (or his own) cannot be decided here. For this depends on a series of intricate points such as the promisee's accountability to the third party, the relevance of direct third party rights, and so forth. Suffice it, however, to say that a majority in *Panatown* denied recovery of damages on both grounds where the third party could sue himself, regardless of the theoretical basis of the promisee's remedy. In the present instance, the building owner could have sued on the basis of a so-called duty of care deed. This result seems somewhat harsh. For that limited, direct right of action was merely meant to fill the gap left by *Murphy* and provide protection to subsequent purchasers or tenants (*cf.* Lewis (1997) 13 *Constr LJ* 305) but arguably not to substitute liability under the building contract itself. (*Cf.* Lords Millett and Goff dissents). *St. Martins* also presents an ironical twist. For Lord Clyde saw it as an example of Lord Goff' theory of "transferred loss" (at p. 529). The latter, however, though the inventor of the theory (in *The Aliakmon*), and user of it in *White* v. *Jones* ([1995] 2 AC 207,267) in relation to the construction cases (*St. Martins*), abandoned it in *Panatown* in the belief that he had not used the term with "any great accuracy". (See, p. 557.) One wonders, however, whether the principle of transferred loss should be discarded without more since it performs a useful function. (See, Unberath (1999) 115 *LQR* 535.) Moreover, this "retreat" from the principle of transferred loss is all the more regrettable as that principle shows similarities to the German concept of *Drittschadensliquidation*, at least in so far as its function is concerned. Thus, contrary to Lord Goff's pessimistic statement that "the concept is not an easy one for a common lawyer to grasp", it enhances the comparability of the positions adopted in the two jurisdictions. Lord Goff had himself emphasised this extra judicially (*The Gradual Convergence* (Ed. B Markesinis) (1994) at pp. 129 f.). His hesitation to base his decision on a concept that allowed recovery of third party loss must however be understood in the light of his overall strategy in the latter case. Lord Goff preferred to explain the promisee's remedy as being founded on loss suffered by himself rather than the building owner. The employer did not get what he bargained for: a building according to the specifications of the contract. It would be "absurd" if he could not recover substantial damages (measured by the cost of cure) as a result. Thus Lord Goff followed the direction indicated by Lord Griffiths in *St. Martins*. Seen in this light, his reluctance to adhere to a principle "invented" by him in *The Aliakmon* for taking care of third party losses, was understandable.

13. In any event, the solution favoured by Lord Goff is not far removed from the German approach, as the learned Lord was ready to admit. For he pointed out that the rights of a building

employer under §§ 633–639 BGB were vested in the customer and that there was no indication that the situation was different if a third party owned the property on which the work was done. Certainly the right to have the defect remedied by the builder, restitution *in lieu* of termination, price reduction are not dependent upon the building employer having sustained a financial loss as a result of a defective performance. (The position is more difficult to ascertain in relation to the right to recover damages.) Thus far then we can indeed observe that the solutions of the two systems coincide. There is only a conceptual difference in that the employer's right is according to Lord Goff framed in terms of a right to substantial damages measured by the cost of cure while the rights mentioned above are not rights which entitle the promisee to recover damages, especially the right to have the defect cured is a variant of specific performance. The rationale behind this approach has been best described by Professor Treitel in the *International Encyclopedia of Comparative Law* Vol. VII chap. 16 (1976) p. 6 as the concept of "enforced performance". From this point of view Lord Goff's approach constitutes a remarkable step towards protecting the right to the performance of a contract and a departure from a mere loss focussed theory of contractual remedies. In respect of the right to recover damages for defective performance the position of German law is more difficult to ascertain. It should be noted however that German courts also allow recovery of damages in respect of a third party's loss (the site owner) in contract. Cases 25 and 26 illustrate this point. Case 25 first of all shows that such claims by a promisee on behalf of a third party are meant to enable the promisee to enforce the contract and therefore are not excluded by a direct right in tort. One might add for the sake of completeness that in carriage of goods (by land) situations German law combines the contract for the benefit of a third party with third party loss recovery and as a consequence allows recovery of damages on behalf of a third party even if the third party has a direct action in contract (§ 421 HGB; *cf*. Basedow *Münchener Kommentar zum HGB* vol. 7 (1997) § 429 Rn. 52; Herber *NJW* 1999, 3297, 3302; Helm *Haftung für Schäden an Fracht-gütern* (1966) 164). Case 26 suggests that even though German law follows the principle accurately described as enforced performance it is sometimes nevertheless necessary to allow recovery of damages in respect of a third party's loss, for instance in the case at hand as far as consequential loss is concerned. We can note that overall German law is characterised by a great degree of flexibility with regard to the rights of a promisee to enforce the contract but also regarding recovery of third party loss. One caveat must be added. The concept of *Drittschadensliquidation* is confined to particular types of situations and is not freely available to third party claimants (see cases 13 and 61 which contain guidelines as to when it is available, and pp. 64 ff.). It has for instance not been applied to problems of product liability or the negligent misstatements situations discussed above, for they do not involve a transfer of a loss to a different person than the contracting party but increase the risk of liability: the product or the statement might cause loss to the contracting party but also to a *per se* indeterminate number of third parties. Therefore, additional controlling factors are necessary which reasonably limit liability and which are not and cannot be provided by the more limited and special principle of transferred loss (see notes 1–5 above).

Finally, it is important to stress that Lord Clyde, as well, drew comparisons with German law. He referred to German law in order to underline that the concept of a contract for the benefit of a third party may provide a satisfactory solution in certain so-called "homely" examples, for instance in the notorious *Jackson v. Horizon Holidays Ltd.* [1975] 1 *WLR* 1468 situation. (*Cf*. Law Com. No. 242 (1996) para. 7.40). Lord Clyde's comments must be welcomed. For English law, after its over due abolition of the traditional doctrine of privity can benefit from the experience that German law has gained by working on this concept over many decades. (*Cf*. Steyn's LJ, strongly expressed dissatisfaction with the traditional doctrine of privity in *Darlington BC* v. *Wiltshier Northern Ltd.* [1995] 1 *WLR* 68, 76).

14. So let us conclude by returning to our starting point, namely to the interrelation between economic loss and contract. These two developments in contemporary English law—the privity reform and the increased availability of contractual remedies where third parties are affected by the defective performance of a contract for the performance of a service—reveal an important reversal. (Especially if compared with the pre-*Murphy* v. *Brentwood District Council* [1991] 1 AC 398

state of affairs.) The conservative approach to economic loss in that case has been weighed down by an unforeseen extension of contractual devices. This interrelationship between contract and tort (in the area of economic loss) is reinforced more specifically by the observation that the extension in the area of construction was prompted by the change of approach to economic loss in *Murphy*, itself.

However, one should bear in mind that the thesis of an expanding tort law before *Murphy* and an expanding contract law after *Murphy* have to be understood as mere generalisations of a general trend to which well-established exceptions existed and continue to exist. First, as far the period before *Murphy* is concerned, it is crucial to note that in the area of carriage of goods the "primacy" of contract was not successfully challenged. The attempt by Lord Goff in *The Aliakmon* to establish a limited exception to the exclusion of economic loss for a case of relational economic loss was not followed by the House of Lords in the light of the already existing flexibility of contractual solutions. Against this background the recent construction cases appear merely as a natural development, as a rediscovery of the already developed flexibility of contractual remedies in the area of shipping law. Secondly, the contractual solutions developed by English law do not seem to be available to litigants in the area of negligent misstatements; in as much the existing tort law approach founded on *Hedley Byrne* retains its importance. The Contracts (Rights of Third Parties) Act 1999 will, likewise, rarely apply to *Hedley Byrne* situations. The other contractual device, the rule in *The Albazero*, will also be of limited assistance, as was suggested in *White* v. *Jones* which will be discussed in more detail in the next part. *White* v. *Jones* is, itself, typical of the pre-*Murphy* period in that the tort solution adopted in that case was preceded by an extensive discussion of the inadequacy of contractual remedies. There is thus room for further expansion and, more importantly, creative comparative thinking.

Addendum 1

Extracts from *Caparo Industries Plc* v. *Dickman*, House of Lords [1990] 2 AC 605

LORD BRIDGE OF HARWICH [After considering the general approach to the duty of care, his Lordship continued:]

The damage which may be caused by the negligently spoken or written word will normally be confined to economic loss sustained by those who rely on the accuracy of the information or advice they receive as a basis for action. The question what, if any, duty is owed by the maker of a statement to exercise due care to ensure its accuracy arises typically in relation to statements made by a person in the exercise of his calling or profession. In advising the client who employs him the professional man owes a duty to exercise that standard of skill and care appropriate to his professional status and will be liable both in contract and in tort for all losses which his client may suffer by reason of any breach of that duty. But the possibility of any duty of care being owed to third parties with whom the professional man was in no contractual relationship was for long denied because of the wrong turning taken by the law in *Le Lievre* v. *Gould* [1893] 1 QB 491 in overruling *Cann* v. *Wilson* (1888) 39 Chap. D 39. In *Candler* v. *Crane Christmas &Co* [1951] 2 KB 164 Denning J, in his dissenting judgment, made a valiant attempt to correct the error. But it was not until the decision of this House in *Hedley Byrne & Co Ltd* v. *Heller & Partners Ltd* [1964] AC 465 that the law was once more set on the right path.

[His Lordship reviewed the subsequent authorities and continued:]

The salient feature of all these cases is that the defendant giving advice or information was fully aware of the nature of the transaction which the plaintiff had in contemplation, knew that the advice or information would be communicated to him directly or indirectly and knew that it was very likely that the plaintiff would rely on that advice or information in deciding whether or not to engage in the transaction in contemplation. In these circumstances the defendant could clearly be expected, subject always to the effect of any disclaimer of responsibility, specifically to anticipate that the plaintiff would rely on the advice or information given by the defendant for the very purpose for which he did in the event rely on it. So also the plaintiff, subject again to the effect of any disclaimer, would in that situation reasonably suppose that he was entitled to rely on the advice or information communicated to him for the very purpose for which he required it. The situation is entirely different where a statement is put into more or less general circulation and may foreseeably be relied on by strangers to the maker of the statement for any one of a variety of different purposes which the maker of the statement has no specific reason to anticipate. To hold the maker of the statement to be under a duty of care in respect of the accuracy of the statement to all and sundry for any purpose for which they may choose to rely on it is not only to subject him, in the classic words of Cardozo CJ, to "liability in an indeterminate amount for an indeterminate time to an indeterminate class" (see *Ultramares Corp.* v. *Touche* (1931) 255 NY 170 at 179), it is also to confer on the world at large a quite unwarranted entitlement to appropriate for their own purposes the benefit of the expert knowledge or professional expertise attributed to the maker of the statement. Hence, looking only at the circumstances of these decided cases where a duty of care in respect of negligent statements has been held to exist, I should expect to find that the "limit or control mechanism . . . imposed on the liability of a wrongdoer towards those who have suffered economic damage in consequence of his negligence" (see the *Candlewood* case [1986] AC 1 at 25) rested on the necessity to prove in this category of the tort of negligence, as an essential ingredient of the "proximity" between the plaintiff and the defendant, that the defendant knew that his statement would be communicated to the plaintiff, either as an individual or as a member of an identifiable class, specifically in connection with a particular transaction or transactions of a particular kind (e.g. in a prospectus inviting investment) and that the plaintiff would be very likely to rely on it for the purpose of deciding whether or not to enter on that transaction or on a transaction of that kind. . . .

[His Lordship reviewed other authorities, and then considered the position of auditors in relation to the shareholders of a public limited company arising from the provisions of the Companies Act 1985.]

No doubt these provisions establish a relationship between the auditors and the shareholders of a company on which the shareholder is entitled to rely for the protection of his interest. But the crucial question concerns the extent of the shareholder's interest which the auditor has a duty to protect. The shareholders of a company have a collective interest in the company's proper management and in so far as a negligent failure of the auditor to report accurately on the state of the company's finances deprives the shareholders of the opportunity to exercise their client powers in general meeting to call the directors to book and to ensure that errors in of skill management are corrected, the shareholders ought to be entitled to a remedy. But in practice no problem arises in this regard since the interest of the shareholders in the proper management of the company's affairs is indistinguishable from the interest of the company itself and any loss suffered by the shareholders, e.g. by the negligent failure of the auditor to discover and expose a misappropriation of funds by a director of the company, will be recouped by a claim against the auditor in the name of the company, not by individual shareholders.

I find it difficult to visualise a situation arising in the real world in which the individual shareholder could claim to have sustained a loss in respect of his existing shareholding referable to the negligence of the auditor which could not be recouped by the company. But on this part of the case your Lordships were much pressed with the argument that such a loss might occur by a negligent undervaluation of the company's assets in the auditor's report relied on by the individual shareholder in knew deciding to sell his shares at an undervalue. The argument then runs thus. The shareholder, qua shareholder, is entitled to rely on the auditor's report as the basis of his investment decision to sell his existing shareholding. If he sells at an undervalue he is entitled to recover the loss from the auditor. There can be no distinction in law effect between the shareholder's investment decision to sell the shares he has or to buy would additional shares. It follows, therefore, that the scope of the duty of care owed to se for him by the auditor extends to cover any loss sustained consequent on the purchase of additional shares in reliance on the auditor's negligent report.

I believe this argument to be fallacious. Assuming without deciding that a claim by a shareholder to recover a loss suffered by selling his shares at an undervalue attributable to an undervaluation of the company's assets in the auditor's report could be sustained at all, it would not be by reason of any reliance by the shareholder on the of the auditor's report in deciding to sell: the loss would be referable to the depreciatory effect of the report on the market value of the shares before ever the decision of the sundry shareholder to sell was taken. A claim to recoup a loss alleged to flow from the purchase urn, in of overvalued shares, on the other hand, can only be sustained on the basis of the for an purchaser's reliance on the report. The specious equation of "investment decisions" to sell or to buy as giving rise to parallel claims thus appears to me to be untenable. Moreover, the loss in the case of the sale would be of a loss of part of the value of the shareholder's existing holding, which, assuming a duty of care owed to individual shareholders, it might sensibly lie within the scope of the auditor's duty to protect. A loss, on the other hand, resulting from the purchase of additional shares would result from a wholly independent transaction having no connection with the existing shareholding.

I believe it is this last distinction which is of critical importance and which prove demonstrates the unsoundness of the conclusion reached by the majority of the Court of Appeal. It is never sufficient to ask simply whether A owes B a duty of care. It is always necessary to determine the scope of the duty by reference to the kind of damage from which A must take care to save B harmless:

"The question is always whether the defendant was under a duty to avoid or prevent that damage, but the actual nature of the damage suffered is relevant to the existence and extent of any duty to avoid or prevent it."

See *Sutherland Shire Council* v. *Heyman* (1985) 60 ALR 1 at 48 per Brennan J.

Assuming for the purpose of the argument that the relationship between the auditor of a company and individual shareholders is of sufficient proximity to give rise to a duty of care, I do not understand how the scope of that duty can possibly extend beyond the protection of any individual shareholder from losses in the value of the shares which he holds. As a purchaser of additional shares in reliance on the auditor's report, he stands in no different position from any other investing member of the public to whom the auditor owes no duty.

I would allow the appeal and dismiss the cross-appeal.

LORD OLIVER OF AYLMERTON: [After considering the general approach to the duty of care, his Lordship said:]

What can be deduced from the *Hedley Byrne* case . . . is that the necessary relationship between the maker of a statement or giver of advice (the adviser) and the recipient who acts in reliance on it (the advisee) may typically be held to exist where (1) the advice is required for a purpose, whether particularly specified or generally described, which is made known, either actually or inferentially, to the adviser at the time when the advice is given, (2) the adviser knows, either actually or inferentially, that his advice will be communicated to the advisee, either specifically or as a member of an ascertainable class, in order that it should be used by the advisee for that purpose, (3) it is known, either actually or inferentially, that the advice so communicated is likely to be acted on by the advisee for that purpose without independent inquiry and (4) it is so acted on by the advisee to his detriment. That is not, of course, to suggest that these conditions are either conclusive or exclusive, but merely that the actual decision in the case does not warrant any broader propositions. . . . My Lords, no decision of this House has gone further than *Smith* v. *Eric S Bush*, but your Lordships are asked by Caparo to widen the area of responsibility even beyond the limits to which it was extended by the Court of Appeal in this case and to find a relationship of proximity between the adviser and third parties to whose attention the advice may come in circumstances in which the reliance said to have given rise to the loss is strictly unrelated either to the intended recipient or to the purpose for which the advice was required. My Lords, I discern no pressing reason of policy which would require such an extension and there seems to me to be powerful reasons against it. As Lord Reid observed in the course of his speech in the *Hedley Byrne* case [1964] AC 465 at 483, words can be broadcast with or without the consent or foresight of the speaker or writer; and in his speech in the same case Lord Pearce drew attention to the necessity for the imposition of some discernible limits to liability in such cases. . . .

In seeking to ascertain whether there should be imposed on the adviser a duty to avoid the occurrence of the kind of damage which the advisee claims to have suffered it is not, I think, sufficient to ask simply whether there existed a "closeness" between them in the sense that the advisee had a legal entitlement to receive the information on the basis of which he has acted or in the sense that the information was intended to serve his interest or to protect him. One must, I think, go further and ask, in what capacity was his interest to be served and from what was he intended to be protected? A company's annual accounts are capable of being utilised for a number of purposes and if one thinks about it is entirely foreseeable that they may be so employed. But many of such purposes have absolutely no connection with the recipient's status or capacity, whether as a shareholder, voting or non-voting, or as a debenture-holder. Before it can be concluded that the duty is imposed to protect the recipient against harm which he suffers by reason of the particular use that he chooses to make of the information which he receives, one must, I think, first ascertain the purpose for which the information is required to be given. Indeed, the paradigmatic *Donoghue* v. *Stevenson* case of a manufactured article requires, as an essential ingredient of liability, that the article has been used by the consumer in the manner in which it was intended to be used (see *Grant* v. *Australian Knitting Mills* Ltd [1936] AC 85 at 104, and *Junior Books Ltd* v. *Veitchi Co Ltd* [1983] 1 AC 520 at 549, 552). I entirely follow that if the conclusion is reached that the very purpose of providing the information is to serve as the basis for making investment decisions or giving investment advice, it is not difficult then to conclude also that the duty imposed on the adviser extends to protecting the recipient against loss occasioned by an unfortunate investment decision which is based on carelessly inaccurate information. . . .

I do not believe and I see no grounds for believing that, in enacting the statutory provisions, Parliament had in mind the provision of information for the assistance of purchasers of shares or debentures in the market, whether they be already the holders of shares or other securities or persons having no previous proprietary interest in the company. It is unnecessary to decide the point on this appeal, but I can see more force in the contention that one purpose of providing the statutory information might be to enable the recipient to exercise whatever rights he has in relation to his proprietary interest by virtue of which he receives it, by way, for instance of disposing of that interest. I can, however, see no ground for supposing that the legislature was intending to foster a market for the existing holders of shares or debentures by providing information for the purpose of enabling them to acquire such securities from other holders who might be minded to sell. . . .

In my judgment, accordingly, the purpose for which the auditors' certificate is made and published is that of providing those entitled to receive the report with information to enable them to exercise in conjunction those powers which their respective proprietary interests confer on them and not for the purposes of individual speculation with a view to profit. The same considerations as limit the existence of a duty of care also, in my judgment, limit the scope of the duty and I agree with O'Connor LJ that the duty of care is one owed to the shareholders as a body and not to individual shareholders.

To widen the scope of the duty to include loss caused to an individual by reliance on the accounts for a purpose for which they were not supplied and were not intended would be to extend it beyond the limits which are so far deducible from the decisions of this House. It is not, as I think, an extension which either logic requires or policy dictates and I, for my part, am not prepared to follow the majority of the Court of Appeal in making it. In relation to the purchase of shares of other shareholders in a company, whether in the open market or as a result of an offer made to all or a majority of the existing shareholders, I can see no sensible distinction, so far as a duty of care is concerned, between a potential purchaser who is, vis-à-vis the company, a total outsider and one who is already the holder of one or more shares. I accordingly agree with what has already fallen from my noble and learned friend Lord Bridge, and I, too, would allow the appeal and dismiss the cross-appeal.

Addendum 2

BILY v. ARTHUR YOUNG AND CO.[1]

834 P.2d 745 (Cal. 1992)

Supreme Court of California,

In Bank.

27 Aug. 1992.

LUCAS, Chief Justice.

We granted review to consider whether and to what extent an accountant's duty of care in the preparation of an independent audit of a client's financial statements extends to persons other than the client. . . .

I

Summary of Facts and Proceedings Below

This litigation emanates from the meteoric rise and equally rapid demise of Osborne Computer Corporation (hereafter the company). Founded in 1980 by entrepreneur Adam Osborne, the company manufactured the first portable personal computer for the mass market. Shipments began in 1981. By fall 1982, sales of the company's sole product, the Osborne I computer, had reached $10 million per month, making the company one of the fastest growing enterprises in the history of American business.

In late 1982, the company began planning for an early 1983 initial public offering of its stock, engaging three investment banking firms as underwriters. At the suggestion of the underwriters, the offering was postponed for several months, in part because of uncertainties caused by the company's employment of a new chief executive officer and its plans to introduce a new computer to replace the Osborne I. In order to obtain "bridge" financing needed to meet the company's capital requirements until the offering, the company issued warrants to investors in exchange for direct loans or letters of credit to secure bank loans to the company (the warrant transaction). The warrants entitled their holders to purchase blocks of the company's stock at favorable prices that were expected to yield a sizable profit if and when the public offering took place.

Plaintiffs in this case were investors in the company . . . Several plaintiffs purchased warrants from the company as part of the warrant transaction. Others purchased the common stock of the company during early 1983 . . .

The company retained defendant Arthur Young & Company (hereafter Arthur Young) . . . to perform audits and issue audit reports on its 1981 and 1982 financial statements . . . In its role as auditor, Arthur Young's responsibility was to review the annual financial statements prepared by the company's in-house accounting department, examine the books and records of the company, and issue an audit opinion on the financial statements.

Arthur Young issued unqualified or "clean" audit opinions on the company's 1981 and 1982 financial statements. Each opinion appeared on Arthur Young's letterhead, was addressed to the company, and stated in essence: (1) Arthur Young had performed an examination of the accompanying financial statements in accordance with the accounting profession's "Generally Accepted Auditing Standards" (GAAS); (2) the statements had been prepared in accordance with "Generally Accepted Accounting Principles" (GAAP); and (3) the statements "present[ed] fairly" the company's financial position. The 1981 financial statement showed a net operating loss of approximately $1 million on sales of $6 million. The 1982 financial statements included a "Consolidated Statement of Operations" which revealed a modest net operating profit of $69,000 on sales of more than $68 million. . . .

---

[1] Text abbreviated by omission of a number of paragraphs from the text of the majority judgment, most of its notes, and the text of the dissent.

II

The Audit Function in Public Accounting

Although certified public accountants (CPA's) perform a variety of services for their clients, their primary function, which is the one that most frequently generates lawsuits against them by third persons, is financial auditing. . . ." In an audit engagement, an accountant reviews financial statements prepared by a client and issues an opinion stating whether such statements fairly represent the financial status of the audited entity." (Siliciano, 86 *Mich.L.Rev.* at p. 1931.) . . .

For practical reasons of time and cost, an audit rarely, if ever, examines every accounting transaction in the records of a business. The planning and execution of an audit therefore require a high degree of professional skill and judgment. Initially, the CPA firm plans the audit by surveying the client's business operations and accounting systems and making preliminary decisions as to the scope of the audit and what methods and procedures will be used. The firm then evaluates the internal financial control systems of the client and performs compliance tests to determine whether they are functioning properly. Transactions and data are sampled, vouched for, and traced. Throughout the audit process, results are examined and procedures are reevaluated and modified to reflect discoveries made by the auditors. . . .

The end product of an audit is the audit report or opinion. The report is generally expressed in a letter addressed to the client. The body of the report refers to the specific client-prepared financial statements which are attached. In the case of the so-called "unqualified report" (of which Arthur Young's report on the company's 1982 financial statements is an example), two paragraphs are relatively standard.

In a scope paragraph, the CPA firm asserts that it has examined the accompanying financial statements in accordance with GAAS. GAAS are promulgated by the American Institute of Certified Public Accountants (AICPA), a national professional organisation of CPA's, whose membership is open to persons holding certified public accountant certificates issued by state boards of accountancy. . . .

In an opinion paragraph, the audit report generally states the CPA firm's opinion that the audited financial statements, taken as a whole, are in conformity with GAAP and present fairly in all material respects the financial position, results of operations, and changes in financial position of the client in the relevant periods. . . .

Arthur Young correctly observes that audits may be commissioned by clients for different purposes. Nonetheless, audits of financial statements and the resulting audit reports are very frequently (if not almost universally) used by businesses to establish the financial credibility of their enterprises in the perceptions of outside persons, e.g., existing and prospective investors, financial institutions, and others who extend credit to an enterprise or make risk-oriented decisions based on its economic viability. The unqualified audit report of a CPA firm, particularly one of the "Big Six," is often an admission ticket to venture capital markets-a necessary condition precedent to attracting the kind and level of outside funds essential to the client's financial growth and survival. As one commentator summarizes: "In the first instance, this unqualified opinion serves as an assurance to the client that its own perception of its financial health is valid and that its accounting systems are reliable. The audit, however, frequently plays a second major role: it assists the client in convincing third parties that it is safe to extend credit or invest in the client." (Siliciano, 86 *Mich.L.Rev.* at p. 1932.)

III

Approaches to the Problem of Auditor Liability to Third Persons

The complex nature of the audit function and its economic implications has resulted in different approaches to the question whether CPA auditors should be subjected to liability to third parties who read and rely on audit reports. Although three schools of thought are commonly recognised, there are some variations within each school and recent case law suggests a possible trend toward merger of two of the three approaches.

A substantial number of jurisdictions follow the lead of Chief Judge Cardozo's 1931 opinion for the New York Court of Appeals in *Ultramares, supra,* 174 N.E. 441, by denying recovery to third parties for auditor negligence in the absence of a third party relationship to the auditor that is "akin to privity." (See part III (A), *post.*) In contrast, a handful of jurisdictions, spurred by law review commentary, have recently allowed recovery based on negligence to third parties whose reliance on the audit report was "foreseeable." (See part III (B), *post.*)

Most jurisdictions, supported by the weight of commentary and the modern English common law decisions cited by the parties, have steered a middle course based in varying degrees on Restatement Second of Torts section 552, which generally imposes liability on suppliers of commercial information to third persons who are intended beneficiaries of the information. (See part IIIC, *post.*) Finally, the federal securities laws have also dealt with the problem by imposing auditor liability for negligence-related conduct only in connection with misstatements in publicly filed and distributed offering documents. (See part III (D), *post.*)

A. Privity of Relationship *(In this section the CJ considers the Ultramares ruling and its subsequent (slight) enlargement by the Credit Alliance case; see notes above.)*

B. Foreseeability (This section reviews the case law of those courts which have opted for the most "liberal" approach which lays great store on the notion of foreseeability. On the judicial studies, one of its greatest advocates was Judge Wiener in "Common Law Liability of the Certified Public Accountant for Negligence Misrepresentation, 20 *San Diego L. Rev.* 233.)

C. The Restatement: Intent to Benefit Third Persons
Section 552 of the Restatement Second of Torts covers "Information Negligently Supplied for the Guidance of Others." It states a general principle that one who negligently supplies false information "for the guidance of others in their business transactions" is liable for economic loss suffered by the recipients in justifiable reliance on the information. (*Id.,* subd. (1)) But the liability created by the general principle is expressly limited to loss suffered: "(a) [B]y the person or one of a limited group of persons for whose benefit and guidance he intends to supply the information or knows that the recipient intends to supply it; and (b) [T]hrough reliance upon it in a transaction that he intends the information to influence or knows that the recipient so intends or in a substantially similar transaction." (*Id.,* subd. (2).) To paraphrase, a supplier of information is liable for negligence to a third party only if he or she intends to supply the information for the benefit of one or more third parties in a specific transaction or type of transaction identified to the supplier. . . .

Although the parties debate precisely how many states follow the Restatement rule, a review of the cases reveals the rule has somewhat more support than the privity of relationship rule and much more support than the foreseeability rule. At least 17 state and federal decisions have endorsed the rule in this and related contexts.[2] Whatever the exact number of states that have endorsed it, the Restatement rule has been for many, if not most, courts a satisfactory compromise between

---

[2] *Bethlehem Steel Corporation v. Ernst & Whinney* (Tenn.1991) 822 S.W.2d 592 (modified Restatement test adopted); *First Fla. Bank N.A. v. Max Mitchell & Co., supra,* 558 So.2d 9; *Badische Corp. v. Caylor* (1987) 257 Ga. 131, 356 S.E.2d 198; *Pahre v. Auditor of State* (Iowa 1988) 422 N.W.2d 178; *Law Offices of Lawrence J. Stockler, P.C. v. Rose* (1989) 174 Mich.App. 14, 436 N.W.2d 70, 81–82, leave to appeal denied, 434 Mich. 862 (1990); *Bonhiver v. Graff* (1976) 311 Minn. 111, 248 N.W.2d 291; *Aluma Kraft Mfg. Co. v. Elmer Fox & Co.* (Mo.Ct.App.1973) 493 S.W.2d 378; *Thayer v. Hicks* (1990) 243 Mont. 138, 793 P.2d 784; *Spherex Inc. v. Alexander Grant & Co.* (1982) 122 N.H. 898, 451 A.2d 1308; *Raritan River Steel Co. v. Cherty, supra,* 367 S.E.2d 609; *Haddon View Inv. Co. v. Coopers & Lybrand* (1982) 70 Ohio St.2d 154, 436 N.E.2d 212; *Shatterproof Glass Corp. v. James* (Tex.Civ.App.1971) 466 S.W.2d 873; *Haberman v. Pub. Power Supply Sys., supra,* 744 P.2d 1032; *First Nat7 Bank v. Crawford, supra,* 386 S.E.2d 310; *First Nat'l Bank of Commerce v. Monco Agency Inc., supra,* 911 F.2d 1053 (Louisiana law); *Ingram Indus., Inc. v. Nowicki* (E.D.Ky. 1981) 527 F.Supp. 683 (Kentucky law); *Bunge v. Eide* (D.N.D.1974) 372 F.Supp. 1058; *Rusch Factors, Inc. v. Levin* (D.R.I.1968) 284 F.Supp. 85 (Rhode Island law).

their discomfort with the traditional privity approach and the "specter of unlimited liability." (*Briggs* v. *Sterner* (S.D.Iowa 1981) 529 F.Supp. 1155, 1177.)

In attempting to ascertain the presence of an intent to benefit third parties from the facts of particular audit engagements and communications with auditors, the Restatement rule inevitably results in some degree of uncertainty. Dean William L Prosser, the Reporter for the Restatement, reflected on the difficulty of formulating a comprehensive rule in this area: "The problem is to find language which will eliminate liability to the very large class of persons whom almost any negligently given information may foreseeably reach and influence, and limit the liability, not to a particular plaintiff defined in advance, but to the comparatively small group whom the defendant expects and intends to influence. Neither the Reporter, nor, it is believed, the Advisers nor the Council, is entirely satisfied with the language of Subsection (2); and if anyone can do better, it will be most welcome." (Rest.2d Torts, Tent. Draft No. 11 (Apr. 15, 1965) § 552, p. 56.)

D. Federal Securities Law (This section reviews the additional ground of liability under Federal legislation for fraud or gross negligence.)

IV

Analysis of Auditor's Liability to Third Persons for Audit Opinions

"Every person is bound, without contract, to abstain from injuring the person or property of another, or infringing upon any of his rights." (Civ.Code, § 1708; all further statutory references are to this code unless otherwise indicated.) Civil liability for injury to others is imposed based on causes of action in tort, which include, insofar as relevant to this case: negligence, negligent misrepresentation, and fraud. . . .

A. Negligence
The threshold element of a cause of action for negligence is the existence of a duty to use due care toward an interest of another that enjoys legal protection against unintentional invasion. (Rest.2d Torts, § 281, subd. (a); 6 Witkin, Summary of Cal. Law (9th ed. 1988), Torts, § 732, p. 60.) Whether this essential prerequisite to a negligence cause of action has been satisfied in a particular case is a question of law to be resolved by the court. (6 Witkin, *supra*, § 748 at p. 83.)

A judicial conclusion that a duty is present or absent is merely " 'a shorthand statement . . . rather than an aid to analysis. . . . '[D]uty,' is not sacrosanct in itself, but only an expression of the sum total of those considerations of policy which lead the law to say that the particular plaintiff is entitled to protection.'" (*Dillon* v. *Legg* (1968) 68 Cal.2d 728, 734, 69 Cal.Rptr. 72, 441 P.2d 912, quoting Prosser, Law of Torts (3d ed.) pp. 332–333.) . . .

We have employed a checklist of factors to consider in assessing legal duty in the absence of privity of contract between a plaintiff and a defendant. In *Biakanja* v. *Irving* (1958) 49 Cal.2d 647, 320 P.2d 16, a notary public undertook to prepare a will for the decedent and then negligently failed to have it properly attested. We allowed the decedent's brother, the sole beneficiary under the will, to recover from the notary public. In permitting negligence liability to be imposed in the absence of privity, we outlined the factors to be considered in making such a decision: . . . (Id. 49 Cal.2d 647 at pp. 650–651, 320 P.2d 16.) . . .

Viewing the problem before us in light of the factors set forth above, we decline to permit all merely foreseeable third party users of audit reports to sue the auditor on a theory of professional negligence. Our holding is premised on three central concerns: (1) Given the secondary "watch-dog" role of the auditor, the complexity of the professional opinions rendered in audit reports, and the difficult and potentially tenuous causal relationships between audit reports and economic losses from investment and credit decisions, the auditor exposed to negligence claims from all foresee-able third parties faces potential liability far out of proportion to its fault; (2) The generally more sophisticated class of plaintiffs in auditor liability cases (e.g., business lenders and investors) permits the effective use of contract rather than tort liability to control and adjust the relevant risks through "private ordering"; and (3) The asserted advantages of more accurate auditing and more efficient loss spreading relied upon by those who advocate a pure foreseeability approach are unlikely to occur; indeed, dislocations of resources, including increased expense and decreased availability of auditing services in some sectors of the economy, are more probable consequences of expanded liability.

In a broad sense, economic injury to lenders, investors, and others who may read and rely on audit reports is certainly "foreseeable." Foreseeability of injury, however, is but one factor to be considered in the imposition of negligence liability. Even when foreseeability was present, we have on several recent occasions declined to allow recovery on a negligence theory when damage awards threatened to impose liability out of proportion to fault or to promote virtually unlimited responsibility for intangible injury.

In placing explicit limits on recovery for negligent infliction of emotional distress by accident bystanders, we commented: "'[Foreseeability'. . . 'is endless because [it], like light, travels indefinitely in a vacuum.'" (*Thing* v. *La Chusa* (1989) 48 Cal.3d 644, 659, 257 Cal.Rptr. 865, 771 P.2d 814.) "'[It] proves too much. . . . Although it may set tolerable limits for most types of physical harm, it provides virtually no limit on liability for nonphysical harm.' . . . It is apparent that reliance on foreseeability of injury alone in finding a duty, and thus a right to recover, is not adequate when the damages sought are for an intangible injury. In order to avoid limitless liability out of all proportion to the degree of a defendant's negligence, and against which it is impossible to insure without imposing unacceptable costs on those among whom the risk is spread, the right to recover for negligently caused emotional distress must be limited." (Id. at pp. 663–664, 257 Cal.Rptr. 865, 771 P.2d 814, citations omitted.)

Emphasising the important role of policy factors in determining negligence, we observed that "there are clear judicial days on which a court can foresee forever and thus determine liability but none on which that foresight alone provides a socially and judicially acceptable limit on recovery of damages for [an] injury." (*Thing* v. *La Chusa, supra,* 48 Cal.3d at p. 668, 257 Cal.Rptr. 865, 771 P.2d 814; see also *Nally* v. *Grace Community Church* (1988) 47 Cal.3d 278, 297, 253 Cal.Rptr. 97, 763 P.2d 948 ["Mere foreseeability of the harm or knowledge of the danger, is insufficient to create a legally cognisable special relationship giving rise to a legal duty to prevent harm."]; *Elder* v. *Sheldon* (1988) 46 Cal.3d 267, 274, 250 Cal.Rptr. 254, 758 P.2d 582 ["[P]olicy considerations may dictate a cause of action should not be sanctioned no matter how foreseeable the risk . . . for the sound reason that the consequences of a negligent act must be limited in order to avoid an intolerable burden on society."].)

In line with our recent decisions, we will not treat the mere presence of a foreseeable risk of injury to third persons as sufficient, standing alone, to impose liability for negligent conduct. We must consider other pertinent factors.

1. Liability out of proportion to fault

An auditor is a watchdog, not a bloodhound. *(In re Kingston Cotton Mill Co.* (1896) 2 Ch. 279, 28S.) As a matter of commercial reality, audits are performed in a client-controlled environment. The client typically prepares its own financial statements; it has direct control over and assumes primary responsibility for their contents. (See *In re Interstate Hosiery Mills, Inc.* (1939) 4 S.E.C. 721 ["The fundamental and primary responsibility for the accuracy [of financial statements] rests upon management,"].) The client engages the auditor, pays for the audit, and communicates with audit personnel throughout the engagement. Because the auditor cannot in the time available become an expert in the client's business and record-keeping systems, the client necessarily furnishes the information base for the audit. . . .

Client control also predominates in the dissemination of the audit report. Once the report reaches the client, the extent of its distribution and the communications that accompany it are within the exclusive province of client management, Thus, regardless of the efforts of the auditor, the client retains effective primary control of the financial reporting process.

Moreover, an audit report is not a simple statement of verifiable fact that, like the weight of the load of beans in *Glanzer* v. *Shepard, supra,* 233 N.Y. 236, 135 N.E. 275, can be easily checked against uniform standards of indisputable accuracy. Rather, an audit report is a professional opinion based on numerous and complex factors. . . .

2. *The prospect of private ordering*

Courts advocating unlimited auditor liability to all foreseeably injured third parties often analogise the auditor's opinion to a consumer product, arguing that the demise of privity as a barrier to recovery for negligence in product manufacture implies its irrelevance in the area of auditor liability as well. (See, e.g., *Rosenblum* v. *Adler, supra,* 461 A.2d at pp. 145–147.) Plaintiffs advance similar arguments. The analogy lacks persuasive force for two reasons. Initially, as noted above, the maker of a consumer product has complete control over the design and manufacture of its product; in contrast, the auditor merely expresses an opinion about its client's financial statements—the client is primarily responsible for the content of those statements in the form they reach the third party.

Moreover, the general character of the class of third parties is also different. Investors, creditors, and others who read and rely on audit reports and financial statements are not the equivalent of ordinary consumers. Like plaintiffs here, they often possess considerable sophistication in analyzing financial information and are aware from training and experience of the limits of an audit report "product" that is, at bottom, simply a broadly phrased professional opinion based on a necessarily combined examination.

In contrast to the "presumptively powerless consumer" in product liability cases, the third party in an audit negligence case has other options—he or she can "privately order" the risk of inaccurate financial reporting by contractual arrangements with the client. (Siliciano, *86 Mich.L.Rev.* at pp. 1956–1957.) For example, a third party might expend its own resources to verify the client's financial statements or selected portions of them that were particularly material to its transaction with the client. Or it might commission its own audit or investigation, thus establishing privity between itself and an auditor or investigator to whom it could look for protection. In addition, it might bargain with the client for special security or improved terms in a credit or investment transaction. Finally, the third party could seek to bring itself within the *Glanzer* exception to *Ultramares* by insisting that an audit be conducted on its behalf or establishing direct communications with the auditor with respect to its transaction with the client. (Siliciano, *86 Mich.L.Rev.* at pp. 1956–1957.)

As a matter of economic and social policy, third parties should be encouraged to rely on their own prudence, diligence, and contracting power, as well as other informational tools. This kind of self-reliance promotes sound investment and credit practices and discourages the careless use of monetary resources. If, instead, third parties are simply permitted to recover from the auditor for mistakes in the client's financial statements, the auditor becomes, in effect, an insurer of not only the financial statements, but of bad loans and investments in general.[3]

3. *The effect on auditors of negligence liability to third persons*

Courts and commentators advocating auditor negligence liability to third parties also predict that such liability might deter auditor mistakes, promote more careful audits, and result in a more

---

[3] The dissent argues that unsophisticated third parties who rely on audit reports are left unprotected by our decision. In our view, the argument itself poses a dilemma. If a third party possesses sufficient financial sophistication to understand and appreciate the contents of audit reports (which often include complex financial data and accounting language as well as technical terms like "Generally Accepted Accounting Principles" and "Generally Accepted Auditing Standards"), he or she should also be aware of their limitations and of the alternative ways of privately ordering the relevant risks. If, on the other hand, a third party lacks the threshold knowledge to understand the audit report and its terms, he or she has no reasonable basis for reliance. In either event, there is no sound basis to extend potentially unlimited liability based on any alleged lack of sophistication.

efficient spreading of the risk of inaccurate financial statements. For example, the New Jersey Supreme Court reasoned: "The imposition of a duty to foreseeable users may cause accounting firms to engage in more thorough reviews. This might entail setting up stricter standards and applying closer supervision, which would tend to reduce the number of instances in which liability would ensue. Much of the additional cost incurred because of more thorough auditing review or increased insurance premiums would be borne by the business entity and its stockholders or its customers. . . . Accountants will also be encouraged to exercise greater care leading to greater diligence in audits." *(Rosenblum* v. *Adler, supra,* 461 A.2d at p. 152.)

We are not directed to any empirical data supporting these prognostications. From our review of the cases and commentary, we doubt that a significant and desirable improvement in audit care would result from an expanded rule of liability. Indeed, deleterious economic effects appear at least as likely to occur.

In view of the inherent dependence of the auditor on the client and the labor-intensive nature of auditing, we doubt whether audits can be done in ways that would yield significantly greater accuracy without disadvantages. (Siliciano, 86 *Mich.L.Rev.* at pp. 1963–1968.) Auditors may rationally respond to increased liability by simply reducing audit services in fledgling industries where the business failure rate is high, reasoning that they will inevitably be singled out and sued when their client goes into bankruptcy regardless of the care or detail of their audits. As a legal economist described the problem: "The deterrent effect of liability rules is the difference between the probability of incurring liability when performance meets the required standard and the probability of incurring liability when performance is below the required standard. Thus, the stronger the probability that liability will be incurred when performance is adequate, the weaker is the deterrent effect of liability rules. Why offer a higher quality product if you will be sued regardless whenever there is a precipitous decline in stock prices?" (Fischel, *The Regulation of Accounting: Some Economic Issues* (1987), 52 *Brooklyn L.Rev.* 1051. 1055.) Consistent with this reasoning, the economic result of unlimited negligence liability could just as easily be an increase in the cost and decrease in the availability of audits and audit reports with no compensating improvement in overall audit quality. (*Id.* at pp. 1055–1056; Siliciano, 86 *Mich.L.Rev.* at pp. 1960–1965.) . . .

[4] For the reasons stated above, we hold that an auditor's liability for general negligence in the conduct of an audit of its client financial statements is confined to the client i.e., the person who contracts for or engages the audit services. Other persons may not recover on a pure negligence theory.[4]

There is, however, a further narrow class of persons who, although not clients, may reasonably come to receive and rely on an audit report and whose existence constitutes a risk of audit reporting that may fairly be imposed on the auditor. Such persons are specifically intended beneficiaries of the audit report who are known to the auditor and for whose benefit it renders the audit report. While such persons may not recover on a general negligence theory, we hold they may, for the reasons stated in part IV (B) *post*, recover on a theory of negligent misrepresentation.

B. Negligent Misrepresentation

One difficulty in considering the problem before us is that neither the courts (ourselves included), the commentators, nor the authors of the Restatement Second of Torts have made clear or careful distinctions between the tort of negligence and the separate tort of negligent misrepresentation.

---

[4] In theory, there is an additional class of persons who may be the practical and legal equivalent of "clients." It is possible the audit engagement contract might expressly identify a particular third party or parties so as to make them express third party beneficiaries of the contract. Third party beneficiaries may under appropriate circumstances possess the rights of parties to the contract. (See *Martinez* v. *Socoma Companies, Inc.* (1974) 11 Cal.3d 394, 400–403, 113 Cal.Rptr. 585, 521 P.2d 841; *Outdoor Services, Inc.* v. *Pabagold, Inc.* (1986) 185 Cal. App.3d 676, 681–684, 230 Cal.Rptr. 73; see also § 1559.) This case presents no third party beneficiary issue. Arthur Young was engaged by the company to provide audit reporting to the company. No third party is identified in the engagement contract. Therefore, we have no occasion to decide whether and under what circumstances express third party beneficiaries of audit engagement contracts may recover as "clients" under our holding.

The distinction is important not only because of the different statutory bases of the two torts, but also because it has practical implications for the trial of cases in complex areas such as the one before us.

Negligent misrepresentation is a separate and distinct tort, a species of the tort of deceit. "Where the defendant makes false statements, honestly believing that they are true, but without reasonable ground for such belief, he may be liable for negligent misrepresentation, a form of deceit." (5 Witkin, Summary of Cal.Law (9th edn. 1988) Torts, § 720 at p. 819; see also § 1572, subd. 2 ["The positive assertion, in a manner not warranted by the information of the person making it, of that which is not true, though he believes it to be true"]; § 1710, subd. 2 ["The assertion, as a fact, of that which is not true, by one who has no reasonable ground for believing it to be true"].)

[6, 7] Under certain circumstances, expressions of professional opinion are treated as representations of fact. When a statement, although in the form of an opinion, is "not a casual expression of belief" but "a deliberate affirmation of the matters stated," it may be regarded as a positive assertion of fact. (*Gagne* v. *Bertran* (1954) 43 Cal.2d 481, 489, 275 P.2d 15.) Moreover, when a party possesses or holds itself out as possessing superior knowledge or special information or expertise regarding the subject matter and a plaintiff is so situated that it may reasonably rely on such supposed knowledge, information, or expertise, the defendant's representation may be treated as one of material fact. (*Gagne* v. *Bertran, supra,* 43 Cal.2d at p. 489, 275 P.2d 15; *Cohen* v. *S & S Construction Company* (1983) 151 Cal.App.3d 941, 946, 201 Cal.Rptr. 173; see also 5 Witkin, Summary of Cal.Law, *supra,* Torts § 680 at pp. 781–782; BAJI No. 12.32.) There is no dispute that Arthur Young's statements in audit opinions fall within these principles.

But the person or "class of persons entitled to rely upon the representations is restricted to those to whom or for whom the misrepresentations were made. Even though the defendant should have anticipated that the misinformation might reach others, he is not liable to them." . . .

Of the approaches we have reviewed, Restatement Second of Torts section 552, subdivision (b) is most consistent with the elements and policy foundations of the tort of negligent misrepresentation. The rule expressed there attempts to define a narrow and circumscribed class of persons to whom or for whom representations are made. In this way, it recognises commercial realities by avoiding both unlimited and uncertain liability for economic losses in cases of professional mistake and exoneration of the auditor in situations where it clearly intended to undertake the responsibility of influencing particular business transactions involving third persons. The Restatement rule thus appears to be a sensible and moderate approach to the potential consequences of imposing unlimited negligence liability which we have identified.

We recognise the rule expressed in the Restatement Second of Torts has been criticised in some quarters as vague and potentially arbitrary. In his Article advocating a foreseeability rule, Justice Wiener generally criticised the Restatement rule as resting "solely on chance considerations" and "fortuitousness" (e.g., the "state of the mind of the accountant" and the scope of his engagement) having, in his view, nothing to do with increasing the flow of accurate information. (Wiener, *supra,* 20 *San Diego L.Rev.* at p. 252.)

We respectfully disagree. In seeking to identify a specific class of persons and a transaction that the supplier of information "intends the information to influence," the authors of the Restatement Second of Torts have applied basic factors of tort liability recognised in this state and elsewhere (see *Biakanja, supra,* 49 Cal.2d 647, 320 P.2d 16). By confining what might otherwise be unlimited liability to those persons whom the engagement is designed to benefit, the Restatement rule requires that the supplier of information receive notice of potential third party claims, thereby allowing it to ascertain the potential scope of its liability and make rational decisions regarding the undertaking. The receipt of such notice justifies imposition of auditor liability for conduct that is merely negligent.

Moreover, the identification of a limited class of plaintiffs to whom the supplier itself has directed its activity establishes a closer connection between the supplier's negligent act and the recipient's injury, thereby ameliorating the otherwise difficult concerns of causation and of credible evidence of reliance. Finally, no unfairness results to those recipients who are excluded from the class of beneficiaries because they have means of private ordering—among other things, they can establish direct communication with an auditor and obtain a report for their own direct use and benefit. For these reasons, the rule expressed in the Restatement Second of Torts represents a reasoned, not an arbitrary, approach to the problem before us.

Additional criticism has been leveled at the Restatement approach because of the vagueness of its "intent to benefit" language. As we read section 552 of the Restatement Second of Torts, it does not seek to probe the state of mind of the accountant or other supplier of information. Rather, it attempts to identify those situations in which the supplier undertakes to supply information to a third party whom he or she knows is likely to rely on it in a transaction that has sufficiently specific economic parameters to permit the supplier to assess the risk of moving forward. As the authors of section 552 observe, liability should be confined to cases in which the supplier "*manifests* an intent to supply the information for the *sort of use* in which the plaintiff's loss occurs." (*Id.*, com. (a), italics added.) This follows because the "risk of liability to which the supplier subjects himself by undertaking to give the information . . . *is vitally affected by the number and character of the persons, and particularly the nature and extent of the proposed transaction.*" (*Id.*, com. (h); italics added.)

The "intent to benefit" language of the Restatement Second of Torts thus creates *an objective standard* that looks to the specific circumstances (e.g., supplier-client engagement and the supplier's communications with the third party) to ascertain whether a supplier has undertaken to inform and guide a third party with respect to *an identified transaction or type of transaction.* If such a specific undertaking has been made, liability is imposed on the supplier. If, on the other hand, the supplier "merely knows of the ever-present possibility of repetition to anyone, and the possibility of action in reliance upon [the information] on the part of anyone to whom it may be repeated," the supplier bears no legal responsibility. (Rest.2d Torts, § 552, com. (h).)

The Restatement Second of Torts approach is also the only one that achieves consistency in the law of negligent misrepresentation. Accountants are not unique in their position as suppliers of information and evaluations for the use and benefit of others. Other professionals, including attorneys, architects, engineers, title insurers and abstractors, and others also perform that function. And, like auditors, these professionals may also face suits by third persons claiming reliance on information and opinions generated in a professional capacity. . . .

By allowing recovery for negligent misrepresentation (as opposed to mere negligence), we emphasise the indispensability of justifiable reliance on the statements contained in the report. As the jury instructions in this case illustrate, a general negligence charge directs attention to defendant's level of care and compliance with professional standards established by expert testimony, as opposed to plaintiff's reliance on a materially false statement made by defendant. The reliance element in such an instruction is only implicit—it must be argued and considered by the jury as part of its evaluation of the causal relationship between defendant's conduct and plaintiff's injury. In contrast, an instruction based on the elements of negligent misrepresentation necessarily and properly focuses the jury's attention on the truth or falsity of the audit report's representations and plaintiff's actual and justifiable reliance on them. Because the audit report, not the audit itself, is the foundation of the third person's claim, negligent misrepresentation more precisely captures the gravamen of the cause of action and more clearly conveys the elements essential to a recovery. (*Garcia* v. *Superior Court, supra,* 50 Cal.3d at pp. 737, 741–744, 268 Cal.Rptr. 779, 789 P.2d 960.)[5]

[5] The dissent argues that auditors should be subject to liability to all foreseeable users of audit reports because auditors can simply insert blanket disclaimers of third party liability in their reports. We perceive no reason to require auditors to disclaim liability to unknown persons who are not intended beneficiaries of their reports in the first instance. An audit report is directed primarily to the client. In this case, Arthur Young's report was specifically addressed to: "The Board of Directors, Osborne Computer Corporation." Under the rule we adopt, if the auditor knows of a third party transaction or type of transaction which the audit report has been commissioned to influence, the report is also necessarily directed to that specific third party. Because its report is directed to no one else, an auditor need not attempt to communicate with other persons by means of a disclaimer of liability.

[9] Based on our decision, the California standard jury instructions concerning negligent misrepresentation should be amended in future auditor liability cases to permit the jury to determine whether plaintiff belongs to the class of persons to whom or for whom the representations in the audit report were made. For the guidance of trial courts, we suggest the jury be instructed on the elements of negligent misrepresentation as set forth in BAJI No. 12.45 with the addition of the following instruction in lieu of BAJI No. 12.50:

"The representation must have been made with the intent to induce plaintiff, or a particular class of persons to which plaintiff belongs, to act in reliance upon the representation in a specific transaction, or a specific type of transaction, that defendant intended to influence. Defendant is deemed to have intended to influence [its client's] transaction with plaintiff whenever defendant knows with substantial certainty that plaintiff, or the particular class of persons to which plaintiff belongs, will rely on the representation in the course of the transaction. If others become aware of the representation and act upon it, there is no liability even though defendant should reasonably have foreseen such a possibility."

Addendum 3

Extracts from the Contracts (Rights of Third Parties) Act 1999

1. (1) Subject to the provisions of this Act, a person who is not a party to a contract (a "third party") may in his own right enforce a term of the contract if—

    (a) the contract expressly provides that he may, or

    (b) subject to subsection (2), the term purports to confer a benefit on him.

(2) Subsection (1)(b) does not apply if on a proper construction of the contract it appears that the parties did not intend the term to be enforceable by the third party.

(3) The third party must be expressly identified in the contract by name, as a member of a class or as answering a particular description but need not be in existence when the contract is entered into.

(4) This section does not confer a right on a third party to enforce a term of a contract otherwise than subject to and in accordance with any other relevant terms of the contract.

(5) For the purpose of exercising his right to enforce a term of the contract, there shall be available to the third party any remedy that would have been available to him in an action for breach of contract if he had been a party to the contract (and the rules relating to damages, injunctions, specific performance and other relief shall apply accordingly).

(6) Where a term of a contract excludes or limits liability in relation to any matter references in this Act to the third party enforcing the term shall be construed as references to his availing himself of the exclusion or limitation.

(7) In this Act, in relation to a term of a contract which is enforceable by a third party—

    "the promisor" means the party to the contract against whom the term is enforceable by the third party, and

    "the promisee" means the party to the contract by whom the term is enforceable against the promisor.

2. (1) Subject to the provisions of this section, where a third party has a right under section 1 to enforce a term of the contract, the parties to the contract may not, by agreement, rescind the contract, or vary it in such a way as to extinguish or alter his entitlement under that right, without his consent if—

    (a) the third party has communicated his assent to the term to the promisor,

    (b) the promisor is aware that the third party has relied on the term, or

    (c) the promisor can reasonably be expected to have foreseen that the third party would rely on the term and the third party has in fact relied on it. . . .

3. (1) Subsections (2) to (5) apply where, in reliance on section 1, proceedings for the enforcement of a term of a contract are brought by a third party.

    (2) The promisor shall have available to him by way of defence or set-off any matter that—
        (a) arises from or in connection with the contract and is relevant to the term, and
        (b) would have been available to him by way of defence or set-off if the proceedings had been brought by the promisee.
    (3) The promisor shall also have available to him by way of defence or set-off any matter if—
        (a) an express term of the contract provides for it to be available to him in proceedings brought by the third party, and
        (b) it would have been available to him by way of defence or set-off if the proceedings had been brought by the promisee.
    (4) The promisor shall also have available to him—
        (a) by way of defence or set-off any matter, and
        (b) by way of counterclaim any matter not arising from the contract,
that would have been available to him by way of defence or set-off or, as the case may be, by way of counterclaim against the third party if the third party had been a party to the contract.
    (5) Subsections (2) and (4) are subject to any express term of the contract as to the matters that are not to be available to the promisor by way of defence, set-off or counterclaim.
    (6) Where in any proceedings brought against him a third party seeks in reliance on section 1 to enforce a term of a contract (including, in particular, a term purporting to exclude or limit liability), he may not do so if he could not have done so (whether by reason of any particular circumstances relating to him or otherwise) had he been a party to the contract.

4. Section 1 does not affect any right of the promisee to enforce any term of the contract.

5. Where under section 1 a term of a contract is enforceable by a third party, and the promisee has recovered from the promisor a sum in respect of—
    (a) the third party's loss in respect of the term, or
    (b) the expense to the promisee of making good to the third party the default of the promisor,
then, in any proceedings brought in reliance on that section by the third party, the court or arbitral tribunal shall reduce any award to the third party to such extent as it thinks appropriate to take account of the sum recovered by the promisee. . . .

7. (1) Section 1 does not affect any right or remedy of a third party that exists or is available apart from this Act. . . .

Addendum 4

Extracts from *Alfred McAlpine Construction Ltd.* v. *Panatown Ltd.* [2001] 1 AC 518

[Panatown employed McAlpine to build a building on land owned by UIPL. The work was defective. Panatown did not suffer any financial loss itself. UIPL owned the defective building, which required a significant expenditure for its repair, and was unable for a considerable period to put the building to a profitable use. Panatown sought to recover, by way of an arbitration, from McAlpine the loss which UIPL had suffered. The appeal thus concerned the circumstances in which the employer in a contract of services may claim from the contractor on the ground of breach of contract damages in respect of a loss which has been suffered by a third party. However, in addition to the contract with the employer, the building contractor, McAlpine, also entered into a duty of care deed (DCD) with the site-owner, UIPL. By that deed the owner acquired a direct remedy against the contractor in respect of any failure by the contractor to exercise reasonable skill in relation to any matter within the scope of the contractor's responsibilities under the contract. The arbitrator rejected the building contractor's objection that the employer, having suffered no loss, was not entitled to recover substantial damages under the contract. The judge reversed that ruling and the Court of Appeal restored the arbitrator's decision. The House of Lords allowed McAlpine's appeal by a majority (Lord Goff of Chieveley and Lord Millett dissenting). There were mainly two routes of recovery. Under the so-called narrow ground Panatown would recover substantial damages on behalf of the building owner. This route was somewhat problematic since in previous cases it had been suggested that if the third party can sue himself the narrow ground ceases to apply and in the present instance the building owner could have proceeded directly on the basis of the DCD. The alternative route, the so called "broader ground" would allow Panatown to recover as building employer substantial damages because it did not get what it bargained for regardless whether Panatown suffered any financial loss as a result of the defective performance, this principle had however never been unequivocally established by the House of Lords. The DCD appeared much less relevant according to this latter approach. The House of Lords was divided in several respects. Lord Clyde rejected the broad ground, Lords Goff and Millett did not apply the narrow ground, while Lord Jauncey of Tullichettle and Lord Browne-Wilkinson rested their decision on both grounds but somewhat surprisingly came to the conclusion that the availability of a direct action under the DCD also excluded the application of the broader ground.]

LORD CLYDE:

. . . The proposition which I refer to as *The Albazero* exception, as described by Lord Diplock (at p. 844), was:

> "that the consignor may recover substantial damages against the shipowner if there is privity of contract between him and the carrier for the carriage of goods; although, if the goods are not his property or at his risk, he will be accountable to the true owner for the proceeds of his judgment."

If by a special contract the goods were the property or at the risk of the consignor then the loss would be his. That indeed was recognised in *Dunlop*. The second part of the passage which I have quoted however advances beyond such a position. What is there propounded is, as was noticed by my noble and learned friend Lord Goff of Chieveley in *White* v. *Jones* [1995] 2 AC 207, 267, a case of transferred loss. This is not a situation where the loss is that of the promisee. It is a loss suffered by the third party but transferred to the promisee who is then accountable to the third party. Thus the loss becomes that of the employer instead of and in place of the third party, a point emphasised by Hannes Unberath in his recent Article in (1999) 115 *LQR* 535. The promisee is deemed to have suffered the loss so that it is he and not the third party who is able to pursue the remedy in damages.

The justification for the exception to the general rule that one can only sue for damages for a loss which he has himself suffered was explained by Lord Diplock in *The Albazero* [1977] AC 774, 847. His Lordship noted that the scope and utility of what he referred to as the rule in *Dunlop* v. *Lambert* 6 Cl. & F. 600 in its application to carriage by sea under a bill of lading had been much reduced by the passing of the Bills of Lading Act 1855 and the subsequent development of the law, but that the rule extended to all forms of carriage, including carriage by sea where there was no bill of lading:

> "and there may still be occasional cases in which the rule would provide a remedy where no other would be available to a person sustaining loss which under a rational legal system ought to be compensated by the person who has caused it."

The justification for *The Albazero* exception is thus the necessity of avoiding the disappearance of a substantial claim into what was described by Lord Stewart in *J. Dykes Ltd.* v. *Littlewoods Mail Order Stores Ltd.* 1982 S.C. (HL) 157, 166 as a legal black hole, an expression subsequently taken up by Lord Keith of Kinkel in this House at p. 177. . . .

The Albazero exception will plainly not apply where the parties contemplate that the carrier will enter into separate contracts of carriage with the later owners of the goods, identical to the contract with the consignor. Even more clearly, as Lord Diplock explained at p. 848, will the exception be excluded if other contracts of carriage are made in terms different from those in the original contract. In *The Albazero* the separate contracts which were mentioned were contracts of carriage. That is understandable in the context of carriage by sea involving a charterparty and bills of lading, but the counterpart in a building contract to a right of suit under a bill of lading should be the provision of a direct entitlement in a third party to sue the contractor in the event of a failure in the contractor's performance. In the context of a building contract one does not require to look for a second building contract to exclude the exception. It would be sufficient to find the provision of a right to sue. Thus as my noble and learned friend Lord Browne-Wilkinson observed in the *St. Martins* case [1994] 1 AC 85, 115:

> "If, pursuant to the terms of the original building contract, the contractors have undertaken liability to the ultimate purchasers to remedy defects appearing after they acquired the property, it is manifest the case will not fall within the rationale of *Dunlop* v. *Lambert* 6 Cl. & F. 600. If the ultimate purchaser is given a direct cause of action against the contractor (as is the consignee or endorsee under a bill of lading) the case falls outside the rationale of the rule."

In the *St. Martins* case the employer started off as the owner of the property and subsequently conveyed it to another company. In the present case the employer never was the owner. But that has not featured as a critical consideration in the present appeal and I do not see that that factor affects the application of the exception. . . . I have no difficulty in holding in the present case that the exception cannot apply. As part of the contractual arrangements entered into between Panatown and McAlpine there was a clear contemplation that separate contracts would be entered into by McAlpine, the contracts of the deed of duty of care and the collateral warranties. The duty of care deed and the collateral warranties were of course not in themselves building contracts. But they did form an integral part of the package of arrangements which the employer and the contractor agreed upon and in that respect should be viewed as reflecting the intentions of all the parties engaged in the arrangements that the third party should have a direct cause of action to the exclusion of any substantial claim by the employer, and accordingly that the exception should not apply. . . .

I turn accordingly to what was referred to in the argument as the broader ground. But the label requires more careful definition. The approach under *The Albazero* exception has been one of recognising an entitlement to sue by the innocent party to a contract which has been breached, where the innocent party is treated as suing on behalf of or for the benefit of some other person or persons, not parties to the contract, who have sustained loss as a result of the breach. In such a case the innocent party to the contract is bound to account to the person suffering the loss for the damages which the former has recovered for the benefit of the latter. But the so-called broader ground involves a significantly different approach. What it proposes is that the innocent party to the contract should recover damages for himself as a compensation for what is seen to be his own loss. In this context no question of accounting to anyone else arises. . . .

The loss of an expectation which is here referred to seems to me to be coming very close to a way of describing a breach of contract. A breach of contract may cause a loss, but is not in itself a loss in any meaningful sense. When one refers to a loss in the context of a breach of contract, one is in my view referring to the incidence of some personal or patrimonial damage. A loss of expectation might be a loss in the proper sense if damages were awarded for the distress or inconvenience caused by the disappointment. Professor Coote ("Contract Damages, Ruxley, and the Performance Interest" (1997) C.L.J. 537) draws a distinction between benefits in law, that is bargained-for contractual rights, and benefits in fact, that is the enjoyment of the fruits of performance. Certainly the former may constitute an asset with a commercial value. But while frustration may destroy the rights altogether so that the contract is no longer enforceable, a failure in the obligation to perform does not destroy the asset. On the contrary it remains as the necessary legal basis for a remedy. A failure in performance of a contractual obligation does not entail a loss of the bargained-for contractual rights. Those rights remain so as to enable performance of the contract to be enforced, as by an order for specific performance. . . .

At the heart of the problem is the doctrine of privity of contract which excludes the ready development of a solution along the lines of a jus quaesitum tertio. It might well be thought that such a solution would be more direct and simple. In the context of the domestic and familial situations, such as the husband instructing the repairs to the roof of his wife's house, or the holiday which results in disappointment to all the members of the family, the jus quaesitum tertio may provide a satisfactory means of redress, enabling compensation to be paid to the people who have suffered the loss. Such an approach is available in Germany see W. Lorenz "Contract Beneficiaries in German Law" in The Gradual Convergence: Foreign Ideas, Foreign Influences, and English Law on the Eve of the 21st Century ed. Markesinis (1994), pp. 65, 78, 79. It may also be available in Scotland (*Carmichael* v. *Carmichael's Executrix* 1920 S.C. (HL) 195). But we were not asked to adopt it in the present case and so radical a step cannot easily be achieved without legislative action. Since Parliament has recently made some inroad into the principle of privity but has stopped short of admitting a solution to a situation such as the present, it would plainly be inappropriate to enlarge the statutory provision by judicial innovation. The alternative has to be the adoption of what Lord Diplock in *Swain* v. *The Law Society* [1983] 1 AC 598, 611 described as a juristic subterfuge "to mitigate the effect of the lacuna resulting from the non-recognition of a jus quaesitum tertio." The solution, achieved by the operation of law, may carry with it some element of artificiality and may not be supportable on any clear or single principle. If the entitlement to sue is not to be permitted to the party who has suffered the loss, the law has to treat the person who is entitles to sue as doing so on behalf of the third party. As Lord Wilberforce observed in *Woodar Investment Development Ltd.* v. *Wimpey Construction UK Ltd.* [1980] 1 WLR 277, 283, "there are many situations of daily life which do not fit neatly into conceptual analysis, but which require some flexibility in the law of contract."

It seems to me that a more realistic and practical solution is to permit the contracting party to recover damages for the loss which he and a third party has suffered, being duly accountable to them in respect of their actual loss, than to construct a theoretical loss in law on the part of the contracting party, for which he may be under no duty to account to anyone since it is to be seen as his own loss. The solution is required where the law will not tolerate a loss caused by a breach of contract to go uncompensated through an absence of privity between the party suffering the loss and the party causing it. In such a case, to avoid the legal black hole, the law will deem the innocent party to be claiming on behalf of himself and any others who have suffered loss. It does not matter that he is not the owner of the property affected, nor that he has not himself suffered any economic loss. He sues for all the loss which has been sustained and is accountable to the others to the extent of their particular losses. While it may be that there is no necessary right in the third party to compel the innocent employer to sue the contractor, in the many cases of the domestic or familial situation that consideration should not be a realistic problem. In the commercial field, in relation to the interests of such persons as remoter future proprietors who are not related to the original employer, it may be that a solution by way of collateral warranty would still be required. If there is an anxiety lest the exception would permit an employer to receive excessive damages, that should be set at rest by the recognition of the basic requirement for reasonableness which underlies the quantification of an award of damages. . . .

LORD GOFF OF CHIEVELEY:

. . . There are, as I understand the case, essentially two questions which your Lordships have to consider: (1) whether Panatown is entitled to recover substantial damages from McAlpine in respect of the assumed breaches by McAlpine of the building contract, notwithstanding that at all material times Panatown had no proprietary interest in the site of the development; and (2) if so, whether the existence of the direct right of action by the owners of the site, UIPL, against McAlpine under the DCD precluded Panatown from recovering substantial damages from McAlpine.

I turn therefore to the first question. Here Panatown presented its case primarily on the basis of Lord Griffiths' broader ground in the *St. Martin's* case [1994] 1 AC 85; though in the alternative it was prepared, if necessary, to fall back on the rule in *Dunlop* v. *Lambert*, 6 Cl. & F. 600 as adopted by the majority of the Appellate Committee in the *St. Martin's* case. It was, however, submitted on behalf of McAlpine that it was not open to Panatown to invoke the broader ground. Its submission was that the prospect of imminent legislative reform of the privity rule, in the form of the

Contract (Rights of Third Parties) Bill already before Parliament, both removed the need for, and rendered illegitimate, any further judicial activism in the field which was subject of the appeal; and that the present case therefore fell to be decided solely on the basis of the exception to the "privity/loss rules" as laid down in the *The Albazero* [1977] AC 774, and explained and applied by Lord Browne-Wilkinson in the *St. Martin's* case. There is, I believe, little doubt that the choice by the parties of their respective grounds was largely dictated by the possible impact of the DCD upon Panatown's claim to substantial damages under the building contract. On McAlpine's approach, it was open to it to argue that, by reason of the exception identified by Lord Diplock in *The Albazero*, the existence of the DCD precluded any claim by Panatown to substantial damages for breach of the building contract; whereas, by invoking Lord Griffiths' broader ground, Panatown could at least avoid that trap, though a claim on the broader ground presented its own difficulties.

Two questions therefore arise at the threshold of the argument in this case: (1) Which is the preferable approach to the appeal? And (2) What is the impact, if any, of the imminence of statutory reform of the old privity rule? I shall now consider the first of these two questions, which is a fundamental question which lies at the heart of the case. The second question I shall postpone to a later stage.

(A) As we all know, from an early time the common law adopted a rule of privity of contract, by virtue of which only a party to the contract could enforce the contract. The rule, seen in the abstract, is rational and very understandable in a law of contract which includes the doctrine of consideration; but it has given rise to great problems in practice—because, both in commerce and in the domestic context, parties do enter into contracts which are intended to confer enforceable rights on third parties, and a rule of law which precludes a right of enforcement by a third party can therefore fail to give effect to the intention of the contracting parties and to the reasonable expectations of the third party. The existence of these problems led first of all to the recognition of a number of exceptions to the rule and ultimately, only last year, to its abolition by the Contracts (Rights of Third Parties) Act 1999.

(B) "There is, or is widely thought to be, a general rule that, where A commits a commits a breach of his contract with B, then B can recover damages only in respect of his own loss and not in respect of loss suffered by a third party, C." I adopt the words of Professor Treitel in (1998) 114 *LQR* 527, because, as I have already indicated, I share his scepticism about the existence of this "rule." Plainly it is right that a contracting party should not use the remedy of damages to recover what has been described by Oliver J (as he then was) in a notable judgment (in *Radford* v. *De Froberville* [1977] 1 WLR 1262, 1270 as "an uncovenanted profit," or indeed to impose on the other contracting party an uncovenanted burden. But if the supposed rule exists, it could deprive a contracting party of any effective remedy in the case of a contract which is intended to confer a benefit on a third party but not to confer on the third party an enforceable right. It is not surprising therefore to discover increasing concern on the part of scholars specialising in the law of contract that the supposed rule, if rigidly applied, can have the effect of depriving parties of the fulfilment of their reasonable contractual expectations, and to read of doubts on their part whether any such rule exists.

It is, I believe, important to keep these two problems distinct in our minds when addressing the basic question which arises in the present case. With this distinction in mind, let us look first of all at the rule in *Dunlop* v. *Lambert* 6 Cl. & F. 600. As Lord Diplock himself explained, this rule should be seen in context of commercial contracts concerning goods, and in particular of contracts for the carriage of goods by sea. It is a commonplace of such contracts that the goods may be shipped pursuant to a contract of sale, under which the property in the goods may pass to the consignee while the goods are in transit. However, the rule of privity of contract requires that, if the contract of carriage is (as it usually is) made between the consignor and the carrier, it can be enforced only by the consignor and not by the consignee. This creates manifest problems where the goods are lost or damaged in transit after the property in them has passed to the consignee. The rule in *Dunlop* v. *Lambert* provided a practical solution to these problems by giving the consignor the right to recover damages for such loss or damage for the benefit of the consignee, to whom he was accountable. The shortcoming of this rule must, I imagine, have been that it left the initiative with the seller, rather than with the consignee who was the person who had suffered the loss of or damage to the goods. It is not surprising, therefore, that Parliament intervened only fifteen years later, in 1855, to pass the Bills of Lading Act of that year, under section 1 of which a person to whom the property in the goods had passed upon or by reason of the consignment to him of the goods or the indorsement to him of the bill of lading acquired a direct right of action against the shipowner on the terms of the bill of lading. (The Act of 1855 has recently been repealed and replaced by the Carriage of Goods by Sea Act 1992.) The more effective remedy given by statute must have meant that the useful life of the rule in *Dunlop* v. *Lambert* was relatively short. For present purposes, however, the important point is that the function of the rule was to escape the undesirable consequences of the privity rule in a particular context, though it had the incidental effect that, if there is a rule that a party can only recover damages for breach of contract in respect of his own loss, then the rule in *Dunlop* v. *Lambert* constitutes an exception to that rule.

Let me turn next to consider in this context Lord Griffiths' broad ground in the *St. Martin's* case. It is at once plain that Lord Griffiths was not concerned with a problem of privity of contract; on the contrary, he was concerned that a contracting party who contracts for a benefit to be conferred on a third party should himself have an effective remedy. He was moreover addressing not a special problem which arises in a particular context, such as carriage of goods by sea, but a general problem which arises in many different contexts in ordinary life, notably in the domestic context where parties may frequently contract for benefits to be conferred on others, though it may well arise in other contexts, such as charitable giving or even, as the present case shows, a commercial transaction. His problem was not, therefore, privity of contract; it was the rule, or supposed rule, that a party can only recover damages in respect of his own loss.

The purpose of this analysis is to demonstrate that, in my opinion, the invocation of the rule in *Dunlop* v. *Lambert* 6 Cl. & F. 600 in the present context is, I believe, inapposite. This is because we are not here addressing a problem of privity of contract. The problem is not that UIPL had no enforceable rights against McAlpine arising under the building contract: it was the evident intention that UIPL should not have such rights, its rights against McAlpine being restricted to different rights under a separate contract, the DCD. That the rule in *Dunlop* v. *Lambert* is inapposite in the present context is illustrated in particular by the irrelevance, in this context, of any contemplation that the property of the contracting party should be transferred to a third party—a feature which was regarded by Lord Diplock as a prerequisite of the application of the rule in *Dunlop* v. *Lambert*, and was fortuitously present in the *St. Martin's* case [1994] 1 AC 85. An indication that any such prerequisite is irrelevant in the present context may be derived from the fact that, in the next case in which the *St. Martin's* case was applied, *Darlington Borough Council* v. *Wiltshier Northern Limited* [1995] 1 WLR 68, there was no such feature and yet its absence was ignored by the Court of Appeal, no doubt because they felt that it did not matter. The same applies to the judgment of the Court of Appeal in the present case. In truth, what we are concerned with here is the effectiveness of the rights conferred on Panatown under the building contract itself. . . .

It follows, in my opinion, that the principal argument advanced on behalf of McAlpine is inconsistent with authority and established principle. This conclusion may involve a fuller recognition of the importance of the protection of a contracting party's interest in the performance of his contract than has occurred in the past. But not only is it justified by authority, but the principle on which it is based is supported by a number of distinguished writers, notably Professor Brian Coote and Mr Duncan Wallace QC.

However, as I have already recorded, it was the submission of McAlpine that your Lordships should regard any such development in the law as a matter for legislation, presumably after a reference to the Law Commission. This submission was made on the basis that the Lord Chancellor had introduced into Parliament a Bill—the Contract (Rights of Third Parties) Bill, based on a Report by the Law Commission, designed to bring about a radical reform of the privity rule, and that the prospect of this imminent legislation rendered illegitimate any further judicial activism in the field which was the subject of the present appeal. That Bill is now on the statute book: see the Contracts (Rights of Third Parties) Act 1999.

I am unable to accept this submission. As I have previously explained, this case is not concerned with privity of contract. There is no question of a third party here seeking to enforce a jus quaesitus tertio—i.e., of UIPL enforcing a right arising under the contract between McAlpine and Panatown. On the contrary, the reason why Panatown contracted as employer under the building contract with McAlpine was so that UIPL, although the owner of the site, should not do so. Even if the new Act had been in force at the material time, it would not have given UIPL any right to enforce the building contract, or any provision of it, against McAlpine. . . .

Furthermore, as I have just indicated, full recognition of the importance of the performance interest will open the way to principled solution of other well-known problems in the law of contract, notably those relating to package holidays which are booked by one person for the benefit not only of himself but of others, normally members of his family (as to which see *Jackson* v. *Horizon Holidays Ltd.* [1975] 1 WLR 1468), and other cases of a similar kind referred to by Lord Wilberforce in his opinion in the *Woodar Investment* case at p. 283—cases of an everyday kind which are calling out for a sensible solution on a principled basis. Even if it is not thought, as I think, that the solution which I prefer is in accordance with existing principle, nevertheless it is surely within the scope of the type of development of the common law which, especially in the law of obligations, is habitually undertaken by appellate judges as part of their ordinary judicial function. That such developments in the law may be better left to the judges, rather than be the subject of legislation, is now recognised by the Law Commission itself, because legislation within a developing part of the common law can lead to ossification and a rigid segregation of legal principle which disfigures the law and impedes future development of legal principle on a coherent basis. It comes as no surprise therefore that, in its Report on "Privity of Contract: Contracts for the Benefit of Third Parties, (1996) (Law Com. No. 242) para. 5.15, the Law Commission declined to make specific recommendations in relation to the promisee's remedies in a contract for the benefit of a third party (here referring to *The Albazero* [1977] AC 774 and *Linden Gardens Trust Ltd.* v. *Lenesta Sludge Disposals Ltd.* (the St. Martin's case) [1994] 1 AC 85 as cases in which "the courts have gone a considerable way towards developing rules which in many appropriate cases do allow the promisee to recover damages on behalf of the third party"), and stated that the Commission "certainly . . . would not wish to forestall further judicial development of this area of the law of damages." This certainly does not sound like a warning to judicial trespassers to keep out of forbidden territory; see also para. 11. 22, concerned with the problem of double liability—which I shall have to consider at a later stage.

The present case provides, in my opinion, a classic example of a case which falls properly within the judicial province. I, for my part, have therefore no doubt that it is desirable, indeed essential, that the problem in the present case should be the subject of judicial solution by providing proper recognition of the plaintiff's interest in the performance of the contractual obligations which are owed to him. I cannot see why the proposed statutory reform of the old doctrine of privity of contract should inhibit the ordinary judicial function, and so prevent your Lordships' House from doing justice between the parties in the present case. As I have said, the principal function of this submission of McAlpine appears to have been to restrict the argument of Panatown to the narrower ground in *Dunlop* v. *Lambert* 6 Cl. & F. 600 and by so doing to enable McAlpine to argue that, on that basis, the cause of action by Panatown under the building contract was excluded by the separate contractual right afforded to the building owner, UIPL, under the DCD. That is a matter which I will have to address when I come to consider the second issue in the case. . . .

Your Lordships were assisted by a presentation by Mr Jeremy Nicholson, junior counsel for Panatown, on the applicable German law, for which I was grateful. This was founded upon advice received from Hannes Unberath, recently a graduate student at Worcester College, Oxford, and the author of an interesting case note on the present case in the Law Quarterly Review: see (1999) 115 *LQR* 535. His thesis is that, in Germany, the present case would be decided in favour of Panatown on the basis of a principle called Drittschadenliquidation, which has been loosely translated into

English as "transferred loss"—an expression which I have myself adopted from time to time, though not I fear with any great accuracy. Indeed the concept is not an easy one for a common lawyer to grasp; and, with all respect to Unberath, I do not feel sufficiently secure to adopt it as part of my reasoning in this opinion. Even so, I find it comforting (though not surprising) to be told that in German law the same conclusion would be reached as I have myself reached on the facts of the present case. I have however also been struck by the provisions of paras. 633 and 635 of the BGB, falling within the Seventh Title entitled *Contract for Work*. I note (from Ian Forrester's translation of 1975) that the remedies under these two paragraphs (for defective work and for non-fulfilment) are vested in "the customer," and that there is no indication that the situation might be different if the property on which the work is to be done is vested in a person other than the customer. . . .

LORD MILLETT

. . . In the *St. Martins* case [1994] 1 AC 85, 96–98 Lord Griffiths refused to accept the proposition that in the case of a contract for work, labour and the supply of materials the recovery of more than nominal damages should depend on the plaintiff having a proprietary interest in the subject matter of the contract at the date of breach. He observed that in every day life contracts for work and labour are constantly placed by persons who have no proprietary interest in the subject matter of the contract. He instanced the common case where the matrimonial home is owned by the wife, the couple's other assets belong to the husband and he is the sole earner. The house requires a new roof and the husband places a contract with a local builder to carry out the work. The husband contracts as principal and not as agent for his wife because only he can pay for the work. The builder fails to repair the roof properly and the husband has to call in and pay another builder to complete the work. Lord Griffiths considered that it would be absurd to say that the husband has suffered no loss because he does not own the property. He suggested that the husband has suffered loss because he did not receive the bargain for which he contracted with the first builder and the measure of damages is the cost of securing performance of that bargain by having the repairs done properly by the second builder. . . .

To my mind the most significant feature of the academic literature is that no one has suggested that the adoption of the broad ground would have any adverse consequences on commercial arrangements. Nor, despite every incentive to do so, has McAlpine been able to suggest a situation in which it would cause difficulties or defeat the commercial expectations of the parties. In my view it would help to rationalise the law and provide a sound basis for decisions like *Ruxley Electronics and Construction Ltd.* v. *Forsyth* [1996] AC 344 and *Jackson* v. *Horizon Holidays Ltd.* [1975] 1 WLR 1468. If it is adopted, it will be for future consideration whether it would provide the better solution in cases such as *St. Martin* also. . . .

It must be wrong to adopt a Procrustean approach which leaves parties without a remedy for breach of contract because their arrangements do not fit neatly into some pre-cast contractual formula. When such arrangements have been freely entered into and are of an everyday character or are commercially advantageous to the parties, it is surely time to re-examine the position.

This is the product of the narrow accountants' balance sheet quantification of loss which measures the loss suffered by the promisee by the diminution in his overall financial position resulting from the breach. One of the consequences of this approach is to produce an artificial distinction between a contract for the supply of goods to a third party and a contract for the supply of services to a third party. A man who buys a car for his wife is entitled to substantial damages if an inferior car is supplied, on the assumption (not necessarily true) that the property in the car is intended to vest momentarily in him before being transferred to his wife, whereas a man who orders his wife's car to be repaired is entitled to nominal damages only if the work is imperfectly carried out. This is surely indefensible; the reality of the matter is that in both cases the man is willing to undertake a contractual liability in order to be able to provide a benefit to his wife.

The idea that a contracting party is entitled to damages measured by the value of his own defeated interest in having the contract performed was not new in 1994. A strong case for its adoption in the case of consumer contracts was made in an important Article "The Consumer Surplus" [1979] 95 *LQR* 581, in which the authors explained that this would make a significant difference only in a minority of cases. As I shall show, the language of defeated expectation has been employed in the context of building contracts, at least in ordinary two-party cases like *Ruxley*, since the nineteenth century. . . .

8. ECONOMIC LOSS (LEGAL MALPRACTICE)

Case 27

BUNDESGERICHTSHOF (SIXTH CIVIL SENATE) 19 JANUARY 1977
NJW 1977, 2073 = VersR 1977, 638

The defendant is an attorney who represented the plaintiff's father in divorce proceedings. In January 1972 the plaintiff's father and mother met in the defendant's office, where they signed a divorce agreement drawn up by the defendant. It contained the following clause:

§ 6. As to the house, the parties agree that the half belonging to Mrs M is to be transferred to the three children in equal parts. Mr M hereby agrees not to sell his half but to transfer it to his present legitimate children. An appropriate notarial contract to this effect is to be concluded immediately after the divorce is final. Mr M further promises that once the divorce is final he will indemnify Mrs M against any liabilities arising from the house or its construction. . . .

A divorce decree was granted in February 1972, and the defendant, in the name of the plaintiff's father, thereupon waived any rights of appeal, as did the mother's attorney. The plaintiff's mother now refuses to transfer her interest in the property to the plaintiff and his siblings.

The plaintiff claims damages for breach of the defendant's duty as attorney. The Landgericht rejected the claim but the Oberlandesgericht allowed it. The defendant was permitted to appeal, but his appeal was dismissed.

I. [the reasoning of the Court of Appeal.]

II. Despite the appellant's contentions, this reasoning is sound in law.

1. [The defendant was in breach of his duty as attorney.]

2. Nor is there anything wrong in law with the Court of Appeal's holding that although there was no contract between the plaintiff and the defendant, the plaintiff could sue the defendant for damages for his faulty breach of contract.

(*a*) The Court of Appeal found that there was here a contract with protective effect for third parties and that the plaintiff's claim arose therefrom. We do not have to decide whether this is so.

(*aa*) Certainly an important factor pointing in that direction is that the plaintiff was the son of the attorney's client and was entitled to care and protection from him (compare BGHZ 61, 227, 233). The usual problem in cases of contracts with protective effects for third parties is whether the victim was someone the debtor could expect to be harmed by a breach of the contract. That is not the problem here. The very words of § 6 of the divorce agreement drawn up by the defendant show that the children were its sole beneficiaries, the only people apt to suffer if the agreement proved invalid.

The only question here is how far the protective effect of this contract works in favour of the children, in particular whether they have any claim for damages for breach of contract in their own right. Now the contract between client and attorney is such, given its nature and structure, that it can only be very seldom, whether one interprets the contract extensively or invokes § 242 BGB (see BGHZ 56, 269, 273; NJW 1975, 977), that the duties it generates can be sued on by third parties, for the fiduciary relationship between client and attorney makes it strongly bilateral and self-contained [references omitted]. Thus the fact that third parties have an interest in what an attorney does will not normally lead to any extension of his liability, even if those persons are named or known to him. However, an exception must be made where a contract drafted by the attorney is designed to vest rights in third parties specified therein, especially third parties who, as in the present case, are represented by the client. It is true that most of the cases where the courts have granted third parties a claim for damages arising out of a contract to which they were not parties have involved personal injury or property damage and its consequences (BGHZ 49, 350, 355; NJW 1955, 257; [other references omitted]), but it is not impossible for a third party to have a personal claim for economic loss caused by breach of subsidiary contractual duties (NJW 1968, 1929; BGH NJW 1975, 344). In drawing the line here one must certainly apply an especially stringent test: the circle of persons to whom the protective effect of a contract extends is to be narrowly drawn, so as to avoid blurring the line between contractual and tortious liability in an unacceptable manner (BGHZ 66, 51, 57; NJW 1974, 1189). It must always be borne in mind, in claims for purely economic loss, that the debtor is not to be made liable for the mere ricochet effect of his conduct on third parties.

(*bb*) Despite this, we cannot, on the special facts of the present case, fault the Court of Appeal's holding that the plaintiff was drawn into the protective ambit of the attorney's contract. The respondent invokes a decision of this court of 6 July 1965 (NJW 1965, 1955), but this is not quite in point. The court there did allow the daughter of a client to sue the attorney although she was not herself a party to the contract, but the court was reluctant to categorise the contract as one with protective effect for third parties [references omitted]. Contracts with protective effect for third parties are concerned with breach of subsidiary duties by the contractor (see BGH NJW 1975, 344), whereas in that case the question was really whether the attorney could be made liable towards the client's daughter, the third party, for a breach of specific duties of performance [reference omitted]. Our case is clearly distinguishable.

(*b*) The plaintiff might also base his claim here on the concept of *Drittschadensliquidation*, a doctrine which borders on, if it does not actually overlap, the area of application of the doctrine of contracts with protective effect for third parties (see BGHZ 49, 350, 355). It would have been quite proper for the defendant's client to indemnify his son, the plaintiff, for the harm he had suffered, and one could then infer from the fact that he brought suit as his son's statutory representative that he was making an assignment of his own claim which the plaintiff, on the threshold of majority, could implicitly accept. But we need not pursue the matter here.

(*c*) In whatever legal or doctrinal category one puts the present litigated facts, the result must be that the plaintiff has a direct claim against the defendant attorney for compensation for the harm which he suffered as a result of the defendant's failure to tell his father of the need to implement the agreement in § 6 of the divorce document. Any other conclusion would be inconsistent with the meaning and purpose of the attorney's contract here and of the father–son relationship between the client and the plaintiff of which the defendant was well aware.

Notes to Case 27

1. Lawyers can through their negligence harm the interests of: (i) their clients and (ii) third parties. Increased litigation under the first heading, spurred no doubt by liability insurance becoming compulsory (as it is in Germany or France) or widespread (as it is in England and the USA), has led in some countries (e.g. the USA) to the flourishing of courses on Professional Responsibility. England, on the other hand, has for a long time refused to follow suit, steadfastly clinging to archaic immunities accorded to barristers (but not solicitors who, in fact, were the first that had to be insured) for work done in court (see *Rondel* v. *Worsley* [1969] 1 AC 191). Recently the House of Lords departed from *Rondel* v. *Worsley* in *Arthur JS Hall & Co* v. *Simons* [2000] 3 WLR 543. Lord Steyn's speech in particular contains some insights which are especially interesting from a comparative perspective. Their Lordships acknowledged that in the light of changes in the law of negligence, the functioning of the legal profession, the administration of justice, and public perceptions towards lawyers, the time had come to reconsider the immunity of advocates from suit. It was thus held that none of the reasons once advanced in favour of immunity (e.g. "cab rank" rule; the analogy to immunity of witnesses; the duty advocates had towards the court; and the public policy against re-litigating a decision) could nowadays justify it in relation to civil proceedings. A minority was also prepared to abandon the immunity in the context of criminal proceedings Lord Millett remarked (at p. 623): "I think the public would at best regard such a result [majority] as incomprehensible and at worst greet it with derision". It is worth noting perhaps that English barristers, unlike their colleagues on the Continent, do not enter into contracts with their clients (or solicitors); and they may not sue for their fees. Therefore, the principle established in *Hedley Byrne & Co Ltd* v. *Heller & Partners Ltd* [1964] AC 465 provides the only route of recovery available against barristers. In that case the rule was established that, irrespective of contract, if someone possessed of a special skill undertakes to apply that skill for the assistance of another who relies upon such skill, a duty of care will arise. Seen in a Commonwealth context, the decision of the House of Lords is remarkable. For the High Court of Australia in *Gianarelli* v. *Wraith* (1988) 165 CLR 543, and the Court of Appeal of New Zealand in *Rees* v. *Sinclair* [1974] 1 NZLR 180, had come to the conclusion that public policy considerations justified the immunity and had followed the *Rondel* case. Canada on the other hand "had got on perfectly well without an immunity for over a hundred years", as was pointed out by Lord Hoffmann, at p. 567. So the decision not only brings English law closer to Continental European practice than it was before; it also confirms the current trend of disunity in the Common law. Notwithstanding the above result in practice, the attempt to draw on the experience of Continnental Europe did not meet with wide approval. The main objection against drawing on the experience of civil law systems was derived from the difference in legal culture. The most sceptical of their Lordships was the Scottish judge, Lord Hope of Craighead, who although in the end also argued against the immunity rule, stressed that "the much wider scope which is accorded to the judicial function under the continental systems makes it very difficult to draw any useful comparisons." (at p. 593). At the other end of the spectrum was Lord Steyn who, as has already been noted, is a keen student of comparative law. The learned Law Lord was thus prepared to downplay the cultural differences between Common and modern civil law because he could see that the absence of an immunity has not caused any practical difficulties in other countries in the European Union. (Lord Hoffmann used the same argument by looking at the Canadian experience.)

For reasons of space we cannot engage in a comprehensive comparison of this point, but a number of observations can be made that would suggest that the divergence between Common and modern civil law may have been somewhat overstated by their lordships. Thus, it is certainly true to say that the control of a civilian judge over the proceedings is greater than that exercised by a judge in England. (See Kötz "Zur Funktionsteilung zwischen Richter und Anwalt im deutschen und englischen Zivilprozeß" in Graveson (ed.) *Festschrift für Imre Zajtay* (1982) 276–293 who points out that the German system with its proactive judge is geared towards dealing with small claims as well.) The *Zivilprozeßreformgesetz* of 27 July 2001, which comes into force on 1 January 2002, deepens this divergence by further widening the powers of the judge, thus giving him even more control over the proceedings. But, as Lord Steyn remarked, in the light of the Woolf reforms, the difference as to the role of the judge between England and the Civilian systems may become less significant. (At p. 552.) To this one might add that although the role of the Continental judge is a more interventionist, the ultimate control over the proceedings is entirely in the hand of the parties—a point often either missed or under-estimated by Common lawyers. (*Dispositions-maxime*; Zöller-Greger *Zivilprozeßordnung Kommentar* (22nd edn. 2001) vor § 128 Rn. 9.) Thus, the subject matter of the proceedings is defined by the parties, § 308 ZPO; and the judge, though managerial in his role, also has to exercise self-restraint in giving directions or hints to the parties: § 139 ZPO. The civilian judge will also take careful account of the legal arguments made before him just as much the judge in England will do. The BVerfG recently reaffirmed (WuM 1999, 383) that it is the court's duty to apply and interpret the law according to the principle of *iura novit curia*. However, the Constitutional court was also keen to stress that if one party puts forward a specific interpretation of the law the court has to take account of its submissions and deal with them in the reasons it gives in its decision. If it does not, it treats the parties as mere objects of the judicial process and violates their rights under Article 103 I GG ("rechtliches Gehör").

A second allegedly crucial difference between the two systems is this. Lord Steyn accepted that the duty of an advocate in a civilian system was less extensive than in England. For instance, in Germany there is no duty to refer the court to adverse authorities. (See at p. 553.) However, the advocate in Germany assumes a position which (in theory at least) goes beyond that of a mere "service provider" to his client. § 1 *Bundesrechtsanwaltsordnung* (BRAO) thus states that the *Rechtsanwalt* is an "independent agent in the development of the legal order" (*Organ der Rechtspflege*). The advocate thus has to exercise his profession in the light of the trust that is placed upon him in his capacity as advocate. (§ 43 BRAO.) The law imposes a number of restrictions on freedom of contract in this area; for instance it prohibits contingency fees (§ 49b II BRAO) or fees that are below the level prescribed by statute (§ 49b I BRAO). The breach of some of the advocate's duties also entails criminal sanctions in addition to possible civil liability towards his own client. For an advocate may not act, even indirectly, for both parties at the same time, § 356 StGB; and he must not knowingly make false statements to the court. This brief survey demonstrates that German advocates do owe duties not only to their clients but also to the public at large, even though in some respects they may be less pronounced than the duties that an English barrister may owe to the court. Finally, it is ironic to note that while the German advocate does not owe the court a duty to refer it to authorities that go against the interests of his client—because the court is supposed to know the law—he breaches his duty *towards the client* if he ignores such authorities and as a result does not accurately advise him as to the outcome of the litigation. The standard applied by German courts in this respect is so high that it has attracted criticism from some authors as being excessive and controversial. (See, Vollkommer *Anwaltshaftungsrecht* (1989), 63 with references.)

2. In those cases, where liability is possible in theory (but by no means easily engaged in practice), two problems have attracted the attention of the courts. The first is connected with the difficulties of assessing what would the chances have been of the disgruntled client/plaintiff but for the negligence of his legal adviser. The second is connected with the curious, if not unjustified, willingness of some American courts to set the standard of expected care at a very low level (note, for example, *Lucas* v. *Hamm* 56 Cal. 2d 583, 364 P. 2d 685 (1961) where the court was prepared to characterise as non-negligent an attorney who failed to take proper notice of the rule against

perpetuities on the ground that it is widely misunderstood by the profession!). (For a comparative study of the problems of professional malpractice (including medical malpractice which is treated with less indulgence by the courts) see chapter 6 of vol. XI of the International Encyclopedia of Comparative Law.)

3. Case 27 deals with a different problem: can a lawyer owe a duty to third persons who are not his clients? The German decision invites comparison with such cases as *Biakanja* v. *Irving* 49 Cal. 2d 647, 320 P. 2d 16 (1958) (pleaded in tort), *Lucas* v. *Hamm*, above, (pleaded in contract *and* tort) and *Heyer* v. *Flaig* (74 Cal. Rptr. 225; 449 P. 2d 161 (1969)) decided in tort in the USA, and *Ross* v. *Caunters* [1980] Ch. 297 and *White* v. *Jones* (pleaded in tort only) in England. Similarities and differences must again be stressed.

(i) The first point to note is, again, the tendency of German law to base its solution on contract. That contract cannot easily explain all such cases is obvious not only by the court's own review of the precedents but also by a certain unease it experiences in utilising the notion of contract with protective effects *vis-à-vis* third parties or the theory of "transferred loss" (*Drittschadensliquidation*), both briefly explained above (chapter 2, section A, 2 (*d*) (*iii*) (*e*)). The first German decision on the subject—BGH NJW 1965, 1955; JZ 1966, 141 note Lorenz—relied on the notion of contract with protective effects *vis-à-vis* third parties and found for the plaintiff, though one is inclined to believe that the theory of transferred loss might have been an even more appropriate device. (This case is discussed in English by Lorenz in "Some Thoughts about Contract and Tort" *Essays in Memory of Professor F. H. Lawson* (1986) 86 ff.) Incidentally, the granting of an action against the attorney (for a sum equal to the void legacy) can in practice result in a "double-legacy"—a point that has troubled some commentators. (See Kegel, "Die 'lachenden Doppelerben': Erbfolge beim Versagen von Urkundspersonen", *Festschrift für Flume* (1978) I, 545. This argument, however, has been rejected both in England (*White* v. *Jones, supra*) and in Germany (see: BGH 12 June 1979, *Zeitschrift für das Gesamte Familienrecht* 1980, 133 and Lorenz and Markesinis (1993) 56 *MLR* 558 *et seq.*)

(ii) The contract versus tort approach must not only be noted but also examined, especially since some American decisions (e.g. *Heyer* v. *Flaig*, 74 Cal. Rptr. 225; 449 P. 2d 161 (1969)) have gone as far as suggesting that the distinction may be meaningless. It is submitted that it is not, and American law may be the poorer for ignoring some of the practical consequences of a proper doctrinal characterisation. Here are some:

(*a*) *Jurisdiction*. The choice-orientated approach adopted by conflicts rules in cases of contract seems more appropriate in these types of cases than the *locus* of the accident tort approach. In any event, it would be odd if the dispute between plaintiff and defendant/debtor were subject to one rule and the relationship between defendant/debtor and creditor were governed by a different law. (See Fig. 2.) We can, of course, again allow the contractual relationship to influence the tort action (as Tobriner J. suggested in *Heyer* v. *Flaig* 74 Cal. Rptr. 225, 449 P. 2d 161 (1969)); but why not opt more openly for the more straightforward contractual reasoning? (The potential impact that the choice of contract or tort can have on jurisdiction can be seen in factual variations of cases such as *Bryant Electric Co.* v. *City of Fredericksburg*, 762 F. 2d 1192 (1985) and *Blake Construction Co.* v. *Alley*, 353 SE 2d 724 (1987) both of which represent variations on the *J'Aire* and *Junior Books* theme.)

(*b*) *Liability for omissions*. Traditional tort theory would deny liability where the debtor/defendant has remained inactive rather than acted badly. A contractual solution could make the defendant/debtor liable both for non-feasance and misfeasance. Should this be regarded as excessively onerous for the defendant/debtor it may still be avoided through the use of *Drittschadensliquidation* or the German notion of contract with protective effects *vis-à-vis* third parties, since this, it will be remembered, makes the debtor liable only for the bad or delayed performance of the *secondary* obligations of the contract. (The first German case was one of omission: BGH NJW 1965, 1955; JZ 1966, 141 (with note by Lorenz). Cf. the factually almost identical cases of *Gartside* v. *Sheffield Young and Ellis* [1983] NZLR 37 and Hof Amsterdam, NJ 1985, 40—the last two resorting to tort doctrine.)

(*c*) *Measure of damages.* The tort and contract measure of damages probably remains different despite Lord Denning's attempt to propose a compromise in *H Parsons (Livestock) Ltd.* v. *Uttley Ingham and Co. Ltd.* ([1978] QB 791). A contractual solution would favour the award of full expectation damages to the plaintiff/third party and this, again, is supported by German law. In the USA a tort solution would further justify a claim for punitive damages. Such a ridiculous claim was, in fact, made in *Heyer* v. *Flaig.*

(*d*) *The limitation period.* Both the length and starting point of the limitation period differ in contract and tort. It is submitted it would be impracticable if one relationship (plaintiff–defendant/debtor) were subject to one rule and the other relationship (debtor–creditor) governed by a different rule. This appears to be in principle the correct starting point but it must be admitted that in some cases it may cause problems. Thus, in the frustrated beneficiary type of case the right of the beneficiary to sue the testator lawyer is not identical to that of the testator since the harm suffered by each is different. Also, if the contractual period of limitation were to apply in exclusion of all tort remedy, it could harm the beneficiaries' interests in those systems where the contractual period of limitation is not substantially longer than the tort period of limitation.

(*e*) *The standard of care.* Few lawyers in England or in the USA seem to have considered points (*a*)–(*d*). More concern, however, has been shown about the standard of care that would be appropriate to the tort action and whether it would be different from that found in the debtor–creditor (contractual) relationship. German law, proceeding on contract theory, has not experienced this difficulty; and German writers, considering a hypothetical (for them) tort action have had no difficulty in saying that the tort standard of care should be determined by the contract. (Schlechtriem, Lorenz, *op. cit.*) American courts have taken a similar view; and both Lord Roskill (in *Junior Books*) and Robert Goff LJ (in *The Aliakmon*) saw little difficulty in adopting this reasoning in English law. Of course, the contractual solution avoids at a stroke these real or imaginary difficulties.

(*f*) *Exemption clauses/defences.* As a general rule in German law the contractual debtor can oppose against the third party/plaintiff all defences, etc., he may have against the contractual creditor (§ 334 BGB, but see now case 23, BGHZ 127, 378, above, as to the possibility of a waiver of this defence). The same reasoning applies where the action is in tort but the defendant is protected by an exclusion clause contained in a contract with protective effects towards third parties (case 57). The contractual solution makes this answer indisputable. In an *obiter dictum* in *The Aliakmon* Robert Goff LJ suggested that something similar should happen where the action was founded in tort ([1985] QB 350 at pp. 397–8) but details have not been worked out. Strangely enough, at least one first instance judgment in England has considered a variant to this problem and, incidentally, suggests a misunderstanding as to how contracts in favour of third parties work.

(iii) In *Southern Water Authority* v. *Carey* ([1985] 2 All ER 1077) the court was not asked to decide whether the defendant sub-contractor (debtor) could oppose against the owner/plaintiff (third party) the exemption clauses that he (the sub-contractor) had in his contract with the main contractor (creditor); instead the court was faced with a claim by the sub-contractor to oppose against the owner a clause which the main contractor had in his contract with the owner. The court thought he could do so and, I believe, the solution displays a misunderstanding of how this triangular relationship should work. It is submitted that had a contractual explanation been used this misunderstanding would not have occurred.

In *Carey* the plaintiffs (or, rather, their predecessors in title) engaged the first defendants as consulting engineers and the second defendants as main contractors in the building of certain sewage works. The second defendants in turn engaged the third and fourth defendants as sub-contractors. Clause 30 of the work contract between the plaintiffs and the second defendants (main contractors) contained an exemption clause. Subsection (VI) of this clause stated that "for the purposes of this sub-clause the Contractor contracts on his own behalf and on the behalf of and as trustee for his sub-contractors, servants and agents". The main contractors having ceased trading, the action for defective workmanship and materials proceeded against the two sub-contractors. At this stage it is worth noting that while the fourth defendant/sub-contractor had in his contract with the main contractor a term almost identical to Clause 30 of the main contract, the third defendants/sub-contractors, when negotiating with the main contractor, had insisted on their own, different, limitation clause. (Though we are nowhere told in what respect the two sets of terms differed, one must assume that the contractor's terms were more advantageous to the defendants/ sub-contractors than their own terms, for otherwise why did they try to invoke their protection?) The Court, applying the tort reasoning of *Junior Books*, accepted that the plaintiff had a cause of action. Unlike *Junior Books*, however, the plaintiff was faced with a defence put forward by the defendant. This was based on an exclusion clause contained not in his (the sub-contractor's) contract with the main contractor (in which case the position could have been similar to *The Aliakmon*), but on the exclusion clause contained in the contract between the plaintiff and the main contractor (and which the third defendant/sub-contractor had, as stated, rejected). Diagrammatically the difference from *The Aliakmon* case can be shown as in Fig. 2.

As stated, the court was prepared to allow a tort action by the employer against the sub-contractor but was also willing to give the latter the protection of the clause contained in the contract between employer and main contractor. One reason was that the nature of this limitation clause was relevant in defining the scope of the duty of the sub-contractor in tort. Another explanation was the use of the notion of *volenti*. The judge expressly excluded the latter concept (*ibid.* at p. 1085a); but later in his judgment he appears to have come very close to accepting it (or something very similar to this concept) since he said: "As the plaintiffs . . . did . . . choose to limit the scope of the sub-contractor's liability, I see no reason why such limitation should not be honoured." (*Ibid.* at pp. 1086 f.) Is the reasoning of this decision and its result acceptable? I confess I have doubts as to both.

It is first of all interesting to note that in *Carey* the court did not follow *The Eurymedon* (*New Zealand Shipping Co. Ltd.*) v. *A. M. Satterthwaite and Co. Ltd*, [1975] AC 154) reasoning in order to achieve its result. The artificiality of the contractual reasoning in that case has been noted by many lawyers; but it was reaffirmed by the Privy Council in *Port Jackson Stevedoring Pty. Ltd* v. *Salmond and Spraggon (Australia) Pty. Ltd., The New York Star* ([1981] 1 WLR 138) so the judge in *Carey* was obviously anxious not to challenge it openly. On the other hand, it was not used either, so those opposed to *The Eurymedon* result and reasoning might be able to argue that in future it may be

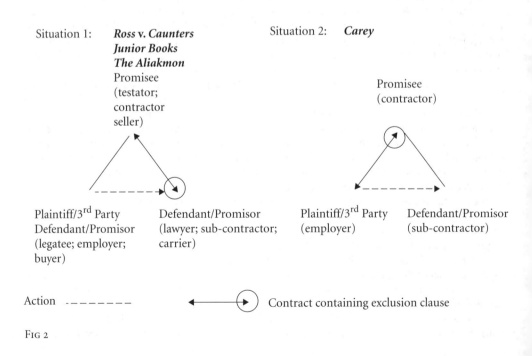

Situation 1:   ***Ross v. Caunters***
                 Junior Books
                 The Aliakmon
                 Promisee
                 (testator;
                 contractor
                 seller)

Situation 2:   ***Carey***
                 Promisee
                 (contractor)

Plaintiff/3rd Party
Defendant/Promisor
(legatee; employer;
buyer)

Defendant/Promisor
(lawyer; sub-contractor;
carrier)

Plaintiff/3rd Party
(employer)

Defendant/Promisor
(sub-contractor)

Action - - - - - - -   ◄———————►) Contract containing exclusion clause

FIG 2

limited to the special shipping context of such cases. This still, however, leaves open the question of how to explain *Carey*.

One could, nowadays, construe *Carey* as a case of contract in favour of third party (and, for brevity's sake we include in this term the contract with protective effects *vis-à-vis* third parties). After all, *Carey* is, in one respect, very similar to *Junior Books*; the owner could be seen as the third party beneficiary of the contract between sub-contractor (promisor) and main contractor (promisee). This construction, of course, was for a long time unacceptable *de lege lata* given the traditional English notion of privity. It is now, under Contracts (Rights of Third Parties) Act 1999 s. 1, conceivable to apply a solution which is very similar indeed to the solution developed by the German courts on the basis of the contract with protective effects towards third parties. (See case 57 which is best understood in conjunction with case 110 concerning liability regimes in labour law). This is somewhat ironic, for the Law Commission indicated that it was not its intention to extend the reform to situations that fall under the German concept of a contract with protective effects (Law Com No 242 (1996) 2.14 n. 22). The present instance is an example where the scope of the contract with protective effects and the 1999 Act overlap. However, this statement retains its validity with regard to other situations such as in *White* v. *Jones* and similar cases which are traditionally solved by applying the principle in *Hedley Byrne*. (See, for instance, example 16, Law Com No 242 (1996) para. 7.43. B & Co's standard form of building contract contains an exclusion clause which excludes the liability of "all agents, servants, employees and subcontractors" engaged by B & Co in the performance of the contract. A & Co, a developer using B & Co's services, discovers that the building is defective. The surveyor engaged by B & Co to carry out the site survey, Mr C, has been negligent. Mr C seeks to claim the benefit of the exclusion clause in A & Co's contract with B & Co to prevent A & Co from recovering against him in tort for negligence. The Commission suggests that "Mr C would succeed under the first limb of our test or, on the basis that the exclusion clause is a promise to confer a benefit (the exclusion of liability) on Mr C, who is expressly identified by class, under the second limb.")

But even if it were accepted it would still not explain the second part of *Carey* namely the allowing to the promisor the defences that the promisee had against the third party. For in contracts in favour of third parties it is the reverse that is allowed: namely the promisor can oppose against the third party the defences *he* has in *his* contract with the promisee.

Can one then justify the outcome through tort reasoning? The judge in *Carey* did so by allowing the tort action to be shaped by the contract to which the plaintiff was a party but the defendant was not. In this he was clearly influenced by certain dicta contained in Lord Roskill's judgment in *Junior Books* v. *Veitchi*. (Lord Roskill refers there to "a relevant exclusion clause in the *main* contract".) With respect I do not find Lord Roskill's dicta as obvious as that, my inclination being to interpret them as referring to the *second* contract (sub-contractor–main contractor) and *not* to the *first* contract (between contractor and owner). I incline in favour of this view largely because Lord Roskill seemed to rely heavily in his relevant passage on *Hedley Byrne*; and there, apart from the fact that there were no contractual relations *stricto sensu*, the exemption clause was inserted by the second bank/defendant when replying to the plaintiff's bank and not by the plaintiff's bank (which was merely transmitting the information) to the plaintiff. The clause, in other words, was in the second not the first relationship. My own understanding of the Roskill dictum is also shared by the Court of Appeal in *Muirhead* v. *Industrial Tank Specialities Ltd.* ([1986] QB 507; Reynolds in (1986) 10 *LMCLQ* 97, 106 probably agrees). On the other hand, it must be admitted that this is not how the judge understood it in *Carey*; and his interpretation also has the important support of Professor Treitel (in (1986) 10 *LMCLQ* 294, 302). Clearly, therefore, the dictum has led to some confusion and should be clarified at the earliest possible opportunity. Nevertheless, even if it were eventually to be classified in the way it was understood in *Carey* it still does not, in my opinion, justify the actual outcome *in that case*. For in that case we were in fact faced with an interesting variant to the problem we have been discussing. Because in *Carey* the judge was faced with *two* sets of exemption clauses, one in the contract between owner and main contractor and one in the contract between main contractor and sub-contractor; and he allowed the sub-contractor the benefit of the first clause even though at the time of conclusion of the relevant contracts the sub-contractor had rejected it in favour of his own clause. I see no commercial reason justifying this result; nor do I think we can say that the plaintiff assented to a limited liability when the defendant, at the time of the making of the contracts, rejected the relevant limitation clause.

4. Contract or tort, the new action must be kept under control, especially where third parties/non-clients are concerned. American decisions are legion—see, for example: *Victor* v. *Goldman,* 74 Misc. 2d 685, 344 NYS 2d 672 (1973); *Pelham* v. *Griesheimer,* 93 Ill. App. 3d 751, 417 NE 2d 882 (1981), aff'd. 92 Ill. 2d 13, 440 NE 2d 96 (1982); *Guy* v. *Liederbach,* 459 A. 2d 744, 501 Pa. 47 (1983); *Needham* v. *Hamilton* 459 A. 2d 1060 (DC App. 1983); *Flaherty* v. *Weinberg,* 303 Md. 116, 492 A. 2d 618 (1985); *Walker* v. *Lawson,* 514 NE 2d 629 (Ind. App. 1987); *Stinson* v. *Brand,* 738 SW 2d 186 (Tenn., 1987); *Mentzer and Rhey, Inc.* v. *Ferrari,* 367 Pa. Super. 123, 532 A. 2d 484 (1987); *Hale* v. *Groce* 304 Or. 281, 744 P. 2d 1289 (1987); *Simon* v. *Zipperstein* 32 Ohio St. 3d 74, 512 NE 2d 636 (1987). *Schreiner* v. *Scoville,* 410 N.W. 2d, 679 (Iowa: 1987); *Licata* v. *Spector,* 225 A. 2d. 28 (Ct.1966) 61 ALR 4th 63–501 suggests that a majority of jurisdictions now favour plaintiffs—at least in the *Ross* v. *Caunters* type of situation. The end result, however, is not all that different from the more restrictive European (German and English) approach. Nevertheless the question remains whether the multi-criteria test enunciated in *Biakanja* v. *Irving* is more workable and (on balance) fairer than the contractual third party beneficiary doctrine. In this context consider: (i) why the six factors mentioned in *Biakanja* (320 P. 2d 16, 19) were subsequently reduced to five (the requirement that "moral blame [be] attached to the defendant's conduct" has been dropped); (ii) whether the various criteria are cumulative or whether one of them is particularly important; (iii) that equal uncertainty seems to prevail on the requirements needed to be satisfied for the invocation of the third party beneficiary doctrine. In particular, who must intend to confer a benefit on the third party: the promisee (better view) or the promisee *and* the promisor? From the vast literature see: Bauman, "Damages for Legal Malpractice", 61 *Temple L. Rev.* 1127 (1988); idem, "Lawyer Liability to Non-Clients", 97 *Dickinson L. Rev.* 267 (1993); Boston, "Liability of Attorneys to Non-Clients in Michigan: a re-examination of *Fridman* v. *Dozore* and a rule of limited liability", 68 *Univ. of Detroit L. Rev.* 307 (1991); Dugdale, "Solicitors' Liability to Third Parties" [1984] *NZLJ* 316 ff.; Eisenberg, "Attorneys' Negligence and Third Parties" 57 *NYUL Rev.* 126 (1982); Gross, "Contractual Limitations on Attorney Malpractice Liability: An Economic Approach" 75 *Kentucky LJ* 793 (1986–7); Hazard, "Lawyer Liability in Third Party Situations: The Meaning of the *Kaye Scholer* Case", 26 *Akron L. Rev.* 395 (1993); Hilliker, "Attorney Liability to Third Parties: A Look to the Future" 36 *Depaul L. Rev.* 41 (1986); Keeton, "Professional Malpractice" 17 *Washburn LJ* 445 (1978); Markesinis, "Fixing Acceptable Boundaries to the Liability of Solicitors" 103 (1987) *LQR* 346; idem, "Doctrinal Clarity in Tort Litigation: A Comparative Lawyer's Viewpoint", 25 *The International Lawyer* 953 (1991); Morley, "Privity as a Bar to Recovery in Negligent Will-Preparation Cases" 57 *Univ. of Cincinnati L. Rev.* 1123 (1989); Peterson, "Extending Legal Malpractice Liability to Non-clients" 61 *Wash. L. Rev.* 761 (1986); Probert and Hendricks, "Lawyer Malpractice: Duty Relationships Beyond Contract" 55 *The Notre Dame Lawyer* 708 (1980); Rolph, "Solicitors' Liability to Non-clients in Negligence", 15 *The Advocates' Quarterly,* 129 (1993); Rubenstein, "Attorney Malpractice in California: The Liability of Who Drafts an Imprecise Contract or Will" 24 *UCLA Law Review* 422 (1976); Walker, "Attorney Liability to Third Parties for Malpractice: The Growing Acceptance of Liability in the Absence of Privity" 21 *Washburn LJ* 48 (1981–2). Gates, "Lawyers' Malpractice" 37 *Mercer L. Rev.* (1986) gives interesting statistical information.

5. *Murphy* v. *Brentwood District Council* [1991] 1 AC 398 undoubtedly marks the end of the expansive period of the tort of negligence that was initiated by *Anns* v. *Merton London BC* [1978] AC 728, but it did not put into question the principles established in *Hedley Byrne*. Thus the criteria of "reasonable reliance" and "assumption of responsibility" have remained a potential source for further expansionist tendencies. Indeed, in the nineties, the House of Lords made use of this possibility. Thus, once again, a series of decisions revealed a tendency to advance the frontiers of liability in negligence by applying *Hedley Byrne* beyond its factual limitations to performance of services. (Only this time the expansion followed the directions given in *Murphy* and *Caparo* and

was attempted incrementally) *White* v. *Jones* is one example, but there are others. The most important must surely be *Henderson* v. *Merrett Syndicates Ltd* [1995] 2 AC 145, though *Spring* v. *Guardian Assurance Plc* [1995] 2 AC 296 is also noteworthy. (In that case the "statement", a reference about an employee, was not addressed to the plaintiff but to his future potential employers. The plaintiff could thus not be said to have relied on the reference). In the *Henderson* case, the plaintiffs, underwriting members ("Names") at Lloyd's, brought proceedings against the defendant underwriting agents in which they alleged that the defendants were negligent in their conduct of the Names' underwriting affairs and in breach of their legal obligations. The plaintiffs' claims concerned the liability of members' agents and of managing agents (to whom the performance of services had been delegated) towards Lloyd's Names (so called "direct Names" and "indirect Names", the latter are indirect Names in relation to managing agents since they do not enter into a contract with them).

The House of Lords held that a duty of care was owed by the agents in tort both to direct Names and indirect Names. The existence of such a duty of care was not excluded by virtue of the relevant contractual regime and that the Names were free to pursue their remedy either in contract or in tort. Lord Goff, who delivered the leading speech, explained the *Hedley Byrne* principle in the following—broad—way (at p. 180). "We can see that it rests upon a relationship between the parties, which may be general or specific to the particular transaction, and which may or may not be contractual in nature. All of their Lordships spoke in terms of one party having assumed or undertaken a responsibility towards the other. On this point, Lord Devlin spoke in particularly clear terms in both passages from his speech which I have quoted above. Further, Lord Morris spoke of that party being possessed of a "special skill" which he undertakes to "apply for the assistance of another who relies upon such skill." But the facts of *Hedley Byrne*, itself, which was concerned with the liability of a banker to the recipient for negligence in the provision of a reference gratuitously supplied, show that the concept of a "special skill" must be understood broadly, certainly broadly enough to include special knowledge. *Hedley Byrne* was, of course, concerned with the provision of information and advice. But the example given by Lord Devlin of the relationship between solicitor and client, and his and Lord Morris's statements of principle, show that the principle extends beyond the provision of information and advice to include the performance of other services. It follows that in the case of the provision of information and advice reliance upon it by the other party will be necessary to establish a cause of action (because otherwise the negligence will have no causative effect). Nevertheless, there may be other circumstances in which there will be the necessary reliance to give rise to the application of the principle. In particular, as cases concerned with solicitor and client demonstrate, where the plaintiff entrusts the defendant with the conduct of his affairs, in general or in particular, he may be held to have relied on the defendant to exercise due skill and care in such conduct." The similarity to the criteria developed by the German courts in cases 19–24 and case 27, though obvious, must be stressed again.

6. As far as statements are concerned reliance is crucial to establish the statement's causative effect: words rarely cause loss directly. It is, therefore, natural to take into account the range of persons who will *rely* on the statement by acting on it. The problem of an incremental extension of *Hedley Byrne* to deeds which cause loss more easily, is that "reasonable reliance" does not have the same limiting power. (Cf. *White* v. *Jones* [1995] 2 AC 207, 272 per Lord Browne-Wilkinson.) As Bingham LJ, as he then was, remarked in *Simaan General Contracting Co.* v. *Pilkington Glass Ltd.* *(No. 2)* [1988] QB 758, 775: "There is, of course, a sense in which it can be said that every successful plaintiff in an action of negligence has relied on the defendant not to be negligent, as every motorist relies on every other motorist in the vicinity to drive carefully." Lord Goff, himself, (in the passage quoted above) defined reliance in such a week sense that it can be hardly distinguished from the formulation of the "assumption of responsibility" principle. Accordingly, additional limiting factors are necessary and it is mainly due to Lord Goff's approach that the principle of assumption of responsibility came to be viewed as the guiding one. But it should be noted that the principle is controversial. It has thus been often suggested that—being too vague and open-textured to provide a proper criterion of liability—it is merely a label for a conclusion reached on

other grounds. (See, for instance, Lord Griffiths in *Smith v. Eric S Bush* [1990] 1 AC 831, 862. See, also, Cane *Tort Law and Economic Interest* (2nd ed, 1996), 185 and Whittaker (1996) 16 *OJLS* 191, 204–205, who prefers limited exceptions to privity to the tort route). Also, the interrelationship with the (though similarly vague) three-stage test in *Caparo* (foreseeability, proximity, policy) is not easy to ascertain. In *Phelps v. Hillingdon LBC* [2000] 3 *WLR* 776 the allegations concerned an educational psychiatrist who gave advice in the knowledge or expectation that the plaintiff would rely upon it. The case was argued on the *Hedley Byrne* principle.—In his judgment, Lord Slynn of Hadley stressed that the *Caparo* approach served to establish a sufficient nexus to give rise to a duty of care, while the "phrase of assumption of responsibility" meant "simply" that "the law recognises that there is a duty of care". Responsibility was thus not deliberately assumed by the professional person but imposed by law under an objective test. (At p. 791.) In Lord Clyde's view (at p. 807) the question did not arise in the present case, but he conceded that the expression may be "descriptive rather than definitive". Lord Goff also stressed in *Henderson* (at p. 181) that the test was objective. However, he also added that, "once the case is identified as falling within the *Hedley Byrne* principle, there should be no need to embark upon any further enquiry whether it is "fair, just and reasonable" to impose liability for economic loss".

7. Finally, *Henderson v. Merrett* (extracts are reproduced below) deserves special attention since it established that where both routes of recovery are available in principle a claimant can choose whether he frames his action in tort or contract. Lord Goff in this respect followed expressly the German model. His observations repay careful reading, not least because they trace the development of English law back to the abolition of the form of actions in the nineteenth century. To avoid a duplication of the arguments pro and con in relation to concurrence of actions, it may be sufficient to deal with one possible objection recently formulated by Mr Weir "The Staggering March of Negligence" in Cane and Stapleton (edd.) *The Law of Obligations—Essays in Celebration of John Fleming* (1998) 97 at pp. 118 ff. He pointed out that English law now in effect combined the French approach of allowing recovery of pure economic loss in tort with the German principle of concurrency of actions. "England has gone much further than either neighbour" since neither allowed a combination of both aspects. However, it should be clear from the examination of the contract with protective effects that according to that principle of German law liability is just as much imposed by law as it is under the *Hedley Byrne* principle of assumption of responsibility or reasonable reliance. As was emphasised by way of introduction to the notes to the cases on negligent misstatements, the different conceptual compartmentalisation does not fully reveal the principles in operation in this intricate area of the law. But if one adopts a functional approach, as we have attempted to do throughout these notes, then the alleged difference between English and German is less significant than it might appear at first sight. Outside the *Hedley Byrne* type of liability however, both English and German law, deny liability for pure economic loss in tort.

Addendum 1

Extracts from *White v. Jones* House of Lords [1995] 2 AC 207

Facts

The testator had two daughters: Carol White and Pauline Heath. When his wife died in January 1986 a family quarrel ensued as a result of which the testator proceeded to cut both his daughters out of his estate. In his will, executed in March 1986, he distributed his rather modest estate in various ways among three of his grandchildren and Mrs White's first husband. Soon afterwards a reconciliation took place and the testator, regretting his rash action, informed his two daughters of the will and of his intention to change it. Both he and Mr Heath (a different son-in-law) contacted Mr Jones of the firm of defendant solicitors and gave both oral and written instructions for a new will under which the two daughters would inherit approximately two-thirds of the estate, the remainder being equally divided among all (five) grandchildren. Despite repeated communications, Mr Jones remained inactive though, in mid-August, and before leaving for his annual holiday, he did write an internal memo to a member of the firm's probate division informing him of the need to prepare a new will. A proposed meeting with the testator on 17 September never took place since the latter died a few days earlier. The two daughters, having failed to reach an amicable settlement between them as to the way the estate should be divided, sued the solicitors. At First Instance, Turner J dismissed their action, holding that though the solicitors had committed a serious wrong, they owed no duty of care to the plaintiffs. A unanimous Court of Appeal (consisting of the Vice Chancellor, and Lord Justices Farquarson and Steyn) reversed the decision. The House of Lords, by a majority, dismissed the appeal.

LORD GOFF OF CHIEVELEY

. . . I turn to the principal issue which arises on the appeal, which is whether in the circumstances of cases such as *Ross* v. *Caunters* and the present case the testator's solicitors are liable to the disappointed beneficiary. As I have already stated, the question is one which has been much discussed, not only in this country and other common law countries, but also in some civil law countries, notably Germany. There can be no doubt that *Ross* v. *Caunters* has been generally welcomed by academic writers (see *eg Salmond and Heuston on the Law of Torts.* (20th edn, 1992) pp. 215, 217, *Winfield and Jolowicz on Tort* (13th edn, 1989) pp. 88–89, 96, 106, *Fleming on Torts* (8th edn, 1993) p. 184 and *Markesinis and Deakin on Tort Law* (3rd edn, 1994) pp. 95–98). Furthermore, it does not appear to have been the subject of adverse comment in the higher courts in this country, though it has not been approved except by the Court of Appeal in the present case. Indeed, as far as I am aware, *Ross* v. *Caunters* has created no serious problems in practice since it was decided nearly 15 years ago. . . .

The conceptual difficulties

Even so, it has been recognised on all hands that *Ross* v. *Caunters* raises difficulties of a conceptual nature, and that as a result it is not altogether easy to accommodate the decision within the ordinary principles of our law of obligations. . . .

They are as follows. (1) First, the general rule is well established that a solicitor acting on behalf of a client owes a duty of care only to his client. The relationship between a solicitor and his client is nearly always contractual, and the scope of the solicitor's duties will be set by the terms of his retainer; but a duty of care owed by a solicitor to his client will arise concurrently in contract and in tort (see *Midland Bank Trust Go Ltd* v. *Hett, Stubbs & Kemp (a firm)* [1979] chapter 384, recently approved by your Lordships' House in *Henderson* v. *Merrett Syndicates Ltd* [1994] 3 WLR 761). But, when a solicitor is performing his duties to his client, he will generally owe no duty of care to third parties. Accordingly, as Nicholls V-C pointed out in the present case, a solicitor acting for a seller of land does not generally owe a duty of care to the buyer: see *Gran Gelato Ltd* v. *Richcliff (Group) Ltd* [1992] Ch 560. Nor, as a general rule, does a solicitor acting for a party in adversarial litigation owe a duty of care to that party's opponent: see *AI-Kandari* v. *J R Brown & Go (a firm)* [1988] QB 665 at 672 per Lord Donaldson MR. Further, it has been held that a solicitor advising a client about a proposed dealing with his property in his lifetime owes no duty of care to a prospective beneficiary under the client's then will who may be prejudicially affected: see *Clarke* v. *Bruce Lance & Go (a firm)* [1988] I WLR 881.

As I have said, the scope of the solicitor's duties to his client are set by the terms of his retainer; and as a result it has been said that the content of his duties is entirely within the control of his client. The solicitor can, in theory at least, protect himself by the introduction of terms into his contract with his client; but, it is objected, he could not similarly protect himself against any third party to whom he might be held responsible, where there is no contract between him and the third party.

In these circumstances, it is said, there can be no liability of the solicitor to a beneficiary under a will who has been disappointed by reason of negligent failure by the solicitor to give effect to the testator's intention. There can be no liability in contract, because there is no contract between the solicitor and the disappointed beneficiary; if any contractual claim was to be recognised, it could only be by way of a ius quaesitum tertio, and no such claim is recognised in English law. Nor could there be liability in tort, because in the performance of his duties to his client a solicitor owes no duty of care in tort to a third party such as a disappointed beneficiary under his client's will.

(2) A further reason is given which is said to reinforce the conclusion that no duty of care is owed by the solicitor to the beneficiary in tort. Here, it is suggested, is one of those situations in which a plaintiff is entitled to damages if, and only if, he can establish a breach of contract by the defendant. First, the plaintiffs claim is one for purely financial loss; and as a general rule, apart from cases of assumption of responsibility arising under the principle in *Hedley Byrne* & *Co Ltd* v. *Heller* & *Partners Ltd* [1964] AC 465, no action will lie in respect of such loss in the tort of negligence. Furthermore, in particular, no claim will lie in ton for damage in respect of a mere loss of an expectation, as opposed to damages in respect of damage to an existing right or interest of the plaintiff. Such a claim falls within the exclusive zone of contractual liability; and it is contrary to principle that the law of ton should be allowed to invade that zone. Of course, Parliament can create exceptions to that principle by extending contractual rights to persons who are not parties to a contract as was done, for example, in the Bills of Lading Act 1855 and the Carriage of Good by Sea Act 1992. But as a matter of principle a step of this kind cannot be taken by the Courts, though they can redefine the boundaries of the exclusive zone, as they did in *Donoghue* v. *Stevenson* [1932] AC 562.

The present case, it is suggested, falls within that exclusive zone. Here, it I impossible to frame the suggested duty except by reference to the contract between the solicitor and the testator—a contract to which the disappointed beneficiary is no a party, and from which, therefore, he can derive no rights. Second, the loss suffered by the disappointed beneficiary is not in reality a loss at all; it is, more accurately, failure to obtain a benefit. All that has happened is that what is sometimes called spes succesionis has failed to come to fruition. As a result, he has not become better off; but he is not made worse off. A claim in respect of such a loss of expectation falls it is said, clearly within the exclusive zone of contractual liability.

(3) A third, and distinct, objection is that, if liability in tort was recognised in cases such as *Ross* v. *Caunters*, it would be impossible to place any sensible bounds t cases in which such recovery was allowed. In particular, the same liability should logically be imposed in cases where an inter vivos transaction was ineffective, and the defect was not discovered until the donor was no longer able to repair it. Furthermore, liability could not logically be restricted to cases where a specific named beneficiary was disappointed, but would inevitably have to be extended to cases in which wide, even indeterminate, classes of persons could be said to have been adversely affected—

(4) Other miscellaneous objections were taken, though in my opinion they were without substance. In particular—(a) Since the testator himself owes no duty to the beneficiary, it would be illogical to impose any such duty on his solicitor. I myself cannot however see any force in this objection. (b) To enable the disappointed beneficiary to recover from the solicitor would have the undesirable, and indeed fortuitous, effect o substantially increasing the size of the testator's estate— even of doubling it in size; because it would not be possible to recover any pan of the estate which had lawfully devolved upon others by an unrevoked will or on an intestacy, even though that was not in fact the testator's intention. I cannot however see what impact this has on the disappointed beneficiary's remedy. It simply reflects the fact that those who received the testator's estate, either under an unrevoked will or on an intestacy, were lucky enough to receive a windfall; and in consequence the estate is, so far as the testator and the disappointed beneficiary are concerned, irretrievably lost.

(5) There is however another objection of a conceptual nature, which was not adumbrated in argument before the Appellate Committee. In the present case, unlike *Ross* v. *Caunters* itself, there was no act of the defendant solicitor which could be characterised as negligent. All that happened was that the solicitor did nothing at all for a period of time, with the result that the testator died

before his new testamentary intentions could be implemented in place of the old. As a general rule, however, there is no liability in tortious negligence for an omission, unless the defendant is under some pre-existing duty. Once again, therefore, the question arises how liability can arise in the present case in the absence of a contract. . . .

[After describing as obiter dicta remarks made by the House of Lords in *Robertson* v. *Fleming* (1861) 4 Macq 167, remarks which clearly supported the defendants' case, his Lordship continued:]

The impulse to do practical justice Before addressing the legal questions which lie at the heart of the present case, it is, I consider, desirable to identify the reasons of justice which prompt judges and academic writers to conclude, like Megarry V-C in *Ross* v. *Caunters*, that a duty should be owed by the testator's solicitor to a disappointed beneficiary. The principal reasons are, I believe, as follows.

(1) In the forefront stands the extraordinary fact that, if such a duty is not recognised, the only persons who might have a valid claim (ie the testator and his estate) have suffered no loss, and the only person who has suffered a loss (ie the disappointed beneficiary) has no claim: see *Ross* v. *Caunters* [1980] Ch 297 at 303 per Megarry V-C. It can therefore be said that, if the solicitor owes no duty to the intended beneficiaries, there is a lacuna in the law which needs to be filled. This I regard as being a point of cardinal importance in the present case.

(2) The injustice of denying such a remedy is reinforced if one considers the importance of legacies in a society which recognises (subject only to the incidence of inheritance tax, and statutory requirements for provision for near relatives) the right of citizens to leave their assets to whom they please, and in which, as a result, legacies can be of great importance to individual citizens, providing very often the only opportunity for a citizen to acquire a significant capital sum; or to inherit a house, so providing a secure roof over the heads of himself and his family; or to make special provision for his or her old age. In the course of the hearing before the Appellate Committee Mr Matheson (who was instructed by the Law Society to represent the appellant solicitors) placed before the Committee a schedule of claims of the character of that in the present case notified to the Solicitors' Indemnity Fund following the judgment of the Court of Appeal below. It is striking that, where the amount of the claim was known, it was, by today's standards, of a comparatively modest size. This perhaps indicates that it is where a testator instructs a small firm of solicitors that mistakes of this kind are most likely to occur, with the result that it tends to be people of modest means, who need the money so badly, who suffer.

(3) There is a sense in which the solicitors' profession cannot complain if such a liability may be imposed upon their members. If one of them has been negligent in such a way as to defeat his client's testamentary intentions, he must regard himself as very lucky indeed if the effect of the law is that he is not liable to pay damages in the ordinary way. It can involve no injustice to render him subject to such a liability, even if the damages are payable not to his client's estate for distribution to the disappointed beneficiary (which might have been the preferred solution) but direct to the disappointed beneficiary.

(4) That such a conclusion is required as a matter of justice is reinforced by consideration of the role played by solicitors in society. The point was well made by Cooke J in *Gartside* v. *Sheffield Young & Ellis* [1983] NZLR 37 at 43, when he observed:

"To deny an effective remedy in a plain case would seem to imply a refusal to acknowledge the solicitor's professional role in the community. In practice the public relies on solicitors (or statutory officers with similar functions) to prepare effective wills."

The question therefore arises whether it is possible to give effect in law to the strong impulse for practical justice which is the fruit of the foregoing considerations. For this to be achieved, I respectfully agree with Nicholls V-C when he said that the court will have to fashion "an effective remedy for the solicitor's breach of his professional duty to his client" in such a way as to repair the injustice to the disappointed beneficiary (see [1993] 3 WLR 730 at 739).

Ross v. Caunters *and the conceptual problems*

In *Ross* v. *Caunters* Megarry V-C approached the problem as one arising under the ordinary principles of the tort of negligence. He found himself faced with two principal objections to the plaintiff's claim. The first, founded mainly upon the decision of the Court of Appeal in *Groom* v. *Crocker* [1939] 1 KB 194, was that a solicitor could not be liable in negligence in respect of his professional work to anyone except his client, his liability to his client arising only in contract and not in tort. This proposition Megarry V-C rejected without difficulty, relying primarily upon the judgment of Oliver J in *Midland Bank Trust Go Ltd* v. *Hett, Stubbs & Kemp* [1979] Ch 384 (recently approved by this House in *Henderson* v. *Merrett Syndicates Ltd* [1994] 3 WLR 761). The second, and more fundamental, argument was that, apart from cases falling within the principle established in Hedley Byrne no action lay in the tort of negligence for pure economic loss. This argument Megarry V-C approached following the path traced by Lord Wilberforce in *Anns* v. *Merton London Borough* [1978] AC 728 at 751–752; and on that basis, relying in particular on *Ministry of Housing and Local Government* v. *Shah* [1970] 2 QB 223 (which he regarded as conclusive of the point before him), he held that here liability could properly be imposed in negligence for pure economic loss, his preferred basis being by direct application of *Donoghue* v. *Stevenson* [1932] itself.

It will at once be seen that some of the conceptual problems raised by the appellants in argument before the Appellate Committee were not raised in *Ross* v. *Caunters*. Others which were raised plainly did not loom so large in argument as they have done in the present case. Thus the point founded on the fact that in cases of this kind the plaintiff is claiming damages for the loss of an expectation was briefly touched upon by Megarry V-C and as briefly dismissed by him (see [1980] Ch 297 at 322), but (no doubt for good reason, having regard to the manner in which the case was presented) there is no further analysis of the point. It is however my opinion that, these conceptual arguments having been squarely raised in argument in the present case, they cannot lightly be dismissed. They have to be faced; and it is immediately apparent that they raise the question whether the claim properly falls within the law of contract or the law of tort. This is because, although the plaintiffs' claim has been advanced, and indeed held by the Court of Appeal to lie, in the tort of negligence, nevertheless the response of the appellants has been that the claim, if properly analysed, must necessarily have contractual features which cannot ordinarily exist in the case of an ordinary tortious claim. Here I refer not only to the fact that the claim is one for damages for pure economic loss, but also to the need for the defendant solicitor to be entitled to invoke as against the disappointed beneficiary any terms of the contract with his client which may limit or exclude his liability; to the fact that the damages claimed are for the loss of an expectation; and also to the fact (not adverted to below) that the claim in the present case can be said to arise from a pure omission, and as such will not (apart from special circumstances) give rise to a claim in tortious negligence. Faced with points such as these, the strict lawyer may well react by saying that the present claim can lie only in contract, and is not therefore open to a disappointed beneficiary as against the testator's solicitor. This was indeed the reaction of Lush and Murphy JJ in *Seale* v. *Perry* [1982] VR 193, and is one which is entitled to great respect.

It must not be forgotten however that a solicitor who undertakes to perform services for his client may be liable to his client for failure to exercise due care and skill in relation to the performance of those services not only in contract, but also in negligence under the principle in *Hedley Byrne* v. *Heller* (see *Midland Bank Trust Go Ltd* v. *Hett, Stubbs & Kemp* [1979] Ch 384) on the basis of assumption of responsibility by the solicitor towards his client. Even so there is great difficulty in holding, on ordinary principles, that the solicitor has assumed any responsibility towards an intended beneficiary under a will which he has undertaken to prepare on behalf of his client but which, through his negligence, has failed to take effect in accordance with his client's instructions. The relevant work is plainly performed by the solicitor for his client; but, in the absence of special circumstances, it cannot be said to have been undertaken for the intended beneficiary. Certainly, again in the absence of special circumstances, there will have been no reliance by the intended beneficiary on the exercise by the solicitor of due care and skill; indeed, the intended beneficiary may not even have been aware that the solicitor was engaged on such a task, or that his position might be affected. Let me take the example of an inter vivos gift where, as a result of the solicitor's negligence, the instrument in question is for some reason not effective for its purpose. The mistake comes to light some time later during the lifetime of the donor, after the gift to the intended donor should have taken effect. The donor, having by then changed his mind, declines to perfect the imperfect gift in favour of the intended donor. The latter may be unable to obtain rectification of the instrument, because equity will not perfect an imperfect gift (though there is some authority which suggests that exceptionally it may do so if the donor has died or become incapacitated: see *Lister* v. *Hodgson* (1867) LR 4 Ex 30 at 34–35 per Lord Romilly MR). I, for my part, do not think that the intended donor could in these circumstances have any claim against the solicitor. It is enough, as I see it, that the donor is able to do what he wishes to put matters right. From this it would appear to follow that the real reason for concern in cases such as the present lies in the extraordinary fact that, if a duty owed by the testator's solicitor to the disappointed beneficiary is not recognised, the only person who may have a valid claim has suffered no loss, and the only person who has suffered a loss has no claim. This is a point to which I will return later in this opinion, when I shall give further consideration to the application of the Hedley Byrne principle in circumstances such as those in the present case.

The German experience

The fact that the problems which arise in cases such as the present have troubled the courts in many jurisdictions, both common law and civil law, and have prompted a variety of reactions, indicates that they are of their very nature difficult to accommodate within the ordinary principles of the law of obligations. It is true that our law of contract is widely seen as deficient in the sense that it is perceived to be hampered by the presence of an unnecessary doctrine of consideration and (through a strict doctrine of privity of contract) stunted through a failure to recognise a jus quaesitum tertio. But even if we lacked the former and possessed the latter, the ordinary law could not provide a simple answer to the problems which arise in the present case, which appear at first sight to require the imposition of something like a contractual liability which is beyond the scope of the ordinary jus quaesitum tertio. In these circumstances, the effect of the special characteristics of any particular system of law is likely to be, as indeed appears from the authorities I have cited, not so much that no remedy is recognised, but rather that the system in question will choose its own special means for granting a remedy notwithstanding the doctrinal difficulties involved.

We can, I believe, see this most clearly if we compare the English and German reactions to problems of this kind. Strongly though I support the study of comparative law, I hesitate to embark in an opinion such as this upon a comparison, however brief, with a civil law system; because experience has taught me how very difficult, and indeed potentially misleading, such an exercise can be. Exceptionally however, in the present case, thanks to material published in our language by distinguished comparatists, German as well as English, we have direct access to publications which should sufficiently dispel our ignorance of German law and so by comparison illuminate our understanding of our own.

I have already referred to problems created in the English law of contract by the doctrines of consideration and of privity of contract. These, of course, encourage us to seek a solution to problems of this kind within our law of tortious negligence. In German law, on the other hand, in which the law of delict does not allow for the recovery of damages for pure economic loss in negligence, it is natural that the judges should extend the law of contract to meet the justice of the case. In a case such as the present, which is concerned with a breach of duty owed by a professional man, A, to his client, B, in circumstances in which practical justice requires that a third party, C, should have a remedy against the professional man, A, in respect of damage which he has suffered by reason of the breach, German law may have recourse to a doctrine called Vertrag mit Schutzwirkung für Dritte (contract with protective effect for third parties), the scope of which extends beyond that of an ordinary contract for the benefit of a third party: see Professor Werner Lorenz in *The Gradual Convergence* edited by Markesinis (1994), pp. 65, 68–72.) This doctrine was invoked by the German Supreme Court in the *Testamentfall* case (BGH 6 July 1965, NJW 1965, 1955) which is similar to the present case in that the plaintiff, C, through the dilatoriness of a lawyer, A, (instructed by her father, B) in making the necessary arrangements for the father's will, was deprived of a testamentary benefit which she would have received under the will if it had been duly made. The plaintiff, C, was held to be entitled to recover damages from the lawyer, A. Professor Lorenz has expressed the opinion (p. 70) that the ratio of that case would apply to the situation in *Ross* v. *Caunters* itself. In these cases, it appears that the court will examine "whether the contracting parties intended to create duty of care in favour of" the third person (BGH NJW 1984, 355, 356), or whether there is to be inferred "a protective obligation . . . based on good faith . . ." (BGHZ 69, 82, 85 *et seq.*). (Quotations taken in each case from Professor Markesinis's Article on "An Expanding Tort Law—the Price of a Rigid Contract Law" (1987) 103 *LQR* 354, 363, 366, 368.) But any such inference of intention would, in English law, be beyond the scope of our doctrine of implied terms; and it is legitimate to infer that the German judges, in creating this special doctrine, were extending the law of contract beyond orthodox contractual principles.

I wish next to refer to another German doctrine known as *Drittschadensliquidation*, which is available in cases of transferred loss (*Schadensverlagerung*). In these cases, as a leading English comparatist has explained:

"the person who has suffered the loss has no remedy while the person who has the remedy has suffered no loss. If such a situation is left unchallenged, the defaulting party may never face the consequences of his negligent conduct; his insurer may receive an unexpected (and undeserved) windfall; and the person on whom the loss has fallen may be left without any redress:" see *Markesinis, The German Law of Torts*, 3rd ed. (1994), p. 56.

Under this doctrine, to take one example, the defendant, A, typically a carrier, may be held liable to the seller of goods, B, for the loss suffered by the buyer, C, to whom the risk but not the property in the goods has passed. In such circumstances the seller is held to have a contractual claim against the carrier in respect of the damage suffered by the buyer. This claim can be pursued by the seller against the carrier; but it can also be assigned by him to the buyer. If, exceptionally, the seller refuses either to exercise his right for the benefit of the buyer or to assign his claim to him, the seller can be compelled to make the assignment: see Professor Werner Lorenz in *Essays in Memory of Professor F H Lawson* (1986), pp. 86, 89–90, and in *The Gradual Convergence*, pp. 65, 88–89, 92–93; and Professor Hein Kötz in *Tel Aviv University Studies in Law* (1990), vol. 10, pp. 195, 209. Professor Lorenz (*Essays*, at p. 89) has stated that it is at least arguable that the idea of Drittschadensliquidation might be "extended so as to cover" such cases as the *Testamentfall* case, an observation which is consistent with the view expressed by the German Supreme Court that the two doctrines may overlap (BGH 19 January 1977, NJW 1977, 2073 = VersR 1977, 638: translated in Markesinis, *The German Law of Torts*, p. 293). At all events both doctrines have the effect of extending to the plaintiff the benefit of what is, in substance, a contractual cause of action; though, at least as seen through English eyes, this result is achieved not by orthodox contractual reasoning, but by the contractual remedy being made available by law in order to achieve practical justice.

Transferred loss in English law

I can deal with this topic briefly. The problem of transferred loss has arisen in particular in maritime law, when a buyer of goods seeks to enforce against a shipowner a remedy in tort in respect of loss of or damage to goods at his risk when neither the rights under the contract nor the property in the goods has passed to him (see *Leigh and Sillavan Ltd.* v. *Aliakmon Shipping Co. Ltd.* [1985] QB 350, 399, *per* Robert Goff LJ and [1986] AC 785, 820, *per* Lord Brandon of Oakbrook). In cases such as these (with all respect to the view expressed by Lord Brandon [1986] AC 785, 819) there was a serious lacuna in the law, as was revealed when all relevant interests in the city of London called for reform to make a remedy available to the buyers who under the existing law were without a direct remedy against the shipowners. The problem was solved, as a matter of urgency, by the Carriage of Goods by Sea Act 1992, I myself having the honour of introducing the Bill into your Lordships' House (acting in its legislative capacity) on behalf of the Law Commission. The solution adopted by the Act was to extend the rights of suit available under section 1 of the Bills of Lading Act 1855 (there restricted to cases where the property in the goods had passed upon or by reason of the consignment or endorsement of the relevant bill of lading) to all holders of bills of lading (and indeed other documents): see section 2(1) of the Act of 1992. Here is a sweeping statutory reform, powered by the needs of commerce, which has the effect of enlarging the circumstances in which contractual rights may be transferred by virtue of the transfer of certain documents. For present purposes, however, an important consequence is the solution in this context of a problem of transferred loss, the lacuna being filled by statute rather than by the common law. Moreover this result has been achieved, as in German law, by vesting in the plaintiff, who has suffered the relevant loss, the contractual rights of the person who has stipulated for the carrier's obligation but has suffered no loss.

I turn next to English law in relation to cases such as the present. Here there is a lacuna in the law, in the sense that practical justice requires that the disappointed beneficiary should have a remedy against the testator's solicitor in circumstances in which neither the testator nor his estate has in law suffered a loss. Professor Lorenz (*Essays in Memory of Professor F H Lawson*, p. 90) has said that "this is a situation which comes very close to the cases of 'transferred loss,' the only difference being that the damage due to the solicitor's negligence could never have been caused to the testator or to his executor." In the case of the testator, he suffers no loss because (in contrast to a gift by an inter vivos settlor) a gift under a will cannot take effect until after the testator's death, and it follows that there can be no depletion of the testator's assets in his lifetime if the relevant asset is, through the solicitors' negligence, directed to a person other than the intended beneficiary. The situation is therefore not one in which events have subsequently occurred which have resulted in the loss falling on another. It is one in which the relevant loss could never fall on the testator to whom the solicitor owed a duty, but only on another; and the loss which is suffered by that other, i.e. an expectation loss, is of a character which in any event could never have been suffered by the testator. Strictly speaking, therefore, this is not a case of transferred loss.

Even so, the analogy is very close. In practical terms, part or all of the testator's estate has been lost because it has been dispatched to a destination unintended by the testator. Moreover, had a gift been similarly misdirected during the testator's lifetime, he would either have been able to recover it from the recipient or, if not, he could have recovered the full amount from the negligent solicitor as damages. In a case such as the present, no such remedies are available to the testator or his estate. The will cannot normally be rectified: the testator has of course no remedy: and his estate has suffered no loss, because it has been distributed under the terms of a valid will. In these circumstances, there can be no injustice if the intended beneficiary has a remedy against the solicitor for the full amount which he should have received under the will, this being no greater than the damage for which the solicitor could have been liable to the donor if the loss had occurred in his lifetime.

A contractual approach

It may be suggested that, in cases such as the present, the simplest course would be to solve the problem by making available to the disappointed beneficiary, by some means or another, the benefit of the contractual rights (such as they are) of the testator or his estate against the negligent solicitor, as is for example done under the German principle of *Vertrag mit Schutzwirkung für Dritte*. Indeed that course has been urged upon us by Professor Markesinis in "An Expanding Tort Law" (1987) 103 LQR 354 at 396–397, echoing a view expressed by Professor Fleming in "Comparative Law of Torts" (1986) 4 OILS 235 at 241. Attractive though this solution is, there is unfortunately a serious difficulty in its way. The doctrine of consideration still forms part of our law of contract, as does the doctrine of privity of contract which is considered to exclude the recognition of a jus quaesitum tertio. To proceed as Professor Markesinis has suggested may be acceptable in German law, but in this country could be open to criticism as an illegitimate circumvention of these long-established doctrines; and this criticism could be reinforced by reference to the fact that, in the case of carriage of goods by sea, a contractual solution to a particular problem of transferred loss, and to other cognate problems, was provided only by recourse to Parliament. Furthermore, I myself do not consider that the present case provides a suitable occasion for reconsideration of doctrines so fundamental as these.

The Albazero principle

Even so, I have considered whether the present problem might be solved by adding cases such as the present to the group of cases referred to by Lord Diplock in *The Albazero, Albacruz (cargo owners)* v. *Albazero (owners)* [1977] AC 774 at 846–847. In these cases, a person may exceptionally sue in his own name to recover a loss which he has not in fact suffered, being personally account-able for any damages so recovered to the person who has in fact suffered the loss. Lord Diplock was prepared to accommodate within this group the so-called rule in *Dunlop* v. *Lambert* (1839) 6 CI & Fin 600, 7 ER 824 on the principle that —

"in a commercial contract concerning goods where it is in the contemplation of the parties that the pro-prietary interests in the goods may be transferred from one owner to another after the contract has been entered into and before the breach which causes loss or damage to the goods, an original party to the contract, if such be the intention of them both, is to be treated in law as having entered into the breach of contract the actual loss sustained by those for whose benefit the contract is entered into." . . . (See [1977] AC 774 at 847.)

Furthermore, in *Linden Gardens Trust Ltd* v. *Lenesta Sludge Disposals Ltd* [1994] I AC 85 your Lordships' House extended this group of cases to include a case in which work was done by the defendants under a contract with the first plaintiffs who, despite a contractual bar against assign-ment of their contractual rights without the consent of the defendants, had without consent assigned them to the second plaintiffs who suffered damage by reason of defective work carried out by the defendants. It was held that, by analogy with the cases referred to in *The Albazero* the first plaintiffs could recover the damages from the defendants for the benefit of the second plain-tiffs. In so holding, your Lordships' House relied upon a passage in Lord Diplock's speech that —

"there may still be occasional cases in which the rule [in *Dunlop* v. *Lambert*] would provide a remedy where no other would be available to a person sustaining loss which under a rational legal system ought to be compensated by the person who has caused it." (See [1977] AC 774 at 847.)

The decision is noteworthy in a number of respects. First, this was a case of transferred loss; and Lord Diplock's dictum, as applied by your Lordships' House, reflects a clear need for the law to find a remedy in cases of this kind. Second, your Lordships' House felt able to do so in a case in which there was a contractual bar against assignment without consent; and as a result, unlike Lord Diplock, did not find it necessary to look for a common intention that the contract was entered into for the benefit of persons such as the second plaintiffs, which in this case, having regard to the prohibition against assignment, it plainly was not. Third, the consequence was that your Lordships' House simply made the remedy available as a matter of law in order to solve the problem of transferred loss in the case before them.

Even so, the result was only to enable a person to recover damages in respect of loss which he himself had not suffered, for the benefit of a third party. In the present case, there is the difficulty that the third party (the intended beneficiary) is seeking to recover damages for a loss (expecta-tion loss) which the contracting party (the testator) would not himself have suffered. In any event, under this principle, the third party who has suffered the loss is not able to compel the contract-ing party to sue for his benefit, or to transfer the right of action to him; still less is he entitled to sue in his own name. In the last analysis, this is because any such right would be contrary to the doctrine of privity of contract. In consequence a principle such as this, if it could be extended to cases such as the present, would be of limited value because, quite apart from any other difficulties, the family relationship may be such that the executors may be unwilling to assist the disappointed beneficiary by pursuing a claim of this kind for his benefit. Certainly, it could not assist the plaintiffs in the present case, who very understandably are proceeding against the solicitors by a direct action in their own name.

The tortious solution

I therefore return to the law of tort for a solution to the problem. For the reasons I have already given, an ordinary action in tortious negligence on the lines proposed by Megarry V-C in *Ross* v. *Caunters* [1980] Ch 297 must, with the greatest respect, be regarded as inappropriate, because it does not meet any of the conceptual problems which have been raised. Furthermore, for the reasons I have previously given, the *Hedley Byrne* principle cannot, in the absence of special circumstances, give rise on ordinary principles to an assumption of responsibility by the testator's solicitor towards an intended beneficiary. Even so, it seems to me that it is open to your Lordships' House, as in *Linden Gardens Trust Ltd* v. *Lenesta Sludge Disposals Ltd* [1994] 1 AC 85, to fashion a remedy to fill a lacuna in the law and so prevent me injustice which would otherwise occur on me facts of cases such as me present. In the *Lenesta Sludge* case, as I have said, me House made available a remedy as a matter of law to solve the problem of transferred loss in the case before them. The present case is, if anything, a fortiori, since me nature of me transaction was such that, if the solicitors were negligent and their negligence did not come to light until after the death of the testator, there would be no remedy for the ensuing loss unless the intended beneficiary could claim. In my opinion, therefore, your Lordships' House should in cases such as these extend to the intended beneficiary a remedy under the *Hedley Byrne* principle by holding that the assumption of responsibility by the solicitor towards his client should be held in law to extend to the intended beneficiary who (as the solicitor can reasonably foresee) may, as a result of the solicitor's negligence, be deprived of his intended legacy in circumstances in which neither the testator nor his estate will have a remedy against the solicitor. Such liability will not of course arise in cases in which the defect in the will comes to light before the death of the testator, and me testator either leaves the will as it is or otherwise continues to exclude the previously intended beneficiary from the relevant benefit. I only wish to add mat, with me benefit of experience during the 15 years in which *Ross* v. *Caunters* has been regularly applied, we can say with some confidence that a direct remedy by the intended beneficiary against the solicitor appears to create no problems in practice.

That is therefore the solution which I would recommend to your Lordships.

As I see it, not only does this conclusion produce practical justice as far as all parties are concerned, but it also has the following beneficial consequences.

(1) There is no unacceptable circumvention of established principles of the law of contract.

(2) No problem arises by reason of me loss being of a purely economic character.

(3) Such assumption of responsibility will of course be subject to any term of the contract between the solicitor and the testator which may exclude or restrict the solicitor's liability to the testator under the principle in *Hedley Byrne*. It is true mat such a term would be most unlikely to exist in practice; but as a matter of principle it is right mat this largely theoretical question should be addressed.

(4) Since the *Hedley Byrne* principle is founded upon an assumption of responsibility, the solicitor may be liable for negligent omissions as well as negligent acts of commission: see *Midland Bank Trust Go Ltd* v. *Hett, Stubbs & Kemp* [1979] Ch 384 at 416 per Oliver J, and my own speech in *Henderson* v. *Merrett Syndicates Ltd* [1994] 3 WLR 761 at 777. This conclusion provides justification for the decision of the Court of Appeal to reverse the decision of Turner J in the present case, although this point was not in fact raised below or before your Lordships.

(5) I do not consider that damages for loss of an expectation are excluded in cases of negligence arising under me principle in *Hedley Byrne*, simply because the cause of action is classified as tortious. Such damages may in principle be recoverable in cases of contractual negligence; and I cannot see mat, for present purposes, any relevant distinction can be drawn between the two forms of action. In particular, an expectation loss may well occur in cases where a professional man, such as a solicitor, has assumed responsibility for the affairs of another; and I for my part can see no reason in principle why the professional man should not, in an appropriate case, be liable for such loss under the *Hedley Byrne* principle.

In the result, all the conceptual problems, including those which so troubled Lush and Murphy JJ in *Seale* v. *Perry* [1982] VR 193, can be seen to fade innocuously away. Let me emphasise that I can see no injustice in imposing liability upon a negligent solicitor in a case such as the present where, in the absence of a remedy in this form, neither the testator's estate nor the disappointed beneficiary will have a claim for me loss caused by his negligence. This is the injustice which, in my opinion, the judges of this country should address by recognising that cases such as these call for an appropriate remedy, and that the common law is not so sterile as to be incapable of supplying mat remedy when it is required.

Unlimited claims

I come finally to the objection that, if liability is recognised in a case such as the present, it will be impossible to place any sensible limits to cases in which recovery is allowed. Before your Lordships, as before the Court of Appeal, Mr Matheson conjured up the spectre of solicitors being liable to an indeterminate class, including persons unborn at the date of the testator's death. I must confess that my reaction to this kind of argument was very similar to that of Cooke J in *Gartside* v. *Sheffield Young & Ellis* [1983] NZLR 37 at 44, when he said that he was not "persuaded that we should decide a fairly straightforward case against the dictates of justice because of foreseeable troubles in more difficult cases". We are concerned here with a liability which is imposed by law to do practical justice in a particular type of case. There must be boundaries to the availability of a remedy in such cases; but these will have to be worked out in the future, as practical problems come before the courts. In the present case Nicholls V-C observed that, in cases of this kind, liability is not to an indeterminate class, but to the particular beneficiary or beneficiaries whom the client intended to benefit through the particular will. I respectfully agree, and I also agree with him that the ordinary case is one in which the intended beneficiaries are a small number of identified people. If by any chance a more complicated case should arise to test the precise boundaries of the principle in cases of this kind, that problem can await solution when such a case comes forward for decision.

Conclusion

For these reasons I would dismiss the appeal with costs.

Addendum 2

Henderson v. Merrett Syndicates Ltd House of Lords [1995] 2 AC 145

LORD GOFF OF CHIEVELEY

The impact of the contractual context
All systems of law which recognise a law of contract and a law of tort (or delict) have to solve the problem of the possibility of concurrent claims arising from breach of duty under the two rubrics of the law. Although there are variants, broadly speaking two possible solutions present themselves: either to insist that the claimant should pursue his remedy in contract alone, or to allow him to choose which remedy he prefers. As my noble and learned friend, Lord Mustill, and I have good reason to know (see *J. Braconnot et Cie.* v. *Compagnie des Messageries Maritimes (The Sindh)* [1975]

1 Lloyd's Rep. 372), France has adopted the former solution in its doctrine of non cumul, under which the concurrence of claims in contract and tort is outlawed (see Tony Weir in XI *International Encyclopedia of Comparative Law.*, chapter 12, paras. 47–72, at paragraph 52). The reasons given for this conclusion are (1) respect for the will of the legislator, and (2) respect for the will of the parties to the contract (see paragraph 53). The former does not concern us; but the latter is of vital importance. It is however open to various interpretations. For such a policy does not necessarily require the total rejection of concurrence, but only so far as a concurrent remedy in tort is inconsistent with the terms of the contract. It comes therefore as no surprise to learn that the French doctrine is not followed in all civil law jurisdictions, and that concurrent remedies in tort and contract are permitted in other civil law countries, notably Germany (see paragraph 58). I only pause to observe that it appears to be accepted that no perceptible harm has come to the German system from admitting concurrent claims.

The situation in common law countries, including of course England, is exceptional, in that the common law grew up within a procedural framework uninfluenced by Roman law. The law was categorised by reference to the forms of action, and it was not until the abolition of the forms of action by the Common Law Procedure Act 1852 (15 & 16 Vict. c. 76) that it became necessary to reclassify the law in substantive terms. The result was that common lawyers did at last segregate our law of obligations into contract and tort, though in so doing they relegated quasi-contractual claims to the status of an appendix to the law of contract, thereby postponing by a century or so the development of a law of restitution. Even then, there was no systematic reconsideration of the problem of concurrent claims in contract and tort. We can see the courts rather grappling with unpromising material drawn from the old cases in which liability in negligence derived largely from categories based upon the status of the defendant. In a sense, we must not be surprised; for no significant law faculties were established at our universities until the late 19th century, and so until then there was no academic opinion available to guide or stimulate the judges. Even so, it is a remarkable fact that there was little consideration of the problem of concurrent remedies in our academic literature until the second half of the 20th century, though in recent years the subject has attracted considerable attention.

In the result, the courts in this country have until recently grappled with the problem very largely without the assistance of systematic academic study. At first, as is shown in particular by cases concerned with liability for solicitors' negligence, the courts adopted something very like the French solution, holding that a claim against a solicitor for negligence must be pursued in contract, and not in tort (see, e.g., *Bean* v. *Wade* (1885) 2 TLR 157); and in *Groom* v. *Crocker* [1939] 1 KB 194, this approach was firmly adopted. It has to be said, however, that decisions such as these, though based on prior authority, were supported by only a slender citation of cases, none of great weight; and the jurisprudential basis of the doctrine so adopted cannot be said to have been explored in any depth. Furthermore when, in *Bagot* v. *Stevens Scanlan & Co. Ltd.* [1966] 1 QB 197, Diplock LJ adopted a similar approach in the case of a claim against a firm of architects, he felt compelled to recognise (pp. 204–205) that a different conclusion might be reached in cases "where the law in the old days recognised either something in the nature of a status like a public calling (such as common carrier, common innkeeper, or a bailor and bailee) or the status of master and servant." To this list must be added cases concerned with claims against doctors and dentists. I must confess to finding it startling that, in the second half of the twentieth century, a problem of considerable practical importance should fall to be solved by reference to such an outmoded form of categorisation as this.

I think it is desirable to stress at this stage that the question of concurrent liability is by no means only of academic significance. Practical issues, which can be of great importance to the parties, are at stake. Foremost among these is perhaps the question of limitation of actions. If concurrent liability in tort is not recognised, a claimant may find his claim barred at a time when he is unaware of its existence. This must moreover be a real possibility in the case of claims against professional men, such as solicitors or architects, since the consequences of their negligence may well not come to light until long after the lapse of six years from the date when the relevant breach of contract occurred. Moreover the benefits of the Latent Damage Act 1986, under which the time of the accrual of the cause of action may be postponed until after the plaintiff has the relevant knowledge, are limited to actions in tortious negligence. This leads to the startling possibility that a client who has had the benefit of gratuitous advice from his solicitor may in this respect be better off than a client who has paid a fee. Other practical problems arise, for example, from the absence of a right to contribution between negligent contract-breakers; from the rules as to remoteness of damage, which are less restricted in tort than they are in contract; and from the availability of the opportunity to obtain leave to serve proceedings out of the jurisdiction. It can of course be argued that the principle established in respect of concurrent liability in contract and tort should not be tailored to mitigate the adventitious effects of rules of law such as these, and that one way of solving such problems would no doubt be to rephrase such incidental rules as have to remain in terms of the nature of the harm suffered rather than the nature of the liability asserted (see Tony Weir, XI *International Encyclopedia of Comparative Law* chapter 12, para. 72). But this is perhaps crying for the moon; and with the law in its present form, practical considerations of this kind cannot sensibly be ignored.

Moreover I myself perceive at work in these decisions not only the influence of the dead hand of history, but also what I have elsewhere called the temptation of elegance. Mr Tony Weir (XI *International Encyclopedia of Comparative Law* chapter 12, para. 55) has extolled the French solution for its elegance; and we can discern the same impulse behind the much-quoted observation of Lord Scarman when delivering the judgment of the Judicial Committee of the Privy Council in *Tai Hing Cotton Mill Ltd.* v. *Liu Chong Hing Bank Ltd.* [1986] AC 80, 107:

"Their Lordships do not believe that there is anything to the advantage of the law's development in searching for a liability in tort where the parties are in a contractual relationship. This is particularly so in a commercial relationship. Though it is possible as a matter of legal semantics to conduct an analysis of the rights and duties inherent in some contractual relationships including that of banker and customer either as a matter of contract law when the question will be what, if any, terms are to be implied or as a matter of tort law when the task will be to identify a duty arising from the proximity and character of the relationship between the parties, their Lordships believe it to be correct in principle and necessary for the avoidance of confusion in the law to adhere to the contractual analysis: on principle because it is a relationship in which the parties have, subject to a few exceptions, the right to determine their obligations to each other, and for the avoidance of confusion because different consequences do follow according to whether liability arises from contract or tort, e.g. in the limitation of action."

It is however right to stress, as did Sir Thomas Bingham MR in the present case, that the issue in the *Tai Hing* case was whether a tortious duty of care could be established which was more extensive than that which was provided for under the relevant contract.

At all events, even before the *Tai Hing* case we can see the beginning of the redirection of the common law away from the contractual solution adopted in *Groom* v. *Crocker* [1939] 1 K.B. 194, towards the recognition of concurrent remedies in contract and tort. First, and most important, in 1963 came the decision of your Lordships' House in *Hedley Byrne & Co. Ltd.* v. *Heller & Partners Ltd.* [1964] AC 465. I have already expressed the opinion that the fundamental importance of this case rests in the establishment of the principle upon which liability may arise in tortious negligence in respect of services (including advice) which are rendered for another, gratuitously or otherwise, but are negligently performed—viz., an assumption of responsibility coupled with reliance by the plaintiff which, in all the circumstances, makes it appropriate that a remedy in law should be available for such negligence. For immediate purposes, the relevance of the principle lies in the fact that, as a matter of logic, it is capable of application not only where the services are rendered gratuitously, but also where they are rendered under a contract. Furthermore we can see in the principle an acceptable basis for liability in negligence in cases which in the past have been seen to rest upon the now outmoded concept of status. In this context, it is of particular relevance to refer to the opinion expressed both implicitly by Lord Morris of Borth-y-Gest (with whom Lord Hodson agreed) and expressly by Lord Devlin that the principle applies to the relationship of solicitor and client, which is nearly always contractual: see pp. 465, 497–499 (where Lord Morris approved the reasoning of Chitty J in *Cann* v. *Willson* (1888) 39 Ch.D. 39), and p. 529 (*per* Lord Devlin).

The decision in *Hedley Byrne*, and the statement of general principle in that case, provided the opportunity to reconsider the question of concurrent liability in contract and tort afresh, untrammelled by the ancient learning based upon a classification of defendants in terms of status which drew distinctions difficult to accept in modern conditions. At first that opportunity was not taken. *Groom* v. *Crocker* [1939] 1 K.B. 194 was followed by the Court of Appeal in *Cook* v. *Swinfen* [1967] 1 *WLR* 457, and again in *Heywood* v. *Wellers* [1976] QB 446; though in the latter case Lord Denning MR, at p. 459, was beginning to show signs of dissatisfaction with the contractual test accepted in *Groom* v. *Crocker*—a dissatisfaction which crystallised into a change of heart in *Esso Petroleum Co. Ltd.* v. *Mardon* [1976] QB 801. That case was concerned with statements made by employees of Esso in the course of precontractual negotiations with Mr Mardon, the prospective tenant of a petrol station. The statements related to the potential throughput of the station. Mr Mardon was persuaded by the statements to enter into the tenancy; but he suffered serious loss when the actual throughput proved to be much lower than had been predicted. The Court of Appeal held that Mr Mardon was entitled to recover damages from Esso, on the basis of either breach of warranty or (on this point affirming the decision of the judge below) negligent misrepresentation. In rejecting an argument that Esso's liability could only be contractual, Lord Denning MR dismissed *Groom* v. *Crocker* [1939] 1 K.B. 194 and *Bagot* v. *Stevens Scanlan & Co. Ltd.* [1966] 1 QB 197 as inconsistent with other decisions of high authority, viz. *Boorman* v. *Brown* (1842) 3 QB 511, 525–526, *per* Tindal CJ, and (1844) 11 Cl. & F. 1, 44, *per* Lord Campbell; *Lister* v. *Romford Ice and Cold Storage Co. Ltd.* [1957] AC 555, 587, *per* Lord Radcliffe; *Matthews* v. *Kuwait Bechtel Corporation* [1959] 2 QB 57 and *Nocton* v. *Lord Ashburton* [1914] AC 932, 956, *per* Viscount Haldane LC He then held that, in addition to its liability in contract, Esso was also liable in negligence. The other members of the Court of Appeal, Ormrod and Shaw L JJ, agreed that Mr Mardon was entitled to recover damages either for breach of warranty or for negligent misrepresentation, though neither expressed any view about the status of *Groom* v. *Crocker* [1939] 1 K.B. 194. It was however implicit in their decision that, as Lord Denning MR held, concurrent remedies were available to Mr Mardon in contract and tort. For present purposes, I do not find it necessary to comment on the authorities relied upon by Lord Denning as relieving him from the obligation to follow *Groom* v. *Crocker*; though I feel driven to comment that the judgments in *Esso Petroleum Co. Ltd.* v. *Mardon* [1976] QB 801 reveal no analysis in depth of the basis upon which concurrent liability rests. That case was however followed by the Court of Appeal in *Batty* v. *Metropolitan Property Realisations Ltd.* [1978] QB 554, in which concurrent remedies in contract and tort were again allowed.

The requisite analysis is however to be found in the judgment of Oliver J in *Midland Bank Trust Co. Ltd.* v. *Hett, Stubbs & Kemp* [1979] chapter 384, in which he held that a solicitor could be liable to his client for negligence either in contract or in tort, with the effect that in the case before him it was open to the client to take advantage of the more favourable date of accrual of the cause of action for the purposes of limitation. In that case, Oliver J was much concerned with the question whether it was open to him, as a judge of first instance, to depart from the decision of the Court of Appeal in *Groom* v. *Crocker* [1939] 1 K.B. 194. For that purpose, he carried out a most careful examination of the relevant authorities, both before and after *Groom* v. *Crocker*, and concluded that he was free to depart from the decision in that case, which he elected to do.

It is impossible for me to do justice to the reasoning of Oliver J, for which I wish to express my respectful admiration, without unduly prolonging what is inevitably a very long opinion. I shall therefore confine myself to extracting certain salient features. First, from his study of the cases before *Groom* v. *Crocker*, he found no unanimity of view that the solicitor's liability was regarded as exclusively contractual. Some cases (such as *Howell* v. *Young* (1826) 5 B. & C. 259) he regarded as equivocal. In others, he understood the judges to regard contract and tort as providing alternative causes of action (see *In re Manby and Hawksford* (1856) 26 L.J.Ch. 313, 317 and *Sawyer* v. *Goodwin* (1867) 36 L.J.Ch. 578, 582, in both cases *per* Stuart V.-C., and most notably *Nocton* v. *Lord*

Ashburton [1914] AC 932, 956, *per* Viscount Haldane L.C.). However *Bean* v. *Wade* (1885) 2 T.L.R. 157, briefly reported in the Times Law Reports and by no means extensively referred to, provided Court of Appeal authority that the remedy was exclusively contractual; and it was that case which was principally relied upon by the Court of Appeal in *Groom* v. *Crocker* [1939] 1 K.B. 194 when reaching the same conclusion. Oliver J put on one side those cases, decided for the purpose of section 11 of the County Courts Act 1915, under which a different statutory test had to be complied with, viz. whether the action was one "founded on a contract" or "founded on a tort."

It is evident that the early authorities did not play a very significant part in Oliver J.'s decision (see [1979] chapter 384, 411C–D). He loyally regarded *Groom* v. *Crocker* as prima facie binding upon him. His main concern was with the impact of the decision of this House in *Hedley Byrne* [1964] AC 465, and of subsequent cases in the Court of Appeal in which *Hedley Byrne* had been applied. As he read the speeches in *Hedley Byrne*, the principle there stated was not limited to circumstances in which the responsibility of the defendant had been gratuitously assumed. He referred in particular to the statement of principle by Lord Morris of Borth-y-Gest, at pp. 502–503, which I have already quoted, and said, at p. 411:

> "The principle was stated by Lord Morris of Borth-y-Gest as a perfectly general one and it is difficult to see why it should be excluded by the fact that the relationship of dependence and reliance between the parties is a contractual one rather than one gratuitously assumed, in the absence, of course, of contractual terms excluding or restricting the general duties which the law implies."

Oliver J went on, at p. 412, to quote from the dissenting judgment of Denning L.J. in *Candler* v. *Crane, Christmas & Co.* [1951] 2 K.B. 164, 179–180 (a passage approved by Lord Pearce in *Hedley Byrne* [1964] AC 465, 538) and said, at p. 413:

> "Now, in that passage, I think that it is abundantly clear that Denning LJ was seeking to enunciate a general principle of liability arising from the relationship created by the assumption of a particular work or responsibility, quite regardless of how the relationship arose. . . . The inquiry upon which the court is to embark is 'what is the relationship between the plaintiff and defendant?' not 'how did the relationship, if any, arise?' That this is so appears, I think, with complete clarity from subsequent cases."

Later he said, at p. 415:

> "The matter becomes, in my judgment, even clearer when one looks at the speech of Lord Devlin in the *Hedley Byrne* case [1964] AC 465, for he treats the existence of a contractual relationship as very good evidence of the general tortious duty which he is there discussing.

He said, at pp. 528–529:

> 'I think, therefore, that there is ample authority to justify your Lordships in saying now that the categories of special relationships which may give rise to a duty to take care in word as well as in deed are not limited to contractual relationships or to relationships of fiduciary duty, but include also relationships which in the words of Lord Shaw in *Nocton* v. *Lord Ashburton* [1914] AC 932, 972, are "equivalent to contract," that is, where there is an assumption of responsibility in circumstances in which, but for the absence of consideration, there would be a contract.'"

He expressed his conclusion concerning the impact of *Hedley Byrne* on the case before him in the following words, at p. 417:

> "The case of a layman consulting a solicitor for advice seems to me to be as typical a case as one could find of the sort of relationship in which the duty of care described in the *Hedley Byrne* case [1964] AC 465 exists; and if I am free to do so in the instant case, I would, therefore, hold that the relationship of solicitor and client gave rise to a duty in the defendants under the general law to exercise that care and skill upon which they must have known perfectly well that their client relied. To put it another way, their common law duty was not to injure their client by failing to do that which they had undertaken to do and which, at their invitation, he relied upon them to do. That duty was broken, but no cause of action in tort arose until the damage occurred; and none did occur until 17 August 1967. I

would regard it as wholly immaterial that their duty arose because they accepted a retainer which entitled them, if they chose to do so, to send a bill to their client."

I wish to express my respectful agreement with these passages in Oliver J's judgment.

Thereafter, Oliver J proceeded to consider the authorities since *Hedley Byrne*, in which he found, notably in statements of the law by members of the Appellate Committee in *Arenson* v. *Arenson* [1977] AC 405 and in the decision of the Court of Appeal in *Esso Petroleum Co. Ltd.* v. *Mardon* [1976] QB 801, the authority which relieved him of his duty to follow *Groom* v. *Crocker* [1939] 1 K.B. 194. But I wish to add that, in the course of considering the later authorities, he rejected the idea that there is some general principle of law that a plaintiff who has claims against a defendant for breach of duty both in contract and in tort is bound to rely upon his contractual rights alone. He said, at p. 420:

"There is not and never has been any rule of law that a person having alternative claims must frame his action in one or the other. If I have a contract with my dentist to extract a tooth, I am not thereby precluded from suing him in tort if he negligently shatters my jaw: *Edwards* v. *Mallan* [1908] 1 K.B. 1002; . . ."

The origin of concurrent remedies in this type of case may lie in history; but in a modern context the point is a telling one. Indeed it is consistent with the decision in *Donoghue* v. *Stevenson* [1932] AC 562 itself, and the rejection in that case of the view, powerfully expressed in the speech of Lord Buckmaster (see, in particular, pp. 577–578), that the manufacturer or repairer of an Article owes no duty of care apart from that implied from contract or imposed by statute. That there might be co-existent remedies for negligence in contract and in tort was expressly recognised by Lord Macmillan in *Donoghue* v. *Stevenson*, at p. 610, and by Lord Wright in *Grant* v. *Australian Knitting Mills Ltd.* [1936] AC 85, 102–104. Attempts have been made to explain how doctors and dentists may be concurrently liable in tort while other professional men may not be so liable, on the basis that the former cause physical damage whereas the latter cause pure economic loss (see the discussion by Christine French in (1981–84) 5 Otago LR 236, 280–281). But this explanation is not acceptable, if only because some professional men, such as architects, may also be responsible for physical damage. As a matter of principle, it is difficult to see why concurrent remedies in tort and contract, if available against the medical profession, should not also be available against members of other professions, whatever form the relevant damage may take.

The judgment of Oliver J. in the *Midland Bank Trust Co.* case [1979] chapter 384 provided the first analysis in depth of the question of concurrent liability in tort and contract. Following upon *Esso Petroleum Co. Ltd.* v. *Mardon* [1976] QB 801, it also broke the mould, in the sense that it undermined the view which was becoming settled that, where there is an alternative liability in tort, the claimant must pursue his remedy in contract alone. The development of the case law in other common law countries is very striking. In the same year as the *Midland Bank Trust Co.* case, the Irish Supreme Court held that solicitors owed to their clients concurrent duties in contract and tort: see *Finlay* v. *Murtagh* [1979] I.R. 249. Next, in *Central Trust Co.* v. *Rafuse* (1986) 31 D.L.R. (4th) 481, Le Dain J, delivering the judgment of the Supreme Court of Canada, conducted a comprehensive and most impressive survey of the relevant English and Canadian authorities on the liability of solicitors to their clients for negligence, in contract and in tort, in the course of which he paid a generous tribute to the analysis of Oliver J in the *Midland Bank Trust Co.* case. His conclusions are set out in a series of propositions at pp. 521–522; but his general conclusion was to the same effect as that reached by Oliver J. He said, at p. 522:

"A concurrent or alternative liability in tort will not be admitted if its effect would be to permit the plaintiff to circumvent or escape a contractual exclusion or limitation of liability for the act or omission that would constitute the tort. Subject to this qualification, where concurrent liability in tort and contract exists the plaintiff has the right to assert the cause of action that appears to be the most advantageous to him in respect of any particular legal consequence."

I respectfully agree.

Meanwhile in New Zealand the Court of Appeal had appeared at first, in *McLaren Maycroft & Co.* v. *Fletcher Development Co. Ltd.* [1973] 2 N.Z.L.R. 100, to require that, in cases where there are concurrent duties in contract and tort, the claimant must pursue his remedy in contract alone. There followed a period of some uncertainty, in which differing approaches were adopted by courts of first instance. In 1983 Miss Christine French published her Article on "The Contract/Tort Dilemma" in (1981–84) 5 Otago L.R. 236, in which she examined the whole problem in great depth, with special reference to the situation in New Zealand, having regard to the "rule" in *McLaren Maycroft*. Her Article, to which I wish to pay tribute, was of course published before the decision of the Supreme Court of Canada in the *Central Trust* case. Even so, she reached a conclusion which, on balance, favoured a freedom for the claimant to choose between concurrent remedies in contract and tort. Thereafter in *Rowlands* v. *Callow* [1992] 1 N.Z.L.R. 178 Thomas J, founding himself principally on the *Central Trust* case and on Miss French's Article, concluded that he was free to depart from the decision of the New Zealand Court of Appeal in the *McLaren Maycroft* case and to hold that a person performing professional services (in the case before him an engineer) may be sued for negligence by his client either in contract or in tort. He said, at p. 190:

> "The issue is now virtually incontestable; a person who has performed professional services may be held liable concurrently in contract and in negligence unless the terms of the contract preclude the tortious liability."

In Australia, too, judicial opinion appears to be moving in the same direction, though not without dissent: see, in particular, *Aluminium Products (Qld.) Pty. Ltd.* v. *Hill* [1981] Qd.R. 33 (a decision of the Full Court of the Supreme Court of Queensland) and *Macpherson & Kelley* v. *Kevin J Prunty & Associates* [1983] 1 V.R. 573 (a decision of the Full Court of the Supreme Court of Victoria). A different view has however been expressed by Deane J in *Hawkins* v. *Clayton* (1988) 164 C.L.R. 539, 585, to which I will return later. In principle, concurrent remedies appear to have been accepted for some time in the United States (see *Prosser's Handbook on the Law of Torts*, 7th ed. (1984), p. 444), though with some variation as to the application of the principle in particular cases. In these circumstances it comes as no surprise that Professor Fleming, writing in 1992, should state that "the last ten years have seen a decisive return to the 'concurrent' approach" (see *The Law of Torts*, 8th ed. (1992), p. 187).

I have dealt with the matter at some length because, before your Lordships, Mr Temple, for the managing agents, boldly challenged the decision of Oliver J in the *Midland Bank Trust Co.* case [1979] chapter 384, seeking to persuade your Lordships that this House should now hold that case to have been wrongly decided. This argument was apparently not advanced below, presumably because Oliver J's analysis had received a measure of approval in the Court of Appeal: see, e.g., *Forster* v. *Outred & Co.* [1982] 1 WLR 86, 99, *per* Dunn LJ Certainly there has been no sign of disapproval, even where the *Midland Bank Trust Co.* case has been distinguished: see *Bell* v. *Peter Browne & Co.* [1990] 2 QB 495.

Mr Temple adopted as part of his argument the reasoning of Mr J.M. Kaye in an Article "The Liability of Solicitors in Tort" (1984) 100 LQR 680. In his Article, Mr Kaye strongly criticised the reasoning of Oliver J both on historical grounds and with regard to his interpretation of the speeches in the *Hedley Byrne* case [1964] AC 465. However, powerful though Mr Kaye's Article is, I am not persuaded by it to treat the *Midland Bank Trust Co.* case [1979] chapter 384 as wrongly decided. First, so far as the historical approach is concerned, this is no longer of direct relevance in a case such as the present, having regard to the development of the general principle in *Hedley Byrne*. No doubt it is correct that, in the nineteenth century, liability in tort depended upon the category of persons into which the defendant fell, with the result that in those days it did not necessarily follow that, because (for example) a surgeon owed an independent duty of care to his patient in tort irrespective of contract, other professional men were under a similar duty. Even so, as Mr Boswood for the Names stressed, if the existence of a contract between a surgeon and his patient did not preclude the existence of a tortious duty to the patient in negligence, there is no reason in principle why a tortious duty should not co-exist with a contractual duty in the case of the broad duty of care now recognised following the generalisation of the tort of negligence in the twentieth century.

So far as Hedley Byrne itself is concerned, Mr Kaye reads the speeches as restricting the principle of assumption of responsibility there established to cases where there is no contract; indeed, on this he tolerates no dissent, stating (at p. 706) that "unless one reads [Hedley Byrne] with deliberate intent to find obscure or ambiguous passages" it will not bear the interpretation favoured by Oliver J I must confess however that, having studied yet again the speeches in Hedley Byrne [1964] AC 465 in the light of Mr Kaye's critique, I remain of the opinion that Oliver J's reading of them is justified. It is, I suspect, a matter of the angle of vision with which they are read. For here, I consider, Oliver J was influenced not only by what he read in the speeches themselves, notably the passage from Lord Devlin's speech at pp. 528–529 (quoted above), but also by the internal logic reflected in that passage, which led inexorably to the conclusion which he drew. Mr Kaye's approach involves regarding the law of tort as supplementary to the law of contract, i.e. as providing for a tortious liability in cases where there is no contract. Yet the law of tort is the general law, out of which the parties can, if they wish, contract; and, as Oliver J demonstrated, the same assumption of responsibility may, and frequently does, occur in a contractual context. Approached as a matter of principle, therefore, it is right to attribute to that assumption of responsibility, together with its concomitant reliance, a tortious liability, and then to inquire whether or not that liability is excluded by the contract because the latter is inconsistent with it. This is the reasoning which Oliver J, as I understand it, found implicit, where not explicit, in the speeches in Hedley Byrne. With his conclusion I respectfully agree. But even if I am wrong in this, I am of the opinion that this House should now, if necessary, develop the principle of assumption of responsibility as stated in Hedley Byrne to its logical conclusion so as to make it clear that a tortious duty of care may arise not only in cases where the relevant services are rendered gratuitously, but also where they are rendered under a contract. This indeed is the view expressed by my noble and learned friend, Lord Keith of Kinkel, in Murphy v. Brentwood District Council [1991] 1 AC 398, 466, in a speech with which all the other members of the Appellate Committee agreed.

An alternative approach, which also avoids the concurrence of tortious and contractual remedies, is to be found in the judgment of Deane J in Hawkins v. Clayton, 164 C.L.R. 539, 582–586, in which he concluded, at p. 585:

"On balance, however, it seems to me to be preferable to accept that there is neither justification nor need for the implication of a contractual term which, in the absence of actual intention of the parties, imposes upon a solicitor a contractual duty (with consequential liability in damages for its breach) which is coextensive in content and concurrent in operation with a duty (with consequential liability in damages for its breach) which already exists under the common law of negligence."

It is however my understanding that by the law in this country contracts for services do contain an implied promise to exercise reasonable care (and skill) in the performance of the relevant services; indeed, as Mr Tony Weir has pointed out (XI International Encyclopedia of Comparative Law., chapter 12, para. 67), in the nineteenth century the field of concurrent liabilities was expanded "since it was impossible for the judges to deny that contracts contained an implied promise to take reasonable care, at the least, not to injure the other party." My own belief is that, in the present context, the common law is not antipathetic to concurrent liability, and that there is no sound basis for a rule which automatically restricts the claimant to either a tortious or a contractual remedy. The result may be untidy; but, given that the tortious duty is imposed by the general law, and the contractual duty is attributable to the will of the parties, I do not find it objectionable that the claimant may be entitled to take advantage of the remedy which is most advantageous to him, subject only to ascertaining whether the tortious duty is so inconsistent with the applicable contract that, in accordance with ordinary principle, the parties must be taken to have agreed that the tortious remedy is to be limited or excluded.

In the circumstances of the present case, I have not regarded it as necessary or appropriate to embark upon yet another detailed analysis of the case law, choosing rather to concentrate on those authorities which appear to me to be here most important. I have been most anxious not to overburden an inevitably lengthy opinion with a discussion of an issue which is only one (though an important one) of those which fall for decision; and, in the context of the relationship of solicitor and client, the task of surveying the authorities has already been admirably performed by both Oliver J and Le Dain J. But, for present purposes more important, in the instant case liability can, and in my opinion should, be founded squarely on the principle established in *Hedley Byrne* itself, from which it follows that an assumption of responsibility coupled with the concomitant reliance may give rise to a tortious duty of care irrespective of whether there is a contractual relationship between the parties, and in consequence, unless his contract precludes him from doing so, the plaintiff, who has available to him concurrent remedies in contract and tort, may choose that remedy which appears to him to be the most advantageous.

9. "OTHER RIGHTS" (FAMILY RELATIONSHIPS)

Case 28

BUNDESGERICHTSHOF (FOURTH CIVIL SENATE) 30 JANUARY 1957
BGHZ 23, 215 = NJW 1957, 670 = JZ 1957, 342

The parties married in 1941. On 24 March 1949 a child was born. Thereupon the plaintiff husband petitioned for a divorce, the wife cross-petitioned, and the marriage was dissolved on the ground that both were to be blamed, in the case of the wife because she had committed adultery. After the divorce, the plaintiff sought and obtained a decree to the effect that the child was illegitimate.

The plaintiff now claimed DM 1130.05 from the defendant representing the legal costs of the bastardy proceedings.

The Court of First Instance rejected the claim. An appeal to the Court of Appeal of Schleswig and a second appeal to the Bundesgerichtshof were without success for the following

Reasons

The Court of First Instance and the Court of Appeal have rejected the plaintiff's claim for damages representing his costs arising out of the bastardy proceedings on the ground that civil law does not allow a claim for damages in respect of such costs against a spouse who is guilty of a breach of fidelity.

I. The question was already debated at the time when the Civil Code was being drafted as to whether a spouse who was not the guilty party to a divorce should be allowed compensation in respect of those losses suffered by him as a result of the other spouse's dereliction of marital obligations. The Report of the Committee drafting the Civil Code (Motive) [reference] shows that the answer at the time was negative, principally because it was thought that such claims were incompatible with the nature of marriage and that to allow them would be tantamount to a penalty for a divorce; the latter had been deliberately omitted from the Civil Code contrary to its treatment in previous laws. The Reichsgericht adopted this view in its decision reported in [reference] and it was mainly followed by the literature and by the practice of the courts [references].

After the collapse in 1945 an opinion to the contrary made itself felt [references].

II. This Division considered as early as 21 March 1956 [reference] the question as to whether in addition to the claims which the civil law makes available in its provision on family law for the violation by a spouse of the duty of fidelity, further claims can be based on such a violation. This Division gave a negative answer in so far as the application of § 823 BGB was concerned. Although this decision has been criticised, this Division, having examined the question afresh, sees no reason for abandoning this practice. The following are the principal considerations that apply.

1. Civil law contains numerous provisions dealing with the duties arising from marriage and with their contravention [references]. Their specific regulation indicates a general principle that thereby the question was to be solved exclusively and finally as to what are the consequences of a violation of marital obligations.

2. The conclusion is in accordance with the ideas aired at the time when the Civil Code was drafted and as they are set out in the Report of the Committee drafting the BGB [reference].

3. That the provisions in the title on family law are exhaustive is borne out by the consideration that the regulation of the patrimonial relations between spouses would lose much of its meaning, if §§ 823 ff. BGB were to apply. For the duty to pay damages in accordance with the rules on obligations would much exceed the duties laid down by the provisions regulating family law. As a result the provisions regulating family law would become largely superfluous.

4. It is true that the conclusion of a marriage has consequences bearing on family law as well as on the law of property. In principle, however—in accordance with the principle which also found expression in § 888 II of the Code of Civil Procedure—a distinction must be drawn between the duties of the spouses which concern family law and those which involve proprietary rights resulting from the marriage. Those which are purely in the nature of family law, such as the duty to live together and the duty of fidelity, are confined to conduct in accordance with these duties, and if any consequences are to accompany their violation, they cannot be found in the law of obligations; instead, having regard to the nature of the marriage, they must be contained in the provisions of family law proper dealing with such violations. It is incompatible with the nature of marriage as well as with present-day moral sentiment which has not changed in this respect since the time when the Civil Code was drafted, to equate marriage with a transaction in the nature of property law.

5. It is true that in principle an interpretation of the law must be approved which serves to maintain a marital community in keeping with the solemn vows of marriage. This Division has constantly emphasised that aspect, particularly in its practice dealing with § 48 of the Marriage Act. However, to apply the rule on damages of the law of obligations to conjugal misconduct leads to undesirable results.

(*a*) First of all, an award for damages for a violation of matrimonial duties would equal a penalty in practice. For example, as a result of the unjustified refusal of the wife to cohabit, the blameless husband is forced to rely on a paid help to run the household, and the court gives judgment against the wife on the ground of a violation of § 1353 BGB to make monthly payments to the husband which correspond approximately to the cost of the help until cohabitation is resumed. This would mean in effect that by means of fines the wife is being compelled to resume cohabitation, with the difference that the money does not accrue to the State, as it does in the cases enumerated in § 888 I of the Code of Civil Procedure, but to the husband, and that in addition § 888 I of the Code of Civil Procedure would cease to have effect.

(*b*) It must be admitted that there are no reasons in equity why a guilty spouse should not bear the costs of proceedings to contest the legitimacy of the child conceived in adultery. The extent of the liability to damages of the guilty spouse is not, however, limited to this aspect, for this liability can only be either recognised or denied in principle. Consequently, if recognized, the blameless spouse could demand in accordance with the principle laid down in § 249 BGB to be placed in every respect in the same position as would have existed if the occurrence which gave rise to the claim for damages, and therefore also the ensuing divorce, had never taken place. The blameless party would be entitled not only to adequate or equitable maintenance by the guilty spouse but to a sum which enables him, contrary to the provisions on maintenance in §§ 58 and 59 of the Marriage Act, to maintain the same living standard as if the marriage still subsisted. In addition the blameless spouse would be entitled on the death of the guilty spouse to be treated as regards the estate of the latter as if the marriage had still existed at that time, leaving open the question as to whether in relation to the estate the blameless spouse is to be regarded as an heir or only as entitled to a compulsory portion (*Pflichtteilsberechtigter*).

(*c*) Among those who hold that claims for damages lie, some deny that they lie against a guilty spouse, among them in particular Schwab, while Boehmer, modifying his previous opinion [reference], now wishes to restrict it to the situation where the marriage subsists [references]. Leaving aside the consideration that the law of obligations hardly supports the distinction introduced by Boehmer, the refusal to allow a claim for damages against the guilty spouse is ineffective as soon as the co-respondent is sued for damages; the latter, who would be jointly liable in tort together with the guilty spouse, could claim a contribution from the guilty spouse under § 426 BGB. In this connection the question would arise further as to whether § 254 BGB may be applicable with the result that possibly the guilty spouse must shoulder the greater part of the damages or even the total amount.

(*d*) To allow a claim for damages may lead to the abuse of the grounds for divorce for base motives in order to make personal gains, a not unusual phenomenon, as the Report of the Committee drafting the Civil Code pointed out.

(*e*) Another consequence will be in all probability that the number of lawsuits between spouses will increase greatly. In many instances the proceedings for divorce and those for maintenance, if any, will be followed by an action for damages.

(*f*) In the proceedings for damages the need will arise frequently to make, first of all, exact findings concerning the history of the marriage and the conduct of the spouses. For contrary to the opinion of Boehmer it is common experience that in many cases a divorce is granted not on the ground of adulterous relations with a third party, but despite the existence of such relations for other reasons connected with the person of the guilty spouse alone, such as persistent refusal to comply with matrimonial duties.

(*g*) Apart from the fact that such suits for damages are prosecuted in a manner which is far from pleasant and constitute an excessive burden for the parties and the courts, the accusatorial character of the proceedings does not offer the same degree of reliability as do divorce proceedings.

(*h*) Finally, as the Report of the Committee drafting the Civil Code has equally pointed out, the assessment of damages in respect of the loss caused by the adulterous conduct and by the divorce must always remain more or less arbitrary. This, however, makes the law extraordinarily uncertain.

6. Boehmer's reference to § 893 of the Code of Civil Procedure does not convince. This provision does not create an independent right to damages but only makes it clear that the right to damages existing according to the rules of civil law is not affected by the rules on levy of execution laid down by the Code of Civil Procedure [reference].

III. The foregoing considerations, which lead to the rejection of a claim for damages based on § 823 BGB, apply also if it is alleged, as indeed it is in the present case, that the adulterous conduct constitutes an intentional infliction of damage contrary to decent morals. It is true that as early as in its decision in [reference] the Reichsgericht had admitted that a married woman may be liable under § 826 BGB, and in its decision in [reference] it has accepted the application of § 826 BGB in a case where a married woman had committed adultery resulting in the birth of a child, a consequence which the wife and the co-respondent had considered possible. The practice of the courts and the literature have also followed this opinion of the Reichsgericht to a considerable extent [reference].

The present Division cannot accept this view. It is contradicted by the fact that the provisions dealing with family law regulate exhaustively the consequences of the violation of matrimonial duties and of a divorce. Instead this Division agrees with the opinions of Giesecke [reference] and of Boehmer [reference] that, if claims for damages for violation of marital duties brought on the basis of § 823 BGB are to be rejected having regard to the provision dealing with family law, the same must apply to claims brought on the strength of § 826 BGB. This Division has already held in its decision [reference] that provisions dealing with family law may also exclude the application of § 826 BGB.

Case 29

BUNDESGERICHTSHOF (FOURTH CIVIL SENATE) 8 JANUARY 1958
BGHZ 26, 217 = NJW 1958, 544 = JZ 1958, 247

The defendant entertained an adulterous association with the plaintiff's wife over a lengthy period, and a child was born on 21 September 1953. By a judgment of 17 May 1955 it was declared that the child was not the legitimate issue of the plaintiff and on 11 November 1955 the defendant, by a public document, recognized the child as his own and undertook to pay a monthly sum of DM 50 as maintenance. The marriage of the plaintiff with the mother was dissolved on 5 January 1956 by a decree which declared both to be guilty; but the wife's degree of blame was held to be predominant.

The plaintiff claimed DM 1457 from the defendant consisting of his expenses in connection with the birth of the child, its maintenance, the costs of the action to have it declared illegitimate, and reimbursement of his repayments to the city of Nürnberg of a child's allowance.

The Court of Appeal of Nürnberg allowed the claim. Upon appeal the decision below was reversed in part only for the following

Reasons

I. . . .

II. According to § 1715 BGB the natural father is under an obligation to reimburse the mother for the expenses of her delivery. The expenses of the delivery were paid by the plaintiff in ignorance of the fact that the defendant was the real father of the child. By these payments the obligations of the defendant towards the child's mother were also discharged. It is true that in principle a natural father is not relieved of his obligation under § 1715 BGB by the fact that a third party has paid the expenses of the delivery. However, considering the purpose of this provision, which only envisages the normal case of the delivery of an unmarried woman, different considerations must apply if and to the extent that the expenses of the delivery have been paid by the husband of the woman. Thus as a result of the plaintiff's payment the defendant has been saved the payment of the expenses of delivery, without good legal reason, and at the plaintiff's cost. In accordance with § 812 BGB the defendant must therefore reimburse the plaintiff for this sum . . .

III. On the other hand the appeal is justified in respect of the expenses, claimed by the plaintiff, for the perambulator, the baby's bed, its clothes, the contributions to the sickness insurance totalling DM 210 since these expenses must be regarded as part of the expenses of maintaining the child (§ 1708 I, second sentence) and since under § 1710 I BGB maintenance is to be provided by means of money payments; for the period in question these expenses are already covered by the maintenance payments awarded above (**I**). The plaintiff cannot either claim these expenses on the ground that they represent damages in tort; in this respect the observations set out below apply here as well . . .

IV. Further, the appeal is well founded in so far as the defendant has been condemned to reimburse the plaintiff for the costs arising from the proceedings to contest the legitimacy of the child.

This Division has already dealt several times with the question as to whether a third party can be held liable for the pecuniary losses caused to one spouse as a result of the relations of a third party with the other spouse which are adulterous or in violation of matrimonial fidelity. This Division has denied that such a claim for damages exists [references]. These decisions have been criticized by writers [references]. However, these attacks do not provide any reason for this Division to change its previous practice. Instead the following comments may be made.

1. The decision of 6 February 1957 is being misinterpreted if it is understood to lead to the inevitable conclusion that no damages can be claimed for injuries to a spouse, such as infection with a venereal disease of a wife who had been the victim of rape, even if the requirements of §§ 823 ff. BGB have been complied with. As the reasons set out in para. 3 of this decision [reference] show clearly, this Division has only rejected claims for damages in so far as they are derived from "the destruction of the marriage". If, however, no liability in damages arises from the "destruction of the marriage", it is irrelevant whether the damage caused by the destruction of the marriage is adequate or not.

2. The marital duties which arise mutually between spouses, in particular the duty of fidelity, are personal obligations of the spouses, having regard to the nature of marriage. Therefore they can only be violated by a spouse and not by a third party [reference].

3. § 172 of the Criminal Code, which only provides the possibility for punishing adultery, does not offer any guidance as to the existence of a duty to pay damages. Other violations of marital duties are not punishable according to German criminal law.

4. It is true that in principle a duty to contribute presupposes a duty to pay damages on the part of the person found to contribute [references]. Boehmer affirms in principle that a spouse is liable in damages, but wishes to prevent any enforcement while the marriage persists, with the result that the principles established by the Bundesgerichtshof [reference] would apply without difficulty. However, as Beitzke remarks appositely, the principle of § 242 BGB requires that if a claim lies against the third party involved in the break-up of the marriage in respect of the loss suffered by the other spouse in consequence of the break-up, the third party must not bear the payment of these damages alone; instead his associate, namely the other spouse, who as a rule is principally to blame, must bear his share (see the case decided by the Bundesgerichtshof in [reference] where an exemption clause agreed between the spouses could not deprive the third party of his right to contribution). It is generally agreed that in assessing the amount of contribution the principle of § 254 BGB applies [reference].

5. The provision of § 1359 BGB does not provide any guidance, since in principle it does not bear upon the duty of marital fidelity; it is also impossible to assume that as regards the latter, a spouse is only liable to apply the same degree of diligence as he applies to his own affairs. If this were so, the guilty spouse to a divorce would also have to be held responsible for every other pecuniary damage which the other spouse suffers as a result of the divorce. This conclusion is ruled out in all likelihood, despite the aim stressed generally by Beitzke "to tie a person to the marriage, once it has been concluded, by the threat of liability in damages".

6. The liability to pay damages laid down by § 1298 BGB in respect of breach of promise referred to by Beitzke does not assist either. On the contrary, the fact that the legislature deemed it necessary to insert this provision appears to indicate that in principle claims for damages arising out of duties imposed by family law are to lie only when the law so provides expressly.

7. The enactment of this provision also militates against the assumption that a general duty to pay damages exists in family law, as Boehmer suggests now, while denying that liability in damages arises under §§ 823 ff. BGB in the case of a guilty spouse. However, until now such claims for damages, as well as those for the violation of other protected interests, have been based exclusively on these provisions, unless allowed expressly by other rules, and claims for damages have been denied in principle where § 1353 BGB has been violated [reference]. Provisions such as those contained in section 151 of the Swiss Civil Code are unknown in German law.

8. Article 6 of the German Constitution (Fundamental Law) does not support a claim to damages either. Leaving aside that the marriage as such is not directly affected by the fact whether damages are paid after its breakdown or not, Article 6 of the Constitution does not concern the personal relationship between the spouses. Boehmer, too, believes that

by allowing claims for damages "no tendency towards the enforcement of the duty to comply" is being shown.

9. Equally nothing can be deduced from the rules on maintenance after divorce; in so far as they concern the position of the wife, Beitzke describes them as being in total contradiction to Article 3 of the Constitution. The question is, however, irrelevant in the present case, since the claims here are not brought by the wife.

10. Finally it remains uncertain, despite the arguments of Boehmer, how the amount of damages is to be assessed when a marriage has been broken up culpably. If the duty to reimburse the costs of the proceedings to contest the legitimacy of the child is to be based on the protective function of § 1353 BGB, as Boehmer seems to hold, no persuasive reason exists for denying the existence of a duty to pay damages for any other pecuniary losses arising from the break-up of the marriage, a result which Boehmer himself regards as "impossible". Any general requirement such as that "the damages claimed must be limited to the protective purpose of the protective rule in question does not permit a clear assessment of the damages. The likely consequences of such a view would be many disputes, the outcome of which must be quite uncertain; such a result does not seem to be desirable for the law's sake as well."

V. The Court of Appeal holds that a claim for damages against the defendant in respect of the costs of the proceedings to contest the legitimacy of the child cannot be supported in law as distinct from the costs of divorce proceedings; in the latter case the mutual relations between the spouses provide the basis, the husband is faced in the first instance with his unfaithful partner, with whom prima-facie matrimonial matters should be thrashed out alone while the co-respondent figures behind the wife and can only be reached through the latter. On the other hand, the co-respondent was directly involved in the claim for damages in respect of the procreation of the child, and in the triangle formed by the relationship between the husband, the child, and the third party, the wife figured either not at all or only as a fictional centre. Therefore the issue was not the protection of the marriage as a community of life but the legal relationship between father and child. Moreover, the attack on the legitimacy of the child and the ensuing consequences were independent of the continuation of the marriage.

These considerations, too, cannot support a claim for damages against the defendant based on the costs of the proceedings to contest the legitimacy of the child. First of all, in considering the relations between the husband, the child, and the third party, the wife cannot be excluded; for these relations cannot exist without the wife and her unfaithful conduct, just as the third party and his adulterous relationship with the wife were decisive in the case of the divorce. Claims arising out of the procreation of the child fall therefore into the sphere of family law, just as much as those based on adultery and on a divorce ensuing therefrom. The fact that a marriage may continue independently of an act of adultery and of the bastardisation of a child does not alter the nature of the claims arising therefrom which fall within the sphere of family law. Finally, if the third party were to be held liable in damages, the wife would be under a duty to contribute, as explained in **IV**(4), above.

Case 30

BUNDESGERICHTSHOF (SIXTH CIVIL SENATE) 22 FEBRUARY 1973
JZ 1973, 668 (with approving note by Manfred Löwisch) = NJW 1973,
991 = VERSR 1973, 442

Facts

The plaintiff married in 1965 and was still married at the time of the action, living together with his wife. From 1 October 1968 until 10 October 1968 the wife remained absent from the marital home at the invitation of the defendant with whom she stayed in his flat. It was not disputed that acts incompatible with marital fidelity occurred during the time; according to the plaintiff's allegation adulterous intercourse occurred as well.

The plaintiff contended that by the adulterous conduct of the defendant his general right of personality and his right to the undisturbed existence of the marital community had been violated. He claimed DM 10,000 with interest as "compensation and satisfaction" to be paid either to himself or alternatively to a charity. The claim was rejected in all three instances for the following

Reasons

I. The Court of Appeal assumes, in accordance with the plaintiff's pleadings, that the plaintiff's wife and the defendant committed adultery. Nevertheless, it rejected the claim and held as follows:

The plaintiff was wrong in referring to the practice of the Bundesgerichtshof according to which a person whose right of personality had been injured can in certain circumstances demand pecuniary damages as compensation for his non-pecuniary damage. This claim too—like that for pain and suffering—was a claim for *damages*, while its function of providing satisfaction was only ancillary. No room existed in addition for a separate claim for satisfaction as understood by the plaintiff. A claim for damages—on whatever grounds—was excluded since special family relations were involved. To this extent the Court of Appeal follows the practice initiated by the decision of the Bundesgerichtshof [reference] and holds that the same principles must apply to non-pecuniary and pecuniary damage (and injury to health). Above all, the damage alleged to be suffered by the plaintiff was caused by the unfaithful conduct of his own wife.

The Court of Appeal believes that any payment to the plaintiff is ruled out in particular for the reason that his marriage continues. The fact that the payment would inevitably also benefit indirectly the wife, who was equally or principally to blame, was clearly unacceptable.

Similarly payment to a third party was excluded. According to the Court of Appeal, it would amount to the imposition of a penalty upon the defendant which was not supported in law.

The Court of Appeal admitted that an intrusion into marital life of the kind alleged in the present case constitutes a violation of the general right of personality of the deceived spouse. However, here again the considerations applied which also excluded other claims based on tort.

II. These considerations cannot be faulted, at least in the result.

1. The plaintiff bases his claims on the fact that the defendant was an accomplice to the breach of fidelity for which the plaintiff's wife was to be blamed. According to a constant practice of the Bundesgerichtshof, maintained until now in the face of attacks by some writers [references], no claims in tort are allowed by the law in force in cases of "intrusion of a marriage" either against the guilty spouse or against the intruding third party. The Fourth Division of the Bundesgerichtshof last reaffirmed this practice in its decision of 3 November 1971 [reference] supported by detailed reasons and accompanied by an account of the present views of writers. In that decision the Fourth Division has given a comprehensive account of its reasons for denying unconditionally and generally that matters of intrusion into marriage involve legal interests protected by the law of tort under § 823 I BGB. The Fourth Division points out that without the co-operation of one of the spouses no interference with the marriage can occur and that, therefore, it constitutes essentially an internal marital matter, which is not sought to be protected by inclusion among the situations attracting liability in tort. In view of its strong link with the conduct of the unfaithful spouse the participation of the third party must be coloured by it as well. It is inadmissible to divide their activities into misbehaviour of the spouse governed by matrimonial law and a tort committed by the third party rendering him liable to pay damages. The Fourth Division has pointed out further that it is difficult, having regard to the multiplicity of possible acts of interference with marital relations, to establish suitable limits for any such liability and that the necessary enquiries, as required in the individual case, would have undesirable effects in various respects. For this reason disputes arising out of marital misconduct are treated exclusively as matrimonial matters, even where third parties are involved. The Division sees no reasons for deviating from these principles. They militate also against the present claim for payment as satisfaction for the non-pecuniary loss of the offended spouse. Even among those writers who are opposed to the practice of the Bundesgerichtshof only very few believe that such a payment is allowed by the law as it stands [references].

2. Contrary to the appellant's main contention, the claim cannot succeed either if in applying § 823 I BGB emphasis is placed on the violation of the plaintiff's general right of personality rather than on that of the integrity of the marital community. It is true that according to the practice of the Bundesgerichtshof, particularly of this Division, a claimant whose general right of personality has been severely infringed may be awarded pecuniary damages for his non-pecuniary loss, provided that additional conditions have been met [references]. However, in so far as the right of personality of a spouse has been infringed because a third party acting together with the other spouse has interfered with the right to the integrity of the marital community, as in the present case, any claims for damages in tort must be denied for the reasons stated above which rule out liability in tort when the right to the integrity of the marital community has been violated. In many cases where a marriage has been subject to interference, and probably in all cases of adultery, the conditions enumerated above will exist for holding that the right of personality has been severely infringed. Therefore, the Court of Appeal, too, assumes that such a violation of the right of personality has occurred. To take such a view of the law would, however, run contrary to the requirements based on the evaluation of the narrower sphere of family law [reference]. This applies at any event in those cases where, as in the present, the violation of the right of personality is restricted to an interference with the

matrimonial community of life and fidelity by a third party with the necessary participation of the other spouse.

3. Contrary to the plaintiff's contention no reason exists for taking a different view of the law either because of a fundamental change of public opinion, or because of a conflict with the values expressed by superior norms of the Constitution.

(a) The refusal to enforce matrimonial conduct by public measures, already apparent in the Preparatory Materials for the BGB [reference], has been reinforced still further. An enforceable claim for damages would be equal to such a measure; for this reason it has been recommended expressly as a means of "deterrence" [reference]. The increased aversion of the legislature to such measures is shown by the fact that the provision of a penalty according to the former § 172 of the Criminal Code—which had been hedged around already by narrow conditions (not applicable here)—was abrogated; it is irrelevant in the present connection that this change in the law only took place after the alleged act of adultery.

(b) The rejection of the claim for damages in a case such as the present does not contravene either the values of superior norms of the Constitution on which the Bundesgerichtshof relied in its practice relating to the right of personality. The limits of the general right of personality recognised and protected by § 823 I BGB are flexible. They can always be drawn only with reference to other areas which are protected by law. In the present case these emerge from the observations made above.

The legislature has refrained from enforcing proper marital conduct directly or indirectly by public measures (see also § 888 II of the Code of Civil Procedure), including any penalties and equivalent measures for adultery, and has contented itself with the protection provided by family law. Having regard to the special character of this subject matter, it cannot be included that the importance of the protection of the personality has been misunderstood and has not been taken into account sufficiently. Instead it expresses the conviction that highly personal relations should not be regulated by law, which is at least compatible with constitutional law and corresponds to modern ethics.

(c) Finally, a conclusion to the contrary cannot be based either on the protection of marriage provided by Article 6 I of the Constitution, which the appellant rightly does not cite. Admittedly, marriage is a human institution which is regulated by law and protected by the Constitution and which, in turn, creates genuine legal duties. Its essence, however, consists in the readiness, founded in morals, of the parties to the marriage to create and to maintain it. The provision of Article 6 I of the Constitution is only intended to protect and to promote this unit, which has its origins in a sphere which precedes law; Article 6 does not refer to the personal relations between spouses [references]. Consequently it does not support any demand for the punishment of marital infidelity, nor of third parties who are indispensable participants. It need not be examined here whether different considerations might apply in respect of totally different attacks against the sexual integrity of a spouse (by threats, fraud, or force) if the general law should not provide adequate remedies for compensation.

Case 31

BUNDESGERICHTSHOF (FOURTH CIVIL SENATE) 19 DECEMBER 1989
NJW 1990, 706 = FAMRZ 1990, 367

Facts

The parties, married in 1953, were divorced by judgment of 24 April 1959 on the ground of the fault of the present plaintiff (then defendant). During the marriage two daughters were born, first B and then, on 22 March 1957, S. After the divorce custody of the daughters was awarded to the defendant, and acting as their statutory representative, she sued the present plaintiff for maintenance payments in 1960, 1964 and 1965. In 1960 she garnished the plaintiff's earnings as well as the disability pension which the plaintiff received while occasionally unemployed through TBC. From the summer of 1966, the plaintiff paid maintenance money for the children by agreement and without court order. In 1986 the plaintiff sued for a declaration that S was illegitimate, and the Amtsgericht in W held that S was not the child of the plaintiff.

The plaintiff now sues the defendant for damages in respect of the maintenance payments he has made since the divorce in respect of the child who was not his and whom he was not bound to support. He alleged that in making the claim for maintenance as the daughter's legal representative, the defendant had represented that he was the father of the child. The defendant replied that she had never doubted the legitimacy of S, and had never noticed the lack of resemblance between her and the plaintiff, which was not at all obvious. The Landgericht dismissed the claim, and the Oberlandesgericht dismissed the plaintiff's appeal, as did the Bundesgerichtshof.

Reasons

I. The court below held it doubtful that the plaintiff had any tort claim for economic loss against his ex-wife on the ground of the illegitimacy of the child S. Founding on the constant decisions of the Bundesgerichtshof the court inclined to the view that the sanctions for anti-matrimonial conduct were to be found in family law exclusively, and that the law of delict afforded the plaintiff no further claim.

Even had claims for damages not been excluded by the provisions of family law, the court below would have dismissed the claim, for the defendant had not deceived the plaintiff in such a way as to render her liable in damages, either by making the claims for maintenance which, until the finding of illegitimacy, were vested in her daughter S, or through any culpable failure to disclose: the defendant was under no duty to confess her adultery or admit the possibility that S might have another father. Finally, claims in tort failed for lack of the requisite *mens rea*: it had not been shown that the defendant had appreciated that the plaintiff was not the father of S, and the mere fact of promiscuity, as to which no findings were made as regards the time of conception, did not establish that she had.

II. We agree with the result reached by the court below.

1. There is no doubt that the plaintiff has suffered economically as a result of the defendant's conduct: for years he has been paying maintenance which he did not owe. As the apparent father of S he was burdened with paying for her upkeep, until the judgment of 25 March 1987 finally declared that S was illegitimate and that it was her true father who had always been liable to make the payments [references].

2. Nevertheless, the law of tort does not permit the plaintiff to sue his ex-wife for this economic loss (BGHZ 80, 235 [238] = NJW 1981, 1445).

(*a*) When the BGB was in draft the question was already being ventilated whether an innocent spouse (as the law then was) could claim compensation for harm due to breach by the other spouse of the duties assumed on entering the marriage, and since that time it has often been the subject of judicial decision and academic discussion.

Such a claim was originally rejected as incompatible with the nature of marriage, on the view that to grant it would amount to penalising divorce in a way which the BGB, in conscious deviation from prior law, had elected not to follow (see BGHZ 23, 215 [216] = NJW 1957, 670 = LM § 823 (Af) BGB no. 5, with references to the Motive to the BGB, vol. 4, p. 615).

In its first decision on the matter (31 March 1956), the Bundesgerichtshof declared that claims for damages for spousal infidelity under § 823 BGB were ousted by the provisions of family law regarding such conduct. This was criticised, but in BGHZ 23, 215 ff. = NJW 1957, 670 the court adhered to its view, and relied *inter alia* on the following considerations: The BGB contains many provisions on the duties assumed on marriage and the consequences of their breach (especially the Marriage Act, and §§ 1353, 1361, 1933, 2077, 2335 BGB); the very existence of this special set of rules indicates that in principle the consequences of a breach of spousal duties are to be determined exclusively in terms of those rules. It is true that the personal and economic consequences of getting married must be kept distinct. Those which appertain purely to family law, such as the duty to live together and the duty of fidelity, are fulfilled by appropriate conduct. Should such duties be breached, the consequences are to be drawn not from the law of obligations but, consistently with the nature of marriage, from the provisions of family law relating to such breaches.

In its judgment of 6 February 1957 (BGHZ 23, 279 ff. = NJW 1957, 671) the court applied to the third party adulterer the principle that the anti-matrimonial conduct of a spouse did not give rise to any claim for damages in the law of obligations independently of the provisions of family law, especially the Marriage Law (and compare BGHZ 26, 217 ff. = NJW 1958, 544). Again it stated: "Although anti-matrimonial conduct can undeniably cause harm to the 'innocent' spouse, especially if it leads to divorce, the law does not afford any compensation outside the provisions of family law, so anti-matrimonial conduct cannot be treated as an unlawful act grounding a claim for damages under §§ 823 ff. BGB."

In 1971 the BGH returned to the question (BGHZ 57, 229). Again it rejected the view expressed by academics [Boehmer in many articles, Beitzke, Dölle, Gernhuber and Jayme] that breaches of marriage vows should trigger liability under § 823 I BGB, and asserted that marriage is not one of the relationships whose breach can give rise to general claims for compensation for economic harm. In more detail it confirmed that it would adhere to the view that marriage vows were not among the rights protected by the law of tort in § 823 I BGB. Since the consortium of the spouses could only be disrupted by the participation of one of them, such breaches constitute essentially a matter internal to the marriage, not under the intended protection of the law of torts (BGHZ 57, 229 [232] = NJW 1972, 199).

In a judgment of 22 February 1973 (NJW 1973, 991), the Sixth Civil Senate of the Bundesgerichtshof adopted the view of the Fourth Senate (as it then was). Then the question was whether damages could be claimed on the basis of an invasion of the right of human personality rather than an invasion of the integrity of the community of marriage. The court refused to allow this, on the ground that the rather fluid limits to the general right of human personality had to be drawn in the light of other legal provisions, in this case the considerations stated by the Fourth Civil Senate (as in BGHZ 57, 229 = NJW 1977, 199), and though in many cases of anti-matrimonial behaviour there would be a serious invasion of the right of personality—perhaps always in the case of adultery—yet to impose liability in tort would conflict with the more specific prescriptions of family law.

(b) In BGHZ 80, 235, the mother of a child conceived out of wedlock made false representations to the father and thereby induced him to marry her. This senate made the general observation, in line with the decisions of the Bundesgerichtshof, that obligational claims, especially tort claims for damages, are ousted by the exclusive special rules of family law, the Supreme Court having uniformly held that a husband whose wife had committed adultery and borne a child could not bring an action in tort against the wife or the third party for compensation for the economic harm he suffered as a result of the apparent legitimacy of the child (BGHZ 80, 235 [238] = NJW 1981, 1445). Because of the peculiar facts in that case, however, the point did not fall for decision, but in the present case it does. A pointer in the same direction is the decision of this court on 4 November 1987 (NJW 1988, 2032) that the personal duties arising from the community of marriage can only be fulfilled by the free moral choice of the parties, and that even indirect compulsion by the state, such as a penalty clause or damages, must be excluded.

In this case, where after a divorce the apparent father is suing his ex-wife (not the real father) for damages in respect of the maintenance he has for years been paying for a child not his, this senate has again considered the matter afresh. We adhere to the holdings which the Supreme Court has increasingly confirmed since the introduction of the BGB (on the significance of continuity of holdings and legal certainty, see Grosser Senat, BGHZ 85, 64 [66] = NJW 1983, 228). We endorse the view that matrimonial difficulties which affect the inner social and sexual life of the partners, adultery being the chief of these, represent a matter internal to the marriage which is not within the protective ambit of the rules of tort [references].

This view was formed by the Bundesgerichtshof under the previous law of marriage; ideas have changed, but the view is even more strongly justified after the first reform law of marriage. Whereas under prior law (§ 58 I and II Marriage Act) the party whose adultery led to divorce and who was solely or principally at fault faced sanctions in regard to maintenance—either the loss of a claim for maintenance or liability to provide it—under the present law "fault" which leads to the breakdown of the marriage does not in principle bar the "guilty" spouse from claiming maintenance if in need, save under § 1579 nos. 6 and 7 BGB in cases of hardship. If there was no liability in tort for adultery under prior law which provided for financial sanctions for such conduct, there is no reason now that the fault principle has given way to the principle of the breakdown of marriage to deviate from the previous decisions and allow claims for damages in tort for conduct which impairs the marriage. This senate therefore adheres all the more strongly to its previous position that it is incompatible with the essence of marriage to apply the law of damages to internal matrimonial matters; marriage and family law oust the law of tort.

Thus not only claims based on § 823 II BGB but all suchlike claims in tort between divorced spouses are excluded if the right alleged to be invaded is the "very core of marriage" and the "interest it seeks to protect" or "marriage as an ideal legal interest" (Gernhuber) or the "personal moral bond of marriage" (Soergel-Lange), the "right to fidelity in marriage" (Gernhuber, Enneccerus-Lehmann) or "the maintenance of sexual fidelity" (Wacke), the "right to the protection and continuance of the matrimonial community of living" (Berg, Lüke), the "absolute right of the spouses to complete and exclusive consortium" (Dölle) or—based on § 1353 BGB—a "claim to enjoin conduct which disturbs the marriage in the area of personal duties of marriage" (Jayme).

The sanctions of tort law may, by contrast, apply to marriage in its external objective and spatial aspects (BGHZ 6, 360 ff. = NJW 1952, 975; BGHZ 34, 80 ff. = NJW 1961, 504), normally vulnerable only by third parties, or, as the Fourth Senate (as it then was) stated in BGHZ 26, 217 [221] = NJW 1958, 544, to the invasion of other legal rights, as for example damage to the health of a spouse through infection resulting from adultery (see Tiedemann, NJW 1988, 729).

But as to the internal mutual relations of the spouses inherent in their matrimonial and sexual community, claims for damages in tort are excluded for the reasons given. Thus adultery by itself cannot be treated as conduct generating liability in damages. If, as in the present case, the wife breaches her duty of fidelity, commits adultery and conceives a child which, until a declaration of illegitimacy, rates as the child of the husband who then pays for her maintenance, he cannot after successfully establishing the illegitimacy of the child use the law of tort to claim compensation for the expense he has been put to because the child was apparently his (BGHZ 80, 235 [238] = NJW 1981, 1445).

3. (a) But the fact that claims for damages under the general law of tort in respect of the consequences of adultery are ousted by the provisions of marriage and family law does not mean that if there are further aggravating factors the special tort rule of § 826 BGB may not be applicable. § 826 BGB is a "rule of law at a higher level", providing a general standard applicable throughout the whole of private and public law, and comparable in this respect with the all-pervasive principle of § 242 BGB. It is true that the former Fourth Civil Senate deviated from the jurisprudence of the Reichsgericht (RGZ 152, 397 ff.) and held that claims arising from anti-matrimonial conduct were barred under § 826 BGB as well (BGHZ 23, 217 [221] = NJW 1958, 544), but that was a case in which there were no special circumstances over and above the adultery which, combined with it, constituted causing harm *contra bonos mores*. Such factors were, by contrast, present in the case decided by the Reichsgericht (Warn. 1935 no. 184) where the adulterous wife and her lover conspired by false statements to procure the dismissal of the husband's claim for a declaration of the illegitimacy of the adulterine child. The Reichsgericht was right to allow a claim for damages under § 826 BGB in that case (and see RGZ 152, 397 [400]). In exceptional cases, therefore, § 826 BGB can apply to disruption of the internal and sexual relationship of husband and wife, especially through adultery, if in addition to the adultery the errant spouse is guilty of further immoral damaging conduct, characterised by an intention, albeit a qualified intention, to cause harm. Whether conduct is immoral under § 826 BGB depends on the standards inherent in that text, not on those appropriate to the spousal community. This is not the case when the wife merely fails to make spontaneous avowal of her act of adultery and leaves the husband in the belief that the child is his. The mere fact that the wife concealed her infidelity does not amount to an immoral wrong in the sense of § 826 BGB, for there is no duty, sanctioned by the law of damages, to tell one's spouse of one's adultery (RGZ 152, 397 [401]). To require a spouse to make such disclosure would normally be excessive, especially as she would quite often find herself in an insoluble dilemma, for disclosure would not only affect her own interests but also imperil the child's interest in maintenance.

There might, by contrast, be a claim under § 826 BGB if a wife who had conceived a child in adultery made false statements or outright denials in order to dispel her husband's doubts about its paternity, or if she prevented her husband by deceit or otherwise, say by duress, from pursuing a claim for a declaration of illegitimacy.

(*b*) No such conduct by the defendant has been established in this case or appears from the facts in evidence.

(*aa*) The plaintiff himself has not alleged that during the period when he was in contact with the child S he ever expressed any doubts about her paternity which the defendant allayed by false statements or otherwise. He rather claims to have been deceived by the fact that the defendant "never made an issue of paternity" and did not volunteer an admission of her adultery. This is not enough to meet the requirements of § 826 BGB.

(*bb*) Nor does the conduct of the defendant in "energetically asserting the apparent rights" of her daughter in several court cases constitute an immoral wrong under § 826 BGB, as the plaintiff alleges.

As the statutory representative of S the defendant sued in April 1960 for monthly maintenance payments of DM 75, which the plaintiff had earlier agreed in writing to make. In 1964 the defendant sought an increase to DM 100 per month and in May 1965 a further increase to DM 130, as well as demanding a like sum for her daughter B, who was four years older. The total sums claimed were in line with the figures in the Düsseldorf Tables for the maintenance by persons in the second and third income groups of children between six and ten years old (S) and between ten and fourteen (B), and the amounts were manifestly reasonable.

Nor is § 826 BGB satisfied by the defendant's conduct in garnishing the plaintiff's wages and then his pension when he did not punctually pay the sums he had agreed or been ordered to pay. The daughter S needed the payments to meet her living needs. Until declared illegitimate, she ranked as the legitimate child of the plaintiff (§ 1593 BGB) and he was liable for her maintenance under §§ 1601, 1602, 1603 BGB. As the child's statutory representative, the defendant was bound to see to making these claims in the interests of the child, and in making and enforcing the maintenance claims she was acting in justified pursuance of the interests of the child. If, instead of parental control being vested in the defendant, a curator had been appointed (§ 1629 II, 1795 I no. 3, 1903 BGB) to claim the maintenance payments and resist the claim for a declaration of illegitimacy, such curator would likewise have been bound, until the illegitimacy was established, to sue the defendant for the maintenance payments if necessary, and to enforce them by execution if not voluntarily met (§ 1915, 1793, 1833 BGB). Such conduct by the curator would not have been essentially different from what the defendant did. This shows that in pursuing maintenance claims for S the defendant remained within the limits of the means and methods provided by the legal system and that she cannot on that ground be found guilty of an immoral wrong under § 826 BGB.

(*cc*) Alternatively the appellant seeks to found his claim for damages on the principles developed by this court in BGHZ 80, 235 ff. = NJW 1981, 1445. He alleges that the defendant's failure to make requisite disclosure and her implicit assertion of his paternity by suing for maintenance prevented the plaintiff from seeking an earlier declaration of illegitimacy, and that this was in law tantamount to the fraudulent inducement to marry in that case.

This is not acceptable. In BGHZ 80, 235 = NJW 1981, 1445 the defendant had conceived the child before marriage and not as a result of adultery in breach of marriage vows, so the facts there were essentially different from this case, where the central question is whether breach of the marriage vows can generate a claim in tort. Furthermore, in that case the mother of the child had expressly and indeed in writing misrepresented the facts by assuring the plaintiff that during the statutory period of conception she had had congress "with him and him alone" and so deliberately allayed his doubts about the paternity of the child about to be born. She thus induced the plaintiff to enter the marriage and procured that the child was born legitimate and would be maintained by the plaintiff until a declaration of illegitimacy. Such deceitful conduct on the part of the mother constituted conduct apt to generate liability in damages for intentionally causing harm in an immoral manner under § 826 BGB as explained. No comparably harmful conduct apart from the adultery itself can be laid at the door of the defendant here.

Notes to Cases 28–31

1. The fourth book of the BGB deals with family law, but problems of family life have also tried to penetrate the law of torts under the heading of "other rights" of § 823 I BGB. (The first decision on the matter was decided by the BGH on 26 June 1952 (BGHZ 6, 360 = NJW 1952, 975) and it was rendered as a result of an action brought by a betrayed wife who sought an injunction to stop her husband's mistress from residing in the marital home. Though the court recognised that delictual protection should be afforded to the spatial and material sphere of matrimony—*räumlich-gegenständlicher Bereich der Ehe*—it did not decide whether this should be achieved by means of § 823 I BGB or through the direct application of Article 6 of the Constitution by virtue of Article 1 III of that enactment. As a result of this, wives have been given the right to enter the premises of a company run by the husband (BGHZ 34, 80, 87) or to insist that they be allowed to work at the family bakery (BGHZ 35, 302, 304).) Such attempts have, on the whole, met with varied, perhaps modest success but this has not discouraged litigation. The proper role of tort law in the context of disrupted family relations has also given rise to a lively literature which can be found (along with a neat summary of the various views) in Medicus, nos. 616 *et seq.* Cases 28–31 come from this area of the law and also show how German judges bring together different parts of their Code and thus try to retain an "internal balance" in the Code. (Earlier cases are reviewed by Markovitz, "Marriage and the State: A Comparative Look at East and West German Family Law" 24 *Stanford L. Rev.* 116 (1971).) Overall, however, the BGH—rejecting academic suggestions—has shown a preference for the view that "marriage is not one of the relationships whose breach can give rise to general claims for compensation for economic harm". (See BGHZ 27, 229; BGH NJW 1973, 991; BGHZ 80, 235; BGH NJW 1990, 706 = Case 31, above.)

2. The "innocent spouse's" losses can be pecuniary or non-pecuniary. The former include such items as the cost of delivery of the child (discussed in case 29), its maintenance, the cost of illegitimisation (not allowed by cases 28 and 30), and of divorce proceedings; the latter can refer to the breakdown of the marriage or nervous or other illness resulting from such upheavals. Those who argue against the trend shown in the cases reproduced above are really arguing in favour of a wider recognition of the first type of loss, not the second.

3. These and other analogous cases raise many points. Here are some: If the "innocent husband"/plaintiff pays for the cost of delivery of the child, the natural father is enriched by a corresponding amount and must, therefore, pay the former that amount. The reasoning given for this in case 29, BGHZ 23, 215, (but not the final result) has been doubted (see Medicus, no. 618). Likewise, maintenance paid by the "innocent husband"/plaintiff for an illegitimate child may be claimed from the natural father *after* the child has been declared as illegitimate. But a husband's tort action against a divorced wife for the economic loss due to his making maintenance payments to an apparently legitimate daughter (who was actually the product of the wife's adultery) will fail. So held the BGH in NJW 1990, 706, Case 31 above, restating its motto: "Marriage and family law oust the law of tort." A claim under § 826 BGB might, however, succeed if the requirement of immorality *of this provision* were satisfied. Mere marital infidelity will, thus, not do. It would be

otherwise, however, if, for example, it could be proved that the woman and her lover had conspired to procure the dismissal of the husband's claim for a declaration of illegitimacy: RGZ 152, 397 which, apparently, is still good law. (For further details, the reader must consult books on family law.) BGH NJW 1990, 706 contains some interesting dicta which explain this pre-eminence of § 826 BGB. The costs of divorce are usually shared by the spouses—§ 93a I ZPO—but the "innocent spouse" can subsequently claim his share of the divorce costs from the "marital intruder". But no damages can be claimed for the act of infidelity (case 31).

4. Some of these points may not arise at all in Common law jurisdictions; others do, and often receive similar solutions. In the US, for example, attorneys' fees are borne by the parties unless otherwise provided for by statute. To that extent, therefore, case 28 has no equivalent. In England there seems to be no case which has awarded costs or compensation for the expense of proving a child to be illegitimate, though *Halsbury*, vol. 13, 4th edn., § 970, does not in terms exclude the possibility. Disavowing a child born in legal wedlock can also receive a different treatment. In England it is possible but not easy, there being a presumption of legitimacy. In the United States the answers are more varied, some States adopting irrebuttable presumptions of legitimacy, others imposing a short period of time following birth within which the illegitimisation proceedings must be brought (*Pounds* v. *Schori* 377 So. 2d 1195 (La. 1979) (six months); *cf. Singley* v. *Singley* 140, So. 2d 546 (La. App. 1962) where a child was born more than three hundred days after separation of husband and wife and the husband was permitted to disavow). (See Clark, *Law of Domestic Relations*, 172 (1968).) But if the father refuses to disavow a child, no one else will normally be allowed to do so. (See *Petitioner F.* v. *Respondent R.* 430 A. 2d 1075 (Del. 1981), where a natural father, who sued for custody of the child which was conceived while its mother was married to another man, had his action dismissed for lack of standing to sue.)

5. The problem discussed in case 30, BGH JZ 1973, 668, is still known in some American jurisdictions under the name of criminal conversation. *Kremer* v. *Black* 201 Neb. 467, 268 NW 2d 582 (1978) is an example. But most States have abolished such actions and much criticism is still made against those who recognise it. The action is no longer known in English law. (It was abolished by the Law Reform (Miscellaneous Provisions) Act 1970, section 5.) In the Commonwealth, the action for enticement was abolished somewhat later. Thus in Australia this was done by the Family Law Act 1975, section 120. In New Zealand on the other hand the action for enticement was enshrined in legislative form as late as 1975 (see Domestic Actions Act 1975, section 3); but it was abolished five years later by the Family Proceedings Act 1980, section 190. For further discussions one must consult family law textbooks as well as older editions of Tort treatises.

10. "ESTABLISHED AND OPERATING BUSINESS"

Case 32

REICHSGERICHT (FOURTH CIVIL SENATE) 27 FEBRUARY 1904
RGZ 58, 24

Three designs were entered in the Register of Designs on behalf of the defendant firm . . . In the summer of 1901 the defendant, under threats of an action for damages and a criminal prosecution, forbade the plaintiff to copy the designs. He did so, at all events by a letter of 2 September concerning carpets, mats, and rugs made of jute pile and, under the same date, by letters to two of the plaintiff's weaving managers. The plaintiff alleged that the defendant had also forbidden the manufacture at an earlier date. In consequence the plaintiff had already, on 10 June 1901, discontinued the manufacture of jute pile in his business. On 15 September 1901 the defendant prosecuted the plaintiff for an offence against section 10 of the Act of 1 June 1891, whereupon a preliminary enquiry was insti-tuted against the plaintiff.

Before that enquiry was concluded the plaintiff sued the defendant claiming that he should (i) agree to a cancellation of the design and (ii) pay compensation for the damage arising from the prohibition against manufacture and the prosecution. The claim under (i) was based on the fact that the design was already, at the time of the notice, a matter of common knowledge. The defendant admitted that claim.

The Landgericht granted the claim. On appeal by the defendant the Oberlandesgericht made the order to pay compensation depend on the failure of the proprietor of the de-fendant firm to deny on oath his knowledge of the design when the notice was sent. On application for review that judgment was set aside for the following

Reasons

The Court of Appeal starts with the statement that the plaintiff ceased manufacturing the Articles corresponding to these designs in consequence of the defendant's demand refer-ring to their registration and that, as a result, the defendant was not entitled to contend that the plaintiff was not forced to accede to his demand. No precise moment is indicated when the demand and the cessation occurred and it is left undecided whether they had not, as the plaintiff alleged, already taken place before the defendant's letter of 2 Septem-ber 1901 to the plaintiff and his weaving managers. The Court of Appeal finds that the defendant's designs had been wrongly registered since they were not entitled to protec-tion and that, therefore, the defendant had no right to prohibit the plaintiff's business activity. For the damage, however, occurring to the plaintiff from the stopping of pro-duction and the prosecution, the court is prepared to make the defendant liable only if there was knowledge of the lack of justification and not merely negligent ignorance. It considers that the evidence so far obtained does not point to knowledge at the critical time and so decides to tender an oath to the defendant proprietors of the firm. Accord-ing to the original form of the oath, each of the two partners was to swear that on 2 September 1901 he did not know that the registered article was a matter of previous knowledge. The form of the oath was later modified to read that each of them should swear that "It is not true that at the time when the plaintiff was required by our company to stop manufacturing the objects protected by our designs nos. 156083, 156084 and 156465, I knew . . .". Even if one assumes that the appellate judge's view of the law is to be approved, this form of oath must still give rise to doubt. For no precise moment is indi-cated to the swearer as to which he must affirm on oath the truth of the fact of his igno-rance; it is left to his conscience to consider which moment to specify among several possible incidents to which his sworn ignorance would refer. Thus the formulation of the oath contains a serious degree of subjective uncertainty. Whether that alone would suffice to justify setting aside the appellate decision may be left undecided. But there are further grounds. The compensation to which the plaintiff is entitled as a result of the prosecu-tion also depends on the oath. According to the accompanying criminal records the prose-cution bears the date 4 September 1901. Hence that moment is decisive for liability under the prosecution. The present uncertain form of oath has its basis in the fact that so far there has been no finding about the factual correctness of the disputed allegation of the plaintiff that the stopping of production consequent on the defendants' demand had already taken place on 10 June 1901. If now the oath is refuted, so that the bad faith of the defendant partners is established, there is clearly no interest in specifying more closely the moment when their knowledge began. Assuming, however, that the oath is sworn and also that the request mentioned in the oath occurred *before* 4 September, in particular on 10 June 1901, it is obvious that the earlier moment of ignorance would be quite irrelevant to the claim for compensation arising out of the prosecution. These considerations would be enough to lead to a setting-aside of the contested judgment.

The setting-aside, however, must also result for a second and more comprehensive reason. The Court of Appeal makes an error of law when it denies the applicability of § 823 I BGB and, therefore, is prepared to make the defendants' liability depend only on their knowledge that their design lacks protection. At the time when the defendants, invoking their right to have their design protected and threatening civil and criminal proceedings, forbade the production of the jute pile in question, the plaintiff had already taken up the manufacture of those objects in its business, although there is up to now no certainty of the extent to which that had happened. The defendants, therefore, are chargeable with having encroached on the established business of the plaintiff by virtue of a right that did not belong to them and hence in a manner contrary to law. The plaintiff, who claimed that he already at that time had ten looms devoted to the manufacture and would, but for the prohibition, have extended the application to 50 looms, believes that the defendant's conduct constitutes also an invasion of his property rights, in that it had unlawfully hindered the full use of manufacturing installations owned by him. That view can indeed not be approved. Against the property itself of the plaintiff, which was never in question, no invasion was intended or directed. It was and remained in its content and legal signification the same as if the plaintiff had done his manufacturing not on his own but on some one else's looms. On the other hand, it is both accurate and to the point when the appellant, associating itself with the plaintiff's explanation of first instance, adopts the point of view that the business was disturbed.

§ 823 I BGB obliges anyone who recklessly or negligently injures the life, body, health, freedom, property, or other right of another contrary to law to make good all damage that ensues.

It is acknowledged that it is not the liability for doing economic damage as such that is here in question, but only that economic damage which is a consequence of the violation of the particular legal interests and rights specified by the Code. Hence the question is whether the defendants have violated such a particular legal interest or right of the plaintiff.

One can first of all consider the injury as an interference with the plaintiff's freedom inasmuch as the plaintiff was reduced by outside interference with his will to discontinue the manufacture of jute pile. But this point of view would not lead to the desired result. Admittedly, in the dispute about the meaning attached to freedom by the Code, notable authors have expressed the view that it must be understood quite generally as the free exercise of the will. But even if one were willing to follow that broadest interpretation, finding a basis for compensation would always presuppose an unlawful injury to the free exercise of the will, and it is out of the question that the Code intends to declare the encroachment on another's will unlawful for the reason only that there is no particular right so to encroach. The encroachment on the free exercise of the will would acquire the character of unlawfulness only through the form in which it occurs, such as deceit, threats, force, and these facts would also have to include, as in § 826 BGB (which was applied by the Court of Appeal), at least the defendant's consciousness of the legal invalidity of the registration of the designs. (*cf.* Decisions of the Reichsgericht in Civil Cases, vol. 48, 123.)

Then there is the view that the law raised the interests mentioned by it (life, body, health, and freedom) to the status of objects of an especial right to them and through the words "or a similar right" intended to extend its protection beyond those expressly mentioned to other vital interests. This did not find favour in the case-law of the Reichsgericht. It has been held already that the theory which wished to construct from the not yet limited range of particular interests, special rights to personality and individuality to an extent which has not yet been determined finally does not appear particularly suitable as a basis for interpreting the law. Thus, for instance, it has been denied that either the freedom to do business or the faculty to exploit one's labour without hindrance is protected by § 823 I BGB. There is no need to go further into this matter. For as distinct from the legal possibility of pursuing the occupation of one's choice, as it is accorded generally by § 1 of the Gewerbeordnung, it has already been accepted in several decisions of different Senates that a subjective right is to be recognised to an actually established and active business which is capable of being directly infringed. And, it has already been held that attacks on the exercise of a business can lead to an injunction [references follow]; but they can also found a claim for compensation arising from injury to the exercise of a business. This view formed the basis, in part, of the judgment delivered by the Senate on 25 June 1891 (RGZ 28, 248, especially 247, 249) before the enactment of the Wettbewerbsgesetz (Act on Unfair Competition). That the exercise of a business can be the object of legal advice under § 823 I BGB was decided by the IV Civil Senate in a judgment of 6 March 1902 and the VI Civil Senate in a judgment of 29 May 1902 (RGZ 51, 369, in particular 373), and also in a judgment of 14 December 1903 (RGZ 56, 271) though with some reservations. This Senate believes that it ought in principle to take the same position. That the established independent exercise of a business not only involves the free manifestation of the will of the person exercising it, but that will has also found in it its embodiment as an object, is the firm foundation for the acceptance of a subjective right to that exercise. Disturbances and encroachments aimed directly against the exercise of a business may therefore be looked upon as injuries falling under § 823 I BGB. Such an attack, directed against the exercise of a business, clearly exists when the legal admissibility of that exercise is denied to a certain extent and its restriction demanded on the ground of an industrial property right to the contrary. That attack is, however, contrary to law when the alleged protected industrial property right does not in truth exist, because it is no longer a question of permitted competition. The law under certain conditions puts at the disposal of persons exercising a business valuable exclusive rights in the form of the protection of patents and designs, by virtue of which they can secure the products of their inventive activity against attacks by way of parallel competition and reserve them for their own advantage. It is only a counterpart of their privileged position that they also answer for the existence of the right they enjoy to the self-seeking restriction of the free exercise of their business by their opponents, and must not only enjoy the advantages but also bear the risks that are involved in the assertion of such exclusive rights to patents and designs. In taking that view this Senate believes that it does not dissent from the opinion expressed by the VI Senate especially in the second of its decisions, mentioned above. Admittedly the protection of the exercise of a business against unfair competition is said in that decision to be found according to positive law in the provisions of the Wettbewerbsgesetz, of § 823 II BGB in combination with the penal rules concerning defamation and undermining credit, as well as in §§ 824 and 826 BGB, whereas the notion is rejected that any disturbance or encroachment on another person in the exercise of his business constitutes a violation of a law falling, as contrary to law, under § 823 I BGB. That, however, is not to deny that in some circumstances such an attack may be seen to be an injury contrary to law. The VI Civil Senate did not, as now, have to decide the particular case where the encroachment of another's exercise of his business was based on an alleged exclusive industrial property right that did not in reality exist.

Accordingly, the contested judgment cannot be upheld, since by not applying § 823 I BGB it contravenes the law. But on the merits itself no decision is possible. The Court of Appeal has so far only found that, apart from the results of the submission to the oath, the knowledge of the invalidity of their design on the part of the defendants has not been proved. On the other hand the question whether that ignorance is to be treated as negligence or whether there is a sufficient excuse has not yet been examined. Even so the Court of Appeal has indeed affirmed the causal connection between the demand of the defendants which, as stated before, remained somewhat uncertain, and the suspension of the plaintiff's business. It will, however, have to be investigated in addition whether on this occasion the plaintiff's conduct also constitutes contributory negligence that would justify the application of § 254 BGB. Wherein the legal defect in the defendants' design consisted has not yet been sufficiently elucidated. According to certain indications it does not appear to be excluded that already from the start the plaintiff at least suspected the invalidity of the registration and in course of time soon obtained a more exact knowledge of it . . .

Case 33

REICHSGERICHT (SIXTH CIVIL SENATE) 19 DECEMBER 1918
RGZ 94, 248 = JW 1919, 247 and approving note by Kirchenbauer

On 10 June 1908 a design was entered in the designs register of the Patent Office under no. 342454 on behalf of defendant 2a for socks, the upper portions of which were in whole or in part made of wool, but the lower portions of non-woollen material. The defendant transferred his right to that design to defendant 1, the partnership H. B., which he operated in common with defendant 2b. On 21 March 1911, defendant 1 sent to the firm L. & S. in D, which had obtained from the plaintiff the right to retail his socks, a letter in which, referring to the registered design, it warned them against retailing the socks received from the plaintiff, ordered them to withdraw the offers made by them, and threatened them with a claim for compensation. According to the plaintiff's allegation defendant 1 had sent letters to the same effect to two other firms whom the plaintiff had appointed retailers of his socks. The plaintiff also asserted that defendant 1 had completely succeeded in the aim pursued in his letter, since his customers had, in consequence of defendant 1's letters, cancelled their substantial orders.

The plaintiff also alleges that in consequence he has suffered substantial damage. He demands RM 16,000 in part payment for the damage averring that the proprietors of defendant 1, namely the defendants 2, had known when sending the letters that their design was not entitled to protection, since, *inter alia*, it lacked novelty.

The defendants, who allege that they were convinced of the validity of the design when they sent the letters and are even now convinced of it, demand the dismissal of the action and offer to show that the plaintiff has no claim whatever against the defendants.

The Landgericht declared the claim justified in principle, but the Court of Appeal invited both defendants 2 to swear upon oath that they were unaware, when they warned the firm L. & S. and two other firms against infringement of the design no. 342454, that already before giving notice of the design socks were being manufactured and put into circulation of which the upper portion was of whole or part made of wool and the lower portion of non-woollen material. If the two defendants swear the oath, the action should be dismissed; if they do not, the claim should be declared justified in principle.

On the plaintiff's application for review, the appeal of the defendants against the judgment at first instance was rejected for these

Reasons

1. The Court of Appeal, in agreement with the judge at first instance, starts correctly from the position that the defendants' conduct constituted an attack on an established business and that this must be regarded as a legal interest protected by § 823 1 BGB. That view conforms to the standing case-law of the Reichsgericht (*cf.* RGZ 58, 24; 64, 52).

The Oberlandesgericht then sets out the content of the defendants' design and finds that in preliminary proceedings brought by the defendants 1 and 2a against the present plaintiff before the Landgericht of Chemnitz, defendant 2a was ordered to approve the cancellation of the registered design no. 342454.

The Court of Appeal attaches no importance to that condemnation for the purposes of the present dispute. In particular it holds that the judgment in that preliminary proceeding, both at first instance and on appeal, ordered the cancellation of defendant 2a's design only because the inventive idea constituted by the socks had not been disclosed in the notice. It followed that the defendants could not have known this legal reason for the invalidity of the design; and, accordingly even apart from the presence of especial circumstances the existence of which was not alleged, they were not bound to make enquiries in that direction.

These considerations should obviously serve to deny negligence in what the Court of Appeal regarded as the objectively unlawful conduct of the defendants. Even so far the explanations of the Court of Appeal do not seem free from objection. It looks as though the Oberlandesgericht attaches to the registration of a design an importance that it does not possess.

In contrast to principles of patent law, whereby the grant of a patent (and the consequent entry in the patent register according to § 19 of the Patents Act) confers on the patent-holder without more ado the exclusive right to manufacture industrially the object of the invention, to put it into circulation, and sell it (§ 4 Patents Act), the person on whose behalf a design is entered in the register of designs acquires an exclusive right to copy the design industrially and put it in circulation only if it serves the purpose of work or use by a new structure, arrangement, or preparation. In other words, the entry in the register of designs confers on the person entering it no right of exclusive use that could empower him to invade another's established business unless the presuppositions exist that are set out in § 1 GebrMustG.

There can therefore be a negligent attack on another's business if anyone on whose behalf a design is registered forbids a tradesman only on the basis of that fact to retail such objects to which the design refers. Whoever makes himself guilty of an attack on another's business on the basis of a design registered for him can therefore in certain circumstances even act negligently within the meaning of § 823 I BGB if he does not convince himself of the efficacy of his design before he seeks registration. For, in contrast to the provisions of §§ 20 ff. of the Patents Act governing the grant of a patent, this is not ordered on the basis of an official examination into whether the material presuppositions exist on which § 1 GebrMustG affords to a design a claim to legal protection. The Patent Office must under § 3 GebrMustG order the entry of the design in the register of designs as soon as only the formal presuppositions of § 2 of the Act are fulfilled (*cf.* also the Reichsgericht decision of 27 February 1900, Via. 347/99).

2. It now appears from the foregoing reasons that the Court of Appeal's opinion that the defendant cannot be charged with negligence on the ground that he had not known of the legal inefficacy of this design is not free from objection. Moreover, its further considerations give occasion for appreciable legal doubt.

In particular, the Court of Appeal went on to say that in both the sets of preliminary proceedings concerning the design no. 342454 brought by the defendants against B1 (Landgericht Köln) and the present plaintiff (Landgericht Chemnitz) it was alleged that the object of the design was not new at the time of the notice. But in both cases that question did not give rise to a judicial decision. The proceedings against B1 ended with a settlement and in that against the present plaintiff, the newness of the design was assumed. In the proceedings against B1, the witnesses K and Sch. had indeed said at their examination of April 1911 that as long ago as twenty-five years their range had included socks of which the lower portion was made of cotton and the upper of woollen yarn. From that the Court of Appeal drew the further conclusion that the evidence of the two witnesses proved the lack of newness of the object of the design here in question. Since, however, their examination took place only after defendant 1's warning letter was sent out, since the latter was under no obligation to enquire what those witnesses would say, and since the defendants could not be held to blame for not waiting for the examination of the witnesses before sending out their warning letter, they could not be charged with negligent behaviour. Nor were they bound, once they knew what the witnesses had said, to withdraw their warning by a corresponding recall, since it appears to be excluded that the statements of the witnesses K and Sch. would have shaken their conviction of the newness of their design. Thus, the defendants were not shown to be negligent in failing to withdraw their warning once they knew of the witnesses' statements.

In these statements it appears even more clearly than in the considerations of the Court of Appeal discussed under (1) that it misunderstood the meaning of the registration of a design. Since that registration conferred on the person registering only a purely formal, but not a material right, he exercised it, as the Senate has already declared in its judgment of 3 July 1916, at his peril and responsibility, in so far as concerns the newness and previous use of the design. Hence "anyone who in reliance on a design encroaches on another's business by a trenchant prohibition against producing and selling the wares and thereby causes damage must constantly examine with the utmost care whether and for how long he is entitled to do it."

If one starts from this fundamental standpoint the conduct of the defendant 1 is already shown to have been negligent by the fact that, although in the preliminary proceedings against B1 the witnesses K and Sch. had alleged that the object of the design had been openly used in Germany, they had nevertheless sent out the warning letters here in question. For the defendants were bound to take into account that witnesses K and Sch. would confirm the correctness of the then defendant B1's statements.

However, the defendants were guilty of a quite exceptionally gross negligence when, after the examination in April 1911 of the witnesses K and Sch. . . . the absence of newness in the object of the design was established, all the same they did not withdraw their warning.

The Court of Appeal, which considers the defendants not obliged to make such a recall, thereby contradicts its own explanations. In particular it lays especial and decisive emphasis on the fact that the warning had already been sent out before the examination of the witnesses K and Sch. From that it follows that even from the Court of Appeal's standpoint the warning letters should not have been sent after the examination of the witnesses. But if that is correct, a recall of the warning letters was under all circumstances essential once the examination of the witnesses had taken place.

The appellate decision, which thereby wrongly denied the negligence of the defendants, is therefore set aside for infringement of § 823 BGB.

Case 34

BUNDESGERICHTSHOF (FIRST CIVIL SENATE) 26 OCTOBER 1951
BGHZ 3, 270 = NJW 1952, 660 = JZ 1952, 227 and partially approving and partially critical note by H Kleine

The ladies' journal "C" is published by the plaintiff. The defendant is the publisher of the weekly *Church and Life*, the church bulletin for the bishopric of M. Each issue of this journal includes for each deanery a "supplement" composed and printed locally, in which notices, mainly of religious services and other deanery news, are published. In the deanery supplement for O, an article was published entitled "The Select Readings of the P. Circle for Every Family", in which the moral conduct of the illustrated journals appearing in the post-war period was criticised. The article contains, *inter alia*, expressions to the effect that the publishers exploited the apparent collapse of the concepts of decency and dignity, had replaced honest commercial competition and market calculation by unscrupulous reliance on the primitive instincts of a wearied people; the plaintiff's ladies' journal "C" was described very critically; Christian readers of the ladies' journal "C" in receiving the journal, neglected their duty towards the honour of their wives and daughters, and the upbringing of their adolescent children. In addition it states that a Christian could obtain from other journals a picture of the world and a new point of view towards such matters. For the last few months there appeared regularly each week at the wish of the bishop the "Select Readings of the Circle" which, in richness, up-to-dateness, and make-up is not inferior to the products of other enterprises and are more value for money. It then names a number of journals which form a "medley" which offered every responsible thinking Christian joy and relaxation by providing moments of reflection in the evenings and on holidays. Information about these Select Readings was available at each parish office or the headquarters of the P. Circle.

The "Select Readings of the P. Circle" mentioned in that article is distributed by the "Catholic L. e.V." in M, which receives the net profit if any. The "P. Circle" and the "Catholic L. e.V." are economically independent of the defendant.

The above-mentioned article in the deanery's supplement appeared anonymously. The plaintiff company holds the defendant company answerable for the statements made against itself and its journal contained in that article, charging the defendant with breaches of certain statutory regulations [references]. The defendant first knew of the article objected to after its appearance, but has declared that it entirely agrees with the article and declines to withdraw the criticism of the plaintiff's journal printed in it.

The plaintiff claimed that the defendant be ordered to refrain from making and to recall the above-mentioned statements. The plaintiff also asked for a declaration that the defendant is liable to pay compensation and the right to publish the judgment.

Both instances below dismissed the action. The application for review led to the decisions being set aside and the case referred back to the lower court for these

Reasons

The applicant for review cannot successfully object that the Court of Appeal looked upon the statements in dispute as comments and not allegations of fact in the sense of § 14 UWG (*Unlauterer Wettbewerbsgesetz*), § 824 BGB, §§ 186, 187 StGB. The Court of Appeal did not fail to perceive that an allegation of a fact can be hidden under the form of a comment. Even if the protection of a reputation intended by the legislator requires the fluctuating boundary between allegations of fact and value-judgments or mere statements of opinion to be drawn as broadly as possible in favour of allegations of fact, since every comment rests ultimately on external or internal facts, yet it remains a prerequisite that the disapproving judgment takes as its starting-point tangible occurrences susceptible of proof, since otherwise a proof of truth or falsehood, as it is envisaged by § 186 StGB, § 824 BGB, and § 14 UWG, is logically excluded. The applicant starts from the position that no evidence whatever can be adduced for the truth of the contested statements. Comments, however, which do not admit of proof of truth, which are not related to definite probable acts, are not allegations of fact in the sense of the above-mentioned statutory provisions. It must, indeed, be conceded to the applicant that the complaint of exploitation can contain an allegation of fact. However, in the present case that complaint does not rest on specifically detailed acts but alleges that the apparent collapse of "decency and dignity" is being exploited. If one connects this statement with the further complaints, according to which the personalities standing behind the plaintiff are accused of "unscrupulous exploitation of the instincts of a wearied people", the view taken by the Court of Appeal must be approved that the expressions in question do not so much conceal a complaint of provable business dishonesty, but rather amount to a moral judgment on the general behaviour and business activity of the persons in question, and, therefore are value-judgments unaccompanied by examinable facts.

The same applies to the further critical statements of the plaintiff's journal and of the statement that "Christian readers of the journal in receiving the journal neglected their duty towards the honour of their wives and daughters and the upbringing of their adolescent children". In agreement with the principles established by the Reichsgericht's decisions in civil and criminal cases on distinguishing between value-judgments and allegations of fact, the Court of Appeal has quite accurately regarded those utterances as general expressions of disapproval, which have not for their object examinable acts of those involved [references follow].

III. In examining, however, the question of who may be sued, the Court of Appeal allows itself to be influenced by erroneous considerations of law which affect its further legal assessment of the facts. Neither the defendant's responsibility under press legislation nor its declaration of willingness to hold itself responsible for the article published without its knowledge justifies the Court of Appeal in assuming that the defendant must be treated as though it composed or authorised the article. The Court of Appeal failed to realise that the provisions of the Press law bear only on criminal law, not on civil law. The civil liability of the publishing house for infringements committed by its publications is defined by the general principles (RGZ 50, 109, 110; RG JW 1917, 713). In this purpose it is to be assumed that the publisher of periodicals is normally not in a position, and is also not in general bound, to scan the publication before it appears. As a rule responsibility for the contents is borne by the editor, whose name must appear on each number under the strict provisions of § 7 of the Press Act. The publisher, however, is liable for a fault of the editor, if the latter is subject to his instructions, and it is therefore a question of employer's liability. He may then try to prove that he is not to be blamed under § 831 BGB (RGZ 148, 154, 161). The publisher who did not know before publication of an injurious utterance made public by a periodical published by him is, as a rule, liable in damages only in so far as general provisions make him responsible for the faults of third persons. The publisher is, however, independently of any question of fault, the right defendant in a claim for an injunction under § 1004 BGB, against a disturber if a leaflet which is inserted in his publication unlawfully affects a third person and that injurious result is at least indirectly traceable to his will, since he has the possibility of exercising influence on the content of the sale of the inserted leaflet [references follow].

. . . The defendant's declaration that makes the contested utterances her own, combined indeed with an approval of all the circumstances under which the Article complained of appeared, is not without importance for the decision of the claim for an injunction. The defendant has refused to tone down the criticism of the plaintiff's journal in the article in the deanery supplement and has expressed the view that the criticism was, even in its present rigour, required by its opposition to the plaintiff's journal, and was covered by the protection of justified interests. It has also announced that it considered itself justified in publishing similar or equivalent statements in the future. That, however, makes it a "disturber" in the sense of § 1004 BGB, since it has made these declarations in knowledge of the attacks, which have already occurred and must here be assumed to have been unlawful—and does not deny its ability to prevent the insertion of deanery supplements with a content not approved by it. From that admission of the defendant there follows a risk of further impairment and thereby its liability to be made defendant in proceedings for an injunction, without any need so far to examine its responsibility for the existing publications.

IV. The Court of Appeal denied any infringement of provisions protecting competition on the ground that those provisions presuppose acting with a competitive purpose, whereas the defendant in its conduct complained of acted not with a competitive intention but exclusively on religious ground without a gainful purpose.

The contention of the applicant for review, that the Court of Appeal misunderstood the concept of acting with a competitive purpose, is unfounded. Relying on a decision of the Reichsgericht [reference], the applicant puts forward the view that where business men were engaged in a competitive struggle any act which is objectively apt to further one's own or another's competition suffices to fulfil the factual characteristics of acting for competitive purposes, without any need to examine the subjective disposition of the actor. The applicant fails here to recognize that the Reichsgericht, in the decision referred to, treated the knowledge that another's competition was being furthered only as an indication that the then defendant was pursuing, along with other aims, also competitive purposes. That additional presupposition, however, was required because according to a constant practice concept "with competitive purposes" requires a subjective intention directed towards competition [references].

The Senate cannot accept the dissenting view put forward by Reimer [reference] in view of the wording of the Act. Although an intention directed to furthering competition by oneself or another does not need to be the only or an essential aim of the act, yet that competitive purpose must not be neglected as completely irrelevant compared with the principal motives [references].

It may, indeed, generally be correct that experience points to a competitive intention when competitors make statements in commercial intercourse which are objectively apt to further one's own or another's competition. It is not, however, a mistake of law when the Court of Appeal does not consider this evidentiary rule, which is not imperative and is merely found empirically to correspond as a rule to the truth, to be decisive in the particular case which concerns information in a church bulletin.

Whether the factual characteristics of acting "for a competitive purpose" are fulfilled is a matter for the unfettered appreciation of the judge of fact. The Court of Appeal was not wrong in inferring from the circumstance that no reference to the church bulletin published by the defendant was contained in the article and that no financial connection exists between the defendant and the "P. Circle" or the "Catholic L. e.V." selling its select readings that there was no intrinsic probability of a competitive intention to be proved by the defendant. When accordingly, the Court of Appeal—starting from the pastoral duties of the bishop, on whose instructions the defendant acted as the publisher—came to the conclusion that the controversial article would, according to the honest conviction of the defendant, serve only its fight against what it considered the extraordinarily corrupting and dangerous world of journals and magazines, those considerations did not offend against the legal principles laid down by the Reichsgericht for the subjective requirement of acting for competitive purposes [reference].

On the other hand the applicants' complaint for review is well founded that the Court of Appeal ought not to have neglected to take up the offer to provide evidence of the testimony of named witnesses that the controversial article was prepared on the defendant's instructions by the publicity manager of the "P. Circle" for competitive purposes and was provided for the deanery supplement [details follow].

V. The considerations also by which the Court of Appeal rejects §§ 823 I and II, 826, in combination with § 1004 BGB, as grounds of claim do not stand up to legal review.

. . . First it must be objected that the Court of Appeal regards as decisive whether the defendant acted with a defamatory intent—a question which can be relevant only when the protection of reputation is in issue—without examining whether there was a direct attack on the plaintiff's business through an unlawful impairment of its business activity, which falls within § 823 I BGB. Even utterances which do not fulfil the requirements of defamation but describe the position of a business undertaking, its products, or other performance and thereby disturb the free development of the undertaking, can constitute a direct attack on the right protected by § 823 I BGB to carry on an established business. Since § 14 UWG and § 824 BGB only allow claims arising from allegations of fact, legal protection against injurious comments which do not bear the taint of immorality and therefore do not fall within the general clause of § 1 UWG, § 826 BGB would be incomplete if they could not be treated as injurious acts violating the right to conduct a business.

The Reichsgericht, it must be admitted, affirmed the existence of that right in its earlier decisions only when the attack was aimed directly against the existence of the business. A diminution of the economic profit or of the prospects of gain was not regarded as sufficient [references]. Yet, in later decisions the Reichsgericht went further in the field of the law of trade marks and competition and considered, for the purpose of an injunction, that any unlawful impairment of business activity was sufficient, if it constituted a direct interference with the sphere of the business [references].

But there remains no substantial reason to restrict the concept of the protection of business activity to the field of competition and industrial property. Just as property is protected by § 823 I BGB against direct attack, in all its individual emanations—for instance the impairment of the unrestricted power of disposal—so also, according to this protective provision, the right to an established and active business must be protected against direct disturbances not only in its substance but also in its individual aspects, including the whole field of business activity.

The contested Article which, supported by the highest ecclesiastical authority, strongly warns everyone, but especially the Christian reader, against the plaintiff's journal, and couples that warning with a derogatory reference to the persons behind the plaintiff. It displays a direct attack on the plaintiff's protected right to an undisturbed development of its business activity. This interference with the protected legal sphere of the plaintiff, which infringes the protection of business activity afforded by the law, would only not be illegal if the defendant had a special justification for the interference [references].

For this purpose, contrary to the view of the Court of Appeal, it is not of vital importance whether the facts point to punishable defamation, for it is not the protection of a reputation but the plaintiff's right to unimpeded business activity that is in question. If aspects of unfair competition are absent, such as attach as a rule to a critical comparison of industrial products for competitive purposes, an objective criticism of the plaintiff's journal would not be contrary to law even if it had adverse consequences for the plaintiff since Article 5 of the Constitution allows anyone to express such criticism in the exercise of his right to the free expression of his opinion. But comments disturbing business, which depart from the field of objective criticism, are only not illegal if in accordance with their content, form, or accompanying circumstances they are objectively necessary to protect legally approved interests.

§ 193 StGB, it is true, provides a justification only where defamation is concerned. Yet that rule governs the special case of conflicts of interests which can arise in the protection of reputation, in accordance with an overriding legal doctrine which assumes importance wherever in a conflict between different interests the injury to one legal interest must be accepted. All comments affecting a business which factually fall within § 823 I BGB can be justified as protecting justified interests if the protection keeps within the limits fixed by law. These limits must be drawn according to the principle of balancing interests and duties that govern all conflicts of interests [references].

The conflict between the interest pursued and the legally protected interest that is to be sacrificed to it must be balanced by observing the principles that the Reichsgericht has developed for overriding necessity. The conflict of values can only be resolved in this way, whereby he who can effectively protect a justified interest only by interfering with another's legally protected interest must choose the least violation of law, the most considerate means. Thus injurious utterances are covered by the protection of justified interests only if according to their content, form, and accompanying circumstances they constitute the indicated and necessary means of attaining the legally approved purpose [references].

A mistake as to the need for the severity and extent of the attack on a protected legal good, if innocent, only excludes fault and thereby liability for damages, but not the substantial unlawfulness of the attack [references follow].

It is to be noted that whoever proposes to encroach on another's legal sphere for the sake of his own interests, or of those especially dear to him, must carefully examine whether the injury which he proposes to inflict is necessary as to severity and extent in order to further those interests appropriately. If he neglects that examination, which must take into account the scale of protection of the legal interest under attack, an excessive amount of injury, which is always illegal, cannot be excused even if there is a mistake as to its necessity.

These legal principles were misunderstood by the Court of Appeal. It assumed, indeed quite rightly, that the defendant, as publisher of a bulletin issued by a high ecclesiastical dignitary, held no exceptional legal position, but that its conduct was to be judged according to all applicable legal provisions. The Court of Appeal is also correct in holding that the interests involved in the struggle of the Church against a degenerate Press of which it disapproved affected so closely the defendant as publisher of the Church bulletin that it must be accorded an especial right to protect those interests (RGSt 63, 229 [231]; RGZ 115, 77 [80]). But the Court of Appeal misunderstands the limits to the pursuit of justifiable interests when it considers that the assumed excess in degree of injury is justified on the ground that the defendant acted exclusively for an ethically objectionable purpose and not with a defamatory intent. Even moral motives afford no right to sacrifice the protected interests of another beyond the necessary limits. The view of the law taken by the Court of Appeal, which makes the unlawfulness of the utterances in issue depend on the personal convictions and intentions of the injuring party, would render the right to reputation and the right to an established business defenceless against the grossest attack, if the perpetrator acted not for objectionable reasons but only with the aim of enforcing more effectually the interest pursued by him by excessive attacks which are objectively unnecessary. The Court of Appeal overlooks the fact that the decisions of the Reichsgericht which it cites in support of its opinion to the contrary (RG JW 1914, 368, 371; RGSt 40, 317), deal only with criminal liability—which always presupposes fault—but not with the objective unlawfulness of unduly injurious utterances.

It is also a matter for criticism that the Court of Appeal, contrary to its opinion that the defendant must be treated as though it had prepared or occasioned the article, chooses to justify the conduct of the defendant within the scope of § 193 StGB by the particular state of conflict in which it found it after the publication of the article. If the defendant had no right to express its condemnation in its existing form at the time the article appeared, that right, which the defendant claims also for future publications, cannot be deduced from its position after the publication. The defendant could, when the plaintiff approached it with a request for the withdrawal of the article, reflect at leisure whether the utterances objected to exceeded the measure permitted for the furtherance of its interests; as a champion of ecclesiastical interests its special concern should have been to examine carefully whether the general character of the plaintiff's journal justified such a severe denigration combined with a general attack on the reputations of its publisher and distributors. If the attack was objectively excessive, the defendant, which approved that excess, is in no way excused, as the Court of Appeal wrongly assumes, by the fact that, even if the form of expression were toned down, an objectively necessary contravention of law remains; for only an objectively necessary attack on the interests of others not the unnecessary, so-called excess is justified by the protection of justified interests.

Whether an injurious attack goes beyond the degree objectively permitted for the protection of interests is a question of fact. The Court of Appeal made no finding on it.

Starting from its mistaken opinion that for the utterances complained of also to be objectively unlawful only the subjective conviction of the defendant was decisive that they were necessary, the Court of Appeal considered that the question was irrelevant whether an objectively unnecessary excessive attack existed. In this connection the Court of Appeal is of the opinion that it could not be its task "to take up a position in the fight between two contesting philosophies of life represented here in the publications in question (the plaintiff's journal and the article for which the defendants were responsible) to examine the correctness of the value-judgments contained in them". That is correct only in so far as the Court of Appeal is not bound to press judgment on the worth or worthlessness of the philosophical aims pursued by the parties, in so far as they are in opposition. If, however, it must be conceded to the plaintiff's journal, as is to be inferred from the reasoning in the judgment under appeal, that it may discuss questions relating to the philosophy of life, the Court of Appeal cannot refuse to decide whether the attack directed by the defendant against this journal, objectively considered, in respect of its content, form, and accompanying circumstances, falls within the limits of legally permitted promotion of interests. In this connection it is to be noted that the permitted degree of attack is to be determined differently when it is directed against a journal with a generally licentious content from when it concerns a journal whose pursuit of serious endeavours is—in whole or in part—not to be denied. For that determination the decisive factor is not single contributions to the journal but its general character. When dealing afresh with the dispute, the Court of Appeal must . . . examine . . . whether the plaintiff's journal (if assimilated to magazines generally regarded as of a scandalous type) has exploited in an unscrupulous and ethically reprehensible way the moral decline of the population for selfish and mercenary ends. In this connection the Court of Appeal will also have to consider that the wide-ranging moral condemnation of the persons behind the plaintiff and its publishing enterprise has been published in the defendant's periodical. Press attacks, however, have such incalculable and profound effects that the limits within which other legal interest may be violated by the promotion of interests of one's own must be drawn especially narrowly (RGSt 63, 92 [94]).

On this view of the law it can be left undecided whether the plaintiff as a company can be regarded as capable of being defamed. It is true that the doubts expressed by the Landgericht in that regard cannot be regarded as removed by the formal assignment, since the claim to forbear from uttering defamatory statements, being of a highly personal nature, cannot be assigned [reference]. Yet, if the unlawfulness of the statements in dispute is established, a basis is provided for an action under § 823 I BGB, so that no discussion is needed as to whether the defendant also infringed a statute serving to protect the plaintiff in the meaning of § 823 II BGB, since no wider claims would arise from that protective provision.

Case 35

BUNDESGERICHTSHOF (SIXTH CIVIL SENATE) 13 OCTOBER 1998
NJW 1999, 279 = JZ 1999, 625

Facts

The claimant runs a car hire business in O and claims an injunction preventing the defendant—a large insurance company undertaking—from statements and actions damaging its business. The claimant alleged that the defendant's experts had in a number of cases told accident victims who had hired cars from the claimant that there had frequently been problems with the claimant's car hire charges and they had tried to persuade them to return vehicles and hire cheaper cars from a firm named by the defendant. The claimant sought an injunction to prevent such action in business contacts for competition purposes and an injunction in the same terms but without the reference to competition. The Landgericht ordered the defendant not (1) to tell the claimant's customers that there were frequent problems in relation to the claimant's car hire charges and not (2) to recommend accident victims who had already hired a vehicle from the claimant (referring to their duty to mitigate their loss) to return it and to hire another with the firm E or another firm in O.

On appeal by the defendant, the Oberlandesgericht rejected the whole of the claim. By its appeal in law the claimant had the judgment of the Landgericht reinstated.

Reasons

I. The appeal court proceeded on the basis that the claimant had accepted the dismissal of its principal applications in competition law. It now only concerned itself with the claimant's claims based on tort law, which had been successful at first instance. It considered these claims not to be acceptable.

Insofar as the claimant objected to the statement that there were often problems with the invoicing of its car hire costs, only § 824 of the BGB needed to be considered as the basis of the claim; it was not possible in this respect to fall back on the framework definition of an interference with an established and functioning business. The prerequisites for a claim based on § 824 of the BGB were not however fulfilled, as here it was question of assertion of true facts by the defendant's experts. Problems with the claimant's invoicing had existed as a matter of fact. These resulted from the defendant, as a leading insurance undertaking, taking the view that the victim of an accident was in principle required, in view of the duty to mitigate loss, to hire a replacement vehicle at the cheapest available hire price on the market. As the defendant had been confirmed in this view by several court decisions in the O Landgericht area and the claimant was not one of the cheap suppliers, the invoicing problems were obvious. Whether the defendant's legal view was accurate, was not of importance; for the question of the alleged invoicing problems, it was only actual implementation mattered. However, not only was there no assertion put forward which was contrary to the truth in the sense of § 824 of the BGB; the defendant and the victims also had a justified interest in the sense of § 824 (2) of the BGB in the communication to which objection was made. It was virtually a requirement for the defendant to mention in good time that it was only ready to allow the hire car costs on the basis of the cheapest supplier and that accordingly there would be problems if cars were hired at higher prices.

The recommendation given to the victims to give back the hired car to the claimant and to hire a vehicle elsewhere was not open to objection on legal grounds either. No illegal interference with the claimant's established and functioning business was to be seen in this. There was no incitement to the victims to break their contracts with the claimant, for the simple reason that the hire contracts were terminable at any time. The proprietor of a business must as a rule accept inducements to cancel contracts without their being breached. Different considerations could only apply if special circumstances were found which amounted to dishonesty. Such a case was not however present here, as the advice given by the defendant's experts to the victims with regard to the invoicing problems with the claimant had been accurate and it had been in the interests of both sides that these problems had been mentioned in connection with the negotiations about the loss.

II. The judgment of the appeal court does not stand up to the arguments contained in the appeal in law. The claimant is entitled to the claims which have been made for an injunctive relief and which formed the basis of the judgment of the Landgericht.

1. Contrary to the view of the appeal in law, the appeal court was admittedly correct in not including the principles for the claim under competition law in its judgment. Possible claims by the claimant for injunctions under §§ 1 and 3 of the UWG (Unfair Competition Act) were, in view of the position here in procedural law, not the subject of dispute at the level of the first appeal.

No final decision is needed on the question of whether, under what conditions and in what manner a party can in principle, in cases in which claims arise under competition law on the one hand and tort law on the other, restrict the legal examination to the one or the other basis of claim. In any case, in the circumstances given here, the claimant has effectively limited the object of the dispute to be decided by the appeal court at second instance to the examination of claims to injunctive relief in tort law, to which it is entitled from the facts put forward which support the judgment at first instance.

. . .

2. The appeal in law correctly objects to the fact that the appeal court considered to be unfounded the claims for injunctive relief in relation to the statement that there had often been problems with the invoicing for the claimant's hire car prices in the context of the calculation of hire car costs in the accident replacement business (no.1a of the judgment of the Landgericht, concerning the claimant's first alternative application), and the recommendation to the victims, referring to their duty to mitigate loss, to give back the claimant's hired vehicle and to hire a vehicle of the same value from another firm instead (no.1b of the judgment of the Landgericht, concerning the claimant's second alternative application).

In both respects, the request for an injunction is justified from the point of view of an interference by the defendant with the claimant's established and functioning business.

(a) The considerations which formed the basis of the appeal court's dismissal of the first alternative application under § 824 of the BGB meet with objections. The appeal court says that the statement that there were problems from time to time with the claimant in the context of calculating car hire costs in the business of accident replacement is about a true fact, since calculation of loss between the defendant and each victim did not actually take place in this respect without problems. Admittedly, this must be agreed. But contrary to the view of the appeal court, this was not the whole content of this statement, as the appeal in law correctly points out. The average victim (whose understanding is what matters here) would have understood this statement as meaning that the claimant was responsible for the invoicing problems which had occurred, because it charged hire car costs at a level not fully recoverable in compensation law. According to the findings made in the appeal judgment, however, the invoicing problems in reality arose because the defendant—inappropriately in law—holds the view that the accident victim was in principle required, from the viewpoint of the duty to mitigate loss, to hire a replacement vehicle at the cheapest hire price obtainable on the market and the victim could not therefore demand compensation for hire prices going beyond this. Such a invoicing practice does not however satisfy the actual legal position (references omitted). Contrary to what the victims would naturally infer from the statement objected to, it was thus primarily the defendant itself which was responsible, by its conduct in relation to the invoicing, for the problems which arose. It can however remain undecided whether one should proceed here on the basis that the defendant was making an incorrect assertion of facts in the sense of § 824 of the BGB or whether this cannot be so because value judgments, namely views of the defendant on the legal position, substantially shaped the statement to which objection is made.

(b) This is because insofar as a claim under § 824 of the BGB is to be denied, the claimant can base its request for an injunction on § 823 (1) of the BGB in combination with § 1004 of the BGB because of the interference with an established and functioning business. It is possible to fall back on this basis of claim if the tort under § 824 of the BGB is not relevant (references omitted).

(aa) The protection of businesses in tort is aimed at business related interferences which concern the business organism or entrepreneurial freedom of decision and go beyond mere nuisance or hindrances which are normal in society (references omitted). An interference of this kind is present here. If the defendant communicates with the claimant's car hire customers as accident victims in the context of its concept for calculating loss, and refers them, in the way it has done, to problems with invoicing for the claimant's car hire prices, this amounts to a deliberate interference with the claimant's business relationships with its customers. This is so even if the defendant's motivation for action of this kind is based on keeping its own insurance payments as low as possible. In view of the fact that the defendant is one of the leading insurance undertakings and accident replacement business is of considerable importance for car hire businesses like the claimant's, action of this kind by the defendant, must lead to a distinct uncertainty on the part of customers in their relationship with the claimant. It interferes with the claimant's protected commercial enterprise in a manner which has legal implications.

(bb) This interference is also to be regarded as illegal. This follows from balancing the interests of the parties, taking into consideration their respective positions as protected not only in civil law but also in constitutional law and especially the basic right of the defendant under Article 5 of the Constitution (references omitted).

The defendant can admittedly not in principle be forbidden to disseminate a legal view held by it, even if this view should be regarded as inaccurate measured by the standards of the case law of the court dealing with appeals in law. Nor is the defendant prevented, within the framework of its own business activity (which includes calculating loss cases under insurance law) from approaching the victims, in order to ensure with them that treatment and invoicing is as efficient as possible and corresponds to the legal duties of all participants. But even taking these principles into consideration, the action of the defendant objected to here should not be regarded as lawful.

The defendant's experts had represented that in the area of calculating car hire costs in the accident replacement business there were problems from time to time in the invoicing of the claimants' car hire prices. The defendant thereby gives to the victims as car hire customers of the claimant the impression that by hiring a vehicle from the claimant they had incurred the risk of having to bear part of their costs themselves. The business relationship with the claimant is thus represented to these customers as an economic risk. But according to the findings which have been made, this action by the experts is based, as already mentioned, on the defendant's view that in principle it must as a vehicle liability insurer only reimburse the car hire costs which arose by hiring a replacement vehicle at the cheapest hiring price available on the market. As this view of the law does not correspond with the legal position and the problems which have occurred on this basis with the invoicing of the vehicles hired by the victims from the claimant are the responsibility of the defendant itself, the statement by the defendant's experts to the victims which is the subject of objection lacks a satisfactory basis.

The defendant has no justified interest in deliberately, on the basis of an inaccurate view of the law (the incorrectness of which, however, remains concealed from the victims), inducing uncertainty in the victims—using the authority of a large insurance undertaking responsible for adjusting the loss of those affected—in their business relationships as car hire customers of the claimant, as has happened here, and thus seriously endangering these relationships to the disadvantage of the claimant's commercial enterprise. By the defendant's action, the victims, who are not as a rule familiar with the law and will be frequently inclined to avoid differences with the defendant in order to ensure speedy loss adjustment, see themselves exposed to pressure not justified by the real legal situation, which affects their behaviour as car hire customers of the claimant, as the defendant intends it should.

In this situation it is not possible to set against the claimant's protected interest in the integrity of its commercial enterprise an interest of the defendant of equal value in the statement by their experts to the claimant's car hire customers who were accident victims, which is the subject of objection here. The interference in the commercial enterprise, for which the defendant cannot in these circumstances rely on its basic right of freedom of expression of opinion, is to be regarded as unlawful.

(cc) No different conclusion can be drawn from the fact that various courts in the Landgericht district of O share (or at least, at the point in time of the statements objected to, shared) the legal view of the defendant as described, on the duty to mitigate the loss of accident victims on the hiring of a replacement vehicle. Contrary to the view of the appeal court, the issue of the alleged invoicing problems is by no means only a question of factual implementation and the local practice of the courts. It is the real legal situation which is decisive. Only implementation which corresponds with this should be regarded as lawful; only references to invoicing problems arising on lawful loss adjustment would be in the justified interest of a party. On the other hand, the legal order cannot recognise any justified interest on the part of someone involved in legal transactions in orientating himself to a practice which is incorrect in law, even if this is supported—temporarily—by locally competent courts.

(dd) The argument that the defendant could not in law be accused of fault in respect of the conduct to be assessed here, because he could refer to a corresponding local court practice at that time and the Senate decision [reference omitted] was not then available, is not of importance in this case. For the claim to injunctive relief (which is the only claim made here), the fault of the defendant is not the issue. The illegality of the interference is the only decisive factor. In this connection danger of repetition in the future must be assumed; from the findings which have been made and the parties' submissions referred to, no sufficient grounds are evident for proceeding on the basis that the danger of repetition has been dispelled.

3. The claimant's request for injunctive relief to prevent the defendant recommending the claimant's car hire customers to give back the claimant's hired vehicles and to hire vehicles of equal value with another (cheaper) firm instead, in view of their duty to mitigate their loss, was dismissed by the appeal court. The appeal in law successfully challenges this. In this respect also, the claimant's claim to injunctive relief is justified from the point of view of the interference with their established and functioning business.

(a) It can remain undecided whether the hire contracts concluded by the victims with the claimant are terminable at any time, which is the view of the appeal court, or whether, as the appeal in law points out, this can be otherwise, at least when the victim has hired a car for the length of his vehicle's repair. This is because the question of whether the defendant is to blame for encouraging the victims to break their contracts, which could be the case for hire contracts which were not appropriately terminable, does not matter in the present case.

(b) The recommendation which, according to the findings made in the appeal judgment, was given by the defendant to the victims represents a business related interference in the claimant's commercial enterprise under the circumstances present here. It is true that a commercial enterprise as such is not in any way generally protected in tort law against inroads into its circle of customers. But here it is a question of a deliberate action by the defendant as a leading insurance undertaking which must inevitably—if the defendant wants to achieve its goal that victims only hire a vehicle with the cheapest supplier—lead to a substantial interference with the claimant in its accident car replacement business. The defendant's action is directed towards making victims decide to behave to the claimant's disadvantage, within the framework of the already existing of business relationships with the claimant, by using its position as liability insurer in relation to loss adjustment.

(c) This interference by the defendant with the claimant's commercial enterprise must be regarded as unlawful. On the balancing of the justified interests of the participants which is required here, the principle must be borne in mind that, within the framework of an order based on a market economy, an interference in the contractual relationships of others is only to be considered as impermissible if special circumstances forming the basis of unfairness are established (references omitted). Contrary to the view of the appeal court, such circumstances forming the basis of unlawfulness are present here.

(aa) The defendant's action which is to be assessed here rests—as must be deduced from the findings which have been made—on the incorrect legal view that the accident victim was required in principle, in view of the duty to mitigate loss, to hire a replacement vehicle at the cheapest obtainable hire price on the market; and could ask for no compensation for hire prices going beyond this. The defendant cannot be allowed any justified interest in implementing a legal opinion of this kind, which contradicts the real legal position, by means of recommendations to the victims and—as already discussed—in particular not even if and in so far as their legal opinion has found recognition in local court practice. An accident victim who has hired a replacement vehicle, within the framework of the so-called accident compensation rates, in such a way that there are no effective legal objections to the full compensatibility of his costs according to the principles of the judgment of the Senate (reference omitted) is not required by the duty to mitigate loss to change to another car hire firm if he subsequently hears of a cheaper offer. The defendant's action is therefore also not lawful from the point of view that it seeks retrospectively to put the victims as it were "in bad faith" by naming the cheapest supplier of hire vehicles.

(bb) The recommendation made to the victims, who as a rule cannot recognise the incorrect approach in the defendant's opinion, gives them the inaccurate impression that they are under a duty to hire their replacement vehicle with the cheapest supplier named to them by the defendant and that they had committed a mistake by hiring from the claimant; and that this must now be corrected to avoid them suffering economic disadvantages, namely having to bear the hire car costs themselves in so far as they are higher than the cheapest supplier's prices. The victims are bound to fear difficulties based on an invoicing practice not in harmony with the real legal position. They are thereby put under pressure to behave in accordance with the defendant's recommendation to the claimant's detriment. This action is unlawful and in particular in the relationship to the claimant with regard to its commercial enterprise protected in tort law. The claimant does not need to accept such action, if the business relationships which it has entered into with its hire car customers are endangered by pressure being exerted on its contractual partners in a way which does not correspond to the legal position.

(d) Fault on the part of the defendant does not matter as here also it is only a question of a request for injunctive relief. The danger of repetition is in this respect to be assumed, as contrary findings have not been made and furthermore the defendant considers its action to be permissible.

Notes to Cases 32–35

1. These four cases deal with the "right of an established and operating business" which the German courts have added to the list of protected interests mentioned in § 823 I BGB. A brief account of the emergence of this new right can be found above in chapter 2, section A. 2 (e) (iii). As in all judge-made rights one finds here, on the one hand the desire to expand the law and, on the other, the need to set workable and reasonable limits. The element of "directness" is here relied upon and is extensively discussed in case 11, above. In the end, however, there is little doubt that policy dictates the results. Case 14, above, is also interesting in so far as it shows that the courts treat this as a residual right to be invoked only where there is no other remedy available to a deserving plaintiff. (A point clearly established in the important decision of 21 June 1966, BGHZ 45, 296 = NJW 1966, 1617 = JZ 1967, 174.) If, however, a particular factual situation is covered by a specific statutory rule (say, § 824 or § 826 BGB), then that rule must be applied; and if one of its conditions is not satisfied, one cannot fall back on this new right. As already stated, only "business-connected" interests will be protected by this right. What exactly this means is difficult to say and, ultimately, it is for the courts to decide. Thus, see Deutsch in JZ 1984, 308, 309. The decision in case 35, though it did not alter the law or develop it further, should be seen as an example of how the concept of an established and operating business is applied in practice. (The importance of competition law in this field is stressed by Helle JZ 1999, 628). As was explained above (chapter 2 A. 2 (e) (iii)), the element of unlawfulness has to be established positively in each case. The present decision also illustrates the balancing act involved though one should note that the approach is flexible. (The balancing act can also take place in defining the protected interest: see BGH NJW 1998, 2141). The case also highlights the need to justify the solution against the background of the constitutional rights of the actors (generally speaking, criticism of a competitor is, of course, allowed as a corollary of freedom of speech: Article 5 I GG). The actual decision must be understood in connection

with case 151 (BGHZ 132, 373), and concerns the relationship between insurer and care hirer. As will be explained in the notes to the latter case, the insurance companies complained about the inflated tariffs for accident car replacement vehicles. The BGH however (unlike the House of Lords) held that such costs were recoverable. As a result, the call for a boycott of such care hire companies could not be justified. The decision leaves open how far insurance companies can go in warning potential claimants. The better view seems to be that they ought to be allowed to make specific proposals and advise the claimant that he has to mitigate his loss. (See Teichmann *LM* BGB § 823 (Ai) Nr. 74.)

2. The cases reproduced above have no exact equivalents in the Common law, the points they raise falling to be discussed under different headings of the law. Thus *Kaplan* v. *Helenhart Novelty Corp.* 182 F. 2d 311 (2nd Cir. 1950) is, to a point, factually analogous to cases 32 and 33, though the decision in that case went in favour of the defendant who had acted in good faith when he gave notice of an alleged infringement of the patent. For further discussion see Choate and Francis, *Patent Law* (2nd edn., 1981) and Rosenberg, *Patent Law Fundamentals* (2nd edn., 1980). Case 34, on the other hand, would raise issues which the Common law would, in part at least, discuss under the heading of defamation and freedom of expression. Many cases discussed in the next section (*Constitutionalisation of Private Law*) deal with this issue. See, for example, BVerfGE 25, 256; BGH NJW 1984, 1956; BGH NJW 1985, 1620.

11. THE "CONSTITUTIONALISATION" OF PRIVATE LAW

Case 36

BUNDESVERFASSUNGSGERICHT (FIRST DIVISION) 15 JANUARY 1958
BVerfGE 7, 198 = NJW 1958, 257

1. Basic rights are primarily to protect the citizen against the state, but as enacted in the Constitution (GG) they also incorporate an objective scale of values which applies, as a matter of constitutional law, throughout the entire legal system.

2. The substance of the basic rights is expressed indirectly in the rules of private law, most evidently in its mandatory provisions, and is best effectuated by the judges' use of the general clauses.

3. Basic rights may be infringed by a judicial decision, which ignores the effect of basic rights on private law (§ 90 Act on Constitutional Court Procedure (BVerfGG)). Judicial decisions on private law are subject to review by the Constitutional Court, only in respect of such infringements of basic rights, not for errors of law in general.

4. Rules of private law may count as "general laws" which may restrict the basic right of freedom of expression under Article 5 II GG.

5. Such "general laws" must be interpreted in the light of the especial significance in a free democratic state of the basic right to freedom of expression.

6. The basic right in Article 5 GG protects not only the utterance of an opinion as such, but also the effect it has on others.

7. The expression of an opinion favouring a boycott does not necessarily infringe proper conduct (*boni mores*) under § 826 BGB; depending on all the circumstances such an expression may be justified as a matter of constitutional law.

Disposition

The decision of the Landgericht Hamburg of 22 November 1951 infringes the complainants' basic right under Article 5 I, 1 GG and is therefore vacated. The matter is remitted to the Landgericht Hamburg.

Reasons

At the opening of "German Film Week" on 20 September 1950 the complainant, then a Senator of the Free and Hanseatic City of Hamburg and Head of the State Press Office, gave an address, in his capacity as President of the Hamburg Press Club, to an audience of film distributors and directors. He said, *inter alia*:

> The person least likely to restore the claim to morality which the German film forfeited during the Third Reich is the man who directed "Jud Süss" and wrote the script for it. If this very man is chosen to represent the German film industry, who can tell what harm we may suffer throughout the world? True he was acquitted in a formal sense in Hamburg, but substantially the judgment was a condemnation. We must call on the distributors and cinema owners to show character—not cheap, but worth the price. And I want the German film to show character as well. If it shows character in its imagination, visual daring and sterling craftsmanship, it will merit every assistance and achieve what it needs in order to survive: success with the public here in Germany and abroad.

Domnick-Film-Produktion GmbH immediately challenged the complainant to justify these charges against Veit Harlan, under whose direction and with whose screen-play they were making "Unsterbliche Geliebte".

On 27 October 1950 the complainant released an "open letter" to the Press by way of reply which contained the following:

> The court did not gainsay the fact that for much of the Hitler régime Veit Harlan was the "Nazi film-director no. 1" or that his film "Jud Süss" showed him to be a committed exponent of the Nazis' murderous purge of the Jews. Some businessmen here and abroad may not be opposed to Veit Harlan's re-emergence, but the moral integrity of Germany must not be destroyed by hard-faced money-makers. Harlan's return can only reopen wounds barely healed, and resuscitate diminishing distrust fatal to German reconstruction. For all these reasons it is not only the right but the duty of all decent Germans to protest against, and even to boycott, this ignominious representative of the German film industry.

Domnick-Film-Produktion GmbH and Herzog-Film GmbH (the distributor of "Unsterbliche Geliebte" in the Federal Republic), obtained an interlocutory injunction from the Landgericht Hamburg ... and the Oberlandesgericht dismissed the complainant's appeal. At the complainant's request the two film companies were required to bring suit within a certain time. They did so, and on 22 November 1951 the Landgericht Hamburg issued the following judgment:

> The defendant is ordered, on pain of fine or imprisonment as determined by the court, to refrain (1) from calling on theatre managers and film distributors not to programme the film "Unsterbliche Geliebte" and (2) from calling on the German public not to go to see the film ...

B. I.

The complaint is admissible since the preconditions for the application of § 90 II, 2 BVerfGG are satisfied (decision before exhaustion of legal remedies).

II.

The complainant alleges that the Landgericht's judgment infringes his basic right to free expression of opinion as laid down in Article 5 I, 1 GG.

The judgment of the Landgericht, an act of the public power of *judicature*, could infringe the complainant's basic right by its *content* only if the court was bound to take account of the complainant's basic right.

By enjoining the complainant from making statements apt to lead others to endorse his views about Harlan's re-emergence and to follow him in discriminating against Harlan's films, the judgment clearly restricts the complainant's freedom of expression of opinion. The Landgericht granted the injunction as a matter of private law order on the basis that the complainant's statements were tortious under § 826 BGB. Thus the public power has restricted the complainant's freedom of expression on the basis of the plaintiff's private law claim. This can constitute an infringement of the complainant's basic right under Article 5 I, 1 GG only if the applicable rules of private law are so substantially affected that they can no longer support the judgment.

The question whether basic rights affect private law, and if so in what manner, is much debated [references]. The extreme positions are, on the one hand, that basic rights constrain only the state, and, on the other, that basic rights (or at any rate the most important of them) prevail against everyone in private legal relations. Previous decisions of this Court support neither of these extreme positions, the conclusions drawn by the Federal Labour court in its decision of 10 May 1957 (NJW 1957, 1688) from our decisions of 17 and 23 January 1957 (BVerfGE 6, 55 and 6, 84) being unwarranted. Nor is it necessary today to deal with all aspects of the debated question of the "effect on third parties" (*Drittwirkung*) of basic rights. The matter can be properly resolved by the following considerations:

1. There is no doubt that the main purpose of basic rights is to protect the individual's sphere of freedom against encroachment by public power: they are the citizen's bulwark against the state. This emerges from both their development as a matter of intellectual history and their adoption into the constitutions of the various states as a matter of political history: it is true also of the basic rights in the Basic Law, which emphasizes the priority of human dignity against the power of the state by placing the section on basic rights at its head and by providing that the constitutional complaint (*Verfassungsbeschwerde*), the special legal device for vindicating these rights, lies only in respect of acts of the public power.

But far from being a value-free system [references] the Constitution erects an objective system of values in its section on basic rights, and thus expresses and reinforces the validity of the basic rights [references]. This system of values, centring on the freedom of the human being to develop in society, must apply as a constitutional axiom throughout the whole legal system: it must direct and inform legislation, administration, and judicial decision. It naturally influences private law as well; no rule of private law may conflict with it, and all such rules must be construed in accordance with its spirit.

The legal content of basic rights as objective norms informs private law by means of the rules which directly control this area of law. Just as new rules must conform to the value-system of the basic rights, so existing and older rules receive from it a definite constitutional content which thereafter determines their construction. From the point of view of substantive and procedural law a dispute between private citizens on the rights and duties that arise from rules of conduct thus influenced by the basic rights remains a dispute of private law. It is private law which is interpreted and applied even if its interpreters must follow the public law of the constitution.

The influence of the value-system of the basic rights is clearest in those rules of private law which are mandatory (*zwingendes Recht*) and form part of *ordre public* in the wide sense, i.e. those rules which in the public interest apply to private legal relations whether the parties so choose or not. Such provisions, being functionally related and complementary to public law, are especially exposed to the influence of constitutional law. "General clauses", such as § 826 BGB, by which human conduct is measured against extralegal standards such as "proper conduct" (*gute Sitten*), allow the courts to respond to this influence since in deciding what is required in a particular case by such social commands, they must start from the value-system adopted by the society in its constitution at that stage of its cultural and spiritual development. The general clauses have thus been rightly described as "points of entry" for basic rights into private law [references].

The judge is constitutionally bound to ascertain whether the applicable rules of substantive private law have been influenced by basic rights in the manner described; if so, he must construe and apply the rules as so modified. This is what is meant by saying that the civil judge is bound by the basic rights (Article 1 III GG). If he issues a judgment which ignores this constitutional influence on the rules of private law, he contravenes not only objective constitutional law by misconceiving the content of the objective norm underlying the basic law, but also, by his judgment, in his capacity as a public official, contravenes the Constitution itself, which the citizen is constitutionally entitled to have respected by the judiciary. Quite apart from any remedies he may have to correct this error in the courts of private law, the citizen can invoke the Federal Constitutional Court by means of a *Verfassungsbeschwerde*.

The Constitutional Court must determine whether the reach and effect of the basic rights in private law has been correctly ascertained by the regular courts. But this is also the limit of its investigation: it is not for the Constitutional Court to check judgments of civil courts for errors of law in general; the Constitutional Court simply judges of the "radiant effect" of the basic rights on private law and implements the values inherent in the precept of constitutional law. The function of the *Verfassungsbeschwerde* is to test *all* acts, whether of the legislature, the executive or the judiciary, for "compatibility with the Constitution" (§ 90 BVerfGG). The Federal Constitutional Court is certainly not to act as a court of review, much less over-review, for the civil courts, but neither may it abjure consideration of such judgments entirely or leave uncorrected any instance which comes to its notice of the misapplication of the rules of basic rights.

2. The basic right to freedom of expression of opinion (Article 5 GG) seems to pose special problems with regard to the relationship between basic rights and private law. As in the Weimar Constitution (Article 118), this right is constitutionally guaranteed only within the limits of "general laws" (Article 5 II GG). Before inquiring what laws are "general laws" in this sense, one might suppose that the constitution's reference to such laws must be to such laws as judicially construed, with the result that no judicial construction of such a law which limited the basic right could be regarded as a "breach" of the basic right.

This is not, however, the sense of the reference to "general laws". The basic right to freedom of expression, the most immediate aspect of the human personality in society, is one of the most precious rights of man (Declaration of the Rights of Man and Citizen (1789) Article 11). It is absolutely essential to a free and democratic state, for it alone permits that constant spiritual interaction, the conflict of opinion, which is its vital element (BVerfGE 5, 85 (205)). In a certain sense it is the basis of freedom itself, "the matrix, the indispensable condition of nearly every other form of freedom" (Cardozo).

Given this fundamental importance for the free democratic state of freedom of expression of opinion, it would be illogical for a constitution to make its actual scope contingent on mere statute (and thus necessarily on the holdings of courts construing it). What was said earlier about the relationship between basic rights and private law applies here also: general laws which have the effect of limiting a basic right must be read in the light of its significance and always be construed so as to preserve the special value of this right, with, in a free democracy, a presumption in favour of freedom of speech in all areas, and especially in public life. We must not see the relationship between basic right and "general laws" as one in which "general laws" by their terms set limits to the basic right, but rather that relationship must be construed in the light of the special significance of this basic right in a free democratic state, so that the limiting effect of "general laws" on the basic right is itself limited.

In its function as ultimate guardian of the basic rights through the medium of the *Verfassungsbeschwerde*, the Federal Constitutional Court must therefore have the power to supervise the decisions of courts whose application of a general law in this area may unduly restrict the scope of the basic right in the individual case. This Court must be competent to uphold as against *all* organs of public power, including the civil courts, the special value it represents for a free democracy, and thus to reconcile, as required by constitutional law, the conflicting restrictive tendencies of the basic right and the "general laws".

3. The concept of "general" law has always been controversial. Leaving on one side the question whether the concept may not be due to an error in the drafting of Article 118 of the 1919 Constitution [reference], we may note that it was then construed to include all which "do not forbid an opinion as such and do not envisage the expression of opinion as such", but rather "serve to protect a legal interest which deserves protection without regard to any particular opinion", and protect "a community value superior to the activity of freedom of opinion" [reference]. Exponents of the Grundgesetz agree with this [reference: "laws which do not inhibit the purely intellectual effect of a mere expression of opinion"].

If the term "general laws" is so understood, we may state the protection of the basic right as follows:

It is unacceptable to hold that the Constitution protects only the expression of opinion, and not its inherent or intended effect on others, for the whole point of an expression of *opinion* is to have "an effect on the environment of ideas" [reference]. Thus value judgements, which always have an intellectual aim, namely to persuade others, are protected by Article 5 I, 1 GG; indeed it is the stance of the speaker as expressed in the value-judgment by which he hopes to affect others which is principally protected by this basic right. To protect the expression and not to protect its effect would be a nonsense.

In this sense the expression of opinion is free in so far as its effect on the mind is concerned; but that does not mean that one is entitled, just because one is expressing an opinion, to prejudice interests of another which deserve protection against freedom of opinion. There has to be a "balance of interests"; the right to express an opinion must yield if its exercise infringes interests of another which have a superior claim to protection. Whether such an interest exists in a particular case depends on all the circumstances.

4. From this point of view the rules of private law may perfectly well be ranked as "general laws" in the sense of Article 5 II GG. If this has not been done by commentators hitherto [reference], that is simply because basic rights have been considered good only as against the state, so it was natural to consider as "general laws" having limiting effect only those laws which regulated state activity *vis-à-vis* the individual, that is, laws of a public law nature. But if the basic right to free expression of opinion affects relations of private law as well and favours free expression of opinion against the fellow-citizen also, then rules of private law which operate to protect superior legal interests must also be taken into account as possibly limiting the basic right. After all, if provisions of criminal law designed to protect honour or other essential aspects of human personality can set limits to the exercise of the fundamental right to freedom of expression, it is not obvious why similar provisions of private law should not equally do so.

Case 37

BUNDESVERFASSUNGSGERICHT (FIRST DIVISION) 24 FEBRUARY 1971
BVerfGE 30, 173 = NJW 1971, 1645 = JZ 1971, 544

Reasons

The complainant seeks constitutional review of the injunction obtained by the adopted son and sole heir of Gustaf Gründgens, actor and theatre director, against the printing, distribution, or publication of a book by Klaus Mann entitled *Mephisto, a Novel, or How to Get on in the World.*

The author left Germany in 1933 and published the novel in Amsterdam in 1936 (Querido Verlag). Seven years after his death in 1949 it was published in East Germany.

The novel portrays the rise of Hendrik Höfgen, a talented actor who in order to make a career for himself as an artist in collusion with Nazi powers, is false to his true political leanings and rides roughshod over all human and ethical considerations. The psychological, intellectual, and sociological factors which made such a career possible are all laid out.

The model for Hendrik Höfgen was the actor Gustaf Gründgens, one of the Hamburger Kammerspieler in the 1920s, when he was a friend of Klaus Mann and briefly married to his sister Erika. Gründgens and his career are reflected in numerous characteristics of Hendrik Höfgen, including his physical appearance, the plays he acted in, and his appointments as State Councillor and Director-General of the State Theatre of Prussia.

Of the relationship between the fictional Höfgen and the real Gründgens Klaus Mann wrote in *The Turning Point* (New York, 1942):

I visualise my ex-brother-in-law as the traitor *par excellence*, the macabre embodiment of corruption and cynicism. So intense was the fascination of his shameful glory that I decided to portray Mephisto-Gründgens in a satirical novel. I thought it pertinent, indeed, necessary to expose and analyse the abject type of the treacherous intellectual who prostitutes his talent for the sake of some tawdry fame and transitory wealth.

Gustaf was just one among others—in reality as well as in the composition of my narrative. He served me as a focus around which I could make gyrate the pathetic and nauseous crowd of petty climbers and crooks.

In the revised version which appeared in Germany in 1948 (*Der Wendepunkt*), we find at p. 334:

The third book published during my exile, in 1936, *Mephisto*, deals with an unsympathetic character. Why did I write it? The actor I portray has talent, but not much else going for him. He has none of those moral qualities which form what is commonly spoken of as "character". Instead of "character" Hendrik Höfgen has only ambition, vanity, passion for publicity and desire for effect. He is not a man but a posturer.

Was such a figure worth writing a novel about? Yes, indeed. For the posturer represents and symbolises the regime, posturing, false and unrealistic. In a state run by liars and dissemblers the actor has a triumphant role. *Mephisto* is the story of a career in the Third Reich.

In a perceptive review in *Das Neue Tagebuch* in 1937 Herman Kesten rightly suggested that perhaps the author wanted to show a real actor among the bloody amateurs in the horror play. He went on: "The author goes further: he gives us a paradigm of the 'fellow-traveller', one of the millions of petty crooks who themselves commit no grand crime but sup with murderers, not principals but accessories after the event; they do not kill but conceal the corpse, and in order to get more than they deserve lick the blood of the innocent from the boots of the mighty. This host of petty toadies and bootlickers are the prop of the powerful."

This is exactly the type I wanted to draw: I couldn't have stated my intentions better myself. *Mephisto* is not, as some people have maintained, a *roman-à-clef*. The infamously brilliant and cynically ruthless go-getter, who is the central figure of my satire may have certain traits in common with a certain real actor still allegedly with us. Is my character Councillor and Director-General Höfgen a portrait of the friend of my youth, Councillor and Director-General Gründgens? Not entirely. There are many differences between Höfgen and my erstwhile brother-in-law. But even if the character were closer to the original than it is, Gründgens is not the "hero" of my tract for the times, since it is not about an individual at all but about the type. Others could have served as a model just as well. My choice fell upon Gründgens not because he was outstandingly awful (indeed he was rather better than many another idol of the Third Reich) but simply because I happened to know him well. It was precisely our earlier acquaintance which led me to make a novel out of the incredible, fascinating and fantastic story of his rise and fall.

II.

1. In August 1963 the complainant announced the publication of *Mephisto*, and suit was brought by the adoptive son and sole heir of Gustaf Gründgens, who died in October 1963. The claim alleged that anyone at all familiar with German theatre in the 1920s and 1930s would link Höfgen with Gründgens; that in addition to many recognisable facts the novel contained many hurtful fictions which helped to give a false and highly derogatory picture of Gründgens's character. The novel was not a work of art but a *roman-à-clef* written to avenge Gründgens's marriage to Mann's sister Erika, which he believed dishonourable.

The plaintiff sought an injunction forbidding the reproduction, distribution, and publication of *Mephisto* on pain of punishment.

The claim was rejected by the Landgericht Hamburg. Thereupon, in September 1965, the complainant published the novel with a foreword stating "All characters in this novel are types, not portraits. K. M." On 23 November 1965 the plaintiff obtained an interlocutory injunction from the Hanseatic Oberlandesgericht in Hamburg and the following foreword was included:

TO THE READER

Klaus Mann wrote this novel in Amsterdam in 1936, having left Germany voluntarily on grounds of conscience. In it he gives a critical view, animated by his hatred of Hitler's

dictatorship, of contemporary conditions in the German theatre. While there are undeniable resemblances to actual figures of the day, the characters are primarily creatures of
the author's imagination. This is especially true of the principal character, whose conduct
and beliefs are at any rate largely imaginary. That is why the author prefaced the book
with the explanation: "All characters in this work are types, not portraits."

. . .

This Court must determine whether in applying the rules of private law the judicial decisions under attack misconceived the meaning of the basic rights of whose infringement
the complainant complains or infringed the basic rights themselves [references]. Such
constitutional "fall-out effects" depend principally on the scope of the right to artistic
freedom (Article 5 III, 1 GG) and the right to freedom of expression (Article 5 I GG), and
especially on the relationship between these rights and the protection afforded by these
decisions to the human personality of the late Gustaf Gründgens under Article 1 I and 1
II, 1 GG.

III.

Article 5 III, 1 GG declares that along with science, research, and teaching, art is free. By
its terms and intention the guarantee in Article 5 III, 1 is an objective value-laden basic
norm regulating the relationship between art and the state. It also guarantees the individual freedom of the artist.

1. The field of "art" must be determined by the distinctive structural features of the artistic enterprise. The essence of artistic endeavour lies in the free creative process whereby
the artist, in his chosen communicative medium, gives immediate perceptible form to
what he has felt, learnt, or experienced. Artistic activity involves both the conscious and
the unconscious, in a manner not rationally separable. Intuition, imagination, and knowledge of the art all play a part in artistic creation; it is not so much communication as
expression, indeed the most immediate expression of the artist's individuality.

The freedom guaranteed covers the artistic creation as regards both the work produced
and the effect produced by it. The two form an indissociable unity. The exhibition and
dissemination of the work are as important as its creation for art as the specifically artistic enterprise; indeed, the "area of effect", public access to the work of art, is the ground
in which Article 5 III GG is rooted. A glance back at the artistic policy of the Nazi regime
shows that to guarantee merely the individual rights of artists cannot ensure the freedom
of art: the basic right would prove hollow unless it extends from the personal zone of the
artist to the area of impact.

2. It is not here possible to give an exhaustive definition of the scope of the constitutional
guarantee of freedom of art in all its various forms. Nor is it necessary for the case in
hand, since it is common ground in the courts below, between the parties and probably
all experts, that the novel in question ranks as a work of art. We may therefore concentrate on factors relevant to the appraisal of an example of the narrative art which by
dealing with actual events courts the risk of conflicting with the rights and interests of
the persons portrayed.

In putting real events in a work of art the artist "recreates" them for he sunders them
from their actual context and places them in a novel setting dominated by his concern
for striking presentation rather than by their own actuality. Artistic unity may, and sometimes must, prime the truth of the occurrence.

The role and purpose of Article 5 III, 1 GG is above all to give protection against encroachment by the public power on any specifically artistic undertakings, actions, and decisions. One cannot without inhibiting the free development of the creative artistic endeavour prescribe how the artist should react to reality or reproduce his reactions to it. The artist is the sole judge of the "rightness" of his response. To this extent the guarantee of artistic freedom means that one must not seek to affect the manner in which the artist goes about his business, the material he selects, or the way in which he treats it, and certainly not seek to narrow the area in which he may operate or lay down general rules for the creative process. As to narrative works of art the constitutional guarantee means that the artist must be free to choose and treat his topic free from attempts by the state to limit the area of specifically artistic judgement by rules or binding value-judgements. This applies also, indeed especially, when the artist is dealing with actual events: "committed art" is not excluded from the constitutional guarantee.

3. Article 5 III, 1 GG is a comprehensive guarantee of the freedom of artistic activity. Thus where intermediaries are needed in order to establish relations between the artist and the public they too are protected by the constitutional guarantee. As a product of the narrative art needs to be reproduced, distributed, and published in order to have any effect on the public, the publisher's function as intermediary is indispensable, so the constitutional guarantee extends to his activity as well. Thus, as publisher of the novel, the complainant may invoke the basic right contained in Article 5 III, 1 GG (see also BVerfGE 10, 118, (121); 12, 205 (260) on the freedom of the Press).

4. Art having its special nature and rules, its guarantee by Article 5 III, 1 GG is absolute. The clear terms of that provision foredoom any attempt to limit it, whether by narrowing the idea of art in the light of one's value judgements or by extending or invoking the limitations applicable to other constitutional provisions.

The Bundesgerichtshof was quite right to state that Article 5 II GG which limits basic rights under Article 5 I is inapplicable here. The different guarantees in Article 5 GG are systematically separated, and this shows that the limitations in Article 5 II are inapplicable to matters covered by Article 5 III, since Article 5 III is a *lex specialis* in relation to Article 5 I. Nor is it acceptable to sever parts of a narrative work of art, call them expressions of opinion under Article 5 I and then apply to them the limitations laid down in Article 5 II. Nor do the *travaux préparatoires* of Article 5 III support the view that the authors of the Constitution regarded freedom of art as a subspecies of freedom of expression or opinion.

. . .

Nor can one accept that the freedom of art is limited under Article 2 I, 2 GG by the rights of others, by the constitutional order or by the moral law. Such a view would be incompatible with the constant holding of this Court that Article 2 I GG is subsidiary and the individual freedoms special [references] in a manner which bars the extension of the community priority of Article 2 I, 2 GG in the light of the use of Article 2 I GG. Nor are these limitations applicable to the area of effect of works of art.

5. Yet there are limits to this freedom. The freedom incorporated in Article 5 III, 1 GG, like all basic rights, is rooted in the Constitution's conception of man as a responsible person free to develop within society [references]. The absolute nature of the guarantee of artistic freedom means that its limits are to be found only within the Constitution

itself. The freedom of art is not subject to mere statute, it cannot be qualified by the general legal system or be at the mercy of any vague clause about essential interests of state and society which lacks constitutional basis and is uncontained by the rule of law. If the guarantee of artistic freedom gives rise to any conflict, it must be resolved by construction in terms of the order of values enshrined in the Basic Law and in line with the unitary system of values which underlies it. As part of this system of basic rights the freedom of art is co-ordinate with the dignity of man as guaranteed by Article 1 GG, the supreme and controlling value of the whole system of basic rights (BVerfGE 6, 32 [41]; 27, 1 [6]). Given the effect which a work of art may have on the social plane, the guarantee of artistic freedom may come into conflict with the area of human personality, equally protected by the Constitution.

A person's claim to respect and value may be affected by an artist's use of details of character and career of actual people as in addition to being an aesthetic reality, such a work also has existence in the realm of social facts and the social effects are not dissipated by being artistically transmuted. Such social effects while taking place beside the artistic effects must nevertheless be appraised with regard to the scope of the guarantee of Article 5 III, 1 GG, since in the work of art the "real" and "aesthetic" worlds are unified.

6. The courts below were right in this connection to invoke Article 1 I GG in their appraisal of its protective effect on the area of personality of the late actor Gustaf Gründgens. It would be inconsistent with the constitutional mandate of the inviolability of human dignity, which underlies all basic rights, if a person could be belittled and denigrated after his death. Accordingly an individual's death does not put an end to the state's duty under Article 1 I GG to protect him from assaults on his human dignity.

In addition the Bundesgerichtshof and Oberlandesgericht held that Article 2 I GG also had radiant protective effects in private law for Gründgens, though to a degree diminished by his death. However, only a living person is so entitled: the right of personality cannot survive death. An essential precondition of the basic right under Article 2 I GG is the existence of at least a potential or a future person. It is irrelevant that a person may be affected during his lifetime by what the legal situation will be after his death, though this weighed with the Bundesgerichtshof. It is no derogation from the freedom of action and self-determination guaranteed by Article 2 I GG to hold that the protection of the personality expires on death.

7. The resolution of the tension between the protection of the personality and the right to the artistic freedom cannot turn solely on the "social" effects of a work of art but must also take account of specifically aesthetic considerations. The conception of man which underlies Article 1 I GG is as much infused with the guarantee of freedom in Article 5 III, 1 GG as the latter is influenced by the value implicit in Article 1 I GG. The individual's claim to social respect and value is not superior to artistic freedom, but neither can art simply ignore the individual's claim to proper respect.

Only by weighing all the circumstances of the given case can one decide whether the publication of a work which artistically deploys true details about an actual person poses a serious threat of encroachment on the protected area of his personality. One consideration must be whether and how far the artistic treatment of the material and its incorporation into the work as an organic whole have made the "copy" independent of the "original" by rendering objective, symbolical, and figurative what was individualised, personal, and intimate. If such an aesthetic appraisal reveals that the artist has indeed produced, or even intended to produce, a "portrait" of the "original", the outcome will depend on the extent of the artistic alienation and how seriously the "falsification" damages the reputation or memory of the subject.

IV.

This Court must therefore decide whether in balancing the protection afforded by Article 1 I GG to the personality of the late Gustaf Gründgens and his adopted son against the guarantee of artistic freedom under Article 5 III, 1 GG the courts below have upheld the principles just stated. However, in this Court the opinions on that matter are equally divided, so it cannot hold that the decisions under attack infringed the Constitution (§ 15 II, 4 BVerfGG).

. . .

3. This Court has always held that a *Verfassungsbeschwerde* empowers it to review judicial decisions only within narrow limits, and that in particular it cannot review the facts as found and evaluated, the construction of mere law or its application in the individual case, which are matters for the regular courts [references]. These principles apply equally when review is sought of the balancing of the protection afforded to the parties to a civil suit by Article 1 I of Article 5 III, 1 GG.

. . .

This Court is not, like a court of appeal, empowered to substitute its own opinion of the case for that of the proper judge. In cases like these it can only hold that the basic right of the losing party has been infringed if the judge has either failed to recognise that it is a case of balancing conflicting basic rights or has based his judgment on a fundamentally false view of the importance, and especially the scope, of either of those rights.

When the judgements under attack are so tested, it emerges that the Oberlandesgericht and the Bundesgerichtshof recognised that a balancing act was required in order to resolve the tension between the rights emanating from Article 1 I GG and Article 5 III, 1 GG, and that the judgments as a whole do not seem to be based on a fundamentally erroneous view of the importance or scope of the two basic rights.

Case 38

BUNDESVERFASSUNGSGERICHT (FIRST DIVISION) 14 FEBRUARY 1973*
BVERFGE 34, 269 = NJW 1973, 1221 = JZ 1973, 662

The plaintiff is Princess Soraya, the ex-wife of the Shah of Iran. At the time in question, after her divorce from the Shah, the plaintiff resided in Germany. The defendants are the publisher and chief-editor of an illustrated weekly paper, which is distributed throughout Germany and known to specialise in sensational society stories.

In April 1961, defendants' paper carried a front-page story purporting to be the transcript of an interview with the plaintiff. The interview, which appeared to reveal much of plaintiff's private and very private life, was wholly fictitious, i.e., it was totally and freely invented by its author, a freelance journalist. Defendants published the story without

---

* This text is reproduced from R Schlesinger, H Baade, P Herzog, and E Wise, *Comparative Law* (6th edn., 1998) pp. 697–709.

investigating whether the interview had actually taken place. In July, 1961, defendants' paper carried another story dealing with Princess Soraya, and as a part of that new story the defendants published a brief statement by the Princess to the effect that the alleged April interview had not taken place.

In the present action, the plaintiff seeks damages for "violation of her personality rights." The Landgericht as court of first instance awarded her DM 15,000. The Oberlandesgericht and the Bundesgerichtshof affirmed, and the defendants brought the case before the Federal Constitutional Court by way of a constitutional complaint.

In order to understand the thrust of defendants' constitutional arguments, we must take a brief look at the development and present status of the rules of substantive law which the plaintiff successfully invoked in the courts below.

Apart from a section protecting a person's right to his name, the German Civil Code contains no specific provisions concerning the subjects which we would label as defamation or invasion of privacy. In Germany, as in France, defamation traditionally has been thought of as a crime rather than a tort. Under this traditional view, defamation actions normally have to be brought in the criminal courts, even though such an action ordinarily has to be prosecuted by the victim rather than the public prosecutor. The public prosecutor brings such an action only if this is required in the public interest. German law generally vests the prosecutor with little or no discretion, and requires prosecution whenever there is reasonable cause to believe that the defendant has committed a crime. This general rule, however, is subject to exceptions in the case of certain relatively minor offences, such as defamation. If the defendant is convicted in such a criminal proceeding, he will be fined, or (in a very serious case) subjected to a jail sentence; but the victim cannot recover substantial damages in that proceeding.

Until after World War II, attempts to bring civil actions for defamation or invasion of privacy found little favour with the German courts. The first paragraph of § 823 of the Civil Code authorises tort recovery only if the plaintiff can show injury to his "life, body, health, freedom, property, or some other (similar) right." In order to bring cases of defamation or invasion of privacy within the ambit of this code provision, plaintiffs often argued that a person's interest in his reputation and privacy should be regarded as his "personality right" and should be protected as one of the "other rights" mentioned in § 823. But throughout the periods of the Empire, the Weimar Republic and the Third Reich, the courts essentially rejected that argument.

A different judicial approach to the problem emerged after World War II, and after the adoption of the new West German Constitution, which contains the following provisions: [citation of Articles 1 and 2 follows]

During the 1950s the BGH, explicitly invoking these constitutional provisions, gave up the former narrow interpretation of § 823 of the Civil Code and repeatedly held that a plaintiff's "personality right" is one of the "other rights" which are protected by § 823 against intentional or negligent infringement. This was an important development. It meant that—in contrast to prior law—the German courts now were treating injuries to a person's reputation or privacy as actionable torts. (For a full account, see Harry D Krause, "The Right to Privacy in Germany–Pointers for American Legislation?" 1965 *Duke L.J.* 481, and most recently Karl-Nikolaus Peifer, "Persönlichkeitsschaden und Geldersatz", 96 *Zeitschrift für vergleichende Rechtswissenschaft* 74 (1997), also discussing parallel developments in Italy at 76–82.)

Even after this judicial breakthrough, however, a difficult issue remained to be resolved regarding the kind of damages for which recovery could be allowed under German law in cases of injury to the plaintiff's "personality right." The difficulty was caused by one of the Civil Code's provisions dealing with damages. [There follows the citation of some relevant provisions of the Code, including the one of § 253 given above.]

There are a few limited and narrowly defined cases in which an express provision of written law (within the meaning of § 253) permits the victim of a tort to recover money damages for an injury to non-pecuniary interests; the prime example is the case of personal injury, with respect to which § 847 of the German Civil Code explicitly authorises the recovery of money damages for pain and suffering. The draftsmen of the Civil Code clearly regarded this provision of § 847 as an exception to the general rule laid down in § 253: that no money damages can be recovered for an injury to non-pecuniary interests. (See Palandt, *Burgerliches Gesetzbuch*, § 847, Anno. la (53rd edn., 1994). Some additional exceptions are provided for in auxiliary statutes. See *ibid.*)

Neither the Civil Code nor any auxiliary statute provides for the recovery of non-pecuniary damages by a person whose "right of personality" has been injured. Thus when the tort of injury to a person's "personality right" was first developed by the German courts, it was initially thought that a plaintiff, while perhaps entitled to the publication of a retraction or to similar non-monetary relief under § 249, could not recover money damages without proof of what we would call "special damage," i.e., loss of his job, loss of customers, or the like. The plain language of § 253 indeed appears to preclude the plaintiff in such a case from recovering "general" damages for his soiled reputation and injured feelings.

In 1958, however, the German courts broke away from this restriction seemingly imposed by § 253. The occasion was the so-called *Herrenreiter* case (the case of the gentleman horse-back rider). That case involved a picture of the plaintiff, a well-known equestrian, elegantly positioned on horse-back while jumping over a hurdle. Without plaintiff's authorisation, the picture was publicly and widely disseminated by the defendant as part of an advertisement promoting a sexual stimulant. The plaintiff's "personality right" was seriously injured by this advertisement, not only because it conveyed the impression that the plaintiff had sought to commercialise his great reputation as a sportsman, but also because it implied that he needed and used sexual stimulants.

The lower courts awarded the plaintiff a substantial sum of money as damages for the injury to his reputation and feelings. The BGH affirmed, essentially on the ground that § 847 of the Civil Code should be extended by analogy to cover the case at hand. This analogy argument was questionable, because the word "only" in § 253 explicitly prohibits an analogical extension of provisions, such as § 847, which engraft exceptions upon the general rule of § 253. Recognising this, the BGH subsequently abandoned the analogy argument; but the result reached in the Herrenreiter case was reaffirmed in later cases, on the ground that in many situations the tort of injury to a person's "personality right"— a tort developed in response to value judgments expressed in the Constitution—would be without an adequate remedy if the victim of such a tort could not recover money damages for the violation of his non-monetary interests.

The BGH limited the breadth of these rulings by further holding that such a cause of action for money damages should be recognised only if (a) the injury to the plaintiff's "personality right" is substantial, and (b) the defendant's act is sufficiently culpable to justify the rendition of a money judgment in a sizeable amount. According to the BGH, both conditions, (a) and (b), are clearly satisfied in a case in which a defendant, by way of large-scale promotion of his own commercial interests, has wantonly violated the plaintiff's "personality right." The repetition of such intolerable conduct, the BGH held, should be prevented by announcing a rule of tort law which makes it clear to would-be violators that such conduct is costly for them.

In the decisions dealing with this question, the BGH also pointed to the drastic technological and social changes that have taken place since the enactment of the Civil Code. The development of mass media, hardly predictable in 1900, makes the protection of an individual's personality right more important and more difficult in our day. Therefore, the BGH held, a court which takes the value system of the Constitution seriously can no longer feel bound by § 253 of the Civil Code insofar as that provision denies recovery for non-pecuniary damages even in cases of grave injuries to an individual's personality right.

The lower courts, after some initial reluctance on the part of some of them, generally followed these holdings of the BGH, which were approved, also, by the majority of the commentators. In the instant case, both the lower courts and the BGH itself based their decision on those previous holdings.

The defendants' constitutional complaint was based mainly on the following provisions of the German Federal Constitution:

Article 5. . . . Freedom of the press and freedom of reporting by broadcast and film are guaranteed. . . .

These rights are limited by the provisions of general (written) laws, by statutory measures for the protection of juveniles, and by the right of personal honour. . . .

Article 20. . . . All of the State's power originates with the People. Such power can be exercised by the People through elections and ballots, and by special organs of the legislative, executive and judicial branches of the government.

The legislature is bound by the constitutional order. The executive and the judiciary are bound by statute and law.

In particular, the defendants argued that the substantive rule pursuant to which the lower courts ordered them to pay money damages to the plaintiff had been created by the courts in violation of the principle of separation of powers laid down in Article 20 of the Constitution. The BGH, they argued, had acted contra legem when it developed the right to money damages for violation of an individual's "personality right." This, it was contended, was a usurpation by the courts of legislative power.

The defendants did not question the constitutionality of the view that the personality right of a person is one of the "other rights" mentioned in the first paragraph of § 823 of the Civil Code. Their attack was directed only against the decisional rule which—contrary to the language of § 253 of the Civil Code—permits a plaintiff whose personality right has been gravely injured to recover a money judgment for non-monetary damages.

The defendants did not deny that the recognition of plaintiff's personality right as one of the "other rights" protected by § 823 of the Civil Code was in part dictated by Articles 1 and 2 of the Constitution. But they argued that the rights derived from Articles 1 and 2, like other human rights protected by the Constitution, are essentially defensive in nature. For this reason, the defendants contended, it is not possible to treat those constitutional provisions as the direct foundation of a cause of action for money damages.

In addition, the defendants argued, the money judgment rendered by the courts below violated the constitutional principle of freedom of the press. In the defendants' view, the money damage rule developed by the courts and applied in this case did not constitute the kind of "general (written) law" which pursuant to Article 5 of the Constitution may be used by the law-giver to limit the freedom of the press.)

In holding that the constitutional complaint was unfounded and that the "ordinary" judges were entitled to (re-interpret) § 253 the way they did in the *Professor of Canon law* decision the Constitutional court included in its judgment the following crucial paragraph.

"occasionally, the law can be found outside the positive legal rules erected by the state; this is law which emanates from the entire constitutional order and which has as its purpose the 'correction' of written law. It is for the judge to 'discover' this law and through his opinions give it concrete effect. The Constitution does not restrict judges to apply statutes in their literary sense when deciding cases put before them. Such an approach assumes a basic completeness of statutory rules which is not attainable in practice . . . The insight of the judge may bring to light certain values of society . . . which are implicitly accepted by the constitutional order but which have received an insufficient expression in statutory texts. The judge's decision can help realise such ideas and give effect to such values."

Notes to Cases 36–38

1. The constitutionalisation of private law is an important and modern development of the law which, on the whole, though studied by national lawyers (especially in Germany and the USA) has, until recently, been receiving, little attention from comparatists. In England, with one notable exception—Andrew Clapham, *Human Rights in the Private Sphere* (1993)—the *Drittwirkung* debate was totally ignored until the Human Rights Act 1998, and some articles written on it, made lawyers wake up to the prospect of *Drittwirkung* coming to our shores. How soon this will happen, is difficult to predict; but those who wish to accept it or reject it, would be arguing their respective positions better if they took into account the views expressed in Germany. One reason for the neglect of this topic and, indeed, the general unwillingness to accept that constitutional law ideas nowadays inform much of the debate in private law, may be due to the fact that comparatists have, traditionally, been private lawyers. (Even their groupings of legal systems into families, has been attempted with private law primarily in mind with the result that existing classifications are not always convincing.) Clearly, in a casebook on tort, one cannot give this topic the attention it deserves. But continuing the innovative approach adopted in the 1994 edition of this book, we provide in the following paragraphs a summary of the German position on this topic. The reader should thus read these three decisions in conjunction with the brief comments contained in paragraph six of Chapter 1 and treat them as providing the constitutional background to the privacy cases discussed in the next section. For in all of these we see a clash of the rights of one individual against another and yet the outcome is largely determined by the Constitution.

2. Though the significance of the *Drittwirkung* doctrine has been felt strongly in the area of speech and privacy rights, the importance of the above cases, especially *Lüth* (case no. 36), goes beyond the facts of the dispute which that Court had to resolve. Indeed, the ramifications of the ruling are gradually engulfing much of the traditional area of private law. Arguably, the most important part of *Lüth* is its "doctrine of interaction" (*Wechselwirkungslehre*) which shows that the basic human rights contained in Articles 1–19 of the Constitution of Bonn of 1949 do not directly affect relations between private citizens. Rather, the impact is indirect and is manifested largely through the mandatory rules (*ius cogens*) of private law and, especially, the various general clauses of private law (e.g. §§ 138, 242, 823 I and 826 BGB) which must be interpreted in conformity with the fundamental values of the Constitution. The practical result is that the judge balances the various competing interests before reaching his decision, freedom of expression (Article 5 of the Constitution) being a cardinal but not absolute value (as this is made clear by para. II of that same article, as well as by Article 20). The *Lüth* doctrine was finally and conclusively incorporated into the civil law by the *Höllenfeuer* decision of 21 June 1966 (BGHZ 45, 296 = NJW 1966, 1617 = JZ 1967, 174). The case, which was encountered when discussing the right of an established and operating business in chapter two, above, shows how this (private law) right had to cede precedence to free speech when the latter is exercised in the public interest. (As always, the nuanced judgment repays careful reading.) The result of the above is that in a public law action between an individual and

the state, a constitutional right will directly override an otherwise applicable rule of public law. The constitutional right will also override a statutory provision of *private* law if it contravenes a constitutional right. This has occurred for instance in the fifties with regard to (pre-constitutional) family law provisions which could not be reconciled with Art 3 GG (equal treatment). However, in private law disputes between individuals where the applicable provisions are not unconstitutional as such constitutional rights [are] said to "influence" rules of civil law rather than actually to override them. It is the duty of the court to adopt an interpretation of private law provisions which is in conformity with the constitutional rights. A certain intellectual content "flows" or "radiates" from the constitutional law into the civil law and affects the interpretation of existing civil law rules. In such cases the rules of private law are to be interpreted and applied in [the] light of the applicable constitutional norm, but it is nonetheless the civil law rules that are ultimately to be applied. A doctrine such as the above, may be condensed (with dangers) within a few lines; but its birth still needs an explanation. More precisely, does it find any basis in the Constitution?

3. There is little doubt that the traditional understanding of human rights is that they apply vertically i.e. bind the Sate in its relations with its citizens but do not have any horizontal effect, affecting the relations of private individuals. Most German scholars would accept this and would also agree that the text of the Basic Law (Constitution) is ambiguous on the question whether its Human Rights articles (mainly Articles 1–19) are also meant to regulate the relations between private individuals. Apart from invoking the wider philosophical argument that it was not for the state to interfere with the rules of private law which enshrine the belief in "private autonomy", opponents of any horizontal extension also argued that where constitutional rules were meant to cover private relationships as well, the constitutional draftsman had said so explicitly. But this argument cuts both ways; and the fact that a horizontal extension was not meant to be prohibited by the Constitution is reinforced by the positive and declarative form given to many of its key articles. (For instance Article 2 (1): "Everyone has the right to the free development of his personality . . ." Likewise with Article 1 (1).) This point is backed by the discussions of the *Herrenchiemsee* drafting committee, which are all the more significant given that the same debate (about horizontally) had plagued the previous Constitution of Weimar. (*Bericht über den Verfassungskonvent auf Herrenchiemsee vom 10. bis 23 August 1948, 2 Akten und Protokolle,* 513, 580. On the other hand Hermann von Mangoldt's authoritative *Das Bonner Grundgesetz,* vol. I (1953), 34–42, argues that the Constitutional Convention, which from 1 September 1948 continued in Bonn the work of the *Herrenchiemsee* Committee of experts, did not believe that the Basic Law was meant to apply to relations between individuals.) On the other hand, the underlying issues, as we are now coming to realise in our country, are not susceptible to unequivocal answers. In retrospect, it was thus not surprising that a storm of protest broke out when the Federal Labour Court, under the influence of its first President Nipperdey, jumped the gun and declared that freedom of expression had an *unmittelbare Drittwirkung*—i.e. a direct limiting effect—on the acts of private parties. (BArbGE 1, 185, (1954)) In actual fact, Nipperdey the judge was only following Nipperdey the scholar who, four years earlier on, had in a seminal and still cited article argued in favour of direct horizontality. ("Gleicher Lohn der Frau für gleiche Leistung. Ein Beitrag zur Auslegung der Grundrechte", *Recht der Arbeit* 1950, 121 ff. The literature, which followed the decision of the Federal Labour Court, was enormous. Sharply critical was Ehmke in *Wirtschaft und Verfassung*, 78 ff. (1961). But Nipperdey struck back in "Grundrechte und Privatrecht", *Festschrift Molitor*, 17–33 (1962). In its subsequent decisions, however, the Federal Labour Court has modified its language and brought it closer to that used by the Constitutional Court in *Lüth*. See: BArbGE 47, 363 (1984).) So, what was the reasoning that brought such a sea change?

In its barest outlines Nipperdey's argument posits that since the eighteenth and nineteenth centuries new threats have arisen to human rights. Whereas before the industrialisation of our society the function of human rights was to protect the freedoms of the individual from incursions by the state, by the time the twentieth century had arrived, new forces had established themselves within society. These were often as powerful as the state, itself; and certainly equally able to determine (adversely) people's lives. This was certainly true of the modern Press and large employers who, through their action, could stifle speech rights. Thus, for Nipperdey, "The basic right to free expression . . . would be rendered largely ineffective . . . if . . . *individuals and others with economic and social power . . . were in a position by virtue of that power to restrict it at will.*" (BArbGE 1, 185, 192.) The fact thus was that in the twentieth century, in parallel with industrialisation, the democratisation of society and the rise of popular sovereignty had changed the role and scope of constitutions. For, where formerly they had been "granted" *(oktroyiert)* by the monarch (or, in the traditionally decentralised Germany, the college of reigning princes), constitutions were now seen as the freely agreed fundamental norm which regulated all life in society. Constitutional provisions, therefore, had to be given the widest possible application. In principle, therefore, no area of life could be exempt from their scope.

Nipperdey's second argument pointed out that in some cases the Constitution itself expressly provides for the horizontal application of human rights. Article 9 (3) GG is a case in point: "Agreements restricting or intended to hamper [the right. to form associations in order to safeguard and improve working and economic conditions] shall be null and void; measures to this end shall be illegal." The open-ended wording of Article 3 (3) GG—"*no one* shall be prejudiced . . ."—could be taken to point to the same conclusion: what is illegal need not expressly be declared void. Moreover, in the light of what immediately preceded the Constitution of Bonn was it possible for discrimination based on race, political opinion, faith, or sex, to be accepted under any circumstances? In any event, as the state nowadays employs decreasing numbers of civil servants, and the majority of the population works in the private sector, to exempt the terms of private employment from the application of the relevant article would reduce its significance to an unacceptable level. If this sounded convincing in 1950 it is all the more so now, as the new century has dawned.

The latter (teleological) argument is reinforced rather than contradicted by the provisions of Article l GG which is, by its position at the beginning of the Constitution no less than because of its content, marked out as the bedrock of the whole Constitution: "(I) Human dignity is inviolable. To respect and *protect* it is the duty of all state authority. (2) *The German people* therefore uphold human rights as *inviolable and inalienable* and as the *basis of every community*, of peace and justice in the world." These sonorous proclamations conclude with the more pragmatic order contained in § (3) of this article which states that 'The following basic rights shall *bind the legislature, the executive, and the judiciary* as directly enforceable law. (Italics supplied.)

Since the judiciary is, according to Article 1 (3) GG, bound by Article 3 (3) GG it cannot, Nipperdey argued, uphold contracts or unilateral acts discriminating on grounds outlawed by the Constitution without itself violating its provisions. The fact that the German *people*, not merely the German *State*, uphold human rights as the basis of their community must also mean that each and every individual must respect the human rights of others. Similarly, given that the state has to protect human dignity, from which all, specific human rights flow, no public authority could endorse any practice that violated human dignity. The same is true of agreements between private parties; as human rights are inalienable, they must not be abrogated by contract.

These conclusions are not, however, limited to Article 3 (3) GG and the principle of equal pay for equal work. Every single human right protected by the Constitution has to be scrutinised with a view to determining whether it is directed exclusively against the state. This would certainly be the case where incursions by private parties are inconceivable. For instance, individuals can neither grant nor withdraw citizenship, retention of which is protected under Article 16 (1) GG. Where, on the other hand, this is not the case but, on the contrary, freedom needs protection against wider societal forces, the basic rights have to inform private law relationships as well.

4. *Lüth* accepts that even in such cases the dispute "remains substantially and procedurally a dispute of civil law" (BVerfGE 7, 198, 205–6). What, then, is the precise role of the Constitutional Court? The answer is not, apparently, entirely clear. According to the *Mephisto* case (BVerfGE 30, 173, 197) the "evaluative" process of the competing interests was to be left to the civil law judges, with the Constitutional Court retaining the right to intervene only if the civil law decision was based on a fundamental misconception of the basic rights and their radiating effect. In some subsequent decisions, however, the Constitutional Court has permitted itself greater latitude for

review, especially whenever there was a "serious" invasion of a basic right. See the *Deutschland-Magazin* case (BVerfGE 42, 143) where the civil court's decision was not disturbed and the *Echternach* decision (BVerfGE 42, 163) where the State Court decision was reversed. As the court put it (*ibid.* 168), "The more a civil court's decision infringes the predicates of free existence and action that are protected by a basic right, the more searching must be the Constitutional Court's investigation to determine whether the infringement is constitutionally justified." (Translation by P Quint, *op. cit.*, 322.) Such a willingness to "intervene" has been manifested in "speech cases" with the result that this interest has received growing protection during the last thirty years or so. These and subsequent important decisions (notably in the *Böll* case (BVerfGE 54, 208) and the *Wallraff* case (BVerfGE 66, 131),) *Strauss Placard* case (BVerfGE 82, 43 (1990)) and *Soldiers are Murderers* case (BVerfGE 93, 266 (1995)), are discussed in Markesinis, "Privacy, Freedom of Speech and the Horizontality of the Human Rights Bill" *1998 Wilberforce Lecture*, 115 (1999) *LQR* pp. 47–88.

5. *Lüth*, still regarded as the leading case, can be compared with *NAACP* v. *Claiborne Hardware Co.*, 458 US 886 (1982). Note, however, that the careful evaluative process advocated by *Lüth* (and also found in the *Lebach* case) is absent from *Claiborne*. This preference for *ad hoc* balancing techniques has not, on the whole, found much favour with American courts in first amendment disputes. Thus, in *Konigsberg* v. *State Bar*, 366 US 36, 61, (1961), Mr Justice Black said: "I believe that the First Amendment's unequivocal command that there shall be no abridgement of the rights of free speech and assembly shows that the men who drafted our Bill of Rights did all the 'balancing' that was to be done in this field . . .". What are the merits and demerits of these differing approaches? What other differences with US law do these German decisions reveal? Consider, for example, the following remarks made by Professor Quint in his thoughtful comparative study, *op. cit.* 247, 273–5 (notes omitted):

[A comparative] examination . . . indicates that the force of the American Constitution in disputes between individuals is in some instances weaker and in some instances stronger than the effect of the German Basic Law under the doctrine of the *Lüth* case. In those actions between individuals in which state action is found to exist, the United States Constitution supersedes the "private law". In contrast, in German cases involving disputes between individuals, the Basic Law only "influences" the rules of private law. The values of private law remain present in the balance and must be accommodated. Moreover . . . the fact that the action remains a private law action may have a significant limiting effect on the scope of the Constitutional Court's review. In these respects, therefore, the impact of the Basic Law on disputes between individuals appears weaker than the impact of the American Constitution in those disputes in which state action would be found under American doctrine.

In contrast, in those private disputes in which state action does not exist under American doctrine, the impact of the German Basic Law becomes stronger than that of the United States Constitution. Where there is no state action in American law, the United States Constitution ordinarily has no effect at all (or, if there is any indirect constitutionalisation, it takes place through different concepts or doctrines). Under American doctrine, therefore, if there is state action, constitutional rights theoretically apply with full vigour; if there is no state action, there are no constitutional rights. Under the German Basic Law, however, the fact that a certain dispute of private law lies beyond where the state action would be drawn under the United States Constitution has no particular meaning. The rules of private law are still "influenced" by the basic rights of the Constitution. Thus the German Constitution continues to have an impact in cases in which no state action would be found under American law. This difference between German and American doctrine is perhaps most notable in the area of contractual relations—particularly private employment contracts—in which the United States Constitution generally has no impact (or, as stated, has so in an indirect, even invisible manner). In these cases the German Basic Law can have some force. A decision of the Federal Labour Court of 1984 offers an excellent illustration. (BArbGE 47, 363 (1984)) In that case a printer working in a private concern refused to take part in the printing of a book which, in his view, glorified war. Though his action was motivated by deeply held beliefs he was dismissed by his employers and sued for reinstatement. The Labour court took the view that the case raised serious issues relating to Article 2 of the Constitution, which guarantees freedom of conscience. This constitutional provision, for the reasons already noted in the area of free speech, exerts an influence on private law which meant that the "reasonableness" of the employer's action had to be tested against the wider constitutional background. The court thus resorted to the by now familiar test of balancing. It took the view that the employee's views were deeply held and the book in question did, indeed, glorify war. More importantly, the Court held that the employer had over-reacted by dismissing the employee instead of assigning another employee to perform the said task. The Court thus came down in favour of the (dismissed) employee. Though the decision is interesting in that it used the *Lüth* reasoning (and not the direct effect reasoning of Nipperdey), in its results it is consistent with a long line of cases, which have used the Constitution to affect private law arrangements. Thus, in BArbGE 1, 185 (1954) condemned the firing of a (private) employee because his employer disagreed with the former's political statements. BArbGE 4, 274 (1957) invalidated a contractual provision which allowed the employer to dismiss his employee if and when the latter married. Thus, the "influence" of the German Constitution on the norms of private law may in some circumstances, lead to something that looks very much like the judicial creation of a constitutional tort action by one private person against *another private person* to redress a constitutional violation. With respect to the right of free speech, this result was first suggested by the *Blinkfüer* case, a decision that resembles *Lüth* in certain important respects [BVerfGE 25, 256].

However, note that American law may, at times, be achieving *Drittwirkung* results via different concepts. On this suggestion, see Markesinis, "Our Debt to Europe: Past, Present and Future" in *The Coming Together of the Common Law and the Civil Law, The Clifford Chance Millennium Lectures*, (2000) pp. 37–66 where cases such as BArbGE 1, 185 are compared to factual American equivalents such as *Novosel* v. *Nationwide Insurance Company*, 721 F. 2d 894 (1983).

6. The *Lüth* and *Mephisto* cases give some indication of how this balancing act is carried out. The first case deals with speech which may affect—indeed aims at affecting—another person's economic interests; the second involves reputation. There is a third category of cases which deals with internal security, treason, and sedition in relation to free speech. This is exemplified by the *Spiegel* seizure case of 5 August 1966 (BVerfGE 20, 162). Cases like this, as well as decisions banning extreme political parties, e.g. the neo-Nazi party (BVerfGE 2, 1) or the Communist party (BVerfGE 5, 85) invite comparison with Anglo-American law. Many could be taken to suggest that the suppression of extreme political activity, even in the absence of "imminent lawless action" (*cf. Brandenburg* v. *Ohio*, 395 U.S. 444, 447 (1969)), may be the result of the German experience in the 1930s. Clearly, at first sight German law appears to be less tolerant than American law; but, it must be stressed again, the decisions of the Federal Constitutional Court must always be seen against the background of the German experience between the two Wars *and* Article 21 II of the Constitution of 1949, which enables the banning of political parties which aim at abolishing the existing liberal-democratic order. Lack of space makes the further examination of this topic impossible.

7. *Lüth* (case 36), as stated, was a case dealing with an invitation to boycott films made by a former Nazi sympathiser. Lüth won, and in the balancing process the "purity" of his motives (the wish to protect the cultural interests of the community rather than to make money for himself) seemed to have weighed heavily in his favour. In other instances, however, where excessive economic pressure was applied and monetary gain was at stake, the courts, though following the *Lüth* dictate that the relevant interests should be balanced, in the end showed less favour for free speech. The *Blinkfüer* case of 26 February 1969 (BVerfGE 25, 256) is a case in point where the Axel Springer Publishing House tried to stop news dealers from handling a left-wing periodical by threatening to stop supplying them their papers if they continued to handle the periodical in question. The action for damages by the owners of the periodical—desisted on grounds that it impinged on Springer's freedom of expression—failed in the civil courts but succeeded in the Constitutional Court for the reasons indicated above. Other cases, dealing with boycotts and illustrating the courts' balancing process, include BGH NJW 1985, 1620 = JZ 1985, 587; BGH NJW 1984, 1956.

8. The *Mephisto* case (case 37) is different, dealing with protection of reputation and the clash this can provoke with free speech. Like other cases, e.g. the *Schmid–Spiegel* decision of 25 January 1961 (BVerfGE 12, 113), it contrasts sharply with cases like *New York Times Co.* v.

Sullivan, 376 US 254 (1964). Before the reader draws any adverse comparative conclusions, however, he should bear in mind the more detailed, complicated, and inter-related provisions of the German Constitution.

Freedom of expression is limited by Article 5 II of the Constitution by the "provisions of the general laws"—in practice §§ 185–7 of the Criminal Code which deal with the crimes of insult and defamation. But it may also be limited by other constitutional provisions e.g. Article 1 (protecting the inviolable dignity of human beings) and Article 2 (protecting the free development of personality). *Lüth* required the courts to balance freedom of expression and personal reputation given the facts of each case. In *Mephisto* the Constitutional Court is balancing two different *constitutional freedoms* and by a narrow majority came down in favour of human dignity enshrined in Article 1 of the Constitution—a protection that endures even after death. (In another important case involving the well-known writer Heinrich Böll (BVerfGE 54, 208) the action was based on both Articles 1 and 2 of the Constitution. See, also, JZ 1990, 37—a case concerning the painter *Emil Nolde*. For a further discussion of *Mephisto* in English see, Markesinis, "Privacy, Freedom of Speech and the Horizontality of the Human Rights Bill" *1998 Wilberforce Lecture*, 115 (1999) *LQR*, pp. 47–88.)

9. These cases and the Privacy decisions reproduced in the next section, require frequent references to the human rights provisions of the Constitution, so the reader must read the cases that follow in conjunction with the relevant articles of the Constitution which were reproduced in chapter one, above. (The translations are by the Press and Information Office of the Federal Government in Bonn and were kindly supplied by the Cultural Office of the German Embassy in London.) Teachers should also set them in their proper historical context in which the ghosts of the Nazi period, combined with the cold-war climate of the 1950s and 1960s, provided an environment which Anglo-American scholars may often find difficult to appreciate. Thus the *Lüth* controversy was provoked by Veit Harlan's record as a film director during the Nazi era. One of his films in particular, apparently produced under the general overview of Josef Goebbels (the propaganda minister of the Third Reich), was so violently anti-Jewish that its circulation was, in the post-war era, treated as a criminal offence. Such a record led another post-war criminal court to find Harlan guilty of crimes against humanity, though in the end he was acquitted on the ground that he was acting under "duress". He was also classified as "exonerated" in the de-Nazification proceedings and, after a brief interlude, attempted to re-enter the cinema world with the (politically innocuous) film that provoked the present litigation. The facts of the *Mephisto* novel, written by Klaus Mann, son of the well-known author Thomas Mann, are given in the judgment. But the character in the novel was largely modelled on Gustaf Gründgens (an actor and, ultimately, director of the Prussian State Theatre) who was a protégé of Hermann Göring. Gründgens, along with many others (including some eminent academics) who collaborated, benefited, or willingly tolerated the Nazi regime survived, often completely unaffected, into the post-war era. Gründgens, in fact, died naturally in 1963 whereas Klaus Mann committed suicide in 1949. Interesting historical background can be found in: K Mann, *Der Wendepunkt: Ein Lebensbericht* (1981).

10. For further reading see: Dürig in Maunz/Dürig *Grundgesetz Kommentar*, Article 1, Abs 3, nos. 129–30. Zöllner, "Regelungsspielräume im Schuldvertragsrecht", *AcP* 196 (1996), 1; Oeter, "'Drittwirkung' der Grundrechte und die Autonomie des Privatrechts", *AöR* 119 (1994), 529. Roellecke, "Das Mietrecht des BVerfG", *NJW* 1992, 1649; Medicus, "Der Grundsatz der Verhältnismäßigkeit im Privatrecht", *AcP* 192 (1992), 35. Quint, *"Free Speech and Private Law in German Constitutional Theory"* 48 *Maryland L. Rev.* 247, 263 (1989) A compressed but interesting comparative account of American, English, and German law can be found in Barendt's *Freedom of Speech* (1985) (paperback with an updating postscript 1987); Humphries, *Media and Media Policy in West Germany. The Press and Broadcasting since 1945* (1990); Kommers, *The Constitutional Jurisprudence of the Federal Republic of Germany* 2nd ed. (1997). For English views on *Drittwirkung* see, *inter alia*, Sir William Wade, "Horizons of Horizontality", (2000) 116 *LQR*, 217 ff. (with references to his earlier works on the subject) and Murray Hunt "'The Horizontal Effect' of the Human Rights Act" [1998] *PL* 423. Both favour (some form) of the German doctrine being adopted by our law. Contra, Lord Justice Buxton, "The Human Rights Act and Private Law" (2000) 116 *LQR* 48, who seems to regard it with

suspicion given that human rights (originally at any rate) were meant to be protected against encroachments by the superior power of the State. For yet another approach see, Lord Lester of Herne Hill and David Pannick in (2000) 116 *LQR*, and Sir William Wade's repost in Appendix 2, pp. 982–4, of his *Administrative Law*, 8th edn. By H. W. R. Wade and C. F. Forsyth, (2000).

12. PERSONALITY AND PRIVACY RIGHTS

Case 39

BUNDESGERICHTSHOF (FIRST CIVIL SENATE) 25 MAY 1954
BGHZ 13, 334 = NJW 1954, 1404 = JZ 1954, 698
(with an approving note by Helmut Coing)

The D Company published on 29 June 1952 in its weekly journal . . . an article by KB with the title "Dr HS & Co." and the sub-title "Political considerations concerning the foundation of a new bank". The article contained a comment concerning the new Bank for Foreign Trade founded by Dr S in H, and expressed itself in that connection in opposition to Dr S's political activity during the national-socialist regime and the years after the war.

On the instructions of Dr S the plaintiff, an attorney, sent to the defendant company a letter of 4 July 1952, saying, *inter alia*:

I represent the interests of Dr S. In terms of § 11 of the Press Act I hereby require the following correction of the above-mentioned article in your issue of Sunday the 6th instant:

1. It is incorrect that . . .

2. . . .

This claim for correction is made under the Press Act, in combination with the BGB, and also the law of copyright.

I ask you to inform me by telephone or in writing on or before midday Saturday 5 July 1952, of your confirmation of the unrestricted execution of the required correction, failing which legal proceedings will be taken.

The defendant company gave the plaintiff no answer. But in the issue of 6 July it published, along with sundry expressions of opinion by readers on KB's article, the following under the heading "Letters from Readers".

Dr HS & Co.

To the . . . [name of journal]

I represent the interests of Dr HS

1. It is incorrect . . .

2. . . .
   Dr M, Attorney

In the contents of 1 there was no reproduction of or extracts from the appropriate Nuremburg judgment concerning Dr S which the plaintiff had introduced in his letter of 4 July 1952. Otherwise they were unaltered.

The plaintiff sees in this kind of publication an injury to his right of personality. The publication of his letter, written in his capacity of attorney for Dr S, under the heading "Letters from Readers" and with its contents falsified by the omissions and the choice of title, constitutes a deliberate misleading of the public. The incorrect impression was thus created that this was a mere expression of opinion by a reader on the previous article on Dr S, as was the case with other readers' letters printed under the same rubric. The plaintiff, however, had kept clear of taking any political attitude and had acted only as an attorney within the scope of his instructions. From a professional standpoint alone the conduct of the defendant company was intolerable. An attorney must be able to ensure that demands for correction made in his client's name must not be circulated in a misleading manner.

The plaintiff demanded that the defendant company be ordered to recall in its next issue under "Letters from Readers" its statement that the plaintiff had sent a reader's letter to the defendant company in the matter of "Dr HS & Co.".

The defendant company takes the view that it was not bound to agree to the plaintiff's demand for a correction, because his letter did not conform to the requirements set out in § 11 of the Press Act. It lay therefore within its discretion whether and at what place in its journal to print the communication.

The Landgericht granted the claim under § 823 II BGB, in combination with §§ 186, 187 StGB. The Oberlandesgericht rejected the claim. According to the Court of Appeal's opinion there was, in the abbreviated publication of the plaintiff's letter under the rubric "Letters from Readers", no lawful disparagement of the plaintiff. The method of this publication certainly contained an incorrect statement of fact. The incorrect statement that the plaintiff had sent a reader's letter to the defendant company was, however, not apt to injure his credit, nor to bring him into contempt or lower his dignity in public opinion.

The appeal led to a restoration of the Landgericht's judgment for these

Reasons

The Court of Appeal was in error in failing to examine whether the plaintiff's claim was justified on the basis of a disparagement of his personality rights. It dismissed the action only because it did not consider as proved the objective presuppositions (elements) of a delict in the sense of §§ 823 II, 824 BGB in combination with §§ 186, 187 StGB. This objection is rightly made in the appeal.

It can be left undecided whether the plaintiff's letter of 4 July 1952 was a written work in the sense of § 1 of the Copyright Act and hence fell within the protection of copyright. The Reichsgericht has, indeed, constantly made the protection of correspondence to depend on whether it showed the individual form required for the protection of copyright (RGZ 41, 43 [48]; 69, 401 [403]). On the other hand it has been rightly pointed out in the academic literature that a need for the recognition of a personality right in respect of the use of one's own notes exists equally even when that protection cannot be derived from the personality right of the author, on the ground that they do not possess the form given by an individual intellectual activity . . . The Reichsgericht believed that it must deny such a protection of personality independent of copyright to publications of correspondence because the German law then in force contained no positive statutory provisions on a general personality right (RGZ 79, 397 [398]; 82, 333 [334]; 94, 1; 102, 134; 107, 277 [281]; 113, 414; 123, 312 [320]). It has indeed, in many decisions on § 823 BGB, approved of the protection of personality rights (RGZ 72, 175; 85, 343; 115, 416; 162, 7), but in principle it has recognised personality rights with an absolute power of exclusion only for certain specified personality interests. In the literature, Gierke and Kohler had already pleaded for the recognition of a comprehensive personality right . . .

Moreover, now that the Basic Law [Constitution of 1949] has recognised the right of a human being to have his dignity respected (Article 1), and also the right to free development of his personality as a private right, to be universally respected in so far as it does not infringe another person's right or is not in conflict with the constitutional order or morality (Article 2), the general personality right must be regarded as a constitutionally guaranteed fundamental right.

No further discussion is needed here of whether and how far the protection of this general personality right, the limitation of which requires a balancing of interests, is restricted in particular cases by justified private or public needs, which outweigh the interest in the inviolability of the exclusive sphere of personality; for in this present case it is not evident that the defendant company has any interests worth protecting, which it could use to justify the conduct objected to by the plaintiff. On the contrary, by the defendant company's choice of a way of publishing the request for correction, omitting essential parts of the letter, interests of the plaintiff in the nature of personality rights have been infringed.

Every verbal expression of a definite thought is an emanation from the author's personality, even when the protection of copyright cannot be attributed to its form. It follows that in principle only the author is entitled to decide whether and in what form his notes are communicated to the public; for every publication of the notes of a living person under his name is rightly regarded by the public as proceeding from a corresponding direction of his will. The nature of the notes and the method of their communication is subject to the criticism and valuation of public opinion, which draws conclusions from those circumstances about the author's personality. While an unauthorised publication of private notes constitutes—as a rule—an inadmissible attack on every human being's protected sphere of secrecy, a modified reproduction infringes the personality rights of the author because such unauthorised alterations can spread a false picture of his personality. In general, not only unauthorised omissions of essential parts of the author's notes are inadmissible, but also additions through which his notes presented for publication only for certain purposes acquire a different colour or tendency from what he expressed in the form chosen by him and the kind of publication he had allowed.

In so far as they concern works protected by copyright, those legal principles have long been inferred by the courts from the creator's enjoyment of the personality right of an author, which is only a particular phenomenon of the general personality right (RGZ 69, 242 [244]; 79, 397 [399]; 151, 50). As regards the protection of personality the interest of the author in notes which are protected by copyright is essentially the same.

In the present case the plaintiff had unambiguously sent to the defendant company only a demand for correction and, indeed, in his character as attorney for Dr S. Thereby the defendant company was only empowered by the plaintiff either to publish the text in an unshortened form or, restricting itself to the required correction, to make clear that there had been a demand for correction. Since the plaintiff does not ask for his original desire for correction to be carried out, it is unnecessary for the purpose of this decision to consider whether his letter of 4 July 1952 conformed to the conditions of the Press Act. If, in agreement with the Court of Appeal, this had to be denied, the only consequence would be that the defendant company had a right to refuse altogether to publish the letter. But it was not entitled to publish it under the rubric "Letters from Readers" and, moreover with the omission of the passages that would clearly show that the plaintiff was not putting forward his personal opinion in favour of Dr S but wished to obtain a correction under the Press law.

The Landgericht's decision is to be approved, that this mode of publication—and also the placing of the correction side by side with five other letters on the article on Dr S published by the defendant company—was bound to produce the impression on an impartial reader that the plaintiff's letter gave his personal attitude to the controversy about Dr S. That misleading impression was also not dispelled by the literal reproduction of the plaintiff's introductory sentence; for that sentence, in its generally accepted character, told the reader only that the sender was Dr S's attorney. It did not make sufficiently clear that the content also of the letter in question referred to his instructions as attorney and that it had been composed by him not as a private person but in the exercise of his profession.

Accordingly the Court of Appeal was not in error in holding that the publication of the letter of corrections in shortened form under the rubric "Letters from Readers" contained an untrue statement of facts. This also means that through the mode of publishing it, the letter acquired a meaning not in conformity with its original composition and that this form of publication did not correspond to what the plaintiff had alone given permission for, namely broadcasting to the public the letter of correction in the form he had chosen.

The Landgericht was right in regarding the publication complained of, which according to its findings had become known to an extraordinarily wide circle of persons, as a continuing disparagement and therefore that the demand for revocation was justified.

Case 40

BUNDESGERICHTSHOF (FIRST CIVIL SENATE) 14 FEBRUARY 1958
BGHZ 26, 349 = NJW 58, 827 (with a partially approving and
partially critical note by Larenz = JZ 1958, 571 and
an approving article by H Coing in JZ 1958, 558)

The plaintiff is co-owner of a brewery in X. He is active as a gentleman show-jumper ("*Herrenreiter*"). The defendant Limited Partnership is the manufacturer of a pharmaceutical preparation which is widely reputed as being able to increase sexual potency. To advertise this preparation in the Federal Republic, and in particular in K, it disseminated a poster with the picture of a show-jumper. Its basis was an original photograph of the plaintiff, which had been taken by a press agency at a show-jumping competition. The plaintiff had not given permission for the use of his portrait.

The plaintiff claimed damages from the defendant for the damage which he suffered as a result of the dissemination of the poster. He alleged that in the given circumstances he could only claim as damages what he would have obtained if he had allowed the defendant to use his portrait. As his professional and social position did not allow him, and his financial means did not compel him, to dispose of his portrait for advertising purposes, and in particular for the defendant's preparation, he would have done this, if at all, only for a fair price, at a rough estimate DM 15,000 at the very least.

The plaintiff applied for an order that the defendant pay by way of damages a fair sum to be fixed by the court.

The defendant denied any fault and pleaded that, after touching up, the plaintiff's features were not recognisable in the poster; and that it had not itself designed or produced the poster nor obtained the portrait from S, but had ordered it from the H advertising agency, which it had trusted as a respectable, competent, and reliable firm, not to injure the rights of third persons. The defendant could not have known that the poster had been designed on the basis of a photograph, or that the photograph showed a "gentleman" rider. Only as the case developed did it discover that it really concerned a portrait of the plaintiff. Thereupon it prohibited without delay any further use of the advertisement.

The Landgericht ordered the defendant to pay DM 1,000 to the plaintiff by way of damages. The Oberlandesgericht ordered the defendant to pay DM 10,000 to the plaintiff. The defendant's further appeal was unsuccessful for these

Reasons

I. The Court of Appeal, in agreement with the Landgericht, found that the depiction of the rider in the poster allowed the plaintiff's person to be recognised despite the retouching. It rightly concluded that the dissemination of the poster without the plaintiff's permission injured his personality rights, namely his right to deal with his portrait, and that the defendant must compensate him under § 823 II BGB in combination with § 2 of the Act on Artistic Creations, if it was found to blame (*cf.* RG JW 1929, 2257, BGHZ 20, 345, 347 ff.). The Court of Appeal came to that conclusion seeing that the defendant had not observed the care required in the circumstances, since it had obtained in the course of its business the poster prepared by the H advertising agency without making certain that the person depicted had agreed to the intended use of his portrait.

The appellant's attacks on these findings must fail [further discussion not reproduced].

II. In awarding compensation to the plaintiff the Court of Appeal had in mind the licence fee which he could have demanded if a suitable contract had been arrived at between the parties. It held that it was justified in applying a method of assessing damages developed for breaches of copyright, because it was hard for the plaintiff to show whether and to what degree there had been any pecuniary loss. In contrast to the Landgericht, which had thought DM 1,000 to be sufficient, the Court of Appeal decided that DM 10,000 was the more appropriate figure.

Although the appeal is unsuccessful in the result, it must be conceded that the Court of Appeal's reasoning is not entirely appropriate to the peculiar facts of the case.

1. The appellant does not dispute that, even where there is an injury to the personality right to one's portrait, the damage can be estimated according to the payment that would presumably have been arranged if there had been a contract. Nevertheless the appellant argued that this method of assessing damages, which the Senate in its judgment of 8 May 1956 (BGHZ 20, 345 ff.—Dahlke) declared admissible for the unauthorised publication of a portrait, could not be used if it was established that the person portrayed would, for special reasons, never have allowed his portrait to be used for advertising purposes.

If in the case under appeal pecuniary damage had actually been in question, this attack would not have been well founded. For according to settled case-law and academic opinion, where a claim to an appropriate compensation, is recognised, it is not a question of applying the *general* provisions of the law of damages but of its customary supplementation to make good injury to valuable exclusive rights, based on the equitable consideration that the defendant should not be better off that he would have been if his application for permission had been granted. The claim to appropriate compensation is therefore granted in all cases of unpermitted invasion of exclusive rights where permission is usually made dependent on payment and where, having regard to the kind of the right which has been violated, the invasion is habitually allowed according to the customs of daily life only—if at all—against compensation (BGHZ 20, 345, 353 ff.). It is not at all necessary for a contract actually to have come into existence if the invader's conduct was otherwise unobjectionable.

2. It must, however, be agreed that the Court of Appeal, by the method of assessment it chose, did not really try to work out the economic loss to the plaintiff, but rather to adjust the satisfaction due to him to his non-material disparagement. In particular the reasoning by which it arrived at the amount of the damage to the plaintiff shows that according to its opinion also he did not suffer any tangible pecuniary loss. In truth he claims not compensation for a non-existent pecuniary loss but an appreciable satisfaction for an unlawful attack on his personality protected by § 22 of the Act on Artistic Creations and Articles 1 and 2 of the Constitution. He demands satisfaction for the fact that a widely disseminated poster, by making him, one might almost say, "ride" for the purpose of advertising the defendant's tonic—and a sexual one at that—humiliated him and made him an object of ridicule. In such a situation it is absurd to award damages on the basis of a fictitious licence agreement. This way of estimating damage is appropriate only if one can start with the doing of some kind of pecuniary damage and all that is left is to alleviate the often difficult task of proving its amount. It fails if no pecuniary prejudice at all is in question. It fails also in the present case because it would assume that the plaintiff had done something that not only he, but all others of the same professional and social standing, must consider harmful and as a continuing degradation of his personality. It must convey an imputation that the plaintiff would, after all, voluntarily and for a large sum of money place himself in the unworthy position against which he is defending himself.

The plaintiff's claim therefore cannot be supported by the Court of Appeal's chosen method of assessment, helped out by the fiction of a loss of licence fee.

3. Moreover, basing the claim on unjustified enrichment is precluded because the plaintiff did not experience any pecuniary disadvantage and there is thus no pecuniary shift of the kind envisaged by §§ 812 ff. BGB.

4. If, therefore, the kind of assessment adopted by the Court of Appeal fails, and it is shown that the plaintiff in truth suffered no pecuniary damage, the decisive question comes to be whether he can demand compensation for the immaterial damage which he has suffered as a result of the invasion of his personality following the appearance of his picture in the advertisement. On the facts before it the Senate answers that question in the affirmative.

This Senate has already said in its decision in BGHZ 13, 334, 338 that the sacredness of human dignity and the right to free development of the personality protected by Article 1 of the Constitution are also to be recognised as a civil right to be respected by everyone in daily life, in so far as that right does not impinge upon the rights of others and is not repugnant to constitutional order or the moral law. This so-called general right to one's personality also possesses legal validity within the framework of the civil law and enjoys the protection of § 823 I BGB under the designation of "other right" (*cf.* also BGHZ 24, 12 ff.).

Articles 1 and 2 of the Constitution protect—and indeed must be applied by the courts in the administration of justice—what is called the concept of human personality; they recognise in it one of the supra-legal basic values of the law. Thereby they are directly concerned with the protection of the inner realm of the personality which, in principle, only affords a basis for the free and responsible self-determination of the individual and an infringement of which produces primarily so-called immaterial damage, damage expressed in a degradation of the personality. To respect this inner realm and to refrain from invading it without authorisation is a legal command issuing from the Basic Law itself. And it follows from the Constitution that in cases of invasion of this sphere, protection must be given against damage characteristic of such an invasion.

On the limited field of portrait protection this was established in 1907 by the special rules contained in §§ 22 ff. of the Act on Artistic Creations, long before the Constitution came into force and at a time when the civil law did not as yet protect a general personality right. For the protection afforded by § 22, according to which portraits may be distributed or shown publicly only with the subject's consent, rests in essence on the fundamental principle of a person's freedom in his highly personal private life, in which the outward appearance of human being plays an essential part. The unauthorised publication of a portrait constitutes, as has long been recognised in legal literature, an attack on the freedom of self-determination and the free expression of the personality. The reason why a third person's arbitrary publication of a portrait is not allowed is that the person portrayed is thereby deprived of his freedom to dispose by his own decision of this interest in his individual sphere.

Once the violation of the right to one's picture is seen as affecting one's personality it is possible to seek an answer to the question how to compensate immaterial damage in § 847 BGB. This allows an equitable compensation in money for non-pecuniary loss in cases of "deprivation of liberty". It is true that deprivation of liberty is here understood to mean deprivation of freedom of bodily movement, as well as compulsion to act, by means of force or threats, whereas § 22 of the Act on Artistic Creations deals with deprivation of the free and responsible exercise of will. Already, however, before the Basic Law came into force, the opinion was often expressed that any attack on the undisturbed exercise of the will was to be regarded as an injury to freedom in the sense of § 847 BGB. Now that the Constitution guarantees a comprehensive protection to the personality and recognises human dignity and the right to free development of the personality as a fundamental value, it has done away with the dogma held by the original draftsmen of the BGB that there can be no civil law protection of general personality right; and since a protection of "inner freedom" without a right to compensation for immaterial damage would be in great part illusory, it would be intolerable to refuse compensation for that immaterial damage. Moreover, there is no obvious reason why § 847 BGB should not be extended by analogy to such attacks as injure the right to free exercise of the will, especially where that deprivation of intellectual liberty, just like deprivation of bodily freedom, renders natural restitution impossible. Where such blameworthy depreciations of the personality right are in question, the effective legal protection offered by the Constitution can, in the absence of any special legal provision, be attained only through its inclusion in the injuries mentioned in § 847 BGB, since their injurious consequences are of necessity primarily immaterial.

This view is not at variance with the sense of § 35 of the Act on Artistic Creations. Of course the injured party can claim under it a penalty for the injury to his right to his portrait, and with it to have his immaterial loss made good, only in criminal proceedings and on condition that the injury was intended; but that special provision shows only that as early as 1907 the legislator regarded an infringement of § 22 as so far-reaching and threatening that it was considered necessary to grant expressly to the injured party a claim to compensation for the disparagement. The restriction of the criminal law claim for a penalty to intentional injuries accords with the legislator's limitation of the threat of punishment for an infringement of § 22 to intentional interference. However, that does not mean that the same must apply to the civil law claims to compensation that are not regulated in the Act on Artistic Creations. On the contrary, since the Constitution now recognizes the general personality right as significant for civil law and has afforded a general civil law protection appreciably exceeding the narrow regulation of § 35 of the Act on Artistic Creations, the special provision of § 35 can no longer be cited in opposition to a more extensive civil law protection of the right to one's portrait. The general provisions of the BGB concerning delicts come into operation instead. That means that, at any rate since the Constitution came into force, by an analogous application of § 847 BGB, any blameworthy injury to the right to one's own portrait involves a duty to make good immaterial damage also.

In so far as the Senate, following the case-law of the Reichsgericht, decided in the *Dahlke* case (BGHZ 20, 345, 352 ff.) that immaterial damage cannot give rise to a money claim in the absence of express legal provision, its opinion cannot be upheld in the light of the foregoing discussions. The statement was *obiter*, since the facts disclosed pecuniary damage, which could be estimated on the basis of the usual licence fee.

III. The compensation to be paid to the plaintiff was fixed by the Court of Appeal at DM 10,000. Although starting from a possible assessment according to the satisfaction that might have been paid in a case of contract on the usual terms, the court's arguments fully apply also to fixing the amount of an equitable compensation under § 847 BGB. They also show that the court really awarded the plaintiff compensation for the immaterial damage that had resulted.

As the Grosse Zivilsenat explained in its decision of 6 July 1955 (BGHZ 18, 149), the claim for damages for pain and suffering offers the injured party an appropriate compensation for the depreciation of life (or personality) which is not of a pecuniary kind. But it also takes account of the notion that the doer of damage owes the injured party satisfaction for what he has done to him. It was emphasised in the decision that "satisfaction", which forms an integral part of the award for compensation for immaterial damage, must take into account all the relevant circumstances. This Senate adheres to this view in this present case. If one therefore moves on from that position, it follows that the Court of Appeal was not in error in taking all the relevant circumstances into account in fixing the amount of damages. In particular, that court explained that the fact that the plaintiff had never been ready to take part in any advertising must be a factor in deciding the amount to be paid. It considered it especially serious that the advertisement was for an aphrodisiac, and so was not to be compared with advertisements for other products. The court was right in taking the view that persons would be unlikely to allow their likeness to be used on a poster for this purpose and so run a risk of being recognised by a wider or narrower public, exposing themselves to the innuendos to which the defendant's preparation would give rise. The Court of Appeal also took the plaintiff's social and business position into account, pointing to the fact that he moved in a social circle the members of which were for the most part known to each other and where the risk of making oneself an object to ridicule was especially great. When, after considering and giving weight to all these special circumstances relevant to amount of damages for pain and suffering, the Court of Appeal regarded the sum of DM 10,000 as appropriate compensation (§ 287 ZPO), it cannot be found to have acted contrary to law.

Case 41

BUNDESGERICHTSHOF (SIXTH CIVIL SENATE) 19 SEPTEMBER 1961
BGHZ 35, 363 = NJW 1961, 2059 (with approving notes by W Rötelmann = NJW 1962, 736 and H Hubmann = VersR 1962, 350, 562)

The plaintiff is a professor in the law faculty of the University of G at which he holds a chair of international and ecclesiastical law. From a stay in Korea he had brought with him a ginseng root, which he placed at the disposal of his friend Professor H, a pharmacologist, for research. The latter mentioned in a scientific article on ginseng roots that he had come into possession of genuine Korean ginseng roots "through the kind assistance" of the plaintiff. This led to the plaintiff being described in a popular scientific article, which appeared in the year 1957 in the *H and W* journal, along with Professor H and other scientists, as one of the best-known ginseng researchers of Europe.

The defendant company dealt in a tonic containing ginseng. In its advertisement for this tonic the plaintiff was referred to as an important scientist expressing an opinion on its value, and in an editorial note, printed in immediate connection with an advertisement in another journal, allusion was made to its use as an aphrodisiac. Both the advertisement and the journal were very widely distributed.

The plaintiff claimed that he had suffered an unauthorised attack on his personality right; and that the advertisement gave rise to the impression that he had, for payment, issued an opinion on a controversial topic in a department of knowledge not his own, and unprofessionally lent his name to advertising a doubtful product. He had suffered damage to his reputation as a learned man and been made an object of ridicule to the public and above all to his students. In reliance on BGHZ 26, 349 (*Herrenreiter*) he claimed DM 10,000 as satisfaction for the harm done to him.

The Landgericht awarded him DM 8,000 as damages for pain and suffering. The appeals to both the Court of Appeal and the Bundesgerichtshof were unsuccessful for these.

Reasons

1. By invoking the plaintiff's scientific authority in it's advertising to encourage belief in the effectiveness of its preparation for the mentioned purposes, the defendant company unlawfully disparaged his personality right (§ 823 I BGB). The reference to researches by the plaintiff, which lacked any objective foundation, was in the circumstances calculated to make him an object of ridicule in society and lessen his scholarly reputation. Moreover, he was bound to feel outraged by the way his name was used in advertising a preparation recommended as a sexual stimulant. The defendant company's conduct was also blameworthy. Before using the plaintiff's name for its advertisement it ought to have sought his agreement or at least to have ascertained whether and where he had stated what was asserted in its advertisement. The information in a popular article in the

H and W journal ought in no way to have been adopted unseen; it was moreover substantially altered. The Court of Appeal rightly characterised the defendant's conduct as irresponsible. Likewise approval must also be given to the Court of Appeal's finding that the defendant company was also responsible for the note in the *M* journal which adopted in somewhat modified form the contents of the advertisement. Even if it was the advertising agency employed by the defendant company that caused the note to appear, the information contained in it depended on material supplied by the defendant company. At the very least, the defendant company had not supervised the advertising agency as was necessary.

2. The senate also agrees with the Court of Appeal's view that the plaintiff has a claim to compensation for immaterial damage. The case is, in its main lines, very similar to those decided by the Bundesgerichtshof and reported in BGHZ 26, 349 (*Herrenreiter*) and 30, 7. In both cases the way a product was advertised attacked the protected sphere of the personality right of persons who claimed compensation for the unlawful injury. In both the conditions for compensation for material damage were absent or at any rate not proved. If, in the circumstances, no permission to use a name or portrait for advertising purposes is in question, it is not possible to estimate pecuniary compensation on the lines of a licence fee according to the principles governing so-called unilateral acquisition without permission. The First Civil Senate awarded damages for pain and suffering to the plaintiff in the case decided by it and reported in BGHZ 26, 349 and also regarded an award of so-called "immaterial damages", with its function of satisfaction, as the adequate compensation that the law must afford to a plaintiff for the violation of his personality right. From the decision reported in BGHZ 30, 7 it must be taken that the standpoint of the Fourth Civil Senate is at least not at variance with that of the First Civil Senate.

This Senate agrees with the First Civil Senate that satisfaction may be awarded to a person affected by the blameworthy infringement of his personality right. It is indeed stated in § 253 BGB that money compensation can be claimed for non-pecuniary damage only in cases expressly designated by the law. When the BGB established that enumeration principle, the high value of the protection of human personality and its special sphere had not received the recognition that it enjoys according to Articles 1 and 2 I of the Constitution. From the standpoint of the BGB, the protection of property interests always stood in the foreground, whereas the personal worth of a human being received only insufficient and fragmentary protection. In recognising a general personality right of mankind and granting it the protection of § 823 I BGB, the courts drew for civil law purposes the consequences resulting from the rank the Constitution assigned to the worth of human personality and the protection of its free development. That protection, however, would be incomplete and full of loopholes if an infringement of the personality right did not give rise to a sanction adequate to the violation. Just as the restriction of protection by the law of delict to specific legal interests of a human being has proved too narrow to afford the protection of personality required by the Constitution, so a narrowing of immaterial damages, for immaterial loss to cover only injury to specifically mentioned legal interests, no longer conforms to the value-system of the Constitution. For Article 1 declares it to be an urgent obligation on the public power to protect the sacred dignity of the human being. Article 2 I puts the right of a human being to free development of his personality at the head of the fundamental rights. If the law of delict, in protecting the personality right in the non-material realm, retreated completely to a position where it merely protected the particular personality interests mentioned in Article 2 II, which are emanations from the personality right, the civil law would not be paying attention to the value-decision of the Constitution. The elimination of damages for immaterial loss from the protection of personality would mean that injury to the dignity and honour of a human being would remain without any sanction of the civil law, which deals with the disturbance of essential values and makes the doer of injury owe satisfaction to the victim for the wrong done to him. The law would then renounce the strongest and often only instrument calculated to ensure respect for the personal worth of the individual.

3. That does not mean that the legal consequences of injuries to body, health, and freedom on the one hand and the violation of the personality sphere on the other hand must be exactly the same or at least largely correspond to each other. A need for differentiation is already indicated by the fact that the factual aspect of an injury to a general personality right is much less specific than where body, health, or freedom is injured. That means that there are many marginal cases where the question is whether the case is one included in the generalised description of violation of the personality and whether, if it does, the unlawfulness is not excluded by the competing rights of the "offender", among which the right to free expression of opinion deserves particular attention. It is precisely where a so-called balancing of interest must take place that the limits of what is allowed are not always easy to fix. If for every overstepping of the limits, however petty, compensation for immaterial loss were to be awarded to the person affected, there would be a danger that unimportant injuries would be used inappropriately to make a gain. The purpose of awarding satisfaction would then be stultified. It must further be observed that it is more difficult to apply the general criterion of monetary value to measure immaterial injuries to the personality right than the consequences of bodily injuries. In injuries to the general personality right the satisfaction function of damages for pain and suffering advances into the foreground as that of compensation recedes. Hence it will always be necessary to look at the kind of injury to the personality right to see if the person affected, whose injury cannot otherwise be redressed, should be granted satisfaction for the wrong he has suffered. That will in general only be the case when the doer of damage is blamed for a serious fault or when an injury to a personality right is objectively significant. Only when such disturbances are serious may the civil law, taking seriously the protection of personality and its value as such, react against the injury by granting satisfaction to the person affected. Insignificant injuries do not call for satisfaction. Having regard to the special character of an injury to a personality right Swiss law, which has devoted greater attention than the BGB to legal protection of the personality (cf. Article 49 I of the Swiss Code of Obligations) also restricts damages for immaterial loss to serious cases.

4. The conditions for an award of immaterial damages especially occur when—as in a present case—there is a wanton attack on the personality right of another person out of a desire to increase the force of one's commercial publicity. Such an unfair attempt to succeed can be effectively countered only if it is burdened with the risk of an appreciable loss, and on the other hand, anyone who seeks to make money out of an unfair invasion of the sphere of another's personality must not feel hurt if he is forced to pay a money compensation. For the plaintiff the outrage inflicted—in particular since the object was recommended for specific purposes—was not at all insignificant, the more so because he ran the risk of readers assuming that he had lent his name for a money

consideration. The award of a money compensation by way of satisfaction was justified by the seriousness of the attack as well as by the seriousness of the fault.

The amount of satisfaction to be given was for the judge of fact to assess. It could be attacked on appeal only if it rested on an incorrect finding of the applicable law or if the judge of fact overlooked essential points of view. No such defects, however, are here apparent. The Court of Appeal did right in attaching importance to the spread of publicity, which extended to Austria and Switzerland. It was also an essential factor in fixing the amount of the satisfaction that the defendant company continued the advertising complained of even *after* being warned by the plaintiff, thus displaying an especially reckless attitude. On the other hand, the Court of Appeal observed in the defendant company's favour that the mention of the name in the advertisement was not especially prominent, so that it might not have been noticed by the cursory reader.

Case 42

BUNDESVERFASSUNGSGERICHT (FIRST DIVISION) 5 JUNE 1973
BVERFGE 35, 202 = NJW 1973, 1227

The petitioner had participated in an armed robbery of an arsenal of the German armed forces in the course of which several soldiers on guard duty were killed or severely wounded. The culprits were arrested after a prolonged search and were convicted. The petitioner was convicted as an accessory and sentenced to six years' imprisonment. A German television station commissioned a documentary play based on the crime, its planning, and detection and the background of the culprits, including the petitioner whose homosexual tendencies were stressed. The play showed a likeness of the petitioner and mentioned him frequently by name. The petitioner who had served two-thirds of his sentence and was soon to be released sought an injunction prohibiting the television company from broadcasting the play pending a decision on the merits of his claim that the play violated his right of personality.

The District Court of Mainz dismissed the action for an injunction on the grounds that the petitioner was "relatively a personality of contemporary history" and could therefore not rely on the right to the protection of his personality. The Court of Appeal of Koblenz [reference] affirmed this decision by weighing the respective interests of an individual to be protected against the unauthorised publication of his likeness in accordance with §§ 22 and 23 of the Act on the Protection of the Copyright in Works of Article and Photographs (henceforth cited as KUG) as a projection of the right to his personality covered by Articles 1 and 2 I, of the Constitution on the one hand and the need for objective pictorial information concerning persons in public life, which is recognised in § 23 KUG and must be interpreted in the freedom to express opinions and the liberty of broadcasting stations to provide information, protected by Article 5 I of the Constitution on the other hand. The Court of Appeal held that in this conflict the right to provide information must prevail, especially since the trial had been concluded. The petitioner was "relatively a personality of contemporary history"; his interest in social reintegration had to give way to the interest of the public in general to receive a truthful account of the facts and the persons involved . . .

The German Federal Constitutional Court quashed the decisions of the two courts below on the ground that Article 2 I in conjunction with Article 1 I of the Constitution had been violated and issued a temporary injunction prohibiting the broadcasting of the play in question to the extent that it mentioned the petitioner by name and reproduced a likeness of him.

Reasons

A. ...

B. ...

II. For the present case the Court of Appeal has held correctly that several fundamental rights affect the application of private law and that they lead in opposite directions. The right to one's personality guaranteed by Article 2 I in conjunction with Article 1 I of the Constitution conflicts with the freedom of broadcasting stations to provide information, in accordance with Article 5 I, sentence 2 of the Constitution.

1. On the one hand, a televised broadcast of the kind in issue here concerning the origins, execution, and detection of a crime which mentions the name of the criminal and contains a representation of his likeness necessarily touches the area of his fundamental rights guaranteed by Article 2 I in conjunction with Article 1 I of the Constitution. The right to the free development of one's personality and human dignity safeguard for everyone the sphere of autonomy in which to shape his private life by developing and protecting his individuality. This includes the right "to remain alone", "to be oneself" within this sphere [reference], to exclude the intrusion of or the inspection by others [reference]. This includes the right to one's likeness and to one's utterances [reference] and even more to the right to dispose of pictures of oneself. Everyone has the right in principle to determine himself alone whether and to what extent others may represent in public an account of his life or of certain incidents thereof.

However, according to the constant practice of the Federal Constitutional Court, not the entire sphere of private life enjoys the *absolute* protection of the above-mentioned fundamental rights [references]. If an individual in his capacity as a citizen living within a community enters into relations with others, influences others by his existence or activity, and thereby impinges upon the personal sphere of other people or upon the interests of communal life, his exclusive right to be master of his own private sphere may become subject to restrictions, unless his sacrosanct innermost sphere of life is concerned. Any such social involvement, if sufficiently strong may, in particular, justify measures of public authorities in the interest of the public as a whole—such as the publication of pictures of a suspect person in order to facilitate a criminal investigation (§ 24 KUG). However, neither the interest of the State to clear up crimes nor any public interest always justifies an infringement of the personal sphere [reference]. Instead, the pre-eminent importance of the right to the free development and respect of personality, which follows from its close connection with the supreme value enshrined in the Constitution, i.e. human dignity, demands that any intrusion of the right of personality which may appear necessary to protect such interest, must always be balanced against the protective rule laid down in Article 2 I in conjunction with Article 1 I of the Constitution. Accordingly, it must be determined in the individual case by weighing the particular interests whether the pursuit of the public interest merits precedence generally and having regard to the features of the individual case, whether the proposed intrusion of the private sphere is required by this interest in this form and extent, and whether it is commensurate with the importance of the case [references].

These principles, which were developed by the courts in respect of measures taken by public authorities, must be observed equally when the courts have to determine conflicting interests on the basis of private law. In the course of such a determination the courts are not precluded from taking into account the special position accorded to the media represented by broadcasting and television by virtue of their organisation regulated by public law and their public functions.

2. In this respect the consideration is decisive, as the Court of Appeal has pointed out correctly, that the broadcast in dispute serves a function, the free exercise of which on its part is directly protected by a provision in the Constitution. Freedom of information by broadcasts in accordance with Article 5 I, second sentence of the Constitution (freedom to broadcast), like the freedom of the press, of expression and information is a basic constituent element of a liberal-democratic order [references] . . .

Only when the exercise of the freedom to broadcast conflicts with other protected legal interests, the purpose of the individual broadcast, the manner of its presentation, and its actual foreseeable effect may become relevant. The Constitution has regulated possible conflicts between the freedom to broadcast and the interests of individual citizens, of groups and of the community as a whole, by referring to the legal system as a whole; according to Article 5 II of the Constitution the emission of broadcasts is subject to the restrictions imposed by the general law. According to the constant practice of the Federal Constitutional Court the need expressed by this provision to take other protected legal interests into account must not render the freedom to broadcast a relative one; instead the laws which restrict the freedom to broadcast must in turn be interpreted in the light of the constitutional guarantee and must, if necessary, be equally restricted in order to ensure that the freedom of broadcasting is safeguarded adequately [reference]. Consequently the opposing protected legal interests must be balanced against each other in each individual case in the light of general and specific considerations.

III. 1. The general laws referred to by Article 5 II of the Constitution include also the provisions of §§ 22, 23 of the Act on the Copyright in Works of Plastic Article and Photography of 9 January 1907 (RGBl. 1907) maintained by § 141 no. 5 of the Copyright Act of 9 September 1956 (BGBl. I 1273), which formed the basis of the judgment in issue before this court. These provisions, the wording and the original purpose of which related originally to the right to one's own likeness, have for a long time been interpreted by the courts and by writers to apply also to reproductions of one's likeness, whether accompanied by the person's name or not, as well as to the representation of a person by an actor on a stage [references]. The general approach to these provisions has changed since the Constitution came into force to the effect that the right to one's likeness is regarded as an aspect, as a special feature of the general right of personality which was derived from Articles 1 and 2 of the Constitution [references].

These provisions are in accordance with constitutional law; their somewhat flexible character gives sufficient scope for applying them in keeping with the Constitution and it has been shown in practice that it is possible, in balancing the interest, as required by § 23 KUG, to take sufficient account of the reflex effect of the relevant fundamental rights. In this context, it is irrelevant from the point of view of constitutional law which factual element of § 23 KUG serves as the balancing factor [references].

2. In cases of conflict, such as the present, the general principle applies, on the one hand, that in applying §§ 22 and 23 KUG to televised broadcasts the freedom to broadcast must not be restricted excessively. On the other hand, as distinct from other general laws in the meaning of Article 5 II of the Constitution, it is a special feature of the present case that the restriction of the freedom to broadcast serves in turn to protect an important concern of the Constitution; the interest of the person affected to prohibit the publication of his likeness or any representation of his person, which must be protected with the frame-work of § 23 KUG, is directly enhanced by the constitutional guarantee of the protection of personality. In solving this conflict it must be remembered that according to the inten-tion of the Constitution both constitutional concerns are essential aspects of the liberal-democratic order of the Constitution with the result that neither can claim precedence in principle. The view of humanity taken by the Constitution and the corresponding structure of the community within the State require both the respect for the independ-ence of individual personality and the guarantee of a liberal social atmosphere; the latter cannot be realised at the present time unless communications are unimpeded. In case of conflict both concerns of the Constitution must be adjusted, if possible; if this cannot be achieved it must be determined which interest must be postponed having regard to the nature of the case and to any special circumstances. For this purpose, both concerns of the Constitution, centred as they are on human dignity, must be regarded as the nucleus of the system of constitutional concerns. Accordingly, the freedom to broadcast may have the effect of restricting any claims based on the right of personality; however, the damage to "personality" resulting from a public representation must not be out of proportion to the importance of the publication upholding the freedom of communication [reference]. Furthermore it follows from these guiding principles that the required weighting of inter-ests must take into account the intensity of the infringement of the personal sphere by the broadcast on the one hand; on the other hand, the specific interest which is being sensed by the broadcast and is capable of being thus served, must be assessed and exam-ined as to whether and to what extent it can be satisfied even without any interference—or a less far-reaching interference—with the protection of personality.

IV. 1. In the light of these general principles the following criteria are relevant from the point of view of constitutional law in assessing televised broadcasts of the kind in issue here.

(a) A public report of a crime in which the name, a likeness, or a representation of the culprit is provided will always constitute a severe intrusion of his personal sphere, seeing that it publicises his misdeeds and gives from the outset a negative slant to his person in the eyes of those to whom the report is addressed. It may be different if the report is designed to create sympathy for the culprit, as for instance in order to achieve a new trial, a pardon, or some other assistance . . .

(b) Disregarding the possibility of an additional infringement by the manner of the representation (polemics, falsification), even a report which seeks to be objective and factual, if televised constitutes normally a much greater invasion of the private sphere than an oral or written report published in the press or over the radio. This is so, in the first place, because the visual impression and the combination of a picture and word is much stronger, but mainly because television commands a much greater audience than the cinema and the theatre, resulting in a special position. Consequently there is a special reason "for watching over the observation of the limits established by the law and to prevent an abuse [sic] of the right of personality which had become more vulnerable. In this respect the law must not give way to technical developments" [reference].

(c) If for the above-mentioned reasons alone a special need exists for protection against violations of the right of personality by televised broadcasts reaching such a wide audience, it must be remembered that the broadcast performance of a documentary play entails specific dangers . . .

In conclusion it can be stated that television broadcasts reporting on a crime naming, depicting, or representing the culprit, especially in the form of a documentary play, will normally constitute a serious invasion of his sphere of personality.

2. On the other hand weighty considerations suggest that the public should be fully informed of the commission of crimes including the person of the culprit, and of the facts which led to them. Crimes, too, are part of contemporary history, the presentation of which is altogether the task of the media. Moreover the violation of the general legal order, the infringement of protective legal interests of the citizens involved or of the community, sympathy with the victims and their relatives, fear of the repetition of such crimes, and the desire to prevent them create a fully justified interest in receiving detailed information concerning the deed and the criminal. This interest will be all the greater the more the criminal act is unusual having regard to the special features of the object of the attack, the manner in which it was carried out, or the severity of the consequences. Where serious crimes of violence are involved, such as that represented in the play in issue, the interest to receive information is based not only on general curiosity and sensationalism but on serious reasons for asking who were the perpetrators, what were their motives, what was done to detect and to punish them, and for preventing similar crimes. For this purpose the desire to know only the facts will be predominant, but as time passes the interest increases to receive a more searching interpretation of the deed, its background, and its social setting. Not least is the legitimate democratic desire in determining to control the organs of the State and public authorities responsible for security and order, the prosecution and the criminal courts . . .

3. In balancing generally the interest in receiving information as circumscribed above by televised reporting within these limits against the invasion of the sphere of personality of the culprit which must follow inevitably, the interest in receiving information must generally prevail in so far as current reporting of crimes is concerned. He who breaks the peace established by law, attacks or violates by his act and its consequences his fellow citizens or legally protected interests of the community, must not only suffer the criminal punishment provided by the law. He must also accept, as a matter of principle, that the public interest in information caused by himself by his own deed is being satisfied in the usual manner in a community which observes the principle of freedom of communication. Moreover, the control of the prosecution and of the criminal proceedings which is assured thereby also benefits the culprit. However, the interest to receive information does not prevail absolutely. The importance of the right to personality, which is a cornerstone of the Constitution, requires not only that account must be taken of the sacrosanct innermost personal sphere [reference] but also a strict regard for the principle of proportionality. The invasion of the personal sphere is limited to the need to satisfy adequately the interest to receive information, and the disadvantages suffered by the culprit must be proportional to the seriousness of the offence or to its importance otherwise for the public. Consequently, it is not always admissible to provide the name, a picture, or any other means of identifying the perpetrator.

It is obvious that the right of personality is only postponed if the reporting is objective and if the interpretation is serious; it is different if the account seeks to be sensational, is intentionally one-sided or misleading. On the other hand, objective reporting of a serious crime justifies not only the publication of the name or of a likeness of the perpetrator; it also includes his personal life in so far as it is directly connected with the act, provides clues about his motive or the setting, and seems relevant for assessing the guilt of the perpetrator in the light of modern criminal law. The actual question as to where the limits are to be drawn in fact seeing that in principle the interest to receive information by reports of contemporary events must prevail, can only be answered having regard to the circumstances of the individual case.

4. The reflex effect of the constitutional guarantee of personality does not, however, allow the media of communication, apart from contemporary reporting, to deal indefinitely with the person of the criminal and his private sphere. Instead, when the interest in receiving information has been satisfied, his right "to be left alone" gains increasing importance in principle and limits the desire of the mass media and the wish of the public to make the individual sphere of his life the object of discussion or even of entertainment. Even a culprit, who attracted public attention by his serious crime and has gained general disapproval, remains a member of this community and retains his constitutional right to the protection of his individuality. If with the prosecution and conviction by a criminal court the act attracting the public interest has met with the just reaction of the community demanded by the public interest, any additional continued or repeated invasions of the personal sphere of the culprit cannot normally be justified.

5. (*a*) The time-limit when the reporting of current events which is admissible in principle becomes subsequently an inadmissible account or discussion cannot be stated generally; certainly it cannot be stated in months and years so as to cover all cases. The decisive criterion is whether the report concerned is likely to cause the culprit considerable new or additional harm, compared with the information which is already available.

(*b*) In order to determine the time limit more clearly, the interest in reintegrating the criminal into society and to restore his social position may be treated as the decisive point of reference.

(*c*) Altogether a repeated televised report concerning a serious crime which is no longer justified by the interest to receive information about current events is undoubtedly inadmissible if it endangers the social rehabilitation of the culprit. The vital chance necessary for the existence of the culprit and the interest of the community to restore his social position must prevail in principle over the interest in a discussion of the crime. Whether and to what extent any exceptions are conceivable such as in the case of an overriding historical interest, of scholarly or other broadcasts which are addressed to a limited range of viewers need not be examined here.

V. 1. Examined in the light of the criteria of constitutional law, the decisions appealed against cannot be maintained. The district court has sought to balance the interests of the petitioner and the broadcasting station exclusively by reference to §§ 22, 23 KUG without taking notice of the reflex effect of the fundamental rights contained in Article 2 I in conjunction with Articles 1 and 5 I of the Constitution.

The Court of Appeal did realise that a conflict exists between the freedom to broadcast by virtue of Article 5 I of the Constitution and the guarantee of personality by virtue of Article 2 I and Article 1 of the Constitution; in balancing, having regard to § 23 KUG, between the right to one's likeness and the interest of the public to receive information it did take the reflex effect of these fundamental rights into consideration. In solving this conflict it did not, however, apply correctly the criteria which are to be derived from the existing constitutional provisions for the determination of cases such as the present, but have not been formulated hitherto by the Constitutional Court; above all, it did not attribute to the interest in rehabilitation the importance which it deserves from the point of view of constitutional law.

2. If sufficient account is taken of the effect of the provisions of the Constitution which are relevant in the present case upon the general law the conclusion must be reached that the petition of the complainant must succeed . . .

Case 43

OBERLANDESGERICHT OF COLOGNE (FIFTEENTH CIVIL SENATE) 2 JUNE 1987
NJW 1987, 2682

Facts

The plaintiff had been a city official and director of the city's Office for Foreigners. In this capacity, he granted residence permits to a number of Syrians who, it emerged, were planning terrorist activities in the Federal Republic. The State Prosecution Authorities decided to investigate the plaintiff's conduct on the suspicion that he had taken a bribe. The investigations were carried out on behalf of the city authorities . . . by the Federal Office of Criminal Investigations (BKA). This body produced its final report in April 1983. After further investigations, the State Prosecution Authorities began proceedings against the plaintiff in January 1985. The Landgericht and the Oberlandesgericht, as the appellate court, rejected the charge at a preliminary stage, refusing to allow it to be taken to trial. A key sentence in the decision of the LG which was approved by the OLG ran as follows: "Above all there is absolutely no evidence which could form the basis at trial of proof of payments of money to the accused in exchange for certain actions which were in breach of his conditions of service."

The defendant is the publisher of a major news magazine. In its issue of 21 February 1983 an article appeared concerning the plaintiff under the title "In the Foreigners Office there is lively trade in illegal residence permits. Amongst those who have benefited from this are Syrian terrorists." The article contained a picture of the plaintiff with the side-line: "Suspended Office Director—did he know about the terrorist activities?". The text of the article began with a paragraph about a "three-man Syrian commando group" and its tasks. Then it continued: "Commando chief F knew his way around the border city in North Rhine-Westfalia. For DM 3,000, he bought himself a thirteen-month residence permit . . .". Later on in the article appeared the following statement: "An internal enquiry conducted by the Federal Office of Criminal Investigations (BKA) is investigating how the applications came to be made and the permits granted". A Director of Criminal Investigations had informed the Federal Office for the Protection of the Constitution, the Federal Information Service, the Interior Ministry, and the criminal authorities of the *Land*, that "the Syrian terrorist R had been able, using intermediaries, to obtain a residence permit from the Foreigners' Office in Aachen for a payment of DM 300 before his arrival in Germany." The article went on a few lines later: "In fact, when a raid was conducted at the offices, documents about the expelled Syrians R and A were discovered. The Director had once more granted the permits personally. Whether he knew of the terrorist activities of both Syrians is not yet known." The plaintiff brought an action claiming that he was innocent of the accusations and that the article represented a serious invasion of his general right of privacy. He claimed damages for pain and suffering of at least DM 10,000, plus interest.

The LG rejected the claim. The plaintiff's appeal was successful for the following.

Reasons

1. The defendant publishing company published a picture of the plaintiff, identified him by name, position, place of work, and age, and also alleged that he provided residence permits in return for money in his capacity as Director of the city's Foreigners' Office. This insulting allegation is to be considered under § 823 II BGB, read in conjunction with § 186 of the Criminal Code. It is not covered by the defence of legitimate interest (§ 193 of the Criminal Code). The allegation is also to be seen as untrue, since the plaintiff asserts this point and the defendant, who carries the burden of proving that the allegation is true, has not been able to discharge it, nor will he be able to do so following the result of the criminal proceedings. The defendant has further infringed the plaintiff's right to his own image (§ 22 KUG) and thus committed a tortious act within the meaning of § 823 I BGB. The question whether a picture of a city official who is suspected of bribery but for which there is no proof, is a picture in the "public domain" (§ 23 I Nr. 1 KUG) [and thus a defence under this Act] need not be decided. For in any case the defendant has infringed a legitimate interest of the plaintiff within the meaning of § 23 II KUG in so far as it published the picture together with the improper text. The picture and text together represented a publication which claimed that the plaintiff was guilty before he had been judged by the competent criminal court and, consequently, infringed the general right of privacy in the form of the presumption of innocence guaranteed by Article 6 II of the European Convention on Human Rights.

2. The words accompanying the text require closer scrutiny.

(*a*) This contains the allegation that the plaintiff has taken bribes and gives details of this allegation. It is to be found in the headline itself, which talks of a lively trade in residence permits within the Office for Foreigners. Although the headline does not use the plaintiff's name, the reader is nonetheless alerted to his identity by the picture and the sideline that accompanies it. This contains his name and then asks the question whether he has been aware of the terrorist activities. It is presumed that all along he was responsible for the "trade in residence permits", and the only doubt that is allowed is related to whether he knowingly took bribes from terrorists. According to the standard established by the OLG (AfP 1976, 132), the headline contains a separate statement. It represents a brief report which is intended to make the reader curious about the text that follows but which is capable of independent evaluation, particularly if taken in conjunction with the picture and the picture sideline. Consequently, it can be expected that readers will have relied on this brief report. Of course it is possible to assume that the average reader of the magazine will be a careful and critical reader. However, it is unrealistic to assume that, given the quantity of information offered by each issue of the magazine, readers will only ever read the headlines *in conjunction* [emphasis added] with the full text which accompanies them. The allegation in the headline is, moreover, formulated in such a way that the meaning it conveys can no longer be altered by the rather weaker comments made in the text. Such a text would, at most, be a contradiction of the headline.

However, there is in fact no contradiction between the headline and the text. The text contains what is promised by the headline, provided one does not only read those comments which could be put forward to support the defendant's case, but rather reads it in context.

Immediately after the alarming warning that a Syrian terrorist commando armed with explosives has penetrated the Federal Republic, comes the news that the commando chief R is very familiar with the border city in North Rhine-Westfalia, and has bought himself a thirteen-month residence permit for DM 3,000. The fact that the "seller" was the plaintiff is suggested not only by the headline, but also by the picture and the sideline that accompanies it since the linking element is the "Syrian terrorists" and the "terrorist activities". In this way the idea of a "lively trade" is fleshed out with these details.

Later in the article the same events are related in a different form. A Director of Criminal Investigations at the BKA had "informed" the Office for the Protection of the Constitution, the Federal Information Office, and the criminal authorities of the *Land* that the Syrian terrorist R had obtained a residence permit with the help of intermediaries at the Office for Foreigners having paid them DM 300 before he entered the Federal Republic. This is apparently one and the same set of events which are referred to in the two quite separate parts of the text. The attentive reader will recognise this fact, even though in the second discussion the Syrian is referred to by only one of the three parts of his name and the DM 3,000 is reduced to DM 300, perhaps as a consequence of an oversight. The text employs in this instance a different method of relating the story, compared to the account of the same facts in the earlier part of the article. Whereas in the headline and the earlier part of the article the perspective is that of an author who is precisely informed about the events and who is establishing what has occurred, here it is the Director of Criminal Investigations who is the mouthpiece. It would be quite wrong to conclude from this that the author and the defendant have done no more than communicate, in an impartial manner, a few details from amongst the many uncovered by the investigations. That would contradict not only the clear meaning which is given to the article by the headline and the first paragraphs, but is also something which is denied by the defendant itself. For the telex sent by the BKA Director is announced as an internal communication on the part of the BKA which "reveals" the ways in which the applications came to be made and the permits granted. And revealing means exposing what actually occurred. The style of presentation chosen thus gives the impression that the defendant is only alleging later in the article what the Director has "stated". The figure of the "Director of Criminal Investigations" thus lends an appearance of authenticity to the allegation.

The fact that it was the plaintiff, himself, who was involved in the trade in residence permits and not, for example, another employee of the Office for Foreigners is made clear once more. For, not only is he presented as the Director of the Office for Foreigners who [personally] made the decision on 70 to 80 per cent of the applications made by Arabs; but also that the documents pertaining to the Syrians R and A were discovered when his offices were raided by the police; the Director, once more, granted the permits personally.

The fact that the Syrians R and A, who are both terrorists, are mentioned in the same context gives the reader the impression that both R and A bribed the plaintiff.

The allegation that the plaintiff had taken bribes from Syrian terrorists is in no way diminished or weakened by another statement contained in the Article that the State

Prosecution Authorities are conducting, with the support of the BKA, a wider criminal investigation against a further eleven defendants for bribery, corruption and breach of the Act on Foreigners, and that these defendants included the previous Director of the Foreigners' Office. This part of the text may be unobjectionable since, while it identifies the defendants, it does not prejudice their cases. However, it does not have the effect of reversing the content of the whole of the rest of the article by stating that the investigations are yet to reveal whether the plaintiff has in fact committed the criminal offences of which he is accused.

In fact, the shadow is further cast on the plaintiff as a result of a further statement that "the investigators thought" that, beyond the permits granted to the Syrian terrorists A and R, the plaintiff may have received further payments of between DM 500 and 3,000 per permit "generously" granted to other Turks, Iranians, and Syrians. Of course, this in no way revokes or qualifies the allegation regarding bribery by the two Syrians. What must be assessed is whether the author and the defendant are not themselves adopting what the investigators "believe" in the same way that they allowed the "Director of Criminal Investigations" to speak for them. This point should not, however, be regarded as being at the heart of the decision, for it is not relevant to the decision.

The LG based its rejection of the claim principally on the fact, also referred to by the defendant in its defence, that it was apparent from the article that the plaintiff was still being investigated but that his guilt was not yet definitively established. It is true that the article does not refer to a completed process of investigation, and so does not state that it can with certainty be expected that the plaintiff will be found guilty. This, however, is not the issue. What is decisive is that the defendants in some parts of the article make allegations about the guilt of the plaintiff with the—understandable—encouragement to the readers that they should believe them. Furthermore, these allegations are made without any reference to the fact that (first) the plaintiff contested his guilt or (secondly) to the points which he was putting forward in his own defence.

(b) The defendants did not act in the defence of legitimate interests.

(aa) They did not examine with necessary care the truth of its allegation. On the contrary they made this allegation despite having insufficient information at their disposal. In their written statements the defendants relied upon the following matters:
— a criminal investigation was being conducted into the plaintiff's activities in 1982 on the grounds of suspicion of bribery;
— the investigations were conducted not only by the state prosecuting authorities but also by the Federal Office of Criminal Investigations (BKA);
— the plaintiff was removed from his position as Director of the Foreigners' Office and moved to another office;
— he was later (although after the appearance of the article) temporarily suspended from office.

The defendants could have reported all these matters without infringing the duty to check the truth. These matters did not represent, however, the basis for alleging that the plaintiff had been bribed by Syrian terrorists and for fleshing out this allegation with further details.

During the litigation, the defendants did not say what other information they had at their disposal. The article indicates that the defendants had succeeded in discovering certain details from the investigation documents. It must be doubted whether "the inves-tigating authorities", that is the state prosecuting authorities or the officials of the BKA, had told the defendants what they "believed". The final report of the BKA was not yet available. As the decision of the Chamber in Case No. 15 U 177/85 indicated, it was only completed in April 1983. After the report was issued, the state prosecuting authorities continued their investigations for a further two years before they decided to initiate criminal proceedings, which eventually were not allowed to develop into a full trial. As it appears from the decisions of the LG and the OLG which did not allow the case to go to full trial, there was no proof in the form of witnesses or documentary evidence of the allegation that the plaintiff had taken money. The defendant should have concluded, from what it read in the investigation documents, that the grounds for suspicion were not sufficient in order to allege publicly that the plaintiff had been bribed by Syrian terrorists. Once the criminal proceedings were brought, the defendant could have reported these (i.e. the nature of the charges).

In circumstances where the investigatory authorities are considering in depth the sus-picion that a criminal act has been committed, and that point is not contested by the defendant but rather confirmed, the duty incumbent upon the media to check the truth of what they report does not allow them to elaborate the grounds for suspicion which they have not gleaned from their own research, but merely derived in a partial and fragmentary manner from the documents relating to an investigation into specific allegations about the guilt of the person in question. This is no longer a case where the media is trying to rouse the awareness of the public in order to bring the truth to light. Consequently, it can only be said that there is a legitimate public interest in the information in so far as the public should be informed of the investigatory activities of the authorities, which was one of the issues covered by the defendant in a short para-graph in its article. To run ahead of the investigating authorities and to communicate its own conclusions from the investigations, even before the authorities have themselves formed a final conclusion, includes a significant risk of misinformation without a corresponding recognisable utility in the provision of such information even though it might be more attractive for readers to be given definite results rather than questions and problems.

Even where an investigation is still in the process of being conducted, there may be situations in which the media may go beyond the information provided to them in this context. This would be the case, for example, where the media are criticising the authorities for dragging their feet in an investigation, or where they are objecting to the presence of irrelevant influences upon the investigation, or the withholding of certain evi-dence. None of these factors apply here. The defendant only sought to publish the infor-mation which it had discovered from the investigation documents and which it had prepared in its own way for publication.

The defendant may not derive a defence from the fact that after extensive further inves-tigations the state prosecuting authorities did decide to bring proceedings against the plaintiff and in fact did seek to claim that the plaintiff was guilty of the acts which the defendant had earlier "established". At the time of the publication of the article these allegations were not allowed to be made. Nor is it permissible from today's perspective to repeat them. The intervening time is irrelevant.

Should these arguments be considered incorrect, it is likewise possible to argue that the defendant did not act, from a wider legal perspective, in the defence of a legitimate interest.

(*bb*) The standard which governs press, radio, and television reports of criminal activities which certain (identified) persons are said to have committed, where these persons are the subject of criminal investigations, is increasingly the standard of the "presumption of innocence" [references omitted]. The presumption of innocence is a principle recognised in all states which adhere to the rule of law, and it has been defined more precisely in Article 6 II European Convention on Human Rights (ECHR). This provision is applicable law in the Federal Republic. The addressees of this provision are, *inter alia*, criminal judges and the investigation authorities, which, for example, must exercise a corresponding degree of caution when making statements to the press; the media are not covered by this provision. However, the effects of the presumption of innocence extend into the realm of privacy and demand that this right is formulated in such a way as to protect the presumption of innocence and that consequently the presumption of innocence is seen as a protected interest for all persons. If the right of personality is understood in these terms, it places limits upon reports of criminal activities, as a counterbalance to the freedom of the press. It was in this sense that this court applied the presumption of innocence in its earlier decision (AfP 1985, 293) which considered proceedings brought by the same plaintiff against another newspaper.

Under Article 6 II ECHR the presumption of innocence operates in favour of the "accused person". This phrase should not, however, be understood in a strictly technical sense as it is under the rules of criminal procedure. Undoubtedly a suspect is also covered by this provision. Furthermore, the practice of the European Court of Human Rights would appear to cover also an accused person ("*Beschuldigter*") as defined by the rules of criminal procedure (see Peukert, EuGRZ 1980, p. 260 who argues that the presumption of innocence should also apply in the preliminary proceedings). In any case, there is no cause for regarding the presumption of innocence, as one aspect of the general right of personality, as arising only once the proceedings themselves begin, since the particular need for protection of a person subject to criminal investigation, who will be required to defend himself in criminal proceedings, arises already at an earlier stage of the procedure, in particular because prejudgments made by the press can have an effect beyond the official inquiries. The plaintiff, who was a person under suspicion at the time when the article was published, was therefore under the protection of the presumption of innocence. This has the effect that when the press alleges the guilt of such a person, and base that allegation on substantial grounds of suspicion, it will not itself be acting on the basis of a legitimate interest. It even follows from the presumption of innocence that such allegations are unlawful right up to the time when the criminal court makes its decision, regardless of whether they are true or untrue. The civil law cause of action which forms the basis for resisting prejudicial statements is consequently to be derived from §§ 823 I and 1,004 BGB. A reason for such a strict application of the presumption of innocence can be found *inter alia* where the criminal proceedings are not yet concluded and where the proceedings are for an injunction or for some other form of interim order. The fact that the question of truth is irrelevant means that the person who has undermined the presumption of innocence cannot bring evidence that the person who is subject to investigation is in fact guilty. This prevents a situation in which parallel and competing investigations into the guilt of that person are undertaken in the context of the civil and criminal proceedings; it also prevents the judge in the civil proceedings coming to a different conclusion to the criminal court.

Where, however, the criminal proceedings conclude, as here, in favour of the accused, whether he is found not guilty or whether the proceedings never come to trial, then there are no grounds for not including the question of truth. An untrue presumption of guilt constitutes a particularly serious breach of the presumption of innocence. Only on this basis can the severity of the invasion of the right of privacy be evaluated. The appropriate provision for such a case, which is a *lex specialis vis-à-vis* § 823 I, is therefore § 823 II BGB read in conjunction with § 186 of the Criminal Code; from this conclusion follows a reversal of the burden of proof. The presumption of innocence must be assessed as a matter of law in the context of the defence of legitimate interests and must therefore be evaluated against the fundamental principle of the freedom of the press; this evaluation will generally result in the conclusion that the press is not acting in the defence of legitimate interests where it is alleging the guilt of the person under investigation.

There may be exceptions to this principle where there are circumstances of particular urgency which influence the conduct of the press. For example, those cases which were mentioned above as regards the question of qualifications of the duty to check the truth of statements could be repeated here. However, it must be stated that in this case there are no grounds for recognising an exception. The defendant did not act in the defence of legitimate interests when it alleged that the plaintiff had been bribed by Syrian terrorists.

3. The tort committed by the defendants represents a serious breach of the right of privacy, which justifies the award of damages for pain and suffering under § 847 BGB. The effects of the breach were serious for the plaintiff. This is all the more so since, apart from the words and text, he was exposed to public scrutiny and a negative judgment by the public as a result of the publication of his picture. This makes the interference with the right of privacy more serious than it would have been had it involved the mere citation of a person's name. Also, the fault of the defendant, or more precisely the negligence of those who acted on their behalf, is also to be seen as gross. This is the case because its actions went beyond those laid down in No. 12 of the Press Code established by the German Press Council, which is to be seen as the correct measure of journalistic care. The interference suffered by the plaintiff cannot be made good by any means other than the award of damages for pain and suffering. The short report printed in the "*Rückspiegel*" in Issue No. 20/86, which stated that the OLG had finally rejected the admissibility of the proceedings had only a very small compensatory effect.

4. The defendants are responsible for the unlawful and negligent acts of the persons who acted on their behalf. In the case of this Article, the story was of a highly sensitive nature, and a constitutionally appointed representative under § 31 BGB should have been required to check it, for which the defendant is unconditionally liable. § 31 BGB is applicable to *Kommanditgesellschaften*. It is not clear whether this control actually took place. If it did not, then the fault of the defendants lies in an organisational failure for which the defendants are responsible by virtue of § 823 BGB. In addition, the defendant is responsible for the departmental editor under § 831 BGB.

5. Damages for pain and suffering in the amount of DM 10,000 appear to be appropriate in all the circumstances.

Case 44

OBERLANDESGERICHT HAMBURG (THIRD CIVIL SENATE) 21 MAY 1987
NJW-RR 1988, 737 = AFP 1988, 247

Facts

The plaintiff claims damages for immaterial harm resulting from a headline in the defendant's national daily newspaper. The Landgericht allowed the claim in part. The plaintiff's appeal was allowed in part, and the defendant's appeal was dismissed.

Reasons

I. The defendant is guilty of a culpable invasion of the plaintiff's right of personality (§ 823 I BGB).

1. The principal invasion of the plaintiff's right consists in the fact that the main headline in the 19 May 1986 issue of the defendant's newspaper B was so drafted as to suggest that the plaintiff would accept or had accepted DM 80,000 in return for being portrayed in the nude. This would be the impression received by any reader of this number of the newspaper who did not go on to read the full text of the article on the front page. The Landgericht was right to state that such readers would be very numerous. Headlines in this newspaper are set up in order to stimulate interest and curiosity about the article in question and induce readers to buy the paper. That is clear from the layout in this issue. The main headline can be read from quite a distance and can therefore be taken in by a person seeing the paper on a news-stand or being read by someone else.

The front page is so laid out that the reader learns the truth very gradually. The words "K Nude—DM 80,000" were readable from a great distance. Persons closer-to could see the text "K Nude. She wants DM 80,000." Adjoining the headline is a coloured picture of the plaintiff unclad down to the bosom; only closer inspection reveals this to be a drawing. Below the picture one sees, in somewhat larger letters, the words "No smile, the cool look—K in the P-Calendar". Even this does not tell the reader that there was no question of the plaintiff seeking a fee for publicity. The reader is throughout led to believe what the headline suggests. Only when the small print begins does the reader learn the truth, and then only if close enough to read it. The great majority of those unable to read this small print, especially those who do not buy the paper, will conclude to the discredit of the plaintiff that she was ready for a fee to display her body in the nude, partly because of what they have read, but partly also because they expect sensations from the B newspaper. Most readers will never learn the unsensational fact of the matter, namely that the plaintiff was actually claiming damages for having been so portrayed.

Even those who read the text below the drawing would have the same impression, for in the main they would conclude that the plaintiff allowed herself to be portrayed in the nude in the P-Calendar and was now demanding a fee for it. It is quite unlikely that anyone who did not have the paper in his hands would read the full text on page one and appreciate the truth of the matter, which was revealed only in its final sentence.

2. As drafted—and the defendant is responsible for its drafting—the headline invaded the rights of the plaintiff. It is true that any newspaper report is capable of being misunderstood by a cursory reader or of giving rise to false inferences. That is why this court has decided that one must put up with such negative reactions if a press report is

accurate and not misleading; on a balancing of the interests involved, such invasions of the personality are not unlawful, for it would constitute a grave constraint on the basic right of freedom of the press if publishers were held responsible for misinterpretations which are, after all, hardly foreseeable. This applies particularly to readers who simply go by the titles of articles in the middle of a paper or journal and pay no heed to the text; the press need not concern itself with such cursory readers.

But it is different when headlines on the front page are calculated to excite the interest of people with no mind to read anything else in the paper, such as those who are wondering whether to buy the paper or glancing at a copy read by someone else in a train or a bus. Such a headline must be considered on its own, independently of the body of the article it heralds, for it can be foreseen that it will often be read cursorily in this way, and the press must certainly strive to avoid recognisable risks of likely misunderstandings, as indeed this court had already said. That is the case here.

3. The defendant was at fault. There was an obvious risk that the mention of the well-known plaintiff's name in conjunction with the idea of nudity and a sum of money would conjure up derogatory assumptions affecting her right of personality. Yet gravely at fault though the responsible editors were, it is not established with sufficient certainty that they deliberately intended to cause the harm.

II. An award of damages for pain and suffering (*Schmerzensgeld*) is justified in this case.

1. The Bundesgerichtshof has always held that even where there has been an unlawful and culpable invasion of the right of personality, the victim can claim money damages for immaterial harm only when the gravity of the invasion makes such a *solatium* absolutely necessary. Whether such an invasion is sufficiently grave depends on all the facts of the case, including the seriousness and intrusiveness of the invasion, the dissemination of the publication, the duration of the harm to the victim's interests and reputation, the nature of and reasons for the defendant's conduct and the degree to which he was to blame.

2. Given the very wide circulation of the B newspaper, the headline must have been taken in by a very large number of people who read no further. Thus the misapprehension we have indicated must have been very widely disseminated. The harm to the plaintiff's reputation as a political figure well-known at home and abroad was grave and long-lasting, and her name in the leading headline of the B paper, which would immediately command attention, placed her in a context highly prejudicial to her honour as a woman, diminished her seriousness as a politician and reduced her standing as a public figure. Apart from this, what was published in the B newspaper was not independently defamatory: it was the way the front page was laid out which induced the false impression of what the article went on to state.

The wrong was not, however, as great as might be expected from publication in the B newspaper, for anyone who read the whole of the front page would learn the truth of the matter.

The informational value of the fact that the plaintiff was claiming damages from P cannot be invoked here, for it was trivial. This fact could have been communicated quite licitly without infringing the plaintiff's rights at all, but the fact that the infringement might have been avoided does not mitigate the infringement which occurred. It is, on the other hand, relevant that the B newspaper did publish a correction on the front page of its edition of 24 July 1986. This certainly amounts to an attempt to allay the consequences so far as those who were misinformed by the headline are concerned, but it cannot be said that it significantly diminished, much less neutralised, the effect of the publication in invading the plaintiff's rights: the correction was published in an unobtrusive manner which had none of the dramatic effect of the original publication, and in any case it can have reached only B's regular readers, and not the many other people who were affected by the original invasion of the plaintiff's right of personality.

III. The appropriate sum to award by way of solatium is DM 10,000. The proven defamation is a weighty one, which set the plaintiff as a woman and well-known public person in a most degrading light. Those who read the headline and not the full article were left with the impression that the plaintiff was ready to let herself be portrayed in the nude for a fee—an impression quite at variance with the public esteem in which the plaintiff was held. This was calculated to do lasting harm to the plaintiff's reputation and standing. This needs no elucidation. It is equally obvious that because the plaintiff is a prominent politician, the adverse effect on her is much greater than it would be on a simple citizen known only to a few intimates. Finally, one must remember that those who drafted the headline must have been aware, had they been taking the proper care, of the grave risk of invading the plaintiff's right of personality. On the other hand, this invasion was not the result of a report which was actually false, as we have said above, and this also must be taken into account in determining the amount of solatium. Given that in this case the true facts were given to those who read the newspaper, the invasion was not as serious as it would have been had it resulted from false statements in *both* the headline *and* the text. Further, the defendant's published correction went some way towards reducing the damage. Taking all these points into consideration, we must say that the sum awarded by the Landgericht does not seem adequate compensation for the way the plaintiff's right of personality has been infringed. On the other hand, the plaintiff's demand for at least DM 30,000 does not seem appropriate on the facts of this case.

Case 45

BUNDESGERICHTSHOF (SIXTH CIVIL SENATE) 19 DECEMBER 1978
BGHZ 73, 120 = NJW 1979, 647 = JZ 1979, 349

Facts

On the 3 of October 1974, the first claimant, the chairman of the CDU [the Christian Democratic Union], had had a telephone conversation with the then general secretary of that party, the second claimant, which without the knowledge of either of them was "bugged" by an unknown person and recorded or taken down in shorthand. A written record of the conversation was received, with an anonymous letter posted in Kaiserlautern on the 2 June 1975, at the editorial office of "stern" Illustrated produced in the publishing house of the first defendants, whose editor-in-chief is the second defendant. The second claimant was told about this at an interview with two editors of "Stern". As the editor-in-chief (who was the second defendant) would not give to the claimants the confirmation they requested that publication would not take place, they obtained an interim injunction prohibiting the printing of the telephone conversation. But in the meantime an article about the "bugging affair" had already been printed (with the co-operation of an editor who was the third defendant) with the full content of the conversation and almost completely delivered, so that the claimants could no longer prevent its appearance.

In their claim they ask for the defendants to be prevented from publishing the telephone conversation between them, the claimants, in whole or in part, or otherwise passing it on to third parties.

The Landgericht and the Oberlandesgericht allowed the claim. The defendants' appeal in law, which is admissible, was unsuccessful.

Reasons

1. By publishing the telephone conversation, for which the first defendant as publisher and the second and third defendants as editors are indisputably responsible, the claimants' personalities have been affected in two overlapping protected areas.

(a) Firstly, the publication interferes with the interest of the claimants in not allowing the *content* of their conversation to reach the public.

Their interest in keeping it secret arose simply because the subject matter of the conversation made it part of their personal sphere. Two friends in the party [the CDU], both in prominent positions within it, were discussing the emergence of the first claimant as a candidate for chancellorship in the face of attacks against him in this context, in particular by "Stern" Illustrated. Their critical concern was the attitude of the leadership and the grass roots of the party to this candidature. They were talking about indiscretions which had resulted in internal party matters reaching the press, and about measures to combat these. Quite personal things were spoken about, even though they referred to the claimants' work in the public sphere. In the conversation, thoughts and feelings were expressed, which a person would only make so frankly to a confidant whose discretion can be trusted, and which he would not let the public hear in that form, even if he had no adverse consequences to fear for himself on this account.

The claimants have also left the defendants in no doubt about their wish for the maintenance of secrecy.

(b) The extent of the interference which the claimants have suffered to their personalities by the publication is not, however, limited to their interest in keeping the content of their conversation secret. Their personalities were adversely affected more strongly than by an indiscretion, because of the area of the personality exposed by the publication of the transcript of the telephone conversation. The individual is especially reliant on this area being protected from the public in order to safeguard and develop his individuality.

Everyone, even a politician appearing in the public arena and seeking publicity, has in principle a claim protected by Articles 1 and 2 of the Basic Law to the safeguarding of his private sphere, to which others only have access insofar as he allows them to see it. In this private sphere he must be safe from control and censorship by the public, otherwise the basis on which his personality can be realised and develop would be endangered. All the events and expressions of life of this personal sphere are in principle protected by the right of the personality to self-determination in this way. This is above all true of a private conversation like the telephone call between the claimants, which did not lose its private character through the political aspect of the conversation. This is because what is said and how it is said depends a great deal on who is taking part in the conversation; a person can only participate uninhibitedly if he has control over the participants or at any rate knows them. This protection is removed if such a confidential conversation is secretly recorded and embodied in a transcript which is made available to the public. In a publication of this kind, therefore, the personality of the person affected is more strongly assailed than if merely something about the content of the conversation gets out; the reason is that it brings the personal sphere in all its complexity into the public eye. The recording does not only fix the content of the statements but also the expressions which the persons themselves have used in the conversation. Moreover, expressions acquire an importance of their own through a recording. All that was associated with the transitory nature of words in conversation and its own "dynamics" is, by being fixed in the transcript, transposed into a "static" condition, which can be accessed and repeated at any time for a completely different circle and a different situation, with a claim to authenticity. It is obvious that the personality in its intrinsic value is, even for that reason, considerably more strongly affected by such objectification, than by a mere indiscretion about a confidential conversation.

In order to protect the personality from such exposure and objectification of its sphere, everyone has the right guaranteed by virtue of the Constitution (and now actually extensively protected in criminal law (§ 201 of the StGB)) that in particular private conversations cannot in principle be recorded on a sound recording system nor played from this and transmitted by third parties without his consent (references omitted). It is also recognised on the same ground that recordings of a confidential character may in principle be published only with the agreement of the author and only in a manner approved by him (references omitted). The case law on the protection of the personality from publication of pictures without approval rests in the end on this basis as well (references omitted).

In the case in dispute it is admittedly not a question of a secret tape recording or the use of it; however, the personality must be protected to the same extent against publication of a written record of a telephone conversation. This is because the personal nature of such a record is scarcely less significant than for a tape recording. It makes the same claim to authentic recording of the individual sphere of the persons participating in the conversation, even though it does not reproduce the sound of the voice. At the same time, the fact that the reader is limited to what he sees carries with it the danger that the transcript acquires an importance of its own which is alien to the personality, and in which sharpening and weakening effects which are only expressed through speech are lost. Therefore, because of this special personal connection, the person affected must in principle keep control over who obtains insight by means of the transcript into his individual sphere and thereby the power of disposition over it.

2. Admittedly the personality is not *absolutely* protected either against indiscretions about confidential private conversations nor from exposure of its private sphere by an unauthorised record of a conversation, insofar as it is not a question of the inviolable area of the intimate sphere, which is not affected here. In particular, in relation to a press publication, the right of personality guaranteed by the Constitution comes into tension with freedom of the press, which is guaranteed with equal status by the Basic Law (Article 5 para. 1 sentence 2 of the Basic Law). The scope of protection of the personality is therefore to be determined as against that freedom on the basis of a balancing of rights and interests. This has to be orientated to the personal interests of the claimants which are affected and those interests of the press in publishing of the conversation which are

worthy of protection, and it must take into account all the circumstances of the actual case (references omitted).

In the end result, the appeal court correctly gave priority to the claimants here over the interest of the defendants in publication. Its statements need clarification, however, in order to avoid misunderstandings.

(a) An absolute ban on use which prevented the press publishing any information from their conversation without regard to its value for the public, because of the claimant's interest in keeping their conversation secret, was not imposed on the defendants. This was not even to be the case if their informant himself had obtained the recording by a sound recording system or a bugging device in a criminal manner. Indisputably, the defendants did not participate in this invasion of the sphere of confidentiality, even though they reaped the benefits of the breach of confidentiality. As the appeal court correctly recognised, their action was therefore not even open to a criminal law conviction; the criminal law protection of § 201 of the StGB did not cover their conduct (references omitted). It is admittedly beyond question that the claimants do not have to accept it simply on that account. Yet the gap which the criminal law creates here indicates that the interest in keeping secret the *content* of the conversation is not to be simply equated with the interest in the preservation of the confidentiality of the spoken word, as the appeal court possibly thought. The right of personality cannot give absolute protection from indiscretions by the press either. It is true that such limitation may not be required by the mere fact that protection of this kind would scarcely be realisable because the diverse secret areas are of very different structure and the varied ways in which secrets get out can frequently not be investigated. But the need for such limitation follows from the fact that inalienable free communication would be burdened more heavily than in case of indiscretions if it were to be subject to a comprehensive legal control. In this respect the appeal in law refers pertinently to the fact that the constitutional guarantee of a free press would be limited to a questionable extent if publication of information which originates from invasion of the sphere of confidentiality was simply forbidden. It must, especially in questions which must interest the general public, also be allowed to report on events worthy of publicity which are not released for publication by the persons affected, even if they come from private areas which are not automatically accessible to the public.

Even for information which, like the telephone transcript sent to the "Stern", has been obtained by invasion of the sphere of confidentiality which is especially protected in constitutional law by the secrecy of telecommunications (Article 10 para. 1 of the Basic Law), there can in principle be no difference, insofar as the press does not itself participate in this invasion. It can be left undecided here in what way and to what extent the special value which the Basic Law attributes to the inviolability of this area of secrecy has an effect on the legal relationships between private individuals (reference omitted). At any rate, assessment of the question of whether such information is barred from the press because of the constitutional law guarantee of the secrecy of telecommunications must take into consideration the tension with the constitutional guarantee of press freedom. Communication takes place largely in areas which are protected by secrecy of letters, post and telecommunications. To exclude in a quite general or absolute way news from such occurrences from publication in the press would be to reduce the contribution of the press to the formation of opinion (which freedom of the press is to guarantee) to an extent which would not correspond to the status of this basic right. The constitutional law guarantee for the citizen "to inform himself unrestrictedly from generally accessible sources" (Article 5 para. 1 sentence 1) likewise does not put such limits on the press (references omitted). The citizen's freedom of information does not, of course, coincide in subject matter and content with the right to information guaranteed by press freedom (references omitted). It is intended to protect the formation of the citizen's opinion from state limitations, but not to limit the sources of information of the press to "generally accessible" ones. The obtaining of information from not generally accessible sources as well—even if it is by exploiting a breach of confidence by its informant in which it did not itself take part— is not simply "unsuitable" for the press (reference omitted) so long as it keeps itself in this connection within the limits which are drawn for it under Article 2 of the Basic Law.

(b) On the other hand, the knowledge that the information published by the press has been obtained, even if without its help, by invasion of the sphere of confidentiality requires a special degree of consideration towards the person affected.

(aa) As has already been stated, the sphere of confidentiality not only underlines the private character which the statement has according to its content, but this is also to be respected by the public as a part of the personal sphere. The press must take also into account the interest which exists in being able to withdraw oneself from the public eye and which is worthy of protection. The fact that it did not force its way into the sphere of confidentiality itself does not free it from this responsibility. Publications from this area document and deepen the invasion; they also put the person's individual sphere in question. And not least the press must keep in mind that by taking up such information it can encourage third parties to invade that individual sphere.

In balancing the competing interests it is therefore in such cases not only necessary to look at the content of the information (references omitted). The way in which their informant has obtained the information can also limit the right and duty of the press to publish. That does not, however, mean that information obtained illegally may only be published if the general public has a fundamental interest in being informed, as the appeal court seems to assume (references omitted). There is likewise no room for parallels which can be drawn in this connection from the relationship of *state power* to the citizen, for instance on the limitations on the secrecy of telecommunications by the statute of the 13th August 1968 based on Article 10 of the Basic Law (reference omitted), because here it is a question of the tension between the basic freedoms of the personality and the *press*, which assumes a different form. As already explained, the press cannot simply be barred from taking up information illegally obtained if it would thereby contribute to formation of opinion in a question which interests the public. Respect for the area of confidentiality from which the information comes, however, requires a limitation of the publication interest to information with a "publicity value" which exceeds the interests worthy of protection in the personal sphere, the preservation of which must matter not only for the person affected but also all citizens. This is especially so if a third party has made an unauthorised invasion of this area and the publication must therefore inevitably strengthen the effects of this illegal invasion. The stronger the private character of the information, the closer the link to it of personal interests in maintaining secrecy and the greater the disadvantages which the person affected has to fear from a publication, the more permanent must its "publicity value" be, if the press wants to disregard his wish not to let it reach the public.

The judge must admittedly take into account the right of the press, likewise guaranteed with press freedom, not to expose its informant insofar as he, in this balancing operation which the judge has to undertake, is required, in favour of the person affected, to investigate the ways in which the information from his sphere of confidentiality reached the press. If the claimant refers to an invasion of his sphere of confidentiality, the proof which he has to provide of this cannot be made easier or even waived just because the defendant is not prepared to substantiate his opposition to such a claim (§ 138 of the Civil Procedure Code). Nor can the judge lay the press open in some other way to the necessity of exposing its information source, in order to protect itself from disadvantages. Otherwise the work of the press, which enjoys the protection of Article 5 para. 1 of the Basic Law in the procuring of information, would be exposed to burdens which come into conflict with the freedom of the press guaranteed by virtue of the Constitution.

(bb) In the case in dispute, the personal interests of the claimants are, as in particular the Landgericht has correctly emphasised, primarily affected by the fact that their personal sphere has been exposed to the public with special intensity by the printing of the record of the conversation. Such exposure is as a rule not offset by the desire of the press to report about the statements of leading politicians as comprehensively as possible. Consideration of the special value which the Constitution attributes to the non-disposability of the personality, requires, as has been explained, that only a very serious need for information on the part of the public can justify assailing a person in this way. But the defendants have not demonstrated such an interest in the publication of the telephone transcript.

They themselves say that the telephone call was even rather boring for a outsider from the point of view of its content. They wanted to publish it in order to show what language the first claimant, as a candidate for the chancellorship, used when he was not standing in front of a microphone; next, to reduce speculation about the "bugging affair" to a factual basis; and finally because of passages in which the other party to the conversation had criticised "Stern" Illustrated. These are not however prevailing grounds justifying the exposure of the individual sphere in this way. The actual personality of a leading politician in the centre of the public interest is affected by throwing open his private conversation for discussion, against his will, by means of a transcript of the conversation, to such an extent that it needs more to justify such an action than a certainly widely held interest in getting to know him in his private surroundings as well. Also the fact that politicians are discussing political and social questions in their private sphere does not of itself give the public access to this area; otherwise there would be no protected private sphere for politician and this should be undeniable for them also (reference omitted). The same applies for the claimants' criticism of "Stern". Such private opinions are quite common. Thus here also they were not so capable of making an impact in characterising political views and intentions of the critic which were of possible interest to the public that they therefore deserved the status, in public debate, of defining his position. There is also the fact that the defendants could get a public discussion going about the claimants' statements regarding "Stern" (if it had to be recognised that they had interests worthy of protection in the matter in this respect) even without printing the telephone transcript, especially as this issue only formed a proportionately small part of the conversation. Their objection, that they could by means of the transcript describe the facts in the greatest detail, is not acceptable; that does not justify them in exposing the personalities of the claimants in their private dealings with each other to such a wide extent. The fact that the telephone conversation in this respect revealed personal relationships and necessarily gave insights into the claimants' personalities could not be overlooked by the defendants; they have themselves admitted that this had been one of the grounds for their decision to publish the conversation.

The fact that the confidentiality of the conversation has since been removed, after it was published, does not prevent a ban on publication or other transmission of the telephone transcript. This is because it emerges from the above considerations that the defendants do not have to enforce the interests of the claimants in keeping the *content* of the telephone conversation secret but their right that the individual sphere of their personality embodied in the telephone transcript should only be dealt with their agreement. Every unauthorised further use of the recording by the defendants violates this right. The finding of the appeal court that there is in this respect a danger of repetition is likewise not open to objection under the law to be applied in the appeal in law.

Case 46

BUNDESGERICHTSHOF (SIXTH CIVIL SENATE) 19 DECEMBER 1995
BGHZ 131, 332 = NJW 1996, 1128 = JZ 1997, 39

Facts

In these proceedings the plaintiff, Caroline of Monaco, is objecting to the publication of certain photographs distributed in Germany and France by the defendant, the publishers of the magazines F and B. In issue no. 30 of the F magazine, dated 22 July 1993, the defendant published a total of five so-called "paparazzi" photographs which show the plaintiff with the actor Vincent Lindon in a garden restaurant in S. (France). On the front page, next to a large photograph of the plaintiff (the use of which is not impugned in these proceedings) is a photograph of her, accompanied by reference to an Article entitled "The most tender photographs of her romance with Vincent". The series of four photographs on pages 4 and 5 is entitled "These photos are proof of the most tender romance of our time". In issue no. 32, dated 5 August 1993 of the illustrated magazine B, the defendant published on page 88 a photograph of the plaintiff on horseback and on page 89 a photograph of the plaintiff with her children P. and A.; these photographs belong to an Article entitled "Caroline: I don't think I am the ideal wife". In issue no 34 of the B magazine, dated 19 August 1993, the defendant published an Article with several photographs entitled "Simple happiness", showing the plaintiff with her daughter in a paddling boat, going for a walk alone, carrying a wicker basket, riding a bicycle, together with Vincent Lindon in a pub, with Lindon and her son P., and, finally, with another woman in the market. After a lengthy dispute over the admissibility of these publications, the defendant brought an action against the claimant before the Landgericht of Munich requesting that the Court make a declaratory judgment to the effect that the defendant need not in future abstain from publishing these photographs. By these proceedings the plaintiff, who claims that the publication of these photographs infringes her right to personal privacy, requests under German and French law that the defendant in future abstain from any further publication of the photographs. The plaintiff claims that even as an "absolute person of contemporary history" she does not have to put up with the publication of photographs of herself. All of these photographs had been taken from a great distance, without her knowledge, and are said to belong to her private life. The plaintiff is constantly followed by photographers leaving her in no peace outside of her home. Even for her, there must be a protected private area outside of her own home.

The Landgericht found in favour of the plaintiff as far as the distribution within France is concerned but otherwise rejected the claim. The plaintiff appealed against this decision, and the defendant cross-appealed. The Oberlandesgericht has rejected the claim. The further appeal, in so far as it was accepted, is partially successful.

Reasons

III. The reasoning of the Appeal Court is, in legal terms, partly flawed. The further appeal rightly claims that the photographs which show the plaintiff in an outdoor restaurant with Vincent Lindon fall into the sphere of her private life. Their publication infringes her right to personal privacy and is thus prohibited. The other photographs are legally unobjectionable.

A. 1. As far as the distribution of the magazines in Germany is concerned, the Appeal Court has rightly based its decision on German law. According to the principles of international private law, for claims based on tort and therefore, as here, claims to desist from certain actions (Unterlassungsanspruch) said to violate the right to one's own personality (references omitted), the law of the place where the tort was committed applies. For products of the newspaper industry, the place of commission is the place where the product was published and every other place where it was distributed (Senate, NJW 1977, 1590 with further references). As regards the magazines distributed in Germany, the place of commission and the place where the effects of the tort were felt are both in Germany, so that German law applies at least for the German area of distribution. . . .

2. According to German law, the distribution of the photographs referred to above is illegal. In particular, it is not covered by the guarantee of press freedom set out in §§ 22, 23 of the Artistic Creations of the Act (KUG) or Article 5 I, Constitution.

(a) In principle, pictures of a person may only be distributed with the permission of the person depicted (§ 22 KUG). The right to one's own image forms a particular aspect of the general right to one's own personality. It follows that basically only the person depicted is entitled to decide whether and in what way his picture will be shown to the public (references). There is no doubt that the plaintiff has not given such permission.

(b) Pictures belonging to the sphere of contemporary history may, however, be distributed or shown without permission of the person involved, unless legally protected interests of the person depicted are thereby infringed (§ 23 I, No.1, II KUG). Pictures of persons regarded as "absolute contemporary persons" form part of contemporary history. The plaintiff belongs to this group of persons. The further appeal wrongly disputes this fact. Decisive for the classification of a person as an absolute person of contemporary history is the fact that the public regards his pictures as important and worthy of note just because of the particular person shown. The public has a justified interest, based on a real need for information, in seeing pictures of these persons (BGHZ 20, 345, 349 *et seq.*; Senat, NJW 1996, 985). In particular Monarchs, Heads of State, and eminent politicians belong to this group (see KG JW 1928, 363—Kaiser Wilhelm II; AG Ahrensboeck DJZ 1920, 596—Reichspräsident Ebert and Reichswehrminister Noske; Senat NJW 1996, 593—Bundeskanzler; OLG München UFITA 41 [1964] 322—Kanzlerkandidat). As the eldest daughter of the reigning Prince of Monaco, the plaintiff belongs to this circle of persons as she, herself, has acknowledged. The Senat's decision of 12 December 1995 (NJW 1996, 985) is based on this view.

(c) There are, however, limits to the publication without permission of pictures of persons who form part of contemporary history. According to § 23 II KUG publication is prohibited where the justified interests of the person shown outweigh the other interests at stake. Whether or not this is the case here, must be decided through a process of weighing up the various rights and interests involved so that in each individual case it is established whether the public interest in information protected by the freedom of the press (Article 5 of the Constitution), which the defendant can cite as justification, has precedence over the plaintiff's right to her personality (Article 2 GG) to which she refers. (BVerfGE 34, 269, 282; BVerfGE 35, 202, 221; Senat, NJW 1994, 124; BGHZ 128, 1, 10.)

(aa) The protection of a person's private sphere of life is of special importance when the two legal interests are weighed against each other. The right to respect one's own private sphere of life is an emanation of the general right to one's own personality, which grants every person an autonomous area of personal life within which he can develop and experience his own individuality, free from the interferences of others. The right to be left alone and "to belong to oneself" forms part of this area (BVerfGE 34, 238, 245 et seq.; BVerfGE 35, 202, 220; for the right to be left alone as part of the right to privacy under American law see Katz v. United States 389 Supreme Court (1967), 347, 350 et seq.; Warren/Brandeis, 4 Har. L. Rev. [1980] 193 et seq.; Götting Persönlichkeitsrechte als Vermögensrechte, 1995, 168 et seq., 174). As a result, since 1954, the German courts have, especially in the area of civil law consistently given particular weight to the right to respect one's own private sphere of life, i.e. treated it as a basic right, guaranteed by the constitution, which includes the right to one's own image (BVerfGE 27, 1, 6; BVerfGE 34, 269, 282 et seq.; BVerfGE 35, 202; BVerfGE 44, 353, 372; BGHZ 24, 200, 208 et seq.; BGHZ 27, 284, 285 et seq.; BGHZ 73, 120, 122 et seq.; Senat JZ 1965, 411, 413—Gretna Green; OLG Hamburg UFITA 78 [1977] 252, 257; OLG Hamburg UFITA 81 [1978] 278, 285; OLG Hamburg, NJW 1970, 1325—Haus Hohenzollern).

(bb) The right to respect one's own sphere of private life can be claimed by anyone, and can therefore be claimed by the plaintiff, even if she is a person of contemporary history. For even such persons need not tolerate pictures which depict central aspects of their private life, for instance their domestic surroundings, being taken for later publication without their permission (BGHZ 24, 200, 208; BGH GRUR 1962, 211, 212—Hochzeitsbild; BGH NJW 1965, 2148—Spielgefährtin). Only in exceptional circumstances, can the distribution of pictures from this area be permissible, i.e. where an overriding public interest justifies such an intrusion (see Senat JZ 1965, 411, 413—Gretna Green; OLG Hamburg UFITA 78 [1977] 252, 257—Grace Kelly; OLG Hamburg UFITA 81 [1978], 278, 285; OLG Hamburg NJW 1970, 1325; OLG München UFITA 41 [1964] 322, 324).

(d) The Appeal Court applied these principles. But it was of the opinion that the public's justified interest in information ends "at the doorstep" of the person depicted and, therefore, extends to places open to anyone, e.g. as here, "in front of" a garden restaurant which is open to public view. The Appeal Court, therefore, restricted the private sphere of life to places inside people's homes from which the public is excluded. This view has been widely adopted by the courts and is shared by the legal literature. (KG in, Schulze UrhRspr. KGZ 14; Schricker/Gerstenberg, UrheberR, 1987, § 23 KUG, n. 35; Wenzel Das Recht der Wort-und Bildberichterstattung, 4. edn. [1994], n. 5.46 and 5.60; Evers, Privatsphäre und Ämter für Verfassungsschutz, p. 44.)

This Division cannot share this view. A spatial restriction of the private sphere of life to the domestic area cannot have been intended under the KUG, since the explanatory notes to that Act state that the safeguards of the justified interests of the person depicted, set out in § 23 II KUG, were intended "especially to prevent events being shown to the public which pertain to the personal and domestic life" of that person (reference). This formulation in no way limits the protection of the private sphere of life to the domestic area but, rather, leaves room for a wider interpretation. The necessity of protecting the private sphere of life outside the domestic area is also partially recognised by legal writers, though for different reasons and with varying intentions (Allfeld DJZ 1920, 702; Evers *Privatsphäre und Ämter für Verfassungsschutz*, 44; Hubmann *Das Persönlichkeitsrecht*, 2d edn., (1967), p. 322; Helle *Besondere Persönlichkeitsrechte im Privatrecht*, 1991, 180; Paeffgen JZ 1978, 738, 740; Prinz NJW 1995, 817, 820; Siegert DB 1958, 419, 421; Siegert NJW 1963, 1953, 1955. Likewise LG Köln AfP 1994, 166, 168; see also BGHSt 18, 182, 186— Callgirlaffäre). This Division shares the view that there is a private area worthy of protection outside that of the purely domestic area. This is the case, where a person has retreated to a place of seclusion where he wishes to be left alone, as can be ascertained by objective criteria, and in a specific situation, where he, relying on the fact of seclusion, acts in a way in which he would not have done so in public. An unjustified intrusion into this protected area takes place where pictures of that person are published if taken secretly or by stealth.[1]

(aa) Like anyone else, persons who are part of contemporary history have the right which must be respected by all third persons to retreat to places outside their own home where they wish to be alone or, at least, left secluded from the general public. This can even occur in places which are open to the public, i.e. in public places. But this presupposes that in the place and at the point in question the person "shut himself off" somewhat from the public at large; and this seclusion from the public must have been objectively obvious to third persons. This can, for instance, be the case in separate rooms of a restaurant or in hotels, sports grounds, telephone booths, under certain circumstances even in the open, as long as the person does not appear more than just another member of the public.

(bb) Moreover, the right to demand that other persons respect one's privacy presupposes that the situation in which the person [observed] finds himself is one of a typically private nature. This is the case where a person, relying on the seclusion of the specific place where he finds himself in, behaves in a manner which he would not normally adopt in full view of the public. This may be the case whenever [the observed person] expresses personal emotions which are clearly not intended for the eyes of third persons or is acting in an "unrestrained" manner. Only in such situations can it be assumed and objectively verified that the person did not intend to allow other persons sharing the moment. In such circumstance he is entitled to have the chosen seclusion respected.

---

[1] Compare the above statement with the following opinion expressed by the Supreme Court of Iowa in *Stressman* v. *American Black Hawk Broadcasting Co.*, 416 N.W. 2d 685, 687 (Iowa 1987): "It is not inconceivable that Stressman was seated in the sort of private dining room offered by many restaurants. To film a person in a private dinning room might conceivable be a highly offensive intrusion upon that person's seclusion . . . the mere fact a person can be seen by others does not mean that that person cannot legally be "secluded . . . Further, plaintiff's visibility to some people does not strip him of the right to remain secluded from others." These are not isolated dicta and strongly suggest that the German reasoning should not be dismissed by any English lawyer as Germanic or un-transplantable. There is no room for prejudice in comparative law; only opportunity to consider (and if necessary reject) new ideas by others.

(cc) It is an unjustified infringement of the sphere of privacy which is worthy of protection if, for reasons of personal gain, pictures are taken/published which exploit the innocence of the person depicted who believes himself unobserved. This is always the case where the person is observed almost as if through a keyhole, or is surprised by the surreptitious taking of the pictures. The same applies where the picture is taken openly but so suddenly that the person photographed has no time to prepare himself. A restriction of the prohibition to these particular circumstances is justified because protection of the private sphere of life is here extended to places which are in theory open to everyone. In these cases the person's privacy is only unjustly infringed where the intrusion happened surreptitiously or by surprise. The courts have always held that the surreptitious taking of photographs by secret means is illegal (BGHZ 24, 200, 208; Senat NJW 1966, 2353, 2355—Vor unserer eigenen Tür; OLG Frankfurt NJW 1987, 1087; see also BGHZ 27. 284—Tonbandaufnahme; BGHZ 73, 120—Telefonabhören; BAG JZ 1988, 108). Up to now, this only applied to the private domaine within one's home, where the depicted person's consent was always required for the taking of photographs. But the same protection can legitimately be demanded in circumstances where persons, so to speak, transfer their private sphere of life to a place outside of their home. For the same reasons, photographs may then and there be taken, and later published, only if prior consent was given.

3. In the light of these principles, the weighing up of the rights and interests involved in this case leads to the conclusion that the plaintiff's protected sphere of privacy was violated by photographs taken in a garden restaurant and published in issue no. 30 of the magazine F. under the headline "These photos are the proof of the most tender romance of our time". The plaintiff can prohibit any future publication of these pictures. . . .

(b) When weighing up the various interests involved, the information value of the events depicted plays a significant role. The greater the interest of the public in being informed, the more the protected interests of the person of contemporary history must recede in favour of the public's need for information. Conversely, the need to protect the depicted person's privacy gains in weight as the value of the information which the public obtains from the photographs decreases. In this case, the photographs which show the plaintiff with Vincent Lindon in a garden restaurant contain little, if anything of value. Here, according to the Appeal Court, mere prying and sensationalism, and the public's wish to be entertained, outweighed all other considerations. Such motives, especially the mere wish of the public to be entertained, which is to be satisfied by pictures of totally private events of the plaintiff's life, cannot be recognised as worthy of protection. Our courts have repeatedly acknowledged this. (BVerGE 34, 269, 283; BGHZ 24, 200, 208; BGHZ 128, 1, 12; BGH NJW 1965, 2148, 2149; BGH JZ 1965, 411; OLG Hamburg AfP 1992, 376, 377).

4. However, the further appeal is unsuccessful in respect of the photographs in the other magazines since these are not concerned with the plaintiff's protected private sphere of life.

(a) . . . The plaintiff cannot prohibit the publication of such pictures. As a person of contemporary history, she must accept that the general public has a justifiable interest in knowing where she goes and how she behaves herself in public, be it during shopping trips in the market square, in a cafe or during sporting or other activities of daily life.

This includes the picture reproduced in the issue no. 34 of the magazine B, taken in a restaurant and showing the plaintiff sitting at a table with other persons. This picture differs from the ones taken in the garden restaurant because here the characteristics which made the other ones an unjustifiable intrusion are missing. For here, the plaintiff had not retreated to a place secluded from the general public, and secondly the situation in which she was photographed was not of a somewhat private nature in the sense outlined above. The fact that the plaintiff was not aware of being photographed does not, in itself, provide a reason for demanding that the photo remain unpublished, since persons of contemporary history must normally tolerate unnoticed or even clandestine photographs of themselves if they appear in public (Frank *Persönlichkeitsschutz heute*, 1985, p. 118, n. 280).

(b) However, what all these pictures have in common is the fact that they do not show the plaintiff performing a public function. They are, instead, concerned with her private life in the wider sense of the term. The plaintiff wishes to prohibit generally the publication of these photographs in Germany and France. But this is not possible under German law. In France under Article 9 of the Code Civil, which is intended to protect private life (*vie privée*), the publication of a picture requires in principle the consent of the person shown. This can even apply to monarchs and other public figures, unless they are shown performing a public duty (see Cour de Cassation, Bulletin des arrêts Chambres civiles, No 98, p. 67—Farah Diba; Tribunal de grande instance de Paris Recueil Dalloz Sirey 1977, Jur. p. 364 *et seq*.—Caroline de Monaco; see also Hauser, GRUR Int. 1988, 839, 840; Ehlers/Baumann ZvglRWiss 1978, 421 *et seq*; Codes Dalloz, Code civil, 92. ed., [1992–1993], Article 9, n. 9).

Under German law (§ 23 KUG), this result is not possible. As this Division stated in its judgment of 14 November 1996 (NJW 1996, 539), under German law the public can have an undisputed interest in seeing photographs of an "absolute person of contemporary history". There is no further requirement that that person be performing a public function. As a consequence, within the scope of § 23 I No. 1 KUG, the public's interest in information which is worthy of protection can be assumed even where the photograph merely shows how a well-known person acts in normal public surroundings, i.e. when not performing public functions. This interest in being informed only needs to give way where, in quite specific situations, the justified interests of the person shown take precedence (s. 23 II KUG). This does not, however, apply to the photographs shown in issues nos. 32 and 34 of the magazine which are in fact quite flattering.

B. As far as distribution of the magazines in France is concerned, contrary to the plaintiff's contentions in this further appeal, the Court need not decide whether or not the plaintiff's claim would succeed if French law were applied.

1. As the Appeal Court rightly held, to apply French law in deciding in favour of a claim for an order to abstain from an action is barred by Article 38 EGBGB. According to this provision, claims based on tortious acts committed abroad against a German citizen are limited to the remedies available under German law. This principle also applies in favour of the defendant, a legal person domiciled within Germany (RGZ 129, 385, 388; OLG Hamburg IPRspr. 1930, No. 155; see also BGHZ 86, 234, 237). A comparison of the results under German and French law is thus superfluous when it is clear, as here, that German law provides no basis for a claim BGHZ 71, 175, 177; BGHZ 86, 234, 237; BAG NJW 1964, 990, 991; *Prof. v. Bar* JZ 1985, 961, 963.

Case 47

BUNDESVERFASSUNGSGERICHT (FIRST DVISION) 15 DECEMBER 1999
BVerfGE 101, 361 = NJW 2000, 1021 = VersR 2000, 773

Headnote

1. The private sphere protected by the general right of personality in Article 2 para. 1 in combination with Article 1 para. 1 of the Basic Law is not limited to the home. The individual must in principle have the opportunity of moving around in other places which are obviously secluded without being pestered by press photographers.

2. The general right of personality is not guaranteed in the interest of commercialisation of that personality. The protection of the private sphere from the taking of pictures takes second place insofar as someone shows himself to be in agreement with certain material usually regarded as private being made public.

3. The protective content of the general right of personality of parents or a parent is strengthened by Article 6 paras. 1 and 2 of the Basic Law, insofar as it concerns publication of pictures which have as their object specific parental attention to children.

4. The guarantee of press freedom contained in Article 5 para. 1 sentence 2 of the Basic Law includes publications and contributions in the nature of entertainment as well as their illustrations. This also applies in principle to the publication of pictures which show people in public life in everyday or private contexts.

Judgment

The judgments of the Bundesgerichtshof of 19 December 1995—VI ZR 15/95—, of the Hanseatic Oberlandesgericht of Hamburg of 8 December 1994—3 U 64/94—and of the Landgericht of Hamburg of 4 February 1994—324 O 537/93—infringe the complainant's basic right under Article 2 paragraph 1 in combination with Article 1 paragraph 1 of the Basic Law insofar as her claim in relation to three pictures published in the Illustrated "Bunte" no. 32 of 5 August 1993 and no. 34 of 19 August 1993 which show the complainant with her children was refused. In this respect and in relation to the decision about costs the judgment of the Bundesgerichtshof is quashed and the case referred back to it.

In other respects the constitutional complaint is rejected.

The German Federal Republic must reimburse the complainant for a third of the necessary expenses.

Reasons

A.

The constitutional complaint concerns the publication of photographs from the everyday and private lives of prominent figures.

I.

1. The defendant in the original proceedings, Burda GmbH, publishes the magazines "Freizeit Revue" and "Bunte". In these magazines, photographs of the complainant Princess Caroline of Monaco were published in various articles. She claimed an injunction to prevent publication of these.

The subject of the original proceedings included at first five photos which were printed in the "Freizeit Revue" no. 30 of 22 July 1993. The complainant could be seen in them together with the actor Vincent Lindon at a table in a garden café in Saint-Rémy (France) in the evening. The photos are advertised on the title page as "The tenderest photos of her romance with Vincent" and show Vincent Lindon kissing the complainant's hand. As the complainant was successful in obtaining from the Bundesgerichtshof an injunction to prevent future publication of these photos, they are not the subject of the constitutional complaint.

The defendant then published in the Illustrated "Bunte" no. 32 of 5 August 1993 the article "Caroline: I don't believe that I can be the ideal wife for a man", in which parts (mostly in indirect speech) of a book about the complainant which appeared in Spain are reproduced. Several photos illustrated the article. A photo on p. 88 shows the complainant riding a horse in a paddock. No other people can be seen in the picture. It has the caption: "Caroline and melancholy. Her life is a novel with countless misfortunes, says the author, Roig". P. 89 contains a photo of the complainant with her children Pierre and Andrea with the caption "Caroline with Pierre and Andrea, her children". In the photo, three people are visible in the foreground; in the background there are vehicles. The complainant is wearing sunglasses.

In no. 34 of the Illustrated "Bunte" of 19 August 1993, an article under the title "Simple Happiness" appeared on pp. 44 to 52 with several photos. On the first page of the article, the complainant can be seen together with her daughter in a canoe, in a close up. The accompanying text to the side states: "It is a hot day this summer. Princess Caroline paddles with her daughter on the Sorgues. This is a small river not far from St-Rémy, the village in Provence where Caroline lives. From New York to London, the rich and beautiful whisper about the Caroline style. A canoe instead of a yacht. A sandwich instead of caviar".

A further photo shows her with a basket slung round her on her way to the market. It includes an accompanying text in small print. "Housewife Caroline Casiraghi. She loves doing the shopping herself". The accompanying text at the side in large print states: "On Wednesday, it's market day. The Caroline style is copied world-wide. Her strap sandals which she wears to the flower market, her pareo which she wears as a skirt". In other photos—not the subject of challenge—within this frame, there are two shops in which the complainant allegedly make purchases, the bistro in which she usually drinks coffee and her country house.

The next photo objected to shows the complainant and the actor Vincent Lindon sitting side by side in a guest house, with other guests around them. The text in small print in the right hand lower corner says: "Every Saturday evening table no. 3 here on the right of the entrance is reserved for Caroline". The accompanying text in large print states: "In the evenings, people sit in the "Sous les Micocouliers" and drink the light red summer wine. Caroline and Vincent Lindon are guests like the baker, the olive farmer or Father Philippe of the Church of St Martin".

A photo also shows the complainant cycling alone on a track across the fields. The text in small print for this photo says: "Caroline cycles home. Her mas (house or farm in southern France) lies at the end of the bumpy track, the 'Chemin du Pilou'". It is supplemented by the larger accompanying text: "The end of loneliness approaches. The Caroline style attracts the beautiful and the rich. Lady Di should have instructed an estate agent to find a property for her. Julio Iglesias is also looking".

The photo on p. 51 shows the complainant together with Vincent Lindon, her son Pierre and another child. It is a close up and shows these persons from behind or from the side as they turn to the child. The text in small print says: "Caroline's youngest, Pierre, 6, has bumped himself. Vincent and Caroline comfort him".

The last photo shows the complainant wearing sunglasses with a female companion in the market by a flower stall. The text accompanying the photo states: "Caroline's body-guard is a woman. She even looks like the princess. They mostly go to the market together".

2. The determining factor for the assessment of these photos by the civil courts was §§ 22 and 23 of the Statute as to Copyright in Works of Article and Photography of 9 January 1907 ([reference omitted]; from now called the Kunsturhebergesetz—KUG). These provisions state as follows:

§ 22

Pictures of people can only be disseminated or displayed publicly with the consent of the persons portrayed. In cases of doubt, consent is to taken as having been given if the person portrayed received a payment for letting himself be portrayed. After the death of the person portrayed, the consent of the relatives of the person portrayed is needed until 10 years have elapsed . . .

§ 23

(1) The following may be disseminated and displayed without the consent necessary in accordance with § 22:
    1. Pictures of people from the realm of contemporary history;
    2. Pictures in which the persons only appear as accessories near a landscape or other locality;
    3. Pictures of meetings, processions and similar events in which the persons depicted have taken part;
    4. Pictures of people which are not made to order insofar as the dissemination or display serves a higher interest of art.

(2) The authorisation does not however extend to dissemination or display which violates a justified interest of the person portrayed or, if he has died, his relatives.
    (a) The Landgericht allowed the claim insofar as it concerned the publication of the photos in magazines sold in France. In other respects it rejected the claim.

. . .

    (b) The Oberlandesgericht rejected the appeal of the complainant, revised the judgment at first instance on the cross appeal of the defendant and rejected the claim insofar as the Landgericht had allowed it (reference omitted).

3. The Bundesgerichtshof quashed the judgment of the Oberlandesgericht in part, and revised the judgment of the Landgericht in part, so that the defendant in the original

proceedings was ordered to refrain from fresh publication of the photographs printed in the magazine "Freizeit Revue" with the picture of the complainant. The remainder of the appeal in law was rejected.

. . .

II

The complainant contests all the civil court decisions, insofar as future dissemination of the photos was not forbidden, on the ground that they are violations of Article 2 para. 1 in combination with Article 1 para. 1 of the Basic Law, in particular of the right to pictures of oneself and the right to respect for the private sphere.

. . .

B.

The constitutional complaint is in part well founded.

I.

The judgments under challenge affect the complainant's general right of personality under Article 2 para. 1 in combination with Article 1 para. 1 of the Basic Law.

1. The protection of the general right of personality extends to pictures of a person by third parties.

(a) The basic right has the task of guaranteeing elements of the personality which are not the object of the special guarantees of freedom in the Basic Law but which are just as important as these in their constitutive significance for the personality (references omitted.) There is a need for such a guarantee to close up the gaps, particularly in view of new types of danger to the development of the personality which mostly arise with scientific and technical progress (references omitted). The assignment of an actual desire for legal protection to the different aspects of the right of personality must therefore be made with the danger to the personality to be deduced from the actual circumstances of the case primarily in mind.

(b) Authority to publish photographs showing persons in private or every day contexts is to be measured by the right to pictures of oneself and the guarantee of the private sphere which are concrete forms of the general right of personality.

(aa) Contrary to the view of the complainant, Article 2 para. 1 in combination with Article 1 para. 1 of the Basic Law does not contain a general and comprehensive right of control over pictures of oneself. Insofar as she seeks to deduce such a right from earlier decisions of the Federal Constitutional Court (references omitted), this is an incorrect generalisation of the protective content of the basic right guarantee which is formulated in the light of the actual cases. As the Federal Constitutional Court has already emphasised many times, the general right of personality does not give the individual a claim only to be portrayed by others in the way in which he sees himself or wants to be seen (references omitted). A wide protection of this kind would not only exceed the objective of avoiding endangering the development of the personality, but would also make deep inroads into the area of freedom of third parties.

The complainant also does not find any fault with the way she is portrayed in the disputed photos, which the civil courts have regarded as in every respect favourable.

She is much more concerned with whether photographs of her ought to be taken and published at all, when she was not acting in an official function but in a private capacity or every day context in public. The answer to this question is to be deduced from those expressions of the general right of personality which protect the right to pictures of oneself and the private sphere.

(bb) The right to pictures of oneself (references omitted) guarantees to the individual the opportunity to influence and make decisions about the making and use of photographs or drawings of himself by others. Whether these show the individual in a private or public context does not in principle play any role here. The need for protection arises instead principally from the possibility of removing the image of a person in a certain situation from this situation, recording it as data, and reproducing it at any time before an enormous number of people. (This is similar to the "right to one's own words", and the right to pictures of oneself entered the constitutional case law following on from that right.) This possibility has grown even further through progress in photographic technology, which permits the taking of pictures from a great distance (recently even from satellite) and in bad light.

With the help of reproduction technology, the kind of public before which the individual appears can be changed. In particular, the visible public in which one moves in normal public appearances can be replaced by the media public. Thus for instance the public in court, ie the audience present in the court room, differs from the media public produced by television, because the audience experiences events itself and can itself be seen and assessed by the parties to the proceedings (reference omitted). Besides this, the message conveyed by pictorial statements can change, or even be intentionally changed, with the change of the context in which a picture is reproduced.

Out of the different protective aspects of the right to pictures of oneself, though, the only one which is significant here is the one which concerns the production of certain photos and conveying them to a larger public. It is not a question of manipulated photos or falsifications by a change of context, which is the primary object of the protection. On the contrary, the complainant takes as a basis the fact that the photos which are the subject of the dispute (and the accompanying article, which is likewise relevant to their content) reproduce situations from her life accurately and in a manner in which observers who were present could have seen them. She merely does not wish these situations to be recorded in pictorial form and presented to a wider public, because in her opinion they belong to her private sphere.

(cc) In contrast to the right to pictures of oneself, the protection of the private sphere (which is also rooted in the general personality right) does not refer specially to pictures but is determined thematically and spatially. It includes on the one hand matters which are typically classified as "private" because of their information content, because public discussion or display of them is regarded as improper, or because revelation of them is felt to be embarrassing or produces adverse reactions from the surrounding world, as is for instance the case with soliloquies in diaries (reference omitted), confidential communications between married couples (reference omitted), the realm of sexuality (reference omitted), socially deviant behaviour (reference omitted) or illnesses (reference omitted). If there is no protection from the desire of others for knowledge here, soliloquies, uninhibited communications between close relations, sexual development or the obtaining of medical help would be interfered with or made impossible even though conduct protected by a basic right was involved.

On the other hand the protection extends to a spatial area in which the individual can sort himself out, unwind or even let go (reference omitted). It is true that this area also gives the opportunity to behave in a manner which is not intended for the public and for it to be seen or portrayed by outsiders would be embarrassing or disadvantageous for the person concerned. But in essence it is a question of a space in which the individual can be free from public observation and therefore from the self control which this imposes, but without him necessarily behaving differently there than in public. If such areas of retreat no longer existed, the individual could be psychologically overtaxed, because he would always have to be paying attention to the effect he has on others and whether he is behaving correctly. He would lack periods for being alone and adjusting which are necessary for the development of the personality and without which it would suffer lasting damage.

Such a need for protection also exists for people who are subject to special public attention because of their rank or reputation, their office or influence, or their capabilities or actions. A person who, whether willingly or unwillingly, has become a figure in public life does not thereby lose the right to a private sphere which remains concealed from the eyes of the public. This also applies for democratically elected office holders, who admittedly are publicly accountable for the conduct of their office (and must put up with public attention in this area), but not for their private lives in so far as these do not affect the conduct of their office.

The home is generally recognised as constituting such a protected sphere. But because of the reference to the development of the personality, the area of retreat cannot from the outset be limited to it. This is so because the functions which it serves are only fulfilled if it does not end at the walls of the house or the boundaries of the garden. The free development of the personality would be substantially hindered if the individual could only escape from public curiosity in his own house. Necessary relaxation from a public which is marked by the pressure of functions and the presence of the media is to be obtained in many cases only in the seclusion of a natural environment, perhaps in a holiday resort. The individual must therefore in principle be able also to move in open but secluded countryside or in places which are clearly secluded from the general public in a manner free from public observation. That applies in relation to photographic techniques which surmount the spatial seclusion without the person affected being able to notice this.

It cannot be determined in a general and abstract manner where the boundaries of the protected private sphere run outside the house. They can only be determined on the basis of the nature of the place to which the person affected goes. The decisive factor is whether the individual finds or creates a situation in which he may reasonably (and therefore in a manner recognisable to third parties) proceed on the basis that he is not exposed to the eyes of the public.

Whether the prerequisites for seclusion are fulfilled can only be assessed in the situation in question. The individual can in one and the same place justifiably feel himself to be unobserved at times and not at other times. Being in an enclosed area also definitely does not always equate with seclusion. As the question is whether the individual may reasonably expect to be unobserved or whether he has gone to places where he will be in the public eye, seclusion, which is the prerequisite for protection of the private sphere outside one's own home, may also be lacking in enclosed areas.

Places in which the individual finds himself amongst many people lack from the outset the prerequisites for private sphere protection in the sense of Article 2 para. 1 in combination with Article 1 para. 1 of the Basic Law. They cannot fulfil the need for retreat and therefore do not warrant the basic right protection, which this need serves on the grounds of development of the personality. The individual also cannot define such places as part of his private sphere by, for instance, conduct, which would typically not be exhibited publicly. It is not his conduct, either alone or with others, which constitutes the private sphere, but the objective facts about the locality at the time in question. If he therefore behaves as if he was not being observed, in places which do not have the characteristics of seclusion, he will himself remove the need for protection for types of behaviour which do not in themselves concern the public.

The protection of the private sphere from public attention also does not apply when the individual himself indicates his agreement with certain matters, which usually count as private, being made public, for instance by concluding exclusive contracts about reporting on his private sphere. The protection of the private sphere in constitutional law under Article 2 para. 1 in combination with Article 1 para. 1 of the Basic Law is not guaranteed in the interests of a commercialisation of the personality. Certainly no-one is prevented from such exploiting of private areas. But he cannot simultaneously appeal for the protection of the private sphere, which is concealed from the public. The expectation that the outside world will not, or will only to a limited extent, take note of matters or types of behaviour in an area which has the function of a retreat must therefore be expressed in a manner which is consistent and covers situations comprehensively. That also applies for the case where the decision to allow or to accept the reporting of certain events relating to one's own private sphere is made retrospective.

(dd) The Federal Constitutional Court has not yet decided what the protection of the private sphere means for family relationships between parents and children. But it is recognised that children need special protection because they must first develop into autonomous persons (references omitted). This need for protection also exists in view of the dangers resulting from the interest of the media and users of the media in portrayal of children. This can disturb the development of their personalities more severely than those of adults. The area in which children feel themselves free from public observation and may develop must therefore be more comprehensively protected than that of adult persons.

Parents are primarily responsible for the development of the personalities of children. Insofar as upbringing depends on undisturbed relationships with children, the special basic right protection of children does not merely have a reflexive effect in favour of the father and the mother (references omitted). Instead specifically parental turning attention to the children falls in principle within the protective area of Article 2 para. 1 in combination with Article 1 para. 1 of the Basic Law. The protective content of the general right of personality is then strengthened by Article 6 paras. 1 and 2 of the Basic Law which puts the state under a duty to secure those conditions of life for children which are necessary for their healthy development, and to which, in particular, parental care belongs (references omitted).

How the strengthening of protection of the personality by Article 6 of the Basic Law should take effect in detail cannot be generally and abstractly determined. Certainly there will as a rule be no need for protection if parents deliberately enter the public arena with their children, for instance by participating together in public events or even taking a position in the centre of such events. In this respect they lay themselves open to the conditions of public appearances. In other respects the protection of the general right of personality can also however apply in principle in favour of specific parent-child relationships where the prerequisites for local seclusion are absent.

2. The decisions under challenge interfere with the complainant's general right of personality. As the pictures enjoy the protection of this basic right, the judicial finding that they may be published against her will curtails the protection which she can claim the courts should respect even in private law disputes (see BVerfGE 7, 198 [207]).

II.

The judgments under challenge do not completely fulfil the requirements of Article 2 para. 1 in combination with Article 1 para. 1 of the Basic Law.

1. The provisions of §§ 22 and 23 of the KUG on which the civil courts have based their decisions are certainly reconcilable with the Basic Law.

According to Article 2 para. 1 of the Basic Law, the general right of personality is only guaranteed within the framework of the constitutional order. The provisions about the publication of photographs of persons in §§ 22 and 23 of the KUG are included in this. The regime goes back to a scandal (photographs of Bismarck on his deathbed [reference omitted]) and the ensuing legal and political debate (reference omitted) and seeks to establish an appropriate balance between regard for the personality and the interests of the general public in information (reference omitted).

According to § 22 sentence 1 of the KUG, pictures may only be disseminated or publicly displayed with the consent of the person portrayed. § 23 (1) of the KUG exempts, amongst other things, pictures from the realm of contemporary history (no. 1) from this principle. However, according to § 23 (2) of the KUG, this does not apply for a dissemination by which a justified interest of the person portrayed is violated. By this graduated concept of protection, the regime takes sufficient account of the need for protection of the person portrayed as well as of the public's wishes for information and the interests of the media who satisfy these wishes. That has already been established by the Federal Constitutional Court (reference omitted).

The view of the defendant that the regime contravenes the freedom of the press, because it amounts to a ban with a proviso for permission, gives no cause to assess the matter differently. There is no such ban, simply because the norms merely balance different legally protected interests of private persons. The regime here does not give a one-sided preference to protection of the personality. Admittedly it takes account primarily of the need for protection of the person portrayed at the first and third stages (§ 22 sentence 1 and § 23 (2) of the KUG). But the interests of press freedom (and the freedom to form opinions which lies behind this) come into play sufficiently at the second stage (§ 23 (1) of the KUG). Likewise it offers with its open formulations sufficient room for an interpretation and application which is in accordance with the basic rights.

2. The interpretation and application of the provisions do not however satisfy the requirements of the basic requirements in every respect.

(a) The interpretation and application of provisions of the civil law which are in accordance with the constitution is a matter for the civil courts. They must however, in this connection, have regard to the meaning and scope of the basic rights affected by their decisions, in order that the significance of those rights in prescribing values is preserved even at the level of application of the law (see BVerfGE 7, 198; constant case law). For this purpose a balancing is necessary between the conflicting protective interests under the basic rights. This is to be undertaken within the framework of the features of the civil law provisions which are capable of being interpreted and has to take into consideration the special circumstances of the case (references omitted). But as the legal dispute remains, in spite of the basic right influence, a private law one, and finds its solution in private law (interpreted as guided by the basic rights) the Federal Constitutional Court is limited to examining whether the civil courts have had sufficient regard to the basic right influence (reference omitted). On the other hand, it is not the business of the Federal Constitutional Court to dictate to the civil courts how they have to decide the case in question in its outcome (reference omitted).

A violation of the basic rights will only lead to objection to the decisions under challenge if the fact that basic rights were to be complied with in interpreting and applying provisions of private law which were in conformity with the Constitution has been overlooked; or if the protected area of the basic rights to be complied with has been determined incorrectly or imperfectly or their weight has been incorrectly assessed so that the balancing of the legal positions on both sides within the framework of the private law regime suffers as a result (references omitted) and the decision is based on this mistake.

(b) In the present case, not only is the general right of personality but also the freedom of the press guaranteed in Article 5 para. 1 sentence 2 of the Basic law (which is likewise affected by these provisions) to be taken into consideration in interpreting and applying §§ 22 and 23 of the KUG.

In the centre of the basic right guarantee of freedom of the press is the right freely to determine the type, orientation, content and form of a publication (references omitted). Included in this is the decision whether and how a publication is to be illustrated. The protection is not limited to certain subjects for illustration. It also includes the portrayal of persons. The protection does not depend on the particular nature or the level of the publication or of the report in detail (references omitted). Every difference of this kind would amount in the end to assessment and control by state authorities which would contradict the essence of this basic right (reference omitted).

Press freedom serves the free, individual and public formation of opinion (reference omitted). This can only succeed under conditions of free reporting for which certain objects or methods of presentation are neither prescribed nor excluded. In particular, formation of opinion is not limited to the political realm. It is true that it is of special importance there in the interest of a functioning democracy. Yet the political formation of opinion is embedded in a comprehensive multiply interlinked communication process which cannot be split into relevant or irrelevant zones either from the point of view of personal development or from that of democratic government (reference omitted). The press must be able to decide according to journalistic criteria what it considers to be worthy of the public interest and what it does not.

The fact that the press has to fulfil a function of forming opinion does not exclude entertainment from the constitutional functional guarantee. Formation of opinion and entertainment are not antitheses. Even contributions of an entertaining kind can form opinions. They can in certain circumstances stimulate or influence the formation of opinion even more permanently than exclusively factual information. In addition a growing tendency can be observed in the media of removing the division between information and entertainment in relation to a publication as a whole as well as in the individual contributions and to disseminate information in an entertaining form or to mix it with entertainment ("infotainment"). Many readers consequently obtain the information which appears to them to be important or interesting from entertaining contributions (reference omitted).

But the reference to freedom of formation of opinion cannot be denied from the outset even to mere entertainment. It would be unbalanced to assume that entertainment merely satisfies the wish for diversion, relaxation, flight from reality and distraction. It can also convey images of reality and makes available subjects for conversation. Ongoing discussions and unifying events which refer to attitudes to life, stances about values and behaviour patterns can be linked into this. Entertainment in this respect fulfils important social functions (references omitted). Entertainment in the press, measured by the protective purpose of freedom of the press, is therefore not insignificant or even worthless and is also included in the basic right protection (reference omitted).

This also applies to news reports about people. Personalisation forms an important journalistic means for arousing attention. It awakens interest in problems in many cases for the first time, and creates the wish for factual information. Participation in events and situations is also mostly communicated by personalisation. Besides this, prominent people stand for certain value concepts and stances about life. They therefore provide many people with a means of orientation in relation to their plans for their own lives. They become crystallisation points for agreement or disapproval and fulfil the functions of a model or a contrast. The public interest in the most varied aspects of such persons' lives is based on this.

For persons in political life, such an interest on the part of the public has always been recognised as legitimate from the point of view of democratic transparency and control. It cannot however in principle be disputed for other people in public life. In this respect, description of people which is not confined to certain functions or events is in line with the tasks of the press and therefore likewise falls within the protected area of press freedom. Balancing against the conflicting rights of personality is needed to determine whether there is a serious and relevant discussion of questions which substantially concern the public or merely dissemination of private matters which only satisfy curiosity (reference omitted).

(c) The judgement of the Bundesgerichtshof overwhelmingly satisfies constitutional law examination in the end result.

(aa) There is no objection in constitutional law to the fact that the Bundesgerichtshof has determined the prerequisites of the definition in § 23 (1) no. 1 of the KUG according to the standard of the general public's interest in information; and on this basis has regarded publication of pictures of the complainant even outside her representative function in the principality of Monaco as permissible.

§ 23 (1) no. 1 of the KUG exempts the publication of pictures of people from the area of contemporary history from the requirement of consent in § 22 of the KUG. The provision according to its legislative intention (reference omitted) and according to the sense and purpose of its regime takes into consideration the general public's interest in information and the freedom of press. The interests of the public are therefore to be observed in the interpretation of the features of this definition. This is because pictures of people who are not important in terms of contemporary history may only be made freely available to the public, with the consent of the persons affected. The further feature contained in the definition in § 23 (2) of the KUG of the "justified interest", which is open to the influence of the basic right, only refers from the outset to persons of importance in terms of contemporary history and cannot consequently sufficiently uphold the interests of press freedom if these interests have been left out of consideration previously by the delimitation of that group of persons.

The concept of contemporary history in § 23 (1) no. 1 of the KUG does not, according to the standard of a judicial determination as to its content, only encompass for instance events of historical or political importance, but is determined by the interest of the public in information (reference omitted). This takes account of the meaning and scope of freedom of the press without cutting down disproportionately on protection of the personality. It is part of the core of freedom of the press and free formation of opinion that the press possesses sufficient leeway within the statutory boundaries within which to decide, according to its journalistic criteria, what the public interest claims; and that it will emerge in the process of formation of opinion what a matter of public interest is. Contributions in the form of entertainment are not, as has been explained, excepted from this.

There are further no grounds for objection to the fact that the Bundesgerichtshof also allocates to the "area of contemporary history" in accordance with § 23 (1) no. 1 of the KUG pictures of persons who have not attracted the public interest to themselves by a certain isolated event of contemporary history but who attract general public attention on the basis of their status and importance, independently of individual events. In this connection, the increased importance which applies to photographic reporting today, in comparison to the time when the Artistic Copyright Act was enacted, is significant. The concept of an "absolute person of contemporary history", which is usually regarded as related in this connection by the case law and the literature, admittedly does not necessarily arise either from statute law or from the Constitution. It is understood by the Oberlandesgericht and the Bundesgerichtshof as shorthand for persons whose image the public finds worthy of attention because of the person portrayed. The concept is not however open to objection from the point of view of constitutional law as long as there is a balancing related to the individual case between the public's interest in information and the justified interests of the person portrayed.

The general right of personality does not require limitation of publications not needing consent to pictures which show persons of importance in the context of contemporary history exercising the function which they fulfil in society. A frequent characteristic of the public interest which such persons claim is that it does not only hold good for the exercise of the function in the narrower sense. Instead it can, because of the distinctive function and the effect which this has, extend to information about how these persons generally behave in public, and therefore outside their respective functions. The public has a justified interest in learning if such persons, who are often regarded as idols or examples, bring their functional and personal behaviour convincingly into line.

A limitation of publication of images to the function of a person of importance in contemporary history would on the other hand not take sufficient account of the public interest which such people justifiably arouse. It would also encourage a selective presentation which would prevent the public from making assessments which are necessary in respect of persons of socio-political life because of their role function as models and their influence. This does not open up to the press unlimited access to pictures of persons of contemporary history. Instead § 23 (2) of the KUG gives the courts sufficient opportunity to put into effect the protective requirements of Article 2 para. 1 in combination with Article 1 para. 1 of the Basic Law (reference omitted).

(bb) In principle, the criteria which the Bundesgerichtshof has developed in interpretation of the feature of "justified interest" in the definition in § 23 (2) of the KUG are not open to objection in constitutional law.

According to the judgment under challenge, the private sphere which deserves protection (which the so-called absolute person of contemporary history is also entitled to) presupposes a secluded space into which someone has withdrawn in order to be on his own there in a manner recognisable to others; and in which, trusting in this seclusion, he behaves in a way in which he would not when in the public eye. The Bundesgerichtshof assumes a violation of §§ 22 and 23 of the KUG if pictures are published which have been taken of the person affected in such a situation secretly or by using surprise tactics.

The criterion of spatial seclusion takes account on the one hand of the purpose of the general right of personality of securing for the individual a sphere outside his own home in which he knows he will not to be under continual public observation. He does not therefore have to control his behaviour in view of this observation, but has the opportunity to relax and come to himself. On the other hand it does not restrict the freedom of the press excessively, because it does not completely remove the everyday and private life of persons of contemporary history from photographic reporting, but only makes it accessible for portrayal where it takes place in public. In a case of paramount public interest in receiving information, freedom of the press can even take precedence over the protection of the private sphere, according to this case law (references omitted).

The Bundesgerichtshof might also regard the behaviour of the individual in a certain situation as having the indicative effect that he obviously finds himself in a sphere of seclusion. It is true that protection from portrayal in this sphere does not only start when the person affected behaves in a way in which he would not when in the public eye. The spatial seclusion only fulfils its protective function for the development of the personality when it secures for the individual a place for relaxation regardless of his behaviour at the time, in which he does not have continually to expect the presence of photographers and cameramen. But it does not matter in the present case because according to the findings on which the Bundesgerichtshof based its decision, the first condition for protection of the private sphere is absent.

Finally there are no grounds for objection in constitutional law to the fact that, in the balancing exercise between the public interest in information and protection of the private sphere, importance is attached to the method of obtaining information (reference omitted). There are doubts however about whether the private sphere outside the home can only be violated by photography by secrecy or surprise. In the light of the function which this sphere should fulfil from a constitutional point of view and in the light of the fact that it often cannot be seen from a picture whether it has been taken secretly or by surprise, an impermissible invasion of the private sphere can be found even when these characteristics are not present. As the Bundesgerichtshof has however already denied that there was a sphere of seclusion for the disputed photographs, these doubts do not affect the outcome of its decision in this respect.

(cc) The constitutional law requirements are not however fulfilled insofar as the decisions challenged have paid no attention to the fact that the complainant's protected position in relation to her right of personality is strengthened by Article 6 of the Basic Law in the case of family contact with her children.

(dd) The following details result from this for the different photographs:

The decision of the Bundesgerichtshof in relation to those photographs which show the complainant on her way to the market, with a bodyguard at the market and with a companion in a well patronised café gives no cause for objection by the Constitutional Court. In the first two cases it is a question of places visited by the general public, which are not secluded. In the third case it is admittedly a question of an area which is spatially enclosed; but it is one in which the complainant is under the eyes of the members of the public who are present. For this reason the Bundesgerichtshof did not dispute the prohibition on dissemination of photos from the garden café which are admittedly a subject of the decisions challenged, but not of the constitutional complaint. The place which the complainant took there with her companion showed all the characteristics of seclusion. The fact that the photographs have obviously been taken from a great distance additionally points to the fact that the complainant might assume she was not exposed to the eyes of the public.

The decision is also not open to objection insofar as it concerns the photos in which the complainant is shown alone when riding and cycling. The Bundesgerichtshof on the basis of its view of the matter likewise attributed them not to the sphere of local seclusion but to the public sphere. That is not open to objection in constitutional law. The complainant herself counts the photographs as belonging to the secluded private sphere only because she let her wish be known to be alone. But according to the criteria which have been explained, it does not merely depend on her will.

On the other hand, the three photos in which the complainant is shown together with her children call for a renewed scrutiny from the constitutional law viewpoints which have been set out above. It cannot be ruled out that scrutiny on the basis of these standards will lead to another result in relation to individual photos or all of them. In this respect the judgment of the Bundesgerichtshof is to be quashed and the case referred back to it for a new decision.

(d) As to the judgments of the Landgericht and the Oberlandesgericht which have been challenged, a violation of the basic right follows from the fact that they have limited the private sphere protected by Article 2 para. 1 in combination with Article 1 para. 1 of the Basic Law—admittedly in harmony with the case law at the time—to the area of the home. But it is not necessary to quash the decisions because the violation has been cured in this respect by the Bundesgerichtshof and the matter is in other respects been referred back to it.

Case 48

BUNDESVERFASSUNGSGERICHT (FIRST DIVISION) 24 MARCH 1998
BVerfGE 97, 391 = NJW 1998, 2889 = JZ 1998, 1114

Facts

The complainant, who is now 41, is no longer capable of earning, and still bears her maiden name. She alleged first to friends in 1973, and later in 1986 to doctors who were treating her for, amongst other things, compulsive gambling, that her father had sexually abused her. She first wrote to her father about this in March 1987, claiming he had driven her to addiction. She also told the Youth Welfare Department, in order to protect her niece who was sometimes looked after by him. In 1990 she wrote to her father to say she forgave him. But she spoke about the abuse in a television broadcast in January 1991 and in a later programme. She also offered to a magazine an article about claims for compensation for psychological harm consequent on sexual abuse. Her father demanded that she should stop accusing him to others of sexual abuse, but she refused to comply. He then started a claim for an injunction alleging he had never sexually abused her; and that the real reason for the accusations was his refusal to pay for her gambling debts. The Landgericht found that he had sexually abused her regularly from the age of eight onwards; and perhaps from the age of twelve onwards by having sexual intercourse with her. It rejected his claim, on the basis that injunctions could only be used to prevent statements injurious to honour if they were untrue. When he appealed, the Oberlandesgericht ordered her not to make statements, using his name or her name, to the effect that he had sexually abused her. It held that regardless of the truth of the statements, such an order could be made under §§ 1004 and 823 para. 1 BGB because of the violation of his right of personality. He could not prevent her allegations to state or judicial authorities that he had sexually abused her where she had a justified interest in making these allegations. But he did not have to put up with being denounced by name in public.

The constitutional complaint by the complainant against this judgment was successful.

Reasons

B. The constitutional complaint is well founded. The judgment of the Oberlandesgericht violates Article 5 (1) and Article 2 (1) in combination with Article 1 (1) GG.

I. These basic rights are affected by the decision which is being challenged.

1. The use of one's own name in connection with a statement comes within the protection of freedom of opinion.

The basic right of freedom of opinion protects statements of opinion of all kinds and assertions of fact as well as other forms of statement, at any rate if they are a prerequisite for the formation of opinions [references omitted]. The use of one's own name in connection with a statement is neither a form of independent statement nor a component of the statement in the narrow sense. Its content stands alone. But this does not mean that the giving of a name falls outside the protective area of the basic right. It is of substantial importance for the statement itself as well as for the individual and public process of opinion formation to which it contributes.

Freedom to state opinions is "the most direct expression of the human personality in society" (BVerfGE 7, 198 [208]). The name of the originator gives the connection between the person and the statement is made in a recognisable way. If the person making the statement adds his own name [to his statement], he shows that he wants to make the statement known as his personal opinion or description and is ready to vouch for it; and in the case of an assertion of facts, to be answerable personally for its truth. It is precisely in relation to those statements with which the speaker very fully identifies himself or which present his own story that the use of a name is one of the prerequisites of the communication of the sense of the statement.

Besides this the name of the person making the statement can contain messages which go beyond the simple content of the statement. Thus it is possible, for instance, that the personal description of oppressive experiences will encourage others affected to break their silence. Such a message could not be communicated in the same way without the use of one's own name and the associated disclosure of personal involvement. That applies especially if communication of certain events is subject to a taboo. Personal confession to the public can help in this case to break through the attribution of guilt often associated with social taboos.

However, the purpose of a statement is not fulfilled in making known personal views or communications. Statements are directed at others and as a rule are destined to have an effect on them in forming opinions or motivating to action. Article 5 (1) sentence 1 GG therefore does not only protect statements in the dimension of their dissemination but also in the dimension of their effect (see BVerfGE 7, 198 [210]). Freedom of opinion includes the right of the person making the statement to choose for his statement those forms and circumstances which ensure the greatest possible effect for it [reference omitted]. But the effect of a statement on third parties depends substantially on whether its originator is identifiable or not. Anonymous statements frequently lack that degree of authenticity and credibility that gives them the desired influence or causes a reaction.

Finally the effect of a statement is not limited to its reception and assimilation by third parties. Just as the statement will usually be connected with preceding communications, so it will in turn trigger further communications. In striving to guarantee free formation of opinions by the individual and the public Article 5 (1) GG is therefore not limited to protecting the individual statement. It also ensures the preconditions for the establishment and maintenance of the communication process in which every statement is embedded [reference omitted]. The use of a name is important for this likewise because it is only such use that makes it possible for participants in the communication process to refer to one another or make contact with each other.

2. The use of one's own name also falls into the protective area of the general right of personality arising from Article 2 (1) in combination with Article 1 (1) GG.

The name of a human being does not only have the function of creating order and differentiation. It is also the expression of identity and individuality. Therefore the individual can require the legal order to respect and protect his name. This protection has so far only become relevant in constitutional case law in relation to change of name on marriage as prescribed by the state [references omitted]. But it is also related to the wish not to use a name (which is not as such in dispute) in certain circumstances or to replace it by a pseudonym. As a name is an expression of identity and individuality it cannot be changed at will. It accompanies the life history of the person who bears it. This is recognisable as connected with [the concept of] a name. To give up the use of one's name does not therefore leave one's personality unaffected.

This also applies to the use of a name in connection with a statement. Statements do not fulfil their purpose in the passing on of a certain communication content. They are at the same time the expression of the personality of the person making the statement. By his statements he presents himself to third parties as a person. Other people identify him with them. On the basis of the use of a name third parties can not only attribute statements to their originator but also categorise him by the type of personality that they make him out to be. At the same time they get the opportunity to assess the person who stands behind the statement alongside its contents. If someone is obliged to refrain from using his name in connection with statements which he sees as personal and which he thinks it important to attribute to himself, such an obligation is to be measured against Article 2 (1) in combination with Article 1 (1) GG.

3. On the other hand, freedom of the press is not relevant. The question of the permissibility of a particular statement is to be judged in accordance with Article 5 (1) GG, independently of whether it is made or is to be made through a medium which enjoys the protection of press freedom. This will only come into play where it is something more than individual statements of opinion—where the press is important for the formation of individual and public opinion [references omitted]. That is lacking here.

4. Freedom of opinion and the right of personality have been limited by the complainant's obligation not to use her name when she speaks in public about sexual abuse by her father. The fact that the statement may incidentally be disseminated further in public does not change anything in view of the inclusion of the use of the name in the protective area of both basic rights.

II. The decision under challenge is not reconcilable with the basic right of freedom of opinion and the general right of personality.

1. Both basic rights are certainly subject to statutory limits. Freedom of opinion is, according to Article 5 (2) GG only guaranteed within the framework of the general laws, the statutory provisions for the protection of the young and the right to personal honour. Development of the personality is according to Article 2 (1) GG confined within the boundaries of the constitutional order. This is to be understood as including all legal norms that are formally and materially in harmony with the Basic Law [reference omitted]. That is the case with the provisions of §§ 823 and 1004 of the BGB on which the Oberlandesgericht based the judgment under challenge.

2. But their application does not comply with the requirements of the basic rights.

(a) The interpretation and application of the civil law provisions are just as much a matter for the civil courts as the establishment of the facts and the assessment of the evidence. But if, during the course of the application of norms of civil law which are unobjectionable in constitutional law, positions protected by the basic rights are affected, the civil courts must take account of the importance and scope of the basic *rights*. This is to guarantee their importance in setting values at the level of application of the law as well (see BVerfGE 7, 198 [205 ff.; constant case law). That requires as a rule a balancing operation, to be undertaken within the framework of the features of the statutory definition, between [two aspects of the matter]. On the one hand there is the significance in the actual case of the basic right which has been limited for the person entitled to it as well as the extent of the interference with it to which he has to submit. On the other hand there is the significance of the legal interest protected by the statute which is being applied and the severity of the interference with it by the exercise of the basic right. In this connection, the courts must have sufficient regard to both positions and bring them into a relationship that takes appropriate account of them. There will, in particular, be a violation of a basic right which the Federal Constitutional Court has to correct if the civil court has not considered the influence of the basic right at all or has evaluated it inappropriately and the decision is based on a misunderstanding of the influence of the basic right [reference omitted].

(b) In this connection, on the complainant's side it must above all be taken into account, from the point of view of freedom of opinion and the right of personality, that the statement in dispute has an accentuated relationship with the personality. The prohibition on giving of [the complainant's] name would to a large extent cause it to lose the effect hoped for in the process of communication.

This statement, which the complainant is only allowed to make in public if she does not use her name, does not relate to some subject with which she only has a distant connection, but concerns her highly personal life story. On the basis of the facts as established by the civil courts, from which the Federal Constitutional Court has to proceed, it relates to an extremely serious experience that had a decisive influence on her physical and emotional development. Every person has the freedom to decide whether he turns to others or to the public with experiences of this kind. If he decides to do so, the prohibition on describing a story of the most personal kind in a personalised form contains as a rule a drastic interference with opportunities for communication and with development of the personality.

Nothing is changed by the circumstance that the judgment under challenge does not prevent the complainant from speaking about the abuse under her own name in the context of private contacts or therapeutic treatment. This is because she is still prevented from widening the radius of those with whom she can communicate beyond the circle of her personal acquaintances or persons professionally concerned with the development of her personality. The complainant can no longer appear before the public as an identifiable person, vouch for her story with her own name and meet directly any reactions of third parties to it.

The effect of her story on persons in a similar situation or a public disturbed by the problem of sexual abuse of children is also reduced because there is a danger of the story failing to acquire the credibility and authenticity generally associated with the use of a name. The encouragement which public analysis of one's own story can have for people in a similar situation is also reduced. Likewise feedback to the complainant who wants a response is made more difficult by the prohibition on the use of her name. Furthermore she loses the opportunity to get over her past experiences with the help of third persons who have only become aware of her through the statement.

It is clear that this experience which has had a decisive effect on the complainant and which she wants to speak about publicly is indissolubly linked with the person of her father. This has to be considered; but it has to be borne in mind that the complainant is reporting about the plaintiff in the initial proceedings from the perspective of the victim of his actions. The statement cannot therefore be understood just as an exposure of the father. It must also be seen in context of overcoming her status of a victim. This victim status (which the courts have found to be a necessary starting point) would be further reinforced if the victim were to be prevented from giving an account in a personalised form. In this respect her interest in making a statement is to be rated more highly than that of third persons or of the media who want to name the persons involved when they make statements about these kinds of events.

(c) On the side of the plaintiff in the initial proceedings weight must be given to his right of personality protected under the basic rights. §§ 823 and 1004 of the BGB give expression to this in civil law. It certainly does not give to the person entitled to it a claim only to be represented to the public in a manner which corresponds to his self-image or which is pleasant for him. It does however protect him against representations which distort or falsify as well as against representations which can substantially interfere with the development of his personality [reference omitted]. Personality interests must as a rule take second place to freedom of opinion if the disputed statement has as its subject facts which are to be regarded as true.

But this principle is not without exceptions. In particular true stories can injure the right of personality of the person affected if the consequences of the representation are serious for the development of the personality and the need for protection outweighs the interest in the [making the] statement. Thus the Federal Constitutional Court in the Lebach judgment (BVerfGE 35, 202 = NJW 1973, 1226) granted personality interests priority over broadcasting freedom, because the transmission of a docudrama about a sensational crime was at a point very close in time to the release of one of the perpetrators from imprisonment. The widespread impact and suggestive power of television would also have made the reintegration of the person affected into society substantially more difficult, if it did not entirely prevent it.

It is true that things are different here to the extent that it is a question not of a report by the media but by the victim. There is therefore no need to decide what the position would be if when the victim tells her story, the media expand this by their own reports from the perpetrator's background. Unlike the *Lebach* case, no independent danger for the plaintiff in the initial proceedings arises here from the point in time of the statement. Nor is it a question of documentation about his conduct identifying him, but merely of the possibility of a conclusion being drawn because he has the same name as the complainant.

Nevertheless, the consequences for the plaintiff in the initial proceedings are serious. This is associated with the accusation of sexual abuse of his own child, which is regarded as an especially abhorrent crime. Reports of conduct of this kind mostly lead to stigmatisation of the perpetrator. Stigmatisations [of this kind] can lead to withdrawal of social recognition and social isolation of and fundamental loss of assurance and self-devaluation by the person affected in numerous areas of his life. This is based on assessment and behaviour mechanisms which are social and therefore not solely attributable to the responsibility of the person affected. The free development of the personality is thereby permanently impeded; and this cannot be treated as due to the usual limits to development opportunities or the unfavourable reactions of others which one has to accept as the consequence of one's own decisions or forms of behaviour.

The protection which Article 2 (1) in combination with Article 1 (1) GG gives in this respect is not dependent on the statements about a person being untrue. It also applies if the statements are true and for this reason become a cause of a social exclusion and isolation. As the protection of the personality has as its goal the maintenance of the basic conditions of social relationships between the person entitled to the basic right and his environment [reference omitted] it is also independent of whether it is the victim himself or third persons who speak about the facts.

The protective effects of the general right of personality are not ruled out simply because the use of the complainant's name cannot from the outset, in her view, affect her father's rights. The protection of the personality does not only apply to the content of an assertion, but also to the consequences which the assertion has as information for others. Therefore it is a question of the information and the chances of identification which the addressees of the statement receive. The possibility that an assertion can be related to a certain person and that this person will be exposed to consequences from which the constitutional law right of personality grants protection does not therefore only exist if his name is mentioned but also if other details facilitate his identification.

On the other hand, the weight of the infringement of the basic right depends upon the breadth of the impact of the discriminatory consequences. This can work out differently according to the extent to which the person affected is known. It must further be considered whether the effects of the statement are limited because of the commonness of the name. If it is a widely used name, the effects of the statement only occur with those persons who know the speaker and his family and therefore can deduce the identity of the perpetrator from his public appearance under his own name. With a television appearance, the interference with the personality by the mention of the name decreases further, because in this case the conclusion is possible even without the mention of the name.

(d) These points of view which are to be taken into account in the context of the basic rights did not sufficiently influence consideration of the matter in the Oberlandesgericht.

The Oberlandesgericht has, in harmony with the civil law case law, considered the complainant's statement to have the effect of "pillorying" the plaintiff in the initial proceedings. This would have serious consequences for the development of his personality and therefore must only be accepted if weighty reasons on the opposite side argue for the publication of the assertion in a form which permitted his identification. There is no objection to this from a constitutional point of view.

However, the Oberlandesgericht did not have sufficient regard to the reasons which argue in favour of publication using the complainant's name. Its decision raises doubt as to whether it was conscious of the fact that the use of the complainant's name in connection with her statement falls under the protection of freedom of opinion and the general right of personality. In any case the complainant's interests protected by these basic rights have not entered sufficiently into the balancing operation. The court merely touched on the subject with the comment that a denunciation of the plaintiff in the initial proceedings could not be justified by the argument that the complainant as a victim was looking after supposed general information interests about the abuse of children in society because the use of a name was not as a rule necessary for this.

In particular there is here no consideration (taking account of the requirements of Article 5 (1) GG) of the functions which use of one's name for one's statements can have and which mean that the name cannot simply be left out or replaced. Thus the court has not considered the question—which is relevant also from the point of view of the right of personality—of whether and to what extent the complainant wants to overcome the experiences of abuse by presenting them to the public as her own experiences and under her own name.

Further, it did not discuss to what extent the adding of a name is needed for statements about the abuse to acquire the character of an authentic communication for the complainant as well as for the recipient of the statement. It did not consider whether the use of a name is needed in the given situation to communicate the contents of the statement to the recipients in the desired fashion and so that they obtain the opportunity of establishing contact with the complainant. The point of view, relevant in the context of formation of public opinion, that personifying the experience of sexual abuse can help to counteract a social taboo and encourage others affected to speak and act themselves, was also left out of consideration.

The Oberlandesgericht did not carry out the necessary evaluation because it did not adequately concretise those interests which are important from the point of view of freedom of opinion and the right of personality. The court did not address the fact that the using of one's own name for one's own statements is the part of freedom of expression of opinion which is close to the personality and an obligation to refrain from doing so therefore represents an especially intensive interference. It also did not take into account that sexual abuse of children is a question substantially affecting the public so that the interest of society in being informed from the perspective of the victim about such acts and their consequences increases the weight to be given to freedom of opinion.

On the other hand the court did not address the question of how great the danger of identification was on the basis of the name in the actual case, to what extent the consequences of an identification would affect him and whether he would have any opportunity to avoid these. This is relevant to the severity of the interference with those interests of the plaintiff in the initial proceedings which are protected by the basic rights.

(e) The judgment under challenge is founded on these defects. The Oberlandesgericht gave priority to protecting the plaintiff in the initial proceedings from social stigmatisation because it did not make a sufficient determination of the protected interests of the complainant and therefore did not adequately consider her basic right position. It cannot therefore be excluded that the court, if it had considered the requirements of the basic rights, would have made a decision, which was more in the complainant's favour.

Case 49

BUNDESGERICHTSHOF (SIXTH CIVIL SENATE) 29 JUNE 1999
NJW 1999, 2893 = VERSR 1999, 1250

Facts

The claimant, a representative of the House of Hanover and prince of Great Britain and Ireland, asks the defendant, a German publishing company, to refrain from publishing certain parts of a report about his divorce.

The marriage of the claimant was dissolved on the 10th September 1997 in public proceedings before the High Court of Justice in London. From the divorce papers which, according to English law, are usually available to the public and press, it appears that the claimant had admitted to having committed adultery with an unnamed woman. The English news agency Reuters reported on the divorce on the same day, giving the ground for the divorce. This news was published on the 11th September 1997 by the "Daily Mail" newspaper. On the 13 September 1997 a report about the divorce appeared in issue no 39/97 of the magazine "Das Neue" published by the defendant. The Article, in which several meetings by the claimant with Princess Caroline of Monaco were mentioned and which included two photographs of these, stated (making reference to a press agency) that family judge A had given as a ground for the divorce that the German prince had committed adultery with an unnamed woman.

The claimant feels that his right of personality has been violated by the publication by the defendant of the ground for the divorce. He has applied for an order that the defendant refrain from disseminating the statement, making reference to a press agency, that he has committed adultery with an unnamed woman.

The Landgericht allowed the claim. The Oberlandesgericht rejected the defendant's appeal. In the appeal in law (which is admissible) the defendant seeks the rejection of the claim.

Reasons

I.

The appeal court, applying the (German) law of the place of commission of the act, adjudges the part of the publication objected to by the claim to be unlawful and therefore, on appropriate application of §§ 823 para 1 and 1004 of the BGB, an interference by the defendant in the claimant's general right of personality from which the defendant must refrain. The mention of adultery as the ground for divorce would give the impression to the average reader that such adultery had actually taken place. This statement was highly prejudicial to the claimant. In the required balancing of the claimant's right of personality with the public's justified interest in information, the claimant's interest in the protection of his private sphere prevailed. The public's interest in the claimant, which arose in view of the fact that he was the great-grandson of the last German Kaiser (and in substance from the significance and position of his ancestors and relations) could not justify the giving of the ground for the divorce. The position did not have to be assessed differently either because of the association of the claimant with Princess Caroline of Monaco nor because the dissolution of the claimant's marriage took place at a public hearing, adultery was expressly named then as a ground for divorce, and the divorce papers could be seen by third parties under English law. (The latter point is inconsistent with the standards applying to German courts) . . .

II.

The judgment of the appeal court does not stand up to legal scrutiny.

1. The considerations which the appeal court uses with reference to the fundamentals of its decision are admittedly not open to objection.

(a) . . .

(b) . . .

(c) The appeal court further thought it necessary to decide on the claim on the basis of balancing the claimant's general right of personality (protected in constitutional law in accordance with Article 2 para. 1 in combination with Article 1 para. 1 of the Basic Law) against the defendant's right to freedom of speech and freedom of the press (which likewise enjoys constitutional rank in accordance with Article 5 para. 1 of the Basic Law) (on the requirement for such a balancing, see [references omitted]). There are no legal objections to this approach. Such a balancing cannot be dispensed with here on the ground that an interference by the defendant with the claimant's right of personality is lacking. It is true that, as stated above, a report had already lawfully been made by an English news agency and an English newspaper about the ground for the claimant's divorce. But this circumstance cannot remove from the publication of it by the defendant for the first time in Germany the character of an interference. A balancing of interests is therefore correctly considered by both parties to be required.

(d) The approach of the appeal court is also to be taken as a starting point in relation to the circumstances to be included in the balancing exercise.

(aa) First, the content of the statement in the defendant's news report as interpreted by the appeal court is not open to objection. Assessing the announcement that the English judge had given the claimant's adultery as the ground for the divorce as meaning that such adultery had in fact taken place, should therefore also be a basis for the appeal in law proceedings. But it is not necessary to examine the additional claim of the reply to the appeal in law that the photo accompanying the news report with the caption "Ernst August and Caroline kiss each other" had also amounted to an innuendo by the defendant that the claimant had committed adultery with Princess Caroline of Monaco. This is because the claimant does not ask the defendant to refrain from a statement to this effect.

(bb) The appeal court, without any error of law, further proceeds on the basis that the claimant is affected in his private sphere by the defendant's publication. This categorisation which means that the claimant's intimate sphere (which as such would enjoy absolute protection) is not affected (references omitted) has its legal basis in the fact that the defendant's news report only announced the fact of the adultery but not details about it (references omitted).

2. However, the appeal court cannot to be followed in how it weights the circumstances to be included in the balancing exercise and in the priority it derives from this for the claimant's right of personality.

(a) It was argued (to the defendant's disadvantage) that the announcement about the claimant's adultery had no actual interest for the public, even though he belonged to the German and British nobility and was the great-grandson of the last Kaiser. This is based on a legally incorrect view.

(aa) In the context of this qualification, the appeal court failed to pay sufficient attention to the fact that it is not only "valuable" items of information given by the press which fall within the freedom of the press in Article 5 para. 1 sentence 2 of the Basic Law. This freedom in principle also exists in favour of the tabloid and sensational press and thereby also for news which primarily satisfies the need of a more or less broad readership for superficial entertainment (references omitted).

(bb) In the case in question, there is the additional fact that the claimant attracts the attention of a broad readership not only because of his ancestry but also as companion of Princess Caroline of Monaco, who is continually in the glare of publicity (reference omitted). Even if the interest of this readership may not be described as particularly valuable, contrary to the view of the appeal court the need for its satisfaction cannot be excluded from the protected area of press freedom (which is simply constitutive for the free democratic order (reference omitted)) as unjustified. Instead, it is precisely in the case of the press that the need for limiting the freedom of news reporting must be convincingly proved (reference omitted).

(b) Further, much too little weight has, to the defendant's disadvantage, been given by the appeal court to the fact that the announcement about the claimant's adultery, even with the content which the court of appeal ascribes to it, involved the assertion of a true fact. Nor does the reply to the appeal in law question this. It is true that a balancing of the basic rights positions on both sides is still required in principle for a true statement (reference omitted); such a statement however must, even if it is disadvantageous for the person affected, be more readily accepted (references omitted). This is particularly the case when it does not represent an especially intensive interference with the right of personality, like the mere general announcement of a formal ground for divorce in the case in question.

(c) Finally the appeal court did not sufficiently consider the fact that the news about the dissolution of the claimants' marriage, with the giving of adultery as the ground for the divorce, had been published already by the news agency Reuters and the "Daily Mail" newspaper before publication by the defendant. It had thereby become known already to a large number of persons, who could then pass it on to others. This further reduces the gravity of the defendant's interference with the claimant's private sphere to a considerable extent (reference omitted).

3. Following all this, the result of the balancing of the basic rights positions of the parties by the appeal court cannot be left to stand. As the facts to be assessed are established, a further elucidation of the matter is therefore not necessary and the senate can finally decide itself on the basis of its own balancing exercise. In this connection it reaches the conclusion, in the light of the lesser weight of the interference with the claimant's right of personality stated under no. 2, as against the freedom of speech and freedom of the press claimed by the defendant, that the announcement by the defendant about the claimant's adultery as a ground for divorce does not appear to be unlawful and therefore must be accepted by the claimant. His claim must therefore be rejected.

Notes to Cases 39–49

1. The first of these cases marks a real turning point in German tort law by creating the new all-embracing right of personality and privacy (*cf.* Larenz/Canaris, II 2, § 80 I 3*a*, p. 492). Some writers have even described it as the most important case in German tort law during this century. It is derived from a somewhat strained—but in the event successful—interpretation of the Constitution of Bonn of 1949 the relevant provisions of which were reproduced towards the end of chapter one, above. The linking of the development of the civil law with the Constitution has already been noted. Here suffice it to mention two further points of interest. First, it reveals that both in Germany and in the United States the constitutional background has had a marked but different influence on the law of defamation and privacy. Thus, whereas in Germany this has often led to a greater protection of privacy, in America the emphasis on freedom of speech has often had the reverse effect. We shall return to this important point later on. Secondly, the interaction of public and private law has been maintained through these years, the Constitutional Court often being called to decide disputes which involved privacy questions. Thus, in BVerfGE 34, 269 (Case 38, above) it was called upon to consider the constitutionality of the award of monetary compensation in cases of infringement of this new right (see above, chapter 2, section A.2(*e*)(iv)); BVerfGE 35, 202, is reproduced above as case 42. Two further decisions of the Constitutional Court can also be found above as cases 47 and 48.) For other instances see BVerfGE 54, 129; BVerfGE 54, 148; BVerfGE 54, 208; BVerfG NJW 2001, 2957 etc.

2. At the risk of becoming repetitive one must stress that these judgments, and indeed the constitutional provisions mentioned above, can only be fully understood if one bears in mind the utter contempt shown towards human dignity by the Nazi regime. It was ironical therefore that the breakthrough decision of 1954 was indirectly connected with one of its former sympathisers. (BVerfGE 7, 198 and BVerfGE 30, 173 also involved former Nazis.) For the mysterious Dr S of that judgment was Dr H H G Schacht, an undoubtedly distinguished economist and financier who

played an important role in the restoration of a stable currency after the devastating German inflation of 1923. From 1923 to 1930 he served as president of the Reichsbank and became a supporter
of the Nazi party, even urging the ageing President Hindenburg to appoint Hitler as Reichs
Chancellor (which, eventually, happened in 1933). When Hitler came to power, Schacht played a
leading role in the rearmament programme, but from 1938/9 onwards he was urging Hitler to
reduce expenditure for armaments as the only way to balance the budget and reduce inflation which
had begun to rise again. In July 1944 he was confined to a concentration camp until the end of the
war and then he was one of the principal accused at the first Nuremberg trial. He was acquitted at
the trial only to be brought subsequently before the German People's court at Stuttgart under the
"denazification" laws which attempted to try "lesser" collaborators of the Nazi regime. Sentenced
to eight years' detention in a labour camp, Schacht successfully appealed against his conviction and
resumed a highly successful and respected career as a financier.

3. Soon after the first decision, the BGH reaffirmed its stand in an interesting case brought as a
result of the publication of Cosima Wagner's private letters and diaries (BGHZ 15, 249); and, again,
two years later in the *Dahlke* case (BGHZ 20, 345). A year later, the BGH declared its willingness
to take the same stand when the interference with the plaintiff's privacy was merely negligent. There
followed the landmark case of the *Gentleman rider* (BGHZ 26, 349, case 40). This decision, along
with the case of the Professor of Canon law (BGHZ 35, 363, case 41), settled the problem of the theoretical basis of monetary compensation for violations of the new right, which had not been
decreed until that moment. They also completed the judicial revolution started by the *Schacht* case
for now the courts had given teeth to the new right. During these years litigation increased at a
considerable rate and in the process a number of issues were clarified. The following are but illustrations. BGHZ 24, 72 (communication of medical reports without the patient's consent may
amount to a violation of the right). BGHZ 27, 284 (recording a conversation with the speaker
without his knowledge and consent may also infringe the new right). BGH NJW 1965, 685 (*fictitious* interview with a well-known figure of international society). BGHZ 39, 124 (statements made
about a television broadcaster can be actionable under this heading even though they could also
have founded an action on defamation (§ 185 StGB in conjunction with § 823 II BGB)). *Vis-à-vis*
this last point, however, there is a view that argues that an action for violation of the right of privacy
has a residual character and will, normally, be available only if there is no other specific rule that
covers the point. (E.g. protection of name (§ 12 BGB); artistic creations, etc. § 97 of the Copyright
Act). (BGHZ 30, 7, 11). § 823 I BGB will also be chosen instead of § 823 II BGB in conjunction with
the Criminal Code as the only way of awarding "pain and suffering" damages (*Schmerzensgeld*; §
847 BGB) to the victim (cf. OLG Düsseldorf NJW 1980, 599). For further amusing instances see
OLG Frankfurt NJW 1982, 648: defendant produced a sticker depicting *two* cranes, copulating,
accompanied by, *inter alia*, the word "Lusthansa"; Lufthansa, which has a crane as an emblem, sued
but failed. In OLG Frankfurt NJW 1985, 1649 a different company produced a sticker with the letters
BMW accompanied by the words "Bumms Mal Wieder". In one sense this could be taken to mean
"Bump [or bang] once again", but *bummsen* can, in colloquial German, mean "to fuck" so the
famous motor car company *successfully* sued for an injunction. Though the decision was reversed
on appeal (see BGHZ 91, 117; 98, 94), the extension of these rules to cover legal (as well as physical) persons is not in doubt: BVerfGE 21, 362; BGH NJW 1974, 1762; BGH NJW 1975, 1882; BGHZ
78, 24; BGH ZIP 1994, 648. For further casuistry, see also, the discussion in chapter two, above.)

4. If, in accordance with the above, it is established that the plaintiff's claim can proceed on the
grounds that his right of privacy has been interfered with, then the court is obliged to consider the
merits of the claim in the light of all the surrounding circumstances. The difficulties involved in
balancing competing values are fully exposed and considered in case 42 which shows *inter alia* that
not only celebrities but also ex-convicts have, in certain circumstances, rights of privacy. Finding
the via media in such circumstances is by no means an easy task; but it is one which, overall, is
performed with admirable clarity and courage of opinion by the Constitutional Court. The
approach in such matters being casuistic, it is difficult to state hard and fast rules. Nevertheless,
three threads of thought are discernible in the judgments. First, freedom of expression will, on the

whole, prevail over the right of privacy where the publication, broadcast, etc. aim at educating and informing the public rather than pursuing mere sensationalism or trying to satisfy the public's taste for gossip. (This, incidentally, is what Lord Bingham of Cornhill thinks will happen in English law, as well, after the Human Rights Act 1998 comes to be applied. See his evidence before the House of Commons Select Committee in Home Affairs on 17 March 1998). However, when human dignity is (grossly) violated and not only incidentally affected there is no room for a balancing process; human dignity prevails. (See e.g. BVerfG NJW 2001, 2957, 2959.) Secondly, the chances of success of a privacy claim tend to decrease as the public profile of the plaintiff increases. But even public figures can seek protection of their privacy in appropriate circumstances. (See BGHZ 73, 120 case 45; BGH NJW 1996, 1128, case 46; BVerfGE 101, 361, case 47.) Finally, not every kind of speech receives the same, preferential treatment. Thus, speech that promotes the public good or is in the public interest will receive much greater protection than self-serving speech. (For instance, see the *Höllenfeuer* decision of 21 June 1966 (BGHZ 45, 296 = NJW 1966, 1617 = JZ 1967, 174. Also important dicta in BGH 12 October 1993, NJW 1994, 124.) The above comments are noteworthy for their seriously question the accuracy of statements repeatedly made by the English Press—broad sheet as well as tabloid—about the extent of the protection given to speech rights in contemporary Germany. What is said in various parts of this book should dispel this myth. Here, however, are some notable extracts that give the lie to such assertions.

(i) "The basic right to freedom of expression, . . . is one of most precious rights of man. [This right] is absolutely essential to a free and democratic state, for it alone permits that constant spiritual interaction, the conflict of opinion, which is its vital element. In a certain sense it is the basis of freedom itself . . . freedom of expression is the matrix, the indispensable condition of nearly every other form of freedom." *Lüth* judgment of the Constitutional Court, BVerfGE 7, 192.

(ii) "Especially in public debate, criticism, even in exaggerated and polemical form must be accepted if one is to avoid limiting the process by which public opinion is formed." *Stern-Strauss* judgment of the Constitutional Court, BVerfGE 82, 272 (1990).

(iii) "Where the person expressing the opinion is not pursuing objectives of self-interest, but rather contributing to the public debate on a question of substantive concern to the public, then there is a presumption that the expression of opinion is permissible; an interpretation of the laws restricting freedom of opinion which makes excessively high demands as regards the permissibility of public criticism is not compatible with Art. 5 (1) GG." BGH 12 October 1993, NJW 1994, 124 (translation N. Sims from van Gerven, *Tort Law*, 2nd ed. (2000), 149.)

(iv) "Contrary to the view of the complainant, Article 2 para. 1 in combination with Article 1 para. 1 of the Basic Law does not contain a general and comprehensive right of control over pictures of oneself. Insofar as she seeks to deduce such a right from earlier decisions of the federal Constitutional Court . . . this is an incorrect generalisation of the protective content of the basic guarantee, which is formulated in the light of actual cases. As this court has already emphasised many times, the general right of personality doe not give the individual a clam only to be portrayed by others in the way in which he sees himself or wishes to be seen by others . . . A wider protection of this kind would only exceed the objective of avoiding endangering the development of the personality, but would also make deep inroads into the area of freedom of third parties." *Caroline* judgment of the Constitutional Court of 15 December 1999, BVerfGE 101, 361 (case 47).

(v) "In the centre of the basic right of guarantee of freedom of the press is the right freely to determine the type, orientation, content, and form of a publication . . . Included in this right is the decision whether and how a publication should be illustrated. . . . The press must be allowed to decide according to journalistic criteria what it considers to be worthy of the public interest and what it does not". *Caroline* decision of the Constitutional Court of 15.12. 1999, BVerfGE 101, 36.

(vi) "It is not only 'valuable' items of information given by the press that falls within the freedom of the press in Article 5 para. 1 of the basic law The freedom in principles also exists in favour of the tabloid and sensational press and thereby also for news which primarily satisfies the need of a more or less broad readership for superficial entertainment." *Prince Ernst August of Hanover* judgment of Federal Court of 29 June 1999, NJW 1999, 2893 (case 49).

One does not expect much accuracy from those who write for the tabloid press; but in an age of high information technology, the broad sheets should be better informed.

5. German law on disclosure of true private facts is particularly interesting not least because its position is so diametrically different from that found in the USA. It thus offers excellent material for reflective comparisons about the basic values and attitudes of these two societies. Two points deserve particular attention. First is the Germanic tendency to distinguish the disclosed facts according to whether they belong to (a) the "intimate" (b) the "private" or (c) the "social" sphere of the plaintiff—the first receiving almost total protection, the last little or none. Though the need to make such distinctions is accepted both by academics and courts (see *Münchener Kommentar*-Schwerdtner, 3rd edn., I (1993), § 12 BGB no. 215; *Palandt*-Thomas § 823 BGB, no. 178; Ricker in *NJW* 1990, 2098) it will also strike Common lawyers as Germanic in its approach and unworkable in practice since the difficulty here is not so much in drawing up these categories but in slotting the facts of each case into the appropriate pigeonhole. On the other hand the German material should also prompt reflection on the merits of according—even to public figures—some degree of privacy and seclusion. Two decisions of the Federal Court, dealing with the unauthorised tapping of a telephone conversation between two prominent leaders of the Christian Democratic party, clearly illustrate these points. In the first (BGHZ 73, 120 = JZ 1979, 349, case 45, above) the Court held that even politicians are entitled to rights of privacy, and granted an injunction preventing the dissemination of the content of the conversation, whereas in the second (BGH JZ 1979, 351) which concerned the same parties, the plaintiffs were awarded DM 10,000 each in damages for the violation of their right of personality. These rights would be overridden only where there was a real and serious interest to inform the public (which was not the case in that litigation.) First Amendment admirers may cringe at such decisions; but in the light of many successes of investigative journalism directed against German public figures, any outright condemnation of German law would be unfounded.

6. Monetary compensation is often the plaintiff's main demand. The difficulties created here by § 253 BGB—overcome by cases 40 and 41 (and approved by BVerfGE 35, 202, case 42) and not to be found in any other system—have been discussed above (chapter 2, section A.2(*e*)(iv)). The BGH started out to work with an analogy to § 847 BGB, but today damages for immaterial harm in this area are directly based on Art 1 I and Art 2 GG. This claim is a claim *sui generis*. But the intrusion into the plaintiff's privacy must also be grave and objectively serious, otherwise the courts would be inundated with frivolous claims; the point is raised in chapter 4, section A.3(*e*), and is illustrated by case 145, below. Moreover, the size of the monetary compensation (whenever it is sought which is by no means always) is modest as is shown by an analysis of all published cases for the period 1980 to 2000, though growing (see below subsection 8).

7. Injunctive relief, though not specifically provided for by the tort provisions of the Code, has for a long time now (see RGZ 60, 6) also been available on the analogy of § 1004 BGB (taken from land law). Indeed, the Code of Civil Procedure (ZPO) in a number of provisions (e.g. 920 II, 935, 937 II, 940, 944 etc.) contains rules which are meant to facilitate the granting of this remedy which, however, does not resolve the merits of the dispute but only provides interim relief. Thus the procedure can be quick, entirely oral, and in very urgent cases even oral argument may be waived (§ 937 II ZPO). Again, in cases of urgency, the remedy can be granted by the Presiding judge sitting alone (§ 944 ZPO) and even the plaintiff's burden of proof may be eased in various ways. This remedy, undoubtedly suffers from one practical drawback: it can only be claimed in those cases where the plaintiff has advance warning of an imminent publication of offending material. Nonetheless, the way it has been shaped by German law seems sufficiently interesting to warrant more attention by English specialists than it has hitherto received. (For details on this subject see: *Münchener Kommentar*-Schwerdtner, 3rd edn. I, (1993) § 12 BGB no. 322; Zöller, *Zivilprozessordnung* 22nd edn. (2001), commentary on the paragraphs mentioned above.) *Douglas* v. *Hello Ltd.* [2001] 2 *WLR* 992 suggests that these ideas may be transplantable to England, especially under the new regime of the Human Rights Act 1998. On the other hand, the idea of a pre-emptive injunction is unlikely to appeal to American lawyers who, in their desire to leave the Press totally

unfettered can (in the eyes of a foreign observer at least) appear to be excessively worried by *all* notions of "prior restraint". This may well explain the paucity of the American material which, especially of read with the history of each dispute, seems inconclusive at best. Thus, see: *Julian Messner, Inc. Spahn*, 393 U.S. 818 (1968); 393 U.S. 1046 (1969); *Roe v. Doe*, 417 U.S. 907 (1974); 420 U.S. 307 (1975); *Wiseman v. Massachusetts*, 398 U.S. 960 (1970); 400 U.S. 954 (1970).

8. Some seven years ago, as the third edition was about to go to print, the Lord Chancellor's department issued a Consultation paper entitled *Infringement of Privacy*. It provided a full and readable account of this topic and, in its recommendations, it went beyond the Calcutt suggestions by advocating the introduction (subject to some important constraints) of a general right of privacy. Just as importantly, it contained a number of subsidiary points and assumptions that could (to some extent) be tested by applying the comparative method. Thus, first it gave a "guesstimate" of the number of cases that were likely to come before the English courts if the new right was recognised. These were estimated to be "in the hundreds rather than the thousand" (p. 52). Secondly, while not suggesting a mandatory figure of damages, the paper implied (at p. 45) that a sum in the region of $3,000 might be an appropriate guideline for judges. Finally (at p. 42) the paper boldly recommended the availability of injunctions, though it remained conscious of the "chilling effect" this remedy might have on investigative journalism. The following data, derived from *all* published German decisions handed down between 1980 and 1993 offers one way of testing the assumptions and predictions made in the valuable (but subsequently discarded) Report. Thus:

First, the total number of cases for this period of thirteen years is 122. Given that the German right of privacy is not "hedged" in by the kind of limitations proposed by the Lord Chancellor's paper, the estimates of litigation contained in the latter document may, in the light of the German experience, be on the pessimistic side. Overall, however, it is unlikely that the new right of privacy will create an excessive load for the courts or an unbearable burden on the Press.

Secondly, in 25 cases "moral damages" were granted by the German courts showing, as the Lord Chancellor's paper implicitly suggests, that damages may not, necessarily, be the remedy most sought after by affected plaintiffs. These are the following (amount—in DM—awarded is given in parenthesis after the reference): LG Stuttgart, 1983 AfP 292 (5,000); OLG Stuttgart, 1983 AfP 291 (10,500); OLG Düsseldorf, 1984 AfP 229; BGH, 1985 AfP 111 (10,500); OLG Frankfurt, 1986 AfP 140 (2,000); OLG Köln, 1987 AfP (10,000); OLG Frankfurt, 1987 AfP 526 (10,000); OLG Köln, 1986 AfP 347 (10,000); LG Hamburg, 1987, AfP 633 (5,000); LG München, 1987 AfP 634 (20,000 to two plaintiffs); OLG Köln, 1987 AfP 602 (5,000); LG Lübeck, 1987 AfP 721 (1,600); OLG Hamburg, 1987 AfP 703 (3,000); OLG Hamburg, 1988 AfP 247 (10,000); OLG Köln, 1987 NJW 2682 (10,000); BGH, 1988 AfP 30 = 1988 VersR 497 (amount to be fixed); BGH, 1988 AfP 34 (amount to be fixed); AG Kaufbeuren, 1988 AfP 277 (500); OLG Oldenburg, 1989 AfP 556 = 1989 NJW 400 (4,000); OLG Karlsruhe, 1989 VersR 1097 (3,000); LG Köln, 1991 AfP 757 (8,000); OLG Frankfurt, 1992 NJW 441 (2,000); LG Köln, 1992 AfP 83 (6,000); OLG Hamburg, 1992 AfP 376 (10,000); LG Bonn, 1992 AfP 386 (10,000). At (approximately) DM 7–7,500 the average German figure is almost identical to the amounts envisaged by the Lord Chancellor's paper. Damages for pain and suffering and "moral damages" are discussed in more detail in ch. 4 section 3(c).

Thirdly, these sums refer to damages for "moral damages". Where plaintiffs can prove additional, pecuniary losses they, too, may be recoverable. Thus in OLG München 1988 NJW 915, the plaintiff complained of being photographed while sunbathing in the nude in the famous *Englischer Garten*. It was alleged that the subsequent publication of the photograph in a local paper resulted in the plaintiff failing to obtain a wage increase which was in the pipeline. The lost "benefit" was awarded in the form of damages. No doubt, the same solution should be adopted by English law as well.

Fourthly, in some cases where the complaining plaintiff has not suffered any loss but the defendant has made a gain (at the expense of the former), the measure of damages may be restitutionary rather than compensatory, recovery being allowed on the basis of § 812 BGB. Thus see: OLG Hamburg, 1983 AfP 282 (DM 4,000); BGH 1987 GRUR 128 (5,500); LG München, 1987 AfP 634 (1360); OLG Karlsruhe, 1989 AfP 558 = 1989 VersR 259 = 1989 NJW 401 (500); BGH, 1993 VersR 66 (amount to be fixed). Sometimes, such actions for account succeed under different provisions (e.g. the Copyright Act). See: BGH, 1987 AfP 508. An equal number of courts, however, have failed to make an award under this heading. See: OLG Frankfurt, 1984 AfP 115; OLG Hamburg, 1985 AfP 120; AG Bonn, 1990 AfP 64; AG Hamburg, 1991 AfP 659; OLG Hamburg, 1992 AfP 159.

Fifthly, in 30 cases injunctions were sought and granted, sometimes initially following the expedited procedure described above. There are some lessons here for English law; and some key structural differences with American law must also be noted. The cases granting injunctions were: OLG Hamburg, 1981 AfP 356; OLG München, 1981 AfP 360; OLG München, 1982 AfP 230; LG Köln, 1983 AfP 414; OLG München, 1985 AfP 209; OLG München, 1986 NJW 1260; OLG Hamburg, 1987 AfP 518; OLG Frankfurt, 1987 AfP 528; LG Oldenburg, 1987 NJW 1419; BGH, 1987 AfP 508; OLG Hamburg, 1987 AfP 703; LG Oldenburg, 1987 AfP 537; OLG Hamburg, 1988 AfP 143; LG Berlin, 1988 AfP 168; OLG Hamm 1988 AfP 258; BVerfG, 1990 NJW 1980; OLG Hamburg, 1989 GRUR 666; OLG Hamburg, 1991 AfP 437 (partial granting of injunction); OLG München, 1991 AfP 435; OLG Frankfurt, 1991 GRUR 49; BGH, 1990 AfP 209; OLG Hamburg, 1991 AfP 626; OLG Hamburg, 1991 AfP 537; LG Köln, 1991 AfP 757; OLG München, 1992 AfP 78; OLG Hamburg, 1991 AfP 537; OLG Hamburg, 1993 AfP 576; BGH, 1993 VersR 614; BVerfG, 1993 NJW 1463; LG Hamburg, 1993 AfP 679.

Finally, an almost equal number of decisions have refused plaintiffs the injunctions they had sought, demonstrating that German courts take the balancing act they are expected to perform between the competing interests very seriously. These are: BGH, 1980 AfP 154; OLG Hamburg, 1982 AfP 177; OLG Hamburg, 1983 AfP 466; OLG Köln, 1985 AfP 293; OLG Oldenburg, 1988 AfP 82; LG Oldenburg, 1987 AfP 720; LG Oldenburg, 1988 AfP 167; OLG Frankfurt, 1989 AfP 402; OLG Karlsruhe, 1989 AfP 542; OLG Celle, 1989 AfP 575; LGBerlin, 1989 AfP 59; OLG München, 1989 AfP 570; LG Köln, 1989 AfP 766; OLG Köln, 1989 AfP 764; OLG München, 1990 AfP 214; BGH, 1990 AfP 209; BVerfG, 1990 AfP 192; OLG Frankfurt, 1990 AfP 229; OLG Hamburg, 1991 AfP 533; OLG Düsseldorf, 1991 AfP 424; OLG München, 1991 AfP 534; BGH, 1991 AfP 410; BGH, 1991 AfP 416 = 1991 VersR 433; OLG Hamburg, 1992 AfP 279; BGH, 1992 AfP 140; OLG Celle, 1992 AfP 295; KG Berlin, 1992 AfP 302; BGH, 1993 VersR 66; OLG Hamburg, 1992 AfP 267.

9. The English Report met with the fate that is reserved for all proposals that do not meet with the approval of the Press: it was binned. But in Germany the law remained on course and despite fears expressed by some that the *Caroline* cases may have disturbed the status quo, the famous floodgates of litigation never opened. Nor was the average level of damages increased in a way that dislocated the newspaper industry or deterred from doing its appointed task. Prophets of doom are rarely proved right that is why they are invariably forgotten. So here, once again, is this valuable data for the period 1993–2000 so that bona fide researchers can draw meaningful conclusions about the future state of English law.

I. Total number of cases reported during the years 1993–2000: 101

II. Cases where plaintiff won (55)

(a). Non-pecuniary damages were awarded in 16 cases, namely: LG Hamburg, 1994 AfP 163 (25,000); LG Berlin, 1994 AfP 324 (6,000); OLG Karlsruhe, 1994 NJW 1963 (60,000); OLG München, 1996 NJW-RR 539 (8,000); OLG Hamburg, 1995 AfP 508 (5,000); BGH, 1994 AfP 142 (10,000); OLG Bremen, 1996 NJW 1000 (30,000); LG Oldenburg, 1995 AfP 679 (15,000); AG Berlin-Mitte, 1996 AfP 188 (1,500); OLG München, 1997 AfP 811 (5,000); OLG Saarbrücken, 1997 NJW 1376 (7,000); OLG Koblenz, 1997 NJW 1375 (20,000); OLG Hamm, 1998 AfP 304 (20,000); OLG München, 1999 AfP 71 (10,000); BAG, 1999 AfP 290 (4,000); LG Berlin, 1999 AfP 381 (30,000);

(b). Damages were calculated on a quasi "restitutionary" basis in 8 cases, namely: BGH, 1995 NJW-RR 1112 (250); LG Hamburg, 1995 AfP 526 (30,000); BGH, 1996 AfP 137 (amount to be fixed); BGH, 1996 AfP 138 (amount to be fixed); OLG Karlsruhe, 1996 AfP 282 (amount to be fixed); OLG Hamburg, 1997 AfP 538 (180,000); LG Düsseldorf, 1998 AfP 238 (10,000); OLG Karlsruhe, 1998 AfP

326 (155,000); The term "restitutionary" must be viewed with caution. For the BGH (NJW 1996, 985) stressed that the claim was *not* simply for restitution of profits. Rather the amount of compensation under § 823 I BGB in conjunction with Art 1 I, Art 2 GG depended on various factors such as the profits made, the preventive effect of the claim for future market behaviour, intensity of the violation of the right of personality;

(c). Injunctions were granted in 26 cases, namely: OLG Naumburg, 1994 AfP 306; OLG Hamburg, 1995 AfP 665; LG Köln, 1994 AfP 165; OLG Hamburg, 1994 AfP 232; BGH, 1994 AfP 306; BGH, 1995 AfP 411 = 1995 NJW 861; BGH, 1994 VersR 1116; OLG München, 1995 AfP 658; BGH, 1996 AfP 140 (partly) = 1996 NJW 1128; OLG Hamburg, 1996 AfP 154 (partly); LG Hamburg, 1996 AfP 185; LG Lübeck, 1996 AfP 406; OLG Hamburg, 1997 AfP 535; LG München I, 1997 AfP 559; LG München I, 1997 AfP 827; LG Berlin, 1997 AfP 938; OLG Koblenz 1998 AfP 328; OLG Hamburg, 1998 AfP 643; OLG Hamburg, 1999 AfP 68; LG Berlin, 1999 AfP 191; OLG Karlsruhe, 1999 AfP 489; OLG München, 1999 AfP 507; LG Berlin, 1999 AfP 525; BGH, 1999 NJW, 2736; BGH, 2000 AfP 88; BGH, 2000 NJW 656;

(d). Finally, in five cases successful plaintiffs obtained both damages and injunctions. These were: LG Hamburg, 1994 AfP 64 (40,000); BGH, 1994 AfP 411 (§ 812, amount to be fixed); LG Hamburg, 1994 AfP 243 (15,000); BGH, 1996 AfP 144 (30,000); BGH, 1997 AfP 700 = 1997 NJW 1148 (amount to be fixed);

III. In 46 cases the plaintiffs' claims was dismissed. These were: LG Baden-Baden, 1994 AfP 59; LG Frankfurt am Main, 1995 AfP 687; OLG Bremen, 1994 AfP 145; LG München I, 1994 AfP 162; BGH, 1995 AfP 495; OLG Hamburg, 1995 AfP 504; LG Lübeck, 1994 AfP 166; LG Hamburg, 1994 AfP 321; OLG Hamm, 1995 NJW 2859; OLG Brandenburg, 1995 AfP 520; OLG Hamburg, 1996 AfP 69; LG Köln, 1996 AfP 189; OLG München, 1996 AfP 391; OLG Köln, 1996 AfP 399; OLG Nürnberg, 1996 NJW, 530; OLG Brandenburg, 1996 NJW 1002; BGH, 1997 AfP 634; OLG München, 1997 AfP 636; OLG Karlsruhe, 1997 AfP 721; LG Berlin, 1997 AfP 732; LG Berlin, 1997 AfP 735; OLG Celle, 1997 AfP 819; KG Berlin, 1997 AfP 926; LG Paderborn, 1998 AfP 331; BGH, 1998 AfP 399; OLG München, 1998 AfP 409; LG Berlin, 1998 AfP 417; LG Berlin, 1998 AfP 418; BGH, 1998 AfP 506; LG Berlin, 1998 AfP 525; OLG Karlsruhe, 1998 AfP 639; OLG Dresden, 1998 NJW, 616; OLG Brandenburg, 1999 NJW 3339; OLG Hamburg, 1999 NJW 3343; LG Berlin, 1999 AfP 91; OLG Hamburg, 1999 AfP 175; KG Berlin, 1999 AfP 361; OLG Zweibrücken, 1999 AfP 362; KG Berlin, 1999 AfP 369; OLG München, 1999 AfP 506; LG Hamburg, 1999 AfP 523; LG Berlin, 1999 AfP 525; LG Waldshut-Tiengen, 2000 AfP 101; BGH, 2000 AfP 167; OLG München, 2000 AfP 174; OLG Frankfurt am Main, 2000 AfP 185.

10. English law, on the whole, compares unfavourably with German law (though the fear of legislation, has forced the Press Complaints Commission to move in the direction of German law. (See *The Times*, 28 June, 2000, reporting Lord Wakeham's latest speech on the matter. See, also, the current set of "Guide Lines" contained in the Code of Conduct of the Press Commission—a document which is reproduced below as Appendix 6. Its text is remarkable for at least two broad reasons. First, because it shows a move towards some of the ideas long established in Germany; e.g. dislike of use of telephoto lens, a shift grudgingly made as a result of public outcry following successive incidents of Press misbehaviour. Secondly, it also reveals the main weakness of the English system of self-regulation: in the event of finding that its code of practice has been violated, the Commission's only power is to direct the broadcaster to publicise its decision. But there is no power to order an apology (let alone to insist that it gives it the same prominence as the offending publication itself); nor can the offender be ordered to make any monetary amends.

The harsh condemnation of English law, should be mitigated by the fact that many aspects of the human personality and privacy do receive some or adequate protection through a multitude of existing torts and specific statutes (e.g. the Data Protection Acts 1984, 1998). But the way the protection is afforded is, itself, defective having emerged from accidents of history. Briefly, this means fitting the facts of each case in the pigeonhole of an existing tort, the process often involving strained constructions or, even, leaving deserving plaintiffs without a remedy. Thus, trespass or nuisance may, at times, help though they may also prove futile because of some technicality.

(See, for instance, *Bernstein of Leigh* v. *Skyviews & General Ltd.* [1978] QB 479). For these old torts have their own limitations (e.g. actions in nuisance are only available to persons having an interest in land). Other illustrations could be given. Thus, an ingenious attempt to extend the tort of passing-off met with only a cautious response (*Sim* v. *Heinz (HJ) Co. Ltd.* [1959] 1 *WLR* 313). Defamation will, more often, be invoked, though this again will not always work (especially when the defence of truth is available). In the celebrated case of *Tolley* v. *Fry* [1931] AC 333, an amateur golfer was depicted without his permission on a poster advertising chocolate bars while playing golf. He was not described as a bad golfer; nor was he made to advertise a cheap product. But his action succeeded because the court was able to discover an innuendo: the advertisement conveyed the impression that he had "prostituted" his amateur status for gain, something which carried (carries?) a stigma in the English way of thinking. That this was really a "privacy" case, however, can be demonstrated by asking what the position would have been if the golfer depicted on the poster had been a celebrated professional. *De lege ferenda* he, too, should have received some legal protection against the unauthorised use of his picture; but the way the *Tolley* decision was phrased suggests that this action would have failed—and if this is so the tort of defamation is clearly inadequate for this purpose. The limitations of the tort of defamation also become obvious where the defence of truth is available. If, for example, a case like *Melvin* v. *Read*, 112 Cal. App. 285, 297 P. 91 (1931) were to arise in England the plaintiff would almost certainly be left without protection. Likewise with facts similar to those in *Briscoe* v. *Reader's Digest Association Inc.*, 483 P. 2d 34 (1971). English law thus does not encourage citizens to forgive even once, let alone seventy times seven! *Re X* ([1984] 1 WLR 1422) is, perhaps, the case that best brings out the unforgiving and casuistic mentality of English law.

10. In 1968, Mary Bell, a juvenile, was convicted of manslaughter and sentenced to detention for life. In 1984, she was released on licence and, some time later, gave birth to a daughter who was made a ward of court at the initiative of the local authority. Somehow this became known to the Press and an application was made by her mother and the local authority to the High Court for an injunction prohibiting the disclosure of the identity and present whereabouts of *both* child and parents. The application, made on the ground that any such disclosure would be detrimental to the family's newly found peace and stability, was accepted by Balcombe J and an order prohibiting publication of the said information (but not of the fact of the birth) was duly granted.

In an earlier wardship case (*Re X* [1975] Fam. 47) the first attempt was made to use the wardship jurisdiction in this type of situation in order to prohibit the publication of a book concerning the ward's deceased father. This was because the book contained material which, as the defendants conceded, was likely to cause X serious psychological damage if it ever came to her notice. A unanimous Court of Appeal took the view that freedom of speech should prevail. In the event, therefore, the carefully balanced judgment of the trial judge was reversed, Lord Denning MR declaring that "it would be extending the wardship jurisdiction too far and infringing too much upon the freedom of the Press for us to grant an injunction in this case" (*ibid.* 59). Roskill LJ echoed similar views, though he felt that in appropriate circumstances a balancing of the competing interests might have to be attempted. Sir John Pennycuick was also anxious to preserve, at least "in exceptional circumstances" (*ibid.* 61), the right to make such an order in favour of the ward. In his view, it was the courts' clear duty to attempt to balance the competing interests, even though in this instance freedom of speech prevailed.

One could of course try to reconcile these decisions by reference to their particular facts, even though to the reader of the law reports a clear distinction is not all that obvious. (The preference for free speech in the earlier *Re X* case is even more remarkable considering that the offending parts of the book—a mere eight pages—could have been removed at a very small cost which the parents of the ward were more than willing to meet.) Could one then look at the second *Re X* decision, delivered almost ten years after the earlier one, as reflecting a greater sensitivity to human privacy, especially in the light of adverse reactions—national and international—to the telephone tapping case of *Malone* v. *Metropolitan Police Commissioner* (No. 2) [1979] Ch. 344? Linking these two cases may strike some people as odd; but, it is submitted, one can legitimately treat *Re X* as a privacy case or, more precisely, as a case dealing with that type of privacy which Judge Cooley described as "the right to be let alone" (*Tort* (2nd edn., 1889), 29).

Seen in this light, *Re X* is a remarkable decision since it protects the anonymity of the (innocent) child and, at the same time, the anonymity of the mother/ex-criminal. Remarkable and yet typical of the way that protection is afforded by pushing into existing pigeonholes certain fact situations. And where tort law cannot afford a remedy, the unusual attempt was made to extend an inherent jurisdiction which was meant for many things but was hardly devised as a substitute for a non-existent tort of violation of privacy.

Re X, however, also makes the patchy nature of the protection most obvious. Thus, the mother's anonymity is only incidentally protected. And once the wardship ends (through the death of the child or its reaching the age of 18), the protection will disappear. The Rehabilitation of Offenders Act 1974 will in this case afford no protection (s. 5); and mother and child will run the risk of having their lives destroyed because some popular tabloid feels that the revelation of their new identity may interest its gossip-thirsty readership. The limited nature of the protection is also obvious when one considers that the nature of the infringement of the judge's order would render liable for contempt proceedings only those who were aware of it in the first place. To put it differently, a publication of the identity of Mary Bell by another newspaper, which independently made the same discovery and published it before the delivery of the judgment would go unpunished. Are these really acceptable results? Should a young girl of 17 be entitled to protection against her mother's distant past but lose it once she has become 18? Should an ex-criminal—*par excellence* of the Mary Bell type—who committed the crime just barely after attaining the age of criminal capacity (10), be haunted by it for the rest of her life?

11. Sections of the Press have shown equal insensitivity in another area where, it is submitted, the plaintiff's right to be left alone should prevail over the public's interest to know. This involves the identification of victims of sexual offences.

The development of the law in this area is typical of the incremental growth of the Common law. First, no anonymity whatsoever was granted to these unfortunate victims. Then section 4 of the Sexual Offences (Amendment) Act 1976 granted anonymity to victims of rape offences (as defined narrowly by s. 7(2) of the Act). Victims of "lesser" sexual offences (such as unlawful sexual intercourse, incest, or buggery), anxious to be left alone to forget their traumatic experiences, were, in fact, left unprotected as far as their privacy was concerned. The Criminal Justice Act 1987 extended anonymity to cases involving conspiracy to rape and burglary with intent to rape; but in the House of Lords the Minister from the Home Office thought that any further extension of the anonymity laws would be "the thin end of the wedge". The Calcutt Report disagreed, but the Home Office was, mysteriously it would seem, adamant. And then, quite unexpectedly and with very little publicity, the official attitude changed. The Sexual Offences (Amendment) Act 1991 made it possible to extend by statutory instrument anonymity to all cases of sexual offences; and Statutory Instrument 1336/1992 brought this protection into existence in October 1992. In this branch of the law, the incremental growth of English law has, surely, not been one of its strengths; and the adverse consequences that both the media and anonymous government circles feared would follow any extension of the anonymity laws have failed to materialise. (For further details on the absurdities of the old law see the second edition of this book, pages 320–1; for comparisons with US law see below. See, also, Villa-McDowell, "Privacy and the Rape Victim: The Inconsistent Treatment of Privacy Interests in The Recent Supreme Court Cases" 2 *Southern California Review of Law and Women's Studies*, 293 (1992).)

12. Telephone tapping, sophisticated eavesdropping, and data banks can also make great intrusions into human privacy. *Malone* v. *Metropolitan Police Commissioner* [1979] Chapter 344 considers the first type of intrusion and after a long, erudite, but timid judgment reaches a negative result. This unfortunate conclusion was partly the result of the maxim that anything that is not specifically made illegal should be treated as being allowable, though the main argument against recognition of a new right was that such a step could only be taken by the legislator. (A favourite posture for many of our judges in their contemporary and timid mood.) Five years later the European

Court ruled that telephone tapping was contrary to Articles 8 and 13 of the European Convention ((1984) 7 EHRR 14); and the legislator had to fall into line with the passing of the Interception of Communications Act 1985. American readers of *Roberson* v. *Rochester Folding Box Co.*, 171 NY 538, 64 NE 442 (1902) will find nothing novel in this. But tort students should ask themselves whether it is acceptable in the light of Parliament's inability or unwillingness to face up to the problem. Justice—a non-political pressure group for law reform—had this to say in 1970 about English law. "English law does . . . provide a remedy for some kinds of intrusion into privacy, but it is certainly not adequate to meet activities of a society which is perfecting more and more sophisticated techniques for intrusion. The present law in the field of privacy is uncoordinated and unsatisfactory, and a strong case . . . exists for the creation by means of statutory provision of comprehensive protection for the right of privacy." In 1993, despite increasing concern and an ever-growing literature, the position remains the same. (For a comparison with American law see Brittan, "The Right of Privacy in England and the USA" 37 *Tul. L. Rev.* 235 (1963). For a fuller account of English law see Seipp, "English Judicial Recognition of a Right of Privacy" *Oxford J. L. Studies* (1983) 324 ff.)

13. The patchiness of English law just described may be in keeping with its casuistic nature; but it is not to everyone's liking. More importantly, even judges are beginning to wonder whether the time has not come to synthesise this rich case law. In *R* v. *Kahn*, for instance, ([1997] AC 558 at 582–3) Lord Nicholls of Birkenhead wondered "whether the present, piecemeal protection of privacy [may] have now developed to the extent that a more comprehensive principle can be seen to exist." In the view of these writers, such an outcome us desirable. Yet it is unlikely that a new tort of privacy will emerge overnight. The tort of breach of confidence may thus prove the most pliable of existing torts in the inevitable albeit gradual expansion of the protection of human privacy in English law. (In this sense, Sir Brian Neill "Privacy: A Challenge for the Next Century" in *Protecting Privacy* (Basil S Markesinis ed.) 1999, pp. 1 ff.) To be sure, this tort is not without its limitations. (They were clearly set out in a leading case: *Coco* v. *A.N. Clark Engineers Ltd* [1969] R.P.C. 41 at 47). These are that the information must (a) have the "necessary quality of confidence about it", (b) it must "have been imparted in circumstances importing an obligation of confidence" and (c) there must have been an "unauthorized use of that information to the detriment of the party communicating it". The merit of using this tort as a springboard for further expansion of protected privacy lies not only in the predilection of English judges to expand their law incrementally but also in the fact that during its long history the tort has proved itself capable of expansion. Thus, the *Spycatcher* (*AG* v. *Guardian Newspaper Ltd* (No. 2) [1990] 1 AC 109) litigation proved beyond doubt that confidence does not depend, as was once thought to be the case, on the commercial value of the imparted information. (See Lord Keith's words in the *Spycatcher* case at p. 255.) A number of cases have also shown that the confidential relationships, from which the obligation may spring, can be varied and expand. They will thus include contract (*BSC* v. *Granada Television* [1981] 1 All ER 417), domestic relationships (*Argyll* v. *Argyll* [1967] Ch. 302) and other relationships which may give rise to a reasonable expectation of privacy such as doctor/patient, lawyer/client and homosexual or extra-marital relationships. (*Stephens* v. *Avery* [1988] 2 All ER 477.) But the criteria set out in the *Coco* case also demonstrate the existing limitations of the protection. This is well illustrated by the recent case of *Douglas and others* v. *Hello! Ltd* ([2001] 2 WLR 992—a case concerned with a request for an interim injunction and thus inconclusive on substance). For there the plaintiffs case (arising from a prohibited taking of a photograph at their wedding reception) cannot stand on breach of confidence, alone, if it is established at the trial that the prohibited photographs were taken not by guests of the couple but by "intruders" at the wedding reception. If, on the other hand, a wider notion of privacy were found to exist, then it would "accord recognition to the fact that the law has to protect not only those people whose trust has been abused but [also] those who simply find themselves subjected to an unwarranted intrusion into their personal lives." (*Douglas*, per Lord Justice Sedley at p. 1025.) That is why the learned Judge, after a careful scrutiny of the Human Rights Act 1988, was finally prepared to accept that the plaintiffs "have a powerful prima facie claim to redress for invasion of their privacy as a qualified right recognised and protected by English law." (*ibid.* at p. 1029.) Other celebrated cases could also be seen as suggesting that current

protection of human privacy may be unacceptably patchy and even defective. (Thus, see, *R* v. *Secretary of State for the Home Department ex parte Amnesty International and others* (un-published report of the Queen's Bench Division, 15 February 2000) where the former President's confidential medical records were revealed to his opponents who were trying to have him tried in the UK. In this case the English court, arguably, succumbed to the particular publicity and related "pressures" that arouse out of this unusual and controversial litigation. *Earl Spencer and Countess Spencer* v. *the UK* (1998) 25 EHRR CD 113, involving the photographing of the Countess of Spencer with telephoto lens while walking in the grounds a private clinic, also seems a flawed decision or, rather, one that owes its existence to successful advocacy rather than any inherent sense of justice.

14. The comparison of German and American Law is, in more ways than one, an intellectually rewarding exercise. For both systems present considerable similarities (e.g. both have a written Constitution and both can claim a prodigious literature on the subject). And both can claim even greater differences in outcome (which can, again, be traced to their Constitutions and the fact that each was attempting to address problems relevant to their particular political backgrounds). The following summary of the law in the United States is taken from an Excursus that Professor David Anderson of the University of Texas at Austin contributed to chapter seven of Markesinis and Deakin, *Tort Law* 4th edn. (1999). We are grateful for his permission to reproduce here.

"Invasion of privacy"

Although it has no counterpart in English law, the American tort law of invasion of privacy is related closely enough to defamation. . . . Many libel suits in the United States are combined with claims for invasion of privacy. To some extent privacy law is an outgrowth of changes in the law of defamation. At one time a truthful statement made without adequate justification might have been actionable as defamation in either the United States or England, but as truth became an absolute defence, at least in the United States, the need for some other remedy became apparent. "Invasion of privacy" is an umbrella term encompassing four distinct American torts. In addition, American law recognises other "rights of privacy" that are not torts and are beyond the scope of this discussion. For example, a constitutional "right of privacy" protects against governmental interference in such personal matters as abortion and contraception (*Roe* v. *Wade*, 410 US 113 (1973); *Griswold* v. *Connecticut*, 381 US 479 (1965).), and "privacy" statutes restrict governmental acquisition and use of certain types of personal information. (E.g. Privacy Act of 1974, 5 USC, s. 552a (1992).)

Of the four privacy torts, the one closest to the core of the privacy concept is the cause of action for public disclosure of embarrassing private facts. A person may recover damages for a disclosure that would be highly offensive to a reasonable person and is not of legitimate public concern. (Restatement (Second) of Torts, s. 652D (1977).) Sexual activities and medical abnormalities are among the kinds of disclosures that are most often litigated. The matter need not have been completely secret before the defendant's disclosure. Even the most intimate secrets usually are known to one's closest friends and family, so it is enough that the defendant has disclosed publicly a matter that previously was known only to such a limited circle. (*Sipple* v. *Chronicle Publishing Co.*, 154 Cal.App.3d 1040, 201 Cal.Rptr. 665 (1984); *Dias* v. *Oakland Tribune, Inc.* 139 Cal. App.3d 118, 188 Cal.Rptr. 762 (1983); *Melvin* v. *Reid*, 112 Cal.App. 285, 297 P. 91 (1931).) On the other hand, matters of official record may be disclosed with impunity, even if they were previously unknown by the public. (*Howard* v. *Des Moines Register & Tribune Co.*, 283 NW2d 289 (1979), cert. denied 445 US 904 (1980).)

The central issue is what facts are "private", and the law has defined that term so narrowly—and the concept of legitimate public concern so broadly—that very few disclosures are actionable. Courts look to contemporary mores to determine what reasonable people would find highly offensive. From that point of reference, disclosures of such matters as one's income or net worth, (*Wolf* v. *Regardie*, 553 A.2d 1213 (DC.App. 1989); *Schoneweis* v. *Dando*, 231 Neb. 180, 435 NW 2d 666 (1989).) personal idiosyncrasies, (*Virgil* v. *Time, Inc.*, 527 F. 2d 1122 (9th Cir. 1975), cert. denied 425 U.S. 998 (1976); *Sidis* v. *F.-R. Publishing Corp.*, 113 F.2d 806 (2nd Cir.), cert. denied 311 US 711 (1940).) illegitimacy, (*Heath* v. *Playboy Enterprises Inc.*, 732 F. Supp. 1145 (1990).) or medical diagnosis (*Davis* v. *Monsanto Co.*, 627 F.Supp. 418 (1986); *Child Protection Group* v. *Cline*, 350 SE 2d 541 (1986); *Meetze* v. *Associated Press*, 230 SC 330, 95 SE 2d 606 (1956).) usually are held not to be sufficiently offensive.

The concept of legitimate public concern is inspired by First Amendment values, and therefore is interpreted expansively. The public usually is held to have a legitimate interest in the identity of victims of crimes (including rape and other sex offences), *The Florida Star* v. *BJF*, 491 US 524 (1989); *Cox Broadcasting Corp.* v. *Cohn*, 420 US 469 (1975).) the sexual activities and medical problems of public officials, (*Hubert* v. *Harte-Hanks Texas Newspapers Inc.*, 652 SW 2d 546 (1983); *Kapellas* v. *Kofman*, 1 Cal.3d 20, 81 Cal. Rptr. 360, 459 P.2d 912 (1969).) and the marital difficulties of celebrities. (*Carlisle* v. *Fawcett Publications Inc.*, 201 Cal. App. 2d 733, 20 Cal.Rptr. 405 (1962).) Courts are reluctant to second-guess an editor's judgement that a matter is of legitimate public concern; some judges have gone so far as to say they will defer to the editor's judgement unless it is one no rational editor could have made. (*Gilbert* v. *Medical Economics Co.*, 665 F.2d 305 (10th Cir. 1981).)

In a society in which free flow of information is treated, judges find it difficult to as a paramount value impose liability for disclosing truth. The tort of public disclosure of truthful but embarrassing private facts, therefore, exists more in theory than in practice; claims are numerous, but they almost never succeed.

The second American privacy tort is a cause of action for publications that depict a person in a false light. The falsehood need not be defamatory, but it must place the person in a false light that would be highly offensive to a reasonable person. For example, affixing the plaintiff's byline to a sensational "first-person" account that he did not write gave rise to a cause of action for false-light invasion of privacy. (*Dempsey* v. *National Enquirer*, 702 F.Supp. 934 (D.Me. 1989).)

The tort is a cousin to defamation, and is subject to many of the same state law restrictions. (*Fellows* v. *National Enquirer Inc.*, 42 Cal.3d 234, 721 P.2d 97, 228 Cal.Rptr. 215 (1986).) Similar constitutional restrictions also apply. A plaintiff who is a public official or public figure must show that the defendant published with reckless disregard of the possible falsity. (*Cantrell* v. *Forest City Publishing Co.*, 419 US 245 (1974).) Private plaintiffs probably must prove at least that the defendant was negligent with respect to the falsity, and sometimes have been required to meet the same standard as a public plaintiff. (*Lovgren* v. *Citizens First National Bank*, 126 Ill.2d 411, 534 NE 2d 987 (1989).)

Because of these restrictions and the necessity of showing a high degree of offensiveness, false-light cases rarely succeed. Some states have refused to recognise the tort at all, (*Renwick* v. *The News and Observer Pub. Co.*, 310 NC 312, 312 SE 2d 405, cert. denied 469 US 858 (1984).) and there is considerable scholarly debate about its legitimacy. (See e.g. Diane Zimmerman, "False Light Invasion of Privacy: The Light that Failed", 64 *NYULR* 364 (1989).)

The two remaining privacy torts are of more practical significance. One is a cause of action for intentional and highly offensive intrusion into a person's private life. This tort supplements the law of trespass in two principal ways. First, it provides a remedy where the intrusion is physical but does not occur on plaintiff's premises. Thus, President Kennedy's widow was able to stop the famous "paparazzo" Ron Galella from shadowing her and her children to photograph them in public parks, restaurants, and schools. (*Galella* v. *Onassis*, 487 F.2d 986 (2d Cir. 1973).) Secondly, it provides a remedy where the intrusion is accomplished without physical invasion, for example, by electronic surveillance or telescopic lenses. (*Dietemann* v. *Time Inc.*, 449 F.2d 245 (9th Cir. 1971).)

The intrusion branch of privacy provides a more effective remedy for media invasions of personal privacy than the other branches. In part, this is because the First Amendment provides less protection for newsgathering activities than for publication. An important California Supreme Court decision illustrates this. A television cameraman accompanied a helicopter rescue crew to the site of a highway accident, outfitted the flight nurse with a microphone, and filmed the rescue of a woman who was seriously and permanently injured in the wreck. The woman sued for both the intrusion and the subsequent broadcast of video showing her begging to be allowed to die. The court held that the First Amendment barred the woman's claims for public disclosure of the sounds and images because those were a matter of legitimate public concern, but did not bar her claim for the TV crew's intrusion into a situation in which she had legitimate expectations of privacy.

With two dissenting votes, the court rejected the defendants' argument that they had a First Amendment right to intrude to obtain information that was of legitimate public concern. (*Shulman* v. *Group W. Productions*, 18 Cal. 4th 200, 74 Cal. Rptr. 843, 955 P. 2d 469 (1998).)

This decision was based on common law, but the California legislature subsequently created a stronger statutory remedy. The statute makes it a tort to trespass or use a "visual or auditory enhancing device"—e.g., a telephoto lens or a directional microphone—to film or record a person engaging in personal or familial activities under circumstances in which the person had a reasonable expectation of privacy. A person violating the statute is liable for up to three times the amount of special and general damages, plus punitive damages, and also may be enjoined. (Cal.Civil Code s. 1708.8. The same remedies are available against a publisher or broadcaster who induces another person to violate the statute, and if the image or recording is published or broadcast, the plaintiff may recover the profits gained thereby.)

The final privacy tort, which generates more successful claims than the other three branches combined, provides a remedy for commercial exploitation of a person's name or likeness. It arose from the un-consented use of a person's photograph or testimonial in advertisements, (*Pavesich* v. *New England Life Insurance Co.*, 122 Ga. 190, 50 SE 68 (1905).) but it now extends to unauthorized use of a person's distinctive nickname, *Hirsch* v. *S C Johnson & Son Inc.*, 90 Wis. 2d 379, 280 NW 2d (1979).) slogan, (*Carson* v. *Here's Johnny Portable Toilets Inc.*, 698 F.2d 831 (6th Cir. 1983).) or costume, (*Motschenbacher* v. *R J Reynolds Tobacco Co.*, 498 F.2d 821 (9th Cir. 1974).) or to the use of a model who looks like the plaintiff, (*Onassis* v. *Christian Dior-New York Inc.*, 122 Misc.2d 603, 472 NYS 2d 254 (trial court 1984), aff'd., 110 AD 2d 1095, 488 NYS 2d 943 (1985).) or a singer who imitates plaintiff's vocal style. (*Midler* v. *Ford Motor Co.*, 849 F.2d 460 (9th Cir. 1988), cert. denied 503 US 951 (1992).)

This branch of the tort has produced an entire industry based on the value of celebrity endorsements, and often seems to have more to do with commerce than with personal privacy. Indeed, the interest it protects is sometimes called a "right of publicity" rather than a right of privacy. Unlike the other privacy torts, which are personal to the victim and cannot be assigned or enforced after death, the right to control commercial exploitation is assignable *inter vivos*, (*Factors Etc. Inc.* v. *Pro Arts Inc.*, 579 F 2d 215 (2d Cir. 1978), cert. denied 440 US 908 (1979).) and in most jurisdictions is held to be a descendible interest enforceable at least for a number of years after the person's death. (*Martin Luther King Jnr., Centre for Social Change Inc.* v. *American Heritage Products Inc.*, 250 Ga. 135, 296 SE 2d 697 (1982).)

The tort is not conspicuously effective in protecting personal privacy because it covers only exploitation for commercial purposes, and most uses of personality for purposes even tangentially related to journalism or entertainment are not considered commercial. It is not actionable for a television station to use film of a bleeding accident victim to promote a documentary about emergency medical treatment, (*Anderson* v. *Fisher Broadcasting Co. Inc.*, 300 Or. 452, 712 P.2d 803 (1986).) or for a magazine that had published photos of a sports hero to republish the photos in advertisements promoting the magazine. (*Namath* v. *Sports Illustrated.*, 80 Misc. 2d 531, 363 NYS 2d 279 (Sup. Ct. 1975), aff'd., 48 AD 2d 487, 371 NYS 2d 10, 352 NE 2d 584 (1976).)

Thus, despite the existence of four rather elaborate privacy torts, American law rarely provides a remedy for persons who believe their privacy has been invaded by media or others. Many of the criticisms by Sir David Calcutt and others of England's failure to protect privacy could be made of American law as well.

Addendum 1

Cox Broadcasting Corp. v. *Cohn*, 420 US 469 (1975).

MR JUSTICE WHITE delivered the opinion of the court.

The issue before us in this case is whether consistently with the First and Fourteenth Amendments a State may extend a cause of action for damages for invasion of privacy caused by the publication of the name of a deceased rape victim which was publicly revealed in connection with the prosecution of the crime . . .

In August 1971, appellee's 17-year-old daughter was the victim of a rape and did not survive the incident. Six youths were soon indicted for murder and rape. Although there was substantial press coverage of the crime and of subsequent developments, the identity of the victim was not disclosed pending trial perhaps because of Ga. Code ann. § 26–9901 which makes it a misdemeanour to publish or broadcast the name or identity of a rape victim. In April 1972, some eight months later, the six defendants appeared in court. Five pleaded guilty to rape or attempted rape, the charge of murder having been dropped. The guilty pleas were accepted by the court, and the trial of the defendant pleading not guilty was set for a later date.

In the course of the proceedings that day, appellant Wassell, a reporter covering the incident for his employer, learned the name of the victim from an examination of the indictments which were made available for his inspection in the courtroom. That the name of the victim appears in the indictments and that the indictments were public records available for inspection are not disputed. Later that day, Wassell broadcast over the facilities of station WSB-TV, a television station owned by appellant Cox Broadcasting Corporation, a news report concerning the court proceedings. The report named the victim of the crime and was repeated the following day.

In May 1972, appellee brought an action for money damages against appellants, relying on § 26–9901 and claiming that his right to privacy had been invaded by the television broadcast giving the name of his deceased daughter. Appellants admitted the broadcasts but claimed that they were privileged under both state law and the First and Fourteenth Amendment. The trial court rejecting the appellants' constitutional claims and holding that the Georgia statute gave a civil remedy to those injured by its violation, granted summary judgment to appellee as to liability, with the determination of damages to await trial by jury.

On appeal, the Georgia Supreme Court, in its initial opinion, held that the trial court had erred in construing § 26–9901 to extend a civil cause of action for invasion of privacy and thus found it unnecessary to consider the constitutionality of the statute (231 Ga. 60, 200 SE 2d 127 (1973)). The court went on to rule, however, that the complaint stated a cause of action "for the invasion of appellee's right of privacy, or for the tort of public disclosure" a "common law tort exist[ing] in this jurisdiction without the help of the statute that the trial judge in this case relied on (231 Ga. 52, 200 SE 2d 130 (1973)). Although the privacy invaded was not that of the deceased victim, the father was held to have stated a claim for invasion of his own privacy by reason of the publication of his daughter's name. The court explained, however, that liability did not follow as a matter of law and that summary judgment was improper; whether the public disclosure of the name actually invaded appellee's "zone of privacy", and if so, to what extent were issues to be determined by the trier of fact. Also, "in formulating such an issue for determination by the fact-finder, it is reasonable to require the appellee to prove that the appellants invaded his privacy with wilful or negligent disregard for the fact that reasonable men would find the invasion highly offensive" 231 Ga. 64, 200 SE 2d 131. The Georgia Supreme Court did agree with the trial court, however, that the First and Fourteenth Amendments did not, as a matter of law, require judgment for appellants. The court concurred with the statement in *Brisco v. Reader's Digest Association Inc.* 4 Cal. 3d 529, 541 93 Cal. Rptr. 866, 874, 483 P. 2d 34, 42 (1971), that "the rights guaranteed by the First Amendment do not require total abrogation of the right to privacy. The goals sought by each may be achieved with a minimum of intrusion upon the other."

Upon motion for rehearing the Georgia court countered the argument that the victim's name was a matter of public interest and could be published with impunity by relying on § 26–9901 as an authoritative declaration of State policy that the name of a rape victim was not a matter of public concern. This time the court felt compelled to determine the constitutionality of the statute and sustained it as a "legitimate limitation on the right of freedom of expression contained in the First Amendment". The court could discern "no public interest or general concern about the identity of the victim of such a crime as will make the right to disclose the identity of the victim rise to the level of First Amendment protection" (231 Ga. 68–9, 200 SE 2d 133–4).

We postponed decision as to our jurisdiction over this appeal to the hearing on the merits (415 US 912 (1974)). We conclude that the court has jurisdiction and reverse the judgment of the Georgia Supreme Court . . .

Georgia stoutly defends both § 26–9901 and the State's common law privacy action challenged here. Her claims are not without force, for powerful arguments can be made, and have been made, that however it may be ultimately defined, there is a zone of privacy surrounding every individual, a zone within which the State may protect him from intrusion by the press, with all its attendant publicity. Indeed, the central thesis of the root article by Warren and Brandeis, "The Right of Privacy" 4 Harv. L. Rev. 193, 196 (1890), was that the press was overstepping its prerogatives by publishing essentially private information and that there should be a remedy for the alleged abuses.

More compelling, this century has experienced a strong tide running in favour of the so-called right of privacy. In 1967, we noted that "[i]t has been said that a 'right of privacy' has been recognised at common law in 30 States plus the district of Columbia and by statute in four States" (Time, Inc. v. Hill 385 US 374, 383 n. 7 (1967)). We there cited the 1964 edition of Prosser's Law of Torts. The 1971 edition of that same source states that "[i]n one form or another, the right of privacy is by this time recognised and accepted in all but a very few jurisdictions". Prosser, id. (4th ed. 1971), at 804 [footnote omitted]. Nor is it irrelevant here that the right of privacy is of recent arrival in the jurisprudence of Georgia, which has embraced the right in some form since 1905 when the Georgia Supreme Court decided the leading case of Pavesich v. New England Life Inc. Co. 122 Ga. 190, 50 SE 68 (1905).

These are impressive credentials for a right of privacy, but we should recognize that we do not have at issue here an action for the invasion of privacy involving the appropriation of one's name or photograph, a physical or other tangible intrusion into a private area, or a publication of otherwise private information that is also false although perhaps not defamatory. The version of the privacy tort now before us—termed in Georgia "the tort of public disclosure", 231 Ga. 62, 200 SE 2d 130—is that in which the plaintiff claims the right to be free from unwanted publicity about his private affairs, which, although wholly true, would be offensive to a person of ordinary sensibilities. Because the gravamen of the claimed injury is the publication of information, whether true or not, the dissemination of which is embarrassing or otherwise painful to an individual, it is here that claims of privacy most directly confront the constitutional freedoms of speech and press. The face-off is apparent, and the appellants urge upon us the broad holding that the press may not be made criminally or civilly liable for publishing information that is neither false nor misleading but absolutely accurate, however damaging it may be to reputation or individual sensibilities.

It is true that in defamation actions, where the protected interest is personal reputation, the prevailing view is that truth is a defence; and the message of New York Times v. Sullivan 376 US 254 (1964); Garrison v. Louisiana 379 US 64 (1964); Curtis Publishing Co. v. Butts 388 US 130 (1967), and like cases is that the defence of truth is constitutionally required where the subject of the publication is a public official or public figure. What is more, the defamed public official or public figure must prove not only that the publication is false but that it was knowingly so or was circulated with reckless disregard for its truth or falsity. Similarly, where the interest at issue is privacy rather than reputation and the right claimed is to be free from the publication of false or misleading information about one's affairs, the target of the publication must prove knowing or reckless falsehood where the materials published, although assertedly private, are "matters of public interest" (Time Inc. v. Hill, above, 385 US 387–8).

The court has nevertheless carefully left open the question whether the First and Fourteenth Amendment require that truth be recognized as a defence in a defamation action brought by a private person as distinguished from a public official or public figure. Garrison held that where criticism is of a public official and his conduct of public business, "the interest in private reputation is overborne by the larger public interest, secured by the Constitution, in the dissemination of truth", 379 US 72–3 [footnote omitted], but recognised that "different interest may be involved where purely private libels, totally unrelated to public affairs, are concerned: therefore, nothing we say today is to be taken as intimating any views as to the impact of the constitutional guarantees in the discrete area of purely private libels", id., at 72 n. 8. In similar fashion, *Time* v. *Hill*, above, expressly saved the question whether truthful publication of very private matters unrelated to public affairs could be constitutionally proscribed (385 US 383 n. 7).

Those precedents, as well as other considerations, counsel similar caution here. In this sphere of collision between claims of privacy and those of the free press, the interests on both sides are plainly rooted in the traditions and significant concerns of our society. Rather than address the broader question whether truthful publication may ever be subjected to civil or criminal liability consistently with the First and Fourteenth Amendments, or to put it another way, free from unwanted publicity in the press, it is appropriate to focus on the narrower interface between press and privacy that this case presents, namely whether the State may impose sanctions on the accurate publication of the name of a rape victim obtained from public records—more specifically, from judicial records which are maintained in connection with a public prosecution and which themselves are open to public inspection. We are convinced that the State may not do so.

In the first place, in a society in which each individual has but limited time and resources with which to observe at first hand the operations of his government, he relies necessarily upon the press to bring him in convenient form the facts of those operations. Great responsibility is accordingly placed upon the news media to report fully and accurately the proceedings of government, and official records and documents open to the public are the basic data of governmental operations. Without the information provided by the press most of us and many of our representatives would be unable to vote intelligently or to register opinions on the administration of government generally. With respect to judicial proceedings in particular, the function of the press serves to guarantee the fairness of trials and to bring to bear the beneficial effects of public scrutiny upon the administration of justice. [Reference.]

Appellee has claimed in his litigation that the efforts of the press have infringed his right to privacy by broadcasting to the world the fact that his daughter was a rape victim. The commission of crime, prosecutions resulting from it, and judicial proceedings arising from the prosecutions, however, are without question events of legitimate concern to the public and consequently fall within the responsibility of the press to report the operations of government. . . .

The developing law surrounding the tort of invasion of privacy recognizes a privilege in the press to report the events of judicial proceedings. The Warren and Brandeis article, *supra*, noted that the proposed new right would be limited in the same manner as actions for libel and slander where such a publication was a privileged communication: "the right to privacy is not invaded by any publication made in a court of justice . . . and (at least in many jurisdictions) reports of any such proceedings would in some measure be accorded a like privilege."

Addendum 2

The Florida Star v. *B.J.F.* Supreme Court of the United States, 1989. 491 US 524, 109 S.Ct. 2603, 105 L.Ed. 2d 443, 16 Med. L. Reptr. 1801.

JUSTICE MARSHALL delivered the opinion of the Court.

Florida Stat. s. 794.03 (1987) makes it unlawful to "print, publish, or broadcast . . . in any instrument of mass communication" the name of the victim of a sexual offence. Pursuant to this statute, appellant *The Florida Star* was found civilly liable for publishing the name of a rape victim which it had obtained from a publicly released police report. The issue presented here is whether this result comports with the First Amendment. We hold that it does not.

I. *The Florida Star* is a weekly newspaper which serves the community of Jacksonville, Florida, and which has an average circulation of approximately 18,000 copies. A regular feature of the newspaper is its "Police Reports" section. The section, typically two to three pages in length, contains brief articles describing local criminal incidents under police investigation. On October 20, 1983, appellee BJF reported to the Duval County, Florida, Sheriff's Department (the Department) that she had been robbed and sexually assaulted by an unknown assailant. The Department prepared a report on the incident which identified BJF by her full name. The Department then placed the report in its press room. The Department does not restrict access either to the press room or to the reports made available therein.

A *Florida Star* reporter-trainee sent to the pressroom copied the police report verbatim, including BJF's full name, on a blank duplicate of the Department's forms. A *Florida Star* reporter then prepared a one-paragraph article about the crime, derived entirely from the trainee's copy of the police report. The article included BJF's full name. It appeared in the "Robberies" subsection of the "Police Reports" section on 29 October 1983, one of fifty-four police blotter stories in that day's edition. The article read: "[BJF] reported on Thursday, 20 October, she was crossing Brentwood Park, which is in the 500 block of Golfair Boulevard, enroute to her bus stop, when an unknown black man ran up behind the lady and placed a knife to her neck and told her not to yell. The suspect then undressed the lady and had sexual intercourse with her before fleeing the scene with her 60 cents, Timex watch and gold necklace. Patrol efforts have been suspended concerning this incident because of lack of evidence."

In printing BJF's full name, *The Florida Star* violated its internal policy of not publishing the names of sexual offence victims.

[BJF sued both the newspaper and the Sheriff's Department. The latter settled for £2,500. The *Star*'s motion to dismiss was denied.]

At the ensuing day-long trial, BJF testified that she had suffered emotional distress from the publication of her name. She stated that she had heard about the article from fellow workers and acquaintances; that her mother had received several threatening phone calls from a man who stated that he would rape BJF again; and that these events had forced BJF to change her phone number and residence, to seek police protection, and to obtain mental health counselling. In defence, *The Florida Star* put forth evidence indicating that the newspaper had learned BJF's name from the incident report released by the Department, and that the newspaper's violation of its internal rule against publishing the names of sexual offence victims was inadvertent.

At the close of BJF's case, and again at the close of its defence, *The Florida Star* moved for a directed verdict. On both occasions, the trial judge denied these motions. He ruled from the bench that s. 794.03 was constitutional because it reflected a proper balance between the First Amendment and privacy rights, as it applied only to a narrow set of "rather sensitive . . . criminal offences." At the close of the newspaper's defence, the judge granted BJF's motion for a directed verdict on the issue of negligence, finding the newspaper per se negligent based upon its violation of s. 794.03. This ruling left the jury to consider only the questions of causation and damages. The judge instructed the jury that it could award BJF punitive damages if it found that the newspaper had "acted with reckless indifference to the rights of others." The jury awarded BJF £75,000 in compensatory damages and £25,000 in punitive damages. Against the actual damage award, the judge set off BJF's settlement with the Department.

The First District Court of Appeal affirmed in a three-paragraph *per curiam* opinion. . . . The Supreme Court of Florida denied discretionary review.

The Florida Star appealed to this Court. We noted probable jurisdiction, and now reverse.

II. The tension between the right which the First Amendment accords to a free press, on the one hand, and the protections which various statutes and common-law doctrines accord to personal privacy against the publication of truthful information, on the other, is a subject we have addressed several times in recent years. Our decisions in cases involving government attempts to sanction the accurate dissemination of information as invasive of privacy, have not, however, exhaustively considered this conflict. On the contrary, although our decisions have without exception upheld the press's right to publish, we have emphasized each time that we were resolving this conflict only as it arose in a discrete factual context.

The parties to this case frame their contentions in light of a trilogy of cases which have presented, in different contexts, the conflict between truthful reporting and state-protected privacy interests. [The Court briefly reviewed *Cox Broadcasting, Oklahoma Publishing*, and *Daily Mail*.]

Appellant takes the position that this case is indistinguishable from *Cox Broadcasting*. Alternatively, it urges that our decisions in the above trilogy, and in other cases in which we have held that the right of the press to publish truth overcame asserted interests other than personal privacy, can be distilled to yield a broader First Amendment principle that the press may never be punished, civilly or criminally, for publishing the truth. Appellee counters that the privacy trilogy is inapposite, because in each case the private information already appeared on a "public record," and because the privacy interests at stake were far less profound than in the present case. In the alternative, appellee urges that *Cox Broadcasting* be overruled and replaced with a categorical rule that publication of the name of a rape victim never enjoys constitutional protection.

We conclude that imposing damages on appellant for publishing BJF's name violates the First Amendment, although not for either of the reasons appellant urges. Despite the strong resemblance this case bears to *Cox Broadcasting*, that case cannot fairly be read as controlling here. The name of the rape victim in that case was obtained from courthouse records that were open to public inspection, a fact which Justice White's opinion for the Court repeatedly noted (noting "special protected nature of accurate reports of *judicial* proceedings") (emphasis added). Significantly, one of the reasons we gave in *Cox Broadcasting* for invalidating the challenged damages award was the important role the press plays in subjecting trials to public scrutiny and thereby helping guarantee their fairness. That role is not directly compromised where, as here, the information in question comes from a police report prepared and disseminated at a time at which not only had no adversarial criminal proceedings begun, but no suspect had been identified.

Nor need we accept appellant's invitation to hold broadly that truthful publication may never be punished consistent with the First Amendment. Our cases have carefully eschewed reaching this ultimate question, mindful that the future may bring scenarios which prudence counsels our not resolving anticipatorily. See, e.g., *Near* v. *Minnesota* (hypothesising "publication of the sailing dates of transports or the number and location of troops"); see also *Garrison* v. *Louisiana* (endorsing absolute defence of truth "where discussion of public affairs is concerned," but leaving unsettled the constitutional implications of truthfulness "in the discrete area of purely private libels"); *Landmark Communications Inc.* v. *Virginia*, 435 US 829, 838 (1978); *Time, Inc.* v. *Hill*, 385 US 374, 383, n. 7 (1967). Indeed, in *Cox Broadcasting*, we pointedly refused to answer even the less sweeping question "whether truthful publications may ever be subjected to civil or criminal liability" for invading "an area of privacy" defined by the State. Respecting the fact that press freedom and privacy rights are both "plainly rooted in the traditions and significant concerns of our society," we instead focused on the less sweeping issue of "whether the State may impose sanctions on the accurate publication of the name of a rape victim obtained from public records—more specifically, from judicial records which are maintained in connection with a public prosecution and which themselves are open to public inspection." We continue to believe that the sensitivity and significance of the interests presented in clashes between First Amendment and privacy rights counsel relying on limited principles that sweep no more broadly than the appropriate context of the instant case.

In our view, this case is appropriately analysed with reference to such a limited First Amendment principle. It is the one, in fact, which we articulated in *Daily Mail* in our synthesis of prior cases involving attempts to punish truthful publication: "[I]f a newspaper lawfully obtains truthful information about a matter of public significance then state officials may not constitutionally punish publication of the information, absent a need to further a state interest of the highest order." According the press the ample protection provided by that principle is supported by at least three separate considerations, in addition to, of course, the overarching "public interest, secured by the Constitution, in the dissemination of truth." The cases on which the *Daily Mail* synthesis relied demonstrate these considerations.

First, because the *Daily Mail* formulation only protects the publication of information which a newspaper has "lawfully obtain[ed]," the government retains ample means of safeguarding significant interests upon which publication may impinge, including protecting a rape victim's anonymity. To the extent sensitive information rests in private hands, the government may under some circumstances forbid its non consensual acquisition, thereby bringing outside of the *Daily Mail* principle the publication of any information so acquired. To the extent sensitive information is in the government's custody, it has even greater power to forestall or mitigate the injury caused by its release. The government may classify certain information, establish and enforce procedures ensuring its redacted release, and extend a damages remedy against the government or its officials where the government's mishandling of sensitive information leads to its dissemination. Where information is entrusted to the government, a less drastic means than punishing truthful publication almost always exists for guarding against the dissemination of private facts. See, e.g., [*Landmark Communications*] ("much of the risk [from disclosure of sensitive information regarding judicial disciplinary proceedings] can be eliminated through careful internal procedures to protect the confidentiality of Commission proceedings"); [*Oklahoma Publishing*] (noting trial judge's failure to avail himself of the opportunity, provided by a state statute, to close juvenile hearing to the public, including members of the press, who later broadcast juvenile defendant's name); [*Cox Broadcasting*] ('If there are privacy interests to be protected in judicial proceedings, the States must respond by means which avoid public documentation or other exposure of private information').

A second consideration undergirding the *Daily Mail* principle is the fact that punishing the press for its dissemination of information which is already publicly available is relatively unlikely to advance the interests in the service of which the State seeks to act. It is not, of course, always the case that information lawfully acquired by the press is known, or accessible, to others. But where the government has made certain information publicly available, it is highly anomalous to sanction persons other than the source of its release. We noted this anomaly in *Cox Broadcasting*: "By placing the information in the public domain on official court records, the State must be presumed to have concluded that the public interest was thereby being served." The *Daily Mail* formulation reflects the fact that it is a limited set of cases indeed where, despite the accessibility of the public to certain information, a meaningful public interest is served by restricting its further release by other entities, like the press. As *Daily Mail* observed in its summary of *Oklahoma Publishing*, "once the truthful information was 'publicly revealed' or 'in the public domain' the court could not constitutionally restrain its dissemination."

A third and final consideration is the "timidity and self-censorship which may result from allowing the media to be punished for publishing certain truthful information". *Cox Broadcasting* noted this concern with over deterrence in the context of information made public through official court records, but the fear of excessive media self-suppression is applicable as well to other information released without qualification, by the government. A contrary rule, [denying] protection to those who rely on the government's implied representations of the lawfulness of dissemination, would force upon the media the onerous obligation of sifting through government press releases, reports, and pronouncements to prune out material arguably unlawful for publication. This situation could inhere even where the newspaper's sole object was to reproduce, with no substantial change, the government's rendition of the event in question.

Applied to the instant case, the *Daily Mail* principle clearly commands reversal. The first inquiry is whether the newspaper "lawfully obtain[ed] truthful information about a matter of public significance." It is undisputed that the news article describing the assault on BJF was accurate. In addition, appellant lawfully obtained BJF's name. Appellee's argument to the contrary is based on the fact that under Florida law, police reports which reveal the identity of the victim of a sexual offence are not among the matters of "public record" which the public, by law, is entitled to inspect. But the fact that the state officials are not required to disclose such reports does not make it unlawful for a newspaper to receive them when furnished by the government. Nor does the fact that the Department apparently failed to fulfil its obligation under s. 794.03 not to "cause or allow to be ... published" the name of a sexual offence victim make the newspaper's ensuing receipt of this information unlawful. Even assuming the Constitution permitted a State to proscribe *receipt* of information, Florida has not taken this step. It is clear, furthermore, that the news article concerned "a matter of public significance," in the sense in which the *Daily Mail* synthesis of prior cases used that term. That is, the article generally, as opposed to the specific identity contained within it, involved a matter of paramount public import: the commission, and investigation, of a violent crime which had been reported to authorities. See *Cox Broadcasting* (article identifying victim of rape-murder); [*Oklahoma Publishing*] (article identifying juvenile alleged to have committed murder); [*Daily Mail*] (same); cf. [*Landmark Communications*] (article identifying judges whose conduct was being investigated).

The second inquiry is whether imposing liability on appellant pursuant to s. 794.03 serves "a need to further a state interest of the highest order." [*Daily Mail*] Appellee argues that a rule punishing publication furthers three closely related interests: the privacy of victims of sexual offences; the physical safety of such victims, who may be targeted for retaliation if their names become known to their assailants; and the goal of encouraging victims of such crimes to report these offences without fear of exposure.

At a time in which we are daily reminded of the tragic reality of rape, it is undeniable that these are highly significant interests, a fact underscored by the Florida Legislature's explicit attempt to protect these interests by enacting a criminal statute prohibiting much dissemination of victim identities. We accordingly do not rule out the possibility that, in a proper case, imposing civil sanctions for publication of the name of a rape victim might be so overwhelmingly necessary to advance these interests as to satisfy the *Daily Mail* standard. For three independent reasons, however, imposing liability for publication under the circumstances of this case is too precipitous a means of advancing these interests to convince us that there is a "need" within the meaning of the *Daily Mail* formulation for Florida to take this extreme step. *Cf. Landmark Communications* (invalidating penalty on publication despite State's expressed interest in non dissemination, reflected in statute prohibiting unauthorised divulging of names of judges under investigation).

First is the manner in which appellant obtained the identifying information in question. As we have noted, where the government itself provides information to the media, it is most appropriate to assume that the government had, but failed to utilise, far more limited means of guarding against dissemination than the extreme step of punishing truthful speech. That assumption is richly borne out in this case. BJF's identity would never have come to light were it not for the erroneous, if inadvertent, inclusion by the Department of her full name in an accident report made available in a press room open to the public. Florida's policy against disclosure of rape victims' identities, reflected in s. 794.03, was undercut by the Department's failure to abide by this policy. Where, as here, the government has failed to police itself in disseminating information, it is clear under *Cox Broadcasting*, *Oklahoma Publishing*, and *Landmark Communications* that the imposition of damages against the press for its subsequent publication can hardly be said to be a narrowly tailored means of safeguarding anonymity. Once the government has placed such information in the public domain, "reliance must rest upon the judgment of those who decide what to publish or broadcast," [*Cox Broadcasting*] and hopes for restitution must rest upon the willingness of the government to compensate victims for their loss of privacy, and to protect them from the other consequences of its mishandling of the information which these victims provided in confidence.

That appellant gained access to the information in question through a government news release makes it especially likely that, if liability were to be imposed, self-censorship would result. Reliance on a news release is a paradigmatically "routine newspaper reporting techniqu[e]." [*Daily Mail*] The government's issuance of such a release, without qualification, can only convey to recipients that the government considered dissemination lawful, and indeed expected the recipients to disseminate the information further. Had appellant merely reproduced the news release prepared and released by the Department, imposing civil damages would surely violate the First Amendment. The fact that appellant converted the police report into a news story by adding the linguistic connecting tissue necessary to transform the report's facts into full sentences cannot change this result.

A second problem with Florida's imposition of liability for publication is the broad sweep of the negligence per se standard applied under the civil cause of action implied from s. 794.03. Unlike claims based on the common law tort of invasion of privacy, civil actions based on s. 794.03 require no case-by-case findings that the disclosure of a fact about a person's private life was one that a reasonable person would find highly offensive. On the contrary, under the per se theory of negligence adopted by the courts below, liability follows automatically from publication. This is so regardless of whether the identity of the victim is already known throughout the community; whether the victim has voluntarily called public attention to the offence; or whether the identity of the victim has otherwise become a reasonable subject of public concern—because, perhaps, questions have arisen whether the victim fabricated an assault by a particular person. Nor is there a scienter requirement of any kind under s. 794.03, engendering the perverse result that truthful publications challenged pursuant to this cause of action are less protected by the First Amendment than even the least protected defamatory falsehoods: those involving purely private figures, where liability is evaluated under a standard, usually applied by a jury, of ordinary negligence. See *Gertz* v. *Robert Welch, Inc.* We have previously noted the impermissibility of categorical prohibitions upon media access where important First Amendment interests are at stake. See *Globe Newspaper Co.* v. *Superior Court*, 457 US 596, 608 (1982) (invalidating state statute providing for the categorical exclusion of the public from trials of sexual offences involving juvenile victims.) More individualised adjudication is no less indispensable where the State, seeking to safeguard the anonymity of crime victims, sets its face against publication of their names.

Third, and finally, the facial under-inclusiveness of s. 794.03 raises serious doubts about whether Florida is, in fact, serving, with this statute, the significant interests which appellee invokes in support of affirmance. Section 794.03 prohibits the publication of identifying information only if this information appears in an "instrument of mass communication", a term the statute does not define. Section 794.03 does not prohibit the spread by other means of the identities of victims of sexual offences. An individual who maliciously spreads word of the identity of a rape victim is thus not covered, despite the fact that the communication of such information to persons who live near, or work with, the victim may have consequences equally devastating as the exposure of her name to large numbers of strangers.

When a State attempts the extraordinary measure of punishing truthful publication in the name of privacy, it must demonstrate its commitment to advancing this interest by applying its prohibition even-handedly, to the small time disseminator as well as the media giant. Where important First Amendment interests are at stake, the mass scope of disclosure is not an acceptable surrogate for injury. A ban on disclosures effected by "instrument[s] of mass communication" simply cannot be defended on the ground that partial prohibitions may effect partial relief. See [*Daily Mail*] (statute is insufficiently tailored to interest in protecting anonymity where it restricted only newspapers, not the electronic media or other forms of publication, from identifying juvenile defendants); *id.*, at 110 (Rehnquist, J., concurring in judgment) (same); *cf. Arkansas Writers' Project, Inc.* v. *Ragland*, 481 US 221, 229 (1987); *Minneapolis Star & Tribune Co.* v. *Minnesota Comm'r of Revenue*, 460 US 575, 585 (1983). Without more careful and inclusive precautions against alternative forms of dissemination, we cannot conclude that Florida's selective ban on publication by the mass media satisfactorily accomplishes its stated purpose.

III. Our holding today is limited. We do not hold that truthful publication is automatically constitutionally protected, or that there is no zone of personal privacy within which the State may protect the individual from intrusion by the press, or even that a State may never punish publication of the name of a victim of a sexual offence. We hold only that where a newspaper publishes truthful information which it has lawfully obtained, punishment may lawfully be imposed, if at all, only when narrowly tailored to a state interest of the highest order, and that no such interest is satisfactorily served by imposing liability . . . under the facts of this case. The decision below is therefore reversed.

Addendum 3

S. D. Warren and L. D. Brandeis, "The Right to Privacy" 4 *Harv. L. Rev.* 193 (1890).

Of the desirability—indeed of the necessity—of some such protection, there can, it is believed, be no doubt. The press is overstepping in every direction the obvious bounds of propriety and of decency. Gossip is no longer the resource of the idle and the vicious, but has become a trade, which is pursued with industry as well as effrontery. To satisfy a prurient taste the details of sexual relations are spread broadcast in the columns of the daily papers. To occupy the indolent, column upon column is filled with idle gossip, which can only be procured by intrusion upon the domestic circle. The intensity and complexity of life, attending upon advancing civilisation, have rendered necessary some retreat from the world, and man, under the refining influence of culture, has become more sensitive to publicity, so that solitude and privacy have become more essential to the individual; but modern enterprise and invention have, through invasions upon his privacy, subjected him to mental pain and distress, far greater than could be inflicted by mere bodily injury.

Nor is the harm wrought by such invasions confined to the suffering of those who may be made the subjects of journalistic or other enterprise. In this, as in other branches of commerce, the supply creates the demand. Each crop of unseemly gossip, thus harvested, becomes the seed of more, and in direct proportion to its circulation, results in a lowering of social standards and of morality. Even gossip apparently harmless, when widely and persistently circulated is potent for evil. It both belittles and perverts. It belittles by inverting the relative importance of things, thus dwarfing the thoughts and aspirations of a people. When personal gossip attains the dignity of print, and crowds the space available for matters of real interest to the community, what wonder that the ignorant and thoughtless mistake its relative importance. Easy of comprehension, appealing to that weak side of human nature which is never wholly cast down by the misfortunes and frailties of our neighbours, no one can be surprised that it usurps the place of interest in brains capable of other things. Triviality destroys at once robustness of thought and delicacy of feeling. No enthusiasm can flourish, no generous impulse can survive under the blighting influence.

Addendum 4

Gordon Kaye (by Peter Froggatt his next friend) v. *Andrew Robertson and Sport Newspapers Ltd.* Court of Appeal 23 February 1990

JUDGMENT

GLIDEWELL LJ

The Plaintiff, Mr Gordon Kaye, is a well-known actor, the star of a popular television comedy series. This formed the basis of a stage show in which the Plaintiff was appearing in January 1990. The show finished its run in London on 27 January 1990. Thereafter it was due to appear in Australia with the Plaintiff in the lead.

Mr Peter Froggatt is a theatrical agent and a personal friend of Mr Kaye. Since Mr Kaye is at present incapable of managing his own affairs, in this action Mr Froggatt is his next friend.

On 25 January 1990 Mr Kaye was driving his car on a road in London during a gale, when a piece of wood became detached from an advertisement hoarding, smashed through the windscreen of the Plaintiff's car and struck him on the head. The Plaintiff suffered severe injuries to his head and brain. He was taken to Charing Cross Hospital where he was on a life support machine for three days. He was then in intensive care, until on 2 February he was moved into a private room, forming part of Ward G at the hospital.

It was apparent that there was intense interest amongst Mr Kaye's fans and consequently in many newspapers and in television in Mr Kaye's progress and condition. For fear that his recovery might be hindered if he had too many visitors, and to lessen the risk of infection, the hospital authorities placed notices at the entrance to the ward asking visitors to see a member of the staff before visiting. Mr Froggatt agreed with the hospital authorities a list of people who might be permitted to visit Mr Kaye, and this was pinned up outside his room. A similar notice to that outside the ward was pinned on the door of the room itself.

The first Defendant is the editor and the second Defendant company is the publisher of *Sunday Sport*, a weekly publication which Mr Justice Potter, from whose decision this is an appeal, described as having "a lurid and sensational style". A copy of a recent edition of *Sunday Sport* which was put in evidence before us shows that many of the advertisements contained in it are for various forms of pornographic material. This indicates the readership it seeks to attract.

Until 13 February 1990, Mr Kaye had not been interviewed since his accident by any representative of a newspaper or television programme. On that day, acting on Mr Robertson's instructions, a journalist and a photographer from *Sunday Sport* went to Charing Cross Hospital and gained access to the corridor outside Ward G. They were not seen nor intercepted by any of the hospital staff. Ignoring the notices on the door to the ward and on the Plaintiff's door, they entered the Plaintiff's room. Mr Kaye apparently agreed to talk to them and according to a transcript that we have heard of a taped record they made of what transpired, did not object to them photographing various cards and flowers in his room. In fact a number of photographs, both in colour and monochrome, were taken of the Plaintiff himself showing the substantial scars to his head amongst other matters. The taking of the photographs involved the use of a flashlight.

After some time members of the nursing staff of the hospital learned what was happening. They attempted to persuade the journalist and the photographer to leave, but without success. Security staff were called, and the representatives of *Sunday Sport* were ejected.

Medical evidence exhibited by Mr Froggatt to his affidavit in this action says that Mr Kaye was in no fit condition to be interviewed or to give any informed consent to be interviewed. The accuracy of this opinion is confirmed by the fact that approximately a quarter-of-an-hour after the representatives of *Sunday Sport* had left his room, Mr Kaye had no recollection of the incident.

According to Mr Robertson's affidavit, he regards what he and his staff had achieved as, "A great old-fashioned scoop". He makes it clear in his affidavit that he realised that a number of newspapers were interested in interviewing and taking photographs of Mr Kaye, and some of them would "pay large sums of money for the privilege". He says, disingenuously, "I do not think it unreasonable to attempt a direct approach in order to get a free interview. The Plaintiff only had to refuse".

The Defendants made it clear that they intended to publish an article in *Sunday Sport* about the interview with the Plaintiff, using one or more of the photographs that had been taken. A draft of the article as originally prepared is exhibited to Mr Robertson's affidavit. It was intended to be in two parts, a front page lead with a banner headline and a full story inside the newspaper. The wording of both parts of the article made it clear that the Defendants were saying that Mr Kaye had agreed to be interviewed and to be photographed and described the interview and pictures as exclusive to *Sunday Sport*.

On Friday, 16 February, 1990, upon Mr Froggatt undertaking by Counsel to issue by noon on Monday, 19 February, 1990 and serve on the Defendants the writ in this action together with an undertaking in the usual form as to damages, Mr Justice Potter on an application made on behalf of the Plaintiff by Mr Froggatt granted an injunction against the Defendants in the following terms:

> "1. The Defendants and each of them whether by themselves, their servants or agents or otherwise be restrained from publishing, distributing, or causing to be published or distributed by any means howsoever or by otherwise exploiting:
>
> (a) any photographs or part of any photographs taken of the Plaintiff at the Charing Cross Hospital on 13 February 1990;
>
> (b) any statement made by the Plaintiff in the presence of any servant or agent of the Second Defendants at Charing Cross Hospital on 13 February 1990 or any summary or record thereof until trial or further order;

2. The Defendants and each of them be restrained whether by themselves, their servants or agents or otherwise from passing off any photograph or part of a photograph taken of the Plaintiff at Charing Cross Hospital on 13 February 1990 as a photograph consented to by the Plaintiff and from passing off any statement made by the Plaintiff in the presence of any servant or agent of the Second Defendants in Charing Cross Hospital on 13 February 1990 as a statement voluntarily given by the Plaintiff to *The Sunday Sport* until trial or further order;

3. The Defendants and each of them be restrained whether by themselves, their servants or agents or otherwise from publishing or causing to be published any statement to the effect that the Plaintiff had posed for a photograph for publication in *The Sunday Sport* and/or had given an interview to *The Sunday Sport* while in Charing Cross Hospital for treatment until trial or further order;"

The Judge also ordered the Defendants to deliver up "any tape-recording, notes of interview or photographs obtained or taken by any servant or agent of the second Defendants in Charing Cross Hospital on 13 February 1990 and any copies of negatives thereof".

The Defendants appealed against the Judge's order. We heard the appeal on Friday, 23 February, 1990. At the conclusion of the hearing we announced our decision which was to the effect that the appeal was allowed to the extent that we discharged the order made under heads 1 and 2 set out above, and that we substituted for the order under head 3 an order in the following terms:

"The Defendants and each of them be restrained until trial or further order whether by themselves their servants or agents from publishing, causing to be published or permitting to be published anything which could be reasonably understood or convey to any person reading or looking at the Defendants' *Sunday Sport* newspaper that the Plaintiff had voluntarily permitted any photographs to be taken for publication in that newspaper or had voluntarily permitted representatives of the Defendants to interview him while a patient in the Charing Cross hospital undergoing treatment".

In place of the order for delivery up, we accepted an undertaking from the Defendants' solicitors

"that the material referred to in paragraph 4 of the aforesaid order will be kept in safe custody by the Defendants' Solicitors with the proviso that they shall be entitled to release it to the 1st Defendant to be used in any way which complies with the terms of the injunction aforestated".

I now give my reasons for arriving at this decision.

It is well-known that in English law there is no right to privacy, and accordingly there is no right of action for breach of a person's privacy. The facts of the present case are a graphic illustration of the desirability of Parliament considering whether and in what circumstances statutory provision can be made to protect the privacy of individuals. In the absence of such a right, the Plaintiff's advisers have sought to base their claim to injunctions upon other well-established rights of action. These are:

1. Libel
2. Malicious falsehood
3. Trespass to the person
4. Passing off.

The appeal canvassed all four rights of action, and it is necessary to deal with each in turn.

1. *Libel* The basis of the Plaintiff's case under this head is that the article as originally written clearly implied that Mr Kaye consented to give the first "exclusive" interview to *Sunday Sport*, and to be photographed by their photographer. This was untrue: Mr Kaye was in no fit condition to give any informed consent, and such consent as he may appear to have given was, and should have been known by *Sunday Sport*'s representative to be, of no effect. The implication in the article would have the effect of lowering Mr Kaye in the esteem of right-thinking people, and was thus defamatory.

The Plaintiff's case is based on the well-known decision in *Tolley* v. *JS Fry & Sons Ltd* [1931] AC 333. Mr Tolley was a well-known amateur golfer. Without his consent, Fry published an advertisement which consisted of a caricature of the Plaintiff with a caddie, each with a packet of Fry's chocolate protruding from his pocket. The caricature was accompanied by doggerel verse which used Mr Tolley's name and extolled the virtues of the chocolate. The Plaintiff alleged that the advertisement implied that he had received payment for the advertisement, which would damage his reputation as an amateur player. The Judge at the trial ruled that the advertisement was capable of being defamatory, and on appeal the House of Lords upheld this ruling.

It seems that an analogy with *Tolley* v. *Fry* was the main plank of Mr Justice Potter's decision to grant injunctions in this case. Mr Milmo for the Defendants submits that, assuming that the article was capable of having the meaning alleged, this would not be a sufficient basis for interlocutory relief. In *William Coulson & Sons* v. *James Coulson & Co* [1887] 3 TLR 46 this court held that, though the High Court has jurisdiction to grant an interim injunction before the trial of a libel action, it is a jurisdiction to be exercised only sparingly. In his judgment the Master of the Rolls said:

"Therefore to justify the court granting an interim injunction it must come to a decision upon the question of libel or no libel, before the jury decided whether it was a libel or not. Therefore the jurisdiction was of a delicate nature. It ought only to be exercised in the clearest cases, where any jury would say that the matter complained of was libellous and where if the jury did not so find the court would set aside the verdict as unreasonable".

This is still the rule in actions for defamation, despite the decision of the House of Lords in *American Cyanamid* v. *Ethicon* [1975] AC 396 in relation to interim injunctions generally. This court so decided in *Herbage* v. *Times Newspapers Limited and others*, unreported but decided on 30 April 1981.

Mr Milmo submits that on the evidence we cannot be confident that any jury would inevitably decide that the implication that Mr Kaye had consented to give his first interview to *Sunday Sport* was libellous. Accordingly, we ought not to grant interlocutory relief on this ground.

It is in my view certainly arguable that the intended article would be libellous, on the authority of *Tolley* v. *Fry*. I think that a jury would probably find that Mr Kaye had been libelled, but I cannot say that such a conclusion is inevitable. It follows that I agree with Mr Milmo's submission and in this respect I disagree with the learned Judge. I therefore would not base an injunction on a right of action for libel.

2. *Malicious Falsehood* The essentials of this tort are that the Defendant has published about the Plaintiff words which are false, that they were published maliciously, and that special damage has followed as the direct and natural result of their publication. As to special damage, the effect of s. 3 (1) of the Defamation Act 1952 is that it is sufficient if the words published in writing are calculated to cause pecuniary damage to the Plaintiff. Malice will be inferred if it be proved that the words were calculated to produce damage and that the Defendant knew when he published the words that they were false or was reckless as to whether they were false or not.

The test in *Coulson* v. *Coulson* applies to interlocutory injunctions in actions for malicious falsehood as it does in actions for defamation. However, in relation to this action, the test applies only to the requirement that the Plaintiff must show that the words were false. In the present case I have no doubt that any jury which did not find that the clear implication from the words contained in the Defendant's draft article were false would be making a totally unreasonable finding. Thus the test is satisfied in relation to this cause of action.

As to malice I equally have no doubt from the evidence, including the transcript of the tape-recording of the "interview" with Mr Kaye in his hospital room which we have read, that it was quite apparent to the reporter and photographer from *Sunday Sport* that Mr Kaye was in no condition to give any informed consent to them interviewing or photographing him. Moreover, even if the journalists had been in any doubt about Mr Kaye's fitness to give his consent, Mr Robertson could not have entertained any such doubt after he read the affidavit sworn on behalf of Mr Kaye in these proceedings. Any subsequent publication of the falsehood would therefore inevitably be malicious.

As to damage, I have already recorded that Mr Robertson appreciated that Mr Kaye's story was one for which other newspapers would be willing to pay "large sums of money". It needs little imagination to appreciate that whichever journal secured the first interview with Mr Kaye would be willing to pay the most. Mr Kaye thus has a potentially valuable right to sell the story of his accident and his recovery when he is fit enough to tell it. If the Defendants are able to publish the article they proposed, or one anything like it, the value of this right would in my view be seriously lessened, and Mr Kaye's story thereafter be worth much less to him.

I have considered whether damages would be an adequate remedy in these circumstances. They would inevitably be difficult to calculate, would also follow some time after the event, and in my view would in no way be adequate. It thus follows that in my opinion all the preconditions to the grant of an interlocutory injunction in respect of this cause of action are made out. I will return later to what I consider to be the appropriate form of injunction.

3. *Trespass to the Person* It is strictly unnecessary to consider this cause of action in the light of the view I have expressed about malicious falsehood. However I will set out my view shortly. The Plaintiff's case in relation to this cause of action is that the taking of the flashlight photographs may well have caused distress to Mr Kaye and set back his recovery, and thus caused him injury. In this sense it can be said to be a battery. Mr Caldecott, for Mr Kaye, could not refer us to any authority in which the taking of a photograph or indeed the flashing of a light had been held to be a battery. Nevertheless I am prepared to accept that it may well be the case that if a bright light is deliberately shone into another person's eyes and injures his sight, or damages him in some other way, this may be in law a battery. But in my view the necessary effects are not established by the evidence in this case. Though there must have been an obvious risk that any disturbance to Mr Kaye would set back his recovery, there is no evidence that the taking of the photographs did in fact cause him any damage.

Moreover, the injunction sought in relation to this head of action would not be intended to prevent another anticipated battery, since none was anticipated. The intention here is to prevent the Defendants from profiting from the taking of the photographs, i.e. from their own trespass. Attractive though this argument may appear to be, I cannot find as a matter of law that an injunction should be granted in these circumstances. Accordingly, I would not base an injunction on this cause of action.

4. *Passing off* Mr Caldecott submits (though in this case not with any great vigour) that the essentials of the tort of passing off, as laid down by the speeches in the House of Lords in *Warnink v. J Townsend & Sons* [1979] AC 731 are satisfied here. I only need say shortly that in my view they are not. I think that the Plaintiff is not in the position of a trader in relation to his interest in his story about his accident and his recovery, and thus fails from the start to have a right of action under this head.

Forms of Injunction

Before I turn to consider the form of an interim injunction which should be granted, I must comment that apart from the initial draft of the article intended to be printed in *Sunday Sport* which was before the Judge, two other versions have subsequently appeared. A second was put before Mr Justice Potter, and a third before us. Both the second and third versions use words which do not imply so clearly as did the original version of the article that the Plaintiff consented to be interviewed and photographed by *Sunday Sport*. Nevertheless, in my view the later articles are irrelevant for present purposes. The fact that at one time the Defendants envisaged printing the original article is sufficient to entitle the Plaintiff to an injunction which prohibits the Defendants from publishing an article which contains the implication which was to be read into that original article.

In relation to the injunctions granted by Mr Justice Potter, the wording of the first injunction was in my view wider than was necessary to prevent the Defendants doing that which was objectionable, i.e. publishing material from which the objectionable implication could be drawn.

The second injunction granted by Potter J. was based upon the tort of passing off. I have already said that in my view the evidence does not prove the commission of this tort. It was for these reasons, that in common with my brethren, I took the view that the first and second injunctions should be discharged. We considered that the third injunction was in general satisfactory but needed some amendment, and basing ourselves on the Plaintiff's right of action in malicious falsehood, we granted the injunction in the terms set out above.

I therefore concluded that, to the extent I have indicated, the Defendants' appeal should be allowed, but that they should be subject to an injunction in the terms which we have already announced.

BINGHAM LJ

I have had the benefit of reading in draft the judgment prepared by Glidewell LJ. I agree with it, and with the order made.

Any reasonable and fair-minded person hearing the facts which Glidewell LJ has recited would in my judgment conclude that these Defendants had wronged the Plaintiff. I am therefore pleased to be persuaded that the Plaintiff is able to establish, with sufficient strength to justify an interlocutory order, a cause of action against the Defendants in malicious falsehood. Had he failed to establish any cause of action, we should of course have been powerless to act, however great our sympathy for the Plaintiff and however strong our distaste for the Defendants' conduct.

This case nonetheless highlights, yet again, the failure of both the Common law of England and statute to protect in an effective way the personal privacy of individual citizens. This has been the subject of much comment over the years, perhaps most recently by Professor Markesinis (*The German Law of Torts*, 2nd edn. 1990 page 316) where he writes:

> "English law, on the whole, compares unfavourably with German law. True, many aspects of the human personality and privacy are protected by a multitude of existing torts but this means fitting the facts of each case in the pigeon-hole of an existing tort and this process may not only involve strained constructions; often it may also leave a deserving Plaintiff without a remedy."

The Defendants' conduct towards the Plaintiff here was "a monstrous invasion of his privacy" (to adopt the language of Griffiths J in *Bernstein* v. *Skyviews Ltd* [1978] QB 479 at 489G). If ever a person has a right to be let alone by strangers with no public interest to pursue, it must surely be when he lies in hospital recovering from brain surgery and in no more than partial command of his faculties. It is this invasion of his privacy which underlies the Plaintiff's complaint. Yet it alone, however gross, does not entitle him to relief in English law.

The Plaintiff's suggested cause of action in libel is in my view arguable, for reasons which Glidewell LJ has given. We could not give interlocutory relief on that ground. Battery and assault are causes of action never developed to cover acts such as these: they could apply only if the law were substantially extended and the available facts strained to unacceptable lengths. A claim in passing off is hopeless. Fortunately, a cause of action in malicious falsehood exists, but even that obliges us to limit the relief we can grant in a way which would not bind us if the Plaintiff's cause of action arose from the invasion of privacy of which, fundamentally, he complains. We cannot give the Plaintiff the breadth of protection which I would, for my part, wish. The problems of defining and limiting a tort of privacy are formidable, but the present case strengthens my hope that the review now in progress may prove fruitful.

LEGGATT LJ

I agree with both judgments that have been delivered. In view of the importance of the topic I add a note about the way in which the Common law has developed in the United States to meet the need which in the present case we are unable to fulfil satisfactorily.

The recognition of a right to privacy seemed to be in prospect when Lord Byron obtained an injunction to restrain the false attribution to him of a bad poem: *Byron* v. *Johnston* [1816] 2 Mer. 29. But it was not until 1890 that in their article *The Right to Privacy* 4 *Harv. L. Rev.* 193 Warren and Brandeis reviewed a number of English cases on defamation and breaches of rights of property, confidence and contract, and concluded that all were based on a broader common principle. They argued that recognition of the principle would enable the courts to protect the individual against the infliction by the press of mental pain and distress through invasion of his privacy. Since then the right to privacy, or "the right to be let alone", has gained acceptance in most jurisdictions in the United States.

It is manifested in several forms: see Dean Prosser, *Torts*, 4th edn., 1971. One example is such intrusion upon physical solitude as would be objectionable to a reasonable man. So when in *Barber v. Time Inc.* [1942] 159 S.W. 2d 291 the Plaintiff was confined to a hospital bed, the publication of her photograph taken without consent was held to be an invasion of a private right of which she was entitled to complain. Similarly, a so-called "right of publicity" has developed to protect the commercial interest of celebrities in their identities. "The theory of the right is that a celebrity's identity can be valuable in the promotion of products, and the celebrity has an interest that may be protected from the unauthorised commercial exploitation of that identity. 'The famous have an exclusive legal right during life to control and profit from the commercial use of their name and personality'": *Carson v. Here's Johnny Portable Toilets Inc.* [1983] 698 F. 2d 831 at page 835.

We do not need a First Amendment to preserve the freedom of the Press, but the abuse of that freedom can be ensured only by the enforcement of a right to privacy. This right has so long been disregarded here that it can be recognised now only by the Legislature. Especially since there is available in the United States a wealth of experience of the enforcement of this right both at common law and also under statute, it is to be hoped that the making good of this signal shortcoming in our law will not be long delayed.

Addendum 5

The impact of the Kaye decision on the English law of privacy

1. Used skilfully the *Kaye* decision offers an excellent starting point for a comparative discussion of the protection of privacy and its clash with the interest of free speech. Consider the following points. *First*, the argument advanced by the media that a law protecting privacy would bar them from investigating suspect conduct by politicians (*The Times*, 28 November 1989, leading article) is clearly inapplicable in cases such as *Kaye* which involved an ordinary citizen's moral right "to be let alone by strangers with no public interest to pursue [while recovering in hospital] from brain surgery and in no more than partial command of his faculties." (*per* Bingham LJ, p. 103 of the Calcutt Report). If the two situations require a different treatment (and in most respects they do though remember that German law allows even public figures a degree of privacy), it is for lawyers and the Press to try and devise rules that can distinguish between them rather than for the latter to foil all efforts by the former to regulate the problem. *Secondly*, the valiant attempts of the Court of Appeal to come up with some protection are notable for revealing the contortions that have to be undertaken in order to provide a remedy. This must, *thirdly*, lead us to consider the limitations of the traditional torts. Trespass, for example, has been advocated by one leading practitioner (see: Prescott, (1991) 54 *MLR* 802). But how effective would it be, especially in light of the restricted availability of punitive damages in English law? *Fourthly*, one must consider whether other systems (such as the German and French) are worse off for having provided a remedy in precisely this kind of situation (for illustration see Markesinis, (1990) 53 *MLR* 802; (1992) *MLR* 118). *Fifthly*, consider the refusal of the English courts to create a right of privacy. Does this conform with the view widely held on the Continent of Europe (and, indeed, among many Common lawyers) that our courts can create new law or adapt outdated solutions when circumstances require it? Thus, is our law any worse off for the fact that this timid approach was ignored on many occasions when there was a need for modernisation (*cf.*, for example, the transformation of English administrative law in the sixties and seventies)? *Sixthly*, consider the proven ability of the Press to frustrate the six attempts (made in England between 1961 and 1989) to legislate on this matter. Is this a healthy state of affairs? The answer must surely be negative, especially when one takes note of the intemperate language

used by some newspaper editors to express their distrust of our judiciary. And is not the Press adopting double standards when it asks for judicial intervention whenever it wishes to avoid high jury awards in defamation cases? Moreover, it must be the height of hypocrisy to express distrust towards *both* judges and jury and then to claim that the Press, itself, is the best judge of its own misconduct.

2. The timing of the *Kaye* litigation, arguably, had a decisive impact on the drafting of the Calcutt Report ("Report of the Committee on Privacy and Related Matters", Cm. 1102) which was published in June of 1990. The recommendations of this (first) Report, referring to the creation of new criminal and civil offences, are reproduced in paragraph 4, below (for reasons of space, its other recommendations, referring to the regulation of Press conduct and Press complaints, have been omitted). But this document, coupled with the follow-up Report prepared by Sir David Calcutt (entitled "Review of Press Self-Regulation" Cm. 2135, January of 1993, and essentially reconfirming its earlier recommendations and concluding that self-regulation is not working) and a "Consultation Paper" published by the Lord Chancellor's Department in July 1993 (entitled "Infringement of Privacy" and going a step further by recommending the establishment of a general tort of privacy) provide some of the most recent and thorough discussions of this topic and can be read with profit by lawyers from most systems that have to face these issues. The specific recommendations they make may provide the last chance (for the foreseeable future) to regulate this topic in a more balanced way. If the Press succeeds in frustrating this attempt, the ball will be back in the judges' court. If they then decide to act, history will justify their intervention; Continental European law could inspire it; and the average citizen would probably welcome it.

3. For further readings see: Bedingfield, "Privacy or Publicity? The enduring confusion surrounding the American tort of invasion of privacy" (1992) 55 *MLR* 111; Louciades, "Personality and privacy under the European Convention on Human Rights" (1990) *B.Y.B.I.L.* 175; Markesinis, "Subtle ways of legal borrowing: some reflections on the Report of the Calcutt Committee 'On Privacy and Related Matters'"; *Festschrift für Werner Lorenz zum siebzigsten Geburtstag* (1990) 717; *idem*, "Our patchy law of privacy—time to do something about it" (1990) 53 *MLR* 802; *idem*, "The Calcutt Report must not be forgotten" (1992) 55 *MLR* 118.

4. *Calcutt Committee Report: Summary of Recommendations*

Physical intrusion
1. The following acts should be criminal offences in England and Wales:
    (a) entering private property, without the consent of the lawful occupant, with intent to obtain personal information with a view to its publication.
    (b) placing a surveillance device on private property, without the consent of the lawful occupant, with intent to obtain personal information with a view to its publication; and
    (c) taking a photograph, or recording the voice, of an individual who is on private property, without his consent, with a view to its publication and with intent that the individual shall be identifiable.
2. It should be a defence to any of these proposed offences that the act was done:
    (a) for the purpose of preventing, detecting or exposing the commission of any crime, or other seriously anti-social conduct; or
    (b) for the protection of public health or safety; or
    (c) under any lawful authority.
3. An individual having a sufficient interest should be able to apply for an injunction against the publication of any material obtained by means of any of these criminal offences or, if the material has already been published, for damages or an account of profits.
4. Further consideration should be given to the extent to which the law in Scotland needs to be extended to cover the proposed offences and civil remedy and how this might best be done.

Legal restrictions on press reporting

5. Consideration should be given to amending the legislation on the non-identification of minors in England and Wales to eliminate any inconsistencies or uncertainties.

6. The statutory prohibition on identifying rape victims in England and Wales should be extended to cover the victims of the sexual assaults listed at Appendix H.

7. In any criminal proceedings in England and Wales, the court should have the power to make an order prohibiting the publication of the name and address of any person against whom the offence is alleged to have been committed, or of any other matters likely to lead to his or her identification. This should only be exercised if the court believes that it is necessary to protect the mental or physical health, personal security or security of the home of the victim.

8. After consulting the press and broadcasting authorities, the Press Complaints Commission (see 11 below) should issue early guidance on jigsaw identification.

Right of reply

9. A statutory right of reply should not be introduced.

Tort of infringement of privacy

10. A tort of infringement of privacy should not presently be introduced.

Press Complaints Commission

11. The press should be given one final chance to prove that voluntary self-regulation can be made to work.

12. The Press Council should be disbanded and replaced by a Press Complaints Commission.

13. The Press Complaints Commission should concentrate on providing an effective means of redress for complaints against the press.

14. The Press Complaints Commission should be given specific duties to consider complaints both of unjust or unfair treatment by newspapers or periodicals and of unwarranted infringements of privacy through published material or in connection with the obtaining of such material.

15. The Press Complaints Commission should publish, monitor and implement a comprehensive code of practice for the guidance of both press and the public.

16. The Press Complaints Commission should operate a hot line for complainants on a 24-hour basis.

17. Press Complaints Commission adjudications should, in certain cases, include a recommendation that an apology be given to the complainant. The precise form of the apology, including whether it should be given publicly or privately, could also be prescribed. Where a complaint concerns a newspaper's refusal to give an opportunity to reply to an attack made on a complainant or to correct an inaccuracy, the Press Complaints Commission should be able to recommend the nature and the form of reply or correction including, in appropriate cases, where in the paper it should be published.

18. The Press Complaints Commission should have an independent chairman and no more than 12 members, with smaller sub-committees adjudicating on complaints under delegated powers.

19. Appointments to the Press Complaints Commission should be made by an Appointments Commission with explicit freedom to appoint whoever it considers best qualified. The Appointments Commission itself should be independently appointed, possibly by the Lord Chancellor.

20. The Press Complaints Commission should have clear conciliation and adjudication procedures designed to ensure that complaints are handled with the minimum of delay. Whenever practical it should first seek conciliation. There should also be a fast track procedure for the correction of significant factual errors. The Commission should also have a specific responsibility and procedure for initiating inquiries whenever it thinks it necessary.

21. Complaints committees should have delegated power to release adjudications, subject to a right of appeal for either party to the full Press Complaints Commission before publication.

22. The Press Complaints Commission should not operate a waiver of legal rights.

23. If the industry wishes to maintain a system of non-statutory self-regulation, it must demonstrate its commitment, in particular by providing the necessary money for setting up and maintaining the Press Complaints commission.

Statutory complaints procedures

24. If the press fails to demonstrate that non-statutory self-regulation can be made to work effectively, a statutory system for handling complaints should be introduced.

25. If maverick publications persistently decline to respect the authority of the Press Complaints Commission, the Commission should be placed on a statutory footing. It should be given sufficient statutory powers to enable it to require any newspaper, periodical or magazine to respond to its enquiries about complaints and to publish its adjudications as directed. It should be able to recommend the payment of compensation.

26. The Government should set the budget for any statutory Press Complaints Commission and provide the money which it should then reclaim from the industry. The industry should set up a funding body which would apportion the cost between, and collect the money from, various industry bodies or individual publications.

Press Complaints Tribunal

27. Should the press fail to set up and support the Press Complaints Commission, or should it at any time become clear that the reformed non-statutory mechanism is failing to perform adequately, this should be replaced by a statutory tribunal with statutory powers and implementing a statutory code of practice.

28. There should be two separate triggers for the replacement of the Press Complaints Commission by a Press Complaints Tribunal.

29. A Press Complaints Tribunal should perform two distinct functions. First, it should attempt conciliation and investigate complaints. Secondly, where necessary, it should resolve disputes by ruling whether there had been a breach of the code of practice. This should be reflected in its structure and procedures.

30. The Press Complaints Tribunal should be able to award compensation. Unless the complainant can show financial loss, the amount of compensation should be limited by statute. This limit should be periodically reviewed.

31. In privacy cases, the Press Complaints Tribunal should be able to restrain publication of material in breach of the code of practice by means of injunctions. No injunction should be granted if the publisher could show that he had a good arguable defence.

32. The Tribunal chairman should be a judge or senior lawyer appointed by the Lord Chancellor. He should sit with two assessors drawn from a panel appointed by the Home Secretary.

Addendum 6

Press Complaints Commission Code of Practice

1. Accuracy
    (i) Newspapers and periodicals should take care not to publish inaccurate, misleading or distorted material including pictures.
    (ii) Whenever it is recognised that a significant inaccuracy, misleading statement or distorted report has been published, it should be corrected promptly and with due prominence.
    (iii) An apology must be published whenever appropriate.
    (iv) Newspapers, whilst free to be partisan, must distinguish clearly between comment, conjecture and fact
    (v) A newspaper or periodical must report fairly and accurately the outcome of an action for defamation to which it has been a party.

2. Opportunity to reply
A fair opportunity for reply to inaccuracies must be given to individuals or organisations when reasonably called for.

3. Privacy
  (i) Everyone is entitled to respect for his or her private and family life, home, health and correspondence. A publication will be expected to justify intrusions into any individual's private life without consent
  (ii) The use of long lens photography to take pictures of people in private places without their consent is unacceptable.

Note—Private places are public or private property where there is a reasonable expectation of privacy.

4. Harrassment
  (i) Journalists and photographers must neither obtain nor seek to obtain information or pictures through intimidation, harassment or persistent pursuit
  (ii) They must not photograph individuals in private places (as defined by the note to clause 3) without their consent; must not persist in telephoning, questioning, pursuing or photographing individuals after having been asked to desist; must not remain on their property after having been asked to leave and must not follow them.
  (iii) Editors must ensure that those working for them comply with these requirements and must not publish material from other sources which does not meet these requirements.

5. Intrusion into grief or shock
In cases involving personal grief or shock, enquiries should be carried out and approaches made with sympathy and discretion. Publication must be handled sensitively at such times but this should not be interpreted as restricting the right to report judicial proceedings.

6. Children
  (i) Young people should be free to complete their time at school without unnecessary intrusion.
  (ii) Journalists must not interview or photograph a child under the age of 16 on subjects involving the welfare of the child or any other child in the absence of or without the consent of a parent or other adult who is responsible for the children.
  (iii) Pupils must not be approached or photographed while at school without the permission of the school authorities.
  (iv) There must be no payment to minors for material involving the welfare of children nor payments to parents or guardians for material about their children or wards unless it is demonstrably in the child's interest.
  (v) Where material about the private life of a child is published, there must be justification for publication other than the fame, notoriety or position of his or her parents or guardian.

7. Children in sex cases
1. The press must not, even where the law does not prohibit it, identify children under the age of 16 who are involved in cases concerning sexual offences, whether as victims or as witnesses.
2. In any press report of a case involving a sexual offence against a child—
  (i) The child must not be identified.
  (ii) The adult may be identified.
  (iii) The word "incest" must not be used where a child victim might be identified.
  (iv) Care must be taken that nothing in the report implies the relationship between the accused and the child.

8. Listening Devices
Journalists must not obtain or publish material obtained by using clandestine listening devices or by intercepting private telephone conversations.

9. Hospitals
  (i) Journalists or photographers making enquiries at hospitals or similar institutions should identify themselves to a responsible executive and obtain permission before entering non-public areas.

(ii) The restrictions on intruding into privacy are particularly relevant to enquiries about individuals in hospitals or similar institutions.

10. Reporting of crime
(i) The press must avoid identifying relatives or friends of persons convicted or accused of crime without their consent.
(ii) Particular regard should be paid to the potentially vulnerable position of children who are witnesses to, or victims of, crime. This should not be interpreted as restricting the right to report judicial proceedings.

11. Misrepresentation
(i) Journalists must not generally obtain or seek to obtain information or pictures through misrepresentation or subterfuge.
(ii) Documents or photographs should be removed only with the consent of the owner.
(iii) Subterfuge can be justified only in the public interest and only when material cannot be obtained by any other means.

12. Victims of sexual assault
The press must not identify victims of sexual assault or publish material likely to contribute to such identification unless there is adequate justification and, by law, they are free to do so.

13. Discrimination
(i) The press must avoid prejudicial or pejorative reference to a person's race, colour, religion, sex or sexual orientation or to any physical or mental illness or disability.
(ii) It must avoid publishing details of a person's race, colour, religion, sexual orientation, physical or mental illness or disability unless these are directly relevant to the story.

14. Financial journalism
(i) Even where the law does not prohibit it, journalists must not use for their own profit financial information they receive in advance of its general publication, nor should they pass such information to others.
(ii) They must not write about shares or securities in whose performance they know that they or their close families have a significant financial interest without disclosing the interest to the editor or financial editor.
(iii) They must not buy or sell, either directly or through nominees or agents, shares or securities about which they have written recently or about which they intend to write in the near future.

15. Confidential sources
Journalists have a moral obligation to protect confidential sources of information.

16. Payment for articles
(i) Payment or offers of payment for stories or information must not be made directly or through agents to witnesses or potential witnesses in current criminal proceedings except where the material concerned ought to be published in the public interest and there is an overriding need to make or promise to make a payment for this to be done. Journalists must take every possible step to ensure that no financial dealings have influence on the evidence that those witnesses may give.

(An editor authorising such a payment must be prepared to demonstrate that there is a legitimate public interest at stake involving matters that the public has a right to know. The payment or, where accepted, the offer of payment to any witness who is actually cited to give evidence should be disclosed to the prosecution and the defence and the witness should be advised of this).

(ii) Payment or offers of payment for stories, pictures or information, must not be made directly or through agents to convicted or confessed criminals or to their associates—

who may include family, friends and colleagues—except where the material concerned ought to be published in the public interest and payment is necessary for this to be done.

13. UNLAWFULNESS AND FAULT

Case 50

REICHSGERICHT (FIRST CIVIL SENATE) 14 JANUARY 1928
RGZ 119, 397 = JW 1928, 1049 with approving note by M. Pappenheim

On 23 October 1921 at noon, the German three-masted schooner *Lisbeth*, on a journey through the English Channel to Göteborg, ran aground on the northern tip of the Dutch island of Texel on a sandbank. On 26 October it became a total loss. The plaintiff owner of the vessel sued the defendant captain of the ship claiming damages on the ground that he negligently caused the loss of the vessel. The District Court of Altona and the Court of Appeal of Kiel rejected the claim. Upon a second appeal the judgment of the Court of Appeal was confirmed for the following

Reasons

The Court of Appeal has found as a fact that during the voyage when the accident occurred, the defendant had not handled the vessel in accordance with the practice of an experienced and able captain of a sailing-ship applying normal care. If the defendant had applied that care required in the circumstances of a normal, proper, and conscientious captain of a sailing-ship, the stranding could have been avoided. However, the defendant lacked the necessary experience and could not possess it in view of his education and previous activity. The plaintiff, himself an old and experienced captain of sailing-vessels, had been well aware of the limits of the defendant's capacity when he appointed him. In particular the plaintiff had known that the defendant was not sufficiently qualified for discharging the specialized task of commanding the sailing-vessel *Lisbeth* and was completely inexperienced, especially for navigating in the North Sea. It was true that the plaintiff had not believed that he would suffer damage by appointing the unsuitable defendant; he had, however, been grossly negligent in failing to perceive the danger to the ship as a result of the defendant's lack of qualification. In so far as the defendant in his written application for the post had stated that he had been in possession of a schooner and was experienced in handling vessels of this kind, the plaintiff had by no means been misled thereby. Considering that the plaintiff was fully cognisant of the extent of the nautical qualification of the defendant, the defendant's own statement was of little importance. It offended against good faith if the plaintiff, who was well aware when he appointed the defendant that the latter, a young captain without any experience in navigating sailing vessels in the North Sea, would be unable to deal with difficult situations, having regard to his training and experience, now claimed damages against him because the defendant had proved unequal to the task. This held good too if the standard of care required of the defendant was put as that of a normal, proper, and conscientious captain of a sailing-vessel, without regard to the degree of experience possessed by men such as the defendant.

These statements of the Court of Appeal are mainly factual . . . On the strength of these facts the Court of Appeal could conclude, without violating the law, that the defendant was not liable to the plaintiff. The facts as found by the Court of Appeal show that in concluding the contract appointing the defendant the plaintiff knew of the particular personal circumstances of the defendant and took them into account. This indicates a tacit agreement to the effect that in assessing the duty of care incumbent upon the defendant in relation to the plaintiff, the latter's special circumstances are of essential importance [reference]. As between the parties, the plaintiff could only demand such nautical activities of the defendant which did not exceed the degree of nautical capacity and experience which was known to the plaintiff. The defendant is not liable for any circumstances resulting in damage which arise outside these limits, having regard to the special nature of the contract between the parties. It makes no difference that the defendant . . . should have known that he was not equal to the appointment assumed by him. The findings of the fact by the Court of Appeal show clearly that the accident could not have been avoided even if the defendant, conscious of his nautical deficiencies, had acted with special precaution and care, seeing that objectively he lacked the capacity for doing so. On the other hand, the plaintiff in deciding to appoint the defendant, was fully aware of the extent of the defendant's nautical qualifications and was not influenced by the fact that he applied for the post and accepted it without reservations.

These observations suffice to support the judgment appealed against. It may be observed, however, that the additional considerations of the Court of Appeal are not free from error. The Court of Appeal states that, leaving aside the special character of the relationship of the parties in issue, according to the general principles of law the defendant had not acted culpably because he had applied all that care expected of a person with his nautical experience.

The Court of Appeal bases its opinion on the view that within the circle of the captains of sailing-ships several groups exist, graded according to their nautical experience. A person belonging to the group of nautical experience similar to that of the defendant could not have avoided the mistakes which caused the accident, even if he had applied the proper standard of care. These considerations conflict with the dominant view in practice and in the literature. This holds that the term "the care required in human relations" must be determined according to an objective standard, which is the requirement in regular and proper human relations, having regard to the individual circumstances. Thus the justified demands of human relations determine what measure of circumspection and care must be applied in order to avoid damage. It is normally to be gauged by reference to the view of a certain limited circle of persons and by the typical qualities of the group of persons who represent a specific range of human relations [references]. Accordingly § 511 of the Commercial Code requires the care of a proper "sailor". If, as in the present case, the command of a sailing-vessel is in issue, the special features of navigating a sailing-vessel and the care of a proper captain of a sailing-vessel is required. Since the just and reasonable requirements of trade form the basis, it is evident that neither the care of a particularly experienced nor that of an inexperienced captain of a sailing-vessel can serve as a standard. Instead that standard of care is decisive which a proper and conscientious captain of a sailing-ship, endowed with normal knowledge, capacity, and experience, is accustomed to apply. If the circle of captains of sailing-ships as defined above were to be divided into groups according to the degree of nautical experience of individual members, the objective standard would become distorted by the introduction of personal circumstances. A group of experienced captains of sailing-vessels, who are incapable of measuring up to serious tasks and who fail in case of need would be useless in trade . . . Although the reasoning of the Court of Appeal contains an error of law, no ground exists for questioning its decision which, as shown above, is supported by other legally valid reasons.

Case 51

BUNDESGERICHTSHOF (SIXTH CIVIL SENATE) 9 JUNE 1967
JZ 1968, 103 = VERSR 1967, 808

On 6 January 1961 early in the morning, while it was still dark and raining slightly, R, a miner aged 27 years, was cycling to his place of work on an illuminated road. Shortly before he had reached a turning, the defendant motorist ran into R from behind, cata-pulting him onto the side of the road where he was hit and killed by a motor car travel-ling in the opposite direction.

The plaintiffs, assignees by subrogation of the claims of R's widow born in 1936 and of his two children born in 1954 and 1958, sued the defendant on the ground that he was alone responsible for the accident, having driven without due care and with a dirty wind-screen. The defendant denies any responsibility. He had been blinded by an oncoming car owing to defective vision, of which he had been unaware hitherto and therefore failed to see R. Moreover, R was himself to be blamed because he was cycling without an illu-minated rear light and was too far left on his side of the road.

The District Court, relying on the Road Traffic Act, gave judgment for the plaintiffs, limited to the amount payable under that Act, and granted a declaration asked for within the limits of liability set by the Road Traffic Act. On appeal by the plaintiffs the Court of Appeal of Hamm held the defendant liable to pay full damages on the ground of liability for negligence and rejected the plea of contributory negligence. A second appeal by the defendant was unsuccessful for the following

Reasons

I. 1. The Court of Appeal starts from the premise that prima facie the defendant appears to have been negligent. The defendant, driving with dimmed lights, ran into the cyclist because he did not see him. In these circumstances common experience leads to the conclusion that the defendant acted negligently inasmuch as he drove either without sufficient care or at a speed incompatible with his field of vision.

2. The defendant does not contest this prima-facie evidence. He only questions the view taken by the Court of Appeal that the defendant had not discharged the burden of proof incumbent upon him thereafter to show as a serious possibility that the events may have taken place without any negligence on his part.

(*a*) The Court of Appeal assumes in favour of the defendant that owing to the special light conditions at the time of the accident he was blinded due to a defect of vision of which he was ignorant. Nevertheless it held that he had not discharged his burden of proof. The Court of Appeal held correctly that the test is whether the defendant could at least realize the limits of his vision, and it is convinced that he could.

This conclusion is based on the consideration that like every motorist the defendant must at least be aware of his individual powers of vision [references]. In determining neg-ligence it is therefore irrelevant in law what the circumstances are which affect an abnor-mal individual vision. Thus a motorist so affected is treated no differently from one whose vision is perfect. The latter, too, is expected to know the limits of his vision, a knowledge obtained not by means of exact figures, but through his own experience. In determining whether the defendant was negligent the question is therefore not whether he knew or ought to have known of his defect of vision . . . but whether he ought to have known the effect of this defect and therefore the limits of his individual capacity to see. The Court of Appeal has answered this in the affirmative without committing an error of law. This determination is all the more valid since according to the experts the defendant was born with this defect of vision and as he had driven a motor car since 1956.

If, however, the defendant could recognise that his personal vision was limited he could and should have so adjusted his driving, especially his speed so as to satisfy the requirements of traffic and to be able to stop, if necessary. The Court of Appeal has held correctly that the defendant has not shown that he has complied with this requirement.

II. The Court of Appeal rules out any contributory negligence on the part of the cyclist R.

1. The Court of Appeal was unable to find that the rear light of the bicycle did not show. It has also not blamed R for having ridden too far left on his side of the road. The judge of fact adopted the allegation of the plaintiffs that R wanted to turn left into the side street and had therefore moved to the middle of the road. The District Court had pointed out that R took this route daily on his way to work . . .

2. The further allegation of the defendant that R had not indicated his intention to turn left by raising his left arm was rejected as irrelevant by the Court of Appeal because on the defendant's own admission he had not seen R at all.

The defendant objects that the presumed conduct of R had been dismissed as the cause of the accident. He argues that it was not decisive that he had failed to see the cyclist but that it was decisive whether he would have seen R if he had indicated his intended change of direction by raising his left arm. Common experience supported this conclusion; moreover a presumption operated against the cyclist since the latter had violated § 11 I of the Traffic Regulations (StVO), i.e. had failed to indicate his direction.

In the result the Court of Appeal was right. The purpose of § 11 I of the Road Traffic Regulations is to eliminate the dangers which threaten—apart from the person making the turn—the traffic behind and in the opposite direction. It is intended to draw the attention of these road-users to the imminence of the traffic manœuvre, to make them use care, and thereby to avoid the danger of accidents. This was not the case here. The collision did not occur because the defendant in his motor car overtook the cyclist on his left side without noticing the latter's intention to turn; it occurred because in proceeding straight ahead he did not see the cyclist . . . It is not, however, the purpose of the protective rule which imposes the duty to indicate a change of direction, to ensure that the person subject to this duty is noticed in the traffic irrespective of his intention to make a turn.

Case 52

BUNDESGERICHTSHOF (SIXTH CIVIL SENATE) 7 FEBRUARY 1984
BGHZ 90, 96 = NJW 1984, 1395 = JZ 1984, 629

On 3 July 1979 the plaintiff was admitted to the S hospital of the defendant Regional District for unexplained pain in his right femur. The first examination was carried out by Dr K, the Duty Doctor. He also discussed with the plaintiff that in order to exclude the possibility of a tumour, a colonoscopy was indicated. Subsequently it was carried out by Dr B, the Senior Medical Officer. In the course of it, the sigmoid colon was perforated and the defendant abandoned the investigation. After an X-ray picture had confirmed the injury, the plaintiff was operated on immediately—complications subsequently occurred.

The plaintiff sued the defendants for adequate damages for pain and suffering as well as for a declaration that they were liable to compensate him for all present and future material and mental damage. He stated that he had not effectively agreed to the colonoscopy and alleged that he had not been informed sufficiently of the character of the investigation or of any possible risks nor that it might be accompanied by considerable pain. He had suffered much pain when the instrument had been inserted in the intestine and had said so at the time. The perforation of the intestine had been caused by a culpable mistake of the second defendant in carrying out the colonoscopy.

The defendant contended that before the colonoscopy the investigation had been sufficiently explained to the plaintiff. They were of the opinion that in view of the fact that complications occurred extremely rarely, it had not been necessary to inform the plaintiff of the risk of a perforation of the intestine. They denied that by this treatment they committed a medical error.

The District court held that "the claim raised in the action is justified in principle". The Court of Appeal dismissed the appeal of the defendants, declared that the plaintiff's claim for damages for pain and suffering was justified in principle and allowed the action for a declaration in respect of material damage; as regards mental injuries in the future, it referred the case back to the District court. Upon a second appeal by the defendants the case was referred back to the Court of Appeal.

Reasons

I. The Court of Appeal has interpreted the judgment of the District Court to the effect that it decided not only the claim for damages for pain and suffering by an interim judgment in principle, but also the plaintiff's action for a declaration. Contrary to the District Court, which held the second defendant to have committed an error in his treatment, it regards the claim as well founded on the ground that the medical investigation which resulted in the injury to the plaintiff was illegal because the plaintiff had not been given sufficient information and because therefore his consent was invalid. In so holding, the Court of Appeal argued essentially as follows: It is possible to agree with the District Court that the information had to be given concerning the risk of a perforation of the intestine as a result of a colonoscopy since complications occurred seldom. However, the plaintiff should have been informed that in certain circumstances the investigation could cause the plaintiff considerable pain. This should have been done, in particular because the diagnostic measure was not of vital importance. No such information had been given. Without having to consider the question as to whether the plaintiff had risked his consent during the colonoscopy or whether the second defendant had, in treating the plaintiff, committed an error, he was liable according to §§ 823 I, 847 BGB to pay damages for pain and suffering. The defendant Regional District was liable according to § 831 BGB for the second defendant as its agent in performing his duties. It was not sufficient for the Regional District to plead as a defence that the second defendant was a specially competent doctor of long experience; nor was the fact that the medical heads of department had regularly called together the doctors working in their department, including the second defendant, for instruction and further education. A proper organisation of a hospital required also that the doctors should be given advice concerning the general principles governing the duty to provide information and to control their observation by random inspection. This had been omitted. In addition, the liability of both defendants for the material damage resulted from a violation of the contract for medical treatment. As regards future mental damage, a further investigation of a factual kind was necessary.

II. The reasoning of the decision under appeal cannot stand up to legal scrutiny.

1. The Court of Appeal has held rightly that the information given to the plaintiff about the proposed colonoscopy was incomplete because she did not also tell the plaintiff that this diagnostic investigation might have disagreeable effects, psychological as well as physical. The plaintiff was aware of this having learnt about the technique of colonoscopy. However, he should also have been told that in certain circumstances this might cause him considerable pain.

A patient who has not experienced colonoscopy previously and has not heard about it from others could not expect this or even regard this as normal. For a patient to decide whether to consent to a physical investigation, it is relevant, among other considerations, what he must accept in the course of it and what pain he will have to suffer which exceeds that to be expected in connection with a diagnostic medical examination. This knowledge must not be withheld from him merely because he might be frightened and might object to what is normally a harmless investigation or because he may stiffen and thereby make the investigation more difficult for himself and the doctor. It is for the doctor to calm a frightened patient and so to explain to him the need for a painful investigation that he can be certain of the patient's consent and co-operation. In the case of a colonoscopy this may include the information that the doctor would immediately abandon the investigation should he find the pain intolerable. Since neither the duty doctor at first examination nor the second defendant before the start of his investigation told the plaintiff what might ensue, the plaintiff's consent was invalid and the colonoscopic investigation was illegal because he was not aware of all the circumstances affecting his decision.

2. It does not necessarily follow therefrom, as the Court of Appeal assumes incorrectly, that the second defendant is vicariously liable for the injuries to the person of the plaintiff as a result of the perforation of the intestine. The facts as found by the Court of Appeal so far are insufficient for holding the second defendant liable for having provided defective information concerning the unpleasantness of a colonoscopy.

(*a*) In as far as the required information of the patient was held to have been incomplete because he was not told before the proposed diagnostic investigation of the possibility of considerable pain (without resulting in a serious and permanent injury to his health), it is not immediately obvious that the patient, if correctly informed, would have declined the investigation. It is even less obvious in the case of a patient who is not normally given to complain of pain. In the present case the plaintiff has described himself in the course of proceedings as a man who is not really hypersensitive; moreover, he has not argued that he had been insufficiently informed because he had not been told of the possibility of pain in the course of the investigation. In these circumstances the mere allegation by the plaintiff that he would have declined to undergo the investigation for fear of pain would be insufficient to accept this account (see the decision of this Senate of 7 February 1984, reported below, BGHZ 90, 103 and the order of this Senate of 27 October 1981—VI Z R 63/81, VersR 1982, 74, 75 = NJW 1982, 700). Since the plaintiff made no such allegation, the fact that the defendants have not pleaded expressly that the plaintiff would have consented to the investigation in any case, cannot be held against them. Instead, the plaintiff's pleadings until now are insufficient to support the conclusion that his right to decide himself whether to agree to the investigation had been violated on the legal ground relied upon by the Court of Appeal.

(*b*) In addition, this Court must accept that in the view of the Court of Appeal the risk of which the plaintiff should have been informed, namely that the investigation might be accompanied by considerable pain, did not materialise in his case. It is true that the plaintiff has made allegation to this effect, but to the detriment of the defendants, who denied from the outset that the investigation had been accompanied by considerable pain; the Court of Appeal did not make any findings to this effect. Evidence taken on this question was not taken into account by it. If, however, the colonoscopy did not cause the plaintiff considerable pain, the investigation also did not cause him any injury. Even if his right to determine himself whether to agree to the investigation has been violated in some respects, he did not suffer any personal injury for which compensation would have to be paid. This conclusion is not vitiated by the fact that in carrying out the colonoscopy leading to the perforation of the sigmoid colon an entirely different and remote risk materialised provided that the latter did not have to be disclosed (for details see *infra* III). The reason is that the damage arising therefrom falls outside the sphere of protection of the rule establishing liability which imposes a duty upon the doctor to pay damages for a physical investigation which is illegal in the absence of a valid consent by the patient.

(*aa*) It is unnecessary in the present case to determine the question of law as to whether no connection exists between the illegality of the physical investigation of the patient in the absence of effective information and the resulting physical injury whenever culpably the basic risks inherent in the investigation have not been set out, but another link has materialised which did not have to be explained to the plaintiff (affirmatively the Court of Appeal Karlsruhe, Med. R. 1983, 180, 192 with a concurring note by Kern; Kern-Laufs, *Die ärztliche Aufklärungspflicht*, 1983, p. 151 ff.; *contra*: Mutons in *Münchener Kommentar* p. 823 no. 423). Certain objections could be raised against this view because in the case of medical investigations involving risks which are not quite inconsiderable, the right of the patient to determine himself whether to agree to the investigation and who also agrees without any knowledge and without any information, always includes his freedom of decision for or against an investigation covering his body as a whole.

(*bb*) The objections set out here do not apply in the present case.

Admittedly, the action of the second defendant does not cease to be illegal for the reason only that the plaintiff's consent certainly covered an investigation free of pain. The consent of a patient to a medical investigation is not a declaration of intent which can be divided into one concerning the violation of personal integrity on the one hand and another, on the other hand, which involves exposing oneself voluntarily to danger by accepting certain possible risks (see however Kern-Laufs *loc. cit.* and Med. R. *loc. cit.*). It is true that in substance it covers both (see Deutsch, NJW 1982, 2585 and in *Arztrecht und Arzneimittelrecht* p. 42 no. 42), but this only defines the legal significance of the declaration of intent. However, it has no bearing on the question as to what is the substance of the declaration made to the doctor in consenting to the medical investigation. The substance is clear: if the consent is valid, it applies without restriction. If it is refused (or what is the same, if it is invalid for failure to receive sufficient information), the declaration of intention means, and cannot be interpreted otherwise, that the patient will not agree to the medical measures, as advised, that is to say in their entirety (similarly Mertons in *Münchener Kommentar loc. cit.*). The motives for his refusal are legally irrelevant as is the question whether hypothetically he would consent to all investigations without complications. If he did not give his consent, he did not consent either to an investigation which was illegal and to which he did not agree, but which was successful. At best the disregard of his right to determine himself whether to undergo the investigation did not result in any damage.

It is possible, however, that in such cases the claim for damages may not succeed for a different legal reason. The duty to supply information concerning the remote damages of considerable pain is designed to protect the patient's right to decide freely whether he will consent to the medical investigation, having regard to the advantages of a diagnostic assessment of his state of health and to the physical unpleasantness which he will experience if he undergoes the investigation.

The medical duty of contract which is to provide information concerning the potential danger of considerable pain is therefore not designed to facilitate the independent decision of the patient whether he is willing to accept possible dangers to his health. Instead it is to enable the patient to decide whether he is willing to face a potential temporary impairment of his well being as a result of sudden pain. In such cases, a connection between the illegality consisting of the doctor's neglect of his duty and that consisting of the violation of the patient's right to determine himself whether to undergo a medical investigation exists only if the risk of a painful treatment has materialised. If apart from this no risk of any damage to health exists, having regard to the fact that the investigation does not present any danger of which the patient should have to be informed, the failure to inform him of the possibility of pain cannot form the basis of liability in respect of a complication which occurred nevertheless in the course of the diagnostic investigation (see Steffen in *Verhandlungen des 52. Deutschen Juristentags* vol. II Part I p. 15; similarly in another connection Giesen, *JZ* 1982, 448, 454 with reference to the decision of this Senate of 16 June 1981, VI I R 38/40 = VersR 1981, 954—NJW 1981, 2513; for criticism of the denial of a link of illegality in general see Mertens *loc. cit.*).

In the present case the plaintiff cannot, therefore, base his claims for damages on the ground that he was not informed of possible pain in the course of the colonoscopy.

Case 53

BUNDESGERICHTSHOF (SIXTH CIVIL DIVISION) 9 DECEMBER 1958
BGHZ 29, 46 = JR 1959, 418

The plaintiff was a patient in the hospital for nervous diseases in L. He claims damages against the local authority in respect of the consequences of electric-shock treatment.

The plaintiff was a chronic alcoholic. When his mental powers continued to deteriorate, he received unsuccessful treatment for alcoholism in the summer of 1954. He was then received by the hospital for nervous diseases. There medicinal treatment had no lasting effect. For this reason the assembled medical staff suggested that the plaintiff should receive a series of electric-shock treatments. Dr N, the head of the neurological psychiatric department, discussed this method of treatment in October 1954 with the plaintiff's brother and sister and with his wife. They consented to the electric-shock treatment. The parties disagree as to what was said during the remaining part of this discussion.

After receiving shock treatment on five occasions without incident, the plaintiff suffered a complicated comminuted fracture of the head of the left femur when he received his sixth and last treatment on 2 November 1954. As a result his left leg, which was already deformed since birth (club-foot and atrophy), was shortened. In addition a so-called false joint appeared in the area of the head of the femur.

The plaintiff contends as follows: he had been given shock treatment without his consent and had not been informed of the dangers of this treatment. Moreover he had not consented validly since he had lacked the capacity at the time. A guardian, who would have acted in his place, had not yet been appointed. His brother and sister and his wife had not consented validly either to the shock treatment since they, too, had not been informed of the nature and the attendant danger. The plaintiff continued, further, that the treatment had been carried out inexpertly; in particular no drugs relaxing the muscles had been administered, although this was necessary in order to prevent injuries resulting from cramp.

The plaintiff has asked that the defendant should pay DM 2,931 as compensation and an adequate sum for pain and suffering. He has asked, further, for a declaration that the defendant is obliged to compensate him for all damage which may arise in the future.

The defendant contends as follows: The plaintiff and his relatives had agreed to the shock treatment. They had been warned that this treatment carried a certain risk. No duty to provide this information existed, for the methods of shock treatment had been greatly improved since the early days when this treatment was first applied, and the danger of injurious consequences was extremely low. The treatment had been carried out correctly and with the help of the most modern appliance, . . . which caused a mild effect of the cramps. Any use of muscle relaxing drugs had been ruled out because the plaintiff's heart, his circulation, his liver, and his lungs had not functioned properly.

The District Court of Landau dismissed the claim. In the course of his appeal the plaintiff abandoned his claim for pain and suffering but maintained his claim for damages amounting to DM 2,931 and for a declaration. The Court of Appeal of Neustadt allowed the claim to the extent that it had not passed to the Social Insurance by way of subrogation and granted the declaration. On the second appeal by the defendant, the judgment of the Court of Appeal was quashed and the case referred back for the following

Reasons

I. The Court of Appeal starts from the proposition that by accepting the plaintiff in their hospital in L a contract had been concluded between the parties. By virtue of this contract the plaintiff was entitled, as against the defendant authority responsible for the hospital, to be treated expertly by the doctors employed by it. This proposition cannot be faulted, nor has the appellant done so. According to the Court of Appeal the evidence does not disclose any violation of the standards of medical care . . .

The Court of Appeal regards the doctor who administered the treatment as liable on the ground that he acted in the absence of a legally valid consent. The Court of Appeal left it undecided whether the plaintiff was legally capable of acting or physically capable of expressing his wishes and therefore able to give a valid consent. The Court of Appeal believes that the question as to whether the plaintiff consented is irrelevant, because he had not been informed of the possible danger accompanying the treatment. In considering the duty of a medical practitioner to inform the patient, the Court of Appeal relied on the principles enunciated by this Division [reference] following the practice of the Reichsgericht and held that the plaintiff or his legal representative should have been informed of the risks connected with shock treatment. It is not clear whether the plaintiff's wife and his brother and sister were given sufficient details of the danger. It seems that the Court of Appeal regarded this question as irrelevant, because none of those persons had been appointed the plaintiff's guardian at that time. As a result the Court of Appeal held that Dr N had acted negligently and in breach of contract for having administered electro-shock to the defendant without any real consent; the defendant was responsible for his according to § 278 BGB.

II. . . . Doctors and lawyers agree that the consent of the patient is required before medical treatment can take place, especially if it interferes with the body. Apart from special, exceptional cases, none of which is in issue here (e.g. where there is danger in delay), any interference with the body of a patient is only lawful if the patient consents. This follows from Article 2 II of the Constitution which guarantees integrity of the person to everybody. A right to compel treatment, as it was being discussed under National Socialism, but as always rejected by the Reichsgericht [reference], is not being called for by anybody today.

Opinions are divided as to the nature of this consent, whether and to what extent it presupposes, in particular, that the patient is aware of his condition and whether, therefore, he must be informed of the nature of his illness as well as of the character, importance, and possible deleterious consequences of the treatment. This question of the duty of a medical adviser to give information . . . can no longer be answered by relying on the advice of Hippocrates to conceal most from the patient and not to tell him anything of what awaits or threatens him. This advice cannot be reconciled with modern ideas about the calling of a medical practitioner and the right of patients to self-determination [reference]; also it no longer serves as a guideline for medical conduct . . .

It is unnecessary in the present case to decide to what extent the patient must be informed, for if it is correct . . . that the plaintiff was capable of acting, he was informed of the nature of his illness and also of the nature of the treatment, at least at the start of the sixth application of the electro-shock treatment which led to the injury and is therefore essential for the present purpose. The discussion can therefore be limited to the question which has given rise to most doubts, as to whether and to what extent the information to be given to the patient must also include the potentially dangerous consequences of the treatment.

1. In response to the demand for such information it is pointed out in medical circles, first of all, that a patient is often incapable of understanding the nature and the consequences of the treatment; that since any serious illness affects the person as a whole and causes a disturbance, not only physically but also emotionally, he is unable to assess rationally the advantages and the disadvantages of the proposed medical treatment or to force himself into reaching a decision free from uncontrollable moods, fears, and prejudices [references]. This aspect is important in assessing the legal position in as much as naturally the information is only indicated if the patient is capable of appreciating the kind, purpose, and consequences of the treatment and to come to a decision, for only a patient who is able to do this can validly consent to the proposed treatment. These problems did not arise in the case decided previously by this Division, for it was found in that

case that the patient was able to consent validly to the electro-shock treatment because his state of depression did not affect his judgment or his ability to act freely . . . [reference].

The question whether a sick person can act freely in the sense set out above is primarily one to be answered by the medical profession. In most cases a court cannot decide it without medical witnesses or experts. However, even if a patient lacks the ability to act freely, the need for consent remains. This must be given by the person who, after having been given the necessary information, must decide instead of the patient himself whether the operation should take place. According to the opinion of some medical practitioners the nearest relatives of the sick and incapable person are not necessarily qualified to do so. It is true that they are the persons with the strongest and humanly closest interest in the well-being of the patient. However, as long as the law has not conferred upon them the right to decide upon the treatment of a patient who is incapable of acting himself, the practice current in many hospitals to obtain the consent of the nearest relative to the treatment of the patient cannot suffice, even if a consultation with the relatives, where danger exists in delay, may be a relevant means of ascertaining the presumed intention of the patient. In the *absence* of a dangerous situation which requires immediate or speedy action, it is necessary to appoint a guardian for the patient, who must decide in the place of the sick person whether the planned medical action is to take place. Such an appointment of a guardian is possible under § 1910 BGB if the sick person is unable as a result of his infirmity to handle his affairs in the particular circumstances . . .

2. . . . as regards information to be given to a patient, the position of the doctor has been compared with that of the lawyer. It is said that it is unsatisfactory to treat the relationship between medical adviser and patient as a contract of service, seeing that the relationship is distinguished by a special human characteristic and often touches the deepest and most confidential areas of human feeling. It is alleged that a legal relationship *sui generis* is created in which the personality of the patient plays an important role which must not be overlooked and that the personal relationship between doctor and patient is the basis of a successful treatment . . . lawyers are said to be too formalistic and do not consider sufficiently the real situation.

. . . observations to this effect cannot be accepted. It is unimportant for the purpose of the problem of a medical practitioner's duty of information whether in law the relationship between doctor and patient is regarded as a contract of service or as a relationship *sui generis*. For, irrespective of the legal characterisation of this relationship a court cannot and must not, in examining this question, regard the doctor and the patient merely as parties to a private law contract. If a court wishes to ascertain the nature and extent of the duty to provide information required by a doctor, all the circumstances of the individual case must be assembled and considered. The court must not overlook either that the relationship between doctor and patient presupposes profound confidence, that it is strongly based on a human relationship, in which the doctor comes to the aid of the patient, and that, therefore, it constitutes much more than a contractual relationship. . . .

The health of the patient is the doctor's principal concern. It is his duty to restore it and to preserve it. It is reasonable that a conscientious doctor often regards himself as entitled, or even as obliged, to assist by interfering physically if the life and the health of his patient is at stake. Nevertheless, these efforts must find their limit if they conflict with the right of the patient to determine the fate of his body. This situation can arise if the doctor begins a treatment without having informed the patient of its nature and consequences [reference].

It is true that a sick person, who consults a medical practitioner or visits a hospital in order to seek relief for his illness also often consents in advance to a limited extent to the administration of physical treatment which is necessary as a means of recovery. It cannot be concluded therefrom, however, that the patient is not interested in being told in broad terms about the proposed treatment, the usual development, the likely result, and possible danger to his health arising from this treatment. Not being an expert in medical matters, the patient also regards the doctor as an adviser and expects normally to be instructed by him in these matters and to be advised. Only if the patient is aware of his situation, and knows broadly what his consent to the administration of physical medical treatment implies can his consent satisfy the meaning and purpose which is to absolve the administration of physical treatment from the charge of illegality and to shift part of the doctor's responsibility to the patient.

It is true that cases will arise in which the patient wishes to be relieved of his sufferings in all circumstances and indicates clearly that he places his full confidence in the doctor. In such a case the doctor may be justified, in view of the clear wish of the patient, in omitting to provide further information. In such a case . . . the patient looks to the doctor as the authority which relieves him from considering the matter on his own and assuming responsibility himself. The patient does not really wish to know but wants to comply. This does not, however, apply normally, for in many, if not most cases the patient wants to know his situation and thus the prognosis and the risks of the intended operation or of another medical administration of physical treatment and wants to decide himself whether this treatment is to take place. If the doctor respects the patient's right to decide himself, the confidence of the latter in the doctor will be enhanced rather than diminished. A sick person may have very good reasons . . . for refusing to undergo an operation and thus possibly for accepting responsibility for a considerable shortening of his life [reference]. The freedom and dignity of human personality require that this wish of the patient is to be respected.

All this shows that in protecting the freedom of a patient to decide for himself, the courts are far from paying homage to what is a formal principle only. On the contrary, they protect a right enshrined in the Constitution, which is to be respected and applied as much as the right to health. In the present context of the decision concerning the duty of a medical adviser to provide information too, much more is at stake than purely formal matters, for in this connection, too, substantive considerations are in issue as to how the responsibility for treatment is to be decided reasonably and justly between doctor and patient [reference].

3. . . . attention has been drawn . . . to the dangers to the health and to the recovery affecting in particular those suffering from psychosis, if they are informed of their illness. It is said, *inter alia*, that only the medical expert and not the court can decide, having regard to the special situation in the individual case, to what extent a patient can be informed of the risks involved in the administration of physical treatment. It was the duty of the medical practitioner to calm the patient and to dispel the fear of an operation and not to produce the opposite effect by providing detailed information. Unrestricted information concerning possible complications would so deter and frighten a sufferer from a psychosis who was willing in principle to undergo the treatment that in most cases he would

refuse his consent to shock treatment and would thus deprive himself of the chance of recovery [reference].

In determining the duty to provide information the above-mentioned consideration cannot be attributed the degree of importance which the medical profession ascribes to it. If the provision of information to a patient who is capable of acting is unlikely to endanger his health or his recovery, and if only the serious possibility exists of the patient refusing his consent to the treatment, contrary to his true interest, it follows that the medical adviser is not relieved of his duty to draw the patient's attention to the typical dangers connected with the treatment . . . the information serves to invite the patient to decide himself. In making up his mind he is to be given the opportunity of considering not only the chances of recovery but also the deleterious effects of the treatment which are not too remote. Only if the patient knows this too, can his consent relieve the doctor of part of his responsibility. Admittedly the doctor must seek to calm the patient and to set his mind at ease, following the information. The doctor may also seek to influence him to undergo urgently needed treatment by patient persuasion and by a discussion of his fears and objections, as well as by pointing out forcibly the disadvantages if the treatment does not take place. On the other hand, the medical adviser must not seek to influence the decision of the patient by concealing relevant facts from him [reference].

The real difficulty is presented by the problem . . . whether and to what extent the duty to provide information must give way to other duties and interests, if serious objections exist against informing the patient having regard to his personality and his mental state, especially if by providing the information his health or even his life may be endangered. The previous decision of this Division has been understood wrongly to state that the Federal Supreme Court regards this circumstance as irrelevant. Admittedly it is stated in the reasons given by the judgment, following the practice of the Reichsgericht [reference]: if, as a result of the information the mood or the general well-being of the patient should be affected adversely, this fact must be accepted as an inevitable disadvantage. The passage in question does not state, however, as has been thought erroneously, that exhaustive information is to be given even if, as a result, the life or the health of the patient is seriously endangered. The principle has been stated meanwhile by this Division in its decision of 10 February 1956 [reference] where it is stated that a doctor is not obliged to prejudice recovery by excessive information. The question as to how such a case is to be judged in law [reference] and how the doctor must act in this situation was irrelevant in the previous case. It need not be decided here either, for, then as now, neither the defendant nor the doctor in charge has pleaded that in this respect doubts existed as to whether the patient should be informed. If a medical adviser has failed to point out the typical dangers connected with the administration of physical treatment, the burden of proof is on him to show good reasons for having omitted to provide information [reference].

This court cannot agree with the claim of the medical profession to decide on their own whether and to what extent in the individual case a patient is to receive information if it is implied thereby that the courts are precluded altogether from reviewing the medical decision. The question as to whether in a particular case the patient received sufficient information touches upon the sphere of law; upon it depends the determination of the legal question, to be decided by the court, as to whether he has validly consented to the treatment. Naturally, the court in determining questions of this kind, will rely extensively on expert medical assistance. This is true . . . in particular in assessing the capacity of the patient to give his consent, but also when the question is whether complete information would have resulted in injury to the plaintiff's health or would have seriously endangered recovery. The court cannot be deprived of the power to review the question whether the doctor has complied with his duty to provide information and whether the patient has validly consented to the treatment.

4. According to the judgment of the Federal Supreme Court, information must only be provided where typical dangers exist inherent in the treatment, that is to say dangers which are normally connected with it and the occurrence of which can be expected according to medical experience and research. . . . The assumption is incorrect that the Federal Supreme Court requires a sick person to be made aware of every possible side effect of the treatment. No such requirement has ever been laid down. Instead it is acknowledged that a doctor is not obliged to draw the patient's attention to those dangers which can be avoided without difficulty, having regard to modern standards of operating techniques [reference]. Nor is he required to advise the patient that in unfavourable conditions even the smallest operation may result in some complications, despite all precautionary measures. Generally every patient knows this, and no special warning is necessary [reference].

5. In conclusion, it appears that the problem of the duty to provide a patient with information incumbent upon medical advisers as a condition for the validity of the patient's consent to the treatment continues to be governed basically by the principles which predominate in practice and in the literature.

III. In applying these principles to the facts of the present case the Court of Appeal rightly assumed that according to medical experience complications may arise in the course of electro-shock treatment. . . . Even incurable mental disease can be alleviated thereby at a stroke and sometimes cured; an electric current causes a cramp, accompanied by a sudden cramp-like contraction of all the muscles of the body and by a temporary loss of consciousness. This cramp-like tension can result in damage to joints and bones . . .

In its previous decision the Federal Supreme Court assumed on the basis of the expert evidence and of the factual findings of the Court of Appeal that at the time of the treatment then in issue, i.e. in the year 1951, complications arose in seven per cent of the cases of electro-shock treatment and that, consequently, it was normally required to inform the patient of this possibility . . . in the present case the question is only what the rate of complications appeared to be in 1954, when the plaintiff received electro-shock treatment. As regards this question the plaintiff, in agreement with statements made by some doctors, has argued as follows: like every therapeutic measure shock treatment had become less dangerous with increasing experience and with improvements in technical handling. For some time, and certainly in 1954, complications had become extremely rare and only occurred in one out of a thousand cases of shock therapy. This objection is relevant, for it is correct that the dangerous nature of the physical treatment cannot be assessed by reference to the frequency of complications during the early stages of a new therapy, when the necessary experience was still lacking. Instead the state of medical science and experience is determining which exists at the time of the particular medical treatment in issue [reference]. The Court of Appeal, too, adopted this view. It stated:

The court realises that the dangers arising from shock treatment may have been less in 1954 than in 1951. . . . In examining the question of the need to provide information it is impossible to rely on the positive experience of one medical expert which, moreover, extends to the present time. It must be considered that at the relevant time, in 1954, the Siemens-Convulsator III which was used in treating the plaintiff was . . . a new instrument, the effects of which had not yet been tested by an extensive practice. In determining a duty to provide information and the extent of the information to be provided, the state of experience at the particular time must supply the standard. Even if in 1954 fractures, injuries to the spine, and other damage had become so rare as no longer to count as typical, they still occurred to an extent which made it appear necessary to draw attention to them.

These observations of the Court of Appeal give rise to legal criticism. Even if in 1954 the application of shock methods as practised in the hospital for nervous diseases led only very seldom to complications, these complications nevertheless remain typical of shock treatment, for injuries of this kind . . . occur precisely on the occasion of this treatment, and at no other. This does not, however, assist in determining the duty of the medical adviser to inform the patient, for it is also unnecessary to draw attention to typical injuries, if they occur in extremely rare cases only and if it can be assumed that a reasonable patient would not consider such injuries seriously in deciding to give his consent. This would be the case if, as the defendant contends, in 1954 complications occurred in less than one in a thousand cases of shock treatment where the Siemens-Convulsator III was used. In such cases information must only be given if the patient enquires specifically about possible dangers. Since the Court of Appeal has found that this did not happen, it should have ascertained the rate of complications in 1954 accompanying this method of treatment. . . . The fact that the Court of Appeal came to the conclusion, without exhausting [these] sources of further evidence, that injuries still occurred at that time to an extent which made it necessary to inform the patient to this effect discloses . . . an error of law. Consequently the judgment under appeal cannot be upheld on the basis of the reasons set out therein . . .

Case 54

BUNDESGERICHTSHOF (SIXTH CIVIL SENATE) 21 NOVEMBER 1995
NJW 1996, 776 = JZ 1996, 518

Facts

The claimant's big toe was fractured on 26 January 1991. He was fitted with a leg plaster, which permitted walking, at the clinic of the former co-defendant, on the orders of the second defendant (hereafter called the defendant) who was a doctor. At the same time he was given a leaflet about what to do if there were complications with the plaster cast. It mentioned the danger of interference with blood circulation. The claimant had pressure pains and called at the outpatients department on 6 February 1991. Small pressure marks on his heel were revealed on removal of the plaster, so no new plaster was put on, and he was given crutches instead. He then came to an appointment in outpatients on 20 February 1991, complaining of severe calf pains. Vein thrombosis was diagnosed, which was treated in hospital, but it could not be healed operatively or with drugs, as it was several days old. The claimant sued the defendant and the former co-defendant for compensation for defective treatment and insufficient explanation.

The claim failed at both earlier instances. The claimant lodged an appeal in law but withdrew it against the former defendant. It led to quashing and reference back.

Reasons

. . .

II. These statements do not stand up to legal examination in the appeal in law.

1. . . .

2. The appeal in law is correct in objecting to the fact that the appeal court did not regard an explanation to the claimant about the risk of thrombosis as necessary. According to the case law of the Senate, the doctor must give an explanation to a patient about the specific risks of a treatment if they would severely cramp his lifestyle if they were realised. These dangers include those of deep leg vein thrombosis. The appeal court obviously proceeds on this basis. It considers however that here no explanation was needed at the point in time of the treatment, because "the danger of a thrombosis from immobilisation on outpatient treatment and therefore the prophylaxis in this situation" was "admittedly under discussion but was not in any way the norm"; the patient did not need an explanation about a step which was not the medical norm. The appeal in law correctly disputes this view as erroneous in law.

The assumption of the appeal court is flawed from the outset. The appeal court takes into account according to the nature of the case that the prophylaxis for thrombosis was not yet at that time the medical norm. But the duty to explain is not about the necessity of a prophylaxis to avert the risk of thrombosis nor about whether such a step was already at that time the medical norm or not. The question of the necessity for an explanation about the risk of thrombosis is only about whether the danger of a thrombosis arising on the prescribing in outpatients of a plaster permitting walking, as here, was sufficiently known in medical circles at that time.

As the Senate decided in its judgment of 12 December 1989, the medical duty of explanation presupposes that the particular risk concerned is known according to the state of medical experience at the point in time of the treatment (reference omitted). In any case, in cases in which, as here, alternative treatments were available, like the prescribing of crutches or of a special shoe, it is not necessary for this purpose that the scientific discussion about particular risks of a type of treatment is already closed and has led to generally accepted conclusions. It will then suffice that serious opinions in medical science indicate definite dangers connected with the treatment, which cannot be merely dismissed as insignificant outsider opinions, but must be regarded as important warnings (reference omitted). Thus in the case in question even an ongoing discussion in medical science about the dangers of thrombosis and the possibilities of combatting it by prophylaxis with drugs in outpatients would suffice to trigger the duty to explain. This is because in such cases the patient's right of self-determination requires the dangers possibly associated with the chosen treatment methods to be communicated to him, and for it at the same time to be indicated to him that such dangers can be avoided or reduced by the other treatment methods which are available . . .

III. Because of all this, the disputed judgment must be quashed in so far as it concerns the defendant, in order that the appeal court can make the necessary findings about whether and to what extent the risk of thrombosis was serious and under discussion (and in a way that the defendant could recognise) at the time of the treatment.

Case 55

BUNDESGERICHTSHOF (SIXTH CIVIL SENATE) 15 FEBRUARY 2000
BGHZ 144, 1 = NJW 2000, 1784 = JZ 2000, 898

Facts

The claimant, who was born on 8 February 1994, seeks compensation from the defendant paediatrician for harm caused by vaccination. The claimant was brought by her mother to the defendant on 11 May 1994 for a routine child care investigation. She gave her a primary immunisation against a number of diseases and a threefold live oral vaccine against poliomyelitis, with the agreement of her mother. The defendant's receptionist gave the mother beforehand a leaflet about the vaccinations which she looked at in the waiting room and gave back again without signing it. The side effects of the vaccination against poliomyelitis were stated in the leaflet, amongst others, to be that: "Feverish reactions seldom arise, and paralyses extremely rarely (one case in five million vaccinations)". The defendant asked her if she had read the leaflet and she said she had. After examining the claimant, the defendant said a vaccination was now possible if the mother wanted it. On 13 June 1994 the mother came to the defendant again because the child had a skin rash, and the second vaccination against poliomyelitis was then carried out. On 18 June 1994 she was found to have fever and on 25 June restraint in the use of her left leg. Investigations revealed that she was suffering from poliomyelitis. The social security office at F found harm caused by vaccination with a reduction in ability to work of 80 per cent, and awarded a vaccination benefit. The claimant claimed defective treatment and insufficient explanation resulting in no effective consent; and that there was no consent by the father either. She claimed damages for pain and suffering of at least DM 100,000 and a declaration that the defendant was under a duty to compensate for all consequential harm.

The *Landgericht* rejected the claim. The *Oberlandesgericht* allowed it in substance, awarding damages for pain and suffering of DM 80,000.

The appeal in law by the defendant was successful.

Reasons

I. . . .

II. These statements do not stand up to legal examination in the end result. The claimant is not entitled to a claim to compensation against the defendant for unlawful harm to her health. The appeal in law is right in objecting to the fact that the assumption by the appeal court that the claimant's mother did not effectively consent to the vaccination because of the lack of sufficient explanation by the defendant was based on requirements which were too strict.

1. The appeal court has admittedly correctly stated that an effective consent was not lacking simply because the claimant's father had not agreed to the vaccination. It is true that in cases in which, as here, parental care belongs to both parents jointly (§§ 1626 ff. of the BGB), the consent of both parents is needed for a medical operation, which also includes a medical vaccination. But it will in general be possible to proceed on the basis that the parent appearing at the doctors with the child has the power to give consent to the medical treatment on behalf of the absent parent as well; and the doctor may rely on

this within limits, as long as no circumstances which would indicate the contrary are known to him. This applies, as the Senate has already stated in its judgment of the 28 June 1988 (reference omitted), and it adheres to this, at any rate in routine cases, which include routine injections.

The oral vaccination against poliomyelitis with live attenuated polio pathogens carried out in the first half year of 1994 is a routine vaccination, as the appeal court has stated without legal error. It was recommended a long time ago by the Standing Vaccination Committee of the Federal Health Office (references omitted) and was also publicly recommended in Baden-Württemberg by the relevant health authority in accordance with § 14 (3) of the *BSeuchG*, in particular in 1994 (reference omitted). It had been carried out millions of times since the introduction of oral polio vaccine in 1962. The question of undertaking of such vaccinations arises for everyone having custody of children in the first months of a child's life (reference omitted) and usually on the occasion of the routine child care investigations of babies and small children, and this was generally known. On a vaccination recommended in this way, which a large number of parents let their children receive, the defendant might therefore rely on the fact, in the absence of concrete indications to the contrary, that the claimant's mother made her decision in favour of vaccination with the father's authority, especially as the mother—as the appeal court correctly observes—always (and this included previous occasions) appeared alone with the claimant at the surgery.

2. The appeal court further correctly assumes that the consent given by the claimant's mother to the vaccination was only effective if the risks associated with it had been previously explained to her. Such an explanation of the risks is also necessary for a voluntary vaccination and even when the vaccination is publicly recommended (references omitted). The necessity for an explanation about the danger that a person who has been vaccinated might contract spinal poliomyelitis because of vaccination with living polio viruses did not—contrary to the view of the appeal in law—cease to apply simply because it was an extremely rare consequence of vaccination. The appeal court, referring to *C. Braemer* (reference omitted) took as a basis a frequency of harm of 1:4.4 million. In the leaflet given by the defendant to the claimant's mother a risk of 1:5 million is given. Although the reply to the appeal in law claims that these figures are incorrect, and that on first vaccinations the risk in fact rises to 1:750,000 vaccinations, no more precise clarification of the frequency of harm is necessary as statistical risk figures have a comparatively low value (references omitted). The decisive factor for determining whether there is a medical duty to advise is not a particular degree of risk, and especially not a particular statistic; it is whether the risk concerned is specifically attached to the operation and on the realisation of the risk it would be especially burdensome to the patient's lifestyle (references omitted). The Senate therefore adheres to the view that in principle even extremely uncommon risks of this kind must be explained. Contrary to the view of the appeal in law and statements to the same effect in the academic literature (reference omitted) this applies also for publicly recommended vaccinations, for which the primary immunisation of the whole population is in the public interest in order to prevent an epidemic spread of a disease. In cases of public recommendation of vaccination, it is true that the health authorities have already balanced the risks of vaccination for the individual and his environment on the one hand, and the dangers threatening the general public and the individual in the case of non-vaccination on the other hand. But that does not change the fact that the vaccination is nevertheless voluntary, and the individual person

receiving the vaccination can therefore also decide against it. This person must therefore not only be aware of the voluntariness of the vaccination (reference omitted), which, in relation to the claimant's mother, is not questioned here. He must also make a decision about whether to take the risks associated with the vaccination or not. This presupposes knowledge of these risks, even if they are only realised extremely rarely; they must therefore be communicated to him by medical explanation.

3. The Senate also agrees with the appeal court that the written advice on vaccination against poliomyelitis in the leaflet which was given to the claimant's mother is not open to objection as to its content.

(b) ...
(aa) ... According to the case law of the Senate, the patient only needs explanation about the chances and risks of the treatment "by and large". Exact medical description of the risks coming into consideration is not necessary ...

Although the reply to the appeal in law mentions other risks (meningo-encephalitis, convulsions etc., see (reference omitted)) which had not been explained, this does not justify any different conclusion. If, as in the present case, the precise risk which had to be explained, and actually was explained, has in fact been realised, it does not as a rule matter whether other risks needed to be mentioned as well in the explanation. The patient has given his consent in the knowledge of the risk which was realised, so for this reason no liability can arise from the operation. Considerations as to whether he would possibly have refused approval on being advised of another risk are necessarily speculative and can therefore not be the basis of a claim for compensation ...

4. However there are serious reservations about the view of the appeal court that the explanation could not be regarded as having been given in time, having regard to the manner in which it was made ...

(b) The appeal court is exaggerating the requirements for an explanation to be given in time in connection with a routine vaccination, as the appeal in law correctly argues. According to the established case law, an explanation on the day of the operation in principle suffices in the case of outpatient operations (references omitted). The only case when that does not apply is if the explanation only occurs so immediately before the operation that the patient is under the impression that he can no longer extricate himself from a course of events already set in motion (e.g. an explanation at the door to the operating theatre).

The multiple vaccination undertaken here did not require an explanation at some earlier point in time, separated from the vaccination. In particular, no requirement can be made (as the appeal court thought was necessary) for the leaflet to be given to the mother to take home, so that she could read and consider it there in peace, and for the vaccination then to be carried out on a separate date. This places excessive requirements on the doctor.

The oral vaccination, even if it was not completely free from risk, did not present the parents with difficult decisions which would first have needed thorough weighing up and careful consideration. It was a question, as has been observed, of a routine vaccination in connection with which the element of conflict in the decision was to a large extent removed from the parents by the balancing of the advantages and disadvantages undertaken by the health authorities and the recommendation for vaccination made by them.

The necessity for vaccination had been generally recognised for a long time amongst the population and parents everywhere saw to it that it was done to their children, in order to avoid the feared disease of poliomyelitis. In this situation the defendant could assume that the claimant's mother was familiar with the vaccination and was in the picture about the generally accepted need for it. If a person having custody of a child should in such a case exceptionally want a period for reflection, then he could be expected to state this to the doctor and to decline an immediate vaccination.

(c) The explanation which had been given to the claimant's mother was also not insufficient simply because the defendant did not make it in a personal conversation about the vaccination and its risks. According to the case law of the Senate "conversation based on trust between the doctor and the patient" is admittedly necessary for the purpose of making an explanation (reference omitted). That however does not in any way exclude the use of leaflets in which the necessary information about the operation, including its risks, is set out in writing. Written advice of this kind is normal today to a large extent and has the advantage of giving a precise and comprehensive description of the subject of the explanation, as well as providing the doctor with substantial means of proof. It is in particular appropriate for routine treatments and therefore also for publicly recommended protective vaccinations.

Such leaflets can admittedly not replace the necessary discussion with the doctor (reference omitted), in which the doctor must satisfy himself as to whether the patient has read and understood the written advice, and which gives him the opportunity to go into the individual interests of the patient and answer possible questions. But this requirement of an explanatory conversation, which must be adhered to in principle, does not require an oral explanation of the risks in every case. In certain circumstances, as with the present facts, having regard to the routine character of the publicly recommended vaccination, the doctor can by way of exception proceed on the basis that the patient does not attach any importance to an additional presentation of the risks in discussion. For such routine treatment, it can suffice if, after a written explanation, opportunity is given to the patient for further information by a conversation with the doctor . . .

Case 56

BUNDESGERICHTSHOF (SIXTH CIVIL SENATE) 15 APRIL 1975
NJW 1975, 1161 = JZ 1975, 535 = VERSR 1975, 831

The defendants accuse the plaintiff of having offered indecent periodicals and picture magazines on their railway bookstalls. After the third defendant, a student of theology, had lodged a complaint with the police he went on the morning of 4 July 1971 together with the other defendants, a lawyer and two acquaintances, to the railway bookstall of the plaintiff in B and invited the sales assistant to remove from the shelves within one hour those publications which he described as indecent. When he found upon his return that they had not been removed, the third defendant took twenty-four newspapers and periodicals from the shelves and from a stand and took them in front of the railway station, where the fourth defendant defaced them with paint. In addition he wrote in paint on the display window of the kiosk "Away with filthy pornography". Meanwhile the first defendant, in the presence of the second defendant, engaged in discussion with passers-by.

On the same evening the first and third defendant went to the plaintiff's kiosk at the railway station in H and made the same demand that all the publications described by them as pornographic were to be removed within an hour. Finding upon their return that their demand had not been complied with, the third defendant began to go through the papers on the newsstand, as a result of which some periodicals fell onto the ground. Using a megaphone he invited passers-by to lodge a complaint against the plaintiff. The first defendant protested against the sale of pornographic publications by holding up a poster.

The plaintiff demands that the defendants should be prohibited from removing from their outlets publications or other objects without any intention of purchasing them, from soiling or damaging them or from affecting them physically.

The district court allowed the claim. The defendants appealed unsuccessfully to the Court of Appeal of Karlsruhe. Their further appeal was rejected for the following

Reasons

The Court of Appeal regards the claim for an order of prohibition as justified under §§ 823 I, 1004 I BGB. It holds correctly that the defendants, acting together, violated the plaintiff's property and interfered with his established and operating business. The appellants do not contest that they acted as trespassers in the meaning of § 1004 I BGB, even if they did not themselves act against the plaintiff. It is only disputed whether the defendants acted illegally and whether a danger exists of a repetition. The Court of Appeal answered both questions in the affirmative. It held that the acts of the defendants were not justified as self-defence nor as permissible defence of others, even if . . . the publications concerned were indecent in the meaning of the wording then in force of § 184 of the Criminal Code and were therefore a danger to young persons according to § 6 of the Act against the Distribution of Publications Endangering Young Persons. In the opinion of the Court of Appeal the infringements of the law committed so far and the conduct of the defendant indicated the likelihood of a repetition. In the result the appeal must fail.

I. 1. The Court of Appeal holds correctly that the defendants cannot seek to justify their acts by relying on the right of self-defence or the defence of others (§ 227 BGB) even if the plaintiff . . . should have contravened § 84 of the Criminal Code or the Act against the Distribution of Publications Endangering Young Persons by displaying and selling the publications to which the defendants took exception. This right of self-help does not enable citizens to maintain morals and order, even if the order is protected by criminal law. Their maintenance is the task of the competent organs of the State; the ordinary citizen must not assume their function. In a State governed by law it is indispensable that the maintenance and protection of orderly community life is to be entrusted primarily to the organs of the State bound to observe the Constitution and not to private initiative [references].

As a matter of principle, an individual can only confront actively a disturbance of public order, even if it involves a criminal act, by relying on his right of self-defence or of defending others . . . if the perpetrator of the disturbance attacks at the same time individual interests which are protected as such [references].

(*a*) Contrary to the contention of the appellants this is not necessarily the case if § 184 of the Criminal Code or §§ 3, 4, 6 of the Act against Distribution of Publications Endangering Young Persons are infringed. Certainly § 184 of the Criminal Code in the wording of 20 July 1971, which applies in the present case, punishes advertising and selling indecent publications in order to protect modesty, morals, and decency in sexual matters in the interest of the community as a whole [references]. The penal sanction sought to protect the sexual feelings current in the community, not the particular notion of morals and decency held by an individual, which may even clash with the sanction. The individual was included in the sphere of protection of the sanction indirectly only inasmuch as normally he benefits from it too. For this reason he was not accorded the right, in the case of contraventions of § 184 of the Criminal Code, to avail himself of the right under § 172 of the Code of Criminal Procedure to apply for the initiation of proceedings to force a prosecution.

Similarly, the Act against the Distribution of Publications Endangering Young Persons in providing for the protection of children and adolescents only serves the State as a guardian. It is the function of the State, not of the individual citizen, to safeguard the order which these provisions seek to protect.

(*b*) Naturally this does not rule out the possibilities that an infringement against these provisions may coincide with an attack against individual interests "susceptible of self-defence" with the result that the citizen concerned himself or another may intervene in order to fend off *this* attacker. However, this presupposes a situation in which precisely the protected individual interests are affected by the dangers connected with the "attack" and that thus the protected sphere of the individual is touched by the coincidence of "attack" and individual interest; the fact alone that the order protected by the criminal law has been disturbed is insufficient. Those relying on the right of self-defence or to defend others must prove that a conflict of the kind described above exists.

The Court of Appeal holds correctly that the pleadings of the defendants are deficient in this respect. In particular they cannot rely on the argument that merely by offering for sale in their kiosks at railway stations publications—assumed to be a criminal act—they have directly violated the right of personality of the defendants by attacking their honour or otherwise, even if the defendants may have regarded the display of such publications as a sufficient slight of their person, as a threat to their intimate feelings or to their family life.

It is unnecessary in the present case to examine the restrictions imposed by our law upon the trade in pornography by the protection of the personality of the individual and of its dignity [references]. In the present case . . . periodicals and picture magazines, the publication of which was prohibited and punishable, are said to have been offered for sale on the shelves of the premises together with the usual range of publications available at a railway bookstall. However, no customer was compelled against his will to take more than fleeting notice of these publications; his personal attention was not drawn to them, nor were they advertised obtrusively. The personality of the individual which is protected by the Constitution was only affected by this confrontation quantitatively and qualitatively as part of an anonymous public, no more than an individual member of the community is troubled by disturbances of public order. The personality of the customer is neither disregarded nor injured in an insulting manner, nor are his protected intimate feelings injured, even if it is remembered that the protection of personal integrity, both physical and mental, must be rated highly.

It is true that human personality and its free expression through self-determination and self-reliance, guaranteed by the Constitution and the legal order, also requires citizens among themselves to respect the innermost sphere of the individual [references].

This precept does not imply, however, that every citizen who is worried or disturbed by a public disregard of general morals and of criminal law by another is entitled for *this reason only* to proceed against the attacker by way of self-help, unless the attack is directed against himself; in the present case an individual citizen has first sought a confrontation in order to make public interests his own private affair. Such an assumption of an "office of censor" would indeed run counter to the constitutional guarantee. Instead it must remain for the State itself, which is primarily charged with adjusting such tensions, to select the place, the time, and the extent of any action against the violation of morals and of law within the community.

(*bb*) The same applies to the claim of the fourth defendant, the father of the child, who relies on the right of self-defence or of the defence of others, on the ground that the attack is directed against the right to educate a child (see Article 6 of the Constitution). In this respect, too, no evidence has been adduced to show that the conduct of the plaintiff constitutes a direct danger to the task of the fourth defendant to educate his child . . .

(*cc*) This Division does not agree with the arguments of the appellants that the courts, by decreeing the prohibition asked for by the plaintiff, would protect a criminal activity by the plaintiff. The question whether the competent public authorities can proceed against the plaintiff, having regard to his trade in the publications objected to, is not affected by a judgment in the terms applied for. This judgment is confined to preventing conduct by the defendants which is to be disapproved by law for the sake of orderly community life and against whom the plaintiff may defend himself by a claim to desist placed at his disposal by private law. Nor is it an abuse of law if the plaintiff resorts to the courts by bringing an action against the defendants.

Addendum 1

Extracts from *Sidaway* v. *Bethlehem Royal Hospital and Maudsley Hospital* [1985] AC 871 House of Lords

This was an appeal from the Court of Appeal which had dismissed an appeal from a decision of Skinner J who had dismissed the appellant's action.

LORD BRIDGE OF HARWICH: . . . The appellant underwent at the hospital for which the first respondents are the responsible authority an operation on her cervical vertebrae performed by a neurosurgeon, since deceased, whose executors are the second respondents. The nature of the operation was such that, however skilfully performed, it involved a risk of damage to the nerve root at the site of the operation or to the spinal cord. The trial judge described that risk as "best expressed to a layman as a 1 per cent or 2 per cent risk of ill-effects ranging from the mild to the catastrophic". The appellant in fact suffered, without negligence on the surgeon's part in the performance of the operation, a degree of damage to the spinal cord of which the effects, if not catastrophic, were certainly severe. Damages have been agreed, subject to liability, in the sum of £67,500.

The appellant denied that she had seen the surgeon at all before the operation was performed. This evidence the judge rejected. He found that, before the appellant consented to undergo the operation, the surgeon explained the nature of the operation to her in simple terms and warned her of the possibility and likely consequences of damage to the nerve root, but did not refer to the risk of damage to the spinal cord. Most unfortunately, the surgeon who performed the operation died before these proceedings were instituted. Accordingly, the trial judge, the Court of Appeal and your Lordships' House have all been denied the advantage of what would clearly have been vital evidence on the issue of liability, not only the surgeon's own account of precisely what he had told this appellant, but also his explanation of the reasons for his clinical judgment that, in her case, the information he gave her about the operation and its attendant risk was appropriate and sufficient. The judge was thus driven to base the finding, to which I have earlier referred, in part on inference from documents, but mainly on the evidence of other doctors as to what they knew of the deceased surgeon's customary practice when discussing with patients an operation of the kind the appellant was to undergo. The result is that liability falls to be considered, in effect, in relation to that customary practice, independently of the vitally important individual doctor/patient relationship which must play so large a part in any discussion of a proposed operation with a patient. That introduces an element of artificiality into the case which we may deplore but cannot avoid.

There was a difference of opinion between the neurosurgeons called as expert witnesses whether they themselves would, in the circumstances, have warned the appellant specifically of the risk of damage to the spinal cord. But the one expert witness called for the appellant agreed readily and without reservation that the deceased surgeon, in omitting any such warning, would have been following a practice accepted as proper by a responsible body of competent neurosurgeons.

Broadly, a doctor's professional functions may be divided into three phases: diagnosis, advice and treatment. In performing his functions of diagnosis and treatment, the standard by which English law measures the doctor's duty of care to his patient is not open to doubt. "The test is the standard of the ordinary skilled man exercising and professing to have that special skill." These are the words of McNair J in *Bolam* v. *Friern Hospital Management Committee* [1957] 1 WLR 582 at 586, approved by this House in *Whitehouse* v. *Jordan* [1981] 1 WLR 246 at 258 per Lord Edmund-Davies and in *Maynard* v. *West Midlands Regional Health Authority* [1985] 1 All ER 635 per Lord Scarman. The test is conveniently referred to as the *Bolam* test. In *Maynard's* case Lord Scarman, with whose speech the other four members of the Appellate Committee agreed, further cited with approval the words of the Lord President (Clyde) in *Hunter* v. *Hanley* 1955 SLT 213 at 217:

> "In the realm of diagnosis and treatment there is ample scope for genuine difference of opinion and one man clearly is not negligent merely because his conclusion differs from that of other professional men . . . The true test for establishing negligence in diagnosis or treatment on the part of a doctor is whether he has been proved to be guilty of such failure as no doctor of ordinary skill would be guilty of if acting with ordinary care. . . ."

The language of the *Bolam* test clearly requires a different degree of skill from a specialist in his own special field than from a general practitioner. In the field of neuro-surgery it would be necessary to substitute for the Lord President's phrase "no doctor of ordinary skill", the phrase "no neurosurgeon of ordinary skill". All this is elementary and, in the light of the two recent decisions of this House referred to, firmly established law.

The important question which this appeal raises is whether the law imposes any, and if so what, different criterion as the measure of the medical man's duty of care to his patient when giving advice with respect to a proposed course of treatment. It is clearly right to recognise that a conscious adult patient of sound mind is entitled to decide for himself whether or not he will submit to a particular course of treatment proposed by the doctor, most significantly surgical treatment under general anaesthesia. This entitlement is the foundation of the doctrine of "informed consent" which has led in certain American jurisdictions to decisions and, in the Supreme Court of Canada, to dicta on which the appellant relies, which would oust the *Bolam* test and substitute an "objective" test of a doctor's duty to advise the patient of the advantages and disadvantages of undergoing the treatment proposed and more particularly to advise the patient of the risks involved.

There are, it appears to me, at least theoretically, two extreme positions which could be taken. It could be argued that, if the patient's consent is to be fully informed, the doctor must specifically warn him of *all* risks involved in the treatment offered, unless he has some sound clinical reason not to do so. Logically, this would seem to be the extreme to which a truly objective criterion of the doctor's duty would lead. Yet this position finds no support from any authority to which we have been referred in any jurisdiction. It seems to be generally accepted that there is no need to warn of the risks inherent in all surgery under general anaesthesia. This is variously explained on the ground that the patient may be expected to be aware of such risks or that they are relatively remote. If the law is to impose on the medical profession a duty to warn of risks to secure "informed consent" independently of accepted medical opinion of what is appropriate, neither of these explanations for confining the duty to special as opposed to general surgical risks seems to me wholly convincing.

At the other extreme it could be argued that, once the doctor has decided what treatment is, on balance of advantages and disadvantages, in a patient's best interest, lie should not alarm the patient by volunteering a warning of any risk involved, however grave and substantial, unless specifically asked by the patient. I cannot believe that contemporary medical opinion would support this view, which would effectively exclude the patient's right to decide in the very type of case where it is most important that he should be in a position to exercise that right and, perhaps even more significantly, to seek a second opinion whether he should submit himself to the significant risk which has been drawn to his attention. I should perhaps add at this point, although the issue does not strictly arise in this appeal, that, when questioned specifically by a patient of apparently sound mind about risks involved in a particular treatment proposed, the doctor's duty must, in my opinion, be to answer both truthfully and as fully as the questioner requires.

The decision mainly relied on to establish a criterion of the doctor's duty to disclose the risks inherent in a proposed treatment which is prescribed by the law and can be applied independently of any medical opinion or practice is that of the District of Columbia Circuit Court of Appeals in *Ganterbury* v. *Spence* 464 F 2d 772 (1972). The Judgment of the court (Wright, Leventhal and Robinson JJ), delivered by Robinson J expounds the view that an objective criterion of what is a sufficient disclosure of risk is necessary' to ensure that the patient is enabled to make an intelligent decision and cannot be left to be determined by the doctors. He said (at 784):

"Respect for the patient's right of self-determination on particular therapy demands a standard set by law for physicians rather than one which physicians may or may not impose upon themselves."

In an attempt to define the objective criterion it is said (at 787) that—"the issue on non-disclosure must be approached from the viewpoint of the reasonableness of the physician's divulgence in terms of what he knows or should know to be the patient's informational needs."

A risk is required to be disclosed—"when a reasonable person, in what the physician knows or should know to be the patient's position, would be likely to attach significance to the risk or cluster of risks in deciding whether or not to forego the proposed therapy."

The judgment adds (at 788): "Whenever non-disclosure of particular risk information is open to debate by reasonable-minded men, the issue is for the finder of facts,"

The court naturally recognises exceptions from the duty laid down in the case of an unconscious patient, an immediate emergency or a case where the doctor can establish that disclosure would be harmful to the patient.

Expert medical evidence will be needed to indicate the nature and extent of the risks and benefits involved in the treatment (and presumably of any alternative course). But the court affirms (at 792): "Experts are unnecessary to a showing of the materiality of a risk to a patient's decision on treatment, or to the reasonably, expectable effect of risk disclosure on the decision." In English law, if this doctrine were adopted, expert medical opinion whether a particular risk should or should not have been disclosed would presumably be inadmissible in evidence.

I recognise the logical force of the *Canterbury* doctrine, proceeding from the premise that the patient's right to make his own decision must at all costs be safeguarded against the kind of medical paternalism which assumes that "doctor knows best". But, with all respect, I regard the doctrine as quite impractical in application for three principal reasons. First, it gives insufficient weight to the realities of the doctor/patient relationship. A very wide variety of factors must enter into a doctor's clinical judgment not only as to what treatment is appropriate for a particular patient, but also as to how best to communicate to the patient the significant factors necessary to enable the patient to make an informed decision whether to undergo the treatment. The doctor cannot set out to educate the patient to his own standard of medical knowledge of all the relevant factors involved. He may take the view, certainly with some patients, that the very fact of his volunteering, without being asked, information of some remote risk involved in the treatment proposed, even though he describes it as remote, may lead to that risk assuming an undue significance in the patient's calculations. Second, it would seem to be quite unrealistic in any medical negligence action to confine the expert medical evidence to an explanation of the primary medical factors involved and to deny the court the benefit of evidence of medical opinion and practice on the particular issue of disclosure which is under consideration. Third, the objective test which *Canterbury* propounds seems to me to be so imprecise as to be almost meaningless. If it is to be left to individual judges to decide for themselves what "a reasonable person in the patient's position" would consider a risk of sufficient significance that he should be told about it, the outcome of litigation in this field is likely to be quite unpredictable.

I note with interest from a learned article entitled "Informed Consent to Medical Treatment" (1981) 97 *LQR* 102 at 108 by Mr Gerald Robertson . . . that only a minority of states in the United States of America have chosen to follow *Canterbury* and that since *1975* "there has been a growing tendency for individual states to enact legislation which severely curtails the operation of the doctrine of informed consent." I should also add that I find particularly cogent and convincing the reasons given for declining to follow *Canterbury* by the Supreme Court of Virginia in *Bly* v. *Rhoads* 222 SE 2d *783* (1976).

Having rejected the *Canterbury* doctrine as a solution to the problem of guarding the patient's right to decide whether he will undergo a particular treatment advised by his doctor, the question remains whether that right is sufficiently safeguarded by the application of the *Bolam* test without qualification to the determination of the question what risks inherent in a proposed treatment should be disclosed. The case against a simple application of the *Bolam* test is cogently stated by Laskin CJC, giving the judgment of the Supreme Court of Canada in *Reibi* v. *Hughes* (1980) 114 DLR (3d) I at 13:

"To allow expert medical evidence to determine what risks are material and, hence, should be disclosed and, correlatively, what risks are not material is to hand over to the medical profession the entire question of the scope of the duty of disclosure, including the question whether there has been a breach of that duty. Expert medical evidence is, of course, relevant to findings as to the risks that reside in or are a result of recommended surgery or other treatment. It will also have a bearing on their materiality but this is not a question that is to be concluded on the basis of the expert medical evidence alone. The issue under consideration is a different issue from that involved where the question is whether the doctor carried out his professional activities by applicable professional standards. What is under consideration here is the patient's right to know what risks are involved in undergoing or foregoing certain surgery or other treatment."

I fully appreciate the force of this reasoning, but can only accept it subject to the important qualification that a decision what degree of disclosure of risks is best calculated to assist a particular patient to make a rational choice whether or not to undergo a particular treatment must primarily be a matter of clinical judgment. It would follow from this that the issue whether nondisclosure in a particular case should be condemned as a breach of the doctor's duty of care is an issue to be decided primarily on the basis of expert medical evidence, applying the *Bolam* test. But I do not see that this approach involves the necessity "to hand over to the medical profession the entire question of the scope of the duty of disclosure, including the question whether there has been a breach of that duty". Of course, if there is a conflict of evidence whether a responsible body of medical opinion approves of non-disclosure in a particular case, the judge will have to resolve that conflict. But, even in a case where, as here, no expert witness in the relevant medical field condemns the nondisclosure as being in conflict with accepted and responsible medical practice, I am of opinion that the judge might in certain circumstances come to the conclusion that disclosure of a particular risk was so obviously necessary to an informed choice on the part of the patient that no reasonably prudent medical man would fail to make it. The kind of case I have in mind would be an operation involving a substantial risk of grave adverse consequences, as for example the 10 per cent risk of a stroke from the operation which was the subject of the Canadian case of *Reibi* v. *Hughes* (1980) 114 DLR (3d) 1. In such a case, in the absence of some cogent clinical reason why the patient should not be informed, a doctor, recognising and respecting his patient's right of decision, could hardly fail to appreciate the necessity for an appropriate warning.

In the instant case I can see no reasonable ground on which the judge could properly reject the conclusion to which the unchallenged medical evidence led in the application of the *Bolam* test. The trial judge's assessment of the risk at 1 per cent or 2 per cent covered both nerve root and spinal cord damage and covered a spectrum of possible ill-effects "ranging from the mild to the catastrophic". In so far as it is possible and appropriate to measure such risks in per centage terms (some of the expert medical witnesses called expressed a marked and understandable reluctance to do so), the risk of damage to the spinal cord of such severity as the appellant in fact suffered was, it would appear, certainly less than 1 per cent. But there is no yardstick either in the judge's findings or in the evidence to measure what fraction of 1 per cent that risk represented. In these circumstances, the appellant's expert witness's agreement that the non-disclosure of neurosurgical opinion afforded the respondents a complete defence to the appellant's claim.

LORD SCARMAN: . . . The issue is whether Mr Falconer failed to exercise due care (this was not challenged) in the advice which he gave his patient when recommending an operation; I use the word "advice" to cover information as to risk and the options of alternative treatment. Whatever be the correct formulation of the applicable law, the issue cannot be settled positively for or against the doctor without knowing what advice, including any warning of inherent risk in the operation, he gave his patient before she decided to undergo it and what was his assessment of the mental, emotional and physical state of his patient. The trial judge derived no help on these two vital matters from the evidence of the appellant. Mr Falconer was not an available witness, having died before trial, and the medical records afforded no sure guide on either matter. Regrettable though a "non-proven" verdict is, it is not, therefore, surprising. Where the court lacks direct evidence as to the nature and extent of the advice and warning (if any) given by the doctor and as to his assessment of his patient the court may well have to conclude that the patient has failed to prove her case.

This lack of evidence is unsatisfactory also from a purely legal point of view. I am satisfied, for reasons which I shall develop, that the trial judge and the Court of Appeal erred in law in holding that, in a case where the alleged negligence is a failure to warn the patient of a risk inherent in the treatment proposed, the *Bolam* test, (see *Bolam* v. *Friern Hospital Management Committee* [1957] 1 WLR 582) . . . is to be applied. In my view the question whether or not the omission to warn constitutes a breach of the doctor's duty of care towards his patient is to be determined not exclusively by reference to the current state of responsible and competent professional opinion and practice at the time, though both are, of course, relevant consideration[s], but by the court's view whether the doctor in advising his patient gave, the consideration which the law requires him to give to the right of the patient to make up her own mind in the light of the relevant information whether or not she will accept the treatment which he proposes. This being my view of the law, I have tested the facts found by the trial judge by what I believe to be the correct legal criterion. In my view the appellant has failed to prove that Mr Falconer was in breach of the duty of care which he owed to her in omitting to disclose the risk which the trial judge found as a fact he did not disclose to her. [Was the judge in *Bolam*] correct in treating the "standard of competent professional opinion" as the criterion in determining whether a doctor is under a duty to warn his patient of the risk, or risks, inherent in the treatment which he recommends? Skinner J and the Court of Appeal have in the instant case held that [he] was correct. Bristow J adopted the same criterion in *Chauerton* v. *Gerson* [1981] 1 All ER 257; [1981] QB 432. The implications of this view of the law are disturbing. It leaves the determination of a legal duty to the judgment of doctors. Responsible medical judgment may, indeed, provide the law with an acceptable standard in determining whether a doctor in diagnosis or treatment has complied with his duty. But is it right that medical judgment should determine whether there exists a duty to warn of risk and its scope? It would be a strange conclusion if the courts should be led to conclude that our law, which undoubtedly recognises a right in the patient to decide whether he will accept or reject the treatment proposed, should permit the doctors to determine whether and in what circumstances a duty arises requiring the doctor to warn his patient of the risks inherent in the treatment which he proposes.

The right of "self-determination", the description applied by some to what is no more and no less than the right of a patient to determine for himself whether he will or will not accept the doctor's advice, is vividly illustrated where the treatment recommended is surgery. A doctor who operates without the consent of his patient is, save in cases of emergency or mental disability, guilty of the civil wrong of trespass to the person; he is also guilty of the criminal offence of assault. The existence of the patient's right to make his own decision, which may be seen as a basic human right protected by the common law, is the reason why a doctrine embodying a right of the patient to be informed of the risks of surgical treatment has been developed in some jurisdictions in the United States of America and has found favour with the Supreme Court of Canada. Known as the "doctrine of informed consent", it amounts to this:

where there is a "real" or a "material" risk inherent in the proposed operation (however competently and skilfully performed) the question whether and to what extent a patient should be warned before he gives his consent is to be answered not by reference to medical practice but by accepting as a matter of law that, subject to all proper exceptions (of which the court, not the profession, is the judge), a patient has a right to be informed of the risks inherent in the treatment which is proposed. The profession, it is said, should not be judge in its own cause; or, less emotively but more correctly, the courts should not allow medical opinion as to what is best for the patient to override the patient's right to decide for himself whether he will submit to the treatment offered him.

In a medical negligence case where the issue is as to the advice and information given to the patient as to the treatment proposed, the available options and the risk, the court is concerned primarily with a patient's right. The doctor's duty arises from his patient's rights. If one considers the scope of the doctor's duty by beginning with the right of the patient to make his own decision whether he will or will not undergo the treatment proposed, the right to be informed of significant risk and the doctor's corresponding duty are easy to understand, for the proper implementation of the right requires that the doctor be under a duty to inform his patient of the material risks inherent in the treatment. And it is plainly right that a doctor may avoid liability for failure to warn of a material risk if he can show that he reasonably believed that communication to the patient of the existence of the risk would be detrimental to the health (including, of course, the mental health) of his patient.

My conclusion as to the law is therefore this. To the extent that I have indicated, I think that English law must recognise a duty of the doctor to warn his patient of risk inherent in the treatment which he is proposing; and especially so if the treatment be surgery. The critical limitation is that the duty is confined to material risk. The test of materiality is whether in the circumstances of the particular case, the court is satisfied that a reasonable person in the patient's position would be likely to attach significance to the risk. Even if the risk be material, the doctor will not be liable if on a reasonable assessment of his patient's condition he takes the view that a warning would be detrimental to his patient's health.
[Having applied the principles in his speech, LORD SCARMAN was in favour of dismissing the appeal.]

[LORD KEITH OF KINKEL agreed with LORD BRIDGE OF HARWICH. LORD DIPLOCK and LORD TEMPLEMAN delivered speeches in favour of dismissing the appeal.]
Appeal dismissed.

Addendum 2

Extracts from *Bolitho* v. *City and Hackney Health Authority* House of Lords [1998] AC 232

LORD BROWNE-WILKINSON: . . . The locus classicus of the test for the standard of care required of a doctor or any other person professing some skill or competence is the direction to the jury given by McNair J in *Bolam* v. *Friern Hospital Management Committee* [1957] 1 *WLR* 583 at 587:

> "I myself would prefer to put it this way: a doctor is not guilty of negligence if he has acted in accordance with a practice accepted as proper by a responsible body of medical men skilled in that particular art . . . Putting it the other way round, a doctor is not negligent, if he is acting in accordance with such a practice, merely because there is a body of opinion that takes a contrary view."

My Lords, I agree with [leading counsel for the appellant's] submissions to the extent that, in my view, the court is not bound to hold that a defendant doctor escapes liability for negligent treatment or diagnosis just because he leads evidence from a number of medical experts who are genuinely of opinion that the defendant's treatment or diagnosis accorded with sound medical practice. In *Bolam's* case [1957] 1 WLR 583 at 587 McNair J stated that the defendant had to have acted in accordance with the practice accepted as proper by a "*responsible* body of medical men" (my emphasis). Later he referred to "a standard of practice recognised as proper by a competent *reasonable* body of opinion" (see [1957] 1 WLR 583 at 588; my emphasis). Again, in *Maynard* v. *West Midlands Regional Health Authority* [1985] 1 All ER 635 at 639, Lord Scarman refers to a "respectable" body of professional opinion. The use of these adjectives—responsible, reasonable and respectable—all show that the court has to be satisfied that the exponents of the body of opinion relied on can demonstrate that such opinion has a logical basis. In particular, in cases involving, as they so often do, the weighing of risks against benefits, the judge before accepting a body of opinion as being responsible, reasonable or respectable, will need to be satisfied that, in forming their views, the experts have directed their minds to the question of comparative risks and benefits and have reached a defensible conclusion on the matter.

There are decisions which demonstrate that the judge is entitled to approach expert professional opinion on this basis. For example, in *Hucks* v. *Cole* (1968) (1993) 4 Med LR 393, a doctor failed to treat with penicillin a patient who was suffering from septic places on her skin though he knew them to contain organisms capable of leading to puerperal fever. A number of distinguished doctors gave evidence that they would not, in the circumstances, have treated with penicillin. The Court of Appeal found the defendant to have been negligent. Sachs LJ said (at 397):

> "When the evidence shows that a lacuna in professional practice exists by which risks of grave danger are knowingly taken, then, however small the risks, the court must anxiously examine that lacuna—particularly if the risks can be easily and inexpensively avoided. If the court finds, on an analysis of the reasons given for not taking those precautions that, in the light of current professional knowledge, there is no proper basis for the lacuna, and that it is definitely not reasonable that those risks should have been taken, its function is to state that fact and where necessary to state that it constitutes negligence. In such a case the practice will no doubt thereafter be altered to the benefit of patients. On such occasions the fact that other practitioners would have done the same thing as the defendant practitioner is a very weighty matter to be put on the scales on his behalf; but it is not, as Mr Webster readily conceded, conclusive. The court must be vigilant to see whether the reasons given for putting a patient at risk are valid in the light of any well-known advance in medical knowledge, or whether they stem from a residual adherence to out-of-date ideas . . ."

Again, in *Edward Wong Finance Co Ltd* v. *Johnson Stokes & Master (a firm)* [1984] AC 296, [1984] 2 WLR 1, the defendant's solicitors had conducted the completion of a mortgage transaction in "Hong Kong style" rather than in the old-fashioned English style. Completion in Hong Kong style provides for money to be paid over against an undertaking by the solicitors for the borrowers subsequently to hand over the executed documents. This practice opened the gateway through which a dishonest solicitor for the borrower absconded with the loan money without providing the security documents for such loan. The Privy Council held that even though completion in Hong Kong style was almost universally adopted in Hong Kong and was therefore in accordance with a body of professional opinion there, the defendant's solicitors were liable for negligence because there was an obvious risk which could have been guarded against. Thus, the body of professional opinion, though almost universally held, was not reasonable or responsible.

These decisions demonstrate that in cases of diagnosis and treatment there are cases where, despite a body of professional opinion sanctioning the defendant's conduct, the defendant can properly be held liable for negligence (I am not here considering questions of disclosure of risk). In my judgment that is because, in some cases, it cannot be demonstrated to the judge's satisfaction that the body of opinion relied on is reasonable or responsible. In the vast majority of cases the fact that distinguished experts in the field are of a particular opinion will demonstrate the reasonableness of that opinion. In particular, where there are questions of assessment of the relative risks and benefits of adopting a particular medical practice, a reasonable view necessarily presupposes that the relative risks and benefits have been weighed by the experts in forming their opinions. But if, in a rare case, it can be demonstrated that the professional opinion is not capable of withstanding logical analysis, the judge is entitled to hold that the body of opinion is not reasonable or responsible.

I emphasise that, in my view, it will very seldom be right for a judge to reach the conclusion that views genuinely held by a competent medical expert are unreasonable. The assessment of medical risks and benefits is a matter of clinical judgment which a judge would not normally be able to make without expert evidence. As . . . Lord Scarman makes clear [in *Maynard's* case] it would be wrong to allow such assessment to deteriorate into seeking to persuade the judge to prefer one of two views both of which are capable of being logically supported. It is only where a judge can be satisfied that the body of expert opinion cannot be logically supported at all that such opinion will not provide the bench mark by reference to which the defendant's conduct falls [His Lordship then concluded that this was plainly not "one of those rare cases".]

[LORD SLYNN OF HADLEY delivered a speech in which he agreed with LORD BROWNE-WILKINSON'S analysis of the question to be decided in this sort of case and of the correct approach in law to them. LORD NOLAN, LORD HOFFMANN and LORD CLYDE agreed with LORD BROWNE-WILKINSON'S speech.]

Notes to Cases 50–56

1. These cases illustrate certain problems that German law discusses under the headings of "unlawfulness" and *culpa* (very loosely translatable as fault). Their theoretical treatment has been sketched above (chapter 2, section A.3) but it is, again, at the level of concrete cases and specific issues that concept is concretised and the similarities become obvious and any comparison with the Common law becomes meaningful. A number of points call for special comment.

2. The standard of care expected of the defendant is discussed in cases 50 and 51. In case 50 (RGZ 119, 397) the plaintiff's claim failed because he himself knew that the defendant was not fully competent. A second reason why the claim failed can be traced in the facts as found by the lower courts: the accident would have occurred even if the defendant had been properly qualified. In other words, the defendant's negligence is not even a condition (let alone a legal cause) of the harm. (See chapter 2, section A.5 (a), and English cases cited there.) But the importance of the judgment is in its second half where (as in case 51) it is stated that the standard of care will be determined objectively by reference to the behaviour of the reasonable man. Here, the basic idea is the same in American, English, and French law, though many formulations have been proposed and the terminology is slightly different. (The Common law searches for the behaviour of the "reasonable man" who, in the context of the tort of defamation, becomes the "ordinary man" in order to accommodate a certain amount of loose thinking (note that in these days of proclaimed sex equality lawyers have still to introduce the notion of the "reasonable woman"), while the civil law systems

refer to the "*bonus pater familias*".) In practice, however, these are merely expressions of the anthropomorphic conception of justice as perceived by judges and/or juries.

Numerous statements can be quoted showing that no legal system expects the behaviour of the model citizen who is the paragon of all true virtue. Equally, however, no system is prepared to countenance the attitudes of the most callous, timorous, or indecisive members of its society. As Harper, James Jr., and Gray put it (*The Law of Torts* 2nd edn. (1986) 389–90): "As everyone knows, this reasonable *person* [*sic*] is a creature of the law's imagination. He is an abstraction. He has long been the subject of homely phrase and witty epigram." (Equally, however, courts have applied the ordinary standards of care even to persons of exceptional skill and perception, *Fredericks* v. *Castora*, 241 Pa. Super. 211, 360 A. 2d 696, (1976).) In *Hall* v. *Brooklands Club* [1933] 1 KB 205, 224, Greer LJ stressed the need to remain in touch with the average community standards when he described the reasonable man as " 'the man in the street' or 'the man in the Clapham omnibus', or, as I recently read in an American author, 'the man who takes the magazines at home, and in the evening pushes the lawn-mower in his shirt sleeves' ". However, the reader must also take note of the clear trend discernible in all systems to raise standards in an effort to keep abreast with the quicker tempo and increased hazards of modern life. Thus, in certain areas of tort law—notably traffic accidents that account for a major part of litigation in all advanced legal systems—the presence of obligatory insurance may be the reason of an almost complete equation of negligence with near-strict liability. Case 51 (BGH JZ 1968, 103) is a good illustration of this tendency and one can find even clearer examples in French (Grenoble, 4 décembre 1978, *JCP* 1980, II, 19340) and English law (*Roberts* v. *Ramsbottom* [1980] 1 WLR 823). In the latter case the English court held "negligent" a 75-year-old man who had a stroke a few minutes before setting off on a drive that was to lead to a series of accidents culminating in his being taken to hospital where his brain haemorrhage (of which he had had no previous forewarning) was finally discovered. In the court's view nothing less than a complete loss of consciousness would have sufficed to exculpate him from liability. (*Cf.* *Breunig* v. *American Family Insurance Co.*, 173 NW 2d 619 (1970): defendant lost control of her car believing that God had taken control of the steering wheel. He had not, and the plaintiff was injured. The plea of insanity was rejected and defendant was held liable.) Other cases like *Henderson* v. *Jenkins* [1970] AC 282 (car brakes defective due to an undiscoverable hidden defect which led to an accident) and *Nettleship* v. *Weston* [1971] 2 QB 691 (learner-driver held to be "negligent" for failing to attain the standard of competence of an experienced driver; likewise with American law: Gregory *et al.*, 152) lend credence to theories which attempt to ascribe such *perversions* of traditional concepts to modern insurance practice. (In this sense B S Markesinis, "La Perversion des notions de responsabilité civile délictuelle par la pratique de l'assurance" (1983) *Rev. int. dr. comp.* 301.) In America standards have also been dramatically raised in cases involving children causing accidents while engaged in "adult activities". *Dellwo* v. *Pearson*, 259 Minn. 452, 107 NW 2d 859 (1961) is such a case and has proved particularly influential in automobile cases. See *Prichard* v. *Veterans Cab. Co.*, 63 Cal. 2d 727, 408 P. 2d 360 (1965); also Henderson and Pearson, 363–4 with further references. Children are judged by adult standards when they are defendants. By what standards should they be judged when they are the plaintiffs and a question of contributory negligence arises? See *Reiszel* v. *Fontana*, 35 AD 2d 74, 312 NYS 2d 988 (1970).

3. For fuller discussions of American law see Franklin, 43 ff.; Henderson and Pearson, 319 ff.; Epstein, 129 ff.; Franklin and Rabin, 31 ff; Prosser, *et al.*, 137 ff. For England see Clerk and Lindsell *on Torts*, 18th edn. 4–55 ff (for children) and 7–159 ff for a more general But detailed) discussion of the expected standard of care. The impact of modern insurance on the modern law of torts has been the subject of an excellent dissertation by Professor Viney of the University of Paris in the mid-sixties (*Le déclin de la responsabilité individuelle* (1965)). The theme is taken up again in her most recent treatise on the subject, *Traité de droit civil* (ed. J Ghestin IV), *Introduction à la Responsabilité* 2nd ed (1995). Finally, for an excellent comparative discussion of the notion of fault and the changed attitudes towards it see Tunc, *La responsabilité civile* (1981).

4. Case 53, BGHZ 29, 46, (and, indeed, case 99, BGH NJW 1959, 1106, below) touches upon one of the most troublesome aspects of medical malpractice law—a topic which has generated heated

debates and lends itself for inclusion in courses on advanced torts. The early American literature can be found in such works as Wadlington, Waltz, and Dworkin, *Cases and Materials* on *Law and Medicine* (1980), and Curran and Shapiro, *Law, Medicine and Forensic Science* (3rd edn. 1982). *Making Health Care Decisions, President's Commission for the Study of Ethical Problems in Medicine*, US Government Publishing Office (1982) is a three-volume report full of useful information on the subject. *Comment to Medical Care* is the title of an interesting study published by the Law Reform Commission of Canada in 1980. English law, woke up to these problems later; and this belated interest was first captured by Margaret Brazier's *Medicine, Patients and the Law*, now in its 2nd edn. (1992) provides a most readable introduction to the whole subject. Mason and McCall-Smith's *Law and Medical Ethics* 5th ed. (1999) gives a good summary (at 140–59), on the whole, supportive of the current rather conservative approach of the English courts. By contrast Ian Kennedy's stimulating Note in 47 *MLR* 454 (1984) is critical of this attitude. (See also Kennedy's excellent essays collected under the title *Treat Me Right* (1988).) Well worth reading also is Robertson's "Informed Consent to Medical Treatment" 97 *LQR* 102 (1981) and Andrew Grubb's "A Survey of Medical Malpractice Law in England: Crisis? What Crisis?", 1 *Journ. of Contemporary Health Law and Policy* 75 ff. (esp. 93–111) (1985). For a comparative study of English and American law on this point see: Schwartz and Grubb, "Why Britain Can't Afford Informed Consent", 15 *Hastings Center Report* (1985); for Anglo-German law see Shaw, "Informed Consent: A German Lesson", 35 *ICLQ* 864 (1986). Kennedy and Grubb's *Principles of Medical Law* (1998) is now the main treatise on English law but is also replete with references to other Common law jurisdictions. The subject is also discussed in the growing books on professional negligence.

5. Lawful consent is required for otherwise the interference with the patient's body would be "unlawful" according to the view taken by German case-law (*contra* Laufs in *NJW* 1969, 529 arguing that in this case the doctor's conduct is not objectively aimed at "injuring" the body but as "curing" and that, therefore, § 823 I BGB is inapplicable). Unlike the English Common law, which expects the patient to prove non-disclosure, German law casts on to the doctor the burden of proving the patient's consent. (Deutsch, *Arztrecht und Arzneimittelrecht*, 2nd edn. (1991) 39.) The action will, typically, be based on § 823 I BGB. In the Common law systems on the other hand total absence of consent or fraudulently obtained consent will justify an action in battery. In practice, however, negligence actions are much more common than trespass to the person because: (i) the rules on limitation and causation in trespass are thought to be too oppressive to defendant/doctors and (ii) intentional torts are usually not covered by insurance. See *Cobbs* v. *Grant*, 8 Cal. 3d 229, 502 P. 2d 1 (1972); likewise in England, though see *Freeman* v. *Home Office* [1983] 3 All ER 589. Consent is thus crucial, but the problems it raises are far from solved. One could, perhaps, categorise the cases into three groups.

The first includes situations where the answers are *reasonably* clear. For example, in the case of an infant or a young child consent must come from those responsible for his care (usually the parents) §§ 1626, 1631 BGB (Germany); *Zoski* v. *Gaines* 271 Mich. 1, 260 NW 99 (1935) (USA); *S* v. *McC*; *W* v. *W* [1972] AC 29, 37 (per Lord Hodson) (England). Older children, mature enough to understand the implications of their consent, are free to give it themselves: *Lacey* v. *Laird* 166 Ohio St. 12, 139 NE 2d 25 (1956) (USA); BGHZ 29, 37 (Germany); *Family Law Reform Act 1969*, § 8 (16 years) (England). On this see Skegg in 36 *MLR* 370 (1973) and [1969] *Recent Law* 295 (NZ). An operation on an unconscious adult will usually be defended on the grounds of necessity.

A second group of cases are controversial (and have this in common with the next group); but they also deal with problems which are relatively new to medical science and social life in general. For example, whose consent is necessary for the prescription of a contraceptive pill: parent's or child's? In *Gillick* v. *West Norfolk and Wisbech Area Health Authority* the Court of Appeal ruled that no contraceptive, abortion advice, or treatment could be given to a girl under 16 years of age without her parents' consent save in a case of an emergency or after a court order (*The Times* 21 December 1984) but the decision was overruled by the House of Lords by a three to two majority: [1985] 3 All ER 402; [1986] AC 112 discussed by Professor Glanville Williams in 1985 *New Law Journal* pp. 1156 ff.; Kennedy, "The Doctor, the Pill, and the Fifteen-Year-Old-Girl" in *Treat Me Right* (1988)

52 ff. Transplant surgery can also raise nice problems. See, for example, *Hart* v. *Brown*, 29 Conn. Supp. 368, 289 A. 2d 386 (1972).

Two related issues have also occupied modern courts and received similar answers. The first is connected with abortion and the father's "rights" or "interests". Can he seek an injunction—acting in his own right or on behalf of the foetus—and prevent the mother from aborting? (If the foetus were viable, the father's action could also be seen as attempting to prevent the commission of a crime.) Two courts—in *Paton* v. *British Pregnancy Advisory Service* [1979] 276, involving an action by a *husband*, and in *C* v. *S* [1987] 1 All ER 1230, involving an action by the *boyfriend* of the mother—have shown a marked reluctance to challenge a medical decision, properly reached, about an abortion; and, in general, would prefer to leave it to the criminal law to challenge the legality of such a decision in the criminal courts where a jury would make the decision and not a judge sitting alone. The European Commission on Human Rights agreed, 3 EHRR 410 (1980).

What of a girl under age who wishes to have an abortion? Is her parents' consent necessary? The answer would appear to be negative so long as the girl is mature enough to understand what is being proposed: *Re P (a Minor)* (1981) 80 LGR 301. In some systems statutes have made it clear that such consent can be given after the age of sixteen. (England: Family Law Reform Act 969, section 8; Australia: Minors (Contracts and Property) Act 1970; New Zealand: Guardianship Act 1968.) But if the law appears to be settled, the ethical controversies are unlikely to end that easily. See Kennedy, "A Husband, a Wife, and an Abortion", in *Treat Me Right* (1988) 42 ff.

The third group of cases deals with what is, perhaps, the thorniest aspect of the problem of consent—what exactly need be disclosed for consent to be valid? "Medicine", wrote an international expert on this subject, "is a discipline which is enriched by . . . joint international contribution. . . . The same is true of the law governing medical practice." (Giesen and Hayes, "The Patient's Right to Know—A Comparative View" (1992) 21 *Anglo-American L.R.* 101–22. See also, Giesen, "Zwischen Patientenwohl und Patientenwille", *JZ* 1987, 282). Judicial decisions from both Canada and, especially, the antipodes, confirm the accuracy of the statement and the value of the method, so the summary that follows is comparative in nature and not focused on one system in particular.

To the question of how much information must be disclosed to the patient before his consent to medical treatment can be legally valid three answers are possible. The first, basically, leaves the decision to "a responsible body of medical men skilled in that particular art." This is known as the *Bolam* test from the leading English case of *Bolam* v. *Friern Hospital Management Committee* [1957] 1 WLR 582 and is the most paternalistic in nature. This test was, essentially, re-affirmed by four out of five law lords in *Sidaway* v. *Royal Bethlehem Hospital Governors* [1985] 1 AC 871. (Reproduced in part as *Addendum 1* above.). Lord Scarman dissented in favour of the doctrine of informed consent. Though three of the judges (Lords Bridge, Keith and Templeman) made comments which have encouraged those who believe that English law is too indifferent to the patients' interests, the tone of the judgment was set by Lord Diplock who insisted that medical opinion remained "determinative" in such matters. This can be seen by the next important case—*Gold* v. *Haringey Area Health Authority* [1988] QB 481 where the Court of Appeal overruled a more pro-plaintiff judgment by Schiemann J ([1987] 1 FLR 125) by insisting that "the Judge was not free, as he thought, to form his own view of what warning and information ought to have been given, irrespective of any body of responsible medical opinion to the contrary." (Per Lloyd LJ at p. 490.) One reason why English law takes such a conservative view was given by Lord Denning in *Whitehouse* v. *Jordan* [1980] 1 All ER 650, 658, and is connected with the fear of increased malpractice litigation. However, such statistics as do exist in America and Germany do not seem to support this fear and further empirical studies are needed before a conclusive view can be expressed. Decisions such as *Bolitho* would suggest that a shift of emphasis is taking place even in English law; and the new Human Rights Act (and growing "rights" culture) can only accelerate this move towards a more balanced view of the patient's rights and the doctor's obligations. (See, also, *Addendum 2* containing extracts from *Bolitho* v. *City and Hackney Health Authority* [1998] AC 232.)

This English position is rejected by most Common law jurisdictions which adopt the so-called doctrine of "informed consent" taking the view that the doctor must disclose as much information as a reasonable patient would require to make an informed choice and frequently add, for good measure, that the doctor "should not lightly make the judgment that the patient does not wish to be fully informed." This last quotation comes from the leading Australian case of *F* v. *R* (1983) 33 SASR 189, 193; and the same ideas are, essentially, found in many American jurisdictions (for example *Canterbury* v. *Spence*, 464 F 2d 772 (1972); *Crain* v. *Allison*, 443 A. d 558 (1982)) and Canada (*Reibl* v. *Hughes* [1980] 2 SCR 880; *White* v. *Turner* 120 DLR 3d 269). Both these positions have been rejected by many decisions of Continental European systems on the grounds that they violate the patient's right of self-determination. (Rich references to French, German, and Swiss law are given by Giesen and Hayes, *op. cit.*, above, in notes 70–72; and the whole matter is exhaustively considered by Giesen in *International Medical Malpractice Law* (1988). For details on French law see: Guillot, *Le Consentement éclaire du patient: autodétermination ou paternalism* (1986).) This position has, as stated, been forcefully stressed by German courts which, in the light of the recent past, have been only too conscious of the dangers of ignoring human dignity and not preventing unwarranted medical interferences with the body and health of human beings. Thus, from the beginning of the post-War period, courts have stressed that "proper respect for the patient's right of self determination will further rather than damage the patient's trust in his doctor" and "to respect the patient's own will is to respect his freedom and dignity as a human being." (BGHZ 29, 46, 53–56. See, also, BGHZ 90, 96; 90, 103.) Thus, the principle of full disclosure is repeatedly stressed (see BGH VersR 1980, 428, 429; NJW 1984, 1397); and in one case, involving *diagnostic* treatment, the court took the view that even a 0.5 per cent chance of a particular risk occurring should be disclosed (OLG Hamm VersR 1981, 68). In the case of *therapeutic* operations disclosure will be geared to the patient's individual circumstance such as his level of understanding (BGH NJW 1980, 633) and even the attending doctor's degree of experience (OLG Köln VersR 1982, 453). The urgency of the situation is also a factor that can be taken into account (BGH VersR 1972, 153); and even the defence of "therapeutic privilege" (no revelation of risks since patient might not be able to "handle" adverse news) has been treated with caution, as a decision of the BGH of 28 November 1957 clearly shows. (BGHSt 11, 111, 114 and compare similar statements in *Meyer Estate* v. *Rogers* (1991) 6 CCLT 2d 114.) Beyond stating the above general, guiding principles, one must advise the reader to consult particular instances where the courts have applied them to different factual situations. The following are recent illustrations. (See for details *Staudinger*-Hager, 13th edn. (1999), § 823 section I, no. 76–133.)

(i) A patient must, as a general rule, be warned of the possibility of stiffening of the shoulders as a result of an injection containing cortisone, even if this is a very slight risk; but he need not be informed of the remote danger of fatal sepsis: BGH NJW 1989, 1533.

(ii) A doctor who wishes to undertake a vaginal delivery, even though the danger to mother and child dictates a caesarean operation, has a duty to warn the expecting mother of the accompanying risks. If the doctor maintains that the expecting mother refused a caesarean section, he has the burden of proving that he furnished her with the required warning: BGH NJW 1992, 741.

(iii) If a doctor fails to provide the patient with the required information concerning the nature and the difficulty of an operation, he is not free from liability merely because the harm which actually occurs is not one against which the doctor was obliged to warn: BGH NJW 1991, 2346.

(iv) Before performing cosmetic surgery a doctor must inform the patient especially carefully and thoroughly of the odds of the operation failing to produce the desired results (in this case removing wrinkles under the chin): BGH NJW 1991, 2349. Properly informing a patient about an operation entails explaining to him the urgency of such an operation.

(v) The doctor has the burden of proving that he provided a thorough and accurate explanation: BGH NJW 1990, 2928. In more recent decisions the BGH has continued this trend and emphasised repeatedly the patient's right of self-determination.

(vi) Thus, in BGH NJW 1996, 776, case 54, the court held that where a number of alternative methods of treatment were available, it was not enough to inform the patient only about the orthodox and established methods. Even if a new method has not yet been fully worked out (in the instant case it could have avoided the risk of thrombosis) it must still be brought to the attention of the patient so long as some experts regard it as a serious and appropriate treatment. The decisive criterion in determining the scope of the duty to inform is thus giving the patient all the necessary information to make an informed choice for, in the end, it is the patient who will have to bear the consequences (see Giesen JZ 1996, 519 with further references).

(vii) A more restrictive approach was adopted in BGH NJW 2000, 1784, case 55, (note by Deutsch JZ 2000, 902). This case, involving a routine vaccination (against polio), raised two interesting points. First the plaintiff submitted that the defendant was liable. For though the risk which materialised had been brought to the attention of the patient, other risks, which should also have been mentioned, had not been mentioned to him. The BGH denied liability on the basis that the patient gave his consent knowing about the risk that did in fact materialize. Whether or not he would have not given his consent had he been informed of the other risks was a matter for speculation and could not be taken into account in the instant case. The second aspect concerns the question whether it was sufficient that the information about the risk was in written form and the patient was given the opportunity to clarify doubts in a personal conversation with the doctor. It was held that such an (informal) procedure was adequate at least as far as routine measures were concerned. Finally, it is interesting to note that German courts are not impressed by the statistical probability of a certain risk, a point also confirmed in the decision in question. Whether the risk is regarded as material depends on the circumstances of the individual case, the nature of the treatment, the seriousness of the risk. Overall, these decisions demonstrate that German courts have succeeded in striking a workable balance between the patient's right of self-determination and the need to control in a reasonable way the extent of medical liability so that the profession is not unduly burdened by excessive costs. (For further discussion of these topics see: Deutsch, NJW 1980, 1305; idem, NJW 1984, 1802; Laufs and Kern, JZ 1984, 631. More detailed discussions can also be found in the standard treatises written by Professor Deutsch, *Medizinrecht—Arztrecht, Arzneimittelrecht und Medizinprodukterecht*, 4th edn. (1999); and Professor Giesen, *Arzthaftungsrecht*, 4th edn. (1995).)

One further point related with informed consent which has troubled the courts of many systems is linked to the problem of causation that arises in such cases. For, once it has been decided that inadequate information has been given to the patient, the next point that arises is whether had there been proper disclosure this particular patient would have gone ahead with the proposed medical treatment. Once again, the doubt has centred as to how this question should be answered: objectively, by discovering the reaction of the hypothetical, reasonable man? Or by finding how this particular patient would have reacted. It would be impossible to deny that the question does not lend itself to an easy answer. Equally, however, it is noteworthy that despite the dangers of self-serving evidence (which arise if the test is to be subjective) many courts have adopted it as the right criterion. Thus see: New Zealand: *Smith* v. *Auckland Hospital Board* [1964] NZLR 191 CA; Australia: *Ellis* v. *Wallsend District Hospital* (1989) 17 NSWLR 553, 560; *Rogers* v. *Whittacker* (1991) 23 NSWLR 601; Germany: BGHZ 90, 103, 111, 112; BGHZ 90, 96, 101, 102. Indeed, German courts have tried to counter the argument that patients may, with hindsight, attempt to manipulate the evidence so they insist that it is for the patient to substantiate his allegation that he would not have consented to the operation even if properly informed "in those [cases] where the reasons adduced [by the patient] for refusing treatment are not altogether comprehensible in the light of the specific facts of the case." In other words, in such cases it is for the patient to come up with plausible reasons for refusing the treatment had he known the risks in advance.

6. Non therapeutic treatments—such as sterilisation operations—have been particularly controversial. In some systems—e.g. Australia (*Secretary, Dept. of Health* v. *JWB* (1992) CLR 218—they require a court order. In other systems—e.g. Canada *Re Eve* [1986] 2 SCR 388—even a court order is insufficient. In England, a court order seems to be deemed desirable but not essential. *In re F (Mental Patient)* [1990] 2 AC 1. The legal outcome may be more controversial depending upon whether the person that is about to be sterilised is a minor, an adult, or an adult of diminished intellectual abilities. The irreversible nature of the operation makes the decision that much more sensitive.

7. German law recognises the privilege of self-defence against persons, § 227 BGB (*Notwehr*) and the defence of necessity, § 904 BGB (*Notstand*). In § 228 BGB it also recognises (in certain circumstances) the right of a person to interfere with objects which belong to another person and from which the danger emanates in order to prevent harm to his own interests or those of others. Where this is the case the "unlawfulness" of the act disappears and the actor cannot be sued under § 823 I BGB. We are here talking of situations which have exact counterparts in the Common law. See, for example, Fleming, 78–80, 90–2; and Prosser and Keaton, 124 ff.

Case 56, BGH NJW 1975, 1161, however, attempts to put the privilege of self-defence to a novel use and the dislike of the legal order for self-help is clearly shown in the judgment of the German court. Compare in this respect § 140 of the *Restatement Second, Torts*, which also states that there will be no privilege to use force to prevent the commission of a misdemeanour.

Problems not dissimilar to those faced by the court in the above case have arisen in the US in the context of occupations of nuclear plants by nuclear protestors, but the defence of "competing harms" raised by the intruders has met with the same fate. An interesting case with such facts is *Commonwealth* v. *Bregman*, 13 Mass. App. Ct. 373, 433 NE 2d 457 (1982).

14. DUTIES OF CARE

Case 57

BUNDESGERICHTSHOF (SEVENTH CIVIL SENATE) 7 DECEMBER 1961
JZ 1962, 570

Facts

The claimant, as insurer, is pursuing an alleged claim of its policy holder ("the Company") which the claimant considers has passed to it in accordance with § 67 (1) sentence 1 of the VVG (Insurance Contracts Act). In 1957 the Company carried out installation work on the territory of the W excavation plant on their behalf and stationed there two vehicles used for carrying personnel and equipment. It transferred the surveillance of these by a contract of the 1 August 1957 to W ("the Surveillance Service"), the employer of the defendant. Its conditions of business, which were quoted on the contract document, stated, amongst other things: "The Surveillance Service is liable for harm which arises through the intentional conduct or gross negligence of its employees in the exercise of their duties . . . Harm which arises in the operation and guarding of machines, heaters, boilers and heating devices . . . is excluded from the liability . . .". The Surveillance Service employed the 71 year old defendant to guard the vehicles. During his duties he generally stayed in one of the vehicles. A stove was burning in it at night, in order to keep the space warm for the defendant. In the evening of the 7 January 1957, the foreman of the Company informed the defendant that the Company's workers had hung out their wet clothes to dry near the stove; he should take care that nothing caught light. At about 21 hours the defendant put some coals in the stove and went out. When he came back again at about 22 hours, the vehicle was on fire; it was destroyed with all its contents. The claimant paid for the Company's damage. The Landgericht allowed the claimant's applications and the Oberlandesgericht those of the defendant. The claimant's appeal in law was unsuccessful.

Reasons

The Oberlandesgericht rejected the claim because it assumed that the exemption from liability agreed between the Company and the Surveillance Service also extended to the defendant. This clause is contained in the "Special Terms" of the Surveillance Service. The Senate, contrary to the view held by the parties, has to interpret them freely (details are given). The appeal court's finding that the Surveillance Service has exempted itself from liability for cases of the present kind should be agreed (details are given).

The decision thus depends on whether the defendant has been included within the protected area of the exemption from liability agreed between the Surveillance Service and the Company. The Senate has, in agreement with the Oberlandesgericht, confirmed this.

Admittedly the "Special Terms" contain no express provisions about this. Further, it is correct that such clauses contained in general conditions of business are to be construed narrowly and, in case of doubt, against the person who has drawn them up and whom they benefit. But that alone is not decisive. It is not the wording of the exemption from liability but its sense and purpose, as recognisable to the other party to the contract, which are decisive. If there are no doubts in this respect, an appropriate amplification in accordance with § 157 of the BGB is not only permissible but required (reference omitted).

1. The assumption that the Surveillance Service wanted to extend the protection of the clause to its employees seems appropriate for the simple reason that the Surveillance Service could be held to this on the basis of the duty of care which it owed. It undertook the task of protecting from harm the objects which it guarded. It regarded the risk here as so significant that it thought it ought to limit its liability in relation to the guarding and operation of heaters, so that it did not have to take responsibility for gross negligence by its employees. To have shifted this risk which it recognised from its own shoulders and yet to have wished to burden its employees with it would be incomprehensible. They were weaker economically and still less in a state than their employers to bear the consequences of their failings resulting from general human weakness. In these circumstances, simply the duty of care which the Surveillance Service owed required it to include its employees in the protection which it considered necessary. It is to be assumed, in the absence of grounds indicating the contrary, that it wanted to fulfil this duty by the exemption from liability clause.

2. The same consequence follows from another consideration.

(a) It is recognised in the case law that, in the case of so-called danger-prone activity, the employee can in certain circumstances ask his employer to release him from his duty to compensate third parties who have been harmed. That can even fall to be considered if the employee has acted with gross negligence; admittedly in that case a complete release of the employee is generally ruled out (reference omitted). These principles are applicable here. It is true that the guarding of a burning stove is in general not exactly difficult. Experience has however taught that damage here is no rarity and that it can be very extensive.

Therefore the activity assigned to the defendant is to be regarded as "danger-prone" in the normal sense.

(b) In this legal situation the Surveillance Service would not or would only imperfectly have attained the goal pursued by it if it had not extended the protection of the release to its employees as well. The reasons for this is that if claims could be made against them, they would in certain circumstances have had a claim to release against their employer. That would have contradicted the sense and purpose of the exemption from liability. Even on this ground it must be assumed that the Surveillance Service, in order to attain its goal, wanted at the same time to exempt its employees by the clause in question.

(c) The appeal in law takes the view that no release from the employee's liability for gross negligence can be derived from the principles repeated above, because in such a case the employer does not need to release him. Here, in its view, the defendant has acted with gross negligence. The objection is unsuccessful. Even its starting point is not correct. This is because even gross negligence on the part of the employee does not, as already explained, exclude the possibility that the employer has to release him from liability at least in part. Apart from this, it must be assumed to be the self-evident will of the employer that a release agreed by it for its employees should have no smaller extent than its own. Merely the idea of the duty of care, as indicated above, leads to this conclusion.

3. The desire of the Surveillance Service to include its employees within the protection of the release is admittedly only of significance if it was sufficiently recognisable to the other party to the contract. But the Senate has no doubts in confirming recognisability. The Company is an employer itself. For it, therefore, those considerations were obvious, just as for all other clients of the Surveillance Service finding themselves in a similar position. It must also not be assumed that a contacting party which agrees to such comprehensive limitations of liability as have been agreed here, has the intention of releasing the wealthy partner to the contract and yet of holding its economically weaker employees to the stricter liability. . . .

Case 58

BUNDESGERICHTSHOF (SIXTH CIVIL SENATE) 19 FEBRUARY 1991
NJW 1991, 2340 = VERSR 1991, 559

Facts

The plaintiff sues the defendant for breach of his duty of safety. On 17 May 1986, when the plaintiff was barely six years old, he was playing on an undeveloped building-plot of land belonging to the defendant and suffered serious injuries in an accident when a concrete ring on the land, about 1.2 metres broad and weighing 750 kg., fell on him. The land was readily accessible at the time. The plaintiff suffered a double fracture of the pelvis and damage to his urinary tract. The injury to his sphincter has caused incontinence. The plaintiff claimed DM 50,000 as damages for pain and suffering in addition to a further appropriate sum of at least DM 50,000. In addition, he claims DM 12,209.10 in respect of costs incurred by his parents in visiting him in hospital (travel DM 6,463.10, increased maintenance expenses DM 5,246 and overnight accommodation DM 500) as well as DM 40,800 lost earnings by the father and DM 9,768 as the value of the housework foregone by the mother while making the visits. For private medical treatment as an outpatient, not made good by the Krankenkasse, he claims DM 1,759.56, and a lump sum of

DM 500 for incidental expenses. He also claims a declaration that the defendant is liable for any further harm, material or immaterial.

The Landgericht rejected the claim. The plaintiff's appeal succeeded in part: the Oberlandesgericht granted the declaration, and awarded the plaintiff DM 25,000 as damages for pain and suffering plus a lump sum DM 200 for incidental costs. His further appeal was also successful in part. The case was remanded for reconsideration of the unliquidated claim for damages for pain and suffering as well as the special damages of DM 38,968.66.

Reasons

I. 1. The court below accepted that the defendant was in breach of his duty of safety to the plaintiff (§ 823 I BGB):

The defendant's land was dangerous to children, since wedges holding the concrete ring could easily be removed and the ring set in motion. It was the dangerous insecurity of the concrete ring which injured the plaintiff. The land was readily accessible, either by a garden gate from the property leased by the plaintiff's parents, or by a lane. Furthermore, the fence dividing it from the highway was broken at this point, and cars were actually being parked on the land.

2. On the view that the defendant's fault was not very grave, the court below held that DM 25,000 was an appropriate sum for damages for pain and suffering, notwithstanding that the claim had been certified at first instance as worth DM 100,000.

3. There was no sufficient legal basis for the mother's claim for the value of the housework she had been prevented from doing, and the court below held that the plaintiff must further specify and prove the other unadmitted items of loss.

II. Some of the appellant's criticisms of the judgment of the court below are sound.

1. The grounds on which court below concluded that the defendant was liable under § 823 I BGB were quite correct. If the owner of land knows or ought to know that, notwithstanding his prohibitions, children use his land as a playground and may play with dangerous objects there and get injured by them, he must take effective steps and lasting precautions to save them from the consequences of their inexperience and fecklessness [references]. The facts found by the court below justify the conclusion that the defendant, who admitted to knowing that children often played on the land and climbed over the things on it, was in breach of this duty of safety. He should also have realised that the concrete ring which injured the plaintiff was so placed and so insecurely fixed that despite its great weight children could set it in motion, as occurred, and be exposed to great danger, and it should have been obvious that notwithstanding the danger, children would play with so inviting an object.

2. As to the material loss claimed, the court below was correct to reject the claim in respect of the father's loss of earnings and the value of the housework the mother was unable to do. However, the total rejection of the claims for travel costs, increased maintenance, and overnight accommodation was not justified.

(*a*) The law of tort is based on the principle that a claim may be brought only by the person whose interests are protected by the rule infringed, and then only to the extent that he personally suffers harm. Only in the exceptional cases provided by §§ 844, 845

BGB may there be compensation for economic losses resulting "indirectly" from the invasion of the interests of others. The Bundesgerichtshof has, however, regularly made an exception for the cost of visits by close relatives to the sickbed of the injured party and, because of their intimate connection with the cost of the victim's recovery, treated them as part of the injury to *his* health (most recently BGHZ 106, 28 [30] = NJW 1989, 706; NJW 1990, 1037 = VersR 1989, 1308).

(*b*) We adhere to the principle of these decisions, especially as it has long become established in practice. It remains the case, however, apart from the exceptional cases where a third party has a statutory right to sue (§§ 844, 845 BGB), that the victim's claim for damages in tort basically covers only compensation for harm suffered by him personally, so claims for expenditure by a visitor depend essentially on who the visitor is. The mere fact that a third party is affected economically is not enough. Clearly no claim lies in respect of visits by persons not in the near family who attend out of a sense of social or similar duty. The rule of tort is not intended to compensate for such expenditures. But even as regards the expenses of those within the class of "near family" there are limitations. It must always be borne in mind that such expenses, which do not cost the injured victim himself anything, are only exceptionally and on special factual grounds chargeable to the person causing the injury, for otherwise the door would be opened, *contra legem*, for the compensation of mere economic harm suffered by persons only "indirectly" affected by the tort.

Previous decisions have therefore always restricted compensation to claims by the "nearest family" in respect of visits to a patient actually hospitalised, for only such visits can properly be regarded as both necessary for the recovery of the victim and also intimately connected with the cost of his cure, and so distinguished from expenses incurred either in law or in fact by those "indirectly" affected as a result of the injury to the victim, which are not compensable under the law of tort. Indeed, the only visiting costs incurred by close relatives which can be compensated consistently with the Code are those which are medically necessary for the recovery of the patient in his existing condition, and only those which are unavoidably incurred. Where there is no such medical necessity, hospital visits even by close relatives cannot be compensated, however desirable as regards the psychic or physical condition of the patient, and the same is true of expenses which might have been avoided. Here the general rule laid down in §§ 249 ff. BGB is not the sole consideration; the limits must be more tightly drawn because the law of tort is in principle restricted to the "direct" victim. Previous decisions of this Senate which go any further than this will no longer be followed.

(*c*) The detailed result of this in relation to the holdings below which are criticised by the appellant is as follows:

(*aa*) *Travel costs* form an expense necessarily involved in hospital visits, provided the cheapest means of transport is used and other economies observed. The court below regarded such expenses as harm to the plaintiff only to the extent that they had been met by the Krankenkasse, but as the appellant argues, this is inconsistent with § 287 Code of Civil Procedure, as the court did not ask why the Krankenkasse limited its payments or whether its limits were in line with the criteria of tort law as explained. The vouchers tendered by the plaintiff in support of this claim seem an adequate basis for evaluation under § 287 Code of Civil Procedure, at any rate so far as the number of visits is concerned.

(*bb*) Exceptionally a claim may be made for *overnight accommodation* in connection with visits, provided it is unavoidable. The documentation of such expenses tendered by the plaintiff is sufficient to permit evaluation under § 287 Code of Civil Procedure.

(*cc*) The *cost of meals* taken by close relatives while visiting hospital out of town depends essentially on the individual needs of the visitor. These determine whether in fact the cost of meals was "greater" than those taken at home. In order to respect the non-compensability of the loss incurred by "indirect" victims, compensation here must be limited to the unavoidable *increase* in the cost of meals. Only such increase is intimately enough connected with expenditures for the cure of the primary victim to be brought within § 823 I BGB. From this point of view the court below must evaluate the harm under § 287 Code of Civil procedure, on further evidence supplied by the parties, if necessary.

(*dd*) As to the claim for DM 40,000 in respect of the father's *loss of earnings*, the following applies: This Senate has repeatedly held that loss of earnings suffered by the visitor is capable of being regarded as part of the cost of cure of the injured party for which the person causing the injury must pay, subject to the general duty to mitigate damage, which requires, *inter alia*, that a self-employed person change his hours of work within reasonable limits (see NJW 1985, 2757 = VersR 1985, 784 [785]). Recovery for such losses is however limited to those so closely related to the cost of curing the victim that they can be seen as being truly costs of the visit; examples might be the loss by an employee of remuneration or perquisites if he can take time off work only on unpaid leave and cannot make it up later, or loss by a self-employed person directly attributable to the hospital visit and incapable of being made good in any other way. Beyond this, loss of income resulting from the fact that visiting hospital made the work more difficult cannot be treated as part of the victim's costs of cure to be made good under the law of delict, for this would, contrary to the Code, amount to liability for harm suffered by persons only indirectly affected.

In the present case, according to the plaintiff, the father, in employment as a manager, lost income because the hospital visits hindered him in developing a parallel practice as an independent accountant and tax adviser. Such a loss cannot be treated as part of the loss to the plaintiff which has to be made good. Leaving aside the question whether it was medically necessary for the patient to have the father by his side at the very time the latter needed to devote to his practice, losses such as these which are attributable to the fact that the visits to hospital left less time for the rapid development or extension of his business cannot be regarded as costs of the visit in the sense mentioned. The same would be true of delay in advancement or preferment in office. Such economic losses are harm suffered by third parties which is not compensable by the law of delict.

(*ee*) Nor can *interruption of housework* by the mother be taken into account. The appellant refers to the decision of the Senate of 10 October 1989 (VersR 1989, 1247), but in that case the expenditure claimed was in respect of nursing the victim, an increase in his need which was compensable under § 843 BGB. Here the plaintiff claims compensation for the time his mother could not spend on housekeeping because she was visiting him in hospital. In accordance with the principles just laid down for treating lost time at work as one of the costs of the visit, compensation in tort cannot be given when work lost through the visit can be made up before or afterwards. This was obviously possible in this case, since no substitute home help was employed.

(*ff*) In rejecting the plaintiff's claim for damages in respect of the *cost of private medical treatment* the court below insisted on too stringent a proof of the expenditures and thus misapplied § 287 Code of Civil Procedure. Whether a person who has statutory health insurance may claim the cost of private medical treatment depends on the circumstances of the individual case (VersR 1970, 129; VersR 1989, 54), and the decisive point is whether a reasonable man in the position of the victim would regard such private medical treatment as necessary. The nature of the injury and the victim's standard of living are especially relevant, but the court below did not consider these points, nor did it investigate the plaintiff's assertion that doctors had advised him to go to a "special clinic" for private medical treatment.

(*gg*) The fact that the court below allowed the plaintiff a lump sum in respect of incidental expenses of only DM 200 discloses no errors of law in the plaintiff's disfavour, and his appeal made no further mention of it.

3. The appellant is correct in arguing that as regards the quantum of damages for pain and suffering the court below misapplied § 287 Code of Civil Procedure.

(*a*) It is true that the judge of fact has a good deal of discretion in determining damages for pain and suffering, and his award cannot normally be criticised simply as being too high or, as here, too low. But this judicial discretion has its limits: the judge must show that in trying to reach a figure appropriate to injuries of that kind and duration he took all the relevant circumstances into account, and he must respect rules of law, canons of logic and the teachings of experience. The judge must also state the factual basis of his evaluation so that it may be seen that he has kept within these limits (invariable holdings, most recently NJW 1989, 773 = VersR 1988, 943).

(*b*) The appellant is right to complain of the way the court below dealt with his claim for damages for pain and suffering. This is especially true as regards the declaration of the Landgericht on 21 August 1989 when it gave full reasons for adopting the figure of DM 100,000 as the value of his claim under this head. On the plaintiff's appeal, the court below agreed that this sum was appropriate, thereby adopting the reasons given, which thus ceased to be the mere assertions of the plaintiff, as the court below later held in the judgment under appeal. While it was not finally bound to this sum, the court should certainly have indicated in the judgment under appeal why it had come to so very different a conclusion on unchanged evidence. If in the absence of different evidence a later evaluation of the damages differs widely from an earlier one, the law of procedure as well as candour to the parties requires the court to indicate at least the critical points of difference. Only so can a court on appeal ascertain whether the court below regarded its earlier judgment as lying outside the discretion proper to the judge of fact or whether both sums lay within it (see NJW 1989, 773 = VersR 1988, 943). Since such considerations are lacking in the judgment of the court below, it must therefore be vacated as inconsistent with § 287 Code of Civil Procedure, without prejudice to the power of the court on remand, if it gives sufficient reasons, again rejecting the claim for unliquidated damages for pain and suffering.

Notes to Case 58

1. This line of cases demonstrates a degree of judicial creativity which Common lawyers do not often ascribe to civilian judges. To understand the problem let us restate the basic stance of German tort law: negligently inflicted pure economic loss is not recovered under § 823 I BGB. Relational

economic loss of third parties, consequent upon injuries to one of the interests of another—the direct—victim are also not covered by § 823 I BGB. The BGH recently emphasised the importance of this general rule. (NJW 2001, 971.) The case concerned a claim for economic loss brought by the parents of a young man killed through the defendant's negligence. Because of his death, the farm run by the victim ceased to operate and this, in turn, caused pecuniary loss to the parents. Given there was no interference with the right of an "established and operating business" since the accident did not involve a direct interference (see ch. 2 A (e)(iii)), and since this was not the type of loss envisaged by §§ 843 ff. BGB, the suing parents were denied recovery. However, in some cases interfering with a person's physical integrity may cause economic loss to third parties and it would not be "fair, just and reasonable" to deny this person any recovery. This was recognised by the fathers of the BGB; and they introduced limited exceptions to the above-mentioned general rules found in §§ 843–846 BGB (wrongful death situations: see ch. 2 A 2.a.). The most important is that the tortfeasor is liable to those of the dependants of the deceased victim who were entitled to receive maintenance from him. A different and, in one sense, the reverse situation, is illustrated by case 51. The victim's injuries prompt close relatives to come to his aid in various ways such as visiting him in hospital, helping him cope with his disabilities and otherwise looking after him. As the present case demonstrates, if the recovery period of the victim is long, the relatives who provide this assistance may suffer considerable losses. However, the fathers of the BGB did not provide for this eventuality as they did for the cases envisaged by §§ 843–844 BGB (wrongful death). These exceptions, being by their very nature exceptions to a given rule, cannot be applied by analogy to a different situation. Nevertheless the BGH has got round this difficulty by pretending that the costs incurred by the relatives can be seen as being part and parcel of the injury to the victim himself.

2. English courts have experienced similar difficulties in establishing a duty of care in comparable cases. (See Markesinis and Deakin *Tort Law* (4th edn. 1999) pp. 754 ff.) They also analyse the problem as one of the extent of the duty of care owed to the "direct" victim. It should be noted that in England these cases are usually discussed in relation to the principle of *res inter alios acta*. (See *McGregor on Damages* (16th edn. 1997) para. 9–18; Lewis, *Deducting Benefits from Damages* (1999) para. 1.10.) The general rule appears to be that services provided by close family members (especially nursing care) do not diminish the loss of the direct victim (here the loss is analysed as that of the victim: see *Liffen* v. *Watson* [1940] 1 KB 556.) More recently, a source of difficulties has arisen in connection with the question whether there is an obligation to account to the third party. Such an obligation (which—not surprisingly—has been found to stem from a trust) proceeds on the footing of a more realistic view and accepts that the victim is in fact recovering damages in respect of a third party's (financial) loss. (See *Hunt* v. *Severs* [1994] 2 AC 350, which makes recovery dependant on such an obligation, and, earlier, Lord Denning's approach in *Cunningham* v. *Harrison and Others* [1973] QB 942.) This latter aspect does not appear to have surfaced in the German case law, presumably because recovery is limited to losses sustained by close relatives.

3. German courts have allowed recovery of travel expenses, cost of staying at a hotel (and the like) and lost earnings, caused by the visits to the hospital. Even the cost of a babysitter has been held to be recoverable (For references to the rich case law see, Emmerich *JuS* 1992, 75). The present—restrictive—decision, however, shows that the BGH feels uneasy with the current state of affairs, largely because of the doubtful theoretical basis of such claims. It is thus at pains to stress the exceptional nature of the recovery. Accordingly, this tends to be limited in the following way. First, costs incurred by close relatives by visiting the victim (travel, overnight accommodation, increased maintenance costs, loss of earnings) can be included as part of the cost of the *victim's* treatment and claimed under § 823 I BGB provided such visits are medically necessary and the expense unavoidable. The guiding (legal) principle is that of causation. Secondly, loss of earnings and housework done for the victim is compensatable only if the work could not be done before or after the visit. Finally, further economic losses are not compensatable. Whether these restrictions introduce greater consistency into the rich case law remains open to doubt. Thus, some

authors have criticised the decision for being overly restrictive and argued that we have not yet heard the last word on this matter. (See, for instance, Grunsky *JuS* 1991, 907).

Case 59

BUNDESGERICHTSHOF (SIXTH CIVIL SENATE) 13 FEBRUARY 1990
NJW-RR 1990, 726 = JZ 1990, 1087

Facts

The plaintiff is a firm trading under the name of Margot H, its owner. Mrs H and her husband were joint owners of a detached house which was built by the defendant in 1977/78. From 1980 onwards, the plaintiff firm was running a kitchen furniture studio from the basement rooms of the house which it rented from the owners. In the time that followed there were repeated leakages of water into these rooms. On 26 July 1982 water again leaked into the basement of the house and damaged the show furniture and associated display items. The plaintiff calculated the loss which it had incurred at DM 53,385. It claimed compensation from the defendants in this amount, arguing that the defendant had defectively constructed the basement floor and basement walls which had caused the leakages. Both the Landgericht and the Oberlandesgericht rejected the claim. The plaintiff appealed to the BGH which quashed the judgment of the Court of Appeal and referred the case back to the lower court.

For the following

Reasons

I. The OLG rejected both the contractual and the tortious claims brought by the plaintiff.

It held that the plaintiff was not a party to the oral building contract concluded with the husband alone. As a commercial tenant, she was also not covered by the protective scope of this contract; for the defendant could not have foreseen that the basement rooms of a detached house which were intended to be used for leisure purposes (e.g. fitness training, hobbies or parties) would be used for the display of furniture. The OLG argued that the plaintiff had no claim in tort because, after the earlier numerous leakages of water, she had acted at her own risk when she once again displayed furniture in the basement and should have foreseen further danger of water damage. Her careless conduct amounted to such a degree of contributory negligence that the defendant was wholly exonerated from responsibility.

II. The appeal decision cannot be upheld on all counts.
1. The OLG is correct to reject the contractual claims for damages brought by the plaintiff.

(*a*) It is not contested that when the husband concluded the building contract with the defendant, he did not say expressly that he was acting as the plaintiff's representative. As the OLG found, it could not be implied from the circumstances (§ 164 I 2 BGB) that the contract was also intended to be concluded in the name of the plaintiff. The plaintiff's appeal did not contest this evaluation of the facts as flawed in law; rather it sought merely to contrast its own evaluation which is basically irrelevant from the perspective

of this court's task as an appellate body. Contrary to the view put forward by the appellants, it was not sufficient for there to be a contract concluded in the name of the plaintiff that she was the joint owner of the land on which the house was built [references
omitted], especially since it is not contested that at the time of the conclusion of the building contract the defendant did not know this fact.

(b) There are, further, no grounds in law for challenging the view of the OLG that there
were no protective effects to be derived from the building contract (concluded between
the husband of the plaintiff and the defendant) in favour of the plaintiff, giving her
autonomous contractual claims against the defendant in respect of the damage caused to
the furniture and display items brought into the basement rooms.

(aa) It may be left open for the purposes of this decision whether in the case of
a building contract concluded in respect of the construction of a dwelling house, the
relatives of the [builder's] client as well as any joint owners of the land to be built
upon will always fall within the protective scope of the contract [references omitted].
For such protection can only be of significance in respect of the infliction of loss
which results from the fact that the persons in question come into contact with the
work of the building contractor precisely in their capacity as family members or joint
owners. This was not the case here. The plaintiff suffered the damage to the furniture
and display items in the basement for which she seeks compensation neither in her
capacity as a joint owner of the house, nor in her position as the wife of the client, but
as the commercial tenant of the basement.

(bb) In its judgment of 28 October 1986 (NJW 1987, 1013) [other references omitted]
this Division left open the question of whether the tenant is covered by the protective
scope of a contract concluded between the client and an architect for the construction
of a building [references omitted]. This question should be answered in the negative
in respect of a contract with a building contractor such as the one in question here.
First, there is no need for such a person to be covered, because in these circumstances
the tenant will normally enjoy sufficient protection through his contractual claims
against the landlord [references omitted]. Second, any other conclusion would mean
that the contractual obligations of the building contractor would be unreasonably
extended to cover risks which were not foreseeable for the contractor, without there
being the possibility of the obligations being subject to clear delimitation on the basis
of standards capable of being measured objectively [references omitted].

(cc) Since in the instant case the contractual claims would fail because there
was insufficient proximity between the legal interests of the plaintiff which were
impaired by the leakage of water and the contractual obligations of the defendant, it
is no longer decisive in this context for the court to determine whether a commercial
usage of the basement rooms by the plaintiff constituted a breach of the building
regulations.

2. The conclusion of the OLG that the plaintiff has no claim in tort does not withstand
legal scrutiny. The BGH must assume that the defendant was negligent in constructing
the basement floor and the basement walls defectively, since the OLG left this matter open,
and it must also assume that this breach of duty was the cause of the leakage of water on
26 July 1982 which resulted in a flood of water several centimetres deep in the basement.

(a) The OLG correctly assumes, on the basis of the judgment of this Chamber of
28 October 1986 (NJW 1987, 1013) [other references omitted], that the defendant is in

principle subject to a tortious duty of care in respect of the items of property brought into the basement by the plaintiff.

(*aa*) In that case this Chamber held that an architect of a house was in principle liable in tort to the tenant in circumstances where, as a result of the defective performance of his duties in respect of the house, he did not offer the type of protection which is to be expected against bad weather. As a result of damp caused by rain, damage was caused to the tenant's property. The position in law of the building contractor must be just the same. His duty of care is likewise not restricted to those risks arising directly from the house and endangering those who use the house and their property. For the building should, in normal circumstances at least, provide protection against threatening external dangers and the users of the house bring their property into the building precisely in reliance upon such protection. There may be an exception in cases of special circumstances involving, for example, the use of the cheapest method of construction (see the judgment of 28 October 1986). However, there were no factual circumstances in the present case requiring the application of this exception. On the contrary, in the application made by the plaintiff to this court, the building was described as "one of the most generously proportioned and most luxurious properties" in the area.

(*bb*) In these circumstances, in matters of liability one must basically apply the same principles related to the performance of the duties owed by both the architect and the building contractor under their respective contracts for work and services as those which apply to the manufacture and dissemination of products which are intended to eliminate certain dangers but which are unsuitable for this purpose [references omitted]. For just as in the case of such products, where the purchaser takes no other precautionary measures in respect of his interests in reliance upon the protective effects of the product he has bought, so the owner or tenant of a building will regard his property as adequately protected from the effects of bad weather if they have been brought indoors, and he would not think of taking additional measures. Of course, it is the case that it is only the law of contract which protects the interest of use or financial interest of the plaintiff ("*Nutzungs- oder Äquivalenzinteresse*"); a mere interference in *this* interest will not give rise to a claim in tort [references omitted]. If, however, the construction of a house is also intended to eliminate dangers threatening those interests of the plaintiff which are given absolute protection, then any impairment of these interests attributable to the defective performance of a duty will amount to an interference in the integrity of the plaintiff's property ("*restitutio in integrum*"), and will be actionable under § 823 I BGB.

(*cc*) There is no need in this case for a final decision to be made on whether the building contractor can only be exonerated from his liability in tort where he makes good the defects in the work by providing a performance which is intended to eliminate the danger in question, even where the client no longer has an effective contractual claim to the removal of the defect because the time limit for bringing such an action has expired, or whether the (additional) responsibility of the contractor also lapses where he has given unambiguous information to persons relying upon the security provided by the performance of his duties that the work in question would provide only inadequate protection [references omitted]. For it is not in dispute in this case that the defendant had not clearly informed either the plaintiff or her husband before the leakage of water on 26 July 1982 that the floor and walls were unsuitable for the purposes of eliminating the dangers resulting from water entry.

(*dd*) The existence of the defendant's duty of care in tort is likewise not undermined by his claim that the plaintiff had used the basement rooms for displays in contravention of the building regulations. This fact does not place the plaintiff, who was using the basement to the house on the basis of a valid tenancy agreement, outside the sphere of persons whom the defendant should have protected against water damage occurring in the vicinity of the basement by building in a workmanlike fashion [reference omitted].

(*b*) The plaintiff's application is right to question the view of the OLG that she had no claims for compensation in tort against the defendant because she had acted at her own risk by bringing kitchen furniture into the basement rooms and that notwithstanding the fault of the defendant, she was overwhelmingly contributorily negligent.

(*aa*) The fact that the OLG denied the plaintiff's claims for compensation stating that she had acted at her own risk and did not balance her fault against the (assumed) negligence of the defendant, indicates that the OLG has followed the later case law of the Reichsgericht [references omitted] which saw "acting at one's own risk" as a form of consent to the interference with the plaintiff's interests which acts as a justification. This interpretation has already been held by this Division in its judgment of 14 March 1961 (BGHZ 34, 355 at 360) [other references omitted] as appropriate for use only in exceptional cases such as dangerous sports, as a realistic and legally correct evaluation of conscious risk-taking. If there is no such exceptional situation, as in this case, then according to the established case law of the Chamber there is merely a question to be assessed under § 254 I BGB, as to what extent the victim through his conduct has contributed to the dangerous situation in which the defendant's own conduct led to the occurrence of damage [references omitted]. In contrast to the view put forward by the OLG, this makes it necessary for the court to weigh up against each other the causally relevant contributions made by each party in order to assess the degree to which the defendant is liable.

(*bb*) The arguments so far advanced here do not provide a justification, on the basis of the passing comments made by the OLG as regards the matter of the plaintiff's contributory negligence, for an evaluation of the respective contributions to conclude in a complete exoneration of the defendant from liability. Of course it is only the role of this court, when reviewing the decision of the judge of fact, merely to assess whether he has fully and correctly taken into account all relevant circumstances within the framework of § 254 I BGB, and has not breached any rules of logic or empirically derived principles [references omitted]. The OLG has not, however, remained within these limits as so defined.

3. (*a*) The OLG assumes that after the leakages of water on 18 May 1981, as well as on 7 and 10 August 1981, which preceded the occurrence of damage on 26 July 1982, in each case the defendant carried out repair work. However, even taking this as a starting point, there is insufficient basis for the conclusion that in July 1982 the plaintiff no longer relied upon the basement area being waterproofed. For the plaintiff, whom the OLG was prepared to acknowledge in its judgment of 22 July 1988 in the context of proceedings brought in respect of the water leakages of 7 and 10 August 1981 was still relying on the basement

being waterproof after the leakage of 18 May 1981, argued in this case that the defendant had stated that the cause of the water leakages in August 1981 was a wall duct for pipes which was not waterproof. Since the OLG both accepted that the fact that the wall being not waterproof was the cause of that loss and also assumed that the defendant had undertaken damp-proofing work on the wall duct in order to remove the defect, there exist no sufficient grounds in fact for the view that in July after the repair work the plaintiff should have expected the basement area no longer to be watertight. The OLG was wrong to state that this point could be derived from the fact that previous renovation works undertaken by the defendant had proved to be inadequate. In the first place the repair works, as the OLG itself accepted, were carried out on other weaknesses in the damp-proofing; second, even multiple unsuccessful attempts to carry out repairs by a contractor do not as such destroy the reliance of the client that the work previously undertaken to eliminate the defect will have finally succeeded.

(*b*) It was in truth appropriate for the plaintiff to rely as such upon the ultimate elimination of the danger from water, since the defendant, as the plaintiff stated in her claim and as she sought to prove in her application for a hearing of witnesses, "announced to the plaintiff that the waterproofing was complete" after finishing the improvement work following the water entry of August 1981, and "guaranteed to the plaintiff that the basement was now waterproof". It is a breach of the principle of good faith (§ 242 BGB) for the defendant to argue that the plaintiff could not rely upon such statements. The statements by the plaintiff were, despite the views of the OLG, sufficiently substantiated, all the more since it was principally the task of the defendant to demonstrate the circumstances in which the plaintiff could be said to be contributorily negligent. In any case, the OLG should not have reached the conclusion, as the plaintiff's appeal correctly asserts, that the plaintiff should have anticipated future dangers arising from water, before it had evaluated the witness testimony offered by the plaintiff.

Case 60

BUNDESGERICHTSHOF (SEVENTH CIVIL SENATE) 11 OCTOBER 1990
NJW 1991, 562 = WM 1991, 202

Facts

In 1979/80, the plaintiff and his wife had a new building built on a piece of land belonging to them. The first defendant was responsible for carrying out the structural work on the building. The supervision of the building work on site was entrusted to the second defendant, an architect. Since no proper damp insulation was fitted, the basement of the building became very damp. The plaintiff had rented this and other parts of the building to a company (F Ltd), which he ran. F Ltd had stored machines in the damp rooms, and these rusted as a result of the damp. The plaintiff claimed compensation from the defendant for the loss which he suffered as a result of the defective building work. He calculated his loss to be DM 139,697.84. In so far as the plaintiff sought to claim in respect of damage, which had accrued to F Ltd, his claim rested upon a deed of assignment dated January 18, 1982 the text of which covered only the claims against the first defendant.

The Landgericht held the defendants liable for the defects and held them to be jointly and severally liable in the amount of DM 19,298.93. The plaintiff appealed claiming a further DM 91,793.22 in damages. The Oberlandesgericht accepted the appeal in part, holding the defendants liable for a further DM 31,381.03. The second defendant appealed to the Bundesgerichtshof, and the appeal was accepted to the extent that he had been held liable for damages in the amount of DM 31,022.50 in respect of the damage to the machines. His appeal against the finding of liability failed.

Reasons

I. The OLG is of the view that the defendant is liable to the plaintiff, and that he must pay 50 per cent of the compensation in respect of the damage caused to the machines.

1. The external insulation of the walls of the basement in contact with the ground was said to be defective. As the architect responsible for on-site supervision of the work, the defendant breached his duty to supervise adequately the performance of the damp-proofing work which experience had taught was particularly delicate and significant in terms of the loss which would be caused by defective work. He was, therefore, jointly responsible for the defective damp-proofing. The defendant's appeal concedes this point.

2. The OLG further held on the basis of expert reports and witness statements that the defects in the damp-proofing, taken in conjunction with certain other defects, had caused the damp in the basement and that it was to this that the rust on the machines was attributable. [Procedural point omitted].

II. The OLG also stated that the plaintiff could claim compensation from the defendant in respect of the damage caused to his property, either through the principles of *Drittschadensliquidation*, or on the basis of the claims duly assigned to him by F Ltd on the basis of a contract with protective effects for third parties or on tortious grounds. The plaintiff has, it is said, become the owner of the claim against the defendant as a consequence of the assignment; this was the appropriate interpretation of the deed of assignment. The final point was that assignment did not contravene the prohibition on contracting with oneself.

1. The Court leaves open the question of whether the damage to the machines may be claimed from the defendant according to the principles of *Drittschadensliquidation*. It may also remain open whether F Ltd may derive claims as a third party on the basis of the protective effects of the construction contract concluded between the parties.

2. It is clear in any case that the plaintiff has a tortious claim. The defendant has breached the duty of care which he owed to F Ltd in that he did not ensure, when performing the role of supervising the building work which was entrusted to him, that the first defendant installed the damp insulation in the basement free from defects.

(*a*) According to the case law of the BGH, an architect may be liable in tort on the basis of a breach of his supervisory obligation for the loss thereby caused. Thus, for example, the architect responsible for the building work was held liable in tort for the loss caused by the collapse of a roof or ceiling [references omitted]; the same applies to the damage caused to a person using a staircase which proved to be unsafe [references omitted]. The tortious responsibility of the architect was also accepted for loss caused by damp to the property of third parties resulting from inadequate damp-proofing or a defective roof [references omitted]. This tortious responsibility of the architect is derived from the fact that during the construction process he not only owes duties on the basis of the contract with the builder, but he also owes duties of care in tort to third parties who are expected to come into contact with the building. For, in the normal course of events, such persons may rely on the architect carrying out in the proper way those tasks which will secure their protection against loss in the future [reference omitted]. That, also, applies to the tenant of a building. The fact that such a person may be, in certain circumstances, less worthy of protection than other third parties who only occasionally come into contact with the building, is no obstacle to a finding that the architect is liable. Of course, in normal circumstances the tenant will have a claim for compensation against the landlord where loss is inflicted by events such as those at issue. That factor makes no difference, however, to the architect's duty of care. Even for the builder himself, claims in tort are not in principle excluded by the fact that there are parallel claims in contract [references omitted]. Nor, however, is the tenant prevented from pursuing claims in tort against the architect, even though he may have a contractual claim against the land-lord. The contractual liability of the landlord is not intended to exclude tortious claims against other persons who inflict loss on the tenant.

The liability of the architect is not excluded by the fact that it is in the first instance the main building contractor who is responsible for the building works. The Division has rejected this argument also to the extent that the architect owes a duty of care to safe-guard the building site [references omitted]. Just as the architect may be responsible for the safety of the building site within the framework of the tasks which he has undertaken to perform, so the supervisory obligations which are intended to protect the residents of the building and their property may generate a duty of care.

This line of case law is likewise not challenged in the literature [references to literature omitted]. While it is possible to find in the literature signs of a move towards restricting the duty of care [references to literature omitted], there is no need in this case to take a definitive position on this matter. It may be doubtful in individual cases how far the duty of care of the architect extends. The Sixth Division has already referred to this point [reference omitted]. In any event, there is such a duty where the supervisory obligations in respect of the building work are specifically intended to avoid the occurrence of particularly dangerous types of errors on the part of the building contractor which are likely to arise.

(b) In this case the defendant was obliged, with respect to the protection of the tenant, to ensure that the damp-proofing was properly carried out. As a type of building work which is particularly risky, the architect was under a duty to take special care [references omitted]. The fact that the damp-proofing was not carried out properly was particularly likely to cause unexpected damage which could be significant to the property of those using the building.

(c) The liability of the architect is likewise not excluded by the fact that the defendant stated in his pleadings that the use of the storage rooms in question for commercial pur-poses was a breach of the planning regulations. It is not necessary to decide whether and in what conditions the protective scope of the defendant's duty of care is limited by the fact that the storage of the machines was prohibited under the planning regulations and was therefore unlawful. For in these circumstances there is no justification for a restric-tion upon the defendant's liability because the use of the rooms for storage was provided for under planning regulations and other local bye-laws. On the facts as given, it cannot make a difference whether the damage occurred to machines used for commercial pur-poses, the storage of which was not permitted, or to machines stored for other purposes, which were permitted. The decisive factor is rather that the rooms in question were not fit for the purpose which they were intended—as storage space.

(*d*) The liability is further not excluded because F Ltd may have occupied the rooms in question before they had been inspected in accordance with either the contract or the relevant building regulations. It is possible for liability based on the breach of a duty of care to be restricted where the activity in question has occurred without the knowledge or intention of the person subject to the duty. Such is not the case here. It is not alleged that the defendant was not in agreement with the occupation of the rooms or that he warned against it.

(*e*) The OLG was also right to hold that the plaintiff did not have to inform the defendant of the intention to store items intended for use in his business in the basement. The defendant must have anticipated the usage of the basement for these purposes.

3. The claim for compensation brought by F Ltd is restricted to the claim for so-called *restitutio in integrum* [references omitted]. The plaintiff claimed no more with his request for the recovery of the costs of repair and the costs of providing an expert report. The deliberations of the OLG concerning the contributory negligence of F Ltd contain no errors of law and there is no appeal against them.

15. PRODUCT LIABILITY

Case 61

BUNDESGERICHTSHOF (SIXTH CIVIL SENATE) 26 NOVEMBER 1968
BGHZ 51, 91 = NJW 1969, 269 (with approving notes by
Diederichsen = JZ 1969, 387 and E Deutsch = VERSR 1969, 155)

On 19 November 1963 the plaintiff, who ran a chicken-farm, had her chickens inoculated against fowl pest by the vet, Dr H. A few days later fowl pest broke out. More than 4,000 chickens died and over 100 had to be slaughtered.

The plaintiff claimed compensation for the damage from the defendants, vaccine manufacturers, whose vaccine XY had been used by the vet. This he (the vet) acquired from the defendants in 500 cm bottles at the beginning of November 1963. The bottles came from batch ALD 210, which the defendant company had had inspected on 18 October 1963 at the public Paul-Ehrlich Institute in Frankfurt-am-Main; and the batch had been released by them for public use. The defendant had subsequently and in the course of its business poured the contents into receptacles normally used in commerce. As regards receptacles with lower than 500 cm capacity that is done by airtight closure under negative pressure; larger bottles were filled by the defendants "openly" but in a closed room under ultraviolet radiation.

When a few days later, on 22 November 1963, Dr H inoculated the chickens at R's farm, fowl pest broke out there. At about this time fowl pest also broke out in three other poultry farms in Württemberg which had had their chickens inoculated with the defendant company's vaccine from batch ALD 210. When the Stuttgart Veterinary Inspection Officer had several bottles of that batch inspected by the Federal Research Institute for virus diseases in animals, there were found in some bottles bacterial impurities and still active

ND (Newcastle Disease) viruses, which had not been sufficiently immunised. Moreover, the Paul-Ehrlich Institute established that some of the bottles sent to it for inspection were not sterile and ND virus could be detected in them.

The defendant company disputed the claim that the outbreak of fowl pest was to be traced to the use of its vaccine; and in any case the defective sterility of the bottles was not the cause. For this it invoked the opinion supplied to it by Dr E of the Federal Research Institute for Virus Diseases. It put forward evidence exonerating it from liability for its workers in and the director of its virus section.

The Landgericht and the Oberlandesgericht declared the claim well founded. The defendant company's appeal was unsuccessful for the following

Reasons

The Court of Appeal started by finding that the vaccine supplied to Dr H was contaminated by bacteria, and that the outbreak of fowl pest was to be traced to it. Even the defendant company's expert, Professor Dr E, could not exclude the possibility that the contamination had arisen through carelessness on the part of persons employed by the defendant company in the bottling. For their fault the defendant company must be liable under § 278 BGB to the vet, the buyer of the vaccine. He, however, was entitled to be compensated for the damage done to the plaintiff. Since he had assigned his claim for compensation to the plaintiff, the action was well founded.

I. The principles governing the claims for damage suffered by a third person (*Drittschadensliquidation*) cannot be applied to the present case.

1. In principle, the only person who can claim compensation for damage under a contract is the one to whom the damage occurred in fact and who, in law, has to bear it. If the damage occurs to a third party, the doer of it is liable to him—apart from certain exceptions—only in delict. This distinction between the more favourable liability in contract and the more restricted liability for delict is imbedded in the existing system of liability law and is not a mere theoretical dogma. Only in special cases have the courts admitted exceptions, namely where special legal relations between the creditor under the contract and the beneficiary of the protected interest cause the interest to be "shifted" on to the third party, so that as a matter of law the damage is done to him, and not to the creditor. From it the doer can derive no benefit to the third party's detriment: he must make good to the creditor the damage to the third party. That applies—apart from the rare cases of responsibility for risks (BGHZ 40, 91, 100)—where the creditor has contracted for the third party's account (BGHZ 25, 250, 258), or where the thing that the debtor promised to take care of belonged not to the creditor but to the third party (BGHZ 15, 224).

(*a*) This is no such exceptional case. No "union of interests" between the vet (who made the contract) and the third party (i.e. the plaintiff) is created by indirect agency. Dr H had not bought the vaccine to the order or for the benefit of the plaintiff. When he ordered and obtained it from the defendant company he did not yet know for which farmer he would use it. A vet invariably buys his medicines for himself like a contractor in respect of his materials and not for his patients or employers, even if he requires them to perform an order already given to him.

Moreover, this is not one of the cases where the thing placed in the debtor's care belonged not to the creditor but to a third party. Of course Dr H may have had imposed on him a "duty of care" (*Obhutspflicht*) concerning the plaintiff's chickens. But it is a condition for claiming for damage suffered by a third party (*Drittschadensliquidation*) that the duty of care exists between creditor and debtor (BGHZ 40, 101). That was not the case here.

(*b*) The Court of Appeal also acts on these principles. It is also aware that in principle the manufacturer and supplier of a thing which has been sold again to a third party does not need, merely on the basis of the contract of sale, to make good damage occurring to a third party (BGHZ 40, 104, 105). All the same it believed that in the present case it could permit the claim in respect of the damage suffered by the third party. Here the faultless condition of the vaccine was of special interest to the plaintiff, on whose chickens it was to be used. The vet could not check the condition of the vaccine, but had to rely on careful manufacture by the defendant company. The latter must therefore have proceeded on the assumption that a duty of faultless delivery rested on it in favour not merely of the vet but also of whomever happened to keep chickens.

(*c*) These considerations do not justify treating this as a case for claiming damage as suffered by a third party (*Drittschadensliquidation*). Already in its judgment (BGHZ 40, 90) the Bundesgerichtshof has emphasised that a contract of sale cannot be interpreted in accordance with the requirement of good faith so as to afford a basis for compensation to a third party injured through defects in the thing bought. In that decision it departed from the judgment of the Reichsgericht in RGZ 170, 246. The Court of Appeal has also established no concrete basis for holding that the defendant company had been ready and willing to afford to the other party to the contract (namely the vet) claims to compensation more extensive than under the statutory law of sale. Moreover, it is a condition of claiming for damage suffered by a third party that only *one* damage shall have taken place, which would have been suffered by the creditor unless the protected legal interest was that of a third party. There can be no question here of "shifting" the damage. It occurred here to the plaintiff in fact as well as in law, whereas in a genuine "shifting" of damage it occurs to the creditor in fact, though not in law. It could not occur either to the vet or to the chicken-farmer, but only the latter, and not—which is the decisive point—to him instead of the vet.

The cases of claims for damage suffered by a third party (*Drittschadensliquidation*), so far admitted by the courts, cannot be extended to cover a case like the present. Otherwise the manufacturer and supplier of necessaries and luxuries, of toiletries and medicines, etc. would have to make good damage to the ultimate user not only in delict but also on the contract of sale. For he also knows, like this buyer, the wholesaler, intermediate, and retail dealers, that any damage would show itself in the hands not of the dealer, but of the ultimate recipient. This does not lead to the conclusion, however, that the producer is liable in contract to the ultimate recipient. The question how these interests are to be protected cannot, therefore, be solved by allowing a claim for damage suffered by a third party (*Drittschadensliquidation*).

2. The Court of Appeal also based its opinion on the principle that a duty of care on the part of the manufacturer towards the third party arises from the meaning and purpose of the contract. This might be interpreted in the sense that the Court of Appeal is willing to allow the plaintiff a claim to compensation on a *contract with protective effects for third parties*. That consequence also cannot be approved.

(*a*) The Bundesgerichtshof has, indeed, allowed claims to compensation on this legal theory and under specified circumstances to a third person not a party to a contract (BGHZ 33, 247, 249 and 49, 350, 351 with references). Those principles, however, cannot be called in aid here.

In no way can everyone who has suffered damage through a failure of care on the part of a debtor derive his own claim to compensation from the contract between creditor and debtor (Senate judgment of 30 April 1968—VI ZR 29/67 NJW 1968, 1323). The Senate in its judgment of 18 June 1968 (VI ZR 120/67 NJW 1968, 1929) indicated afresh that the law distinguishes between persons suffering direct and indirect damage and that liability under a contract is, on principle, bound up with the bond that binds debtor to creditor (*cf.* also BGH judgment of 9 October 1968—VIII ZR 173/66). Otherwise there is a danger that the debtor can no longer calculate the risk that he undertakes in making a contract. Hence it would no longer accord with the principle of good faith, out of which the contract with protective effect for third parties has been developed, for the debtor to be liable for such extensive consequences of his breach of contract. That can be admitted only if the creditor shares, so to say, in the responsibility for the welfare of the third party, because damage to the latter affects him also, since he is under a duty to afford him care and protection. It is this internal relation between creditor and the third party, ordinarily marked by legal relations of a personal character, and not the relation between the parties to the contract, that is the reason for the protection of the third party. Such a relation does not, as a rule, exist in a contract of sale or a contract for doing a job.

(*b*) Moreover, in the present case there are no such close relations between the creditor (the vet) and his clients.

II. If therefore the judgment under attack cannot be supported by the foregoing reasoning, we must enquire whether it can be upheld on other grounds. The plaintiff not only based her action on claims derived from the contract made by Dr H with the defendant company, but also invoked §§ 823 ff. BGB. In addition, she prayed in aid the question exhaustively argued in recent times, above all at the *Deutscher Juristentag* of 1968, concerning the direct liability of the manufacturer of goods to the ultimate user ("product liability").

1. Even the advocates of an extensive liability of the producer start as a rule from the proposition that it can be based neither on a claim for damage suffered by a third party (*Drittschadensliquidation*) nor on a contract with protective effects for third parties. They prefer to provide the user with his own claim for damages, not one dependent on the contract between the manufacturer and buyer, and not brought against the manufacturer as an "*action directe*"—like the claim for damages based on §§ 823 ff. BGB. But they consider this claim in delict no longer satisfactory or appropriate, because it does not, as a rule, cover purely economic damage and, above all, because it leaves open to the producer the possibility of exonerating himself, especially where there is a mere slip in the productive process.

The case to be considered here affords no occasion for examining the question whether we should adhere to the rule developed by the courts that the producer can invoke § 831 BGB when there are defects in the actual production . . . and that such defects raise no presumption of fault against the manufacturer (Senate judgment of 21 April 1956—VI ZR 36/55). For it is not established here that it was because the defendant company's staff had made a mistake that the vaccine contained reactivated viruses. That may also be due to causes that are inherent in the company's methods of production, and in particular in the method of bottling. In the present case there is no need to adopt a comprehensive attitude to the problems of products liability. Here, only the following considerations apply.

(*a*) The claim in the action could be granted without further discussion if the view of Diederichsen in his *Die Haftung des Warenherstellers* (1967) could be followed, that the manufacturer must be liable for every kind of defects in the product without reference to fault, as in the liability for risks or results ("strict liability"). He believes that this can be derived from the existing law by "considerations of legal sociology or legal theory". It is however doubtful whether his standpoint can be supported on grounds of legal policy and, at any rate, liability without fault is incompatible with the present law of (civil) liability. To extend the liability for risks regulated in particular enactments—mostly subject to different ceilings—to products liability is forbidden to judges. It is rather for the legislator to decide whether or how far a stronger objective liability should be imposed on the manufacturer.

(*b*) Nor is it legally possible—apart from special cases—to afford to the ultimate recipient a direct claim for damages on the assumption that contract of warranty was concluded directly, albeit tacitly, between him and the producer. The fact that the producer allows his goods to be distributed as his invention, that is to say with his label, in original packaging, with his trade name or trademark, and so on, cannot, *as a rule*, be considered as a declaration that he intends to make himself responsible to users for careful manufacture (*cf.* RGZ 81, 1). Normally, even the advertisement of branded goods which are advertised with particular emphasis on the ultimate user, contains no indication of any willingness to be liable for any defects in the goods (BGHZ 48, 118, 122–3). Moreover, that cannot be assumed even when the appreciably wider question is asked whether the manufacturer is willing to be directly liable to the ultimate user of his product.

(*c*) There is also no question of a claim for damages being accorded for a breach of alleged duties of protection consequent on a "social contract". No business relations exist between manufacturer and recipient nor are they intended to be started and, eventually, to be concluded. The relations which certainly exist on the sociological plane have not enough legal weight for claims for liability to be made from a special legal relation. That applies also to Weimer's attempt to derive a producer's liability from the general rule in § 242 BGB.

2. Special consideration is merited by the idea that recognition should be given to a special quasi-contractual relation between manufacturer and user, resting on statute and developed from the notion of confidence. In fact the relations that have come into existence between the buyer of a dangerous product and its manufacturer, before the occurrence of the damage, would seem to be closer than those that bring the latter into relations with "everyman" when—and not before—he is actually injured. As regards the claims for compensation of a buyer, on the other hand, it should be considered whether they also arise from contract law if he bought the goods not directly from the manufacturer but through a dealer.

(*a*) Starting from the special legal relationship between manufacturer and acquirer of goods, Lorenz at the *Karlsruher Forum* 1963 was the first to state the opinion that the manufacturer must be liable under § 122 BGB to answer for the confidence in his product, strengthened by advertising, that he has awakened in its users. Those ideas were mentioned by the Eighth Civil Senate of the Bundesgerichtshof at the close of its judgment of 13 July 1963 (BGHZ 40, 91, 108), but without committing itself to any position. In its judgment BGHZ 48, 118, it declined to accept advertisement as a possible source of liability. In the struggles for the all-important customer (*König Kunde*), advertisements have become more and more extensive and more and more significant from a business point of view. This, however, does not yet mean that they have acquired the meaning of a promise of legal liability. Moreover, no reasonable user understands it to be so: and Lorenz has not followed up his idea.

(*b*) Lorenz's basic idea provided the foundation for the attempts to derive the manufacturer's liability from a duty to satisfy the confidence placed by the user and made the basis for a claim corresponding to the legal principles developed for *culpa in contrahendo*.

It is however doubtful whether these considerations can hold water, so as to afford the user a claim for damages which, like the claim in delict, cannot be excluded automatically, but on the other hand would not be threatened by exoneration under § 831 BGB. The Senate has already, in its judgment of 21 March 1967 (VI ZR 164/65) reacted against the attempts to base the liability of a third person, not a party to a supposed contract, on the fact that his confidence was sought; and it emphasized that they would break, with dire consequences, through the boundary drawn between liability based on a contractual obligation and that arising from delict. Whether the doubt there expressed against an extension of liability for "positive breach of contract" ("*positive Vertragsverletzung*") tells also against a subjection of the producer to a liability on the analogy of contractual liability need not be finally decided in this case. Nor need the question be gone into of how such a quasi-contractual claim should be afforded to a person injured by the product if he did not buy it but damage occurred through its use by himself or another person. In the case now to be decided there is no question of a number of legally successive sale contracts in which the seller, in fact, is often the mere "distributor" of the manufacturer in which case a breaking of the veil suggests itself. Here between the plaintiff and the defendant company stood a vet, who had alone to decide which vaccine to use. The plaintiff had placed confidence in him and not in any advertisement. She was not, herself, in a position to buy the vaccine directly or in the market: the defendant company could deliver it only to the vet and only he might use it . . . That, of itself, excludes the idea that a quasi-contractual relation existed between the parties. The plaintiff was not a "consumer" of the vaccine, nor even a "user" of it, but, from a legal point of view, "only" a sufferer of damage. As such she is limited to her claim in delict.

III. According to the Court of Appeal's finding of fact the conditions of liability under § 823 BGB are fulfilled. The vaccine supplied by the defendant company was defective and the cause of the disease to the chickens. Even if, as explained above, the rules of contract law are not applicable, nevertheless the starting-point must be that the defendant company has committed a fault. If anyone when using an industrial product for its declared purpose suffers injury in one of the legal interests protected by § 823 I BGB, through the defective manufacture of the product, it is for the manufacturer to explain the antecedents that caused the defect and thereby to show that he was not to blame for it.

1. It is not in question that even in "product liability" the injured party must prove that the damage was caused by a defect in the product. The plaintiff had therefore to show

that the fowl pest broke out among her chickens because the vaccine originated with the defendant company and contained active viruses when delivered.

That proof was considered by the Court of Appeal to have been furnished. [An explanation followed.]

2. The Court of Appeal, having to ascertain why the vaccine contained live viruses, started from the fact that both the Paul-Ehrlich Institute and the Federal Research Institute found bacteria in the bottles examined by them. It based its conclusions in essence on Professor Dr E's opinion. He declared it highly probable that the bacteria had found their way into the bottles at the manual pouring of the vaccine from the large containers into the bottles. It has been observed on various occasions that viruses which—as here—have been killed by the addition of formaldehyde can, under certain conditions, become reactivated. It was therefore possible that the bacteria here had reactivated the virus. On the basis of these explanations of the expert, the Court of Appeal believed it could find that the contamination of the bottles by bacteria was the cause of reactivation. It pointed out also that no damage arose from the part of the batch that was not contaminated by bacteria, whereas that was the case with the bottles used by Dr H and in the district of Heilbronn, and in which the bacteria were found. Even Dr E held it possible that the contamination of the vaccine was caused by "human error" on the part of one of the persons employed by the defendant company in bottling the vaccine.

3. The appellant attacked this conclusion of the Court of Appeal, but without success.

It is indeed correct that the Court of Appeal considered no fault of the defendant company itself as proved. It accepted that it was probably only an employee that was to blame for the damage. A liability of the defendant company, cannot, as we have seen, be established by applying the law of contract, as set out in § 278 BGB. That does not, however, necessitate sending the dispute back to the judge of fact. For it would still be for the defendant company to exonerate itself even if the plaintiff can rely on § 823 BGB.

> (aa) This results from the fact that the plaintiff's claim for compensation is also based on § 823 II BGB. For the defendant company, by delivering the dangerous bottles of vaccine infringed a protective enactment. This vaccine, a medicine in the sense of the Medicines Act of 16 May 1961 (§ 3 III AMG), was capable of producing in the chickens injurious, even fatal, effects. § 6 AMG prohibits the putting of such vaccines into circulation. That provision—like § 3 LebMG (cf. RGZ 170, 155, 156 on § 4 LebMG) which applies to foods dangerous to health—constitutes an enactment for the protection of endangered human beings or animals. If, however, an infringement of a protective enactment is proved, it is presumed to be the result of fault. The infringer therefore must produce facts sufficient to disprove his fault (Senate judgment of 12 March 1968— VI ZR 178/66). The owner of the business did not produce that proof so long as a possible cause, falling within the scope of his responsibility and which might point to fault remained unelucidated (Senate judgments of 3 January 1961—VI ZR 67/60 and 4 April 1967—VI ZR 98/65).

> (bb) This rule governing the burden of proof would, however, also apply if the plaintiff could here base a claim for damages only on § 823 I BGB. In that case also it would be for the defendant to exonerate itself. It is true that the injured party who relies on § 823 I BGB will have to allege and if necessary prove not only the causal connection between his damage and the conduct of the doer, but also his fault (BGHZ 24, 21, 29). However, the possibility of proving the subjective conditions depends appreciably on

how far the injured party can elucidate the detailed course of events. That is however especially difficult when it relates to antecedents which played a part in the business of manufacturing the products. The courts for a long time came to the help of the injured party by contenting themselves with proof of a chain of causation, which, according to human experience, indicates an organisational fault in the manufacturer. All the same, one cannot stop at this point in considering claims for damages for "product liability". All too often the owner of a business can show that the defect in the product might have been caused in a way that does not point to his fault—evidence which generally relies on activities in his business and which is difficult for the injured party to disprove. In consequence, when damage has arisen within the range of the manufacturer's business risks, he cannot be regarded as exonerated merely because he points out that the defect in the product might have arisen without any organizational fault of his. This is required in the area of "product liability" in order to protect the interests of the injured party—whether ultimate acquirer, user, or third party; on the other hand, the interests of the producer allow him to demand that he may prove his lack of fault.

This rule of evidence indeed only operates as soon as the injured party has proved that his damage falls within the scope of the manufacturer's organisation and risks, and indeed is satisfied by the existence of an objective defect or of unbusiness-like conduct. This proof is required of the injured party even when he sues the doer of damage for breach of protective and subsidiary duties arising from a contract or the negotiations for one (Senate judgments of 16 September 1961—VI ZR 92/61 and 18 January 1966—VI ZR 184/64). It is the same if he claims against the producer for breach of his duty of care. However, once he has provided this evidence, the producer is better able to explain the facts or to bear the consequences of being unable to offer an explanation. He surveys the field of production, determines and organises the manufacturing process and the control of delivering the finished products. The size of the business, it's complicated, departmentalised organisation, its involved technical, chemical, or biological processes and the like make it practically impossible for the injured party to ascertain the cause of the defect. He is therefore unable to lay the facts before the judge in such a way that he can decide with certainty whether the management is to be blamed for neglect or whether it is a case of a mistake in manufacture for which a workman is at fault, or a single breakdown that may happen at any time, or defect in development that was unforeseeable in the existing state of technology or science. But if the unknown cause lies within the scope of the producer, it is also within the scope of his risks. In that case it is appropriate and expected of him that the risk of not being able to prove his innocence should lie with him.

Such rules of evidence have always been applied to contractual or quasi-contractual relations of a special legal character between injured party (creditor) and doer of damage (debtor) (BGHZ 48, 310, 313). No obvious reason can be given why they should not also apply to delict, if the reasons for them apply. In certain connections § 831 BGB already imposes on the employer the proof of exoneration—the same applies to liability cases under §§ 832, 833, 834 BGB, and above all to §§ 836 ff. Here, indeed, the law requires a person damaged through the collapse of a building to prove that the damage was "the consequence of defective erection or defective maintenance", but lays on the possessor etc. the burden of proving that he had done everything to avoid the dangers that could attach to his building. The reversal of the burden of allegation and proof ordered in these provisions does not always proceed from a presumption of fault in the doer of damage. It rests in the main on the thought that the doer is in a better position than the injured party to throw light on the events relevant to the charge of negligence, so that it is just to impose on him the risk of being unable to do so. The Senate has already in its judgment of 1 April 1953 (VI ZR 77/52) indicated that the plaintiff cannot be required to prove—as a rule an almost impossible task—that the thing that caused the damage came into circulation through the fault of the owner of the business or his agents. Above all, the Senate has already in its judgment of 17 October 1967 (VI ZR 70/66) declared that it is for the producer to exonerate himself, if the injured party can give no detailed information about the management's blameable breaches of duty. The modern development of production, which is distributed among persons or machines that are hard to identify at a subsequent stage and rests on finishing processes capable of being inspected and controlled only by specialists, demands a development of the law of evidence in the direction already indicated in § 836 BGB . . .

In any case—as with the recognised shifting of the burden of proof for "positive breach of contract"—it always depends on the interests at stake in the groups of cases from time to time under consideration. The question whether the assumption of the risk of proof can be imputed in the case of the owner of a small business, where the manufacturing processes can be easily surveyed and examined (family and one-man businesses, agricultural producers, and the like), need not be considered here. In cases of the present kind it is in any case for the manufacturer to exonerate himself.

4. The defendant company has not furnished that proof of exoneration.

(a) According to Professor Dr E's opinion submitted by the defendant company, it is possible that carelessness on the part of someone concerned with the bottling led to the contamination of the bottles. He considered the process of filling containers over 500 ccm by manual pouring and not, as happens with the smaller containers, by means of an apparatus as an "older method" which was indeed "tolerable", but needing improvement. For this manual pouring there must at least be constructed a correspondingly superior "clean work bench" with UV radiation. In addition the "modest apparatus outfit" of the business must be increased by installing dry sterilizers, so that the larger containers could be better sterilised, above all without long interruption. He also pointed out that in the process of autoclave without a temperature and pressure gauge no control could be exercised over whether the high temperature needed for the sterilisation under pressure was really attained. Moreover, he recommended the use of tubes showing changes of colour. He also advised that the filling-room be examined for its germ content from time to time by exposing dishes of agar or blood.

The expert then was of opinion that in spite of these suggestions for improvement, the manufacturing methods of the defendant company were "not unsatisfactory" and fulfilled the "normal requirements". Moreover, the method of bottling guaranteed a sufficient degree of security, even though it needed to be improved. Finally, he was of opinion that the defendant company had not carelessly neglected any of the necessary precautions. The bacterial contamination could indeed have been caused by defective observance of the required precautions, but could have occurred even if they had been observed.

(b) The expert's view of the required degree of care cannot be approved. Even he starts by saying that in the manufacture of vaccines in which the effect of living viruses must be immunised "the highest possible security" must be required. For that very reason vaccine works are subjected to strict public supervision (§ 10 AMG together with the provisions of Land law still operative under § 5). The defects mentioned by him in the equipment of the defendant company's business, above all as regards manual bottling, are in conflict with a finding that the management were not guilty of careless conduct. The improvements recommended by him were not at all far-fetched and imposed on the company requirements that were neither technically nor financially excessive. The possibility cannot be excluded that those additional precautions would have averted the bottling of dangerous vaccine.

Case 62

BUNDESGERICHTSHOF (SIXTH CIVIL SENATE) 11 JULY 1972
BGHZ 59, 172 = NJW 1972, 2217 = VersR 1972, 1075

On 12 October 1961 the plaintiff, a farmer's wife born in 1920, went to a hospital for a minor gynaecological operation to be carried out by its director. Dr M, his assistant, injected the plaintiff with an anaesthetic called Estil to be employed for a short narcosis, which was produced by the defendant. Dr M injected it in the bend of the plaintiff's left arm. By accident, the anaesthetic, which was to be administered intravenously only, was injected into an artery. This led to a serious disturbance of the plaintiff's circulation and necessitated, finally, the amputation of her upper arm.

Beginning in August 1960 Estil had been subject to clinical tests, first in one and then in several hospitals. As early as 8 December 1960 an accidental injection into a patient's artery had resulted in the amputation of an arm. Estil was registered with the Senator for Health in Berlin on 23 January 1961 and was put on sale on 1 April 1961. Instructions attached to each package contained the sentence in bold type: "Intra-arterial injection must be avoided with certainty". After the accident involving the plaintiff, the warning attached to the package was increased twice. On 9 February 1962 the defendant withdrew Estil from sale.

Meanwhile a number of such accidents had occurred, most of them involving the loss of an arm, but also some affecting the kidneys, in one case with lethal effect. The plaintiff claimed damages from the defendant. The Court of First Instance rejected the claim, but the Court of Appeal of Stuttgart allowed it. A second appeal by the defendant was unsuccessful for the following.

Reasons

I. The Court of Appeal holds the defendant to be liable in tort (§ 823 I BGB) because he has caused the loss of the plaintiff's arm by having culpably violated in his capacity of producer of medicines his public duty of care. The appeal against this decision fails in the result.

1. (*a*) The Court of Appeal reaches this view primarily because it holds that thorough clinical tests had not been carried out before Estil was put on the market. Such tests were required in order fully to recognize the dangerous nature of Estil, i.e. its arterial intolerance and the fact that an intra-arterial injection could not be avoided with certainty. If these tests had been carried out, so the Court of Appeal believes, the incident suffered by the plaintiff would not have happened.

(b) This Division agrees with the appellant that the arguments of the Court of Appeal cannot be accepted in their entirety. It may be true that further clinical tests were indicated. It is also clear that if the tests had not yet come to an end, the medicament would not yet have been in free circulation and would not have been administered to the plaintiff. Nevertheless, it seems doubtful whether, regarded from this point of view, the incident which affected the plaintiff can be attributed in law to the defendant as a breach of duty. The incident suffered by the plaintiff was caused exclusively by the arterial intolerance of the medicament, as the Court of Appeal found without committing a mistake of law. In order to obtain further certainty further clinical tests with human beings would hardly have been the most suitable means, especially since incorrect injections are less likely to occur among medical specialists and since greater care is applied in an experimental situation than in general practice, for which the medicament was meant at least as much. However, at the time when it was put on the market, the defendant was not at all in doubt, as the Court of Appeal itself stated in another connection and, as he states, he decided for this reason to include a warning in the notice attached to the package, an unusual measure from his point of view. The general danger of intra-arterial injections by accident, especially in the arterial area, was not to form the object of experiments with human beings, least of all by a medicament which would cause necessarily most severe damage in such circumstances. Moreover, applying that degree of care which must be expected absolutely of a manufacturer of such a medicament, this danger could be gleaned already at that time from the medical literature, as the expert opinions show upon which the Court of Appeal relied in another connection.

2. It is unnecessary to enlarge on this point, since the decision of the Court of Appeal is well founded in law on the ground of insufficient information concerning the dangerous nature of the medicament.

(a) The Court of Appeal holds it against the defendant, above all, that he was content to include a general warning in a notice included in the package and in the prospectus sent to medical men without having indicated in any way the serious, possibly irreparable, consequences of a misdirection of the injection into the artery, although he was well aware of them.

In the opinion of the Court of Appeal, there was all the more reason to do so since according to the unanimous opinion expressed in specialist medical circles an accidental intra-arterial injection could not be avoided with certainty, especially if administered in the bend of the arm; the danger inherent in particular in the bend of the arm in this respect could not have escaped the attention of the research department, directed by a medically qualified person, of the defendant's enterprise. Instead the defendant had recommended for the first time only in the notices dispatched after 16 October 1961—i.e. after the incident involving the plaintiff—to make injections in the lower arm for preference and, moreover, at first only 0.5 ccm as an experimental dose; even then he had not mentioned the nature of the possible danger. He had done so only in the third version of the notice—when called upon by the authorities—from January 1962 onwards, i.e. shortly before the product was withdrawn.

The Court of Appeal found further: If the defendant had, as was his duty, drawn the attention of every medical person to the existing risk in such a forcible manner from the beginning or at least after the Congress of Anaesthetists held on 8 October 1961 (where the Estil incidents were discussed) Dr M would have avoided the bend of the arm, and if he had approached the artery nevertheless, he would have noticed it at any rate while making an experimental preliminary injection. Thus the incident would have been avoided.

(*b*) These arguments cannot be invalidated by the appellant. The opinion of the Court of Appeal cannot be faulted in law that the defendant had violated his public duty of care (duty to inform) as a manufacturer of medicaments [references] inasmuch as he failed to indicate openly in the notice included in the package and in the medical prospectus the absolute arterial intolerance of Estil known to him.

It has been recognised for a long time by the practice of the courts that it is the duty of a manufacturer, the violation of which may render him liable to third parties for any ensuing damages, to give an effective warning of specific dangers emanating from a product brought on the market [references].

The requirements are especially strict for providing information about possible danger connected with medicaments. The Court of Appeal is correct in holding that in the face of this principle any consideration of the interest of the manufacturer to promote sales is excluded. The Court of Appeal was therefore right in requiring as information sufficient for the practising medical profession that the consequences of intra-arterial injections (almost certain total loss of the extremity) should be set out clearly together with the advice that the well-known practice of injecting Estil in the bend of the arm must be abandoned, because in the opinion of all the expert advice at the disposal of the Court of Appeal the danger of a misdirected injection is much increased, given the special nature of the anatomical situation. The Court of Appeal, in so holding, agrees in the essential point with numerous decisions which in deciding claims for damages against medical practitioners have found as a fact that an injection of Estil in the bend of the arm is altogether inappropriate. Several of these decisions have been upheld on appeal to this Division [references].

According to the findings of the Court of Appeal, especially in so far as they are based on expert testimony called for by the court and on its foundations, the arterial intolerance to Estil—which could have been proved easily by experiments carried out on the ear of a rabbit—exceeded by far the dangers which accompany generally an accidental intra-arterial injection with other medicaments. The fact that the same may have been true for a few other medicaments which had to be injected intravenously, such as Presuren, which was no longer advertised for sale later on, makes no difference; in the present case a special source of danger existed which the doctor using the medicament did not expect unless his attention was specifically drawn to it. This is all the more valid since according to its purpose as indicated by the advertisements of the manufacturer (the defendant), the medicament was to be used above all in general practice, i.e. by doctors without special qualifications in anaesthetics. This danger was further increased because Estil, intended for brief narcosis, is subject to a quick breakdown in the body and must be injected quickly in one move by a wide-bore needle and under heavy pressure.

No legal objections can be raised if the Court of Appeal holds in the light of these considerations that medical practitioners ought to have been informed of the full extent of the risk in selecting this medicament because only thus would they have been warned particularly to use the utmost care and not to use it at all in case of doubt.

(*aa*) The appellant fails inasmuch as he wishes to show with reference to the statistical material, previously presented to the judge, but not so found in detail by the latter that on the average other anaesthetic methods disclose for other reasons an even higher quota of incidents. The old medical maxim above all not to create more harm (*primum nil nocere*) militates against the acceptance a priori of a certain quota of incidents. Instead every recognisable source of danger—especially, however, one which is already well known—must be eliminated in dealings with patients, be they diagnostic, anaesthetic, or therapeutic, if and in so far as it can be reasonably avoided; this applies even if actual danger is only to be expected to materialise in relatively few instances. The duty to avoid danger is primarily incumbent upon the doctor, for subject to agreement with the patient, he determines the treatment. However, to impose this duty upon him *alone* would not correspond to the peculiarities of modern pharmaceutical specialisation. Here the responsibility, and with it the duty of care, of the manufacturer increases to the extent in which the production of the medicament is based on development which cannot be repeated easily by the medical practitioner or even understood; also the manufacturer himself, through intensive advertising among the medical profession, seeks and achieves to influence a choice in favour of his medicament and no other.

This Division need not decide whether—as the Court of Appeal finds in the alternative—already at the time of the incident involving the plaintiff it was improper to put Estil on the market because it was known that the danger connected therewith was disproportionately high (see now § 6 I of the Medicaments Act which in this respect merely gives statutory authority to a previously recognised duty of care towards the public). The decision under appeal is already supported by the conclusion that the defendant has not complied sufficiently with his clear duty of care towards the public to inform freely medical practitioners who wish to use the medicament of the specific danger and to warn them against it. Especially if it were conceded in favour of the defendant that the continuing marketing of Estil could still be justified having regard to its special narcotic advantages, it was necessary to acquaint the medical profession clearly and explicitly. Only thus could a medical practitioner balance correctly the risk which is connected to a greater or lesser degree with the use of every medicament against the benefit for the patient hoped for in the individual case, and could, if necessary, give proper advice to the patient in making up his mind. The conditions required for such weighing to take place were not provided by the defendant when he drew attention in bold type for the need to avoid intra-arterial injections with certainty. This is particularly valid because, as the defendant has stressed constantly, this requirement is a matter of course where narcotic medicaments are being used. This notice did not bring home that a special danger was to be avoided or had to be accepted for special reasons.

(*b*) Contrary to the view of the appellant, the Court of Appeal is also not wrong in not conceding to the appellant that he could rely on the publications in medical journals to provide the medical profession with information about Estil. Leaving aside the Court of Appeal's apposite consideration that those general medical practitioners who are mainly concerned with using the medicament do not all read specialised publications regularly, the court could deduce from the files to which it referred that those publications did not justify the defendant to treat them as being of unlimited objectivity, for in accordance with an alleged custom he had inspired these reports himself and had paid for them . . .

(*c*) As regards the question whether the insufficient information was the cause of the damage, the Court of Appeal concluded that a warning of the kind which it regarded as indicated would have prevented the incident involving the plaintiff.

(*aa*) This, too, cannot be faulted in law as far as the result is concerned. It could be expected that, as a typical and intended consequence of an adequate notice, no conscientious doctor would have made an injection in the bend of the elbow, but would on finding another suitable vein, have applied the highest possible attention commensurate with the highly dangerous nature of the remedy and would, in appropriate cases have abandoned the use of the medicament altogether. The latter was particularly appropriate in the present case as the appellant emphasises since . . . the chief medical officer had expected in any case that the well-tried anaesthetic Evipan would be applied.

If this had happened, the typical increase in danger resulting from the failure to give a warning would have been excluded. It was for the defendant to prove that exceptionally, despite the application of extreme care, a misdirected injection would have taken place which according to prevailing medical opinion could never be avoided with *absolute* certainty . . .

(*cc*) Finally the appellant argues, though unsuccessfully, that a manufacturer of medicaments can only be held liable for the application of his product in accordance with its prescribed use; to inject a medicament intended for intravenous application in an artery was to apply it contrary to its prescribed use, the consequences of which could not be attributed to the manufacturer.

This is only correct in so far as an intentional misapplication (e.g. oral, instead of external as prescribed) is in issue. In such circumstances the occurrence of unforeseen acts may break the chain of causation. However, even to that extent the manufacturer is not exempt from giving appropriate warning, as the case may be, against likely wrong use, e.g. by a clear notice "for external use" (see now § 10 VI 3 of the Medicaments Act). Such a duty to give notice is precisely in issue here. It is all the more important where it is necessary to prevent not an intentional but a negligent misapplication ("missing it") if, as found in the present case, this possibility is not totally remote and must have surprisingly severe consequences. The question as to whether the medical practitioner also acted negligently remains irrelevant as long as the manufacturer is to be blamed specifically for not having forestalled such mistakes of the medical attendant which are not beyond all expectation. According to general opinion, which is also supported by the provision of § 840 I BGB, the fact that another person has also caused the illegal act does not exonerate the tortfeasor either altogether or in part. Thus in the result the Court of Appeal has rightly held that the defendant is liable in tort for the incident involving the plaintiff.

II. . . .

Case 63

BUNDESGERICHTSHOF (SIXTH CIVIL SENATE) 15 DECEMBER 1978
BGHZ 75, 75 = BB 1979, 1257 = NJW 1979, 2036

In 1969 the plaintiff gave an order to the G firm to carry out the glazing of his house. Thereupon the firm inserted "I–Glass" units which had been manufactured under licence by the defendant. The delivery took place on 9 October 1969 by way of the F Company, which had ordered the material from the defendant and taken delivery on 7 October 1969. In September 1974 the plaintiff detected condensation on a part of the inserted plates. At the end of October 1974 the defendant was notified of claims by the plaintiff. The defendant, in a letter of November 1974, asserted that the limitation period affecting the warranty had already elapsed. When that letter reached the plaintiff by way of the G firm on 14 November 1974, he learnt for the first time that the defendant included in its publicity a declaration under the heading "warranty", which read, *inter alia*, as follows:

> The manufacturers of "I–Glass" warrant—for five years from the date of the first delivery—that under normal conditions the transparency of "I–Glass" will be vitiated neither by the formation of film nor by the deposit of dust in the space between the plates . . . This warranty creates an obligation only to replace the defective "I–Glass" units . . . The group of European "I" manufacturers . . . have established a warranty fund to insure quality and warranty. This fund serves to provide extraordinary insurance of the "I" warranty and makes it ultimately independent of local conditions and circumstances. The warranty fund therefore supports the warranty issued by each "I–Glass" licensee . . .

The plaintiff in his action begun in January sued the defendant on his producer's warranty. He at first demanded twelve substitute glass units. In May 1977, he had the plates he objected to changed and claimed compensation for the cost of the materials. The lower courts rejected his claim. On his application for review the Bundesgerichtshof set aside the appellate judgment and sent the case back for reconsideration for these

Reasons

1. The Court of Appeal is of opinion that no direct contractual relation came into being between the defendant manufacturer and the plaintiff as ultimate acquirer of the glass plates. Whether that is correct may be left undecided: for the judgment under review cannot be upheld because by virtue of a contract between the defendant and the F Company a warranty came into existence for the benefit of the plaintiff as ultimate acquirer (contract for the benefit of their parties).

(*a*) . . .

(*b*) . . . The defendant's warranty attached on the date of the first delivery, namely that of the glass to the F Company. Thus it is obvious that the contractual intention of the defendant also relates back to that moment. That answers to the interest of the middleman, who acquires advantages for himself as well as from the creation of the warranty in favour of the ultimate acquirer. If, that is to say, one of the defects covered by the warranty occurs, he will be free from his own liability to the other party in so far as the manufacturer is responsible for the defect by virtue of his duty to perform the warranty. Accordingly everything speaks in favour of the F Company's intending to establish the warranty as early as possible, in order to assure itself of the indirect exemption from liability connected therewith and its independence of later contingencies (e.g. the question whether the ultimate acquirer had notice as a third party of the warranty). The fact that the warranty fund set up intended the liability assumed by the defendant to be independent of local conditions and circumstances does not stand in the way. That turn of phrase emphasizes the *material security* of the warranty, but says nothing about the *person to whom* the defendant intended to direct his offer to make good the warranty. The custom sought by the warranty is not put in doubt on the ground that it initially operated on the middlemen in their relations with the manufacturer, for the last middleman will as a rule indicate to the ultimate acquirer the advantages implied in the warranty, in order to obtain a customer.

(c) As the interests of all concerned speak in favour of creating the warranty at once by means of a contract for the benefit of third parties (§ 328 BGB), it must follow that the defendant and the F Company intended to enter into a contract of that kind . . .

That the person of that third party was not ascertained when they made the contract does not affect the result. For the contracting parties the identity of the future ultimate acquirer played (to start with) no role. The agreement that whoever should happen to be the ultimate acquirer should be the third party beneficiary was enough. That made him sufficiently ascertainable.

2. The plaintiff claimed in good time under the warranty offered by the contract for his benefit.

It is true that the defendant learnt of the occurrence to which the warranty applied only after the limitation period had run out. Since the F Company had taken delivery of the glass plates from the defendant on 7 October 1969, the five-year limitation period had already run out when the defendant obtained on 28 October 1974 knowledge of the complaint. That, however, is of no significance since according to the clear wording of the warranty, the period referred to is the period within which the material damage envisaged must occur and not the period within which the claim must be made.

The only decisive factor therefore is that the defect appeared in September 1974—and so within the warranty period. That at that moment the plaintiff's claim against the G firm was already time-barred, because it was based on VOB/B standard contract, is irrelevant. The warranty was to be valid "independent of local conditions and circumstances", and therefore irrespective of the contractual arrangements of the ultimate acquirer with the glazier.

3. If the glass plates manufactured by the defendant turn out to have the defect alleged by the plaintiff (which must be taken for granted for present purposes), it should make no difference to the plaintiff's action that he no longer demands their replacement but compensation.

The defendant's warranty is intended to give greater effect to the claims for defects that the ultimate acquirer has against the person (the glazier) employed by him to do the work. The contract of warranty is, therefore, ancillary to a warranty arising from a contract for work and labour. In the present case the plaintiff's contract with the G firm was one of sale and work concerning non-fungible goods; for the glass plates had been prepared to fit the special dimensions of the window-frames in the plaintiff's house. That the defendant's contract with the F Company is one of sale is irrelevant. The decisive factor is the economic function the warranty has to perform for the ultimate acquirer as third-party beneficiary.

The plaintiff was at liberty to remedy the defects himself—assumed to exist for the purposes of the present appeal—and to demand monetary compensation from the defendant.

4. The plaintiff's claim under the warranty is not statute-barred. As has already been explained, the warranty was intended to give greater effect to the ultimate acquirer's claim for defective delivery based on the contract of work against the builder carrying out his order. In accordance with that purpose, the claim under the warranty becomes statute-barred at the same moment as the corresponding claim of the ultimate acquirer. Here the glazing of all the windows in a house amounts to a building contract. The limitation

period for a contract of work is five years. Accordingly, claims under the warranty also are subject to a five year limitation. That the plaintiff agreed with the G firm that standard conditions of VOB/B should apply makes no difference. The warranty here for the ultimate acquirer was to be "independent of the circumstances of the particular case". It was to give greater effect to his claims of the final acquirer under the warranty arising from the contract of work and therefore according to its sense and purpose should in no way be subject to the agreed curtailment of the limitation period applicable to a contract of work.

The defendant by his warranty agreed to be responsible for all defects appearing within the limitation period. Accordingly, that period for claims under the warranty cannot be taken to run from the delivery, fixing or acceptance of the glass. The better view is that the sense and purpose of the warranty require it to begin only with the discovery of the defect (cf. also BGH NJW 1979, 645). Otherwise defects which were first detected towards the end of the warranty limitation period could in many cases not be successfully invoked before the limitation operated. That is precisely shown in the present case.

The plaintiff here detected the defect in September 1974—within five years from the delivery of the plates—the subject of the action started in January 1977. Thereby the limitation was interrupted in good time.

5. In view of these considerations, the appellate judgment must be set aside. The case must be sent back to the Court of Appeal, which must now inquire whether and how far the plates were defective and what the substitute plates cost.

Case 64

BUNDESGERICHTSHOF (SIXTH CIVIL SENATE) 7 JUNE 1988
BGHZ 104, 323 = NJW 1988, 2611 = JZ 1988, 966

Facts

The defendants manufacture carbonated soft drinks which they bottle in reusable bottles manufactured by DB and Co. and which they market *inter alia* under the trade mark "Fri." The parents of the plaintiff, who, at the time of the accident was three years old, purchased a crate of lemonade produced by the defendants on September 5, 1981 from the drinks retailer F. Two days later, on 7 September 1981, when the plaintiff took one of the bottles out of the crate in the basement of his parents' house, it exploded. The plaintiff lost his right eye and part of the sight in his left eye as a result of injuries received from glass splinters. The remains of the glass were not preserved after the accident.

The plaintiff claimed damages for part of his pain and suffering from the defendants in the amount of DM 6,000. In support of his case he claimed that as manufacturers, the defendants are responsible for an injury to his health which occurred when one of their products was being used for the purposes for which it was intended. He could not be expected to prove that the defect in the bottle occurred after it had been marketed by the defendants, since this would be impossible for him in practice. The numerous other comparable cases in which bottles containing products manufactured by the defendants or other producers of mineral water products had exploded showed that this accident did not merely involve a "stray incident". Rather, they demonstrated that technical precautions which could have been taken in the bottling process were not in fact taken, even though the dangers must have been known.

The defendants contested the plaintiff's description of the accident. In their view the bottle of lemonade did not explode, but rather it either fell out of the plaintiff's hands or was banged against another object when it was lifted out of the crate. The bottle of lemonade was free from defects when it left the defendants' business. This was guaranteed by the technical installations and organisation of the defendants' business. The fact that the cause of the accident could not be clarified since the remains of the bottle were not preserved, was a matter for which the plaintiff must take responsibility.

The LG gave judgment for the plaintiff. The OLG rejected the claim, and allowed the defendants' appeal on the basis that the plaintiff had no claims against the defendants arising from the accident. The plaintiff's application to the BGH was successful and led to the quashing of the judgment and the remittance of the case to the lower court for decision.

For the following

Reasons

I. The OLG considers that it is not proven that the lemonade bottle was already defective when it was marketed by the defendants. In the view of the OLG, the lack of proof falls as a burden upon the plaintiff. The essential findings of that court are as follows: the reversal of the burden of proof developed by the case law for product liability did not extend either to the defective nature of the product or to the proof of a causal link between the defect and the damage which gives rise to liability, but concerns merely the question of fault. There is also no possibility of a lessening of the burden of proof using the rules governing *prima facie* proof. It is true that there is no question of inappropriate handling of the product by the plaintiff. According to the evidence given by the expert witness Dr Sch., what caused the accident was excessive pressure within the bottle as a result of it being insufficiently filled, or an existing crack in the glass which led to the bursting of the bottle as a result of a small increase in pressure caused by the movement of the contents as it was removed from the crate. However, it could not be excluded that the damage to the bottle such as might here be considered to be the causal factor for the explosion of the bottle could have been caused only after the bottle had been marketed by the defendant. Consequently, the plaintiff must incur the typical difficulties regarding proof which are faced by a consumer who is injured by a product which has been passed along a rather lengthy chain of manufacture and distribution. A lessening of the burden of proof can be of no assistance to the victim as regards evidence of the causal connection. That would lead to a form of strict liability for the manufacturer which is not recognised under the present law, since it would be practically impossible for the defendant to provide the necessary proof.

II. The arguments put forward by the OLG are not, as a matter of law, in all respects convincing.
1. The OLG clearly regards the liability of the defendants as being feasible where it could be said that both possible causes which the expert witness said might explain the explosion of the lemonade bottle—namely excessive pressure inside the bottle as a result of it being insufficiently filled or a crack in the glass—were *already* present at the time when the bottle was marketed by the defendant. In reaching that conclusion, the OLG placed limits which were too restrictive upon recovery. At the present time, it cannot be excluded that the defendants as the manufacturers might still be responsible for the explosion of

the lemonade bottle, including an explosion of the violence which caused the severe injuries suffered by the plaintiff in this case, even where the direct cause of the accident was a hairline crack which only appeared in the glass after the bottle had been put into the marketing chain leading to the plaintiff by the defendant. In this case there would be no question of considering the issue which the OLG took to be central, namely the burden of proving whether the defect in question was present or absent at the time when the bottle left the defendant's business.

(a) As the manufacturers of carbonated lemonade, the defendants are subject to a duty under the principles of the law of tort to ensure, within the limits of what is technically possible and economically reasonable, that consumers do not suffer any impairment of their health as a consequence of their products. This duty covers not just the concern that the drink which they manufactured should be fit for consumption; it also makes the defendants responsible for ensuring that the containers in which their lemonade is marketed do not cause injuries, whether to the consumer or to other persons concerned with the transport of the product [references omitted]. This applies also to the danger of the bursting of the glass bottle chosen by the defendants for their product as a consequence of a defect in the material or of excessive pressure which can lead—as the present case shows—to very serious injuries. Those types of accidents may be rare, even when measured against the high turnover in drinks and the common usage of that type of lemonade bottle—even in reusable containers. Still, as the experience of the court and the evidence of the expert witness demonstrate, they do occur and have long been known to the drinks industry as a specific risk inherent in such products.

It was the task of the defendants to deal with this risk within the limits of what was technically possible and financially reasonable. The responsibility of the defendants is not undermined by the fact that in addition to used bottles which it prepared for refilling, it also used brand new reusable glass bottles manufactured by DB and Co for its lemonade. Even with regard to these new bottles, they assumed responsibility for the product when they made use of them; consequently it was for the defendants to ensure that when the bottles were delivered they would withstand the demands of being transported and of being used in the normal way by the purchaser. The defendants were also not solely a bottling concern in respect of which the responsibility for the use of the bottles might have been differently evaluated [reference omitted]. The defendants decided how the drink would be put together, specifying in particular the level of carbonation which in turn determined the degree of pressure in the interior of the bottle; they also specified the type, get up, and usage of the chosen packaging material. Consequently, the defendants are not simply responsible for ensuring that this material and the level of internal pressure to which the bottles were subject once filled were appropriate, but also for ensuring that the composition of the bottles was satisfactory bearing in mind the demands which could be expected to be placed upon them in the context of distribution and consumption. The type of defects which in the view of the expert witness were likely to be responsible for the eye injuries suffered by the plaintiff are amongst those which it is for the defendant, if possible, to eliminate using appropriate methods of production and control.

(b) In this context the defendants must take into account that even if the bottles were not damaged when they left the manufacturer's sphere of control, they may [subsequently] be damaged and left in a state in which they might explode on the way to the consumer. For the product must not only be capable of withstanding impacts arising in the context of normal and intended usage such as knocks, pressures, heat, cold, etc.; such bottles must also be capable of standing up to all types of foreseeable and normal usage [see OLG Frankfurt VersR 1985, 890; Borer, *Produkthaftung: Der Fehlerbegriff nach deutschem, amerikanischem und europäischem Recht* (1986) p. 26]. Of course, it cannot be expected that the manufacturer should take precautions against all types of instances in which its bottles of drink are handled carelessly. The limits of the type of care which the manufacturer would be expected to demonstrate are exceeded in circumstances where the inappropriate handling of the bottle deviates from what is normally foreseeable. However, the defendants must take into account not only the distance which the bottle must travel before it reaches the consumer and the length of time between production and consumption, all of which means that there are uncertainties as to how the bottles will be handled, but also the [possibility of a] great variety of different consumers coming into contact with the bottles. The defendants may not rely upon the fact that the bottles will be sensibly and gently handled during transport and storage.

(c) Of course, the defendants cannot be reproached for having used reusable glass bottles in the first place for bottling their lemonade, even though there remains a residual risk of injury from such bottles, in particular where they are not handled carefully by distributors or consumers. In principle, the defendants are entitled to expect the users, themselves, to take care to avoid injury from glass breakages, because these are inherent risks in the material itself. The same cannot be said of the risks of an explosive breakage of the bottle such as occurred in this case. The average consumer does not anticipate such a risk; even an appropriate warning on the bottle would not change the expectations of consumers in this respect in any lasting way. The consumer cannot in general protect himself against the bottle through acting more carefully where it has already been damaged or where it is subject to excessive internal pressure. The serious injuries which are in particular likely to occur if there is an explosive breakage of the glass are completely disproportionate to the obligations in respect of the product which the consumer can be expected to assume when handling it as an aspect of the general risks of life. It is true that there is much to be said, in the light of the information put forward so far in this case, for the fact that, having regard to the great number of reusable bottles with the same features used by manufacturers of carbonated drinks, there are extremely few accidents caused by exploding bottles which have suffered prior damage. Consequently, there are no grounds for raising legal doubts about the admissibility of using such bottles on the grounds of any general level of risk. On the other hand, the specific risks of an explosive breakage cannot for these reasons simply be ignored by the manufacturer; the consequences of such an accident are too serious for this to be the case. On the contrary, the manufacturer of drinks must be regarded as subject to an obligation within the realms of what is economically reasonable and technically possible to eliminate such specific risks leading to serious injuries in so far as is possible. The type of measures which can be expected of the manufacturer include introducing a significant reduction in the level of carbonation, as was suggested by the expert witness in this case, using a type of bottle which is not as dangerous when it breaks, making use of caps which automatically release excessive pressure, and other appropriate measures.

(d) In this case, it can be concluded from the above that the OLG must first examine the question of whether and to what extent the defendants could be reasonably expected, at the relevant time when the bottle was put on the market, to take these types of precautions against their bottles exploding where the glass was damaged, even if only when it was being transported to the consumer. In judging what it is economically reasonable to expect of the manufacturer it is necessary to take into account *inter alia* the customs of consumers and sales potential for a product altered to take into account these matters. However, it must [also] be taken into account that it is the basic safety needs of consumers which are being counterpoised to these economic factors. The burden of going forward with the evidence and of proving that a method of production which eliminates the risk of lemonade bottles exploding is possible and reasonable and of demonstrating that there is a breach of duty on the part of the defendants falls upon the plaintiff, who is not protected by any easing of the burden in this respect. Should the OLG come to the conclusion that the defendants could have eliminated those types of risks of exploding bottles even at the time of the accident, and that the defendants had negligently closed their minds to this possibility in spite of the risk which had long been known in this branch of industry, then it is clear that the defendants are responsible for the injuries to the plaintiff even where the bottle exploded not because of excessive pressure because it had not been filled up, but because the glass had been damaged, even during transport to the consumer.

2. It is only where it can be said that the defendants are not subject to a duty to take such precautions with a view to eliminating the risk discussed above at the time when the bottle was put into circulation that it would be relevant, for the purposes of determining whether the defendants are liable, to consider the question which the OLG placed at the centre of its analysis. This [question] was whether, alongside the possibility that it was excessive pressure caused by the bottle having been insufficiently filled (which would certainly be a defect in manufacture on the part of the defendants) the other possible cause of the damage (namely a crack in the glass) should also be regarded as occurring in the defendants' sphere of production. To put it differently, did the bottle, when it was put on the market, already have the defect which actually triggered the explosion? However, even in this context the arguments of the OLG are not sustainable.

(*a*) The OLG cannot, without erring in law, exclude the possibility that the lemonade bottle in question was free from defects when it was marketed by the defendants.

(*aa*) The applicants' submissions to this court seek to rely, without avail, upon the rules of *prima facie* proof in order to demonstrate that the defect which led to the breakage of the bottle was already present when the product was marketed. The plaintiff argues that it is possible to see that the occurrence of the loss is typical—a feature which it must display if there is to be an easing of the burden of proof and which is in principle necessary for the purposes of demonstrating a defect in the product [references omitted]—from the fact that there have been repeated similar accidents in the past involving lemonade bottles marketed by the defendants, as well as lemonade and mineral water bottles manufactured by others, but despite this the defendants had not taken any care to ensure that adequate controls were placed upon the bottles which it put on the market. Additionally, the plaintiff argues that it has satisfied the conditions of *prima facie* proof because the defendants have neither identified nor proven a serious possibility of the lemonade bottle suffering damage after it left their business premises.

As this court has repeatedly stated [references omitted], the rules on *prima facie* proof are of no assistance where it cannot be excluded that the condition which caused the danger only arose after the product left the manufacturer's business premises. There is nothing to counter the arguments put forward by the OLG that it could not be excluded that the damage was caused to the bottle after it had been finally marketed by the defendants. There remains the possibility that a third party for whom the manufacturer is not responsible—such as a distributor or a retailer—damaged the lemonade bottle by handling it incorrectly.

(*bb*) Even the arguments led by the plaintiff in his appeal whereby the damaging occurrence resulted in the product destroying itself so that the reasons for the difficulties in proving the case were the responsibility of the defendants do not justify allowing the modifications in the burden of proof sought by the plaintiff. It cannot be said that the *defendants* are frustrating the plaintiff's attempts to prove his case because it cannot be excluded that it was not the defendants but a third party who was responsible for the bursting of the bottle and consequent destruction of the means of proof.

(*cc*) The plaintiff likewise derives no assistance from the reversal of the burden of proof developed in case law of the BGH in particular for cases of medical malpractice involving gross negligence in the treatment process. This case law is based on the proposition that the difficulties experienced by the plaintiff in clarifying exactly what happened during the treatment process which result from the error in treatment can be traced back to the fact that the range of possible causes for the plaintiff's misfortune is either widened or displaced because of the particular likelihood that the error in question would cause loss and to the fact that the failure of the treatment is especially likely as a consequence of the serious medical error [references omitted]. The situation here is not comparable to such a serious error in treatment. The re-use of used lemonade bottles without adequate controls against prior damage to the glass does not in itself represent an elementary error which on these grounds alone would justify an easing of evidentiary difficulties including potentially a shifting of the burden of proof. For it was established by the OLG that the defendants screened the bottles by putting them under an initial pressure of 6.0 bar.

(*b*) It is crucial to determine in this case which party is burdened with the consequences of the fact that the exact cause of the defect and the point at which it arose remain unclarified, and in this context it is correct to adopt the starting point of the OLG, namely that it is in principle the task of the plaintiff not only to prove the defect in the product and the causal link between the defect and the injury to the plaintiff, but also to prove that the defect in question arose within the manufacturer's sphere of control for which the defendants are responsible. The courts have so far always refused to extend the principles of the reversal of the burden of proof regarding the issue of fault to the issue of objective attribution of the injury to the action ("*objektiver Zurechnungszusammenhang*") of loss [references omitted]. A generalised form of reversal of proof would turn the manufacturer's tortious liability into a form of strict liability ["*Erfolgseinstandshaftung*"] for all consequences for which it would be necessary to find some specific legitimation in the substantive law.

However, it does not follow from the above—as the OLG assumes—that modifications of the evidentiary burdens (amounting to a reversal of the burden of proof regarding the attribution of a harmful defect in the product to the manufacturer's sphere of control) are always excluded.

The objections to a presumption of a causal link working against the manufacturer will exceptionally become weaker *inter alia* where the defect in the product which has been established is typically one which arises within the manufacturer's sphere of control. In such cases, and precisely for this reason, the manufacturer (who is required wherever possible to eliminate such risks in order to avoid the infliction of serious loss) is under an obligation, for the sake of the consumer, to assure himself before the product is put on the market that it is free of such defects. This is so where the victim has demonstrated that the manufacturer's attempts to ensure the "safety status" of the product have been inadequate. In such a case there is no significant hardening of the substantive duties imposed upon the manufacturer if he is required to demonstrate—as it were, in order to ensure the performance of the duty to ensure the 'safety status' of the product which he has not so far fulfilled—that the defect occurred only after he had put the product on the market. The manufacturer would be acting in bad faith if, in the context of litigation and in order to exonerate himself, he were able to rely upon the absence of data regarding the state of the products when they were put on the market which should precisely be available by law in order to ensure the substantive protection of the consumer.

(*aa*) By opening up such a possibility of reversing the burden of proof regarding the existence of a causal link in the field of product liability, this court is building on principles which it has already developed regarding the easing of the evidentiary burden within the law of tort. In this context it is not accepted that every breach of duty which leads to the occurrence of damage remaining unexplained will necessarily lead to the imposition of a burden upon the tortfeasor. There is no general rule that the risk of non-clarification will fall upon the party which has caused it as a consequence of a breach of duty [references omitted]. If it were the case that a failure on the part of the defendants to institute adequate controls upon the re-use of bottles in order to ensure that they will not burst merely represented a breach of their general duty of care to manufacture products which can be used without harming the consumer's health, then there would be no reason to relieve the plaintiff, as the victim, of the burden of proving that the non-existent controls were responsible for the accident, simply because of this breach on the part of the defendants of a duty of care to which they were subject [reference omitted].

(*bb*) However, the position is different where the duty on the part of the manufacturer to eliminate the risk is precisely focused on the clarification of an ambiguous state of affairs or an unclarified feature of the product and is a duty which is imposed upon the manufacturer for the protection of the consumer precisely in order to ensure, through a timely and exact investigation and control of the status of the product, that it is free of risks typically found in such products and which can no longer be discovered once the product has been put on the market by the manufacturer. If the manufacturer is in this way required to produce and preserve data on the inquiries made into the safety of the product, because he is not permitted to burden the consumer with the unclarified status of the product and the risks inherent in that status, then this in no way changes the material duties imposed upon the manufacturers, but rather confirms them. This is so where the manufacturer has breached this duty and so carries the burden of proving that the proper provision of data at the time of the inspection of the product would have ensured that it was guaranteed free of defects. To this extent, there is a conflict of interests which is comparable to that arising in those cases in which the doctor is required, for the purposes of protecting his patient, to provide written reports in order to ensure that there is prompt clarification of the patient's state of health. This clarification serves to avoid dangerous developments and cannot be drawn

up belatedly. In these cases, too, this court has imposed upon the doctor who wrongfully fails to ensure that there is such a report the burden of proof in respect of what
actually occurred where as a consequence of the breach of duty the clarification of what
is in any case a probable causal connection between the negligence of the doctor and
the injury to the plaintiff is made more difficult or impossible and the provision of a
report is required precisely because of the increased risk of the procedure undertaken
in that particular case [reference omitted]. The general essence of the principle of law
underlying these decisions can also be applied exceptionally in respect of the constel-
lations of fact described above concerning product liability in order to ease the burden
of proof upon the consumer in respect of the causal connection and can go so far as
to shift the burden of proof upon the manufacturer.

(cc) The preconditions for the application of the principles regarding the reversal
of the burden of proof are fulfilled, having regard to the facts as they are to be understood for the purposes of this appeal hearing. By selling the returnable bottles, the
defendants put on the market a product which, because of its particular features (glass
containers which are used several times and which are subject to considerable internal
gas pressure) reveals an enhanced tendency to cause damage. In respect of such bottles,
which may have been used many times over a period of many years, and which may
therefore have already been damaged and are therefore likely to explode, the defendants, as the manufacturers, are subject to a duty of examination and report preservation in that they must inspect the state of the glass of every bottle before it is put on
the market with a view to ensuring that it is not likely to burst and to ensure that only
undamaged bottles leave the manufacturers' place of business. For if the manufacturer
of soft drinks uses not only new bottles but also, as here, re-used bottles, then if there
is no report preservation there will be no basis for judging the state of the glass and
whether and to what extent it is capable of withstanding not only the high internal gas
pressure to which it will be subjected but also the considerable demands which will be
placed upon it during its journey to the consumer; these are risks which the manufacturer must take into account. It is precisely because serious injuries to the health of a
victim can occur where there has been a prior impairment of the glass leading to a risk
of explosion and because the risk of such impairments is greater where the previously
used bottles are re-used, that the manufacturer is subject to a duty to investigate the
condition of the bottles which is so far unknown to him, and thereby to provide for
himself and for the consumer information regarding the resistance to explosion of the
glass.

It has been established by the OLG that there was no comprehensive method of identifying the already damaged bottles within the defendant's firm; in particular, subjecting
the bottles for a short period of time to pressure of 6.0 bar was not a sufficient form of
control. Consequently, there appears to have been a breach by the defendants of their duty
of report preservation with the resulting possibility of a reversal of the burden of proof.
It is a precondition for this duty to ensure the "safety status" of the bottles that some form
of reliable means of identifying already damaged bottles is both technically possible and
economically reasonable for the defendants; while this can be assumed for the purposes
of this appeal, it has so far not been adequately clarified. If there was such a duty of examination and report preservation, then if it was a hairline crack in the glass which caused
the explosion of the bottle, it is to be assumed until the defendants have proved the contrary that the damage to the bottle existed already before it was put on the market by the

defendants and could have been discovered through a proper inspection [reference omitted].

III. The judgment of the OLG must therefore be quashed and the issue returned to the OLG for a further hearing and decision. It is for the OLG to clarify—where necessary after having heard the parties once again and having taken the advice of an expert witness—whether the defendants could have prevented the explosion of the bottles in the hands of the consumer where the glass had been damaged, by taking reasonable measures in the context of the manufacture of the products (the lemonade) or, if this was neither possible nor reasonable, whether it could have ensured through appropriate and reasonable controls and report preservation that damaged bottles were not once more put on the market. In such a case the defendants, as the manufacturers, are required to prove that the absence of such controls and some means of securing the safety status of the products was irrelevant to the loss which occurred. If, however, at that time it could not be demanded of the defendants that they provide such a "safety status", then the burden resulting from the unexplained cause of the damage will fall upon the plaintiff.

Case 65

BUNDESGERICHTSHOF (SIXTH CIVIL SENATE) 19 NOVEMBER 1991
BGHZ 116, 104 = NJW 1992, 1039 = JZ 1993, 671

Facts

After the wedding breakfast held at the second defendant's restaurant on 29 July 1989, the plaintiff and some of the 54 guests suffered from salmonella poisoning. Germs of *salmonella enteritis* were later found not only in the vanilla ice-cream but also in the pudding and custard prepared the previous evening by the first defendant and her daughter, who were found to be carriers of salmonella. The plaintiff claimed back the DM 3,000 she had paid the second defendant for the wedding feast; from both defendants she claimed damages for pain and suffering in the amount of DM 1,500 and a further DM 800 because the start of the honeymoon was delayed for four days by reason of the illness.

The Landgericht held both defendants jointly and severally liable for DM 1,500 as damages for pain and suffering, but rejected the rest of the claim. All parties appealed to the Oberlandesgericht, which ordered the second defendant to repay the DM 3,000 paid for the wedding feast, but rejected the rest of the claim. On the plaintiff's appeal the decision rejecting the claim for damages for pain and suffering against the second defendant was vacated. The second defendant's ancillary appeal was rejected.

Reasons

A. [Procedural.]

B. The court below dismissed the claim for damages for pain and suffering against both defendants.

It held that the first defendant was not liable under §§ 823 I, II BGB in conjunction with § 230 Criminal Code and/or § 8 LMBG for serving meals contaminated with salmonella, because the plaintiff could adduce no proof that the first defendant was at fault. According to the experts' reports, there were three ways the salmonella could have got into the pudding: from the hands of the salmonella-carriers, from the equipment used in making the pudding or from the ingredients used, especially the eggs. It could be neither proved nor disproved that the salmonella got into the pudding from the hands of the first defendant or her daughter. The rules regarding the burden of proof in cases of product liability did not affect the first defendant since she was not the owner of the restaurant. Nor did they affect the second defendant, since they are inapplicable to the owners of small family businesses, where proof of the subjective elements of delict is not particularly difficult: it is relatively simple to make a pudding and to understand how it is made. Furthermore, the plaintiff could sue the second defendant on the basis of the contract between them. The second defendant could not be made liable under § 831 BGB, for he had shown that he was free from fault as regards the conduct of his wife and daughter. As against this, the claim that the second defendant return the money paid for the wedding feast was allowed on the basis of § 635 BGB. The second defendant had failed to prove that neither he nor any of those who helped him perform the contract were responsible for the salmonella, for it was possible that his wife or daughter had been salmonella carriers before they started to prepare the pudding, and should therefore have washed their hands more carefully. Although there was nothing wrong with the rest of the meal and only a few of the guests were rendered ill, the entire sum paid could be reclaimed since the feast was to be regarded as a single event.

The court below rejected the claim for damages in respect of the lost honeymoon as not representing an economic loss.

II. The plaintiff's appeal.

1. The plaintiff's appeal from the dismissal of his claim for damages for pain and suffering against the second defendant is justified (a), but the court below was right to reject the similar claim against the first defendant (b).

(*a*) *The second defendant's liability.* The reasons given by the court below for denying the second defendant's liability for the immaterial harm suffered by the plaintiff are not good in law.

(*aa*) In providing food infected with salmonella, the second defendant as owner of the restaurant contributed to the injury to the plaintiff's health. Liability under §§ 823 I, 847 BGB must therefore be considered, as it was by the court below. It is a precondition of liability under these provisions that the defendant be chargeable with some fault. The burden of proof of fault normally lies on the victim, but in the area of product liability the Bundesgerichtshof has developed the exceptional principle that if a product is defective when he puts it into circulation the producer must establish and prove by evidence that he was not at fault as regards the defect in the product which harmed the consumer (BGHZ 51, 91 [103 ff.] = NJW 1969, 269; BGHZ 80, 186 [196 ff.] = NJW 1981, 1603). For the purposes of product liability the second defendant was unquestionably the producer of the meals prepared in his restaurant, so the application of this principle falls for consideration. This is not a case, to use Brüggemeier's words (VersR 1983, 116 ff.) of 'transferring the rules of product liability to the providers of services', for the wedding feast involved much more than the mere provision of services: services were indeed involved, but the main thing was the supply of the meals.

When the burden of proof in the area of product liability was first reversed in the so-called *"chicken-pest"* case (BGHZ 51, 91 = NJW 1969, 269), the Bundesgerichtshof took into account the evidentiary difficulty which a plaintiff normally faces in a suit against a manufacturer. The court based its reversal of the burden of proof on the fact that since the producer oversees the sphere of production and organises the production process and quality control, he is in much the better position (*"näher dran"*) to explain what actually happened and to bear the consequences of lack of proof. If the cause of the lack of explanation falls within the producer's area of responsibility, it seems appropriate and fair under these decisions that he bear the risk of being unable to prove that he was not at fault (BGHZ 51, 91 [105] = NJW 1969, 269; for comparable conflicts of interests, see BGHZ 67, 383 [387] = NJW 1977, 501, etc.).

(*bb*) In the *"chicken-pest"* case, which certainly involved industrial production, the court deliberately left open the question whether the risk of inability to disprove fault should also be imposed on the owner of a small business—a family operation or one-man concern—where the methods of production are uncomplicated and simple to understand. In its judgment of 30 April 1991 (BGHZ 114, 284 = NJW 1991, 1948—Aids) the court again declined to decide whether the principle as to proof applies only to industrial mass production, but it did hold it applicable in a case where an infusion solution for use in a hospital became un-sterile either during or after the preparation (BGH NJW 1982, 699), and the Eighteenth Civil Senate of the Oberlandesgericht Frankfurt has applied it in a case, rather like the present, of a gypsy salad infected with salmonella in a restaurant (19 February 1979, VersR 1982, 151).

Writers are divided on the question, but by far the majority opinion is that in cases like the present, the burden of proof should be reversed [references]. This court is of the view that there is no compelling reason to exempt small businesses such as personally-run restaurants and cafés from the evidential burden.

The underlying idea which gave rise to this reversal of proof in cases of product liability, namely the consumer's ignorance of how the producer manufactures his products or organises his business, is of general application, whether the business is big or small, the method of production industrial or personal. It is quite true that what happens in a family-run café is more easily understood than what goes on in a factory geared to mass production. It is also true, as the court below noted, that making a pudding is quite a simple operation calling for no specialist knowledge, comprehensible even by the injured customer. But that does not alter the fact that production takes place in the owner's area of control, and that the restaurateur can monitor the process more easily than the customer. He is in the better position to discover and investigate sources of error. The consumer is an outsider who is normally in no position to know how individual dishes are prepared, what ingredients the patron uses or where he obtains them, nor can he tell what steps are taken to maintain hygiene in the kitchen. Given these considerations, it seems right and fair to put on the second defendant the burden of disproving fault.

This court is well aware that it may seem harsh to place the burden of proof on small businesses which cannot be expected to have the same facilities for control as a big industrial concern, but this difference is largely offset by the fact that it is much easier for the owner of a small business than for the manager of a large industrial concern to oversee its organisation, to discover any faults in the system of production and to adduce the necessary proof.

Another consideration is that there are no really satisfactory criteria for distinguishing sensibly between large and small and middle-sized businesses. To go by the number of employees would lead to capricious results, especially as there is often little relation between the size of the workforce and the structure of the enterprise. Indeed, in family and one-man businesses it is often immaterial whether any person outside the family is employed or not.

The Product Liability Act of 1 January 1990, based on principles applicable throughout the EC, does not draw any distinction between large and small businesses or make liability turn on whether the production is industrial or personal [references]. To draw such a distinction in claims for immaterial harm which are not covered by the Act and still fall under § 823 BGB would not be right.

(*cc*) The court below gave a further reason for not reversing the burden of proof in this case, namely that the plaintiff had a contractual claim against the "producer". This is an error. The Bundesgerichtshof decided in the "*Schwimmerschalter*" case (BGHZ 67, 359 [362 f.] = NJW 1977, 379) that the reversal of the burden of proof is not excluded by the mere fact that consumer and producer were in contractual relations; to hold otherwise would lead to unacceptably capricious results, as it is often a matter of mere chance whether there is any contract between the victim and the producer, whether any contractual claim has prescribed (§§ 477, 638 BGB) or whether a contractual claim would be barred by an exclusion clause. Cases in the Supreme Court have consistently held that claims in contract and tort co-exist, each following its own rules (BGHZ 67, 359 [362] = NJW 1977, 379; BGHZ 86, 256 [258] = NJW 1983, 810). In the present case, the reversal of the burden of proof in tort cannot depend on whether the plaintiff or other wedding guests have contractual claims for damages against the second defendant.

The court below was therefore wrong to hold that the plaintiff had the burden of proving that the second defendant failed to show the care required by the circumstances. It should rather have inquired whether the second defendant had managed to exculpate himself.

(*dd*) The mere fact that the food provided for the wedding guests was infected with salmonella does not of itself demonstrate any fault on the part of the second defendant. As has been said, the court below was unable to determine how the salmonella got into the pudding and custard, in which it was undoubtedly present, whether from the eggs or some other source. In particular, it is not known whether or not the first defendant and her daughter were already carriers of salmonella when they prepared the pudding. Infection from the kitchen equipment, according to the court below, "could be ruled out", but there is the possibility that the salmonella got into the pudding from ingredients bought in by the second defendant.

In such a case, what matters is what steps the second defendant took to ensure a properly hygienic method of preparation. On this point the court below found, in connection with another matter, that the second defendant had exculpated himself, and the appellant does not question this. But the court below did not advert to the precautions taken by the second defendant to minimise the use of tainted ingredients, or ask what checks the patron of a restaurant should make on the products he buys in. The duties imposed on the producer and retailer of food products are onerous (constant holding, see BGHSt 2, 384 etc.), but only within the limits of what is possible for the defendant. A small business cannot be treated just like a large one (references). This does not relieve the small café proprietor of responsibility towards his guests: if with the means at his disposal he cannot ensure that the food he serves is wholesome, then he may have to stop serving it. In general, however, if he obtains his supplies from a reliable source, he need go in for quality control only when on the particular facts a test is called for. This matter requires further elucidation on remand.

(b) *Liability of the first defendant*. The plaintiff's appeal from the dismissal of his claim for damages for pain and suffering against the first defendant must fail.

(aa) The first defendant cannot be made liable under § 823 I BGB because the plaintiff cannot prove that she was at all at fault in preparing the infected pudding. The mere fact that it was infected does not establish fault. Nor is the burden of proof reversed against the first defendant since she did not own the restaurant and therefore was not the "producer" of the noxious sweet. Only the owner is affected by such reversal: it does not apply to subordinate employees, nor even to all managers, but only to those whose role and position in the firm is such that they can be seen as its representative [references], especially those with a capital stake in the business, such as partners (see BGH NJW 1975, 1827).

(bb) Nor can the first defendant be made liable under § 823 II BGB in relation to § 21 8 no. 1 of the Food Act. Not only is it doubtful whether she can be said to have "produced" the pudding, but there was no proof of fault, as the court below was right to find. The appellant blames the defendant for not using a recipe which would have heated the pudding to over 75 degrees and thus have killed all the germs. This does not establish fault. Like the court below, we can leave aside the question whether the risk of salmonella poisoning makes it obligatory for cafés to heat puddings above 75 degrees, for in view of the possibility that the dishes in which the pudding was placed were infected by the hands of the defendant or her daughter, it was not shown that cooking the pudding as recommended by experts would have prevented the spread of the salmonella. Contrary to the view of the appellant, the fact that there was a breach of § 8 Food Act does not imply any negligence on the part of the second defendant. The decisions do hold that where a protective law has been infringed, it is usually for the defendant to assert and prove facts which repel an inference of negligence (BGHZ 51, 91 [103 ff.] = NJW 1969, 269; BGH VersR 1967, 685; BGH NJW 1985, 1774 = VersR 1985, 452, 453), but this only applies when the protective law is so detailed in its prescriptions that one can properly infer that there must have been negligence (BGH VersR 1984, 270 [271]). If the protective law merely prohibits a stated injurious result, the mere fact that such a result occurs is no indication of negligence.

That is the situation here. § 8 Food Act simply forbids the preparation and circulation of noxious food products. It contains no detailed prescriptions of conduct whose neglect might indicate fault, so one cannot infer any fault on the part of the second defendant from the mere fact of the infraction. It follows that the plaintiff must adduce full proof of the intentional or negligent failure by the first defendant to take the precautions required by the circumstances.

2. The appellant must also fail in her appeal against the rejection of her claim for damages for the delay to the honeymoon. The court below was right to deny that this constituted economic harm. As this court held in BGHZ 86, 212 = NJW 1983, 1107, the pleasure of a

holiday foregone owing to personal injury is not to be commercialised, though it may be taken into account as an element of damages for pain and suffering . . .

Case 66

BUNDESGERICHTSHOF (SIXTH CIVIL SENATE) 9 MAY 1995
BGHZ 129, 353 = NJW 1995, 2162 = JZ 1995, 1060

Facts

The defendant bottled and distributed carbonated mineral water in returnable glass bottles, either "standard spring-water bottles" or bottles of thicker glass and different shape. On 27 June 1990 the plaintiff, then nine years old, was fetching two bottles of the latter type from the cellar of her parents' house. She had placed them on the floor outside the cellar in order to close the door and was about to pick them up when one of the bottles exploded. Splinters of glass entered her left eye and caused serious injuries which despite an operation reduced her sight to 60 per cent and left her with astigmatism.

When bottles were to be refilled in the defendant's factory the following process took place. Cases of empties were put on rollers and carried to a conveyor belt, where the bottles, still in the cases, were visually inspected by two of the defendant's operatives, whose job it was to discard any intrusive or damaged bottles. Then a grab armed with rubber bulbs picked up the bottles, three at a time, and transported them to the washing point, where they were repeatedly sprayed with water. On leaving the washing point, still on the conveyor belt, they were inspected again visually by another employee. They then passed through the bottle-inspection unit, an electronically-operated machine which passed a beam of light through the base and mouth of each bottle, and if this disclosed any damage in those parts, the bottle was discarded. There was then a further visual inspection before the conveyor belt carried the bottles to the filling station. Before entering the filling station they were subjected to yet another visual inspection, and then entered the pressure chamber, where they were subjected to a pressure of 5 bar, a pressure one-third greater than would be exerted by the contents of the bottle once filled. On leaving the pressure chamber the bottles were filled, visually checked once again, and then labelled. The conveyor belt then carried them to the packing station where rubber grips lifted them and placed them in cases for consignment. About 15,000 bottles per hour were processed in this manner.

The plaintiff, relying on the report of the national materials laboratory in D which he put in evidence, maintained that there was a fault in the glass at the site of the fracture—a chip about 4 mm. broad, which may well have existed at the time the bottle was delivered.

For her pain and suffering the plaintiff claimed an appropriate capital sum plus monthly instalments of DM 500. She also claimed a declaration that the defendant was bound to make good to her any material loss she might suffer as a result of the accident on 27 May 1990, except in so far as her claims may have vested in third parties.

Both lower courts dismissed her claim. Her appeal was now allowed.

Reasons

The court below, whose decision is published in VersR 1995, 103, accepted the evidence that explosions of glass bottles filled with carbonated water are always due to damage to the surface of the bottle, and that spontaneous explosions occur through the spread of a very fine hairline crack. The very slightest physical contact, even, under certain circumstances, that of a warm hand, may be enough to cause the bottle to break. The court below held that in this case the bottle had such a hairline crack in it and that the defendant should have withdrawn it during the production process, but that it was at fault in failing to do so and letting the bottle get into circulation. Accordingly the precondition of a claim for damages for pain and suffering, namely that the defendant have been culpably in breach of a duty of care towards the public, was not satisfied. The explosive bottle was one which unavoidably "got away" despite the exercise of all appropriate precautions. Certainly before a manufacturer puts into circulation a product which entails particular risks he must take every care to make sure that it has no defect. But the defendant's techniques of quality control were, according to the experts, up to the state of the art, and no system of control could absolutely ensure that no bottle with a hairline crack left the factory. According to the experts there was an irreducible residual risk in refilling glass bottles, and this case was an instance of it.

The court below was also of the view that the defendant was not liable for the future material loss of the plaintiff under the Product Liability Law of 15 Dec. 1989 (BGBl. I, 2198), since it followed from the reasons given for dismissing the claim in tort that in the current state of scientific and technical knowledge the defect in the bottle could not have been detected (II no. 5).

The appellant's criticisms of the judgment below are justified.

1. The court below was wrong to dismiss the plaintiff's claim for damages for her material harm under 1 of the Product Liability Law.

(a) The plaintiff rightly objects on procedural grounds to the finding that there was a hairline crack in the bottle, which exploded in the plaintiffs' hand. There was no basis for such a finding. The plaintiff's case was that there was a 4 mm. chip off the surface of the bottle, and this was confirmed by the report from the national materials laboratory in D which was put in evidence. The report was to the effect that this fault, which could have arisen shortly before the bottle broke, was the direct cause of the explosion. Furthermore V stated in his expert testimony that the explosion could be assumed to have occurred at the place of the fault. If so, the bottle had at the time of the accident a defect, which caused the bottle to explode.

If it was by reason of the chipping that the bottle exploded, then the defendant is liable for the consequent material harm to the plaintiff under 1 I (1) of the Product Liability Law. Liability could only be avoided if the defendant could prove (1 IV (2)) that at the time the bottle was put into circulation it did not have the defect, which caused the damage (1 II (2)). No such proof was adduced by the defendant in this case. It asserted only, by reference to the expert opinion of C, its production manager, that if the bottle had been chipped when it was in the factory, it would have exploded in the pressure chamber, an assertion which does not exclude the possibility that the bottle was chipped after being filled but while it was still in the defendant's sphere of influence and risk.

On such facts there would be no room for the defence under 1 II no. 5 of the Product Liability Law: there is no difficulty in detecting such a chip.

(b) But even if, as the court below evidently supposed, the bottle broke not in the area of the chip but elsewhere, by reason of a hairline crack, it was still no defence to a claim under 1 I (1) of the Law that the current state of science and technology did not permit the defect to be detected.

(aa) As the court below rightly held, a product is defective under 3 I of the Law if it does not afford the safety which in all the circumstances can justifiably be expected, and consumers expect soda water bottles to be free from faults such as hairline splits and microfissures which could make them explode. The consumer's expectation that the bottle be free from faults would not be diminished even if it were technically impossible to identify and remove such faults. The presence of such a hairline crack constitutes, as the court below rightly held, a manufacturing fault, even if it is one which "got away". (see BGHZ 51, 91 [105] = NJW 1969, 269—the "chicken-pest" case).

(bb) Manufacturing defects which "get away" do not, simply because they cannot be avoided by any proper precautions, constitute defects unascertainable in the current state of scientific or technical knowledge in the sense of Art. 7(e) of the Directive or of 1 II no. 5 of the Law which transposes the Directive into German law.

The purpose of the rule in both instances is merely to exclude liability for what are termed development risks [references to literature]; the term covers only cases where at the time a product was put into circulation none of the means offered by the current state of science and technology rendered it possible to detect its dangerous quality. [More references]. The strict liability of the producer is to be limited by what is objectively possible in the light of the knowledge of risks available at the time the product is put into circulation. [Reference]. The only dangers to be treated as development risks are dangers inherent in the design and construction of the product, which in the current state of technology could not be avoided, not those that were inevitable at the stage of production. When the EC Directive on product liability was being fashioned it was agreed that the defence under art. 7 (e) should apply not to manufacturing defects, but only to defects of design and construction [references], and the only dangers emanating from a product which the German legislator wished to exempt from the scope of the Product Liability Law were dangers, undetectable even with the exercise of all possible care, arising at the stage of design and construction. Liability is to be excluded "only if the potential danger of the product was unrecognisable by reason of the fact that at the time of circulation it was not yet possible to recognise it" [official explanation (*Gesetzeserläuterung*) of the draft Product Liability Law]. It is no longer a defence to this strict liability that the defective product "got away".

The potential danger of returnable glass bottles filled with carbonated liquids has long been recognised and has indeed frequently engaged the courts [references]. As the lower court found, the danger of such glass bottles lies in the fact that even a tiny hairline crack which spreads can cause it to explode. Such a defect may arise at the stage of filling or pre-exist unnoticed, but in neither case is it a fault of design or construction, so liability in respect of it cannot be excluded under 1 II (5) of the Product Liability Law. In such a case the liability of the producer under 1 I (1) of the Law can only be avoided if it appears that the hairline crack was not in the bottle when it had been refilled and put into circulation. No such proof has been adduced by the defendant.

(c) There is no need to refer the matter to the Court of Justice of the European Communities. It is true that the concept of "the state of science and technology" in 1 II no. 5 of the Product Liability Law comes from Art. 7 (e) of the EC Directive and must be interpreted in a similar manner in all member states [reference]. It is also true that if the interpretation of a concept of community law is in issue the court of last resort in a member state must in principle refer the matter to the Court of Justice (Art. 177 II EC). But in the present case there is no occasion to construe the concept of "the state of science". The question is rather whether and how far the German legislator has utilised the freedom allowed by Art. 15 I (b) of the Directive to deviate from Art. 7(b) and make the producer liable, and this is a question for the national courts. Indeed, even where a concept in a Directive is in issue, a reference to the Court of Justice is required only if its interpretation is disputed in the literature or the case-law [reference] or if the court wishes on a point material to the case to deviate from the holding of the Court of Justice (see BVerfG NJW 1988, 2173). Neither of these is the case here.

2. The appellant is also right to criticise the court below for rejecting her claim in tort for damages for pain and suffering.

(a) The court below correctly held that on the question whether a particular defect, such as the chip or hairline crack in this case, arose or even remained undiscovered while it was in the producer's sphere of responsibility the burden of proof can be reversed if the producer was in breach of his *Befundsicherungspflicht*, his duty to ascertain the condition of his product and correct it if defective (BGHZ 104, 323 [330]; BGH NJW 1993, 528). [See note, below.] It also rightly held that users of returnable bottles are bound to have a control system which so far as is possible and reasonable in the light of the latest technology checks the condition of every bottle and takes out of circulation any bottles which might be dangerous.

(b) The court below concluded that in this case the defendant had fulfilled its *Befund-sicherungspflicht*, but there are procedural objections to the way in which it reached its conclusion.

(aa) Despite the appellant's complaint, there was no need for the court below to inquire whether the defendant excluded bottles which had been in prolonged use, since even if such a duty was broken, the breach was not causative of the harm in issue. The evidence of the national materials laboratory in D was that the general condition of the bottle that exploded indicated that it had been used relatively infrequently. So the court below could properly suppose that the defendant was not in breach of its *Befundsicherungspflicht* for failing to remove from circulation, on the ground of its prior use, the bottle which injured the plaintiff.

(bb) But the court below failed to obtain the further expert opinion demanded by the plaintiff on the question whether the pressure of only 5 bar in the chamber through which the bottles were passed prior to being refilled was adequate. This was a procedural lapse (references) which the plaintiff is right to criticise. The particular reason for obtaining such a report in this case is that standard spring-water bottles, which are made of thinner glass than the bottle which injured the plaintiff, are exposed to a pressure of 5.5 to 6 bar, and even this is inadequate to exclude all bottles which are apt to explode (reference). In principle the extra thickness of the bottle in question may have increased the resistance of the glass (reference), as is indeed indicated by the defendant's assertion that 25 bar was needed to make their bottles explode. The court below should therefore have called for direct evidence on the question whether the pressure chosen by the defendant for its bottles of thicker glass was adequate to produce the desired effect of excluding damaged bottles. It was not bound to raise the pressure so high as to cause all bottles with hairline cracks to explode, for the precautions which a defendant must take in order to avoid a reversal of the burden of proof need not totally exclude the chance of explosion of bottles when handled by the consumer: it is enough if they would significantly reduce the risk of this happening (reference).

(cc) The court below was also wrong to ignore the plaintiff's evidence that the production methods used by the defendant and its system of control were inadequate to disclose existing defects such as the possible chipping of the bottle in question.

Having found that the defendant's electronic bottle inspection unit could recognise a blemish only if it was apparent at the base or neck of the bottle, the court should not have been satisfied by the expert opinion of V. that it would be impossible to construct a machine which could detect other faults. As this court has already held (NJW 1993, 528) a mineral water company's *Befundsicherungspflicht* requires it to provide a control system which reveals the condition of every single bottle and guarantees, within the limits of what is technically feasible, that dubious bottles are not reused. This does not mean that it is enough for the company to use the best possible machinery in its control procedures. If defects in bottles undetectable by machinery could be seen by human beings, the company is under a duty to arrange for a visual inspection of every single bottle. Here the defendant admittedly had the bottles inspected visually several times both before and after they were filled, but it is not clear that every bottle was so inspected, especially as during the first inspection the bottles were still in cases, and the two inspectors had to remove not only damaged bottles but also those of a different sort. Again, seeing that the throughput was 15,000 bottles per hour the subsequent inspectors had to check four bottles every second, and to check them not only for faults but also to see that they were clean, duly filled and properly labelled: it is highly unlikely that they could be expected to discover all possible faults, including a chip only a few millimetres in size.

III. This being so, the decision below must be reversed. The plaintiff's claim for material harm is ripe for final decision. The evidence shows that the explosion which damaged the plaintiff was due either to a chip or to a hairline crack, both of which are defects under 3 of the Product Liability Law so that the defendant is liable under 1 for all material harm and the declaration sought can be made. There is no case for restricting the quantum of damages since the harm suffered by the plaintiff falls below even the individual limit under 10 I of the Law.

The plaintiff's claim for damages for pain and suffering must be reheard and decided afresh.

In the further proceedings the following must be noted. Should the court accept that the bottle was chipped, as the plaintiff claims, and the question is whether the chipping occurred during carriage or within the parents' sphere of control and responsibility, this would be a matter for the defendant to prove if it emerged that it was in breach of its *Befundsicherungspflicht*. If the defendant cannot discharge that burden, it will be liable even if the explosion was not due to the chip but to a hairline crack elsewhere in the bottle: its failure to keep the bottle out of circulation would constitute a cause of the injury, and damage due to its exploding because of a hairline crack would fall within its area of responsibility since the exclusion of bottles with external damage helps protect consumers from injury through explosion. Should it transpire that the bottle was not chipped but that the explosion was due to a tiny hairline crack invisible to the human eye somewhere else on the bottle, then if the defendant has fulfilled its *Befundsicherungspflicht* by having adequate pressure in the pressure chamber and keeping the bottle exposed to it for long enough, it will not be liable for the plaintiff's pain and suffering.

Case 67

BUNDESGERICHTSHOF (SIXTH CIVIL SENATE) 12 DECEMBER 2000
NJW 2001, 964 = ZIP 2001, 379 = JZ 2001, 711

Facts

The claimant, who was born on 31 August 1982, claims compensation on the ground that his milk teeth "bite" was destroyed. This was because a child tea product made by the former first defendant had been supplied to him for the first two years of his life by a plastic feeding bottle which this defendant sold with the tea without the necessary warnings.

In 1985 dentists told the claimant's mother that his tooth damage could be due to the tea. In the autumn of 1993 she was referred to the relevant local health insurance scheme about the possibility of a claim. She then took legal advice.

The claim, lodged on 4 January 1996, sought compensation from the former first defendant and from its leading employees sued as the second to the sixth defendants. The claimant considers these latter defendants are jointly responsible (partly as members of the board of directors and partly as authorised signatories, departmental managers etc) for the development, production and sale of the children's tea and for consequential breach of duties in liability law to consumers.

The *Landgericht* rejected the claim on the basis of a limitation defence. The claimant's appeal was unsuccessful. He withdrew his appeal in law against the first defendant, but is pursuing it against the second to sixth defendants.

Reasons

I. The appeal court considers—in agreement with the *Landgericht*—that the claims made in the statement of claim are time barred. The three year limitation period in § 852 of the BGB had begun to run from 1 January 1986 at the latest. The claims had therefore become time barred on 31 December 1988 as no interruption of the limitation period took place within the permitted time.

The claimant's mother—according to the relevant indications given by the dentists giving treatment—had had the necessary knowledge, at any rate by the end of 1985, of the fact that the consumption of children's tea and the manner of its administration had caused the tooth damage. Since this time it had also been possible for her to know that the first defendant as manufacturer of the tea and marketer of the feeding bottles fell to be considered as a tortfeasor. But in fact the mother was completely unaware that the claimant, as a person suffering harm, could have looked to the defendants for compensation. However, this circumstance did not prevent the running of the limitation period. This was because the running of the period would not be delayed until the time when the person suffering harm or his legal representative had legal knowledge that he had a claim to compensation. If, on the other hand, he had no knowledge at all of a possible claim to compensation and if this lack of knowledge formed the hindrance to obtaining knowledge of the tortfeasors, the running of the limitation period would begin with the knowledge of the harm. . .

2. The judgment of the appeal court (which is no longer the object of the appeal in law proceedings) that possible claims by the claimant against the first defendant as producer and seller of the children's tea and the feeding bottle were time barred has no legal effects on the claims which now still remain against the other defendants. The appeal in law correctly alludes to the fact that the prerequisites for the running of the limitation period and the expiry of the limitation period are to be tested independently for each defendant.

(a) The beginning of the running of the limitation period is dependent, according to § 852 (1) of the BGB, on the knowledge of the person suffering harm not only of the harm but also of the identity of the person obliged to compensate. If several people are to be considered as tortfeasors, the beginning of the limitation period is to be determined as against each of these persons who are possibly liable according to the point in time when the person suffering harm has obtained knowledge of the identity of the tortfeasor concerned (references omitted). Accordingly the limitation period can, in relation to several persons obliged to compensate, begin and end at different points in time, even if they are simultaneously responsible for the same harm arising out of the same event.

(b) Contrary to the view of the reply to the appeal in law, the position is no different in this respect when the several persons coming under consideration as responsible under a duty to compensate are on the one hand an undertaking (carried on in the form of a legal person) and on the other hand persons who are its organs or (managing) employees, for whom the undertaking has to assume liability under § 31 of the BGB or § 831 of the BGB. The employee liable according to § 823 (1) of the BGB and the proprietor of the business who is responsible for him according to § 831 of the BGB are joint debtors to the person suffering the harm (§ 840 of the BGB) just as much as the legal person liable under § 31 of the BGB and its directly responsible organ in tort are (reference omitted). Consequently a claim can only become time barred against the joint debtor as to whom each of the prerequisites are established (§ 425 (2) of the BGB). The personal responsibility of the person who acts directly tortiously exists not only in the case of § 831 of the BGB but also in the framework of liability for organs under § 31 of the BGB as separate and independent liability beside that of the undertaking (see for the case of the director of a company [references omitted]); here also automatic parallel treatment of the prerequisites for limitation does not come into consideration.

3. The limitation period for possible claims by the claimant against the second to sixth defendants could therefore only begin to run from the point in time from which the claimant (or his mother who was entitled to care for him) had the necessary knowledge in relation to the identity of these persons who were possibly liable to compensate. He or she would therefore have to know their names, addresses and the nature of their work in the business in each case (references omitted). Even for the organ of a legal person, responsibility in tort law for injury to the legal interests of third parties can in fact depend

to a considerable extent on the division of competences and work in the business (references omitted).

The appeal court made no findings at all on the question of the date from which the claimant's mother had the knowledge about the second to sixth defendants which was necessary in this respect. There is nothing evident which indicates that this could have been the case earlier than three years before the filing of the claim.

4. It has to admitted in favour of the reply to the appeal in law that exceptionally—following the legal concept of § 162 of the BGB—the limitation period can also begin in the sense of § 852 (1) of the BGB if the person suffering harm did not positively possess a state of knowledge which would trigger the running of the period, but certainly had the opportunity of obtaining the necessary knowledge in a reasonable way and without significant difficulty (references omitted). But this only applies when the person suffering harm effectively closes his eyes in the face of unavoidable knowledge and neglects to take advantage of a more or less obvious opportunity for knowledge so that an appeal to lack of knowledge appears to be mere formalism because any other person in the position of the person who has suffered harm would have had the knowledge under the same concrete circumstances (references omitted).

It is not possible to assume such a case, not even in relation to those defendants who at the point in time of the harm were not only managing employees but members of the board of directors of the former first defendant. No grounds at all can be deduced from the findings which have been made for saying that the claimant's mother could at any time have discovered the names, addresses and areas of competence of the members of the board of directors coming under consideration for liability in the present context in a manner so simple and obvious to everyone that reliance on the absence of knowledge could appear to be impermissible. This would apply especially in relation to those defendants who—without being members of the board of directors—were engaged in the production and sale of tea products as departmental managers or authorised signatories.

5. It is to be deduced from the judgment on appeal that the appeal court did not consider findings about the actual knowledge of the identity of the second to sixth defendants as persons under a duty to compensate to be necessary on legal grounds, because the claimant's mother simply did not know that the claimant as the person suffering harm could have looked to these defendants for compensation. The appeal court takes the view that the limitation period would begin to run immediately on knowledge of the harm when the person suffering harm had no knowledge at all of a possible claim to compensation and this absence of knowledge constituted the hindrance to obtaining knowledge of the persons causing harm. The appeal in law successfully contests these arguments.

The view of the appeal court cannot be supported by the decision of the *Bundesgerichtshof* of the 17th March 1966 (reference omitted) cited in the appeal judgment on this issue. That judgment takes into account the fact that in the area of § 852 of the BGB also the legal maxim that absence of knowledge of the law always and in all circumstances causes prejudice does not apply without exception. In particular it does not apply when the absence of knowledge of legal maxims and principles forms the hindrance to knowing the identity of the person obliged to compensate. It would admittedly work to the disadvantage of the person suffering harm if the identity of the person obliged to compensate was actually known and nothing was lacking for the making of the claim to compensation other than the knowledge of the legal norm which permitted proceeding against the tortfeasor. From these principles, it follows for the present case:

> If the claimant's mother had actually known the names and addresses of the second to sixth defendants and their business positions, it would not have been relevant to the running of the limitation period that she had refrained from making a claim to compensation through lack of legal knowledge. But so long as she did not know the names, addresses and positions of these defendants (and this has to be assumed here, in the absence of contrary findings for the period up to three years before the lodging of the claim), the situation is still that the limitation period did not begin to run through lack of the required knowledge of the identity of the person causing the harm. In such a state of affairs it has no legal effect whether or not the person suffering the harm had the necessary legal knowledge for the pursuit of possible claims. § 852 (1) of the BGB makes the beginning of the limitation period dependent on the required knowledge of the facts; if this is lacking, no hypothetical conclusions can be drawn as to how the person suffering the harm—on whatever grounds—would have behaved if he had had the knowledge.

Notes to Cases 61–67

1. Traffic accidents, product liability, medical malpractice: this surely must be the trilogy of tort subjects that attracts most attention these days—at any rate in terms of volume of litigation. (The trilogy would be a tetralogy but for the fact that "accidents at work" have in some systems (e.g. French, German, and to some extent in the USA) effectively been removed from the province of the law of tort. See chapter 3 section A.3., below). The practical importance of these topics is indisputable—though the first two provide some of the most often litigated. The theoretical importance of these subjects is also considerable as attested by the fact that much of the modern economic analysis of tort law has grown from the academic works dealing with these two areas of tort law. The economic point is already obvious in the pioneering judgment of Traynor J. in *Escola* v. *Coca-Cola Bottling Co. of Fresno* 150 P. 2d 436 (Cal.1944); and, nearly thirty years later, it also became a central theme in such celebrated and controversial books as Calabresi's *The Costs of Accidents* (1970). And as if all this were not enough, product liability sits uneasily on the boundary between contract and tort, in a way which makes the traditional strict dichotomy of these two parts of the law of obligations look more than usually questionable.

Not surprisingly the literature on the subject is enormous. In the US, in addition to the two major treatises of Hursh and Bailey, *American Law of Products Liability* (1974) and Furmer and Friedman's *Products Liability* (rev. edn., 1974) (both of which have regularly published supplements) the subject receives particular attention in all the textbooks. Thus Franklin and Rabin, 473–587 (a particularly good section of this excellent case-book); Epstein, 611–729 ff.; Henderson and Pearson, 707–841; Posner, 633 ff.; and Prosser, Wade and Schwartz, 696–852 (a most systematic and informative account). Outside the US the literature is poorer but growing. Waddams's *Products Liability* (Toronto, 1974) is a doctrinally interesting but now somewhat dated monograph. Fischer and Powers, *Products Liability: Cases and Materials* contains much material and thoughtful comments and questions. Miller and Lovell's *Products Liability* (Toronto, 1977) was, until recently, the only monograph in English law but Professor Stapleton's, *Product Liability* (1994) can now claim to contain one of the most doctrinally interesting accounts of this subject. Markesinis and Deakin, *Tort Law* (4th edn. 1999) gives an account of the contract and tort solutions of English law and also cites further literature, while Miller's *Product Liability and Safety Encyclopedia* (1979) addresses itself more to the practitioner (while also quoting many of the European proposals). The German law is discussed in chapter 2, section A.4(*c*), above, where one can find extensive bibliographical references to German literature. The cases reproduced here must, therefore, be read in close conjunction with the above and these notes are, for reasons of space, kept to a minimum.

2. In this area of the law more than in others, the student of German law will be irresistibly tempted to make comparisons with developments in the US. Many reasons can be adduced to explain this.

First, it is a matter of fact that German academics have used American law quite extensively in their writing in this area of tort law. The interest first manifested itself in the early 1930s when the great Ernst Rabel encouraged two of his most brilliant students—Kessler (subsequently Professor at the Yale Law School) and Wahl—to take note of the emerging American doctrines (*Die Fahrlässigkeit im nordamerikanischen Deliktsrecht* (1932) and *Vertragsansprüche Dritter im französischen Recht* (1935) published in vols. 6 and 9 of the *Beiträge zum ausländischen und internationalen Privatrecht*). By the 1960s this approach received further impetus—with the work of Professor Lorenz (in *Festschrift Nottarp* (1961), 59) leading the way—as the belief grew that the richness of American law might be of use to the emerging German law of product liability (Lorenz's many articles on the subject clearly show this influence). The American influence on current European proposals for law reform is also noticeable.

A second reason which invites comparison between German and American (but not English) law is the willingness of both systems to experiment with contractual notions and devices in an attempt to satisfy the ever-growing demands of modern consumers. Thus contractual experiments are discussed in case 43 and the concepts used are explained chapter 2, section A.4(*c*), above. This leading case may—to the approval of most commentators—have turned attention away from contract to tort; but contractual solutions—especially in the form of "implied warranties" are still alive as case 45 shows. This use of contract, on occasion, offered procedural and substantive advantages to plaintiffs; and it may still provide the better answer in certain cases of damage *to* the product (i.e. cases of purely economic loss). *Cf.* on this the decision of the US Supreme Court in *East River SS Corp.* v. *Transamerica Delaval* 476 US 858, 106 S. Ct. 2295, and decisions nos. 68–75. But it also has its drawbacks when physical injury or property damage is involved as the Americans discovered after *Henningsen* (*Henningsen* v. *Bloomfield Motors, Inc.* 161 A. 2d 69 (N.J.1960)). See *Greenman* v. *Yuba Power Prods, Inc.,* 377 P. 2d 897 (Cal.1963).

3. Treating the ultimate purchaser as a third-party beneficiary—as case 63, BGHZ 75, 75, does—can also involve an obvious fiction (see Traynor's remarks in the *Escola* case, above). But such fictions are impossible in English law where contractual warranties in the absence of any privity and contracts in favour of third parties have been denounced (until recently at any rate) as a result of a rigid adherence to the doctrine of consideration. If such notions were known to English law they would explain in a satisfactory manner cases like *Junior Books Ltd.* v. *Veitchi Co. Ltd.* [1983] AC 520, and avoid some of the problems created by that decision (*cf.* Weir, *A Casebook on Tort* (5th edn., 1983), 33–4); but to treat the ultimate consumer as a third-party beneficiary of the contract between the manufacturer and the wholesaler or retailer would involve an impossible stretching of that notion (Weir, *op. cit.,* 21).

On the other hand, American law, which has freed itself from the shackles of consideration, accepts the notion of warranty without privity; and section 2–318 of the UCC (reproduced below) expressly authorises such contractually flavoured actions. As we shall see, its use is considerable where the damage is *to* the product and the usual tort remedies are not (according to the prevailing view) appropriate or available. By means of a short digression, it is also worth noting that the French law of products liability was, for many years, based largely on the extension of the original contractual action between seller and buyer to cover even the ultimate purchaser. (On this see J Ghestin, *Conformité et garanties dans la vente* (1983) and the earlier contributions of Professors Ghestin and Viney in *La responsabilité des fabricants et distributeurs,* collection of essays published by *Economica* (1975).) The national legislation that has been inspired by the European Directive has now, of course, based liability in tort.

4. The comparison of German and American law also reveals some differences. Some, e.g. the use of civil juries, the contingent fee system of remuneration of attorneys, the absence of a developed welfare system, the role of the pro-plaintiff bar and judiciary (on which, *inter alia*, see Neely, *The Product Liability Mess* (1988))—may account for larger awards and increased litigation. (John Fleming's *The American Tort Process* (1988) admirably explains how the institutional framework in the USA has influenced the development of American tort law and made it so different from English law.) Others, concerning warning notices, for example, are on questions of emphasis in degree. Yet others may be more apparent than real. In this group one could place the discussions about the *nature* of liability. For, as we have seen in German law, it was, until recently, fault-based liability and not, as now provided by the American *Restatement (Second), Torts* § 402A (reproduced below), strict liability. In one sense it is churlish to minimise this difference between the two systems since some German writers (e.g. Kötz) have argued that the reluctance of German law to acknowledge openly a risk-based liability can only help increase costs and complicate matters in an area of the law which is in any event not known for its simplicity. On the other hand even Kötz admits that the burden of proof cast by German law is a *probatio diabolica*, in effect making this a strict liability subject. And in the USA there is by no means unanimity that the introduction of strict liability has led to a decrease in the complexity of product liability litigation. See Ver Steeg, "Strict Liability and Judicial Resources" 3 *J. Legal Studies* 217 (1974). Moreover, in practice, negligence and strict liability are almost always pleaded in the alternative in a way that would make it a mistake to assert that strict liability has completely displaced the older rules of negligence. See Rheingold, "Proof of Defect in Product Liability Cases" 38 *Tenn. L. Rev.* 325 (1971). (The main advantage for the plaintiff of winning the case on negligence rather than on strict liability is, of course, that he is entitled to claim huge punitive damages.)

5. Traditonally, in product liability cases the victim had to prove that the defect in the product which was the cause of the injury arose in the producer's organisational area, before the product left the defendant's factory. Case 66 (BGH NJW 1995, 2162) lowers further the hurdle for the victim. For in that case the BGH alleviated this difficult burden of proof by imposing on the defendant a *Befundsicherungspflicht*. This means that there is a presumption that the defect arose in the producer's organisational area unless he can prove that he took all possible and requisite measures of quality control to ensure that the product was free from defects. The term *Befundsicherungspflicht* has perplexed some commentators. Literally it signifies a duty to keep a record of the results of an investigation, such as a doctor's note of his diagnosis, a meaning quite appropriate to its function of reversing the burden of proof in cases where the defendant can adduce relevant evidence more easily than the claimant. But the term is here used to mean a duty not just to ascertain the condition of the product but also to correct it if faulty, i.e. effectively to operate an extremely good system of quality control. As the BGH said in another case: "The producer's duty to ascertain and assure the result of the investigation is neither a duty to "keep a record of the evidence", nor a (non-existent) duty of documentation. In this context *Befundsicherung* applies to all bottles being reused, not in the sense of making a list of the results of checking each bottle, but rather in the sense of establishing and operating a control procedure which permits the ascertainment of the physical condition of each bottle and ensures that, so far as technically possible, all bottles which are in any way faulty are kept out of further use." (BGH NJW 1993, 529.) Finally, one should note that the device is necessary only where a claim is brought for pain and suffering under the BGB (§ 847 BGB). The Directive, and the laws which implement it, make it clear that it is for the defendant to prove that the established defect was not present in the product when it was put into circulation. (Interesting is also the restrictive reading given to § 1 II Nr. 5 ProdHaftG—Article 7e of the Directive: the exclusion for some defects that could not be avoided according to the present state of science was limited to defects in the design of the product but did not apply to defects in its construction, *Ausreißer*).

6. Case 67 (BGH NJW 2001, 964) could be seen as a sequel to the "baby bottle" cases. In these cases the sugary content of the baby bottle caused tooth decay when the bottle was used regularly and for longer periods of time. The BGH (JZ 1995, 902) required that crystal clear warning notes

had to be attached to the product if liability was to be avoided. It also held a company liable which, although being in fact a retailer, could nevertheless be treated as if it were the producer of the product since it was the exclusive retailer (so-called *Quasi-Hersteller*) of this product (Milupa AG in that case). The decision highlights a different aspect of product liability. As was explained in chapter 2, section A.4(*c*) the codal provisions, unlike the Directive, do not adequately reflect that the duties imposed in the context of product liability are primarily addressed to the manufacturer and not to the individual employee or manager. Thus, the process of production has to be organised in such a way as to ensure that dangerous products are not put into circulation. Clearly, it is impossible for an individual employee to comply with these requirements. Against this background the interesting question arises whether employees can, nevertheless, be held liable. For the reason already given, the BGH used to reject such a possibility. (See e.g. BGH ZIP 1987, 1260.) However, in BGH NJW 1992, 1039 (case 65) the court, arguably, established two new principles. First the rules of product liability (*Produzentenhaftung*) under § 823 I BGB, (namely the reversed burden of proof for a deficient organisation of the production process) apply also to minor companies—in this instance, a catering company. Secondly, and this is important in the present context, it held that an employee could also be liable if the defect occurred in his sphere of responsibility. This was a qualified liability in so far as the burden of proof for fault was not reversed for the employee (the chef of the catering company in that case). In BGH NJW 2001, 964 the court confirmed this line of reasoning in respect of an employee (who had a higher position in the company) and the management without clarifying the exact conditions of their liability. The decision, although highly legalistic in tone, is nevertheless noteworthy for two reasons that are not immediately apparent from its wording. First of all the external liability of employees of a company is not self-evident. (*Cf.* Brüggemeier *ZIP* 2001, 381, with references, who suggests that such liability should be subsidiary as is the case of civil servants under § 839 BGB). Secondly, one must note the potentially far-reaching implications of this decision. For if one accepts that both management and employees may be liable under the heading of product liability, the limitation period (§ 852 I BGB, three years; now contained in §§ 195, 199 I BGB, see ch. 1 section 10) can in practice be considerably prolonged. In the present case the Court of Appeal found that the limitation period of the action against the company had run out on 31 December 1988. But it also held that the action against the managers and the (appropriate) employee had also become time-barred as the plaintiff knew at an early stage of the injuries caused by the sugary tee in the baby bottle. The BGH quashed this decision and explained that for the limitation period to commence, it was not sufficient to know that the damage was caused by the company's product. In addition, it was necessary to show that the victim knew the identity, function in the company, and address of the potential defendant. (The rule that the limitation period may be different for each severally liable debtor is contained in § 425 II BGB.) The claimant does not even have to undertake any special effort to find this out, but can rely on channels of information open to everyone. Given that the defendant/employee may be able to claim an indemnity from his employer (under the principles contained in case 110, below), one can thus see how, in effect, the present decision undermines the limitation period of three years that affects the company itself. We are thus confronted here by yet another judicial extension of product liability in the interest of the "consumer". This is a noteworthy observation. For one can try to imagine how the CBI or some other such organisation would react to a similar decision handed down by the House of Lords. Almost certainly, there would be an outcry, condemning the effect that such a decision would have on the competitiveness of British industry. Perusing the German Press, one found no such reaction. Is this because the British industrialists are accustomed to a legal regime that is solicitous of their interests or is it because its German counterpart has found ways of coping with the economic consequences of such decisions?

7. The classifications made in German law between defect in construction (case 61, BGHZ 51, 91, and 68, BGHZ 67, 359), defect in design, defect in marketing (warnings etc.) (case 62, BGHZ 59, 172), and development risks have exact equivalents in American law. Reference must thus be made to the cases extracted and noted in the case-books quoted above, § 1, and in the early exposition of German law (above, chapter 2, section A.4(*c*)).

16. DAMAGE CAUSED *TO* THE PRODUCT

Case 68

BUNDESGERICHTSHOF (EIGHTH CIVIL SENATE) 24 NOVEMBER 1976
BGHZ 67, 359 = NJW 1977, 379 = JZ 1977, 343 (with critical notes
by M Lieb and B Rengier = VERSR 1977, 358)

Facts

The D firm—insured by the plaintiff company—were manufacturers among other things of tin covers for transformers. The defendant produces cleansing and degreasing apparatus for industrial products, in which through heating and evaporation perchlorhylene oil is washed out and separated from the parts to be cleansed. A ballcock connected to a switch, which the defendant alleges to have obtained from a foreign supplier, prevents the filaments, normally covered with fluid, from being exposed to the air.

After the D firm had, on 29 January 1969, ordered such cleansing apparatus for about DM 20,000, the defendant confirmed the order on 4 February 1969 with the addition: "Warranty: according to our enclosed conditions of sale and delivery."

No. VIII of those conditions of delivery—in so far as is relevant here—runs as follows:

VIII. liability for defective delivery:

1. All those parts are to be made good or replaced without charge at our choice to be exercised fairly, which within twelve months of the delivery are proved unusable or the usefulness of which is seriously affected in consequence of circumstances existing before the passing of the risk—in particular owing to defective design, inferior materials, or defective construction . . .

9. Further claims of the buyer or the party giving the order, in particular a claim for compensation for damage caused not to the delivered object itself but by the latter indirectly will in no case be accepted by us.

After the apparatus had been set up and put into operation at the beginning of June 1969 the used oil in the apparatus ignited because a switch operated by a ballcock had not switched off the filaments in time and they had become overheated. The plaintiff company, which had paid to the D firm, its insured, a sum of DM 70,971, made a claim for compensation against the defendant on the ground that the switch had failed in consequence of a defect in manufacture or construction; the D firm had had to spend that amount for the repair of the cleansing and electrical apparatus as well as the elimination of corrosion of the metal stocks. The defendant stated that the fire had happened only through an excessive supply of petroleum, and denied that it was liable for the damage caused by the fire, and in addition points to the formal exclusion of liability for all claims for compensation and in that respect invokes the operation of prescription in that the order for payment was first made on 23 June 1972.

Both courts below rejected the claim. Upon the plaintiff company's application for review, the judgment of the court was quashed and the case referred back to the Court of Appeal for the following

Reasons

I. ...

II. ...

1. The decision of the Court of Appeal must be opposed in the result to the effect that the plaintiff company's claims in contract for damages did not exist according to its pleadings, because they were time-barred under § 477 BGB. [Details follow.]

2. On the other hand, the further considerations of the Court of Appeal that also from the delictual point of view the plaintiff's action is without foundation according to its own pleadings, does not stand up to legal examination.

(*a*) An objective breach of duty by the defendant causing damage resulting from a fire by delivering defective cleansing apparatus has been sufficiently established by the plaintiff company and proved by experts. [Details follow.]

(*b*) Since to this extent the plaintiff company claims against the defendant as the producer of the apparatus, it was for the latter, regarded from the point of view of so-called "product liability", to exculpate itself by proving absence of fault, a circumstance that lay entirely within its sphere of influence and of which the plaintiff who could rely only on conjecture, could not be unaware (BGHZ 51, 91; Senate judgments of 28 September 1970—VIII ZR 166/68 = WM 1970, 1418, 1420—LM BGB § 433 no. 36 and of 24 November 1971—ZR 81/70 = WM 1972, 106 = NJW 1972, 251). In this connection, it can be assumed in favour of the defendant that the ballcock switch, the failure of which, according to the plaintiff's account, started the fire, was obtained from a third party and only incorporated in the apparatus manufactured by it. If that switch was of itself free from defect, but its performance was too weak or otherwise unsuited for the apparatus, it is a matter of a so-called defect of the construction, characteristic "product liability" (see judgment of 20 September 1970). But even if there was nothing wrong with the construction and only the switch showed a defect, the defendant would be required—without prejudice to the question which additional claims the plaintiff might perhaps have against the producer of the switch—to exculpate himself from any fault in respect of such defect of production; for after the defendant ordered and incorporated this switch which was necessary for the operational safety of the apparatus to be sold, the responsibility for a defect-free working of the switch—as between the parties—fell exclusively within the ambit of the defendant, who alone could control the workmanship and incorporation of the switch, whereas the D firm was deprived of such a possibility of examining it.

(*c*) The Court of Appeal's view based on that of the Landgericht, that the "legal institution of product liability" had been developed for a disposition of goods involving several stages and could not therefore be applied if—as here—direct contractual relations existed between producer and ultimate consumer, is at variance with the law. A genuine concurrence existed between a claim for damages for breach of contract and that for a tort, with the consequence that each claim follows its own legal rules and the injured party is, as a matter of principle, free to choose the basis on which to put forward his claim. In particular he is not prevented from falling back on delictual liability, if contractual claims are no longer available either because the period of limitation has run out or because an exemption clause is restricted to contractual liability (*cf.* the applicability of § 852 BGB alongside of § 477 BGB dealt with in the judgment of the Senate of 24 May 1976 = BGHZ

66, 315 = WM 1976, 839). If the injured party bases his claim on a tort of the producer, the mere circumstance that direct contractual relations exist between them or in any case have existed, does not exclude the application of the principles of concurring the reversal of the burden of proof of fault developed for claims against a producer (*cf.* also the judgment of the Senate of 28 September 1970—VIII ZR 166/68). In so far as in this connection Count von Westphalen in his criticism (*BB* 1976, 1097) of the judgment of the Senate of 24 May 1976 openly expresses the opinion that the Senate, on facts like the present, has retreated from the principles of evidence governing product liability, overlooks the fact that the subject of the dispute then decided was a typical case of a claim arising out of a chain of dealings against a firm which had neither manufactured the product nor had distributed it as a detached agency of the manufacturing firm, and that for this reason there was no room to introduce the principles of product liability; that was also to be deduced from the unabridged statement of facts in the judgment reported in WM 1976, 839.

(*d*) Contrary to the view of the Court of Appeal the plaintiff has also alleged in sufficient detail the existence of the property of the D firm and damage resulting from it. [Details follow.]

(*e*) The Court of Appeal declares as regards the cost of repairing the cleansing apparatus, that in any case there was no interference with property, because, according to the plaintiff's statement, the apparatus was originally delivered in a defective condition and therefore the D firm was never the possessor or owner of an object free from defects. This view is based on a mistake of law. It is indeed correct that both the Reichsgericht (RG JW 1905, 367) and the Bundesgerichtshof (BGHZ 39, 366) denied a claim of the owner of a building for damage to property based on the defective erection of a building (§ 823 I BGB) in respect of that particular building, when the materials used in the building were defective and when, with the completion of each phase, each time a further defectively produced portion passed into the landowner's ownership (*cf.* also OLG Karlsruhe 1956, 913; Schäfer in *Staudinger, BGB*, 10/11 edn. § 823, n. 49). It is essential in these cases that the defect in the object transferred was inherent beforehand to the object as such; it was therefore completely useless to the owner from the start and that the defect was identical with the damage complained of (*cf.* Duns/Kraus, *Haftung für schädliche Ware* (1969) p. 66). In such a case the damage to an object of another is in fact already excluded conceptually; only economic damage exists for which § 823 I BGB does not provide redress (BGHZ, above).

That is however not so here. Apart altogether from the fact that the above-mentioned considerations of the Court of Appeal concern only the damage to the cleansing apparatus itself, but not the damage caused by the fire to other property of the D firm, the defendant here had transferred to the D firm the ownership of an apparatus which was otherwise free from fault and only contained a regulating device which was defective as regards a limited function—the failure of which caused further damage to the whole apparatus after ownership has passed. In such a case it does not matter that from the formal point of view the purchaser only acquired property which was defective at the outset (*cf.* Diederichsen, *VersR* 1971, 1078, 1098; Schlechtriem, *VersR* 1973, 581, 589). Instead, it is decisive that the danger arising from the accompanying delivery of the switch resulted in damage exceeding that represented by the defect only after title had passed and thereby the property of the purchaser, otherwise from defect. (Duns and Kraus, *op. cit.*, 66; Schmidt-Salzer, *Entscheidungssammlung Produkthaftung*, 30 ff.). In cases of that kind—

especially when the injured party has acquired the ownership on the basis of a contract of sale—there is no reason to restrain him from having recourse to claims in tort. That is true all the more so since, if the injured party wishes to retain the apparatus (perhaps in order to maintain production) and only wants compensation for the cost of repairs, he cannot rely on a contractual claim to compensation because the law of warranties in sale (§§ 459 ff. BGB) does not provide for damages beyond the express warranties of quality (§§ 463, 480 II BGB). Moreover, claims for breach of contract by a positive act (*positive Vertragsverletzung*), arising out of the delivery of defective objects, are restricted to compensation for damage caused to other legally protected interests but do not cover damage to the object of the sale itself [reference]; thus, to that extent the buyer would be largely without a remedy if he could not fall back on claims in tort.

The Senate does not fail to recognize that in some cases the boundary may be difficult to draw between a defect affecting the transferred object as a whole and a limited defect which later on causes new damage to the object transferred which was otherwise free from defect, as for instance when what was to begin with a limited defect expands like a "creeping disease" and afterwards takes hold of the entire object (*cf.* Schlechtriem, *op. cit.* 589; Duns/Kraus, *op. cit.*, 66 fn. 7). In the present case it is not necessary to set down unambiguous criteria for delimiting the two given the small value of the ballcock and the total value of the cleansing apparatus sold for some DM 20,000.

(*f*) Finally, the claim for compensation put forward by the plaintiff, in so far as it is based on tort, is not excluded on legal grounds. The short period of limitation of § 477 BGB is not applicable to such a claim (see judgment of this Senate of 24 May 1976—ZR 10/74). The same applies to the disclaimer of liability regulated in section VIII no. 9 of the defendant's general conditions of delivery, which it may be assumed in the defendant's favour, were incorporated in the contract. Whether such a disclaimer also includes claims in tort, in so far as they are connected with the defective performance, is a question of interpretation in the light of the individual case (*cf.* BGH judgment of 23 April 1970—VII ZR 150/68 = JZ 1970, 903). Since the Court of Appeal—consistently with its point of view—did not attempt an interpretation of the general delivery conditions, this Senate can itself interpret this clause (see Senate judgment of 25 June 1975—VIII ZR 244/73 = WM 1975, 895 = NJW 1974, 1693). For this purpose it must be taken into account not only that exemption clauses being exceptions from liability provided by dispositive law—must in principle be construed narrowly, but also in the present case that according to the so-called "obscurity rule" any remaining doubts as to the extent of the provisions contained in the general conditions of trade must be interpreted against the party who drafted them and makes use of them. In the present case the exemption clause is found in a section of the general conditions of trade which is headed "Liability for defects in delivery" and which regulated in particular the contractual warranty by the seller, and therefore by modifying §§ 450 ff. BGB and §§ 377 ff. HGB regulates the contractual claims for a warranty. It need not be decided whether the buyer's or contracting party's disclaimer which is mentioned only in no. 9 also includes claims for compensation for breach of contract by positive act arising from a defective delivery. In any case there is no sufficiently clear provision that claims for a blameworthy injury to the legal interests protected by § 823 I BGB are to be excluded. If this had been the defendant's intention, it ought to have been indicated to the D firm by an unambiguously formulated clause that the latter's legal position was being further restricted to an appreciable degree, for example as regards any claims arising from a negligent bodily injury or a destructive threatening the existence of an entire business.

In so far as this Senate stated in the decision BGHZ 64, 355 that the exclusion of liability contained in section II no. 5 of the "General Conditions for the supply of Electrical Power from the Low Tension Network (AVB)", embraces not only contractual but also delictual claims for damage arising from the break in the supply of current, those statements relate to a state of facts and interests which is not comparable with the present case. Quite apart from the fact that the AVB are regarded as a legal enactment (BGHZ 9, 390) and that for this reason the so-called "obscurity rule" cannot be invoked for its interpretation (*cf.* judgment of the Senate of 21 October 1958—VIII ZR 145/57 = NJW 1959, 38), the exclusion of liability in no. II 5 AVB takes account of the circumstance that the energy undertakings can only perform the task allotted to them of providing the public with cheap current, if they are as far as possible exempt from liability; this particular task demands the widest possible exemption from liability with the consequence that—as far as admissible—claims for compensation are included in whatever legal form (judgment of this Senate of 9 June 1959—VIII ZR 61/58 = NJW 1959, 1423 = LM BGB § 138 [Cc] no. 2). On the other hand in the present case, which involves a shift from the seller to the buyer by means of general trade conditions, these considerations do not apply.

III. The decision of the dispute depends therefore on whether the plaintiff succeeds in proving that a defective or unsuitable switch caused the fire. To that extent the dispute requires a further clarification of facts.

Case 69

BUNDESGERICHTSHOF (EIGHTH CIVIL SENATE) 11 JANUARY 1978
NJW 1978, 1051 = JR 1978, 240

Facts

The defendant ran a sandpit. On 1 February 1973 she delivered to the plaintiff six cubic metres of sand which was intended to be used as the outer cladding to the plaintiff's newly constructed house. The plaintiff had the outer cladding applied in spring 1973, and subsequently damage in the cladding began to appear which were attributable to certain mineral impurities present in the sand delivered by the defendant. Alleging that the defendant had quarried the impure sand, which was unsuitable for use as an outer cladding, out of a new sandpit without first examining it to see whether it was pure, the plaintiff brought a claim for compensation against the defendant on 8 January 1974. Notice of the claim was served upon the defendant on 21 February 1974. The LG rejected the claim on the grounds that it was barred by the statute of limitations. The OLG rejected the plaintiff's appeal. The permitted appeal to the BGH was likewise unsuccessful.

For the following

Reasons

[In Point **I**, the court agreed with the conclusion of the OLG that the plaintiff had no claim against the defendant in respect of the delivery of the impure and therefore defective sand based on the statutory guarantees applicable to the sale of goods, either because such a claim was not possible, or because it was no longer possible since the time limit for bringing the action had expired (§ 477 BGB).]

II. Finally, the plaintiff also has no claim based on *damage to his property* (§ 823 I BGB) which is not subject to brief limitation periods and which is consequently not out of time (§ 852 BGB [references omitted]). The question which has been debated in the literature and which the plaintiff's application places at the forefront of this case concerns the circumstances in which a client has claims against a building contractor for damage to his property based on defects in the construction of a building. Such a general question, however, is not at issue here because the defendant was not working as a building contractor but had only delivered the defective sand on the basis of a contract of sale, and it was the plaintiff who then used the sand, mixed with other building materials, to apply the cladding to his house which was previously unclad [references omitted]. Even the judgment of this court of 24 November 1976 (BGHZ 67, 359 [other references omitted]) and the question which arose in that case as to whether a purchaser, who had bought a technical installation from the seller which contained no defects, with the exception of a faulty safety switch, could bring a claim against the seller when the failure of the switch resulted in damage to the installation itself, concerns an entirely different set of factual circumstances which do not apply here.

What is decisive here is that according to the findings of the OLG, which are correct in law, the plaintiff's building, which previously did not have an external cladding, did not suffer a reduction in value as compared to what it was previously worth, as regards either its physical substance or use as a dwelling house. Accordingly, the present case is to be distinguished also from factual circumstances which were present in the judgment of the BGH of 6 November 1963 (BB 1964, 65). The plaintiff's application is incorrect on this point. For that case involved a finished house which already had an outer cladding, but which subsequently suffered a reduction in its value as a result of damage from smoke and soot emanating from neighbouring land. The financial burden suffered by the plaintiff, as a consequence of what he argued was the need to remove the cladding, therefore represents pure economic loss and therefore represents an interference with an interest which is not protected by § 823 I BGB. Since, moreover, the mere fact of delivering what was, from the beginning, defective sand does not in itself represent property damage to this building material, then the only remaining question is whether the plaintiff has suffered property damage as regards those building materials (chalk, cement) which originally belonged to him and which were mixed with the defective sand to form the outer cladding, and which consequently became worthless. The OLG correctly denied this claim. The plaintiff overlooks the fact that when the outer cladding was manufactured, his original property interest in the building materials which he provided lapsed as a consequence of the mingling (§ 948 BGB) and the processing (§ 950 BGB) of the materials, and that he acquired a new, albeit impaired, property interest in the cladding material. Therefore there is no loss which can be defined as property damage affecting the plaintiff in respect of which he could claim compensation under § 823 I BGB [reference omitted].

Case 70

BUNDESGERICHTSHOF (EIGHTH CIVIL SENATE) 5 JULY 1978
NJW 1978, 2241 = JR 1979, 199

On 21 January 1975 the plaintiff bought a used motor car from the defendant. A so-called "Order Form" in standard form provided that the motor car was being delivered as "used, as inspected, every warranty being excluded". A handwritten addition noted ". . . is being delivered in an unexceptionable technical condition". On the reverse side of the form the defendant's general conditions of trade were set out which are provided in Article VII [Warranties].

1. No warranty is given in respect of the objects sold. This does not apply if and to the extent that the seller has provided a warranty in writing by a separate letter of guarantee.

2. No right exists to demand a return of the price in return for the goods [*Wandelung*], a reduction of the price [*Minderung*] or damages.

On 28 March 1975 the plaintiff, while driving the motor car, suffered an accident due to a blow-out of a rear tyre which was not of the type required by law to be fitted to this type of car. He sued the defendant for damages. The latter pleaded *inter alia* that the period of limitation had run.

The Court of First Instance and the Court of Appeal of Bamberg allowed the claim. A second appeal was rejected for the following

Reasons

I. The appeal is rejected. The appellant is correct, it must be admitted, in objecting to the view of the Court of Appeal that the defendant is liable to pay damages to the plaintiff under § 463 I BGB. For that claim is caught by the period of limitation, contrary to the opinion of the Court of Appeal.

1. (*a*) The Court of Appeal is right in regarding the statement that the motor car was being delivered in an unexceptional technical condition as a guarantee of a quality in the meaning of § 459 II BGB, i.e. as a guarantee that at the time of delivery the vehicle is technically in order, ready to be used and safe in operation. The question as to whether such details contained in a contract of sale of the object sold only serve to describe it (§ 459 I BGB) or whether they warrant a certain quality (§ 459 II BGB) is a matter of factual appreciation in the individual case, provided that—as in the present case—the statements are not of the type which are normally made in connection with such transactions. The interpretation reached by the Court of Appeal is possible, conforms to the principles laid down by the practice of the courts concerning the assurance of the existence of certain qualities [references], and therefore binds this court. Moreover it is convincing. A purchaser from an appointed dealer of a certain manufacturer of a used car of this particular make is interested, above all, that the car should at least conform to the official rules for permitting the car to be used on the roads (§§ 18 ff. of the Decree concerning the Admission of Motor Vehicles for Use on Roads) and can be put into operation without any hesitation. If the dealer in used cars, contrary to the practice in the trade with second-hand cars, confirms in addition that the car's condition is technically unexceptionable, it is at least likely that he undertakes thereby to be responsible for any possible damage, if those conditions are not present. The argument of the appellant is inapposite to the effect that

it cannot possibly be assumed that the defendant intended to warrant the technically unexceptionable condition of *all* parts of the used car, seeing that thereby the plaintiff would be in a much more advantageous position than if he had bought a new car. Clearly the Court of Appeal did not wish to attribute to the contractual statements of the defendant such an extensive meaning; it interpreted them and could interpret them to warrant *operational readiness and safety* . . .

Since by fitting tyres which did not conform to the permit for operating the car, the permit had become invalid (§§ 18(1), 19(2), 21 of the Decree concerning the Admission of Motor Vehicles for Use on Roads) and since, moreover, the vehicle . . . fitted with tyres which did not comply with the legal requirement, was no longer operationally safe, the defendant is liable to pay to the plaintiff damages for having failed to perform the contract (§ 463 first sentence BGB).

(*b*) The Court of Appeal is also correct in holding that the liability of the defendant for promised qualities has not been excluded either by the standard clause "used, as inspected, every warranty being excluded" or by the exemption clause of the general conditions of trade reproduced on the reverse side of the standard contract. This Division has stated repeatedly that an exemption clause in a standard contract does not affect the liability of a seller for the absence of stipulated qualities [references]. If the seller is unwilling to remain subject to the risk of liability in accordance with the provisions of the law, he must indicate this unequivocally and in a manner intelligible to the buyer—with particular reference to the promises made—in the text of the contract or otherwise at the conclusion of the contract [reference]. This had not happened in the present case. Therefore, the defendant cannot plead either that his declaration, which amounts to a stipulation as to quality, was not made in the form prescribed by Article VII no. 1 of its general conditions of trade (". . . by a separate letter of guarantee") [reference].

2. However, the claims for damages available to the plaintiff under § 463 I BGB are caught by the period of limitation. The Court of Appeal believes that the period of limitation amounting to six months according to § 477 I BGB had only begun to run when the plaintiff was able to perceive the cause of the accident with the necessary degree of certainty following the receipt on 23 September 1975 of the written information by the manufacturer of the tyre. However, this view of the law is erroneous.

(*a*) It is true that this Division has raised the question several times—although it was not decisive in the final resort—whether in certain circumstances in order to prevent gross injustice or a curtailment of buyers' rights the period of limitation for claims for damages in respect of warranties arising out of a sale, instead of beginning to run from the delivery of the object sold, should not start at a later moment only, e.g. when the damage occurred, when the buyer could become aware of it, or quite generally when it becomes possible in the individual case to raise such claims so as to interrupt the period of limitation [references]. These considerations, however, concerned without exception the question of liability for damage arising out of defects of the goods sold (*Mangelfolgeschäden*). In typical cases this often manifests itself in other legally protected assets of the buyer only a considerable time after the object sold has been delivered, or the damage may only occur at a later time.

In the present case, however, the issue is exclusively one of damages for *failure to perform*. It is unnecessary to dilate on this in respect of costs of repair, reduced value, and loss of use; the same applies to the cost of expert opinions relating to the existence of defects, for these are necessarily the consequences of defects, they are directly connected with remedying the defects, and—like profits lost as a result of the defects [references]—they reduce the value of the consideration received by the buyer in return for the price [reference].

(b) It need not be decided here as to whether to this extent, despite the clear wording of § 477 I BGB, a case exists in certain circumstances for postponing to a later date the moment when the period of limitation begins to run [references]. For even if this were to be assumed in favour of the plaintiff, the time for bringing a claim would have passed . . .

II. Since the contractual claims of the plaintiff against the defendant are caught by the period of limitation, the reasons given by the Court of Appeal do not support the decision under appeal. However, the decision is right for different reasons. The claim is well founded in tort (§ 823 I BGB); in this respect the defence that the period of limitation has run is ineffective, since the claim in tort is not subject to the short period of limitation [reference].

1. The Court of Appeal expresses doubts as to whether an action in tort lies—without going into details—because the plaintiff had acquired the motor car in a defective condition. His property was threatened from the outset with the danger of further losses through an accident. The fact that this threat had materialized did not constitute a separate violation of property. This view cannot be accepted.

(a) It is true that in the decision referred to by the Court of Appeal [reference] the Bundesgerichtshof rejected the claim of the owner of a building based on the violation of his property because the building has been badly constructed (§ 823 I BGB); it rejected the claim in respect of this building in particular, if the materials used for the building were defective and if, as the building work progressed, each time another defectively constructed section became the property of the owner of land [reference]. These cases are characterised by the fact that the defect of the object delivered was inherent in it as a whole, that the latter was therefore altogether useless to the owner from the beginning and that the defect was identical with the damages claimed [reference].

(b) With reference to this case, this Division in its decision of 24 November 1976 [case 48, above] has distinguished the case where the seller transferred to the buyer title in an object which was unexceptionable in general and merely included a defective control instrument (a safety switch)—the function of which was limited—the failure of which after title has passed caused further damage to the installation as a whole. In that case this Division accepted that property had been damaged illegally. It regarded as decisive that the cause of the danger represented by the contemporaneous supply of a defective switch had only materialised in damage exceeding the defect itself after title had passed and that as a result the property of the buyer, which was in every other respect free from defects, had been damaged as a whole. Rengier [reference] and Schubert [reference] criticize this decision on the ground that even small, limited defects render the entire object sold defective from the outset, as well as useless having regard to the danger of its destruction connected therewith. Weitnauer [reference] does not deny that property has been violated—illegally on the facts—but argues that a subsequent destruction of the installation does not constitute damage; in his opinion the latter event had only laid bare damage which had occurred previously. The value of an installation, the self-destruction of which as a result of a defect could be expected, was "nil" from the beginning.

These objections—which are substantially identical—are not convincing in the opinion of this Division and do not persuade it to abandon its position in [reference]. Above all, it is not correct that in commerce a danger-ridden installation is treated as valueless. This might perhaps be so if the defect in question is absolutely incapable of detection and must lead to the destruction of the entire installation. No such case is in issue here. As Rengier and Schubert have pointed out, it may be difficult in individual cases to distinguish between a defect which affects the object transferred in its entirety from the beginning and a limited defect which only later on caused additional damage to an object which is otherwise free from defect. This Division has already stressed this in its decision of 24 November 1976 [reference], but the unequivocal facts of that case did not make it necessary to establish detailed criteria of delimitation. This Division is also not persuaded by the view of Rengier and Schubert that in allowing a claim in tort, the Bundesgerichtshof undermines the provisions of the law of sale concerning damages for non-performance (§ 463 BGB) as well as the rule concerning the limitation of this action laid down in § 477 BGB. A real concurrence of actions exists between the claim for damages for breach of contract and that in tort; in the latter case—leaving aside the special aspects of products liability—the claimant bears the burden of proof that the tort-feasor is to be blamed, unlike in the case of a claim in contract (§ 282 BGB). It follows that each of these two claims is governed by its own rules [reference]. In cases such as that which this Division had to decide [reference] no reason exists for denying the injured party recourse to claims in tort and thus for placing the party causing the damage in a better position than a third party who had incorporated a defective individual part into an object of a sale after its delivery to the buyer which led to the destruction of the latter.

(c) The case to be decided now—damage to a purchased motor vehicle arising out of an accident due to the fitting of a tyre contrary to the regulations—must in the opinion of this Division be treated similarly. On the one hand, the motor car which the plaintiff bought from the defendant was defective as far as the rear tyres were concerned. On the other hand, the car as a whole remained a valuable asset. Only after ownership had passed, a cause of danger resulting from this defect resulted in different and much higher damage compared with the original defect when an accident occurred in actual circulation. If the course of events had been different, especially if the tyres had been changed in time, this damage, which is different in substance from that of having tyres fitted which were contrary to the regulations, would have been avoided. Therefore it must be held that the defendant has violated the plaintiff's property illegally ... It would seem that also the Sixth Division of the Bundesgerichtshof in its decision of 30 May 1978 [reference], which is to be published, proceeded from the above-mentioned view of this Division.

2. (a) [The court considered the culpability of the defendant] ...

(b) [The court considered the contributory negligence of the plaintiff] ...

3. Finally, faced with a claim for damages based on tort (§ 823 I BGB) the defendant cannot rely either on the exemption clause in the standard contract form (Article VII of the defendant's general conditions of trade) and on the fact that the plaintiff bought the vehicle "as inspected". It is true that in all trade with second-hand cars a very wide exclusion of liability accords with the customs of this branch of business; this Division has

described it as "more or less a requirement of economic reason" [reference]. On the other hand, in the present case the defendant gave an express assurance by a personal statement that the used car was in an "unexceptional technical condition". If the defendant also intended to exclude similar claims for damages based on tort, thus rendering his assurance largely ineffective in this area of liability and therefore of no value for this buyer, he should have stated this unequivocally. The simple reference, made in standard form in connection with the arrangement concerning contractual warranties to the effect that "no right exists to demand . . . damages" is certainly insufficient to embrace such an extensive exclusion of liability, having regard to the special features of the present case. The further question can remain undecided as to whether generally, even in the absence of special assurances, exemption clauses of the kind employed here in the trade with second-hand cars also cover claims for damages in tort [reference].

Case 71

BUNDESGERICHTSHOF (SIXTH CIVIL SENATE) 18 JANUARY 1983
BGHZ 86, 256 = NJW 1983, 810 = JZ 1983, 499

A motor car manufactured by the defendant was sold by the L garage to the plaintiff in February 1976. The throttle on this car was defective in that the accelerator-pedal did not always spring back after being depressed. On 12 May 1976 the plaintiff tried to repair it, but in vain. In June 1976 the gas-pedal broke off and he installed another pedal of his own devising.

On 5 July 1976 the plaintiff had an accident in B, allegedly because the car accelerated after he had removed his foot from the pedal. The front of the car was damaged. The plaintiff had the car repaired, and a new gas-pedal from the factory was installed. A few weeks later there was another accident when the car struck a fence while being reversed by the plaintiff's wife, then his fiancée. This accident also, according to the plaintiff, was due to the fact that the vehicle accelerated unexpectedly because the gas-pedal stuck. This time it was the rear end of the car which was damaged. The cost of repairs to the plaintiff's car on these two occasions totalled DM 3,742.

[Here follow technical details of the defect, according to the two expert reports procured by the plaintiff.]

The plaintiff argues that the damage was due to a defect in construction and that the defendant is liable therefore: in respect of the repairs to his car and the garden fence, as well as the cost of the two expert reports, he claims a total of DM 4,443. The Landgericht rejected his claim for the cost of repairing the car (in the amount of DM 3,742). The plaintiff's appeal was dismissed. On his further appeal to this court, the decision below is reversed and the case remanded.

Reasons

The judgment of the Court of Appeal is wrong in law.

1. Certainly the Court of Appeal was right to hold that where a purchased chattel suffers damage because of the faulty construction or manufacture of a component part, its purchaser may have a claim in tort against the manufacturer on the basis of an invasion of his rights as property-owner (§ 823 I BGB).

(*a*) It is true that tortious duties are not imposed, like guarantees in the law of sales, in order to protect a contractor's expectations of utility and value in the acquisition of an undefective thing (see BGHZ 77, 215, 218 with references; BGHZ 80, 186, 188). They rather relate to the interest which people have in the integrity of their belongings or possessions, in not having them adversely affected by the chattel which the manufacturer puts into commerce (*Integritätsinteresse*). Such tortious duties to guard against damage or disturbance may be imposed on the manufacturer not only as regards other property of the acquirer which may be imperilled by faults in construction or production of the manufactured item, but also as regards that item itself. In principle, the purchaser's interest in having the purchased item undamaged and undisturbed is as much worth protection as his interest in the safety of the rest of his property; the manufacturer must therefore respect this interest as well (see Brüggemeier *WM* 1982, 1294, 1303). Accordingly, it is not a precondition of tortious liability that other goods or interests of the consumer or of third parties should necessarily have been affected by the thing which is put into commerce with a defective component (*contra*, Schlechtriem [reference omitted]). The manufacturer may be held liable to the consumer in tort if the impairment or disturbance of the manufactured item constitutes harm which it was the manufacturer's duty under the law of tort to avoid out of respect for the interest of the owner or possessor in the safety of his property.

(*b*) Where the loss due to the defective nature of the thing simply reflects the acquirer's interest in its utility and value, the case is different, for as we have said, duties in tort are not imposed in order to reinforce the purchaser's expectation that he will have the value and use of an object without a defect. This expectation is protected by the law of contract exclusively, save in cases under § 826 BGB where the harm is caused deliberately. It would be wrong to say that whenever a person acquires a defective thing his rights as owner are thereby invaded, and thus invoke the law of tort. Such harm cannot, as is generally acknowledged, ground a claim in tort (see RG JW 1905, 367, 368; compare BGHZ 39, 366; 55, 392; 67, 359, 364; BGH judgments of 11 Jan. 1978, NJW 1978, 1051; 5 July 1978, NJW 1978, 2241, 2242). If the only harm in issue is the undervalue due to the original defect and existing from the time of acquisition, that is simply a case of disappointed contractual expectations, and the law of tort has no role to play (so Duns/Kraus, *Haftung für schädliche Waren* (1969), 66). But the harm may not be *substantially identical* (*stoffgleich*) with the undervalue of the thing in that the defect impairs the owner's interest in its value and usability; it may take the form of an invasion of the consumer's interest in the integrity of his property and possessions which the manufacturer may in the circumstances be under a duty to respect. The manufacturer can then in principle be subjected to delictual products liability, and this is so even when there is a concurrent contractual claim under the law of warranty or replacement [references omitted], for it is accepted law that the rules of tort and contract apply concurrently and independently neither excluding the other (BGHZ 67, 359, 362; constant holding).

Of course liability in tort must not be permitted to unhinge the law of contract. But that will not happen in cases like the present if tort liability is carefully restricted to the integrity interest, appropriately distinguished in each case from the interest in usability and value. There is no conflict with the refusal of courts to impose liability in damages for positive breach of contract in cases of so-called consequential loss due to defects except where the purchaser has suffered damage to property other than the purchased item (BGHZ 77, 215, 217; so, too, for the contract of services, BGH 4 March 1971, NJW 1971,

1131, not reported on this point in BGHZ 55, 392). This judicial extension of warranties in sales (§§ 459 ff. BGB) was undertaken in order to reinforce, not to exclude, in cases where a special relationship existed, the protection of integrity provided by the law of tort. The tort liability of the supplier or manufacturer for damage due to defects in the purchased thing is not thereby blocked off (*contra*, apparently, Diederichsen, *NJW* 1978, 1281, 1286 [other references omitted]).

2. We realise that there will occasionally be practical difficulties in distinguishing the case where the harm in suit is substantially identical with the diminution in value of the thing due to an original defect which, as we have said, should be dealt with by the law of contract, from the case, subject to the law of tort where the damage or disturbance to the thing, defective owing to the manufacturer's negligence, goes beyond the owner or possessor's interest in the usability and value of the thing and affects his interest in the integrity of his property. Sometimes the defect will be so radical that from the very beginning the thing is really worthless and that therefore the "damage" to the thing when the defect manifests itself is "substantially identical" (see the cases in RG JW 1905, 367 and BGHZ 39, 366). Such cases will be relatively rare. Much commoner will be the case where the defect originally affects a more or less distinct part of the thing. Even so, one must find criteria of distinction which are of practical utility [reference omitted].

(*a*) In BGHZ 67, 359 the thermostat in a dry-cleaning machine was defective and unable to perform its safety function with the result that the machine overheated and burnt out. The Eighth Civil Senate allowed a claim in tort essentially because the defective thermostat was functionally distinct and, in relation to the machine as a whole, relatively trivial in value. These criteria may or may not be capable of extrapolation beyond the facts of that case [references omitted], but as the court below clearly recognized, they certainly cannot of themselves determine when the supplier or manufacturer of a partially defective product is liable. The manufacturer's liability cannot depend solely on the relatively accidental consideration of how the component parts are put together [references omitted]. But it is clear that the Eighth Civil Senate was dealing only with the case before it and had no intention of laying down definitive tests, as is shown by its subsequent decision of 5 July 1978. Then it allowed the purchaser of a used car to sue the seller in tort for the harm suffered in an accident due to the fact that the rear tyres were not in conformity with regulations. In both decisions the court expressly stated that it was not laying down definitive criteria.

(*b*) The adoption of a common-sense or economic standpoint will often enable one to say whether the harm in suit is substantially identical with the undervalue due to the original defect [reference omitted]. Thus substantial identity will be found where the defective component is so integrated into the composite or so unified with the part now damaged but originally undefective that separation is impossible without great economic loss (BGH 24 June 1981, NJW 1981, 2248, 2249). So, too, where it would make no economic sense to make the defect good (this may have been the case in the decision of the Seventh Civil Senate on 25 May 1972 (BauR 1972, 379) where the foundations underneath the whole of the extension were inadequate). Other cases where the distinction is hard to draw must be determined in accordance with the principles stated in 1(*b*) above, taking into account the nature and extent of the damage in suit, the nature of the defect to which it was due, the effect of the defect on the condition of the thing, and, as reflected in these factors, the extent of the manufacturer's duty in tort which here, as in other cases, is affected by the purpose of the product, the consumer's expectations of it and even, under certain circumstances, its price [reference omitted].

(*c*) In this case we need not ask whether the throttle was a functionally distinct component of the motor car in the sense of BGHZ 67, 359, or whether the Court of Appeal was right to suppose that it was not. For the purposes of this appeal we must take the accident to have been caused by a defect which inhibited the flow of petrol, and in such a case the common-sense observer could disregard the nature and origin of that defect and say that the harm to the car was substantially different from the undervalue which the defect caused to the owner's interest in its being worth what he paid for it. The critical feature in this case is that the vehicle remained roadworthy despite the defect in the throttle, which by no means rendered the vehicle valueless from the outset, and that the inherent risk of damage could have been allayed by prompt discovery of the defect and its repair at little cost and without damage to other parts of the car. The accident to the car was far from being a necessary manifestation of the undervalue of the car owing to the defect in the petrol supply; the harm was rather due to the concurrence of regrettable circumstances which could and would have been avoided had the plaintiff become conscious of the danger in good time.

We need not decide whether the manufacturer's liability for property damage resulting from a defect exists only if the damage or disturbance occurs in a *violent* manner (for example, through fire, explosion, or similar events) [reference omitted]. But certainly when the defect in a component is apt to lead to the destruction of a valuable chattel such as a motor car or damage to it in a "violent" manner such as occurred here, then this clearly speaks for the liability of the manufacturer: the duty breached by the manufacturer in putting into circulation a vehicle with such a noxious defect was imposed on him not just because people are interested in the usability and value of their chattels but also because the owner or possessor has an interest in their well-being.

Case 72

BUNDESGERICHTSHOF (SIXTH CIVIL SENATE) 14 MAY 1985
NJW 1985, 2420 = VERSR 1985, 837

In April 1980 the plaintiff bought a compressor from the defendant manufacturer. In March 1982 its diesel motor suffered considerable damage, because it had run for a time without lubricant. This was because oil had leaked out owing to the fracture of the oil-conduit at the point where it joined the sump. The plaintiff maintains that it was a fault in design that the oil-conduit was fixed at only one point, namely where it entered the motor—or compressor—housing, and that it would not have broken under the vibrations set up by the prolonged running of the motor if it had been affixed to the chassis as well.

The plaintiff claimed damages of DM 5730.28 for damage to property (cost of substitute motor, expenses of experts, and rental of replacement).

Reasons

1. The Court of Appeal was of the opinion that, accepting the plaintiff's allegations as true, the damage to the compressor's motor was not damage to the plaintiff's interest in

the integrity of his property such that the defendant was under a tort duty to take care to avoid it. If, as he alleged, the compressor was unfit for prolonged use as envisaged, he must bring a claim in respect of his interest in the usability and value of a merchantable compressor.

II. The judgment of the Court of Appeal is unsound in law.

1. The first points made by the Court of Appeal are correct enough.

(*a*) The Court of Appeal followed decisions of this Division to the effect that the manufacturer of a product can be liable under § 823 I BGB for harm to a consumer's property if the damage to or destruction of the property represents damage which it is the duty of the manufacturer to take care to avoid in the interest of the acquirer in the integrity of his property [references].

(*b*) The Court of Appeal correctly distinguished those cases where the damage consisted simply of the fact that the defect in the thing made it less valuable and constituted an infringement of the acquirer's interest in usability and value for money, since it is not the function of duties imposed by the law of tort to protect a purchaser's interest in having a thing to use which is free from defects.

(*c*) As to whether or not the damage represented an invasion of the plaintiff's interest in the integrity of his property the Court of Appeal was right to adopt the test whether the damage was identical with the loss of value of the compressor due to its initial defect, i.e. whether it was "substantially similar' to the loss in value *quoad* usability and value for money represented by the defect.

2. The Court of Appeal was nevertheless wrong to infer from the fact that the initial defect in the compressor only manifested itself in the loss of its value the conclusion that in this case there was no invasion of the plaintiff's interest in the integrity of his property.

(*a*) The Court of Appeal was wrong to suppose that the primary test as to whether the harm which later manifests itself is identical with the loss of value due to an initial defect, that is, whether they are "substantially similar", is whether the thing was fit for prolonged use. What really counts is the comparison between the damage which is in issue and the disvalue of the product at the time of transfer, namely the amount by which the defect renders it less valuable. The diminution in value due to the defect and consequently the harm to the interest in value for money can be tested by the principles applied when abatement of the price is sought for breach of warranty (§ 472 I BGB) [references]. While it is true that in making this assessment the fact that the defect will reduce the useful life of the product can materially increase the initial shortfall in value, it is only if the entire thing or component for which compensation is sought is affected from the economic point of view by the non-durability that the short life expectancy will be *fully* expressed in the diminution of value and thus establish *complete* "substantial similarity" between loss of value and damage to the thing. Where the initial defect which carries the risk of premature breakdown affects only part of the product and is quite curable, and only later destroys the product or damages other parts of it, the undefective part of the product has a value sufficiently distinct from the shortened life due to the defect that there is no complete identity between the damage and the shortfall in value.

That was the case here. Taking the material facts as found below, the component parts of the compressor which the plaintiff bought from the defendant manufacturer were individually faultless and it was initially quite functional. The only trouble was the inadequate anchorage of the oil-pipe which rendered it likely to break under the stress of operation and let the oil escape. This could have been avoided by the simple welding job of making an additional fixing to the chassis. Only the oil-pipe was non-durable, not the compressor as a whole or even the motor. As the defect, viz. the inadequate and easily curable fixing of the oil-pipe, could only damage the motor if its fracture and the consequent loss of oil remained unnoticed, the loss of value due to the defect at the critical moment, namely the transfer of ownership, was limited to the cost of occasional replacement of the pipe during the normal life of the compressor, or alternatively the cost of installing an additional fixing.

(*b*) Contrary to the view of the Court of Appeal, the plaintiff's claim is not simply for an invasion of his interest in the usability and value for money of a functioning compressor. This case differs from the "*hydraulic jack*" case, cited below, in which this Division dismissed a damages claim for damage to property where the jack was not usable (NJW 1983, 812 = VersR 1983, 346). A point sometimes overlooked by critics is that the defendant in that case had restored the jack to its original condition after the collapse of one of the supports, so that the plaintiff was in possession of a jack with just the original defect and no more, namely the design or construction fault in its undercarriage. It is true that as this defect was not remedied by the manufacturer the plaintiff did not use the jack for a long time for fear that a support might again give way under the weight of the vehicle. In such a case the purchaser suffers no harm over and above the original defect in the product, whereas in our case, as explained above, the damage is significantly greater. This demonstrates that the plaintiff here is not complaining simply of an invasion of his interest in having a functional compressor to use.

(*c*) This case differs in two respects (neither of which affects the outcome) from previous decisions of this Court where it was held that there had been an invasion of the plaintiff's interest in the integrity of his property (BGHZ 67, 359 = NJW 1977, 379 (thermostat); BGHZ 86, 256 = NJW 1983, 810 (accelerator pedal); NJW 1978, 2241 = BB 1978, 1491 (rear tyres)).

(*aa*) In the accelerator pedal case "a risk of accident arose through a combination of unfortunate circumstances". As the court below correctly held, that was not the case here.

It cannot be a precondition of a damages claim that *further* special circumstances be required before any damage occurs [reference]. Even in the absence of further special circumstances defect and harm lack "substantial identity" if, as explained above, a curable defect initially affects only a particular part of this product.

Furthermore, it must be irrelevant to the question of the congruence of initial defect and subsequent harm whether or not the harm occurs by means of an accident or results from a "violent" occurrence. This senate in BGHZ 86, 256 (273) = NJW 1983, 810 left it open whether it was only in such circumstances that the manufacturer's liability arose. But just as tort liability cannot depend on whether the defect in part of a product endangers *other* interests of the consumer or third party, that is, poses a risk to the environment and not just to the product itself (BGHZ 86, 256 (258) = NJW 1983, 810, criticized by Hager, *AcP* 184, 417), so it cannot be relevant to liability that the harm occurs by means of an "accident" or by "violent" damage to or destruction of other parts of the product. That would introduce into the law of tort a criterion foreign to its general principles.

The principle is that the acquirer's interest in the thing not being damaged or destroyed by reason of a fault of design or manufacture deserves as much protection as his interest that such fault not damage other property acquired elsewhere, and the manufacturer's liability cannot sensibly depend on whether the defect in manufacture damages other property of the consumer or only the product itself [references]. Likewise, the victim's interest in the integrity of his property and its protection by the law of tort cannot depend on whether the thing is damaged or destroyed "violently" or gradually over a period of time. After all, the manufacturer's liability for damage to other property of the consumer does not depend on whether the damage is sudden or gradual; nor does it where the damage is to the product itself. For damage to the product the manufacturer is liable in tort as well as in warranty unless the plaintiff never had an undamaged product and so cannot complain of any impairment in his interest in the product remaining undamaged, that is, unless the subsequent damage was so inherent in the original undervalue of the product that any damages awarded must be for his failure to acquire an undamaged thing rather than for invasion of his interest in the thing not being damaged.

(*bb*) Finally it is immaterial that in this case the damage to the compressor's motor occurred through the *absence* of an *additional* fixing for the oil-pipe, rather than through the presence of a defective or unsuitable component which threatened the whole. Here the damage was as much an invasion of the plaintiff's interest in the integrity of his property, which the manufacturer was under a duty to respect, as in cases where an original defect in a component affects the whole or other parts of the thing. The case is like those in which a thing is badly constructed because one of its parts is too weak to work or otherwise unsuitable (BGHZ 67, 359 (362) = NJW 1977, 379). This distinction can have no effect on tort liability.

Reversed and remanded for further findings of fact.

Case 73

BUNDESGERICHTSHOF (SIXTH CIVIL SENATE) 24 MARCH 1992
NJW 1992, 1678 = VERSR 1992, 758 = ZIP 1992, 704

Facts

The plaintiff brought an action for damages against the defendants arguing that he had suffered an interference with his property interest in a car engine which had been damaged as a consequence of a faulty mounting by the defendant. On 8 April 1989 the plaintiff purchased a car engine from Firm P which an acquaintance then installed in his motor vehicle. This engine had previously been given a general overhaul by the defendants and delivered by them as a so-called replacement engine to Firm P. After 9,500 km had been registered on the clock, serious damage to the engine occurred on January 18, 1990. The plaintiff attributes the occurrence of loss to the fact that the defendants had not put in place the fastening screw of the camshaft driving wheel, so that this slipped off the camshaft. He claimed compensation from the defendant in the amount of DM 6,870.39, covering the costs of repair and the provision of an expert report, damage resulting from loss of use, and telephone expenses.

The LG rejected the claim. The plaintiff's appeal to the OLG was unsuccessful. His further appeal to the BGH resulted in the quashing of the judgment and its remission to the lower court for reconsideration.

For the following

Reasons

The OLG found a failure of the pleadings to state a cause of action as a matter of law. In its view the defendants are to be seen as the manufacturers of the engine. However, they are not liable on the basis of § 823 I BGB because only the plaintiff's financial interest ("*Äquivalenzinteresse*") and not his interest in the integrity ("*Integritätsinteresse*") of his property were affected. There was an "identity of substance" between the damage and the alleged defect in the product. In other words, the initial loss in value corresponded to the loss which occurred.

The initial lack of value of the engine was not restricted to the costs of putting in place the missing fastening screw. Such an approach would only be appropriate where the absence of the screw was known or should have been apparent in the context of the normal usage of the motor, for example, during a service. According to the pleadings of the plaintiff, this was precisely what did not happen. The subsequent sequence of events— the slippage of the camshaft drive wheel—was inevitably going to occur. A defect which is not discoverable cannot be removed. In that case, therefore, the plaintiff's financial interest coincided in full with the subsequent (large scale) loss. In addition, it was relevant that from the beginning the plaintiff had not acquired a properly functioning engine, since the risk of the destruction of the engine existed at all times. The drive wheel, which was only secured by the cable attached to the camshaft, could have fallen off immediately after the engine was put into service, so that this was not a case of "creeping loss".

II. The judgment of the OLG is incorrect in law and must be quashed. The plaintiff has implicitly satisfied the basic conditions of an adequate plea for damages based on § 823 I BGB.

1. Any person who manufactures a product may be liable in damages in respect of loss which occurs to the product itself after it has been delivered on the grounds that the property of the purchaser has been damaged in accordance with § 823 I BGB. This is the case where the damage to or destruction of the product results in a form of damage (creeping loss) which, because of the purchaser's interest in the integrity of his property, should have been avoided by the producer who is under a duty to take care. In contrast, there is no right to compensation in tort in respect of losses which merely represent a "lack of value" of the product and which merely affect the purchaser's interest in usability and financial interest as a consequence of the defect in its condition [references omitted].

The OLG likewise based its decision on these principles. In that context it was right to hold that the defendant is subject to a tortious duty of care in respect of the engine to which it had given a "general overhaul", which it sold and delivered as a "replacement engine" and which it guaranteed as being free from defects. This is the case irrespective of whether the defendant had renewed only a limited number or all of the components of the engine in the context of the overhaul and in so doing had made use of materials supplied by third parties; for the defendant in any case took responsibility for the assembly of the components which it had prepared [references omitted].

2. However, the arguments on the basis of which the OLG reached the conclusion that there was no interference with the plaintiff's interest in the integrity of his property— namely that the ultimate damage (damage to the engine) and the defect in the product (the missing fastening screw) are "identical in substance", and that therefore the "lack of value" corresponded to the loss which occurred are not free of errors in law.

(*a*) In its case law, this court has described the financial destruction of the interest of the purchaser which was already disappointed when the property was acquired [reference omitted] as "identical in substance" to the initial "lack of value" [references omitted]. Consequently, there will be "identity of substance" where, viewed from an economic perspective, the initial defect affects the whole object in respect of loss for which compensation is now claimed [reference omitted] because for instance the object as a whole from the beginning is not at all or only in part usable for the purpose for which it was intended because of the defect [references omitted]. In this category are included also the cases in which the elimination of the defect (even if it only affects a part of the object) is not technically possible; the same view is gaining ground in respect of those cases where the defect cannot reasonably be eliminated without excessive expenditure [references omitted]. If, however, the defect is confined to a part of the product and is therefore capable of rectification according to the principles set out here and if it only subsequently leads to the destruction of the product or to damage to other parts of it, then that part of the object which was not initially tainted by the defect has its own value; the "lack of value" does not therefore correspond to the damage [reference omitted].

(*b*) The OLG correctly uses these principles as the basis for its judgment, but makes the mistake of treating the absence of the fastening screw on the camshaft driving wheel as a defect which cannot be rectified, which leads to the view that the damage is identical to the "lack of value" attributable to the defect. The conclusion of the OLG cannot be followed where it essentially focuses on whether the defect could have been discovered in the context of the normal use of the engine, for example, during a service.

It is not, in legal terms, of relevance for the question whether it is the purchaser's interest in the integrity of his property or only his financial interest in the usability of the product which has been impaired, whether he could or could not have discovered the defect before the loss occurred in normal circumstances; the subjective ability to discover is not relevant. What is essential is that the defect—from an objective technical standpoint—could have been identified even if only when it was specifically being sought, so long as that would not have involved a disproportionately high cost in terms of time and expenditure. Only from the latter perspective can it be relevant to the economic value of a defect in what circumstances a presumed defect can be discovered. For in the case of a defect which can only be identified with difficulty, as defined here, the possibility of rectifying the defect can be challenged on technical or economic grounds [reference omitted]. The initial "lack of value" and the damage will coincide where the search for the defect and its elimination cause costs which are, for example, equal to or even greater than the cost of the whole product [reference omitted].

(*c*) The factual circumstances based on the plaintiff's pleadings which the OLG uses as the basis for its decision do not justify the conclusion that the defective securing of the camshaft driving wheel could not have been eliminated on technical or economic grounds. The OLG bases the adoption of this position solely on the allegation made by the plaintiff that the absence of a screw on the camshaft would not have become apparent if the servicing of the engine had been carried out in accordance with the instructions given in the service booklet.

It is incorrect to conclude that there is a defect the elimination of which is excluded on technical or economic grounds and which consequently taints the whole product with an initial "lack of value", simply because it is not known whether the product actually has a defect or because the defect did not become apparent in the context of normal servicing work which the manufacturer would expect to be undertaken, in other words, in the context of normal usage. As the BGH decisions on "creeping loss" have so far shown this will normally be the case [reference omitted].

There is in this case no support to be derived from the findings of the OLG or from the pleadings of the parties, which are focused purely on the foreseeable servicing work, that the absence of the fastening screw could not have been discovered without economically disproportionate expense.

3. This court is also unable to follow the arguments of the OLG to the effect that the engine delivered by the defendants was entirely unusable from the outset, because from the beginning there was an inherent danger of its destruction thus making this not a case of "creeping loss" and that it was coincidental that the initial propensity of the product to be damaged was only subsequently realised. It is true that the engine was defective in the sense that it lacked a screw which should have secured the driving wheel to the camshaft. The rest of the engine, however, was fit and had, as a whole, considerable value. The defect affected only a small portion of the product at first—namely the driving wheel which was not properly secured and which therefore ran the risk of breaking away from the camshaft—but not the product as a whole, even if—as is, in fact, always the case with "creeping loss"—there is from the outset the risk of significant damage to the whole product (which is otherwise free from defects). The question of when this risk might be realised, and in particular the question of whether the defect might be timely discovered and eliminated (for instance in the context of repair work otherwise necessitated) was uncertain. The facts of the case, on which the OLG based its decision having regard to the pleadings of the plaintiff, show that the damage to the whole product did not in fact occur immediately after it was put into operation, but the engine proved capable—for whatever technical reasons—of providing 9,500 km of usage over 19 months. In these circumstances, it cannot be said that the "lack of value" of the engine from the outset was so high that the damage which later occurred could be regarded as "identical in substance" with this "lack of value" and as merely the expression of the plaintiff's financial interest.

III. The OLG also concluded—logically from its standpoint—that it should leave open the question disputed by the parties as to whether in fact the fastening screw for the camshaft driving wheel was in fact missing when the defendant delivered the engine. The appeal judgment must therefore be quashed and the decision sent back to the OLG so that the necessary findings of fact can be made.

Case 74

BUNDESGERICHTSHOF (THIRD CIVIL DIVISION) 27 MAY 1963
BGHZ 39, 358 = NJW 1963, 1821 = JZ 63, 707 (with a critical note by
H H Rupp = VERSR 1963, 973)

The plaintiff site-owner claimed damages from a local authority which had issued a building permit without adequately checking the architect's calculations regarding the load-bearing capacity of the foundations, as marked on the plan. Because of this error, the building collapsed while in process of construction, and both the builder and the architect were insolvent.

The plaintiff's claim was dismissed by the trial court and his appeal was also dismissed for the following

Reasons

1. The trial court was correct to hold that in checking and authorising the plans for the building, the supervisory authorities are exercising a governmental function. In consequence, as the Appeal Court agrees, the plaintiff's claim against the defendant can only be based on the rules relating to the liability of officials (§ 839 BGB in connection with Art. 34 GG); it must be shown that one of the defendant local authority's officials in the exercise of the public function attributed to him was in breach of an official duty which he owed to the plaintiff . . .

2. In approaching the question whether, in giving building permission when it should not have done so, the local authority was in breach of official duties owed to the plaintiff, the trial court correctly started by considering the purpose served by the official duty [reference]. In the first instance, official duties are imposed in the interest of the State and the public. If the sole function of an official duty is to promote public order, the general interest of the commonwealth in orderly and proper government, the satisfaction of exigencies within the service, or the maintenance of a properly organised and functioning administration, then there is no question of any liability to third parties for its breach, even if its exercise has adversely affected them or their interest. Liability exists only where the official duty which was broken was owed by the official to the third parties themselves. Whether this is so and how wide the range of protected persons may be are questions which must be determined in accordance with the purpose served by the official duty. This purpose is to be inferred from the provisions on which the official duty is based and by which it is delimited, as well as from the particular nature of the official function in question. If, in addition to satisfying the general interest and public purposes, the official duty has the further purpose of safeguarding the interests of individuals, this is sufficient, even if the affected party had no legal claim that the official act in question be undertaken (BGHZ 35, 44, 46–47; BGH VersR 1961, 944).

Before a building permit is issued, the plans must be checked for conformity with all building regulations of public law (§ 2 II Provincial Building Ordinance). Such an investigation must encompass the structural safety of the building (§ 15 I e, § 61 Provincial Building Ordinance); as the Court of Appeal was right to emphasise, with reference to Pfundtner/Neubert [reference omitted], concern for safety is one of its most important aims, since unsafe buildings pose a direct threat to life and health, the value of physical property and safe conduct of business. The supervision of buildings thus permits the avoidance of dangers (BGHZ 8, 97, 104; see Baltz/Fischer, *Preussisches Baupolizeirecht* I ff.). The provisions requiring the verification of the calculations concerning the load-bearing capacity of buildings are directed to the dangers which threaten the public from the collapse of unsafe constructions. While these provisions and the official duties which they impose serve the protection of the public—the "public interest" (Baltz/Fischer, *ibid.*)—they also protect every individual member of the public who might be threatened by its unsafe condition, that is, every person who comes into contact with the building as inhabitant, user, visitor (RG Recht 1929 no. 757, SeuffArch 83 no. 134; JW 1936, 803,

BGHZ 8, 97, 104), neighbour (BGH VersR 1956, 447), passer-by (LM to BGB § 839 Fe no. 1), or workman, and who relies on its being safe. The owner or developer may also be a beneficiary of this protective function if he suffers damage to his body, health, or property as a result of a collapse while he is visiting the building or inhabiting it, but only if the harm is a consequence of the danger from which it is the function of the official verification of the technical specifications to protect the public and hence the individual endangered. That is not the case here. It is true that the plaintiff has suffered damage as a result of the collapse of the building, but he is not a victim of the danger from which, as a member of the public, he was entitled to be protected by the official duties and the provisions which created them, since it was only the building itself and no other property of his which was damaged.

Case 75

BUNDESGERICHTSHOF (SEVENTH CIVIL SENATE) 30 MAY 1963
BGHZ 39, 366 = NJW 1963, 1827 = VERSR 1963, 933, 1024

In 1951 the plaintiff contracted with the defendant builder to have a house built on his land and with the defendant architect to have the construction supervised. Cracks appeared in the ceilings because the concrete used was well below the requisite strength. The plaintiff claimed damages for the reconstruction of the ceilings which were in danger of collapse. Because he was out of time for a contract claim the plaintiff based his claim on the delictual provisions § 823 I BGB and § 823 II BGB in connection with § 330 of the Criminal Code (StGB) or § 367 no. 15 StGB.

Reasons

The Court of Appeal was right to find that the facts disclosed no tort on which the plaintiff's claim for damages could be based.

1. There is no question of a claim for damages under § 823 I BGB on the basis that the plaintiff's property (*Eigentum*) has been damaged by fault. The land owned by the plaintiff, as compared with what it was, has suffered no harm through the defective method of construction. In so far as the land has been built on, as the Court of Appeal rightly stated, the plaintiff never owned it in an undefective condition. As the building proceeded, the plaintiff's ownership attached to each part of the building as it was constructed in the condition in which it was constructed, with all the qualities and defects resulting from the incorporation of the building materials. To make someone the owner of a defective building is not to invade an already existing ownership (compare RG JW 1905, 367; OLG Karlsruhe NJW 1956, 913).

The decision of the Senate in LM no. 4 to § 830 BGB was a different case; there defective concrete balconies which had been built onto the top storey caused the collapse of the whole building.

2. The Court of Appeal was also right to reject the claim for damages based on § 823 II BGB in connection with § 330 StGB. Under this last-named provision a person "who in supervising or erecting a building in breach of generally recognised rules of building practice acts in such a way as to cause danger to others' is guilty of an offence. The trial court found that a danger existed within the meaning of this provision and this finding is not

subject to review. But as the Court of Appeal stated, § 330 StGB is solely designed to protect the lives and health of individuals [references]. It is only to this extent that the provision is a protective statute whose breach can give rise to a claim for damages under § 823 II BGB. Damages can only be claimed under this text if the harm takes the form of the invasion of a legal interest for whose protection the rule of law was enacted (BGHZ 19, 114, 126; 28, 359, 365 f.). The claim before us is for compensation for harm to an interest other than the legal interest protected by § 330 StGB.

Nor is the claim for those damages justifies by the consideration that the replacement of ceilings which are in danger of collapse is necessary to save the users of the rooms from imminent danger. It still remains the case that the cost of rendering the ceilings represents a harm which affects only the pecuniary interests of the plaintiff. This is evident if one imagines that a ceiling collapses and injures an individual; then certainly the harm attributable to the personal injuries must be compensated under § 823 II BGB and § 330 StGB; but there would still remain the material harm requiring the replacement of the ceilings, and this would still affect only the economic interests of the plaintiff.

3. The plaintiff finally relies on § 823 II BGB in connection with § 367 I no. 15 StGB. This provision provides, *inter alia*, that it is an offence for a builder or building worker to construct a building in deliberate deviation from the building plan approved by the authority. According to the plaintiff, an offence was here committed because the approval of the plan was based on specific calculations, incorporated in the submission, relating to the load-bearing capacity of the construction, and these calculations were in turn based on the quality of the concrete to be used.

It is not necessary to decide whether the use of concrete inferior to that on which the stress calculations were based constitutes a deliberate deviation from the authorised plan. We agree with the Court of Appeal that § 367 I no. 15 StGB is not designed to offer protection against harm of the sort for which the plaintiff claims damages.

It is true that in its decision reported in LM no. 1 § 823 (Bb) BGB the Bundesgerichtshof recognised that § 367 I no. 15 StGB was a protective statute; that case, however, involved personal injuries suffered by a worker employed on the building site.

In the view of the Court of Appeal, § 367 I no. 15 StGB is like § 330 StGB in offering protection only to the human person.

This view is open to criticism. The final Courts of Appeal have accepted that the cognate provision of § 367 I no. 14 StGB exists for the protection of property as well and that a breach of the provision may also give rise to claims for damages in respect of property damage under § 823 II BGB (RGZ 51, 177–8, BGH, LM no. 2 to § 823 Bd BGB). Both these decisions were concerned with harm caused to neighbouring buildings adjoining the building site and vested in third parties.

Thus it may be taken that the protective purpose of § 367 I no. 15 StGB is also to be construed to guard against damage to property as well as damage to persons. In the present case, however, as has already been stated, there is no damage to property but a pecuniary loss attributable to the defective execution of the building work in breach of contract . . .

Notes to Cases 68–75

1. Cases 68–73 deal with damage *to* the product and not damage caused *by* the product and must be compared with the decision of the US Supreme Court in *East River* reproduced in *Addendum 2*

to this section. The questions here are basically two: (i) is this economic loss or physical damage and (ii) should the answer be left to the law of contract or be found in an extended law of tort? If the answer favours tort, should the tort duty be determined, both in its scope and extent, by the underlying contract? Cases 74 and 75 face an analogous problem in the context of immovables.

Case 75, BGHZ 39, 366, concerned the question whether a defective design could as such lead to damage to property in the meaning of § 823 I BGB. The court denied this: "The land owned by the plaintiff, as compared with what it was, has suffered no harm through the defective method of construction." The plaintiff never owned it in a non-defective condition. This restrictive approach must now however be approached with caution. For in BGH, 12 December 2000, NJW 2001, 1361, the BGH held that in principle the criteria developed in cases 68–73 in relation to chattels could be applied by analogy to immovables. Yet, in the case at hand it denied liability under § 823 I BGB. The (simplified) facts were these. The plaintiff bought a site from the defendant and erected buildings on it. The defendant had filled the site with slag that made the site unsuitable for building. Within a couple of years cracks appeared in the buildings. The plaintiff sought a declaratory judgment that the defendant was liable in tort for the cost of repair of the buildings. The BGH held that the plaintiff never owned the building in a non-defective condition. It was of central importance that the site was from the outset unsuitable for building. The defect "attached" to the whole property and could not be confined to one of its "components". The mere fact that the buildings were not defective when build (but became so only subsequently) did not indicate otherwise. Thus, where the building is "doomed" from the outset, whether because of a defective design (here the court relied on case 75) or unsound foundations as in the present case, § 823 I BGB cannot be relied on. In the final analysis one wonders, however, whether this new approach will substantially increase the use of tort law in this area. Purchasers of buildings or building employers will have difficulties to show that they ever owned the land in a non-defective condition. Thus, the main remedy for plaintiffs in such situations will lie in the law of contract, which is not without its pitfalls, given the shorter limitation periods which are "objective" in the sense that they do not depend on whether the plaintiff knew or could have known of the defect. (See, also p. 39)

Plaintiffs who have a cause of action against a local authority for negligently granting permission to build on a site unsuitable for building are, at least in theory, in a better starting position. (This is the situation in case 74, BGHZ 39, 358.) For here, under § 839 BGB, the plaintiff can recover damages also for *pure* economic loss. This is not say, however, that the plaintiff will recover easily, as case 74 illustrates. For such liability to arise the plaintiff must establish that the local authority violated a duty that *specifically* protected the plaintiff's interests. This was denied in case 74. In assessing whether such a duty of care was breached, as will be further explained in Ch. 4 section A 2b, there is ample room for policy considerations. Foreseeability of loss is not a sufficient condition of liability. The courts have, after much hesitation, allowed claims (also for pure economic loss) where the health of potential occupants of a licensed building was potentially affected (e.g. because the building was erected on an abandoned and temporarily forgotten waste damp). The first decision in which the BGH adopted a more generous approach, and in which it awarded damages to a purchaser of a building that was inhabitable because it was erected on polluted soil, was BGH, 26 January 1989, BGHZ 106, 323. Damages were assessed on this basis. The plaintiff's investment in the site and the building was frustrated. Accordingly, it could be recovered, minus what the land was actually worth. The case law that followed is rich and not easy to reconcile. See, BGH, 6 July 1989, BGHZ 108, 224; BGH, 21 February 1991, BGHZ 113, 367; BGH, 14 October 1993, BGHZ 123, 363; and BGH, 29 July 1999, BGHZ 142, 259. See, also, annotations by Ossenbühl, JZ 1989, 1125; JZ 1991, 922. A detailed examination of these cases at the borderline between public (building) law and the law of delict must be reserved to a specialised treatise. Here, suffice it to make three general observations. *First*, the factual background of this line of cases was a growing awareness of environmental issues, in particular, of the dangers posed by old waste damps and the like. *Secondly*, generally speaking, the courts confined this new head of liability to cases where the planning authority (city or district councils) neglected health risks. This enabled the courts, *thirdly*, to limit liability for pure economic loss to a clearly identifiable, small group of victims. This is achieved by confining the protective scope of the duty of care to those persons who intend to live in a building that is not inhabitable because of the negligent planning. Occasionally, the courts departed from this bright line rule, not always consistently. For instance the BGH awarded damages to a developer who never had the intention to live in the building himself but to sell the property to third parties. (BGHZ 108, 224). In the same case however the court refused to award damages to investors or banks who are, in the court's view, not included in the protective scope of the duties that the local authority must respect in the course of planning.

2. First, as to defective premises since German law seems quite settled on this point: *Dutton v. Bognor Regis UDC* ([1972] 1 QB 373) held that the ultimate purchaser of a house that had been built on a rubbish tip and subsequently developed cracks had suffered material damage that could be claimed in tort. (A key extract from Lord Denning's judgment is reproduced below in *Addendum 3*.) The House of Lords, in those days in frequent disagreement with the Court of Appeal, approved: *Anns v. Merton London Borough Council* ([1978] AC 728). These cases stand in stark contrast with the German decisions whose reasoning was: (*a*) superior and (*b*) transplantable. In fact English law has, thirteen years later, moved much closer to the German approach, though it has done so gradually (some would say confusingly slowly) and in much more expansive judgments. (See: *Peabody Donation Fund v. Sir Lindsay Parkinson & Co. Ltd.* ([1985] AC 210); *Curran v. Northern Ireland Co-Ownership Housing Ass'n Ltd.* ([1987] AC 718); *D & F Estates Ltd. v. Church Comm'rs* ([1988] 3 WLR 368; and, most significantly, in *Murphy v. Brentwood DC* [1991] 1 AC 398). The basic tenets nowadays are clearly two: (*a*) the harm suffered by the plaintiffs in these cases is pure financial harm and not, as originally believed, property damage, and (*b*) the purpose behind the supervisory powers over building operations conferred by the legislature on local authorities is to protect occupiers of buildings and the public against dangers to their health and personal safety and nothing more.

3. On the *Dutton, Anns, Murphy* problem, American courts have not been able to come up with a uniform answer, so all one can do here is to warn of the diversity of answers. Thus, at one end of the spectrum, many state courts have allowed recovery of economic losses resulting from defects in buildings. See: *Sewell v. Gregory* 371 SE 2d 82, 84–5 (W.Va. 1988); *Cincinnati Riverfront Coliseum v. McNulty and Co.*, 504 NE 2d 415, 419 (Ohio, 1986); *Keel v. Titan Constr. Corp.*, 639 P. 2d 1228 (Okla. 1981). Probably more courts have opted for the exact opposite view, denying all recovery. See: *Atherton Condo. Apartment-Owners Ass'n Bd of Dir. v. Blume Dev. Co.*, 799 P. 2d 250, 262 (Wash. 1990); *Ellis v. Robert C. Morris, Inc.*, 513 A. 2d 951 (N. H. 1986). Cf., however, *Lempke v. Dagenais*, 547 A. 2d 290 (N.H. 1988) (allowing recovery for breach of warranty even in the absence of privity). In between these two extremes, one also finds compromise permutations—for instance recovery for remedial work for life-threatening defects. See: *Council of Co-Owners Atlantis Condo., Inc., v. Whiting-Turner Constr. Co.* 517 A. 2d 336, 344–5 (Nd. 1986). These problems are discussed by Jones, "Economic Loss Caused by Construction Deficiencies: the Competing Regimes of Contract and Tort", 59 *U. of Cin. L. Rev.* 1051 (1991); Libertucci, "Builders' Liability to New and Subsequent Purchasers", 20 *SW. U. L. Rev.* 219 (1991); Yuen, "Absent Privity of Contract Contractors may not Recover Economic Damages caused by an Architect's Negligence", 60 *U. Cin. L. Rev.* 565 (1991).

4. These cases, however, also show that accidents cannot always be neatly categorised. A television set explodes and injures my child: this is product liability and the damage is clearly personal injury (if it damages my table, it is property damage). The same television does not function when switched on. This (according to the better view) is economic loss and the remedy should best be sought in the law of sales, the UCC etc. In this sense: *Spring Motors Distrib. Inc. v. Ford Motor Co.*, 489 A. 2d 660 (N.J. 1985); *Henry Heide, Inc. v. WRH Prods. Co., Inc.*, 766 F. 2d 105 (3rd Or.1985). For a systematic analysis see *Two Rivers Co. v. Curtiss Breeding Serv.*, 624 F. 2d 1242 (5th cir.1980). For Germany see Hager, "Zum Schutzbereich der Produzentenhaftung", AcP 184 (1984), 413.

5. In between are cases like 68–73 where a defective component causes further damage to the product but no other damage to persons or other property. This borderline case has caused its problems; and it is here that tort is increasingly used to invade the province of contract law. This

unease is reflected in the German cases reproduced in this book. (Note, for example, case 68 and, incidentally, note how superficially (by English standards) earlier case law is brushed aside. This "summary" way that earlier "precedents" are handled by German courts is a subject worthy of further study.) Thus it is said that if the defect and the damage caused by it are not "substantially the same" then recovery for the latter is possible in tort. And conversely, if there is "substantial identity" (*Stoffgleichheit*) between defect and subsequent harm, then no tort action will be allowed. So where asbestos tiles attached to the plaintiff's house released in rainy weather a substance which silted up his windows, a tortious claim was successful (BGH NJW 1981, 2250). But in another case (BGH NJW 1981, 2248) insulation material built into a roof caused it to crack as temperature variations produced expansion and contraction. The defect and the damage it caused were here considered to be "substantially the same" so the tort action failed.

6. Decisions such as the above provide illustrations (see also BGH NJW 1983, 812); but the criterion of "substantial identity" has much troubled the German courts as cases 68–73 clearly show. Their study makes hard reading but, basically, one detects an unease with the whole subject evidenced by changing tests and underscored by academic doubts (see, for example, Deutsch, *JZ* 1984, 308, 311; Stoll, *JZ* 1983, 501). Thus, originally, the defective part had to be a "functionally limited unit" of the whole product in order to be classed as damage to property when it spread and "infected" the rest of the product. In the *Gaszugfall* case (71, BGHZ 86, 256) the court decided that one should not focus exclusively on the idea of a "functionally limited unit" but one should, instead, adopt an economic approach. The question to be asked was thus whether the defective part could be separated from the rest of the product without considerable economic loss (see section II.2(*b*) of case 71). The *Kompressorfall* case (72, BGH NJW 1985, 2420) now introduces a new test which requires the court to compare the defect of the product when acquired with the damage done when the defect has spread.

7. This German case law has proved highly controversial with academics, but their criticisms have left the judges unmoved. In the light of this, an outside observer must be cautious in expressing his views and should, perhaps, limit his observations to three points. Thus, *first* comes the advice to the reader to familiarise himself with as much of this literature as possible. The references given in the next paragraph (8.) are meant to assist this process; and the study of foreign laws can only enrich this understanding. *Secondly*, the reader will be assisted in his task by the comments that Professor Kötz volunteered (in a private letter to the author; *Addendum 1*) and which refer to the *Schwimmerschalter* case (68, BGHZ 67, 359, above). The main thrust of his objections (and further references) can also be found in his invaluable *Deliktsrecht*, pp. 27 *et seq. Finally*, despite the force of these arguments, the reader will also benefit from looking at these developments from a broader perspective. Thus, another distinguished comparatist, (Professor Fleming in (1989) 105 *LQR*, 508–511; *Addendum 2*) seems to regard this case law as a reaction (perhaps inept but, arguably, inevitable) to the restrictive regime that the Code has adopted towards the problem of pure economic loss. Seen in this light, these developments may thus also contain important lessons for Common lawyers. (See p. 39 as to the consequences of the latest BGB-reform).

8. See, more recently: BGH VersR 1989, 91 (*Fischfutter*); BGH NJW 1990, 908 = VersR 1980, 204 (*Weinkorken*); BGH VersR 1990, 1283 (with disapproving note by E. Lorenz); BGH VersR 1992, 758 (*Nockenwellensteuerrad*); BGH VersR 1992, 837 (*Kondensator*); Steffen, "Die Bedeutung der 'Stoffgleichheit' mit dem 'Mangelunwert' für die Herstellerhaftung aus Weiterfresserschäden", VersR 1988, 977; Kullmann, "Die Rechtsprechung des BGH zum Produkthaftpflichtrecht in den Jahren 1991/92", *NJW* 1992, 2669; v. Bar, "Probleme der Haftpflicht für deliktsrechtliche Eigentumsverletzungen," *Mannheimer Vorträge zur Versicherungswissenschaft* (1992).

Addendum 1 (From Professor Dr Hein Kötz)

"It might shed some . . . light on the *Schwimmerschalter* decision if one bears in mind that the parties in that case were the buyer and the seller of the product in question and that the buyer had lost his contractual remedy only because he had failed to bring his action within the six-month period laid down in § 477 BGB. Nobody would have raised an eyebrow if the Court had said: 'We are sorry that we cannot help the plaintiff since he failed to bring his action within the limitation period of § 477 BGB.' Nobody would have raised an eyebrow if the Court had added: 'This is a harsh result since in this case a reasonable man would have been unable to detect the defect before the end of the six-month period, let alone bring an action before that date. We cannot do anything about it, but we ask Parliament to look at the problem and devise a solution, perhaps along the lines of Art. 39 of the Vienna Sales Convention.' It would have been somewhat bolder but perfectly acceptable if the Court had said: 'We interpret § 477 BGB restrictively so as to let the six-month period start running not at the time of the delivery of the product but, in the event of a reasonably undetectable defect, at the date at which the buyer did detect it or, as a reasonable man, should have been able to detect it.' The Federal Court, however, did not choose any of these solutions, but came up, quite unexpectedly, with a disastrous fourth solution.

In later cases, the Federal Court applied the *Schwimmerschalter* rule to cases in which the parties were not linked by a contract but the plaintiff was a buyer further down stream. It follows that a seller may do what he pleases in order to exempt himself from both contractual and tort liability by way of a contractual agreement with his direct customer. All this, however, will not help him at all if a downstream buyer suffers damage to the defective product itself. Let me add that the limitation period for a tort claim is of course three years after detection of the damage and the [identity of the] person responsible for it (§ 852 BGB). In my view, this makes no sense."

Addendum 2 (Professor John Fleming)

"This line of attack [contained in the *Kompressor* case] is reminiscent of the equation of 'property damage' with structural change in the pre- *D & F Estates* cases, also of Justice Traynor's view in the leading American case of *Seeley* v. *White Motor Co.* 403 P.2d 145 (Cal.1965) distinguishing between a claim by a purchaser of a defective truck for the cost of repairs in a causally related accident and a claim for loss of profit due to inability to haul the expected quantity of loads.

What is at issue here is not so much the precise formula suggested by the German court as its willingness, indeed eagerness, to extend tort protection for damage to the defective thing itself. It is the more remarkable because of the Civil Code's categorical exclusion of tort damages for purely economic loss and the great weight reputedly given by German law to theoretical orthodoxy over pragmatism. Clearly English law would not have to go to the same pains to justify similar results: only traditionalists have to seek refuge in abstractions. The answer is found in a search not for what the law had been thought to be, but what we want it to be. There clearly are options."

Addendum 3

1. Extract from Lord Denning MR's judgment from *Dutton* v. *Bognor Regis UDC* (CA) [1972] 1 QB 373, 396.

Mr Tapp [attorney for the defendant local authority] submitted that the liability of the council would, in any case, be limited to those who suffered bodily harm: and did not extend to those who only suffered economic loss. He suggested, therefore, that although the council might be liable if the ceiling fell down and injured a visitor, they would not be liable simply because the house was diminished in value. He referred to the recent case of *SCM* (*United Kingdom*) *Ltd.* v. *W. J. Whittal & Son Ltd.* [1971] 1 QB 337.

I cannot accept this submission. The damage done here was not solely economic loss. It was physical damage to the house. If Mr Tapp's submission were right, it would mean that if the inspector negligently passes the house as properly built and it collapses and injures a person, the council are liable: but if the owner discovers the defect in time to repair it—and he does repair it—the council are not liable. That is an impossible distinction. They are liable in either case.

I would say the same about the manufacturer of an Article. If he makes it negligently, with a latent defect (so that it breaks to pieces and injures someone), he is undoubtedly liable. Suppose that the defect is discovered in time to prevent the injury. Surely he is liable for the cost of repair.

2. Uniform Commercial Code, § 2–318
Third-Party Beneficiaries of Warranties Express or Implied

Alternative A

A seller's warranty whether express or implied extends to any natural person who is in the family or household of his buyer or who is a guest in his home if it is reasonable to expect that such person may use, consume, or be affected by the goods and who is injured in person by breach of the warranty. A seller may not exclude or limit the operation of this section.

Alternative B

A seller's warranty whether express or implied extends to any natural person who may reasonably be expected to use, consume, or be affected by the goods and who is injured in person by breach of the warranty. A seller may not exclude or limit the operation of this section.

Alternative C

A seller's warranty whether express or implied extends to any person who may reasonably be expected to use, consume, or be affected, by the goods and who is injured by breach of the warranty. A seller may not exclude or limit the operation of this section with respect to injury to the person of an individual to whom the warranty extends. As amended 1966.

3. *Restatement Second, Tort*, § 402A
Special Liability of Seller of Product for Physical Harm to User or Consumer

(1) One who sells any product in a defective condition unreasonably dangerous to the user or consumer or to his property is subject to liability for physical harm thereby caused to the ultimate user or consumer, or to his property, if
   (*a*) the seller is engaged in the business of selling such a product, and
   (*b*) it is expected to and does reach the user or consumer without substantial change in the condition in which it is sold.

(2) The rule stated in subsection (1) applies although
   (*a*) the seller has exercised all possible care in the preparation and sale of his product, and
   (*b*) the user or consumer has not bought the product from or entered into any contractual relation with the seller.

Addendum 4

East River S.S. Corp. v. *Transamerica Delaval*, 476 US 858, 106 S. Ct. Rep. 2295 (1986)

JUSTICE BLACKMUN delivered the opinion of the Court.

In this admiralty case, we must decide whether a cause of action in tort is stated when a defective product purchased in a commercial transaction malfunctions, injuring only the product itself and causing purely economic loss. The case requires us to consider preliminarily whether admiralty law, which already recognises a general theory of liability for negligence, also incorporates principles of products liability, including strict liability. Then, charting a course between products liability and contract law, we must determine whether injury to a product itself is the kind of harm that should be protected by products liability or left entirely to the law of contracts.

I. In 1969, Seatrain Shipbuilding Corp. (Shipbuilding), a wholly owned subsidiary of Seatrain Lines, Inc. (Seatrain), announced it would build the four oil-transporting supertankers in issue—the TT Stuyvesant, TT Williamsburgh, TT Brooklyn, and TT Bay Ridge. Each tanker was constructed pursuant to a contract in which a separate wholly owned subsidiary of Seatrain engaged Shipbuilding. Shipbuilding in turn contracted with respondent, now known as Transamerica Delaval, Inc. (Delaval), to design, manufacture, and supervise the installation of turbines (costing $1.4 million each, see App. 163) that would be the main propulsion units for the 225,000-ton, $125 million (*ibid.*) supertankers. When each ship was completed, its title was transferred from the contracting subsidiary to a trust company (as trustee for an owner), which in turn chartered the ship to one of the petitioners, also subsidiaries of Seatrain. Queensway Tankers, Inc., chartered the Stuyvesant; Kingsway Tankers, Inc., chartered the Williamsburgh; East River Steamship Corp. chartered the Brooklyn; and Richmond Tankers, Inc., chartered the Bay Ridge. Each petitioner operated under a bareboat charter, by which it took full control of the ship for 20 or 22 years as though it owned it, with the obligation afterwards to return the ship to the real owner. See G Gilmore and C Black, Admiralty §§ 4–1, 4–22 (2nd edn. 1975). Each charterer assumed responsibility for the cost of any repairs to the ships. Tr. of Oral Arg. 11, 16–17, 35.

The Stuyvesant sailed on its maiden voyage in late July 1977. On 11 December of that year, as the ship was about to enter the Port of Valdez, Alaska, steam began to escape from the casing of the high-pressure turbine. That problem was temporarily resolved by repairs, but before long, while the ship was encountering a severe storm in the Gulf of Alaska, the high-pressure turbine malfunctioned. The ship, though lacking its normal power, was able to continue on its journey to Panama and then San Francisco. In January 1978, an examination of the high-pressure turbine revealed that the first-stage steam reversing ring virtually had disintegrated and had caused additional damage to other parts of the turbine. The damaged part was replaced with a part from the Bay Ridge, which was then under construction. In April 1978, the ship again was repaired, this time with a part from the Brooklyn. Finally, in August, the ship was permanently and satisfactorily repaired with a ring newly designed and manufactured by Delaval.

The Brooklyn and the Williamsburgh were put into service in late 1973 and late 1974, respectively. In 1978, as a result of the Stuyvesant's problems, they were inspected while in port. Those inspections revealed similar turbine damage. Temporary repairs were made, and newly designed parts were installed as permanent repairs that summer.

When the Bay Ridge was completed in early 1979, it contained the newly designed parts and thus never experienced the high-pressure turbine problems that plagued the other three ships. Nonetheless, the complaint appears to claim damages as a result of deterioration of the Bay Ridge's ring that was installed in the Stuyvesant while the Bay Ridge was under construction. In addition, the Bay Ridge experienced a unique problem. In 1980, when the ship was on its maiden voyage, the engine began to vibrate with a frequency that increased even after speed was reduced. It turned out that the astern guardian valve, located between the high-pressure and low-pressure turbines, had been installed backwards. Because of that error, steam entered the low-pressure turbine and damaged it. After repairs, the Bay Ridge resumed its travels.

II. The charterers' second amended complaint, filed in the United States District Court for the District of New Jersey, invokes admiralty jurisdiction. It contains five counts alleging tortious conduct on the part of respondent Delaval and seeks $3.03 million in damages, App. 73, for the cost of repairing the ships and for income lost while the ships were out of service. The first four counts, read liberally, allege that Delaval is strictly liable for the design defects in the high-pressure turbines of the Stuyvesant, the Williamsburgh, the Brooklyn, and the Bay Ridge, respectively. The fifth count alleges that Delaval, as part of the manufacturing process, negligently supervised the installation of the astern guardian valve on the Bay Ridge. The initial complaint also had listed Seatrain and Shipbuilding as plaintiffs and had alleged breach of contract and warranty as well as tort claims. But after Delaval interposed a statute of limitations defence, the complaint was amended and the charterers alone brought the suit in tort. The non-renewed claims were dismissed with prejudice by the District Court. Delaval then moved for summary judgment, contending that the charterers' actions were not cognisable in tort.

The District Court granted summary judgment for Delaval, and the Court of Appeals for the Third Circuit, sitting *en banc*, affirmed. *East River SS Corp.* v. *Delaval Turbine, Inc.*, 752 F. 2d 903 (1985). The Court of Appeals held that damage solely to a defective product is actionable in tort if the defect creates an unreasonable risk of harm to persons or property other than the product itself, and harm materializes. Disappointments over the product's quality, on the other hand, are protected by warranty law. Id., at 908, 909–10. The charterers were dissatisfied with product quality: the defects involved gradual and unnoticed deterioration of the turbines' component parts, and the only risk created was that the turbines would operate at a lower capacity. Id., at 909. See *Pennsylvania Glass Sand Corp.* v. *Caterpillar*

Tractor Co., 652 F. 2d 1165, 1169–70 (3rd cir. 1981). Therefore, neither the negligence nor the strict liability claims were cognisable.

III. ...

B. [2] The torts alleged in the first, second, third, and fifth counts clearly fall within the admiralty jurisdiction. ...

C. [3] With admiralty jurisdiction comes the application of substantive admiralty law. ... Absent a relevant statute, the general maritime law, as developed by the judiciary, applies. ... Drawn from state and federal sources, the general maritime law is an amalgam of traditional Common-law rules, modifications of those rules, and newly created rules. ...

[4] The Courts of Appeals sitting in admiralty overwhelmingly have adopted concepts of products liability, based both on negligence ... and on strict liability. ...

We join the Courts of Appeals in recognising products liability, including strict liability, as part of the general maritime law. ... Our incorporation of products liability into maritime law, however, is only the threshold determination to the main issue in this case.

IV. Products liability grew out of a public policy judgment that people need more protection from dangerous products than is afforded by the law of warranty. See *Seely* v. *White Motor Co.*, 63 Cal. 2d 9, 15, 45 Cal. Rptr. 17, 21, 403 P. 2d 145, 149 (1965). It is clear, however, that if this development were allowed to progress too far, contract law would drown in a sea of tort. See G. Gilmore, *The Death of Contract*, 87–94 (1974). We must determine whether a commercial product injuring itself is the kind of harm against which public policy requires manufacturers to protect, independent of any contractual obligation.

A. [5] The paradigmatic products-liability action is one where a product "reasonably certain to place life and limb in peril", distributed without reinspection, causes bodily injury. See e.g. *MacPherson* v. *Buick Motor Co.*, 217 NY 382, 389, 111 NE 1050, 1051, 1053 (1916). The manufacturer is liable whether or not it is negligent because "public policy demands that responsibility be fixed wherever it will most effectively reduce the hazards to life and health inherent in defective products that reach the market". *Escola* v. *Coca Cola Bottling Co. of Fresno*, 24 Cal. 2d, at 462, 150 P. 2d, at 441 (concurring opinion).

For similar reasons of safety, the manufacturer's duty of care was broadened to include protection against property damage. See *Marsh Wood Products Co.* v. *Babcock & Wilcox Co.*, 207 Wis. 209, 226, 240 NW 392, 399 (1932); *Genesee County Patrons Fire Relief Assn.* v. *L Sonneborn Sons, Inc.*, 263 NY 463, 469–73, 189 NE 551, 553–5 (1934). Such damage is considered so akin to personal injury that the two are treated alike. See *Seely* v. *White Motor Co.*, 63 Cal. 2d, at 19, 45 Cal. Rptr., at 24, 403, P. 2d, at 152.

In the traditional "property damage" cases, the defective product damages other property. In this case, there was no damage to "other" property. Rather, the first, second, and third counts allege that each supertanker's defectively designed turbine components damaged only the turbine itself. Since each turbine was supplied by Delaval as an integrated package, see App. 162–3, each is properly regarded as a single unit. "Since all but the very simplest of machines have component parts, [a contrary] holding would require a finding of 'property damage' in virtually every case where a product damages itself. Such a holding would eliminate the distinction between warranty and strict products liability." *Northern Power and Engineering Corp.* v. *Caterpillar Tractor Co.*, 623 P. 2d 324, 330 (Alaska 1981). The fifth count also alleges injury to the product itself. Before the high-pressure and low-pressure turbines could become an operational propulsion system, they were connected to piping and valves under the supervision of Delaval personnel. See App. 78, 162–3, 181. Delaval's supervisory obligations were part of its manufacturing agreement. The fifth count thus can best be read to allege that Delaval's negligent manufacture of the propulsion system—by allowing the installation in reverse of the astern guardian valve—damaged the propulsion system. *Cf. Lewis* v. *Timco, Inc.*, 736 F. 2d 163, 165–6 (CA5 1984). Obviously, damage to a product itself has certain attributes of a products-liability claim. But the injury suffered—the failure of the product to function properly—is the essence of a warranty action, through which a contracting party can seek to recoup the benefit of its bargain.

B. The intriguing question whether injury to a product itself may be brought in tort has spawned a variety of answers.[3] [Footnote omitted.] At one end of the spectrum, the case that created the majority land-based approach, *Seely* v. *White Motor Co.*, 63 Cal. 2d 9, 45 Cal. Rptr. 17, 403 P. 2d 145 (1965) (defective truck), held that preserving a proper role for the law of warranty precludes imposing tort liability if a defective product causes purely monetary harm. See also *Jones and Laughlin Steel Corp.* v. *Johns-Manville Sales Corp.*, 626 F. 2d 280, 287 and n. 13 (CA3 1980) (citing cases).

At the other end of the spectrum is the minority land-based approach, whose progenitor, *Santor* v. *A and M Karagheusian, Inc.*, 44 NJ 52, 66–7, 207 A. 2d 305, 312–13 (1965) (marred carpeting), held that a manufacturer's duty to make nondefective products encompassed injury to the product itself, whether or not the defect created an unreasonable risk of harm. See also *LaCrosse* v. *Schubert*, 72 Wis. 2d 38, 44–5, 240 NW 2d 124, 127–8 (1976). The courts adopting this approach, including the majority of the Courts of Appeals sitting in admiralty that have considered the issue, e.g., *Emerson GM Diesel, Inc.* v. *Alaskan Enterprise*, 732 F. 2d 1468 (CA9 1984), find that the safety and insurance rationales behind strict liability apply equally where the losses are purely economic. These courts reject the *Seely* approach because they find it arbitrary that economic losses are recoverable if a plaintiff suffers bodily injury or property damage, but not if a product injures itself. They also find no inherent difference between economic loss and personal injury or property damage, because all are proximately caused by the defendant's conduct. Further, they believe recovery for economic loss would not lead to unlimited liability because they think a manufacturer can predict and insure against product failure. See *Emerson GM Diesel, Inc.* v. *Alaskan Enterprise*, 732 F. 2d, at 1474.

Between the two poles fall a number of cases that would permit a products-liability action under certain circumstances when a product injures only itself. These cases attempt to differentiate between "the disappointed users . . . and the endangered ones", *Russell* v. *Ford Motor Co.*, 281 Or. 587, 595, 575 P. 2d 1383, 1387 (1978), and permit only the latter to sue in tort. The determination has been said to turn on the nature of the defect, the type of risk, and the manner in which the injury arose. See *Pennsylvania Glass Sand Corp.* v. *Caterpillar Tractor Co.*, 652 F. 2d 1165, 1173 (CA3 1981) (relied on by the Court of Appeals in this case). The Alaska Supreme Court allows a tort action if the defective product creates a situation potentially dangerous to persons or other property, and loss occurs as a proximate result of that danger and under dangerous circumstances. *Northern Power and Engineering Corp.* v. *Caterpillar Tractor Co.*, 623 P. 2d 324, 329 (1981).

We find the intermediate and minority land-based positions unsatisfactory. The intermediate positions, which essentially turn on the degree of risk, are too indeterminate to enable manufacturers easily to structure their business behaviour. Nor do we find persuasive a distinction that rests on the manner in which the product is injured. We realise that the damage may be qualitative, occurring through gradual deterioration or internal breakage. Or it may be calamitous. Compare *Morrow* v. *New Moon Homes, Inc.*, 548 P. 2d 279 (Alaska 1976), with *Cloud* v. *Kit Mfg. Co.*, 563 P. 2d 248, 251 (Alaska 1977). But either way, since by definition no person or other property is damaged, the resulting loss is purely economic. Even when the harm to the product itself occurs through an abrupt, accident-like event, the resulting loss due to repair costs, decreased value, and lost profits is essentially the failure of the purchaser to receive the benefit of its bargain—traditionally the core concern of contract law. See E Farnsworth, *Contracts* § 12.8, pp. 839–40 (1982).

We also decline to adopt the minority land-based view espoused by *Santor* and *Emerson*. Such cases raise legitimate questions about the theories behind restricting products liability, but we believe that the countervailing arguments are more powerful. The minority view fails to account for the need to keep products liability and contract law in separate spheres and to maintain a realistic limitation on damages.

C. Exercising traditional discretion in admiralty, see *Pope and Talbot, Inc.* v. *Hawn*, 346 US 406, 409, 74 S. Ct. 202, 204, 98 L. Ed. 143 (1953), we adopt an approach similar to *Seely* and hold that a manufacturer in a commercial relationship has no duty under either a negligence or strict products-liability theory to prevent a product from injuring itself.

"The distinction that the law has drawn between tort recovery for physical injuries and warranty recovery for economic loss is not arbitrary and does not rest on the 'luck' of one plaintiff in having an accident causing physical injury. The distinction rests, rather, on an understanding of the nature of the responsibility a manufacturer must undertake in distributing his products." *Seely* v. *White Motor Co.*, 63

Cal. 2d, at 18, 45 Cal. Rptr., at 23, 403 P. 2d, at 151. When a product injures only itself the reasons for imposing a tort duty are weak and those for leaving the party to its contractual remedies are strong.

The tort concern with safety is reduced when an injury is only to the product itself. When a person is injured, the "cost of an injury and the loss of time or health may be an overwhelming misfortune", and one the person is not prepared to meet. *Escola* v. *Coca Cola Bottling Co. of Fresno*, 24 Cal. 2d, at 462, 150 P. 2d, at 441 (concurring opinion). In contrast, when a product injures itself, the commercial user stands to lose the value of the product, risks the displeasure of its customers who find that the product does not meet their needs, or, as in this case, experiences increased costs in performing a service. Losses like these can be insured. See 10A Couch on Insurance §§ 42: 385–42: 401, 42: 414–17 (2nd edn. 1982); 7 Benedict on Admiralty, Form no. 1.16–7 (7th edn. 1985); 5A Appleman, Insurance Law and Practice § 3252 (1970). Society need not presume that a customer needs special protection. The increased cost to the public that would result from holding a manufacturer liable in tort for injury to the product itself is not justified. *Cf. United States* v. *Carroll Towing Co.*, 159 F. 2d 169, 173 (CA2 1947).

Damage to a product itself is most naturally understood as a warranty claim. Such damage means simply that the product has not met the customer's expectations, or, in other words, that the customer has received "insufficient product value". See J White and R Summers, Uniform Commercial Code 406 (2nd edn. 1980). The maintenance of product value and quality is precisely the purpose of express and implied warranties. See UCC § 2–313 (express warranty), § 2–314 (implied warranty of merchantability), and § 2–315 (warranty of fitness for a particular purpose). Therefore, a claim of a non-working product can be brought as a breach-of-warranty action. Or, if the customer prefers, it can reject the product or revoke its acceptance and sue for breach of contract. See UCC §§ 2–601, 2–608, 2–612.

Contract law, and the law of warranty in particular, is well suited to commercial controversies of the sort involved in this case because the parties may set the terms of their own agreements. The manufacturer can restrict its liability, within limits, by disclaiming warranties or limiting remedies. See UCC §§ 2–316, 2–719. In exchange, the purchaser pays less for the product. Since a commercial situation generally does not involve large disparities in bargaining power, *cf. Henningsen* v. *Bloomfield Motors, Inc.*, 32 NJ 358, 161 A. 2d 69 (1960), we see no reason to intrude into the parties' allocation of the risk.

While giving recognition to the manufacturer's bargain, warranty law sufficiently protects the purchaser by allowing it to obtain the benefit of its bargain. See J White and R Summers, *supra*, ch. 10. The expectation damages available in warranty for purely economic loss give a plaintiff the full benefit of its bargain by compensating for forgone business opportunities. See Fuller and Perdue, "The Reliance Interest in Contract Damages" *1*, 46 *Yale LJ* 52, 60–3 (1936); R Posner, *Economic Analysis of Law* § 4.8 (3rd edn. 1986). Recovery on a warranty theory would give the charterers their repair costs and lost profits, and would place them in the position they would have been in had the turbines functioned properly. See *Hawkins* v. *McGee*, 84 NH 114, 146 A. 641 (1929). Thus, both the nature of the injury and the resulting damages indicate it is more natural to think of injury to a product itself in terms of warranty.

A warranty action also has a built-in limitation on liability, whereas a tort action could subject the manufacturer to damages of an indefinite amount. The limitation in a contract action comes from the agreement of the parties and the requirement that consequential damages, such as lost profits, be a foreseeable result of the breach. See *Hadley* v. *Baxendale*, 9 Ex. 341, 156 Eng. Rep. 145 (1854). In a warranty action where the loss is purely economic, the limitation derives from the requirements of foreseeability and of privity, which is still generally enforced for such claims in a commercial setting. See UCC § 2–715; J White and R Summers, Uniform Commercial Code 389, 396, 406–10 (2nd edn. 1980).

In products-liability law, where there is a duty to the public generally, foreseeability is an inadequate brake. *Cf. Petitions of Kinsman Transit Co.*, 388 F. 2d 821 (CA2 1968). See also Perlman, "Interference with Contract and Other Economic Expectancies: A Clash of Tort and Contract Doctrine" 49 *U. Ch. L. Rev.* 61, 71–2 (1982). Permitting recovery for all foreseeable claims for purely economic loss could make a manufacturer liable for vast sums. It would be difficult for a manufacturer to take into account the expectations of persons downstream who may encounter its product. In this case, for example, if the charterers—already one step removed from the transaction—were permitted to recover their economic losses, then the companies that subchartered the ships might claim their economic losses from the delays, and the charterers' customers also might claim their economic losses, and so on. "The law does not spread its protection so far." *Robins Dry Dock and Repair Co.* v. *Flint*, 275 US 303, 309, 48 S. Ct. 134, 135, 72 L. Ed. 290 (1927).

And to the extent that courts try to limit purely economic damages in tort, they do so by relying on a far murkier line, one that negates the charterers' contention that permitting such recovery under a products-liability theory enables admiralty courts to avoid difficult linedrawing. *Cf. Ultramares Corp.* v. *Touche*, 255 NY 170, 174 NE 441 (1931); *State of Louisiana ex rel. Guste* v. *M/V Testbank*, 752 F. 2d 1019, 1046–52 (CA5 1985) (*en banc*) (dissenting opinion), cert. pending, no. 84–1808.

D. For the first three counts, the defective turbine components allegedly injured only the turbines themselves. Therefore, a strict products-liability theory of recovery is unavailable to the charterers. Any warranty claims would be subject to Delaval's limitation, both in time and scope, of its warranty liability. App. 78–9. The record indicates that Seatrain and Delaval reached a settlement agreement. Deposition of Stephen Russell, p. 32. We were informed that these charterers could not have asserted the warranty claims. See Tr. of Oral Arg. 36. Even so, the charterers should be left to the terms of their bargains, which explicitly allocated the cost of repairs.

In the charterers' agreements with the owners, the charterers took the ships in "as is" condition, after inspection, and assumed full responsibility for them, including responsibility for maintenance and repairs and for obtaining certain forms of insurance. Tr. of Oral Arg. 11, 16–17, 35; App. 86, 88, 99, 101, 112, 114, 125–6, 127. In a separate agreement between each charterer and Seatrain, Seatrain agreed to guarantee certain payments and covenants by each charterer to the owner. App. 142–6. The contractual responsibilities thus were clearly laid out. There is no reason to extricate the parties from their bargain.

Similarly, in the fifth count, alleging the reverse installation of the astern guardian valve, the only harm was to the propulsion system itself rather than to persons or other property. Even assuming that Delaval's supervision was negligent, as we must on this summary judgment motion, Delaval owed no duty under a products-liability theory based on negligence to avoid causing purely economic loss. *Cf. Flintkote Co.* v. *Dravo Corp.*, 678 F. 2d 942 (CA11 1982); *S. M. Wilson and Co.* v. *Smith International, Inc.* 587 F. 2d 1363 (CA9 1978). Thus, whether stated in negligence or strict liability, no products-liability claim lies in admiralty when the only injury claimed is economic loss.

While we hold that the fourth count should have been dismissed, we affirm the entry of judgment for Delaval.

17. CAUSATION

Case 76
REICHSGERICHT (THIRD CIVIL SENATE) 13 OCTOBER 1922
RGZ 105, 264

On 2 January 1920, as the plaintiff's husband was about to alight from a tram, he was shot in the arm above the elbow by a policeman aiming at an escaping criminal. He was taken to hospital, contracted influenza (then prevalent in the hospital), and died on 18 March of a suppuration which developed in the chest in connection with the influenza. The plaintiff claims from the Prussian State under the Act of 1 August 1909 compensation for the loss arising from the death of her husband, caused by the fault of the policeman. The Landgericht granted her claim in part; the Court of Appeal rejected it completely. The plaintiff's application for review succeeded for these.

Reasons

The Court of Appeal agreed with the Landgericht in finding it proved that the policeman who shot the plaintiff's husband was guilty of a negligent breach of his official duty. Unlike the Landgericht, however, it denied the causal connection between that shooting and the husband's death. It regarded the influenza, from which the victim died, as a mere "subsequent accidental illness" and continued: At a time when the influenza epidemic was so widespread throughout Germany, no particular causal significance can be attached to the fact that at that time the influenza was fiercely raging in the hospital and especially in the ward into which the plaintiff's husband was taken. The risk of infection was the same inside the hospital as it was outside. Moreover, it is generally accepted that in hospitals the better hygienic arrangements and the continuous medical assistance if anything reduce such risks. Further, the applicant's case was not strengthened by the argument that the weakening of the victim's system by the shooting affected his resistance to infection or the illness that followed it.

The applicant rightly complains that in this way the Court of Appeal makes too rigorous demands for the acceptance of a causal connection. There is no doubt that between the shooting and the death of the plaintiff's husband a causal connection in the natural, mechanical sense does exist: the plaintiff's husband was taken into the hospital because he was shot. In the hospital he was attacked by the outbreak of influenza and succumbed to that illness. That causal connection was not excluded by the mere possibility that he could have contracted influenza elsewhere, and also without the shooting.

Moreover, according to case-law the causal connection—the so-called adequate connection—exists here. The taking of the injured person to the hospital was an unobjectionable (even though not absolutely necessary), appropriate, and normal consequence of the injury. However, once in hospital he was, contrary to the opinion of the Court of Appeal, exposed to the risk of infection by a complaint prevalent to a particularly high degree because he could not escape from the company of the sick, as he might otherwise have done. He had to stay night and day in the ward where the influenza raged. That fact involved an enhancement of the risk of infection, according to human experience, and cannot be outweighed by any hygienic arrangements in the hospital or the care of the doctors and nurses. It must also be accepted that an injury, such as here existed, even if its cure progressed favourably, is in general not without effect on the resistance of the injured person against otherwise injurious influenza and that, therefore, the risk of an infection and its consequences is much greater than if there had been no injury. Accordingly, in agreement with the Landgericht, the shooting must be in law found to have been a contributory cause of the death of the plaintiff's husband.

Case 77

REICHSGERICHT (SIXTH CIVIL DIVISION) 22 JUNE 1931
RGZ 133, 126

Reasons

The only point in dispute in the appeal is whether the fault of the plaintiff contributed as a cause to the automobile accident of 9 November 1928 (§ 9 Automobile Act, § 254 BGB). The Court of Appeal, which decided in the plaintiff's favour, denied this for the following reasons. Admittedly he acted carelessly, for that as a pedestrian he failed, before crossing the road, to ascertain whether an automobile was approaching. The co-defendant driver, however, was not prevented from avoiding the accident, which he could easily have done, and which was his duty. No adequate causal connection, therefore, existed between the plaintiff's conduct and the accident.

The complaint that in these explanations the concept of adequate causal connection was misunderstood is well founded. There can be no doubt that a natural causal connection existed between the plaintiff's conduct and the accident, for if he had not crossed the street at the very moment that the defendant's automobile overtook J's cart, he could not have been struck by it. That was apparently the view of the judge of First Instance. But the facts must also be regarded as showing an adequate causal connection. Such a connection exists where an act or omission, generally, not only under especial and quite improbable circumstances which are not to be anticipated in the regular course of things, is capable of producing the result that occurred [references]. But in view of present traffic conditions, it cannot be accepted as inconceivable, that at the moment a pedestrian crosses the road, an automobile will pass over the same spot. The appellate judges seem to have been of the same mind; for they found a lack of foresight in the plaintiff's not looking round for any approaching automobiles, and therefore held him to have been at fault (§ 276 BGB).

Accordingly, the causation and fault of both parties must be balanced against each other according to § 9 of the Automobile Act and § 254 BGB. This balancing is essentially a matter for the trial judge and is reserved to the court below.

Case 78

REICHSGERICHT (SIXTH CIVIL SENATE) 26 APRIL 1937
RGZ 155, 37

[The facts of the case are not entirely clear but what appears to have happened is that the plaintiff suffered from morbid disturbances which impaired her earning capacity. The part of the judgment that is reproduced here discusses a causal point, namely whether her state is due to the defendant's negligence or should be attributed to her nervous disposition induced by her pregnancy.]

1. ...

2. ...

3. ...

4. The plaintiff submits the opinion and report of the director of a university women's clinic and has nominated him as a witness. Although a judge of fact is entrusted with the choice of experts the Court of Appeal in the present case has rejected the request with a reasoning extracted from the factual content of the opinion, but which is legally objectionable. That reasoning is, according to the final sentence of the opinion, that the plaintiff's present state is conditioned by the pregnancy that produced twins. The expert's explanation must however be understood in its context. He says: the possibility remains open that the lady, affected mentally and bodily by the accident, was burdened by the beginning of the pregnancy, in which she was carrying twins, to quite an exceptional degree; but one can best account for the plaintiff's condition by assuming that she had received severe damage by the accident, especially to her nerves. Moreover, there were also some slight bodily changes. So the opinion says: "If the lady with her delicate constitution had not become pregnant, all consequences of the accident would probably have been made good. However, her present state is conditioned by the pregnancy, especially as she was carrying twins." It would follow from this that the accident was still *one*

condition of the plaintiff's present state. The pregnancy would indeed have affected the course of her state of health; but her present state would not have come into existence without the accident. That the causal connection was broken by the pregnancy cannot be said: the cause of her present state can still be adequately linked to the accident.

5. The Court of Appeal further admits that the origin of nervous disturbance which really existed, is to be traced to the accident, that the plaintiff, however, had a nervous predisposition and that it combined with her fantasies to affect the extent of the disturbances. The Court of Appeal is only willing to take all these disturbances into account down to the end of July 1933, in assessing medical expenses relying for that on the opinion of the expert K. Indeed, he too admits that the accident precipitated in the susceptible patient a lively "mental reaction" with various morbid excitable states, but is of the opinion that the accident was not responsible for the plaintiff's especial mental disposition which was at the root of her nervous disturbance. This view is based on a legal error. If any accident strikes a person in a weakened state of health and the consequences have been so serious because of that state of health that his earning capacity is diminished, the law treats that diminution entirely as a consequence of the accident; in other words: anyone who commits an unlawful act against a person in weakened health has no right to be placed in the same position as if he had injured a person in perfect health.

Case 79

REICHSGERICHT (EIGHTH CIVIL SENATE) 29 APRIL 1942
RGZ 169, 117

On 20 January 1937 the plaintiff (a chimney-sweep) was struck down by a lorry owned by the second defendant and driven by the first; he suffered various injuries. The accident was caused by unlawful driving on the part of the first defendant, who was convicted of an offence under § 335 StGB. The plaintiff claims damages for this accident; he demands RM 6000 for pain and suffering and RM 1725 for loss of earnings until 30 June 1938 and monthly payments of RM 100 from 1 July. The Landgericht allowed the claim in general but fixed the damages for pain and suffering at RM 3000. On appeal by the defendants, the Oberlandesgericht reduced the damages for pain and suffering and the compensation for the period until 30 June 1938 to one-half, the monthly payments for the period from 1 July to 31 December 1938 to RM 50, from 1 January 1939 to 30 June 1940 to RM 17.50, from 1 July to 30 November to RM 10.50, and from 1 December 1940 onwards to RM 7.50.

On the plaintiff's application for review, the Landgericht's decision was restored as regards the capital payments claimed; as regards the monthly payments the case was sent back to the Oberlandesgericht for these.

Reasons

The defendants no longer object to the order obliging them to pay compensation for the damage done by the accident; nor is any doubt cast on the first defendant's conviction. The dispute between the parties is limited to whether the pain and suffering and loss of earning capacity are to be traced to the accident. While the Landgericht recognized this to the full extent, the Oberlandesgericht, on the basis of a fresh expert opinion of University Professor Dr von G, adopted a division of percentages. According to that opinion, the plaintiff suffered from a disease called *arthrosis deformans* (deforming arthrosis with degeneration of the joints), which is to be traced to a predisposition. But, in addition, down to the end of 1938 there were signs of so-called arthritis which arose from the accident. Moreover, sciatica on the left side, which also occurred down to the end of 1938, was produced by a predisposition but was brought into the open as an illness by the accident. According to the expert's opinion, the sick state of the plaintiff was traceable in equal shares to his predisposition and the accident. With this predisposition the plaintiff's illness was suddenly brought into the open by the accident which he suffered; besides, experience shows that those signs appeared in much greater degree, developed more quickly, and resulted as a rule in a more protracted illness than if it had developed only from the predisposition. Accordingly, the expert holds that down to the end of 1938 the illness was due about 50 per cent to the predisposition, the rest to the accident. Afterwards, when the arthritic complaints faded away, he traces the plaintiff's condition as 75 per cent to his predisposition and only 25 per cent to the accident. According to his opinion even without the accident, which brought it into the open, his illness would conceivably have broken out in the course of 1937 or 1938 from some other cause (by catching a cold or the like). In accordance with this opinion, the Oberlandesgericht awarded to the plaintiff, who had had to employ an assistant because of his illness, only half the damages for pain and suffering, assessed at RM 3000, and half of the expense of employing assistants in 1937 and 1938, and as regards the monthly payments demanded for the following period only 25 per cent of his shortfall, which it assesses at 70 per cent of the payments demanded.

The applicant for review rightly takes objection to this partition of the damage suffered by the plaintiff. The Court of Appeal misunderstands the concept of causal connection, as it has been shaped by the writers and the courts. The court has to answer the question of causal connection not only according to the view of the medical expert but independently by having regard to the relevant legal prerequisites, which may lead to deviations from the medical view (*JW* 1938 (no. 4), 105; SeuffArch. 95, no. 9). It is recognised that even illnesses that are brought to light by an accident, only because there was a predisposition thereto in the injured person, are treated by the law as consequences of the accident to their full extent; anyone who commits an unlawful act against a person in weak health has no right to be treated as though he had injured a completely healthy person (RGZ 151, 283; 155, 41; SeuffArch. 95, no. 9). The causal connection between the act of the person inflicting the damage and the damage is also not excluded because the particular consequence that followed from the injurious act could have occurred through another event that definitely happened later on (RGZ 141, 365; 144, 80 and 348; similarly *Kommentar zum ABGE* 4, n 1*d* to § 1294). For that other event, the occurrence of which without the injurious act of the first defendant the Court of Appeal regards as certain in agreement with the expert opinion (catching cold and the like), would not have deprived the first defendant's act of its causal responsibility for the damage; instead that act has prevented the second event from being itself the cause of the damage. The accident to the plaintiff, which induced the illness, must, therefore, be looked upon as itself causing the damage that occurred in full even if the consequences could have been produced without the accident by a cold or the like because of the plaintiff's predisposition—an occurrence which the Court of Appeal took into account without more ado. The plaintiff's predisposition is important only in so far as, like advancing old age, in course of time and without the intervention of anything particularly inducing illness, reduces earning capacity and so influences the amount of damage. Only with this limitation is it right for the appellate judge to form the opinion that, where symptoms of illness are brought to light by an accident which triggered them off, the person to blame can be made liable only for the portion of its consequences that can be traced to it but not for those that are brought about by the predisposition. A partition of the consequences of an accident by percentages, as where the injured party shares the blame, is quite impossible in such cases.

In the present case the damage to the plaintiff consists in his no longer being able to undertake the heavier work of chimney-sweeping, in particular climbing up the chimney and therefore being greatly hindered in the exercise of his craft since bent chimneys (*Schiefkamine*) are common. To carry on with his business he has had to employ an assistant. It is a question of how long the plaintiff would have been able to expect to carry on his business without help but for the accident, and when therefore his predisposition would, even without the accident, have made it impossible for him to attend the cleaning of *Schiefkamine*. According to the expert's opinion the arthritic symptoms which made him unable to work are traceable to the accident. These symptoms, which must be judged to be a development of the pre-existing arthrosis—which did not affect his ability to work—lasted until the end of 1938. Since then only the arthrosis remains to which, though its effects were exacerbated by the accident, he is substantially predisposed. Hence it can now be said that the damage sustained by the plaintiff down to 30 June 1938 is traceable to its full extent to the accident and must, therefore, be made good by the defendants. The same applies to the damages the plaintiff claims for pain and suffering. The judgment appealed against, which remains unaltered in so far as it orders payment by the defendants, must therefore be modified as regards the damages for pain and suffering and the amounts claimed for the period down to 30 June 1938. As concerns the monthly payments for the period from 1 July 1938 onwards, further elucidation is needed up to what time the plaintiff might have been expected, without the accident, to be in a position to devote himself without assistance to his occupation, and from what date the natural development of his predisposition to arthrosis would have made it impossible for him to carry on his business without assistance. Up to that moment he must be awarded the monthly payments that he claims, the Court of Appeal having fixed the cost of an assistant at over RM 100 a month; for the subsequent period (irrespective of the amounts already awarded him with final effect) he has no longer a claim.

Case 80

BUNDESGERICHTSHOF (FIRST CIVIL SENATE) 23 OCTOBER 1951
BGHZ 3, 261 = VERSR 1952, 128

On 27 July 1948 six ships entered down stream the Datteln lock of the Lippe Side Canal. The first, the tug *Dollart*, was moored to barges *Gesine* and *Heinrich Hirdseg* (*HH9*), which were moored behind each other to the south wall. In the fourth place followed the MS *Edelweiss*, laden with 360 tonnes of wheat, on the way from Bremen to Rüdesheim. The *Edelweiss* lay on the starboard side of the *HH9* and was moored to the north wall. Finally came the motor ships *Weser I* and *Nixe* moored behind each other to the north wall. The walls of the Datteln locks are strengthened towards the bottom so that their chambers have a conical instead of a rectangular cross-section. As the water-level then stood, with a difference of 7.46 m between high and low water, the clear distance between the wall diminished from 12.77 m above to 12.31 m below. For that reason the lock personnel were instructed to pass through ships side by side of the overall breadth of 11.75 m only.

In the absence of the lock-keeper, the lock was operated by the subordinate T. He asked the skippers of *HH9* and *Edelweiss* beforehand about the breadth of their craft. *Edelweiss* gave her breadth correctly as 6.67 m, whereas the skipper S gave the breadth of *HH9* incorrectly as 5 m. It was actually 5.87 m. The pump operator M received the same answers to his questions. The subordinate T accepted the declared overall breadth as satisfactory, shut the upper gate, and emptied the lock chamber. As the water dropped, *Edelweiss* and *HH9*, which originally floated freely, were pressed together and also left rubbing marks on both walls. They were disregarded and the process was continued until the lower water level was reached. It was only when the skipper of the tug *Dollart* tried to drag the barges *Gesine* and *HH9* that it was noticed that the latter was stuck fast to the *Edelweiss* and could not be moved. So *Dollart* dragged only *Gesine* out. Thereupon T and M, in the lock-keeper's absence, decided to free the ships by raising the level of water in the lock chamber. The lower gate was shut and the sluice-boards of the upper gate raised 19 cm. The water level rose at a rate of 25 cm in a minute and a half. But the boats that were stuck together did not float up evenly. They were lifted like a roof along their common surface of contact but with their other surfaces listed, hanging on the lock walls. The *Edelweiss*, which had only a 15 cm freeboard, was threatened with flooding. Despite persistent danger signals the lock personnel failed to stop the rush of water in time. The *Edelweiss* filled with water and sank. Only the crew could be saved.

The plaintiff, who had insured the owner of the *Edelweiss*, indemnified him and claimed DM 103,605 as compensation from the defendant as owner of the *HH9*, on the ground that the damage had been caused by its skipper's incorrect statement of its breadth. The defendant rejected the claim, disputing the causality of the incorrect statement and attributed the damage exclusively to the unskilful steps taken by the lock personnel.

The Navigation Court declared the claim (originally only for a part claim amounting to DM 10,000) against the defendant and the skipper S justified in full against the latter, but limited as to the defendant to the ship and cargo or their value. Only the plaintiff and the defendant appealed. The Court of Appeal allowed in full the claim, extended in the second instance to the total damage, and now directed only against the defendant, and rejected the defendant's appeal.

The application for review resulted in the decision being quashed and the case being referred back for the following.

Reasons

The Court of Appeal holds that the master's incorrect statement of the *HH9*'s breadth was the immediate and adequate cause, not only of the jamming together of the ships, but also of the additional damage that arose from the loosening of the ships from the jam. It went on to say that jamming on leaving a lock, though infrequent, was not extraordinary, and that the instructions to the lock personnel took account of such an occurrence. In any case, the removal of the jam by letting the water in was not an extraordinary but the only solution. Risks in operating locks are always a matter of practical experience. These risks are multiplied if one of the foreseen dangers, here the jamming, intervenes and must be removed in a usual way, in accordance with practical experience. In so doing increased account must be taken of a failure, at the same time both human and technical in character. That is not at all improbable and should, according to general human experience, have been recognized by the bargemaster. Accordingly, the failure of the lock personnel was not enough to break the causal connection between the incorrect information about the breadth and the sinking of the *Edelweiss*.

It must be conceded to the applicant that the statements concerning the causal connection as a presupposition of the defendant's liability are not free from legal error. To begin with, the assumption that the blameworthy conduct of the master S was the immediate cause of the damage is not correct. S did nothing to lay *Edelweiss* alongside *HH9* and thereby provide the first condition for the subsequent jamming. The choice of the berth depended on the free decision of the master of *Edelweiss*. Likewise, the placing of the boat at that spot depended on the decision of the lock personnel, who alone had to determine the occupation of the lock and approved the laying side by side, so as to make better use of the space. However, S's incorrect statement of the breadth led to that decision and in that way indirectly caused the jamming. It is certain that the lock personnel would not have allowed the boats to be placed side by side, if they had known the correct breadth of the *HH9*. The incorrect information was therefore, in spite of its merely indirect operation, a *conditio sine qua non* of the further course of events.

However, this alone does not prove that S caused the damage in such a way as to incur liability. It has long been undisputed in legal literature and case-law that the scope of such natural logical causes is commonly far too wide for all their consequences to be imputed to the person causing them. Hence the jurists have elaborated the concept of adequate causation, which, according to the Reichsgericht's decision of 18 November 1932 [reference],

should make it possible to exclude some conditions, which from the point of view of natural science were conditions of a certain consequence, and without whose existence the consequence would not have occurred, for the purpose of causal connection in a legal sense; and the conditions which are logically most remote from the consequence should be excluded, because a consideration of those conditions would also lead to legal results that are at variance with equity.

Adequate cause has been formulated mainly by von Kries, Rümelin, and Traeger (*cf.* summary in Lindenmaier, "Adequate cause and proximate cause" in *Festschrift für Wüstendörfer, Zeitschrift für das gesamte Handelsrecht und Konkursrecht* 113, Heft 3/4 (Stuttgart 1950)). Common to these formulations is the valuation of a concrete *conditio sine qua non* on the basis of its tendency to favour the consequence according to general standards. They differ according to the point of view from which the valuation is undertaken. While von Kries, the creator of the concept of adequate cause, prefers to undertake a valuation on the basis of all circumstances known or knowable individually to the originator of the condition at the time of its entry (*ex ante*), and also taking into account general practical knowledge (*ex post*) based on experience, Rümelin puts forward the theory of "objective hindsight". For the formation of a judgment of possibility he prefers to have regard to the whole empirical knowledge of mankind and all the circumstances anywhere to hand at the time the condition occurred, whether they were recognizable by the most superior discernment or had first become recognisable *ex post* from events following the condition in question.

Von Kries's individual foresight proved to be too narrow for private law cases of objective strict liability and contractual liability, Rümelin's objective hindsight too wide, to exclude with certainty the inequitable results of the condition theory. Rümelin himself accordingly found it necessary to curtail his doctrine, in so far as by the condition in question the injured party was brought into contact in time or in space with the damage-producing event. Traeger avoided the defects in both formulations with the following formulation (*Kausalbegriff im Zivil- und Strafrecht* (1904), 159): An event is an adequate condition of a consequence if it has in a general and appreciable way enhanced the objective possibility of a consequence of the kind that occurred. In making the necessary assessment account is to be taken only of:

(*a*) all the circumstances recognisable by an "optimal" observer at the time the event occurred,

(*b*) the additional circumstances known to the originator of the condition.

The factual situation so established is, according to Traeger, to be examined by applying the whole human experience available at the time a decision is made to see whether it appreciably favoured the occurrence of the damage-producing event (*cf.* Lindenmaier, *op. cit.*, 223–6).

Traeger's formulation has been followed in essentials by the Reichsgericht since the decision in RGZ 133, 126, 127, more recently in the form that there is an adequate connection "if a fact in general and not under special peculiar quite improbable circumstances, to be disregarded according to the regular course of things, was apt to produce a consequence".

This formulation expressed until now unaltered in essentials in many decisions (RGZ 133, 126; 135, 154; 148, 165; 152, 49; 148, 38; 168, 88; 169, 91) has also been followed by this Senate, maintaining the grounds for decision laid down by Traeger. Admittedly—as Lindenmaier points out (*op. cit.*, 239, 241)—one must not forget the starting-point of the inquiry: namely the search for a corrective that restricts the scope of the purely logical consequences, in order to produce an equitable result to the imputable consequences. Only if the courts are conscious of the fact that it is a question here not really of causation but of the fixing of the limits within which the originator of a condition can equitably be presumed liable for its consequences, and therefore of establishing in reality a positive condition of liability (Larenz, *Vertrag und Unrecht* 12, 14; Lindenmaier, *op. cit.*, 239, 241–2), will the danger of a schematisation of the formula be avoided and correct results be guaranteed.

That in the case before us the jamming of the boats was an adequate consequence of the incorrect information (concerning the breadth of the vessel) was accepted by the Court of Appeal without error of law. But the jamming produced no provable damage, since matters were at a standstill and the boats lay quietly on an even keel in the lock chamber. However, the first real damage-producing consequence came later, and in assessing them the Court of Appeal did not pay sufficient attention to the possibly necessary restriction of liability, when, while recognizing it the court declined to consider the failure of the lock personnel. It is true that the Reichsgericht has repeatedly recognized that anyone who has caused an accident must also answer for such consequences as are first produced in the course of conduct made unavoidable by the accident, through an intervening lack of skill, because according to human experience it must be taken into account that not all conduct will necessarily be perfect and accompanied by the desired result (RGZ 102, 230; 105, 264; 119, 204; RG HRR 28, 831; RG JW 1911, 755). This principle, however, does not apply without exception and cannot lead to saddling the person responsible for an accident indiscriminately with all consequences that, without his doing, are brought about in a completely unusual and inappropriate way by persons who are completely unauthorised to intervene (*cf.* the aforementioned decisions RGZ 102, 230 and JW 1911, 755).

The defendant had pointed out that such an unusual and grossly incorrect intervention of the lock personnel did occur and the Court of Appeal should therefore have made a detailed examination of their behaviour, instead of contenting itself with the remark that "no matter how significant the signs of the failure of the lock personnel they did not suffice for a break in the causal connection, above all because there could be no question of the accident being intentionally brought about by the lock personnel".

The question raised by the concept of intentional conduct has no place in this connection, which is concerned only with the concept of causation. It requires only an examination of whether an "optimal" observer would normally have been able to take into account the behaviour of the lock personnel as it is presented—and, for the most part, undisputed—at the moment the condition on which liability was based—i.e. the incorrect declaration of breadth—occurred. The omission of that examination not only justifies the procedural objection raised by the application for review that the factual situation was not exhaustively dealt with, but leads to a recognition that the Court of Appeal did not apply the correct standard for distinguishing between imputable and inadequate consequences.

Among the circumstances which could form independent causes of damage according to the factual situation, the following were to be examined:

1. the fact that the lock-keeper neglected, contrary to § 2 no. 2 of the service instructions, to supervise the operation of the lock in person, that he left the operation to the subordinate who had not been appointed as his representative and who had continued it although the marks of rubbing on the lock walls ought to have made him notice that the boats were jammed;

2. the fact that after the jamming the lock personnel and the pump engineer had, of their own volition and contrary to an express prohibition in the service instructions, tried to break the jam by letting in the water, without warning the lock-keeper, who was alone empowered to do so by the instructions, and leaving to him the removal of the obstacle, and all of it although there was no occasion for precipitate action, since the course of events had come to a standstill once the lower water-level had been reached;

3. the fact, asserted by the defendant and established by evidence, that the lock-keeper would have been able to break the jam without danger to the boats, as he had done on several previous occasions, perhaps by removing obstacles created by good fenders and coverings and by carefully raising the water-level, if need be by manually working the sluice-boards;

4. the fact that the raising of the water-level was so quick that within one and a half minutes the freeboard of the *Edelweiss*, which was only 15 cm high, was bound to be flooded if the jam were not broken and the boats did not float up as intended;

5. the fact of the failure in the electricity supply, which remains unexplained, when and why it happened . . .

It may be that one or even several of these facts fall within the scope of the dangers which experience would lead one to expect, so that their foreseeability, taken one by one, could be affirmed. Nevertheless it should have been examined whether the coincidence of these manifold conditions, in part possibly accidental, were not unusual and outside the scope of normal risks. In that connection it should be noted that conditions were under consideration which reinforced each other and only in combination led to the perilous aggravation of the situation that had little to do with the original creation of the jam.

The Court of Appeal's findings of fact do not go far enough to enable the court of review to decide finally the question of causal connection. The part played by the lock personnel in the course of the accident must be elucidated, if need be with the help of independent experts, and then a fresh conclusion reached on the responsibility of the defendant.

Case 81

BUNDESGERICHTSHOF (SIXTH CIVIL SENATE) 12 MARCH 1996
BGHZ 132, 164 = NJW 1996, 1533 = JZ 1996, 1178

Facts

The claimant Land ("the claimant") is suing the defendant (on the basis of a right acquired by subrogation from the police officer W) for costs of medical treatment (DM 77,572.73) salary (DM 67,191.43) and damaged uniform (DM 300). The police officers W and M had brought the defendant (then nearly 17 years old) and Ü (also a juvenile) before a magistrate. They had been arrested on suspicion of car break-ins and house thefts. They had numerous previous convictions. After their judicial examination, they escaped through a window about 4 metres above the ground on the first floor of the court building. Ü jumped first. M ran down the stairs in pursuit but W ran to the window. The claimant says he could have caught the defendant there, but the defendant pulled him down with him. The defendant claims that he was about 10 metres away from the building when W jumped after him. Ü was uninjured but the defendant broke his arm. W fractured both legs. He was treated in hospital for about 6 months, and was unfit for work for about a year and a half altogether.

The Landgericht allowed the claim. The appeal of the defendant was unsuccessful. His appeal in law led to quashing and reference back.

Reasons

I. The appeal court left undecided the question of whether the defendant pulled W down with him through the window opening, or whether W jumped after the defendant. Even in the latter case it considered that the defendant would be obliged to provide compensation for harm under § 823 (1) of the BGB in combination with § 95 of the NdsBG. This was because W would then have been provoked by the defendant, in such a way as to give rise to liability, to jump after him. The defendant should in all the circumstances have reckoned on the police officer jumping after him. Admittedly, W also laid himself open to the accusation of negligence, as he must have known that he was exposing himself to a substantial risk by jumping from a height of 4 metres. But this did not lead to a limitation of the defendant's liability, because he had created the quite decisive cause of W's injury.

II. The appeal court judgment does not withstand the arguments against it in the appeal in law in every respect. On the basis of the defendant's claim, assumed by the appeal court to be correct, that W jumped after him through the window opening when he was escaping, the appeal court's view that W's injuries arising from the jump were to be attributed to the defendant in liability law admittedly reveals no error of law. But the appeal court's reasoning, that W was not guilty of any contributory fault which would affect the outcome of the case is not legally tenable.

1. According to the constant case law of the Senate, someone who by his reprehensible conduct provokes another person to behaviour which endangers that other person can be obliged in tort law to provide compensation to him for the harm which has arisen as a consequence of the risk which was increased by the provocation (references omitted). The claimant's voluntary decision must however be based on motivation which deserves approval at least to some extent. The Senate has found tortious liability on such a basis, in particular in cases in which someone seeks to escape from arrest, or provisional arrest, by police officers, or other persons authorised to make an arrest, by flight. The flight has provoked these persons in a reprehensible manner to a pursuit which endangers them and in which they have then suffered harm because of the increased risk (references omitted). In these kinds of cases, motivation deserving approval causing the pursuer to rush after the fugitive in spite of the special associated dangers, can, as the Senate has repeatedly emphasised, can be based, amongst other things, on the official duties of the officer responsible for guarding the fugitive (references omitted). The Senate adheres to this case law.

(a) The appeal in law unsuccessfully objects (referring to Steffen [reference omitted]) to the fact that, in cases of the kind present here, the risk associated with the pursuit by the police officer is part of the risks of his employment commitment, and that duties to compensate for harm cannot therefore be based on the behaviour of the fugitive. Undoubtedly for a police officer, the risk involved in the employment commitment covers the "normal" risk of injury which is not especially based on the circumstances of the pursuit (and therefore is part of the general risks of life) and the harm which may result to the pursuer. For a police officer therefore there may be no transfer of the risks to the escaping criminal unless the necessary internal connection with the pursuit exists (references omitted). On the question of transferring to the fugitive an "increased" risk associated with pursuit, (and the case in dispute is only about the realisation of this) it admittedly must be borne in mind that an officer whose official tasks include pursuing criminals in the public interest may feel himself called on to undertake greater risks, in his efforts to fulfil his duty carefully to a greater extent than other people (reference omitted). But, in the Senate's view, this does not lead, when the necessary boundary is drawn between the areas of risk of the pursuer and the pursued, to an unreasonable transfer of risks to the fugitive, if he knows that his pursuer, or potential pursuer, is a person whose job requires him to act in this way. This is because the fugitive must in this case take into account that the pursuer may undertake a higher risk and this may possibly result in the fugitive having to assume an increased responsibility. He can take that into account by behaving in a way which prevents such risks arising. Admittedly on a just division of the risks of a pursuit, it should not be forgotten that the transfer of the increased risk will not lead to the fugitive being liable for the realisation of those dangers to which it was completely inappropriate for the pursuing officer to expose himself (references omitted). The assumption of responsibility for physical injury which arose from increased risk of this kind would not be covered by the protective purpose of § 823 (1) of the BGB.

Whether and to what extent an escaping criminal or suspect has accordingly to bear an increased risk of pursuit is determined by the peculiarities of each individual case; the prerequisites for a division of loss in accordance with § 254 of the BGB can also be fulfilled here. This will need more precise application in the case in question at a later juncture. It must however be emphasised here that, contrary to the view of the appeal in law, even with officers (in particular police officers), the risk they bear because of their work commitment does not exclude the transfer of the increased risk associated with pursuit to a fugitive.

(b) The appeal in law argues that the fugitive, could not be made responsible for harm which befell his pursuer during the pursuit, because action in one's own interest is not criminal. This objection is misconceived. Admittedly a criminal has no legal duty to give himself up to criminal prosecution. But the ground for civil law liability does not lie in the escape as such, as the appeal in law in the end does not fail to recognise. It is based instead on the fact that the fugitive, by the manner of his flight, has in a reprehensible manner provoked the pursuer to a reaction which endangers himself. The conduct of the fugitive which is contrary to duty consists in this pressure at a psychological level, causing the decision to make a pursuit which is required by duty (or which is at any rate desired by the legal order) with the special potential for danger which it holds (references omitted).

2. In the case in dispute, the factual findings of the appeal court support its legal assessment that W's injuries caused by the pursuit are objectively to be attributed to the defendant.

(a) Admittedly (and the appeal in law uses this as an argument) the Senate making the decision in its judgment of the 13 January 1976 (reference omitted) approved the decision at previous instance in that case, that a juvenile sought for the serving of a weekend detention who fled from a toilet window situated at a height of 4.05 metres did not have to assume liability for the fracture of the heel bone of a police officer who leapt after him, which this officer had sustained on impact with the asphalt yard. But this is not inconsistent with an affirmation of the defendant's liability in the present case. For one thing, the facts of each case differ. Apart from the fact that the appeal court did not establish the presence here of an asphalt or similar hard landing surface, there is a substantial difference from the above mentioned Senate's judgment. In the present case it was not merely a matter of arresting a juvenile whose home and place of residence were known for the serving of a weekend detention, but of resolving and punishing serious crimes, namely breaking into cars and house theft. As the two persons arrested had been punished for such crimes on numerous occasions, the commission of further crimes of the same kind was likely following a successful escape. The appropriate relationship between purpose and means, i.e. that the risks of pursuit should not be out of proportion to the goal of apprehending the fugitive, is, however, the essential gauge when examining the prerequisites for provocation to pursue and the transfer of the increased risk of injury to the fugitive (references omitted). If such proportionality is not maintained, physical injury of the pursuer, as already stated, will not fall within the protected area of the liability norm.

When comparing the present case with the Senate's decision of 13 January 1976 (reference omitted), it must finally be considered that the Senate making the decision did not actually deny objective attribution of the physical injury, in spite of the fact that the jump was from a height of 4.05 metres, but left the issue undecided. It let the liability on the part of the fugitive fail on subjective grounds, namely for lack of fault.

(b) On the question of the objective attribution, cases of the kind present here can on other grounds as well take into account other factors besides the height of the jumping-off point (which would in this respect perhaps be entirely a matter of a certain number of centimetres). Admittedly the transfer of the risk of injury to the fugitive is dependent on whether the pursuer should have felt himself called on to jump in pursuit, which, with unusually great heights, is not the case. In the critical area, which covers the present case of a height of about 4 metres, the special circumstances of the case in question must however in the end be the decisive factor. In this connection, besides the nature of the jumping-off point already mentioned above, amongst other things the age and physical condition of the person jumping in pursuit are also of importance. According to the findings of the appeal court, these factors in the present case gave no cause for the 31-year-old W to refrain from jumping.

(c) In examining the question of objective attribution, the court must finally also bear in mind (as did the appeal court) that W, in pursuing the defendant, had to make up his mind very quickly about whether to jump after him; and that therefore, as the appeal court explains, there was scarcely any time and opportunity left for him to weigh up the risks of a jump. On that account also, the requirements for deciding whether he was justified in feeling called on to act cannot be too high. For W, the way the situation presented itself was that two people had already jumped out of the window in front of him and both had then still been able to run away. The fact that in these circumstances W thought the danger of a substantial injury was not great enough to prevent him from jumping justifies (contrary to the view of the appeal in law), in the context of the peculiarities of the present case set out above under a and b, the appeal court's view that W could have felt himself to be called on to pursue in the sense of the case law on this subject.

3. The appeal court made no legal error in also attributing the physical injuries of W to the defendant in a subjective sense.

(a) The subjective side of the liability, i.e. the accusation of having culpably caused the physical injury of his pursuer, assumes that the fugitive had to take into account that he was being followed, and that he could also foresee that his pursuer might be harmed in the pursuit. It is not a necessary prerequisite for his liability that the fugitive was actually aware of the pursuit as such (reference omitted). The conduct which has provoked a pursuer (prepared to pursue out of motives deserving approval) to a reaction which endangers himself is no less in breach of duty just because the fugitive rushes away so fast that he cannot see whether the person he provokes actually commences pursuit. The fugitive can also be the "controller of events" in the sense of the case law (reference omitted) by forcing special potential for danger on his pursuer, if he prevents the person provoked by his escape from being able to consider carefully before going into a situation of increased danger. For this very reason he must take into account the possibility of a pursuit even into these special dangers. Any different view would, especially in relation to a jump from a window, as here, (where the fugitive himself can possibly not be aware of the pursuit at all) not take proper account of the fact that he has reprehensibly exposed his pursuer to an increased potential danger. Accordingly, the Senate making the decision has always considered as the only decisive factor the question of whether the fugitive by running away created, in a way that was attributable to and recognisable by him, a situation of increased risk of injury for the pursuer and whether he should have taken pursuit into account (references omitted). Even if the defendant therefore (on the basis of the description of the facts assumed by the appeal court, that he had already distanced himself 10 metres from the building when W jumped after him) was not to know of the pursuit by W, this is not a barrier to liability on his part.

(b) The appeal in law challenges the finding of the appeal court that the defendant should have taken into account that the police officer would jump after him, simply by reference to the special danger of a jump from a height of 4 metres. But this argument was already considered above not to be effective, when examining whether W ought to have felt himself to be provoked to make the jump. The grounds mentioned there suggested that, for the defendant (who of course exposed himself to the risk of injury from jumping), W, who was responsible for guarding him, would not be any less likely to do the same. The danger that W could be injured in so acting was likewise known to the defendant; it is also described by the appeal in law as clearly recognisable and obvious.

4. The judgment under challenge cannot however stand in relation to the appeal court's reasoning in refusing to divide the loss on the basis of § 254 (1) of the BGB.

(a) The appeal court proceeded without legal error on the basis that the accident was partly caused by W's fault. The fact that the defendant, as has been explained, provoked him in a reprehensible manner to jump after him and therefore in such a way as to oblige him to pay compensation, is not inconsistent with this. The connection in liability law between the psychological pressure to pursue and the injuries to the pursuer which occurred in the pursuit does not only exist when the person pursued is solely responsible for the harm. Allocation of the loss in cases of psychological causation admittedly assumes, as the Senate has stated on a number of occasions, that the person intervening ought to feel himself to be called on to act not merely in a general sense, but exactly in the way he chose (references omitted). But this limitation is only to exclude those cases in which the person intervening has taken on a risk which is so excessive that allocating it in law to the person who set the chain of causation in motion would cause the risk of liability to become infinite (reference omitted). For cases of the present kind, it does not follow from the above that, on a jump from a window from up to a certain height, the fugitive should be fully liable for his pursuer's injuries, and where this height is exceeded he should not be liable at all. Instead there remains room, as the Senate has already stated (where the pursuit should have been foreseen by the fugitive and its potential for harm does not exceed the unacceptability threshold mentioned above) for balancing the special circumstances of its actual execution in accordance with § 254 of the BGB (reference omitted). An "all-or-nothing" principle in such cases would often prevent a just assessment of each individual case, because a differentiated balancing exercise could not take place (reference omitted). The Senate making the decision has therefore already repeatedly approved decisions in which the judge of fact divided the loss on such a basis (references omitted).

(b) In the present case the facts established by the appeal court justify its view that W was partly responsible for his injuries. The fact that, as explained above, he had to decide very quickly whether he should jump after the defendant through the window opening, or perhaps like his colleague M take up the pursuit by the stairs, admittedly diminished the requirement for the care to be expected from him within the framework of § 254 of the BGB (reference omitted). But this did not relieve W of every duty of care in respect of his own interests (references omitted). He could also therefore, despite the required haste, recognise and bear in mind in his decision that the window was a considerable height above the ground and that a jump from the first storey of the building gave rise to a risk of not inconsiderable injuries, even though the defendant, and earlier the co-suspect Ü, survived their jumps apparently without serious injury. Therefore, as the appeal court explains, on careful consideration there were reasons for W not taking the risk of injury associated with the jump. Admittedly no protracted consideration was needed for the protection of his own interests which was required of him within the framework of § 254 of the BGB. But even with the need for a rapid decision, W could have considered and avoided the potential for danger which would come to mind with a jump from a height of 4 metres. The fact that W did not take account of this justifies the accusation of contributory fault.

(c) The partial responsibility which W bears cannot, however, on the basis of the considerations on this issue laid down by the appeal court, be regarded as so insignificant that it could be left entirely out of consideration within the framework of the balancing exercise under § 254 of the BGB for the allocation of loss. In taking the view that the defendant was solely liable, because he had provoked W and thereby created the quite decisive cause of his injury, the appeal court did not consider all the circumstances of the present case which were relevant in this respect, and this issue is subject to re-examination in the appeal in law (reference omitted). As the Senate has explained in its judgment of 12 July 1988 which has just been mentioned, in relation to division of liability under § 254 of the BGB it should be taken into account as a decisive factor whether the behaviour of the one or other party made the onset of the harm probable to a significantly higher degree. Here this requires balancing the extent to which the defendant and W could recognise and avoid of the risk of injury, according to an attribution appraisal, and this has not so far been undertaken by the appeal court. It also requires an explanation evaluating the grounds for saying whether and to what extent the defendant's provocation to take increased risks (as against W's exposing himself to a position of danger) made the onset of harm more probable.

III. The judgment of the appeal court relieving W from any participation in the harm must therefore be quashed and the matter referred back to the appeal court. The Senate making the decision cannot make a conclusive decision itself under § 565 (3) no. 1 of the Civil Procedure Code. For one thing the balancing of the responsibilities under § 254 of the BGB is for the judge of fact to assess and this information is only available to the court dealing with the appeal in law to a limited degree (reference omitted). For another thing, the appeal court has left open so far whether the defendant pulled W down with him when he jumped. As this could lead to full liability on the defendant's part, the appeal court will also have to make the necessary findings on this point, insofar as this should in its opinion now be material.

Case 82

BUNDESGERICHTSHOF (SIXTH CIVIL SENATE) 24 APRIL 1952
NJW 1952, 1010 = VERSR 1952, 352

The husband/father of the plaintiffs was in 1937 struck by an automobile belonging to the defendant. In consequence of the accident, his right leg was amputated; he bore therefore an artificial leg and had to walk with the aid of two sticks. In a lawsuit it was established that the defendant was obliged as a joint debtor to make good all the damage arising from the accident of 1 February 1937.

In 1945 the husband/father of the plaintiffs was injured by artillery fire and died of that injury. He used at the time in question to set out in the evening to go to a bunker with the plaintiffs. In the afternoon of 31 March 1945 the place lay under artillery fire. The plaintiffs' family first stayed at home, and only when the firing stopped, set out for the bunker. While the three of them were on their way, the firing suddenly started up again. The first plaintiff ran to a house where he took shelter. The second plaintiff hurried to the bunker. The husband/father of the plaintiffs set out on the road but could cover the ground only slowly because of his lameness. Before he reached either a house or the bunker he was injured by a shell fragment.

The plaintiffs, considering the death of their husband/father as a further consequence of the 1937 automobile accident, demanded of the defendant compensation for the support they were deprived of in consequence of the death.

Reasons

Even if the laming of the first plaintiff's husband is looked upon as a *conditio sine qua non* (BGHZ 2, 138, 140 ff. = NJW 51, 711) for the injury from the shell fragment, it cannot be the basis for the defendant's liability, for there is no adequate causal connection between the laming due to the accident and the death resulting from the artillery fire. An adequate connection exists only "if according to general experience and not under especially peculiar, quite improbable circumstances, not to be contemplated according to the regular course of things, were apt to produce a consequence" (RGZ 113, 126, 127 and the later constant case-law of the RG). Whether there is "adequacy" is not really a question of causation but of setting the limits within which liability can equitably be attributed to the originator of the condition. Since in so doing we are concerned with an assessment which of its nature affords some room for judicial discretion, an element of uncertainty cannot be excluded, especially at the lower limit, in deciding whether the condition favoured the result to an appreciable degree. Such an uncertainty cannot be avoided either by applying other important legal concepts such as offending against good morals, important reason and, above all, against the principle of good faith. Only the idea of adequate causation can provide a sufficient guide. The question whether and in what measure a causal connection induces liability can never be exhaustively answered by abstract rules but can be decided in doubtful cases only by the judge according to his unfettered discretion having regard to all the circumstances; and only when it is borne in mind that the doctrine of adequate causation as a way of limiting liability is based on § 242 BGB, will the danger of schematising the formula be avoided and correct results obtained (BGHZ 3, 261, 267; Lindenmaier in *Zeitschrift für das gesamte Handelsrecht und Konkursrecht* 113, 239–43).

In agreement with both courts below, an adequate causation must be rejected, without any need to go into the formulations set out in the books, which are concerned with whether foreseeability of the consequence must be required and by what rules it must be determined. "Adequacy" is here excluded because the laming, by its general nature, did not enhance in what experience would show to be an appreciable degree, the probability of being struck by artillery fire. For a causal connection exists in a legal sense, as has already been mentioned, only when the condition originated by the person doing the damage is in a general way apt to produce the damage in question—especially peculiar and quite unusual circumstances which would not be taken into account in the regular course of things, being excluded. In examining, therefore, the facts, it must be determined whether a "general" favourable tendency exists, but a tendency will be disregarded which is so considerable that no account would be taken of it in ordinary experience (Lindenmaier, *op. cit.*, 227; Enneccerus-Lehmann, *Schuldrecht* (13th edn., 1950) 63, fn. 6). Such a consequence, outside ordinary probability, must be treated as accidental and not imputable. That is so in the present case because a laming as such cannot in any case according to general experience be regarded as enhancing to an appreciable extent the danger of being wounded. Shell fire may make anyone, even healthy persons, liable to be hit. It is in no way foreseeable how hostile fire may be directed. For the civil population being struck by a shell was a "new and independent event" of a purely accidental character. The danger might be avoided to a certain extent by seeking shelter at once. Whether it was generally "right" to run to a neighbouring house or a bunker could be at least doubtful. The probability that the plaintiffs could be hit, when they ran to seek shelter, was, according to general experience, not less than the danger for the injured party in case he remained standing or lying down. In view of this "accidental effect" of a few shots happening at short intervals, running away might have proved "wrong" and standing or lying down "right". In view of the combinations of purely accidental conditions the injury to the first plaintiff's husband from shell fragments can no longer be regarded as an imputable consequence of the 1937 traffic accident.

Case 83

BUNDESGERICHTSHOF (THIRD CIVIL SENATE) 25 SEPTEMBER 1952
BGHZ 7, 198 = NJW 1953, 700 = VERSR 1952, 430

The orphan plaintiffs claim compensation from the defendant for the damage they suffered from their mother's death as the consequence of an abortion carried out by the defendant. She felt herself pregnant in May 1949 as a result of intercourse with Sp. The defendant, who practises as a doctor, was at her request ready to perform an abortion in consideration for a fee. For that purpose he visited Frau S at Sp's home and with his help operated on her. He felt, but misunderstood, a peculiar structure in her womb and thought he noticed the remains of an afterbirth. After douching the womb with Sp's help he placed the patient on a sofa, and ordered her to rest in bed for three days and to see him in his surgery in 14 days. He left the house a few minutes before 4 p.m. Some 20 to 25 minutes later the patient complained of severe pains in her abdomen. At her request, Sp. hurried to the defendant's surgery, reported that Frau S was in pain, and obtained from him a pain-killer. When, after about an hour's absence, he came home, he found that her condition had deteriorated further. When a gynaecologist was eventually called in, arriving about 6 p.m., he found a severe internal haemorrhage, so he arranged for an immediate transfer to a hospital; and after about three-quarters of an hour he operated and found a rent in the womb and ascertained that the womb artery had been torn. Although he bandaged the source of blood and made a blood transfusion, the plaintiffs' mother died before the operation was complete.

The plaintiffs claimed compensation from the defendant in contract and delict for medical and hospital expenses together with payment of an annuity and also a declaration that they were entitled to be compensated for all further damage.

Both instances rejected the claim; the appellants demanded the case be sent for reconsideration.

Reasons

1. The Court of Appeal agreed with the Landgericht that the defendant caused the death of Frau S from loss of blood by piercing the wall of her womb and thus damaging the womb artery. It came, however, to the conclusion that he was not at fault in causing the injury.

The experts were unanimously of the opinion that an injury such as happened here could have been inflicted by even the most conscientious and experienced medical man in the course of an abortion; in following it the Court of Appeal made no mistake of law. Thus, such an injury *could*, but *need not*, have resulted from a careless and improper use of the instruments. The Court of Appeal acted consistently in examining whether such a careless act of the defendant in the present case was to be inferred either according to the prima-facie evidence or by way of circumstantial evidence. It said no to both questions.

(*a*) Whether this was a typical course of events affording sufficient *prima facie* evidence required, in the first place, a formulation of the results of experience and then its application to the present situation. Such a formulation is a conclusion of fact inferred from general circumstances and can, in these proceedings, be checked for correctness only in so far as it is drawn from established facts. The facts themselves cannot be checked; they must be proved by the person who seeks to found on them a *prima facie* case. The burden of proof is thus on the plaintiffs just as the other party must prove the possibility of a deviation from the typical course of events. When, therefore, the Court of Appeal reached the result, on the basis of expert opinions, that "no formulation from the results of experience can be established that the piercing of a womb in an abortion can as a rule be traced to a careless use of instruments by a doctor", the unassailable finding of fact followed, that according to medical experience the injury in question was "possible even with a careful use of instruments" and could "find its explanation in the peculiar characteristics, not visible to the doctor, of the womb". That under these circumstances experience afforded no prima-facie evidence was based on no error of law.

(*b*) The Court of Appeal considered that the defendant was at fault in not affording the required medical care after finishing the operation. But it declined to attribute fault to the general conduct of the defendant, which would also provide, as the plaintiffs contend, *prima facie* evidence of a faulty use of the instruments and therefore of his being to blame for the injury.

The court took into account various surprising and irregular circumstances such as the use of a camphor injection before the operation; the suspicion that a miscarriage was beginning; the failure to recognise the rupture of the artery; the leaving of an alleged afterbirth in the womb; and finally the omission still to be discussed, of an immediate reference to a hospital. While it adhered to the opinion that they did not constitute errors in medical practice, it saw in both of the last circumstances two blameworthy omissions; yet it considered that they did not disclose a general prolonged lack of medical conscientiousness or care, and that there was, as a whole, no typical conduct justifying a prima-facie presumption that the defendant did the injury to the wall of the womb and the opening of the artery through a careless use of instruments.

Here also no objection can be taken on legal grounds to the Court of Appeal's decision . . .

(c) It is on the other hand possible to treat fault in such a situation as an indication that the doctor was not careful in the operation itself. That point also was not missed by the Court of Appeal. But it considered the evidence insufficient to afford it the necessary certainty. It considered that the proved omissions predominantly disclosed a lack of conscientiousness in the *after-care* of the patient, whereas a fault in the abortion itself would consist in lack of care in the use of the instruments. The basis of the fault in the two cases would be too different to enable secure enough conclusions to be drawn from the one to the other. The court was entitled to value the indication as a means of information, and that valuation could not be checked in these proceedings, so that no legal error can be found to exist in its judgment.

II. The Court of Appeal, however, rightly found that the defendant was at fault in his neglectful conduct after finishing the actual operation. He ought not to have left a doubtful situation without getting rid of the afterbirth, and he ought, by that time, to have had the patient sent at once to a hospital. That he did not do so was described by the expert, Professor Ph., as "unintelligible", and the Court of Appeal rightly agreed with him. Complications had ensued which required further treatment in hospital, in relation to which it was irrelevant whether the defendant was to blame for them or not.

The Court of Appeal likewise declined to infer liability for the consequences because it denied causality. It inferred indeed from the opinions of the experts that an immediate transfer to the hospital would have improved the patient's chances of survival. But it held that death might have occurred even if there had been immediate transfer after the abortion and an operation without delay. It could "not decide beyond reasonable doubt that if the defendant had done his duty immediately after the operation or even when informed by Sp. that the patient was in pain, her life would have been saved".

These considerations do not make it quite clear whether the Court of Appeal had sufficiently in mind what was needed to prove causation. According to longstanding case-law it is not the strict rule of evidence in § 236 ZPO but that in § 287 that applies here . . . Under § 287 ZPO the court is not prevented from being convinced by the evidence and the circumstances that there is an adequate causal connection, even if the possibility cannot without reasonable doubt be excluded that the damage could have occurred without the defendant's fault. If, as here, the blameworthy conduct consisted in an omission, the question of adequate causation ought to be formulated as "whether that omission was in the ordinary way capable of producing a result, and not only under peculiar, quite improbable circumstances, not to be contemplated in the normal course of events". It is not, therefore, a question of whether other, not remote circumstances could have produced the result, but whether the injurious consequence could not have occurred in the normal course, or rather would have been produced only by special circumstances of that kind. Here the Court of Appeal had merely found that a dutiful conduct would not certainly have prevented the result, and that finding cannot be regarded as sufficient to exclude the omission as the cause of the result. The Court of Appeal ought to have considered in accordance with § 287 ZPO—if need be after further questioning the experts— whether it could have produced such a result.

III. The Court of Appeal started from the position that the operation was an unlawful attack on the mother's bodily integrity, and therefore an infringement of the protective enactments §§ 223, 218 StGB. Yet, it was unwilling to infer any liability from them because it did not see any causal connection between the operation and its fatal outcome. It explained that the defendant undertook the abortion as a doctor and carried it out according to the rules of medical art and science. Permitted abortions with the object of saving the life and health of the patient would be conducted in the same way. According to the expert, Professor Ph., injuries could occur outside the actual purpose of treatment. The doctor need not, however, as a rule take account of them when he started. In particular, complications dangerous to life were conditional on the intervention of peculiar or unfortunate circumstances, such as an opening of the womb artery through an injury to or spontaneous cleavage of the wall of the womb, which must in the normal course be disregarded. Even when such dangerous circumstances occur, the doctor would have means at his disposal to prevent a fatal outcome with some, though not absolutely sure, prospect of success. Thus, the possibility that an abortion undertaken by a doctor would lead to a patient's death was too remote for the assumption of a causal connection, giving rise to liability, between the operation and its fatal outcome.

1. These explanations exaggerate the requirements for adequate causation . . . It need not be decided whether there are medical operations in which complications dangerous to life can be produced only through the intervention of quite unique, quite improbable circumstances which can be disregarded according to the regular course of things. For an operation such as an abortion this was evidently assumed neither by the expert nor the Court of Appeal, for both reckoned with the possibility of such dangers and omitted to consider them only because in this case the doctor had appropriate means at his disposal, to which however the Court of Appeal accords only "some, though not a certain prospect of success".

If one starts from the position—as one must—that the entry of the aforementioned dangerous circumstances falls within the adequate consequences of an abortion, the further adequate causal connection cannot be denied on the ground that there was some possibility of preventing the fatal outcome. This denial of a causal connection is based on a fallacy similar to that which appeared in relation to the causality of the delayed transfer to the hospital. Once a danger to the patient's life appeared in any way, no peculiar and quite improbable circumstances were needed to lead to death, but, on the contrary, medical skill was needed to prevent it. Whether the prospects of success in those attempts to avert it were more or less great cannot alter the fact that a failure is the adequate consequence of a danger to life.

2. Moreover, the liability of the defendant cannot be denied on the ground that there was no causal connection between the illegal operation and its fatal outcome. That connection would be unimportant only if the operation was not illegal on the ground that the deceased not only agreed to but expressly wished it. The Court of Appeal was able to refuse to go more deeply into the question of what significance that wish had. It confined itself to the statement that consent to an abortion is forbidden and therefore legally inoperative . . . A consent is inoperative not only when influenced by a defect of the will, but also when it is repugnant to a legal prohibition or good morals and is therefore invalid (§§ 134, 138 BGB). That presupposition is here affirmed by the Court of Appeal on the ground that an infringement of § 218 StGB makes both the doctor and the patient punishable.

It is also not a defence to a claim that a plaintiff is acting deceitfully and in bad faith if he claims damages from a person whom he asked to afford a particular kind of medical assistance, so long as he keeps within what he was asked for. This invocation of good faith must also be denied to one who so severely infringes a prohibition of the Criminal Code. The legal position is not altered by the fact that a portion of the public, for various reasons, demands an abolition of the prohibition.

3. By undertaking the operation, the defendant not only deliberately injured the body of Frau S, but also infringed the protective enactments contained in §§ 233, 218 StGB. Although the second paragraph aims in the first place at protecting the living embryo, it serves also to protect the pregnant woman; and that is enough to satisfy the conditions of § 823 II BGB. If, however, they are satisfied, it follows, as the Reichsgericht has pertinently said . . . that the defendant is liable for all the injuries caused by his operation, even if they are not his fault. That, contrary to the Court of Appeal's opinion, there was a causal connection between the death of Frau S and the operation is shown above at (1).

For these reasons also the legal dispute is not yet ripe for decision, since the defendant can rely on the consent and wish of the deceased in so far as that, too, implied fault in the undertaking of the operation. As matters stood, if she had not energetically desired the operation, the defendant would not have performed it . . . That fault will have to be balanced against the defendant in respect of causality (§ 254 BGB), and the defence arising from it must affect the plaintiffs also in accordance with § 846 BGB.

Case 84

BUNDESGERICHTSHOF (THIRD CIVIL SENATE) 17 OCTOBER 1955
BGHZ 18, 286 = JZ 1956, 177 (with approving note by K Sieg)

In 1946 the husband and the father of the plaintiffs had to undergo the general inoculation against typhus, which was carried out in virtue of an ordinance of the Oberpräsident of the then province of Hanover of 22 January 1946 with the approval of the British military government. He had three inoculations in all, after which he suffered an illness, in the course of which a malignant swelling appeared. On 27 February 1948 he died.

The plaintiffs claimed compensation from the defendant State on the ground of its breach of official duty and—in a subsidiary way—for public sacrifice in being deprived of their right to support by the death of their breadwinner. They alleged that the death of their husband and father was caused by the typhus inoculation and the doctor was to blame for the death.

The lower courts applying the rules on sacrifice for the public good declared the claim justified in principle but otherwise dismissed the action.

The defendant's application for review failed for these

Reasons

I. . . .

II. In agreement with the Landgericht the Court of Appeal finds it proved, on the basis of the evidence adduced, that the typhus inoculations applied to the deceased produced a staphylococcus suppuration which within $1\frac{1}{2}$ to 2 years developed into a malignant swelling of sarcoma appearance, from which death resulted. Against this interpretation of the evidence no doubt is raised by the applicant. An attack is made on the view taken by the Court of Appeal that the inoculation constitutes not only an incontrovertible condition in the physical sense (*conditio sine qua non*) for the death, but also the cause in the legal sense, i.e. an adequate condition for the occurrence of the death. That attack is, however, unfounded. In this connection it is of importance—as the Court of Appeal conclusively observed—that the inoculation led to the death not through the intervention of independent acts of third persons or the deceased himself, but that death ensued without the co-operation of any further intervening causes. Admittedly the findings of the Court of Appeal must lead to the conclusion that a staphylococcus suppuration only seldom results from a typhus inoculation and also, in particular, that the development of such a suppuration into a fatal sarcoma belongs to the class of rare medical phenomena. All the same, neither such a suppuration nor its further development into a fatal sarcoma can be regarded as circumstances outside all medical experience which, according to the case-law of the Reichsgericht, further developed by the Bundesgerichtshof (*cf.*, e.g., BGHZ 3, 261, 265–7) could not be described as an adequate casual connection. It must be noted that the question of adequacy between condition and consequence cannot be answered in a purely logical, abstract way by numerically computing the frequency of the occurrences of such a consequence, but that in a value-judgment those out of the many conditions in a physical sense must be excluded which on a reasonable view of things cannot be regarded as circumstances giving rise to liability; in other words, the limit must be found by a value-judgment "up to which a liability for the consequences of a condition can be equitably imputed to its originator" (BGHZ 3, 267). In making such a value-judgment it must be of importance (for the purposes of setting the limits of liability) whether the originator of the condition consciously took into account the more or less remote possibility of damage resulting from it or would not have acted otherwise if he had thought of the possibility of such damage. In that case the limit of liability may be set relatively wide. There would have been no decision not to order a general typhus inoculation if a possibility—though extremely rare—of death had been envisaged. Accordingly, the typhus inoculation (carried out in virtue of an official ordinance) must be imputed to the State as the cause creating the death, even though the manner in which the inoculation led to the death belonged to the class of exceptional medical phenomena.

Moreover, for the following reasons a liability-creating causal connection between the inoculation and the death cannot be called in question: That an inoculation—whatever be the kind—leads to the death of the person inoculated does not lie beyond the bounds of experience. That is the ground for example for § 6 of the North Rhine–Westphalian Act on Inoculation Injuries of 10 February 1953 (GVBI 166). If, therefore, an inoculation has directly caused a death, i.e. without the co-operation of further intervening causes, an adequate causal connection between inoculation and death must be said to exist irrespective of the precise manner in which it came about (e.g. through infection, as in this case, or because of a particular predisposition of the inoculated person).

III. The applicant goes on to object that the Court of Appeal granted to the plaintiffs a claim for compensation, as only indirectly injured, by an analogous application of § 844 BGB. The Senate, however, shares the Court of Appeal's opinion.

The right to compensation is, indeed, governed by the principle that only the person directly injured is entitled to compensation. None the less we have here to do with the exceptions contained in §§ 844, 845 BGB. These exceptional provisions, which in the case of a person's death afford compensation to persons who suffer indirect damage, correspond to the quite general opinion prevalent before the BGB came into force, which developed at a very early date in modification of Roman law and had already found a place in the positive law of different countries (*cf.* for the historical development RGZ 7, 139, 141–4). Parties of the kind of interest here, who have suffered only indirect damage are allowed damages not only in the case of culpable unlawful acts but also where the duty to compensate rests exclusively on strict liability (§ 3 II Haftpflichtgesetz: § 10 II StrVerkG; § 21 II LuftVerkG of 21 August 1936). Further, the principles laid down in §§ 844, 845 BGB apply, if not generally, certainly partly to the law of contract by virtue of express provisions (§ 618 III, § 62 III, § 76 I BGB) and are to that extent regarded as capable of an analogous application (RGZ 167, 85, 89; BGHZ 5, 62 ff., with further references). Likewise, it is generally recognised that these principles are also to be applied in the sphere of public law (RGZ 11, 22, 23 and 112, 290, 297); Enneccerus-Lehmann, *Recht der Schuldverhältnisse* (1954) 971). Our law is accordingly widely governed by the principle that, where compensation is payable to the injured party for bodily injury, compensation must also be afforded in a case of death to those deprived of their legal right to maintenance. This principle, according to what has been said, cannot without further ado be applied to all cases in which compensation would have to be paid for a mere bodily injury (e.g. not simply in the field of pure contract law). If, however, in general a claim for compensation is afforded for violent attacks on bodily integrity, then within the scope of compensation claims a corresponding application of § 844 BGB to killing cannot be refused. The state of facts that gives, outside all contractual relations, a claim for compensation on the ground of sacrifice for the public good for attacks on bodily integrity are from the points of view of interest here so close, both in law and in fact, to the states of fact in which compensation is to be paid for similar damage under §§ 823 ff. BGB or on the basis of strict liability that those who are legally entitled to support in case their breadwinner is killed cannot in any circumstances be denied redress for the loss of their right to support. The legal result is unacceptable that, on the one hand, interference by a public authority with corporal integrity leading to an injury must be compensated while, on the other hand, if the interference leads not only to corporal injury but to death, and the person concerned has made a far bigger "sacrifice" the relatives entitled to maintenance, who are only affected indirectly but particularly hard by this sacrifice should be left wanting. Such a result would also, as the Court of Appeal has already conclusively remarked, be incompatible with the principle of a social law-abiding State (Article 20 GG) and would clash with the constitutionally guaranteed protection of the family (Article 6 GG). The Court of Appeal, therefore, rightly awarded to the plaintiffs (i.e. the widow and the sons of the deceased) compensation on the ground of sacrifice for the public good in compliance with § 844 BGB.

The amount of compensation to be awarded to those entitled to support in accordance with the general rules on sacrifice for the public good by the analogous application of § 844 BGB, already limited by § 844 to the actual loss of support cannot—as the applicant would wish—be further limited quite generally by the courts, to conform to the corresponding rules of social insurance law. That can only be done by express legislative provision, such as is, for example, contained in § 6 of the North-Rhine–Westphalian Act on Inoculation Injuries.

Case 85

BUNDESGERICHTSHOF (SIXTH CIVIL SENATE) 22 APRIL 1958
BGHZ 27, 137 = NJW 1958, 1041 = JZ 1958, 742 (with lively
approving article by G Boehmer)

The plaintiff's motor cycle collided on a main road passing through a village with a motor-car coming in the opposite direction which belonged to the defendant's husband, since deceased, as the latter turned left to enter a side street. The plaintiff was injured. Both vehicles were damaged.

Criminal proceedings were instituted against both drivers. The defendant's husband was convicted of causing bodily harm in a negligent manner but then died. The death was not connected with the accident and occurred before the order of the court could be served upon him. The plaintiff was also sentenced by the Amtsgericht to pay DM 30 for speeding. On appeal the Bavarian Oberstes Landesgericht quashed this judgment and remitted the case to the Court of First Instance for rehearing. The plaintiff was then acquitted for lack of evidence.

He claimed from the defendant, as heir of her husband, compensation for the costs he had incurred in defending himself in the criminal proceedings.

The Landgericht declared his claim justified as to four-fifths and rejected any further claim. On appeal by the defendant, the Oberlandesgericht rejected the claim for the costs. The plaintiff lost his appeal against the decision for the following.

Reasons

The parties are still in dispute only over the question whether the defendant must also pay the plaintiff four-fifths of the costs which he had to pay to defend himself in the criminal proceedings. The Court of Appeal gave a negative reply on the ground that no causal connection existed between the bad driving of the defendant's husband and the incurring of the defence costs. Whether the attacks against this decision of the Court of Appeal are justified may be left undecided since in any case the view of the Court of Appeal that this claim for compensation of the plaintiff is to be rejected must in the result be approved.

A finding of adequate causation is not decisive for the decision of the dispute. The current mode of thought which looks at the question of limiting liability only from the point of view of adequate causation is not always capable of providing a proper solution . . . In previous judgments the Bundesgerichtshof has already made clear its view that the formula of adequate causation does not suffice to solve the problem of limiting liability (*cf.* BGHZ 8, 325, 329; 10, 107, 108; 20, 137, 142, 143). In a search for other means, von Caemmerer has justly focused on the question whether the facts for which compensation is demanded lie within the area of the protection of the rule that has been broken. This formulation of the question is commonly applied and recognised in determining liability for breach of a protective statute (§ 823 II BGB). Here, as this Senate also declared in its judgments (BGHZ 12, 213, 217 and 19, 114, 126), following the case-law of the Reichsgericht, it is a condition of liability that the damage lies within the scope of the interests protected by the protective enactment, that is to say that the damage arises from the injury to a legal interest for the protection of which the rule was made. This limitation applies no less, if, as here, claims are raised under § 823 I BGB. Here, too, it must first be asked whether the damage in question lies within the protective purpose, in other words whether it concerns dangers which fall within the scope of the risks for which the rule was made. For this reason the sense and scope of the rule violated by the defendant must first be inquired into . . .

The plaintiff, in demanding compensation for his defence costs, in claiming that damage be made good that he suffered in his estate, that is to say economic damage. It is generally accepted that by § 823 I BGB, under which he primarily makes his claims, the estate as such is not protected. The only question therefore is whether the damage falls within another aspect of the field of dangers dealt with in § 823 I BGB, namely the integrity of the body, health, and property. Its intention is to protect against all risks that arise from an infringement of those rights. Only the consequences of that infringement are imputed to the wrongdoer and only within that scope are the interests of the injured party protected by it.

If anyone, like the plaintiff, is injured in an accident and his motor vehicle is damaged, the costs of restoring his health and repairing the vehicle are undoubtedly within the protective purpose of § 823 I BGB. That applies also to his loss of earnings, because his injury makes him unable to continue his calling, and also to the loss of the use he makes of the vehicle in his business. All of these are consequences of the accident which are connected with the personal injury and the damage to the vehicle. Although to some extent economic damage is involved, they fall within the protection of § 823 I BGB. It is quite different with the expenditure the criminal proceedings brought upon the plaintiff. So far no dangers that were protected against by the law have materialised through the accident. This had nothing to do with the personal injury and property damage suffered by him through the accident, for it arose from his being suspected of committing a criminal offence and from the decision of the prosecuting authority to institute proceedings against him. The risk of becoming involved in criminal proceedings is a general risk that affects every citizen. It is independent of the personal injury and property damage suffered in an accident, for it occurs even where an accident produces neither of them, and even when the driving complained of leads to no accident at all. The risk of having to spend money in defending oneself against a criminal charge is not one that the law intends to avert when casting the protection of § 823 I BGB over the integrity of health and property. Thus that provision disappears as a foundation for a claim to have that damage made good, irrespective of whether there is an adequate causal connection between the conduct of the wrongdoer and the damage done by him.

Moreover, the plaintiff cannot claim compensation for his defence costs under § 823 II BGB, in combination with § 13 StVO. For § 13 StVO . . . apart from protecting the orderly movement of traffic, also protects only the health and property of those engaged in it, but not their economic interests. The only damage that is still in dispute, the defence costs, touches neither the health nor the property of the plaintiff, but interests that are not protected by it . . .

None of the legal considerations that have been adduced support the plaintiff's claim to have his defence costs made good.

Case 86

BUNDESGERICHTSHOF (SIXTH CIVIL SENATE) 16 FEBRUARY 1972
BGHZ 58, 162 = NJW 1972, 904 = JZ 1972, 559 (and important article
by E Deutsch in JZ 1972, 551 = VERsR 1972, 560)

On 21 June 1968 there was a traffic accident on L Street in B. A lorry of the Dutch armed forces, in an attempt to overtake an automobile which was in course of parking, collided with an oncoming car. Both drivers left their vehicles in the narrow passage made by the parking vehicle, waiting for the arrival of the police. In consequence the highway was, for the time, blocked for the following car drivers. Thereupon several drivers, who could not make headway because of the lorry in front of them, drove round on to the sidewalk to the right of the scene of the accident. About fifteen minutes later, when the police arrived, substantial damage had been done to the sidewalk. The city of B, as owner of the highway, had to spend DM 1736.58 to clear it up.

The drivers who drove on the sidewalk have not been identified.

The Bundesrepublik, under the provisions of NATO Armed Forces Statute, compensated the owner of the car struck by the army lorry. The plaintiff city contended that the Bundesrepublik must also make good the damage done by those drivers in driving on the sidewalk.

Whereas the Landgericht rejected the claim, the Oberlandesgericht allowed it.

On appeal, by leave of the Oberlandesgericht, the Bundesgerichtshof restored the judgment of the Landgericht for the following.

Reasons

The Federal Republic, as is agreed between the parties, has, under the provisions of the NATO Armed Forces Statute, assumed liability for damage done by the lorry of the Dutch armed forces as if it had been done by a lorry of the German forces. The claim is based on § 839 BGB, in combination with Article 34 of the Constitution, so that liability under §§ 831, 823 BGB combined with the provisions of the Road Traffic Ordinance is excluded. According to the second sentence of § 839 I BGB, the plaintiff city would have had to show that it could not have obtained compensation in any other way for the damage— in particular, not from the drivers who had actually caused the damage and who, if they had been ascertained, would doubtless have had to make it good.

There is no dispute between the parties that the conditions for this liability are satisfied. For, as the judgment under attack establishes, the driver of the lorry was even at fault, since the strict liability is not excluded by unavoidable circumstances (§ 7 II StVG). The only question is whether the damage that the drivers who were forced to halt behind the lorry did in driving round on the sidewalk would be traced back to a conduct giving rise to liability, in this case the occupational hazard of this lorry, for which the operator is responsible. The Court of Appeal said yes.

II. This standpoint cannot be accepted.

1. Admittedly, approval must be given to the Court of Appeal's holding that the causal connection between the conduct of the lorry-driver and the damage to the sidewalk was even in this case adequate (the decision of the District Court of Düsseldorf in the "Greenbelt" case, is, to this extent, sound). It is well known that in cases like this drivers

constantly—no doubt in breach of traffic regulations and subject to punishment for malicious damage (§ 303 StGB)—do not wait long enough for passage to be possible or for a diversion to be allowed by the traffic police. In view of the experience that the conduct of such drivers will always recur, it may also be assumed that a driver must foresee that an accident caused by him in the flow of traffic may lead to such reactions on the part of following drivers, with ensuing damage to the public streets, private front gardens, fences, and so on. Nevertheless, in the present case, there is no absolute need to discuss fault as a ground for liability, because the plaintiff city can base its claim on § 7 StVG.

The appeal wrongly casts doubt on the view of the Court of Appeal that the lorry was "in operation" when such drivers passed over the sidewalk. The lorry had not been taken out of circulation when it came to a stop but prevented other vehicles from going forward. For the purposes of § 7 StVG the operation of an automobile lasts as long as the driver leaves it in circulation and the danger involved by it persists (BGHZ 29, 163, 166). More-over, the diversion made by the impatient drivers is still in close connection, in both time and place, with the collision caused by the lorry (cf. BGHZ 37, 311, 318). If a following automobile, in an attempt to avoid striking the lorry in front of it, braked and skidded and so invaded the sidewalk, the damage caused would certainly fall within the operational hazard of the lorry. Nor would it be different if a following driver, in order not to collide or not to be overrun by subsequent participants in the traffic, had deliberately turned on to the sidewalk.

2. If, therefore, the adequate causal connection and the connection with the operational hazard of the lorry are admitted to exist, the decision of the dispute depends on whether such consequences also can be imputed to a causer of damage as rest upon the "free" decision of a third party (so-called "breach of the causal connection" or "no recourse"). That question does not depend, in cases of this kind, on whether the injured party bases his claim on § 823 II (in combination with the provisions of the StVG) or on § 823 I BGB or on § 839 BGB or, as here on the ground that the highway was blocked by an automobile, on §§ 7, 18 StVG.

(a) Despite the contention of the appellant this imputation is not to be rejected on the ground that such impatient drivers acted deliberately and unlawfully in driving on the sidewalk.

The imputation of damage is not automatically excluded by the intervention of a third party (BGHZ 12, 206, 211; 17, 153, 159; 24, 263, 266). Only when the causal nature of the first state of facts is completely irrelevant to the second event can it be said that the causal connection is "broken" (BGHZ 3, 261, 268; 17, 159). That is not the case here. That such drivers caused the damage unlawfully does not stand in the way of the imputation. Whether the intervention of the third party was unlawful is of no decisive importance for the question of imputation.

Just as irrelevant is it that a person is acquitted of liability for damage done by a third party on the ground that the latter acted wilfully. Accordingly, the driver and operator, whose automobile collided with a lorry so that its load fell on to the highway, must com-pensate not only for the goods that were damaged by the fall, or could not be put in safe-keeping, but also the goods stolen from among those strewn on the highway. There the person liable for the fall cannot refer the injured party to his claim against the thieves; that damage also may be imputed to him, on the ground that he created the danger of their being stolen. That those consequences of his conduct causing liability (that is to say

the operation of the damage-causing automobile, or the traffic blunder of his driver)
no longer fell into the class of risks for the avoidance of which rules of liability are
prescribed (§§ 7, 18 StVG; §§ 823 ff. BGB, in combination with the provisions of the StVG),
cannot be accepted (*cf.* BGHZ 27, 137, 140). Such duties to assume risks may also be
established by statute. Thus, under certain circumstances, the duty of care of a person
participating in traffic may extend so far that he must take care that he does not, by
defective behaviour, induce third parties to contravene wilfully the road traffic rules.
Above all, the operator of an automobile is answerable for all damage that is connected
with the operation of his vehicle, irrespective of the way its dangerous character has
caused damage in a particular case; he is liable also for damage a joy-rider knowingly and
deliberately causes by his vehicle, even for the reckless killing of a human being (BGHZ
37, 311, 316/317).

(*b*) On mature consideration, however, the case to be decided appears to be different.
The drivers, once they came to a halt on the road, drove onto the sidewalk of their own
free will. That was connected with the accident, and so with the manner of driving the
lorry and the operational hazard involved in it, only so far as the accident and its blocking of the road provided an occasion for the behaviour of the drivers. This was, however,
no more than an external circumstance which gave the motivation for wilful conduct,
without regard for the public safety, of the drivers. It cannot, therefore, be regarded as a
sufficient foundation for an imputable connection (*cf.* also BGHZ 25, 86, 90; Senate decision of 12 February 1963—VI ZR 181/62). Above all, it cannot be said here that the conduct
of the lorry-driver and the blocking of the highway "provoked" the conduct of the drivers
(*cf.* BGHZ 57, 25, 28). The blocking of the highway did not constitute such a situation
compelling the intervention of the third parties. As regards the damage to the border
strip, the impatient drivers alone, and not the lorry-driver, were "masters" of their
injurious conduct. Accordingly, the present case affords no opportunity for examining
whether, in discussing "provocation" of the reckless conduct of a third party, effect should
be attributed to the degree and importance of the danger caused to the property of others.
The decision of the dispute follows from the principle that the activities which are important in deciding the imputation of a damage must always be made the subject of a valuation (BGHZ 18, 286, 288; 30, 154, 157; Senate decisions of 8 January 1963—VI ZR 80/62
and 12 February 1963—VI ZR 181/62—823 BGB).

In making the valuation there is no connection sufficient to ground liability between
the conduct of the lorry-driver and the damage, even if, in the plaintiff's interest, attention is focused not only on § 7 StVG, but also on the fault of the lorry-driver which led
to the collision. Here the law, and above all the traffic ordinance, clearly distinguished the
spheres of liability: the driver and operator of the lorry were liable for the collision and
its consequences to others involved in the accident as well as for all objects thereby
damaged. For the damage to the sidewalk on the other hand, only the drivers who drove
on it are answerable. The current instructions and prohibitions applicable to the lorry-
driver protected the interests of those who, with their property, were near the highway
only to the extent that the driver was not allowed to invade the pedestrian path with his
lorry or to afford an occasion for other vehicles to swerve onto the ground next to the
road in order to avoid a collision. But what happened after the accident, as a result of
other vehicles driving over the sidewalk in order to get on more quickly, does not fall
within his sphere of duty. The lorry-driver was not in a position either in fact or in law
to hinder them. That the imputation made by the Court of Appeal goes too far is also

plain because the plaintiff city, if it were correct, could claim also against the operator of the car with which the lorry collided, if he did not succeed in exonerating himself under § 7 II StVG; and in certain circumstances the concurrent liability of the automobile which was being parked on the right might have to be considered. It would also be going too far to hold an operator liable for the damage done by the following drivers driving onto the sidewalk if, as a result of failure in its equipment, the lorry had slid across the road.

3. After all, it was not here the operational hazard of the lorry or the driver's way of driving that in any imputable way led to the damage of the sidewalk. That might, to be sure, have happened because the driver of the lorry left it standing until the police arrived in answer to their call. If the resulting hindrance to traffic (*cf.* § 1 StVG) had no longer had a reasonable justification, this conduct could have created a liability for the damage done by the impatient drivers (§§ 823 I and II, 839 BGB), so that the operator also (according to § 831 BGB, here the defendant according to Article 34 of the Constitution) might be liable. But a liability on this ground must be legally distinguished from the liability due to the preceding conduct for the actual consequences of the accident. The liability could also affect anyone who blocked the highway not by a vehicle or had not been to blame for the accident.

Under what conditions such a liability should be allowed to exist needs no examination here. The plaintiff city has made no complaint against the driver on these lines.

III. The plaintiff city therefore can have recourse to those drivers only for the damage done by them. It runs the risk, if their identity can no longer be ascertained, of having ultimately to bear the damage. That is, however, a general loss that falls on anyone who has property adjoining a road used for traffic and one that it cannot shift off onto the defendant. In consequence the decision appealed from cannot stand.

Case 87

COURT OF APPEAL OF STUTTGART, 24 NOVEMBER 1964
NJW 1965, 112 = JZ 1966, 189

The defendant drove his car, in which were two workmates, down a street in Heilbronn. Unfit to drive because he had a blood–alcohol proportion of 1.80, he drove into a stationary lorry. In the collision his car caught fire. The plaintiff, who saw the accident from his parents' petrol station, hurried with an extinguisher and, together with a passer-by, rescued the defendant and his two passengers from the burning car . . . He suffered severe burns and was unable to work for two weeks.

The defendant's insurer paid compensation for the pecuniary damage, but denied liability to pay for pain and suffering. The Landgericht rejected the claim, but the plaintiff succeeded on appeal for the following.

Reasons

In so far as compensation was awarded to the plaintiff for his material damage, the judgment was not attacked by the defendant. The plaintiff has appealed against the rejection of his claim to be compensated for his pain and suffering.

Contrary to the view of the Landgericht, the plaintiff is also entitled to be paid for his pain and suffering in delict under §§ 823 I, II, and 847 BGB. The finding that the defendant's driving while unfit to drive did not afford an adequate cause for the plaintiff's injury cannot be accepted. Admittedly, it is not every *conditio sine qua non* that constitutes an adequate cause, but only such a one as, generally and in accordance with an objective judgment or experience, is apt to produce such a consequence, or one that in general appreciably enhances the possibility of its occurrence, and therefore adequate causes do not include conditions which according to general human experience are completely irrelevant to its occurrence that according to common opinion they cannot reasonably be taken into account. All the same, the finding cannot be accepted that in the present case the bodily injuries to the plaintiff lay outside what was to be normally and objectively expected as a consequence of the accident. It is of course true that it occurred here only because of a further act, due to the free decision of the plaintiff, namely his intervention in order to rescue the defendant and his passengers. That does not, however, exclude an adequate causal connection between the unlawful act and the consequences. It is not correct that where there is an independent and voluntary intervention by a third party an adequate causal connection can only be recognised to exist if the intervention served to ward off an especial danger to the public and therefore was in performance of a legal or moral obligation. Admittedly in RGZ 29, 121 and 50, 223, where an adequate connection was held to exist between the insufficient securing of a team of horses drawing a vehicle and the injuries to a person who tried to hold them up, attention was directed to the fact that the rescuer had acted in performance of a legal or moral duty. In RGZ 50, 223 attention was also expressly directed to the fact that the injured party had intervened to avoid a threatened accident to persons in the village street, and especially children coming out of school precisely at that moment. Nevertheless the Bundesgerichtshof in NJW 1964, 1363, when holding that an adequate causal connection existed between the conduct of a hit-and-run driver and an accident to a pursuing driver caused by an increase of speed, expressly said that the recurrent allusion in those decisions of the Reichsgericht to the fact that the rescuer's intervention had been in accord with a legal or moral duty should not be understood to limit liability to such cases, but only to show that in such cases the intervention of the self-sacrificing third person is nearly always automatic, so that the injuries suffered in doing so were undoubtedly adequate consequences of the wrongful act. In the above-mentioned decision, the court drew the conclusion that in less threatening situations it turns on the circumstances whether the situation produced by the wrongdoer is generally to be considered apt to produce rescues by third persons and, if so, in the present form. In the case then decided the court went on to say that after a sufficiently serious traffic accident it is not at all unusual for other drivers to take up the pursuit of a hit-and-run driver independently, and that such traffic camaraderie, even if it may not reach the level of moral duty, is a fact which prevents us from regarding such a pursuit of the escaping driver as the quite improbable and gratuitous intervention of a third party in the causal continuity. Thus, one may start from the position that even where such an intervention is the immediate cause, an adequate connection may be held to exist between the damage and the event that was the initial occurrence, if the conduct of the third person was justifiable. It is therefore irrelevant that in the present case the plaintiff was not expected to assist and, therefore, under no legal duty to help. It can also be left undecided whether there was a moral duty to rescue. In any case there was a justification. Indeed morally his conduct was of a high standard. Although in the circumstances his intervention required considerable courage and intrepidity, one cannot agree with the

Landgericht that the possibility of it must have appeared to an observer so remote that it could not reasonably have been taken into account . . .

Moreover, one cannot agree with the judgment under appeal in regarding the injury to the plaintiff as not an imputable consequence of the defendant's unlawful act . . . It shows a misunderstanding of Larenz's position in invoking his opinion that even where there is an adequate causal connection between the rescue by the plaintiff and the defendant's unlawful act, that act must be regarded as a meaningless condition of the rescue and the ensuing injury to the plaintiff, which must no longer be imputable as a consequence of the unlawful act, since although the defendant could in any case be blamed for negligence in relation to the plaintiff's injuries, the latter bears the full responsibility for his deliberate conduct and therefore a quite predominant share of responsibility falls on him. As the plaintiff in his grounds for appeal aptly says, Larenz was merely upholding the view that even where several persons caused, because they one after another provided conditions for the eventual consequence, one of them can be regarded as its author because he intended the act as his own and thereby reduced the condition that the others provided to the status of an indifferent and legally meaningless condition; side by side therefore with the responsibility of the one who deliberately produced the consequence by his unlawful act, that of another person who merely provided an adequate condition, even though he acted negligently, appears meaningless, so that the consequence cannot be imputed to him as his act. Thus, the Landgericht failed to see that the plaintiff, who, as has already been explained, had a justification for his deliberate intervention, and whose conduct was of a high moral order, acted neither contrary to law nor in blameworthy fashion. Moreover, it failed to see that Larenz, when referring to the above-mentioned decisions of the Reichsgericht in RGZ 164, 125, expressly said that the free but faultless act of a third party did not exclude the imputation to the one who had provided an adequate condition . . . Further, the defendant was also to blame for the damage to the plaintiff through his negligence, because it was foreseeable not only objectively, as has already been said, but subjectively, and here also, just as objective foreseeability is required for an adequate causal connection, infrequent and exceptional consequences are to be taken into account and only quite remote possibilities are to be left out of account. Such a remote possibility, however, as has already been discussed in connection with the intervention of the plaintiff, was, neither objectively nor, from the defendant's point of view, subjectively, in question.

The defendant, therefore, is liable for the damage suffered by the plaintiff under § 823 I and II BGB. The plaintiff, therefore, is entitled to damages for pain and suffering under § 847 BGB. Admittedly, in the cases decided by the Bundesgerichtshof (NJW 1964, 1363) only compensation for material damage was dealt with and not pain and suffering. There was no question at all of personal injury to the driver pursuing the hit-and-run driver, but only damage to his car. This, however, seems immaterial. What is essential is that the court affirmed liability for a delict.

It follows that where a person suffers personal injuries he can claim damages for pain and suffering. Moreover, the Reichsgericht, in the case already mentioned of the rescue of passengers from a burning vehicle (RGZ 164, 125), expressly awarded damages for pain and suffering to the injured rescuer against the objection of the defendant.

Since the plaintiff's claim for damages for pain and suffering is based on an unlawful act, there is no need to go more deeply into whether a claim for damages for pain and suffering also lies under the head of *negotiorum gestio*. [Discussion followed about the amount of damages for pain and suffering.]

Case 88

BUNDESGERICHTSHOF (SIXTH CIVIL SENATE) 30 JUNE 1987
BGHZ 101, 215 = NJW 1987, 2925 = JZ 1988, 150

Facts

When 13 years of age, on 6 February 1976, the plaintiff was injured while engaged in sport. Since it was suspected that her spleen had been damaged the doctor attending the accident sent her to the hospital in E which is run by the rural district. The surgeon Dr H, in his capacity as the Second Senior Registrar acting in the absence of the Chief Surgeon, examined the plaintiff and decided to open the abdominal cavity. Finding that the left kidney had been damaged, he removed it. On the following day the plaintiff was transferred to the University clinic in H as a result of acute renal failure. It was discovered there that she lacked a right kidney from birth and that consequently her only existing kidney had been removed in the District Hospital in E. In the hospital in H she was first treated temporarily by means of an artificial kidney. Upon the advice of the resident medical staff the plaintiff's mother expressed her readiness to donate one of her own kidneys. On 31 March 1976 one of her kidneys was removed and implanted in the plaintiff. At the end of April the plaintiff was sufficiently well to be discharged from the hospital for further treatment at home.

The plaintiff sued Dr H and the District Council for damages in respect of her own economic loss and for pain and suffering. To that extent the action has been concluded. As a result it is also undisputed that the removal of the plaintiff's kidney constituted a negligent course of treatment. If the correct medical procedure had been followed, the kidney could have been saved. The plaintiff now asks for a declaration that the defendant Rural District must compensate her mother for any economic damage which the latter suffered as a result of the removal of her own kidney on 31 March 1976, subject to any assignment of the claim—by operation of law—to the authority administering social security. For this purpose the plaintiff has accepted an assignment of her mother's claims.

The District Court allowed the action for a declaration. The appeal by the defendant was rejected by the Court of Schleswig. At the same time, on an appeal against a supplementary judgment of the Court below it, the Court of Appeal increased the assessment of costs. A second appeal by the defendant against these decisions remained unsuccessful.

Reasons

I. The Court of Appeal, whose decision dated 3 October 1986 was published in FamRZ 1987, 384 and NJW 1987, 710, has held that the mother's claim for damages is well founded. Its conclusions amount in essence to the following:

The action for a declaration was admissible, irrespective of who was entitled to assert the claim. Even if she had not been assigned the claim, the plaintiff had a legal interest of her own in the declaration demanded by her if for no other reason than because she was then potentially exposed to future claims by her mother on the ground of *negotiorum gestio*. The need to avoid that any claims for damages might be caught by the rules on limitation of actions was, in itself, a reason for an immediate declaration. A real possibility existed that the plaintiff's mother would suffer physical damage.

The plaintiff's mother was entitled to damages in her own right against the defendant by virtue of §§ 31, 89, 823 I BGB in respect of that damage which could not be treated as expenses in restoring the plaintiff's health.

The surgeon Dr H, acting on his own responsibility in his capacity of deputy of the chief medical officer of the hospital's surgical department, was to be regarded as a representative of the defendant Rural District which was responsible for his wrongful treatment. As in the cases of action to save a person or to assist in an emergency, considered by the practice of the courts and in the literature, the donation (by the mother) of one of her kidneys was called for by the tort committed against the plaintiff. Despite the voluntary character of the decision of the plaintiff's mother, a causal link (operating mentally) existed between the tort attributable to the defendant, the physical damage resulting from the donation of a kidney, and the requisite connection between them. Nor did the mother's consent to the operation to remove the kidney exclude the illegality of the bodily injury as far as the defendant was concerned.

II. The objections against these conclusions put forward in the second appeal are unfounded. The Court of Appeal has held correctly that the action for a declaration, which has as its object any future physical damage to the plaintiff's mother, is well founded. This Senate also holds that the plaintiff's mother has to this extent a claim of her own for damages according to §§ 31, 89, 823 I BGB which the plaintiff, as an assignee, may pursue by way of an action for a declaration.

1. Contrary to the view expressed by the appellant, no objections exist against the admissibility of the action for a declaration. The fact that the Court of First Instance by its decision, which has since obtained the force of *res judicata*, has held the defendant liable in respect of future physical damage is not an obstacle. It only dealt with damage suffered by the plaintiff, but did not include damage suffered by the plaintiff's mother, which is in issue here. As the Court of Appeal has stated correctly, the plaintiff may, in certain circumstances, be exposed to subsequent claims by her mother based on *negotiorum gestio*, if the latter incurs expenses in consequence of the loss of the kidney which she donated.

2. The question, denied by the Court of Appeal, as to whether the plaintiff's mother also has claims against the defendant based on *negotiorum gestio* in view of §§ 683, 670 BGB in respect of future expenses resulting from the loss of the kidney need not be examined here. As the Court of Appeal has held correctly, she is entitled in any event to claim compensation in tort, according to § 823 I BGB from the defendant in respect of future damage as a result of the physical injury caused culpably by Dr H.

(*a*) Contrary to the view put forward by the appellant, such a claim is not excluded on the ground that the surgeon Dr H was not to be regarded as an organ representing the authority responsible for the hospital where he removed the kidney. In the absence of the chief medical officer of the surgical department, Dr H, in his capacity as the latter's deputy, was charged with the function of a chief medical officer. In law his position does not differ from that of the chief medical officer himself, had he been present. In so far as the appellant doubts whether also the chief medical officer in charge of a department of a hospital (and not only the chief medical officer in charge of the entire hospital) acts as an organ of the authority responsible for the hospital, his references are to a judicial practice which is outdated and has been abandoned [references]. The question, which had been left open by the Federal Supreme Court [reference], has been decided in the meantime by the present Senate to the effect that the heads of individual sections of a hospital must be regarded as the properly appointed representatives of the local authority responsible for the hospital [references]. This certainly holds good as long as the authority responsible for the hospital does not show that in the particular instance the organisation of the hospital must lead to a different conclusion. The defendant has not made any allegations to this effect in the court below dealing with the facts. On the contrary, the liability of the defendant according to §§ 31, 89 BGB for its organs was never disputed in respect of the culpable acts of Dr H.

(*b*) When the Chief Medical Registrar, Dr H, removed the plaintiff's only kidney in violation of a medical practitioner's duty of care, he did not only damage the plaintiff's body and health. In addition he thereby created a dangerous situation which could, above all, cause near relatives of the plaintiff to accept an injury to their own body in order to save the life and health of the plaintiff, by offering a kidney for implanting into the plaintiff. This enforced sacrifice of personal bodily integrity is an injurious act. Leaving aside some special aspects remaining to be discussed, which cannot however lead to a different legal assessment, it can, as in other cases of rescue and emergency, also result in a duty of reparation on the part of the person responsible for the situation calling for rescue or emergency—assistance towards those engaged in the rescue or assistance towards those who suffer injury in the course of it.

(*aa*) There can be no question that a causal nexus, which is relevant for the purpose of legal liability, exists between the removal of the plaintiff's sole kidney, for which the defendant must assume responsibility, and the mother's donation of her kidney. The possibility of a kidney transplant, including a donation by a living person, was known at the time, and the donation of a kidney by a close relative was not so remote as to leave it out of legal consideration. Contrary to the appellant's view, it is to be expected that, upon the advice of medical practitioners, a mother will be prepared to make this sacrifice for her child. Nor is the causal nexus broken by the fact that the donation of the kidney was due to a voluntary decision of the plaintiff's mother; this decision was solely induced by the dangerous situation, for which the defendant is responsible, faced by the mother as a result of the wrong medical treatment, which alone led to the rescuing action. As the practice of this Senate shows [reference], a mentally induced cause can also suffice to establish liability. Writers agree almost unanimously on this. Nor does the appellant challenge this conclusion.

(*bb*) The practice of the Federal Supreme Court, too, has recognised for a long time that the resolution to expose oneself to the risk of injury in order to rescue another who is in danger does not in principle create a new chain of causation which attributes liability for injuries of this kind to the "rescuer" himself and relieves from liability the person who is responsible for endangering the "object of the rescue". On the contrary it was the *Reichsgericht* which extended the liability of the latter to injuries of this kind suffered by the "rescuer", at least in those cases where the act of rescue was not disproportionate to the impending danger and its prevention (RGZ 28, 120 ff.: restraining bolting carriage horses; RGZ 50, 219, 223: restraining bolting riding horses; RGZ 164, 125 ff.: saving passengers in a bus; OLG Stuttgart NJW 1965, 112: saving passengers in a burning motor-car). This Senate followed that practice in the so-called pursuit cases [references]; and at least in principle it is approved unanimously by writers [references]. It is true, as this Senate has made clear on another occasion, that no duty exists to protect others against harming themselves and, conversely, no general prohibition against inducing another to imperial himself [references]. Social co-existence involving manifold contacts between human beings means that one person may influence another in many ways, without having to incur liability. Only if the person causing the injury is to be *blamed* for having created a dangerous situation which is so serious and calls so urgently for action by the rescuer and emergency-helper the risk assumed by the latter, together with the danger created for the person to be rescued, must be attributed to the person causing the injury, having regard to the circumstances. He must be held liable for any self-inflicted injury of the rescuer and emergency-helper. The reason is that he has created a situation which, although the rescuer and emergency-helper are not required to intervene, at least makes such intervention reasonable and praiseworthy. In such circumstances, it is no longer permissible to consider the intervention on the part of the rescuer and emergency-helper in isolation, distinct from the creation of the "aggravated dangerous situation" [reference] by the person inflicting the injury. Thus the present Senate has repeatedly spoken of a culpable "challenge" by the person inflicting the injury to the injured party to imperil himself.

(*cc*) In order to give concrete expression to this assessment of liability this Senate has already formulated a number of principles. The intervention of the rescuer and emergency-helper must not be completely of his own accord; it must have been sug-gested by the initial act and been "challenged" by it, as this Senate has expressed it in the decisions referred to above. In addition the acceptance of the peril and the injury to oneself must be commensurate with the possible success of the intervention, and its motivation must at least be acceptable according to the recognized rules of social conduct [references]. In the absence of these criteria limiting liability, which in their formulation are only defined very generally and require to be developed in greater detail in each individual case, the liability of a person who has injured another for the resulting intervention by a third party would no longer be covered by the protective range of the duty of care not to bring about situations which constitute a call for rescue or emergency aid. Outside this range, the fact that a rescuer or emergency-helper imperils or injures himself will fall within his own sphere of action for which he is only responsible to himself. He acts "at his own risk". (For the neces-sary restriction of liability in the case of a mentally transmitted causality see *inter alia* [references].)

(*dd*) These legal principles permit it, in the case for decision involving the donation of a kidney and the injury to the body and the health of the plaintiff's mother, to attribute legal liability to the defendant in respect of the conduct of the Senior Medical Registrar, Dr H. The donation of the kidney was caused precisely by the fact that Dr H, by injuring the child, placed the plaintiff's mother in a situation in which she may have felt called upon to make such a sacrifice. Undoubtedly her conduct must deserve high praise morally and must therefore be approved and recognised by the law. The attempt, which was medically indicated, to improve the plaintiff's physical and health situation by the donation of a kidney and at least to shorten the period of treatment by dialysis, is reasonably and proportionately commensurate with the injury to herself which the mother accepted. Her decision was based specifically upon the detailed advice by the medical officers attending the plaintiff.

(*ee*) Contrary to the appellant, the causal nexus is not to be denied on the ground that the mother did not make up her mind to donate a kidney under the direct impression of an acute emergency but that she had time to consult the medical officers and could ponder the grounds for and against. If an intervention by the rescuer and emergency-helper is suggested, it is irrelevant whether the latter has acted, so to say, on the spur of the moment or whether he was able to assess in advance the chances and risks of his intervention. This does not alter the "challenging situation" in any respect; and the causal nexus between the damaging act of the injuring person and that by which the rescuer and emergency-helper imperils or injures himself remains in any event. It is not unusual for a rescuer to have sufficient time for reflection. It must be admitted that the notion of "rescue", understood as an induced intervention for the purpose of averting or containing of damage resulting from a perilous situation brought about culpably by the person committing the injurious act, normally does not extend to help in overcoming the damage, especially if it represents mere assistance in restoring it. From the point of view of legal liability, such assistance can no longer be attributed to the damaging act by the person inflicting the injury. The answer to the question as to when the sacrifice by a person who wishes to reduce the actual damage or at least to contain it still amounts to a rescue and to emergency aid requires an assessment which must take into account the intimate relationship with the challenge of the situation and undoubtedly also the connection in time and space. Regarded from this angle, the donation of a kidney by a near relative—in this case by the mother—for the benefit of the injured child can still be held, without straining the argument, to have been a measure, responding to a challenge, of rescuing the child whose life and health was imperilled. The mother's sacrifice is directly connected with the dangerous situation caused by the defendant medical practitioner by removing the child's only kidney. The delay in making the sacrifice is due not so much to the fact that only after the child's health had been damaged remedial measures were initiated, but that in the circumstances the rescuing donation of the organ could not be carried out immediately, but only after some time. For this reason, the donation of the kidney by the plaintiff's mother is to be regarded in the case for decision as a consequence of the injurious act for which the defendant must assume liability. (To the same effect Deutsch, *Arztrecht und Arzneimittelrecht*, 1983, p. 205 marginal note 305; in Anglo-Saxon law on the basis of the "rescue doctrine" *Urbanski* v. *Patel*, Manitoba Queen's Bench, 25 January 1978, 84 DLR 3d 650 on the one hand; *Sirianni* v. *Anna* 21 December 1967, 55 Misc. 2d 553, 285 NYS 2d 709 (1967); *Moore* v. *Shah* 30 December 1982, 458 NYS 2d 33; 90 AD 2d 389 and *Ornelas* v. *Fry*, Court of Appeals of Arizona 6 May 1986, 727 P. 2d 819 (Ariz.1986) on the other hand.) It need not be considered whether the Senior Medical Registrar Dr H or the defendant authority responsible for the hospital were under a legal *duty* to arrange for a kidney transplant. This consideration cannot serve as the criterion whether the plaintiff's mother made an "induced sacrifice".

(*ff*) Contrary to the arguments of the appellant, the claim of the plaintiff's mother does not fail for the reason that she accepted not only the possibility of injuries to herself, as it seems to happen in most cases of rescue and emergency aid, but that she submitted to this injury by donating her kidney, thus sacrificing her health with her eyes open. This fact, too, does not modify in any respect the challenge of the situation nor does it give cause for assessing liability restrictively. Any restriction of liability could only be justified if the self-inflicted injury was disproportionate to the chance of saving the injured person or if the self-inflicted injury exceeded the boundaries of moral approval. Neither is the case here. On the contrary, this Senate has no doubt that the necessary nexus with the tort for which the defendant is responsible is not dispropor-tionate and not reprehensible.

(*gg*) Finally, this Senate cannot accept the appellant's contention that, from the legal point of view the plaintiff's mother has not suffered a bodily injury giving rise to damages because she consented to the operation for the removal of the donated kidney. It is true that therefore the surgical removal of the kidney by the medical practitioner entrusted with this task was lawful. The author of the injurious act who has caused, and is liable for, what from this point of view is a voluntary sacrifice of health and a consensual bodily injury, is precluded on his part from arguing that the bodily injury of the intervener was voluntary and therefore lawful. He cannot do so either if, as in the case, another person must first commit an act of bodily injury in order to enable the rescuer and emergency helper to carry out his rescue operation. In agreeing to the removal of a kidney the plaintiff's mother did not also give her consent to Dr H to being placed in a situation where she had to sacrifice her health in order to save her child. Therefore the tort committed against her retains its illegal character.

Case 89

BUNDESGERICHTSHOF (SIXTH CIVIL SENATE) 29 FEBRUARY 1956
BGHZ 20, 137 = VERSR 1956, 305

The plaintiff, born in 1911, suffered a fractured skull when he was twelve years old. On 2 April 1940, while riding a motor cycle, he collided with a railway belonging to the defen-dant mining company and suffered an injury to the right side of his forehead coupled with a concussion. By a judgment which has the force of *res judicata* it was held that the defendant is liable to pay three-quarters of the damage suffered by the plaintiff. Up to 31 December 1944, the defendant made to the plaintiff periodic payments.

The plaintiff contends that as a result of the accident he became permanently unfit for work and demands a monthly payment of DM 300 from 1 January 1951 until he reaches the age of sixty-five. The defendant alleges that all the effects of the accident had long disappeared and, in particular, that the plaintiff's ability to work is no longer restricted.

The claim was rejected by the District Court of Essen and by the Court of Appeal of Hamm. A second appeal was also unsuccessful for the following

Reasons

1. . . .

2. . . .

3. . . . the question is whether the Court of Appeal, relying on its own findings and of the observations of the expert, Professor Dr K, rightly rejected the plaintiff's claim. The appel-lant denies this and refers to the well-known practice of the Reichsgericht in the matter of accident neurosis. He contends that according to this practice the existence of a causal nexus must be admitted between the accident of 2 April 1940 and the condition of the plaintiff which, while constituting a neurosis inspired by the device to obtain periodical

payments, was nevertheless one which paralysed the plaintiff's working capacity and power of mental resistance.

It is true that contrary to the previous practice of the Reich Insurance Office [reference] the Reichsgericht held in principle that a causal connection exists even if the accident was suffered by a person who, owing to his neurotic and labile condition, could not resist sufficiently purpose-and-desire-inspired fantasies. In particular, the Reichsgericht pointed out repeatedly that it is not possible to limit liability to pay damages to physically ascertainable injuries and to exclude nervous or emotional disturbances caused by the accident on the ground that they are due to a special predisposition of the victim. According to the Reichsgericht, a tortfeasor who has injured a person weakened by bad health cannot expect to be treated as if the victim had been healthy. It made no difference whether the fact of bad health was caused by a physical ailment or by an emotional weakness based on his personal make-up [reference].

This point of view was consistently opposed by the medical profession; the dispute was further seriously complicated by the fact that the two sides relied on different notions of causality. In the face of these attacks and the change in the practice in matters of social insurance the Reichsgericht adhered to its view and pointed out, in particular, that a court must always determine in accordance with legal considerations whether a causal nexus exists. Nevertheless, in special cases the Reichsgericht approved a refusal to grant damages [references] and showed in its decision [reference] a clear tendency to restrict liability in the light of a "purely external nexus" between the accident and the neurotic condition. Further, the Reichsgericht sought to counter an excessively broad liability by relying on § 254 BGB. This Division, in its decision of 8 July 1953 [reference], agreed in principle with the practice of the Reichsgericht and affirmed the possibility that an adequate causal connection can exist between an accident and a "psycho-reaction" initiated by it.

It would be unnecessary to reopen this question if it were evident that the plaintiff consciously practised deception in simulating the existence of complaints . . . However, the observations of the Court of Appeal in connection with the expert evidence appear to permit only the conclusion that the conduct of the plaintiff borders on simulation and conscious aggravation, but yet that it is primarily to be characterised by the fact that the plaintiff, who is emotionally labile, influenced by purpose-and-desire-inspired fantasies had acquired and retained the fixed idea that he suffered from the consequences of an accident and . . . the fluid transition from intentional to automatic effects is characteristic [of this illness]. The exaggerated symptom results finally in a childish psychotic state akin to pseudo-dementia, in which the patient remains caught. It is therefore impossible to reject a claim for damages in reliance on § 254 BGB without further considerations; contributory negligence could only be held to exist if it could be said that a neurotic person is able to control his will in response to the requirements of the situation and to resist effectively his wishful fantasies. Especially those whose neurotic tension makes them take refuge in the fantasy that they are sick and are entitled to claim against the community or against the tortfeasor to have their livelihood guaranteed are unable to exercise this control and to offer this resistance [reference].

This Division reaffirms the principle that a tortfeasor must also pay compensation for any damage resulting from emotional reactions of the victim if the accident constituted the adequate cause. The fact alone that a certain behaviour is interpreted as a psychogene reaction does not necessarily rule out a connection between the occurrence which caused the accident and the condition which inhibits the ability to work and to resist. Much as the courts must familiarise themselves with the new ideas of medical and psychological sciences about the nature and the causes of neurotic conditions of behaviour, it must not be forgotten that the question of causality is a legal question, and from the legal point of view causality is not restricted to the functioning of the body and its organs. The attempt to restrict liability for neurosis on the ground that these are "outwardly connected only" does not supply a test for achieving a correct delimitation. If this should mean that the existing complaint and inhibitions would in all probability have manifested themselves even if the accident had not occurred, the court in the exercise of the power conferred by § 287 of the Code of Civil Procedure to assess the evidence quite independently, in particular the conclusions of the medical experts, can deny the existence of a causal nexus altogether. If, on the other hand, it would appear in favour of the plaintiff that his emotional condition which impedes his integration into working life would not have arisen without the occurrence of the accident, the causal nexus cannot be denied, even if the emotional disposition of the plaintiff was an important contributory factor.

If, therefore, it is useless to attempt to limit liability for neurosis by reference to considerations of causality, it is necessary nevertheless to restrict liability for other reasons. In according a claim for compensation to a victim of a corporeal injury, the law wishes to assist him and to facilitate his speedy recovery. It would be contrary to the purpose of the claim for damages if the fact that another must pay the damages would render integration into social life and obligations more difficult or even impossible. For this reason medical opinion points out regularly that the legal regulation of damages must not result in supporting the flight into illness of neurotics set on obtaining damages by way of pensions and in assisting their "infantile regression . . ." [reference]. If the expert evidence shows that the psychological state of the plaintiff, especially his apathy, is to be explained primarily by his—admittedly unconscious—aim to obtain an advantageous settlement of his livelihood or as a fixation on an imaginary legal position—the accident forming an excuse for avoiding the struggle of daily life—it is equitable not to attribute these consequences to the tortfeasor. For the latter cannot be required to contribute to the perpetuation of a condition which, in the end, is harmful to the physical and mental health of the plaintiff. For this reason claims of neurotics with a fixation on asserting legal rights and damages by way of pensions must be set a limit inspired not by the absence of a causal nexus but by the purpose of compensation owed by equitable considerations. As the First Division of the Federal Supreme Court has pointed out appositely [reference], similar considerations moved legal theory and practice to restrict liability for damages to the adequate consequences of the occurrence which caused the damage, although the Code does not lay down such a restriction. If the principle of liability is not to be extended excessively, as it would if the court were to follow the test of strict causality, liability to pay damages must also be limited correspondingly in the present case. Thus the justified interests of social medicine are also satisfied.

Naturally, only a very detailed and careful assessment of the plaintiff's personality will make it possible to determine correctly the manner and the causes of his neurotic condition. For this purpose, it will be particularly important to establish the boundary between the emotional disturbance caused by the gravity of the accident, the resulting shock, or the physical medical treatment and that which is inspired, following the ensuing legal position, by fantasies of demands [reference].

4. Even if the Court of Appeal has not considered the decisive legal problems correctly in every respect, its findings suffice to enable it to reject the claim for damages in respect

of loss of earning capacity . . . The Court of Appeal was therefore correct in the result in rejecting the claim of the plaintiff for damages in respect of loss of earning capacity.

Case 90

BUNDESGERICHTSHOF (SIXTH CIVIL SENATE) 11 NOVEMBER 1997
BGHZ 137, 142 = NJW 1998, 810 = JZ 1998, 680

Facts

The plaintiff is claiming compensation for a traffic accident of the 3 February 1986, for the consequences of which the defendant has to assume liability under the liability insurance undertaking. In the accident, the car insured with the defendant struck the front of the plaintiff's car obliquely and damaged the side of it substantially, as a result of which the plaintiff who was wearing a seatbelt struck his head on the door frame. A radiological examination in a hospital outpatients department, in findings that are not conspicuous in simple neurological terms, established bruising of the skull with trauma associated with the twisting of the cervical vertebrae but without external injuries or signs of concussion. According to the opinion of the doctor there was a five-day unfitness for work and out-patient GP care would suffice. Subsequently the plaintiff claimed for further physical impairment and symptoms of immobility, which he traced back to the injuries suffered in the accident. On the basis of these disorders in 1987 he gave up a furniture business which he had carried on since 1982. By his claim he asks for refund of his loss of earn-ings of DM 3,360 per month (less monthly payments of pension insurance), and com-pensation for pain and suffering over and above the pre-trial payment of DM 7,000, for which he regards a total sum of DM 50,000 as reasonable. He also seeks a declaration that the defendant was under a duty to provide compensation for future harm, insofar as the claims have not passed to the Department of Social Security.

The *Landgericht* rejected the claim. The Court of Appeal rejected the plaintiff's appeal. His appeal in law led to quashing of that judgment and reference back.

Reasons

1. The Court of Appeal, in contrast to the *Landgericht*, does not regard the plaintiff's claims for compensation for harm as time barred. But it considers that neither his inability to earn nor his further physical infirmities are, in tort terms, traceable to the road traffic accident.

The problems in the region of the lumbar vertebrae were the subject of a predisposi-tion or based on degenerative prior harm. Whether this also applied to the problems in the region of the cervical vertebrae could be left undecided as these problems were in any case not based on organic changes caused by the accident. It was instead a case of psy-chogenic physical disorders. According to the convincing report of the expert witness, the plaintiff had already suffered before the accident from a so-called narcissistic personality disorder which in combination with work and partnership problems had been activated by the accident. The plaintiff had thereby accentuated and extended the problems, which had originally come into existence through the accident injury, in connection with which wishes for security and compensation had played a role. Although the defendant had in principle to be responsible even for adverse psychological effects of the consequences of the accident, and the plaintiff's special susceptibility to harm had also to be accounted for by him, boundaries were nevertheless set to such a liability. Thus case law had denied liability for compensation neurosis or wish neurosis because the plaintiff in his neurotic striving for assistance and security merely took the accident as a pretext for evading the difficulties and burdens of a working life. This was the case if the psychological consequences of the accident had only been produced purely coincidentally by the accident and could possibly also occur in the same or a similar manner through other trivial causes. That was the state of affairs here. As it had been a case of an accident with only quite trivial consequential injuries, the psychological reactions of the plaintiff were in gross disproportion to this cause and were therefore not comprehensible. The plaintiff's existing personality disorders (as well as his work and marriage situation) would also have led to this reaction through other events unavoidably occurring in everyday life, so that the infliction of harm had formed at most a crystallisation point for a wish neurosis. As no further consequences of the accident were to be expected, the request for a declaration could also not be complied with.

II. These deliberations do not stand up to the arguments of the appeal in law.

1. [Paragraph relating to limitation issue omitted].

2. The appeal in law does not question the assessment of the plaintiff's physical harm by the Court of Appeal. However, it successfully claims that the reasoning by which the Court of Appeal has denied attribution in tort terms of his psychological harm is not in accord with the case law of this Senate. The Court of Appeal is, nevertheless, correct in its legal approach when it says that the defendant must in principle also be responsible for adverse psychological effects which have the effect of extending liability, provided there is sufficient certainty that this consequence would not have occurred without the accident [references omitted].

In the judgment of the Senate of 30 April 1996 [references omitted], which is of fundamental importance for the attribution of psychological harm, this Senate explained that the attribution of such harm was not defeated by the plaintiff's particular susceptibility as a result of physical or mental anomalies or dispositions. This was because the defendant had no claim to be put in the same position as if he had injured a person who had been hitherto healthy. But the Senate has set out in more detail in this judgment and in the judgment of 25 February 1997 [references omitted] the cases in which boundaries are set to the attribution in tort law of such harm. The Court of Appeal has failed to recognise the principles developed here. In the case in dispute it confirmed the prerequisites for an exception from liability on the basis of insufficient findings of facts. In this connection the deliberations of the Court of Appeal do not clearly reveal whether it is denying an attribution of liability from the point of view of the triviality of the harm or of a wish neurosis. However, in both cases the reasoning is not able to support the contested judgment.

(a) The Court of Appeal emphasises that it is a question of an accident with quite insignificant consequential injuries and the psychological reaction of the plaintiff to this is in gross disproportion to the cause and not comprehensible. It is true that it is considering here a category of cases for which, according to the principles explained in the judgment of the Senate of the 30 April 1996 [references omitted] the attribution of the harm can be excluded can be excluded in tort. These are cases in which the event causing the harm is quite insignificant in the sense of being a triviality.

(aa) The appeal in law however correctly contests the assumption that the accident in question is to be regarded as a trivial matter in the sense of those principles. As this limitation of liability is obviously an exception from the attribution in liability law of harm connected to the accident, strict requirements must be made for the assumption that the case is trivial. The deliberations of the Court of Appeal do not reveal that it was conscious of this principle. The findings of fact cannot support the assessment of the event causing the harm as completely insignificant.

It is true that account must be taken in this respect only of the primary injury suffered by the plaintiff in the accident. This cannot however be described as insignificant in the sense of trivial harm. The Court of Appeal proceeds on the basis of bruising of the skull with trauma associated with twisting of the cervical vertebrae. Even if these injuries can be healed organically without consequences, they were not in any case, when they arose, as insignificant as would be necessary for an exceptional case in the sense explained. When deciding if the injuries are so insignificant that they can exceptionally involve the exclusion of liability for harmful psychological consequences, the same principles must apply as those which the Senate has developed for the denial of compensation for non-material harm in accordance with § 847 BGB in relation to trivial injuries. This denial, likewise, only applies in exceptional cases. According to these principles, compensation can be denied in the case of insignificant injuries of body or health without substantial prejudice to lifestyle and without lasting consequences. It must only be a case of passing interference with the body or with mental health, typical in daily life and frequently arising from other reasons than a special case of harm. This, therefore, means interferences, which are quite insignificant not only in their intensity but also in the type of primary injury involved. They will normally not make a lasting impression on the plaintiff because he is already accustomed to being exposed to similar disturbances to his situation because of community life with other human beings [references omitted].

But the established injuries of the plaintiff here obviously go beyond such a model of harm, as is evident from the fact that bruising of the skull with trauma associated with twisting of the cervical vertebrae is not typical of daily life. It is always connected with a special case of harm. Here the injury also unquestionably had as its consequence an incapacity for work on the part of the plaintiff, which lasted several days.

(bb) If (contrary to the opinion of the Court of Appeal) one accordingly cannot proceed in the case in dispute on the basis of a completely insignificant occurrence of harm, attribution of liability for harmful psychological consequences is not excluded simply on this account. Therefore the further objection of the appeal in law that the Court of Appeal failed to consider that the defendant had encountered a special predisposition of the plaintiff to harm is immaterial. In this respect it is certainly correct that attribution of harmful psychological consequences can exceptionally be justified if the occurrence causing the harm has encountered a special predisposition to harm on the part of the plaintiff and not merely his general susceptibility to the development of neuroses. This is true even where the harm is trivial in the sense explained, according to the principles in the Senate's judgment of the 30 April 1996. This follows from the fact that psychological harm is in principle equated with physical harm as to which the defendant must likewise accept a special predisposition to harm on the part of the plaintiff.

The allusion to the special predisposition to harm in the literature has been understood to the effect that an attribution of liability is ruled out in cases of insignificance and special predisposition to harm on the part of the plaintiff [reference omitted]. This rests on a misunderstanding of the last-mentioned judgment of the Senate, because according to this such susceptibility can on the contrary exceptionally lead to an attribution of liability. There is of course only room for this additional criterion of special susceptibility to harm if there is some question of excluding liability on account of the triviality of the harm. This is however not the case here.

(b) The appeal in law also successfully contests the view of the Court of Appeal that the plaintiff had a wish neurosis and therefore an attribution of liability could not follow. This assessment is not supported by sufficient factual findings, as the appeal in law correctly argues.

(aa) The Court of Appeal seeks to rely on the case law of this Senate. According to this, the attribution of harmful psychological consequences is ruled out if the plaintiff has a compensation neurosis or wish neurosis. The plaintiff would thus be using the accident merely as a pretext in his neurotic striving for assistance and security in order to evade the difficulties and burdens of the working life [references omitted]. The denial of compensation for harm in the case of such neuroses is based on the idea that the psychological disorder obtains its character from a conscious or unconscious "wish" idea to safeguard one's life or exploitation of an assumed legal position. It is so prominent that the necessary attributable connection with the accident cannot be affirmed. This is so despite the fact that a direct causal connection between such neuroses and the preceding accident exists.

From this starting point, the appeal in law correctly claims that the necessary finding for the assumption of a wish neurosis, i.e. that neurotic striving for assistance and security played a determining part in the degeneration of the plaintiff's mental health, is lacking. It correctly points out that the expert Dr P has merely stated in his opinion that in the face of the plaintiff's work situation in 1986 the possibility could not be dismissed that, besides the remaining symptoms which the expert had discussed in detail, psycho-dynamic desires for security and compensation had played a role. That does not suffice for the assumption of a wish neurosis, especially as the Court of Appeal has made no further findings in this direction beyond [referring to] these statements of the expert. The Court of Appeal's view was that because of the plaintiff's personality disorders and his marriage and work situation, he could have had the same adverse reaction to other unavoidable occurrences in everyday life. This could acquire significance in the legal sense of a hypothetical development of the harm or supervening causality only if the relevant findings of the Court of Appeal were free from procedural errors. However, the appeal in law refers to the fact that the work and marriage difficulties of the plaintiff had first resulted from the neurotic disorder induced by the accident and the plaintiff had also stated this to the expert. The Court of Appeal will therefore have to investigate this further.

(bb) Moreover, the appeal claims that the Court of Appeal has inferred from the statements of the expert that the infirmities are based on a narcissistic disturbance of the plaintiff's personality. These are to be traced back to so-called near-conscious conversions, so that one should not proceed on the basis of a wish neurosis but on the basis of a conversion neurosis. In this respect also the appeal in law reveals extensive doubt about the judgment under challenge.

In the face of the statements of the expert about the neurotic condition of the plaintiff, the Court of Appeal would have had to examine whether the degeneration of his psychological condition does not rather indicate a conversion neurosis in which a mental conflict is changed into physical disorders [references omitted]. Such a neurosis is likewise based on an adverse effect of the accident, which is unconsciously taken as a pretext to compensate for latent inward conflicts, even if, unlike wish neurosis, not actually in respect of the wish not to have to work any more. Here therefore in principle an attribution of the causal connection takes place [references omitted]. Accordingly, it could be decisive for the assessment of liability whether the neurotic condition of the plaintiff is decisively shaped by "wish" ideas.

The expert in the current case on the one hand proceeded on the basis of an—admittedly near-conscious—conversion with the plaintiff, but on the other hand also addressed his wishes for security and compensation as components in the formation of the neuroses. The Court of Appeal ought not therefore simply to have denied the attribution of this neurotic condition to the event causing the harm, but should have subjected this condition to comprehensive elucidation—perhaps by additional questioning of the expert.

A further elucidation of the matter is, according to the above, necessary. In undertaking this, the Court of Appeal will certainly not be able to ignore the fact that according to recent psychological findings, frequently even in cases in which at first a compensation neurosis has been assumed, the wish for compensatory income has certainly been a symptom, though not the substantial or only decisive pathogenic factor. Even with psychologically abnormal behaviour of this kind, the personality structure of the person affected, as well as the adverse effects or substantial stresses in the personal area which could come to the surface through an accident, played a significant role [references omitted].

The appeal in law claims these complicated psychological interrelations in this case and on the basis of the findings of fact so far they cannot simply be dismissed. In the face of these interrelations it may be asked how, in accordance with the exact understanding of the plaintiff's neurotic disorder which is needed, a susceptibility on the part of the plaintiff to "wish" ideas which has possibly been established operates. Taking these considerations into account, it should follow that the disorders asserted by the plaintiff have their foundation not only in unconscious "wish" ideas but also in a conversion-neurosis-type development. But attribution in tort law can still not be denied from the point of view of either compensation neurosis or wish neurosis.

III. The judgment of the Court of Appeal was therefore to be quashed and the matter referred back to the Court of Appeal for further elucidation, in connection with which the Senate making the decision has made use of the possibility of § 565 I 2 ZPO.

The Court of Appeal at this point on the legal basis described and after the further findings to be made might conclude the defendant to be liable for the harm based on the plaintiff's neurosis. It will then have to be taken into consideration that his special psychological characteristics and within this framework also possible "wish" ideas contributing to the neurotic development can be of importance for the calculation of the harm. This is to be ascertained, as to the sum involved, in accordance with § 287 ZPO within the framework of compensation for pain and suffering as well as in connection with the loss of earnings. In calculating compensation for pain and suffering fairly, according to the constant case law of the Senate [references omitted] a special susceptibility to harm on the part of the plaintiff can be considered; this also applies to his psychological disposition and the risks based on it. In ascertaining the loss of earnings, the judge has to undertake a prognosis of the usual course of events, as they would have developed without the accident, taking all points of view into account which were available at the time of the last oral hearing (§ 252 BGB). In this respect it is not only a question of the assessment of possible supervening causalities but also of the ascertainment of harm as such on the basis of the facts of the case as it would probably have presented itself in the future.

Within this framework, it is important to ascertain whether (and with what probability) comparable harmful effects would have sooner or later occurred because of the original psychological condition of the plaintiff even without the actual accident. One must also take into consideration the risk which existed for the plaintiff's future work situation through possible unconscious "wish" ideas as they—as has been revealed in the neurosis—were built into the plaintiff's psychological make-up. In order to elucidate these risks and to obtain a sufficient factual basis for the assessment of the chances for and limitations to the plaintiff's career path, the judge of fact needs to obtain expert advice. He must therefore discuss the questions relating to this in detail with the expert and seek to clarify them.

On the basis of such findings of the facts of the case serious risks may give rise, with a probability which suffices for the purpose of the application of § 287 ZPO, to fears of a substantial strain on his work options in the long term, even independently of an accident. This is because of plaintiff's the inclination to adverse neurotic effects from the various vicissitudes of life and, in some cases also, an unconscious striving to withdraw himself from the "battle of life". The judge of fact must consider this in the prognosis that has to be undertaken for the loss of earnings. This can be important both for the duration as well as for the level of loss of earnings. Just as with difficulties in prediction because of a business life which shows little structure [references omitted], here also consideration can be given to a percentage deduction from the business receipts to be expected without risks of this kind.

Case 91

BUNDESGERICHTSHOF (FIRST CIVIL SENATE) 29 JANUARY 1969
NJW 1969, 789 = VERSR 1969, 406

[A collection of jewellery owned by the plaintiff was being carried in the trunk of a car by their traveller K, then a general agent and now a partner in the firm. In the middle of June 1965 K hired a room in the defendant's hotel, as he had often done before. On returning to the hotel one evening at about 10 p.m., he gave the night porter the keys of the car (including the key of the trunk) and told him to have the car garaged. The garage in question was nearby but it was not part of the hotel: it belonged to B, a firm which serviced and rented cars. If a guest wished his car garaged, this was the garage which the defendant hotel used. The porter called B and had the car fetched by one of his employees.

There were notices in hotel rooms about this service in June 1965. They said "Contract Garaging. Day and Night. Cars Fetched and Returned".

One of B's employees collected the car and the porter handed him the keys of the car and its trunk. The car was returned next morning by a different employee at about 9 a.m. and left in front of the hotel. In the middle of the afternoon K and his colleague T drove to H to see a customer, and when T went to the trunk to collect the jewellery he found it locked. K and T then looked through the collection and saw that a number of wrist-watches had been stolen from it. The lock of the trunk was undamaged, and police enquiries proved fruitless.]

The plaintiff claims compensation both in his own right and as assignee of the rights of K. The Landgericht dismissed the claim and the Oberlandesgericht dismissed the appeal. On the plaintiff's appeal, the judgment below is reversed and the case remanded.

Reasons

I. . . .

II. 1. . . . 2. . . .

3. (*a*) The Court of Appeal clearly assumed that if the defendant were liable in contract for the loss of the wrist-watches the plaintiff could claim for its loss on the basis of an assignment to it by K. This is correct. The principle of *Schadensliquidation des Drittinteresses* is applicable. It is implicit in the agreement between the defendant and K, already a contractual guest in the defendant's hotel, for the deposit of the car for reward, that the defendant's contractual liability for the protection of the car applies even if the car belongs to a third party, it being irrelevant whether the defendant knew or should have known or had any ground for supposing that it did so belong (BGHZ 15, 224, 228).

(*b*) On the other hand, there are objections in law to the view of the Court of Appeal that the contract of deposit in this case did not cover the contents of the trunk. By its very nature the contract of deposit applies to the moveable which is handed over to the depositee for protection as an entirety, whether it consists of a single object, a collection of objects which are legally or physically discrete, or of one single thing which contains a number of objects which are legally or physically separate. So far as can be seen, this has never been doubted before (see BGH NJW 1968, 1718). Thus the defendant's contractual duty extended to safeguarding the contents of the trunk.

Given the findings made by the Court of Appeal, that the watches were stolen while the car was in B's garage, the defendant had the burden of proving that its inability to return the property was not due to matters for which it was responsible (§ 282 BGB). It is not enough for the defendant to prove that it took all necessary care, which in any case it has not yet done. The circumstances here (the trunk being opened without harming the lock, the removal of the more valuable objects from the collection, the employment in the garage of a person who, according to the district attorney was "well known to be a burglar and confidence trickster") strongly suggest that it was the fault of the defendant or one of its agents for performance (§ 278 BGB) that the goods have gone, so the defendant can exculpate himself only by proving what in fact caused their loss (RGZ 149, 284 ff.; BGH NJW 1952, 1170). This has not been done.

(*c*) The outcome of the case now depends on whether the defendant has a total or partial defence on the ground that the plaintiff or its partner K was at fault under § 254

BGB. This defence was raised by the defendant, but the Court of Appeal naturally did not consider it.

As will be seen, this court cannot conclusively apportion responsibility for the harm under § 254 BGB, since the requisite facts have not been found by the Court of Appeal. The judgment of that court must therefore be vacated and the matter remanded to it for further proceedings and decision on the merits and on costs, taking the following considerations into account.

4. The Court of Appeal will have to verify whether fault on the part of K or the plaintiff contributed to the loss in issue, so as to reduce, perhaps to nothing, the damages payable by the defendant (§ 254 BGB). Given such a fault, then the amount of responsibility to be attributed to K and therefore to the plaintiff depends in the first instance on how far the harm was preponderantly caused by one or other party; the critical factor here is whether the conduct of one party not only enabled the harm to occur but made its occurrence substantially more probable than did the behaviour of the other party. The temporal order of the events which caused the harm is not critical (BGH NJW 1952, 537, 539; NJW 1963, 1447, 1449). Only if one cannot conclude from the respective causal efficacy of the conduct of both parties that the harm was preponderantly caused by either of them should the degree of fault of the two parties be considered. Then the first thing to do, before proceeding to apportionment, is to determine the amount of the fault of each party.

The first factor to consider is that K left the jewellery in the trunk of the car without telling the porter or anyone else on the defendant's staff that it was valuable and that the risk of loss was consequently very high (§ 254 II 1 BGB). If the trunk had a separate key— this is not clear—the fact that K gave it as well as the car key to the porter would increase the plaintiff's contribution.

K's behaviour seems intrinsically to be grossly negligent of his own interests, but various considerations, some undisputed, others inferable from the plaintiff's evidence, make it seem less grave. There is the standing of the hotel to be considered and the quality of service which guests would expect. Guests want to be spared the bother of parking their car, but they also expect it to be safeguarded as they themselves would do. According to the defendant, the garage ticket states that no liability is accepted for the contents of the trunk, but since the plaintiff's evidence is that the ticket was not handed to K before, or even at the time when, the car was handed over, the defendant would not be showing the careful service to be expected of such a hotel unless he told K that the garage-owner's exclusion of liability make it risky to leave things in the trunk. There is the further fact in this case, according to the plaintiff, that K had been a frequent guest in the defendant's hotel in recent years. It was known to the hotel staff who looked after him that he carried a valuable collection of jewellery with him in the car and they never sought to dissuade him from leaving it in the trunk, as he sometimes did. Furthermore, on the present occasion the staff knew that K had the jewellery with him. It is true that K did not always leave the jewellery in the car, but he may have been induced to believe that when the car was securely garaged the jewellery in its trunk would also be safe. It is not clear on the evidence whether K knew where the car was garaged or how it was secured, so he could perhaps infer from the information provided in the hotel that his car would be looked after in a manner appropriate to its standing. The Court of Appeal will have to investigate these circumstances, determine the causal potency of the conduct of both parties, and apportion the responsibility between them.

Case 92

REICHSGERICHT (THIRD CIVIL SENATE) 27 JUNE 1913
RGZ 83, 15

In December 1908 the plaintiff, a travelling decorator, suffered an injury to the little finger of his right hand, and went to the defendant for medical treatment. The defendant washed the wound with raw carbolic acid, and put a carbolic acid bandage on it for over twelve hours. As a result there developed a so-called carbolic gangrene which required prolonged medical attention. The fingernail came off and the finger itself became pink and shiny, thick in parts and stiff overall. To the plaintiff's claim for damages the defendant objected that the plaintiff would be able to work just as well as before the accident if only he had the finger amputated. It was clear, according to the defendant, that the plaintiff would have had the finger amputated if the injury had been due to an accident or something of the sort and there were no third party to pay for his loss of earnings. Experts would testify that the operation was simple and free from risk. Of course there was no question of forcing the plaintiff to undergo the operation, but if there was some method by which his loss of earning capacity could be reduced and he chose not to employ it, this must be at his own expense and not at the expense of the defendant. The plaintiff could therefore claim compensation for only such loss of earning capacity as would subsist after such an operation.

The plaintiff contested this defence. Experts would testify that the operation was attended with pain and risk, and that so far from necessarily improving his earning capacity as travelling decorator, it might lead to the whole hand becoming stiff; under these circumstances he could not be expected to expose himself to the danger and trouble of an operation.

The defendant was held liable at first instance and in the Court of Appeal, but his further appeal to this court is now allowed. The decision of the courts below is vacated, and the case is remanded for further proceedings and judgment.

Reasons

The appellant first complains that the Court of Appeal paid no attention to his defence that all or most of the harm in respect of which the plaintiff is suing would have been avoided by the amputation, partial or total, of the useless little finger on his right hand, since such an operation would restore or greatly improve his ability to work . . . This defence the Court of Appeal wholly ignored, to the extent of not even referring to it in its judgment. It will be clear from what follows that the point raised by the defendant cannot be so easily passed over.

In RGZ 60, 147, the Sixth Civil Senate considered the rights of the parties when a person who has been injured in an accident at work refuses to enter a hospital for medical treatment although the prognosis of a cure of great improvement is good. They held that a person who is responsible for the consequences of an accident has a defence under § 254 BGB if a treatment exists which experts agree would lead to a cure or significant diminution of the injury, and if the victim should have been aware of the existence of, and in a position to benefit from, such treatment. If this is established, then a victim who has declined to undergo this treatment must explain why. The court must then weigh his reasons in order to determine whether a reasonable man who was paying due attention to the interests of the party responsible for the harm would likewise refrain from having the treatment in question. A reasonable person would certainly have such treatment if it involves no risk to life, no great bodily pain, and no expense—the expense being borne by another (RGZ 60, 151, 153). The same Senate of the Reichsgericht, in JW 1907, 740 no. 6, applied this principle to operations of the kind in question before us, and approved the formula enunciated by the Court of Appeal: a victim can be expected to undergo an operation if its success is guaranteed—so far as guarantees can exist in medical matters— and if the victim is convinced that the operation is free from risk. The Senate added that all the circumstances of the individual case must be taken into account, including the gravity and danger of the operation and the greater or lesser prospect of success.

These principles must now be amplified and defined with greater particularity. We must remember, when a defendant invokes § 254 II BGB against a victim of personal injuries whose capacity to earn could be restored or improved by undergoing an operation, that the victim has a basic right to decide freely and at his own discretion whether he wishes to undergo such an invasion of his bodily integrity. Before the BGB came into force, lawyers therefore used to hold that it was wrong to treat a victim as being at fault if in the exercise of his free right over his body he refused to undergo a surgical operation simply to reduce the liability of the person responsible for the harm. There was the additional consideration that even in the case of operations which are normally safe, some unforeseen circumstance may cause further harm, even death, and that it may not be as successful as expected. It was thus unjustifiable, they believed, to use the threat of refusing full compensation for all the victim's harm in order to cause him to undergo an operation, even one which is normally safe and effective, just to protect the tortfeasor.

This is a one-sided view which takes account only of the victim's rights, and since the BGB came into force, writers and courts alike have rightly abandoned it. There must be some limit to the victim's right of free self-determination over his body, and that limit is reached when the exercise of this right is purely capricious, a selfish and inconsiderate exploitation of the fact that the defendant is liable. The right is not to be used to equip the victim with the means of living a life of idleness when his capacity to work could be restored by a safe and relatively painless operation. This is required by *Treu und Glauben*, a principle to which the exercise of the right to claim compensation for harm is subject. We can leave aside the question whether a passion for a pension is, as we have recently been taught, an actual disease, so-called compensation hysteria, and to be treated as such. For our purposes the only thing that counts is the objective situation in the individual case.

It follows that certain requirements must be fulfilled before the victim's failure to undergo an operation can constitute a defence. First, the operation must, in the view of experts, be free from danger in so far as in the current state of medical knowledge any operation can be said to be free from danger, that is, it must be safe in the absence of unforeseen circumstances. This removes from consideration immediately any operation which calls for a general anaesthetic, as opposed to a purely local anaesthetic, for with chloroform there is always a risk of death even if the preliminary physical examination of the patient is carried out with scrupulous care. This is in line with the decisions of the *Reichsversicherungsamt* [reference omitted]. Next, the operation must be one which does not involve any significant pain; after all, it is only as a result of some act for which the defendant is responsible that the victim is in the situation where he must take steps to restore his earning capacity, so the principle of *Treu und Glauben* can hardly require him to undergo significant pain for the defendant's benefit. Thirdly, the operation must, on the evidence of experts, be sure to bring about a major improvement in the victim's earning capacity, that is either restore it completely or improve it very greatly. Finally, the defendant must have let the victim know that he is ready to arrange for the operation to be carried out at his expense in an appropriate place and by professional doctors, or to pay the cost of the operation in advance and let the victim arrange it himself; for a victim whose recovery is otherwise complete is not obliged to use money of his own to have an operation carried out simply to reduce the liability of the defendant who, whether he be the person actually to blame or only the party responsible for him, is bound to make good the harm.

Often, it is true, a victim proceeds spontaneously to an operation just to relieve an intolerable physical condition, and then he is personally responsible to the surgeon for the fee; but cases of that sort are not before us now.

It follows that if, contrary to expectation, the operation fails, the defendant is automatically responsible for any further harm it may cause, for such harm is also in a causal relationship with the original injury for which he was responsible. His liability follows naturally from his requiring the victim to undergo the specified operation in order to restore or improve his earning capacity.

If the defendant makes a demand which satisfies these requirements and the victim refuses to undergo the operation in question, the defendant has a good defence to the victim's claim for damages to the extent that the victim's earning capacity would have been restored or improved by the operation. It is then for the victim by way of reply to explain the special reasons for his refusal, as laid down by the Reichsgericht in RGZ 60, 151 ff. . . .

Case 93

BUNDESGERICHTSHOF (SIXTH CIVIL SENATE) 14 MARCH 1961
BGHZ 34, 355 = NJW 1961, 655 = JZ 1961, 602 (with approving note by W Flume)

The plaintiff in this claim for damages was involved in a motor accident when he was sixteen-and-a-half years old. Like the first defendant, then nearly twenty years old, he was an apprentice motor mechanic in a workshop in H. Every week they had to visit D in order to attend the local training college there. On 21 February 1957 they drove to school in a colleague's Volkswagen. The first defendant, who was at the wheel, was the only one with a driving licence. In the lunch break he suggested to the plaintiff and to two other fellow apprentices, the second defendant and J, then nearly seventeen and seventeen-and-a-half years old respectively, that they should drive to V to have lunch with his parents. On the way there, the second defendant entreated the first defendant to allow him to drive the car but the first defendant refused because, like the plaintiff, he knew that the second defendant had no driving licence. On the way back, however, the second defendant renewed his entreaties and the first defendant relented and allowed him to take the wheel for a spell. They changed places with the motor still running. Though the road was quite steep, the second defendant drove down it at about 60 km per hour, and failed to reduce this speed a few hundred metres on where the road curved slightly to the left. He lost control of the car, and it crossed the highway and struck a tree. The second defendant suffered a cranial fracture, the first defendant a knock on the head, and J a bruise to the left eye. The plaintiff suffered brain damage and a severing of the left ocular nerve: vision in his left eye is reduced to about 10 per cent and is unlikely to improve.

The plaintiff alleged that he had warned the second defendant against driving, though only from fear of a police check.

Accepting that he was 20 per cent to blame, the plaintiff claims appropriate damages for pain and suffering from the defendants as common debtors, and seeks a decree that they are liable as common debtors for four-fifths of any harm he may suffer in the future.

The defendants urge that the claim be dismissed on the ground that the plaintiff was acting at his own risk: not only did he consent to the wheel being taken by the second defendant despite his having neither experience nor a licence, but he himself had even sought to drive and so put his companions at risk.

The Landgericht awarded DM 4,000 as damages for pain and suffering and decreed that the defendants were liable as common debtors for two-thirds of any future harm suffered by the plaintiff.

On appeal by the defendants the Court of Appeal dismissed the plaintiff's claim in its entirety. The plaintiff now appeals to this court. The judgment below is vacated and the case is remanded.

Reasons

I. The Court of Appeal held that there was no implied agreement which excluded the defendants' liability in tort, any such agreement by a minor like the plaintiff being in any case invalid without the consent of his legal representative. But the court held that the defendants were nevertheless entitled to be relieved from liability on the ground that the plaintiff had been acting at his own risk. The plaintiff had sufficient insight, so the court found, to appreciate the clear risk involved in the second defendant's taking over the wheel. Just as he himself had been ready to imperil his companions by driving the car, so it was in full knowledge of the risk that he had agreed to the second defendant's attempting to drive despite his lack of skill and experience. Though he objected at first, this was only through fear of a police check, and even this objection he did not maintain. The accident was due exclusively to the second defendant's being an inexperienced and incompetent driver. This being so, it would be contrary to *Treu und Glauben* to hold the defendants liable for the results once the risk materialised. Since it was reasonable that the defendants be released from liability, their release should not be prejudiced by the application of § 107 BGB, which need not be applied where there was a "community of danger among the young", as here. So to hold was consistent with the view recently adopted by the courts, that the effect of a young person's consent to surgery depends not on the law relating to contractual declarations but on his factual ability to appreciate the situation (BGHZ 29, 33).

II. We quite agree with the Court of Appeal that the defendants' liability was not effectively excluded by contract. However, its observations on the doctrine of acting at one's own risk require us to make a decision of principle.

At present lawyers speak of a person as acting at his own risk when, without any sufficient reason, he puts himself in a position of imminent danger although he is aware of the particular circumstances which make for the danger in question. If this risk results in injury, the question arises whether the injured party can claim damages from another person who would otherwise be liable, whether under the law of strict liability or under the rules of contract or tort law. At first the courts applied § 254 BGB in such cases unless they found an implicit contractual exclusion of liability, which they were very reluctant to do. The doctrine of acting at one's own risk only became an independent force in litigation when the Reichsgericht used it to avoid imposing *strict* liability towards a victim who had consciously exposed himself, without any legal, professional, or moral obligation, to a hazard he might well have avoided (RGZ 130, 162). This was a way of avoiding the imposition of strict liability in cases to which the legislative reason for imposing strict liability did not seem to apply. The Reichsgericht adopted the idea that a conscious exposure of oneself to danger might amount to acting at one's *own* risk in order to mitigate strict liability in accordance with the supposed purpose of the legislature. In so doing the Reichsgericht emphasised that when the defendant's liability arose under § 823 BGB, the fact that the plaintiff had acted at his own risk need not necessarily lead to a dismissal of his claim for damages: in such a case there might be an apportionment under § 254 BGB which could take account of the particular facts (RGZ 130, 162, 169; see also RG JW 1911, 28).

Not until its judgment of 19 June 1933 (RGZ 141, 262) did the Reichsgericht . . . adopt the view that a person who rides in a vehicle with knowledge of special attendant dangers thereby consents to any personal injury which may arise therefrom during the journey. If the agreement was valid and relevant, it neutralised the illegal quality of the defendant's conduct with the result that though he caused the harm, he was not liable for it. Such consent to an invasion of a legal interest was a declaration of will, needing to be received by its addressee and, if uttered by a person with limited legal capacity, valid, in view of its adverse effect, only if his statutory representative agreed to it. The Reichsgericht adhered to this view (RGZ 145, 390), and the Third Civil Senate of the Bundesgerichtshof adopted it in BGHZ 2, 159 (see also BGH VersR 1952, 420). This Senate has assumed the soundness of the doctrine that acting at one's own risk is a complete defence, although in none of the cases it has decided were its requirements found to be satisfied. We permitted the plaintiff to appeal in this case because we wish to depart from the decisions of the Reichsgericht and the Bundesgerichtshof.

III. As long ago as 25 March 1958 (NJW 1958, 905), this Senate expressed doubts about the way of treating conscious self-imperilment introduced by the Reichsgericht in RGZ 141, 262, and scholars have increasingly objected to treating a person who "acts at his own risk" as giving a consent to a possible invasion of a legal interest which operates as a justification. They stress that it is artificial and unrealistic to view the situation in this way, that it is inappropriate to employ the concept of the "legal act", and that this construction tends to lead to unsatisfactory results [references omitted]. We agree with these criticisms and now depart from the doctrine of the Reichsgericht.

1. The commonest case involves carriage by an incompetent driver. Here it is clearly unrealistic to suppose that the passenger who is aware of the driver's incapacity is consenting to the personal injuries which may arise during the journey. It is normally a case of conscious negligence rather than of conditional intention, to use a distinction which is drawn when one person injures someone else rather than himself: the passenger is aware of the danger, but hopes that it will not materialise. We blame him because in imperilling himself he is acting recklessly: it is normally a gross fiction to hold that such conduct by the passenger constitutes a consent to personal injury.

2. Furthermore, it is only within the rather narrow limits of §§ 134, 138 BGB and § 226a StGB that any such agreement could serve as a justification for the defendant's conduct.

Should the injury prove fatal, the defendant's conduct clearly cannot be justified by any such agreement (BGHSt 4, 88, 93). And if the resulting personal injuries are serious, especially if they involve loss of vital organs, the victim's agreement still cannot justify their infliction, since this is morally offensive and legally discountenanced, regardless of the victim's consent (see BGHSt 6, 232, 234 [other references omitted]). Thus to treat putting oneself at risk as raising an issue of consent inevitably makes the legal outcome depend on the gravity of the harm, which for tort lawyers should be irrelevant. Furthermore, there is no need for any justification at all in cases of strict liability, since strict liability does not depend on the illegal nature of the conduct (GSZ in BGHZ 24, 21, 26).

3. Another unsatisfactory consequence of treating a person's consent to the invasion of a legal interest as constituting a declaration of will is the requirement that it needs to be received and must therefore "reach" the addressee. There can be no good reason for making the defendant's liability depend on whether *he* knew or could have known that the victim was consciously putting himself at risk (compare the facts of the case before the Senate on 8 December 1954 (VersR 1955, 120)) . . .

4. Nor is the doctrine any better when the victim is under age. Why should liability towards minors, who are themselves capable of being liable in tort, depend on whether their statutory representative consents which is in practice extremely uncommon since normally the decisions involved are sudden and spontaneous?

5. In cases involving drunk-driving the view we now reject meant that whether there was a complete defence or a more elastic apportionment under § 254 BGB depended on whether the passenger, himself often drunk, was conscious of the risk or whether he had simply rendered himself incapable through gross negligence of appreciating it. This is a very subjective matter, and in cases like these where things happen very quickly it is hard to come to any firm conclusion on it. Thus even in the typical case the test which stems from RGZ 141, 262 proved impracticable: applying it led to unpredictable results.

6. We note finally that the view of the Reichsgericht leads to a difference in the way the illegality of an actor's conduct is judged in private and in criminal law. In criminal law the victim's conscious self-exposure to harm is not accorded the same justificatory force where personal injuries are negligently inflicted as it has been in private law since RGZ 141, 262 (see BGHSt 4, 88, 90 [other reference omitted]). Furthermore, in dealing with consent to an invasion of one's corporeal integrity, the criminal law does not invoke the private law principles of *Willenserklärung* at all [reference omitted]. Thus so long as a person's exposure of himself to danger is to be treated as a justificatory declaration of will, our legal system can never achieve a unitary method of judging the illegality of conduct.

IV. In the view of this Senate, the problem under discussion gives rise to issues of illegality and justification only when the victim's conduct really and without any artificial construction amounts to a consent to an envisaged invasion of his legal interest. This may happen in certain dangerous sports (compare BGHSt 4, 88, 92), but in the common case before the courts today the sole question is almost always whether, and if so to what extent, a person's liability in damages is affected by the fact that the victim had consciously exposed himself to the danger when it was imminent. If in such cases it seems more or less offensive that the damage should be shifted from the victim to the other party, that is because in claiming compensation the victim is acting in a manner inconsistent with prior conduct of his own and for which he is answerable. To go against one's own act conflicts with the principle of *Treu und Glauben*, and it is this which makes it wrong for the victim to invoke the liability of the defendant without taking account of the fact that he himself consciously created or helped to create the dangerous situation which enabled the defendant's contribution to it to cause the harm. Once this is realized, we see that the correct way to deal with the problem is by means of the value-judgment expressed in § 254 BGB. This rule, which provides that a defendant's liability may be affected, or even extinguished, if conduct for which the victim is responsible, especially his capricious exposure of himself to danger, contributes to the harm, is essentially based on the concept of inconsistent behaviour which is rooted in § 242 BGB. Specific application of this principle to damages law is found in § 254 BGB [references omitted]. Thus if a judge, in apportioning responsibility under § 254 BGB, gave great weight to the views here put forward, he would not be invoking any consideration extraneous to that rule; on the contrary, if he failed to take sufficient account of the victim's conscious exposure of himself to the danger and his inconsistency of conduct, the judge would not be doing justice to the particular circumstances in which the harm, and responsibility for it, arose.

It is true that if the commonest cases of self-exposure to danger are to be dealt with under § 254 BGB, we will be abandoning the familiar rigid principle that to act in the knowledge of specific existing danger is to act at one's *own* risk and thus to forfeit one's claim to damages. But in our view it will do nothing but good if this principle is abandoned. Even the practice of the courts hitherto has failed to give effect to this principle in a full and logical manner; they have been forced to adopt unrealistic exceptions in order to limit its effect. Furthermore the courts have tended to set almost impossibly stringent requirements for the proof of the plaintiff's knowledge of the special source of danger, simply because they wished to be free to apply § 254 BGB, which they believed to be more appropriate.

As to the question when liability should be *excluded* in a case where the victim has exposed himself to danger, and when there should simply be a *reduction* of the damages, we are of opinion that no precise rule can be laid down. The types of case involving conscious self-endangerment are so various that clarity and certainty of law could not be achieved by any inflexible and uniform rule. Certainly, when a victim has clear knowledge of a specific danger and exposes himself to it without any good reason and is hurt, or indeed when he helps to create the dangerous situation, there will be good reason to relieve the defendant of all liability. But it would be one-sided to concentrate, to the exclusion of all the other features of the individual case, on the fact that the plaintiff voluntarily endangered himself. Other factors may be of great weight, for instance how the danger arose, how much the defendant was to blame for the existence and actualisation of the risk, what the relationship between the parties was, and how obvious the danger was (see also the decision of this Senate on 2 December 1958 (VersR 1959, 368)). A person's psychological state is very hard to ascertain, and a decision which focused exclusively on the plaintiff's attitude at a particular moment of time would often be unrealistic and unfair. § 254 BGB permits the trial judge to do justice in the particular circumstances of the individual case in a judicially responsible manner, and he will be assisted in making a just and proper exercise of his discretion in applying this provision if he pays attention to the principles evolved by the courts in relation thereto and to the principle of inconsistency in conduct.

The Third Civil Senate has stated that it no longer wishes to adhere to the doctrine of "acting at one's own risk" as laid down in BGHZ 2, 159, so it is unnecessary to convoke the Great Senate for Civil Matters under § 136 GVG.

V. It is well-established law that if the victim is a minor, his contributory fault under § 254 BGB is to be judged in accordance with the relevant principles of delictual law. If a sixteen-and-a-half-year-old like the plaintiff is personally at fault in consciously putting himself at risk, one must therefore look to his actual ability to recognise the dangerous nature of his conduct and to behave accordingly. To this extent we agree with the Court of Appeal. But as has been explained in **IV**, above, we cannot follow the Court of Appeal in holding that the defendants must be released from liability just because the plaintiff consciously endangered himself. This very case shows how unjust a result may follow from undue concentration on this point.

The following factors in particular should be noted. It is true that the plaintiff's failure to maintain his objection to the second defendant's taking over the wheel counts against him, as does the fact that he himself was ready to take the wheel in lieu of the second defendant and so imperil his fellow-travellers. On the other hand, the plaintiff was not the first to suggest that someone other than the first defendant should drive. In view of the way young people behave, the conduct of the plaintiff as a whole, while certainly culpable, is not incomprehensible. Young people like the plaintiff are especially ductile if an older comrade sets a bad example. In the circumstances, the plaintiff's fault in remaining in the vehicle when the second defendant was driving it certainly cannot be described as gross. The second defendant, by contrast, was the origin of the suggestion that an unqualified person should drive, and it was his unreasonable and incompetent driving which caused this serious accident. The first defendant was especially to blame, for it was he who had control of the car; furthermore, as the only person with a driving licence, he must have known the probable consequences of letting the second defendant drive; finally, he was the oldest of the group and should have asserted himself more strenuously.

These observations are not intended to prejudge the final decision which in view of the change in the law and the possibility of further evidence must necessarily be left to the trial judge. We make them only in order to show that on the evidence so far adduced it would be wrong that the defendants, who have apparently suffered only slight injuries, should be entirely released from liability to the plaintiff, who is maimed for life. This case is entirely different from the hypothetical case put by the Court of Appeal, where three youths of the same age who do not know how to drive and have no licence take turns at driving a car they have stolen and are badly injured in an accident while one of them is at the wheel. There is really no comparison between the situations. Nor does the very vague idea of "community of danger among the young", which weighed with the Court of Appeal, provide any legal basis for refusing to hold the defendants liable to the plaintiff.

Case 94

BUNDESGERICHTSHOF (SIXTH CIVIL SENATE) 17 SEPTEMBER 1991
NJW 1991, 3275 = VERSR 1991, 1293

Facts

The plaintiff *Land* brought a claim for damages by way of the right of subrogation in respect of injuries suffered by K who was injured in a road accident on 11 February 1962. At the time of the accident, K was employed by the *Land* as a police officer. As a result of the consequences of the accident, K had to take early retirement on 1 February 1964. The defendants in the action were the insurers of R (the other driver), whose responsibility for the accident is not in dispute. As a result of a declaratory binding judgment dated 9 January 1969, the defendants are obliged to compensate the plaintiff *inter alia* for the costs which the latter will incur up to 30 November 2000 in respect of maintenance payments which it must make to K. The amount of the compensation payable is the difference between what K would have earned as a police sergeant and his earnings as a computer programmer. This is because since July 1964 K has been working as a programmer at the firm of T. Soon afterwards K was earning more in his new job than as a police officer. On 1 March 1982, however, he left the employment of T and joined the firm of S, owned by his brother. The intention was that after about one year's experience working for this firm he would take over the management of a newly established subsidiary company of S. Soon after opening, this subsidiary had to cease trading as its economic prospects were poor. K left the employment of S on 30 September 1983. Subsequently, he was employed as a sales representative for a publishing company, and then as an insurance agent. Since 1984 his income has been less than that of a police sergeant. The plaintiff therefore sought to recover in respect of the maintenance payments made between 1984 and 1987, based on the difference between what K actually earned and the earnings of a police sergeant, namely DM 101,219.69.

The LG gave judgment for the plaintiff; the OLG rejected the defendants' appeal. The defendants' appeal to the BGH was successful.

For the following

Reasons

I. The judgment of the OLG is based on the assumption that were it not for the accident, K would have remained in the police force and during the period of time in question would have had the earnings of a police sergeant. The claims for loss of earnings brought by the plaintiff by way of the right of subrogation (§ 99 NRWBG) were losses resulting from the accident. An adequate causal link exists between the loss and the accident. Developments such as those which have occurred in a case like the present one, whereby the professional activity initially taken up is subsequently abandoned with the result that the victim has a lower level of earnings, are not wholly improbable. There were therefore no grounds for the defendants to be exonerated from the duty to make good the damage resulting from K's loss of earnings according to the principles which have been developed by the case law on the protective scope of the norm and on the breaking of the chain of causation.

II. The judgment of the OLG is incorrect in law. The defendants' appeal must succeed and the claim must be rejected.

1. The OLG is correct to affirm that the pre-requisites are satisfied which would normally suffice for the defendants to be liable, such that they would be responsible for the loss of earnings in accordance with the provisions of § 823 I and § 842 BGB read in conjunction with § 3 of the Act on Compulsory Insurance (PflVG). Thus it is not in dispute that the defendants are bound to make good in full the loss of earnings suffered by K as a result of the accident. In contrast to the view put forward at the oral hearing on behalf of the applicants, it must also be assumed that K's accident is a scientific and factual cause of the loss of earnings for which the claim has been brought. For the OLG has established—

and its underlying procedure has not been called into question by this appeal—that this loss would not have occurred but for the road accident. The judgment of the OLG is also correct in holding that there is an adequate causal link between this loss and the accident. It is not wholly improbable (to use the general definition [references omitted]) that a person injured in an accident who can no longer exercise his earlier profession because of the injuries he has suffered and must therefore earn his living in a different way, may also give up this professional activity, even if it is better paid, in order to seek greater job satisfaction elsewhere or in order to earn more, but that the result of the further change in job may be that his earnings fall behind what he was earning previously. Such a chain of events lies within the sphere of what experience has indicated can be expected to occur.

2. These general preconditions for liability will not, as this court has repeatedly stated, suffice in every case as the basis for the tortfeasor's duty to make good a particular consequence of the accident. Even though the loss may have been "adequately" caused by the accident, there may not, in exceptional cases, be the necessary internal connection between the infringement of the legally protected interest and the "resulting loss" as defined by § 823 I BGB for which the injured victim claims compensation required to generate a duty to compensate on the part of the defendants. If, as appears from the evaluation so far made of the facts, there is no more than a purely external, so to speak coincidental connection between the conduct which caused the injury and the consequential loss for which recovery is sought, then there is no relevant justification for attributing responsibility for this consequence of the original accident to the tortfeasor [references omitted]. Such is the case here.

(*a*) The necessary connection, such as is required for there to be a duty to compensate on the part of the defendants, with the range of risks to which the defendants, through their tortious conduct, subjected the victim, may be missing, in particular where the victim himself decides to take a certain course of action and thus himself has been the true cause of the consequential loss for which he now seeks recovery. In such a set of circumstances, an evaluatory assessment can lead to the conclusion that the loss thereby caused belongs exclusively to the normal risks of life of the victim himself. Thus it is recognised that the causal connection with the original tortious act is broken where conduct of the victim which causes the loss is wholly unusual or inappropriate [references omitted]. The same may apply where a decision of the victim which brings about the loss is so far removed from the risk created by the tortfeasor and is embedded within the victim's own sphere of risk such that the tortfeasor cannot legitimately be made liable for this consequence. It was with this reasoning and in the same circumstances as those at issue here, in which the victim of the accident changed job and thus suffered loss, that this court decided that further consequential loss fell outside the sphere of risk for which the defendant was responsible, provided that the change of professional activities was such that the accident was no more than the external trigger for this development (NJW-RR 1991, 854).

Such an exception will only apply subject to strict conditions. The principle of full compensation which applies to the law of damages requires that such an evaluation can only be undertaken in exceptional cases. It is necessary that there is a clear break which is externally visible, which shows that the injured person has accepted as his own the risks resulting from his decision to pursue a different professional goal [reference omitted].

If in a particular case there are unequivocal factors which indicate that with his decision to change careers the victim separated his future professional activities from the accident, then the principle of full compensation does not require the victim to be exonerated from the negative consequences of his career choice or the tortfeasor to take the burden of those consequences which, on an evaluatory assessment, have nothing more to do with the injury which was suffered or with the career change which this brought about, simply because the victim's career took a different path as a consequence of the accident and there is thus a causal connection with the loss. Where there is such a change of career, the victim—who may benefit from increased promotion and earning opportunities without being asked to account for these [references omitted]—acts at his own risk. He is not protected by the liability of the tortfeasor against the effects of all the incorrect vocational decisions he may make or against all the misfortunes which may occur from the moment of the accident to the time when he ceases work.

(*b*) In the case in question, K took up a post as a programmer in Firm T after the accident; he worked there for nearly 18 years. Soon afterwards, he earned more than in his previous job as a police sergeant. It is not claimed, nor is it the case, that K did not feel "wholly valued" in his new job or that he did not have the same social standing as in his previous job [references omitted]. K's decision to leave Firm T in 1982 and to switch to his brother's Firm S was not for instance based on any continuing effects upon his health of the road accident which occurred long before, but was simply based on K's wish to take up a new job which promised success and higher remuneration. These circumstances, taken as a whole and evaluated as this court is entitled to do on the basis of the findings of fact of the first instance court, make it apparent that there is a break in the chain of causation between the road accident on 11 February 1962 and the professional failures of the plaintiff after 1982. By taking a decision, which was no longer influenced by the accident, to leave his established job of 18 years with Firm T and to switch to his brother's firm, K decided to take his subsequent professional fate into his own hands, as would have been the case if any employee of Firm T, regardless of whether he or she had suffered a road accident, had decided to change jobs. So long as he was earning the level of salary paid by Firm T, K was suffering no loss of earnings as a consequence of the accident. There is evidence that this would not have changed up to the end of working life. If, in these circumstances, K were to feel the need to change jobs, then he was free to do so; however, there is no question of him making the person who caused an accident which happened 20 years earlier responsible for his professional failures which were caused by a decision by K which was brought about neither by the injuries caused in the accident, nor by any alleged "lesser value" of his work for Firm T. The road accident and K's subsequent employment at Firm T which was brought about by the accident were only relevant to his renewed decision to change jobs and work for Firm S to the extent that were it not for the accident he would have shied away from the possibility of working in his brother's business, given his permanent position in the public service as a police sergeant. This circumstance alone does not change the position as regards the factors set out above which indicate clearly that K was acting on his own responsibility, and does not undermine the argument that the chain of causation is broken between the road accident and the loss of earnings which is claimed. It follows that the disadvantageous consequences can no longer, with regard to the accident, be construed as "damage arising therefrom".

(*c*) Contrary to the view put forward by the respondent in its argument, it is not necessary to reach a different conclusion on the grounds that his professional situation with

Firm T might have been a contributing factor in K's decision to move to his brother's business and that consequently it was necessary to establish the facts further in this respect. It is not necessary to decide whether the tortfeasor will always be liable in respect of the loss of earnings suffered by the victim which might occur considerably later after his forced change of job as a result of a reorganisation by his new employer. For the decision of the OLG does not leave it open as to whether the reason for K's move to his brother's business was attributable to his professional situation with Firm T, but rather it stated in the grounds for decision—and these were not challenged in the appeal—that K gave up his job as a programmer *in order* to take up a senior post in another business. In addition, as was apparent from the facts presented in the OLG judgment, the plaintiff, himself, did not even argue that K would no longer have been able to work for Firm T when it moved its data processing department, in which he worked, to the town of W; on the contrary, the plaintiff argued that the reason for K's move to his brother's business was that K did not want to move to W. Whether this would suffice as a ground for imposing the burden of the consequential loss of earnings which would have resulted from K's refusal and the subsequent change of job upon the person who caused the accident can be left open in this context since, as was said, the OLG found that the reason for K's change was his decision to take up a senior post in his brother's business. The professional misfortunes which resulted from this decision are, as stated here, no longer attributable to the acts of the tortfeasor.

Notes to Cases 76–94

1. The twenty cases reproduced above deal with various aspects of causation: cases 89, BGHZ 20, 137, and 80, BGHZ 3, 261, contain oft-quoted definitions of the adequate cause theory; cases 85, BGHZ 27, 137, and 86, BGHZ 58, 162, provide the leading examples of the operation of the "scope of the rule theory" of causation; case 78, RGZ 155, 37, deals with the problem of predispositions, while no. 89 discusses the thorny question of accident neurosis; case 87, OLG Stuttgart NJW 1965, 112, looks at the issues associated with rescues; case 92, RGZ 83, 15, deals with the plaintiff's duty to mitigate his loss and so on. All these points have been developed in section A of chapter 2, 5, above; and excellent collections of American materials can be found in: Franklin and Rabin, 293–381; Epstein, 363–459; Henderson and Pearson, 127–174; 521–575; Posner, 543; Prosser, Wade, and Schwartz, 252–355 etc. Dobbs, *The Law of Torts*, 405–492, nowadays provides one of the clearest treatise accounts. All of these also give abundant references to the rich periodical literature, so these notes can be kept to a minimum.

2. The literature may be extensive and some of the problems intellectually fascinating, but causation must be approached with the following warning in mind:

The problem [of causation] is a difficult one, but the length of the treatment in this casebook and the amount of time allocated it in most courses may perhaps give an exaggerated impression of its importance. In the great majority of negligence cases, the problem does not arise at all; it comes up only in the fraction of negligence actions that involve unusual fact situations. (Prosser, Wade, and Schwartz, 349.)

This down-to-earth remark applies equally to German and American law.

Prosser et al. also state in their case-book that "The principle task of the court is to do justice as between these parties in their present situation. For this purpose, a weighing evaluative process is required, rather than a clear-cut rule of law". (pp. 349–50) This is not so different from the point the German Federal Court made in its famous judgment of 23 October 1951, BGHZ 3, 261, (case 80) where, after reviewing the many variants of the adequate cause theory, it concluded that the answer must, in the end, be found in common sense and a reasonable choice between competing policy factors. Once again Americans and Germans are thus not so far apart. For in both these countries academics have not managed to conceal their fascination with the subject which, in the end, they are forced to admit is of relatively small practical value and should be approached in a common-sense way (Hart and Honoré, ch. 2).

3. The differences between adequate causation and foreseeability have been discussed above (chapter 2, section 2.A 5(*b*)). "But foreseeability", to quote Prosser et al. again (*ibid.* 350), "is an accordion concept, depending upon the detail and precision with which foresight is required." In modern times it has thus been stretched (over-stretched in some cases, see, for example, *Meah* v. *McCreamer* [1985] 1 All ER 367), so that it is legitimate to enquire whether it has lost much of its usefulness as a device controlling liability. Was not that one of the reasons why the *Re Polemis* rule [1921] 3 KB 560 was abandoned in England (but not the USA; see Friendly J's remarks in *Petitions of Kinsman Transit Company* 338 F. 2d 708 (1964)) by the *Wagon Mound* (*No. 1*) [1961] AC 388? In Germany, von Caemmerer has reached the same conclusion about the effectiveness of the adequate cause theory ("Das Problem des Kausalzusammenhangs" *Gesammelte Schriften* I, 395, 402, 408); and the German Federal Court is not tuning down its doubts about the concept of adequacy in general (for example see BGHZ 79, 259). Not unnaturally, the search for more normative theories of causation can thus be found in both systems, though once again the similarity between the views of Rabel and Green is, to say the least, coincidental but uncanny. Such theories, as we have seen, can help keep liability under control; but they can also lead to irreconcilable decisions: *cf.*, for example, *De Haen* v. *Rockwood Sprinkler Co.* 258 NY 350, (1932); *Di Caprio* v. *New York Cent. RR Co.*, 131 NE 746 (NY1921); *Kernan* v. *American Dredging Co.*, 355 US 426, 78 S. Ct. 394 (1958) and, of course, the classic English case of *Gorris* v. *Scott*, LR 9 Exch. 125 (1874). Little wonder that in view of such ambiguities and uncertainties some authors have expressed open scepticism about the utility of the notion of causation (see, for example, Coase, "The Problem of Social Cost" 3 *J. Law and Econ.* 1, 2 (1960); Calabresi, *The Cost of Accidents* 6, n. 8 (1970). But can terms like "cheaper cost avoider" avoid causal language?

4. In view of this, the selection of cases translated above more than usually reflects personal tastes and predilection. But even here a note of warning must be sounded. The judgments reproduced usually deal with one facet only of the problem selected for inclusion and discussion. For example, take the rescue case reproduced above (case 87, OLG Stuttgart NJW 1965, 112). This obviously invites comparison with *Wagner* v. *International Ry Co.* 133 NE 437 (NY 1921). The result is the same, since the policy behind the judgments is the same. But the terminology is different (causative language instead of duty of care). The use of the one rather than the other does not really matter, as most American books which discuss the problem say quite categorically. (In any event, terms such as "duty", "foreseeability", "adequate causation" in these cases barely conceal policy dictates.) But the difference in literary style cannot be passed unnoticed. Cardozo's romantic imagery has justly been immortalized; dry causative language, on the other hand, can only make the law appear even more remote from real people and their problems than most of us perceive it to be. But the equivocation between concepts can be found in both systems; and once grasped, makes their comparison much easier in so far as one does not get too hung-up by concepts and notions.

Giving a rescuer an action is right only under certain circumstances. The German judgment, along with other different systems, hints that the solution will be different if his intervention is rash or the result of pure intermeddling with the affairs of others. Other problems arise. What, for example, if the person rescued negligently puts himself in a position of danger? What if the rescuer injures the rescued person or a third person? What about the rescuer's rescuer? In the casuistic Common law, most of these problems have been litigated (see Prosser, Wade and Schwartz, 331–3); in German law the answers are usually canvassed in the literature; but in practice the solutions, again, should not be different, since the same policy issues are at work in both systems. The references given in the principal German case confirm this.

5. Foreseeability and rescue have also been considered in a novel context that has arisen, in part, because the law has not kept up with the rapid forward leaps of medical technology. The point can

be easily put: should a medical practitioner who culpably removes the *sole* kidney of an injured child be liable for the damage which a close relative (typically mother or father) suffers by donating one of his kidneys? Case 88, BGHZ 101, 215, and Canadian law (*Urbanski* v. *Patel*, 84 DLR 3rd 650, 671 (1978)) have said "yes" to such claims—the courts in the USA have decided otherwise. (See *Sirianni* v. *Anna* 285 NYS 2d 709 (1967); *Moore* v. *Shah*, 458 NYS 33 (1982); *Ornelas* v. *Fry*, 727 P. 2d 819 (Ariz.1986).) What are the arguments for and against recovery?

First, there is a hint, but no more than that, to suggest that the donor's intervention may be unforeseeable and unexpected. This must have been particularly true when cases like *Sirianni* v. *Anna* (1967) were decided when organ transplants were still rare. This argument, however, is unlikely to carry much weight today when, as the Canadian Court put it in *Urbanski* v. *Patel*, "a kidney transplant is an accepted remedy in [cases of] renal failure".

A second argument, considered in *Moore* v. *Shah*, was that foreseeability alone is not enough to lead to the discovery of a "duty of care" and thereby to the imposition of liability. This is certainly true as far as English law is concerned though it is somewhat surprising to see it coming from the pen of American judges. For, as Professor John Fleming has put it, "In California [at least] foreseeability has for most purposes become a sufficient test for 'duty'" (*The American Tort Process* (1988), 118). Equally surprising is the fact that American judges, who are in practice quick to usurp the (inactive) legislature's role, are in this context suggesting that if a remedy is needed it should come from the legislator (*Sirianni* v. *Anna* at p. 713).

A third objection considered by the *Moore* court is that the imposition of liability would extend the physician's liability "beyond manageable limits" since they could not "foresee each and every person other than his patient who might conceivably be affected by his negligence". But quite apart from the fact that the floodgates argument has never held out much appeal in instances involving physical injury, the fact is that in these cases one is only concerned with a limited and usually identifiable group of close relatives who, for medical reasons (tissue matching), or from an understandable moral compulsion, are, in practice, the only ones likely to come forward in order to save the injured primary victim. In any event, the floodgates argument seems to be effectively· countered by the criteria which the German courts say must be evaluated *ad hoc* before the rescuer's intervention is deemed worthy of support.

The fourth objection is that in the view of the American courts this situation is incompatible with Cardozo's phraseology in the *Wagner* case. There Cardozo had talked of "the act of rescue, *if only it be not wanton*, is born of the occasion"; and "wanton" was in the kidney cases interpreted to mean "wilful", later elaborated into "wilful, intentional, voluntary". Do you think that is what "wanton" means? Since every rescue, even one attempted on the spur of the moment, is intentional and voluntary, should not "wanton" here be taken to imply "reckless"?

Fifthly, in the USA the rescue doctrine was not applied to the present situation on the grounds that the rescuer/donor had time to reflect on his action. How does the German court counter this point? Which view do you find more convincing?

Finally, the sixth objection against recovery is the presence of consent on the part of the donor/plaintiff. With respect, however, the argument is misleading. For no one is saying that the kidney was removed without consent; if it had been, there would be an action for battery! What one is saying is that the defendant's negligence placed the donor in a position in which, morally and socially, he felt compelled to act the way he did. Indeed, wider policy considerations should encourage such donations, not penalise them by not rewarding them. The German court, influenced by such motives, had no doubt that "consent" could not in this case be used as a defence. Do you agree with its view or do you prefer the American reasoning? How much has policy influenced the outcome of those cases? Which view do you think the English courts should/will adopt?

6. The problem of accident neurosis is represented in this selection by two cases only (no. 89, BGHZ 20, 137, and 90, BGHZ 137, 142) though many have reached the courts. It is best understood if read in conjunction with the cases 1–3 on nervous shock annotated above. The difference here, however, is that the victim, as primary victim, does not need to fulfil any additional criteria ("ties of love and affection" etc.) before he can recover. The main problem in these cases is to exclude

such psychiatric illness as is too remote and ought not give rise to a cause of action. Generally speaking, the tortfeasor has to accept that the victim has a predisposition for the illness; i.e. the harm has only arisen because of the special condition of the plaintiff. A psychological susceptibility, which leads to disorders and consequential harm—perhaps incapacity to work—which would not have occurred in the case of the vast majority of human beings, can be included in these individual conditions. In principle, the plaintiff—according to the *egg shell rule*—has to compensate for such consequential harm. At the same time, it is clear that the law has to impose some limits to the extent of liability. German courts have developed two major exceptions to recovery. The first concerns the so-called "rent neurosis" (*Rentenneurose*. "Rent" must here be understood in the sense of "periodic payments" which is the form that many injury awards take in Germany). In these cases the claimant (whose illness is not in doubt), in his desire for financial security, merely takes the accident as a welcome opportunity to avoid the hardship of having to earn his livelihood in his profession. Awarding compensation in such a case would be counterproductive and would hinder the claimant's recovery (see case 89 above, BGHZ 20, 137 and BGHZ 56, 163). The main problem here is of course to prove that that is the case. The second exception concerns cases where the accident concerns a minor incident (*Bagatelle*). If the psychiatric illness is not due to a clear predisposition of the victim, and there is a clear disproportion between the accident and its consequences, liability will, again, be denied (see BGH NJW 1997, 1640). For a useful summary of the case law see case 90, which also emphasises that the two exceptions mentioned above must be construed narrowly. This case also shows that the BGH, unlike its common law counterparts, is increasingly taking psychiatric illnesses seriously (see Schiemann JZ 1998, 684). Given the limitations of space we cannot go into more details; but this is also regrettable since the interaction of law and medicine is here, as elsewhere, fascinating. The medical aspects of this problem are discussed by a consultant neurologist in a book which is intelligible even to non-specialists (Trimble, *Post Traumatic Neurosis* (1981)); and one of the points made there is that attitudes towards this problem are changing. Thus, while during the nineteenth century stress was put on "organic" material changes, during the greater part of our century the emphasis has shifted to psychological interpretation of the symptoms. More recently, however, there is a certain return towards more "organic" interpretations as the functioning of the human brain becomes better understood. The notion that in most of these cases plaintiffs are not guilty of malingering may (subject to what has been said in relation to the *Rentenneurose*), in part, explain the greater willingness to provide compensation. Certainly medical science has shown that illness following injury seems susceptible to manipulation by compensation factors. Clearly there is here more room for interdisciplinary work (incidentally, the BGH justified its more victim-friendly attitude in BGH NJW 1998, 810 by referring to new medical research). By the way, the same interest in the increased ability of medical science to explain and understand these complaints is also evidenced in the (English) Law Commission's learned report entitled "Liability for Psychiatric Illness" (Consultation Paper No 137, 1995). But this new learning has still failed to budge English judges from their fears of endless litigation. The result? English law on the subject is in a hopeless tangle from which, some judges seem to think, only the legislator can save it.

7. Case 81, BGHZ 132, 164, deals with a different question: under what conditions can liability be imposed if the victim brings the injury upon himself. The aspect of the question we wish to consider has arisen in cases where law enforcement officers are injured while pursuing the perpetrators of crime. Two points must be considered.

In such cases, the first step is to establish in what circumstances the tortfeasor owes a duty of care to his pursuer. The German court suggested that it was not the flight, as such, that created liability but the manner in which it was executed. We have already noted in the context of the nervous shock cases (see notes to cases 1–3, above) that although there is no duty of care to abstain from injuring oneself, the situation might be different where self-harming also causes injuries to another person. Conversely the suspect—assuming the position of the BGH is correct—has no duty to help the police to arrest him. But if he seeks to escape the pursuit, he is under an obligation to do this in a manner that will not endanger the health of the pursuing officers. Since, as is clear to him, it is their duty to enforce the law and to arrest him, the suspect owes them a duty of care not to provoke a dangerous pursuit. The problem has been identified above (chapter 2, section 2.A 5(*a*)) as one of causation while the BGH prefers the language of "objective attribution", *objektive Zurechnung*. (The older case law assumed that the chain of causation was interrupted, see Emmerich *JuS* 1996, 846) This may be more a matter of terminology than substance. Nonetheless, it is remarkable to note how much effort the court expended in trying to define the circumstances under which a duty of care would arise. Equally interesting is the fact that it did not openly analyse the problem as one of causation even though the theory of "the protective scope of the rule" can be framed as a problem of legal cause. This indicates yet again how interchangeable the different approaches really are (scope of the duty owed, duty of care, and causation). One obvious advantage of approaching the case on the basis of § 254 BGB (mitigation) is that it allows a partial reduction of damages (as was actually held in the present case). A causative analysis on the other hand could entail an all or nothing result. (See for a similar approach in English cases, Hart and Honoré *Causation in the Law* (2nd edn. 1985) p. 141.)

The second issue raised by the case is how to weigh the interests involved. It is not necessary to repeat the reasoning of the court, which repays careful reading. Suffice it to say that the BGH requires that the police's decision to pursue is not wholly unreasonable (which is determined by a comprehensive balancing of interests). Additionally, it must be shown that the loss was caused because of the increased danger situation inherent in the pursuit and was not part of the general risks of life (*allgemeines Lebensrisiko*). (For details see Teichmann's note in *JZ* 1996, 1181.) The notions are interesting; indeed, they make much sense. But, as always, the devil lies in the detail.

Maps of Europe and Germany

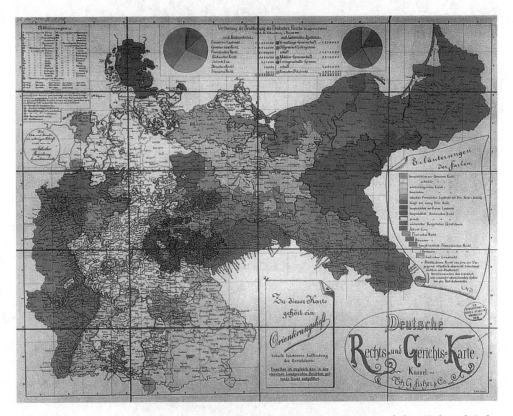

MAP 1. Pre-codification map of Germany reproduced by kind permission of the Niedersächsische Staats-und Universitätsbibliothek in Göttingen.

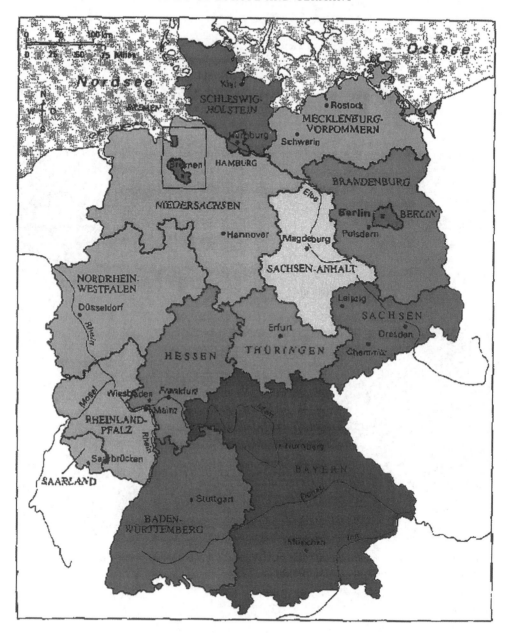

MAP 2. Re-united Germany.

A Note on the Jurists that Follow

Selection is an invidious task; and it becomes almost impossible to perform when the list of distinguished German jurists is so extensive. From the outset, it was clear to me that focusing on the better known names of the 19th century would have been wrong on two counts. First and foremost this is a work on contemporary German law. Secondly, to concentrate on the past would imply that the present offers unworthy successors. This is patently wrong; and a variety of factors, including the cultural "fall out" of the Second World War, can account for the fact that modern German law (and its lawyers) is less known in the university class rooms of today. Incidentally, from the moment the decision was taken to include pictures of distinguished German jurists, I was clear in my mind that I would not include jurists, however distinguished they might have been, who had played an active part in the National Socialist regime in the thirties and early forties.

A second question that had to be resolved was whether this "pantheon" should be limited to academics. Given the strong academic content of German law, such a decision would have been perfectly possible and defensible. Yet one of the theses of this work is that modern German law is highly dependent on its case law. So judges had to be included, though that did not answer the question how to select those who merited inclusion.

The difficulty is caused by the fact that no individual judgments are delivered in the German Courts (except the Constitutional Court); and it is difficult to trace an individual's contribution in a collective judgment. The possibility of finding in German law an individual stylist such as Cardozo's or Holmes', Blackburn, Atkin or Denning simply does not exist. After consulting my German friends, I decided that selecting from those who had served as Vice President's or Presidents of the Federal Supreme Court in the fifties and sixties was an objective a criterion as I could get. Their short biographies that I have prepared to accompany each photography shows that all were not only senior judges but also had impressive academic credentials. If my list is still not to everyone's liking, the possibility of a fifth edition of this book is the only hope of redemption that I can offer.

German Jurists

Friedrich Carl von SAVIGNY (1779–1861). He was a descendant of a well-to-do family from Lorraine, which moved to Germany in 1730 because of its Protestant beliefs. He studied law in Marburg between 1795 and 1799 where he wrote his doctoral dissertation in Latin. He then held Chairs in Marburg (1803), Landshut, in Bavaria (1808), and Berlin (from 1810 where he co-founded the Prussian University and was its first Rector from 1812–1813). He was the founder of the Historical School and the *Zeitschrift der Savigny-Stiftung für Rechtsgeschichte*. He taught the Crown Prince subsequently King Frederick William IV of Prussia. His first major work on *The Law of Possession* appeared during his first year in Marburg. The book was translated forty-five years later into English by Sir Erskine Perry, Chief Justice of Bombay who described it as a "most valuable work to Indian practitioners." This appreciation was later echoed by John Austin who referred to it in his Lectures on Jurisprudence as "of all books upon law, the most consummate and masterly. But Savigny had already won acclaim as polemicist, opposing any rapid moves at German (political) and legal unification. This battle began when, in 1814, Thibaut, a Professor at Heidelberg, wrote his famous tract *Über die Nothwendigkeit eines allgemeinen bürgerlichen Rechts für Deutschland*, proposing a general Civil Code for Germany along the lines of the recently enacted French Code. Savigny replied with his equally forceful tract *Vom Beruf unserer Zeit für Gesetzgebung und Rechtswissenschaft* arguing that the time was not ripe for such a project which should be preceded by a thorough study of the existing, indigenous legal material. Savigny's *magnum opus* was his *System des heutigen römischen Rechts* published in 8 volumes between 1840 and 1849 (the last chapter of which on conflict of laws was translated into English.) Savigny, was remarkable in devoting much time to his friends and among the many beneficiaries of such generosity of spirit was our own John Austin and Jacob Grimm—one of the Brothers Grimm of the *Fairy Tales*—whom he helped by getting him a chair at Berlin. Grimm, whose substantial correspondence with Savigny survives and provides excellent insights into the difficult (and not always compatible) characters and aspirations of both men, repaid the compliment by dedicating to Savigny his *Deutche Grammatik*—one of the most important works ever written for German philology. Savigny's work received State recognition of the award of the *Order Pour le Merit (pronounced in French)*, which was originally instituted by Frederick the Great as a military order but was later extended to cover a very limited number of luminaries from the world of arts and sciences. It is still Germany's highest distinction, held by a limited number of persons at any one time, and thus in many ways analogous to our own Order of Merit.

Rudolph von JHERING (1818–1892) is an ideal subject for biography, especially if his life is examined, as it must be, in close connection with his work and his times. Peripatetic as a student—he studied in Heidelberg, Munich, Göttingen and Berlin—he proved just as mobile as a Professor, confirming the statement that Goethe put in Faust's mouth "It is only through restlessness that one proves one's worth". He thus held chairs successively in Berlin (as an Associate) and then as *ordinarius* in Basel, Rostock, Kiel, Giessen, Vienna (from which, on departure, he was given the Knight's Cross in the Order of Leopold which carried with it the title of *von* which he proudly used ever after) and, finally, Göttingen (while refusing "calls" to Leipzig and Heidelberg). His interests were just as varied, ranging from music to art, gardening, and particularly growing wines. His spread in law was just as impressive, ranging from Roman law—with his *Geist des römischen Rechts* being his most original work—to jurisprudence with his *Kampf ums Recht* where he boldly asserted that law triumphs only when citizens assert their rights. Even more widely acclaimed was his *Der Zweck im Recht*, where he dared to challenge the German establishment's attachment to Hegel and the idea that law was the expression of the general will. (For Jhering, like Ulpian, "*Jus privatum quod ad singulorum utilitatem special.*") But the work is wider than the few lines above suggest, as it contains in its second volume some remarkable views on teleology, the theory of morals, as well as a fascinating study on courtesy—*Höflichkeit*—in relation to manners, dress, symbolism, and speech. Humour is also not absent from his interests, represented by a later work *Scherz und Ernst in der Jurispurdenz*—a work, which also contains some original ideas about the need to maintain a close link between academic law, practice, and legal education. Jhering lived in an era of political giants (Bismarck, was his hero) and legal luminaries of the highest order. (He was almost an exact contemporary of Sir Henry Maine at the time when the latter was doing his best work). As a scholar he may have lacked the precision of Dernburg (whom he followed in his study of the law of possession) or the investigative gifts of Mommsen. But the vivacity of his style and the force with which he put forward his views not only made him a great teacher but the best selling legal author of his time. Moreover, he was a visionary, who did not allow his scholarly interest in Roman law to obscure his conviction that the time had come to go, as he put it, "through Roman law, above and beyond it." This vision is also evident in his attack on parochialism that came with the triumph of the sovereign state of the 19th century, arguably making him a precursor of some contemporary ideas of legal globalisation.

Otto von GIERKE (1841–1921). Son of a Prussian judge who served first as Associate Professor in Berlin (1866) and then as full Professor in Breslau (1872), Heidelberg (1884) and Berlin (from 1887). His principle work was his *Genossenschaftsrecht* in 4 volumes which appeared between 1869 and 1913. He provided a useful contribution to the preparation of the Code through his polemical piece *Der Entwurf eines Bürgerlichen Gesetzbuchs und das deutsche Recht* published in 1889. He was a severe critic of the 19th century bourgeois liberal ideas that came to be enshrined in the Code; and as the leading "Germanist" of his age, he often criticised the predominant influence that Roman law had on the drafting of the new Code.

Hans Carl NIPPERDEY (left) (1895–1968). Started his legal career as an Associate Professor in Jena. His first major work which brought him to national attention was published in 1920 and was entitled *Kontrahierungszwang und diktierter Vertrag*. From 1925 onwards he was Professor at Cologne mainly writing on the General Part of the Civil Code (Ennecerus/Nipperdey *Allgemeiner Teil des Bürgerlichen Rechts*) and (with Alfred Hueck) on labour law (*Lehrbuch des Arbeitsrechts*). From 1954 to 1963 he held the post of President of the (supreme) Federal Labour Court and concentrated his efforts on developing the uncodified labour law on a case-by-case basis, paying particular attention to the constitutionally guaranteed basic rights.

Werner FLUME (right) (1908–). He was a pupil of the famous Romanist Fritz Schulz. In the beginning, his career under Schulz flourished with a scholarly work on the accessory nature of guarantee stipulations in Roman law. After 1933, however, the persecution of Schulz by the Nazis affected his career as well and he had to earn his living as a practising lawyer specialising in business and tax law. Academic recognition finally came in 1945 when he was elected to a Chair in the University of Bonn. Important works followed: in 1948 his *Eigenschaftsirrtum und Kauf* and later (between 1965 and 1977) his three-volume *Allgemeiner Teil des Bürgerlichen Rechts* along with numerous articles on company and tax law. Flume spoke on a number of occasions to the German Association of Lawyers giving his views on many matters of tort law, his severe criticism of the "Gentleman Rider" case being one of them.

Ernst von CAEMMERER (1908–1985). Born and raised in Berlin. Studied law in Munich and Berlin and then became judge at the Berlin Landgericht. Later he became legal adviser to the Dresdner Bank. While in Berlin he met Ernst Rabel and was persuaded to join as an Assistant the famous Kaiser Wilhelm Institut für ausländisches und internationales Privatrecht. In the long run, Rabel's influence on von Caemmerer and his work proved decisive. But in the thirties his association with this great jurist (who had by then sought refuge in the United States) hindered his career which seemed to be grinding to a halt. During the war he served as a naval officer on a mine sweeper. The breakthrough came in 1946 when he completed his *Habilitation* in Frankfurt under Walter Halstein (who was later to become Germany's first Foreign Affairs Minister) and a year later was called to a full Chair in Freiburg where, despite many attempts to entice him away, he stayed for the rest of his life. Von Caemmerer defies the usual pattern of a German academic career depending for advancement on the writing of learned monographs or large treatises. But his influence on the German law of torts, unjust enrichment, and the law of international commerce was enormous and it came through numerous scholarly articles and notes which still attract much attention in Germany.

Robert FISCHER (left) born in 1911 in Hessen studied law in Tübingen and Breslau. His doctoral thesis in 1935 was on a subject of company law which qualified him well for his subsequent work in the Legal Department of the *Deutsche Bank*. From 1945 to 1950 he served as the Director of the Landgericht of Göttingen and then was offered a seat in the Bundesgerichtshof becoming the youngest person ever to reach such a post at the age of thirty-nine. He subsequently turned down an offer of a Chair at Cologne University choosing, instead, to concentrate his efforts on his work as President of the Second Civil Senate. Between 1968 and 1977 he served as President of the entire Federal Court. His influence on the court's case law, especially in the areas of commercial and company law, was very great.

Bruno HEUSINGER (right) (1900–1975). Originated from Lower Saxony. Studied history at the University of Göttingen where he wrote a doctoral dissertation on the *Servitium Regis* (dealing with the economic relations of the German Monarchy between 900 and 1250 A.D.) He later switched to law and from 1929 he served as judge in the Landgericht and later in the Oberlandesgericht of Braunschweig of which he had become president by 1934. In that year, however, the Nazis demoted him to his first rank. It was not until 1948 that he was allowed to return to his earlier judicial post as president of the Court of Appeal, a post which was followed by that of President of the Oberlandesgericht of Celle. Two years later the supreme recognition of a distinguished judicial career finally came with his appointment as President of the Bundesgerichtshof a post which he held until his retirement in 1968.

Fritz HAUSS. Born 1908 in Münster, Westfalia. He studied law in Innsbruck, Münster, Berlin and Marburg where he defended his thesis in 1931 on *Die Pfändung der Eigentümergrundschuld*. His first judicial post was at the Oberlandesgericht of Hamm. In 1952 he was promoted to the Bundesgerichtshof where he was assigned first to the Sixth Civil Senate—where, it is believed, many tort cases dealing with the emerging right of privacy bear his mark—and later made President of the Fourth Civil Senate which deals with problems of family law, succession, and insurance. Between 1971 and 1977 he was Vice President of the entire Bundesgerichtshof and also managed to carry out (on a part time basis) the duties of a Visiting (later Honorary) Professor at Heidelberg. His academic work, which includes many publications on the law of civil liability, has been recognised by an honorary doctorate from the University of Tübingen. Hauss also holds the post of Chairman of the Appellate committee of the German Press Council.

Walter STIMPEL. He was born in 1917 in Saxony and served in the Luftwaffe as officer for "air force personnel". Between 1947 and 1950 he studied law in Kiel and then pursued post graduate studies in the Yale law school in the USA. From 1954 he served as judge in the Landgericht and Oberlandesgericht of Braunschweig. In 1965 he was promoted to the Bundesgerichtshof and assigned to the Second Civil Senate which deals with matters of company law, banking law and maritime law. From 1971 he served as President of that Senate and as Vice President of the entire court. From 1984 he held a teaching position in the University of Heidelberg and, later, was made an honorary Professor of the same University; and his many publications (especially on company law) have also been recognised by the award of an honorary doctorate from the University of Tübingen.

3

Liability for Others, Labour Law, and Stricter Forms of Liability

SECTION A. COMMENTARY

1. §§ 831 AND 278 BGB

Select bibliography

Brüggemeier, "Organisationshaftung—Deliktische Aspekte innerorganisatorischer Funktions-differenzierung", *AcP* 191 (1991), 33; Von Caemmerer, "Wandlungen des Deliktsrechts, Hundert Jahre deutsches Rechtsleben", *Festschrift zum 100 jährigen Bestehen des Deutschen Juristentages* II (1960) 49, 115 ff., reproduced in his *Gesammelte Schriften* (1968) 452; idem, "Reformprobleme der Haftung für Hilfspersonen", *ZfRV* (1973) 241; Deutsch, "Die neuere Entwicklung der Recht-sprechung zum Haftungsrecht", *JZ* 1984, 308, 314 ff.; Diederichsen, "Zum Entlastungsbeweis für Verrichtungsgehilfen", *ZRP* (1968) 60; Hassold, "Die Lehre vom Organisationsverschulden", *JuS* 1982, 583; Helm, "Rechtsfortbildung und Reform bei der Haftung für Verrichtungsgehilfen", *AcP* 166 (1966) 389; Hübner, "Zur Reform von Deliktsrecht und Gefährdungshaftung", *NJW* 1982, 2041; Jakobs, "Über die Notwendigkeit einer Reform der Geschäftsherrenhaftung", *VersR* 1969, 1061; Kiser, "Die Haftung des Fuhrparkhalters nach § 831 BGB hinsichtlich Auswahl und Beauftragung des Fahrers", *VersR* 1984, 213; Kupisch, "Die Haftung für Verrichtungsgehilfen (§ 831 BGB)", *JuS* 1984, 250; E. Schmidt, "Zur Dogmatik des § 278", *AcP* 170 (1970) 502, 520 ff.; Steindorff, "Repräsentan-ten-und Gehilfenversagen und Qualitätsregelungen in der Industrie", *AcP* 170 (1970) 93; Weitnauer, "Aktuelle Fragen des Haftungsrechts", *VersR* 1970, 585, 593 ff. For comparative discussions see Eörsi, in *International Encyclopedia of Comparative Law* XI, chap. 4; Kötz, "Strict Liability in German Law", *In Memoriam Jean Limpeus* (1984) 75 ff.; Lawson and Markesinis, *Tortious Liability for Unintentional Harm in the Common Law and the Civil Law* (1982), I, 163 ff.; Zweigert and Kötz, *An Introduction to Comparative Law* (1998) para. 41, p. 629, with further references to English and French literature.

(a) General observations

Up to now we have been envisaging liability for one's own acts or omissions. Its impor-tance remains crucial in today's world; and in fairly primitive or simple societies, with agrarian economies and a fairly elementary system of labour, it was the *most* crucial form of tort liability. But economic growth, industrialisation, the increase of commerce and of economic activity in general, necessitated the introduction of a more elaborate system of work which enabled one person or business entity to use the services of other persons in the furthering of their economic interests. Since these persons or entities—the masters as they were once called—derived the benefit from the services of those working for them—the "servants" or, nowadays, employees—it was only natural to think of making the former liable for the harmful conduct of the latter. Besides, the masters were often in a position to take steps to prevent the harm or—at a later stage—to carry insurance against the risk. Such a way of looking at things also offered considerable advantages to the victim, for he was thus offered a person worth suing in the place of the often, impecunious servant who had actually caused him the harm. Arguments such as these led to the strengthening and extension of what Common lawyers call vicarious liability; subject to the points made below, they are to be found as much in German law as they are in the other systems.

But the urge to make the "master" liable instead of or in addition to the servant could be approached in two ways. The one most consistent with the reasons we gave above was to make the master liable *strictly* for the faults (or unlawful acts) of the servants. The master's own liability, therefore, was strict in the sense that it did not depend on any fault on his part; but fault there had to be on the part of the servant. (But on this point, as well, note that German law presents a variant.) This is, indeed, the position taken by most of the legal systems of the world. But the German Civil Code opted for a weaker rule of "vicarious" liability: the master's liability would be based on his *own* fault of bad selection or supervision of the servant but it would be rebuttable in accordance with what will be said very shortly. Liability of masters is thus one way of making a person liable for the harm caused by another—§ 832 BGB being the other. (It is discussed below at pp. 700f.)

There are a number of reasons that account for this different approach taken by German law. An historical explanation lies in the fact that the nineteenth-century Pandectists had convinced themselves that the doctrine of *culpa in eligendo*, which they were introducing into § 831 BGB, was the only one known to Roman law. That this was so in a number of individual factual situations is beyond doubt; but to develop from the casuistic Roman approach a generalised doctrine that the master could *only* be liable if he himself was at fault was incorrect. (For more details see Seiler, "Die deliktische Gehilfenhaftung in historischer Sicht" *JZ* 1967, 530; Kaser, *Das römische Privatrecht* (1955) I, 527 ff., and, in English, Lawson and Markesinis, *op. cit.*, I, 160–3; Zimmermann, *Law of Obligations* (1990) 1121–6.)

A more pragmatic objection to the introduction of the "true" notion of vicarious liability was the fear that it would bring in its wake unwanted economic consequences, and in particular, increased economic burdens for small industry. And it was the aspirations and interests of this small industry, populated by the rising middle class, which the Civil Code had at heart. Not for the first time, therefore, the Code was to give effect to these ideas, oblivious to the fact that in the wider industrial field the enactment of such statutes as the Imperial Liability Act of 1871 had imposed strict liability on railway companies and, in this context, completely overtaken the notion of fault. In the end, therefore, the Code chose, as we shall see in section A.3, below, to leave the regulation of special matters to specialised legislation. Instead, it sanctioned as a general principle the idea that the master would be liable for the unlawful conduct of his servants only if fault could be imputed to him, the master, personally, in the choice and supervision of the servants. (If the master was a legal entity, the fault had to be imputed to its "duly" appointed representatives: § 31 BGB.)

We shall discuss this subject under four headings (*b*)–(*f*): (*b*) master–servant relationship; (*c*) damage in the course of employment; (*d*) unlawfulness; and (*e*) the master's exculpatory proof. A concluding section (*f*) will deal with the many ways devised to the unfortunate effects of § 831 BGB.

(b) Master–servant relationship

For the master to be liable, the damage must have been caused by a person to whom the master had "entrusted the performance of a function" (*zu einer Verrichtung bestellt*). Who qualifies as a servant (*Verrichtungsgehilfe*) is a mixed question of law and fact for the court to determine. Often, one encounters the term "dependency" (*Abhängigkeitsverhältnis.* Thus, Esser/Weyers, *op. cit.* II 2, p. 210); but like most of these terms, its utility depends on precise definition and this is not always possible. The most widely applied test, used to determine this relationship, is that of "direction and control" which means that salaried and wage-earning employees will, invariably, be classed as servants. (A classic formulation can be found in RGZ 92, 345, 346.) The limitations of this test, in a society with sophisticated labour and economic relations, have become apparent in Germany as they have elsewhere. The need was thus felt to widen the test so as to render, for example, hospitals liable for the wrongs of their surgeons, anaesthesiologists, and technical staff over whom, obviously, the master (hospital) had no direct and detailed control. Thus, it has on several occasions been stressed that the right to direct and control need not cover details. In one case (no. 104) the court expressly said that the right to give instructions need not cover details. It is sufficient that the master has the right to limit the worker's activity or withdraw it or circumscribe it as to time or circumstances. (BGH 30 June 1966, BGHZ 45, 311, 313. See, also, BGH 25 February 1988, BGHZ 103, 303.) The relaxed way in which the control test has been understood has thus allowed a hospital to be held liable for the harm caused by one of its doctors (BGH 26 April 1988, NJW 1988, 2298) and a doctor for the harm caused by one of his locums. (BGH 16 October 1956, NJW 1956, 1834.) The onus of proving the requisite relationship is on the plaintiff. (BGH 21 June 1994, ZfS 1995, 7.)

Clearly, even this redefined test will not solve all difficulties, and borderline cases will always exist. So, for example, a problem area well known to Common lawyers can be found in cases dealing with "borrowed servants" (usually "let out" by their masters with complicated modern machinery). If they cause damage while operating this machinery, who will be held responsible—the permanent or temporary master? Much will depend on the facts of each case but as in England (see *Mersey Docks and Harbour Board* v. *Coggins & Griffiths* (*Liverpool*) *Ltd.* [1947] AC 1), so in Germany (see BGH VersR 1956, 322), there is a certain tendency to retain the responsibility of the permanent master since he usually retains the greater degree of overall control. The solution adopted sometimes in the USA, to hold *both* employers liable to the employee and then let them sort the situation out among themselves (as in *Strait* v. *Hale Constr. Co.*, 26 Cal. App. 3d 941, 103 Cal. Rptr. 487 (1972)), has thus not found favour. It will be noticed, however, that there is an increasing tendency to think in terms of the possibility of command and not, necessarily, actual command—a development which tends to extend the area of vicarious liability.

This trend is further reinforced by the fact that *actual* and not *legal* subordination will suffice to render the master liable (see Enneccerus, Kipp, and Wolff (Lehmann) 980; *cf. Restatement (Second) of Agency*, (1959) § 220, which talks in terms of "control or *right* to control"). Moreover, the subordination need not be constant: a student working on a part-time basis may render his employer liable and this even if the services he is rendering to him are gratuitous.

Determining whether a person is an employee or, alternatively, what Common lawyers would call an independent contractor is essential, since, in *principle*, there will be no liability for the wrongs committed by the latter category. To achieve this, German lawyers are increasingly following the Common law example and looking at the entire economic relationship, not merely enlarging or adapting the control and direction test. Thus, von Caemmerer has candidly suggested ("Reformprobleme der Haftung für Hilfspersonen" in *Zeitschrift für Rechtsvergleichung* 1973, 241, 254) that this enquiry should be directed towards such matters as which person is in a better position to carry the risk or is economically more suitable to take out insurance. Once again, though individual solutions may occasionally receive a different answer, the German approach is, on the whole, quite similar to that taken by Common law lawyers, so no further details need be given.

This similarity is also to be found in the exceptions to the rule that one is not, in principle, liable for the torts of independent contractors (*Cf.* §§ 410–29 *Restatement (Second) of Tort.*) However, here, too, German lawyers have felt the need experienced by their Common law colleagues to develop rules of responsibility analogous to our non-delegable duties. Thus, the master will be liable under § 823 I BGB if he himself has negligently selected the independent contractor and, on occasion, also if he failed to control him in the exercise of his task. The extent and nature of this duty will vary from case to case, but in cases of large building works—especially when neighbouring buildings or their foundations are endangered—such additional obligations will readily be imposed on the employer of the independent contractor. The decision of the Bundesgerichtshof of 7 October 1975 (JZ 1975, 733) provides another illustration, akin to the English notion of extra-hazardous activities. In that case, a chemical factory engaged a firm of specialist contractors to dispose of some very toxic waste for their benefit. The waste was improperly removed and the chemical factory was held responsible for this bad execution of the work. It will be noticed that, as in English law, these duties are *stricter* than the normal duties of care in so far as they impose a duty to see that care be taken; but that they do not actually impose truly *strict* liability. Some German writers, however, have advocated that a strict duty be imposed in such cases upon the employer (see Vollmer, JZ 1977, 371).

(c) The damage must have been inflicted by the servant "in the exercise of the function assigned to him" (in Ausführung der Verrichtung)

Behind this not very informative expression lies one of the most litigated aspects of the whole law of vicarious liability as Common lawyers who have grappled with the equivalent notion of "course of employment" will readily understand. To solve it the courts have used—as we shall note below—a variety of terms or notions. Perhaps we could attempt to simplify the problem by saying that in practice there is one rule. Either the servant is within the "course of employment" (and so if the other conditions are satisfied will render his master liable), or he is not (in which case there is no liability for the master). Whether he is in the course of his employment or not is really a question of fact. In a sense, the situation here is not dissimilar from that found when discussing the elements of negligence or carelessness. For there, as well, there is a simple rule: if a person has behaved carelessly, he is liable (subject to certain other conditions being fulfilled); if he was not careless, he is not liable. The question whether his behaviour was careless or not is, once again, one of fact. Just as there are guidelines (not rules) to help in determining carelessness, so there are guidelines, and no more, which help in determining "course of employment" (or the equivalent German expression). The decision is, therefore, often impressionistic. The only permissible generalisation is that the area of activity falling within the "scope of employment" seems to be widening. This may be partly as a result of the increase in motor traffic (and the compulsory insurance schemes that go with it) and partly because the scope of acceptable risk has widened as legal entities have taken over from human beings the position of "master".

However, one must immediately qualify the last sentence by pointing out that German law has consistently taken a stricter view on this matter than other systems have done (e.g. the French). It has thus excluded acts done by the servants merely because their employment provided them with the occasion or opportunity for performing these acts (Enneccerus, Kipp, and Wolff (Lehmann) 979; Larenz I, § 20, viii, p. 401; Larenz/Canaris II 2, § 79 III, p. 480; see, also, case 96, BGHZ 49, 19, below). Thus, if the wrong is something incidental to the work assigned (*bei Gelegenheit der Verrichtung*) to the worker, his master will not be "vicariously" liable (under § 831 BGB) for it, unless it can be shown that he himself was at fault (§ 823 I BGB) in introducing this risk. A practical joke played by one employee on another will therefore not justify the employer's vicarious liability though it may attract his own personal liability if it can be shown that he was aware of the employee's mischievous or irresponsible propensities. (For English law see *Hudson* v. *Ridge Manufacturing Co. Ltd.* [1957] 2 QB 348 (personal liability); *Chapman* v. *Oakleigh Animal Products Ltd* (1970) 8 KIR 1063 (vicarious liability).) Once again, however, one can do little more than note the terms and underlying ideas; and then add that in practice one can always find examples where liability is imposed on the employer simply because the employment significantly enhanced the chance of the tort being committed. (Thus, see, BGH 4 November 1953, BGHZ 11, 151 where it was said that a theft committed by an employee working in a building site could render his employer liable.)

On the other hand, the employer's liability may be engaged even if the act accomplished by his employee is not *exactly* the one he was entrusted to perform. For this to happen, however, it must fall within the range of measures which can be properly linked to the exercise of the entrusted functions (see BGHZ 49, 19, 23). Sometimes this idea is also expressed in causal language. This is so whenever the court speaks of an internal, direct connection between the function assigned to the servant and the activity that has caused the harm—(BGH NJW 1971, 31). In practice this means that if the servant's act amounts to a *bad* way of performing the entrusted function (rather than doing something completely different), the master will—all other conditions being satisfied—be liable for the wrongful result. So, using a vehicle of the employer's in a forbidden manner will not necessarily absolve the employer from all liability (see BGH VersR 1966, 1074; BGH NJW 1971, 31). On the other hand, if the servant gives a free ride to the injured plaintiff in the employer's car, despite the latter's express prohibition, then the employer *may* not be liable (BGH NJW 1965, 391). (Compare and contrast the following English cases: *Limpus* v. *London General Omnibus Co.* (1862) 1 H. & C. 526; 158 ER 998 and *Conway* v. *George Wimpey & Co. Ltd.* [1951] 2 KB 266. More recent pronouncements can be found in *Rose* v. *Plenty* [1976] 1 WLR 141.) The same is true of the so-called "deviation" cases where the servant while on duty deviates from the prescribed route or even goes off on a trip of his own and then causes damage. The answer here will largely depend on the extent of the deviation (see RG LZ 1930, 589).

The case law on this topic is, as one would expect, rich (see also RG DR 1942, 1280 and *cf.* OLG Munich MDR 1959, 391) and, it is submitted, not all decisions can be reconciled with one another. On the other hand, as already noted, this is something which should not cause too much consternation; and the Common lawyer will again realise that this is almost inevitable in this area of the law. (For a brief comparison with English (and Commonwealth) law see Fleming, *Law of Torts*, 9th (ed.) (1998), 420 *et seq.*, Markesinis and Deakin, *Tort Law* 4th edn. (1999), chapter 6; for a summary of American law see Dobbs, *The Law of Torts* (2000), 910 *et seq.*)

(d) "Unlawful" damage

§ 831 BGB further requires that the damage caused by the servant be inflicted "unlawfully". The element of unlawfulness and the element of *culpa* (fault, which is *not* mentioned in § 831 BGB) were discussed in chapter 2 under the heading of § 823 I BGB, but since they raise difficult problems in this context as well, they must be re-examined briefly.

It will be remembered that there exist two theories on the definition of "unlawfulness". The traditional one looks at the *result*, and if this is an interference with one of the interests enumerated in § 823 I BGB, then the element of unlawfulness is satisfied. The more modern theory looks at the *conduct* and treats as unlawful only those interferences with the enumerated interests, which also amount to a breach of one of the duties of care. It will be remembered also that we stressed that, according to the traditional theory, the element of *culpa*—fault—is only considered *after* the element of unlawfulness is satisfied in accordance with the above. On the other hand, according to the new theory, unlawfulness and *culpa* tend to be merged into the same phase of the enquiry. Finally, it will be remembered that we said that save in some exceptional circumstances the two theories will, almost certainly, produce the same practical results.

§ 831 BGB is one of those exceptional circumstances where the two theories *could* produce different results. This is because, § 831 BGB, unlike § 823 I BGB, makes no mention of *culpa*—and, apparently, only requires an unlawful infliction of damage on the part of the servant. (Contrast on this point French and English law which require fault on the part of the employee.) If unlawful is taken to mean a simple interference (even if committed without fault) with one of the enumerated interests, then the master will be presumed liable unless *he* can then adduce his exculpatory proof in accordance with what we shall say below under (*e*). To put it differently, a logical application of the traditional theory on unlawfulness would require the plaintiff/victim *merely* to prove that he had been injured, even by a non-faulty act of the servant. Then, and only then, would the presumption of fault (of the master) under § 831 BGB come into play; and it would be for *him* to adduce the exculpatory proof envisaged by this provision.

The new theory on unlawfulness would look at things in a different way. An interference with one of the protected interests of the plaintiff is not, *per se*, unlawful; it will be so if, in addition, the servant does not attain the standard of care required in the circumstances. To put it differently, if the servant's activity was in breach of one of the duties of care and also interfered with an enumerated interest, then and only then, would it be unlawful. Both these things are matters for the plaintiff/victim to prove and only if they are established will § 831 BGB be invoked and the defendant/master will have to produce the required exculpatory proof.

The different distribution of the burden of proof, resulting from the application of one or other of the theories of unlawfulness, could have important practical consequences. A servant/driver, for example, who *through no fault of his own*, injures the plaintiff because black ice forces his car into a skid, will have acted unlawfully if the traditional theory is applicable, but lawfully if the new theory is used to determine the nature of his conduct. Let us take another example from a case decided by the Bundesgerichtshof in 1954. The plaintiff was injured by a telephone post, which collapsed due to a heavy storm. The interference with the plaintiff's life and limb was clear, and according to the traditional view, the element of unlawfulness was satisfied. This means that § 831 BGB should have been applicable, and the defendant/Post Office (owner of the post that had collapsed) should have been called upon to adduce the exculpatory proof envisaged by § 831 BGB. The Bundesgerichtshof, however, felt that this stage had not been reached since the plaintiff had not shown that the accident was also due to a fault on the part of the team of employees responsible for the maintenance of the posts (BGH NJW 1954, 913). Unfortunately, the problem of who has to prove exactly what is not only linked with the view one takes on the notion of unlawfulness. In fact our last illustration reveals the kind of uncertainties and difficulties that persist in this field.

In a decision handed down in 1957, the Great Senate of the Federal Supreme Court had to deal with the following problem (For fuller details, see the judgment reproduced below, case 109, BGHZ 24, 21). The plaintiff was injured while getting into a tram due to the fact that the tram departed before the plaintiff had completed his entry. It could not be established whether the plaintiff's injury was caused because he tried to jump onto the tram after it had started moving, or whether the accident was the result of the conductor giving the departure signal prematurely. If the old theory of unlawfulness was applied, then the servants of the defendant (tram) company had acted unlawfully and the burden of producing the exculpatory proof of § 831 BGB would have shifted to the defendant company. If, on the other hand, the new theory applied, then the defendant would not have to be called to produce such evidence, since the plaintiff had not proved (nor, given the uncertainty we mentioned, could he prove) that the conductor had culpably and prematurely given the departure signal.

The Great Senate clearly opted for the new theory on unlawfulness and, as we have already noted, this has commended itself to most modern lawyers (but not to all lower courts). But when it came to applying it to the burden of proof it did not take the attitude that has been described above but chose, instead, a different manner of distributing the burden of proof. The injured party was thus merely obliged to prove an interference with one of his protected rights. It was then for the *master to prove* that the conduct of his servant was correct in the circumstances and thus *not* unlawful. If he did not do this (and, in the present case, given the uncertainty as to what had happened, he could not), then he would have to rebut the presumption of his own fault in accordance with § 831 BGB.

The convoluted reasoning as well as the result has not been welcomed (except for the part of the judgment that sanctioned the new theory of unlawfulness). The reason is clear. As Professor Kötz has remarked (*Deliktsrecht*, no. 281), "this decision has the absurd consequence that where the facts of the accident are not clear, the injured party will be in a more favourable position if his injuries have been caused by the servant, and not the master himself". For if a pedestrian is run down by a van belonging to a pharmacist and it is not clear whether the accident could be attributed to the driver, the condition of the van, or the pedestrian himself, then the pedestrian's claim may be rejected. This will be the case if the pharmacist (master) was at the wheel, himself, (since the action would then be based on § 823 I BGB) and the plaintiff would have to prove the defendant's fault. (Incidentally, for the reasons we shall give below, section A.5 (iii), the Road Traffic Act

1952 might also not be applicable in this case.) If, on the other hand, the van was being driven by the pharmacist's servant, then the victim would (by invoking § 831 BGB) be able to see his claim succeed *unless* the pharmacist could produce the exculpatory proof provided by this paragraph.

(e) The master's exculpatory proof

If all the above-mentioned conditions are satisfied, the defendant/master will be presumed at fault and will be made liable unless *he* shows one of two things. Thus, he must show that he was careful in the selection, instruction, and training of his servants and that he properly supplied them with the right kind of equipment. Alternatively he must show that the damage or injury would have occurred even if he (the master) had fulfilled the above-mentioned duties. Paragraph 831 BGB thus establishes a simple presumption of responsibility. (*Widerlegliche Vermutung*)

Producing evidence that the servant was properly selected, instructed, and supervised has become an increasingly heavy burden for employers—especially in those cases where the accident is caused in the context of carriage of passengers by buses, trains, trams, and the like. Here, as the cases reproduced below (cases 105 and 106) show, the degree of supervision required is very high and can includes such things as random checks and regular warning notices. (See, for instance, BGH VersR 1966, 364; BGH VersR 1969, 518; KG NJW 1966, 2365. More recently, BGH VersR 1984, 67, contains a good description of the master's duties to select and supervise his employees carefully). When such accidents occur, and the action proceeds on § 831 BGB, the attention of the court is thus switched away from the details surrounding the accident, which the victim could conceivably discover or reconstruct. Instead, it becomes focused on the kind of internal supervision system that the defendant/master had devised in order to avoid or minimise the chance of the accident. In these cases, however, the plaintiff/victim has little knowledge of what has gone wrong. So, often, rather than be faced with such uncertainties and the cost of prolonged litigation, he will settle for the lesser sums provided by the strict liability Acts such as the Road Traffic Act or the Strict Liability Act (discussed below, section A.4 (iii)).

Where large organisations are concerned, proof that *every* employee has been carefully selected or supervised is, of course, impossible. So the practice developed in Germany of allowing the master to show that "leading employees", who stand in a hierarchically intermediate position (for example a foreman who had chosen and was supervising the "guilty" servant), had been properly chosen and supervised. This system of "decentralised exoneration" (*dezentralisierter Entlastungsbeweis*), which substitutes the intermediary employee for the "real" master and makes the former liable instead of the latter, is undesirable both economically and in terms of labour–management relations. Not surprisingly, it has thus not been followed by other systems such as the Swiss which, in this area of tort law, has otherwise closely followed the German model. (Oftinger, *Schweizerisches Haftpflichtrecht* II, I (2nd edn. 1960) 139, 159). But German lawyers, as well, came to realise the unfortunate nature of this rule, and the Supreme Court itself discovered a way to neutralise it by finding fault in the real master for the way he has organised his business and thus made the accident possible. This creation of the *Organisationspflicht*, allowed the German courts to fall back on § 823 I BGB and, in this way, provided a way of bypassing the unfortunate § 831 BGB. (See BGHZ 4, 1, 2 below, case 107. See also BGH VersR 1964, 297 and BGH NJW 1980, 2810.)

(f) Methods developed in order to avoid the effect of § 831 BGB

It will have been noticed that despite the fact that the German courts impose strict requirements for the exoneration of masters, the possibility of such proof being adduced is always there with the result that the victim can then only sue the usually penniless employee. This result is not only incompatible with the rationale of true vicarious liability; it is also economically unsound given the employer's greater ability to insure and to spread the cost with a minimum of social dislocation. For some time now the courts have therefore been eager to discover ways to bypass § 831 BGB and four of them will be discussed here.

The *first* device that neutralises the exculpatory proof available to the master under § 831 BGB originates in labour law. If in the course of his employment an employee negligently causes loss to a third party he acquires, under certain circumstances, a right to an indemnity against his employer in respect of any claim which the victim may have against him, personally. So, in these cases the "innocent master" will shoulder the consequences of the employee's negligence even though his careful selection and supervision of the employee should have, normally, exonerated him (the master) from all liability. The conditions under which the liability is transferred (back) to the employer are examined below in section 3(a). So here suffice to say that once it is established that the conduct of the tortfeasor is sufficiently linked to his employment the courts will be likely to grant the employee the right to an indemnity from his employer. (This is the reverse of a situation better known to the Common law (but also known to German law) and involving the master seeking contribution or a full indemnity from the employee for having been held liable towards a third party because of his employee's fault. In English law this is, nowadays, covered by the so-called "gentlemen's agreement" of 1959 by which employers' insurers waived their entitlement to exercise subrogation rights against the "guilty" employee. It is discussed in (1959) 22 *MLR* 652 and in *Morris* v. *Ford Motor Co* [1973] 1 QB 792. For Australia, see Insurance Contracts Act 1984, section 66; Employees Liability Act 1991 (NSW), section 3 (2).)

The *second* is particularly applicable to legal entities of a private (§ 31 BGB) or a public law (§ 89 BGB) character. (BGH NJW 1985, 1838.) The legal entity's liability for the torts committed by its organs, i.e. members of its board, or other "duly appointed representatives", is absolute without any possibility of exoneration so long as the tort was committed by the representative in the "carrying out of his duties". The potential sphere of application of this provision was, initially, rather limited, but in more recent times it has been expanded considerably, especially by giving a very wide meaning to the phrase "duly appointed representative". Consequently, the original requirement that this liability be applied only for the acts of organs who had a legal power to represent the legal entity in legal transactions was abandoned in favour of a wider definition. (See RG, 25 Oct. 1943, DR 1944, 287; BGHZ 49, 19, 21 reprinted as case 96, below.) Representatives who have the right to make independent decisions in their own sphere of work, subject only to general instructions, will thus be included in the definition. This will be so even though they may not have the wider power of legal representation and their powers are not specifically defined in the articles of association. And the legal entity may also be liable for the torts of persons who have been authorised to act for it *ad hoc* in lieu of the person who should have acted in accordance with its articles (RGZ 157, 228, 235 ff.). Liability of the entity for its *own* defective organisation, in accordance with what is said in the next paragraph, may also be invoked.

The *third* way round § 831 BGB is by discovering a "defect in the structure of the enterprise" for which the master/entity is made liable. We are here talking of liability under § 823 I BGB and no longer of liability under § 831 BGB. Two cases reproduced below (99 and 100) show how effective is this method of bypassing § 831 BGB.

In the first case (BGH NJW 1956, 1106; case 99) the plaintiff was hurt while in the defendant's hospital as a result of risks inherent in the treatment he was receiving but of which he had not been adequately warned. The defendant/hospital was successful in adducing the exculpatory proof required by § 831 BGB but was found liable under § 823 I BGB for its own culpable failure to guide its doctors as to how they should discharge their duties to warn and explain matters to patients. Similarly, in the second case (BGH NJW 1971, 1313; case 100) the defendant's employees carelessly damaged an underground gas-pipe which caused an explosion which led to the destruction of the plaintiff's house. The track record of the employees was perfect and the defendant was able to adduce the exculpatory proof imposed upon him by § 831 BGB. The Supreme Court, however, was not interested in this line of reasoning and chose to hold the defendant liable for his own fault.

It should be noted that though the grounds of liability are distinct, there is no reason why in practice the result could not be based on both. A decision of the Supreme Court in 1955 (BGHZ 17, 214) illustrates this. In that case, the Federal Railways used wagons to transport animal foodstuffs. The wagons had not been properly cleaned and the foodstuffs were contaminated, thereby causing serious damage to the plaintiff's cows. Both the Court of Appeal and the Supreme Court had no difficulty in holding the defendant railway company liable on both grounds, i.e. liable for not properly inspecting their employees (§ 831 BGB) *and* for their own failure to adopt a safe system of work (i.e. liability under § 823 I BGB). The importance of this type of liability for defective organisation of an enterprise cannot be overstated since out of it grew the modern approach to product liability under the heading of *Produzentenhaftung* long before strict liability was imposed on manufacturers (and others) under the ProdHaftG. (See Brüggemeier *Prinzipien des Haftungsrechts* (1999) pp. 116 ff.)

The advantage of the heading "defective organisation of the enterprise" meant that liability could be based on the master's fault (for failing to organise his business properly) independently from his servant's negligence. It was a small step from there to hold the master liable by simply reversing the burden of proof for a deficient organisation of the production process where the injury was caused by a defective product. This heading of liability for faulty organisation of an enterprise emerged as a way of by-passing § 831 BGB. Having achieved this, it was then transplanted to liability for defective products. (This occurred in the famous chicken pest case in 1968, BGHZ 51, 91, reproduced above, as case 61). Shifting the burden of proof was prompted by the kind of considerations that also underlie the presumption of fault of § 831 BGB. For it will be difficult if not impossible for the victim to prove that the organisation of the manufacturing process was defective and ascertain the cause of the product's defect. As the BGH remarked in the "chicken pest" case the manufacturer "surveys the field of production, determines and organises the manufacturing process and the control of delivering the finished products." As a consequence, the manufacturer needs to furnish the proof of exoneration. As in the instances of organisational fault outside the field of product liability, the courts allow the "master" to rely on a system of decentralised exoneration alluded to in the previous section.

2. THE ESCAPE INTO CONTRACT: § 278 BGB

The *fourth* way of evading § 831 BGB is for comparative law purposes the most intriguing. In one sentence, it meant invoking the adaptable law of contract in order to remedy the deficiencies of the law of tort. This, of course, is not the first time a civil law system has had to turn to its law of contract in order to remedy the shortcomings of its law of tort. For example, we have already noted how the non-recognition of purely economic loss as a compensable type of harm under § 823 I BGB forced German (and French) lawyers to "discover" contracts in the negligent misstatement cases which, in the Common law system, are resolved through the law of tort. The converse was true of the Common law systems: the doctrine of consideration—especially where it was taken rather seriously (e.g. in *English* Common law)—meant that contracts could not be discovered where the plaintiff had not "paid" for the information he received. The law of product liability is another example, for in this area as well, civil law has shown a tendency to extend the law of contract to do the work of the law of tort. We have noted (above, chapter 2, section A.4 (*c*)) how German law has moved away from this position. (*Cf.* French law where the ultimate purchaser's rights in product liability cases are still in many instances viewed as an extension of the rights conferred by the law of sale to the immediate purchaser (Articles 1641 ff. French CC) though, in recent times, tort law has reasserted its position.) The problems posed by § 831 BGB provided the third, though by no means least, important impetus to side-step tort law and have recourse to contract; § 278 provided the much-needed escape provision.

§ 278 BGB states that a "debtor"—which in the instances that concern us means the employer—"is responsible for the fault of his statutory agent and of persons whom he employs in fulfilling his obligation, to the same extent as for his own fault". It thus imposes upon the debtor "strict" liability for *faults of the persons he uses in the course of fulfilling his contractual obligations.* The possibility of exoneration, which can be found in § 831 BGB, is absent in this case. Moreover, the terms used in § 278 BGB suggest that the debtor's liability may cover the faults of persons whom he uses in the performance of these obligations, but who may not, strictly speaking, be "servants" (in the sense of § 831 BGB). Both these points, and especially the first, make the plaintiff's position more advantageous than it might otherwise be if his action were based on § 831 BGB. There are other advantages for the plaintiff who can shift in this way the basis of his claim from tort to contract. It will suffice to mention three. First, pure economic loss is more easily recoverable in a contract action. Secondly, the *contractual* period of limitation used to be longer, though not always (see BGHZ 61, 227 and § 558 BGB). (For the recent reform see H P Mamsel, NJW 2002, 89.) Finally, the burden of proof may be more favourable for the plaintiff if the action is based on § 278 BGB (see § 282 BGB and BGHZ 66, 51; BGH NJW 1976, 712, case 90, now § 280 I 2 BGB). But these advantages for the plaintiff are also bought at a price: § 278 BGB will *only* apply in the fulfilment of a *contractual* obligation; and the range of remedies it may offer the victim/plaintiff may be more restricted than it would be if the action were based on tort. These two points require further elaboration.

Since § 278 BGB requires a contract (or, more precisely, a *Schuldverhältnis* = a relationship creating obligations), in order to come into force, the courts set about discovering such contracts where none would be immediately obvious to a Common lawyer. This meant extending the contract to the pre-contractual phase and also extending its scope to include persons other than the immediate contracting parties. Eleven cases dealing with these types of situations are reproduced below (section B.2) so here we shall limit our remarks to a few general points.

The famous linoleum case (RGZ 78, 239, case 111) marks historically the first attempt to extend contractual remedies to the pre-contractual phase of negotiations through the concept of *culpa in contrahendo*. This doctrine was developed by the famous German jurist Rudolf von Jhering. (*Culpa in contrahendo, Schadenersatz bei nichtigen oder nicht zur Perfektion gelangten Vertraegen*, in *Jahrbuecher für die Dogmatik des heutigen römischen und deutschen Privatrechts* (1861).) (See now § 311 II BGB.) It was extended from certain contractual situations to cases, such as the one before the Reichsgericht in 1911, which were essentially delictual in nature. In that case, the prospective purchaser entered the store, asked to inspect some carpets and, while doing so, was injured by two rolls, which fell from the shelf. The court took the view that the demand to see the carpets and the fulfilment of this demand resulted in a relationship preliminary to the sale and similar to a contract and imposed duties of care with respect to the person and property of the parties. The wording of this judgment makes frequent references to the "prospective purchaser" and, therefore, makes it clear that this extension of the "contract" to the pre-contractual phase will not be attempted in all instances. The demarcation line is left for future courts to draw. (See also case 112.) Probably, the same *contractual* protection will be extended to cover not only the prospective purchaser who, for example, is queuing to pay for the goods he has already selected, but also the "potential purchaser" who enters the shop "to look around" but with as yet no fixed intention to purchase anything in particular. The shoplifter, on the other hand, who slips on spilt yoghurt, will not be protected in this way (BGH NJW 1976, 712 *obiter*). In between these "extremes", one can envisage other possibilities, for example the citizen who seeks refuge in the store during a heavy storm. The solution and the casuistic approach of the German courts should neither surprise nor disturb the Common lawyer. Given the greater willingness to discover "duties of care" these days, the answer to our hypothetical problem should be sought in the law of delict and not the law of contract. And the disadvantage that this might create for the plaintiff—the return to § 831 BGB—could be avoided by arguing that the store's potential liability should be justified by reference to § 823 I BGB. In other words, it should be based on the shop keeper's own fault in the running of his business.

The expansion of the contract to the pre-contractual phase was not enough; the protective sphere of the contract had also to be expanded to cover persons other than the immediate contracting parties. In BGH NJW 1976, 712 (case 112) the person injured was not the prospective purchaser but her young daughter who was accompanying her in order to help her with her shopping. In the court's view, good faith required that the child should be included in the protective sphere of the contract (which was *about to be* concluded); indeed, the court felt that even mere "bystanders, who do not themselves participate in a contract", should be included under the contract's protective umbrella. This, of course, is precisely the kind of situation, which could not receive a satisfactory solution through the medium of § 831 BGB. It thus forced the German courts to develop, under juristic guidance, the concept of contract with protective effects towards third parties, which was briefly described in chapter 2.2 (*d*) (iii) above. But resorting to § 278 BGB provided a partial answer at best. For the drawback of § 278 BGB lies precisely in the fact that the nature of the liability established by this provision is contractual. This means that the plaintiff's damages in these cases will be limited to his economic loss *alone*. To put it differently, because of § 253 BGB, the plaintiff who is basing his claim on § 278 BGB will not be allowed to claim damages for pain and suffering. If, on the other hand, the liability could be based on tort (in case a right listed in § 847 BGB has been infringed), then such damages could be claimed (§ 847 BGB establishing a specific exception to § 253 BGB). A decision of the Supreme Court in 1957 brings this point out very clearly (BGHZ 1, 383, case 120; see, also, RGZ 112, 290, case 121, below). In that case the plaintiff was referred to the defendant hospital as an outpatient for a minor ailment in his foot. The second defendant—who was the hospital's chief doctor—administered a mild anaesthetic before attending to the patient's foot but failed to make the plaintiff lie down properly on a couch and instead made him sit temporarily on a narrow kind of settee used for gynaecological examinations. As a result of the injection of the anaesthetic, the plaintiff temporarily lost consciousness and fell off the settee and severely injured his cervical column. He claimed his economic loss *and* compensation for pain and suffering from *both* defendants and the Court of Appeal granted him both these claims. The Supreme Court adopted a more nuanced approach. The contract of hospital treatment was between the hospital/first defendants and the plaintiff's union, who had referred him to the hospital. Yet this was a contract in favour of third parties—with protective effects *vis-à-vis* third parties we would say today—and thus the hospital was liable to the plaintiff for the doctor's careless behaviour under § 278 BGB. This action could cover the plaintiff's economic loss but not—because of § 253 BGB—his claim for pain and suffering. But the plaintiff had a *further* cause of action against the second defendant—the doctor—and since this was delictual in nature, based on § 823 I BGB, it could justify, under § 847 BGB, a claim against *the doctor* (but not the hospital) for compensation for pain and suffering. Before we conclude it may be worth pausing for a moment to consider a possible consequence of the recent reform proposals. If damages for "pain and suffering" become available in contractual actions, it may well be that plaintiffs in cases such as the ones we have been discussing above will have even less of an incentive to base their case on § 823 I BGB. For the contract route, with its more favourable § 278 BGB, will then provide a means of obtaining full compensation, including damages for non-material harm.

3. LIABILITY REGIMES IN LABOUR LAW

Suggested reading

The reader will have a better appreciation of the debate sketched in the next few paragraphs if he consults some of the following works. Blomeyer, "Beschränkung der Arbeitnehmerhaftung bei nicht gefahrgeneigter Arbeit", *JuS* 1993, 903; Brox and Walker, "Die Einschränkung der Arbeitnehmerhaftung gegenüber dem Arbeitgeber", *DB* 1985, 1469; Denck, "Zur betrieblichen Tätigkeit als Voraussetzung für die privilegierte Arbeitnehmerhaftung", *DB* 1986, 590; Dütz, "Gefahrgeneigte Arbeit", *NJW* 1986, 1779; Pfeifer, "Neueste Entwicklungen zu Fragen der Arbeitnehmerhaftung im Betrieb", *ZfA* 1996, 69; Richardi, "Abschied von der gefahrgeneigten Arbeit", *NZA* 1994, 241; Schnauder, "Die Grundsätze der gefahrgeneigten Arbeit", *JuS* 1995, 594; Seewald, "Gefahrgeneigte Arbeit bei allen Tätigkeiten des Arbeitslebens?" *DB* 1986, 1224.

Making the employer of the tortfeasor liable for the damage the latter has caused may provide compensation for the victim and, in that sense, largely fulfil the function of tort law as a system of compensation for accidents. Yet achieving this result will not mark the end of the problems that have to be faced by the law. Thus, further issues have to be resolved which are of interest to tort law and insurance law (should insurers have such subrogation actions? Is this not tantamount to their having their cake (i.e. collecting premiums) and eating it (i.e. being given subrogation claims) unless, perhaps, someone can prove that by having such rights and exercising them they can (and do) keep premiums at lower levels?). But even more questions have to be answered. Should the actual wrongdoer—the employee—go scot-free because policy considerations related to the smooth functioning of labour relations demand this? Will such a solution lead to more accidents by making employees less careful? Is it economically advisable to place part of the risk on a worker who might be without personal insurance? These concerns of *different parts of private law* come together when one sees these cases in the context of increased industrial accidents, modern insurance practices, collective labour agreements, and an ever-increasing volume of litigation with the delays this phenomenon brings in its wake. Little wonder then that this problem of the employee's liability towards his employer has given rise to considerable debate but little agreement in Germany. The *revirement* of the case law of the Bundesarbeitsgericht must be seen in this light. But its understanding will be made easier if we explain first the kind of factual configurations in which these problems arise. They can, in fact, be three.

The first will be easily recognisable to English lawyers. The employer is held liable (either under Common law principles of vicarious liability or under § 831 BGB) for the harm caused to a third party by his employee and then seeks a contribution or an indemnity from the latter.

The second variant, mentioned earlier on, is more Germanic in its nature and stems from the possibility that is open to the employer to avoid liability by invoking the exculpatory proof contained in § 831 BGB (careful selection/supervision of employee.) In this case, the employer may not be liable. But if the employee is sued by the victim and is made liable to him can he—the employee—then seek an indemnity from the employer? As stated, German labour law allows this to happen and, as a result, § 831 BGB is, in practice, circumvented.

The final and in practice most important variant is where the employee negligently causes harm to his employer and, as a consequence is sued by the latter. For instance, the defendant/employee drives mini cabs owned by the plaintiff/employer. Because of the negligence of the defendant, a collision takes place with a third party in which the plaintiff's car is also damaged. Can the plaintiff/employer seek damages from his employee/defendant? (See BAG NJW 1988, 2816. Currently, the governing decision can be found in case 110.) From the discussion that will follow it will be noticed that German law treats—with some measure of justification—all these three variants in the same manner for, in substance, in all three it sets out to alleviate the employees' personal liability. The real question, thus, was how extensive should this "immunity" be? Moreover, a workable method had to be discovered that would distinguish those cases where the employee was liable to pay a contribution or a full indemnity from those where his potential liability could be engaged.

Since the decision of the Great Senate of 25 September 1957 the BAG limited the employee's liability towards his employer where the activity carried out was not "danger-prone". Moreover, liability would follow provided further conditions were satisfied. Notably, it had to be shown that the employee had acted with "gross" negligence. (BAGE 5, 1. The first decision where the criterion of dangerous work was utilised to restrict a worker's liability was ArbG Plauen ARS 29, 62 from 1936).

The partial or total immunity granted to the employee was and still is difficult to reconcile with general principle. More precisely, the fundamental assumption of the rules on reparation and compensation (§§ 249 ff. BGB) is that if the conditions of liability are met (in particular if the tortfeasor is shown to have acted negligently) he will be held liable for *all* the loss caused by the wrong. The only express exception to this doctrine is found in § 254 BGB: contributory negligence. However, in the line of cases examined here it is not contended that the employer contributed negligently to the loss of the third party. The damage is caused exclusively by the fault of the employee. Hence, in 1957 the BAG had to assert that there was in fact a "concealed" gap in the Code and that it was entitled to modify the rules applicable to the special relationship arising by reason of a labour contract (§ 611 BGB).

The reason why German law (especially the BAG) has come to regard the employee's full and unconditional liability as being contrary to equity (*Billigkeit*) is this. The employee acts at the instance and in the interest of the employer. The latter determines the production process or more generally how the company is organised. The employee's pursuit of his job is directed by his integration into the business organisation and the actual conditions of the work process. The employee cannot influence the risk inherent to the activity assigned to him by the employer, and he cannot avoid these pre-determined conditions of work either factually or legally. Nor will his wages normally reflect or cover the risk if anything goes wrong. So, although the employee is under the general legal obligation of *neminem laedere*, German courts have argued, it is justified to limit his liability in specific circumstances.

However, as already suggested, this alleviation of the employee's liability depended—until recently—on whether the employee could establish that his activity was "danger-prone". This requirement was meant to "preserve" an area where the employee could be held accountable. But the criteria for this category became increasingly open-ended once the BAG no longer applied them in an abstract and typified way but took account of the specific circumstance of the individual case. Thus, in one case—case 110—the BAG did not regard the activity of supervising the driver of a bulldozer as dangerous, even though the activity of the driver of the machine was undoubtedly so. (Paradoxically, an earlier decision had treated such supervisory work as inherently dangerous. BAG AP § 611 Haftung des Arbeitnehmers Nr. 80. That (earlier) case was distinguished on the basis that the construction site involved was large and more difficult to organise than the present.) The unworkable nature of the criterion of "danger-prone activity" was also revealed by the tragic case of BAG NZA 1986, 91. There, an experienced nurse accidentally dropped a baby twelve days old. As a result of the fall, the baby suffered a scull fracture. In earlier proceedings the child had sued the nurse and her employer and had been held entitled to recover all losses resulting from the accident. In the case at hand, the nurse sought an indemnity from her employer in respect of the child's claims. The BAG came to the conclusion that in the circumstances the activity of taking a baby out of its bed was *not* "danger-prone". The consequence of such a determination would have been that the nurse would shoulder full responsibility—a result which was widely considered as unacceptable. (The case settled so we do not know what happened in the end.) In its decision of 12 June 1992, BAGE 70, 337 (case 110) the Great Senate of the BAG responded to this wide-spread criticism and decided that the time had come to abandon altogether the criterion of "danger-prone" activity. Since the BGH (in NZA 1994, 270) agreed as to the result, it was not—in the end—necessary for the Common Great Senate of the Supreme Courts to decide the issue. The case thus reproduced in the book reflects the current state of the law.

The criterion that replaces that of the dangerous character of the activity carried out by the employee is that of an intrinsic link between the activity and the duties assigned to the employee. From a methodological point of view it is interesting to note that the BAG felt the need to assert once again its powers to change and develop the law in this area. The irony is that in its latest judgment the BAG was departing from its own jurisprudence and not the rules of the BGB. This is somewhat concealed behind general observations on the role of the judiciary.

Though by its decision the BAG, essentially widened the scope of the employee's immunity, the other conditions of liability remained untouched. This should not, however be taken to indicate that the remaining conditions of liability have not generated their own problems. Evidence of this is provided by the tergiversations of the BAG. The pedigree of the present rules is reflected in the different editions of this book (thus see the decision on page 572 of the second edition which was overruled by the decision on page 762 of the third edition (annotated at pp. 690–692). The first of these decisions (7th Senate, NZA 1984, 83) confined the employee's liability to gross negligence and intentional conduct. The second (8th Senate, NZA 1988, 579) restored orthodoxy and re-established the old threefold approach which hinges on the degree of fault of the employee. (The different forms of negligence are discussed in chapter 2, section 3(b).) The current position of the BAG, found in case 110, confirms the threefold approach.

In the case of gross negligence, the employee must, as a rule, bear the total loss alone. At the other end of the spectrum, in the case of the slightest negligence, he is not liable at all. For normal negligence, the loss is, as a rule, to be divided between the employer and the employee proportionately. In such cases, all the circumstances regarding the causing of the harm and its consequences are to be balanced against each other in a reasonable way and in accordance with the principles of fairness. In weighing up the circumstances of the individual case the following factors can, according to the Great Senate of the BAG, be taken into account. The danger involved in the activity. Whether the risk in question can be taken into account by the employer and covered by insurance. The position of the employee in the business is also important. As are the level of salary (i.e. whether the employee is paid a risk premium) and the personal circumstances of the employee. For instance, how long has he has been part of the business; his age; his family circumstances, as well as the employee's conduct so far under his contract of employment. From these the insurability of the risk by the employer is certainly the most difficult to determine in practice (see Tschöpe and Henninge MDR 1995, 135, 137). In the case of gross negligence it will be decisive whether the remuneration of the employee is out of proportion to the risk of damages that has materialized as a result of the grossly negligent conduct. In BAGE 90, 148 for instance a lorry driver caused an accident because he had ran a red light. His attention was distracted as he was speaking on the mobile phone installed in the cabin. The lorry was damaged and the court found that he had been grossly negligent. The court held him liable to the full extent of the loss because the loss was not out of proportion to his wage (it was less than the sum of three monthly gross wages, which amount is taken as a first indication).

Two further comments are desirable.

First, the theoretical basis of the limitations of the employee's liability towards the employer is now explained by reference to § 254 BGB (which is in fact applied by analogy only given that the employer is not "negligent"). The true basis for the exception can thus be found in the policy considerations outlined in the introductory comments of this section. It is thus quite puzzling that in its most recent pronouncement the BAG sought to justify the exception also by reference to the indirect (horizontal) effect (*mittelbare Drittwirkung*) of Article 2 I GG (personality rights) and Article 12 I GG (free exercise of the employee's vocation). To the extent that this construction is convincing, it can be seen as providing yet another illustration of the constitutionalisation of private law mentioned in the first chapter of this book. Yet this construction may not be without its flaws. For, while the radiating effect of these provisions of the Constitution into labour law is generally accepted, the consequences drawn by the BAG in applying these provisions to the case in point appear questionable. It suffices here to draw the reader's attention to the following argument.

The BAG stated that unlimited liability for all negligently caused harm should not be imposed for otherwise the employee would be burdened with the risk of unreasonable financial burdens and in particular the danger to his economic existence. This would represent a disproportionate infringement of the above-mentioned constitutional rights. However, if the employee is to be protected from the danger to his economic existence, then liability ought to be restricted *irrespective* of the employee's fault to the extent that this danger is imminent. This would be at least the natural consequence of this particular approach. But the BAG does not consider these potentially far-reaching implications of its stance. (The BAG's derivation of the liability regime from the danger to the employee's economic existence was expressly rejected by the BGH in NZA 1994, 270; see also Blomeyer *op. cit.* 906; Richardi *op. cit.* 244; Schnauder *op. cit.* 597.)

Secondly, the brief discussion of the German agonising over this issue also reveals German law to be true to reputed form: theoretical, un-necessarily nuanced, and, in its most recent pronouncements, of dubious wisdom in its attempt to make a difficult subject even more difficult by discovering in it a constitutional dimension. To these doctrinal objections we add one last thought. The obvious favouring of the helpless employee may have much to support it. But it has still to be demonstrated how much it has added to the productions costs of German industry thereby making it internationally less competitive. This is clearly a political and economic issue; yet it is raised here to demonstrate how legal rules, supportable by reasons of fairness or equity may also have political dimensions.

4. OTHER INSTANCES OF PRESUMED FAULT OR STRICT LIABILITY IN THE CIVIL CODE

The Code provides for the reversal of the onus of proof in three more situations; § 832; §§ 833–4, and §§ 836–8 BGB. § 829 BGB imposes an "equitable" obligation to pay compensation independent of culpability.

(i) § 832 BGB makes those who are under a duty to supervise (*Aufsichtspflichtige*) other persons (minors, mentally or physically incapacitated adults, etc.) liable for the damage caused by these persons to third parties or to their property. The obligation to supervise may stem from the law (*kraft Gesetzes*). Persons under such duties include the parents of a child (§ 1626 I; § 1631 I BGB) and the legal guardian (§§ 1793, 1800 BGB). Alternatively, the obligation to supervise may derive from contract (*kraft Vertrages*). This category usually includes those in charge of kindergardens, boarding schools (but not State schools, which are liable, if at all under § 839 BGB: BGHZ 13, 27), holiday camps, orphanages, private nursing-homes, and the like. (For doctors and nurses in psychiatric hospitals see: BGH NJW 1984, 2574; BGH 19 January 1984, NJW 1985, 677). In yet other instances, difficult demarcation problems may arise (e.g. a grandparent or a neighbour looking after a child: is this always a purely factual situation or can it amount to a legal relationship bringing into operation § 832 BGB?) As for those doing an "apprenticeship", the courts seem to distinguish between apprentices who are lodged with their masters and those who are not. In the first case, the master may be liable for all harm caused by his apprentice, while in the second the master's liability may be engaged only if the harm occurred during working hours. (BGH 24 June 1958, VersR 1958, 549.) (On all these points see Larenz/ Canaris, II 2, § 79 IV, p. 485–7 with references. For further details on § 832 see: Albilt, *Haften Eltern für ihre Kinder?* (1987); Rauscher, "Haftung der Eltern für ihre Kinder", *JuS* 1985, 757; M. J. Schmid, "Die Aufsichtspflicht nach § 832 BGB", *VersR* 1982, 822.)

The liability of the supervisor arises the moment the "tortfeasor" has realised the *objective* conditions of a particular rule of liability. If such an unlawful infliction of loss has occurred, the supervisor will be presumed to have culpably failed to discharge his own duty to supervise. He will then be liable to the victim, either solely or jointly with the "tortfeasor" depending on whether the latter is capable of some fault (§§ 827–8 BGB). The supervisor's liability will be avoided only if he proves that he had exercised the requisite standard of care or if he can show that the harm would have occurred in any event.

The requisite standard of care in supervision obviously varies from case to case, the Reichsgericht having stated that it will depend on "the age, disposition, characteristics, development, education, and all other individual features of the minor" (RGZ 52, 73). A "difficult" child will, thus, have to be kept under closer control (BGH 10 July 1984, NJW 1984, 2574). The vagueness and flexibility of such phrases is deliberate but it should not conceal a discernible trend in recent cases to raise the standard of care expected of modern parents. Courts have taken a stern view in cases of damage caused by children playing with matches. (See: BGH 17 May 1983, NJW 1983, 2821; OLG Karlsruhe VersR 1985, 599); in BGH VersR 1983, 734 the court held liable the parents of a seven-year-old child which started a fire having got hold of an easily accessible box of matches. (See, also, BGH 2 May, NJW 1990, 2553.) But no "supervision" duty was imposed on the parents of a fifteen-year-old boy playing football (OLG Stuttgart NJW 1982, 2608); and the courts demonstrate their reluctance to impose such duties as children approach majority and their supervision is accepted as being difficult if not impossible. (BGH 26 November 1979, NJW 1980, 1044.)

If the supervisor succeeds in exculpating himself, and the "tortfeasor" is incapable of all fault according to §§ 827, 828 BGB (and, therefore, not personally liable), the innocent victim might run the risk of being left without any compensation. This, in fact, was the solution adopted by French law until the Court of Cassation changed its case law in 1964 (Cass civ. 2ème 18 déc. 1964, *D.* 1965, J. 191). The German legislator, however, foresaw this eventuality and included a provision in the Code—§ 829 BGB. This enables the judge to take into account the financial position of the parties (including the insurance situation) and to oblige the innocent tortfeasor to pay the equally innocent victim/plaintiff such compensation as equity demands. The factors that are to be taken into account in establishing that the minor is under an equitable obligation to pay compensation are the seriousness of the injury; how close the culpability of the minor was in relation to the threshold of § 828 BGB; and, crucially, the economic situation of the defendant. Two things should be noted in this context.

(ii) § 829 BGB can apply also in the reverse situation where the minor is the victim and where he is not culpable, i.e. contributory "negligent", under § 828 BGB. More important is the second observation. Although this section is often referred to as the "millionaire provision" the minor, himself, need not be wealthy. The question is whether his liability insurance is a factor that can found his liability under § 829 BGB. The role of insurance in the context of § 829 BGB was considered and in principle accepted by the Federal Court in a number of decisions, BGHZ 76, 279; BGH NJW 1958, 1630; BGH NJW 1962, 2201 but never relied on to establish liability. The most recent pronouncement of the BGH in this area, BGH NJW 1995, 452, (reproduced below, case 144) has clarified a number of controversial points and in particular states that liability can flow from the fact that the defendant was insured. There is, however, an important theoretical problem in imposing liability based on the fact that the defendant was insured.

The so-called *Trennungsprinzip* is a fundamental principle of tort law. Indemnity insurance follows liability but liability cannot flow from the fact that the tortfeasor is insured. Therefore, deriving the minor's liability from his insurance amounts to an exception to this principle. The BGH acknowledged this in the recent decision. However, in its view the imposition of liability could be nevertheless justified by a number of considerations. Thus, first, the exception to the principle is confined to mandatory insurance as in the case of traffic accidents. It is noteworthy that the BGH stated that in this field the function of mandatory insurance has undergone a change, now serving mainly to protect the interest of the victim. (Sceptical, Kötz and Wagner, *Deliktsrecht*, no. 328.) Secondly, the insurance factor must not be the only one that points to liability. The situation must be such that in the particular circumstances it would be wholly unsatisfactory not to hold the minor liable. This means thirdly that to the extent that the victim can recover damages on the basis of strict liability imposed by the traffic statute (§ 7 Road Traffic Act—StVG, as to which see below), the victim cannot rely on § 829 BGB. In the present case the defendant was epileptic (which excluded in the circumstances his liability under § 823 BGB according to § 827 BGB but not his liability under the Road Traffic Act). Hence, § 829 BGB will be relevant mainly in relation to damages for pain and suffering (§ 847 BGB) and in cases where the defendant is not liable under the Road Traffic Act (this concerns minors). (See for the interrelations between §§ 829, 847 BGB also below, chapter 3, section 3(c). According to recent reform proposals (discussed below, chapter 4 section A 2(c)), the culpability of minors for traffic accidents (crucial in relation to § 823 I BGB) is relaxed (starting at the age of ten compared to seven at present), which would suggest that § 829 BGB becomes even more important.)

(iii) §§ 836–8 BGB impose a similar (compared to § 832 BGB) presumption of fault in the context of damage or personal injury caused by collapsing buildings, or man-made structures (e.g. walls, fences, flag-poles etc.) (See, BGH WM 1990, 1878.) Responsibility here is placed on a number of persons meticulously defined in §§ 836–7 BGB. Thus, while the person usually liable will be the owner, liability may also be imposed on a mere possessor (§ 836 I and III BGB), a former possessor (§ 836 II BGB), or even a builder or constructor (§ 837 BGB). At Common law some of the above would, for certain purposes, probably be treated as the occupier of the premises and be made liable accordingly.

These provisions, which derive in part from Roman law and can also be found in a less elaborate form in civil codes such as the French, do not impose risk-based liability. In reality, they widen the area of liability for unlawful omissions which is further intensified by a presumption of fault. Thus, the possessor will be held responsible for personal injury and/or property damage suffered by a third party as a result of the collapse of a building on his land. Such liability, however, will be avoided if the possessor proves that he took all necessary steps to avert the danger. Where a former possessor is being sued, he must prove that he took all necessary steps while he was the occupier of the premises or that a later possessor could have avoided the danger by observing the appropriate standard of care. In any event, the liability of the former possessor is potentially limited to damage caused within one year after the termination of his possession (§ 836 II BGB).

The wording of § 836 BGB makes clear its potential limitations. The damage must be the result of the collapse of a building (or part thereof) or some other structure attached to land, and to the consequence of defective construction or inadequate maintenance, not otherwise. Thus, for example, the Federal Supreme Court has ruled that building material falling as a result of *demolition* work will not be included in the protective ambit of this provision (BGH VersR 1978, 1160). In this case liability, if any, will be imposed on the demolition contractor and will be based either on the breach of some statutory duty or the violation of the general duties of care (§ 823 I and II BGB). One must, therefore, be always alert to the in-built limitations of this provision and be prepared to consider the alternative or parallel application of the general rules of liability. All in all, however, the resulting intricate web of overlapping legal rules is not a feature unique to German law. English Common lawyers in particular have faced similar problems. And, they too, have had to combine different torts (like negligence or private or public nuisance) with statutory instruments (like the Occupiers' Liability Act 1956 or the Defective Premises Act 1972) in order to solve the potential liability of owners, occupiers, possessors, or landlords of dangerous or defective premises towards, visitors, next-door neighbours, and users of adjoining public roads.

(iv) §§ 833–4 BGB are the last provisions to be discussed under this subheading. Here a distinction has to be made between § 833 sentence 1 and 2 BGB. For the first imposes genuine risk-based liability (the only one to be found in the Code) for damage caused by certain kinds of animal—luxury animals (*Luxustiere*)—whereas the second merely establishes a rebuttable presumption of fault against the keeper of "domestic or useful animals" (*Haustiere, Nutztiere*). The term "domestic animals" refers not just to tame animals (or animals domesticated in Germany in the sense that the English Animals Act uses this notion) but tame animals that are used "to aid the business, the earnings, or the prosperity of the keeper". Thus a gamekeeper's dog, a farmer's pigs, herd of cows, or working horses, a shepherd's dog, will come under this category; but dogs (generally), cats, or birds, which simply provide for their owner's pleasure, come under § 833 sentence 1 BGB. In between one finds some doubtful cases. For example, there is some ambiguity as to which part of § 833 should apply to a blind man's guide-dog. On the other hand a policeman's dog or horse, assisting him in the execution of his professional duties, have been brought under the second sentence of § 833 BGB (RGZ 82, 226). The privilege afforded to keepers of "useful animals" is no longer justified since a keeper might well be in a position to insure against the risk of being liable. However, the BGH in NJW 1986, 2501 could not bring itself to abolish the distinction and decided that it was the task of the legislator to make the correction. (Comparison with the Common law and the English Animals Act 1971 is fruitful and can reveal some interesting differences but cannot be attempted here. (For an amusing case of strict liability being imposed on the keeper of a dog which destroyed the plaintiff's valuable carpet see LG Karlsruhe, 22 March 1994, *MDR* 1994, 453.)

The liability provided by § 833 BGB falls on the keeper (*Halter*) and that is the person who, irrespective of ownership, is in charge in a real and durable manner of the animal in question. Temporary loss of control will thus not transfer the quality of keeper to another person (BGH 19 January 1988, NJW–RR 1988, 655). It is, however, otherwise, in the case of theft when the thief is likely to be held as the animal's keeper and thus liable for any damage caused while it remains under his control. The keeper is liable for all damage caused by the animal through its own movement or volition (e.g. biting, kicking etc. The term used in German is that the damage must occur "through" the animal: *durch ein Tier*). The injury must be the result of the realisation of a risk specific to animals. In some instances this can be controversial. For instance, a driver attempts to avoid running over an animal that has strayed onto the highway. In the process of so doing, his car capsizes. Subsequently, a second car crashes into the capsized vehicle. The keeper of the animal would be strictly liable to the first car under § 833 BGB; but does his liability under this section extend towards the driver of the second car? Is this risk still peculiar to the animal's movement? (Example taken from Kötz and Wagner, no. 360). But this provision of the Code is inapplicable where the harm was caused by a movement instigated by a human being in control of the animal at the relevant time. (BGH 25 September 1952, NJW 1952, 1329.) Liability in this case will have to be based on some other provision of the Code (typically, § 823 I BGB.) This approach that requires that the damage can be linked to a risk peculiar to the animal is part of a broader concept of legal cause to which recourse is had in order to define and limit effectively the scope of strict liability; see next section 5(b)(iii). In the case of § 833 sentence 2 BGB (domestic or useful animals), the liability of the keeper is presumed, but he can avoid it by proving either he took all care necessary in the circumstances or showing that the harm complained of would have occurred in any event. This defence is, of course, not available to the keeper of a "luxury" animal where liability is strict (§ 833 sentence 1 BGB).

§ 834 BGB imposes a similar liability on the person (*Tierhüter*) who, pursuant to a contract, undertakes to look after an animal on behalf of its keeper. The liability of such a person, however, is the same whatever kind of animal he may happen to be looking after. In this instance, therefore, no distinction is made between house and luxury animals.

For further detailed discussions see: Baumgärtel, "Neue Tendenzen der Beweislastverteilung bei der Tierhalterhaftung", 25 *Jahre Karlsruher Forum, Sonderbeilage zu VersR* (1983) 85; Deutsch, "Die Haftung des Tierhalters", *JuS* 1987, 673; *idem*, "Gefährdungshaftung für laborgezüchtete Mikroorganismen", *NJW* 1976, 1137; Dunz, "Reiter wider Pferd oder Versuch einer Ehrenrettung des Handelns auf eigene Gefahr", *JZ* 1987, 63; Herrmann, "Die Entwicklung der Tierhalterhaftung nach § 833 Satz 1 in der modernen Judikatur und Literatur", *JR* 1980, 489; Honsell, "Beweislastprobleme in der Tierhalterhaftung", *MDR* 1982, 798.)

5. STRICT LIABILITY

Select bibliography

Bauer, "Erweiterung der Gefährdungshaftung durch Gesetzesanalogie", *Festschrift für Ballerstedt* (1975) 305; von Caemmerer, *Reform der Gefährdungshaftung* (1971); Deutsch, "Methode und Konzept der Gefährdungshaftung", *VersR* 1971, 1; *idem*, "Gefährdungshaftung: Tatbestand und Schutzbereich", *JuS* 1981, 317; *idem*, "Das Recht der Gefährdungshaftung", *Jura* 1983, 617; *idem*, "Das neue System der Gefährdungshaftungen: Gefährdungshaftung, erweiterte Gefährdungshaftung und Kausal-Vermutungshaftung", *NJW* 1992, 73; Dunz, "Gefährdungshaftung und Adäquanz in der neueren Rechtsprechung des BGH", *VersR* 1984, 600; Esser, *Grundlagen und Entwicklung der Gefährdungshaftung* (1941); *idem*, "Die Zweispurigkeit unseres Haftpflichtrechts", *JZ* 1953, 129; Filthaut, *Haftpflichtgesetz*, 3rd ed. (1993); Kötz, "Haftung für besondere Gefahr. Generalklausel für die Gefährdungshaftung", *AcP* 170 (1970) 1; *idem*, "Empfiehlt sich eine Vereinheitlichung und

Zusammenfassung der gesetzlichen Vorschriften über die Gefährdungshaftung im BGB" *Gutachten und Vorschläge zur Überarbeitung des Schuldrechts* (1981) 1779; Medicus, "Gefährdungshaftung im Zivilrecht", *Jura* 1996, 561; Stoll, "Nochmals: Gefährdungshaftung und Adäquanz in der neueren Rechtsprechung des BGH", *VersR* 1984, 1133; Ullmann, "Gefährdungshaftung in der Schiffahrt?", *VersR* 1982, 1020. Will, *Quellen erhöhter Gefahr* (1980, with complete comparative references). *In English:* Zweigert/Kötz, para. 42, 646; Lawson and Markesinis, *Tortious Liability for Unintentional Harm in the Common Law and the Civil Law* (1982) I, 142 ff. Finally, for the historical background see Bienenfeld, *Die Haftung ohne Verschulden* (1933); Ogorek, *Untersuchungen zur Entwicklung der Gefährdungshaftung im 19. Jahrhundert* (1975); Rümelin, "Culpahaftung und Causalhaftung", *AcP* 188 (1988) 285.

(a) General observations: the statutory method

Tort liability was in German law traditionally based on fault. This was certainly true of the *lex Aquilia*, in a sense the *fons et origo* of Roman law which, in its turn, became the basis of the *Gemeines Recht* that prevailed in a large part of central Germany during the pre-codification era. The Prussian Code, in force mainly in the north and the east of the country, had also based tort liability on fault; and so, of course, had the French Code which, as we have noted, had also been adopted by yet another group of German States in the Rhine region. Apart from history, logic also dictated—and dictates—that "bad" people must pay for the harm they cause and, usually, the greater the degree of their blameworthiness the greater the amount that they have to pay. (This correlation between degree of blameworthiness and legal consequences is characteristic of criminal law. But it is also used by some tort lawyers to deny tort liability in cases were the consequences are disproportionate to the defendant's fault.) But during the nineteenth century—especially in its latter half—the reverse of this proposition was also advocated by many lawyers: if there was no fault there should be no liability and the loss should be left to lie where it fell. The mixture of moralistic, economic, and other arguments that led to the adoption of this attitude are reviewed by Professor Tunc in his excellent introductory chapter to the tort volume of the *Encyclopedia of International and Comparative Law*. But, as Tunc has shown—and his observations though couched in broad comparative terms, also apply to German law—these arguments are hardly convincing.

It could, of course, be argued that it would be asking too much of the nineteenth-century draftsmen of the German Civil Code to see the weaknesses of the proposition that there can be no liability where there is no fault. The nineteenth century was the century when the fault rule reigned supreme. Yet, interestingly enough, some courts did make limited attempts to introduce strict liability *automatically* by discovering fault in particular activities. (Much later, and in the context of liability towards guest passengers in cars, the French courts adopted the theory of *faute virtuelle* to achieve more or less the same result.) More importantly, during the latter part of the nineteenth century the German Parliament had enacted a number of specific but important statutes, which introduced risk liability (*Gefährdungshaftung*). So, if there was one national legislator in Europe at that time that had realized the limitations of the fault principle, it was the German. The problem of the foundation of tortious liability could thus have received a more unified and innovating treatment than was, in the end, actually accomplished. But legal tradition prevailed. Apart from one minor exception found in the Code (§ 833 BGB) dealing with "luxury animals", the Code refused to be moved from the principle that liability for fault was the only acceptable basis for any obligation to compensate the victim. The specific legislation alluded to above, was treated as exceptional and denied the moral superiority attributed to provisions found in the Code itself. This approach had many consequences. Notable among them are two. First, it set the pattern of the future development of strict liability in German law and in this respect set it apart from other civil law systems, notably the French. Second, it created a dual regime of liability, partly to be found in the Code and partly in specific statutes, with resulting difficult problems of demarcation. The difficulties of demarcation, and the gaps that have resulted from this dual system of treating accidents, will be noted later on as particular aspects of these enactments are considered more closely. Here suffice it to note that the Janus-like nature of the German legislator, displaying a "social" outlook in his special legislation, while remaining strongly "individualistic" in his general Code, did not pass without criticism even at the time. An extract from Gierke's scathing comments brings out clearly the inconsistencies and dangerous consequences of this approach. He wrote:

[I]t is a fatal error—an error committed by the draft of the German Civil Code—to think the social work can be left to special legislation so that the general private law can be shaped, without regard to the task that has thus been shifted, in a purely individualistic manner. There thus exist two systems ruled by completely different spirits: a system of the general civil law that contains the "pure" private law, and a mass of special laws in which a private law, tarnished by and blended with public law, governs. On the one side a living, popular, socially coloured law full of inner stimulus, on the other an abstract mould, romanistic, individualistic, ossified in dead dogmatics. The real and true private law can now develop in all its logical splendour oblivious of the heretical special laws . . . But the general law is the native soil out of which the special laws also grow. By contact with the general law our youth learn legal thinking. The judges take their nourishment from it. What a fatal abyss opens before us! What a schism between the spirit of the normal administration of justice and the administrative jurisdiction that is being extended further and further! What a . . . danger of stagnation and degeneration of jurisprudence . . . (*Die soziale Aufgabe des Privatrechts* (1889) 16–18; trans. by von Mehren and Gordley, *The Civil Law System* (2nd ed. 1977), 693.)

In the remainder of this subsection we shall concentrate on the peculiarly German method of introducing strict liability in the legal system. Then, in the next subsection (ii) we shall note some features shared by these enactments and, finally, in subsection (iii) we shall take a closer look at some of the most important statutes: the Strict Liability Act, the Road Traffic Act, Environmental Liability Act and related statutes, and the Products Liability Act.

The passing of strict liability statutes is not a phenomenon unique to Germany. One can find specific statutory interventions in the Common law system (for example the English Animals Act 1971) and in other civil law systems (for a list of French statutes see Viney, *Les obligations: la responsabilité* (1982) 25 ff.). What is, however, typically German is the development of a legal tradition, going back to the first Prussian Railway Act of 1838, that the introduction of strict liability into the legal order is a prerogative of the legislature. This mentality, along with the carefully, and on the whole restrictively, drafted articles of the Civil Code had an important consequence. It made it difficult for German judges to develop the kind of general, all-embracing rules which their French counterparts were able to create thanks to the wide if not amorphous delict provisions found in their Code. As a result, though there are a number of situations where *fault* can be presumed, there is no general presumption of *liability* for damage caused by things (whether dangerous or not) under one's control analogous to that established by the famous first line of Article 1384 French CC, or in a much more limited fashion in England (*Rylands v. Fletcher* [1868] L.R. 3 H.L. 330), or any general rule dealing with "extra-hazardous" activities. Nor has German law adopted the bold attitude taken by the French Supreme Court in the *Desmares* decision (and subsequently incorporated in the French Road Traffic Act of 5 July 1985) to ignore the contributory negligence of the victim in certain instances of strict liability. Once again, clear statutory provisions to the contrary make this impossible.

The next thing to note is that the introduction of strict liability was the result of different though not necessarily mutually exclusive factors, which influenced the mind of the legislator. (Indeed, looking at the strict liability acts one can trace the evolution of industrial and technological developments in modern Germany.) So, for example, it has for some time now been recognised that the social security legislation of the early 1880s, namely the Sickness Insurance Act of 1883 (*Krankenversicherungsgesetz*) and the Accident Insurance Act of 1884 (*Unfallversicherungsgesetz*), had predominantly political not legal motives. For they were largely prompted by Bismarck's political calculation that the satisfaction of certain legitimate needs of the working classes concerning conditions of work and accident insurance would go a long way in "taking the wind out of the sails" of the socialist movement which was at that time, in Germany and elsewhere, slowly gaining wider political support. (For further details see Lawson and Markesinis, *op. cit.* I, 158.)

In other instances it was the novelty of the danger coupled perhaps with the risk of serious injury resulting from the operation in question. This was so, for example, in the case of the Prussian Railway Act of 1838 (later incorporated in the Imperial Act on Liability of 1871) and the Road Traffic Act (*Strassenverkehrsgesetz*), both of which dealt with potentially dangerous (and, at the time of their enactment, also novel) activities. In all instances, however, the utility of rail and, later, motor vehicle transportation was perceived. Clearly, increased benefit was accompanied by increased dangers. The solution was obviously to permit these activities and, indeed, to encourage them in various ways, but only on condition that they were saddled with the cost of the risks they entailed.

In yet another group of cases the enormity of the possible damage resulting from the activity in question was such that the activity could only be allowed to continue "at a very high price". The "Act Relating to the Peaceful Use of Nuclear Energy and the Protection Against its Dangers" (*Gesetz über die friedliche Verwendung der Kernenergie und den Schutz gegen ihre Gefahren*) 1959—more briefly referred to as the Nuclear Energy Act—therefore imposes absolute liability on the operator of installations which are concerned with nuclear fusion or fission. This is also the case according to § 33 ff. of the Air Traffic Act (*Luftverkehrsgesetz*) of 1936. In both these instances, liability is truly "absolute" in the sense that even the defence of *force majeure* is denied to the "operator" (of the nuclear installation) and custodian (of the aircraft). Finally, the enormity of the potential harm that can be caused by water pollution must explain the (financially) unlimited liability imposed by the Water Supply Act of 1957 (*Wasserhaushaltsgesetz*). This is imposed on anyone who "introduces" substances into water (which includes lakes, rivers, streams, ponds etc.), thereby altering the quality of the water so as to render it harmful.

The Imperial Act on Liability of 1871 (*Reichshaftpflichtgesetz*), originally imposed strict liability for death or personal injury suffered by persons "in the course of operation of a railway" (§ 1). The legislator had a variety of aims in mind when, in 1940 it extended the statute to cover property damage and in 1943 extended it further to cover death or personal injury caused, under certain specific circumstances, by gas, electricity, or steam. (The present version—the *Haftpflichtgesetz* of 1978—includes harm caused by gases, fumes, and piped fluids.) Notable among these aims was the desire to facilitate the evidentiary burden of proof cast on the unfortunate victims of what the French, at that time, called the "anonymous accidents" caused by modern industrial machinery. (See Josserand, *Cours de droit civil positif français* (2nd edn., 1933) ii, no. 415.) To some extent the same is also true of the most recent of these strict liability statutes—the Act on Pharmaceutical Products of 1976 (*Arzneimittelgesetz*). But arguably from the beginning, and certainly, with the passage of time, it became obvious that the imposition of strict liability in the above instances also aimed at placing the risks of these activities on the shoulders of those who could best carry them. For all these industrial concerns were in a far better position to spread the cost of accidents either by reflecting it in the form of minute increases in the cost of their products or, later, by their greater ability to insure. The same motive can also be found in modern product liability law, though the 1989 Product Liability Act had, as its immediate cause, the EEC's desire to try to achieve greater harmonisation of the law of the Member States. Be that as it may, the fact is that in our modern mechanised society a variety of policy aims accounted for the steady increase of legislative enactments, each dealing with a fairly narrowly defined activity or risks emanating from ownership of potentially dangerous things or substances. Some of the problems raised by this patchy growth of the law will be noted in the next subsections.

(b) Some general characteristics shared by all or most of these enactments

(i) Similar or analogous clauses

Though one of the ideas behind specific legislation is to allow the legislator to word his provisions in a way most appropriate to the particular risk or industry being regulated, this has not prevented the appearance in most of these enactments of almost identical provisions. One such provision—imposing maxima for monetary compensation—can be found in all but one of the statutes, and because of its importance it will be discussed separately, below. Another common provision (for example § 12 of the Strict Liability Act 1978; § 16 of the Road Traffic Act 1952) preserves the validity of the "Common law"— which, in effect, means the Civil Code—so that a victim can recover further sums by relying on the fault-based articles of the Code. This, as we shall note, is often necessary. For, first, the monetary maxima imposed by these statutes (and discussed below) may not be sufficient. Secondly, and perhaps more importantly however, is the fact that compensation under these statutes does not include sums for pain and suffering. These can thus be claimed only if the fault-based provisions of the Code can be successfully invoked. (The only exception to this last rule can be found in § 53 III of the Air Traffic Act.) According to recent reform proposals this artificial restriction is abandoned. Damages for pain and suffering will then be available also if the plaintiff bases his claim not on § 823 BGB but on the defendant's strict liability under the various specialized statutes. Details are discussed in chapter 4 section 3 below. At this stage, it is, perhaps, worth observing that other systems, which have on the whole adopted the German way of introducing strict liability by means of specific statutes, have not followed the German example of imposing monetary maxima or excluding from the statutory provisions compensation for pain and suffering. As a result of this arguably more logical approach to the problem, these systems have been able to provide for the exclusion of the ordinary rules of civil responsibility. The Swiss Road Traffic Act—in force in its latest form since 1 August 1975— provides such an example. (For a good summary of Swiss law see Deschenaux and Tercier, *La responsabilité civile* (1975) 138 ff.)

A third type of common clause reduces the liability of the tortfeasor by taking into account the contributory negligence of the victim. (See, for example, § 2*a* of the 1871 Imperial Act on Liability—now § 4 of the 1978 Strict Liability Act; § 27 of the 1959 Nuclear Energy Act.) The reduction of the damages awarded to the victim will be decided in accordance with § 254 BGB after weighing the victim's own fault against the typical risks connected with the activity in question (the so-called "business risk") and the causative connection with the victim's hurt (BGHZ 2, 355). In extreme cases this could mean either that the victim could lose his entire claim for compensation (see, for example, BGH VersR 1963, 874) or the reverse, i.e. receive full compensation despite some negligence on his part (see, for example, BGH VersR 1969, 736). In the context of traffic accidents, the recognition of this defence has meant a net increase in contested cases. For there is hardly an incident in which the keeper of the vehicle will not invoke this defence and start a usually lengthy dispute into the exact facts of the accident. Many of the advantages of a strict liability statute can thus soon be lost in a controversy over facts which have little or reduced significance given today's insurance background. *In this context*, it is therefore important to note with approval the solution advocated by the Court of Cassation in the *Desmares* decision which refuses to take into account the victim's own fault in the realization of his harm. (see Cass. 2ème civ. 21 juillet 1982, *D*. 1982, 449; see, also, the Law of 6 July 1985, reprinted as *Addendum* 2 to B. 3). This approach, however, has not prevailed in Germany, insurers arguing that the abolition of the defence would affect the level of motor insurance premiums. (For a look of the German position by a knowledgeable French insurer see, Margeat, "Nos voisins européens et la protection des victimes de la circulation", *Gaz. Pal.* 31 May/2 June 1992, 3. The text of the French statute is reproduced below at pp. 850 ff.)

(ii) Monetary maxima imposed on compensation paid under these statutes

Save in the case of the Water Act (and also in the case of § 833 BGB) all other strict liability statutes impose maximum amounts, which can be paid in the form of compensation under their respective provisions. However, recourse to the fault-based provisions of the Civil Code for additional compensation for pecuniary losses, as well as for pain and suffering, is in all cases expressly permitted. (See §§ 12 of the 1978 Strict Liability Act; 16 of the 1952 Road Traffic Act; 37 of the Air Traffic Act; 31, 38 of the Nuclear Energy Act.) Here the only limitation on the tortfeasor's liability is, practically speaking, his capacity to pay or, if he is insured, the ceiling of his insurance coverage. Thus, if a person is killed or injured through the operation of electricity, gas, steam, or current escaping from a cable or a pipeline or a plant for the provision of such energy or material (§ 2 of the Strict Liability Act, 1978), then the concern in question will be liable to indemnify to the full his medical expenses (§ 6) and to compensate him for his lost earnings by paying him an annuity of not more than DM 30,000 per annum per victim. And the liability under the Act (§ 10) for property damage will not exceed DM 100,000. (This figure applies even if more than one objects was damaged in the course of the same accident; but it does not apply to damage to buildings.) In the case of motor vehicle accidents, to which the Traffic Act of 19 December 1952 applies, the sums are DM 30,000 in the form of an annuity or a maximum lump sum of DM 500,000. Where several persons are killed or injured in the same accident, the liability of the person responsible cannot exceed in total the amount of DM 750,000. The total liability under the Act for damage to property is, again, DM 100,000 and this even where several objects are damaged in the same accident (§ 12 1;

see also § 37 of the Air Traffic Act and § 30 of the Nuclear Energy Act). It should be noted however that if recent reform proposals become reality these maxima are considerably raised. (The recommended provisions are reproduced alongside the Act). These figures represent true maxima so that if, for example, more than one person or car is injured or damaged in the same accident the total amount available will have to be shared between them all. Who, in the case of a traffic accident, is responsible to pay these sums will be discussed in greater detail in subsection 3, below. Here suffice it to state that since the enactment of the Obligatory Insurance Act in 1939, the "holder" of any car is obliged to take out third-party insurance which, as a *minimum*, covers the above sums. Needless to say, the growing cost of road accidents, coupled with the very real possibility of the "holder" of the car being made *additionally* liable under § 823 I BGB, has meant that insurance policies covering risks in excess of one million marks are increasingly common these days. (In practice the extra coverage, typically of the order of 2 million DM, can be obtained at a very small extra premium.) Incidentally, these maxima can be (and have over the years been) readjusted by governmental decree in order to take into account inflation and other rising costs.

As stated, the regulation of compensation through statutory maxima makes it increasingly likely that in cases of serious accidents the "Common law"—i.e. the BGB—will be invoked. This, of course, means that the victim is then thrown back into the fault system with all the theoretical and practical disadvantages that this entails (delays, costs, uncertainty of result, increasing the load of court work). Even so, the victim's position has, once again, been improved in recent years by the development of three devices. The first is the "discovery of new duties of care" which were discussed above, in chapter 2, A 4). The second way is to treat many of the provisions of the Road Traffic Act as "protective laws" and allow the victim to bring an action under § 823 II BGB (discussed in the next chapter). Finally, the German courts are, in many cases, willing to invoke the doctrine of prima-facie proof—*Anscheinsbeweis*—which is analogous to our doctrine of *res ipsa loquitur*. In practice, this can often result in the surreptitious introduction of strict liability in a system which, judging by the letter of its Civil Code, remains faithful to the idea of fault.

(iii) The courts' role in defining the precise ambit of the statutes

As one would expect, all these enactments contain terms or notions, which though simple and obvious at face value, have given rise to many difficulties of proper demarcation. In the face of these observations, the courts have not been inactive and the rich case law that has emerged clearly presents great interest both to the academic and practising lawyer. Here, for reasons of space, we shall limit our observations to three points. First, is the use of normative theories of causation as a means of defining the proper ambit of the statute in question. Second, comes the occasional tendency to construe narrowly certain provisions. Finally, we note the tendency in other, more numerous, instances to define more widely a particular statutory term and thus, to enlarge the scope of the statute in question. In all these instances we find illustrations of how the courts have exercised the rather limited role ascribed to them by legal tradition in the area of strict liability.

1. Compensation under the strict liability rules will clearly be limited to the extent that the harm complained of represents the realisation of precisely that danger which prompted the legislator to enact the strict liability rule. The search for the protective aim of the violated norm thus becomes as important in this area of the law as it is when

discussing causation problems arising from the violation of fault-based rules (§ 823 I and II BGB; see above, chapter 2, section A.5). The limits of the liability will, therefore, be determined by discovering whether the type of harm in suit and the manner of its infliction was of the kind which the statute wished to prevent. The search for an answer to such questions will, obviously, start by looking at the wording of the relevant statute. For example, was the plaintiff injured "in the course of the operation of a motor vehicle"? (*beim Betrieb des Fahrzeuges*: § 7 I of the Road Traffic Act.) Or was he killed "in the course of the operation of a railway" (§ 1 of the Strict Liability Act)? In all these cases, the end-result will largely be determined by the judge's value judgment of the situation, which will often lead him to an interpretation of the enactment against the background of *contemporary* socio-economic demands. A decision of the German Supreme Court in 1959 brings this point out very clearly (BGH 9 September 1959, BGHZ 29, 163, case 122, below). The court in that case had to decide whether a *stationary* vehicle could be brought under § 7 I of the Road Traffic Act. This, as will be explained below, imposes strict liability upon the keeper of a motor vehicle which "in the course of *operation*" injures or kills another person. In the court's view since

the legislator has not provided any . . . explanation, it is for the judge to interpret this ambiguous rule [accident in the course of operation]. The judge is, therefore, not prohibited from interpreting § 7 StVG broadly if in so doing he conforms to the sense and purpose of the enactment to protect participants in traffic against the dangers of motor traffic. It is therefore entirely within the scope of permissible interpretation if this protection . . . is extended also to the dangers produced by stationary vehicles in present-day traffic conditions.

Clearly, continued the court,

"even if the legislator of 1909 (when the first Road Traffic Act came into force) saw the chief danger of motor vehicles, in their rapid movement due to engine power . . . that would not exclude the adaptation of the concept 'in the operation of a motor vehicle' to the experiences and requirements of present-day traffic".

In the end, therefore, the use of normative theories of causation can lead—as Anglo-American lawyers have also discovered—to a considerable flexibility. In turn, this can produce an extension (and not only a restriction) of liability, rendering the defendant liable for all the "typical" consequences inherent in his business activity. (*Cf.* in this respect the views of Ehrenzweig in his *Negligence Without Fault* (1951) reprinted in 54 *Cal. L. Rev.* 1422 (1966); see also "Vicarious Liability in the Conflict of Laws—Towards a Theory of Enterprise Liability under 'Foreseeable and Insurable' Laws III", 69 *Yale L. J.* 978, 989 (1960).)

2. An example of narrowing liability can be found in the area of application of § 833 BGB in so far as it imposes strict liability. Here, it must be shown that the harm caused was the result of the specific dangers arising from the animal's nature. Damage caused by a bolting horse—even where the cause of its fright is an external noise—or from a biting dog, would clearly be the kind of typical harm that animals of this kind can cause. But the injury suffered by a rider who borrowed from a friend a horse, which he knew to be unruly when ridden by strangers, in order to demonstrate his greater riding skills, would not lead to strict liability of the owner of the horse. (BGH NJW 1974, 234; NJW 1977, 2158). Nor, as Professor Kötz has suggested (*Deliktsrecht*, no. 360), would a cyclist, who collided in darkness with the corpse of a dead dog, be able to sue its owner under § 833 BGB. For in such a case, the hurt of the plaintiff cannot be traced back to a special risk inherent in

the animal. (But see OLG Celle VersR 1980, 431. Liability under § 823 I BGB is another matter.) The example may seem far-fetched; but this kind of reasoning produced the same (negative) conclusion in a case where the plaintiff's cellar was flooded as a result of his drains being blocked by cow-dung from the defendant's cows (LG Köln, 13 July 1960, MDR 1960, 924). Further illustrations were given in the previous section 4(iii).

At this point a brief excursus can show how the same kind of legal reasoning can be found in precisely the same area of the law in the Common law system. Thus, s. 4 I of the Animals Act, enacted in England in 1971, imposes strict liability for "damage" done by straying livestock "to the land or to any property on it". The definition of damage in this section is narrower than the general definition given in s. 11, which includes personal injury and disease. The narrower definition of s. 4 I is generally taken to prevail in this case since it is regarded as *lex specialis.* (For example, Winfield and Jolowicz, *On Tort* (15th edn. by W V H Rogers) 577 and n. 68.) For our purposes, however, it could be seen as a statutory embodiment of the scope of the rule theory. In other words, it can be said that the legislator wished to impose strict liability *only* when the typical consequences resulting from cattle trespassing actually occurred (damage to land, crops etc.). When other harmful consequences flowed from such straying livestock (e.g. human beings were trampled down) then liability should be based on the possible fault of their owner and not on the statute.

A similar narrow interpretation of the rules of strict liability has been adopted in other instances outside the area of the Civil Code. The Water Supply Act imposes, as we have seen, strict liability on anyone who "introduces" (*leitet ein, bringt ein*) substances into water, thereby prejudicially altering its physical, chemical, or biological characteristics. The deliberate discharge by factories of pollutants into nearby rivers, lakes, ponds, or estuaries is, of course, caught by this provision. But so is the discharge of substances, which do not affect the quality of water and marine life therein, even if its effects are not known to the person (legal or physical) who is carrying on these activities. On the other hand, the courts insist that for harmful conduct to be brought under this statute it must be shown that there was "a positive act objectively aimed at the water". As stated, this would include the above activities of "discharge" of substances, but would exclude, for example, a collision between two petrol tankers which led to one of them falling into a nearby river and thereby accidentally emptying its contents into the water. (See Larenz/Canaris, II 2, § 84 V; idem in *VersR* 1963, 593, 602. (In the 12th edn., § 17. ix, p. 731, another illustration is given: bridge collapsing under the weight of a petrol tanker.) See also BGHZ 46, 17; 57, 170, 173; 62, 351, 355. For other examples see the discussion in 3(iii), below.)

3. More often than not, however, the courts use the avowed purpose of the rule imposing strict liability in order to give an extended meaning to a term or phrase to be found in one of the enactments. A number of illustrations will be given in 3(ii), below, when we talk about traffic accidents. Here we shall, therefore, concentrate on one of the best-known examples which can be found in the definition of a "railway" in § 1 of the old Imperial Act on Liability—now included in the 1978 Strict Liability Act.

Today, there is no doubt that "railway" includes all types of transport moving on rails—whether wide or narrow gauge, or moving above or beneath the metal rails in question; indeed, the Strict Liability Act has made this clear by expressly including cable-cars and suspension railways. But the statute also requires that the accident happened "in the course of the operation of a railway . . .". The question thus arises whether this statute can be extended to cover other activities carrying with them risks not unrelated to the kind of dangers peculiar in some sense to the operation of a railway. This question as to whether the accident can be regarded as a "business accident" (*Betriebsunfall*) and thus covered by the statute was, in a sense, linked with the question of proper definition of a railway. Both were raised in one of the early cases that came before the Reichsgericht in 1879 (RGZ 1, 247).

In that case the defendant, a building contractor, was engaged in the business of constructing a railway and was moving earth around in tipping-wagons operated on a narrow-gauge rail when the accident occurred. The Court of Appeal refused to apply § 1 of the Imperial Act on Liability of 1871. Its decision was reversed by the Reichsgericht in a judgment most notable for its polemical style against all attempts (favoured by some judges and academics) to give a narrow interpretation to the recent Imperial enactment. The Supreme Court openly alluded to the policy factor briefly mentioned at the beginning of this paragraph. It concluded that any narrow interpretation of the wording of the statute, of the kind adopted by the Court of Appeal, would lead to the emasculation of the new statute and should, therefore, be rejected. As a result of this bold judgment, and after many others took a similarly broad view of the notion of "business accident", German law has now come to include under the protective ambit of this paragraph not only typical accidents connected with railways, such as deaths or injuries resulting from sudden application of brakes (even where this is caused by the totally unexpected appearance of a child or animal on the tracks: RGZ 54, 404; BGH VersR 1955, 346), swaying or swinging of carriages, derailments, or accidents caused by faulty signalling, but also cases where passengers are injured on platforms when jostled by other passengers during rush-hour. For this to happen, however, there must exist a "direct external local and temporal connection between the accident and a particular business procedure or business installation belonging to the railway" (BGHZ 1, 17, 19). This rather verbose statement can lead to some fine distinctions so that, for example, if the plaintiff's injury is caused by the kind of jostling that takes place in crowded stations or results from an uneven or slippery surface of the platform, the railway concern will be liable. But if the injury resulting from the fall was caused by, say, the presence of black ice, formed by freezing rain, then the liability of the railway would have to be based on fault (i.e. pleaded under § 823 I BGB). However, it is always possible in this case to try and argue that the water that froze, and caused the fall of the plaintiff, came from a railway engine or found its way onto the platform because of a defect in the station roof. If such an allegation is substantiated, then one could again be back under the heading of "business accident" and thus be able to invoke strict liability. Given the desirability of avoiding such niceties and, one might add, given the prevalence of modern insurance, it is not surprising to note a very clear tendency to interpret the statute "generously" and thereby afford maximum protection to victims. A result, one might add, that the French courts have also very largely managed to achieve through the medium of Article 1384 French CC, or the discovery of implied contractual terms (*obligations de sécurité*) in the contract of carriage. (For a summary of the French approach, which moves freely between contract and tort, see Terré, Simler and Lequette, *Droit civil, les obligations*, 5th ed. (1993) nos. 543, 565 and references in note 7.)

(iv) Is analogical extension of the statutory rules possible?

We have already noted how the German courts carved out for themselves an important area of activity in this otherwise statute-dominated part of the law. Yet they stopped short of taking the most vital step, which would have placed them on an approximate par with the legislature, when they refused to arrogate to themselves the right to extend analogi-cally specific statutes to new situations raising similar issues of public policy. The impor-tant judgment of 1912, RGZ 78, 171, that marked the beginning of this judicial attitude towards this matter, is reproduced below as case 128. (For other instances see RGZ 147, 353; BGHZ 54, 332.)

The litigation was provoked by an accident caused when one of Count von Zeppelin's experimental airships was forced by bad weather to land and then broke its moorings, injuring one of the many spectators who had spontaneously gathered to witness this novel sight. An attempt to extend analogically the recently enacted (3 May 1909) Road Traffic Act was rejected by the Supreme Court on the ground of the exceptional nature of this piece of legislation. Yet, the policy reasons behind the legislator's decision to enact the Traffic Act (novel form of transport, increased dangers etc.) were, arguably, equally to be found in airships; and, indeed, other German-inspired systems, such as the Austrian, have allowed their courts to extend statutes analogically, imposing strict liability (see cases cited by Zweigert and Kötz, *An Introduction to Comparative Law*, (1998), p. 657). In 1912, however, the German Supreme Court refused to accept this and has since repeatedly adhered to this position (see, for example, BGHZ 55, 229 and cases cited previously). The "tame" language employed in that famous judgment thus stands in stark contrast to the "bold" approach adopted some thirty years earlier when, for a moment, the court seemed to indicate its willingness to play a part in expanding the grounds of strict liability.

(v) A critical epilogue

Though necessarily brief, our sketch of the German way of introducing strict liability has already revealed some of the system's cardinal weaknesses. The notion that only the leg-islator can introduce strict liability has resulted in a delayed, patchy, and complicated system for handling accidents resulting from new technology and more generally, the risks of modern life. It has been *delayed* because, inevitably, there always was, and always will be, a time-lag between new technological developments and the time when the legislator intervenes in order to regulate them. The result is that until such intervention occurs, the courts have to step in and handle as best they can the problems posed by new technol-ogy. (Some illustrations can be found in RGZ 17, 103 (protection of property before the enlargement of § 1 of the Imperial Act on Liability, discussed in section (iii) and below); RG JW 1938, 1234; RGZ 147, 353 (liability of electricity companies before the 1943 exten-sion of the Imperial Act on Liability); RG DJZ 11, 1316 (car accident before the enactment of the 1909 Road Traffic Act).)

It was *patchy*, since each statute only handled specific problems, on the basis of scien-tific and technological information available at the time of their enactment, while leaving often-related activities or risks outside their purview. The inability to extend these enact-ments analogically, only aggravated the difficulties. Thus Professors von Caemmerer, Kötz, and others have for some time now been pointing out the capriciousness of the existing law and advocating the adoption of a more generalized provision to deal with this subject. So, for example, why cannot the dangers inherent in operating an explosives factory be assimilated to those of the gas industry dealt with by § 2 of the Strict Liability Act? Could it not be said that the operation of a large river dam poses risks broadly anal-ogous to those found in nuclear stations regulated by § 25 of the Nuclear Act? Should the spraying of a poisonous insecticide lead to strict liability only if it contaminates water, in accordance with § 22 of the Water Supply Act, but not when it destroys or dangerously contaminates useful crops? Or why should a contractor using a tipping-wagon for the construction of a *railway* be strictly liable for any damage he causes, but only be liable upon proof of fault if he is simply helping build a *factory* or a large block of *flats*? Other systems have provided for strict liability not only in the case of specifically mentioned activities, but also in all those instances where an activity carries with it an increased danger for others.

Finally, the system is *complicated* because the imposition of maxima for monetary compensation and the exclusion under these statutes of all compensation for pain and suffering often means recourse to the ordinary, fault-based liability rules to be found in the Civil Code. If these "limitations" imposed by the statutes were dictated by fears of unlimited liability and unbearable economic consequences, especially at a time when insurance was not as widely spread as it is today, then the time has surely come to reconsider the validity of this kind of argument. Certainly, the absence of any maxima in compensation paid under the Water Act has caused no problems. In motor vehicle insurance, coverage in excess of the maximum amount provided by the statute (i.e. DM 750,000) is widely obtained without a considerable increase in premium cost. Finally, the Swiss experience, quite different in this respect from the German, has not justified the fears expressed in Germany concerning an extension of the rules of strict liability. A more unified treatment of its problems would, it is submitted, be a considerable improvement on the status quo. But, despite many rumblings, and even more proposals for reform, the present system seems unlikely to be greatly changed in the near future. Thus, in this as in so many other areas of civil liability (e.g. § 831 BGB; express recognition of the right of personality etc.) the codal framework has proved too resistant to much-needed change.

(c) Four specific statutes on strict liability

(i) The Strict Liability Act 1978

It was stated earlier in this section that the history of the German strict liability statutes follows closely the development and expansion of modern industry. The Strict Liability Act of 1978 brings this point out very clearly.

The origin of this Act can, in a sense, be traced back to the 1838 Prussian Railways Act— by any reckoning, a most pioneering enactment. For when it was enacted, the Kingdom of Prussia had less than 100 kilometres of rail tracks so there was really no pressing practical need for such a measure. But capitalism in those days also had its paternalistic aspects; and, in any event, the economic consequences resulting from the imposition of strict liability for harm to persons or property "resulting from carriage on the railway" (§ 35) hardly affected the mainly land-owning dominant class.

The importance of the railway system for the economy and, later, the defence of the realm, was quickly perceived by the German leaders. The investment in an efficient national railway system was considerable and with the unification of the Reich, the 1838 enactment was to serve as the model of the Imperial Insurance Act of 1871. This statute introduced strict liability for railway carriage throughout the entire Reich. But the 1871 version of the statute it was also narrower than its model—which remained in force in Prussia and certain other parts of Germany (and also served as the model of an Austrian enactment of 1869). For § 1 of the 1871 Act limited strict liability to cases of death or personal injury only (and excluded property damage) resulting from the "operating of the railway". This discrepancy between the old, geographically limited but in one respect wider statute and the Imperial enactment posed difficult problems which a number of courts tried to resolve by extending strict liability to property damage caused by the operation of railways (*cf.* RGZ 17, 103). These attempts, however, achieved only limited success and, on the contrary, attracted some hostile academic criticism. It was not, therefore, until the enactment of the 1897 Commercial Code that some measure of uniformity was achieved in the area of liability for carriage of goods. This trend was firmly consolidated in 1940 when a special statute, amending the 1871 Imperial law, introduced strict liability for property damage, as well (*Gesetz über die Haftpflicht der Eisenbahnen und Strassenbahnen für Sachschäden*). This position is, of course, now also clearly reflected in § 1 of the 1978 consolidating enactment.

Apart from this "retrograde" step, connected with the exclusion of property damage from the scope of the 1871 statute, the Imperial Insurance Act was a far-reaching enactment. § 2, for example, imposed what we would call true vicarious liability on the operators of mines, quarries, pits, and factories for the damage caused by the *faults* of their authorised agents or representatives. This was a great step forward for those persons working in these industries and most exposed to their dangers. And the progress was even greater if taken together with another set of provisions of the Act—§§ 6 and 7—which greatly increased the discretion of the courts in evaluating the evidence and the amount of damages to be awarded. This "free evaluation" principle, as it became known was a great innovatory step when compared with the rigid rules of procedure applicable at the time. (It was subsequently widely adopted by the Code of Civil Procedure of 1871 with the result that §§ 6 and 7 of the Imperial Insurance Act became redundant and were abolished.) But the more equitable treatment of industrial accidents did not stop there. The passing of the social security legislation of the early 1880s gave even greater protection to the working classes for accidents at work, and the consolidation of the entire law of social insurance by the 1911 *Reichsversicherungsordnung* removed accidents at work from the province of the law of tort. A bird's-eye view of this system will be given in the next subsection.

The expansion of the Imperial Insurance Act continued well into the twentieth century. Apart from the enlargement that took place in 1940 in order to include property damage, a further amendment was introduced in 1943. This extended the ambit of the statute to cover injury to persons or damage to property resulting from the operation of electricity, gas, steam, or current escaping from cables, pipelines, or plants for the provision of such energy or materials (see § 2 of the 1978 statute). The 1978 *Haftpflichtgesetz* of 4 January 1978 (extended strict liability further so as to include gases, fumes, and piped fluids but in other respects it can be regarded as a consolidating act.

Finally, one should note that the Strict Liability Act contains the usual defences—contributory fault of the victim (§ 4) and *force majeure* (*höhere Gewalt*) (§ 3), which is interpreted in a very stringent manner (and thus is more demanding a test than that of unavoidable event: *unabwendbares Ereignis*). Thus, in one case (BGHZ 7, 338) the young plaintiff was electrocuted when his kite—secured by a metal wire and not, as is usual, by a string—came into contact with an overhead electricity cable. Though the facts of the case were, clearly, very atypical, the Supreme Court refused to treat this as a case of an unavoidable accident and held the electricity operators liable to the victim. (For the full text of the 1978 statute see below, p. 853)

(ii) Accidents at work and social security legislation in modern German law

Since 1884 Germany has had a no-fault compulsory insurance scheme covering accidents at work, *gesetzliche Unfallversicherung* (statutory accident insurance). This has been amended and expanded in various ways by subsequent enactments and now forms part of a wider and more comprehensive system of social security that covers such things as permanent incapacity for work as well as sickness.

Here we shall limit our comments to the treatment given to accidents at work, a phrase which should be taken to include not only injuries sustained while actually at work but also accidents occurring while travelling to and from work. (Hence in practice we have, here, a considerable overlap with the compensation system established by the Road Traffic Act discussed below.)

The importance of this statutory insurance can be seen from the fact that two thirds of the population of Germany are currently covered (Kötz/Wagner, no. 581). Awards are made to all those in paid employment (whether German nationals or not), certain groups of self-employed persons. Since 1971, children and students have been covered by the schemes. The latter group is certainly not negligible: in 1998 alone about 688 million DM were paid out for these so-called "education accidents" (Kötz/Wagner, no. 618).

Compensation in the above cases is made through various schemes which are administered by trade co-operatives or institutes (*Berufsgenossenschaften*) which are separate legal entities, usually in close contact with one another, and under the general supervision and responsibility of the Minister of Labour and Social Security. The institutes function on a territorial basis and are organised to cover different commercial or other activities. There are in all some thirty-four industrial accident insurance institutes; nineteen agricultural institutes; thirteen municipal accident insurance organisations; eleven State funds; four Federal insurance institutes; and a number of other smaller autonomous funds—some ninety institutes in all. The first two of these, however, are the most important, covering between them some 90 per cent of work accident insurance. These institutes are self-governed by boards or councils, usually composed of equal numbers of employers and employees. Every employer is automatically a member of the institute appropriate to his firm's activities in the locality in which it carries on its business. Institutes may provide voluntary insurance for the self-employed in their areas and some actually make this compulsory.

The financing of the various institutes is a complicated affair. Generally speaking, revenue from taxes funds those institutes, which insure public employees; and the funds of agricultural institutes are subsidised by the central (Federal) government. The thirty-four industrial accident insurance institutes, on the other hand, derive their funds entirely from contributions made by employers, though there is the possibility (realised once only) of mutual financial help. The contributions vary depending on the risk factor attendant on the branch of industry to which the member belongs as well as on the risk-rating of the firm in question. These figures are reviewed periodically and contributions tend to vary from 1 to 12 per cent of earnings.

The awards are made by the officials of the appropriate institutes; and there is an intricate system of appeals to local State and Federal courts. A basic assumption of the system is that if an employee is entitled to compensation under SGB VII (for an accident suffered at work), save in cases of intentionally inflicted injury, the injured victim cannot claim any further compensation by relying on the ordinary tort rules of the BGB: the *employer* or any other *colleague* of the victim who may also be responsible for the accident enjoy an immunity (§§ 104, 105 SGB VII. Previously §§ 636, 637 RVO). Hence, this is the only main area in which tort law has been completely replaced by a compulsory and statutory insurance scheme in Germany. It is interesting to note that one of the main objects of tort—to provide incentives to reduce the risk of accidents—has been apparently achieved by other means. In 1976 the institutes running the system introduced a system by which the contribution of the individual employer depended also on the number of accidents in his company. As a result, the overall number of accidents has decreased significantly. (*Cf.* Kötz and Schäfer *AcP* 189 (1989), 501.)

The statutory scheme just described thus provides a number of advantages/incentives to employers. But is the system acceptable also from the employee's perspective? One of the main advantages is that the employee will be able to obtain compensation from a solvent debtor and he will not have to establish the fault of the employer. Nor will his own contributory fault be taken into account to reduce his "damages". This highlights once again the overall aim of social protection of the system. Its main disadvantage is, of course, that the employee cannot recover damages for pain and suffering (§ 847 BGB). On the other hand, the system of awards tends to be closely connected with the victim's pre-accident earnings and the sums recoverable can thus often be quite generous. More precisely, the system of an abstract assessment of the victim's earning disability tends—to some extent—to generate windfall payments. Professor Kötz (*op. cit.* no. 589) gives the example of a legal representative who while on a business trip has an accident and loses his right arm. This means that according to the disability guidelines his earning capacity will be diminished by 75 per cent. Generally speaking, whether or not he subsequently learns to write with his left hand and performs his duties just as he did before the accident will not be taken into account. (Limited exceptions from this are contained in §§ 85, 87 SGB VII.) Moreover, pensions and other periodic payments are index-linked. What is awarded depends largely upon whether the case is one of personal injury or death.

Awards for personal injuries will cover medical costs, including the costs of nursing, convalescence, and rehabilitation. The vast majority of cases will be dealt with under the general sickness insurance schemes (which are financed by contributions from both employers and employees). But the accident insurance institutes will meet all costs after the eighteenth day and, in about 15–20 per cent of the cases, depending on the type and seriousness of the injury, they take over responsibility from the outset and handle the case through their own specialists and hospitals. The institutes will also pay varying sums for loss of wages depending on the degree of invalidity incurred (minimum 20 per cent) and the period it lasts, but during the first six weeks of incapacity the employer remains responsible for paying the victim's wages. Total incapacity will usually produce approximately 65 per cent of the pre-accident wages for the first thirteen weeks of the incapacity and from then onwards a pension equal to two-thirds of the pre-accident wages within certain maximum limits. In the case of partial incapacity, the sums payable represent the proportion of the sum payable in the case of total incapacity that corresponds to the actual degree of incapacity and these sums are increased by small amounts if the injured person has dependants. In the case of fatal accidents, a sum equal to one month's earnings plus the funeral expenses becomes payable immediately. In addition to this sum, a widow would receive a pension, which is usually 30 per cent of the deceased husband's pre-accident income. This sum can be increased to 40 per cent where the widow is over the age of forty-five or her own earning capacity is reduced by at least 50 per cent, or if she has children to look after. Children can also receive a pension, which is higher where both parents are dead and lower if one of the parents has died. The sums are, once again, calculated on the pre-accident earnings of the parent, are index-linked, and cease to be paid when the child becomes eighteen. A widower, too, can claim a pension, but only where he can show that his wife was mainly responsible for the maintenance of the family and that he is, through incapacity, unable to support himself. Naturally, this applies if the wife died in an industrial accident as defined above.

A final issue that is of great practical importance in this context of accidents at work is whether the insurance institution can recoup from the tortfeasor the compensation it has paid to the victim. According to § 110 SGB VII the employer (or another employee) is liable to the extent that the insurer paid the victim; this is however subject to the crucial condition that the accident was caused intentionally or by gross negligence. In the case of a deliberately caused accident this seems perfectly sensible. But this may be more difficult to justify in the case of gross negligence since the advantages of certainty and simplicity of the social security system may thus be undermined. If on the other hand a third party caused the accident negligently then the victim's claim in tort against the third party will be transferred to the insurer (*cessio legis*), § 116 SGB VII. This has given rise to difficulties in cases where both, the employer and a third party, have caused the injuries. The question then is whether the third party is fully liable or whether his liability ought to be limited to his share of the blame. The courts have adopted the latter view (BGH 51, 37; see more recently NJW 1987, 2669). Otherwise the third party (who might be 10 per cent responsible) would be required to pay compensation for 100 per cent of the loss sustained by the victim, while at the same time he could not claim any contribution from the employer, who is 90 per cent to blame, but who enjoys an immunity from liability as against the victim, § 104 SGB VII. This cannot be right. The aim of the statutory insurance scheme is not to deprive third parties of their right to contribution (§§ 840, 426 BGB) but to protect the employer who finances the insurer by paying premiums. Thus, the insurer will be able to recover only 10 per cent of the loss in our example.

It goes without saying, as the example given also shows, that the rights to recoup awards of compensation raise intricate issues and require a special infrastructure to deal with them. In certain areas, where the third party is, himself, insured, the social security institutions sometimes enter into so called general "loss-sharing-agreements" with the private insurer (*Teilungsabkommen*). The claim is then settled on the basis of previous statistical experience without looking at the facts of the individual case. This saves the cost of establishing the respective portions of negligence in the individual case but it also departs from the idea of personal responsibility for one's acts under § 823 I BGB. This is most likely the case in the area of car accidents, for here insurance is compulsory (where the figure of payments under such agreements amounted in 1999 to 2.073 million). (For further details see Kötz/Wagner, no. 614–615 with references.)

(For the historical background of the *Unfallversicherungsgesetz* of 1884: Kaltenborn, "Die Sozialgesetzgebung des Reichskanzlers Fürst Otto von Bismarcks", JZ 1998, 770. The subsequent *Reichsversicherungsordnung* (RVO) was replaced in 1997 by the provisions in Sozialgesetzbuch (SGB) Book VII. Its purpose is to protect employees against risks specifically associated with their activities as employees, namely to suffer an accident at work (*Arbeitsunfall*, § 8 SGB VII), or to sustain an illness that is related to specific health risks of the task assigned to the employee (*Berufskrankheit*, § 9 SGB VII). In the period between 1996 and 1998 there were around two million accidents in employment per annum where the employee was not able to work for more than three days (including roughly 90.000 cases of "professional" illness). See Kötz/Wagner, no. 206.)

(iii) The Road Traffic Act 1952

(*a*) *General observations.* The twentieth century presented tort law with challenges never before encountered during its long history. A set of legal rules, originally devised for human beings, were increasingly applied to legal entities. Rules, which are meant to regulate the consequences of blameworthy conduct were used to determine the allocation of risks. Modern insurance and social security meant that more and more of those who met the cost of accidents were innocent absentees. One could go on and on with this list with the intention either to criticise the "antiquated" tort system and recommend its reform or abolition or, alternatively, to marvel at its ability to survive such changes. This is not the place to do either. But it is, perhaps, appropriate to remind the reader that the topic that has revealed the greater weaknesses of tort law, has prompted some of its most imaginative writing, and has proved a veritable hot-bed for ideas for reform, is the law of traffic accidents.

The practical significance of the topic is undisputed. In Germany, with whose system we are here primarily concerned, the cost of car accidents, in both human and financial terms, is enormous. In 1999 there were about 50 million licensed cars. In the same year the police registered 2.412.641 car accidents in which 7.777 people were killed and 520.902 injured. Given the complexity of the compensation system—which draws its funds both from social security and private insurance—it is difficult to give an accurate idea of the financial cost. What is clear, however, is that insurance payments for personal injury, death, and property damage were around 27.7 billion DM in 1999. (See Kötz/Wagner, no. 207, 511.) Moreover, in the first half of the 1990's, roughly 12 per cent of *all* civil claims brought before the *Amtsgericht* and 8.5 per cent of those brought at the *Landgericht* were related to traffic accidents. See Greger *Haftungsrecht des Straßenverkehrs* 3rd edn. (1997), Einleitung, no. 2.) Whatever else these figures may suggest, they certainly make one wonder whether and to what extent has the strict liability statute succeeded in accelerating compensation for victims of traffic accidents and reducing the volume of civil litigation.

Clearly, the topic is one of those that could justify on its own an "advanced course in tort law". Here we shall only outline the German approach under three headings. In the first we shall sketch briefly the gradual expansion of the statute law in order to assure a more comprehensive protection of victims of car accidents. In the second, we shall describe the main liability provisions of the Road Traffic Act of 1952. In the third, we shall consider some of the shortcomings of the present law in the light of some brief comparative observations. Before tackling these points, however, some reference must be made to the very rich legal literature on this subject.

Further reading

On German law (written in *German*) see Becker-Böhme, *Kraftverkehrshaftpflichtschäden. Die Regulierung in der Praxis*, 20th edn. (1997); Bauer, *Die Kraftfahrtversicherung* (1976); Becker, *Kraftverkehrs-Haftpflichtgesetz* (18th edn., 1992); Birkmann, "Die Rechtsprechung des BGH zum Verkehrshaftpflichtrecht", DAR 1989, 201; Drees/Kuckuk/Werny, *Strassenverkehrsrecht Kommentar* (7th edn., 1992); Gelhaar/Thuleweit, *Das Haftpflichtrecht des Strassenverkehrs* (1969); Gessner/Kötz, "Verkehrsunfälle vor Gericht. Eine rechtstatsächliche Untersuchung", *JZ* 1973, 82; Greger, *Haftungsrecht des Straßenverkehrs*, 3rd ed. (1997); Grossfeld, "Haftpflichtversicherung im Wandel" *VW* 1974, 693; Hanau, "Rückwirkungen der Haftpflichtversicherung auf die Haftung", *VersR* 1969, 291; Jagusch/Hentschel, *Strassenverkehrsrecht* (35th edn. 1998); Weyers, *Unfallschäden, Praxis und Ziele von Haftpflicht und Vorsorgesystemen* (1971); Wussow, *Das Unfallhaftpflichtrecht* (14th edn. 1996).

For a brief account in *English* see Pfennigstorf, "Analysis of the German Auto Accident Compensation System" in *Comparative Studies in Automobile Accident Compensation*, 33 ff., published by the US Department of Transportation in 1970; idem, *German Insurance Laws* (trans. and annotated in English) and published by the American Bar Foundation in 1975 and 1977 (Supplement).

For proposals for reform of the German law see Bollweg, "Gesetzliche Änderungen im Schadensersatzrecht?", *NZV* 2000, 185; von Caemmerer, *Reform der Gefährdungshaftung* (1971); Güllemann, *Ausgleich von Verkehrsunfallschäden im Licht internationaler Reformprojekte* (1969); von Hippel, *Schadensausgleich bei Verkehrsunfällen, Haftungsersetzung durch Versicherungsschutz* (1968); idem, "Schadensausgleich bei Verkehrsunfällen, Mögliche Wege einer Reform", *ZRP* 1973, 27; Kötz, "Empfiehlt sich eine Vereinheitlichung und Zusammenfassung der gesetz lichen Vorschriften über die Gefährdungshaftung im BGB", *Gutachten und Vorschläge zur Überarbeitung des Schuldrechts* (1981) 1779; Krause, *Das Risiko des Strassenverkehrsunfalls, Zuordnung und Absicherung* (1974); Schmeer, "Haftungsersetzung durch Versicherungsschutz?", *VersR* 1973, 390; "Soziale Sicherung gegen Unfälle im Strassenverkehr?" *Verhandlungen der Tagung des Deutschen Sozialgerichtsverbandes in Berlin am 17./18. 10. 1974* (1975).

Finally, excellent comparative law insights can be obtained by reading Professor Tunc's "Traffic Accident Compensation: Law and Proposals" in vol. XI, chapter 14 of the *International Encyclopedia of Comparative Law* (1971) and the most recent collection of essays on his latest proposals on the subject entitled *Pour une loi sur les accidents de la circulation* (1981).

(*b*) *Increasing protection through statutory interventions.* We have already noted that the introduction of strict liability in German law has been a closely guarded legislative prerogative. In this area of the law, legislative intervention on two fronts (the purely delictual and the insurance front) has been coupled with a close regulatory function on the part of the State. In different ways both have tried to improve the protection given to victims, the public in general, and in some cases, the insured keepers of the cars.

The process has been a gradual one. The first attempts to introduce strict liability were made nearly two years after the BGB came into force. A conference of lawyers then passed a resolution demanding the extension of the Imperial Insurance Act of 1871 to motor vehicles (even though at that time there were less than 2000 cars on the road) and, what is particularly interesting, proposing the creation of a mandatory co-operative risk-spreading association. (*Verhandlungen des Sechsundzwanzigsten Deutschen Juristentages* I, 27–55; III, 163–207 (Berlin 1902, 1903).) The idea met with some success with the government, which even went so far as to present Parliament in 1905 with a Bill. But by that time the motor car lobby was also gaining strength. So the Motor Vehicle Act (*Gesetz über Verkehr mit Kraftfahrzeugen*) that was finally enacted on 3 May 1909, was a compromise. For. (i) it introduced maxima for monetary compensation, which the 1871 Imperial Liability Act *in its original form* did not contain; (ii) it included no proposals for some kind of insurance scheme (as proposed by the 1902 conference), and (iii) it excluded from its application death or injuries suffered by the driver or non-paying passengers. The idea behind this last restriction was that the *rationale* of strict liability for car accidents was the danger posed to road-users by fast-moving objects. Strict or stricter forms of liability by means of specific statutes were first introduced by Denmark in 1903 (and were considerably extended by a 1918 amendment). Sweden followed suit in 1906 (and its statute was further amended in 1916), then came Greece in 1911, Norway in 1912, Finland in 1925, Switzerland in 1932, and the Netherlands in 1935. A readable account of the very different evolution of the English Common law during this same period can be found in an Article written by J. R. Spencer in [1983] *Cambridge Law Journal* 65 ff..

After various amendments and re-enactments, the 1909 Motor Vehicles Act became the Road Traffic Act (*Strassenverkehrsgesetz*) of 19 December 1952 and has since then survived basically unchanged. But the introduction of strict liability helps the victims of traffic accidents only so long as the tortfeasors can and will pay. In the absence of obligatory insurance this could not originally be guaranteed, even though many German drivers voluntarily obtained insurance coverage after the enactment of the 1909 Act. In the 1930s, however, a new trend started to manifest itself. In 1931 warehouse operators were, under certain circumstances, obliged to carry insurance; in 1936 the same was true for airplanes. Obligatory third-party liability insurance for cars was clearly not far away. In fact, it became a reality on 7 November 1939, when the first Obligatory Insurance Act came into force imposing on the "keeper" of a motor vehicle an obligation to carry insurance for himself and for the *authorised* driver of his vehicle. But there were still important gaps and, following the 1959 European Convention on Compulsory Insurance against Civil Liability in Respect of Motor Vehicles (*European Treaty Series* no. 29), the 1939 Act was revised and re-enacted under the short title *Pflichtversicherungsgesetz* of 5 April 1965. The main two loopholes that were closed by this enactment concerned (i) uninsured cars and (ii) hit-and-run accidents. In effect, the Act "legalised" an unofficial agreement that the insurance industry had operated since 1955. A private non-profit corporation, controlled and managed by the insurers, was created and compensation was provided out of its funds to the victims of the above-mentioned type of accidents. But compensation from the fund was limited in two important ways. First, it was entirely secondary in nature and could be claimed only if no compensation could be obtained from any other source. Second, it was limited to the statutory maxima (now, as we have seen, DM 750,000) and was and is further limited to claims for actual pecuniary damages arising from death or injury. Property damage, therefore, and pain and suffering are not compensated under this scheme save in very exceptional circumstances of real hardship. The other insurance gap that remained to be filled was connected with the possibility of an insurance company going bankrupt and being unable to meet its obligations. Though not something that has happened frequently—indeed so far as one can discover there exists only a handful of such incidents—German insurers decided to intervene in this area as well. Thus, in 1968 they created a private law corporation known as the Aid for Traffic Victims Fund (*Verkehrsopferhilfe e.V.*) which meets to the full all claims made against insolvent members, subject to a small deduction.

The increased legislative intervention described in the preceding paragraphs has created a regulatory background against which the modern insurance market operates under the supervision of a Federal Office situated in Bonn. The intricate nature of the rules so established stems partly from the need to regulate the interrelationship with the social security system of compensation, notably through the establishment of a complicated system of subrogation. The complexity also becomes inevitable when one remembers that one is here trying to protect at one and the same time the interests of (i) the public at large, (ii) the injured person, and (iii) the insured himself.

The protection of the public at large is assured first of all by the creation of the obligatory system of liability insurance. (Only the Federal State, the States of the Federal Republic and certain public institutions are exempt from this requirement.) Second, this protection is ensured by imposing an obligation on insurers to provide the minimum mandatory coverage (application for insurance coverage cannot be refused except in certain narrowly defined cases given in § 6 of the 1965 Obligatory Insurance Act). Third, the protection is ensured by the establishment of an elaborate administrative system by which no car is put on the road without a valid licence and, for this to be obtained, a valid certificate of insurance must be produced. Operating a car in contravention of the above is made a criminal offence, and penalties are also imposed if the termination of an insurance policy is not notified without delay to the licensing authority.

The protection of the injured person is, clearly, also furthered by all the above rules. In addition, however, since 1965 the victim has been given a direct right of action against the insurer (§ 3 I of the Obligatory Insurance Act, following the French model of the *action directe*). The victim can rely on the insurance policy even after its cancellation, but only if the claim is made within one month from the cancellation being notified to the licensing authority. Moreover, the victim's rights against the insurer are protected against the risk of the contract being void or voidable or the insurer having some other defence against the insured. Defences of the insurer are that the insured failed to pay the insurance premiums on time, or that the insured breached some other collateral "obligation" arising from the internal relationship between the insured and insurer. The most important example of this is found in cases where the insurer claims that the victim increased considerably the risk of an accident by driving under the influence of alcohol or not keeping the car in safe condition for driving. Finally, since 1965 the insurer is also liable for the damage caused by unauthorised drivers of vehicles for which their keeper is not liable under § 7 III of the Road Traffic Act. This is because the insurance covers the respective driver of the insured whether he may be authorised by the keeper or not. As a result of all these statutory provisions, the victim's protection under the compulsory insurance scheme is almost absolute. This can be understood only if one acknowledges that this comprehensive insurance coverage serves mainly a social purpose. This is to protect the injured but at the same time to spread the risk of this immensely useful but also highly dangerous activity to the whole community of those carrying out the activity.

The general rule as to statutory insurance schemes is that the insurer's liability to the victim is limited to the amounts, if any, that the victim cannot recover from other sources—notably the social security system (§ 158c IV VVG, Insurance Contracts Act). It should be noted however that this rule does not generally apply in the context of car insurance. (§ 3 Nr. 6 of the Obligatory Insurance Act.) The insurer's liability is not excluded by the fact that the injured is entitled under a social security system. In these cases the victim's medical expenses and even lost earnings are met by the appropriate social sickness insurance or social accident insurance. Given the dominant role in the compensation system played by the various social security schemes, the insurance companies tend to be brought into the picture at a later phase when the social insurance carrier wishes to be subrogated to the compensation claims of the insured. (The victim's claim is assigned by operation of law to the social security carrier, § 116 I SGB X.) The subsidiary liability of the car insurer is, in turn, subject to an exception where the insured breached one of the collateral "obligations" (*Obliegenheiten*) owed to the insurer, the insurer is then relieved from his liability to the victim. (See Greger *op. cit.* Anh II no. 99–175. A brief description in English of these complicated subrogation agreements can be found in Pfennigstorf's account of German law quoted in the Further Reading above.) Needless to say, an insurer who has paid the victim or his social security carrier may, in his turn, seek reimbursement from the insured person in accordance with the relative insurance laws and will be entitled to do so under § 3 Nr. 9 S. 2 of the Obligatory Insurance Act if the insured breached an obligation owed to the insurer. It should not be overlooked, however, that the insurer's claim against the insured is in most cases limited by statute to an amount of 10,000 DM (§ 5 III 1 KfzPflVV). (There is no such limit in the case of reimbursement claims by social security carriers. Where the injured is covered by social security legislation and in addition the insurer is not liable under § 3 of the Obligatory Insurance Act, the combined effect of the above rules will be that the insured will be held personally liable to the full extent. This is the case if certain obligations owed by the insured to the insurer are breached. See for details Greger *op. cit.* Anh II no. 156 ff.)

In practice, as was already alluded to, the insurer will seek reimbursement from the insured in cases where the insured is in some way in breach of the contract of insurance. This will be the case where, for instance, the car is used by an unauthorised or unlicensed driver, or is used for unauthorised racing. The same would be true if the contract was concluded under fraud or misrepresentation or there was a failure to pay agreed premium etc. Thus, as Professor Kötz points out (no. 419), the rules which govern the question whether the insured is protected by the policy acquire the function of determining whether and to what extent the keeper or driver of the car will be hold *personally* liable for the accident. This is remarkable for this was originally the purpose of the rules governing ordinary delict and strict liability.

Finally, the interests of the insured (and, arguably, once again the public at large) were safeguarded by a stringent supervisory control exercised over the one hundred or so insurance companies that are involved in the car insurance field. This regulatory function was by any standard quite stringent and included such things as the control of the standard terms of insurance contracts as well as an effective control on premiums to be charged and the criteria for differentiating between premiums. Needless to say, this last point had been very controversial, critics of the old regime arguing that it prevented effective competition between insurance companies and thus helped in keeping insurance premiums unrealistically high. (For further details on this see Gärtner, *Privatversicherungsrecht* (1976) 235.) The enactment of the "third generation" Council directive on non-life insurance brought about a major change: control of standard terms by way of authorisation had to be abolished (there is only a post-market abuse control); the same happened with regard to the premiums (they are "controlled" only insofar as they may represent a danger for the financial health of the insurance company). See for details: W.-H. Roth, "Die Vollendung des europäischen Binnenmarktes für Versicherungen", NJW 1993, 3028.

(*c*) *The salient features of the Road Traffic Act 1952.* The leading provision of this enactment is, undeniably, § 7. (The full text of the liability section of the Act is reproduced below, B.4.) § 7 imposes upon the "keeper" or "holder" (*Halter des Fahrzeugs*) of a "motor vehicle" strict liability for personal injury, death, and property damage resulting from the "operation of a motor car". These three terms must be examined more closely.

Motor vehicle. This includes, according to § 1 II of the Act, all land vehicles, which are driven by mechanical force and are not attached to railway tracks. § 8, however, excludes from the purview of the Act all slow-moving vehicles, i.e. those whose maximum speed at ground level does not exceed 20 kilometres per hour (12.5 m.p.h.). Given the evidence that we now have that most lethal traffic accidents occur at speeds of under 30 mph, this provision of the statute seems of dubious validity.

Keeper. The liability is primarily imposed on the keeper of the car. The keeper is the person who uses the car at his own expense and who has the power of disposal that goes with such use (see RGZ 127, 174, 175; BGH 29 May 1954, BGHZ 13, 254 etc.). The owner is usually deemed to be, but need not always be, the keeper. Cars driven by the employees of the keeper and causing damage will render him liable under the Act, the defence of bad selection or supervision, provided by § 831 BGB (discussed in chapter 3, section 3 A.1), not being available in this case. A person using a car on a short-term hire agreement will, usually, not be treated as its keeper (see BGH 23 May 1960, BGHZ 32, 331; 37, 306). But in the case of a long-term hiring agreement, the user of the car may become its keeper if he is saddled with all the running costs. (BGH 22 March 1983, BGHZ 87, 133.) If the car is used with the consent of the keeper, or it has been stolen because the keeper's negligence facilitates such a theft, the keeper (along with the user: *Benutzer*) will remain liable under the Act (§ 7 III). But if the car is used without the keeper's knowledge and consent—by a so-called "joy-rider" (usually a thief)—then that person and not the keeper will be liable under the Act. The danger that could result from this rule to a victim of a car accident (impecuniosity of the "joy-rider" and, hence, inability to meet the victim's claims) has, as we have seen, been removed by the insurance legislation of 1965 which renders the insurer liable. The German statute—unlike those of Austria and Switzerland—also regulates in § 18 the liability of the driver. This, however, is only a *prima-facie* liability, which the driver can rebut by proving that he was not negligent when driving the car. In practice this excul-patory proof is very difficult to adduce, the courts imposing on drivers a very high standard of care indeed, and thus rendering the driver jointly liable with the keeper of the vehicle. When this is so, § 17 is brought into operation and the extent of the com-pensation to be paid as between keeper and driver will be determined in accordance with the usual rules of contributory fault (§ 254 BGB).

Damage caused in the course of the operation (running) of the car (beim Betrieb des Fahrzeuges). This is the last positive requirement for strict liability to be imposed on the keeper. As already indicated, this term has given rise to a very rich case-law which is marked by the courts' desire to extend the protection of the victims of traffic accidents. (Though, once again, their value judgments are often couched in causative language. See, for example, BGH NJW 1972, 1808.) Naturally, the term "in operation" includes the typical way harm is caused, namely through collisions with moving or even immovable objects (other cars, cycles, pedestrians, sign posts etc.). But no contact with the car that causes the injury is required; for example a sudden turn of a car which causes a cyclist, who is coming behind it, to swerve, lose his balance, and fall can render its driver liable under the Act. (BGH 10 October 1972, NJW 1973, 44.) A leakage of oil on the road or dropped cargo, which then causes an accident, can also be brought under this heading. An acci-dent is caused by the "operation" of a car even where the car is stationary and not, strictly speaking, "running" on the road. Abandoned stationary vehicles (because the driver is having a rest or because they have broken down) which have caused an accident have thus also been brought under this heading (see, for example BGHZ 29, 163, case 122); though a police car or a motor cycle which was parked in the middle of the road with its lights on to serve as a "signal" that there was an accident ahead, was not included under the term "in operation" (OLG Celle DAR 1973, 183, 187 cited by Kötz/Wagner no. 388). Like-wise, not in operation (for the purposes of the statute) is a motorcycle placed on the road with its engine running simply in order to use its headlamp in order to light up the path ahead. (BGH VersR 1961, 369) The case law, in its desire to invoke the strict liability of the Act and afford greater protection to victims has, in fact, gone even further than the above examples may suggest (though these results have not escaped criticism). In one case when a tank smashed a paddock fence thereby enabling a horse to escape into the highway causing an accident, it was held that the accident had occurred in the course of "operat-ing a motor vehicle" (OLG Celle NJW 1965, 1719). In another, more extreme case, the same was held to be so when the car that caused the plaintiff's death was deliberately driven into him in order to facilitate the driver's escape from arrest. But it remains very doubtful that this was the type of "mischief" that prompted the legislator to impose strict liability. A proper application of the scope of the rule theory should have then produced the opposite result. Thus, in other cases a more correct result has been reached by observing the proper purpose of § 7 of the Road Traffic Act. One such case is BGH NJW 1975, 1886, which is reproduced below (case 124), not only because it illustrates the point just made, but also because it shows how casuistic the approach of German courts is in this respect. In that case the engine of a stationary specialised motor vehicle was kept "running" in order to help to discharge its cargo in a silo. One of the questions the court had to decide was whether damage caused during this operation could render the keeper of the vehicle liable under § 7 of the Road Traffic Act. The Supreme Court, overruling the Court of Appeal, held that it could not since, in principle, the statute only applied to "such perils . . . which emanate from the motor vehicle in its capacity of an engine serving transport". The court continued, "Since our legal system does not know of a general principle of strict liability for operating engines supplying power at work, § 7 of the Road Traffic Act cannot be applied to accidents which occur in consequence of technical processes which cannot any longer be reasonably connected with the character of the engine employed as part of a motor vehicle."

If the above requirements are satisfied, then the keeper of the vehicle will, usually, be liable to the extent provided by the Act (see §§ 10, 11, and 12) and perhaps, additionally (see § 16 of the Act) in accordance with the general rules of the law of delict (namely § 823 I or II BGB). But the liability under the 1952 Act will be excluded if he, the defendant, succeeds in proving that the accident was caused by an unavoidable event. An "unavoidable event" is defined by § 7 II 2 as "an event that (*inter alia*) . . . is due to the conduct of the injured party or of a third party (who is not an employee) or of an animal and if both the keeper and the driver of the vehicle have applied that care which is required in the light of the circumstances". This concept peculiar to the Road Traffic Act is difficult to classify. For on its face it raises fault connotations that cannot be squared with the nature of strict liability. It cannot come as a surprise therefore that the defence has been interpreted in a very strict way, the courts demanding proof of "extreme concentration and circumspection" on the part of the driver (BGH VersR 1962, 164). And, it is made even harder by expressly stating (§ 7 II 1) that an event is *not* unavoidable if it is due to a defect in the construction of the vehicle or a failure of one of its component parts (e.g. defective axle, brake failure, etc.). Moreover, the courts have assimilated to this "mechanical" failure of the car any "human" failure of its driver so that, for example, the loss of consciousness on the part of the driver, perhaps because of a sudden and unexpected brain haemorrhage, will *not* count as an "unavoidable event" (BGHZ 23, 90). In practice, therefore, adducing this exculpatory proof is difficult though not necessarily impossible, e.g. unexpected appearance of black ice. (See Kötz/Wagner, no. 389 ff. and references given therein.) At the time of writing, the most recent reform proposal of 24 September 2001 (*2. Gesetz zur Änderung schadensersatzrechtlicher Vorschriften*) draws the consequences from this and abolishes the concept of *Unabwendbarkeit*. However, in line with other strict liability statutes, the keeper's liability will not be absolute and the defendant will be able to raise the defence of *force majeure* ("höhere Gewalt"). This, however, does not mean that the plaintiff's overwhelming responsibility cannot be taken account of. His causal contribution to the accident will acquire weight in the context of § 254 BGB (contributory negligence) and, accordingly, his claim can be reduced, in extreme cases to zero. The reform is thus not likely to have a major practical impact—as the proposal readily admits—though it will enhance consistency in the law.

Apart from the above—and the exclusion of the liability of the keeper for damage caused by a "joy-rider"—the Act also contains one more important exceptional case where its application is excluded. This can be found in § 8*a* which states that the Act does not apply (i) to injury or death caused to any non-paying passenger travelling in the car (and this is taken to include the driver—see BGHZ 37, 311, 318) and (ii) to damage to property carried in the car unless it is carried by a paying passenger on himself. Naturally, in these cases the victim's claims can be based on the ordinary provisions of the Code (§ 823 I and II BGB). In this respect, therefore, we note a significant difference between German law and French law, since the latter changed its case law in 1968 on the so-called *transport bénévole*. Otherwise, one should not a considerable convergence between French and German jurisprudence on such key definitions as the involvement (*implication*) of the car in the accident in question. And there is hope for further convergence. For the reform proposal (already referred to in the previous paragraph) proposes the abolition of this peculiarity of German law which can only be explained as a historic relic. (See also the recommendations of the 1995 *Verkehrsgerichtstag*). Thus, it will no longer be material whether the injury occurred while the victim happened to be in- or outside the car.

Finally, as was already alluded to, according to § 9 of the Act, the injured party's contributory fault will also be taken into account. This can mean that, either this fault will be deemed to be the sole or main cause of the accident, or more likely, the victim's fault will be considered as a contributing factor to his hurt and the damages awarded to him will be reduced in accordance with § 254 BGB. It is of first importance to observe how the nature of liability under the Road Traffic Act transforms the defence of § 254 BGB. It is not necessary for the defendant to invoke or establish the *fault* of the other driver or keeper if two or more cars are involved in an accident (§ 17 I of the Act). Decisive is the risk inherent to the respective vehicle in the circumstances (*Betriebsgefahr*). This means that if two cars collided and both drivers were without fault then each driver will be able to recover 50 per cent of his loss from the other provided that the two cars posed roughly the same degree of danger. It should be noted that this is by no means rare. One must consider that fault needs to be proved by the plaintiff and this will be often difficult. Hence, in most cases an (expensive) expert will be instructed by the parties to reconstruct the accident and often it will remain impossible to ascertain the exact degree of negligence involved on either side. The expert will in effect determine the outcome of the trial either way. If fault is established on either side the respective rate of liability will shift accordingly up to a maximum of 100 per cent where the risk peculiar to the plaintiff's car is totally outweighed by the defendant's share of responsibility (for instance because he was grossly negligent). (A detailed account of the jurisprudence is given by Greger, *op. cit.* § 17 StVG, no. 57–155.)

(*d*) *A comparative epilogue.* Despite the fact that over the years a number of loopholes affecting traffic accident victims have been closed, German law on this subject still retains much of its vitality and controversial nature. Many of the criticisms have been voiced in a comparative way and it is appropriate in a book such as this to adopt a similar attitude.

The German approach to traffic accidents via a strict statutory liability is not unique. As already noted, Austria, Greece, the Netherlands, Switzerland, and the Scandinavian countries have all followed the same path and one can find quite similar (though not German-inspired) enactments even in the Common law world (the Saskatchewan Motor Vehicle Insurance Act 1947 being, probably, the best-known example). This way of regulating traffic accidents is markedly different from the French approach through the Code (but see now the 1985 Act at p. 854 below) and the Common law's persistent tendency to treat traffic accidents as a branch of the law of negligence. But in addition to being different, the German approach was, despite gaps, also pioneering in so far as it introduced strict liability at a very early stage in the life of the motor car. (The Scandinavian countries took a similar approach at about the same time.) Yet, even allowing for the progressive closing of the gaps of the original enactment and recognising as undeniable the extension of the protection given to car accident victims, German law still remains, in some respects at least, less wide and less generous to victims than some of the more contemporary European systems. Two of its main weaknesses will be discussed below while a third—the extreme complexity of the compensation system—will be ignored since this accusation can also be levied against the English and French systems.

Subject to the reform proviso explained above the first weakness of German law is the exclusion from the Traffic Act of injuries suffered by non-paying passengers. True, the position of the gratuitous passenger may not be as bad as it can be in some US jurisdictions where his recovery will depend on proof of gross negligence on the part of the driver; but it does remain unjustifiable given modern insurance practice. By contrast, in this area the most conceptually antiquated French system managed to break new ground when in the late sixties it decided to extend the strict liability of Article 1384 CC to such cases. The older arguments invoked against such an extension (consent of the victim; impropriety of suing one's "benefactor" without at least proving some fault on his part), advanced in all systems, have been increasingly recognized for what they are—fictions, appropriate to an era when third-party liability insurance was not compulsory, but objectionable relics now that modern insurance practices have transformed this part of the law. Old practices, however, die hard, especially when the insurance lobby wishes to retain them.

Insurance arguments also point to another weakness of the German system; the decision to reduce (and in extreme cases even eliminate) the victim's damages because of his own contributory fault. The abolition by the courts of this defence is impossible in German law given the express statutory provisions of the main Act; but even the desire to do this has often been lacking. For proposals for reform have always been met with moralistic arguments that any such move would not only increase the number of accidents but it would also sap tort law of much of its moral content. Empirical evidence, however, has shown that the first objection at least is not convincing. Many would thus be prepared to treat the legalistic arguments in favour of retaining the defence of contributory fault as a smoke-screen concealing the vested interests of certain members of the legal profession who vehemently oppose the abolition of this lucrative source of revenue. Tort law is thus increasingly seen in the area of law accidents as little more than a "forensic lottery" (the title of a pioneering monograph by Professor Isson). Tort litigation (especially in France and in Common law jurisdictions) has cluttered the overburdened courts even further. And tort law has itself been forced to encourage the growth of fictions (e.g. the tendency to discover negligence in cases of unfortunate but statistically inevitable inattentions) in order to avoid the harshness of its rules. Here, again, French law has proved its flexibility and given a lead by recently advocating the abandonment of the defence of contributory fault. True, the pioneering decision of the Second Chamber of the Court of Cassation was rendered in a car accident case based on Article 1384 CC; and the problem now exercising the French courts is whether it should be limited (as Professor Viney has argued in *Dalloz Chronique* 1982, 201) to cases where insurance is obligatory or, at least, widely prevalent. That it should is not seriously disputed though *how* this can be achieved, given the wide wording of Article 1384 CC ("One is responsible for the damage caused by the things in one's care"), is another difficult matter (see

Durry, 1983 *Rev. trim. dr. civ.*, 752). But whatever the difficulties of delimitation, the fact remains that the French experiment (which has still to receive the blessing of the plenum of the Court of Cassation) has given an interesting lead and has generated legal literature which can be consulted with profit even by the non-comparatively minded Common lawyer. (See now the 1985 Act reproduced below at p. 850.)

This brings us to the next point that at least American students of the modern civil law should bear in mind. The study of the European systems (including the English), fruitful as it may be, must always be undertaken bearing in mind some essential differences in the legal background. Thus it must be remembered that in Europe (including England) civil action claims arising from car accidents are not tried by juries. Likewise, the American style contingent fee system for legal remuneration is banned, and most importantly, a highly developed social welfare system plays an important part in the overall compensation of car accident victims. All these factors can help to explain the lower levels of awards and other differences in the substantive law. Finally, though Germany (like the USA) is a Federal State, tort law (and hence, traffic accident law) is the same in all the States of the Federation. Thus, one does not find in Germany the regional variations that the American (or Canadian) lawyer has come to accept in his own system.

This comparative epilogue should, perhaps, end by reminding the reader that, once again, the study of the subject can be greatly enhanced by an interdisciplinary approach. The contact with insurance, in particular, must never be forgotten; and it could provide the "unifying link" in any comparative study that sought to argue that legal borrowing is possible even in an area where historical and conceptual differences might at first sight seem to discourage it.

(iv) Environmental liability[1]

Further reading

A. Texts of German Environmental Laws: Kloepfer, Umweltschutz, Textsammlung des Umweltrechts der Bundesrepublik Deutschland (looseleaf collection of virtually all German environmental laws); B. Books: Landsberg and Lülling, *Umwelthaftungsrecht—Kommentar* (1991) (the first and best commentary on the ELA co-written by one of the drafters of the ELA); Salje, *Umwelthaftungsgesetz—Kommentar* (1993); Schmidt-Salzer, *Kommentar zum Umwelthaftungsrecht* (1992); Schmitt, *Haftungs- und Versicherungsfragen bei Umweltrisiken* (1990); C. Articles: Diederichsen, "Die Haftung für Umweltschäden in Deutschland" *Produkthaftpflicht international* (PHI 5/92) (Sept. 1992); Hager, "Europäisches Umwelthaftungsrecht", *ZEuP* 1997, 9; W. Hoffman, "Germany's New Environmental Liability Act: Strict Liability for Facilities Causing Pollution", 28 *Neth. Int'l L. Rev.* 27–41 (1991) (a fully annotated text providing the basis for this note); W. Hoffman, "Environmental Liability and its Insurance in Germany", 43 *Fed'n of Ins. & Corp. Couns. Q.* 147–65 (1993); Michalski, "Das Umwelthaftungsgesetz", *Jura* 1995, 617; Nicklisch, "Umweltschutz und Haftungsrisiken", *VersR* 1991, 1093; Salje, "Die Entscheidungspraxis zum UmweltHG", *VersR* 1998, 797; Wagner, "Die Aufgaben des Haftungsrechts—eine Untersuchung am Beispiel der Umwelthaftungsrechts-Reform", *JZ* 1991, 175.

1. Environmental Liability under German Law Prior to 1991

Environmental liability in the Federal Republic of Germany has been the subject of many provisions widely dispersed throughout public and private law. Numerous public

---

[1] Subject to some updating, this section draws heavily on a note prepared for the third edition of this book by William C. Hoffman, International Legal Counsel, Cologne Reinsurance Co., Cologne, Germany. We are grateful to Mr Hoffman for his assistance in this matter.

law provisions prohibit specific polluting activities, and various civil liability laws require polluters to compensate for losses caused by pollution. See Kloepfer, *Umweltschutz* (collecting texts from over 100 separate pieces of German legislation regulating and providing liability for activities harmful to the environment).

Thus, German environmental law in force prior to 1991 consists of a patchwork of various laws, each having a relatively narrow scope of application. Many individual federal laws regulate single activities, such as construction, mining, railroads, streets, hunting, hotels, x-rays, and the removal of animal bodies, to name only a few. Each law contains restrictions deemed appropriate to curb pollution with respect to the particular activity. As a result, approximately 30 separate federal laws regulate water pollution arising from different sources and activities.

As will be discussed below, the ELA is an attempt to provide a broader and more comprehensive liability scheme supplementing the numerous pre-existing laws. An understanding of the ELA therefore requires a review of the most significant pre-existing laws, including: state police power, § 906 BGB, and special laws providing strict liability for damage caused by water pollution or by certain inherently dangerous facilities.

Police Power to Prevent Pollution

The several states (*Länder*) of the Federal Republic have police power to regulate directly conduct causing pollution, including conduct that threatens to pollute. Liability is strict, and *force majeure* generally is not a defence; in many cases, no proof of causation is required at all. The police power is, however, generally preventative only, and permits State and local authorities only to issue orders enjoining future pollution but not to order the clean-up of past pollution or to order payment of police-response costs. See Schmitt, *Haftungs- und Versicherungsfragen* at 50–3, 58.

In short, while public liability for police-response costs does not exist *per se*, in some cases authorities can, in effect, order "clean-up" operations by reference to a future threat to public health. However, the police power is not a source of tort law, and does not provide for civil damages as compensation for injury to persons or property. For a damages remedy, the claimant must sue under the various liability laws.

§ 906 BGB and the "Common Law" of delict

A claim for nuisance arises under §§ 906, 1004 BGB. Liability for nuisance is strict. The action will lie where one landowner infringes the right of another to make use of the land. Generally, however, the offending neighbour is liable only for emissions that *substantially* deprive the claimant of use of the land. According to § 906 I BGB the landowner cannot prevent emissions of "unweighable materials" (*unwägbare Stoffe*), such as airborne substances, vibration, noise, or similar emissions from another plot that have a negligible impact only on the use of the land (*unwesentlich beeinträchtigt*). If the emissions exceed levels customary for the area, and it is also economically *reasonable* to require the offending landowner to reduce the emissions (§ 906 II 1 BGB), the plaintiff will be granted an injunction (§ 1004 BGB). If on the other hand it is not reasonable to demand that the emissions are reduced, the landowner is required to tolerate the interference under § 906 II 1 BGB. However, in this case § 906 II 2 BGB entitles the land-owner to compensation for the economic consequences of the interference. In the case of certain plants and facilities that are subject to the *Bundesimmissionsschutzgesetz (BImSchG)* § 14 BImSchG is *lex specialis*. Those rules are very similar. If the landowner is not allowed to prevent the emission he will be entitled to compensation.

Thus, § 906 BGB affords protection to private use interests in land and does not extend to other kinds of injuries that pollution can cause. Personal injury or damage to personal property cannot give rise to a claim under § 906 BGB. For example, in the "Smelting Oven" (*Kupolofen*) case from 1985, BGHZ 92, 143, it was held that an industrial landowner was not liable under § 906 for damage which airborne ashes, emitted by its facility, caused to the paint of cars parked on neighbouring industrial property. A further problem is that proving the elements of causation can be exceedingly difficult in environmental cases. § 906 BGB generally defines the unlawfulness of emissions. It acquires thus importance also in the context of claims based directly on § 823 I BGB, which is mainly relied on in claims for personal injury. However, plaintiffs in environmental cases benefit from a (to some extent) reversed burden of proof. For, in analogy to the product liability jurisprudence, the BGH reverses the burden of proof in claims based on § 906 BGB. (See BGHZ 92, 143, 146–147; JZ 1998, 358–359.) It is thus for the defendant to prove that the emissions are *within the limits imposed by law* and/or in that particular area customary. If that is not the case, the operator of the facility must further establish that he has undertaken all reasonable or economically sustainable precautions to prevent any damage that the emissions may cause. The rationale of reversing the burden of proof is clear. (It must be remembered that German law does not normally provide for procedures of pre-trial disclosure.) Only the company running the facility is able to control the emissions and to give evidence whether these have been such that the safety standards have not been violated. If the defendant establishes that the emissions are below certain levels prescribed by statutory instruments, then the plaintiff must prove that the defendant has not done enough in the special circumstances of the case. A third limitation results from the negative criterion that the emissions are customary in the respective area. This, potentially, inhibits the imposition of pro-active measures that increase the safety of the facility. It should be further noted that the main impetus for basing claims in personal injury cases on the general law of delict was § 847 BGB, namely the availability of damages for pain and suffering, which, if the already discussed reform proposal becomes reality, will no longer be the case. Such damages will then be recoverable under the special strict liability statute.

Increasingly, the German legislature responded to the inherent limitations of § 906 BGB and similar provisions by enacting a number of pollution laws of special scope.

Water Resources Act

By far the most significant civil environmental liability act in force prior to 1991 is the Water Resources Act of 1957 (WRA) (*Wasserhaushaltsgesetz*). § 22 WRA imposes strict liability for bodily injury, property damage and—unlike §§ 906 or 823 BGB—pure economic loss resulting from any change in the physical, chemical, or biological composition of a water source. Liability for pure economic loss may arise under the WRA where, for example, water contamination causes a loss of income to a fisherman or to another business dependent on the water source.

§ 22 I WRA provides for non-facility liability and § 22 II for facility liability. The facilities caught by the Act are those which process or store materials that typically pose a danger of pollution to water. This was denied for instance (BGH NJW 1993, 2029; see, also, case 95) in the case of a facility that stored plastic materials to be used in the assembly of caravans. It burned down and dangerous substances escaped together with the water used to extinguish the fire. The material stored in the warehouse did not represent a *typical* danger against which § 22 II WHG afforded protection. As was explained by way of introduction (section 5(b)(iii)) the main control device of strict liability is the concept of legal cause. It focuses on the specific danger which was meant to be prevented by imposing strict liability, and the present case is a further example of this. Multiple tortfeasors are jointly and severally liable. Further, in 1971 the BGH construed the WRA to give rise to a presumption of causation. If the polluting substance is "inherently suited" (*geeignet*) to cause the harm suffered, then causation may be presumed; BGHZ 57, 257, 264. This presumption applies, however, only if it not clear which of several facilities caused the damages. But in relation to a single facility the claimant bears the full burden of proving causation.

Other Facility Liability

Other strict liability laws enacted since the WRA have also used the "facility liability" approach. These laws apply only to certain types of facilities deemed inherently dangerous. Usually, the types or categories of facilities are listed in an appendix to the law. Under the most significant of these laws, strict liability exists for injury or damage arising from mining facilities (*Bundesberggesetz*), from nuclear reactors (*Atomgesetz*), from electricity plants and other energy production facilities (*Haftpflichtgesetz*), and from certain other facilities that release emissions harmful to the environment (*BImSchG*).

2. *The Environmental Liability Act*

As shown, the state of German environmental law in force prior to 1991 was a patchwork of numerous individual provisions enacted piecemeal and each having a relatively narrow objective. This state of the law gave rise to a need for a broader and more comprehensive statute. It will be remembered in particular that the WHG of 1957 covers only damage caused through polluting water.

On 1 November 1986, the Rhine was severely polluted following a fire at a large chemical plant in Schweizerhalle, Switzerland. Water that had been used for extinguishing the fire drained into the river, washing highly toxic substances released during the fire into the environment. As a result, from Basel, Switzerland to Rotterdam in the Netherlands, the Rhine became extremely contaminated and virtually all fish and much other wildlife were destroyed. This event prompted the German government to announce, in 1987, that a strict liability law was desired, not only for water damage but also for damage caused by air and soil pollution.

The act that emerged after a hotly debated legislative process is the Environmental Liability Act of 1990 (*Gesetz über die Umwelthaftung*). This was adopted in spite of harsh criticism by the industry which had feared disadvantages in international competition. However, none of these fears seem to have actually materialized. This may be partly due to the balanced approach adopted by the ELA. Thus, it does not impose liability for abstract "ecological" damage to the environment. For liability to arise, a protected interest (property, life or health) of a particular individual must be violated through the ecological mediums of air and soil (§ 16). The ELA contains a mixture of public, criminal and administrative law but it is also a liability law providing a civil damages remedy for harm caused by pollution of air, soil or water. As such, the ELA has a broader scope than prior liability laws but it does not pre-empt or supersede any of the prior laws. Rather, the ELA coexists with and complements them, although some overlap is apparent.

Nature, Scope and Elements of Liability Under the ELA

The ELA imposes strict liability of up to DM 160 million for bodily injury and DM 160 million for property damage caused by any one environmental impact on air, soil or water. Liable persons are the "operators" (*Inhaber*) of certain facilities listed in Appendix 1 of the Act. Thus, facility operators may be liable for a total of up to DM 320 million per impact, per facility.

Unlike the WRA, however, the ELA does not provide for recovery of damages for pure financial loss or non-material harm. A claimant seeking compensation for pure financial loss must therefore establish liability under other provisions permitting recovery for such losses, such as the WRA (permitting recovery of pure financial loss caused by water pollution) or § 847 BGB (damages for pain and suffering; pending reform).

The nature and scope of liability under the ELA in general are set out in § 1 of the Act, which provides: "If anyone suffers death, personal injury, or property damage due to an environmental impact emitted from one of the facilities named in Appendix 1, then the operator of the facility shall be liable to the injured person for the damages caused thereby." Liability is "strict" under § 1 ELA. Polluters are liable for damage caused by their pollution regardless of whether the environmental impact was intended or negligent, known or unknown, occurred within a short span of a few minutes or over a prolonged period of many years. Causation alone, if proved under the ELA's provisions discussed below, provides the basis of liability. Further, the ELA as enacted contains no development risk exclusion, so that it is no defence against liability to assert that the state of scientific or technical knowledge at the time did not permit the defendant to know of the potential harm to the environment. Moreover, strict liability can attach under the ELA for amounts of pollution that are authorised or tolerated by existing regulatory laws, if the claimant can establish the element of causation.

Liability seems to be joint and several among multiple defendants under the ELA but the issue is controversial. A draft bill containing a pro rata apportionment among multiple defendants was blocked by the Upper House in October 1990, and one of the provisions that were unacceptable to the Upper House was the pro rata provision. That provision was deleted from the ELA as enacted. The better view now seems to be that multiple ELA defendants are subject to general tort principles, including joint and several liability under § 840 BGB. This means that any one of several defendants held to be jointly liable may be liable for the entire amount given by the judgment (regardless of what percentage of the damage that particular defendant might have caused in fact). However, recently the OLG Düsseldorf adopted a different approach. (See its judgment of 19 June 1998, JZ 1999, 684.) In that case, the plaintiff proved that the defendant's emissions caused damage to the paint of his adjoining house and claimed the cost of repainting it. The defendant objected that part of the damage resulted out of the "general pollution" of the air in that particular neighbourhood. The court followed this and apportioned liability, allocating to the defendant a share of 50%. Under § 840 BGB this would not be the case. If other polluters contributed to the damage, then the defendant remains liable in full and may seek contribution from the other polluters. It is clear that identifying the other polluters and holding them responsible would not have been easy in the case at hand. So, on final analysis, the question is who bears the risk of "general air pollution". If one approaches the problem from general principle it should clearly be on the defendant (*cf.* Salje *JZ* 1999, 685 ff.). In tort law it suffices that the defendant contributed to the damage. Furthermore, the operator of the facility alone is able to control the risk of causing the damage by taking protective measure and avoiding that the overall pollution reaches critical levels. It is therefore somewhat puzzling that the court departed from this and in effect seems to have restored the pro rate apportionment principle that had been rejected by Parliament (even though it limited the ruling to the specific case).

Several exclusions from liability delimit the scope of the ELA. § 4 ELA excludes liability for damage caused by *force majeure* (*höhere Gewalt*). Further, § 5 ELA excludes liability for property damage that is "only insubstantial" or that the impairment is "reasonable according to the local conditions" if the facility was "operated properly", i.e., according to all applicable regulations and no interruption of operations has occurred.

In order to establish liability under the ELA, a claimant must prove three elements: (1) that the defendant operates a *facility* named in Appendix 1; (2) that *an environmental impact was emitted* from the defendant's facility; and (3) that this environmental impact *caused* the damage complained of. The following paragraphs examine each of these elements briefly.

Facility

The ELA applies only to a "facility" as defined in its provisions. Because the ELA imposes liability on a "per impact, per facility" basis, the definition of "facility" would play an important role, for example, in determining whether the ELA defendant might be subject to multiple limits of liability, e.g., where more than one "facility" may be said to have given rise to an "environmental impact".

§ 3 II ELA defines "facility" (*Anlage*) to mean a "permanent structure such as a place of business or warehouse". The same provision states that "facility" also includes any "machines, instruments, vehicles and other mobile technical structures", and "outbuildings" which "stand in a spatial or technical relation to a facility or part thereof and could be significant for the occurrence of an environmental impact". Thus, the existence of a "facility" seems to be tied to a structure, vehicle, or instrument of some kind. Under § 2 ELA, uncompleted or unfinished facilities and finished facilities no longer in use are included in the definition.

Appendix 1 of the ELA contains a list of 96 specific types of facilities. These are grouped into ten general categories of facilities engaged in the processing, manufacture, or handling of certain materials and include industries engaged in:

(1) mining, energy and heat production;

(2) the manufacture of products from stone, earth, glass, ceramic, and other construction materials;

(3) the processing and manufacture of steel, iron, and other metals;

(4) the manufacture of chemical, pharmaceutical, or petroleum products or their further processing;

(5) treatment with organic materials and the manufacture of artificial materials;

(6) the processing of wood and wood pulp;

(7) the production of food, feed, and agricultural products;

(8) the treatment of waste;

(9) the storage and disposal of certain materials; and

(10) other facilities, including paint, printing ink, asphalt, etc. production.

This list of facilities is more extensive than prior facilities appendices, and includes certain toxic waste disposal and burning facilities not previously subject to major environmental legislation.

Environmental Impact

§ 3 I ELA defines "environmental impact" (*Umwelteinwirkung*) to mean an impact from "material, vibration, noise, pressure, rays, gasses, steam, heat, or other phenomena which are emitted into soil, air, or water". Thus, the ELA applies to all emissions already specifically prohibited by § 906 BGB, and also overlaps with the remedy for bodily injury and property damage caused by water pollution under the WRA. Strict liability for bodily injury and property damage resulting from impacts on soil and air is, however, new under the ELA.

Causation

The element of causation presents the core problem of proof under the ELA. Causation can present nearly insurmountable difficulties in cases of gradual pollution arising from sources located far away, such as chemical emissions from a distant smokestack, toxic waste seeping into a water source, etc. The drafters of the ELA drew on the experiences from the WRA and attempted to compensate for this difficulty with a presumption of causation.

At the time of its passage through the legislature, the ELA's most controversial provisions were those located in § 6 ELA. § 6 I ELA provides that the element of causation will be presumed upon a prima facie showing that the particular facility is "inherently suited" (*geeignet*) to cause the damage. Thus, the drafters of the ELA codified the judge-made presumption of causation that had its origins under the WRA in the 1971 decision, cited *supra*. This presumption reverses the burden of proof: it eases the claimant's evidentiary burden by shifting to the defendant the task of showing an absence of causation. However, unlike its predecessor under the WRA, the presumption of causation under § 6 I ELA applies equally in cases against single facilities. Once the presumption applies, the defendant may be held liable unless the presumption can be precluded or rebutted.

§§ 6 II, III and IV ELA provide that the presumption of causation set out in § 6 I is precluded from arising, and has therefore no application, if the defendant can show that his facility was "properly operated". "Proper operation" means that the facility fulfilled all "special operational duties" and that no disruption of operations occurred. "Special operational duties" refers to all applicable administrative regulatory duties aimed at preventing pollution. In a sub-presumption aiding the defence, the ELA provides that compliance with a "special operational duty" may be presumed for purposes of excluding the presumption of § 6 I. If (1) documented checks are required by law and (2) such checks do not allow for an inference of a violation, then compliance with the applicable laws will be presumed.

A defendant may rebut the presumption of causation under § 6 I by using the provisions of § 7 ELA. In cases of single or multiple facilities inherently suited to cause the claimant's damage, the presumption of causation is rebutted if another "circumstance" (*Umstand*) also appears "inherently suited" to be the cause.

Substantively, perhaps the most far-reaching effect of the ELA's presumption of causation occurs in connection with joint and several liability. In cases against multiple defendants, the presumption may form the basis of liability as against all defendants who fail to exclude or rebut it.

It must be noted, however, that neither §§ 6 II–IV ELA nor § 7 ELA operates as an absolute defence. In other words, even if a defendant successfully precludes § 6 I's presumption of causation from arising under §§ 6 II–IV, or rebuts it under § 7, this alone will not necessarily relieve a defendant of liability. Rather, the effect of these provisions is merely procedural; the claimant thereby loses the benefit of the reversed burden of proof. In such a case, the claimant bears the full evidentiary burden on the element of causation which, if met, nevertheless establishes liability.

Perhaps the drafters of the ELA did not foresee that § 7 ELA may turn out to be the exception that swallows the rule. The broader the courts construe the language "inherently suited" in § 6 ELA, the easier it will be for a defendant to point to facts giving rise to a "circumstance" to rebut the presumption under § 7. With a little imagination, a clever defendant might easily point to facts raising an issue as to whether another "circumstance" satisfies a broadly construed "inherent suitedness" test. Thus, § 6 I's presumption, together with § 7's rebuttal thereof, could operate to blunt the teeth of the ELA. But these fears have not been confirmed, for the BGH has taken a clear, plaintiff-orientated stance on this matter and has interpreted these exceptions narrowly. However, as the language "multiple facilities" in § 7 makes clear, in no case can another defendant facility be the other "circumstance" justifying the exclusion. Thus, § 7 prevents multiple defendants from using each other to deflect use of that presumption.

It comes as no surprise then that the first BGH decision on liability under ELA deals almost exclusively with this key issue of ecological liability: causation and burden of proof. (BGH, 17 June 1997, NJW 1997, 2748 = JZ 1998, 358, with an approving note by Hager). In this case the plaintiff suffered from headache, insomnia and was feeling unwell for several years. She sued the operator of two varnishing facilities which were located at a distance of three kilometres. The difficulty in this case was that the defendant could prove that, overall, it had respected the limits imposed by statutes on toxic emissions. Accordingly, the claim failed in the lower courts. But the BGH reversed those decisions and remitted the case for re-hearing. The Court of Appeal had not decided whether the emissions were suited to cause the injury and thus whether the presumption of causation (§ 6 I ELA) was raised. For it had stated that in any case the presumption would be rebutted. This provoked harsh criticism from the BGH.

First, as to § 6 II, the court applied a strict approach and required that the judge needed to establish specifically and in detail that the level imposed by law for the respective emissions was respected and that thus the plant was "properly operated". In this context the judge had also to take account of the evidence offered by the plaintiff that the plant was not run properly (this proof is presumably easier to adduce than to establish causation itself).

Secondly, as to § 7, the requirements were also considerably toughened. It does not suffice to refer in a general manner to circumstances that might constitute an alternative (to the emissions of the defendant's facility) cause of the injuries. On the contrary, the alternative cause must be identified and scrutinised specifically before the exception can apply. Again, the proof offered by the plaintiff may be relevant and indeed essential in this context (the lower courts had simply ignored it). (The judgment arrives at remarkably similar distinctions in the context of § 823 I BGB; however, the relevance of this is limited as soon as damages for pain and suffering will become more broadly available).

Right to Disclosure

In a highly unusual provision for German law, the ELA confers on claimants and defendants rights to obtain information pertinent to ELA claims. Generally, German civil procedure does not provide for party-initiated fact gathering. See John H Langbein, "The German Advantage in Civil Procedure", 52 *Univ. of Chi. L. Rev.* 823, 824 (1985). There is a substantive-law-based right to disclosure; but this remedy is a limited one. It will help the plaintiff to calculate the damages, for instance in the field of intellectual property law, where the holder of the infringed right may calculate damages on the basis of the profits made by the defendant.) §§ 8 and 9 ELA grant claimants a right to seek disclosures from facility operators and from administrative agencies. § 10 ELA grants defendant facility operators a similar right. In further provisions, these rights are made subject to other laws, more firmly imbedded in German legal tradition, providing for secrecy. See §§ 8 II, 9, and 10 II ELA.

Mandatory Insurance of ELA Appendix 2 Facilities

§ 19 ELA imposes a provision-of-coverage requirement for the facilities named in Appendix 2 of the Act. The operators of those facilities must ensure that compensation will be provided for losses caused by an environmental impact issuing from such a facility. This § 19 ELA coverage may take the form of (1) a liability insurance provided by an insurance company licensed to do business in Germany; (2) an indemnity agreement with the federal government or a state; or (3) an indemnity agreement with certain credit institutions if the security provided is comparable to an insurance coverage.

The mandatory insurance requirement of § 19 ELA will not come into effect until the Ministry of Justice issues a decree setting the terms of the insurance. The decree has not been issued as of 1 October 1993. When issued, it will establish, for example, what coverage limits will be required. If the recently issued genetic damage insurance regulation is any indication—and some believe that it is—the mandatory minimum amount of coverage might be between 10 million and 30 million DM. On the other hand, one cannot dismiss summarily the view that the special hazards posed by ELA Appendix 2 facilities may prompt the Ministry of Justice to require some higher amount of coverage, particularly since the ELA itself imposes a potentially far greater amount of liability.

The drafters of the decree will also resolve issues arising from the nature of mandatory insurance of ELA Appendix 2 facilities. For example, § 19 I ELA provides in part: "If a facility that is no longer in operation presents a special hazard, the competent public agency may order the person who operated the facility at the time of the ceasing of operations to provide for coverage for a period not to exceed ten years." Based on this provision, the Ministry of Justice could require facility operators to purchase an "extended reporting period" of up to ten years for claims based on damage caused by a facility's operations but discovered after operations cease.

Competence of the Court and Extraterritoriality

Generally, the proper German court for a claim in tort is the *forum delicti commissi*. See Code of Civil Procedure (*Zivilprozeßordnung*) § 32 (the proper court is the court of the district "in which the tort was committed").

This rule does not always designate a single forum in environmental cases because damage occurring in one forum may be due to pollution emitted in another. As with other multi-jurisdictional torts, the *locus delicti* (or "place where the tort occurs") can be either the place of the emission or the place where the claimant's damage is located. A claimant in a border-straddling case therefore may choose the more favourable of two proper courts.

However, the ELA abolished the claimant's choice of forum in domestic cases. The ELA amended the Code of Civil Procedure to provide that an ELA action must be brought in the district court where the facility emitting the pollution is located (§ 32a ZPO). If, however, the facility emitting the pollution is located beyond German borders, then this rule does not apply. Thus, in cases of emissions from abroad causing damage in Germany, the general procedural rule of claimant's choice of forum applies. (Note that Article 5 Nr. 3 of the Brussels Convention or Article 5 Nr. 3 of the Lugano Convention will have to be applied with priority.)

3. *Liability for Genetically Modified Products*

In 1990 the German Parliament also passed the Genetic Engineering Act (*Gentechnikgesetz, GenTG*); (BGBl 1990 I. 1080). This statute mainly regulates the conditions for the licensing of facilities that produce or research genetically modified products. But it also provides for a strict liability regime of such facilities in § 32 GenTG. Like the ELA the statute does not exclude liability for so called "development risks", i.e. risks that could not have been foreseen at the time when the product was put into circulation. Similarly, it is required that physical damage to one of the protected interests (life, health, property) has occurred (§ 32 VII GenTG). According to § 34 I GenTG if the damage was caused by a genetically modified product it is presumed that the damage was caused by the specific alteration of the genetic structure of that product. This presumption is displaced (§ 34 II GenTG) if the damage is likely to have been caused by some other property of the product. The legislator adopted here a far more cautious approach than under the ELA. It may be perhaps due to this restrictive approach that so far there seems to be only one reported case in which a plaintiff sought to establish liability under this provision. In LG Stuttgart NJW 1997, 1860 a farmer claimed the cost of effectuating (precautionary) examinations of the harmful effects of the genetically modified crop growing on the adjoining plot, which was administered by a polytechnic for research purposes. His claim failed as he could not establish that he actually suffered damage.

4. *Conclusion*

Comparatively speaking, Germany is a leader in matters of environmental liability legislation in Europe. Indeed, German law has provided for strict liability for a wide variety of environmentally-related damage since the WRA entered into force in 1960. Thus, German strict environmental liability pre-dates by many years the experience of the United Kingdom under the Environmental Protection Act 1990 and of the United States under the Comprehensive Environmental Restoration, Compensation and Liability Act of 1980 (CERCLA).

However, it must be noted that the patchwork of German environmental laws seems to result in a less comprehensive body of law than, say, in the United States, where civil liability, police power to order clean up, and enforcement provisions are combined in CERCLA. In Germany, civil liability for harm caused by pollution arises under entirely separate laws than does the power to order clean up. Whether or not this patchwork approach makes a substantial difference in the effectiveness of German law to regulate and deter pollution, as well as to compensate for pollution-related harm, is a far more difficult question, the answer to which will have to be based in part on future experience under the ELA.

(v) The products' liability regime (including the Pharmaceutical Products Act)

The Products Liability Act (*Produkthaftungsgesetz*) of 15 December 1989 follows in its structure largely the European Community's Directive of 25 July 1985 to which it aimed to give effect. Products to which it applies includes all moveables, excluding agricultural produce and animals. These products must, further be defective in the sense that they lack the security one is entitled to expect from them. The definition of defect is thus stricter than that found in § 434 BGB of the law of sales which defines the defect by reference to the reduced value or utility of the sold object. This liability envisaged by the statute falls primarily on the manufacturer (*Hersteller*): (§ 4). If more than one is implicated, their liability is *in solidum* (*gesamtschuldnerisch*: § 5). Clearly manufacturers of finished products, component parts, and new materials are subject to the new regime (§ 4 I of the 1989 Act reflecting Article 3(1) of the Directive). But the Directive (Article 3(1)) and the 1989 Act (§ 4 I) resolves an ambiguity that existed in German law prior to 1989 by subjecting anyone "who presents himself as the producer by affixing to a product his name, trade name, or other distinguishing feature". Dealers were also not *normally* liable for not testing products (BGH NJW 1980, 119), though there was a greater inclination to find dealer-importers liable given the difficulty of enforcing judgments against foreign manufacturers. Immunity, however, seemed the rule rather than the exception (BGH NJW 1987, 1009). Again, the new regime is stricter. § 4 III of the 1989 Act thus follows Article 3 III of the Directive, making the supplier liable under the Act whenever the producer cannot be identified.

The Act covers personal injury and damage to (other) property but not economic loss or the so-called, insidious spreading loss (*Weiterfresserschaden*). In the case of death, funeral expenses can also be claimed; and, in what is an interesting illustration of claimable ricochet damage, the statute expressly allows dependants to claim their own loss of support. (§ 7 2). But the victim has to carry himself the first DM 1,125 of his damage. The liability is avoided if one of the six possible defences mentioned in §1 of the statute applies; but all kinds of exemption clauses are null and void. § 13 of the statute, following Article 11 of the Directive, provides that an action under the new law will expire ten years after the producer has put the actual product that caused the harm into circulation. This is the absolute outer limit for § 12 I of the Act (again following the Directive: Article 10) provides for a limitation period of three years from the moment when the claimant knew or ought to have known of the damage (pending reform of the BGB: according to the new § 199 BGB the limitation period will start to run from the end of the year when the plaintiff knew or ought to have known).

The new statutory regime, expressly predicated on no fault liability, does not exclude in any way the application of other rules which may be more favourable to the plaintiff. Thus, if his harm is under the above-mentioned deductible of DM 1,125 an action based on the rules of the "ordinary" law may be the only remedy. The same is true if the exact opposite occurs namely, the plaintiff's damages exceed the maxima provided by the statute (or he wishes to claim money for his non-pecuniary harm such as his pain and suffering.) Recourse to the "ordinary" law here means the law of torts for the German courts, unlike their French counterparts, have not allowed an extension of the contractual remedies. But the obstacles that this might create in terms of fault have been considerably lessened by the presumptions of fault or the reversal of the onus of proof, which the German courts have introduced in a number of cases. The continued vitality of the "ordinary" law, described above in chapter two, remains obvious and, indeed, one is struck by the paucity of decisional law ten years after the coming into effect of the said Act. The reader must read the text of the statute (reproduced below at p. 872) in conjunction with what has been said in the earlier chapter.

Another way in which the plaintiff may choose to base his claim is on one of the other, related statutes of strict liability. The *Gentechnikgesetz* of 20 June 1990 is one (discussed in the previous section (iv)3) at the border line between environmental liability and product liability; the very long (over ninety paragraphs) Law of Pharmaceutical Products (*Arzneimittelgesetz* of 24 August 1976 (BGBl 1976 I. 2445, modified on 9 August 1994, BGBl 1994. I. 2071) is another. All of these statutes have there own "peculiarities" and complexities but, clearly, they represent too specialised an area of tort law practice to warrant a more detailed consideration in a comparative law textbook. For fuller details one must therefore consult such leading treatises as Deutsch, *Arztrecht und Arzneimittelrecht,* 2nd ed, (1991). The periodic literature is also large; and has grown as a result of the AIDS contaminated blood cases which made their appearance all over Europe in the mid 1990's and, *inter alia,* led most European courts to increase considerable their quantum of damages. (On the AIDS cases see: Durquet-Turek, "La responsabilité du fait des produits en Allemagne. Le problème de sang porteur du virus du SIDA", *Gaz, Pal.* 27–29 Sept. 1992, 7. On the case law in general after the coming into effect of the act see: Kullman, "Die Rechtsprechung des BGH zum Produkthaftungsrecht in der Jahren 1994–1995", *NJW* 1996, 18. On the effect of the AIDS cases on the level of damages, von Bar, *Festschrift Deutsch.*

SECTION B. CASES

1. § 831 BGB

Case 95

BUNDESGERICHTSHOF (SIXTH CIVIL SENATE) 7 OCTOBER 1975
NJW 1976, 46 = JZ 1975, 733

The plaintiff, the Gas–Electricity and Waterworks of the City of K, as holders of the right to draw water for their undertaking, claimed damages in respect of expenses incurred or likely to be incurred in the future as a result of the pollution of the water-table by petroleum waste. The plaintiff alleged that the fourth defendant, a petrochemical enterprise, had engaged the first defendant on the recommendation of the second defendant—an independent expert on damage by mineral oil and *de facto* manager of the first defendant—to carry and safely to dispose of their oil waste consisting mainly of a mixture of oil and water. In carrying out this assignment, the first defendant had installed ovens and barrels in a gravel-pit filled with refuse situated in an area which had been designated by the government as a protected water-zone for the use of the waterworks. No licence had been obtained, although the first defendant had been given to understand by the competent authorities that it would be forthcoming, if certain conditions were complied with.

On being alerted by an outsider that the oil waste had not been disposed of expertly, the plaintiff caused boreholes to be sunk and excavations to be made which disclosed that the water-table was covered by an extensive body of oil. In the action against the fourth defendant the plaintiff sought to be reimbursed for the expense of drilling observation wells and of collecting and examining samples of water and soil.

The District Court, by a separate judgment, rejected the claim against the fourth defendant while allowing the other actions to proceed. On appeal by the plaintiff, the Court of Appeal of Cologne quashed the judgment of the District Court and referred the case back. A second appeal was unsuccessful for the following

Reasons

I. The Court of Appeal has held that the fourth defendant is liable in tort (§ 823 I BGB), as well as on the ground that the plaintiff had acted on his behalf in his interests and in accordance with his actual or presumed intention (§§ 683, 677, 670 BGB), to pay the expenses claimed by the plaintiff if further evidence to be obtained by the District Court reveals that the first defendant has contaminated the water-table to the plaintiff's detriment by disposing inexpertly of the waste entrusted to him.

1. The plaintiff's pleadings do not support any liability of the fourth defendant according to the provision of § 22 of the Water Preservation Act (WHG) which establishes extensive strict liability for such expenses in the instances enumerated there.

(*a*) § 22 I WHG cannot serve as a basis of the claim, if for no other reason, because no act of the fourth defendant was objectively capable of allowing the waste produce to seep into the water-table [references]. The fourth defendant has not even envisaged and accepted the possibility that the oil waste might be disposed of in this manner nor were the measures taken by him for the destruction of the waste in fact capable of allowing the waste to seep into the water. The circumstance that by handing the waste over to the first defendant he enabled the latter to dispose of it improperly, contrary to a contractual arrangement, does not suffice to attract liability under § 22 I WHG. This provision was not intended to create such an extensive liability for the unauthorised conduct of third parties . . .

(b) The fourth defendant cannot be held liable under § 22 II WHG because the noxious substances infiltrated into the water-table from the *first defendant's* installation but not from that of the fourth defendant from which they had already been carried away.

2. Liability for damage caused by the fact that waste materials seeped into the water-table is not, however, confined to the situations enumerated in § 22 WHG. This provision was intended to reinforce the protection against interference with the quality of water by introducing strict liability; in the absence of an express statement to this effect this pro-vision, like any other establishing strict liability, does not preclude claims based on tort or on quasi-contract [acting for another without authorization; references].

The Court of Appeal was also correct when considering this ground of liability that the right of the plaintiff enjoyed by virtue of §§ 46 ff., 200, 203 of the Prussian Water Act was not affected by subsequent legislation [references]. The right to extract water is an absolute right in the meaning of § 823 I to be respected by everybody [reference], capable of being violated by the pollution by noxious substances to the water-table in the area of the intake operated by the plaintiff's waterworks [reference]. The Court of Appeal was right in holding consequently that the fourth defendant must prevent as far as possible any such interferences with the right to extract water by waste products and that if he fails to act in accordance with the care required in daily life he must, *inter alia*, pay for the necessary measure to avert the danger to the supply of drinking-water by the water-works as a result of a pollution of the water-table [references].

II. 1. As stated, the producer of such industrial waste which is a source of danger to the environment in the absence of special measures is liable, irrespective of other special rules of conduct and of the legal consequences resulting from their infringement under § 823 I BGB, to take the necessary steps in the execution of the general duty of care to safe-guard the public in general [*Verkehrssicherungspflicht*] derived from § 823 I BGB to avoid that the (potential) danger results in damage to third parties. Just as the producer of goods is subject to this duty in respect of goods introduced into commerce [references] the pro-ducer of industrial waste must also seek to avert within the limits of what is practicable any usual dangers emanating from by-products "of negative value". It is irrelevant in this connection that they are not for sale, as is also that their manufacture is allowed. The fact alone determines that the manufacturer has created the source of danger and must render it safe for third parties within the limits of what is possible and can be expected of him. This general principle of the law of tort [reference] has its counterpart, as regards objec-tive imputation, in the maxim which also dominates in public law relating to the envi-ronment to the effect that he who causes damage to the environment must also pay for it [references] . . .

2. The Court of Appeal has found, without contravening the law, that the waste con-taining petroleum constitutes a special danger for the maintenance of the water-table if

it is stored or destroyed inexpertly. Given the danger to the environment, especially having regard to the quantity of petroleum waste products produced by the fourth defendant (about 570 tonnes in approximately two months), strict care was required in storing and disposing of it. The Court of Appeal stressed correctly in this connection that a harmless disposal of the waste was technically difficult and therefore demanded a special method and a special installation for destroying it if the danger of inexpert or incomplete destruction was to be avoided; and that at least greater storage capacity and longer storage was necessary with its attendant perils.

3. The Court was right, moreover, in holding that the fourth defendant was not obliged to store, and dispose of, the waste himself, but could delegate this task to an independent enterprise which could not be regarded as its aide in the meaning of § 831 [*editor's note*: the judgment refers wrongly to § 832] BGB in the absence of a relationship of dependency. In such circumstances, the fourth defendant was, however, bound to see to it that the necessary safety measures were taken properly in order to prevent damage to third parties by the disposal of the oil waste.

(*a*) Naturally the supervision of a specialized enterprise is limited by the need for a trusting collaboration, and by the independence and the immunity from orders of the agent; it would mean straining excessively the requirements of care in the face of economic and technical reality if the principal were asked to control at every step the manner in which the agent operates. On the other hand, those subject to duties of care to safeguard the public in general are not always released of their responsibility for the sources of danger which they have created if another is equally bound to take safeguarding action by virtue of a contract. Instead they may be obliged, if the circumstances so require—as for instance in an acutely dangerous situation [reference: fireworks] or if serious reasons exist for doubting whether the agent will take sufficient account of the dangers and the need to safeguard against them [reference: Mosel Lock construction]— to control the work by the enterprise entrusted with it or to intervene in case of necessity [reference]. In particular, the duty is not discharged if an enterprise is employed which does not offer a sufficient guarantee that the necessary safety measures will be taken; for in those circumstances the delegation to such an enterprise of the duty to safeguard the public only increases the danger of damages to third parties. In such a case those subject to a duty of care to safeguard the public in general cannot plead that by the interposition of an independent enterprise their power controlling the source of danger has been curtailed. They had the opportunity to select the agent carefully; the more their influence is limited by the independence of the enterprise to which the task is delegated, the more the duty to select the enterprise carefully must be taken seriously. They are liable if the danger materializes, since they themselves brought it about by employing an unreliable enterprise.

(*b*) The appellant argues that petroleum waste is no more dangerous than the petroleum produced by the fourth defendant. Since the fourth defendant cannot be held liable for damage caused by an inappropriate use of the petroleum after it has been delivered to his customers he cannot be liable either if an enterprise engaging in the destruction of waste employed by him disposes of the waste in an improper manner contrary to a contractual arrangement.

This argument cannot be accepted—at least in this generalization. It need not be decided whether and to what extent the manufacturer of goods can also be held liable for damage to third parties when the product is used contrary to its intended use, if the man-ufacturer ought in this respect to have had doubts about the reliability of the customer [references]. In determining and delimiting the respective spheres of liability it is deci-sive that the waste incidental to the manufacture of petroleum and its disposal are, so to say, the "negative aspect" of the manufacture and that, according to the general view, its destruction is and remains a matter for the manufacturer, while the "destruction" of the petroleum is in the hands of the customer according to its purpose. If a manufacturer decides to engage in the production of petroleum, he must provide for safe destruction of waste, the more so since this normally requires special measures; certainly resort may also be had to his liability in private law if somebody is damaged by the waste. If the man-ufacturer employs a third party for the disposal of the waste, he complies with his *own* duty to safeguard the public in general through the interposition of the third party . . .

4. No legal objections exist against the finding of the Court of Appeal that in the course of the enquiries, which were necessary and could be expected to be carried out before delegating the task, the fourth defendant should have realised that the enterprise employed by him did not at the time offer a sufficient guarantee that the waste would be disposed of safely and that, if the enterprise should have disposed of it in the way the plaintiff alleges, dangers did materialise for which the fourth defendant is liable, not having used sufficient care in selecting the enterprise.

(*a*) The Court of Appeal is correct in law when it bases its critical appreciation of the first defendant's action on the primitive conditions in which the installation, established provisionally only, was operated . . . This method did not comply with the provisions of § 34 II 1 WHG according to which even outside a water protection zone materials may only be stored or deposited so as not to create the fear that the water-table may become polluted or that its quality may be affected in any other way. The fact that the installa-tion was set up on a foundation of clay which had been spread over the refuse did not exclude with the necessary degree of certainty a pollution of the water-table—by seeping oil—if only as a result of mixing it with oil [reference], the more so since it was uncer-tain whether the layer was resistant to water and fluids throughout [reference]. For this reason special measures had to be taken for the protection of the water-table so as to prevent effectively that oil should escape because the containers begin to leak as a result of corrosion, of defective materials or construction, or in consequence of spilling in the course of filling or emptying [references] . . .

At all events the fourth defendant should have realised, when he gave the order, that the installation lacked the simplest safety mechanism for protecting the water-table and that in its actual state the harmless destruction of the waste was not guaranteed, keeping in mind the amount of waste to be destroyed. If so, he should have entertained doubts about the reliability of the management of the enterprise which has so flagrantly disre-garded the simplest requirements of safety. In view of such manifest flagrant omissions the fourth defendant could also have foreseen that the first defendant in destroying the oil waste would not seriously consider the protection of the water-table . . .

(*b*) Having regard to its duty to safeguard the public in general [*Verkehrssicherungspflicht*], the fourth defendant was obliged to inform himself of the operational conditions of the first defendant before entrusting him with the waste oil. The fact that at the time malpractices in disposing of industrial waste had not seriously concerned the public and the industries involved, as the appellant contends, does not relieve the fourth defendant; given his experience he must have been aware of the possibility and the resulting danger of an improper destruction of such waste . . .

In agreement with the Court of Appeal it must be held that the fourth defendant could not rely on the recommendations of the second defendant, even if he got to know him as a reliable expert on the prevention of damage by oil and that he had been recommended as such by the water authorities and by the department head of the fourth defendant's insurers. Whether the same considerations would apply also if the second defendant had not been personally connected with the first defendant need not be decided here. At any rate . . . the fourth defendant knew that the second defendant had founded the enterprise together with his wife, who was only nominally the manager, and that in fact he managed the affairs of the first defendant himself.

III. 1. In view of those considerations, the Court of Appeal had held correctly that if the fourth defendant had applied the standard of care required of him, he should not have left it to the first defendant to dispose of the waste, at least not without taking special measures for controlling the destruction. Consequently, the fourth defendant is liable, certainly from the angle of damages due according to § 823 BGB, to compensate the plaintiff for the expenses necessarily incurred in restricting the dangers to the supply of drinking-water, in so far as they are caused by the alleged inexpert operations of the first defendant and would not have occurred if the fourth defendant had properly complied with his duty of care to safeguard the public in general.

Case 96

BUNDESGERICHTSHOF (SEVENTH CIVIL SENATE) 30 OCTOBER 1967
BGHZ 49, 19 = NJW 1968, 391 = VersR 1968, 92

The plaintiff finances hire-purchase agreements of motor-cars by providing loans for the purchasers. The money representing the loans is paid direct to the vendors in discharge of the purchase price. The plaintiff only grants a loan if title to the motor vehicle is transferred to him by way of security, if the seller becomes a surety, and if a report concerning the purchaser's creditworthiness is favourable.

The defendant carries on the business of an information agency with branches in sixteen cities of the Federal Republic. The branch in Bonn was managed from 1955 onwards by Z, its "commercial representative" (until he died in March 1962). For many years Z provided the motor car dealer F—who has since lost his fortune and was adjudicated bankrupt at his request—with "information concerning the financial standing" of about 1500 clients of F. This information was supplied on paper with the name of the defendant at the letter-head. In twenty-six cases the information was invented; the persons did not exist; in five other cases the persons existed, but the information was too favourable. In these twenty-six cases Z wrote the letters at short notice without having engaged in any enquiries or examination, relying exclusively on the information supplied by F, and concealed their existence from the defendant. Using these letters, F deceived the plaintiff into making him pay over the "loan". The District Court found, and it is now undisputed, that Z was aware of the danger to the plaintiff's assets as a result of his conduct, but that he took the risk.

The plaintiff claims from the defendant damages in respect of the loss, alleged to be DM 201,145.08, caused by F and Z. The defendant disputes the claim both as to its basis and its extent. He also pleads contributory negligence . . .

The District Court and the Court of Appeal of Frankfurt rejected the claim. Upon a second appeal the claim was admitted in principle and the case referred back to ascertain the amount for the following

Reasons

The plaintiff argues that the defendant is liable under § 31 BGB for the torts committed by Z to the detriment of the plaintiff. The Court of Appeal denies this.

1. It holds that Z is not the defendant's representative appointed in accordance with the statutes in the meaning of § 31 BGB. He lacked the necessary independence in his dealings with third parties and a sphere of administration of his own within functions of management of the defendant.

These arguments are not free from error in law. The facts as found by the Court of Appeal compel the conclusion that Z was the representative of the defendant in the meaning of § 31 BGB.

(*a*) According to this provision, a legal entity is responsible for the damage to a third party by its representative, appointed in accordance with the statutes, as a result of an act "in the execution of the duties allotted to him" which engages liability to pay damages. The legal concept of "representative appointed in accordance with the statutes" has been extended increasingly in practice and in the literature. The Court of Appeal has overlooked this.

Representatives appointed in accordance with the statutes are not only those persons whose activities are envisaged by the statutes of a legal entity, nor need they possess the right to represent the entity in legal transactions. It is not necessary either that the range of tasks falls within the managerial administration of the legal entity. It suffices if the representative is entrusted with handling important and essential functions of the legal entity by the general system and functioning of the enterprise [references]. In such circumstances it would be inequitable to permit the legal entity to exonerate itself in reliance on § 831 BGB.

(*b*) These conditions were fulfilled in the present case as regards Z.

(*aa*) It is undisputed that he managed the office of the defendant in Bonn as a "one-man business" in complete independence. With the permission of the defendant he described the office as a "branch" of the latter. In agreement with the defendant he used the latter's business stationery and reference forms and a stamp to the same effect. Thus, in his dealings with third parties he clearly did not act as an "independent commercial agent" on behalf of the defendant; the Court of Appeal was wrong in holding that in fact he managed the defendant's office in Bonn as an independent agency of information.

(*bb*) In view of the agreed conduct in dealings with third parties, it is irrelevant that, as between Z and the defendant, their legal relationship was governed by the "contract of agency" of 11 August 1955 in accordance with the law relating to commercial agents. This does not rule out the conclusion that in his relations with third parties Z was the representative of the defendant in accordance with § 31 BGB.

(*cc*) By providing references on paper bearing the letter-head of the defendant, Z made the statements contained therein *in the name of the defendant*. Nothing in these letters indicates that these are not statements of the defendant, but only of Z. Obviously, the value of these references for the recipient consisted in the fact that they emanated from the reputable defendant, a big information agency known throughout the world. It is not disputed that the defendant knew of this general practice of Z, although the particular thirty-one "references" which form the basis of the present claim were concealed from him.

(*dd*) The Court of Appeal has found that the defendant himself engages in the business of an information agency, that he has set up and maintains a network of information offices, that it provides these offices with the sources from which to draw their information and permits these offices to use its business name. In so doing it has, to a wide extent, delegated to the managers of its "offices" the independent discharge of its characteristic functions (to provide information). Thus, the defendant has also delegated to Z the task of supplying references independently in the area of Bonn. It need not be stressed that the provision of references on creditworthiness by an information agency is a very responsible activity; if carried out carelessly much damage can be caused, as the present case shows clearly.

2. By way of a subsidiary argument the Court of Appeal denies that the defendant is responsible for Z under § 31 BGB on the ground that his torts had not been committed "in the execution of the functions allotted to him", but only on their "occasion". This conclusion, too, is wrong having regard to the facts as found by the Court of Appeal.

(*a*) An act is done in the execution of the duties entrusted to a person if it remains within the range of measures which constitute the execution of the functions entrusted to him. The act must be in close objective connection with those measures. The liability is not excluded if the order is exceeded or the power is abused. An international tortious act may well be committed in close objective connection with the allotted functions; this is the case, in particular, if the tortious act violates the allotted specific duties [references].

(*b*) The defendant refers to the decision [references]. However, that case must be distinguished. A credit agent who had been entrusted with a single sale of a motor vehicle had falsely represented to a third party that the order had been carried out, in order to get hold of the moneys involved. In so doing, the agent had severed himself from his allotted range of functions objectively as well. As is pointed out in that decision, the conclusion would have been different if he had sold the vehicle intentionally on his own account and had embezzled the purchase price; this act would still have been sufficiently connected with the functions allotted to him. This is not the case here. It is true that Z gave false references, but they were references and thus he operated exactly within his real sphere of functions. The close objective connection is not destroyed by the fact that he exceeded his powers arbitrarily and intentionally illegally.

3. The Court of Appeal relies on an additional subsidiary argument to the effect that the plaintiff's contributory negligence excludes altogether a possible obligation of the defendant to pay damages . . .

The judgment of the Court of Appeal does not show clearly whether this statement refers only to liability under § 831 BGB or whether the Court of Appeal also wishes thereby to rule out any claim under § 31 BGB which, as was shown here, is alone in issue.

If the latter should be the case, the decision of the Court of Appeal cannot be approved. Faced with intentional acts of representatives appointed in accordance with the statutes in accordance with § 31 BGB, contributory negligence on the part of the injured party can never be regarded as so serious as to preclude a claim for damages altogether.

Case 97

BUNDESGERICHTSHOF (SIXTH CIVIL SENATE) 6 OCTOBER 1970
NJW 1971, 31 = VERSR 1970, 1157

For the purposes of his business the defendant owns a lorry and a lorry-train consisting of a lorry with a trailer. In addition to a number of drivers employed by him, he is assisted by his brother. He instructed the latter on 16 June 1965 to fetch 10 tonnes of coal. The brother used the lorry-train and not the single lorry, which would have required two journeys. Since the trailer was parked on the market in K, he fetched it from there and drove the empty vehicle to the place where the coal was located. On the way he had to pass through a village where the road made a sharp bend to the left. Since the road was wet he braked. As a result the trailer skidded on to the left side of the road and collided with the plaintiff's car. The plaintiff suffered severe injuries, and his car was badly damaged.

The defendant's brother was fined for negligently causing bodily harm. In these proceedings an expert stated that the brakes of the trailer were too weak with the result that it tended to skid on a wet surface and to leave its side of the road. In these circumstances the defendant insurer refused to pay for the entire damage and has only accepted liability in favour of the plaintiff up to DM 150,000 in accordance with §§ 158 ff. of the Act concerning Contracts of Insurance.

The plaintiff sued the defendant's brother and the defendant claiming damages amounting to DM 24,216 and asking for a declaration that both brothers are also liable to compensate him for any other damage arising or likely to arise in connection with the accident. The plaintiff also sued the defendant's brother for damages for pain and suffering.

The District Court, dealing with part of the claim, allowed damages for pain and suffering as well as DM 14,363 in respect of general damages and reserved its decision as regards the remaining DM 9,853. In addition it granted the declaration asked for by the plaintiff.

After the brother of the defendant had paid the sum of DM 14,363, the defendant lodged an appeal limited to the grant of the declaration that he was also liable to the plaintiff in respect of future damage. The Court of Appeal of Düsseldorf rejected the appeal. A second appeal was unsuccessful for the following

Reasons

B. . . .

II. Contrary to the contentions of the appellant, the Court of Appeal applied § 831 BGB correctly.

1. It is undisputed that the defendant, in asking his brother to fetch the coal with the motor vehicle, appointed him to execute a function. The appellant questions, however, whether the brother of the defendant acted illegally in the meaning of § 831 BGB [reference] and argues that the brother had been engaged in a "frolic of his own"

[*Schwarzfahrt*] for which the defendant was not liable. In both respects the Court of Appeal was right.

(*a*) The brother of the defendant has injured the plaintiff illegally. Even if the test employed here is not that of an "effect tort", i.e. whether the plaintiff was injured, the defendant must prove at least that his brother observed "proper traffic practices" when he passed the sharp bend with his lorry-train. This is not, however, the case, even if he had not hit the plaintiff's motor car. If a motor vehicle skids and bars the road, it cannot be said that the driver—whose personal culpability is not immediately relevant in applying § 831 BGB—drove in accordance with "proper driving practices". Even if the defendant's brother had examined the brakes of the trailer before starting and had found them in good order, it has not been shown and proved that his manner of driving at the time of the accident complied with the legal regulation of traffic to such a degree that it could not be condemned as illegal. This would only be the case if the brother of the defendant had acted in a manner which complied entirely with the demands and prohibitions of the traffic regulations [reference]. In the present case the question remains open, to the detriment of the defendant, whether his brother entered the sharp bend at an excessive speed in contravention of § 9 of the Road Traffic Act with the result that despite the dangerous wet road he had to apply the brakes of the lorry-train—with the behaviour of which he was not familiar in any case, as the defendant alleges. The Court of Appeal is therefore justified in stating that the insufficient operation of the trailer's brakes had been a "contributory cause" of the accident.

(*b*) It is true that the reversal of the burden of proof laid down by § 831 BGB only affects the principal if the person entrusted with the execution of a function has caused the damage in the course of executing the function, and not merely on its occasion. A direct intrinsic connection must exist as to manner and purpose between the function entrusted to him, on the one hand, and the injurious act on the other hand [references]. Contrary to the objections raised by the appellant, the Court of Appeal has correctly found that such a connection exists.

It must be admitted that the keeper of a motor vehicle is not liable for a "frolic of his own" by the driver against his will; the principle is that he is not liable either under § 7 of the Road Traffic Act or under § 831 BGB [references]. However, in the present case the brother of the defendant was not on a "frolic of his own"; he had undertaken the journey not against his brother's will, but with his consent; both the time of the journey as well as the route chosen by him corresponded to the latter's intention. It is true that the principal may not be liable in certain circumstances for the faults of his assistant if the damage would not have occurred had the driver followed a certain prohibition imposed by his principal. This Division has so held in a case in which the driver, in disregard of a prohibition, had given a ride to an acquaintance who was injured in an accident [references]. The appellant is mistaken in contending that the present case is similar. In the former case, the injured party had accepted a lift by a driver on a journey on which only goods were to be transported; in the present case the third party was injured not in the course of making use of the vehicle, but as a road-user. It must be assumed in favour of the defendant that his brother fetched the trailer which caused the accident in disregard of the express prohibition by the defendant and connected it. According to a constant practice, however, acts of a person entrusted with the execution of certain functions do not fall outside the range of these functions even if he contravened the principal's orders intentionally and on his own [references]. In the present case, when the brother of the defendant hitched on the trailer contrary to his orders, he did so in order to avoid having to make two journeys, and thus in order to carry out the task more quickly. Therefore this, and in particular the journey, in the course of which the accident occurred, stood in a relation not only of adequate causality but also, which is decisive, of intrinsic connection with his order to fetch 10 tonnes of coal. The fact is irrelevant that the defendant, as he alleges, forbade his brother to take the trailer because he did not wish to entrust him with driving the lorry with a trailer on the grounds of his advanced age.

Case 98

BUNDESGERICHTSHOF (THIRD CIVIL SENATE) 14 JANUARY 1954
BGHZ 12, 94 = NJW 1954, 913

The plaintiff, who was insured by M, while riding his motor cycle at night collided with one of four telegraph poles which were lying across the road and suffered a severe fracture of his skull. The District Court allowed his claim for damages, but the Court of Appeal of Frankfurt rejected it. Upon a second appeal the judgment below was quashed and the case referred back for the following.

Reasons

I. The defendant, the Federal Post, is only liable for the consequences of the accident if the case falls within the ambit of a particular statutory provision. The law in force at present does not provide for liability "according to general principles"; in particular it does not contain a principle that everybody is liable to make good any damage caused by his property unless he can prove that he is not to be blamed for the fact that the location of the property imperilled others. Absolute strict liability of the defendant in respect of the telephone lines maintained by it deserves even less consideration.

II. The plaintiff complains that the defendant did not maintain its installations in a safe condition for traffic and that its employees did not take measures for removing the recent obstacle to traffic. None of these considerations is sufficient to hold the defendant liable under § 839 BGB and Article 131 of the Constitution of Weimar; even in the case of public operations both the duty to maintain an installation adequately for traffic purposes as well as the duty to remove sudden obstacles to traffic are obligations which do not arise out of a special relationship of protection between the public authority and a third party who happens to have been affected accidentally; the real reason is that objectively a dangerous situation has been created. Where such obligations to take safeguarding measures are concerned public corporations are not to be treated differently from private persons, even if the activity in question may bear the character of an act *jure imperii*. The liability of the public corporation is therefore governed by §§ 823, 831 BGB. Following the practice of the Reichsgericht, this Division in its decision [reference] has given detailed reasons for so holding; the observations made there as to the duty to safeguard the public in respect of a public path apply here as well. The appellant is wrong in relying in this connection on the argument that according to the practice of the courts the activity of the Federal Post has been regarded increasingly as being exercised *jure imperii*. The appellant is also wrong in referring to the decision of the Reichsgericht [reference]; it is there stated expressly that the principle set out here applies also to damage caused by the laying of telephone cables; as regards "third-party outsiders" no liability arises under § 839 BGB; liability in the exercise of official functions to protect a third party against damage exists only in favour of those who are obliged, by virtue of the Law concerning Telegraph Lines to suffer interference with their property. However, this is not the case.

III. The Court of Appeal has held correctly that the defendant is not liable for having failed to remove the fallen telegraph poles from the highway in time.

1. The objection of the appellant to the conclusion of the Court of Appeal that the defendant is not liable under § 831 is unfounded.

(*a*) According to a constant practice no liability arises under § 831 BGB, even in the absence of separate evidence in exoneration, if the employee has acted in such a manner as any carefully selected person would have done [reference].

(*b*) The technical supervisor acted, however, as any other employee, including he who acts with the necessary care, would have acted. It may be that the night in question was stormy and that this could also be observed at the Post Office in L. It cannot be said, however, that in these circumstances an employee of the Post Office, acting with the necessary care, on noticing a partial disruption of the telephone lines would have dispatched immediately a repair column during the night. Since only seven out of thirty lines failed to function, it could not be assumed that poles had fallen and that the lines had collapsed. The defendant has stated, and the plaintiff has not disputed it, that such interruption had also occurred previously due to the fact that damp had penetrated the cables and because 'lead fatigue' had affected the strength of the cables. The parties agree that during the night when the accident happened the weather was wet. It is understandable, therefore, that the technical supervisor also attributed this disruption of the lines to the causes which had been observed previously. It must be conceded to the defendants that little purpose would have been served in attempting to remedy this disruption if a repair column had been sent on a search errand during the night. The Act on Telegraph Lines, too, assumes, as § 12 III shows, that disruptions are normally dealt with during daytime only.

2. In these circumstances, the appellant is wrong in contending that the telephone business had been supervised inadequately by the defendant and that it was therefore liable for the damage—directly in accordance with § 823 BGB—thus ruling out the need to prove that one of its organs had been at fault. Such liability has been held by the practice to exist, e.g. if a public corporation has failed to take any measures at all which serve to control its installations in order to ensure the safety of traffic [references]. During the night from 15 to 16 February 1948, too, an employee of the Post Office had been charged with supervising the functioning of the telephone lines. It need not be decided whether the technical supervisor could be regarded as an "organ" of the defendant in the meaning of §§ 89, 30, 31 BGB; the Court of Appeal has rightly denied that he acted negligently. The observations made above in respect of the question whether a carefully chosen employee would have acted in the same way have shown that he did not act culpably. It has not been demonstrated either that during the night when the accident occurred another employee of the defendant or one of his organs negligently omitted to attend to the telephone lines. No claims arise therefore on the ground that the obstacle to traffic had not been discovered and removed in time.

IV. The plaintiff also bases his claim on the ground that the defendant had not maintained its telephone poles properly; the accident had occurred because the storm had felled a rotten pole which by means of the telephone cable had in turn pulled down the other poles which had been secured inadequately. This allegation has not been considered entirely satisfactorily by the court below.

1. The Court of Appeal does not consider this allegation as forming a basis of the claim because in its opinion the fact has not been proved and is incapable of being proved that the accident actually occurred in the way alleged by the plaintiff; the possibility should not be ruled out that an American lorry had collided with a pole and had thus caused the collapse of the telephone lines.

In so far as the appellant argues that the Court of Appeal had misunderstood the burden of proof, seeing that faced with an actual situation in violation of the traffic rules the defendant bore the burden of proof "that it is not responsible for the dangerous condition of its installation", his contention cannot be accepted. It is for the plaintiff to prove that the damage was caused by faulty maintenance of the installation not only where the claim is based on § 823 BGB but also in the case of § 836 BGB [reference]. This follows from the principle that a claimant must prove that the factual conditions exist for the creation of a right.

2. The Court of Appeal overlooks, however, that the defendant may be liable even if an American lorry had collided with the pole, thus leading to the collapse of the telephone lines. The Court of Appeal is of the opinion that the possibility of the lorry by colliding with it made a strong impact on one of the poles is to be ruled out. In the absence of any traces on one of the collapsed poles, experience shows that, if at all, the collision would only have had a weak impact on the pole. If, however, even a slight impact with the pole could have resulted in a complete collapse of a part of the installation, the possibility would exist that inadequate maintenance of the installation was in fact a contributory cause of the accident. It must be considered whether the rotten condition of one of the poles, conceded by the defendant itself, was so considerable and, apart from this the other poles had been secured insufficiently so as to render them no longer safe for traffic. It need not be decided whether the storm or the lorry broke the pole. Neither does a natural event create liability nor does the act of a third party exclude liability in all cases. This principle applies also in respect of § 836 BGB. In dealing with the question of causality, the determining factor is whether the structure was so inadequately maintained or secured that even a minor impact, to be taken into consideration as normal, could lead to its collapse. The "last" cause may perhaps never be ascertained, and yet liability may not be excluded for this reason.

If upon further examination it should appear that the telephone poles were deficient in the sense indicated here, the defendant would be liable under § 823 BGB in conjunction with §§ 89, 31, 30, unless it proves that none of the organs is to blame; the fact alone that another dangerous situation was allowed to persist is a sufficient indication that the care was lacking which is required for safeguarding traffic . . .

In view of the special features of this case, liability under § 823 BGB would exist if it should be established that the telephone lines were inadequately maintained, unless the defendant can exonerate himself. In these circumstances it is unnecessary to discuss the question raised by the appellant as to whether liability under § 836 BGB can arise even if the damage has not been caused by the "mobile force" of the collapsing structure but by the fact that the collapsed structure is allowed to lie on a road which carried public traffic.

§ 836 does not involve a different type of case but only a reversal of the burden of proof [reference]. Thus § 836 can be disregarded if within the framework of § 823 BGB the debtor is called upon exceptionally to prove that he is not to blame.

Case 99

BUNDESGERICHTSHOF (SIXTH CIVIL SENATE) 10 JULY 1954
NJW 1956, 1106

The plaintiff was a patient in the neurological clinic of the Municipal Hospital in B between 25 May 1951 and 9 February 1952. He suffered from introspective-endogenous depressions. On 24 May 1951 he received electro-shock treatment and on 28 May 1951 he underwent a lumbar puncture. On 6 and 7 June the electro-shock treatment was repeated. In the course of it he suffered a fracture of the twelfth vertebra from which he recovered after having lain in plaster for six and a half months. Since then his right leg is paralysed and he suffers from intestinal and heart trouble. The medical expert of the Social Insurance Office of the Land regards him as incapable of work. The Court of Appeal of Bremen allowed the plaintiff's claim for damages against the hospital of the defendant. A second appeal was unsuccessful for the following.

Reasons

The Court of Appeal has found that the plaintiff entered the clinic of the defendant as a patient supported by social security. It has held correctly that in these cases the legal relationship between the municipal hospital or clinic and the patient is of a private law nature. According to a constant practice of the Reichsgericht, followed by the Federal Supreme Court [references], the reception of a patient supported by social security creates a contract with the hospital in favour of the patient with the result that the patient acquires a right of his own to be treated expertly. If a doctor, who has been charged with the treatment of such a patient supported by social security commits a mistake culpably, the defendant as owner of the clinic is liable according to § 278 BGB for the mistake of the doctor appointed by him to perform the duties of the latter.

On the other hand, as the Court of Appeal has pointed out, a claim for pain and suffering against a doctor in charge on the ground of assault causing bodily harm cannot be based on § 278 BGB, but only on § 831 BGB, unless direct liability under § 823 BGB is in issue.

II. 1. The appellant is wrong in alleging that the plaintiff had validly consented to the electro-shock treatment and that this consent could only have been annulled in accordance with §§ 161 ff. BGB. This view would only be correct if

(*a*) the plaintiff had been aware of the typical dangers of electro-shock treatment and, in particular, of a fracture of the spine and if with knowledge of these dangers his consent had included these factors, or

(*b*) the doctor in charge could so understand and interpret the general conduct of the plaintiff in the particular circumstances of the case and having regard to the views current in human relations between reasonable people that the plaintiff was aware in outline of the dangers connected with shock treatment and that he had accepted the risk.

As to (*a*): It is a constant practice in cases where a passenger in a motor vehicle is injured that an exemption from liability based on the assumption of a risk can only be presumed if the victim went on the journey conscious of the possibility of danger and thus consented expressly or tacitly to a possible danger arising out of the driver's conduct, whether culpable or not. Such a consent does not include dangers which the victim merely ought to have noticed [references]. Similarly, the Reichsgericht has pointed out [reference] that physical treatment by a doctor involving the corporeal inviolability of a patient is only covered by the contract and not illegal in so far as the consent of the patient extends to it. According to the Reichsgericht, [reference] before applying any physical treatment the doctor must make certain of the patient's consent, which must be done based upon correct ideas concerning the nature and consequences of the treatment, even if naturally it does not cover all details. In [reference] the Reichsgericht upheld this view. The Federal Supreme Court has affirmed this view [reference], even if in the case before it the existence and the extent of the consent was not in issue, but whether it was void on the ground of illegality or contrary to *bonos mores*. These principles must be applied here. The Court of Appeal agrees [reference] . . . by requiring that a valid consent presupposes that the person who gives it knew the significance and the extent of the physical treatment by the doctor, at least in outline. No objections can therefore be raised against its legal conclusions.

As to (*b*): As the Reichsgericht [reference] and the Federal Supreme Court [references] have stated, the declared and not the subjective intention of the plaintiff counts. The Court of Appeal has found that the doctors administering the treatment assumed that the plaintiff had consented. However, according to the Court of Appeal they should have realised that real consent was lacking. They had therefore assumed negligently that consent had been given. This conclusion cannot be faulted in law. The court has thereby correctly made it clear that all the plaintiff's declarations, oral, tacit, or to be presumed, could not and should not have been regarded by the doctors treating him, having regard to the attendant circumstances and according to good faith, as constituting a valid consent which included the possible dangers connected with the physical treatment . . .

2. The appellant denies that, as the Court of Appeal held, he was obliged to inform the plaintiff of the possible consequences of the electro-shock treatment. The Court of Appeal, in examining whether the doctor was under a duty to give information, rightly relied on the practice of the Reichsgericht according to which the substance and the extent of the duty to inform a patient is influenced by the degree of danger which the physical treatment affecting corporeal inviolability involves.

The duty to respect the freedom to allow physical treatment affecting corporeal inviolability cannot be denied on the ground that the relationship between patient and doctor requires the use of a special standard. It is the ethical task of a doctor to listen to the patient and to inform him in detail about undesirable side-effects of the therapy to be used. If the right of personality is properly appreciated, it cannot be said that this appreciation discloses a tendency, flowing from a mistaken notion of freedom, to enmesh in a network of legal provisions the special relationship between doctor and patient. On the contrary, this duty to give information concerning the possible injurious consequences of the therapy is part of a doctor's calling which must not fail to pay regard to personality and corporeal inviolability. It is no answer to point out that in certain cases it may perhaps be advisable not to enlighten the patient. It is unnecessary here to determine the extent of the duty to provide information as regards diagnosis and therapy and what the doctor can and must say, for in the present case no information was given at all. The Court of Appeal has also rightly referred to the decision of the Reichsgericht [reference] where it is stated that as a matter of principle the individual must remain free to determine the fate of his body even in relation to his doctor [reference]. Naturally the doctor would attempt to spare the patient injurious fear and not to remind him unnecessarily of the possible serious consequences of his illness. However, this consideration had to give precedence to the necessity for the doctor to ensure before any physical treatment is begun that the patient has given clear consent, based upon accurate ideas concerning the kind and the consequences of the corporeal treatment. In so far as the information provided in order to obtain the patient's consent led to a lowering of his mood or even of his health in general, it was an inevitable disadvantage which had to be accepted.

It is unnecessary here to discuss the cases decided by the courts concerning physical treatment without consent where danger lies in delay, for this situation does not arise here. Every doctor knows that physical interference with the inviolability of the patient against his will is not permitted. A doctor may not disregard this even if he disagrees from his professional point of view [reference]. The consent of a patient who is capable of giving it is required and, in principle, is to be obtained by the doctor, but does not, however, extend necessarily to treatment which, according to medical experience, especially in its after-effects, cannot be regarded as relatively harmless. The Court of Appeal has found that electro-shock treatment gives rise to such dangers so as to rule out the possibility of calling them atypical and not worth mentioning . . .

If, therefore, the Court of Appeal speaks in these circumstances of a danger which cannot be regarded as atypical, it has done so without committing an error of law. If, for this reason, it held that the doctor was obliged to inform the plaintiff of the therapy and its consequences, no criticism can arise against this either . . . Since during the period in question electro-shock treatment could not be regarded as harmless according to the details given in the literature, and particularly in the light of the contradictory conclusions about its results, the Court of Appeal has rightly held that the doctors engaged in the treatment were under a duty to inform the patient . . . The treatment in the absence of the consent required in this case, based on adequate information, is therefore illegal. The duty to inform the plaintiff remained, despite his tendency to depressions. It is another question how the patient is to be informed of the consequences, having regard to his personality and what details are to be intimated.

III. It is true that the extent of the duty to inform is disputed. The medical profession points out, in particular, that the relationship of trust between doctor and patient is an important factor. Nevertheless, a doctor cannot take the view, without incurring the charge of negligence, that he need not inform his patient at all about a therapy which is not without danger. Since this is a legal problem, a doctor cannot without further consideration follow the view which is occasionally expressed by medical circles, but is rejected by a constant practice of the courts [reference]. The fact that the plaintiff suffers from a psychotic illness could not induce the doctors to believe that they were entitled to interfere to a considerable extent with his physical inviolability without informing him [reference]. It is irrelevant in this connection whether . . . fractures normally heal without further complications . . . The Court of Appeal has recognised that the information need not always be complete in every detail. However, it holds the doctors responsible for having omitted to give any indications. It has not been suggested that at the time of the electro-shock treatment the clinic had gained special experience of its own which could have justified the opinion that this treatment was entirely free from danger . . . The Court of Appeal was therefore right in holding that the doctors treating the plaintiff had been negligent.

The finding of a causal nexus cannot be faulted either. It need not be decided whether any finding of fact would have been relevant to the effect that the plaintiff would have given his consent, had he been properly consulted, seeing that in the present case an illegal interference with his corporeal inviolability did in fact take place. Since the Court of Appeal was unable to make such a finding, having regard to all the circumstances, it has held correctly that the defendant is liable to the plaintiff for the consequences of the corporeal treatment in accordance with §§ 611, 275, and 278 BGB.

IV. The Court of Appeal was correct in law when it regarded the doctors administering the treatment as persons allotted the execution of a function in the meaning of § 831 BGB. The Court of Appeal credits the defendant with having selected with care the doctors administering the treatment. The Court of Appeal had held, however, with justification that the directors of such a clinic owe a duty of guidance and control, for the violation of which those setting up the clinic are liable. Naturally, purely medical questions of therapy cannot be subject to guidance by the administration in individual cases. The duty to provide information incumbent upon the doctors in respect of therapy . . . is not, however, a purely medical matter, exempt from the duty to give guidance, even if it need not be decided here whether the doctors in its employ must be given guidance as to the extent itself of the information. The Court of Appeal has rightly criticised the absence of all instructions and control in respect of the information to be given to patients. In the present case it has not been established whether a doctor was among the directors. If so, the defendant would be liable for the medical director's failure to give the necessary instructions [references]. However, even if the directors of the clinic did not include a medical expert and only one doctor, in his capacity as chief medical officer, had been entrusted with the control and determination of all questions concerning medical matters, in the absence of any provision in the statutes, the defendant would be liable for the absence of control and for having culpably omitted to provide instructions. This would be all the more the case if neither the directors of the defendant had given the necessary instructions since they were not experts nor had any expert individual been charged with this task. Irrespective of the reason why the necessary control in this case or the instruction concerning the duty to provide information was lacking, the Court of Appeal was correct in also holding the defendant liable to pay damages for pain and suffering.

Case 100

BUNDESGERICHTSHOF (SIXTH CIVIL SENATE) 20 APRIL 1971
NJW 1971, 1313 = VERSR 1971, 741

On 8 July 1964 the first defendant's excavator, used to dig a ditch (for the purpose of moving a new electric-light cable), hit the pipe across the street which connected the house of the plaintiff with the main gas pipeline. Gas escaping into the cellar of the house caused an explosion which damaged the house so severely that it had to be pulled down. The plaintiff sued the defendants as joint and several debtors for compensation in respect of the damage to the house and to his business. The claim against the first defendant was based on his own culpable act (§§ 31, 823 I BGB) as well as on the culpable acts of the second and third defendants (§ 831 BGB).

The Court of Appeal of Koblenz rejected the claim. A second appeal was successful for the following.

Reasons

The Court of Appeal denies that the first defendant as a legal entity is liable under §§ 31, 823 I BGB and holds that it had discharged the burden of proof required to exonerate it from liability under § 831 BGB for the second defendant, the local construction manager, and the third defendant, the chief supervisor of excavations, having regard to what it treats as undisputed pleadings.

1. The Court of Appeal is of the opinion that the second defendant, having been in charge of the local construction works, is liable for the occurrence at the place of construction.

As a graduate civil engineer with considerable experience in road building he had the necessary qualifications to carry out tasks on his own in accordance with the relevant technical guide-lines and restrictions as well as those provided by his firm. He had been in charge of big construction works, showing great circumspection, and was familiar with all construction operations and safety measures connected therewith. He had executed conscientiously many construction works of the first defendant on his own and had never given cause for complaint. The managers and building specialists of the customer of the first defendant regarded him as a particularly reliable and conscientious specialist.

The third defendant, too, who had been in the employ of the first defendant for twenty-seven years, had much experience in civil engineering and had excelled in training younger leading construction workers.

2. These statements do not suffice, however, to show that the first defendant has discharged the burden of proof incumbent upon him for exonerating himself. Instead, the undisputed pleadings themselves disclose that the first defendant's organisation is to blame.

(*a*) According to the practice of the highest courts and to the dominant view in the literature, civil engineers undertaking construction work on public roads of cities must take into account the existence of subterranean service ducts and must exercise the utmost caution in the knowledge of the exceedingly great danger which can be caused if electricity, gas, water, or telephone lines are damaged. The life and health of human beings is imperilled if such works are carried out inexpertly, especially through contact with power cables or the escape of gas. Moreover, the failure of the supply lines often causes considerable damage to industrial and commercial enterprises, to hospitals and others. Consequently, civil engineers whose work brings them into contact with supply lines, especially by the use of excavators and similar heavy gear, are under a particularly heavy duty to make enquiries and to take safety measures concerning any existing supply lines; a civil engineer is obliged to obtain the information within the limits of general technical experience which is necessary for the safe execution of the operations to be carried out [reference].

In this connection a civil engineer is bound, in particular, to acquaint himself adequately with the lay-out of the gas pipes as well as the other supply lines by inquiring at the place where the relevant reliable details are available.

Since supply lines are normally laid down and maintained without the collaboration of the communal building authority, it is not sufficient to make enquiries with the latter; instead, information must normally be obtained from the competent supplier of the services. In a number of cases evidence of this can be found, as is shown by the cable information leaflet of the electricity works of Koblenz . . . These instructions do not have the character of legal rules. They show, however, the extent of the duty to safeguard the public in general (§ 823 I BGB) incumbent upon civil engineers using excavators. If the necessary information cannot be obtained by inspecting the documents in the possession of the supplier of the service, the position of the supply lines must be ascertained by other means before the excavators begin their work . . .

In general, an inspection of these maps will provide the civil engineering enterprise with a sufficient amount of information concerning the position of the subterranean lines and individual connections with houses . . .

It must not be decided either whether their duty to obtain information, which the first defendant had assumed, additionally by contract [reference] is always incumbent upon the management *itself* of the civil engineering enterprise [references]. In the case of enterprises which are as big as the first defendant, this may be difficult, even if the manager of the branch in K should be regarded as its statutory representative. In any event, if the gathering of information is delegated to employees, the civil engineering enterprise must give clear, emphatic instructions to the local construction manager and to the supervising foreman when and how they must ascertain the position and extension of the supply lines, including the individual connections of houses on the basis of reliable documentation by the supply undertakings in question. In view of the particularly grave danger if gas, water, and power installations are damaged, the instructions must point out imperatively not to be satisfied with oral information of a general kind not containing specific figures—especially as to the depth at which the ducts are located—which is clearly not based on maps.

Such a duty to ascertain the location of the existing supply lines must be said to exist where the excavations involve the creation of a ditch to a depth of 0.60 metres, especially if it is to run under the pavement and thus in the neighbourhood of connections with houses; experience shows that the latter run at a lesser depth than the main ducts.

The duty to make enquiries existed even if information was supplied by . . . on the occasion of a previous examination. When as a result of the extension of the order for excavations—as it was in the present case—the danger is increased, the additional operation requires further information if on the previous occasion only oral information of a general kind was provided without precise details and also clearly without the assistance of maps or other papers. Moreover, the first defendant should have given general instructions to the two other defendants concerning the need for a renewed investigation if an additional order of this kind is received.

The defendant failed to give instructions dealing with the various aspects as was required here.

The first defendant would not be exonerated if, as he contends, the connection of the gas pipe with the house was located at a depth of 45 centimetres. It is not true that if a ditch is dug by an excavator to a depth of 60 centimetres, the possibility of hitting a gas pipe could be disregarded altogether . . . [references]. The first defendant should therefore have considered the possibility that gas pipes, particularly connections with houses, may be located at a depth much less than one metre.

(*b*) The failure to give the necessary instructions to the second and third defendants also constituted the cause of the damage which occurred . . .

Case 101

BUNDESGERICHTSHOF (SIXTH CIVIL SENATE) 3 NOVEMBER 1964
NJW 1965, 391

Reasons

. . .

II. The second appeal by the first defendant must succeed.

1. The legal position would be favourable to the plaintiffs (the dependants of O, who was killed), if they could rely on the liability under § 831 BGB. The District Court gave judgment against the first defendant on the basis of this provision. The Court of Appeal did not consider this aspect. In the light of the facts as found it is indeed not possible to hold the first defendant liable on the strength of § 831 BGB (in conjunction with § 844 BGB). It is true that the Reichsgericht has held occasionally that an employed driver continues to act "in the execution of the function entrusted to him", if contrary to his instructions he gives a lift to outsiders in the course of a journey ordered by his employer [references]. In the opinion of this Division it cannot be stated generally, at least, that in such cases the employer is liable for the damage, unless he has been able to exonerate himself. In the present case, the first defendant had ordered the second defendant to *transport goods* and has expressly forbidden him to carry persons other than those connected with the business in his lorry. Having regard to the circumstances of the journey it was not reasonable either for O to assume, without making further enquiries, that the first defendant would agree to it that O would be carried in his lorry over a considerable distance at night. O entrusted himself exclusively to the second defendant, who was an acquaintance of his. In these circumstances the employer of the driver, and owner of the lorry, cannot be held liable for the personal safety of O. If the functions of the driver have been restricted by his employer, these restrictions are also effective in relation to such a user. Consequently a direct connection between the activity entrusted to the driver and the damage cannot be said to exist, even if the journey itself was not undertaken outside the scope of the employment [reference]. Even if in the absence of exoneration (§ 831 I first sentence BGB) the first defendant would be liable to a person in the street who had been injured owing to the negligence of the second defendant, irrespective of the fact that the latter had deviated from the timetable fixed by the office [reference], it does not follow that the first defendant is similarly liable to an unwanted passenger. His position is different; in so far as he is concerned, the employee entrusted with the execution of tasks allotted to him [*Verrichtungsgehilfe*] has exceeded his function, a fact which is relevant in excluding liability, seeing that the passenger's damage falls outside the operational risk attracting liability under § 831 BGB [reference]. Therefore claims by the dependants under §§ 831, 844 BGB are also excluded.

Case 102

BUNDESGERICHTSHOF (SIXTH CIVIL SENATE) 11 DECEMBER 1956
NJW 1957, 499 = VERSR 1957, 165

Reasons

According to § 17 I of the Rules for the Prevention of Accidents issued by the Bavarian Builders' Confederation in the wording of 1 July 1941, then in force, unauthorized persons were to be prohibited by notices from entering a building site. The District Court has found that this was done in the present case. Thereby the builders involved in the conversion of the house have complied with their duty to safeguard the public in general [*Verkehrssicherungspflicht*] in so far as third persons are concerned who were not employed on the building site. By means of the warning notices they indicated in a usual and generally comprehensible way that the parts of the building which were being converted were barred to "unauthorised persons" in view of the danger connected with the building operations. The plaintiff, too, was to be regarded as an unauthorised person, although she came to speak to her husband who was employed on the site. This follows clearly from § 17 II of the Rules for the Prevention of Accidents according to which even insured persons are only permitted to visit building sites if this is necessary in the performance of tasks allotted to them.

No need existed according to § 17 I of the Rules for the Prevention of Accidents cited above to protect the building site against the entry of third parties otherwise than by the erection of warning notices. In particular it was unnecessary to specify particular rooms in the course of conversion or to indicate the particular dangers which threatened unauthorized visitors, for they came within the danger zone if they obeyed the general prohibition of entry. The plaintiff cannot therefore base her claim on § 70 of the Rules for the Prevention of Accidents which requires special safety measures for rooms with ceilings or floors which are not load-bearing; these provisions exist to protect persons who are endangered while entering the room with permission, i.e. primarily workers operating there. It is neither the purpose of the Rules for the Prevention of Accidents to protect unauthorized visitors against the many dangers lurking on a building site, nor can the owner or the builders employed there normally do so or be expected to do so. It is unnecessary to determine here whether stricter requirements exist in special circumstances, as for instance if children play frequently near a building site, for the plaintiff is an adult who could understand the meaning of the warning notices on the building site and who did so, as the Court of Appeal found, despite her simple-mindedness.

Case 103

BUNDESGERICHTSHOF (SECOND CIVIL SENATE) 27 FEBRUARY 1952
BGHZ 5, 321 = NJW 1952, 658 = VERSR 1952, 166

In late November 1946 the plaintiff hurt his right hand and went as a private patient to Dr D, a senior doctor in the defendant hospital. A few days later the plaintiff became an in-patient in the defendant hospital in one of Dr D's private beds. On 9 December he there received a blood transfusion administered on Dr D's instructions by an assistant, Dr J. The donor of the blood was A, who had given blood at the defendant hospital on many previous occasions. In 1948 it was discovered that both A and the plaintiff were suffering from syphilis. A had first given blood at the defendant hospital in early August 1946. On that occasion, the only test administered to him was a Wassermann reaction test, which proved negative: there was no visual inspection or any other kind of examination. Between August 1946 and November 1947, A gave blood on twenty-five occasions for twenty-four different recipients, twenty of these occasions being at the defendant hospital. During this period he had no further tests. Only in the middle of January 1948 did a different doctor cause blood tests to be made on A. In both cases the Wassermann test proved to be extremely positive, a fact which A communicated to Dr J on 14 February. Dr D then examined the plaintiff and ascertained that he too had syphilis.

The plaintiff asserts that his infection resulted from the blood transfusion effected in the defendant hospital on 9 December 1946. He asserts that the defendant was at fault in failing to follow the requirements of the Blood Donor Ordinance of 5 March 1940 [reference omitted] and in particular in failing to give A the prescribed tests. The serious result of this was that the disease was diagnosed in the plaintiff only at a very late stage, when the prospect of cure was much poorer. The plaintiff sought a decree that the defendant hospital, Dr D, and Dr J were liable to him as common debtors in respect of all the resulting harm, as well as for damages for pain and suffering.

The Landgericht held that the claim was well-founded. The Oberlandesgericht dismissed the defendant hospital's appeal by separate decree. The hospital's further appeal is now dismissed for the following.

Reasons

1. The appellant's first objection is to the Court of Appeal's finding that it was under any contractual obligation to the plaintiff regarding the provision of medical treatment. When the plaintiff became one of Dr D's private out-patients in late November 1946, a contract for medical treatment was formed between him and Dr D, a contract which was not terminated on 7 December 1946 when the plaintiff was admitted to the defendant hospital. It followed, according to the appellant, that the contract whereby he was admitted to the hospital did not extend to any medical treatment, the plaintiff's medical treatment being a matter for Dr D alone, but simply called for the provision of bed and board.

We cannot agree with the appellant.

(a) We need not decide whether the contract which the plaintiff made with the hospital on 7 December 1946 was what is called a "total hospital contract" which involves the provision of medical treatment, for even if one accepts the appellant's assertions that in a case like the present the contract formed between doctor and patient before the patient is admitted to hospital is not affected by his admission to the hospital, it does not at all follow that the contract by which the patient later enters the hospital covers only bed and board. On the contrary, the in-patient who has made an independent contract with his doctor for medical treatment and then makes a further contract with a hospital for nursing care expects the hospital to provide him with all necessary medical treatment which is not provided by the doctor himself but is usually provided by hospital staff using hospital equipment. This would include administering drugs, giving injections, taking X-rays, and much else. The hospital itself evidently has the same expectation, since it makes the equipment available and not only performs these tasks but charges for them as well. Into this category fall blood transfusions such as the present plaintiff had, for the apparatus required for blood transfusion is normally found only in hospitals and the transfusion itself is normally performed by someone other than the principal doctor.

There is therefore no doubt that Dr J, the doctor who carried out the blood transfusion in this case, was acting as the defendant hospital's contractual assistant. The defendant is therefore responsible under §§ 276, 278 BGB for any mistakes which Dr J made in carrying out the transfusion.

The Court of Appeal held that in performing the transfusion, the assistant, Dr J, failed to follow the safety procedures laid down in the Decree of 5 March 1940. Like any other doctor in charge of a blood transfusion, Dr J should have been aware not only of how the transfusion should be effected from the technical point of view but also what steps were required for it to be effected with the greatest safety. The Court of Appeal also held that in failing to follow the prescribed tests and other safety measures, Dr J was at fault and that this fault was a cause of the plaintiff's being infected with syphilis. The Court of Appeal was therefore correct to hold that the defendant's liability for faulty breach of its contractual duty to afford the plaintiff proper medical treatment was established.

(b) But the defendant's contractual liability can be based also on the fact that it failed to take care to bring to the notice of the doctors in the hospital the provisions regarding the safety rules to be followed in giving blood transfusion. The failure was due to Dr L, who from 1940 to 1946 was the doctor in charge of the hospital and one of its statutory representatives under § 31 BGB. In this capacity he became aware of the Decree of 5 March 1940 regarding the precautions to be taken in blood transfusions, but he culpably failed to pass this information, which was important to all doctors, to the other departments in the hospital. It was his duty to do this even though his position *vis-à-vis* the other senior doctors was not that of a director. Since the hospital's contractual duty remained unfulfilled by reason of a faulty omission on the part of one of its statutory representatives, the hospital is liable (RG DR 1941, 1937).

The Court of Appeal was thus correct to hold that the failure to inform the doctors in the surgical and gynaecological departments of the hospital of the provisions of the Circular of 5 March 1940 was a cause of A's being used as a blood donor for the plaintiff and also of the plaintiff's being infected by A's blood. This was not, however, as suggested by the Court of Appeal and the appellant, a so-called organisational fault but rather a breach of the defendant hospital's own duty through a member of its executive committee, the said Dr L. This failure is equally a basis for the defendant's liability.

2. But Dr L's negligence renders the defendant hospital liable to the plaintiff not only in contract but also, and more extensively, in tort. The Court of Appeal established that it was because the doctors in the surgical department of the defendant hospital were not informed of the security precautions required by the Minister in cases of blood donors that Dr D and Dr J were insufficiently apprised of these security measures and therefore failed to check that the prescribed tests had been administered to A. It was therefore a cause of syphilis being transferred from A to the plaintiff. It follows that the defendant is liable for the harm suffered by the plaintiff under §§ 31, 843 I, 847 I BGB as well.

Case 104

BUNDESGERICHTSHOF (SEVENTH CIVIL SENATE) 30 JUNE 1966
BGHZ 45, 311 = NJW 1966, 1807 = JZ 1966, 645 = VERSR 1966, 959

Defendants G and T are partners in civil law (*Gesellschafter einer Gesellschaft des bürgerlichen Rechts*) in a motor vehicle garage. The plaintiff had an accident as a result of defects in repairs to his automobile that had been made at the garage. He brought a claim for damages against the defendants. The Oberlandesgericht adjudged G and T liable to pay for only half the damages in view of the contributory fault of the plaintiff. On the revision brought by the defendants, the liability of defendant G for damages was denied.

The court holds that defendant T, who actually repaired the vehicle, is liable under § 823 BGB for defects in the repairs which caused the brake fluid to leak out and the brakes to fail at the time of the accident. The court also holds that defendant G is not liable under § 823 BGB since he did not repair the vehicle, and that he cannot be held liable under § 31 BGB since that section does not apply to his partnership.

Accordingly, [with respect to G] only liability under § 831 BGB comes into consideration. The appellate court held that such liability existed. Nevertheless, the factual basis for imposing it is absent.

One assigned a task within the meaning of § 831 BGB is simply one who is dependent upon the instructions of the person assigning it. The right to give instructions need not extend to details. It is sufficient that the worker's activity may be limited at any time or withdrawn or circumscribed as to time and circumstances. These requirements are not met with regard to the work which defendant T did on the plaintiff's automobile. Dependence in the sense just described cannot be deduced from the fact that both defendants bound themselves to a partnership contract in which each had the obligation to conduct repairs pursuant to the purpose of the partnership. In such cases, as a rule, two prerequisites for imposing liability under § 831 BGB are absent, namely the possibilities of limiting the task by use of an authority to give instructions and of ordering that the task not be performed. [Citations omitted.]

Case 105

BUNDESGERICHTSHOF (SIXTH CIVIL SENATE) 18 FEBRUARY 1969
VersR 1969, 518

A bus owned by the defendant pulled up to a bus-stop without coming close enough to the kerb to enable passengers to step directly from the kerb into the bus. Plaintiff, a sixty-year-old woman, stepped into the street to board the bus and slipped on a patch of ice. As the plaintiff was regaining her feet, the conductor of the bus gave the signal to start the vehicle, the driver set the bus in motion, and the bus struck the plaintiff. She sued the bus company under § 831 BGB for her injuries. The court held that "in view of the great danger of accidents [during departures at icy bus-stops], and especially of accidents caused by inopportunely placing the bus in motion, it is not enough that, as witness J testified, the driver received instructions during his training as to the need for appropriate conduct". The defendant had to supervise the driver and conductor on a continuing basis.

The appellate court correctly reasoned that, from a practical and legal standpoint, the measures for training and supervision demonstrated by the first defendant are insufficient to guarantee sufficiently the proper conduct of bus personnel and, in particular, their conduct in stopping and supervising departures from the bus at icy bus-stops. In view of the great danger of accidents during these departures, and especially of accidents caused by inopportunely placing the bus in motion, it is not enough that, as witness J testified, the driver received instructions during his training as to the need for appropriate conduct. Unless the driver and the conductor were given continual oral reminders, it was at least required that a written notice be kept before them in an accessible place advising them of precisely these dangers and the means for avoiding them. The first defendant, who has the burden of exoneration, has presented no evidence on such measures, and has also failed to prove that the personnel were instructed concerning the special dangers of icy bus-stops.

The appellate court also justifiably criticised the proof offered on the grounds that the inspections, which were only described in the testimony of witness J, should have been directed to the proper starting of the vehicle and to the attention required at icy bus-stops. Finally, the appellate court correctly reproached the defendant for not having been able to present any evidence of both occasional unanticipated inspections and occasional covert inspections (the latter being normally impossible when personnel known to the driver are used). In view of the special responsibility of public commercial enterprises, such inspections by reliable employees cannot be neglected.

Case 106

BUNDESGERICHTSHOF (SIXTH CIVIL SENATE) 25 JANUARY 1966
VERSR 1966, 364

[The first defendant was employed by the second defendant as a butcher boy and driver. While delivering a load of meat and sausage, the first defendant negligently collided with a vehicle parked by the kerb. The owner of the vehicle brought suit, and the second defendant, arguing that his employee had been adequately selected and supervised pursuant to § 831 BGB, prevailed in the lower courts. The plaintiff's *Revision* was unsuccessful.]

Notwithstanding the opinion of the *Revision*, the conclusion of the appellate court that the second defendant adequately supervised his driver can be supported without proof being made of unexpected or covert inspections. The judge of the facts was aware that particular observation of a driver's conduct is frequently necessary in order to satisfy the strict requirements governing supervision of one employed as a driver. He nevertheless held that the question whether such additional measures were taken no longer arises when the employer and his representative—-here the second defendant's brother—-participate in the trips so frequently that their presence is no longer perceived as an inspection and the vehicle driver accordingly drives so as to show his customary behaviour. If no objection arises to his behaviour after this sort of observation, then no further information should be expected from following the driver occasionally in another vehicle, a procedure in which the possibilities for observation are limited. This point of view is in agreement with the decisions of this Senate which have repeatedly emphasised that, although supervision must be strict, it must still be conducted in accordance with what the individual case requires and that no simple catalogue of required measures can be given. Thus, in a very similar case, it was held to be sufficient that the driver had proved his ability by making trips for about two years without any accidents and that the owner or his representative had provided continual supervision by frequently accompanying the driver on these trips. Under such circumstances, it would be exaggerated to require particular inspections in addition, such as those conducted for the most part in large businesses and in any event in public enterprises. It has also been decided that a well-founded belief in the ability of the driver, based on careful selection and supervision, could possibly make exceptional and unexpected inspections unnecessary. The same must apply to the training, instructions, and supervision of speed which the *Revision* asserts is lacking here.

If a need for such measures does not arise when the owner and his representative accompany the driver on trips that are no longer perceived as supervision, then the question whether such additional measures were taken cannot be decisive. The plaintiff has not cast doubt on the fact that the first defendant was actually supervised in the manner alleged without any objections arising to his conduct. Accordingly, there are no legal grounds for objecting to the conclusion of the appellate court that the second defendant has fulfilled his duty of oversight.

Case 107

BUNDESGERICHTSHOF (THIRD CIVIL SENATE) 25 OCTOBER 1951
BGHZ 4, 1 = NJW 1952, 418 = VERSR 1952, 166

The defendant is the owner of an estate. His manager, K, assigned B, a sixteen-year-old agricultural labourer employed on the estate, to transport gasoline. B used a cross-bred horse. The horse bolted and seriously injured the plaintiff.

The defendant contests the plaintiff's claim on the grounds that the horse had been gentle, B had been a careful driver who was accustomed to driving horses, and the horse had pulled a milk wagon every day and was accustomed to jolting vehicles.

The Landgericht denied recovery, the Oberlandesgericht reversed, and the *Revision* results in reversal and remand.

Reasons

The appellate court held that the proof of exoneration required of the defendant had not been made because the defendant had paid no attention to the transport of the gasoline. It held that the defendant has violated the duty of supervision incumbent on him because he himself did not take care that his manager gave adequate instructions to the boy for the particular trip with the cross-bred horse, which was not without its dangers. The appellate court thought it had been demonstrated that manager K told B that he should drive carefully on this trip; however, it is thought that this instruction was not sufficient and that, in view of B's youth, the disused street, and the use of a cross-bred horse (which, as a matter of common experience, is difficult to ride), K ought to have given more particularised instructions.

In so far as the appellate court derived the liability of the defendant from the fact that he did not personally concern himself with the trip, its opinion cannot be accepted.

In the present case, the manager hired B and supervised his work. He intervened as an intermediate party between B, the worker, and the defendant, the proprietor. According to the decisions of the Reichsgericht, the proprietor of a large enterprise is not to be expected to select and supervise the entire personnel. If a number of persons are employed in a manner such that one is subordinate to another, then the employer's proof of care extends only to the selection and supervision of the higher employee chosen by him, the manager.

This easier proof for purposes of § 831 BGB is to be permitted, in the Reichsgericht's view, on the basis of what is equitable and consonant with the section's purpose. It is certainly true that the employer must institute a system of controls sufficient to guarantee reasonable supervision and conduct of business. Even if only the manager were required to exercise immediate personal oversight of the agricultural labourer, it remains the task of the estate owner to attend to the general regulation of the supervision which provides the guarantee for orderly conduct of the enterprise. If there is a defect in the organisational structure, then the employer is liable for negligence in providing general oversight as required by § 823 I BGB.

Some writers have opposed the Reichsgericht's basic principles for the liability of large enterprises. They feel that this easier burden of proof is inequitable and inconsistent with the Code. If an intermediary between the employer and the worker is employed, then it should not be sufficient for the employer to prove that he carefully selected and supervised this intermediary, but he should also prove that the intermediary acted carefully in the selection of subordinate employees. If the employer had appointed a legal representative (*Vertreter*) to make this selection, he would answer for the fault of this representative as though it were his own (§ 278 BGB); otherwise, moreover, one would reach the inequitable result that an entrepreneur with large capital resources could escape liability even though the higher employees were not in a position to pay large damages.

Nevertheless, these objections do not provide a basis upon which the Reichsgericht can discharge its task of deciding cases. Prevailing law distinguishes as to whether the basis for liability for the conduct of employees rests on contractual or on non-contractual principles. If the provisions of § 278 BGB, which pertain to contractual liability, are applicable in a variety of cases involving relationships similar to contracts, such as the public law responsibility for the safekeeping of objects (*Verwahrungsverhältnis*), it is still not possible to expand these provisions to cover the case of tortious liability for which the code has expressly provided the particular dispositions of § 831 BGB. This provision makes it possible for the employer to make a proof of exoneration, and also provides that his liability does not rest on whether his employee has committed a fault. This general principle of § 831 BGB is not dependent on the size of the enterprise. There were large enterprises in existence at the time the Civil Code was enacted, and it was impossible then, in these enterprises, for the selection and oversight of every single employee to be left to the owner or a legal representative (*gesetzlicher Vertreter*) chosen pursuant to § 831 BGB. If establishment of a particular rule governing such enterprises had been desired and, in particular, if the expansion of the legal concept contained in § 278 BGB to include delictual liability had been desired, it would have been expressed in the Code.

Accordingly, in the present case, the principal matter to be demonstrated was whether the defendant used the requisite care in the selection and supervision of his manager K.
. . .

Case 108

BUNDESGERICHTSHOF (SIXTH CIVIL SENATE) 11 NOVEMBER 1956
MDR 1957, 214 (with approving note by Josef Esser)

In February 1952, as the plaintiff was leaving a house on S Street in Hamburg where he had been visiting his sister, he slipped on a walk which bordered the house and was separated from the sidewalk of S Street by strips of greenery, and suffered a compound fracture of the upper thigh. He contends that his fall was caused by a slippery patch of snow. He claims the defendant is liable for his accident as owner of the house and sidewalk because of a violation of a duty to sand the walk. The Landgericht rejected the claim. The appellate court held the claim for damages to be legally grounded. It granted the demand for a fixed sum of money and periodic payments, provided the claim was not paid by a publicly owned insurer. It also entered a judgment subject to the same reservation, declaring the defendant to be liable.

The *Revision* is without success.

Reasons

The appellate court found that it had been demonstrated that the walk had a slippery patch of snow and had not been sanded and that the defendant was under a duty to pay compensation under § 823 BGB because, as owner of the walk which was used by the general public and, in particular, by the residents of neighbouring houses and the customers of three stores located in them, the defendant had a duty to clean and sand the sidewalk according to the provisions of the Hamburg Road Cleaning Ordinance of 10 January, 1940 [reference] and regulations made under this Act on the same day [reference]; and that the responsibility falls on the defendant for not having taken care to fulfil the duty to sand the walk in the required way.

[The court rejects the defendant's contention that sanding the sidewalk was not required on the day of the accident under the Act and regulations just cited, because weather conditions that day would have made the sanding of the walk useless.]

Moreover, the conclusion that the defendant committed a fault stands up against legal scrutiny.

In this regard, the appellate court maintained that the assignment of the duty to clean and sand the walk to a married couple, W, living on the ground floor by a contract of lease had legal effect only in relations between the defendant and these lessees. The prerequisites for finding that the married couple W had a duty with public law effects to clean and sand the sidewalk under the provisions of the Road Cleaning Ordinance are absent. Therefore, as what is involved is a violation of a duty required of the defendant itself, and as the plaintiff's claim for compensation is based on § 831 BGB, the case does not turn on proof of exoneration under § 831 BGB. The defendant, indeed, is a large enterprise, which must employ the help of others to fulfil its duty to sand. The appellate court did not reject that the defendant had entrusted the lessees of the buildings with this task. But it correctly took as its premise that the defendant must organise the carrying out of the duty to sand so as to guarantee that it will be reliably performed.

The appellate court found that the defendant apparently placed the duty to clean and sand walks on the inhabitants of the ground floors of its buildings by simply inserting such provisions in form contracts of lease, and that the married couple W became obligated in this way without regard to whether the wife W, after the death of her husband and after attaining the age of seventy-six, still possessed the physical ability to do the cleaning. The appellate court took the view that the method used by the defendant for the employment of persons for sanding the walk does not satisfy the requirements imposed on him.

The *Revision* contests this view as too extensive, arguing that the customary practice in Germany is for the lessee living on the ground floor to be responsible for the performance of the duty to clean and sand the sidewalks, and that an objection to this practice should not be made if the owner of the building demonstrates that the lessee adequately performs this duty by himself or with the help of a third person.

The question can be left open whether placing the duty to clean and sand the sidewalks on the person living on the ground floor by a form contract of lease is consistent with the content of the duty of care in selecting persons to sand the sidewalks, a duty which concerns the building owner in the area of its responsibility under § 823 BGB to no less extent than the duty of care which falls on the employer under § 831 BGB concerning the selection of an employee. The owner of the building has at the least a duty of supervision which is sufficiently broad for it to be required to ensure that the lessee actually performs—-or has another perform—-the obligations assigned the lessee in a regular manner. The duty of general supervision rests on one who makes a careful selection of persons to whom he, as the one responsible for fulfilling a general duty, assigns the actual performance of this duty. This applies particularly and in very large measure when regard to the competence and reliability of these persons was not a decisive factor at the time they were employed.

According to the findings of the appellate court as to the factual situation, the defendant failed to provide the supervision required of it. The measures taken by the defendant consisted of the employment of a building manager for three different blocks of housing, located six to ten minutes apart and containing a total of thirty separate buildings. It need hardly be argued here that, as a general rule, it must be held insufficient for an enterprise leasing houses to employ only one man for a housing area of this size to supervise the performance of the duty to clean and sand walks by lessees. The manner in which Mrs W performed the duty assigned her of cleaning and sanding the walks had given cause for complaints before the day of the accident—-that the place where the accident occurred was often not adequately sanded. The defendant could not have remained in ignorance of this if it had organised supervision in the manner required by the duty just described to provide oversight. As a result, the conclusion of the appellate court that the plaintiff's accident was caused by the neglect of the defendant must be accepted. The defendant is accordingly liable on the basis of §§ 831 and 823 BGB.

Case 109

BUNDESGERICHTSHOF (DECISION OF THE GREAT SENATE) 4 MARCH 1957
BGHZ 24, 21 = NJW 1957, 785 = JZ 1957, 543 (see article by F Wieacker in
JZ 1957, 535 = VERSR 1957, 288, 517, 783)

Reasons

1. The case submitted to the Great Senate for Civil Cases is based on the following facts:

The plaintiff took part in a family celebration and intended about 1.30 a.m. to return on the tramway run by the defendant enterprise from the "Apotheke" stopping-place. When he tried to mount the forward platform of the tramcar he fell: he was run over by a car and his right foot so severely injured that his leg had to be amputated below the knee. The plaintiff made the defendant, the driver, and the conductor of the vehicle responsible for the damage and put forward the following grounds for his claim:

The fall occurred because the tramcar started too soon. The conductor gave the departure signal and the driver started although both could have seen that the plaintiff was still just about to mount the forward platform. He had stood in front of the door when it started and had already grasped both the entrance handles. The driver did not stop immediately on getting the emergency signal from the conductor.

In his action the plaintiff demanded damages from the defendant, the driver, and the conductor of the tramcar.

The defendant, the driver, and the conductor admitted his claims in part . . . Otherwise they claimed that the action should be dismissed and urged that:

The conductor gave the signal to start and the driver set the tramcar in motion only after the invitation to enter had been given and no one else was prepared to enter. The plaintiff had been standing by a group of persons who had not intended to ride, but had then hurried after the moving tramcar and tried to jump on. When the emergency signal was given the driver stopped at once. The plaintiff had been drunk and had only himself to blame for the fall.

The Landgericht allowed the claim, reduced to one-half.

On appeal by the plaintiff and counter-appeal by the various defendants, the Oberlandesgericht dismissed the action against the driver and conductor and declared the defendant tramway company liable to pay compensation up to two-thirds.

On appeal the defendant company moved for a complete dismissal of the action.

2. It was disputed in the first place whether the defendant company also was liable under § 831 BGB for the damage caused by its employees. This question required examination because the plaintiff's claims were not completely supported by the *Reichshaftpflichtgesetz*, in particular in so far as he demanded damages for pain and suffering.

The Court of Appeal found that the defendant company was responsible under § 831 BGB for the damage to the plaintiff, because the driver, and perhaps also the conductor, had caused the physical injury unlawfully and because the defendant company had not produced the proof necessary for exonerating itself under § 831 I sentence 2, case 1 BGB from liability for its "employees". The Court of Appeal came to the conclusion that the way the fall occurred was not clear. It was possible that the plaintiff's allegations of fact were correct, but it was also possible that the accident happened in the way described by the defendant. In view of this negative result of the evidence, the Court of Appeal felt that the possibility could not be excluded that a causal connection did exist between a presumable failure of choice and supervision on the defendant company's part, and the occurrence of the damage (§ 831 sentence 2, case 2 BGB).

3. The Sixth Civil Senate had doubts whether to follow the Court of Appeal's findings of law. The doubts were directed above all against the view that an "employee" (for the purposes of § 831 BGB) engaged in tramway or railway traffic did damage unlawfully merely by causing physical injury. It is a matter for discussion whether the basis of the unlawfulness must be further gone into in order to show whether the conduct of the employees is objectively contrary to good traffic practice. For that purpose, reference is made to the traffic rules which regulate the conduct of participants in traffic in ever-greater detail. Recourse must also be had to the legal concept of social adequacy and to developments in modern criminal theory, more especially because according to this the concept of negligence includes essential requirements which relate to unlawfulness and not to fault. If a finding of unlawfulness in traffic accidents does not automatically follow from the resulting consequence but (is satisfied) only if a breach of the traffic regulations has occurred, then it seems probable, in view of the report laid before us, that the conception of the burden of proof hitherto followed in applying § 831 BGB can no longer be upheld. That must be true in particular of cases which resemble the one in question and are distinguished by the fact that, in view of the failure to clarify what happened on the occasion of the accident, no objectively irregular conduct on the part of the "employees" can be established.

The Sixth Civil Senate attaches fundamental importance to the clarification of these questions of law. In accordance with § 137 GVG it submits them for decision to the Great Senate for Civil Cases and formulates them as follows:

Does a person employed in tramway or railway traffic do damage unlawfully to another within the meaning of § 831 I BGB merely by injuring his life, body, health, or property? Or is it a further condition of unlawfulness that the participant employed in the traffic conducted himself in an objectively irregular way? Is the employer who fails to exonerate himself from the charge of defective selection or supervision liable under § 831 BGB even if according to the evidence the possibility remains open that the "employee" observed the objective duties of care and, in particular, the rules governing highway or rail traffic?

1. When § 831 BGB makes the employer's liability depend on whether his "employee" did unlawful damage to another person in executing his task, this requirement connects it with the factual situations of the law of delict in which the unlawful acts involving a duty of compensation are described and delimited. Not every doing of damage produces liability, but only such as falls within a liability situation of the law of delict, and, therefore, is an "unlawful act" in the sense of §§ 823 ff. BGB. Accordingly, for the purpose of traffic accidents as here in question, in the first place a reference is needed to § 823 BGB, especially § 823 I. Claims for damages are constantly recurring from injuries to life, body, health, or property in tramway and railway traffic. Now the wording of § 823 I BGB requires that the injury to the enumerated legal interest be unlawful, that is to say repugnant to the legal order. The legislator, however, when describing in legal terms the factual basis of illegality, indicates that he regards the breach of the legal interests listed in § 823 I BGB as normally unlawful. By adding "unlawful", however, he indicates that the mere breach does not necessarily involve unlawfulness, but that unlawfulness can for special reasons not exist. It may be questionable whether that indication was needed. It is certainly useful in applying the law, by making judges attentive to the fact that any factual description of unlawful conduct is bound to be incomplete and that therefore they are under a duty to examine whether a finding of unlawfulness based on a fulfilment of the factual conditions must be withdrawn on special grounds. Further, the BGB does not provide an exhaustive formulation for defining when there is a legal justification. The initial provision about consent as a justification was struck out in the discussion of the draft because it was desired to leave to practice the task of marking out the limits of justification. Moreover, the jurists and judges have also developed slowly those principles to which they may have resort for the purposes of excluding unlawfulness, such as on the basis of *negotiorum gestio*, the protection of vested rights, or the balancing of interests. There is, therefore, no exhaustive legal catalogue of justifications, no *numerus clausus* which would set limits to legal development. Accordingly, the matter must be gone into now that the report of the Sixth Civil Senate has submitted for discussion the question whether, in the special field of tramway or railway traffic, conduct fulfilling on its face the factual condition of § 823 I BGB must no longer be adjudged unlawful if it was in harmony with the legal regulations laid down for the traffic.

The line of thought in that direction found in the report must in principle be approved. The draftsmen of the BGB may indeed not have recognized that these are matters for discussion which concern objective unlawfulness and not merely fault in the sense of personal blameworthiness. Only with the technical development of traffic and the increase in its dangers did modern mass traffic produce problems calling for regulatory legislation. The legislator was faced with the need to regulate by increasingly detailed provisions the duties of participants in traffic, so that the possibilities of danger should be reduced to a minimum. At the same time, the legal provisions dealing with liability for risks were developed in order to apportion with social fairness in their economic effects the dangers and risks rendered inevitable by modern traffic. In the process, it was more and more recognised that what was in question was not a liability for wrong but a duty on those in control of dangerous operations to assume responsibility for certain typical risks. With that legal development there is no longer any place in the law of delict for a doctrine that looks upon unavoidable injuries in tramway and railway traffic as unlawful injuries to persons or property and denies liability only for lack of fault. The legal order, in permitting dangerous traffic and prescribing in detail to its participants how to conduct themselves, declares that conduct conforming to those prescriptions is within the law. It is not right that conduct which takes full account of the orders and prohibitions of the traffic regulations should nevertheless be adjudged unlawful. The actual consequences do not afford sufficient ground for it, for, in deciding whether conduct is unlawful within the meaning of the BGB provisions about delicts, one cannot leave unconsidered the act that produced the consequences. The rule must therefore be laid down that orderly conduct of a participant in tramway or railway traffic conforming to traffic regulations does not produce unlawful damage.

Whether the result implies a special application of the legal idea of so-called social adequacy may be left unanswered. Since the question here is restricted to the field of traffic law, there is also no need to go into whether the same result could equally be obtained through reliance on modern criminal theory, which splits up the concept of negligence by treating the enquiry into the observance of objectively required care as appertaining to unlawfulness, and only the question whether the disapproved conduct should be imputed to *an individual doer* as an inquiry into fault. Doubt must in any case be expressed as to whether, if this complex concept of negligence in modern criminal theory were to be taken over into civil law, in the law of civil responsibility, also, under cover of a special enquiry into fault, a special standard of judgment should be imposed on the conduct of the doer of damage that took account of his personal characteristics. That might, indeed, appear to harmonise the legal concepts, but it would not allow for typical differences which arise from the specific characteristics and purposes of two different branches of the law. In particular, this view would not be in accord with the provisions of § 276 I 2 BGB as it has always been understood in applying the law.

2. The question submitted to the court now makes it necessary to enquire what are the consequences produced by the standpoint adopted for apportioning the burden of proof. Here it must be recalled that the legislator, by establishing a separate factual basis for delicts, intended to lighten the judges' task of examining whether a wrongful act exists or not. Unlike the cases where delict is governed by a general clause, leaving a wide scope for judicial interpretation (§§ 823—25 BGB), in describing casuistically the wrongs giving rise to liability, the legislator affords a solid basis for applying the law, by suggesting, at least provisionally, the criterion of unlawfulness. Thus, an injury to one of the legal interests especially named in § 823 I BGB to which the law affords a preferred protection, needs a special justification if it is not to be adjudged unlawful. That applies irrespective of whether the act was done intentionally. This relation of rule and exception established as part of the system of our law of delict and upheld in its application has, in accord with the recognised principles of the law of evidence, the consequences that the proof of a justification is for the person who infringes a protected legal interest. In this respect, the

justification afforded by conduct according to rules in tramway and railway traffic can claim no separate status.

This apportionment of the burden of proof in applying § 823 I BGB to traffic accidents means that the doer of damage can provide a basis for justification by proving that his conduct conformed to traffic rules. If the proof is supplied, proof of fault ceases to have any substance, because there is to start with no unlawful infliction of injury. If on the other hand the question whether his conduct in traffic was regular is not cleared up, one starts with an unlawful injurious act. The question of liability however is not yet decided; for § 823 I also requires the injurious act to have been intentional or careless. The injured party must therefore prove that the doer acted intentionally or negligently, in the meaning of § 276 I 2 BGB, that is to say omitted to take the care required in daily intercourse. For that enquiry also it will, of course, be essential to know whether the provisions of the traffic regulations have been observed. That the question of conduct according to the traffic rules can be significant for unlawfulness and fault is due to the shape and legal classification of the concept of negligence. For the practical application of the law it remains that the injured party must prove in full the conditions of a claim for compensation under § 823 I BGB and that accordingly—-unless there is a prima-facie case—-an insufficient elucidation of the facts is to his disadvantage.

The apportionment of the burden of proof in applying § 831 BGB is different. There the legislator consciously made the employer's liability depend only on the "employee's" acting unlawfully and not also on his doing the damage intentionally or negligently. In so far therefore as concerns the "employee's" conduct, only those principles governing the burden of proof apply that affect the sphere of unlawfulness. Thus, the injured party must prove that the "employee" by an adequately causal act injured one of the legal interests protected in § 823 I. On the other hand, it is for the employer to prove that the "employee's" conduct was regular, because it conformed to the legal rules of tramway or railway traffic. So far, doubt is to the disadvantage of the employer. On the other hand, if regular conduct of the "employee" is proved, the conditions for a claim under § 831 BGB are unfulfilled, so that there is no longer any need to go into whether proof can be provided that there was no causal connection between the prima-facie presumption of faulty selection or supervision, and the damage. From that last-mentioned point of view the Reichsgericht had denied the employer's liability when the judge was convinced that even a carefully chosen and supervised "employee" could not have acted differently in the given case. That the production of the exoneratory proof under § 831 I and II BGB makes it unnecessary to go into the question of unlawful injury is self-evident.

It is clear that as regards a traffic accident the cause of which remains obscure, the regulation of the burden of proof set out above makes it better for the injured party if the "employee" and not the employer himself has caused the accident. In the latter case the employer's liability is as a rule excluded, because no fault can be established, whereas where it is caused by the employee, the employer is liable if he cannot exonerate himself from the charge of imperfect choice and supervision. This preferential treatment was clearly intended by the legislator, for there is here a certain allowance for the fact that otherwise the injured party's legal position is quite unfavourable because exoneration is possible and usually successful. It is precisely for that reason that it would be wrong in applying the law to do away with the part favourable to an injured party in the regulation of the BGB of delictual liability for "employees". If one observes that emphasis is there placed—-even though incompletely—-on responsibility for enterprise risks, it is not unfair to impose on the one in whose sphere of influence the risk originated the burden of proof about the way the damage occurred, which he is usually, though not always, in a better position to satisfy than the one to whom it occurred. Also so far as the provision of "appliances and implements", which include the means of transport, is concerned, the law has for the same reason imposed on the employer within the framework of § 831 BGB an enhanced duty of elucidation and proof. If the evaluation of the employee's conduct is under discussion, attention must also be paid to the point of view that the employee—-that is the meaning of the reversal of the burden of proof—-must be considered to have been unfit for his task, until the employer proves that he showed the care described more fully in § 831 I 2 BGB.

Case 110

BUNDESARBEITSGERICHT (GREAT SENATE) 12 JUNE 1992
BAGE 70, 337 = NJW 1993, 1732 = JZ 1993, 908 = NZA 1993, 547

Facts

The claimant, who runs a building business, had to build a boundary wall around a house plot. Its foreman for this work was the defendant. Ditches 80 cm deep and 16 cm wide had to be dug with an excavator for the foundations. The claimant's director showed the defendant the site in the presence of a fellow employee. During the excavation, the excavator driver damaged a gas pipe. Gas escaped into the cellar rooms of the house and exploded. Damage amounting to DM 244,263 was done to the house. The claimant seeks compensation from the defendant for the part of the loss not covered by its business liability insurance. It claims that the defendant had been shown the location of the pipe from the gas main to the cellar and that the plan and the street excavation had shown where the house connection ran. The defendant had been advised that in this area the digging ought only to be by hand. Nevertheless, he had failed to instruct the excavator driver accordingly, and told him that he did not need to take care, as there were no pipes there.

The claim was unsuccessful at earlier instances. The *LAG* stated that there was no liability as the defendant was not grossly negligent. It considered that, contrary to the case law of the highest courts, this should also apply to non-dangerous work, as here. The claimant lodged an appeal in law. The 8th Senate of the *BAG* wished to depart from the view of the Great Senate, and apply the principles developed by the case law about limiting employee liability in the case of dangerous work to non-dangerous work as well, if it results from the business and is carried out on the basis of the employment relationship. It has therefore asked the Great Senate of the *BAG* to decide on this legal issue under § 45 (2) sentence 1 of the Labour Courts Act.

Reasons

The Great Senate of the *BAG* agrees with the legal opinion of the 8th Senate to the effect that the limiting of employee liability is not conditional on the dangerous nature of the work. The limiting of employee liability should instead apply in all cases in which an employee causes harm in connection with work which is carried out for business reasons.

I.1. The *BAG* since the decision of its Great Senate of 25 September 1957 (references omitted) proceeds on the basis that, for harm which an employee has negligently caused in the carrying out of dangerous work, he is only liable to his employer in accordance with the following principles: In the case of gross negligence the employee has as a rule to bear the total loss alone. In the case of the slightest negligence he is not liable. For normal negligence the loss is as a rule to be divided between the employer and the employee proportionately and in this connection all the circumstances regarding the causing of the harm and its consequences are to be balanced against each other in a reasonable way in accordance with the principles of fairness (references omitted). But these principles alleviating liability which evolved by development of the law apply (according to the case law so far) only where dangerous work is concerned. The Great Senate considers it necessary no longer to limit the alleviation of liability to cases of dangerous work, because otherwise, under §§ 276 and 249 of the BGB, employees who do not carry on any dangerous activity would in principle have to bear the whole of the loss where there is a violation of duties of care and protection in the employment contract which leads to loss for the employer. To burden an employee with such a risk of liability is not justified, having regard to the possible extent of the harm (and also that present here) and the fact that compensation for it can lead to serious inroads into his lifestyle. It would contradict the principle of proportionality (reference omitted).

2. The Great Senate is authorised, according to Article 20 para. 3 of the Basic Law and § 45 (2) of the Labour Courts Act, to adapt employee liability law to actual business conditions by developing it beyond the existing case law (reference omitted).

(a) The provisions of the BGB do not contain a closed regime for employment contract law (reference omitted).

Even on the enactment of the BGB, a gap in the law was assumed in relation to employee liability. In the materials, a special statutory regime for employment contracts "inclusive of compensation law questions" was demanded "as soon as possible" (reference omitted). In addition to this, employees have been increasingly exposed to liability risks since the time when the BGB came into force. Formerly, harm caused by employees was kept within boundaries, but since those days it has become capable of leading to unreasonable levels of liability for employees because of the substantially higher value of the means of production used by employers. In this respect, because of the gap in the BGB's regime which was present from the outset, there is an obvious defective development which must not be accepted. Not just because of the special nature of work, but also because of the increase in value of means of production, the employee is exposed in the world of work today to a very much higher risk of harm, which in part threatens his very existence.

(b) Until now, in spite of various plans, no statutory liability regime for employees has been enacted nor is this issue at present the subject of pending legislation . . .

II. The Great Senate of the *BAG* takes the view that as to all harm caused by employees in the employment relationship which arises in connection with activities which are business related, limitation of employee liability is required. This view is propounded in the academic literature almost unanimously, although on the basis of differing reasoning (references omitted).

1. According to § 254 of the BGB, the duty to compensate as well as the amount of compensation to be provided depends on the circumstances and in particular on how far the

harm has been caused mainly by the one or the other party. § 254 of the BGB is applied to circumstances beyond its wording (that the person harmed has himself contributed in the origin of the harm) when the person harmed is jointly responsible for the harm which has arisen on the basis of a property or business related danger for which he has to take responsibility. This will occur if he has been involved in the origin of the harm in a way that can be attributed to him. At the same time, it is recognised that a division of the harm can range from full liability of the tortfeasor and his complete exoneration, depending on assessment of the circumstances in the individual case (references omitted).

2. These legal principles also apply in the employment relationship in relation to employee liability. The *BAG* proceeds—admittedly with the further prerequisite of the presence of a dangerous activity—in constant case law (references omitted) on the basis that the business risk has to be considered from the employer's side. The employer cannot simply shift the loss which business risk brings with it on to the employee just because he has entrusted him with the execution of work to be carried out in the interests of the business. As the employer claims the results of the business activity for himself, he must assume liability for the risks associated with it. The business risk relates to the danger of e.g. the production plant, the production itself or the manufactured products and thereby encompasses only part of the sources of business related harm.

3. Over and above this, there is the ground of attributability, and therefore of liability or joint liability, of the employer within the framework of § 254 of the BGB arising from his actual organisational and staff authority and the legal formulation of the employee's personal dependence and responsibility to obey instructions. This justifies also imposing on the employer the organisation risk, as an element of the general risk of the undertaking. The employer puts at the disposal of the business the organisation predetermined by him. He can thereby direct the work process organisationally and technically. The employee is integrated into this business in order to realise, alone or together with the employees employed in the business, the technical work purpose of the business by activity which is directed by instructions. The employer can determine the technical work purpose of the business on his own responsibility, can formulate the business organisation in accordance with his plans and needs, and can exert influence over the employee's activity. The employee's pursuit of his job is directed by his integration into the business organisation and the actual conditions of the work process (e.g. the type of technical plant available (which is often particularly valuable) and the arrangement of the work organisation and of the production process, with qualitative and quantitative requirements in relation to the work products).

The employee cannot avoid these pre-determined conditions of work either factually or legally. The employer, on the basis of his right to give instructions, determines the performance of work owed under the employment contract in a concrete sense. He can decisively influence the conditions of the performance of work (e.g. by organisational or technical measures). He can also authoritatively shape the temporal components of the performance of work within the framework of the maximum permitted limits. And finally he can lay down the place of performance of work in accordance with the regime in the employment contract. The organisation of the business established by the employer thereby determines the risk of liability for the employee. By virtue of his power in the organisation, the employer can create, maintain or alter conditions for risks of harm e.g. he can take steps to prevent danger factors by alteration of the work process, better supervision, safety precautions or other planned risk protection, like effecting insurance. In a risk situation of this kind created by the employer, he himself must allow risks of harm to be attributed to him within the framework of § 254 of the BGB and cannot, or cannot only, offload them on his employee even if the employee is at fault in the causing of the harm.

III. The protective scope of the regime under § 254 of the BGB in the employment relationship is also influenced by constitutional law guarantees under Article 12 para. 1 sentence 2 in combination with Article 2 para. 1 of the Basic Law.

1. According to the constant case law of the Federal Constitutional Court, the basic right norms do not only contain subjective defensive rights of the individual against the state. They also embody at the same time an objective order of values which applies as a basic constitutional law decision for all areas of law and thus also for civil law, and gives directives and impulses for legislation and case law. No civil law provision may exist which contradicts the principles which are expressed in the basic rights. This applies primarily for those provisions of private law which contain compulsory law and therefore set limits to private autonomy (references omitted).

2. The statutory regime under § 254 of the BGB admittedly gives no indication that it intrudes into the basic rights contained in Article 2 para. 1 and Article 12 para. 1 of the Basic Law or that it secures basic right protection. However the scope of the protection which these basic rights are meant to secure can also be affected by provisions which have a close internal connection with the exercise of a vocation and display a tendency to regulate it (references omitted). These prerequisites are present here, because, depending on how employee liability law is formulated legally, there is a tendency for an intrusion into the employer's economic freedom of action and activity, the development of the personality of the employee and the exercise of the vocation of the employer and the employee. If the employee is liable for harm for which he is responsible, this has an effect on the development of his personality and affects the exercise of his vocation. If the employer is liable wholly or partly, this intrudes into his economic freedom of action and activity and the exercise of his vocation.

3. Article 2 para. 1 of the Basic Law guarantees the general freedom of action in the full sense (reference omitted). It includes on the one hand the freedom of economic activity as an employer and at the same time gives with this an appropriate amount of space for development of entrepreneurial initiative (reference omitted). On the other hand this basic right protects the general right of personality (reference omitted) and thereby the development of the personality of the employee. This increases in importance specifically in view of modern developments in working life and the new dangers to the human personality associated with this. The vocational activity for which Article 12 para. 1 sentence 2 of the Basic Law guarantees the necessary scope for the employer as well as for the employee does not only serve the personal development of the working man in society. It also guarantees citizens who have to rely on the use of their capacity to work the possibility to make for themselves an economic basis for existence (references omitted). In the framework of employment law, this typically occurs through contracts in which the employer and the employee reciprocally limit their vocational freedom of action in the exchange of stipulated counter obligations. Vocational freedom under Article 12 para. 1 sentence 2 of the Basic Law thereby protects the exercise of the vocation of the employer

as well as that of the employee with a view to the free development of their individual capacity to earn a living and provide services (reference omitted).

4. Proceeding from this constitutional law basis, an unlimited liability for harm on the part of the employee represents a disproportionate intrusion into the employee's right to the free development of his personality (Article 2 para. 1 of the Basic Law) and into his right to free exercise of his vocation (Article 12 para. 1 sentence 2 of the Basic Law).

(a) The duty of protection under Article 12 para. 1 sentence 2 of the Basic Law to guarantee the exercise of vocation represents a substantial part of the realisation of the right of personality (reference omitted) and, in combination with the social state principle in Article 20 para. 1 of the Basic Law, secures the general requirements for life and the minimum for existence (reference omitted) as the lowest prerequisite for an existence consistent with human dignity. On the basis of the value order of these interests protected by the basic rights, a disproportionate interference with the exercise of the right of vocation must be assumed if, in an employment relationship, unreasonable financial burdens or even danger to the economic existence of the employee can arise through general risks of harm associated with business. This would be so in an employment relationship if the employee had to assume unlimited liability for all negligently caused harm, even where the negligence was only slight. The employer is by the organisation of the work, with regard to the actual and legal arrangement of the activity as well as through integration into the business organisation, exposed to risks which he cannot avoid. These conditions created by the employer and the value of the means of production used by the employer determine the extent and scope of the employee's risks of liability (see, on this issue, II 3 above). With such an extensive determination of the work by another party, the employee's interests protected by the basic rights are violated if the income from the work is substantially disproportionate to the level of the harm to be compensated for, or if the employee's duty to compensate leads to his economic existence being endangered. Such an excessive and therefore disproportionate financial burden for the employee represents an unacceptable disturbance of the relationship of equivalence between salary and harm to be compensated for. It compels the employee and his family to live with the minimum for existence which is determined by the limits to enforcement proceedings for a lengthy or even unforeseeable period. This can have the ultimate consequence of leading to every incentive for a further exercise of the employee's vocation being taken away from him, because it seems to him to be useless.

(b) Over against this, the basic right position of the employer is not unreasonably affected by the imposition of risks of liability in the scope in question here. The employer must put up with limitations of his freedom of economic action and activity (Article 2, para. 1, of the Basic Law) and exercise of his vocation (Article 12, para. 1, sentence 2 of the Basic Law) as protected by the basic rights, because he sets the conditions of work and business himself on his own responsibility and is thereby jointly responsible for the employee's risks of harm (see II 3). In these factual and legal conditions, there is no equality of power between the parties to an employment contract, so through the regime of § 254 of the BGB, a proper balancing of interests by limitation of the employer's freedom of exercise of vocation should be allowed. The possession and use of assets available in the business must take second place to the employee's ability to work and perform services if this is necessary for the protection of his existence. Therefore the attribution of the risk situation created by the employer on his own responsibility should be seen as a socially adequate formulation of the employer's freedom of economic action and activity and exercise of vocation.

(c) Such an attribution is not unreasonable, having regard to the legal position in favour of the employer which is at issue in constitutional law. The question of whether and, if appropriate, in what sum the harm is to be attributed to the employer should be governed by the circumstances of the individual case as a whole having regard to the causes of the harm and its consequences. Besides this, the points of view mentioned in the case law so far (references omitted), insofar as they are based on the work relationship, are to be considered within the framework of § 254 of the BGB, on weighing up the circumstances of the individual case. This includes, for example, the danger involved in an activity, a risk which can be taken into account by the employer and covered by insurance, the position of the employee in the business, the level of salary, the personal circumstances of the employee, as for instance how long he has been part of the business, his age, his family circumstances as well as the employee's conduct so far under his contract of employment.

5. So as not to burden the employer with the general risks in life of the employee, the activity which has led to the harm must be caused in connection with the business and based on the employment relationship. Activities caused in connection with the business are those activities of the employee which have been entrusted to him for business purposes or which he carries out in the interests of the business, which are in close relationship with the business and his area of operation in the business and which in this sense are caused in connection with the business (references omitted) . . .

2. § 278 BGB (OR § 831 BGB)

Case 111

REICHSGERICHT (SIXTH CIVIL SENATE) 7 DECEMBER 1911
RGZ 78, 239 = JW 1912, 191

Reasons

According to the findings of the Court of Appeal the plaintiff, after making several purchases in the defendant company's department store, went to the linoleum department to buy linoleum floor-cover. She mentioned this to W, the sales assistant who served there, and looked through the patterns which he displayed for her to make a choice. W, in order to pull out the roll she pointed to, put two others aside. They fell, hit the plaintiff and her child, and struck both of them to the floor. The purchase of the linoleum was not completed because, in the plaintiff's words, she became seriously disturbed by the fall.

The Court of Appeal rightly attributed the plaintiff's accident to W's fault, on the ground that he had put the rolls, which were not stable enough because of their relatively small bulk, insecurely on one side, instead of furnishing them with lateral protection on leaning them against the wall, and this even though he could have foreseen that the plaintiff, as usually happens with the buying public, would approach the place where the goods she had asked to be displayed were stored. The Court of Appeal's view is comprised in the simple conclusion that the rolls would not have fallen if W had placed them carefully and regularly on one side.

The Court of Appeal's opinion that the defendant company is liable for W's fault under § 278 BGB cannot, in spite of the appellant's contention, be rightly objected to; and it conforms to the case-law of this Senate. W was acting for the defendant company (§ 164 BGB, § 54 HGB) when he entered into negotiation with the plaintiff. The plaintiff had asked for a piece of linoleum to be laid out for inspection and purchase. W had acceded to her request in order to make a sale. The proposal and its acceptance had for their purpose the conclusion of a sale, and therefore the production of a legal transaction. That was no mere factual proceeding, a mere act of courtesy, but a legal relationship came into existence between the parties in preparation for a purchase; it bore a character similar to a contract and produced legal obligations in so far as both seller and prospective buyer came under a duty to observe the necessary care for the health and property of the other party in displaying and inspecting the goods.

The judgments of this Senate have already proceeded on similar grounds, and it has been recognised in several decisions of the Reichsgericht that duties of care for the life and property of the other party can arise from bilateral or unilateral obligations, which have nothing to do with the legal nature of the relation in a narrower sense, but nevertheless follow from its factual character.

The defendant company made use of W's services for the fulfilment of the aforesaid obligation to the prospective purchaser, and is therefore answerable for his fault. This is in line with the thought expressed in § 278 BGB, that whoever himself owes a performance that he must carry out with the required amount of care must, when he makes use of an employee, answer for his careful performance, and that accordingly the other person to whom the performance is due must not be put in a worse position because he does not do it himself but commits it to an employee. It would be contrary to the general feeling of justice if in cases where the person in charge of the business of displaying or laying out goods for exhibition, sampling, trial, or the like carelessly injures a prospective purchaser, the proprietor of the business—with whom the prospector wished to make a purchase—should be answerable only under § 831 BGB and not unconditionally, so that the injured person should, if the proprietor succeeds in exonerating himself, be referred to the usually impecunious employee.

There is no need to go here into the legally questionable view of the Court of Appeal that the mere entry into a department store of a prospective purchaser or even a visitor without any intention of buying creates a contractual relation between him and the proprietor, including the widely discussed duties of care . . .

Case 112

BUNDESGERICHTSHOF (EIGHTH CIVIL SENATE) 28 JANUARY 1976
BGHZ 66, 51 = NJW 1976, 712 = JZ 1976, 776 with approving note by
K F Kreuzer = *VERSR* 1976, 589

The plaintiff, who at the time of the accident was fourteen years of age, went with her mother to a branch of the defendant's, a small self-service store. Whilst her mother, after selecting her goods, stood at the till, the plaintiff went round to the packing counter to help her mother pack the goods. In doing so she fell to the floor and suffered an injury which necessitated lengthy treatment. Alleging that she had slipped on a vegetable leaf, she sued the defendant for breach of his duty to provide safe access. The Court of Appeal, having dismissed as time-barred the claim for damages for pain and suffering, the parties are now in dispute only on the question whether the defendant is obliged to compensate the plaintiff for her economic loss as well as prospective damage.

The Landgericht rejected the claim as time-barred. The Court of Appeal granted it—after deducting one-fourth for contributory fault. The defendant's further appeal was unsuccessful for these

Reasons

I. The Court of Appeal found as proved that the plaintiff slipped on a vegetable leaf lying on the floor near the packing counter and suffered injuries which necessitated the expenditure in question and may possibly lead to future loss. These findings disclose no legal error; they are in fact undisputed on appeal.

II. According to the Court of Appeal's opinion the defendant had not furnished the proof incumbent on him that he had taken all necessary care for the safety of movement in his store and that the accident could only be attributed to the fact that another customer had shortly before let a vegetable leaf fall to the floor. These findings also cannot be faulted legally. They conform to the settled case-law of the BGH (NJW 1962, 31; *cf.* also RGZ 78, 239) both on the duty of a shopkeeper to ensure safety of movement and on the reversal of the burden of proof required by § 282 BGB in cases of claims for damages based on *culpa in contrahendo*. This point also is not contested on appeal.

III. The defendant therefore is liable—so continued the Court of Appeal—after taking the contributory fault of the plaintiff into account, for three-quarters of the existing and prospective loss, and that not only in delict, but also for fault in concluding contract, since in opening the self-service store he infringed the contractual duty of protection and care which he had undertaken to the plaintiff. Moreover, the plaintiff also has a claim for damages under a contract with protective effects towards a third party because her mother was during the accident preparing to contract with the defendant and the plaintiff was being included as an assistant within the scope of that contract-like obligation. For claims, however, arising from fault in concluding a contract the limitation period is thirty years, so that the claim was brought in good time.

IV. These explanations stand up to examination—at least in result. Admittedly, the main line of the Court of Appeal's reasoning, that the defendant is directly liable to the plaintiff for fault in concluding the contract, irrespective of whether a contract with protective effects towards a third party needs to be brought into the picture, gives rise to doubts. Liability for *culpa in contrahendo*, which in cases like the present one is more favourable to a plaintiff than the general liability in delict for breach of the duty to provide safe access—because of the increased liability for employees (§ 278 BGB in contrast to § 831 BGB), the longer limitation period (§ 195 BGB in contrast to § 852 BGB), and the reversal of the burden of proof (§ 282 BGB)—rests on a legal obligation created by way of supplement to the written law. It arises from the process of bargaining for a contract and is largely independent of the actual conclusion or efficacy of a contract (BGHZ 6, 330, 333). The liability for a breach of the duties of protection and care arising from this obligation finds, in cases of the present kind, its justification in the fact that the injured party entered the other party's sphere of influence for the purpose of negotiating for a contract and can therefore rely on an enhanced carefulness in the other party to the negotiation (*cf.* also BGH NJW 1960, 720). This is borne out exactly by the present case in which the mother entered the sales department of the defendant for the purpose of making a purchase and in doing so had to subject herself to a risk involved in the increased congestion, especially near the till, in a self-service store. It is, however, always a presupposition of liability for *culpa in contrahendo* in this type of contract of sale that the injured party enters the sales department with the purpose of contracting or of entering into "business contacts"—and therefore at least as a possible customer, though perhaps without a fixed intention to purchase (*cf.* BGH NJW 1962, 31). It need not be decided whether it is enough, in view of the peculiarities of sale in a self-service store, for a customer (when entering the sales department) to have intended at first only to have a look at the objects offered and be possibly stimulated to buy or only to make a preliminary comparison of prices with those in competing enterprises. In any case there is insufficient justification for a contractual liability for *culpa in contrahendo* stretching beyond liability for delict when the person entering the store never intended to buy, perhaps because—leaving aside the shop-lifter mentioned by the Court of Appeal—he is sheltering from a shower or using the store as a way through to another street or even only to meet other persons. The line may be difficult to draw in particular cases, above all because it depends on the difficult proof of unexpressed intention. In the present case, however, it is beyond dispute that the plaintiff from the start did not intend to make a contract herself but only to accompany her mother and help her in buying. A direct application of liability for fault in concluding a contract with the defendant is therefore excluded.

V. Nevertheless, the appellate judgment is proved right in result, because it is supported by supplementary considerations.

1. If the plaintiff's mother had been injured in the same way as her daughter, there would have been no objection to making the defendant liable for *culpa in contrahendo*—as is also clearly stated in the appeal. In that case nothing need be said about the question, disputed in academic circles, whether in a self-service store the display of the goods constitutes an offer and the contract of sale is concluded by the buyer's accepting it in presenting the selected goods at the till—thus reserving a final decision until that moment—or whether the display of the goods constitutes only an invitation to make offers, which the customer for his part makes by showing them to the cashier and the latter accepts by registering it on behalf of the self-service store. In any case, the general run of the reasons for the judgment, even though it contained no express statement by the Court of Appeal, makes it obvious that at the moment of the accident the goods intended for the purchase had already been finally chosen and a legal obligation already existed between the defendant and the plaintiff's mother justifying liability for *culpa in contrahendo*.

2. It is on the legal obligation that the plaintiff can rely to justify her contractual claim for damages. It accords with the long-standing case-law of this Senate in particular that in special circumstances even bystanders who do not themselves participate in a contract are included in the protection afforded by it, with the consequence that although they have no claim to have the primary contractual duty performed, they are entitled to the protection and care offered by the contract and can make good in their own name claims for damages arising from the breach of those subsidiary duties . . . It is not necessary to

consider here the theoretical question whether such a contract with protective effects toward third parties, on which the courts have proceeded hitherto, is derived from the supplementary interpretation of a contract incomplete to that extent (§§ 133, 157 BGB), or whether, as is increasingly accepted in the literature, direct quasi-contractual claims arise on grounds independent of the hypothetical intention of the parties, perhaps from customary law, or on the basis of legal developments by the courts. In any case, according to both views it is essential that the contract, according to its sense of purpose and the requirements of good faith, demands an inclusion of third parties in its sphere of protection; and that one party to the contract can in honesty—and in a manner discernible by the other party—expect that the care and protection owed to it will be equally extended to a third person. There is no good reason to exclude sales in general from this legally possible configuration as this is shown in particular by sales in shops to which buyers, in certain circumstances, must enter the sphere of influence of the seller. And that is also the view of the Sixth Senate in BGHZ 51, 91, 96.

3. Admittedly the inclusion of third persons in the sphere of protection of a contract—if the contract between contractual and delictual liability established by the legislator is not to be destroyed or blurred—needs to be confined to narrowly defined cases. Whether the mere fact that the customer makes use of a third person in initiating and concluding a purchase in a self-service store is enough for the protected effect to be accepted as possible may be left undecided; for in the present case it must be added that the plaintiff's mother was responsible for her daughter "for better or worse" (BGHZ 51, 91, 96) and therefore—and this should be known to the defendant also—for that reason alone it could reasonably be inferred that the daughter accompanying her should enjoy the same protection as herself. In such a close family relationship the courts have always seen themselves justified in extending contractual protection.

4. That in the present case the sale was not concluded at the moment of the accident is, in the result, unimportant. If one looks upon the duty of protection and care as the determining element of the legal obligation based on negotiating for a contract, and if one considers that the other party owes this duty of care both before and after the conclusion of the contract, the inclusion of third persons (who are equally worthy of protection) in the obligation follows. Moreover, there would be no rational ground for making the contractual liability depend on the chance of whether the negotiations had already led to a contract when the damage occurred; that is impressively shown by the present case, where the "sale negotiations" had, in essence, been completed and the conclusion of the contract—possibly subject to a delay on the mother's part in completing it at the till, and for which the plaintiff's mother was not responsible—was in any case imminent. The appellant's contention that a cumulation of liability for *culpa in contrahendo* and inclusion of a third party in the protective effect of a contract would lead to an unforeseeable widening of the risk on a seller, is directed in principle against justification of both institutions in general. The danger of a flood of litigation, which cannot be dismissed out of hand, has, as has already been explained, long been taken into account by the courts, which have imposed strict requirements on the inclusion of third parties in the protective sphere of a contract. As regards to merely pre-contractual relations some reservation may be indicated. But in any case with so narrow a limitation there is no objection to an extension of protection if—as here—the person causing the damage could not reasonably have opposed any desire expressed by the mother, when negotiating for a contract, to have from the start the same protection expressly given to the child who was subse-

quently injured herself. Finally, in so far as the appellant contends that the long limitation period—combined with the reversal of the burden of proof—would intolerably worsen the evidentiary position of anyone sued for damages in such situations, the remedy must be found in laches (*Verwirkung*) of the existence of which there is no indication in this case.

Case 113

BUNDESGERICHTSHOF (THIRD CIVIL SENATE) 10 MAY 1951
BGHZ 2, 94 = NJW 1951, 596

The plaintiff was leaving the hospital where his wife was a private patient when he fell and suffered concussion, a fractured skull, and a cerebral haemorrhage. He alleged that the accident was due to the dangerous condition of the main entrance of the hospital, and claimed damages from the defendant. So far as his action was based on breach of contract it was dismissed at all levels of jurisdiction.

Reasons

The Court of Appeal held that the defendant was not liable on its contract with the plaintiff for the hospitalisation of the plaintiff's wife. It accepted that under a contract of *lease* the tenant's family have a contractual claim against the landlord if there is a defect in the leased dwelling or its approaches which is attributable to him and they suffer harm thereby; and it agreed that the hospitalisation contract is like a lease in certain respects; it found, however, that the lease features of a hospital contract are really very subsidiary: the patient has no claim to any particular form, and the primacy of the medical treatment reduces the significance of the premises as compared with a contract of lease. Therefore no contractual liability of the defendant arose under § 278 BGB.

In contesting these views, the appellant emphasises the fact that he himself made the contract whereby his wife was taken in by the defendant as a private patient. The contract bound him to pay the hospital bill and bound the defendant not only to care for his wife (§ 328 BGB), but also, as a subsidiary duty, to enable him to visit his wife in safety. Given that he was a principal contracting party, it is irrelevant, says the plaintiff, whether, had he not been, the defendant would be liable to him under § 328 BGB in the way the landlord is liable to the tenant's family.

Contrary to the appellant's view, the contractual liability of the defendant for the accident which the plaintiff suffered as he was leaving the hospital by the front steps cannot depend on whether it was the plaintiff himself or his wife who entered into the hospitalisation contract. It is true that a contract is formed when a private patient is taken into a hospital, even a hospital run by a public body (RGZ 64, 231; 83, 72; 111, 263; see also RGZ 108, 87), and that the plaintiff as husband acquired contractual rights against the defendant (RGZ 64, 233); yet it is not from the formation of the contract but from its content that a duty to take care of the plaintiff's safety must arise. If in addition to the primary obligation towards the patient to give him medical treatment, the terms of the contract include an obligation towards certain third parties, the hospital would be contractually liable to those third parties regardless of whether they had participated in the formation of the contract or not.

The hospitalisation contract is doubtless a contract of services (*Dienstvertrag*) (RG JW 1938, 1246 [other references omitted]), whereby the patient is to be provided with bed and board as well as with medical treatment and care. The medical treatment is, however, the essential and critical element, the bed and board being by contrast rather subsidiary (see RGZ 112, 60 [other references omitted]). There is thus no occasion to infer any subsidiary *contractual duty* to ensure that the patient's husband be safe in visiting the hospital. But the result would be just the same even if one held, in view of the purposes of the hospitalisation contract, that there was an independent contract for lodging and meals collateral to the main contract for medical services; the result would be the same, too, if a separate contract with different terms were made with a doctor (RG JW 1936, 3182 no. 6), for example, if the patient were taken into the hospital on the referral of the doctor treating her so that the treatment could be continued there. For even if there were a separate contract with the hospital for lodging and meals, the plaintiff as husband would have no contractual claim to safe access to his sick wife, despite the lease features of the contract. It is true that under the law of lease the tenant's family have the same rights against the landlord regarding the safety of the premises as the tenant himself (RGZ 91, 21, 24; 102, 232; 152, 177; 169, 87 [other reference omitted]). In accordance with the purpose of the contract, rights are granted under § 328 BGB to those who belong to the tenant's household, members of the family and domestic help; but no such rights are granted to guests: the precondition is living together in the rented premises. The tenant intends (and his intention, though inexplicit, is perceptible by the landlord) to have the lease include the members of his family and respect their needs; to persons outside the home, who stand in no particular relationship to the leased premises, this does not apply. The recognition of the tenant's implicit contractual purpose to put his family in the optimum legal position may have led to giving a child a direct claim for proper medical treatment when the treatment is arranged by its statutory representative (RGZ 152, 175), but even so it is only the child being treated who has a direct claim for the contractual performance arising out of the contract. When the husband takes his wife to hospital, he admittedly has a contractual claim that she be properly treated, but apart from that he is in no special relationship with the hospital and has no contractual claim for care towards his own person; and therefore cannot demand safe access to his wife in the hospital on the basis of the hospitalisation contract. We need not decide whether it would make any difference if the husband, with the consent of the hospital management, had stayed in the hospital, even overnight, in order to be near his wife. On the facts, the plaintiff had no claim against the defendant for breach of a contractual duty of care.

Case 114

OBERLANDESGERICHT DÜSSELDORF, 3 OCTOBER 1974
NJW 1975, 596 = VERSR 1975, 863

The plaintiff's son was stabbed in a brawl and was taken to the defendant's hospital where the chief surgeon saw to the stab wound in the skin and stomach-lining. The youth died. At the post-mortem it transpired that there were other wounds which had not been cared for, in the rear stomach-lining, in the upper and lower intestine, and in the left kidney. The plaintiff asserted that the chief surgeon had caused his son's death by failure to attend to these wounds, and claimed damages for loss of support.

The Landgericht rejected the claim. Before the Oberlandesgericht the plaintiff sought to answer the defendant's proof of exculpation under § 831 BGB, first by asserting that the defendant was also to blame in failing to provide an assistant surgeon for the operation, and then by arguing that the defendant was personally liable in contract and must answer for the fault of the chief surgeon as its agent for performance. The plaintiff's appeal was dismissed.

Reasons

The plaintiff has no claim for damages against the defendant. There can be no claims under §§ 242, 276 BGB for breach of contractual duty since there was no contract between the parties. The hospitalisation contract with the defendant under which the plaintiff's son received medical treatment and care in the hospital was made not with the plaintiff but with the local General Health Insurance Scheme (AOK). It is true that the AOK did not actually refer the plaintiff's son to the hospital—this was an emergency case— but the contract was formed later when AOK agreed to pay the bill. It is not argued that any contractual negotiations took place between the parties, and it is clear that there were none.

Nor did this contract have any protective effect for the plaintiff. Such protective effect only applies to the insured and not to his dependants (RG JW 1937, 926; BGHZ 2, 94). Normally, the protective effect of a contract is limited to those persons who, by their connection with the creditor, come into contact with the debtor's performance, and whose safety is, to the debtor's knowledge, as important to the creditor as his own. This requirement is normally met only when the creditor has a joint responsibility for the protection and care of the third party (BGHZ 51, 91, 96; BGHZ 56, 269; BGH NJW 1959, 1976; 1970, 38). This is not the case with the plaintiff here. The decision of the Bundesgerichtshof to which the plaintiff refers (NJW 1959, 1676) is of no assistance to her, for in that case the third party was one of the plaintiff's employees, that is, a person who came into contact with the debtor's performance through the creditor and to whom the creditor owed a duty of care and protection. These preconditions are not satisfied here: the defendant's performance did not affect the plaintiff and AOK is not bound to afford her care and protection. Nor can it be said that the plaintiff was "close to the performance" (*Leistungsnähe*). The performance which was owed by the defendant, namely medical care and attention in its hospital, did not affect the plaintiff. She was not the patient. Furthermore, the plaintiff in this case was in no relationship to the creditor AOK. She cannot acquire a claim against the defendant by founding it on her relationship with the third party, her son (under § 328 BGB), or on *his* duties towards her . . .

Case 115

BUNDESGERICHTSHOF (SEVENTH CIVIL SENATE) 7 NOVEMBER 1960
BGHZ 33, 247 = NJW 1961, 211 = JZ 1961, 169
(with approving article by W Lorenz)

On 11 April 1953 two adjoining ferro-concrete plates became loose from the 16–18 m high roof of the steelworks at W belonging to the Siemens-Martin-Stahlwerk and fell on two persons at work in the works, namely the works engineer S and the steel-worker L. S died at once, leaving a widow and two children. L was severely injured.

The roof had been erected by the defendant company between October 1952 and March 1953. In making use of the old roof construction, ferro-concrete plates developed by the defendant company were substituted for the former concrete layers (which formed the ceiling).

The plaintiff association claims to be recouped for the payments made as an accident insurer to the surviving relatives of the works engineer S and to L.

It bases its claim on delict and on a "positive breach of contract" (*positive Vertragsverletzung*) (§§ 328, 618 BGB), in each case in combination with § 1542 RVO (right of subrogation).

The defendant company denies that it did an unsatisfactory job in performing the steelworks contract. It pleads in addition that the steelworks were jointly at fault in defectively altering the roof. This share of the fault must be imputed to the plaintiff. The defendant company also pleads that the claim is time-barred.

The Landgericht dismissed the claim. On appeal, the Oberlandesgericht found the claim for payment justified in principle and granted the declarations applied for.

The defendant company's appeal led to the decision being quashed and the case being sent back for reconsideration for the following

Reasons

1. (*a*) The Court of Appeal left open the question whether the claim in delict of the injured parties (and therefore of the plaintiff) was time-barred. It granted them a direct claim against the defendant company on a "positive breach of contract" under §§ 328, 618 I and III, 844 BGB. The contract between the defendant company and the steelworks included a subsidiary duty on the defendant company to see that no damage should occur to the other party in doing the job. That obligation bound the defendant company under § 618 I BGB to the customer's work-force also; they had acquired direct claims for damages through the breach of the obligation.

(*b*) That is in conformity with the opinion developed in the case-law of the Reichsgericht and the Bundesgerichtshof. According to it the basis of this liability is a contract for the benefit of third parties in the sense that in its protection are included the persons to whom the promisee on his part owes essential duties of care and protection.

(*c*) The Court of Appeal was not in error in including those injured in the accident within the circle of those so benefited. That circle must of course be limited and easily ascertainable. But it was so here. Both the victims belonged to the work-force and were employees who were regularly active in the shop roofed by the defendant company. It was a numerically limited and spatially confined group to which the employer owed a special duty of care in fitting out the workshop. It was only that circle that the Court of Appeal included in the protection afforded by the construction contract, not, as is said in the appeal, the several thousand employees of the steelworks' work-force.

2. Nor was the Court of Appeal in error in affirming the transmission of the claims of the injured persons to the plaintiff under § 1542 RVO. That paragraph is, as the Senate has already decided (BGHZ 26, 365), applicable also to claims for contractual damages.

3. The Court of Appeal properly held that the defendant company contributed by its fault to the accident and was therefore bound to make good the damage on the ground of a "positive breach of contract" [point discussed but not reported].

4. It left open the question whether the steelworks contributed at all by their fault to the accident, because in its opinion this was irrelevant.

That was rightly attacked in the appeal.

The question whether in such a case the injured third party must have imputed to him under § 254 BGB a contributory fault of the other party to the contract with the person causing the damage has been answered in the affirmative by the Reichsgericht and the Bundesgerichtshof only where that party is the statutory representative or the employee of the injured party (BGHZ 9, 316; 24, 325; LM No. 2 to § 254 BGB) that "inclusion of the plaintiff in the contractual protection" implies that "he must along with the widening of his legal protection, take into account the legal disadvantages bound up with it" points in this direction and shows also that the solution found here conforms to equity.

It follows that the judgment under attack, in so far as it disregards any contributory fault of the steelworks, cannot be upheld.

5. It could of course stand if the plaintiff's claim could also be supported in delict, for to that extent the contributory fault of the steelworks must not affect the liability of the defendant company.

The Court of Appeal—consistently with its standpoint—did not examine that question. In particular, it had left open the question whether this claim was time-barred. For want of the necessary findings, the Senate is itself not in a position to arrive at a decision.

The judgment under attack must therefore be set aside and the matter referred back to the Court of Appeal.

The view is taken further in the legal literature that the person who owes compensation may quite generally, even when the other party to the contract—as here—is not the statutory representative or the employee of the injured third party, plead against the latter under § 254 BGB the contributory fault of that party to the contract.

That view must—contrary to the Court of Appeal's opinion—be accepted. As in every contract for the benefit of third parties, so also in a contract of the kind in question, the protected third party derives his rights against the doer of the damage only from the contractual relations between the immediate parties. That follows already from the legal principle underlying § 334 BGB, according to which defences under the contract available to the promisor can also be pleaded against the third party. The words in the decision of the Bundesgerichtshof in LM 2 of § 254 BGB(E) that "the inclusion of the plaintiff in the contractual protection" implies that "he must along with the widening of his legal protection take into account the legal disadvantages bound up with it" points in this direction and shows also that the solution found here conforms to equity.

It follows that the judgment under attack, in so far as it disregards any contributory fault of the steelworks, cannot be upheld.

6. It could of course stand if the plaintiff's claim could also be supported in delict, for to that extent the contributory fault of the steelworks might not affect the liability of the defendant company.

The Court of Appeal—consistently with its standpoint—did not examine that question. In particular it had left open the question whether this claim was time-barred. For want of the necessary findings, the Senate is itself not in a position to arrive at a decision.

The judgment under attack must therefore be set aside and the matter referred back to the Court of Appeal.

Case 116

REICHSGERICHT (SIXTH CIVIL SENATE) 10 FEBRUARY 1930
RGZ 127, 218 = JW 1930, 1720 (with approving note by A Elster)

The plaintiff acted from the middle of April until the end of June 1926 as daily help to the widow M. On 10 and 11 August 1926 she was helping Frau M to move to a new dwelling; as from 15 August she had accepted a new post as a maidservant. Frau M had employed the defendant firm to move the gas meter in the bathroom of her new dwelling. At the end of July the firm instructed their leading fitter B to do the job. On 11 August the plaintiff noticed a smell of gas in the dwelling, as she had done the day before. To discover the place of the leak she climbed a ladder in the bathroom and lit the gas burner with a match. The leaking gas was set alight and the plaintiff suffered appreciable damage to the upper part of her body. The gas escape was due to the looseness of an overflow screw on the meter. The screw had been installed by B. The Court of Appeal found that he had been grossly negligent in the unworkmanlike execution of the job.

The plaintiff first sued the widow M for damages in preliminary proceedings. At that stage the present defendant firm appeared as "co-defendant" with Frau M. The action was dismissed on the ground that in any case the plaintiff was predominantly to blame (§ 254 BGB).

The plaintiff now sued the firm B & R and also B as co-defendants for damages and an annuity, and for a declaration of liability for further damage.

The Landgericht found the claim against both defendants justified as to two-thirds. The Oberlandesgericht reduced the award to one-half.

The appeal of the firm B & R (hereinafter called the defendant) was unsuccessful, apart from a determination of the duration of the annuity.

Reasons

The essential grounds on which the Court of Appeal based its judgment were the following. The defendants were strictly liable without exoneration for damage caused by B under the contract made with Frau M. That contract bound the defendants to take the care normally required in carrying out the job; moreover, in performing that duty they made use of their employee B and must therefore take responsibility for him under § 278 BGB. Not only was Frau M entitled as a contracting party to have that care taken, and to be compensated for the damage caused by the neglect of it, but the plaintiff was also entitled in so far as the contract must be taken to have been a contract for the benefit of third parties.

Whether a contract was intended to bring § 328 I BGB into operation, so that the third party should acquire directly a right to claim the promised performance must, under § 328 II BGB and in the absence of any special provision, be decided on the facts of each case, with particular reference to what can be recognised by both parties to have been the purpose of the contract.

The contractual purpose here signifies the objective means of determining the terms of the contract so that an agreement must be taken as covered by the contractual intention which the contracting parties could have arrived at if they had faced up to the elaboration of the details according to the purpose of the contract. Whether the extent of their agreement had actually been realised was beside the point. The application of these principles led to the conclusion that there was here a contract for the benefit of third parties. When a contract is made for the execution of a job in a customer's dwelling the danger is involved for anyone using it, the customer must be assumed to have intended— and this intention is capable of being observed by the contractor—that the interest of relatives living with him would be respected and that they should, for this purpose, have the same rights as he himself has to be compensated for damage done to them through the performance of the job. For without such an extension of the contractual duties, injured dependants would be limited to non-contractual claims. Such a different treatment of the customer and his dependants would offend against a sound instinct for justice and be out of accord with the contractual intent of the customer who, as the contractor must have been aware, would not wish to place his dependants in a worse position than himself as regards claims for compensation.

The position of the customer's domestic servants is the same. Here, too, the intention— capable of being recognised by the contractor—must be implied that he will respect the interest of the domestic staff, who must work on the premises where the contractor does the job and would have a claim to a safe system of work against the customer (§ 618 BGB). Where the customer contracts for a performance of a dangerous character, the contractor must know that he intends the performance to be carried out so as not to cause damage either to himself or to the members of his family or domestic staff, and that he is to stand in no better position than those belonging to his immediate household.

Now the plaintiff was indeed not a domestic servant but only a daily help, and therefore, was not a member of the domestic community. But, when making the contract, the head of the household must have intended—and this intention must have been understood by the contractor—to ensure that, over and above the circle of family dependants and domestic staff, all those persons to whom a master owes a duty of protection shall enjoy the special protection of a personal claim to have care taken of them under § 618 BGB. The daily help belongs to that class. This interpretation, however, must be subject to the limitation that only such persons must be regarded as benefiting from § 618 BGB as stand towards their employer in a relationship of some duration from which arises at least a moral duty on the employer to increase his protection. For a master must not be taken to intend to contract for the benefit of persons who serve only occasionally and temporarily on his premises and with whom he does not form any close attachment, such as arises from a longer use of their services and a more frequent contact, and even the creation of personal relations. The plaintiff stood in no passing relation to Frau M for she was in regular service with her for about a quarter of a year and was also, as is stated more fully, in a long-standing relationship with her.

But even if that no longer applied to 11 August 1926—so says the appellate decision— a contract for the benefit of third parties would exist as regards the plaintiff. For during the removal and the putting in order of the new dwelling, the dangers involved in the furnishing were so much greater than in ordinary housekeeping that the occupier must be taken to have intended to provide special protection to all taking part in the removal. The contract for the benefit of third parties must be taken to have imposed a duty of care upon all taking part in it.

Against this the appeal contends that a contract for a job of work cannot be taken to include the protection of all those permanently or temporarily in a dwelling; for principles worked out for leases cannot be applied to contracts for a job of work.

This attack cannot succeed, in particular because the appellate judge's interpretation of the contract of work between the defendant and the widow M, to the effect that it was a contract of work for the benefit of the plaintiff is free from legal error, above all in his application of §§ 133, 157, 328 BGB. Whether his definition of the circle of those benefited was entirely correct need not be discussed. In any case it includes persons who are entitled to damages from the customer under § 618 BGB.

The fundamental considerations on which the Court of Appeal proceeded are to the point, and are established by case-law of the Reichsgericht. It is in particular correct that the contract for the benefit of a third party can be an implied one and that the decision whether a contract is to be regarded as having been made for the benefit of a third party also and whether the third party shall acquire rights immediately against the promisor depends essentially, in the absence of a special term, on a finding of the facts in each case. For that purpose, regard must be had to the intention of the parties, the purpose of the transaction, and business usages; especial attention must be paid to the supplementary interpretation of contracts. The business intention of the parties provides an objective indication; whether the parties were aware when contracting of the scope of their declarations is irrelevant. Finally, there is no requirement that the identity of the third party should be ascertained when the contract is made; it is enough for it to be ascertainable.

On this basis, more recent judgments of the Reichsgericht have followed its earlier case-law in recognising more and more contracts for the benefit of third parties in cases where a third party has suffered damage [there follows an exposition of the slowly developing practice of the Court].

If, now, one comes to decide the present case, one arrives at the following conclusions. The plaintiff was a daily help in a long-term relationship with the widow M. Accordingly she was entitled and obliged, in the interest of her own health but also in the furtherance of her employer's business, to enter the bathroom from which the smell of gas seemed to come. The gas escape rendered the premises in which she was bound to serve unfit to afford her protection against danger to life and limb. The unfitness was due to the grossly negligent way B, the defendant's "employee", performed the job of fixing the gas meter (§ 278 BGB). Under § 618 BGB Frau M was subjected to obligations which the legislator considered so essential that their exclusion or limitation by contract was made illegal (§ 619 BGB). Under them Frau M was liable to compensate the plaintiff, although she was not herself to blame. For liability under § 618 BGB is contractual and hence § 278 is applicable, so that Frau M had to answer the plaintiff for the defendant's fault.

Now, Frau M's purpose, as the defendant could well realize, in making the contract was to have the gas meter properly fixed, and in particular that the execution of the job should produce no danger to life and limb either to herself or to any persons to whom she might become liable under § 618 BGB. No obligation to point of law can be taken to the further finding that the appellate made in interpreting the contract by way of supplementation, according to § 157 BGB, that Frau M and the defendant would have agreed to the direct liability of the latter for all damage for which Frau M might become liable to compensate persons through an improper fitting of the gas meter, if the parties, when making the contract, had contemplated such a possibility. For Frau M would have made the assumption of such direct liability a term of the contract and the defendant would, in order to get the order, have accepted such a term, all the more so because he had in any case to do a perfect job and it made no essential differences to him whether he exposed himself to a direct claim for damages by the employee of Frau M or for an indemnity by the latter.

Case 117

REICHSGERICHT (THIRD CIVIL SENATE) 3 JUNE 1921
RGZ 102, 232

The plaintiff and her husband lived on the third floor of a house belonging to the defendant and rented from him by the husband. On the morning of 23 October 1918 her husband was found dead and she was found unconscious in their bedroom. This was due to gas poisoning, the gas having come, according to the plaintiff, from the floor below. On the floor below the defendant was having gas replaced with electricity, and had retained G, a master plumber, to remove the gas pipes. At the end of his work on 21 October, one of G's workmen failed to plug the gas pipe leading from the gas meter to the apartment of one Gr., a publican. The gas meter was turned off at the time, but it was turned on by Gr. on 22 October, and gas then flowed out of the unstopped pipe and filtered through the ceiling into the living quarters above, those of the plaintiff and her husband as well as those of Gr. himself.

The plaintiff claimed compensation for her own illness and for the loss she suffered through her husband's death, the claim being based on the contract of lease which her husband had entered as well as on tortious negligence. The defendant denied the plaintiff's assertions about the gas poisoning and contended that the accident had occurred because a gas tap in their apartment had carelessly been left on either by the plaintiff or by her husband.

Both lower courts dismissed the claim, but the plaintiff's appeal was allowed.

Reasons

The Court of Appeal accepted the plaintiff's version of the cause of the gas poisoning. It held, in accordance with decisions of this court (see, for example, RGZ 91, 24), that the contract of lease concluded by the plaintiff's husband was one for the benefit of the plaintiff under § 328 BGB and that therefore the plaintiff had a personal contractual claim against the landlord for breach of his contractual duty of care under §§ 536, 538 BGB. It is held, correctly, that the landlord was contractually bound to each of his tenants not to damage them by works being effected on the premises and to indemnify them for any harm due to culpable breach of his duty. The court nevertheless rejected the plaintiff's claim because the defendant was neither personally at fault nor liable for the negligence of an agent for performance (§ 278 BGB). There was no personal fault in the defendant because the person to whom he had entrusted the work, the master plumber G, was a specialist. He had thereby fulfilled his duty of care to see that the works were carried out properly and in a manner not involving risk to the occupants of the house, all the more so since what was involved was a simple and easy task which the chosen specialist could be expected to carry out properly. It was not common practice for the landlord himself to supervise specialist tasks which he was in no position to evaluate, nor to appoint a representative to do so for him. It therefore could not be expected that the defendant should supervise G's work. Nor was the defendant liable under § 278 BGB, because the work being done on the gas pipes was not in execution of any duty owed by the defendant to the plaintiff, but of a duty owed by the defendant to the occupant of the lower apartment; G and his workmen could therefore not be regarded as the defendant's agents for performance *vis-à-vis* the plaintiff.

The appellant criticises the Court of Appeal's opinion of both points. Criticism of the finding that the defendant was not personally at fault is without merit. In the case of work such as was here entrusted to the master plumber G, the defendant was under no duty, either personally or through a clerk of works, to see that the work was being carried out properly or to check it as soon as it had been completed. A subsequent inspection, perhaps in the defendant's own interest, would not have prevented the accident.

On the other hand, the appellant is right to say that there has been misapplication of §§ 278, 536, 538 BGB. The Court of Appeal itself recognised that the landlord has a contractual duty to all his tenants not to injure them by work being done on the premises. This duty stems directly from the basic duty imposed on the landlord by § 536 BGB, which is not simply to make the rented property available at the outset of the lease in a condition suitable for use in accordance with the contract, but also to maintain it in this condition for the duration of the lease. But this is not a duty merely to avoid doing harmful work on the premises, it is a positive duty to see that the rented property is maintained in a condition suitable for contractual use. It therefore includes the duty to take care that the tenant's use of the premises is not unacceptably affected by any work being done on the premises, including the work done in parts of the building other than those demised to the tenant for his exclusive use. If the landlord allows work to be done in the house which runs the risk of affecting the tenanted premises, he is bound under the contract of lease so to effect these works that this danger is averted, regardless of where in the house or why the work is being done. The landlord of a house whose ground floor needed strengthening or whose gas or water supply was defective at any point would clearly be contractually bound as against tenants anywhere on the premises who were endangered thereby to do any repairs properly. If he entrusts the work to someone else he is using that other person for the performance of his duty towards all such tenants: he must therefore answer for his assistant's fault under § 278 BGB as if it were his own. The same is true if the danger arises from works undertaken in rooms rented to others. For example, suppose a supporting wall on the ground floor is to be removed in order to enlarge the window. The landlord's contractual duty to do these works is owed only to the tenant of the ground floor and not to other tenants, but if he actually engages on the work, he owes to all the tenants in the house a contractual duty so to manage it that the rooms they rent are not adversely affected. To this extent, therefore the workmen whom the landlord employs for modification of the building are his agents for performance under § 278 BGB not only as against the tenants of the ground floor but also as against all tenants whose rooms could be affected by the work of reconstruction. So here, taking the plaintiff's assertions as true, although the defendant was indeed under no contractual duty towards the plaintiff to replace the gas pipes by electric wiring, he was responsible to the plaintiff and to the other tenants in the house for seeing that the gas pipes were removed without risk of gas flowing into their rooms. Those persons to whom the defendant entrusted the removal of the gas pipes were consequently his agents for performance *vis-à-vis* the plaintiff too.

Such an application of § 278 BGB in respect of the landlord's obligation to maintain the leased property so that it remains fit for contractual use is correlative to the tenant's liability for his employees arising from his duty to treat the leased property properly: those whom the tenant engages in the business he runs on the tenanted premises are his agents for performance of his duty to treat the premises properly, even if he owes the landlord no duty whatever to run the business in which those persons are employed (see RGZ 84, 222) . . .

Case 118

REICHSGERICHT (SIXTH CIVIL SENATE) 7 JUNE 1915
RGZ 87, 64 = JW 1915, 1018

On 20 July 1913, there was a collision between a tram belonging to the plaintiff and a taxi belonging to the first defendant and driven by the second defendant. The passengers in the taxi, Sch., an accountant, and his wife and daughter, were injured. They claimed damages from the plaintiff tram company under the Imperial Act on Liability. The plaintiff now alleges that the accident was entirely due to the fault of the second defendant, for which the first defendant is responsible, and seeks a declaration that the defendants are bound to indemnify it for all loss arising from the accident.

The lower courts granted the claim, and the defendant's appeal is dismissed.

Reasons

1. The court below did not misapply § 278 BGB, as the appellant contends. Doubts may certainly be entertained about the reasoning of the Court of Appeal that in a case like the present the taxi-driver may regard all of his passengers as contractors, and may look to each of them for the fare. We need not decide this, however, since in any case there is no doubt that a contract was made with the accountant Sch., who boarded the taxi at the same time as his wife and daughter. But that does not mean that he is the only person with a contractual claim arising out of the contract of carriage. On the contrary, the contract of carriage is a contract in favour of the wife and daughter who were travelling with him; they were "third parties" under § 328 BGB, and acquired a direct right to demand performance, namely proper and safe carriage. There is therefore no reason to doubt the Court of Appeal's conclusion that the first defendant was liable under the contract of carriage to all three passengers, and that he must answer for the fault of the second defendant, who in this respect was his agent for performance under § 278 BGB . . .

Case 119

REICHSGERICHT (THIRD CIVIL SENATE) 5 OCTOBER 1917
RGZ 91, 21 = JW 1918, 95 (with approving note by K Friedrichs)

The male plaintiff is a senior assistant on the railways. When he was moved to J, he was provided with accommodation which had previously been used by Dr, the station supervisor. A few months after moving in, his daughter, the female plaintiff, contracted tuberculosis, and had to go on a voyage for her health. The plaintiffs attribute this illness to the fact that the dwelling was infected with tuberculosis bacilli, Dr's wife having had pulmonary trouble, and that the defendant State failed to disinfect the dwelling until five or six days after they moved in. They therefore claim damages for the loss attributable to the disease, not all of which may have manifested itself.

The Landgericht allowed the claims. The Oberlandesgericht rejected the defendant's appeal in respect of the male plaintiff's claim, but allowed it in respect of that of the female plaintiff, whose claim was therefore dismissed. The female plaintiff's appeal was allowed, and the defendant's appeal was dismissed.

Reasons

On the basis of the evidence, the Court of Appeal concluded that the female plaintiff became ill because the service dwelling in which she lived had been infected with tuberculosis bacilli during the illness of Mrs Dr, but it held that the only person to whom the defendant was liable was the male plaintiff: he had a claim, based on an analogous application of §§ 618, 278 BGB, for the damage he had suffered through his daughter's illness. The court said that the delay in disinfecting the house was due to the fault of Dr D, the railway doctor appointed by the defendant who attended to Mrs Dr. It was the duty of Dr D to inform the railway authorities of all cases of tuberculosis which came to his notice in his capacity as railway doctor, and if he had performed this duty, the house would have been disinfected at the right time. But the Court of Appeal disallowed the female plaintiff's claim for damages on the ground that she had no contractual or similar relationship with the defendant, and that her claim in tort failed because the defendant, having adduced exculpatory proof under § 831 BGB, was not liable for Dr D.

So far as the male plaintiff's rights are concerned, the Court of Appeal was correct in the result but wrong in the reasons, and so far as the female plaintiff's rights are concerned, it was wrong in both regards.

Since the male plaintiff is an official, the solution must be looked for in public law; and since there are no relevant tests, it must depend on the principles which emerge from the nature of the case in the light of the legal ideas which control decisions in analogous relationships subject to private law. It is established by the Reichsgericht that the State and other bodies of public law owe their officials a duty of care such as is implied into the contract of employment by § 618 BGB. Thus it has been held that under the Prussian Act on Conditions of Service of Teachers in Public Schools of 3 March 1897, local authorities are bound to ensure that the accommodation they provide for teachers are safe and properly maintained, and that they are liable for any injury or illness caused to the teacher by culpable breach of this duty (RGZ 71, 243). This duty of care is closely related to the fact that the accommodation is provided so as to enable the occupant to perform his service obligations or to perform them more easily. Being required to use the service dwelling for the performance of his duties, the official can expect the local authority to protect him adequately against defects in the dwelling which imperil his health. This leads to the conclusion that in respect of official accommodation, the State owes the same duty of protection to the dependants whom the official is entitled to lodge in the dwelling as to the official himself. For if the official is bound to use the accommodation provided, so, too, are they, in the interests of maintaining the family community.

So far as the official himself is concerned, the protective duty owed to him means that he can hold the State responsible for its breach, not only when his own health suffers but also when he suffers loss through injury to the health of a dependant. Just as the official's entitlement to compensation when his own health is affected is based on the application of § 618 BGB by analogy so, when a dependant's health is affected, private law powerfully suggests that the dependant has a claim for damages as well as the official himself. If a landlord is responsible for unhealthy conditions on the leased premises and a member of the tenant's family suffers thereby, the tenant can sue the landlord under § 538 BGB for the consequent harm he may suffer (RGZ 77, 99, 101). But in addition the dependant himself can normally sue the landlord for his own harm (though not for his pain and suffering). Unless very peculiar circumstances indicate a different conclusion, the tenant of a family dwelling who concludes a lease must be taken, as the landlord must know, to intend to obtain the maximum protection for the members of his household and to acquire for them the same rights in relation to the safety of the premises as he himself enjoys against the landlord (§ 328 BGB). If the landlord's contractual duties are not extended in this manner, injured dependants would be restricted to claim in tort, and would not have the benefit afforded to the tenant by §§ 278, 538 BGB, that the landlord is strictly liable for any defects in the premises existing at the time of the contract. To give such different rights to the tenant and to his dependants is offensive to proper legal sentiment and false to the tenant's purpose in contracting, for, as the landlord is bound to know, he wants his dependants to be as well placed as himself to sue for damages. So, too, in the contract of employment of private law where the employer provides the employee with a family house so as to facilitate the rendering of the contractual services, the employee must be taken to intend the employer to assume the duty, as regards the condition and maintenance of the living quarters, to protect his dependants from danger to life and limb to the same extent as himself (§ 618 BGB) and to have them acquire rights of their own to this effect. Now, if an official who is directed to live in service quarters could not claim from the State protection against dangerous defects in the living premises for those dependants who are entitled to stay in the dwelling, and if his dependants did not have a claim of their own to the effect, there would be an intolerable difference in the treatment of cognate legal relationships in public and private law. Such differential treatment would be all the more unjustifiable as the official and his dependants do not have the freedom of choice which is open to the tenant or employee and their dependants, but are bound to use the accommodation provided. This extension to the dependants of the State's duty of care is also in line with the development in public law of the state's duty to look after the family of its officials. It is one of the benefits to which officials are entitled, not by way of contractual counter-performance for their services, but as a means of assuring their position in life.

In the case for decision, the State has failed to satisfy its duty of care, since it failed to take steps to ensure that its service accommodations were disinfected sufficiently soon after the departure of an occupant in whose family tuberculosis had broken out. The rules certainly provide that in such a case the station-master is to undertake the disinfection. A duty is also imposed on railway doctors and supervisors to inform the railway authorities of any cases of tuberculosis in the families of railway employees which come to their knowledge. If this duty is performed, the railway authorities would be in a position to give the station-master due notice of any required disinfection. But if no such notification is given, as may easily happen, the regulations make no provision for securing the object in question. The dangers to which officials are exposed in the absence of such notification is such that the defendant should have provided for steps to be taken which would permit the premises to be disinfected at the right time, possibly by making inquiry of the station doctor before assigning accommodation to a new occupant.

Case 120

BUNDESGERICHTSHOF (SECOND CIVIL SENATE) 11 APRIL 1951
BGHZ 1, 383 = NJW 1951, 798

The plaintiff, who had in-growing toe-nails, was referred for out-patient treatment to the defendant city's hospital by the local Medical Union of which he was a member. He was made to sit down on a three-piece settee, about 30 inches high, designed for gynaecological examinations but used as an auxiliary operating table, the back part having been fixed in a horizontal position. The second defendant, who had been the hospital's chief doctor for many years, gave the plaintiff a local anaesthetic, an injection of 2 per cent novocaine solution, in either one big toe or both. While waiting for this to work, the plaintiff suddenly lost consciousness and fell off the settee. He injured his cervical column in the fall, and has since experienced severe stiffness and loss of function in both arms. At the time of the accident, the second defendant was standing at the door of the small operating theatre, speaking to his chauffeur, and the operating sister was quite close to the plaintiff, treating a patient for burns.

The plaintiff claims that the defendants are liable on the following grounds. No one told him to lie down after the injection, so he was still sitting when he suddenly became unconscious. Had he known he should lie down, he would have done so, and not fallen. The second defendant should have realised and guarded against the risk of a sudden faint, in particular by making him lie down, but instead of taking any such steps he left the plaintiff to his own devices after giving him the injection. This was the sole reason for the accident, which had rendered him wholly and, as it seemed, permanently unfit for work. The plaintiff claims an annuity for lost earnings and damages for pain and suffering from both defendants.

The Landgericht rejected the claim, but the Oberlandesgericht held the plaintiff entitled to a monthly sum for loss of earnings and damages for pain and suffering. The defendants' appeal was successful only in part.

Reasons

The plaintiff has a good contractual claim against the first defendant. The Reichsgericht always held that when a General Health Insurance Scheme (AOK) refers a member to a hospital, the contract it makes with the hospital is one in favour of the patient whereby, under § 328 BGB, the patient acquires a direct claim to proper treatment against the operator of the hospital (RGZ 165, 106). The first defendant entrusted to the second defendant the treatment of the National Health patient referred to it, so he became the first defendant's agent for performance and the first defendant is accordingly responsible to the plaintiff under § 278 BGB for any fault committed by the second defendant in the execution of his professional medical activity.

Between the plaintiff and the second defendant there were no direct contractual relations. A hospital doctor's contractual duty to undertake the proper treatment of National Health patients is normally owed only to the hospital which appoints him. But if a hospital doctor actually does embark on the treatment of a union patient and injures him in his health by infringing a widely recognised rule of medical science, he is liable to the patient under §§ 823 ff. BGB, whether or not he has any contract with the patient. It is immaterial whether the fault of the doctor is one of commission or of omission. The doctor may be under no obligation to the patient to treat him at all, but if he does so, he must avoid injuring him in body or health by breach of the rules of medical science [reference omitted].

In the instant case the Court of Appeal was right to find that it was the second defendant's fault that the plaintiff did not lie down after the injection; he should have told him himself or got the operating sister to do so.

The appellant contends that the failure to tell the plaintiff to lie down was not an adequate cause of the consequent harm. This is not so. The decisions of the Reichsgericht cited by the appellant on consequences for which the actor is not responsible because the causal connection is not adequate refer to consequences which occur only under extremely peculiar circumstances and through quite improbable concatenations of events and which can be ignored in the normal course of things. The consequences here, according to the expert, are not of this kind. On the contrary, the expert expressly emphasised that the reason for the good old rule that a patient should always be prone or supine during all manipulations and injections is precisely the possibility of a faint and a fall; it may be true that this rule cannot always be observed in practice and often is not, but such practical considerations cannot relieve the doctor of the charge that he ignored a duty of care. In such a case there can be no question of any interruption of the adequate causal connection. The appellant is also wrong to say that the Court of Appeal pitched the doctor's duty of care too high. The court was right to follow the expert, whose evidence was based on his knowledge of the rules of the medical art, and who stated in clear terms that there was undeniable negligence in this case unless perhaps it could be proved that the sister had been enjoined to attend to the patient and that the patient had disobeyed her instruction to lie down.

It follows that the plaintiff's claim for monthly payments is established against the first defendant under §§ 276, 278 BGB and against the second defendant under § 823 BGB. However, the second defendant alone is liable for the damages for pain and suffering under § 847 BGB. Only under § 831 BGB could the first defendant be held liable for such damages. The defendant city asserts that it has satisfied the requisite exculpatory proof. We agree. It was common ground that the second defendant had been chief doctor in the first defendant's hospital for many years and that the nurse had served as operating sister for nine years without any criticism. The plaintiff did not even assert, much less prove, anything that tended to show that the second defendant had been guilty of any fault during his twenty years' service in the defendant city's hospital. Under such circumstances, the hospital management cannot be expected to adduce any further exculpatory proof.

Case 121

REICHSGERICHT (THIRD CIVIL SENATE) 8 JANUARY 1926
RGZ 112, 290

On 8 January 1919 and the following days several people went to the All Saints Hospital in B to be treated for scabies. They were rubbed with an ointment which, though thought to be the normal sulphur ointment, was in fact extremely poisonous with chromium. The treatment resulted in the death of Joh. Sch. and of Ha., a coachman, whose mother and heirs are respectively plaintiffs, and in severe injury to Miss Ch. H. The fatal ointment had been supplied to the city B by an independent apothecary.

These are suits for damages against the city B. Miss Ch. H seeks an indemnity for her medical expenses, loss of earnings, and damaged clothing, as well as damages for pain and suffering and a decree that the defendant is liable for any future damage due to the chromium poisoning. Mrs Sch. claims burial expenses and an indemnity for the support her son would have provided had he lived. Ha.'s widow and children likewise claim for loss of support.

The Landgericht gave judgment for all the plaintiffs. The Oberlandesgericht dismissed the claims of Ch. H and of Ha.'s heirs, and dismissed also the city's appeal in the case of

Frau Sch. Appeal has been brought to this court by Ch. H, the heirs of Ha., and the city. The judgment below is vacated, and the matter remanded to the Court of Appeal for further proceedings.

Reasons

All Saints Hospital is primarily a charitable institution through which its owner, the city B, performs its public welfare functions by providing poor patients with free medical treatment and, in suitable cases, free board and nursing as well. Its relationship with these patients is purely one of public law with no private law elements. But other patients pay a fee, fixed according to a sliding scale, for treatment and nursing in the hospital, and these people are admitted under a contract of private law, whether of services or of some other kind (see RGZ 64, 231; 83, 71; 91, 134 and 263). Thus the duties of the city and the consequences of their breach are determined for the first class of patients by public law, and for the second class by the contract law of the BGB, unless, of course, tort law applies.

Ch. H, Joh. Sch., and Ha. were treated in the All Saints Hospital with a poisonous chromium mixture instead of the normal sulphur ointment. Sch. and Ha. died, but Ch. H regained her health after a long period in hospital. The fatal ointment was first used on 8 January 1919. According to the Court of Appeal, the mere fact of this occurrence betokens no fault on the part of the city. The court accepted the testimony of Professor J that the nurses who were applying the ointment would not be alerted by the fact that it was greenish in colour rather than yellow: the usual ointment used to vary in colour because the Vaseline used during the war and immediately thereafter was not uniform. The poisonous ointment was purchased from an independent apothecary. Of course, the hospital doctors were not bound to test the ointment before using it: it would take far too much of a doctor's time and energy if he had to check the composition of every medicament he prescribed. For this occurrence, then, only the apothecary is responsible.

But the Court of Appeal found that on the first application of the ointment on 8 January, many of the patients screamed and one of them had a fit of vomiting. Such reactions are normally rare and sporadic, so the number of them on this occasion should have led the nurses to inform Dr U or some other doctor in the hospital immediately, and the doctor should then have had the ointment checked forthwith. Then its odd colour would have confirmed the suspicion that it had been incorrectly made up. Had this happened, the Court of Appeal found, the poisonous quality of the ointment would have been discovered that very day, and the fateful events of the following two days would have been avoided. As it was, either the nurses failed in their duty to inform the doctors, or the doctors failed in their duty to investigate.

Up to this point the views of the Court of Appeal are logical and correct, but hereafter their analysis of the case, both factually and legally, is inadequate.

1. When the clinic accepted Ch. H for treatment as a charity patient, there arose between her and the city a relationship in public law which imposed on the city a public law duty to treat her in an appropriate way without endangering her life and limb, and gave Ch. H a right in public law to have such treatment. Thus there was superimposed on the city's general welfare duties a specific obligation to Ch. H with a defined content such as to render the city liable if this obligation were broken by the fault of the person whose

services the city used in the performance of its obligation. As this Senate held on 11 March 1921 (RGZ 102, 6; see also RGZ 98, 343), the legal idea which applies in private contract law by reason of its expression in § 278 BGB applies in public law relationships as well, unless there is some special feature in a case which excluded its application. No such feature is present here; indeed, to hold that the principle of law contained in § 278 BGB was inapplicable to the public law relationship between a commune and a charity patient in a communal hospital would be to pervert the very notion of welfare.

Ch. H was given the ointment treatment on 8 January, and very early on that day, since she presented herself at the clinic at 7 a.m. and was back home two and a half hours later. As has been established, neither the nurses nor the doctors were negligent in the original treatment, but if the requisite care had been taken and the ointment investigated, then, as the Oberlandesgericht found, the dreadful mistake made by the apothecary would have been discovered that very day. The city should then have informed Ch. H immediately— for her name and address were in their books—of any possible counter- measures. This would have been not just an act of humanity, but part of its public law duty towards her. The judges of fact must therefore investigate, with the aid of experts if need be, whether Ch. H's injuries could have been avoided or reduced if such a communication had been made, that is, whether and how far the failure to make it was a cause of the plaintiff's suf- fering. Even if this question is resolved in favour of Ch. H, however, she will still have no claim for damages for pain and suffering, for according to § 253 BGB, money damages can be awarded for non-economic harm only in the cases prescribed by law. The idea here expressed by the legislator is that in the normal case one does not have to pay for the so- called immaterial harm one may cause. An exception is made in § 847 BGB which imposes an obligation to repair such harm in cases of injury to body and health, but it only applies when such harm results from an unlawful act as laid down in the BGB. Thus § 847 BGB cannot give rise to a claim when the defendant's liability is based only on faulty breach of a contractual obligation (see RGZ 65, 17; JW 1910, 112 no. 13). Just as this exceptional rule cannot be applied by analogy to breach of contractual duties, so it cannot be applied to faulty breaches of public law obligations.

Only if the city were liable in tort as well as for breach of its public law duties would Ch. H's claim for damages for pain and suffering be good. On this point also the views of the Court of Appeal seem inadequate. There is nothing wrong with its finding that the city was free from fault with regard to the provision of the ointment, and in its choice and appointment of its doctors and nurses. There was no need to direct or supervise the application of the ointment, as such a mechanical task was well within the competence of trained nurses. Thus the city cannot be made liable under § 831 BGB. But that does not conclude the matter. One must distinguish between the duty of a business or insti- tution to supervise the performance of individual tasks and its general duty to supervise, monitor, and instruct, for breach of which it may be liable under § 823 BGB, a liability which attaches to a commune if the breach is due to one of its constitutional represen- tatives under §§ 31, 89 BGB. What the precise implications are of this general duty of supervision must depend on the individual case, and especially on whether the execution and supervision of tasks has been entrusted to knowledgeable persons who are familiar with them and who have proved themselves reliable. It will only be very rarely that a busi- ness or institution will be able to exempt itself entirely from its duty to exercise this control (see RGZ 53, 53 and 276; 82, 206; 95, 181; 96, 81; JW 1906, 547 no. 13; JW 1906, 75 no. 16; JW 1909, 659 no. 10).

In the present case, the city is performing a welfare function, and poor patients trust it with their greatest assets, namely their health and life. It follows that the city must issue instructions through its top management that it is the duty of nurses to inform the doctors whenever any medicament has an unexpected effect and whenever anything unusual occurs on its being administered and that it is the duty of the doctors, if so informed, to make an immediate investigation. But this does not exhaust the city's duties in the matter. It is not enough simply to issue these instructions: the city must also see to it by suitable occasional checks that they are being followed. From the opinion below we cannot tell whether the city has satisfied its general duties of instruction and super-vision, any breach and its causal effect being for the plaintiff to establish, with any possible assistance from the rules regarding prima-facie proof. The tort aspects of Ch. H's suit therefore require further investigation.

2. With regard to the death of young Sch., the Oberlandesgericht held that although he paid no fee to the hospital when he was accepted for treatment, he thereupon entered into a private law contract with the city. Were this so, then his mother's suit must fail, for in a contractual claim she could only claim for the harm which her son had suffered as a result of breach by his contractor, and her claim was for a loss which had befallen the mother rather than the son, namely the loss of the support which Joh. Sch. would have been bound to provide had he lived. Such a claim, which is at odds with the general prin-ciple that compensation may be claimed only by the person directly affected, could only be based on § 844 II BGB, and that provision requires that her son's death be attributa-ble to a tort for which the city is responsible through its constitutional organs. § 844 II has no application in the law of contract, any more than § 844 I (see JW 1907, 710 no. 18; JW 1908, 9 no. 9). Now the Oberlandesgericht gave no reason for holding that there was a private law contract in this case. One almost has the impression that the only reason was that unlike Miss Ch. H, Sch. did not return home after the treatment but was kept in hospital while the scabies were to be cured. But gratuitous admission to the hospital is just like gratuitous treatment to an out-patient: it is an act of public law welfare which gives rise to public law relations between the in-patient and the city. But even though the Court of Appeal was wrong to invoke private law, the decision it reached is correct in public law.

The poisonous ointment was applied to Sch. on 9 January, so his death was indubitably due to negligence on the part of either the doctors or the nurses. Now just as the princi-ple that a debtor must answer for the fault of his assistants as he does for his own applies in public as well as private law, so do the legal ideas expressed in § 844 BGB. If it were otherwise, public law would be intolerably and unjustifiably defective. Nevertheless, we cannot yet affirm the decision of the Oberlandesgericht in favour of Frau Sch. since it is possible that even though Sch. did not actually pay the hospital as required by the tariff for money patients, he might nevertheless be under a duty to pay and so have entered into a private law contract with the city. Thus in this case also we need further facts, including whether the city was guilty of any breach of its general duty of supervision (see §§ 823, 31, 89 BGB) . . .

Notes to Cases 95–121

1. Most of these cases illustrate (i) the difficulties experienced by German law as a result of § 831 BGB and (ii) the ways used by the courts to produce a more sensible result. Thus, cases 100,

105, 106, and 107 show how the employer must supervise his employee properly and constantly or otherwise run the risk of being held liable under § 823 I BGB for breach of his own primary duty; case 96 discusses issues relevant to § 31 BGB; cases 98 and 109 discuss the thorny question of "unlawfulness" in the context of § 831 BGB (though much of the reasoning in the latter case appears to have become obsolete); cases 111–121 illustrate what is, perhaps, the most ingenious way of bypassing § 831 BGB, namely by invoking the aid of the law of contract. As Zweigert and Kötz have put it (*An Introduction to Comparative Law*, 2nd ed. II, 147):

The sole purpose of these decisions is to put the accident victim in a better position than if his only claim for damages were based on delict. Under German law, with regard to prescription, burden of proof and especially vicarious liability, a victim is in a much better position to claim damages if he can claim in contract for the harm he has suffered. Not the slightest blame attaches to the German courts for using the contract for the benefit of third parties in order to get round the misconceived legal policy contained in § 831 BGB; nor is there anything wrong with what they have done as a matter of positive law. Nevertheless, it must be seen that these are cases where the harmful consequences of accidents are attributed to the person responsible, not because he is guilty of any breach of specifically contractual duties but because he has committed a breach of general duties of care imposed by the law of delict. The position of German law may be excused by the necessity caused by the unfortunate policy of § 831 BGB, but the comparative lawyer has to classify problems according to the true significance of their actual facts. These cases must therefore be put in the law of tort, as is done everywhere else in the world. In doing so, the comparatist must realise that it may be necessary to study a person's contractual relations with third parties in order to discover *to whom* he owes his delictual duties of care not to cause harm.

But this solution is, at best, only a partial one. Claims formed in contract cannot, because of another troublesome provision (§ 253 BGB), compensate the plaintiff for his pain and suffering (contrast § 847 BGB). The return to the law of delict thus not only produces an intellectually neater classification; it can also benefit the victims (see case 120). The growing tendency to invoke § 823 I BGB, by discovering what the Common lawyers would call non-delegable duties, may then be described as a move in the right direction (for illustrations see cases 95, 101, 114, 115 etc.). From the little said in this paragraph, it should be clear that these cases must be read in close conjunction with the text of Chapter 3, section A.

2. The cases and the preceding commentary make it clear that there exist some important structural differences between German law on the one hand and the Common law on the other. One further difference of classification must also be noted with American Common law: in the latter, vicarious liability is a subject, which is shared between agency and tort and the two relative Restatements. Thus, the master–servant relationship and the notion of "scope of employment" are defined in §§ 220 and 229 of the *Restatement (Second) of Agency*, (and are reproduced below in Addendum 1). On the other hand, liability for independent contractors is treated in §§ 409–29 of the *Restatement (Second) of Torts*. Tort books that discuss (briefly) the matters raised in this chapter include Dobbs, *The Law of Torts* (2000), pp. 905 *et seq.*; Fleming, *The Law of Torts*, 9th ed. (1998), pp. 409 *et seq.*

3. Once the above points are well digested, the comparatist should experience no difficulty in understanding what is happening in "the other system", the differences being differences in emphasis or detail rather than substance. Thus, the rationale for imposing vicarious liability is the same everywhere: the belief that it is more efficient to place the risk on the employer's shoulders than on the employee's. The same rationale also seems to favour the more modern tendency not to allow masters (or, more likely, their insurers) the right to claim contribution or an indemnity from the servant unless the latter's conduct was intentional and grossly negligent. (For English law see Markesinis and Deakin, *Tort Law* 4th edn. (1999), chapter 6; for American law see Comment, 34 *La. L. Rev.* 79 (1973); Note, 53 *Or. L. Rev.* 366 (1974).) The tendency to make employers rather than employees liable also accounts for the increased willingness to give a wide meaning to such inherently ambiguous notions as "course of employment". As already noted, German law is, perhaps, the strictest in this respect, with French and American law showing a clear willingness to include even acts of violence which the servant's employment merely gave him the opportunity to commit. The

French decision which held the employer of a cinema attendant vicariously liable for the latter's rape of a cinema patron (Crim. 5 nov. 1953, D. 1953, J. 698) has happily not been followed in the US: see *Mays* v. *Pico Finance Co.*, 339 So. 2d 382 (La. App. 1976). But there are other just as grotesque examples; thus in *Miller* v. *Keating* 349 So. 2d 265 (La. 1977) the attempted murder of a company employee by some of his co-employees was held to be within the scope of their employment since the corporation (the Common employer) was the beneficiary of the victim's insurance policy—a conclusion which led one commentator to remark that "cynicism reaches new heights when attempted murder becomes regarded as 'fair and reasonably incident' to corporate offences"! (Comment, 52 *Tul. L. Rev.* 443, 450 (1978).) But, as stated in section A of chapter 3, this point need not be laboured too much: aberrant cases can always be found and the vagueness of such notions as "course of employment" may also be their main virtue since it provides the desirable degree of flexibility in decisions. (For French law and the possibility that the insurance factor may in some cases account for such wide interpretations see Hassler, "La responsabilité des commettants" D. Chron. (1980) 125–8; Markesinis, "La perversion des notions de la responsabilité civile délictuelle par la pratique des assurances", *Rev. int. dr. comp.*, 301 (1983).)

4. Lack of space prevents a more detailed annotation of the cases but three more points can be made briefly. First, in the case of borrowed servants, American law until recently took a different view from English and German law and tended to make the "special or temporary employer" liable for the torts of the borrowed servant on the grounds, *inter alia*, that he had (at the moment of the accident) the benefit of the services of the borrowed servant. See *Lewis* v. *Potter*, 149 Mont. 430, 427 P. 2d 306 (1967). Recent decisions, however, suggest an opposite movement (for example, *Salsgiver* v. *E S Ritter Co.*, 42 Ore. App. 547, 600 P. 2d 951 (1979); *LeSuer* v. *LeSuer*, 350 So. 2d 796 (Fla. App. 1977)); and, as stated, Californian courts have favoured plaintiffs further by allowing the victim to sue *both* employers and then let them solve their internal relationship: *Strait* v. *Hale Constr. Co.*, 26 Cal. App. 3d 941, 103 Cal. Rptr. 487 (1972).

Secondly, American courts have developed the family purpose doctrine which, in some circumstances, makes car owners vicariously liable for harm caused by persons to whom the vehicles were loaned or made available. Although attempts to introduce the doctrine in England were made by Lord Denning MR in *Launchbury* v. *Morgan*, they met with the disapproval of the House of Lords which felt that the matter should best be left to the legislator to settle. Needless to say, the legislator these days does not have the time to intervene in such matters of relative detail with the result that in cases such as these the English victim may be in a less favourable position than his American counterpart.

Finally, § 831 BGB and the growth of the non-delegable duty device in Germany and England must be compared carefully with §§ 409–29 of the American *Restatement (Second) of Torts*. The text of the basic rule (§ 409 on liability of torts of independent contractors) and the exceptions are reproduced below in *Addendum 2*. A glance at these rules makes it clear that the exceptions are gradually swallowing up the rule, a result which led one American court to say that ". . . it would be proper to say that the rule is now primarily important as a preamble to the catalog of its exceptions". (*Pacific Fire Ins. Co.* v. *Kenny Boiler & Mfg. Co.*, 277 NW 226 (1937)).

Addendum 1

Restatement (Second) of Agency

§ 220. *Definition of servant*

(2) In determining whether one acting for another is a servant or an independent contractor, the following matters of fact, among others, are considered:

(*a*) the extent of control which, by the agreement, the master may exercise over the details of the work;

(*b*) whether or not the one employed is engaged in a distinct occupation or business;

(*c*) the kind of occupation, with reference to whether, in the locality, the work is usually done under the direction of the employer or by a specialist without supervision;

(*d*) the skill required in the particular occupation;

(*e*) whether the employer or the workman supplies the instrumentalities, tools, and the place of work for the person doing the work;

(*f*) the length of time for which the person is employed;

(*g*) the method of payment, whether by the time or by the job;

(*h*) whether or not the work is a part of the regular business of the employer;

(*i*) whether or not the parties believe they are creating the relation of master and servant; and

(*j*) whether the principal is or is not in business.

§ 229. *Kind of conduct within the scope of employment*

(1) To be within the scope of employment, conduct must be of the same general nature as that authorized, or incidental to the conduct authorised.

(2) In determining whether or not the conduct, although not authorised, is nevertheless so similar to or incidental to the conduct authorised as to be within the scope of employment, the following matters of fact are to be considered:

(*a*) whether or not the act is one commonly done by such servants;

(*b*) the time, place, and purpose of the act;

(*c*) the previous relations between the master and the servant;

(*d*) the extent to which the business of the master is apportioned between different servants;

(*e*) whether or not the act is outside the enterprise of the master or, if within the enterprise, has not been entrusted to any servant;

(*f*) whether or not the master has reason to expect that such an act will be done;

(*g*) the similarity in quality of the act done to the act authorised;

(*h*) whether or not the instrumentality by which the harm is done has been furnished by the master to the servant;

(*i*) the extent of departure from the normal method of accomplishing an authorised result; and

(*j*) whether or not the act is seriously criminal.

Addendum 2

Restatement (Second) of Torts

§ 409. *General principle*

Except as stated in §§ 410–29, the employer of an independent contractor is not liable for physical harm caused to another by an act or omission of the contractor or his servants.

§ 410. *Contractor's conduct in obedience to employer's directions*

The employer of an independent contractor is subject to the same liability for physical harm caused by an act or omission committed by the contractor pursuant to orders or directions negligently given by the employer, as though the act or omission were that of the employer himself.

§ 411. *Negligence in selection of contractor*

An employer is subject to liability for physical harm to third persons caused by his failure to exercise reasonable care to employ a competent and careful contractor

(*a*) to do work which will involve a risk of physical harm unless it is skilfully and carefully done, or

(*b*) to perform any duty which the employer owes to third persons.

§ 412. *Failure to inspect work of contractor after completion*

One who is under a duty to exercise reasonable care to maintain land or chattels in such condition as not to involve unreasonable risk of bodily harm to others and who entrusts the work of repair and maintenance to an independent contractor, is subject to liability for bodily harm caused to them by his failure to exercise such care as the circumstances may reasonably require him to exercise to ascertain whether the land or chattel is in reasonably safe condition after the contractor's work is complete.

§ 413. *Duty to provide for taking of precautions against dangers involved in work entrusted to contractor*

One who employs an independent contractor to do work which the employer should recognize as likely to create, during its progress, a peculiar unreasonable risk of physical harm to others unless special precautions are taken, is subject to liability for physical harm caused to them by the absence of such precautions if the employer

    (*a*) fails to provide in the contract that the contractor shall take such precautions, or

    (*b*) fails to exercise reasonable care to provide in some other manner for the taking of such precautions.

§ 414. *Negligence in exercising control retained by employer*

One who entrusts work to an independent contractor, but who retains the control of any part of the work, is subject to liability for physical harm to others for whose safety the employer owes a duty to exercise reasonable care, which is caused by his failure to exercise his control with reasonable care.

§ 414A. *Duty of possessor of land to prevent activities and conditions dangerous to those outside of land*

A possessor of land who has employed or permitted an independent contractor to do work on the land, and knows that the activities of the contractor or conditions created by him involve an unreasonable risk of physical harm to those outside of the land, is subject to liability to them for such harm if he fails to exercise reasonable care to protect them against it.

§ 415. *Duty to supervise equipment and methods of contractors or concessionaires on land held open to public*

A possessor of land who holds it open to the public for any purpose is subject to liability to members of the public entering for that purpose for physical harm caused to them by his failure to exercise reasonable care to protect them against unreasonably dangerous activities of, or unreasonably dangerous conditions created by, an independent contractor or concessionaire employed or permitted to do work or carry on an activity on the land.

§ 416. *Work dangerous in absence of special precautions*

One who employs an independent contractor to do work which the employer should recognise as likely to create during its progress a peculiar risk of physical harm to others unless special precautions are taken, is subject to liability for physical harm caused to them by the failure of the contractor to exercise reasonable care to take such precautions, even though the employer has provided for such precautions.

§ 417. *Work done in public place*

One who employs an independent contractor to do work in a public place which unless carefully done involves a risk of making the physical condition of the place dangerous for the use of members of the public, is subject to liability for physical harm caused to members of the public by a negligent act or omission of the contractor which makes the physical condition of the place dangerous for their use.

§ 418. *Maintenance of public highways and other public places*

(1) One who is under a duty to construct or maintain a highway in reasonably safe condition for the use of the public, and who entrusts its construction, maintenance, or repair to an independent contractor, is subject to the same liability for physical harm to persons using the highway while it is held open for travel during such work, caused by the negligent failure of the contractor to make it reasonably safe for travel, as though the employer had retained the work in his own hands.

(2) The statement in subsection (1) applies to any place which is maintained by a government for the use of the public, if the government is under the same duty to maintain it in reasonably safe condition as it owes to the public in respect to the condition of its highways.

§ 419. *Repairs which lessor is under a duty to his lessee to make*

A lessor of land who employs an independent contractor to perform a duty which the lessor owes to his lessee to maintain the leased land in reasonably safe condition, is subject to liability to the lessee, and to third persons upon the land with the consent of the lessee, for physical harm caused by the contractor's failure to exercise reasonable care to make the land reasonably safe.

§ 420. *Repairs gratuitously undertaken by lessor*

A lessor of land who employs an independent contractor to make repairs which the lessor is under no duty to make, is subject to the same liability to the lessee, and to others upon the land with the consent of the lessee, for physical harm caused by the contractor's negligence in making or purporting to make the repairs as though the contractor's conduct were that of the lessor.

§ 421. *Maintenance of structures on land retained in lessor's possession necessary to tenant's enjoyment of leased land*

A possessor of land who, having a part of the land, is under a duty to maintain in reasonably safe condition the part retained by him, and who entrusts the repair of such part to an independent contractor, is subject to the same liability to the lessee, and to others upon the retained part of the land with the consent of the lessee, for physical harm caused by the negligence of the contractor in failing to maintain such part of the land in reasonably safe condition, as though the lessor had himself retained the making of the repairs in his own hands.

§ 422. *Work on buildings and other structures on land*

A possessor of land who entrusts to an independent contractor construction, repairs, or other work on the land, or on a building or other structure upon it, is subject to the same liability as though he had retained the work in his own hands to others on or outside the land for physical harm caused to them by the unsafe condition of the structure
  (a) while the possessor has retained possession of the land during the progress of the work, or
  (b) after he had resumed possession of the land upon its completion.

§ 422A. *Work withdrawing lateral support*

One who employs an independent contractor to do work which the employer knows or should know to be likely to withdraw lateral support from the land of another is subject to the same liability for the contractor's withdrawal of such support as if the employer had retained the work in his own hands.

§ 423. *Making or repair of instrumentalities used in highly dangerous activities*

One who carries on an activity which threatens a grave risk of serious bodily harm or death unless the instrumentalities used are carefully constructed and maintained, and who employs an independent contractor to construct or maintain such instrumentalities, is subject to the same liability for physical harm caused by the negligence of the contractor in constructing or maintaining such instrumentalities as though the employer had himself done the work of construction or maintenance.

§ 424. *Precautions required by statutes or regulation*

One who by statute or by administrative regulation is under a duty to provide specified safeguards or precautions for the safety of others is subject to liability to the others for whose protection the duty is imposed for harm caused by the failure of a contractor employed by him to provide such safeguards or precautions.

§ 425. *Repair of chattel supplied or land held open to public as place of business*

One who employs an independent contractor to maintain in safe condition land which he holds open to the entry of the public as his place of business, or a chattel which he supplies for others to use for his business purposes or which he leases for immediate use, is subject to the same liability for physical harm caused by the contractor's negligent failure to maintain the land or chattel in reasonably safe condition, as though he had retained its maintenance in his own hands.

§ 426. *Negligence collateral to risk of doing the work*

Except as stated in §§ 428 and 429, an employer of an independent contractor, unless he is himself negligent, is not liable for physical harm caused by any negligence of the contractor if
    (*a*) the contractor's negligence consists solely in the improper manner in which he does the work, and
    (*b*) it creates a risk of such harm which is not inherent in or normal to the work, and
    (*c*) the employer had no reason to contemplate the contractor's negligence when the contract was made.

§ 427. *Negligence as to danger inherent in the work*

One who employs an independent contractor to do work involving a special danger to others which the employer knows or has reason to know to be inherent in or normal to the work, or which he contemplates or has reason to contemplate when making the contract, is subject to liability for physical harm caused to such others by the contractor's failure to take reasonable precautions against such danger.

§ 427A. *Work involving abnormally dangerous activity*

One who employs an independent contractor to do work which the employer knows or has reason to know to involve an abnormally dangerous activity, is subject to liability to the same extent as the contractor for physical harm to others caused by the activity.

§ 427B. *Work likely to involve trespass or nuisance*

One who employs an independent contractor to do work which the employer knows or has reason to know to be likely to involve a trespass upon the land of another or the creation of a public or a private nuisance, is subject to liability for harm resulting to others from such trespass or nuisance.

§ 428. *Contractor's negligence in doing work which cannot lawfully be done except under a franchise granted to his employer*

An individual or a corporation carrying on an activity which can be lawfully carried on only under a franchise granted by public authority and which involves an unreasonable risk of harm to others, is subject to liability for physical harm caused to such others by the negligence of a contractor employed to do work in carrying on the activity.

§ 429. *Negligence in doing work which is accepted in reliance on the employer's doing the work himself*

One who employs an independent contractor to perform services for another which are accepted in the reasonable belief that the services are being rendered by the employer or by his servants, is subject to liability for physical harm caused by the negligence of the contractor in supplying such services, to the same extent as though the employer were supplying them himself or by his servants.

3. ROAD TRAFFIC ACT OF 19 DECEMBER 1952 [BGB1 I., 837]
(AS AMENDED)

CONTENTS

II Liability

§ 7 Liability of the Keeper of a Vehicle

(1) If in the course of the operation of a motor vehicle a person is killed, the body or the health of a person is injured or an object is damaged, the keeper of the motor vehicle is obliged to compensate the injured party for the damage resulting therefrom.

(2) The duty to compensate is excluded, if the accident was caused by an unavoidable event which is not due to a defect in the construction of the vehicle or to the failure of its mechanism.

An event is deemed to be unavoidable in particular if it is due to the conduct of the injured party or of a third party who is not an employee or an animal and if both the keeper and the driver of the vehicle have applied that care which is required in the light of the circumstances.

(3) If somebody uses the vehicle without the knowledge and consent of the keeper of the vehicle that person is liable to pay compensation for the damage in the place of the keeper; in addition the keeper himself remains liable to pay compensation if the use of the motor vehicle was facilitated by his negligence. The first sentence of this paragraph does not apply if the person using the vehicle was employed by the keeper for the purpose of operating the vehicle or if he was entrusted with the vehicle by the keeper.

§ 8 *Exceptions*

The provisions of § 7 do not apply, if the accident was caused by a vehicle which cannot proceed at a speed exceeding 20 kilometres on level ground or if the injured person was employed in operating the motor vehicle.

§ 8a *Liability to Passengers in the Course of Commercial Transport of Persons*

(1) If a passenger in a motor vehicle has been killed or injured, the keeper of the vehicle is only liable in accordance with § 7 if a commercial transport of passengers for remuneration is involved.

  If an object has been damaged which was carried by a motor vehicle, the keeper of the vehicle is only liable under § 7 if a person who is carried in the vehicle in the circumstances envisaged in § 7 carries the object on himself or with himself.

  The commercial character of a transport of passengers in the meaning of the first and second sentences is not excluded by the fact that the transport is performed by a corporation or institution governed by public law.

(2) The duty of the keeper to pay compensation in respect of the death or injury suffered by a passenger in accordance with para. 1, final sentence, in conjunction with § 7 cannot be excluded or restricted. Any provisions or arguments to the contrary are invalid.

§ 9 *Contributory Negligence of the Injured Party*

If the injured party contributed to the damage by his negligence, § 254 BGB applies with the proviso that if an object was damaged, negligence on the part of the person exercising factual control over the object is treated as equivalent to negligence on the part of the injured party.

§ 10 *Extent of Liability in the Case of Death*

(1) In the case of death, damages to be paid comprise compensation for the expenses of an attempted cure and for the economic loss which the deceased has suffered because his earning capacity was destroyed or reduced during his illness or because his needs were increased. The person liable to pay damages must also reimburse the cost of the burial to the person responsible for it.

(2) If at the time of the injury the deceased stood in a relationship to a third party by virtue of which he was legally bound to maintain the latter, or might become so liable, and if as a result of the death the third party has lost the right to maintenance, the person liable to pay compensation must pay damages to the third party to the extent that the deceased would have been liable to pay maintenance during the probable duration of his life. The duty to compensate arises even if the third party was conceived at the time of the injury, but had not yet been born.

§ 11 *Extent of Liability in the Case of Injury to the Person*

In the case of injury to the person or to health, the damages comprise compensation for the expenses of the cure and for the economic loss which the injured party suffered because his earning capacity was temporarily or permanently destroyed or reduced as a result of the injury or because his needs have increased.

§ 12 *Maximum Amount of Liability*

(1) The person who is bound to pay compensation is liable to pay:

1. Where one person was killed or injured a lump sum of up to DM 500,000 and no more or periodic payments up to DM 30,000 per annum;

2. Where several persons were killed or injured in the same event, notwithstanding the limits laid down in (1), a total lump sum of DM 750,000 and no more or periodical payments of DM 45,000; this restriction does not apply, however, in the cases of § 8*a*, para. 1, first sentence in so far as the liability of the keeper of the vehicle is concerned;

3. Where an object was damaged, up to an amount of DM 100,000 even if several objects were damaged in the same accident.

(2) If the damages to be paid to several claimants involved in the same event exceed in total the maximum amount enumerated in 2., first part of the sentence, or in 3., the damages payable to each individual are reduced in proportion of the total in relation to the maximum amount.

§ 13 *Periodical Payments as Damages*

(1) In the future, damages in respect of the loss or the reduction of earning capacity or because the needs of the injured party have increased as well as the damages due to a third party under § 10, para. 2, must be paid by way of periodical amounts.

(2) The provisions of § 843, II to IV of the BGB apply by way of analogy.

(3) If at the time when judgment was given for periodical payments the judgment debtor was not asked to give security, the person entitled to the payment may demand security nevertheless, if the circumstances of the judgment debtor have deterioriated considerably; in the same circumstances he can demand that the security fixed by the judgment should be increased.

§ 14 *Period of Limitation*

The period of limitation is determined by the analogous application of the rule of the Civil Code governing the limitation of actions in tort.

§ 15 *Duty to Give Notice—Laches*

The claimant for damages forfeits the rights granted by the provisions of this law, unless he had given notice of the accident to the person liable to pay compensation within six months after having ascertained the damage and the identity of the person liable to pay compensation. Forfeiture does not take place if the failure to give notice was due to circumstances for which the claimant for damages is not responsible or if the person liable to pay compensation has come to know of the accident by other means during the period set out above.

§ 16 *Liability due to Other Legal Provisions*

Any Federal provisions are unaffected according to which the keeper of a motor vehicle is more extensively liable for damage caused by the vehicle than according to the provisions of the present law or according to which another person is liable.

§ 17 *Contribution among Several Persons Liable to Pay Compensation*

(1) If damage is caused by several motor vehicles and if the keepers of the vehicles involved are bound by law to pay compensation to a third party, the liability to pay compensation of the keepers of the vehicles and the extent of the compensation to be paid as between themselves depends upon the circumstances, especially according to whether the damage has been caused predominantly by one or the other of the parties. The same applies to the liability of one of the keepers of the vehicles if the damage was caused to another keeper of a vehicle involved in the accident.

(2) The provisions of para. (1) apply by way of analogy if the damage is caused by a motor vehicle and an animal or by a motor vehicle and a railway.

§ 18 *Liability of the Driver to Pay Compensation*

(1) In the circumstances covered by § 7 I, the driver of the motor vehicle is also liable to pay compensation in accordance with the provisions of §§ 8–15. No liability exists if the damage was not caused by the blameworthy conduct of the driver.

(2) The provisions of § 16 apply by way of analogy.

(3) If in the circumstances covered by § 17 the driver of a vehicle is also liable to pay compensation, his liability in relation to the keepers and duties of the other vehicles involved, to a keeper of animals or a railway undertaking is determined by the analysis application of the provisions of § 17.

§ 19 (Abrogated.)

§ 20 *Local Jurisdictions*

Claims based on this Act fall also within the jurisdiction of the court of the district in which the event occurred which caused the damage.

Reform proposal of 24 September 2001 concerning some of the above provisions

§ 7 (1) sentence 2

If the motor vehicle was connected to a trailer at the time of the accident, the keeper of the trailer as well as the keeper of the motor vehicle is obliged to provide compensation to the person suffering harm.

§ 7 (2)

The duty to compensate is excluded if the accident is caused by *force majeure*.

§ 7 (3) sentence 3

Sentences 1 and 2 are to be applied accordingly to the use of a trailer.

§ 8

The provisions of § 7 do not apply,

1. if the accident was caused by a motor vehicle which cannot travel on level ground at a higher speed than twenty kilometres per hour, or by a trailer connected to such a vehicle at the time of the accident,

2. if the injured person was operating the motor vehicle, or

3. if an object has been damaged which was being transported by the motor vehicle or by a trailer connected to it at the time of the accident, unless a person who is being transported is carrying the thing on him or takes it with him.

§ 8a

In the case of commercial transport of persons for remuneration, the duty of the keeper to compensate in accordance with § 7 because of the death or injury of persons transported cannot be either excluded or limited. The commercial character of a transport of persons is not excluded by the fact that the transport is performed by a body or institution governed by public law.

§ 11 sentence 2

In this case, fair compensation in money can also be demanded for harm which is not economic in accordance with § 253 para. 2 of the BGB.

§ 12 (1)

The person who is bound to pay compensation is liable to pay

1. where one person was killed or injured, a lump sum of up to 600,000 Euro or periodic payments of up to 36,000 Euro per annum;

2. where several persons were killed or injured in the same event, notwithstanding the limits laid down in 1, a total lump sum of up to 3,000,000 Euro or periodical payments of up to 180,000 Euro per annum; this restriction does not however apply to a keeper of a motor vehicle who is under a duty to compensate in the case of commercial transport of persons for remuneration;

3. where an object was damaged, a sum of up to 300,000 Euro, even if several objects are damaged in the same event.

§ 12a

(1) If dangerous goods are transported, the person bound to pay compensation is liable to pay

1. where several persons were killed or injured in the same event, notwithstanding the limits laid down in § 12 para. 1 no 1, a total capital sum of up to 6,000,000 Euro or periodic payments of up to 360,000 Euro per annum,

2. where immovable objects are damaged, even if several objects are damaged in the same event, a sum of up to 6,000,000 Euro, in so far as the damage is caused by the characteristics which make the transported goods dangerous. In other respects § 12 para. 1 remains unaffected.

(2) Dangerous goods in the sense of this Act are substances and objects whose transport on the road is forbidden, or allowed only under certain conditions, in accordance with Appendices A and B to the European Convention of 30 September 1957 on the International Carriage of Dangerous Goods by Road (ADR) (reference omitted) in the version applying at that time.

(3) Paragraph 1 is not to be applied in the case of exempted transports of dangerous goods or transports in limited quantities within in the limits laid down in marginal number 10 011 of Annex B to the Convention mentioned in paragraph 2.

(4) Paragraph 1 is not to be applied when the damage on transport has arisen within a business in which dangerous goods are produced, treated, processed, stored, used or destroyed, in so far as the transport takes place on a self-contained site.

(5) § 12 para. 2 applies accordingly.

§ 12b

§§ 12 and 12a are not to be applied when damage is caused by the operation of an armoured caterpillar vehicle.

§ 17 (2)

The provisions of paragraph 1 are to be applied accordingly when the damage is caused by a motor vehicle and a trailer connected to it at the time of the accident, by a motor vehicle and an animal, or by a motor vehicle and a railway.

§ 18 (3)

If in the cases in § 17 the driver of a motor vehicle is also obliged to pay compensation for the damage, the provisions of § 17 are to be applied accordingly to this duty in his relationship with the keepers and drivers of the other motor vehicles involved, with the keeper of the trailer connected to another motor vehicle involved at the time of the accident, with the keeper of the animal or with the railway undertaking.

Case 122

BUNDESGERICHTSHOF (SIXTH CIVIL SENATE) 9 DECEMBER 1959
BGHZ 29, 163 = NJW 1959, 627

The plaintiff's lorry (motor vehicle and two trailers) remained stationary on the right side of the Karlsruhe–Frankfurt autobahn in the night of 7–8 March 1951 because of damage to the engine. About 1.15 a.m. the carrier K—husband of the defendant Sophie K and father of the defendant Herbert Bernhard K—driving a motor lorry with a trailer ran into the plaintiff's stationary lorry. Both lorries sustained considerable damage. K, who had been driving his lorry, suffered such serious injuries that he died on the way to hospital.

The plaintiff contends that the collision is exclusively attributable to the fault of K; for he would have been bound, if he had been attentive enough, to notice the red light of the stationary lorry and the hurricane lantern which had been set up, and could have deviated in time on to the lane for overtaking. He demanded damages from K's heirs.

The District Court upheld the claim in principle. The Court of Appeal, on the other hand, in principle affirmed the defendant's liability in damages, limited only as to one-half. The plaintiff's application for review, in which he sought to have the judgment of the District Court restored, failed for these

Reasons

I. According to the findings of the Court of Appeal the carrier K, with his long-distance lights turned on, ran with the whole width of his vehicle into the stationary lorry, without braking in time or turning off to the left. During the previous one and a half hours several other vehicles had driven past the plaintiff's lorry, whilst it stood on the autobahn. According to the Court of Appeal's view K also would have been bound to notice the stationary lorry if he had been attentive enough, even if it had been completely unlit, and could then still have moved on to the lane for overtaking. It went on to say: the fact that K did not react at all to the obstacle before him proves that he was guilty of gross inattention or, alternatively, that despite his being blinded by the light of oncoming vehicles he drove on with undiminished speed into a space where he could not see. On the basis of the established facts, this view of the Court of Appeal is unexceptional in law. It therefore also held rightly that the defendants, as heirs of K, must under §§ 823, 1967 BGB make good the damage to the plaintiff.

II. The applicant for review objected that the Court of Appeal applied § 17 StVG and awarded to the plaintiff in principle compensation for only half his damage.

He alleges that §§ 7, 17 StVG are not applicable, because the plaintiff's lorry was no longer in operation and urges that a vehicle is no longer in operation, even when it has not reached the end of its journey, if it has come to a full stop from lack of fuel or a mechanical fault. Even if a failure of its engine causes it to stop on a traffic highway and it stays there for a not wholly inappreciable time, it is generally regarded as no longer in operation, since it has lost the capacity to move.

This view of the appellant corresponds in result to the practice of the Reichsgericht and of several Courts of Appeal. According to that practice, a vehicle is no longer in operation in the sense of § 7 StVG if it is reduced to a complete standstill and owing to failure its engine can be set again in operation only after considerable time (e.g. RGZ 122, 270; 333, 132, 262). In so holding, the Reichsgericht also did not start from the engineering notion of operation, according to which a vehicle is in operation only as long as the engine is working directly or indirectly. It preferred the traffic-orientated point of view and even then attributed an accident to the operation of a motor vehicle if it stood in a close local and temporal connection with a particular operation or a particular operating mechanism, irrespective of whether the engine propelled the vehicle or not. According to the Reichsgericht's point of view, approved by the Bundesgerichtshof, the operation of a vehicle is therefore not interrupted as a rule when it stops on the highway with the engine switched off. But even in adopting this traffic-orientated point of view, the Reichsgericht has interpreted the concept of the operation of a motor vehicle strictly, and assumed that the operation comes to an end when, for more than a short time, the vehicle can no longer move under its own power because of engine failure or lack of fuel.

The Bundesgerichtshof is unable to follow this practice of the Reichsgericht because, in view of the enormous increase of motor traffic and its dangers, it no longer conforms to the sense and purpose of § 7 StVG. The purpose of the Act, to protect participants in traffic against the increasing dangers of present-day motor traffic, makes it necessary to give a broad interpretation to the concept "in the operation of a motor vehicle" [references]. In that decision this Senate denied that the vehicle was inoperative and so exempt from strict liability where a driver has left his lorry on the carriageway of a federal highway to have a good night's rest. The Senate also attributed the accident that ensued because a car ran into the stationary lorry to the operation of the stationary vehicle in the sense of

§ 7 StVG. No other conclusion can be reached if similarly an accident occurs because a lorry remains standing for a considerable time on the carriageway of a high-speed highway owing to engine failure. The case that now calls for decision differs from the earlier one only because the lorry here had lost the capacity to proceed under its own power, whereas there, although its engine was turned off, it was ready to move on the highway. That distinction is irrelevant in applying § 7 StVG if one looks at the concept of operation in that provision from the traffic-orientated point of view, as the prevailing opinion now does. The risks which the motor vehicle produces in traffic emanate not only from the engine and its effect on the vehicle but, with the increase of traffic, more and more from its general flow and in particular from motor vehicles which stop or park on the carriageway portion of a high-speed highway. It is precisely on the autobahn on which the present accident occurred that stationary vehicles raise a typical risk for other participants in the traffic. In this case, as the Bundesgerichtshof observed in its judgment of 8 April 1957 [references] the risk of a stationary motor vehicle may even be greater than of a moving one. It is therefore permissible and justified by the sense and purpose of the provisions on liability of the Road Traffic Act to attribute an accident produced by a collision with a stationary vehicle not only to the operation of the moving but also of the stationary vehicle and hence to make both drivers strictly liable in damages. It is irrelevant whether the driver voluntarily pulled up for a break or was forced to stop on the carriageway owing to a defect in the vehicle. The decisive factor is that in both cases other participants in the traffic are put at risk by his vehicle standing on the highway. That an accident due to a defect in the vehicle or a failure of its mechanism should lead to liability of the driver is clear from § 7 StVG which expressly denies that this case constitutes an avoidable event which excludes liability. This liability for accidents which are attributable to a technical defect in the vehicle would, as the Court of Appeal of Karlsruhe (VersR 1956, 260) accurately emphasizes, be rendered nugatory to a considerable extent if it were held that an accident during a halt due to a technical failure was not within the operation of the vehicle and therefore did not lead to liability under § 7 I StVG. The wording of section II of that provision shows that the strict liability established by it extends also to accidents of this kind.

This result follows a line which originated with the decision of the Reichsgericht, RGZ 170, 1. There the Reichsgericht held that an accident was within the course of operation of a lorry in a case where a railway train collided with a lorry stuck in a hole in the road, the left rear part of its loading flap extending over the rails and unable to move under its own power because the lifting arrangement had been torn off. In that case, the Reichsgericht held that the operation of the motor vehicle continued. It explained that the lorry had moved to the place of accident and had thereby in the course of its operation set the cause which produced the collision. It is not essentially different when a lorry, as in the present case, blocks a portion of the highway because of engine failure. Here also the lorry drove up to the place of accident and therefore produced in the course of its operation a situation endangering traffic.

In examining the question whether in such a case § 7 StVG is to be applied, one cannot neglect the criterion of how long a motor vehicle stands on the carriageway. If the defect in the vehicle can be remedied in a short time and it can soon go on its way, it is now generally accepted in accordance with the practice of the Reichsgericht that the operation of the vehicle, for the purpose of § 7 StVG, is not interrupted by that halt (cf. *inter alia* RG JW 1929, 2055 no. 7 in a case where the petrol lead was blocked). If now one considers that the dangers from a stationary vehicle increase the longer it forms an obstacle for other participants in the traffic, it would be illogical from the traffic-orientated stand-point to treat favourably as regards liability the driver of a vehicle which is stationary for a longer period and which therefore creates a greater risk. It is wrong to exempt him from liability while a slighter operative risk of the vehicle attracts strict liability. If, as in the present case, a vehicle must stay for a longer time on the carriageway because it cannot be repaired at once, then if another vehicle collides with the obstacle, that accident must also be attributed to the operation of the stationary vehicle [references]. The operation of this vehicle continues as long as the driver leaves the vehicle in the midst of the traffic and the dangerous situation thus created continues. For the purpose of § 7 StVG the oper-ation is only interrupted when the vehicle is withdrawn from the carriageway and is placed somewhere away from the regular traffic. Only thus the interruption of the operation is made known to others, but also that typical risk is eliminated which arises if motor vehicles are stopped or parked on the fast traffic lane of the carriageway. Whether as Walther [reference] contends, the answer should be different when an unauthorized user leaves a vehicle standing in the middle of the traffic, never to use it again, need not be examined since such a case is not in issue here. In the case for decision the lorry was on the way to a particular place and it was planned to continue the journey.

This view is criticised by Roth Stielow [reference] on the ground that it goes beyond the limits which the judge must observe in interpreting legislation. He starts by assum-ing that there is a "clear statutory direction to the contrary" which it infringes. But this starting-point is wrong. The enactment does not provide a detailed definition of the concept "in the operation of a motor vehicle" and, as Boehmer (*VersR* 1957, 587) correctly explains, says nowhere that it only constitutes an accident within the operation if the vehicle is in motion or its engine is running. But if the legislator has not provided any further explanation, it is for the judge to interpret this ambiguous concept. The judge is therefore not prohibited from interpreting § 7 StVG broadly if in so doing he conforms to the sense and purpose of the enactment to protect participants in traffic against the dangers of motor traffic. It is therefore entirely within the scope of permissible interpre-tation if this protection of the participants is extended also to the dangers produced by stationary vehicles in present-day traffic conditions.

Even if the legislature in 1908 saw the chief danger of motor vehicles in their rapid movement due to engine power and hence regarded the mechanical aspect of the concept of operation as paramount, that would not exclude the adaptation of the concept "in the operation of a motor vehicle" to the experiences and requirements of present-day traffic. As was already emphasized in another connection, according to experience modern traffic risks arise, not only from the engine as such and its effect on the motor vehicle, but from the movement of traffic as a whole. The motor vehicle itself creates a substantial danger as part of the traffic. Accordingly, Wussow [reference] rightly remarks that it is precisely from the point of view of risk, which the legislator takes as his starting-point, that the traffic-orientated aspect becomes much more prominent than the danger produced by the engine. The judge would not be true to his task if under these circumstances he clung to the concept, which is far too narrow, of a mechanical operation. His duty towards legislation and to law (Article 20 II GG) allows him not only to develop the law by interpretation in the direction of its further evolution, but obliges him to do so if the finding of a just decision requires it. The wording of the enactment gives way to its sense and purpose. To give effect to them in applying the law in the individual case and to provide an equitable and reasonable solution to the dispute is the judge's task [references]. As Radbruch [references] expresses it, not only must he follow the thoughts of the legislature, but he must also think them through to their final conclusion. But the judge does nothing else when he adapts the concept of operation in § 7 StVG to the experiences and requirements of the modern age in order to give effect to the legislative intent which is to afford extensive protection against the dangers of motor traffic.

In any case, it cannot be assumed that the characterisation of the concept of operation from the traffic-orientated point of view, which has long prevailed in the courts, conflicts with the intent of present-day legislature, for while it has repeatedly altered other provisions of the Road Traffic Act, it has retained the wording of § 7 I StVG, although it was aware of the long-standing practice concerning the term "in the operation of a motor vehicle".

III. In view of these considerations, the Court of Appeal was right in dividing the damage of the plaintiff according to § 17 StVG, and, when examining how far it was caused predominantly by the one or the other side, considered in the first place the risk arising from the operation of both lorries. [A discussion of the apportionment follows.]

Case 123

BUNDESGERICHTSHOF (SIXTH CIVIL SENATE) 23 NOVEMBER 1955
BGHZ 19, 114 = NJW 1956, 217 = VERSR 1956, 36, 126

On 23 December 1948 the A H Limited Partnership held a Christmas party for its personnel in a restaurant. E, the partner personally responsible, instructed the defendant, a bookkeeper in the firm, to take home two drunken employees, Sch. and H, in the firm's car. The car was struck by a train on a level-crossing and H was killed.

The appropriate professional association claimed from the plaintiff reimbursement of its payment under § 1542 of the Imperial Public Insurance Act (henceforth referred to as RVO) and the provisions of the Reichshaftpflichtgesetz. The plaintiff, the German Federal Railway, met the claim of the professional association. It demands of the defendant compensation for its disbursements on the ground that he had alone caused the accident by his gross negligence.

Its claim for compensation failed in all instances for these

Reasons

I. The Court of Appeal rightly proceeded from the principle that the plaintiff can under § 17 of the Road Traffic Act (StVG) claim from the defendant compensation for the payments made to the professional association only if the defendant as driver of the car involved in the accident was bound by statute to make good the damage suffered by the dependants of the deceased. For that purpose it is material whether H lost his life in an industrial accident and whether the defendant's liability is excluded by § 899 RVO in combination with § 898 RVO.

1. The appropriate professional association acknowledged that the fatal accident of H was an industrial accident requiring compensation. The court is bound by this decision under § 901 RVO.

If the defendant were to be regarded as an agent or representative of the entrepreneur, or as a superintendent of his business and work, he would be liable to H's dependants

under § 899 in combination with § 898 RVO only if it was established in criminal proceedings that he caused the accident intentionally. Since no such finding was made, and
the defendant was only convicted of a criminal act committed negligently, it is necessary
to examine first of all whether the defendants belong to one of the classes of persons who
are assimilated to the entrepreneur in § 899 RVO.

The Landgericht and Oberlandesgericht regarded the defendant as a superintendent of
the business and work. The Court of Appeal came to that conclusion on the basis of the
following findings:

The defendant supervised the whole business in the absence of the managing partner.
He had prepared and carried through the staff Christmas party on the entrepreneur's
instruction. That the managing partner, on leaving the party about four o'clock in the
morning with his co-partners, entrusted to the defendant, and not to one of the professional drivers who were present, the task of taking the drunken employees home was not
only because he seemed to be quite sober but because the whole conduct of the party had
been placed in his hands. The managing partners, on leaving the party, had wished to
hand over the responsibility for its smooth ending to the man who possessed the highest
authority in their absence. By virtue of the order given him, the defendant had to perform
independently and responsibly the task of getting the inebriates properly and safely home
and, in accordance with the entrepreneur's duty of care, to assure the safety of the employees who were his passengers.

Contrary to the view of the applicant for review, these findings justify the conclusion
that the defendant enjoys the protection of § 899 RVO.

The applicant maintains that the Court of Appeal drew the character of superintendent too widely and therefore misunderstood it. That is not correct. In its judgment the
Court of Appeal accurately started from the principles regarding the notion of character
of a superintendent of business and work developed by the Reichsgericht in its decision
RGZ 167, 685 and 170, 159. It did not fail to realize that the only person who can be regarded
as a superintendent is a member of the work-force who has the duty to supervise others
so engaged or at least one of the departments of the enterprise. As the Reichsgericht (RGZ
170, 159) correctly states, he must stand out from among the other employees by the fact
that he must care for the co-operation of several employees or for the smooth interlocking of the establishment and the plant, and therefore for the harmonious interplay of
personal and technical forces and must be responsible for these. It must be conceded to
the appellant that this is of course not generally the case of a car driver who has no other
duties. The performance of the necessary journeys and the care and upkeep of the car are
not a supervisory activity contemplated by § 899 RVO. It is established, however, that the
defendant was not appointed as chauffeur. As the Court of Appeal found, even when he
undertook the fatal journey he did not act only as a chauffeur but was engaged in a task
that exceeded the general duties of a driver. As the Court of Appeal found, he was given
the responsibility for the smooth ending of the party after the managers had left, and
therefore a position was entrusted to him that raised him above the other employees. The
applicant is in error in maintaining that the order did not fulfil the conditions for rendering him responsible for the regular co-operation of several employees or the smooth
interlocking of the establishment and the plant, for such a range of duties demanded
a delegation of at least some duration. There is no need here to decide whether the
position of a superintendent of business and work requires that the responsibility is to
be delegated for a longer period, for in the present case there is a finding, overlooked by
the applicant, that the defendant had the task not only for the time being, but generally

of supervising the business in the managing partner's absence. In this situation the Court of Appeal's characterization of the defendant as a superintendent of business and work is free from objection. It can therefore be left undecided whether he was also an agent in the sense of § 899 RVO, because in driving several employees home on the order of the entrepreneur he discharged the latter's duty of care. In any case, the finding of fact makes it free from doubt that, even on the journey which led to the accident, the defendant acted as a person assimilated to the entrepreneur as mentioned in § 899 RVO.

2. Moreover, the application of §§ 898, 899 RVO is not excluded by § 1 second sentence of the Act of 7 December 1943 (RGBl. I 674) on the extended admission of claims for damages arising out of service and industrial accidents. According to that provision, insured persons and their surviving dependants can make good their claims for compensation without limit against the persons mentioned in §§ 898, 899 RVO, if the accident occurred when they were participating in general traffic. On this point the Court of Appeal followed the case-law of the Supreme Court for the British Zone, according to which there is no participation in the general traffic if the injured person was a passenger in a private vehicle driven by the person who caused the injury and the injured party stood in causal and organic connection with the employment (BGHZ 1, 245 = NJW 1949, 263). It assumed that such was the case here.

The present Senate decided (BGHZ 8, 330, 336 ff.) that so-called works traffic (constant transport of workers in a works vehicle to the place of business) constitutes transport within the business and that the transported workers do not participate in general traffic. It left unanswered the question whether also in the case dealt with in the Supreme Court of the British Zone, in which the entrepreneur took an employee from the place of work in his own car, there was no participation in the general traffic. In the dispute between the present parties there is also no need to decide whether the principle established by the Supreme Court is invariably to be followed. In any event in the present case, in agreement with the Court of Appeal, no participation in the general traffic can be said to have taken place.

The Act of 7 December 1943 deals principally with accidents suffered by a worker on the way from or to the place of work and which count as industrial accidents according to § 543 RVO. If an entrepreneur or a person assimilated to him (§ 899 RVO) should run down an employee on the way to the place of work, §§ 898, 899 RVO would exclude claims of a private law nature against the entrepreneur and the persons mentioned in § 899 RVO, although in such cases only a slight connection exists between the accident and the worker's activity in the business. The Act, according to its preamble, wishes to do away with the unfairness that was produced because in cases of this kind a person injured in the course of service or work is placed in a worse position than other participants in traffic. This unfair disadvantage was to be removed in all cases where the accident occurs in the course of participation in general traffic. As this Senate has already said (BGHZ 8, 330 [337]), in deciding whether there is such participation it must first be asked whether the insured person suffered the accident as an ordinary participant in traffic or as an employee. Whether the former or the latter is the case or predominates must be decided on the facts of the particular case. If an employee, like H in the present case, is driven home after a staff party in a works car on the entrepreneur's order, that journey is occasioned by the operation of the enterprise and is so closely connected with the enterprise and with the injured party's membership of the enterprise that the character of the passenger as a participant in the traffic recedes into the background. That applies especially if the journey, as here, served only to take the employees home and, as the Court of Appeal also found, was ordered out of a feeling of care for the drunken employees. That an insured person in a case of this kind does not participate in the general traffic, in the meaning of § 1 II of the Act on the extended admission of claims for damages arising from service and industrial accidents, conforms to the principles on which both the courts and writers proceed in similar cases. The prevailing opinion recognises that taking an employee home as a passenger from the place of work in the works car is not a participation in the general traffic [references].

The Court of Appeal thus held correctly that the Act of 7 December 1943 on the extended application of claims for damages arising out of service and industrial accidents does not stand in the way of applying §§ 898, 899 RVO in the present case.

II. The applicant for review also asks for an examination as to whether the statutory exclusion of liability in § 898 RVO affects the claim for compensation at all. He refers to the judgment of 3 February 1954 (BGHZ 12, 213) in which this Senate decided that a contractual exclusion or reduction of liability, e.g. between driver and passenger, cannot adversely affect the claim for contribution by a second tortfeasor under § 17 StVG or § 426 BGB. The applicant wishes to apply to the present case the notion that the effectiveness of such an exclusion of liability would stultify the equitable contribution intended by the legislator, and maintains that since the entrepreneurs and those assimilated to them under § 899 RVO are liable to the professional association for his expenditure according to § 903 RVO, the limitation of liability under §§ 898, 899 RVO is only justified in relation to the person directly injured in order to avoid litigation within the enterprise. But the legislator, the applicant continues, cannot have intended by this provision to interfere with the rights of third persons and thus to curtail provisions whose purpose is to produce an equitable compromise. Since the professional association sought the reimbursement of its expenditure from the plaintiff only but did not make any claims against the defendant under § 903 RVO, the plaintiff, who was responsible only on the ground of strict liability, was saddled with the damage, whereas the defendant, who was to blame, was not called upon to pay. The applicant regards this as unfair and as an infringement of §§ 898, 899 RVO and 17 StVG.

These arguments of the applicant for review cannot be of help to it. It may, of course, at first sight appear unfair that the plaintiff, who has to answer for the damage only on the basis of strict liability, must perform in full, whereas the defendant, who was to blame, is relieved of responsibility. But this objection of the applicant does not take sufficiently into account the special conditions of accident insurance law, which consciously aims at protecting the entrepreneur, agent, and business superintendent against claims exceeding the liability under § 903 RVO [reference]. The provisions, indeed, of §§ 898, 899 RVO serve also, as must be conceded to the applicant, the purpose of avoiding, in the interest of industrial peace, disputes between workers and employers over the responsibility for business accidents (BGHZ 8, 330 [339]) . . . It is, however, essential here that the Act has in relation to industrial accidents excluded claims for compensation by injured parties against an entrepreneur because the latter has to bear the burden of accident insurance and because the insured are allowed claims for compensation when the entrepreneur and his agents are not to blame and even if the employer himself has caused the accident through his own negligence. Likewise § 899 RVO in principle relieves agents as well as business and work superintendents of liability towards the workers because under § 903 RVO they must reimburse the professional association the expenses incurred by the latter, if they caused the accident intentionally or by carelessly neglecting their official, professional, or industrial duties. Hence the exemption of the entrepreneur as well as his agents and superintendents from liability towards the injured constitutes a compensation for the latter in return for their statutory liability to the professional association (RGZ 170, 159 [160]; *cf.* also RGZ 153, 38, 41, 42 and BGHZ 8, 330 [338]). This compensation would only be incomplete if the entrepreneur, agents, and superintendent were exposed, along with the liability under § 903 RVO, to a further claim and had to pay damages to a second wrongdoer in whole or in part by way of compensation. That would contradict the purpose of the law of social insurance, for the protection afforded by it to the business entrepreneur and those assimilated to him according to § 899 RVO would in that way be nullified again. That cannot be the intention of the statute. It shows that as a rule the insured has no claim against the individual entrepreneur, agent, or superintendent and that such a claim lies only in the exceptional case, not in issue here, where the entrepreneur, agent, or superintendent causes the accident intentionally (*cf.* RGZ 153, 38 [43]). If, however, the injured party has no claim whatever against them, an essential condition is lacking for a claim to contribution by the second wrongdoer. Contribution is a consequence of the common duty of several wrongdoers to pay damages and hence presupposes as a matter of principle that several wrongdoers are liable as joint debtors for the damage (BGHZ 11, 170 [174] and 12, 213). Since in the case to be decided the liability of the defendant to the injured party's surviving dependants is excluded, a joint debt is lacking and with it the foundation for a claim to contribution.

It is another question whether the plaintiff could have resisted the professional association's claim to payment, on the ground that it would be contrary to good faith, in spite of the possibility of recourse against the defendant (§ 903 RVO) to claim the full payment from the plaintiff. That question, however, need not be decided here.

III. The applicant for review now maintains that the claim has none the less a basis in § 426 II BGB. Both parties are alleged to be liable to the professional association as joint debtors, the defendant under § 903 IV RVO and the plaintiff because the claim of the surviving dependants under § 1542 RVO had been assigned to the professional association. Since the plaintiff has satisfied the association, their claim has passed to the plaintiff under § 426 II BGB.

It must be conceded to the applicant that both parties were debtors of the association for the reasons adduced by it. But that could lead to a duty of contribution between them under § 426 BGB only if to that extent they had stood in a true joint debtor relationship towards the association (BGB RGRK 10 edn. § 426 n. 1 and § 421 n. 1*c*). That, however, is not the case. A true joint debtor relationship presupposes an internal connection of the two obligations in the sense of a legal community of purpose (BGHZ 13, 360 [365], Great Civil Senate with references to practice of the Reichsgericht). That is missing from the obligations on which the claims were based which the association had against parties to the present dispute. It has lodged against the plaintiff a claim of the dependants of the injured party which is based on the Reichshaftpflichtgesetz and falls within the sphere of private law; it had been assigned to the association by operation of law (§ 1542 RVO). On the other hand, the association had against the defendant in its own right a claim to compensation of a special kind based on a statutory provision forming part of public law (§ 903 RVO) against which a contributory fault of the injured party could not be pleaded (RGZ 96, 135; 144, 31 [35]). It is adapted to the structure of accident insurance in the Reich Insurance Ordinance and to the relationship of the association to enterprises belonging to it which must pay contributions and has the purpose of indemnifying the association for its expenditure arising from the accident. Admittedly the existence of a true joint debt is not absolutely excluded by the differing bases of the obligations and of their origins. Instead it is decisive that in the present case an internal connection is lacking between the two obligations in the sense of a legal community of purpose. Both claims stand only in loose economic connection with each other, for they both had for their object the reimbursement of payments which the association was bound to make on the occasion of the accident arising out of the enterprise. The plaintiff and the defendant thus owed identical performance to the same creditor (the professional association) to the extent that the economic purpose of the obligation is attained by a single performance to the creditor who can therefore claim only one payment. This happened, however, without the internal connection required for a true joint debt. Since there was no legal community between the debtors, which is required by § 426 BGB as a presupposition for a duty to contribute (cf. BGHZ 13, 360, 365), only a joint debt in a non-technical sense can be envisaged. §§ 421 ff. BGB, and in particular the regulation of contribution in § 426 BGB, do not cover a relationship of this kind. Hence there is also no room for an analogous application of that provision.

This emerges also from another point of view. The Reichs Insurance Act does not wish to force the professional association to make claims on its members to cover its expenditure if they only acted negligently. Accordingly § 905 RVO provides that the meeting of members of the professional association or, if the by-laws so permit, the directors can renounce their right to recourse. If the directors wish to claim reimbursement, § 906 RVO allows the person liable to appeal to the meeting. Accordingly, the question whether a claim should be made on a member of the association under § 903 RVO is referred to the exclusive decision of the association. If the plaintiff were to be granted a claim for contribution by an analogous application of § 426 BGB, that would indirectly involve an outsider bringing a claim against the tortfeasor indirectly, which the professional association did not wish to make. This would be an admissible attack on the insurer's authority to decide.

This view of the Senate that the plaintiff cannot bring a claim for contribution under § 426 BGB conforms to the practice of the Reichsgericht. It took the same standpoint in its decision in Seuffarch, 65 no. 32; and in its judgment published in DR 1940, 1779 no. 10 dealing with a similar case without, however, going more deeply into the matter it came to the same result that no joint debt and therefore no duty to contribute existed [reference].

IV. Before the Court of Appeal the plaintiff, by referring to the fact that the defendant had endangered transport, also based its claim on § 823 II BGB. The Court of Appeal regarded this as a modification of the claim which was inadmissible owing to irrelevance (§ 264 ZPO). It can be left undecided whether the arguments of the Court of Appeal on this question merit approval, for even from that legal standpoint contrary to the view of the applicant, a claim by the plaintiff for the reimbursement of its expenditure is not well founded.

The plaintiff does not allege that as a result of the defendant's conduct it suffered damage to its locomotive or any other direct damage to itself. It relies only on the damage which is suffered because it was called upon to pay under the Reichshaftpflichtgesetz. A claim for compensation of that damage cannot be derived from § 823 II BGB in combination with §§ 315, 316 StGB. It is true that those criminal law provisions are protective statutes, which also serve to protect the plaintiff. Moreover, the mere circumstances that the sum which the plaintiff claims involves indirect damage does not, contrary to the view of the respondent, lead to a rejection of the claim, since, according to a general principle of civil law, a person who has suffered direct damage can claim compensation not only in respect of any direct but also of any indirect damage which he suffered. It is however always a presupposition that the damage falls within the scope of the interests protected by the protective statute, i.e. that it arose from the invasion of a legal interest for the protection of which the legal rule was enacted [references]. In the case for decision the danger which the protective statute is intended to avert did not in fact arise. The provisions on endangering the operation of a railway (§§ 315, 316 StGB) protect the health and property of railway entrepreneurs and the other persons directly affected by railway traffic, but not their general economic interests [references]. The damage that the plaintiff suffered through the claim for compensation on the basis of the Reichshaftpflichtgesetz affects only its general economic interests and therefore a sphere of interests which is not protected here. Hence § 823 II BGB, in combination with §§ 315, 316 StGB, also fails to provide a legal basis for the claim made in the plaintiff's action.

Case 124

BUNDESGERICHTSHOF (SIXTH CIVIL SENATE) 27 MAY 1975
NJW 1975, 1886 = VERSR 1975, 945

The plaintiff owned a chicken-farm. The hens were housed in a building where they were arranged in so-called batteries. The first defendant supplied the plaintiff with concentrated chicken feed. On 8 September 1969 the second defendant, employed by the first defendant, delivered ten tons of chicken feed loaded on a lorry which was equipped with two tanks in which the feed was contained. The chicken feed was to be deposited in a silo attached to the building. The walls of the silo consisted of chipboard sheets of a thickness of 20 millimetres. On the outside of the silo, a feed-pipe leading to within 70 centimetres below the roof turned vertically into the silo and terminated at a distance of 1.25 millimetres from the opposite chipboard wall. The second defendant connected the tanks of the lorry with the feed-pipe by means of a hose-pipe. Using a compressor attached to the lorry, he blew the feed into the feed-pipe in order to deposit the feed in the silo. The force of the pressure broke the chipboard sheets of the opposite wall and the escaping feed was deposited on the adjacent roof of the building which collapsed under the weight. Many laying hens were killed or had to be destroyed. The plaintiff claimed damages in respect of the damage to the roof and to his livestock.

The Court of First Instance allowed the claim and the Court of Appeal of Aldenburg rejected an appeal by the defendant. Upon a second appeal the judgment below was quashed and the case referred back for the following

Reasons

I. The Court of Appeal left it open as to whether the first defendant is liable in contract, as the Court of First Instance has held. Instead it found that the first defendant was liable under § 7 I of the Road Traffic Act because an object belonging to the plaintiff had been damaged "in the course of operating the defendant's motor vehicle". According to the Court of Appeal, the necessary connection existed in space and time between a certain operational use or installation and the accident, at any rate if, as in the present case, a load was discharged from a vehicle with the aid of a motor, thereby causing an accident.

II. These conclusions cannot be maintained in face of the objections raised by the appellant. It is impossible to accept the view of the Court of Appeal that the accident occurred "in the course of operating a motor vehicle" in the meaning of § 7 I of the Road Traffic Act.

1. According to the so-called engine-orientated view, which was enlarged by the traffic-orientated view first put forward by the Reichsgericht [reference] and subsequently adopted and developed by the Bundesgerichtshof [reference] in respect of certain cases, a motor vehicle is "in operation" if its motor has been started and moves the vehicle or one of its operational parts. To that extent, as the Court of Appeal states correctly, it makes no difference whether during the operational activity the motor vehicle is located on a public highway or (as here) on private land (building site [reference]; works compound [reference]).

As a result of technical developments, the motor power of motor vehicles is being used not only to transport persons and goods, but also for other works processes which can hardly be regarded as merely loading or unloading goods for transport. Thus many specialised vehicles exist today which are constructed for special tasks but serve ordinary purposes at the same time. The heavy goods lorry of the defendant was also such a specialized vehicle, since it was fitted with special containers for transporting feed and was provided, *inter alia*, with a mechanical installation for discharging it. If an accident occurs in the course of employing operational installations of such special vehicles which do not serve directly the purpose of transport, it is not obvious that such an accident has occurred "in the course of operating a motor vehicle" in the meaning of § 7 of the Road Traffic Act. In the present case, this cannot be said to have happened, contrary to the view of the Court of Appeal.

(*a*) The Court of Appeal, too, states that the question is whether the accident is still to be regarded as arising from the operation of the motor vehicle. According to the Court of Appeal the test is whether the accident was "closely connected in space and time with an operational process" of the heavy goods vehicle (for this notion see the decisions of this Division [reference]). This formula indicates, in the first place, that a link of adequate causality must exist between the operation of the motor vehicle and the actual damage. However, the meaning of this formula is not completely expressed thereby. To that extent it only defines a minimum requirement for a causal link to exist. In addition, the effect caused by the operation of the motor vehicle for which damages are to be paid must be covered by the meaning and the purpose of the rule creating liability, i.e. by the protective range of § 7 I of the Road Traffic Act [references]. It is insufficient for the Court of Appeal to argue that the process of discharge falls within the sphere of operation of the lorry because the compressor employed for the purpose of discharging the load was impelled by the motor of the lorry. This establishes only the causal link between the operation of the motor and the damage which, however, cannot be in doubt. On the other hand, contrary to the opinion of the Court of Appeal, the occurrence is not to be attributed to the operation of the lorry, against the danger of which § 7 I of the Road Traffic Act is to provide protection, as the appellant correctly points out.

(*aa*) It is true that in accordance with the recent practice of the Courts of Appeal the discharge of a vehicle with the assistance of its motor constitutes a use of an operative installation corresponding to the purpose of the vehicle and therefore takes place "in the course of its operation" [references—all concerning either the loading or discharging of oil by a tanker lorry]. These decisions are frequently cited in the literature, albeit without a more detailed discussion of possible objections against them [references]. This Division has expressly left the question open in the cases which have come before it hitherto on appeal from the Courts of Appeal of Nürnberg and Hamm as to whether an accident caused on the occasion of oil being loaded or discharged by a road-tanker can be also attributed to the operation of the latter in the meaning of the Road Traffic Act [references]. The decision of this Division dated 25 April 1956 [reference] also does not show any other attitude in principle. It is true that this Division held that a "close connection in space and time with the operational process" existed in the case where a motor lorry dropped its load on a rubbish dump with the help of its engine power and thereby caused an accident. However, in that case, too, this Division observed that no need arose to decide whether such a connection "always" exists when damage is caused on discharging a motor lorry.

(*bb*) Whether, as in the present case, an accident caused in the course of the unloading of a specialised motor vehicle with the assistance of its engine is still to be attributed to the operation of a vehicle in the meaning of the Road Traffic Act depends upon the answer to the question against what perils § 7 of the Road Traffic Act is to provide protection and whether the user of this "operative installation" which led to the accident still falls within this range of protection. Naturally only such perils are involved which emanate from the motor vehicle in its capacity of an engine serving transport (see §§ 1, 2 of the Road Traffic Act). As soon as a connection no longer exists with the purpose of the motor vehicle as a means of transport in traffic, and the motor vehicle is only used as a means of performing work, the danger emanating specifically from a motor vehicle used for its natural purpose has ceased to exist. (See also the Reichsgericht [reference omitted], concentrating on the nature of a motor vehicle as a means of transport.) Since our legal system does not know a general principle of strict liability for operating engines supplying power at work, § 7 of the Road Traffic Act cannot be applied to accidents which occur in consequence of technical processes which cannot any longer be reasonably connected with the character of the engine employed as part of a motor vehicle. As this Division has already stated in its decision of 10 January 1961 [references] it is not decisive that the engine of the motor vehicle has been started up if this is done independently of an operational process characteristic of a motor vehicle for purposes other than moving it [reference]. In the case referred to, the engine of a moped served only to operate its lights which were required as a source of illumination for purposes other than to drive the moped (but see critically Boehmer [reference]).

In what circumstances the power of the engine and the operational installations of the vehicle driven by it have lost their connection with the latter's function as a means of transport and with road traffic, with the result that from the point of view of legal liability only the function of the engines as a source of power is in issue, can only be determined in the individual case, having regard to all the circumstances. If, as in the present case, the engine is used for purposes of unloading, it will be decisive whether the damage was caused by the special construction of the vehicle and the operational installations connected therewith (as for instance in the case of discharging a load with the help of a tipping-device; see the decision of this Division of 25 April 1956 [reference] or in the case of a towing vehicle equipped with a crane or of a vehicle for transporting long loads which is provided with a grip [reference]) or whether its function as a source of working power was predominant, as for instance in the case of a mobile building-crane.

If the present case is examined in accordance with these principles it follows that it is not to be regarded as part of the operation of a motor vehicle if feed is blown into a silo with the engine of the motor vehicle running the compressor. The occurrence of damage is entirely independent, both technically and legally, of the specific peril emanating from a motor vehicle, be it even a specialised vehicle. Instead, the only peril is that flowing from the engine providing power for work, which is supplied by the engine of the motor vehicle. The damage thus caused does not come within the range of protection provided by § 7 of the Road Traffic Act.

(b) The traffic-orientated approach to the term "operation" in § 7 of the Road Traffic Act does not lead to any different conclusion. It was developed for the protection of those involved in traffic in order to cover the after-effects of the perils created by a motor vehicle present in the area of public traffic, even if the motor vehicle which had been put "in operation" had come to a standstill [reference]. A dangerous situation of this kind has not occurred in the present case. The motor vehicle was standing on private land belonging to the plaintiff and did not represent an obstacle for other users of the road in the place where it stood.

Case 125

BUNDESGERICHTSHOF (SIXTH CIVIL SENATE) 6 JUNE 1989
BGHZ 107, 359 = NJW 1989, 2616 = JZ 1989, 1069

Facts

The plaintiff, who suffered from high blood pressure, was involved in a road accident around midnight on 28 April 1984 while driving his wife's car. His car collided with another vehicle driven by M. The liability insurer for this car was the defendant. Soon after the accident had occurred and the police had taken the details of the accident, the plaintiff suffered a stroke. Since then, he has been unable to work and draws disablement benefit. Between the parties it is not disputed that the defendant must compensate the plaintiff for all the damages of the accident. On the basis of these facts, the plaintiff claimed from the defendant compensation for his loss of earnings, a declaration of the defendant's continuing responsibility for the loss since the claim was brought, and damages for pain and suffering; in particular the plaintiff made the following allegations: the stroke, which occurred as a result of the rupture of a blood vessel and a resulting brain haemorrhage, was caused by the excitement brought on by the conduct of M and his three passengers after the accident and the measures taken by the police officer who was at the place of the accident in order to test whether the plaintiff was driving under the influence of alcohol. After the accident, M and his passengers approached the plaintiff in a threatening manner. One of the passengers ran at him and shouted, incorrectly, that he was driving too fast. Another of the persons accompanying M drove his vehicle to the side of the road, so that he feared that it would no longer be possible for the facts of the accident to be clarified. All four occupants of M's vehicle falsely alleged to the police that he was under the influence of alcohol; that caused the police officer to breathalyse him, although the results of the test were negative. As a consequence of this test and the subsequent conduct of M and his fellow passengers, the shock which he had suffered as a result of the accident grew more intense. When he later drove on, he experienced symptoms of paralysis which were the symptoms of his stroke.

The plaintiff's claim was unsuccessful in both lower courts, and his application to the BGH was rejected.

For the following

Reasons

I. [According to the OLG] . . . the claim as a whole had no legal basis. A direct claim against the defendant on the basis of § 3 Nr. 1 PflVG [*Pflichtversicherungsgesetz* = Act Concerning Compulsory Insurance] failed because the loss claimed by the plaintiff was not suffered as a consequence of the operation of the vehicle insured by the defendant (§ 10 I AKB [*Allgemeine Bedingungen für die Kraftverkehrsversicherung* = General Conditions for Motor Vehicle Insurance]). Furthermore, M himself was not liable to the plaintiff. There was no liability under §§ 7 and 18 StVG [*Strassenverkehrsgesetz* = Road Traffic Act] because the invasion of his health alleged by the plaintiff did not occur in the context of the use of the vehicle by M. There was no liability under § 823 I BGB because there was no basis for holding that M was at fault. A claim for compensation based on § 823 II BGB failed because even if there were a breach of a protective law (§§ 164 and 185 *et seq*. StGB = Criminal Code), a reasonable bystander would not have expected the occurrence of a stroke as a consequence of the damage inflicted upon the plaintiff.

II. The plaintiff's appeal fails. The judgment of the OLG is correct in its result, even if not in its reasoning (§ 563 ZPO).

The claim has no basis in law. The prerequisite for a claim against the defendant on the basis of § 3 Nr. 1 PflVG is that the plaintiff has claims for compensation in respect of the alleged loss against M or the keeper of the vehicle driven by M (§§ 823 *et seq*. BGB and §§ 7 and 18 StVG) and that the loss is caused in the context of the operation of the motor vehicle insured by the defendant (§ 1 of the PflVG; § 10 I AKB). That is not, however, the case here.

1. A claim for compensation against M based on tort (§§ 823 *et seq*. BGB), which is the only way a claim for damages for pain and suffering could be justified (§ 847 BGB), has no basis in law.

(*a*) Loss of earnings and non-pecuniary loss on the part of the plaintiff should not be recoverable from M under § 823 I BGB simply because M caused damage to the plaintiff's property as a consequence of the crash caused by his fault and was consequently guilty of an interference in the *ownership* rights of the plaintiff and because the impairments claimed by the plaintiff could be seen as *consequential* loss. First, the property damage caused by M to the car driven by the plaintiff was suffered not by the plaintiff, but by his wife as the owner of the vehicle. Furthermore, there is no evidence from the pleadings that the state of excitement which the plaintiff believes led to his stroke was in any way caused by his being upset by the *damage to the vehicle* [emphasis added].

(*b*) The plaintiff's request for damages is furthermore not justified in so far as it is based on an argument that there was an invasion of the plaintiff's *health* actionable under § 823 I BGB.

(*aa*) Following the plaintiff's arguments, and rejecting the view of the OLG, it must be concluded that M did make a contribution to the injury to the plaintiff's health in so far as he acted unlawfully and negligently by contravening the priority rules (§ 8 StVO = *Strassenverkehrsordnung*) and consequently causing the crash. For by causing the accident he led the plaintiff to become upset and thus created one precondition which, in conjunction with the consequent conduct of M and his passengers, and the attendance at the accident by the police, caused the plaintiff to suffer a critical increase in blood pressure in his brain and led to the rupture of the blood vessel and the consequential brain haemorrhage when the plaintiff later drove away from the accident [references omitted]. It is not relevant to his responsibility in tort that M did not cause the impairment of the plaintiff's health through a physical invasion of his bodily integrity; an invasion of the plaintiff's health can occur, as here, through a psychological impact upon the victim [references omitted].

Contrary to the view of the OLG, it is equally irrelevant to the tortious responsibility of M that the impairment to the plaintiff's health may only have occurred because, unbeknown to M, the plaintiff was suffering from high blood pressure. For it is established case law that a person who causes loss must also take responsibility for those consequences of his actions which are the result of the fact that the victim is already suffering from some form of bodily injury or some other weakness in his constitution [references omitted]. A tortfeasor must always reckon with the possibility that a person affected by his breach of the priority rules may be a person suffering from high blood pressure. It is also not wholly unforeseeable that as a consequence of the upset caused by the accident that such a person may suffer impairment to his health. It is not necessary to foresee the precise circumstances in which this might occur or how the risk might result in the occurrence of damage [references omitted].

(*bb*) The linkage of the invasion of health suffered by the plaintiff and the infringement of the priority rules by M for the purposes of liability is, however, precluded by the fact that this damage in fact only occurred as a result of the conduct of M and his passengers after the accident and the events which occurred when the police attended the scene of the accident. For the traffic rule contained in § 8 StVO breached by M is not intended to provide protection against the possibility that an accident caused by a failure to observe this provision leads to the plaintiff suffering a stroke in the manner alleged by the plaintiff as a consequence of pressures experienced by the victim solely as a result of the upset occurring in the context of the aftermath of the accident.

It is also established case law that in the context of damages claims which are based on § 823 BGB it should be examined whether the event in respect of which compensation is claimed falls within the protective scope of the norm, and thus whether the risks materialised through the event which breached the rule of conduct was intended to protect against [references omitted]. This condition is not satisfied here. For the provision contained in § 8 StVO breached by M is intended, according to the basic principle set out in § 1 II StVO, to protect above all the bodily integrity of other persons; its protective scope extends, however, as is apparent from § 1 I StVO, to cover only the prevention of the risks of accidents and the prevention of injuries to health associated with primary threat to life and health. These can include those injuries which occur in the aftermath of the accident, for example in the context of salvage work or while making the accident report, which themselves constitute the realisation of one of the risks of road traffic at the scene of the accident. It is the view of this court that this argument cannot extend to cover psychological pressures associated with disagreements regarding the clarification of how the accident occurred or regarding the question of fault, such as those which were primarily responsible for the plaintiff's stroke, leaving aside the impairment of his condition caused by the accident itself. In this case the plaintiff, himself, admitted that the breach of the priority rules by M engendered in him merely a state of general excitement which, in itself, did not represent an invasion of his health [references omitted]. The fact that this state of excitement became more intense as a consequence of the subsequent conduct of M and his passengers before and during the presence of the police, and the fact that this led to the plaintiff suffering a brain haemorrhage leading to a stroke, fall beyond the protective scope of § 8 StVO. It is not the task of this provision of road traffic law to protect the person who had priority on the highway against the psychological and physiological impairment which he might suffer as a consequence of a criminal investigation or criminal proceedings being mounted against him, or against his own need to take action in civil or criminal proceedings to recover his loss. Nor is this provision aimed at providing protection against an invasion of the plaintiff's health suffered as a consequence of a state of excitement regarding the police attendance at the accident, whether this is caused by measures taken by the police, or by statements made by the tortfeasor or third parties which make it more difficult to clarify the issue of responsibility. Protection against detriment stemming from errors or attempts to manipulate the facts when the circumstances of the accident are being clarified is subject to separate rules; it is not included within the scope of the rule of conduct contained in § 8 StVO which is intended to ensure the safety of traffic on the roads.

Having regard to the assessment which has been made, it must be concluded that as a matter of the ascription of responsibility, the stroke suffered by the plaintiff was linked to the conduct of M and his passengers *after* the accident. However, even from this perspective the conduct of M cannot give the plaintiff an action for damages under § 823 I BGB. For the fact that, as the plaintiff alleges, M and his fellow passengers might have given an incorrect description of the accident to the police officer charged with making a report after the crash or might have "invented" allegations about the plaintiff having driven too fast or being under the influence of alcohol does not, of itself, render their conduct unlawful. Such an attempt by those using the highway to shift the blame for an accident onto the other side does not in itself violate, in the absence of other circumstances, the standard of conduct which is to be expected of every person who uses the roads but who has no claim for compensation, after an accident. The same applies to the unsubstantiated allegation made by the plaintiff (though only before the OLG) that the passengers in the other vehicle came towards him "in a threatening manner" [references omitted].

Finally, it is not possible to conclude that the conduct of M after the accident was unlawful simply because the OLG, when it was examining the plaintiff's claims which it ultimately rejected, reached the conclusion under § 823 II BGB that M and his passengers had breached the protective laws contained in §§ 164 and 185 *et seq.* StGB as a result of their conduct following the accident. Quite apart from the fact that the defendant, as the insurer, could only be liable for the conduct of M and not for that of his fellow passengers (*cf.* § 10 I d AKB), the findings of the OLG should be viewed as findings of law, not as findings of fact, that is as a presumption of the truth of the plaintiff's allegations. For the facts as pleaded by the plaintiff reveal no evidence of a breach of the provisions of the criminal law by M.

2. As a result, the OLG was correct to deny, on the basis of § 3 Nr. 1 PflVG, a claim for compensation by the plaintiff leading to the liability of the defendant under §§ 7 I and 18 I StVG. Such a claim, which in accordance with § 11 StVG can in any case only extend to compensation for *pecuniary* loss, presupposes that the invasion of the plaintiff's health occurred in the context of the operation of the vehicle driven by M and that the loss claimed by the plaintiff is attributable to the risks associated with the operation of this vehicle. The OLG was wrong to conclude that the first condition was not present; the second requirement is not, however, fulfilled.

(*a*) Damage occurs "in the context of the operation" of a motor vehicle where the risk which emanates from the vehicle as such has had an impact upon how the damage actually happened, and thus where the occurrence of damage has in this way been (partially) shaped by the motor vehicle. Evaluated from this perspective, the case law of this court leads to the conclusion that the condition of liability that the damage must occur "in the context of the operation" of a motor vehicle must in principle be construed extensively in accordance with the broad protective scope of § 7 I StVG [references omitted].

(*b*) In this case, however, as was stated above in the context of liability under § 823 BGB, the accident caused by M's operating the vehicle in breach of the road traffic rules did contribute to the stroke suffered by the plaintiff as a result of the impairment of the general condition of a victim such as the plaintiff who suffered from high blood pressure. However, as with liability in tort, the responsibility of M under §§ 7 and 18 StVG requires that the loss suffered should fall within the protective scope of the norms in question [references omitted]. Any attribution of this loss to the risk of the operation of the vehicle driven by M must, however, be denied on the same grounds as those which justified the refusal to link, as a matter of the law of tort, the loss with the wrongful breach by M of the provisions of § 8 StVO. For since liability under § 7 StVG represents, so to speak, the price for the fact that the use of a vehicle on the roads offers a permissible source of risk, then the responsibility of the keeper and the driver which is based on this provision must be limited to those losses which represent the realisation of precisely those risks which result as such from motor vehicles. It is not possible to establish the necessary internal link between the risks of operation of a motor vehicle and the loss in the form of the plaintiff's stroke and the damaging consequences of that stroke. In this context, rather, it is a separate sphere of risk which is involved also as regards the risk-based liability contained in the Road Traffic Act, and this sphere of risk must, according to the standards imposed for this form of liability, be attributed to the general risks of life.

Case 126

BUNDESGERICHTSHOF (SIXTH CIVIL SENATE) 13 APRIL 1956
BGHZ 20, 259

In order to enter a private driveway, the defendant made a sharp left-hand turn from the right-hand side of the highway. The plaintiff came round a bend behind him on a 490 cc. motorcycle, and struck the defendant's vehicle near the left-hand kerb. The plaintiff was thrown on to the sidewalk and suffered serious injuries.

The Landgericht granted the plaintiff's claim for damages for pain and suffering, and held the defendant liable for all other damage as well. On the defendant's appeal, the Oberlandesgericht held that the claim for damages for pain and suffering should be allowed only as to two-thirds, and that the defendant was liable only for a like proportion of the other harm suffered by the plaintiff. The plaintiff sought to have the decision of the Landgericht reinstated and the defendant sought to have the claims dismissed. Both appeals were unsuccessful.

Reasons

It was alleged that the plaintiff could and should have foreseen the defendant's improper left turn in time to brake or swerve and so avoid the collision. The trial judge, however, held—unobjectionably in law—that this was not established. But an accident does not constitute an "unavoidable event" in the sense of § 7 II KrfzG (Motor Vehicle Act) (now StVG (Road Traffic Act)) just because the plaintiff is not proved to have been at fault in contributing to it. Supposing that the defendant, as is possible, had put out his direction indicator and was proceeding slowly, and that the plaintiff had been driving with abnormally scrupulous care, alertly and attentively focusing all his faculties on the situation (NJW 1954, 185 no. 1), then the plaintiff might, despite the unexpectedness of the defendant's manoeuvre, have avoided the damaging collision by braking or swerving, given that his own speed was perhaps only 20 m.p.h. If in this sense the accident could possibly have been avoided by the plaintiff, the danger attributable to his motorcycle is a factor which must be taken into account in any claim he may make (BGHZ 6, 319).

It is true that some writers have criticized the decisions of the Bundesgerichtshof (BGHZ 6, 319; VersR 1953, 337) to the effect that, except in the case of an unavoidable event, the claim of the injured custodian is subject to reduction by reason of any contribution made to the accident by the danger due to his vehicle (references omitted), but despite these criticisms this senate proposes to adhere to the established case-law. If someone else as well as the custodian of a car is liable to an injured third party and the question is how the loss should be borne as between the two of them, it is quite obvious that the custodian will have to bear part of his loss. The same must apply when the custodian of a vehicle which the legislature has stigmatised as dangerous, suffers damage while in the vehicle whose dangerous nature contributed to the accident, even if he himself was not at fault, or not provably so. Theoretically one might avoid splitting the loss in this way by drawing a distinction between the capacities of custodian and occupant, and attaching strict liability only to the capacity of custodian, but this would be unduly theoretical and quite unrealistic. The danger attributable to the custody of a motor vehicle exists equally if the custodian happens to be in his own car, as passenger or driver, and so in such a case also he must bear the consequences which flow from having it in his custody. It is irrelevant that § 8 StVG exempts him from liability to any other occupant. Berchthold is wrong to draw the conclusion that even a scrupulously careful custodian will always have to bear part of the loss he suffers (see also BGH VersR 5, 251, 253), since if the event is unavoidable, the dangerous nature of the vehicle has no part to play. If the danger does fall to be taken into account, the trial judge must in each case determine whether and to what extent the loss should be divided. Even then, as Gelhaar and Wussow have pointed out with reference to decisions of this senate, the custodian is not inevitably saddled with part of his loss. As against a tortfeasor whose conduct was gross or reckless, it might be right to ignore an insubstantial contributory danger. On the other hand (and this supports the view here put forward), it would not be right to require a person who has been only slightly negligent to bear the whole of the custodian's loss when the custodian's vehicle made a significant contribution to the harm.

The same must apply when a custodian-occupant brings a claim for damages for pain and suffering. It is true that in JW 1931, 3315, the Reichsgericht stated that the loss should not be divided unless the custodian would have been liable to any third party injured in the accident, and it refused to use § 17 KrfzG to curtail the claim for damages for pain and suffering brought by an injured custodian who was responsible for nothing other than the custody of a dangerous motor vehicle. On the other hand, in RGZ 149, 213, the Reichsgericht held that the part of the loss which an injured custodian must bear if he himself was in part responsible was not subject to the monetary limit laid down by § 12 KrfzG. To this extent, therefore, according to the Reichsgericht, different rules may apply on the same facts depending on whether the issue is one of liability to a third person or of the duty to bear part of one's own loss. It is certainly clear that the main reason the legislature set the monetary limit on the strict liability introduced by the KrfzG was to enable custodians of vehicles to insure themselves against liability without undue cost (see RGZ 149, 213, 215 and the reasons there given).

But the idea of so limiting the amount of a claim based on strict liability has no application when the question is whether the plaintiff should bear an appropriate part of his own harm. It would be irrational to say that the custodian need not bear any part of his loss when his claim is based on the BGB (loss of income, § 842; loss of services, § 845; damages for pain and suffering, § 847) but that his claim is reduced if it is based on the StVG when it is in any case limited in quantum (§§ 10–12 StVG). The result would be that a reduction would take place only in those very claims whose satisfaction the legislature thought particularly urgent, as the enactment of the KrfzG/StVG shows. The legislature cannot have intended this result to flow from the limitation on the amount of the defendant's liability. It is rather for the judge whenever the situation is appropriate for a division of the loss between the victim and the person who caused the injury, to apply § 17 I, 1 StVG, which is analogous to § 254 BGB, and decide whether the victim is to bear an equitable part of his own loss.

This conclusion is logically consistent with the decisions of the Bundesgerichtshof on the question of contribution between common debtors liable for the same harm under § 17 StVG (BGHZ 6, 319, 322). The relationship between common debtors and their respective contribution claims depends exclusively on the actual facts, especially the extent to which they respectively contributed to the harm, and not on the basis of their legal liability to the victim; the adjudication of contribution claims is entirely divorced from the legal basis of the individual debtor's liability, to the point where it is irrelevant whether the actual causes of the harm were a ground of liability to the victim (reference omitted). Now, since the same considerations apply, and the results should be the same, when one is weighing up the respective responsibility for harm as between several common debtors on the one hand (§ 17 StVG) and as between those causing and suffering harm on the other (§ 254 BGB), so in the latter case also one should take no account of the basis of liability, but only of the totality of the facts, especially the extent to which each contributed to the harm as a matter of causation (reference omitted). Just as one is to ignore the legal basis of liability in the individual case when it comes to dividing the loss (BGH VersR 5, 163), so one should ignore the question whether the harm is of such a kind that a third party could claim in respect of it. The only safe way to an equitable division of the loss is to have the judge make the custodian bear part of it by applying the standards of § 17 I, 1 StVG, as would be the result of applying § 17 StVG and § 254 BGB [reference omitted].

Accordingly, the Court of Appeal was right to hold that the plaintiff's claim for damages for pain and suffering was also affected by the danger contributed by his motor cycle.

Case 127

BUNDESGERICHTSHOF (SIXTH CIVIL SENATE) 16 JUNE 1959
BGHZ 30, 203 = NJW 1959, 1772

About 9 p.m. on 5 September 1952 the plaintiff was riding his moped out of town on V. St. He crossed the intersection with I. St., and was about to pass the E. gas station on his right when the defendant E. drove out of the gas station in his Opel Olympia 1937 and turned right into V. St. in front of him. In overtaking E.'s car, the plaintiff got between the tramlines in the middle of the highway. He overtook E.'s car but had not yet regained the right hand side of the road when he collided head-on with B.'s Mercedes 170S, 22 metres before the intersection with E. St. The plaintiff suffered serious injuries in the collision, and his left leg had to be amputated.

The plaintiff asserts that E. came out of the gas station right in front of him, so that he was forced to overtake. In doing so the plaintiff had to get between the sets of tramlines in the middle of the road, because E.'s left hand wheels were over the right hand tram lines by reason of cars parked on the right hand side of the road. The plaintiff took some time to overtake because E. accelerated as he was doing so, and he was therefore unable to regain the right hand side of the road in due time. The defendant B. had also crossed the tramlines while overtaking a car in front of him, and would have seen the plaintiff if he had been paying proper attention.

The plaintiff claims compensation from the defendants for one-half of the damage he suffered, and the defendants answer that the accident was entirely due to the plaintiff's fault.

The Landgericht dismissed the claim against E., and granted the claim against B. as to one-fifth of the total damage.

On appeal by the plaintiff and B., the Oberlandesgericht held that both defendants were liable under the Strassenverkehrsgesetz (StVG) for two-fifths of the total harm, and that the defendant B. was also liable under the Civil Code (BGB) for two-fifths of the amount claimed by the plaintiff.

The defendants' appeals were allowed in part, the Bundesgerichtshof holding that while each defendant was liable for one-fifth of the total damage, they were not together liable for more than one-third.

Reasons

The Court of Appeal was right to hold that the defendant E. was liable for one-fifth of the plaintiff's total damage, so E.'s appeal on this point must be dismissed. B.'s appeal equally fails in so far as it argues that he is not liable at all.

The Court of Appeal then added together the two liabilities for one-fifth each, and consequently held the defendants jointly liable for two-fifths of the total harm (four-fifths of the amount actually claimed by the plaintiff, for he claimed for only one-half of his harm). The defendants are right to object to this.

1. The Court of Appeal was right to start out by weighing the plaintiff's contributory fault against each of the defendants separately, and correctly applied § 254 BGB first as between the plaintiff and E., and then as between the plaintiff and B. This separate apportionment is necessary because the plaintiff has an independent claim for compensation against each defendant. Each defendant is responsible for providing an adequate cause of the harm,

and has thereby met the conditions of statutory liability (§ 823 BGB, §§ 7, 18 StVG). Had the plaintiff sued only one of the defendants, he could claim only one-fifth of his total damage (= two-fifths of the sum actually claimed). The fact that he sued both defendants in one suit does not justify an apportionment under § 254 BGB on the basis that the responsibility of the two defendants should be treated as a unit and compared as such with that of the plaintiff.

Where several persons have caused harm, there is only one case where it is right to combine their spheres of responsibility and thus make each responsible for the contribution to the harm made by the others, and that is when the requirements of § 830 I, 1 BGB are met, namely that the various persons causing the harm caused it by means of "a wrongful act committed jointly". There is no question of that here. Indeed, it may be that this provision is inapplicable on the mere ground that whereas E. was guilty of an unlawful act in the sense of § 823 BGB, B. was liable only on the basis of the strict liability in §§ 11, 18 StVG. Be that as it may, there was here no "act jointly committed" by the defendants. True though it is that together they produced the harmful result, this was through different independent individual acts, not through a common act. To several acts of negligence of this kind (*fahrlässige Nebentäterschaft*), § 830 I, 1 BGB is not to be applied [reference omitted]. If in RGZ 58, 357 the Reichsgericht indicated otherwise, this court cannot agree. When the harm has been caused by the concurrence of several individual acts, the fact that these acts may coincide closely in time and place does not justify an apportionment which burdens each debtor with the contributions of the others. Nor did the Reichsgericht itself hold that when several drivers had caused an accident by various independent acts of bad driving they were "joint actors" (*Mittäter*) in the sense of § 830 I, 1 BGB.

2. The Court of Appeal believed that § 840 BGB empowered them to add together the portions of the harm, namely one-fifth each, for which the defendants were responsible. In this they failed to see that since under § 840 I BGB the debtors' obligations must coincide before there can be a relationship of common debt, the defendants could be common debtors only in respect of one-fifth of the plaintiff's harm. In contrast with § 830 I BGB, there is here no legal basis for treating the contributions of the two defendants as a unit imputable to both and opposing it to the plaintiff's quota of responsibility. Such a solution is irreconcilable with the recognised principles concerning the factors relevant to an apportionment under § 254 BGB. It would improperly extend the limits within which the law of tort allows the imputation to one person of another person's fault. And it is inequitable because each of several *defendants* would bear the risk of the insolvency of the others, whereas the *plaintiff* would not be exposed to this risk at all, even though he was equally to blame, if not more so.

3. According to the decisions of the Reichsgericht and those of the Bundesgerichtshof hitherto (BGHZ 12, 213, 220; VersR 1957, 167), several tortfeasors whose liability as a result of the individual weighing process is equal in amount (as with the defendants here, one-fifth each) are liable for that amount as common debtors under § 840 BGB, and the plaintiff must bear the remainder of the loss himself. This is an unsatisfactory solution, because it gives the victim less than he should, if one views the accident as a whole, recover. The example given by Dunz in JZ 1955, 727 makes this quite clear. If ten people, all equally at fault, cause damage to an eleventh, the victim can claim the full amount of his loss from any of the ten. But if one of the ten who are equally careless is himself the victim, the result of the individual weighing is that each of those causing the harm is liable to the

plaintiff for half of his harm. If we apply the rule of common debtors as the courts have done until now, the victim recovers only half of his harm altogether whereas, if all the debtors are solvent, he should get nine-tenths. On the other side, the effect of contribution proceedings would be that each person causing the harm would pay only one-eighteenth of it.

The main reason for the unsatisfactory nature of the law hitherto applied in such cases is that the rules of common debt have been applied too soon and too formalistically. Of course § 840 I BGB applies in the case of several as well as joint tortfeasors (see BGHZ 17, 214). This makes for no difficulty if the several tortfeasors are each liable for the whole harm, for then we have the situation which is characteristic of a common debt, namely that performance by any one debtor satisfies the whole of the creditor's interest. But this identity of the content of performance is lacking to some extent if the victim is himself guilty of contributory fault so that his damages claims against the several tortfeasors fall to be reduced under § 254 BGB. It is also lacking in the case before us today, for the one-fifth for which E. is liable as a result of the individual apportionment is neither economically nor legally identical with the one-fifth of the harm which B. has to pay. Payment of one of these two parts of the harm does not give the victim of the accident all he ought to get from E. and B. together. This is the second reason for the unsatisfactory nature of the law applied until now: the traditional comparison of the contribution of the victim with that of each individual causing the harm fails to give a global view of the accident and leads to a division of the loss which, on a global view, is unsatisfactory.

4. It might seem that one could equitably deal with the consequences of an accident by dividing the harm between the parties involved in the occurrence of the harm in relation to their respective contributions to it, and burdening each only with the appropriate portion of the harm he has caused. In support of such a view one might adduce the idea that all those involved in an accident, including the responsible victim (§ 254 BGB, §§ 7, 17, 18 StVG), form a kind of community, entailing a duty to resolve it so that no member has to bear more of the loss than is appropriate under § 17 StVG or § 254 BGB. Such a method brings the apportionment of the loss between the various persons who caused it (the inner or contribution relationship) into the suit brought by the victim against any or all of the persons causing the harm (external liability). There are several reasons which render this unacceptable.

There is no statutory basis for such apportionment proceedings. In admiralty law, indeed, there is such a rule (§ 736 HGB): if a collision between two or more vessels results from the fault of the crews involved, the owners of these ships are only liable in proportion to the gravity of their respective faults, at any rate so far as concerns damage to the ships themselves or to property on board, personal injury being dealt with otherwise. Here, several liability is introduced in lieu of joint liability, and the division between external liability and internal contribution which the law has maintained for good reason in other areas is abolished. But § 736 I HGB only applies in this particular area of admiralty law: it cannot be applied to the law of road traffic or to the general law of tort. Certainly nothing in § 17 StVG would justify abandoning the distinction between external liability and internal contribution in the case of a collision between motor-cars and making the drivers and custodians involved in the accident liable to the victim only for their several parts (see also BGHZ 15, 123, 135). Several liability such as is exceptionally provided for by § 736 I HGB would often be detrimental to the victim, for it would deprive him of the security and advantages offered to him by the principle of joint liability and by the separation of external liability and internal contribution. To take Dunz's example once again, if several liability existed, the plaintiff could recover only one-tenth of his harm from each person causing it; yet each of them had provided an adequate cause for the harm and was, in relation to the plaintiff, as much to blame for it as the plaintiff himself, so it would seem right to give him a claim for half his harm against each individual causing it. Finally, several liability would greatly complicate the trial of many tort cases. Very frequently, the victim does not sue all those liable for the harm resulting from an accident; to minimise the risk, he often sues only the person whose liability can most easily be established. Now if the principle of several liability applied, one could only decide how much the defendant must pay by ascertaining the extent to which all the other persons responsible for the accident were to blame and contributed to it as a matter of causation. Thus in every traffic accident case, one would have to ask whether anyone not in court might be liable for the harm, though any such determination would lack the force of *res judicata* against such a person. Wide-ranging enquiries would often be necessary although the actual issue was quite simple. To complicate matters like this would conflict with the policy of the Code, especially § 421 BGB, to assist the victim, even when he, too, is at fault, for it is in the victim's interests to limit the issues in trial and to make a quick decision possible.

For all these reasons the principle of several liability does not provide a solution.

5. Solutions are suggested by Dunz (*JZ* 1955, 727 and 1957, 371) and Engelhardt (*JZ* 1957, 369) but as Dunz himself admits in his second Article, they are not ideal.

6. In order to achieve a satisfactory result one must somehow harmonise the principle of common debt (joint liability) with the principle of apportionment of § 254 BGB (§ 17 StVG) and combine the individual apportionment with a global apportionment achieved by looking at the accident as a whole. An example may make this clear. Suppose that A is injured in an accident due to his own carelessness and the careless driving of B and C. If the contribution of all three parties is equal, and the damage suffered by A amounts to DM 3,000, the individual apportionment will be that A's contribution to the accident is equal to that of B (1:1). A may therefore claim DM 1,500 from B. The same applies as between A and C. Now if A claims damages from B and C together, one must follow this individual apportionment by taking a global view of the accident, and asking how much each of them contributed to it. Since from this point of view A, B and C are each responsible for one-third, A should have to bear only one-third of his harm (DM 1,000) and should be able to claim a total of two-thirds (DM 2,000) from the others. The results of these two processes of apportionment (the individual and the global) leads to the conclusion that: "B and C together must pay A total of DM 2,000, but neither of them need pay more than DM 1,500", or, to put it another way: "A may claim DM 1,500 from B, and he may claim DM 1,500 from C, but he may not claim more than DM 2,000 in all." The question of contribution between B and C remains a matter of their relationship *inter se*. If B has paid A the DM 1,500 he owes him, then C owes B DM 500 as contribution under § 17 StVG. C remains liable to A, but only for DM 500, since A has already received DM 1,500 from B.

While maintaining the legal structure of joint liability, this solution accommodates it to the particularities of the law of tort liability arising from the principle of apportionment of § 254 BGB and related provisions, and the solution is a just one in that all those involved in an accident bear the loss in a measure which reflects their responsibility for it. By linking individual and global apportionment, it avoids the disadvantages to which the victim has hitherto been exposed when claiming damages from several defendants (hitherto A has obtained judgment for DM 1,500 against B and C as common debtors, and had to bear half his loss himself). On the other hand, the individual apportionment ensures that no person causing the harm pays more to the victim than is fair in view of their relationship *inter se* (B pays A here DM 1,500, and so does C). So far as these debts overlap, the victim has the security and other advantages which the principle of joint liability is designed to give him (§§ 840, 421 BGB).

The step of making the global apportionment and ascertaining the respective quotas of harm is naturally only to be taken when the victim sues several persons at the same time, or if there are successive suits.

7. We can now apply these principles to the case in hand, taking the individual apportionments made by the Court of Appeal as correct in law. Here as between plaintiff and E. the total harm must be divided in the proportion 4:1, and likewise, under the StVG, in the same proportion of 4:1 as between the plaintiff and B. Taking the global view next, as we must, the harm must be divided between the three parties involved so that the proportion of the harm borne by the two defendants remains the same and that on the other hand the proportion of four to one is maintained both in the relationship between the plaintiff and E., and in the relationship between the plaintiff and B. It follows that the global apportionment must be in the ratio 4:1:1. This means that the plaintiff is responsible for four-sixths (= two-thirds) and the defendants are each responsible for one-sixth. In the end result, the plaintiff will have to bear two-thirds of the total loss, and the defendants must make good one-third, though each defendant is liable only for one-fifth of the harm and B. is liable only under the StVG. The plaintiff's claim being limited to half of his total harm, the end result is that his claim succeeds against E. for two-fifths and against B. for two-fifths under the StVG, subject to this, that the total sum he may recover from both is not to exceed two-thirds of the sum he has claimed.

Notes to the Road Traffic Act

1. Traffic accidents represent a major area of accident compensation; arguably, they have also presented traditional tort law with its major challenge. The result was inevitable: revealing empirical studies, a vast literature, and numerous proposals for reform. Comparing the German law with other systems of compensation (whether in existence or merely proposed) makes it look both pioneering and in need of further reform. But change is hard to achieve and the role of a reformer is rarely a happy one. In some countries such as the USA no-fault statutory schemes have been challenged on constitutional grounds. See, for example, *Kluger* v. *White* 281 So. 2d 1 (Fla. 1973); *Lasky* v. *State Farm Insurance Co.* 296 So. 2d 9 (Fla. 1974). In other countries, like France for example, proposals for reform have met with strenuous if not at times undignified reactions on the part of various specialised pressure groups (insurers, practising lawyers).

2. Any comparative summary of such a topic is bound to be incomplete if not misleading. The decision was thus taken to depart from the pattern adopted throughout this book. Instead of comparing German law with Common law, the reader is invited to look at an imaginative French proposal and then compare it with German law and his own law.

3. The French proposal can be best understood by looking at the French legal background and discovering its own deficiencies. Good brief accounts of this can be found in von Mehren and Gordley's *The Civil Law System, chapter 9,* (2nd ed. 1979), and Lawson and Markesinis, *Tortious Liability for Unintentional Harm in the Common Law and the Civil Law,* chapter 3. Professor Tunc— the author of the proposed French Bill—has also provided more detailed accounts in 31 *Am. J. Comp. Law* 489 (1983) and in 16 *Rev. Jur. Uni. Interam. Puerto Rico* 125 (1981). André Tunc is also

responsible for a masterly comparative account of the subject in vol. XI, chapter 14 of the *International Encyclopedia of Comparative Law*. The literature in French on the Tunc proposals is enormous. One of the most recent and interesting collections of essays on the proposed Bill have been published under the editorship of Tunc under the title *Pour une loi sur les accidents de la circulation* (1981). The reader is invited to compare Tunc's proposals (*Addendum 1*) with (*a*) the *Desmares* decision and (*b*) the 1985 Act (*Addendum 2*). The difficulties caused by some of the Act's terms (particularly the words *faute inexcusable*) have given rise to much case-law reviewed by Margeat, Landel, Thiry, and Besson, *Accidents de la circulation: Loi du 5 juillet 1985—Bilan et perspectives*, published in 1988 by the Gazette du Palais.

Addendum 1

A BILL CONCERNING THE COMPENSATION OF VICTIMS OF ROAD TRAFFIC ACCIDENTS, PROPOSED BY ANDRÉ TUNC

Part I. Obligation to insure

Article 1

Every owner or possessor of a motorised vehicle must, before putting it into "circulation", take out an insurance policy covering, according to the provisions of the present law and despite all contrary clauses, the damages that may result from a road traffic accident in which the said vehicle is involved.

For the purposes of the present law, the word "vehicle" denotes a motorised land vehicle, its trailer, or semi-trailer and their load; any vehicle not immobilised in a private garage is considered to be in circulation.

For the purposes of the present law, public bodies exempted from the obligation to insure their vehicles, will assume with regard to their vehicles the rights and obligations of an insurance company.

Part II. Corporeal damage

Article 2

Every victim of personal injury, resulting from a road traffic accident in which a vehicle has participated, has the right to be compensated in accordance with the provisions of Articles 3–12, below.

Article 3

The victim has a right to be reimbursed for all expenses reasonably incurred as a result of the injury, whether for care, rehabilitation, aid, special equipment for or adaptation of the home, travelling expenses for members of the family, repair or replacement of clothes, or items worn at the time of the accident and damaged as a result of the latter.

Article 4

The victim has the right to be compensated for loss of salary or professional earnings resulting from a temporary disablement.

Article 5

If the victim is permanently disabled, he has the right:

(a) to be compensated for the loss of salary or professional earnings which would arise from the normal course of events concerning a person in the same position as himself;

(b) to compensation for purely physiological harm in accordance with a table taking into account the degree of his disablement and his age—this table, and also the medical scale used to calculate the degree of his disablement, to be established by Decree.

Article 6

Loss of salary or professional earnings in the sense of Articles 4 and 5, above, should be taken to mean only the actual loss not compensated by employers' contributions, social security, or any other organisation for social welfare.

Article 7

Compensation will only be paid for loss of salary and professional earnings not exceeding x times the index-linked minimum wage.

Article 8

When the permanent disability of the victim entails the loss of salary or professional earnings of at least 30 per cent, compensation of this loss will take the form of an index-linked annuity in accordance with the provisions of the law of 27 December 1974, and will be reviewed as the victim's physical condition develops.

This annuity will be liable to be reduced should the beneficiary refuse without valid reason a measure of examination, observation, treatment, or adjustment reasonably suggested by the insurance company.

It will not be subject to attachment any more than would have been the salary or professional earnings it is meant to replace.

Article 9

When the victim dies as a result of the accident, his heirs and next of kin are entitled to be reimbursed for expenses which they must reasonably have incurred as a result of the accident. The persons who paid the funeral expenses are entitled to be reimbursed.

Article 10

The persons who as the result of the victim's death are deprived of (financial) assistance which they were receiving or could reasonably have expected to receive from him are entitled to compensation within the limits provided by Article 7 of the present law. This compensation will take the form of an index-linked annuity in accordance with the provisions of the law of 27 December 1974.

Article 11

The obligation to pay the compensation envisaged in Articles 3–10 of the present law falls upon:

(a) the insurer of the vehicle in which the killed or injured victim was being transported or,

(b) if the victim was not being transported [in a vehicle], the insurer of the vehicle which participated in the accident.

When more than one vehicle has participated in the accident, each insurer will be obliged to compensate the victim (to the full extent), the cost of the damages to be divided either in equal parts or in proportions to be agreed amongst them.

Article 12

When a stolen vehicle has participated in an accident, the thief and the handler of the stolen car forfeit all rights to compensation under the present law.

Part III. Material damage

Article 13

Damage suffered by colliding vehicles is compensated in accordance with percentages determined by types of circumstance fixed by Decree. The same Decree will specify the elements of compensatable loss.

Damage occasioned to goods carried in or on vehicles will only be compensated in cases of collision with or transport by professional carriers and then only within the limits laid down by Decree, subject to any more extensive compensation envisaged by the contract of insurance.

All other material damage caused by a vehicle (to a furnished building) must be compensated.

Part IV. Miscellaneous provisions

Article 14

The rights provided for by the law exclude all other rights of compensation resulting from a road traffic accident with the exception of the following:

(1) the victim has a right to seek further compensation in accordance with the ordinary rules of civil liability against the manufacturer, seller, or repairer of the vehicle;

(2) the insurer, obliged to pay compensation under the provisions of this law, is entitled to be subrogated against:

(a) any person who intentionally caused a type of damage covered by this law;

(b) the manufacturer, seller or repairer of the vehicle, responsible under the ordinary rules of civil liability;

(c) the highway authorities under the ordinary rules of civil liability. These subrogation rights will be for lump sums even where the compensation is to be paid in the form of an annuity.

Article 15

Whenever a person is, because of his involvement in an accident, condemned to imprisonment of ... [a certain period] the criminal court can order as an additional penalty the payment of a sum not exceeding 50,000 fr. to be made to the Fonds de Garantie.

Article 16

The courts cannot be seized of a dispute arising from the application of this law until it has been submitted to a Commission for Reconciliation, the membership and functions of which will be decided by Decree.

Article 17

The actions of personal injury and property damage are statute-barred in three months and one year respectively from the moment the victim becomes aware of the damage.

Article 18

The premium to be paid by the insured will be adjusted every twelve months depending on the number of accidents in which the vehicle has participated. A Decree will regulate such details as no-claims bonuses and upward adjustments of premiums.

Addendum 2

Law no. 85–677 of 5 July 1985
Aiming at the improvement of the position of victims of traffic accidents and the acceleration of the compensation process. (JO of 6 July 1985, 7584.)

Chapter 1. Compensation of traffic accident victims

Article 1

The provisions of the present chapter apply to victims of traffic accidents, whether transported by virtue of contract or not, involving (impliqué) a land motorised vehicle as well as trailers and half-trailers with the exception of trains and trams running on fixed rails.

Section 1. Provisions relating to compensation

Article 2

The driver or guardian of a vehicle mentioned in Article 1 above cannot plead against victims, including drivers, [the defence] of force majeure or act of a third party.

Article 3

Victims, excluding the drivers of motorised land vehicles, are compensated for damage resulting from injuries to their person without it being possible to invoke against them their own fault with the exception of their inexcusable fault [negligence] in so far as it was the exclusive cause of the accident.

The victims designated in the preceding sub-paragraph, whenever they are below the age of sixteen or over that of seventy, or whenever, irrespective of their age, they have at the time of the accident been recognised as suffering from a permanent incapacity or invalidity of at least 80 per cent, will in all cases be compensated for damages suffered as a result of personal injuries.

However, in the cases envisaged in the preceding sub-paragraphs, the victim will not be compensated by the tortfeasor for harm resulting to his person when he voluntarily sought the damage that he suffered.

Article 4

The fault committed by the driver of a motorised land vehicle has the effect of limiting or excluding the compensation of the damages that he has suffered.

Article 5

The victim's [contributory] fault results in the exclusion or limitation of his compensation for damage suffered by his property. However, compensation for supplies and equipment provided on medical prescription is made in accordance with the rules applicable to compensation for personal injury.

Wherever the driver of the motorized land vehicle is not its owner, the fault of such driver can be opposed against the owner for compensation of damages caused to his vehicle. In such cases the owner has a right to sue the driver.

Article 6

The loss suffered by a third party as a result of the damage caused to the direct victim of the traffic accident is made good by taking into account the limitations or exclusions applicable to the compensation of such damage.

Section 2. Provisions relating to insurance and fonds de garantie

Articles 7–11 contain amendments and conditions to the Code of Insurance.

Section 3. Concerning the offer to pay compensation

Article 12

The insurer who guarantees the civil liability resulting from a motorised land vehicle is bound, within a maximum period of eight months from the date of the accident, to make an offer of compensation to the injured victim. In the event of death of the victim, the offer is made to his heirs and, where appropriate, the spouse.

The offer must also be made to the other victim within a period of eight months reckoning from the date of the request for compensation.

The offer includes all compensatable headings of damage including the elements relating to property damage whenever they have not been the object of preliminary settlement.

They may be of a provisional nature whenever the insurer has not, within three months of the accident, been informed of the stabilisation of the state of the victim's [health]. The definitive offer for compensation must in this case be made within five months of the insurer being informed of such stabilisation.

In the case of plurality of vehicles, and if there are many insurers, the offer is made by the insurer authorised by the others.

The preceding provisions are not applicable to victims to whom the accident caused only property damage.

Article 13

On the occasion of his first correspondence with the victim, the insurer is bound [subject to] relative nullity of any agreement that might be reached [result] to inform the victim that he can obtain through a simple request a copy of the report of the police enquiry and to remind him that he may obtain the assistance of a lawyer and, in the case of a medical examination, [the assistance] of a doctor.

Under the threat of the same penalty, the above-mentioned correspondence must inform the victim of the provision of sub-paragraph 4 of Article 12 and of Article 15 [of this law].

Article 14

When the insurer could not, without fault on his part, have known that the accident had occasioned disbursements to the paying third parties envisaged in Articles 29 and 33 of the present law, these [third parties] lose all rights of reimbursement against the insurer and the author of the damage. However, the insurer cannot invoke such ignorance vis-à-vis organisations that make social security payments.

In all cases, failure to produce the claims of paying third parties, within a period of four months from the moment of the request made by the insurer, will entail the forfeiture of their rights against the insurer and the author of the damages.

In the case where the demand that emanates from the insurer does not mention the stabilization of the victim's health, the claims made by the paying third parties may have a provisional character.

Article 15

Whenever, through the conduct of the victim, the paying third parties have not been able to assert their claims against the insurer, they will have a right of recourse against the victim to the extent of the indemnity he has received from the insurer under the same heading of damages and within the limits provided for by Article 31. They must act within a period of two years from the demand of payment.

Article 16

When the offer has not been made within the period allowed by Article 12, the amount of compensation offered to the victim by the insurer or granted to him by the judge, automatically attracts interest at double the rate of the legal interest from the moment of expiry of the permissible period up until the moment when the offer or the judgment becomes definitive. This penalty can be reduced by the judge because of circumstances not attributable to the insurer.

Article 17

If the judge who determines the compensation is of the view that the offer made by the insurer is manifestly insufficient, he will, of his own initiative, condemn the insurer to transfer to the *fonds de garantie* envisaged by Article 420–1 of the Code of Insurance a sum of at [most] 15 per cent of the compensation awarded [by the court] without prejudice to any damages and interest due to the victim for this conduct.

Article 18

The insurer must submit to the *juge des tutelles* or the *conseil de famille*—depending on which of the two is appropriate—all proposals of settlement concerning minors or adults subject to guardianship [*tutelle*]. Similarly, he must give informal notice to the *juge des tutelles*, at least fifteen days in advance of the payment of the first instalment of an annuity or of any sum due to be paid as compensation to the legal representative of the protected person.

Any payment which has not been preceded by the requisite notice or any unauthorized transaction can be annulled at the request of any interested party or one of the *ministère public* but not of the insurer.

Any clause by which the legal representative of a minor or of an adult subject to guardianship, guarantees the ratification [by the said persons] of the acts mentioned in the first sub-paragraph of this Article is void.

Article 19

The victim may, by means of a registered letter accompanied by a request for its receipt, denounce the settlement within fifteen days of its conclusion.

Any provision in the settlement that deprives the victim of this right is void.

The above-mentioned provisions reproduced very clearly in the offer proposing a settlement and in the settlement itself [at the risk of] relative nullity of the latter.

Article 20

Payment of the agreed sums must take place within one month from the expiry of the period within which denunciation is permitted according to Article 19. Sums not paid will automatically [produce] interest at 50 per cent above the legal rate for the first two months [of the delay] and twice the legal amount for any period thereafter.

Article 21

In the event of payment being ordered by the court (even by a provisional decision) the rate of legal interest is increased by 50 per cent after the expiry of two months and it is doubled after the expiry of four months counting from the day when the decision was made whenever the case was contested. In all other cases [time runs] from the day on which the decision was notified [to the defaulting party].

Article 22

The victim can, within the period provided for by Article 2270–1 of the Civil Code, demand from the insurer compensation for the increase of the damage he has suffered.

Article 23

Whenever the insurer invokes an exception of legal or contractual guarantee, he is bound to comply with the provisions of Articles 12 to 20 on account of the party concerned; the resulting settlement can be contested before the judge by the person on whose account it was made without challenging the amount of money allocated to the victim or those deriving rights from him.

Article 24

For the purposes of Articles 12 to 20, the State and all public entities, enterprises or organizations not obliged to carry insurance or having by virtue of Article 211–3 of the same Code obtained [a waiver from the duty to take out insurance] are assimilated to an insurer.

Article 25

The provisions of Articles 12 and 13 to 22 are applicable to the *fonds de garantie* in its relations with the victim and those deriving rights from him. However, the times provided for in Article 12 run against *le fonds* from the day when it has received information justifying its intervention. The application of Articles 16 and 17 are not obstacles to the [specific] provisions that cover actions against the *fond*. Whenever the *fonds de garantie* is bound to pay the interest provided for by Article 17, this is payable to the Treasury.

Article 26

Under the control of public authority a periodic publication will provide an account of the amounts of compensation awarded by the courts or agreed upon as a result of private settlements.

Article 27

A degree of the Council of the State will fix the necessary measures for the application of this section. In particular it will list the causes of suspension and prorogation of the delays mentioned in Article 12 as well as the reciprocal information that must be supplied by insurer, victim and paying third parties.

4. STRICT LIABILITY ACT 1978

HAFTPFLICHTGESETZ OF 4 JANUARY 1978
(BGBL. I, 145—AS AMENDED)

§ 1. Liability of the entrepreneur

(1) If in the conduct of a railway or cable-way a human being is killed or suffers injury to body or health or a thing is damaged, the entrepreneur [the undertaking] is bound to make good to the injured party the damage arising therefrom.

(2) The duty to make good is excluded if the accident was caused by *force majeure.* Nevertheless in so far as the railway was operated within the travelled portion of a public highway, the duty to make good is excluded if the accident was caused by an unavoidable event which is due neither to a defect in the condition of the vehicle or lay-out of the railway nor to a failure of its management. An event is deemed to be unavoidable in particular when it is traceable to the conduct of the injured party or of a third person not concerned in the undertaking or of an animal and both the entrepreneur and the persons engaged in the undertaking observed the care required of them by the circumstances of the case.

(3) The duty to make good is also excluded if:
    1. an object accepted for safekeeping is damaged;
    2. an object being transported is damaged, unless a passenger is wearing or carrying it with him.

§ 2. Liability of the proprietor of an energy establishment

(1) If a human being is killed or suffers injury to body or health or an object is damaged through the operation of electricity, gas, steam, or current escaping from a cable or pipeline or a plant for the provision of such energy or material, the proprietor of the plant is bound to make good the damage arising therefrom. The same applies if the damage, without being due to the operation of the electricity, gas, steam or current, is traceable to the existence of such plants, unless they were in a proper state when the damage was caused. A plant is in a proper state as long as it conforms to the recognised technical rules and is intact.

(2) Subsection 1 does not apply to plants which serve only for the transmission of signs or sounds.

(3) The duty to make good under subsection 1 is excluded:
    1. if the damage occurred inside a building and is traceable to a plant discoverable therein (subsection 1) or if it occurred inside a plot in the possession of the proprietor of the plant;
    2. if the damage was caused by *force majeure,* unless it is traceable to fall of cable wires.

§ 3. Liability of other entrepreneurs

Anyone who operates a mine, quarry, pit, or factory is liable to compensation if an authorised agent or representative or anyone employed in the direction or supervision of the undertaking or of the workmen causes by a fault in the carrying out of the service arrangement, death or bodily injury to a human being.

§ 4. Contributory fault

If a fault of the injured party contributed to the occurrence of the damage § 254 BGB applies; where an object is damaged, the fault of the person who exercises the factual control over it is equivalent to the fault of the injured party.

§ 5. Extent of the compensation for death

(1) In the case of death, compensation must be made by making good the cost of the attempted cure as well as of the pecuniary damage which the deceased has suffered

therefrom by having his earning capacity destroyed or diminished during the illness, or by having his personal needs increased. The person bound to make compensation must also make good the funeral expenses to the person who is under a duty to bear those expenses.

(2) If the deceased at the time of the injury stood to a third party in a relation by virtue of which he was, or could have become under a statutory duty of maintenance, and if the third party is deprived of the right to maintenance as a result of the death, the person bound to make compensation must compensate the third party for the period of the deceased's presumed life expectancy. The duty of compensation arises also if the third party at the time of the injury was conceived but not yet born.

§ 6. *Extent of the compensation for bodily injury*

In case of bodily injury, the compensation (§§ 1, 2, and 3) must be made by making good the cost of cure as well as the pecuniary damage which the injured party suffers by having his earning capacity temporarily or permanently destroyed or diminished or by having his personal needs increased by reason of the injury.

§ 7. *Compulsory law*

The duty of compensation under §§ 1–3 of this Act may not, in so far as personal injury is concerned, be either excluded or restricted for the future. The same applies to the duty of compensation under § 2 of this statute to damage to objects, unless the exclusion or restriction of liability has been agreed to between the proprietor of the plant and a public corporation or fund or a businessman by the terms of a contract relating to the conduct of his business. Provisions and agreements to the contrary are void.

§ 8. *Money annuity or lump sum settlement*

(1) Compensation for destruction or diminution of any earning capacity and for increase in the personal needs of the injured person as well as compensation to be paid to a third party under § 3 II is due only for future losses and payments must take the form of an annuity.

(2) The provisions of §§ 843 II–IV BGB apply *mutatis mutandis*.

(3) If in the sentencing of the person bound to pay a money annuity no decision is made as to the provision of security, the person entitled to compensation can nevertheless demand that such security be provided if the financial status of the person bound to pay it has appreciably worsened; in similar circumstances, he can demand an increase in the security fixed by the judgment.

§ 9. *Limit of liability*

The entrepreneur or the proprietor of the plant indicated in § 2 is liable in cases under § 8 I only up to an annuity of DM 30,000 for each person killed or injured.

§ 10. *Limit of liability for damage to objects by energy plants*

(1) The entrepreneur or the proprietor of a plant listed in § 2 is liable for property damage only up to the sum of DM 100,000, even if several objects are damaged by the same event.

(2) If, by reason of the same event, compensation is payable to several persons, which together exceeds the highest permissible sum of DM 100,000, the individual awards are reduced in the proportion to which their total sum stands to the highest permissible sum.

§ 11. Prescription

With regard to prescription the provisions of the BGB applicable to unlawful acts apply *mutatis mutandis.*

§ 12. Further liabilities

Statutory provisions remain unaffected according to which a person bound to make compensation is liable to a greater extent than under the provisions of this Act or another person is responsible for the damage.

§ 13. Several persons liable

(1) If several persons are bound to make good property damage to a third person, as regards the mutual relations of those bound to make compensation, the duty to compensate and its extent depend on the circumstances, and in particular on how far the damage was caused by one or the other. The same applies if the damage occurred to one of those bound to compensate, to the liability that attaches to another of them.

(2) Subsection (1) applies *mutatis mutandis* where, along with those bound to compensate under §§ 1 and 2, another person is legally responsible for the damage.

§ 14. Optional jurisdiction

Actions based on these provisions may also be brought in the court, in whose district the event causing damage took place.

Case 128

REICHSGERICHT (SIXTH CIVIL SENATE) 11 JANUARY 1912
RGZ 78, 171

On 5 August 1908, while flying from Mainz to Friedrichshafen, the defendant's airship was forced by engine failure to land on a field near Echterdingen. Since thousands flocked to see the sight, the landing area was sealed off by the military, while the fire brigade, and various army units were placed at the defendant's disposal. Around 3 p.m. a sudden storm caused the airship to break loose from its moorings and to be dragged for some 1,200 metres before exploding and burning up. The plaintiff, who was among the spectators standing near the place of anchorage, was struck by the anchor-chain. He sued the defendant for damage alleging that the accident was caused by the defendant's negligence.

Both lower courts rejected the plaintiff's claim and his application for review was denied for the following.

Reasons

1. The claim was considered by the Court of Appeal in the light of §§ 823 and 831 BGB and it refused to consider the applicability of other statutory provisions imposing liab-

ility for dangerous objects (*Gefährdungshaftung*). This conclusion is entirely justified by existing law. In cases such as this, where the plaintiff's injuries have been sustained outside any contractual relations, the provisions of the Civil Code dealing with torts are the only ones that can apply. According to these provisions, however, the defendant can only be liable to the plaintiff if the latter's damage is due to the former's culpable conduct. Special provisions of the Civil Code imposing liability without fault, e.g. § 833 BGB concerning the liability of keepers of animals, the principles of the Imperial Act on Liability (*Reichshaftpflichtgesetz*), or of the statute of 3 May 1909 (*Strassenverkehrsgesetz*) concerning automobile accidents, which (statutes) impose liability based on risk, cannot be applied to aerial navigation given their exceptional character.

2. With regard to liability for damages resulting from illegal acts, the older view can no longer be accepted which postulated with respect to the dangerous nature that constitutes a fault (*Verschulden*). Consequently, it cannot be said that because aerial navigation is fraught with great dangers the defendant, as initiator of this dangerous undertaking, can be regarded as being at fault in the sense required by § 823 I BGB. This approach has not been misapplied by the Court of Appeal taking the view, which pays due attention to the requirements of general safety and which is legally correct, that in the circumstances the defendant was under a duty to take particular care. The Court thus held the defendant was under a duty to take exceptional care, not least because at the time of the accident there was little experience in landing such an airship . . .

3. Given that in view of the above points the position taken by the Court of Appeal is free from legal error, the question arises whether the findings of fact justified it in holding that the defendant had discharged this duty. The plaintiff denies this on two grounds.

(*a*) First, he insists that the defendant was at fault, if for no other reason than the fact that he decided to go ahead with the flight even though he had insufficient experience in landings. In his appeal he therefore alleges that the defendant should not have gone ahead on the assumption that everything would necessarily proceed smoothly. At the very least he should have, from the outset, warned the public of all incidental dangers; and, if common sense and experience suggested that such warning of possible dangers would not be sufficient to avert them, then he should have cancelled the flight altogether.

This argument is misconceived. The facts of this case show that the defendant embarked upon this journey, which would have lasted for several days, in excellent weather conditions and was aided by an experienced crew. As the Court of Appeal suggested, he had every reason to believe that a carefully executed landing would pose no dangers to any crowd assembled for the spectacle. His principles of anchorage were correct and his means for anchoring were ample. And the defendant knew that wherever this happened competent assistance would be on hand. In his opinion his experience in such matters was more than adequate and he entertained no doubt that, even in the event of a storm he would be able to anchor his airship safely. Given all this he could undertake this flight without hesitation. And past experience had also shown that public warnings against possible future risks were ineffective. Instead he is entitled to believe that if need be injuries could be prevented by a cordon and by warning the crowds.

In view of the above no legal error can be found in the conclusion that the defendant's conduct during the preparation of the flight was careful in the sense of § 276 BGB. The applicant's view that the defendant should have had absolute certainty that the flight posed no dangers whatsoever is too far-fetched. Any enterprise of this type is bound to entail some dangers, also for third parties, and this could never be entirely eliminated, even if great care was taken. In the circumstances, therefore, it would be unjust to demand that such flights were banned altogether because their inherent dangers cannot be entirely eliminated. All that one can demand is that all care required in the circumstances should be taken. This, indeed, occurred since the defendant undertook the flight after proper preparations were carried out in accordance with prevailing experience. The flights went ahead when the weather conditions were good and everything could normally be expected to go well and safely. Consequently, he is not guilty of any recklessness constituting a danger to the community nor, indeed, can he be regarded as having carelessly breached his duty to take care.

(b) The applicant's second complaint is against the finding of the Court of Appeal that the defendant took sufficient measures at the landing-field both in respect of his anchoring his airship and in cordoning off the landing-space.

This argument, too, is unacceptable. With regard to the anchoring the Court of Appeal found the following facts. Prevailing experience, on which the defendant was entitled to rely, clearly suggested that since the emergency landing was only expected to last a few hours, the airship was quite properly anchored. Thus at the front, where it pointed downwards, the ship was secured to the ground by means of an anchor and posts and sacks while at the rear end the airship was held down by men, and deliberately kept in suspension so that it could swing in the direction of the wind. Forty men held the anchor rope and the front cabin of the ship while thirty men, properly instructed as to how to handle the side-movements of the airship, controlled the ship's rear cabin. And reinforcements were also at hand should the need arise. When the defendant left the airfield, the weather did not indicate that there might be any change in the direction of the wind, but even if such a change occurred, the airship was sufficiently secured to remain on the ground so long as its back remained free to swing in the new direction of the wind. The Court of Appeal also examined how, despite the above, the airship could cut loose from its anchor. In its view what happened was that the first gust of wind was quite suddenly followed by a second and extraordinarily violent gust which hit the airship on its side before it had time to swing to its direction and raised it with great force. Whatever method of anchorage was adopted there was no absolute proof that it would have managed to secure the ship to the ground.

The applicant is also wrong in arguing that since no one was to be responsible to the defendants for such extraordinary occurrence, he should have taken precautions against such an exceptional situation. This allegation is unsupported by the findings of facts. For given the initially prevailing favourable weather conditions, no sudden changes of wind were foreseeable at the time of the landing; thus, the defendant was not in breach of the duty of care required in the circumstances given that he had anchored his ship in accordance with the dictates of human experience and knowledge believing that his anchor could hold well even in a storm. That the airship was nevertheless torn away, as a result of the unexpected and violent gust of wind, and would probably have been torn away whatever system had been adopted for the anchoring, must be seen as the consequence of an act of God (höhere Gewalt).

As for the cordoning off of the landing-place, the Court of Appeal admitted that the plaintiff would probably not have been hurt if the cordon had been considerably wider. But again it is established that in taking these measures the defendant had done all that could have been expected of him. Thus, towards Echterdingen—from where the wind was blowing—ropes were used and soldiers were employed, while in the direction of

Berhausen soldiers alone were posted at a close distance since no more ropes were available to drive the surging crowds back over and over again.

Nevertheless, the applicant feels that the defendant took insufficient precautions in this respect and insists that ropes should have been used in the direction of Berhausen; and soldiers could also have been used at much shorter intervals. But on the findings of facts this argument, too, fails. For as stated, the defendant cordoned off the place with all disposable means and achieved this as best he could despite the fact that curious crowds kept surging in the direction of the airship. If this forced landing, which was only meant to last for a few hours and carried out in favourable weather conditions, had not been disturbed by an unforeseeable change of weather, taking place against all reasonable expectation, the cordon would have been perfectly sufficient and no accident would have occurred. The defendant had no reason to anticipate that a storm, the result of an act of God, would suddenly blow up and tear his airship away from its moorings and then carry it over the heads of the public at such low height as to cause injury to some bystander. The requisite standard of crew did not, therefore, require the taking of such precautions that might protect the public against dangers which could in no way be foreseen as the likely consequence of a more or less normal forced landing . . .

Notes to the Strict Liability Act

1. Reading the text of the Strict Liability Act in conjunction with the commentary in chapter 3, section A, above, one immediately becomes aware of the considerable historical and methodological differences that exist between the German law on the one hand and the French and Common law on the other in the area of strict liability. For the French, unlike the Germans, have, by skilfully developing—one might even say perverting—an unpromising provision of their Code, brought strict liability within the codal context. This technique, however, has not blinded them to the advantages of special legislation dealing with specific areas where strict liability is desirable.

By contrast, the English Common law has experienced some difficulty in abandoning the idea that where there is no fault there can be no liability. On the whole, the attack on the notion of fault has not been a frontal one, but has taken the form of guerrilla warfare (waged through the concept of *res ipsa loquitur* and the objectivisation of the notion of negligence) thus affecting the fringes only of the notion. The position is considered by many to be unsatisfactory; and the Pearson Committee recommended that strict liability should be introduced in a number of areas of tort law. At the time of writing, however, the prospects of that happening appear slim with the result that in English law strict liability can only be found in a limited number of statutes (e.g., the Nuclear Installations Acts 1959–65); in the rule of *Rylands* v. *Fletcher* (1868) LR 3 HL 330 (considerably restricted over the years by successive timorous judicial pronouncements); and in certain instances of damage caused by animals. Incidentally, this latter subject is now embodied in the Animals Act 1971—a prime example of the long-winded and unnecessarily complicated English drafting techniques.

2. As is often the case, the position in the United States is much more interesting and, indeed, advanced than it is in England. The traditional strict liability areas—animals, *Rylands* v. *Fletcher*—can be found there, as well. But the reception that the latter rule has had in the different parts of the United States has varied depending on the prevailing socio-economic and geographical conditions of the area in question. A well-known extract from *Turner* v. *Big Lake Oil Co.* 62 SW 2d 491 (Tex. App. 1933) makes this clear:

In *Rylands* v. *Fletcher* the court predicated the absolute liability of the defendants on the proposition that the use of land for the artificial storage of water was not a natural use, and that, therefore, the landowner was bound at his peril to keep the waters on his own land [Citations omitted]. This basis of the English rule is to be found in the meteorological conditions which obtain there. England is a pluvial country, where constant streams and abundant rains make the storage of water unnecessary for ordinary or general purposes. When the court said in *Rylands* v. *Fletcher* that the use of land for storage of water was an unnatural use, it meant such use was not a general or an ordinary one, not one within the contemplation of the parties to the original grant of the land involved, nor of the grantor and grantees of adjacent lands, but was a special or extraordinary use, and for that reason applied the rule of absolute liability. This conclusion is supported by the fact that those jurisdictions which adhere to the rule in *Rylands* v. *Fletcher* do not apply that rule to dams or reservoirs constructed in rivers and streams, which they say is a natural use, but apply the principle of negligence. [Citations omitted.] In other words, the impounding of water in streamways, being an obvious and natural use, was necessarily within the contemplation of the parties to the original and adjacent grants, and damages must be predicted upon negligent use of a granted right and power; while things not within the contemplation of the parties to the original grants, such as unnatural uses of the land, the landowner may do only at his peril. As to what use of land is or may be a natural use, one within the contemplation of the parties to the original grant of land, necessarily depends upon the attendant circumstances and condition which obtain in territory of the original grants, or the initial terms of those grants.

In Texas we have conditions very different from those which obtain in England. A large portion of Texas is an arid or semi-arid region. West of the 98th meridian of longitude, where the rainfall is approximately 30 inches, the rainfall decreases until finally, in the extreme western part of the State, it is only about 10 inches. This land of decreasing rainfall is the great ranch or livestock region of the State, water for which is stored in thousands of ponds, tanks, and lakes on the surface of the ground. The country is almost without streams; and without the storage of water from rainfall in basins constructed for the purpose, or to hold waters pumped from the earth, the great livestock industry of West Texas must perish. No such condition obtains in England. With us the storage of water is a natural or necessary and common use of the land, necessarily within the contemplation of the State and its grantees when grants were made, and obviously the rule announced in *Rylands* v. *Fletcher*, predicated upon different conditions, can have no application here.

Again, in England there are no oil wells, no necessity for using surface storage facilities for impounding and evaporating salt waters therefrom. In Texas the situation is different. Texas has many great oilfields, tens of thousands of wells in almost every part of the State. Producing oil is one of our major industries. One of the by-products of oil production is salt water, which must be disposed of without injury to property or the pollution of streams. The construction of basins or ponds to hold this salt water is a necessary part of the oil business. . . .

Other references are given by Leon Green, "Tort Law Public Law in Disguise", 38 *Tex. L. Rev.* 1, 5 (1959), who puts great stress on the "environmental factor". But not all courts have taken such a hostile view and the trend is to adopt in substance, if not always in name, the *Rylands* v. *Fletcher* rule. See, for example, *Cities Service Co.* v. *State* 312 So. 2d 799 (Fla. App. 1975). But if the accumulation and escape of liquid substances have at times left the courts divided, blasting operations have been dealt with greater severity and uniformity. See, for example, *Sullivan* v. *Durham* 161 NY 290, 55 NE 923 (1900) (and many others since). The underlying idea here is that extra-hazardous activities must pay their own way (cf. *Smith* v. *Lockheed Propulsion Co.*, 247 C.A. 2d 774, 56 Cal. Rptr. 128 (1967)).

The *Restatement (Second) of Torts* has phrased the rule, which stems from *Rylands* v. *Fletcher* but is also stripped of many of its limitations, in the following way:

§ 519 (1) One who carries on an abnormally dangerous activity is subject to liability for harm to the person, land, or chattels of another resulting from the activity, although he has exercised the utmost care to prevent such harm.

(2) Such strict liability is limited to the kind of harm, the risk of which makes the activity abnormally dangerous.

§ 520. In determining whether an activity is abnormally dangerous, the following factors are to be considered:

(*a*) whether the activity involves a high degree of risk of some harm to the person, land, or chattels of others;

(*b*) whether the gravity of the harm which may result from it is likely to be great;

(*c*) whether the risk cannot be eliminated by the exercise of reasonable care;

(*d*) whether the activity is not a matter of common usage;

(*e*) whether the activity is inappropriate to the place where it is carried on; and

(*f*) the value of the activity to the community.

3. For further discussion of the rich case law see Franklin and Rabin, 498 ff.; Henderson, Pearson and Siliciano, 481 ff. *Rylands* v. *Fletcher*, and its reception in the USA, has given rise to an interesting socio-legal literature. Thus see, *inter alia*, Bohlen, "The Rule in *Rylands* v. *Fletcher*" 59 *U. Pa. L. Rev.* 298, 373, 423 (1911); Molloy, "*Fletcher* v. *Rylands*—A Re-examination of Juristic Origins" 9 *U. Chi. L. Rev.* 266 (1942). These have, in turn, been scrutinised by Professor Simpson's masterly "Legal Liability for Bursting reservoirs: The Historical Context of *Rylands* v. *Fletcher*" (1984 13 *Jo. LS*, 209, reprinted in a slightly different form as ch. 8 of his *Leading Cases in the Common Law* (1995.)

4. In addition to the above-mentioned developments of "traditional" strict liability doctrines, one can also find in the US new areas of strict liability. The modern law of product liability offers such an example in the key provisions of the *Restatement (Second) of Tort*. Good accounts and further references to this dynamic part of modern tort law can be found in all the textbooks and case-books referred to throughout this work.

One must further note the existence of new compensation systems which have emerged as alternatives to the system of tort liability based on fault. Some of these, e.g. workers' compensation schemes (replacing in all but some isolated instances the Common law tort action) have already acquired a respectable history. The Massachusetts statute enacted in 1911 (Mass. Gen. Laws, ch. 152) is a fairly representative example. No-fault automobile insurance is, on the other hand, a relative newcomer and despite many statutory variations and even more proposals for reform, has never quite aspired to replacing tort law completely. Finally, what was in the 1970s described as the "medical malpractice crisis" prompted many to contemplate the possible advantages of a no-fault system of compensation for this type of injury. An example of such thinking can be found in a feasibility study prepared in 1979 by the American Bar Association on Medical Professional Liability. These "alternatives" discussed at varying lengths by Henderson, Pearson and Siliciano, 721–748; Franklin and Rabin, 785–863; Prosser, Wade and Schwartz, 1190–1214. The American Bar Association also published in 1979 a useful annotated bibliography of the growing literature on this topic under the title *Tort Reform and Related Proposals: Annotated Bibliographies on Product Liability and Medical Malpractice*, (ed. B. A. Levin and R. Coyne) but the literature, which has grown further since those days, must be sought elsewhere.

5. The legal aspects of case 128, RGZ 78, 171, are discussed at p. 723; but its non-legal background is also interesting for the accident described in the case happened in the process of perfecting the lighter than air dirigible aircraft first manufactured by the Frenchman Giffard in 1852—his airship was steam-powered and could travel at 5 m.p.h.—but perfected by the German Count Ferdinand von Zeppelin. (The British did not, initially, enter this Franco-German race; and it was only in 1917 that their first airship—the R33—was successfully launched, though its design was based on a German Zeppelin—the L33—which was brought down in England in September 1916 in an almost intact condition.)

The accident described in the leading case happened as the airship was returning to its base in Friedrichshafen, the old capital of Württemberg, on the north-eastern side of lake Constance where Zeppelin had set up his famous factory. During the First World War the Zeppelin was put to military use; and some fifteen years later, again in Friedrichshafen, another lethal air machine—the Dornier—was manufactured.

The French competed with the Germans not only in the manufacture of these dirigibles but also in making legal history through their misfortunes. See: *Coquerelc. Clément-Bayard*, Cass. Req. 3 août 1915, D.P. 1917, 1. 79.

5. ENVIRONMENTAL LIABILITY ACT OF 10 DECEMBER 1990
(TRANSLATED FROM THE GERMAN BY THE COLOGNE RE.)

With the consent of the *Bundesrat*, the *Bundestag* has enacted the following into law:

Article 1

Environmental Liability Act (ELA)

§ 1. *Facility liability for environmental impacts*

If a person suffers death or injury to his body or health, or if property is damaged, due to an environmental impact that issues from one of the facilities named in Appendix 1, then the operator of the facility shall be liable to the injured person for the damage caused thereby.

§ 2. *Liability for non-operating facilities*

(1) If the environmental impact issues from a facility that is not yet completed and arises from circumstances forming the basis of the hazard posed by the facility after completion, then the operator of the not yet completed facility shall be liable pursuant to § 1.

(2) If the environmental impact issues from a facility that is no longer in operation and arises from circumstances forming the basis of the hazard posed by the facility prior to its ceasing operations, then the operator of the facility at the time of the ceasing of operations shall be liable pursuant to § 1.

§ 3. *Definitions*

(1) Damage arises from an environmental impact if the damage is caused by materials, vibrations, noises, pressure, rays, gasses, steam, heat, or other phenomena that have been dispersed in soil, air, or water.

(2) Facilities are permanent structures such as plants or storage facilities.

(3) Facilities include:
    (*a*) machines, instruments, vehicles and other mobile technical structures, and
    (*b*) ancillary structures
that stand in a spatial or operational relation to the facility or part thereof and could be significant for the occurrence of an environmental impact.

§ 4. *Exclusion of liability*

No liability shall exist insofar as the damage has been caused by *force majeure*.

§ 5. *Limitation of liability for property damage*

If the facility has been operated properly (§ 6 II second sentence), then liability for property damage shall be excluded if the property has only been impaired insignificantly or to a degree that is reasonable according to the local conditions.

§ 6. *Presumption of causation*

(1) If a facility is inherently suited, on the facts of the particular case, to cause the damage that occurred, then it shall be presumed that this facility caused the damage. Inherent suitedness in a particular case is determined on the basis of the course of business, the structures used, the nature and concentration of the materials used and released, the weather conditions, the time and place at which the damage occurred, the nature of the damage, as well as all other conditions which speak for or against causation of the damage in the particular case.

(2) Paragraph (1) shall not apply if the facility has been properly operated. A proper operation is present if the special operational duties have been complied with and no disruption of operations has occurred.

(3) Special operational duties are those duties imposed by administrative permits, requirements, and enforceable administrative orders and regulatory laws, insofar as their purpose is to prevent such environmental impacts that could be considered to be the cause of the damage.

(4) If, for the purpose of supervision of a special operational duty, controls are prescribed in the permit, in requirements, in enforceable administrative orders or in regulatory laws, then compliance with this operational duty shall be presumed, if:

1. the controls were carried out during the period in which the environmental impact in question may have issued from the facility, and these controls give rise to no inference of a violation of the operational duty, or

2. at the time the claim for compensation is made, more than ten years have passed since the environmental impact in question occurred.

§ 7. *Rebuttal of the presumption*

(1) If multiple facilities are inherently suited to cause the damage, then the presumption shall not apply if another circumstance is, on the facts of the particular case, inherently suited to cause the damage. Inherent suitedness in a particular case is determined on the basis of the time and place at which the damage occurred, the nature of the damage, as well as all other conditions which speak for or against causation of the damage.

(2) If only one facility is inherently suited to cause the damage, then the presumption shall not apply if another circumstance is, on the facts of the particular case, inherently suited to cause the damage.

§ 8. *Injured party's right to disclosure from facility operator*

(1) If there are facts justifying the assumption that a facility has caused the damage, then the injured party may demand information from the operator of the facility insofar as this is needed to determine the existence of a claim for damages pursuant to this Act. The demand shall be limited to data about the structures used, the nature and concentration of the substances used or emitted, and other effects issuing from the facility as well as the special operational duties as provided in § 6 (3).

(2) The right to disclosure pursuant to paragraph (1) shall not exist to the extent that the events must be kept secret pursuant to legal norms or the countervailing interests of the facility operator or of a third party requiring secrecy.

(3) The injured person may demand from the facility operator an opportunity to review existing documents insofar as the assumption is justified that the information provided is incomplete, incorrect, or insufficient, or if the information is not provided within a reasonable time. Paragraphs (1) and (2) shall apply accordingly.

(4) §§ 259–261 of the Civil Code shall apply accordingly.

§ 9. *Injured party's right to disclosure from administrative agency*

If the facts justify the assumption that a facility has caused the damage, then the injured party may demand information from administrative agencies that have issued a permit in respect of the facility, that supervise the facility, or that are responsible for recording impacts on the environment, insofar as this is needed to determine the existence of a claim for damages pursuant to this Act. The agency shall not be required to provide information if to do so would impair the performance of the tasks of the agency, if the disclosure would disserve the well-being of the Federal Republic or of a state thereof, or to the extent that the events must be kept secret pursuant to law or due to their nature, in particular due to lawful interests of the parties or of third parties. § 8 I, second sentence, shall apply accordingly for those agencies which have issued a permit in respect of the facility or which supervise the facility; information regarding the name and address of the facility operator, his legal representative, or agent for service of process may be demanded from these agencies.

§ 10. *Facility operator's right to disclosure*

(1) If a claim pursuant to this Act is brought against the operator of a facility, he may demand from the injured person or from the operator of another facility information or an opportunity to review documents or demand information from the agencies named in § 9, insofar as this is needed to determine the scope of his liability to the injured person or of his claim for indemnity against the other operator.

(2) The provisions of § 8 (2), (3) sentence 1, and § 8 (4) shall apply to the right to disclosure from the injured person; § 8 (1) sentence 2 and (2)–(4) shall apply to the right to disclosure from an administrative agency pursuant to § 9.

§ 11. *Contributory negligence*

If the fault of the injured person contributed to the cause of the damage, § 254 of the Civil Code shall apply; in case of property damage, the fault of the person having actual control of the property shall be considered to be the fault of the injured person.

§ 12. *Scope of liability for death*

(1) In case of death, compensation shall be paid for the costs of healing efforts as well as for the financial loss which the deceased suffered because his earning capability was eliminated or diminished or his needs were increased during the illness. In addition, the liable person shall pay funeral costs to the person who has to bear these costs.

(2) If, at the time of injury, the deceased stood to a third party in a relationship whereby he was obligated to that person, as a matter of law, to provide support or could become so obligated, and if the third party is deprived of the right of support as a consequence of the death, then the liable person shall pay to the third party damages to the extent that the deceased would have been obligated to provide support during his presumed lifetime. Liability shall also attach if, at the time of the injury, the third party was conceived but not yet born.

§ 13. *Scope of liability for bodily injury*

In case of bodily injury or injury to health, compensation shall be paid for the costs of treatment as well as for the financial loss which the injured person suffers thereby because his earning capability is eliminated or diminished temporarily or permanently or his needs are increased.

§ 14. *Compensation by annuity*

(1) Future compensation for elimination or diminution of earning capability and for increased needs of the injured person, as well as future compensation to a third party pursuant to § 12 (2), shall be provided by means of an annuity.

(2) § 843 (2) of the Civil Code shall be applied accordingly.

§ 15. *Maximum limits of liability*

The person liable shall be liable for death, bodily injury or injury to health only up to a maximum amount of 160 million Deutsche Mark and also for property damage only up to a maximum amount of 160 million Deutsche Mark, insofar as the damage is caused by a unitary environmental impairment. If the multiple losses to be indemnified on the basis of a unitary environmental impairment exceed the applicable maximum amounts provided in the first sentence, then the amount of each indemnification shall be reduced in the proportion that the total bears to the maximum amount.

§ 16. *Expenses incurred for restoration measures*

(1) If damage to property also impairs nature or scenery, then, insofar as the injured person restores the condition that would exist but for the occurrence of the impairment, § 251 (2) of the Civil Code shall apply, but the expenses incurred for restoring the prior condition shall not be considered unreasonable for the sole reason that they exceed the value of the property.

(2) Upon demand by the person entitled to compensation, the person liable shall make advance payment for the necessary expenses.

§ 17. *Limitation of actions*

The limitation provisions of the Civil Code pertaining to torts shall apply accordingly.

§ 18. *Effect on liability under other laws*

(1) This Act shall have no effect on liability arising under other legal provisions.

(2) This Act shall not apply in case of a nuclear event insofar as the Atomic Act applies in connection with the Paris Convention on Atomic Liability of 29 July 1960 (as

published on 15 July 1985, BGBl. 1985 II p. 963), the Brussels Convention on Reactor-Powered Ships of 25 May 1962 (BGBl. 1975 II p. 957, 977) and the Brussels Convention on the Transportation of Nuclear Materials by Sea of 17 December 1971 (BGBl. 1975 II p. 957, 1026), as amended.

§ 19. *Provision of coverage*

(1) The operators of facilities named in Appendix 2 shall ensure that they are able to fulfil their legal obligation to provide compensation for damages that arise from a person suffering death or injury to his body or health, or from property being damaged, as a result of an environmental impact that issues from the facility (provision of coverage). If a facility that is no longer in operation presents a special hazard, the competent administrative agency may order the person who operated the facility at the time of the ceasing of operations to provide for coverage for a period of up to ten years.

(2) Coverage may be provided

1. in the form of liability insurance issued by an insurance company licensed to do business in the territory in which this Act applies;

2. in the form of an indemnity agreement or guarantee made by the Federal Government or by a state; or

3. in the form of an indemnity agreement or guarantee made by a credit institution licensed to do business in the territory in which this Act applies if such agreement or guarantee provides security comparable to that provided by liability insurance.

(3) The persons named in § 2 (1), Nos. 1 to 5 of the Compulsory Insurance Act as published 5 April 1965 (BGBl. I p. 213), last amended by the Act of 22 March 1988 (BGBl. I page 358), are exempt from the duty to provide for coverage.

(4) The competent administrative agency may prohibit, in whole or in part, the operation of a facility named in Appendix 2 if the operator does not comply with his duty to provide for coverage and fails to prove, within a reasonable time to be set by the competent agency, that coverage has been provided for.

§ 20. *Authorisation to issue executive orders*

(1) The Cabinet shall, with the consent of the Upper House of the German Parliament, issue executive orders regulating:

1. the point in time after which the operator of a facility shall be required to provide for coverage pursuant to § 19;

2. scope and amount of the provision of coverage;

3. the requirements to be set for indemnity agreements and guarantees by credit institutions;

4. the procedures and powers of the administrative agency having jurisdiction to monitor the provision of coverage;

5. the proper office pursuant to § 158 c (2) of the Insurance Contract Act and the giving of notice pursuant to § 158 c (2) of the Insurance Contract Act;

6. the duties of the operator of a facility, of the insurance company, and of a person making an indemnity agreement or guarantee to the administrative agency having jurisdiction to monitor the provision of coverage.

(2) Any executive order shall be presented to the Lower House before presentment to the Upper House. The order may be amended or rejected by resolution of the Lower House. The resolution of the Lower House shall be presented to the Cabinet. If, after three session weeks following receipt of an executive order, the German Lower House has not deliberated on it, the order shall be returned to the Cabinet unamended. The Lower House shall deliberate on an executive order upon petition by the number of members required for forming a parliamentary group.

§ 21. *Criminal penalties*

(1) Any person who

1. fails, wholly or partly, adequately to provide for coverage in violation of § 19 (1), sentence 1, in connection with an executive order pursuant to § 20 (1), No. 1 or 2; or

2. violates an enforceable order issued pursuant to § 19 (1), sentence 2, shall be imprisoned for a term not to exceed one year or fined.

(2) If the violation is committed negligently, the imprisonment shall not exceed six months or the fine shall not exceed 180 day-sentences (*Tagessätze*).

§ 22. *Administrative penalties*

(1) Any person who violates an executive order pursuant to § 20 (1), Nos. 3 to 6, commits an administrative offence insofar as the particular order refers to this provision on administrative penalties for a specific violation.

(2) The administrative offence may be penalized with a fine of up to ten thousand Deutsche Mark.

§ 23. *Transitional provisions*

Where the damage was caused before the entry into force of this Act, this Act shall not apply.

Article 2

Amendment to the Code of Civil Procedure

The Code of Civil Procedure, as revised and published in the *Bundesgesetzblatt*, Part III, 310–14, most recently amended by Schedule 1, chapter III, Area A, Section II No. 1 of the Unification Treaty of 31 August 1990 in connection with Article 1 of the Act of 23 September 1990 (BGBl. 1990 II pp. 885, 921), shall be amended as follows:
The following shall be inserted after § 32:

"§ 32a Jurisdiction in actions against the operator of a facility named in Appendix 1 of the Environmental Liability Act seeking compensation for damage caused by an environmental impact shall be vested exclusively in the court sitting in the district in which the impact issued from the facility. The aforesaid shall not apply if the facility is located abroad."

Article 3

Transitional Provision

Insofar as the damage was caused before the entry into force of this Act, the Code of Civil Procedure, unamended by this Act, shall apply.

Article 4

Amendment to the Federal Emissions Protection Act

The Federal Emissions Protection Act, as published on 14 May 1990 (BGBl. I p. 880), as amended by Schedule 1, Chapter XII, Area A, Section II of the Unification Treaty of 31 August 1990 in connection with Article 1 of the Act of 23 September 1990 (BGBl. 1990 II pp. 885, 1114), shall be amended as follows:

The following § 51b shall be inserted after § 51a:

"§ 51b Provision for service of documents

The operator of a facility for which an operating permit is required shall ensure that certain documents may be served on him within the territory to which this Act applies. If service may be ensured only by the appointment of an agent for service, then the operator shall provide the name of the agent to the competent administrative agency."

Article 5

Entry into force

This Act shall enter into force on 1 January 1991.

6. CONSUMER LEGISLATION AND DEFECTIVE PRODUCTS

(*i*) *EEC Council Directive* of 25 July 1985, on the approximation of the laws, regulations and administrative provisions of the Member States concerning liability for defective products

Article 1

The producer shall be liable for damage caused by a defect in his product.

Article 2

For the purpose of this Directive "product" means all movables, with the exception of primary agricultural products and game, even though incorporated into another movable or into an immovable. "Primary agricultural products" means the products of the soil, of stock-farming and of fisheries, excluding products which have undergone initial processing. "Product" includes electricity.

Article 3

1. "Producer" means the manufacturer of a finished product, the producer of any raw material or the manufacturer of a component part and any person who, by putting his

name, trade mark or other distinguishing feature on the product presents himself as its producer.

2. Without prejudice to the liability of the producer, any person who imports into the Community a product for sale, hire, leasing or any form of distribution in the course of his business shall be deemed to be a producer within the meaning of this Directive and shall be responsible as a producer.

3. Where the producer of the product cannot be identified, each supplier of the product shall be treated as its producer unless he informs the injured person, within a reasonable time, of the identity of the producer or of the person who supplied him with the product. The same shall apply, in the case of an imported product, if this product does not indicate the identity of the importer referred to in paragraph 2, even if the name of the producer is indicated.

Article 4

The injured person shall be required to prove the damage, the defect and the causal relationship between defect and damage.

Article 5

Where, as a result of the provisions of this Directive, two or more persons are liable for the same damage, they shall be liable jointly and severally, without prejudice to the provisions of national law concerning the rights of contribution or recourse.

Article 6

1. A product is defective when it does not provide the safety which a person is entitled to expect, taking all circumstances into account, including:

(*a*) the presentation of the product;
(*b*) the use to which it could reasonably be expected that the product would be put;
(*c*) the time when the product was put into circulation.

2. A product shall not be considered defective for the sole reason that a better product is subsequently put into circulation.

Article 7

The producer shall not be liable as a result of this Directive if he proves:

(*a*) that he did not put the product into circulation; or
(*b*) that, having regard to the circumstances, it is probable that the defect which caused the damage did not exist at the time when the product was put into circulation by him or that this defect came into being afterwards; or
(*c*) that the product was neither manufactured by him for sale or any form of distribution for economic purpose nor manufactured or distributed by him in the course of his business; or
(*d*) that the defect is due to compliance of the product with mandatory regulations issued by the public authorities; or
(*e*) that the state of scientific and technical knowledge at the time when he put the

product into circulation was not such as to enable the existence of the defect to be discovered; or

(*f*) in the case of a manufacturer of a component, that the defect is attributable to the design of the product in which the component has been fitted or to the instructions given by the manufacturer of the product.

Article 8

1. Without prejudice to the provisions of national law concerning the right of contribution or recourse, the liability of the producer shall not be reduced when the damage is caused both by a defect in product and by the act or omission of a third party.

2. The liability of the producer may be reduced or disallowed when, having regard to all the circumstances, the damage is caused both by a defect in the product and by the fault of the injured person or any person for whom the injured person is responsible.

Article 9

For the purpose of Article 1, "damage" means:

(*a*) damage caused by death or by personal injuries;
(*b*) damage to, or destruction of, any item of property other than the defective product itself, with a lower threshold of 500 ECU, provided that the item of property;
  (i) is of a type ordinarily intended for private use or consumption, and
  (ii) was used by the injured person mainly for his own private use or consumption.

This article shall be without prejudice to national provisions relating to non-material damage.

Article 10

1. Member States shall provide in their legislation that a limitation period of three years shall apply to proceedings for the recovery of damages as provided for in this Directive. The limitation period shall begin to run from the day on which the plaintiff became aware, or should reasonably have become aware, of the damage, the defect and the identity of the producer.

2. The laws of Member States regulating suspension or interruption of the limitation period shall not be affected by this Directive.

Article 11

Member States shall provide in their legislation that the rights conferred upon the injured person pursuant to this Directive shall be extinguished upon the expiry of a period of ten years from the date on which the producer put into circulation the actual product which caused the damage, unless the injured person has in the meantime instituted proceedings against the producer.

Article 12

The liability of the producer arising from this Directive may not, in relation to the injured person, be limited or excluded by a provision limiting his liability or exempting him from liability.

Article 13

This Directive shall not affect any rights which an injured person may have according to the rules of the law of contractual or non-contractual liability or a special liability system existing at the moment when this Directive is notified.

Article 14

This Directive shall not apply to injury or damage arising from nuclear accidents and covered by international conventions ratified by the Member States.

Article 15

1. Each Member State may:
   (*a*) by way of derogation from Article 2, provide in its legislation that within the meaning of Article 1 of this Directive "product" also means primary agricultural products and game;
   (*b*) by way of derogation from Article 7(*e*), maintain or, subject to the procedure set out in paragraph 2 of this Article, provide in this legislation that the producer shall be liable even if he proves that the state of scientific and technical knowledge at the time when he put the product into circulation was not such as to enable the existence of a defect to be discovered.

2. A Member State wishing to introduce the measure specified in paragraph 1(*b*) shall communicate the text of the proposed measure to the Commission. The Commission shall inform the other Member States thereof.
   The Member State concerned shall hold the proposed measure in abeyance for nine months after the Commission is informed and provided that in the meantime the Commission has not submitted to the Council a proposal amending this Directive on the relevant matter. However, if within three months of receiving the said information, the Commission does not advise the Member State concerned that it intends submitting such a proposal to the Council, the Member State may take the proposed measure immediately.
   If the Commission does submit to the Council such a proposal amending this Directive within the aforementioned nine months, the Member State concerned shall hold the proposed measure in abeyance for a further period of 18 months from the date on which the proposal is submitted.

3. Ten years after the date of notification of this Directive, the Commission shall submit to the Council a report on the effect that rulings by the courts as to the application of Article 7(*e*) and of paragraph 1(*b*) of this Article have on consumer protection and the functioning of the common market. In the light of this report the Council, acting on a proposal from the Commission and pursuant to the terms of Article 100 of the Treaty, shall decide whether to repeat Article 7(*e*).

Article 16

1. Any Member State may provide that a producer's total liability for damage resulting from a death or personal injury and caused by identical items with the same defect shall be limited to an amount which may not be less than 70 million ECU.

2. Ten years after the date of notification of this Directive, the Commission shall submit to the Council a report on the effect on consumer protection and the functioning of the common market of the implementation of the financial limit on liability by those Member States which have used the option provided for in paragraph 1. In the light of this report the Council, acting on a proposal from the Commission and pursuant to the terms of Article 100 of the Treaty, shall decide whether to repeal paragraph 1.

Article 17

This Directive shall not apply to products put into circulation before the date on which the provisions referred to in Article 19 enter into force.

Article 18

1. For the purposes of this Directive, the ECU shall be that defined by Regulation (EEC) no. 3180/78, as amended by Regulation (EEC) no. 2626/84. The equivalent in national currency shall initially be calculated at the rate obtaining on the date of adoption of this Directive.

2. Every five years the Council, acting on a proposal from the Commission, shall examine and, if need be, revise the amounts in this Directive, in the light of economic and monetary trends in the Community.

Article 19

1. Member States shall bring into force, not later than three years from the date of notification of this Directive, the laws, regulations and administrative provisions necessary to comply with this Directive. They shall forthwith inform the Commission thereof.

2. The procedure set out in Article 15(2) shall apply from the date of notification of this Directive.

Article 20

Member States shall communicate to the Commission the texts of the main provisions of national law which they subsequently adopt in the field governed by this Directive.

Article 21

Every five years the Commission shall present a report to the Council on the application of this Directive and, if necessary, shall submit appropriate proposals to it.

Article 22

This Directive is addressed to the Member States.

(*ii*) *The German Product Liability Act of 15 December 1989*

§ 1. Liability

(1) If, as a result of a defect of a product, a human being is killed, is injured or affected in his health, or a thing is damaged, the producer† is obliged to compensate the person who suffered the damage for the ensuing harm. In the case of damage to property this

rule applies only if an object other than the defective product is damaged and if this object is normally intended for private use or consumption and has been used by the injured party primarily for this purpose.

(2) The obligation to pay damages is excluded if:

1. the producer has not put the product into circulation;
2. it is to be assumed, having regard to the circumstances, that the product was not yet defective when it was put into circulation;
3. the producer has neither manufactured the product for sale or for any other form of distribution for a consideration nor has manufactured or distributed it in the course of his occupational activities;
4. the defect is due to the fact that at the time when the producer put the product into circulation it complied with mandatory legal provisions;
5. the defect could not yet be discerned, having regard to the state of art [literally: science and technique] at the time when the producer put the product concerned into circulation.

(3) In addition, the maker of the part of the product is exempt from the obligation to pay compensation if the defect was caused by the construction of the product into which the part was inserted or by the instructions of the maker of the product. Sentence 1 applies *mutatis mutandis* to a producer of a basic substance (*Grundstoff*).

(4) The person who has suffered the harm has the burden of proving the defect and its causal connection with the harm. In a dispute as to whether the obligation to pay compensation is excluded according to sub-paragraphs (2) or (3), the producer bears the burden of proof.

§ 2. Products

Product in the meaning of this Act includes every moveable object, even if it forms part of another moveable or of an immovable as well as electricity. Produce of the soil, of animal husbandry, bee farming, fishing, and hunting are exempt, unless they have undergone the first stage of processing.

§ 3. Defects

(1) A product is defective if it does not provide that degree of safety which can be justifiably expected, having regard to all the circumstances, in particular

(a) its presentation;
(b) its use which may be reasonably expected;
(c) the time when it was put into circulation.

(2) A product is not defective for the sole reason that later on an improved product was put into circulation.

§ 4. Producer

(1) Producer in the meaning of this Act is the person who has manufactured the final product, a basic substance or a component part of the product. Furthermore, whoever represents himself as a producer by attaching his name, trademark or other distinctive mark is regarded as the producer.

(2) Notwithstanding sub-paragraph 1, a person is also treated as a producer who, within the range of his commercial activity, imports into the area covered by the Treaty for the Establishment of the European Economic Community a product with a view to sale, hire, hire-purchase or any other form of distribution.

(3) If the manufacturer of the product cannot be ascertained, every distributor is treated as its producer, unless he indicates to the injured party within one month of receiving the latter's relevant request who is the producer or the person who supplied him with the product. The same applies to an imported product in respect of which the person referred to in sub-paragraph (2) cannot be ascertained, even if the name of the producer is known.

§ 5. Several tortfeasors

If several producers are co-liable for the damage, they are jointly and severally liable. Between the debtors themselves, in the absence of provisions to the contrary, the liability to pay compensation and its extent depends upon the circumstances, in particular as to whether the damage has been caused predominantly by one or the other of them; furthermore §§ 421–5, 426 sub-paragraph 1, second sentence and sub-paragraph 2 BGB apply.

§ 6. Reduction of liability

(1) If the injured party is partly to be blamed for having caused the damage, § 254 BGB applies; if an object has been damaged, any blame attached to the person exercising physical control over it is treated as that of the injured party.

(2) If the damage has been caused at the same time by a defect of the product and by the act of a third party, the liability of the producer is not reduced. § 5 second sentence applies.

§ 7. Extent of damages in case of death

(1) In case of death, the expenses incurred in an attempt to restore health must be compensated together with the pecuniary loss suffered by the deceased in consequence of the loss or reduction of his earning capacity or of his increased needs. Damages also include the funeral expenses payable to the person responsible for them.

(2) If at the time of injury the deceased was connected with a third party by a relationship which rendered him, actually or potentially, liable by law to maintain that person, and if the third party lost his right to maintenance in consequence of the death, he is entitled to damages in so far as the deceased during the period of his life expectancy would have been liable to maintain him. This liability arises also if the third party was conceived at the time of death but not yet born.

§ 8. Extent of damages in case of injury to the person

If injury was caused to the body or to health, the expenses incurred in restoring health must be compensated together with the pecuniary loss suffered by the injured party resulting from the temporary or permanent loss or reduction of his earning capacity or from his increased needs.

§ 9. Damages by way of periodical payments

(1) Damage arising in the future as a result of the total or partial loss of earning capacity and of increased needs together with the damages payable to a third party in accordance with § 7 sub-paragraph (2) is to be compensated by periodical payments.

(2) § 843 sub-paragraphs 2–4 BGB apply.

§ 10. Maximum rate of damages

(1) If death or injury to the person has been caused by a product or by products of the same kind affected by the same defect, the liability to pay damages is limited to a maximum of DM 160 million.

(2) If the damages payable to several injured parties exceed the maximum rate set out in sub-paragraph (1), the individual damages are reduced in proportion of their total to the maximum rate allowable.

§ 11. Extent of compensation in case of damage to goods

Where goods are damaged, the person who suffered the damage has to bear the loss up to DM 1,125.

§ 12. Limitation of actions

(1) An action according to § 1 shall not be brought after the expiration of three years from the time when the claimant knew or could have known of the damage and of the person liable to pay damages.

(2) Time does not run if negotiations are pending between the persons liable to pay and to receive compensation until the continuation of the negotiations has been abandoned.

(3) Furthermore, the provisions of the BGB relating to limitation of actions apply.

§ 13. Extinction of claims

(1) A claim according to § 1 is extinguished after the expiration of ten years from the date when the producer against whom the claim is made has put the product into circulation. This does not apply where a law suit or summary proceedings are pending.

(2) Sub-paragraph (1), sentence 1 does not apply to a claim which has become *res judicata* or to a claim covered by another executory title. The same applies to a claim which is the subject-matter of an out-of-court settlement or which has been recognised by a legal act.

§ 14. Mandatory character

The liability of a producer in accordance with the Act cannot be excluded or restricted in advance. Any agreement to the contrary is void.

§ 15. Liability according to other legal provisions

(1) If, due to the application of a pharmaceutical product destined for human use and sold in the area of application of the Pharmaceutical Products Act, a person is killed or

his body or health otherwise affected, the provisions of the Product Liability Act will not be applicable.

(2) Liability in accordance with other provisions remains unaffected.

Notes

The Act establishes a parallel regime of liability which can be similar or more extensive to that found in the "Common law" (based on § 823 BGB and described above, ch. 2, section A. 4 (*c*)). Under the Act, liability depends on the product being "defective", i.e. not meeting the degree of safety normally required from such a product. Whether this will *in practice* lead to different results than the case law built on § 823 I BGB is a matter of some doubt. (See Kötz/Wagner, *Deliktsrecht*, no. 461). § 2 of the Act provides a list of situations where liability can be excluded. § 4 is worthy of special attention since it defines the persons likely to be liable; and it *may* be rendering non-manufacturers more extensively liable than they are under the "Common law" regime. Finally, note that (like all German strict liability statutes) the Act sets limits to the amounts of damages that can be claimed under it. Compensation for pain and suffering (immaterial damages) also presupposes that the claim is based on the *tort* provisions of the Code so they are *not* claimable under the Act. For a fuller discussion see references given in ch. 3, section A. 5(*b*). It is, of course, left to the plaintiff to decide whether he will base his claim on the "Common law" regime and/or that established by the Act.

(*iii*) *The [UK] Consumer Protection Act 1987*

I. *Product Liability*

1 (1) This Part shall have effect for the purpose of making such provision as is necessary in order to comply with the product liability Directive and shall be construed accordingly.

(2) In this part, except in so far as the context otherwise requires

"agricultural produce" means any produce of the soil, of stock-farming or of fisheries;
"dependant" and "relative" have the same meaning as they have in, respectively, the Fatal Accidents Act 1976 and the Damages (Scotland) Act 1976;
"producer", in relation to a product, means
(a) the person who manufactured it;
(b) in the case of a substance which has not been manufactured but has been won or abstracted, the person who won or abstracted it;
(c) in the case of a product which has not been manufactured, won or abstracted but essential characteristics of which are attributable to an industrial or other process having been carried out (for example, in relation to agricultural produce), the person who carried out that process;
"product" means any goods or electricity and (subject to subsection (3) below) includes a product which is comprised in another product, whether by virtue of being a component part or raw material or otherwise; and
"the product liability Directive" means the Directive of the Council of the European Communities, dated 25 July 1985, (no. 85/374/EEC) on the approximation of the laws, regulations and administrative provisions of the member States concerning liability for defective products.

(3) For the purposes of this Part a person who supplies any product in which products are comprised, whether by virtue of being component parts or raw materials or other-

wise, shall not be treated by reason only of his supply of that product as supplying any of the products so comprised.

2 (1) Subject to the following provisions of this Part, where any damage is caused wholly or partly by a defect in a product, every person to whom subsection (2) below applies shall be liable for the damage.

(2) This subsection applies to

(a) the producer of the product;

(b) any person who, by putting his name on the product or using a trade mark or other distinguishing mark in relation to the product, has held himself out to be the producer of the product;

(c) any person who has imported the product into a member State from a place outside the member States in order, in the course of any business of his, to supply it to another.

(3) Subject as aforesaid, where any damage is caused wholly or partly by a defect in a product, any person who supplied the product (whether to the person who suffered the damage, to the producer of any product in which the product in question is comprised or to any other person) shall be liable for the damage if—

(a) the person who suffered the damage requests the supplier to identify one or more of the persons (whether still in existence or not) to whom subsection (2) above applies in relation to the product;

(b) that request is made within a reasonable period after the damage occurs and at a time when it is not reasonably practicable for the person making the request to identify all those persons; and

(c) the supplier fails, within a reasonable period after receiving the request, either to comply with the request or to identify the person who supplied the product to him.

(4) Neither subsection (2) nor subsection (3) above shall apply to a person in respect of any defect in any game or agricultural produce if the only supply of the game or produce by that person to another was at a time when it had not undergone an industrial process.

(5) Where two or more persons are liable by virtue of this Part for the same damage, their liability shall be joint and several.

(6) This section shall be without prejudice to any liability arising otherwise than by virtue of this Part.

3 (1) Subject to the following provisions of this section, there is a defect in a product for the purposes of this Part if the safety of the product is not such as persons generally are entitled to expect; and for those purposes "safety", in relation to a product, shall include safety with respect to products comprised in that product and safety in the context of risks of damage to property, as well as in the context of risks of death or personal injury.

(2) In determining for the purposes of subsection (1) above what persons generally are entitled to expect in relation to a product all the circumstances shall be taken into account, including

(a) the manner in which, and purposes for which, the product has been marketed, its get-up, the use of any mark in relation to the product and any instructions for, or warnings with respect to, doing or refraining from doing anything with or in relation to the product;

(b) what might reasonably be expected to be done with or in relation to the product; and

(c) the time when the product was supplied by its producer to another;

and nothing in this section shall require a defect to be inferred from the fact alone that the safety of a product which is supplied after that time is greater than the safety of the product in question.

4 (1) In any civil proceedings by virtue of this Part against any person ("the person proceeded against") in respect of a defect in a product it shall be a defence for him to show

(a) that the defect is attributable to compliance with any requirement imposed by or under any enactment or with any Community obligation; or

(b) that the person proceeded against did not at any time supply the product to another; or

(c) that the following conditions are satisfied, that is to say

(i) that the only supply of the product to another by the person proceeded against was otherwise than in the course of a business of that person's; and

(ii) that section 2(2) above does not apply to that person or applies to him by virtue only of things done otherwise than with a view to profit; or

(d) that the defect did not exist in the product at the relevant time; or

(e) that the state of scientific and technical knowledge at the relevant time was not such that a producer of products of the same description as the product in question might be expected to have discovered the defect if it had existed in his products while they were under his control; or

(f) that the defect

(i) constituted a defect in a product ("the subsequent product") in which the product in question had been comprised; and

(ii) was wholly attributable to the design of the subsequent product or to compliance by the producer of the product in question with instructions given by the producer of the subsequent product.

(2) In this section "the relevant time", in relation to electricity, means the time at which it was generated, being a time before it was transmitted or distributed, and in relation to any other product, means

(a) if the person proceeded against is a person to whom subsection (2) of section 2 above applies in relation to the product, the time when he supplied the product to another;

(b) if that subsection does not apply to that person in relation to the product, the time when the product was last supplied by a person to whom that subsection does apply in relation to the product.

5 (1) Subject to the following provisions of this section, in this Part "damage" means death or personal injury or any loss of or damage to any property (including land).

(2) A person shall not be liable under section 2 above in respect of any defect in a product for the loss of or any damage to the product itself or for the loss of or any damage to the

whole or any part of any product which has been supplied with the product in question comprised in it.

(3) A person shall not be liable under section 2 above for any loss of or damage to any property which, at the time it is lost or damaged, is not

(a) of a description of property ordinarily intended for private use, occupation or consumption; and
(b) intended by the person suffering the loss or damage mainly for his own private use, occupation or consumption.

(4) No damages shall be awarded to any person by virtue of this Part in respect of any loss of or damage to any property if the amount which would fall to be so awarded to that person, apart from this subsection and any liability for interest, does not exceed £275.

(5) In determining for the purposes of this Part who has suffered any loss of or damage to property and when any such loss or damage occurred, the loss or damage shall be regarded as having occurred at the earliest time at which a person with an interest in the property had knowledge of the material facts about the loss or damage.

(6) For the purposes of subsection (5) above the material facts about any loss of or damage to any property are such facts about the loss or damage as would lead a reasonable person with an interest in the property to consider the loss or damage sufficiently serious to justify his instituting proceedings for damages against a defendant who did not dispute liability and was able to satisfy a judgment.

(7) For the purposes of subsection (5) above a person's knowledge includes knowledge which he might reasonably have been expected to acquire

(a) from facts observable or ascertainable by him; or
(b) from facts ascertainable by him with the help of appropriate expert advice which it is reasonable for him to seek;

but a person shall not be taken by virtue of this subsection to have knowledge of a fact ascertainable by him only with the help of expert advice unless he has failed to take all reasonable steps to obtain (and, where appropriate, to act on) that advice.

(8) Subsections (5) to (7) above shall not extend to Scotland.

6 (1) Any damage for which a person is liable under section 2 above shall be deemed to have been caused

(a) for the purposes of the Fatal Accidents Act 1976, by that person's wrongful act, neglect or default;
(b) for the purposes of section 3 of the Law Reform (Miscellaneous Provisions) (Scotland) Act 1940 (contribution among joint wrongdoers), by that person's wrongful act or negligent act or omission;
(c) for the purposes of section 1 of the Damages (Scotland) Act 1976 (rights of relatives of a deceased), by that person's act or omission; and
(d) for the purposes of Part II of the Administration of Justice Act 1982 (damages for personal injuries, etc., Scotland), by an act or omission giving rise to liability in that person to pay damages.

(2) Where

    (a) a person's death is caused wholly or partly by a defect in a product, or a person dies after suffering damage which has been so caused;

    (b) a request such as mentioned in paragraph (a) of subsection (3) of section 2 above is made to a supplier of the product by that person's personal representatives or, in the case of a person whose death is caused wholly or partly by the defect, by any dependant or relative of that person; and

    (c) the conditions specified in paragraphs (b) and (c) of that subsection are satisfied in relation to that request,

this Part shall have effect for the purposes of the Law Reform (Miscellaneous Provisions) Act 1934, the Fatal Accidents Act 1976 and the Damages (Scotland) Act 1976 as if liability of the supplier to that person under that subsection did not depend on that person having requested the supplier to identify certain persons or on the said conditions having been satisfied in relation to a request made by that person.

(3) Section 1 of the Congenital Disabilities (Civil Liability) Act 1976 shall have effect for the purposes of this Part as if

    (a) a person were answerable to a child in respect of an occurrence caused wholly or partly by a defect in a product if he is or has been liable under section 2 above in respect of any effect of the occurrence on a parent of the child, or would be so liable if the occurrence caused a parent of the child to suffer damage;

    (b) the provisions of this Part relating to liability under section 2 above applied in relation to liability by virtue of paragraph (a) above under the said section 1; and

    (c) subsection (6) of the said section 1 (exclusion of liability) were omitted.

(4) Where any damage is caused partly by a defect in a product and partly by the fault of the person suffering the damage, the Law Reform (Contributory Negligence) Act 1945 and section 5 of the Fatal Accidents Act 1976 (contributory negligence) shall have effect as if the defect were the fault of every person liable by virtue of this Part for the damage caused by the defect.

(5) In subsection (4) above "fault" has the same meaning as in the said Act of 1945.

(6) Schedule 1 to this Act shall have effect for the purpose of amending the Limitation Act 1980 and the Prescription and Limitation (Scotland) Act 1973 in their application in relation to the bringing of actions by virtue of this Part.

(7) It is hereby declared that liability by virtue of this Part is to be treated as liability in tort for the purposes of any enactment conferring jurisdiction on any court with respect to any matter.

(8) Nothing in this Part shall prejudice the operation of section 12 of the Nuclear Installations Act 1965 (rights to compensation for certain breaches of duties confined to rights under that Act).

7 The liability of a person by virtue of this Part to a person who has suffered damage caused wholly or partly by a defect in a product, or to a dependant or relative of such a person, shall not be limited or excluded by any contract term, by any notice or by any other provision.

8 (1) Her Majesty may by Order in Council make such modifications of this Part and of any other enactment (including an enactment contained in the following Parts of this Act, or in an Act passed after this Act) as appear to Her Majesty in Council to be necessary or expedient in consequence of any modification of the product liability Directive which is made at any time after the passing of this Act.

(2) An Order in Council under subsection (1) above shall not be submitted to Her Majesty in Council unless a draft of the Order has been laid before, and approved by a resolution of, each House of Parliament.

9 (1) Subject to subsection (2) below, this Part shall bind the Crown.

(2) The Crown shall not, as regards the Crown's liability by virtue of this Part, be bound by this Part further than the Crown is made liable in tort or in reparation under the Crown Proceedings Act 1947, as that Act has effect from time to time.

(*iv*) *Notes on the consumer protection enactments*

1. Individually, each of these texts has inspired many articles in legal journals and many more will no doubt follow. The critical comparison of the texts is, if anything, an even more difficult task and one that cannot be undertaken within the confines of this book. Here, however, are some basic points with the main emphasis naturally being placed on German law (described briefly in section A.4(c) above).

2. The Directive is the progenitor of the three texts reproduced above and is, itself, the result of (*a*) the consumer movement that gained momentum in Europe in the late 1960s and 1970s as well as (*b*) the EC Commission's desire to harmonise the law within the EEC. The first provides the political motive, the second the excuse for the European Community's intervention. Both points are important though the EEC would stress the latter. But have the national laws been harmonised? Cf. for example the attitudes of the Member States towards the defence of the state of art. Existing differences are also (to some extent) maintained where existing laws (e.g. the German Pharmaceuticals Act) are more generous to consumers. Otherwise, has the Directive frozen existing national laws? Put differently, has the national legislator been deprived of the right to pass future legislation that is more generous to the consumer than is the text of the Directive? And what about national case-law? Can it improve the consumer's lot and remain faithful to the spirit of the Directive?

3. The Directive creates no direct rights but obliges the Member States to implement it by national laws. England and Germany are among the countries which have done so. But what if the text of a national law departs from the text (and intentions) of the Directive? For example, s. 4(1)(c) of the UK Act says that the producer is not liable if he proves "that the state of scientific and technical knowledge at the relevant time was not such that a producer of products of the same description as the product in question might be expected to have discovered the defect if it had existed in his products while they were under his control". On the other hand, Article 7(c) of the Directive gives the producer immunity if he proves "that the state of scientific and technical knowledge at the time when he put the product into circulation was not such as to enable the existence of the defect to be discovered". The Confederation of British Industry prefers the subjective wording of the Act; the Directive, by contrast, has opted for an objective wording, while

the UK government has tried to argue that *its* wording states more clearly the intentions of the Directive (see Lord Lucas of Chilworth, HL Deb. vol. 487 c. 785 (14 May 1987)). What do you think? Other (permissible) derogations include the exemption from strict liability for the producers of primary agricultural products (where the farming lobby is strong, as it is in England, this derogation has not been taken up) and the possibility of limiting damages for a particular effect (10 million ECU, or about £40 million).

4. The Confederation of British Industry strongly and successfully opposed the abandonment of the defence of the state of art. One of its arguments was that inventiveness would be stifled and industry would suffer. Has the German pharmaceutical industry—one of the best in the world—suffered by adopting the opposite view? Did anyone do a comparative study of the two systems, look at the insurance situation, study the market? Or do British businessmen like British lawyers go into a tizzy when the words change and reforms are mentioned?

5. The Product Liability law now has many sources. As stated, the old tort rules to some extent remain in force; and they are expected to co-exist along with the new regime. Indeed, the old law is still relevant for damages *to* products and other forms of economic loss. Additionally, contract law remains alive; and here not only liability is strict; it is also not subject to any state of art defence. The different sources of product liability law have also given rise to much confusion in the USA as a quick glance at any specialized book will reveal.

6. Each European state has, following its own drafting techniques, implemented the Directive in a different way. Assuming that this was quite genuinely inevitable and preferable to giving the text of the Directive direct effect, what should happen when there is a significant difference between the wording of the Directive and a national enactment? The Directive, for example, excludes from the regime of strict liability primary agricultural products so long as they have not undergone "initial processing". The UK legislation, on the other hand, has excluded from strict liability agricultural produce before it has undergone an "industrial process". Does the use of hormones, pesticides, fertilisers, additives, etc. remove the exemption and subject these products to strict liability? In the case of the above examples the answer is probably a negative one; but the exception for its strict liability regime must surely be lost when, say, vegetables or fruit are frozen in a factory. Compare the wording of the English, French, and German Acts with the Directive and decide which of them is closer to the "model".

7. In one of the best Hamlyn Lectures ever given, Professor Honoré thundered that "England does not have a genuine legal culture". Anyone who compares academic law in our Universities at the turn of the century with, say, the situation in Germany at that time will immediately appreciate the validity of this condemnation. But Professor Honoré attributes this state of affairs in part to our inability to make laws "as clear, elegant, and rational as they could be". (*The Quest for Security: Employees, Tenants, Wives* (1982), 119.) True though this may be about Common law statutes, what do you think of *modern* civil law statutes? The French text (still not accepted by Parliament) is exceptionally long and complicated. It is also inelegant in that it purports to add 29 product liability articles to the French Civil Code when a mere 5 cover the entire law of torts. Are the French (and the Germans for that matter) following our (bad) example? Compare in this respect the equally long-winded French Road Traffic Act of 1985.

8. There is no doubt that the Directive and its national progenies will add to the complexity of the law; but will the new enactment make it substantially different from how it was before this costly exercise was undertaken? For countries like Germany and France the answer is, on the whole, negative. The Italians and the Greeks, however, may find that membership of the EC also carries with it some responsibilities. Nevertheless, the Directive does take a more open stand on some issues. Here are some:

(*a*) Liability is now strict in theory as well as in practice (except for development risks in non-pharmaceutical products). All that the victim will have to show is that the product was defective and the defect caused his injury. This is not to say that all will be plain sailing since (a) causation (despite presumptions) may be difficult to prove and (b) the Directive (and the national laws) retain quite an array of defences. For details see the texts.

(*b*) When is a product defective? Note again the different national formulations as well as the Directive's emphasis on "user expectations". Can American case law help in this respect?

(*c*) In the many happy hours of reading that will be necessary to understand the emerging law, the following articles in English may help (detailed references to the German literature are given in chapter 2, section A.4(*c*) above): Borrie, "Product Liability in the EEC" 9 *Dublin U. L. J.* 82 (1987); Dielmann, "The European Economic Community's Council Directive on Product Liability" 20 *The Int'l Law* 1391 (1986); Lord Griffiths, De Val, and Dormer, "Development in English Product Liability Law: A Comparison with the American System" 62 *Tul. L. Rev.* 353 (1988); Newdick, "The Future of Negligence in Product Liability" 103 (1987) *LQR* 288; Stapleton, "Product Liability Reform—Real or Illusory?" (1985); Whittaker, "The EEC Directive on Product Liability" *Y. B. of Eur. L.* 233 (1985); Whittaker, "European Product Liability and Intellectual Products" 105 (1989) *LQR* 125.

4

The Remaining Grounds of Liability in the Civil Code and the Law of Damages

SECTION A. COMMENTARY

1. TWO MORE GENERAL CLAUSES

(a) § 823 II BGB

This important provision of the BGB imposes an obligation to make amends on anyone who violates a statutory provision intended for the protection of others. The element of unlawfulness which, as we saw in the context of § 823 I BGB, is defined by reference to the violation of the specifically enumerated interests, the so-called *Rechtsgüter*, is here made to depend upon the notion of a violated protective norm (*Schutzgesetz*). The term *Gesetz*, is taken here widely to refer to statutes (of private and public law), government decrees, local by-laws or ordinances (*Verordnungen*), food and drugs regulations, and police orders. Along with § 823 I BGB, paragraph II of this Article contains the second of the so-called small general clauses of the Code. In its ambit, however, it is both wider and narrower than the first paragraph of the same Article. (Wider since it covers economic loss but narrower since the illegality is defined by reference to the scope of the particular statute (which may be narrow) and not on the consequences of its violation.)

The literature on this important paragraph is extensive. See, *inter alia*: Canaris, "Die Haftung für fahrlässige Verletzung der Konkursantragspflicht nach § 64 GmbHG", *JZ* 1993, 649; Dörner, "Zur Dogmatik der Schutzgesetzverletzung", *JuS* 1987, 522; Kothe, "Normzweck und Interessenabwägung bei der Auslegung des § 823 II BGB", *Jura* 1988, 130; Karollus, *Funktion, und Dogmatik der Haftung aus Schutzgesetzverletzung* (1992); Knöpfle, "Zur Problematik der Beurteilung einer Norm als Schutzgesetz im Sinne des § 823 Abs. 2 BGB", *NJW* 1967, 697; Lutter, "Gefahren persönlicher Haftung für Gesellschafter und Geschäftsführer einer GmbH", *DB* 1994, 129; Peters, "Zur Gesetzestechnik des § 823 II BGB", *JZ* 1983, 913. A list of laws recognised as containing protective norms in the sense of this paragraph can be found in: Palandt, § 823 BGB, no. 145 ff. and *Münchener Kommentar*-Mertens, § 823 BGB, nos. 166 ff. They include certain statutory provisions from the area of company law (e.g. § 92 II *Aktiengesetz*, § 64 I *GmbH-Gesetz*), § 5 of the *Arzneimittelgesetz*, many provisions of the Criminal Code (e.g. §§ 142, 185), and so on. More interesting is the classification of these various *Schutzgesetze* according to their purpose. Thus, according to Professor Medicus these statutes may wish to protect one of three things. First, they may wish to protect the essential legal rights and values (e.g. human freedom, corporeal integrity etc.). Secondly, they may wish to prohibit a dangerous behaviour (e.g. dangerous driving). Finally, they may wish to protect (in a measured way) a person's "estate" (including his economic interests), which, it will be recalled, are not covered by the first paragraph of § 823 BGB. But liability for violation of a protective norm under § 823 II BGB is not exclusive and may overlap with liability arising from the violation of some other provision of the Code. For example, in the chicken-farm case (case 61) we saw that the manufacturer of the defective vaccine that killed the plaintiff's poultry was in breach of a special statute which was held by the court to be a protective statute in the sense of § 823 II BGB. However, readers will also remember that his liability overlapped with liability based on § 823 I BGB and in fact it was this part of the judgment that made history. Sometimes the overlap may exist with the provisions of some other enactment. As already stated, a breach of the Road Traffic Act (or police regulations made pursuant to it) will often be treated as a breach of a protective norm. In such cases liability for a breach of the Road Traffic Act will co-exist with liability based on § 823 II BGB. Indeed, liability may further be based on § 823 I BGB. § 823 II BGB is thus an additional cause of liability, not a reason for excluding liability that may arise from another legal source.

This overlap, however, does not mean that the requirements of liability are the same in all these cases. As we have already noted, liability under the Road Traffic Act does not depend on fault. On the other hand, liability under § 823 I and II BGB is fault-based liability. The second sentence of § 823 II BGB makes this abundantly clear by stating that where breach of a particular statute can engage liability irrespective of fault—something which often happens these days—additional civil liability under § 823 II BGB will be imposed only if some fault can be found in the wrongdoer. In this instance, however, the case law has reversed the onus of proof and placed it squarely on the defendant. (Esser/Weyers, II 2, p. 201.) So fault will be presumed unless the defendant can positively disprove any fault on his part (BGHZ 51, 91; BGH NJW 1968, 1279). In this sense, therefore, § 823 II BGB is more favourable to the plaintiff. But, as stated, it is also more favourable in another respect as well, notably in its recognition of the compensability of purely economic loss. This explains why the plaintiffs in the cable cases, reviewed earlier on (cases 11–13), tried to base their claims on § 823 II BGB. These observations, however, should not be taken to imply that plaintiffs can, as a matter of course, base their claims on this paragraph of the BGB every time there has been a violation of some statute. The requirement that the violated statute is a protective norm provides the greatest obstacle and the most interesting condition of this provision of the Code. It is to this, therefore, that we must now turn our attention.

Now the first thing to note in this respect is that the German legislator expressly states that, subject to what is said below, the breach of a particular statute will always give rise to a civil remedy. By so doing he has successfully avoided one of the problems that has literally plagued the English (and American) courts and forced them to search for the real or imaginary intention of the legislator on this matter. (See in this respect Lord Denning's remarks in *Ex. p. Island Records Ltd* [1978] Ch. 122, 135A.) But the civil remedy will be granted only if the violated norm was a protective statute. This means that the plaintiff must show that the mischief that occurred was in fact the one that the legislator wished to avoid. Moreover, he must show that he himself belongs to the class of persons to which the legislator intended to grant a civil remedy. Both of these propositions are quite simple to state; and they contain nothing that will surprise a Common lawyer. But the answer to these questions is by no means easy to find; it invariably involves difficult questions of statutory construction, which varies from case to case and in practice it has given rise to a very rich case law. The detailed study of this case-law presents little interest to any course of lectures or book that aims at introducing students to the study of foreign or comparative law so we shall limit ourselves to a few illustrations. (For further details see Peters, "Zur Gesetzestechnik des § 823 II BGB", *JZ* 1983, 913.)

When looking at these cases, the first thing one can note is the fact that a statute meant to protect the public at large does not necessarily mean that it was not also intended to include within its protective ambit a particular (legal or physical) person. For example, during the First World War the German Government imposed stringent regulations concerning meat imports. Powers to control such imports, regulate their qualities and internal distribution (in order to avoid food shortages), and if necessary to confiscate illegally imported consignments of meat, were vested in a state-owned Central Purchasing Corporation. On one occasion one of the Corporation's employees, working near the Netherlands border, wrongfully authorised the import of an excessive quantity of meat which reached an accomplice of his and was subsequently sold to their mutual gain. The Corporation's action for damages against both these persons was successfully based on § 823 II BGB in conjunction with the relevant government order that had created the Corporation and vested in it the powers described above (RGZ 100, 142, 146. See, also, BGHZ 46, 23). As the court said, the fact that the order creating the Corporation was issued for the protection of the common well did not prevent it from conferring a special right of action on the Corporation in accordance with § 823 II BGB. It would be wrong, however, to argue the reverse and say that all statutes passed in the interest of the public at large also automatically conferred rights on its individual members. This point was made very clear in one of the cable cases—and which need not be repeated here.

The question whether the particular plaintiff is included in the protective ambit of the violated statute naturally turns on the wording and the often elusive intention of the legislator. The search for this can be aided by consulting the *travaux préparatoires*. If these are ambiguous, and often they are, then "the question must be attacked directly, whether the creation of an individual claim for compensation appears meaningful, sensible, and tolerable in the light of the whole system of liability" (BGHZ 66, 388; see, also, BGH NJW 1980, 1792). Three cases, reproduced below (cases 129–141) provide interesting illustration of how the above guiding principles are applied in practice.

In the first case (BGHZ 26, 42), the defendant was granted under statutory powers a licence to operate a bus service, but was prohibited from operating on a regular line between points A and B. Despite this express prohibition, he did operate that line and was sued by the Federal Railways. One of the questions before the court was whether the Federal Railways could base their claim under § 823 II BGB and the violation of the Act on Carriage of Persons on Land under which the original licence had been granted. The main question was connected with the proper construction of the law subjecting land transport to State licensing and regulation. In the court's view this was meant to protect the interests of the general public in the establishment of an orderly transport system which has always occupied a special position in the country's transport policy. The action by the Railways was thus accepted.

In case 130 (BGHZ 15, 315), an association was formed in order to protect the interests of tenants of leased premises. Among the services that the association provided for its members was the availability of legal advice on legal points and this was done in consideration of a fee which was fixed in accordance with the professional fee-scales applicable to the members of the Bar. The plaintiffs, another association formed to protect the economic and professional interests of the members of the Hamburg Bar, applied for an injunction requesting that the defendant tenants' association cease to provide legal counselling services. Once again, the outcome depended on discovering the purpose of the relevant statute concerning the provision of legal services by qualified members of the Bar. The court took the view that this had a double purpose. The first was to ensure that the public received proper counselling from a well-qualified and disciplined body of professionals. The second was to protect the interests of the Bar against competition coming from persons or bodies who were not subject to the same disciplinary and other restrictions as were professionally qualified lawyers. The claim that the association of tenants could not charge full fees was accepted, though the court also took the view that a more modest charge could be made simply in order to cover the association's expenses.

BGHZ 29, 100 (case 131) is our last example. In that case the plaintiff, an unsecured creditor of a company in liquidation, sued one of its directors alleging that in breach of statutory duty (§ 64 of the Companies Act) he had failed to commence liquidation proceedings at a given date. As a result of this inaction, the plaintiff had suffered financial loss by advancing credit to the company. The defendant's argument, that the obligation to commence liquidation proceedings on time was solely meant to safeguard the public interest, was not accepted. The court took the view that the purpose of this enactment was also to safeguard the position of creditors of the company against precisely this type of risk. Moreover, this was true even for those creditors who had advanced credit *after* the date when the liquidation proceedings ought to have been commenced. (See, further, Medicus no. 622 giving further references. See, also, the more recent decision BGHZ 100, 19.)

It is not enough for the plaintiff to prove that he belongs to the class of persons that the violated statute wished to protect; he must also show that the mischief that has occurred was the one that the statute wanted to avoid. Only if both these points are proved will the plaintiff be able to base his claim on § 823 II BGB.

The liquidation case, mentioned in the previous paragraph, provides an illustration for this point as well. Another and arguably better example can be found in one of the cases discussed earlier under the heading of manufacturers' liability (BGHZ 39, 358, case 74). It will be remembered that in that case a local authority was being sued because cracks appeared in a building, the foundations of which had not been properly inspected. No personal injury or damage to other property was pleaded and the claim was rejected. For the court took the view that the purpose of the statute imposing upon local authorities an obligation to inspect foundations was to prevent injury to human beings and damage to *other* property but not to safeguard potential buyers against the risk of paying an excessive price for a worthless building. (For another illustration see BGHZ 66, 388, BGHZ 19, 114, 125 and cases 12, BGHZ 66, 388, and 123, BGHZ 19, 114, respectively. See, also, Deutsch, *JZ* 1984, 308, 311–12 and *JZ* 1990, 733.)

(b) § 826 BGB

Select bibliography

Braun, *Rechtskraft und Restitution. Erster Teil. Der Rechtsbehelf gem. § 826 BGB gegen rechtskräftige Urteile* (1979); Kohte, "Rechtschutz gegen die Vollstreckung des wucherähnlichen Rechtsgeschäfts nach § 826", *NJW* 1985, 2217; Koller, "Sittenwidrigkeit der Gläubigergefährdung und Gläubigerbenachteiligung", *JZ* 1985, 1013; Larenz, "Grundsätzliches zu § 138 BGB", *Juristenjahrbuch* 7 (1966/7) 98; Prinz/Wanckel, "Vorsätzliche sittenwidrige Schädigung einer Privatbank durch unwahre Presseberichterstattung", *EWiR* 1998, 171; Prütting-Werth, *Rechtskraftdurchbrechung bei unrichtigen Titeln*, 2nd edn. (1994); Sack, "Das Anstandsgefühl aller billig und gerecht Denkenden und die Moral als

Bestimmungsfaktoren der guten Sitten", *NJW* 1985, 761; Simitis, *Gute Sitten und ordre public. Ein kritischer Beitrag zur Anwendung des § 138 I BGB* (1960); Teubner, *Standards und Direktiven in Generalklauseln, Möglichkeiten und Grenzen der empirischen Sozialforschung bei der Präzisierung der Gute-Sitten-Klauseln im Privatrecht* (1971); Wieacker, "Rechtsprechung und Sittengesetz", *JZ* 1961, 337; Wolf, "Der Ersatzberechtigte bei Tatbeständen sittenwidriger Schädigung", *NJW* 1967, 709.

This is the third and last general provision of the Code and was, in fact, intended from the outset as an all-purpose residual provision, able to accommodate future expansion in the growth of the law of torts. In the event, however, the limitations built into this provision did not facilitate such growth. The result was that some of the most significant extensions of tort liability have been achieved either through § 823 I BGB, or the expansion of the law of contract into what otherwise would properly be described as the province of the law of torts.

§ 826 BGB is subjectively the narrowest of the three general provisions, since it will be satisfied only if intention can be shown to exist. For present purposes, mere negligence is thus not an acceptable *mens rea*. Intention is taken to include *dolus directus* and *dolus eventualis*. An example of the first can be found whenever the defendant knows the consequences of his conduct and wishes to bring them about; an illustration of the latter can be seen in those cases where the defendant is aware of the consequences of his conduct which he accepts as inevitable even though he may not specifically desire them. What must be intended is the damage in suit, though its full extent and the precise way it is brought about need not have been specifically anticipated.

Though subjectively narrow § 826 BGB is objectively wide—in fact the most general, indeed amorphous provision of the Code. In this instance the pervading notion of unlawfulness is not determined by reference to the violation of a carefully enumerated list of protected interests; nor is it linked with breaches of statutory provisions to be found outside the Code. Here, the determination of the element of unlawfulness is left to the judge to decide by reference to the flexible notion of *boni mores*. Though as we shall see this does not mean that the outcome depends on the personal views and predilections of the judge, in practice this formula does confer wide praetorian powers.

It will have become obvious from the above that intentionally inflicted loss will not, of itself, bring § 826 BGB into operation. Economic competition—the basis of all modern free economies—often means that the economic ruin of one person is the price of success for the competitor. Though nowadays there is an increasing tendency to limit some of the excesses of capitalism, the fact remains that in all systems intentionally causing economic loss to another person will not alone suffice to create tortious liability. Thus, just as English law imposes the additional requirement that the loss be inflicted "unlawfully", so does German law require that the activity be intentional and *contra bonos mores*. This, then, becomes the crucial notion of this paragraph: crucial and, one should also add, elusive.

The difficulty of definition lies largely in the fact that because of historical reasons, German law chose to cover a multitude of wrongs under one broad and abstract formula instead of treating each factual situation as giving rise to different torts and requiring its own concepts and definitions. To put it differently, this separate pigeonhole approach which can be found in England did not commend itself to the Germans. Thus deceit, passing off, intimidation, procuring a breach of contract, unfair competition, malicious prosecution, etc., which are all actionable as separate torts in the Common law, in German law are brought under one heading. Clearly, these wrongs are so disparate that if one formula is to cover them all it has to be a very wide one. This, as stated, accounts for the different approach and, indeed, has encouraged the abstract if not philosophical writings on the subject. But whatever the merits or demerits of this different approach—and one is inclined to think that in this instance the English casuistry has its advantages—the problems (and often the solutions) are quite similar in both systems. But to return to the basic notion: when is an activity *contra bonos mores*?

Apart from a brief interlude during the Nazi period, when this provision of the Code (as so many others) was subverted to the cause of National Socialism (*cf.* RGZ 150, 1, 4), good morals have received a fairly constant definition. Thus "the sense of propriety of all good and right-thinking members of society" (BGHZ 17, 327, 332) has often been quoted as the yardstick to be used in these cases. This is a flexible test, capable of accommodating change, and particularly useful in the context of problem situations which arise within the context of family life (e.g. RGZ 58, 248; BGH NJW 1962, 958). But in a modern pluralistic and less homogeneous society, is it always possible to discover a prevailing morality? Or is it practicable to introduce "moral" considerations in the most typically litigated disputes involving some kind of excessive or improper competition? Should the actual practice of businessmen be used as the model instead? Or should the standard be derived not from extra-legal rules of morality but from the various rules of the positive legal system, including the Constitution itself? The idea that good morals is a notion much more akin to the English concept of public policy or the French *ordre public* has gained support, and in turn, become the target for criticism. It is difficult—especially for a Common lawyer looking at the German law—to say which of the many theories best explains the case law. It is safer to assert with some measure of confidence that (i) the notion of *boni mores* has undergone some change since the War and, perhaps, (ii) that no one theory can be said to be able to cover the whole spectrum of disparate cases. To use Dean Prosser's description of the tort of nuisance, this is not a tort but a field of tortious liability. Perhaps, therefore, the best one can do is to give a series of examples from actually litigated cases and thus demonstrate to the Common law student the amplitude of this provision. For convenience's sake these illustrations are grouped under four headings. (For a comprehensive account of this very rich jurisprudence *Staudinger*-Oechsler, 13th edn. (1998), § 826 BGB, nos. 145–562.)

(i) Misstatements

1. If a person gives in good faith false information and then subsequently becomes aware of its falsity he may, under certain circumstances, be under a duty to correct it and if he does not do so he will be liable under § 826 BGB (RGZ 76, 318; BGH JZ 1979, 725).

2. If the directors of a company produce what to their knowledge is a false balance sheet in order to attract a potential investor they will be liable under the same paragraph (RG JZ 1908, 448).

3. If an employer intentionally gives to a third party an untrue reference about one of his employees he may be liable to the third party for the loss resulting therefrom (RG DJZ 1905, 697; see also BGH NJW 1970, 2291; BGHZ 74, 281).

4. If a person gives recklessly false information about the credit of a third person he may be liable to the recipient of this information under § 826 BGB (BGH WM 1956, 1229; BGH WM 1979, 428).

5. Failure to disclose relevant information in the course of a business transaction may be actionable under § 826 BGB, especially where the defendant's conduct constitutes an abuse of his dominant economic position. (BGH NJW 1982, 2815.)

6. If a person recklessly issues fictitious receipts and collusively collaborates with the employee of the victim he may be liable to the recipient of the receipt under § 826 BGB (BGH NJW 2000, 2896).

7. For other decisions under this broad heading see: BGH NJW 1983, 1850; BGH WM 1984, 221; BGH NJW 1992, 3167.

(ii) Obtaining a judicial decision by fraud etc

1. If a person perjures himself and thereby causes another to be condemned to pay a debt which that other has in fact already discharged, he will be liable to that person for the loss suffered thereby (RGZ 46, 75).

2. A person who obtains a divorce by fraud can be liable under this paragraph (RGZ 75, 213).

3. A person who executes a judgment which he knows to be wrong can be liable under § 826 BGB, though this heading and the conditions that have to be satisfied, are controversial (BGHZ 50, 115; BGHZ 101, 380; BGHZ 26, 391; BGHZ 112, 54).

(iii) Inducing breach of contract and other trade disputes

Liability under § 826 BGB may be incurred in the following situations:

1. Intimidation of employers by trade unions not to employ non-union members (RGZ 104, 327).

2. Boycott (under certain circumstances) (RGZ 60, 94, 104; 64, 57, 61; 66, 379, 384; 76, 35; 86, 152; 105, 70; BGHZ 19, 72; BGH NJW 1985, 60, 62).

3. Inducing breach of contract (RG JW 1913, 866; RGZ 78, 14, 17; RG JW 1913, 326; BGH NJW 1981, 2184; BGH NJW 1994, 128; BGH JZ 1996, 416). Mere "co-operation" in the breach of a contract with a third party will not suffice (BGH NJW 1969, 1293 ff.). In reaching a decision all the surrounding circumstances must be considered. (BGH NJW 1981, 2184.)

4. Under certain circumstances, strikes can also be caught by this provision (RGZ 130, 98).

5. A person who induces a vendor of sold but undelivered goods to hand them over to him (rather than to their purchaser) (RG JW 1931, 2238; BGHZ 70, 277).

6. Disclosing confidential information acquired during previous employment may be actionable in contract (§ 74 HGB and § 242 BGB) as well as being actionable under § 826 BGB (BAG NJW 1983, 135). BGH NJW 1981, 1089 ("*Wallraff-Fall*") is particularly noteworthy not only because of the public interest it attracted, but also because it discussed the position of § 826 BGB within the context of the wider constitutional order. In that case *Wallraff*—the second defendant—wrote a book, which was to be published by the first defendant, and in which he described how a well-known Hanover newspaper was

run. This information he had acquired while working under a false name for the editor of this newspaper. The latter's action—based *inter alia* on § 826 BGB—to prevent the publication of the said account was dismissed on the grounds that § 826 BGB in this instance had to give way to the constitutionally protected freedom of expression (*Meinungsfreiheit*) (Art. 5 I of the Constitution of Bonn). See BVerfG NJW 1984, 1741.

(iv) Miscellaneous matters

1. Malicious falsehood (RGZ 76, 110).

2. Abuse of rights (BGHZ 26, 391, 396).

3. Passing off (RGZ 144, 41, 45).

4. Malicious prosecution (BGHZ 17, 327; BGH NJW 1951, 597).

5. Wrongful use of monopoly power (RGZ 132, 273; *cf.* BGH MDR 1980, 121).

6. Other underhand activities (OLG Celle NJW 1983, 1065; BGH WM 1984, 850 (touting)).

7. Rejected applications to join business or social "societies" or "clubs" can also under certain circumstances found actions on § 826 BGB (BGHZ 29, 344 ff.; BGH NJW 1969, 316 ff.; BGH NJW 1980, 186; BGHZ 93, 151).

2. OTHER HEADINGS OF TORTIOUS LIABILITY

(a) Some specific torts of the BGB

§ 824 BGB imposes civil liability for oral or written statements which are likely to endanger the credit of another person or otherwise damage his earnings or prosperity. Liability under this heading may overlap with the crime of insult or defamation (§§ 185, 186 StGB) and the civil consequences envisaged by the treatment of these provisions as protective statutes within the context of § 823 II BGB. But § 824 BGB is also wider in so far as it covers (i) intentional and negligent activities and (ii) statements which may endanger a person's credit or economic interests, even if they do not actually affect his reputation.

The statement must refer to an identified or identifiable plaintiff and not merely a wider class to which he belongs. Moreover, § 824 BGB refers to statements of facts and not expressions of opinion or other value judgements. (See BGH NJW 1987, 2225.) The truth of the asserted fact will, normally, provide a full defence. If the facts are untrue—and the burden of proving their inaccuracy lies on the plaintiff—the maker of the statement may still avoid liability if he or the receiver of the communication had a lawful interest in it. But this privilege only applies if the maker of the statement did not know that his statement was incorrect. The defence of "justified interest", as this defence is called, will be upheld only where an "objective assessment of the contents of the communication, its form and all the surrounding circumstances suggest that it is the appropriate and necessary means for achieving a legally acceptable objective" (BGHZ 3, 281). If the elements of liability are satisfied, the plaintiff will, normally, be entitled to demand the retraction of the statement and compensation for costs reasonably incurred in order to mitigate his loss (§ 249 BGB). In some (but not all) of these cases the courts have also allowed the plaintiff the costs of inserting a "correcting statement" in the national press (see on this BGHZ 66, 182, 191 ff.).

§ 825 BGB contains the elements of another specific tort: the unlawful inducement of a woman to extra-marital cohabitation. The gist of the tort lies in the unlawful means used to coerce the woman's will: cunning, threats etc. Compensation for this tort will include economic loss (e.g. medical expenses incurred for curing a sexually transmitted disease; miscarriage or costs of giving birth to a child) as well as appropriate damages for pain and suffering and impairment of the victim's reputation (§ 847 BGB). The anti-quated nature of the tort and the emergence of the new and wider right to one's person-ality have rendered this provision almost entirely obsolete in practice. However, the reform proposal already referred to, suggests that the provision should be extended to males. This seems odd since the Proposal also acknowledges that § 825 BGB has no impor-tance in practice for the reasons mentioned above. Thus retaining the provision must be seen as merely symbolic act of little practical value.

(b) Liability under § 839 BGB

Paragraph 839 BGB—dealing with liability for breach of official duty—is one of the most important "special" provisions of the tort section of the Code and has given rise to a rich case law. Before analysing the elements of liability, three preliminary observations should be made. (For more detailed discussions see Esser/Weyers, II 2, § 59 I, p. 220).

First, one must note that this paragraph provides for the *personal* liability of the of-ficial. In most cases, however, the victim/plaintiff will be anxious to engage the liability of the State (or other local authority or agency). When and how this can be done depends on the *nature of the act* of the official.

This brings us to the second preliminary observation. The official may be exercising a "sovereign act" or he may be pursuing ordinary, private law activities on the part of the State. The distinction between acts *iure imperii* and *gestionis*, never entirely satisfactory, has become more difficult in recent time as the modern State has entered the market place. Nevertheless, as we shall note further on, the distinction is of great significance in the context of § 839 BGB.

Finally, one must always remember that § 839 BGB is a specific enactment and as such overrides the provisions of the other more general clauses of the Code (BGHZ 3, 94, 102; BGH NJW 1971, 43, 44). This is important to bear in mind since often the same act (by the official) can be brought under §§ 839, 823 I or II, or 824 BGB. Where this is the case, § 839 BGB will prevail and this may have serious repercussions on the position of the plaintiff given the various restrictions of liability provided in § 839 BGB. In this sense, therefore, § 839 BGB represents a narrowing of liability. On the other hand, the paragraph is also wider than some of the other general clauses (e.g. § 823 I BGB) in so far as it imposes liability for *any damage* arising from the unlawful conduct of the official. This means that under this heading even claims for negligently inflicted purely economic loss may succeed.

In German law, tort liability of public bodies is widely discussed. Reform has been con-sidered for over twenty years. Its unquestioned aim is a modern, unified responsibility for wrongs committed by public bodies—mostly, but not entirely, independent of fault, and based on statute. At present, however, most of the law is judge-made; it is secreted in many different kinds of causes of action, and it is not always clear. In this book, however, we will concentrate solely on those situations where damages are sought for breach of an official duty (*Amtspflichtverletzung*)—comparable to the factual situations found in many English cases. In this section we will be dealing only with the liability of public bodies and not with the liability of their employees. The latter will result from BGB § 839 only if there is no liability of the public body according to the combined application of Article 34 of the Constitution and BGB § 839 and only if the employee has the status of a civil servant (*Beamter*). Other employees will be liable in accordance with BGB, §§ 823 *et seq.* where no state liability is envisaged.

This liability of public bodies flows from the combined application of Article 34 of the Constitution and § 839 of the BGB. This means that public bodies are liable in damages to individuals injured by their own (or their employees') culpable failure to perform properly any official duty owed to the individual. Liability is excluded where, first, the breach of a duty is due to a negligent act only and the individual injured can obtain redress from another source (§ 839 I 2 BGB). Secondly, liability is also excluded where the victim did not make use of any legal remedy which could have mitigated his damages (§ 839 III BGB). Finally, the same is true where a statute expressly provides for such an eventuality. (For example, BNotO (*Bundesnotarordnung*, which is the Federal Law on Notaries), § 19, which provides for the personal liability of the notary public; RBHaftG *Reichsbeamten-haftungsgesetz* (Law on Liability of Civil Servants), § 5 No. 2, which excludes liability for certain political acts in the diplomatic service; for further discussion especially on the constitutionality of such restrictions on state liability, see Ossenbühl, *Staatshaftungsrecht* 5th edn., 1996, 79 *et seq.*) Here, it will suffice to draw the reader's attention to two elements of the cause of action: "fault" and the fact that "the duty must be owed to the individual plaintiff" and not the public at large.

The requirement of culpability has to be seen against the code's historical background: § 839 BGB was designed originally to cater solely for the liability of a public official himself. The old (Roman law) principle—*si excessit, privatus est*—known also in English law, along with disputes over the legislative competence for state liability rules, induced the draftsmen of the civil code to refrain from any rule on public liability (leaving this issue to the member states), although not from rules on liability of public bodies acting fiscally (see §§ 89, 31 BGB). (For further details, see *Entwurf eines Einführungsgesetzes zum BGB für das Deutsche Reich*, 1. *Lesung nebst Motiven*, (1888), 185.) The central idea (first introduced to the whole of Germany by the *Beamtenhaftungsgesetz* of 1 August 1909 (GS 691) and, subsequently, acknowledged in Article 131 of the Weimar Constitution 1919) was that such an official should bear liability in damages only where he is at fault. Individual responsibility is of less significance where the state takes over liability. In the current debates, over reforms, German writers remain convinced that the fault requirement should be loosened, but there is considerable disagreement as to the extent that this should happen. (*Cf.* Pfab, *Staatshaftung in Deutschland* (1997), passim.) These debates should not, however, conceal the fact that the concept of fault in German civil law (in contrast to the concept of fault in criminal law) is already understood in a very broad way. So, as in English law, the standard of care in cases of negligence is an objective one, concentrating on the reasonable person in general and—with regard to particular groups or professions—on the special high standard of care one can expect from such particular group or profession. In practice, the test thus often comes close to the notion of strict liability; and it has been demonstrated that in most litigation concerning breach of official duty the issue of fault is rarely an obstacle for plaintiffs. *Zur Reform des Staatshaftungsrechts, rechtstatsächliche Erkenntnisse in Staatshaftungssachen, Verwaltungserhebung und Gerichtsauswertung* (1976), edited by the Bundesministerium der Justiz, 34, 202—only 14.1 per cent of the claims failed because of the absence of fault.

Secondly, discretionary acts of public bodies (or their employees) are, in Germany, subject to judicial review to a far greater extent than in English law. Thus, a German judge may rule on and find fault even where the official acted within the ambit of his dis-cretion (as will be shown in detail below). The discretionary character of an act is not in principle, therefore, a bar to justiciability; nor does it hinder the proof of careless decision taking within the ambit of the discretion. The test applied by German courts is much wider than the *Wednesbury (Associated Provincial Picture Houses* v. *Wednesbury Corporation* [1948] 1 KB 223, CA) test of reasonableness that prevails in English law.

If the requirement of fault is no real obstacle to state liability the same is not true of the second element, namely "that the duty must be owed to the individual to protect his interests". This serves as an effective filter to remove from all public wrongs those cases where the state itself might be liable in damages. The duty must not exist solely for the benefit of the general public, but must at least also protect the individual or a class to which the individual/plaintiff belongs. The claimant must thus be such a protected individual or a member of a protected group, and the duty must exist to protect especially those interests of the individual that have been injured. The parallels here with the English requirements of liability for breach of statutory duty are evident. Nevertheless, one must remain conscious of the dangers that would accompany any complete assimilation. Although there are many decisions on this issue leading to some uncertainty over the exact application of this requirement in given cases, the approach of German law seems to be stricter than that found in English cases. Thus, where it is open for policy considerations to play a part in the outcome of a dispute, they tend to focus on the relevance and meaning of the official duty. (*Münchener-Kommentar,* Papier, (3rd edn., 1997) § 839, no. 227; for proposals to streamline the discussion, see: Ladeur, "Zur Bestimmung des drittschützenden Charakters von Amtspflichten im Sinne von § 839 BGB und Art. 34 GG—insbesondere bei Aufsichtspflichten", *DÖV* 1994, 665.) By contrast, less attention is paid to the wider (open ended?) considerations of justice, fairness and economic efficiency which one finds in English decisions. One, therefore, starts with the premise that fairness and justice require the state to be held liable to the individual for public wrong, except where the official duty is owed only to the public at large. Although the element of "duty towards the individual" (*drittbezogene Amtspflicht*) is phrased as a requirement and not only in a negative form as an obstacle to the claim, the relation of rule and exception in English and German law seems in many instances to be the reverse. This is obvious in the decision of the Federal Court of Justice with regard to the banking control system, where the court inferred from the silence of the statutory rule that the duty was owed towards the individual. (BGH 15 February 1979, BGHZ 74, 144, 147 = NJW 1979, 1354; BGH 12 July 1979, BGHZ 75, 120, 122 = NJW 1979, 1879. For doubts on the constitutionality of the amendments of the statute (Kreditwesengesetz, as amended on 20 December 1984), *Münchener-Kommentar,* Papier (3rd edn., 1997), § 839, no. 250, 251.) This may be further illustrated by contrasting the indicators of such a "duty towards the individual" with the requirements of state liability in English law laid down by Lord Browne-Wilkinson in the *Bedfordshire* case.

It is well established that there is a "duty towards the individual" when the (particular) individual has a right to claim performance of that duty (*öffentlich-rechtlicher Erfüllungsanspruch*). Claim of and duty towards the individual are two sides of the same coin. For example, an applicant may claim the issue of a building permission where he has complied with certain requirements. If the permission is not issued, or is issued too late, or is (illegally) made subject to a supplementary condition, a private law cause of action will arise. (BGH 14 December 1978, NJW 1979, 641, 642; BGH 10 March 1994, NJW

1994, 1647; BGH 13 July 1989, NJW 1990, 505 (marriage officer arriving too late in the hospital for the marriage ceremony, the fiancée having died already); compare also BGH 6 May 1993, NJW 1993, 2303, 2304; BGH 24 February 1994, NJW 1994, 2091; *Münchener-Kommentar*, Papier, § 839 no. 228; *Wurm*, JA 1992, 1, 2.) Of course, these situations are less problematic and do not arise frequently in practice because the individual may usually, launch an appeal against the decision and thereby obtain what he or she is entitled to claim. Although not identical, this class of case comes close to those situations in English law where Lord Browne-Wilkinson referred to breaches of statutory duty *simpliciter*. (*X* (*Minors*) v. *Bedfordshire C. C.* [1995] 3 WLR 165, 166).

Another instance giving rise to a duty towards an individual is where the public body and the individual have entered into a special relationship. The duties of protection and care arising from such relationship are owed to the individual and also to third parties included in the realm of protection (*Schutzwirkung zugunsten Dritter*). See for instance: BGH of 20 June 1974, NJW 1974, 1816, 1817—a slaughterhouse owed a duty towards the employee of the butcher, who had to use the slaughterhouse; this notion of third party protection is known not only in tort law but especially in contract law, where contractual duties may involve the protection of persons close to the parties. Another example can be taken from the education context. A school owes a special duty of care towards its pupils. (BGH 27 April 1981, NJW 1982, 37, 38; BGH 10 March 1983, FamRZ 1984, 1211 (both concerning the negligent control of a school bus stop).) In most cases there will be no liability of the school and its responsible body because damage will be covered by statutory insurance against school accidents. This exception will not apply, however, when violations of the right of personality (*Persönlichkeitsrechtsverletzungen*) are at issue and money compensation for pain and suffering is sought: OLG Zweibrücken 6 May 1997, NJW 1998, 995: the responsible body had to pay DM 1,600 to a pupil who had consistently been made fun of by his teacher in front of the class causing the pupil great psychological harm. In addition, a school has the duty to prevent pupils from causing harm to others. Thus, if a pupil damages the car of X during a school excursion, the responsible body may be liable towards the car owner. (LG Hamburg 26 April 1991, NJW 1992, 377; in that case a cause of action against the pupil himself would have been unsuccessful due primarily to his lack of means.) It is tempting here to draw parallels with the *Dorset Yacht* case, although one might also be inclined to compare this element of the "duty towards the individual" with the requirement of proximity found in the *Caparo* test. (*Caparo Industries Plc.* v. *Dickman* [1990] 2 AC 605.) There are also differences, however, insofar as, in general, the required proximity need not exist between the tortfeasor and the injured person but between the injured person and the person protected by a special relationship with the tortfeasor. In addition, this duty has been extended— in contrast to contract law—towards those individuals who come into contact with the person protected: the duty of the public body encompasses the duty to prevent harm from the entrusted person as well as to prevent that person from doing harm to others. Thus, the scope of the duty is much broader than the duty of care considered in the *Dorset Yacht case*.

A "duty towards the individual" will also arise where the public body directly infringes absolute rights of an individual, namely his life, body, health, freedom, property (and other rights or interests of comparable weight, for example the right of personality), but not his purely economic interests (BGH 1 February 1982, NJW 1983, 627, 628; *Münchener-Kommentar*, Papier, § 839, no. 229.)

If none of these indicators are present, a "duty towards the individual" may arise from the protective purpose of the rule (*Schutzzweck der Norm*);—the rule which imposes a certain duty on the public body—must have been created, *inter alia* to prevent the mischief that occurred. But this need not necessarily follow from the express intention of the legislator. It suffices that such protection for the individual arises from the nature of public dealings and the circumstances of such dealings, even if the rule has been laid down primarily for the protection of the public in general. One indicator of the protective purpose of the duty is the availability of a public law remedy for an injured person; another indicator is the special danger for the life and health of an individual resulting from these dealings. If public dealings create a special situation where an individual can rely on the duty of care owed to him by a public body, this indicates that duties arising from public dealings also have the purpose of protecting individuals. But the extent of the protective purpose may be limited to certain goods, especially to absolute rights and interests. This is especially the case with regard to the duty to ensure safe traffic on the roads (*Straßenverkehrssicherungspflicht*). This exists towards every individual road-user, (the German cases differ considerably from the English cases, as exemplified by *Ancell v. McDermott* [1993] 4 All ER 355) but only with regard to life, body, health, liberty, property and other rights and interests of comparable weight. Generally speaking, the duty does not extend to protection against economic loss (BGH 18 December 1972, NJW 1973, 463.) Thus, if traffic lights are installed wrongly and, as a result, an accident occurs which causes injury to individuals and damage to property, the public authority will be liable for all these damages. However if, due to the wrong installation of traffic lights traffic congestion occurs, no liability will arise towards individuals who suffered economic loss because they were caught in the resulting traffic jam were caught in the resulting traffic jam. An interesting example is BGH 26 January 1989, BGHZ 106, 323 = NJW 1989, 976 (*Altlasten*, i.e., planning by local authorities on polluted soil). The protective scope of the duty owed by the local planning authority was geared towards the protection of the health of those who would be living in the respective area. However, it was not regarded as necessary for the liability under § 839 BGB to arise that the inhabitants actually suffered physical damage. The purchasers of the uninhabitable land could recover their purely economic loss. (Contrast case 74, and see, also, notes to cases 68–75, note no. 1, above.)

If there is a duty towards the (respective) individual, and the protected rights and interests of the individual have been injured, there will be no further room for policy arguments and the state will be held liable—provided, of course, that the other requirements mentioned above are fulfilled. No duty towards the individual, however, exists with respect to legislative acts, such as the failure to provide necessary laws or the violation of individual rights by virtue of unjust or improper laws. Legislative acts—in comparison to specific acts towards individuals or groups of persons—are owed only to the public in general and, thus, cannot constitute a duty towards an individual or a violation of an individual's rights, unless specified by administrative or judicial acts. Other principles, however, apply with regard to "legislative wrongs" under European law; see Joined Cases C-6 and 9/90 *Francovich v. Italy* [1991] ECR I-5357.

At the beginning of this section we alluded to the distinction between acts of government and acts of ordinary (commercial) administration. The preceding paragraphs have focused on the state's liability for the first kind of act. We now conclude with some observations about the second.

It is important to note that the liability of the Federal Government (State or other public body) is not limited to the acts of State officials (as the term is defined in administrative law) but can include the conduct of any other person. This includes a private enterprise or private individual, so long as they are performing acts which fall within the realm of "sovereign" activities of the State. The position is different when officials (in the public sense) breach official duties while pursuing the private law interests or obligations of the State. For such acts the State can only be liable, either under § 31 BGB (acts of a constitutionally appointed representative) or under the rules of vicarious liability of § 831 BGB, both of which have been discussed in chapter 3. Whether and how the liability of the State can be engaged will thus depend on how the activity will be characterised. Since the distinction between sovereign and private law acts is not clear, a rich case law has, inevitably, developed in this area. Thus, some activities (e.g. running the police, the post office, etc.) are described as sovereign acts attracting the direct liability of the State under Article 34 of the Constitution, while others (e.g. running the Federal Railways system (but excluding the activities of the railway police), the maintenance of public buildings, operation of State hospitals, etc.) are treated as private law acts leading first and foremost to the liability of the official under § 839 and, possibly, the State under §§ 31 or 831 of the BGB.

Before we conclude it is worth pausing briefly over a reform proposal in the context of state liability that may have wider implications in the context of expert liability. It will be remembered that if an expert makes a false statement to a third party and causes pure economic loss to that party the expert can be held liable by a German court provided he owed a *contractual* duty to the third party. It is interesting to note that the recent reform proposal makes a first inroad into this contractual approach to negligent misstatements. The draft § 839a BGB (reproduced above, p. 21) establishes the expert's liability in tort for negligently prepared reports prepared for a court whilst appointed by it to act as expert. The courts had refused to regard the forensic expert's employment by them as acquiring protective effects towards the actual parties of the proceedings. As a result, at present, the expert is liable only under § 823 II BGB in connection with the criminal provisions that prohibit false statements under oath, § 154 StGB (and § 826 BGB). See for details: *Staudinger*-Oechsler, 13th edn. (1998), § 826 BGB, no. 223. The reform seeks *inter alia* to close this liability gap which arises if and when the expert does not testify under oath. Three features of the draft provision are noteworthy. First, pure economic loss is recoverable in such actions. Secondly, liability is, however, limited to gross negligence, purportedly, to encourage the expert to write the report without "fear" of becoming liable. The real reason, however, must surely be the wish to dissuade the party that lost the case to attempt to reverse the decision by suing the expert. Finally, generally speaking, the expert does not exercise a "sovereign" act. This means in the context of the proposed new section § 839a BGB that the expert's liability would not be transferred to public bodies and does not become state liability under Article 34 GG. So in the end we face here a limited and pragmatic exception to § 823 I BGB which imposes liability for negligent misstatements for pure economic loss *in tort* in an instance where the contractual route that prevails elsewhere was not, or could not be utilised by the courts, thus leaving the parties without protection.

Further reading

The literature on this topic is extensive. The leading treatise is that of Professor Fritz Ossenbühl, *Staatshaftungsrecht*, currently in its 5th edn. (1998). For a comparative account in English see: Markesinis, Auby, Coester-Waltjen, Deakin, *Tortious Liability of Statutory Bodies—A Comparative and Economic Analysis of Five English Cases* (1999). On German law see also e.g.: Detterbeck/Windthorst, *Staatshaftungsrecht* (2000); Ehlers, "Die Weiterentwicklung des Staatshaftungsrechts durch europäisches Gemeinschaftsrecht", *JZ* 1996, 776; Giesberts, "Amtshaftung für überplante Altlasten auf ehemaligen Industrie-, Gewerbe- und Deponieflächen", *DB* 1996, 361; Hidien, *Die gemeinschaftsrechtliche Staatshaftung der EU-Mitgliedstaaten* (1999); Krohn, *Enteignung, Entschädigung, Staatshaftung* (1993); Mader, "Zur Amtshaftung der Gemeinde für rechtswidrige Beschlüsse des Gemeinderats", *BayVBl* 1999, 168; Meysen, "Der haftungsrechtliche Besamtenbegriff am Ziel?", *JuS* 1998, 404; Motsch, "Gedanken zur Staatshaftung aus zivilrechtlicher Sicht", *JZ* 1986, 1082; Windthorst, "Staatshaftungsrecht", *JuS* 1995, 791 and *JuS* 1996, 894.

(c) The remaining provisions of the Code

In an introductory book such as this, the remaining provisions of the Code need not concern us for long. Thus, §§ 827, 828 BGB deal with cases of infliction of damage by persons of diminished responsibility—in the case of the former paragraph because of mental disturbance preventing the free exercise of the will, in the case of the latter paragraph because of youth. Under certain circumstances, no liability will be imposed for harm thus caused, though another person may be made liable for such loss, for example, under § 832 BGB (parents or legal guardians).

§ 828 II BGB stipulates that a person who has completed his seventh but not his eighteenth year is not responsible for any damage which he does to another if, at the time of committing the damaging act, he did not have the understanding necessary for realizing his responsibility. This provision governs also the question of whether the youngster was contributory negligent. But if such a person does realize what he is doing, he may be held liable for the consequences of his behaviour. The imposition of unlimited liability under § 828 II BGB has, in such circumstances, been repeatedly criticised—especially in the context of liability for traffic accidents. (See Bollweg *NZV* 2000, 185, 186 with references). The main argument for reform stems from the insight that children below that age are typically not capable of coping adequately with the demands of everyday traffic even though they have in principle the understanding for realising the fatal consequences of a traffic accident. For instance, they are less able to estimate distances; infants of that age are impulsive, less concentrated and tend to follow the movement of groups. Thus, imposing unlimited liability may violate the infant's personality rights (Article 2 I and 1 I GG). In a decision of 13 August 1998 the BVerfG (*NJW* 1998, 3557) expressed doubts as to whether the unlimited liability of infants according to § 828 II BGB was in conformity with the Constitution but entrusted the task of finding a satisfactory solution to the courts. (See Rolfs, *JZ* 1999, 233 for an overview of how the problem could be solved *de lege lata*—e.g. by regarding the victim's claim against the minor as being contrary to § 242 BGB "good faith", *cf.* Canaris, *JZ* 1987, 993, 1001. An alternative solution would be to restrict the subrogation rights (§ 116 SGB X) of the social security carrier. Under § 76 II Nr. 3 SGB IV such rights may not be enforced if it was not equitable to do so.) However, the details of this development need not detain us here, for the above-mentioned concerns have now been acknowledged in a recent reform proposal which increases the threshold of liability of youngsters for causing traffic accidents to 10 years. (*2. Gesetz zur Änderung schadensrechtlicher Vorschriften*; a translation of the envisaged changes is provided at pp. 21 and 820.) Alternatively, § 829 BGB may be relied upon in order to make the innocent tortfeasor pay the equally innocent victim equitable compensation. Thus, § 829 BGB becomes a central provision for the liability of infants under the age of ten (as was explained in chapter 3 section A 4, above).

§§ 830 and 840 BGB deal with the important practical problems raised by torts committed by several persons, their liability to the victim and their rights and duties against each other.

The first of these paragraphs deals expressly with the problem of joint tortfeasors. This is the case where the parties commit a breach of a joint duty or act in pursuance of a common design. If this element of common design is satisfied it is irrelevant how significant is the contribution of each party in causal terms. Even mental participation in the form of helping out with the planning of the act or merely providing friendly support will suffice. § 830 II BGB treats instigators and accomplices in the same way.

§ 830 I, second sentence, applies the same rule to a different situation where several persons participate in a course of conduct which, though not unlawful in itself, is potentially dangerous to others. The difference between this and the previous situation lies in the fact that whereas in the former case of joint tortfeasors the loss is caused by several persons acting in consort, in the latter case only one person has caused the loss but it is difficult if not impossible to say which one has done so. (The classic illustration is that of the huntsmen who discharge their guns simultaneously and the pellets from one unidentifiable gun hit an innocent passer-by.) In this case, as well, § 830 BGB adopts the same rule and makes all the participants liable to the victim for the full extent of damage.

The problem of several concurrent tortfeasors (*Nebentäterschaft*) does not receive express treatment by the Code but in principle there is little doubt as to how it should be dealt with. In the absence of specific proof showing what damage each tortfeasor caused, the courts will apply the rules stated above and hold them all responsible for the full amount.

§ 840 BGB deals with the status of joint debtors and their internal claims for adjustment. Joint debts will arise in many ways: the tortfeasors may be joint tortfeasors, they may be several concurrent tortfeasors, or they may have participated in a dangerous activity as described in the previous paragraph. Alternatively, the joint debt may arise because of a master–servant relationship (§ 831 BGB) or because one debtor is the owner of an animal (§ 833 BGB) that has caused damage and the other is its custodian (§ 834 BGB). The possessor of a building may also be liable along with a former possessor or a constructor (§ 836 BGB) and the owner of a vehicle may be liable under the Road Traffic Act along with the driver who may be liable under § 823 I BGB (though in this case the first debtor's liability will be subject to the statutory maxima provided by the Road Traffic Act). All of these persons will be liable to the victim for the full amount of his loss. As between themselves, § 426 I BGB envisages equal contributions unless otherwise provided. §§ 840 I and II and 841 BGB do, in fact, specify certain exceptions. (The text of these provisions is set out in chapter 1, section 3, above; and for a fuller discussion of these issues the reader must consult more specialised works. Larenz I, § 37, II; II, § 74 gives further references. For interesting causative explanations of these solutions see Honoré in *International Encyclopedia of Comparative Law* XI, chapter 7 *passim*. For discussions in German see: Bodewig, "Probleme alternativer Kausalität bei Massenschäden", *AcP* 185 (1985) 505; Brambring, *Mittäter, Nebentäter, Beteiligte und die Verteilung des Schadens bei Mitverschulden des Geschädigten* (1973); Brehm, "Zur Haftung bei alternativer Kausalität", *JZ* 1980, 585; Eberl-Borges, "§ 830 BGB und die Gefährdungshaftung", *AcP* 196 (1996), 491; Ries, "Zur Haftung des Nebentäters nach § 830 und § 840 BGB", *AcP* 177 (1977), 543; Weckerle, *Die deliktische Verantwortung Mehrerer* (1974).)

3. COMPENSATION AND SATISFACTION

Select bibliography

Berger, "Abkehr von der konkreten Schadensberechnung?", *VersR* 1985, 403; Däubler, "Sachen und Menschen im Schadensrecht", *NJW* 1999, 1611; Ebel, "Schadensersatz bei Personenschäden (§§ 844–6 BGB)", *Jura* 1985, 561; Flessner, "Geldersatz für Gebrauchsentgang", *JZ* 1987, 271; Gro, "Die Entwicklung der höchstrichterlichen Rechtsprechung im Haftungs- und Schadensrecht", *VersR* 1996, 657; Grunsky, "Neue höchstrichterliche Rechtsprechung zum Schadensersatzrecht", *JZ* 1986, 170; idem, *Aktuelle Probleme zum Begriff des Vermögensschadens* (1968); idem, "Neue höchstrichterliche Rechtsprechung zum Schadenersatzrecht", *JZ* 1983, 372; Lange, *Schadensersatz* (2nd edn. 1990); E. Lorenz, *Immaterieller Schaden und "billige Entschädigung in Geld", Eine Untersuchung auf der Grundlage des § 847 BGB* (1981); Lipp, "Der Ausgleich des Integritätsinteresses im KFZ-Schadensrecht", *NZV* 1996, 7; Looschelders, *Die Mitverantwortlichkeit des Geschädigten im Privatrecht* (1999); Medicus, "Naturalrestitution und Geldersatz", *JuS* 1969, 449; idem, "Schadensersatz und Billigkeit", *VersR* 1981, 593; Mertens, *Der Begriff des Vermögensschadens im bürgerlichen Recht* (1967); Schiemann, *Argumente und Prinzipien bei der Fortbildung des Schadenrechts* (1981); Stürner, "Der Erwerbsschaden und seine Ersatzfähigkeit", *JZ* 1984, 412–16, 461–8; Thüsing, "Das Schadensrecht zwischen Beständigkeit und Wandel", *ZRP* 2000, 126; Wussow/Küppersbusch, *Ersatzansprüche bei Personenschäden* (5th edn., 1990). For comparative analysis see Fleming, "Damages or Rent" 19 *Univ. of Toronto L. Jour.* 295 (1969) and McGregor and Stoll in vol. IX, chs. 9 and 8 respectively of the *International Encyclopedia of Comparative Law.*

(a) Preliminary observations

The concluding section of this chapter deals with the scope and extent of remedial relief that a victim of a proved tort may claim from his tortfeasor. Clearly, the two main issues that have to be discussed here are compensation for personal injury and for damage to property. For reasons of space, injunctive relief and self-help will not be discussed in this book even though in some cases it may provide the most appropriate remedy as far as a particular plaintiff is concerned. Before this is done, however, it is advisable to make a few preliminary observations.

The first thing to notice is that for the traditional Common law everything that pertained to the notions of damage and damages was within the province of the jury and not the judge. As a result, for much of its history the Common law was weak in the elaboration of legal principles; indeed, at times one could have been forgiven to think that they were non-existent. Interestingly enough the same can still be said of French law which gives great powers to the trier of fact (under the rubric *pouvoir souverain du juge*), does not oblige him to give reasons for his assessment of the damage award, and gives restricted possibilities to the *Cour de Cassation* to intervene and correct an award, or establish visible principles of adjudication.

The above statement must now be qualified as far as the English Common law is concerned. The abolition of juries in personal injuries cases may be a comparatively recent phenomenon. (It was decided by the full Court of Appeal in *Ward* v. *James* [1966] 1 QB 273; see especially Lord Denning's reasons at 299–300). Remarkably however, in the thirty five years that have elapsed since this important decision was handed down, a clear body of legal principle has emerged, making the comparison with German law easier than it would have been in days gone by. Indeed, in the pages that follow, the presentation of German law has, once again, been accompanied by frequent excursus into English Common law in order to show how a different history and a different methodological approach have, yet again, failed to produce significant differences in outcome. Indeed, in many respects the similarities between the two systems is quite remarkable; and if a contrast is to be drawn it should with the French law which, to English eyes and for the reasons already given, may even appear to be shrouded in mystery. Overall, one must also note that the levels of compensation are quite similar in both England and Germany.

However, we must immediately stress how very different is the methodological approach adopted by the two systems. German law, a creation of the universities and the product of a constant move towards abstraction and systematisation, immediately reveals these features in its law of damages. For it is these characteristics that account for the reduction of the vast English casuistry into a mere handful of Articles: §§ 842–7 BGB dealing with personal injury; §§ 848–51 BGB dealing with damage to property. However, provisions dealing directly or indirectly with compensation can also be found in the various strict liability statutes. Such are, for instances, the rules found in the Strict Liability Act §§ 5–10; Road Traffic Act §§ 9–13; Air Traffic Act §§ 35–8, 46–51, etc. (Incidentally, one should note that though §§ 842, 843 BGB are in the tort section of the Code, many authors believe that they contain rules of general application and that they are, therefore, also relevant to the law of contract.) And it is the tendency to be ruthlessly systematic and logical that accounts for the fact that the provisions that crucially supplement the above-mentioned Articles of the Code are to be found in the general part of the law of obligations and not in the tort section of the BGB. Thus § 249 BGB states that a person who is obliged to make compensation must restore the situation which would have existed if the circumstances, which render him liable to make amends had not occurred. This provision is to be found in the general part of the law of obligations quite simply because an obligation to pay compensation can arise from breach of contract and/or the commission of a tort. German authors thus apply it directly to tort situations. The second point that must be stressed, therefore, is that once again the Common lawyer must be prepared to find the guiding principles in different parts of the Code. Learning how to jump over these hurdles of classification will resolve much of the apparent difficulty of finding the law in the foreign codes.

A rule that must satisfy both contract and tort inevitably must be widely phrased and abstract. Abstract generalisations may be good for codes. Without more, however, they will be of little use to practitioners. Often they must be transformed into concrete rules of thumb, especially if out-of-court settlements are to be encouraged. Theory must yield to the demands of practice and the codal bones must acquire flesh and muscle before they can function properly. Indeed, the regulation of compensation by the Code hardly does justice to the subject (though, on the other hand, it is infinitely more detailed than the French civil code, which is entirely silent on this as so many other crucial matters. Unjustified enrichment is one example; the rules of formation of contract is another.). This is where the courts come into the picture and it is through their work that the comparative lawyer can start to perceive the real similarities that the abstract apparatus of the Code tends to obscure. Once again the understanding of foreign law is enhanced if it is studied through its case law.

Another area in which the two systems come closer together is where "satisfaction"— a notion taken over from Swiss law but given a different meaning in German law—takes over from "compensation" and the court is instructed by the legislator to weigh all the surrounding circumstances when deciding the level of the award. In those cases, as we shall note later on, insurance considerations at last come to the surface of the German judgments, giving a greater sense of reality to what the judges are really trying to achieve.

The same is true of wider considerations of "equity" or fairness, which are sometimes very obviously taken into account but in most cases tend to be concealed. An excellent example of the former can be found in a decision of the Bundesgerichtshof of 22 June 1993 (MDR 1993, 847). For the decision there, handed down in the aftermath of German re-unification, stated that the calculation of damages had to start by taking into account the practice in the (former) East Germany. But the figure thus reached (for pain and suffering) should then be adjusted upwards to take into account the differing economic realities that had followed re-unification and, in many cases, caused much hardship to the population of the former DDR. Thus, even the judicial literature—traditionally sombre and concept-orientated—can reveal a refreshing interest in the problems of real people and real life. Its famous and earlier attempts to flesh out the famous good faith provision of the Civil Code (§ 242 BGB) has given it, of course, good training!

The third point that must be made absolutely clear is that the advent of social security has dramatically affected the function and purpose of the rules concerning compensation. This is, of course, true in all systems; but it is particularly noticeable in Germany where these days social security covers most of victims' needs and then takes over the tort actions against their tortfeasors. (§ 116 Sozialgesetzbuch Book X.) At this point it is important to stress three points. First, the breadth of this subrogation mechanism is manifest from the range of entities that it covers. Thus, for instance, the statutory health insurance scheme, the retirement pension scheme, and the accidents at work insurance scheme will all, automatically, be subrogated to these claims. Secondly, the reader must realise that this subrogation occurs at the moment of the accident and results in the victim automatically and immediately loosing all control over the claim (or parts of the claim) which he may have. Finally, it might be worth clarifying the fact that we are here talking only of claims for material losses in cases of personal injury. Incidentally, the typical feminine designation of the plaintiff—*die Klägerin*—which usually refers to either *die Kasse* (the social security carrier) or *die Gesellschaft* (the private insurance company), underscores the fact that the bulk of the personal injury litigation is these days undertaken by these two types of subrogees. Or, to put it differently, those who nowadays pay in tort cases are "innocent absentees" namely, social security carriers, insurers and employers. In such circumstances, compensation of the victim can no longer be the prime purpose of the tort rules (even though German judges and jurists, inordinately it would appear, enjoy stressing this function). Rather, seen from a distance, they have come to form a part of the intricate complex of rules, which help allocate risks or, in some cases, seek to promote deterrence. To put it differently, the tort action, when it is taken over by the social security carrier or the insurer, helps to put the cost of accident back on the shoulders of the wrongdoer (or his insurer). Of course, if allocation of risks and costs is nowadays a prime purpose of tort law one should perhaps discuss at the liability phase of the enquiry which of the two parties is in a better position to carry the risk or channel the loss. But with few exceptions, such an open economic approach to tort law does not figure in German tort books; nor is it greatly favoured by the courts. American ideas tend to reach Europe with a jetlag of about twenty years or more. In practice, therefore, actions by injured victims against their wrongdoers only take place whenever the social insurance scheme has not fully covered the actual loss.

Be that as it may, the fact remains that modern tort law has been forced to take into account the fact that its rules are no longer the only ones that determine compensation for loss. The need to regulate the interrelationship between all these disparate rules of compensation has thus arisen in Germany as it has elsewhere. This topic should and has been approached with one guiding principle in mind: the tort victim must be indemnified for his loss but he must not make a profit out of it (e.g. Kötz/Wagner, *Deliktsrecht*, no. 508 *et seq.*). In this respect German law is different from American law since, on the whole, the latter appears to take a very generous view about cumulation of different benefits partially, no doubt, because a substantial part of the award goes towards financing the costs of tort litigation. Though this "background" difference (between English and American law) may thus seriously affect the operation of tort law in practice, it seems rarely to be openly acknowledged. There does, however, exist the occasional, frank judicial admission which makes such an idea plausible and thereby underscores the need to study legal rules within their wider political and socio-legal context in which they operate. In *Helfend v. Southern California Rapid Transit Dist.* (2 Cal. 3d 1, 465 P. 2d 61 (1970)) the Supreme Court of California did just that. It thus argued that: "Generally the jury is not informed that plaintiff's attorney will receive a large portion of the plaintiff's recovery in contingent fees or that personal injury damages are not taxable to the plaintiff and are normally deductible by the defendant. Hence [the plaintiff] rarely actually receives full compensation for his injuries as computed by the jury. The collateral source rule partially serves to compensate for the attorney's share and does not actually render 'double recovery' for the plaintiff."

The general approach of German law is, in this respect, much closer to English law than it is to American law. Historically, however, there were also differences as to how one should avoid double compensation. Thus, originally, English law provided that in the case of certain benefits there should be a partial deduction from damages for personal injury, amounting to half the social security payments made to the plaintiff up to a maximum period of five years from the cause of action. Benefits both paid and likely to be paid after the judgment were deductible, but in calculating future benefit entitlement, no account was taken of likely increases in the levels of payment. The courts read the Act as implying that beyond the five-year period, no deduction was to be made in respect of the specified benefits. (S. 2(1) of the Law Reform (Personal Security) Act 1948). This rule was widely criticised, partially on the ground that it "subsidised" tortfeasors and, eventually, it was replaced by the Social Security Act 1989 which, in s. 22, changed the law by introducing a scheme of state "recoupment" of social security benefits from damages awards above a statutory threshold set initially at £2,500. All the significant benefits which are concerned with income replacement and with the expenses of accident victims are included in the scheme. The court must now disregard these specified benefits when making its assessment of damages. However, the tortfeasor must then pay to the Department of Social Security the full amount of any of the benefits, which the plaintiff has received in respect of his injury or accident. The Department of Social Security is not formally subrogated to the plaintiff's claim (as in German law) but the effect is very similar. Thus, the tortfeasor must now pay in full but, as a result of these reforms, the plaintiff is worse off than he was under the old regime as a complete reduction of benefits is made. This scheme applies to accidents and injuries occurring after 1 January 1989.

As already suggested, this is not the German approach. Here, the entity (social security, insurance) that has compensated the victim will be subrogated to his tort action and will be able to claim from the tortfeasor the full amount that it has paid to the victim. According to the German Insurance Act (*Versicherungsvertragsgesetz*) of 1908 the same, broadly speaking, is true of payments made by a private insurer. The position more precisely is as follows. In respect of certain types of insurance contracts (e.g. loss insurance but *not* personal injury insurance), the rights of the insured are *ex lege* transferred to the insurer to the extent that he has indemnified the latter (§ 67 I 1 VVG). In other types of insurance contracts, however, e.g. medical costs insurance, only "conventional" subrogation is envisaged, i.e. the right of subrogation depends upon the insured having contractually conferred on the insurer a legal right to take over his claim. In this latter case the victim will thus have to cede to the insurer his right of action against the tortfeasor and will not be entitled to cumulate the insurance benefit and the tort damages. The point is widely accepted as just, though one could argue against it that the insurance money is the product of the victim's own thrift and foresight and that it is bad policy to take it away from him. (For further details Kötz/Wagner, nos. 507–12.)

The last preliminary point that has to be made is that the plaintiff's damages will be reduced (and in some circumstances even completely wiped out) in order to take into account his contributory fault. The term "contributory fault" is here used instead of the more familiar Common law term "contributory negligence" not only because it is the one employed by German (and, incidentally, French) law; but also because it is wider than the Common law term in at least two respects. For in the first place contributory fault includes intentional as well as negligent conduct. Secondly and, perhaps, more importantly it includes the conduct of the injured party/plaintiff *after* the occurrence of the initial harm as well as *before* it. However, though the German Code distinguishes the fault of the injured party that positively contributes to his harm and his failure to minimise it once it has happened, it subjects both these types of contributory fault to the same rules.

In the matter of contributory fault, German law departed from the old Roman law rule (also found in pre-1945 English Common law and still accepted by those American jurisdictions that have not introduced the notion of comparative negligence). This rule, as is well known, decreed that the injured party could not recover if his injury was due to his own fault unless the tortfeasor's conduct was intentional. Instead, § 254 I BGB states that "if any fault of the injured party has contributed to the occurrence of the damage, the duty to compensate and the extent of the compensation to be made depend upon the circumstances, especially upon how far the injury has been caused predominantly by the one or the other party". In this respect the German approach could be termed to be more "modern" than that of traditional Common law; but German law has not taken the next step to ignore altogether the fault of the victim. This, it has been noted, has already happened in French law in the context of traffic accidents; and according to the view of some German authors it should also be introduced in German law, especially in the context of injuries caused on the roads. For there appears to be hardly a traffic accident case which in theory should be dealt with expeditiously under the strict liability of the Road Traffic Act but which in practice does not become a prolonged and convoluted affair because the defendant raises the plaintiff's contributory fault. Nonetheless, a move towards the modern French solution has not been made, largely because of feared consequences on the levels of insurance premiums.

When then is there such contributory fault? In Common law there has been some discussion as to whether negligence in the defendant is the same thing as negligence in the plaintiff. The answer is negative since in the former but not the latter case a breach of a duty has to be proved. Likewise, in Germany it has been debated whether fault in the context of § 254 BGB has the same meaning as it has in §§ 823, 276 BGB—the better view being that a negative answer is appropriate since the notion of unlawfulness is relevant only in the latter instance. (See Kötz/Wagner, nos. 552–3.)

The answer to the question when is there fault on the part of the victim depends on the facts of each case. Certain factual situations, however, have come almost automatically to indicate that there is fault on the part of the plaintiff/victim. So, for example, a *motor cyclist* who does not wear a crash helmet will be deemed to be at fault (BGH NJW 1965, 1075) and the same rule applies to mopeds (BGH NJW 1979, 980). But an injured *cyclist* is not guilty of contributory fault if he is not wearing a helmet (BGH NJW 1979, 980). The occupants of a vehicle will also be contributorily negligent if their injury can be partly attributed to not wearing safety belts. (BGH VersR 1979, 536; BGHZ 74, 25.) Nor will a passenger who had not fastened his seat belt have his damages reduced if he can show that his injuries would have occurred even if he had secured his seat belt (BGH NJW 1980, 2125 and *cf. Froom* v. *Butcher* [1976] QB 286). Incidentally, the wearing of seat-belts became compulsory in German law in 1976 (new § 21*a* of the Road Traffic Ordinance (Straßenverkehrs-Ordnung = StVO).

The vast majority of illustrations of contributory fault comes from traffic accident cases but one group of cases which is not always connected with accidents arising from cars deals with incidents involving infants. The case-law is clear that an infant's contributory fault will be taken into account only if he was capable of committing fault in accordance with § 828 II BGB and had acted culpably in the sense of § 276 BGB. § 828 II BGB adopts a rather arbitrary test by providing that "A person who has completed his seventh year but not his eighteenth year of age is not responsible for any damage which he does to another if, at the time of committing the damaging act, he did not have the understanding necessary for realising his responsibility . . .". Academics, on the other hand (e.g. Esser/Schmidt, *Schuldrecht* I, 36), are not so categorical, some arguing that the infant's contributory negligence should be counted against him even where he was incapable of recognizing the danger to himself, while others maintain that policy reasons require that it should be ignored. Recent reform proposals restrict the infant's liability in the context of traffic accidents. See Section 2(c) for details.

Contributory fault may, as has already been stated, arise after the damaging occurrence and will consist in the victim's own failure to mitigate his loss (§ 254 II BGB). Thus, if the plaintiff's vehicle is damaged in an accident and can be repaired he will, normally, have the right to have it repaired at the defendant's expense. But what if the cost of repair significantly exceeds the cost of replacement of the car with another one of approximately the same value? In such cases the plaintiff will be obliged to mitigate his loss and opt for the lower cost of replacement (*cf. Darbishire* v. *Warran* [1963] 1 WLR 1067, which reached the same result and with the same reasoning). Difficulties, however, can arise when the destroyed item is unique and the question how the replacement value will be calculated can also raise nice problems (on which see Kötz, "Die Abwicklung des Kraftfahrzeug-Totalschadens" in *Festschrift Hauss* (1978) 181).

The same duty to mitigate the loss arises in personal injury cases so that, for example, an injured person must where reasonable obtain medical treatment as soon as possible (RGZ 139, 131, 136). This means that he should submit himself to any reasonable operation that could help restore his health (RGZ 129, 398; OLG Oldenburg NJW 1978, 1200). (For further references Stürner, "Der Erwerbsschaden und seine Ersatzfähigkeit" *JZ* 1984, 412 ff. and 461 ff.) What of course is reasonable depends on a variety of factors and will, ultimately, be a question of fact. (BGH 13 May 1953, BGHZ 10, 18.) These facts will include such things as the age of the person injured, the degree of danger involved in the operation, the chances of acquiring alternative employment after the operation (which may depend on the condition of the labour market), and so on. (See, RGZ 129,

398; *cf.* also OLG Oldenburg NJW 1978, 1200). Equally, the injured person must mitigate his loss by seeking alternative employment, which if necessary may even mean changing his profession (BGHZ 10, 18 though this again may raise nice problems). Alternatively, the plaintiff may have to take part in a retraining scheme, naturally at the defendant's expense (RGZ 160, 119; BGHZ 10, 18); and, in another case (BGH VersR 1971, 82) it was said that a self-employed individual may have to employ an assistant rather than give up his business altogether. The similarities here with Common law are such that they need not be laboured any further. On the whole one can match English and German cases fairly neatly.

(b) Personal injury (pecuniary losses)

Personal injury can cause primary and consequential loss. The first term is taken to refer to such items as medical expenses incurred as a result of the injury and compensation for the injury itself (loss of an arm, eye, etc.). On the other hand, the second heading would include future loss of earnings and expenditure incurred as a result of further deterioration in the health of the victim flowing from the accident itself, e.g. subsequent development of epilepsy as a result of severe cranial injuries. This distinction between primary and consequential loss, with its strong causal undertones, is made both in cases of personal injury and damage to property and is usually adopted by textbook writers. Here, however, we shall adopt the English distinction between pecuniary and non-pecuniary losses, partly because it appears to be neater but mainly because it will help in the comparative presentation of the German law. (Another set of terms that might be appropriate is material and non-material harm.) It should also be noted that the following remarks apply equally to claims based on the tort law provisions in the BGB as well as to those based on the provisions of special statutes of strict liability. The technique used in the latter case is one of special provisions and partial cross-referencing linking these statutes to the paragraphs of the BGB on damages. (For instance, see sections 10–13 of the Road Traffic Act). With regard to pecuniary losses, the most important deviation from the general rules of the BGB is found in the imposition of monetary maxima in most cases of strict liability. (For instance, section 12 of the Road Traffic Act and the earlier discussion contained in chapter three.)

When the injured party's loss is pecuniary, i.e. it can be estimated in money terms, then the guiding principle is that of *restitutio in integrum.* This is true of English law (*Livingstone* v. *Rawyards Coal Co.* (1880) 5 App. Cas. 25, 39 per Lord Blackburn) as it is of German law. § 249 sentence 1 BGB expressly authorises the restoration of the position in which the plaintiff would have been in had the injury not occurred, which in personal injury cases means ordering the defendant to meet the plaintiff's costs (see § 249 sentence 2 BGB). It follows that all *reasonably* incurred medical expenses, including such items as hospitalisation, nursing, physiotherapy, radiotherapy, post-operative convalescence, the acquisition of special, e.g. orthopaedic aids, cosmetic surgery etc., will be met by the tortfeasor or, more likely, his insurer etc. (Once again, the position is identical in England: see Markesinis and Deakin, *Tort Law,* 710 *et seq.*) The cost of private medical care may also be claimable if reasonably incurred and is usually claimed and awarded in the more serious types of injury where long and costly treatment or convalescence is necessary (see BGH VersR 1964, 257). In England failure to use the facilities of the National Health Service will not affect the reasonableness of the plaintiff's expenses which will thus be claimable (see *Harris* v. *Brights Asphalt Contractors Ltd.* [1953] 1 QB 617, 635 per Slade J).

In German law medical expenses cannot be claimed if they have not been actually incurred or, at the very least, it can be shown that the plaintiff does not intend to use the money for medical treatment. (14 January 1986, BGHZ 97, 14, case 142.) Prior to this decision, courts had, occasionally, awarded damages for personal injury even though the plaintiff did not intend to spend the money for the required treatment. (For instance, OLG Celle VersR 1972, 468; OLG Stuttgart VersR 1978, 188.) This attitude is dictated by § 253 BGB which excludes, as a general rule, recovery of damages for non-pecuniary losses. If the plaintiff does not use the damages, for instance in order to have cosmetic surgery, but pockets the award, it is argued that he would be in effect receiving compensation for a non-pecuniary loss. However, as we shall see below (section 3 (f)) the rule is different with regard to damage to property; and the most recent case provides plausible (but not overwhelming) reasons for maintaining such a distinction. Some questions, however, still remain unanswered. For instance, what happens if the plaintiff subsequently changes his mind and simply puts the money into his pocket? (Cf. Zeuner, JZ 1986, 640, 641.)

Further limits may be placed by § 242 BGB (good faith) and § 251 II BGB (the cost of the treatment must not be disproportionate). § 251 II BGB provides for monetary compensation if the cost of curing the defect is disproportionate. This presents formidable difficulties in cases of personal injury and in particular where the cost of cosmetic surgery is claimed. For apart from the cost of actually restoring the plaintiff's health, his interest is non-pecuniary. Because of the human dignity one cannot resort to a diminution "in value" measure. At the same time in some extreme cases there may be reasons for rejecting claims for cost of medical treatment for personal injury. The BGH ingeniously solved this problem by relying on § 242 BGB ("good faith") and thus bridged the gap in the Code. On this basis, the BGH, in a decision rendered on 3 December 1974 (BGHZ 63, 295), denied the plaintiff's claim for DM 2,590 requested in order to pay for an operation to remove a 2,5 cm scar located next to his right ear. The BGH stressed that reasonableness depends on the circumstances of each case. Accordingly, a balancing operation had to be undertaken and it would weigh the severity of the injury, the scale of the claimed cost, and the motives of the plaintiff. The court reaffirmed that as a general rule cost of purely cosmetic surgery could be recovered as part of the restoration owed by the defendant under § 249 BGB. But the BGH also accepted the Court of Appeal's finding that awarding compensation would be unreasonable in the present case. It seems that this was because the scar was regarded as insignificant and, in any event, hardly visible and likely to disappear over time. Incidentally, we stress "it seems" for the facts are not fully and clearly stated—something which marks out German from Anglo-American cases which have to consider facts in detail if they are to perform the distinguishing function which is so central to the Common law process of deciding cases. Finally, the court also pointed out that the plaintiff was awarded a correspondingly higher amount of damages for pain and suffering. Hence, the court in effect arrived at a solution which is surprisingly close to § 251 II BGB. Where cost of reinstatement to the status quo ante appears unreasonable, the plaintiff may obtain some other monetary compensation, for instance in the form of an increased award of damages for pain and suffering.

Lost future earnings often form the largest item in the damages packet. According to the figures of insurance payments made in the context of traffic accidents for the year 1999, approximately one billion DM was paid under this heading. This must be compared to 300 million DM paid for the cost of medical treatment. The largest amount of money— 1.7 billion DM—was, however, reserved for compensating pain and suffering. (See Kötz/Wagner, no. 511).

As in English law, the purpose of the award is to put the plaintiff in the same position, financially, as if he had not been injured. Where future lost earnings are claimed the plaintiff is not restricted to restoration of the *status quo ante* but can ask to be put in the (hypothetical) position he would have been in but for the injury. *Therefore* in the calculation of lost future earnings increases in pay, promotions, and the like will be taken into account when deciding the amount of compensation. Where the victim is self-employed, his future prospects will have to be estimated as best as possible. But, in keeping with the pro-plaintiff predilection, some the courts have suggested that "the guessing process" should not be subjected to over rigorous proof at the expense of the plaintiff. (BGH 6 July 1993, MDR 1994, 43.) In any event, all loss of earnings will have to be compensated. (BGH 20 March 1984, VersR 1984, 639.) If the plaintiff/victim, has been forced to settle after his accident for a less well paid job, or has otherwise experienced a loss of gains, he will be allowed to claim these amounts. (BGH 22 February 1973, VersR 1973, 423.) Income from an illegal or immoral source, however, tends not to be taken into account (see, however, the controversial decision of BGHZ 67, 119 dealing with the income of an injured prostitute). Damages are not awarded (or are reduced) if the defendant can show that the injured party/plaintiff would have lost his income in any event, e.g. through an imminent dismissal (BGHZ 10, 6; BGH VersR 1963, 674—predisposition).

Not infrequently, relatives of the victim come to his assistance thereby incurring travelling expenses and often more serious loss of income (e.g. mother giving up her job to look after her injured child). German and English law are, in principle, at one on this by accepting that the victim may recover from the tortfeasor these expenses. (See BGH VersR 1961, 272; VersR 1964, 532 and *cf. Donnelly* v. *Joyce* [1974] QB 454, also BGH NJW 1989, 766; BGH VersR 1991, 559, and Seidel, "Der Ersatz von Besuchskosten im Schadensrecht", *VersR* 1991, 1319). However, a fair number of decisions also seem to take a harsher view on such claims whenever the visits cannot be genuinely linked to the condition of the victim (BGH NJW 1990, 1037; NJW 1991, 2340). Both systems also agree that if compensation is decreed for the victim it is then for him to decide whether he will reimburse these relatives with the sums he has recovered from the tortfeasor. Equally, however, in both systems attempts have been made to impose a *legal* obligation on the victim to reimburse the relatives who have come to his aid and thereby suffered loss. In Germany this could arguably be satisfied by having recourse to § 683 BGB (management without mandate) and in England by utilizing the trust mechanism (see *Cunningham* v. *Harrison* [1973] QB 942, 952 per Lord Denning MR). In both these systems, however, these attempts have met with little success in the courts. The intricacies of this topic come to full light in case 58 and are further discussed in the accompanying notes.

As was explained in the section dealing with "accidents at work" (chapter 3 section A 5(c) (ii)) in this area of the law social security system has almost completely replaced tort law. But even outside this special field, the victim's loss (including his lost earnings) are often met by some social security carrier or insurer who is then subrogated to the victim's tort action to the extent that he has indemnified him. It is clear, however, that the social security systems will provide a minimum coverage regardless whether the victim has a right to compensation against another person. Generally speaking, it is also immaterial whether the injury is caused by a "negligent" conduct of the injured itself (Bundessozialgericht NJW 1986, 1572). Thus, in these cases where the victim is entitled to social security services and payments, the purpose of tort law is, in effect, to determine whether the social security carrier can seek reimbursement from the tortfeasor or his insurance. (*Cf.* Kötz/Wagner, no. 510). In accordance with what was said earlier on, the right of the insurer is here provided by § 116 SGB X. Likewise in England social security benefits, as well as NHS costs of treatment of traffic accident victims, are generally recouped by the State. (*Cf.* R. Lewis *Deducting Benefits from Damages for Personal Injury* (1999) 127 ff., 223 ff.) If the social security carrier has only partially compensated the victim, the latter naturally retains his tort action for the difference. An obvious example is damages for pain and suffering).

The statutory health insurance system is the main social security system which is likely to offer relief to those suffering personal injury. The legal regime that governs these cases is set out in Book V of the *Sozialgesetzbuch*. In 1998 roughly 90 per cent of the population (then 82 million) had potential entitlements under this scheme while out of the remaining 10 per cent a further 7.3 million were privately insured. (Figures from Kötz/Wagner, no. 214.) Victims are entitled to all ambulance and hospital treatment that is necessary and also to the cost of appropriate medication (§ 27 SGB V). In other cases the victim's earning incapacity may be compensated under the retirement insurance scheme (*Rentenversicherung, Sozialgesetzbuch VI*) which applies to employees. (In 1999 44,9 million fell into this category in Germany. Kötz/Wagner no. 224.) If the employee has (totally or partially) lost his earning capacity and has paid premiums for a minimum period of five years he will be entitled to the payment of a rent (annuity) which will be calculated in the usual way. This will be on the basis of his income and the duration of the period during which he paid premiums (§§ 43, 67 SGB VI). German law, also *imposes a legal obligation* on employers to continue paying the wages or salaries of their injured employees for a period of six weeks (See § 3 of the *Entgeltfortzahlungsgesetz* (EFZG) of 1994 (BGBl. I 1014).) After this period has come to an end, the health service will take over and pay normally 70 per cent of the previous income for a further 78 weeks. (§ 47 SGB V). In such cases, therefore, the loss falls on the employer and not the injured employee so it should be the former who should have the right to take over the tort action to the extent that he has paid the victim/employee. This result has been accepted by the courts. (*Cf.* BGHZ 43, 378.) But it did not pass unquestioned by some writers, not least because the loss suffered by the employer (paying wages without receiving any services in exchange) is purely economic loss and, as we have seen, it is not covered by § 823 I BGB. For a time the above undoubtedly sensible result was explained by some arguing that the employee retained his independent action against the tortfeasor but implicitly assigned it to his employer. This "legal construction" means that in the event the tortfeasor is made to pay; the victim was not doubly compensated; and the employer was not left to carry the loss. (*Cf.* BGHZ 7, 30; 42, 76; 43, 378.) The problem, however, has been solved by the aforementioned EFZG of 1994 (§ 6) and the *cessio legis* envisaged by it. It should be noted that in English law *whenever* the employer is under a legal duty to continue paying the wages of the injured employee, the latter cannot claim them from the tortfeasor. (Since it would appear that the employer is equally unable to recover sums thus paid, the only one who stands to gain from such an arrangement is the tortfeasor.) But where the employer has made *ex gratia* payments, these will probably not be set off against the lost earnings (*Dennis* v. *London Passenger Transport Board* [1948] 1 All ER 779; *Cunningham* v. *Harrison* [1973] QB 942. Likewise in German law: RGZ 92, 57; BGHZ 10, 107). However, the BGH recently held that the payment of an early retirement pension made *by the employer* to a disabled employee had to be taken into account in assessing the loss of the victim. (BGH 7 November 2000, NJW 2001, 1274.) This seems at first sight difficult to reconcile with a line of cases where such socially motivated benefits were regarded as collateral benefits and were disregarded when assessing damages. Thus, as we have seen, sick-pay (whether paid by the employer during the first six weeks, or by the health service afterwards) is *res inter alios acta*. (BGHZ 90, 334; 139, 167.) This is also the case with disability pensions under the statutory pension scheme. (BGHZ 10, 107.) In the present case, however, the court stressed that the early retirement pension did not aim at compensating the victim for the consequences of the accident and therefore did not fulfil the function of providing care to victims of accidents. The rent had been granted primarily because the employee was 58 years old and not because of the accident. The policy behind the scheme was to relieve pressure from the labour market. Thus, to the extent that the employee received these payments, he did not suffer a loss of earnings. The practical effect of this is that the employer will not be able to recoup such payments made to the employee from the tortfeasor or his insurer. For if the employee does not have a right of action he cannot assign it to his employer.

In *Parry* v. *Cleaver* [1970] AC 1 a police constable was severely injured by a car driven negligently by the defendant. The plaintiff was entitled to a police pension on discharge for disablement. The House of Lords held that the police pension should be ignored in assessing the plaintiff's loss. It would be unjust that money spent by an injured person on premiums should enure to the benefit of a tortfeasor; and a contributory pension is a form of insurance as also the reward for pre-injury services (at 14, 16 per Lord Reid; at 42 per Lord Wilberforce). This ruling is more favourable to plaintiffs in these kind of cases and would appear to set the two systems apart. Nevertheless, the two legal systems may not be as far apart as they appear to be. For, in the final analysis, both look for the purpose of the payment when determining whether it ought to be taken into account. The object of the retirement pension in the recent BGH case was thus, arguably, of a special nature. (*Cf. Smoker* v. *London Fire and Civil Defence Authority* [1991] 2 AC 502.)

Finally, it should be noted that private accident insurance also plays an increasing role in the compensation of accidents. Professor Kötz has thus estimated that in 1999 40 per cent of the population older than 14 years had a private accident insurance which provides additional coverage of the risk of earning incapacity (*op. cit.* no. 222).

Up to this point the presentation of German law will have caused no difficulties to the Common (especially English) lawyer. When we move, however, to the form of the award and the method of its calculation, some important differences of approach become obvious. Surprisingly, however, once again they seem to be attenuated in practice. The source of the difference lies in the attitude any given system is prepared to take towards lump sum awards and periodical payments. Of course, whenever a debate about this issue takes place one must remember that it refers to the form the compensation will take for *future economic* loss. For no system objects to capitalising earnings lost up to the time of the judgment. And the same is true for sums awarded to "compensate" for pain and suffering—the relevant paragraph of the BGB (§ 847 BGB) being silent on this point. The dispute as to the form the payments should take is thus limited to such items as loss of future earnings, future medical expenses, and in the case of wrongful death loss of future support.

The question "what form should these payments take?" can receive four possible answers. At the one extreme one finds Common law systems with their unequivocal preference for lump sum awards. The task of the court in assessing damages for personal injuries is to arrive at a lump sum which represents as nearly as possible full compensation for the injury which the plaintiff has suffered. However, by Section 2(1) of the Damages Act 1996, a court may make an order for the whole or part of the damages to take the form of periodical payments, provided the parties agree to this. (For American law an illustration can be found in *Slater* v. *Mexican Nat'l RR Co.* 194 US 120, 24 S. Ct.

581 (1904).) At the other end of the spectrum one could find in the past certain socialist systems which only allowed periodical payments or annuities, as they were most commonly called. (Rudden, *Soviet Insurance Law* (1966), chapter 7; *idem*, "Soviet Tort Law" 42 *NYUL Rev.* 583, 609 ff. (1967).) In between lie the vast majority of legal systems, though their approach can be further divided into two categories: the first includes those systems which are, technically speaking, neutral as to what form the award will take, accepting that either lump sums or periodical payments are perfectly acceptable. (France and Switzerland belong to this category.) The systems that belong to the second group, in which we find German law, accept that awards can take either form but expressly state their preference for periodical payments. §§ 843 I BGB and 844 II BGB state this preference in unequivocal terms. (According to §§ 843 II and 760 BGB annuities are paid three months in advance (but monthly annuities are commonly *agreed*). The duration of the annuity will be estimated at the time of the judgment on the basis of his estimated earning years but for the accident: BGH 10 October 1987, VersR 1988, 464.) The only exception to the annuity rule is provided by § 843 III BGB where it is stated that a capital sum can be allowed instead of a periodical payment only if "a serious reason" exists (*ein wichtiger Grund*). Many events or things may amount to a sufficiently "serious reason" to by-pass the rule. Thus, accident neurosis has for a long time been recognised as a sufficient ground for granting a capital sum. (RGZ 73, 418, 420; 136, 373.) The danger of the defendant going bankrupt would also constitute a serious reason: OLG Stuttgart OLGE 2, 440, 441. The victim's wish to use his compensation award to start a new professional life has also been accepted as a good reason for awarding a lump sum (RG JW 1933, 840). So has the fact that the person paying the compensation normally resides abroad or changes his residence permanently, making the collection of the annuity hazardous or difficult. (OLG Nürnberg FamRZ 1968, 476, 478. See also RGZ 93, 209, 210 and Palandt, § 843 BGB, no. 21.) According to Larenz/ Canaris, II 2, p. 587, the cost of retraining for a new job in order to pursue gainful employment after the injury would also justify the demand of a lump sum. But the fact that both parties wish to have the payment take the form of a lump sum is not, in itself, a "good reason" for the judge to make such an award (though if they agree to this extra judicially, the judge will give effect to such an agreement).

This different approach taken by the two systems to the question of how the damages will be paid calls for a number of observations.

The first is to invite the reader to examine the merits and demerits of the lump sum versus the periodical payments method of compensation and consider whether in the light of comparative observations the controversy can be seen in a different light. (For an excellent study see J Fleming, "Damages or Rent" 19 *UTLJ* 295–325 (1969).) Such a comparative approach can reveal that some of the disadvantages of the periodical payments system of compensation (which are correspondingly treated as advantages of the lump-sum method) can effectively be countered in practice. For example, the alleged disadvantage of the annuity system that it can expose the plaintiff to the danger of the defendant going bankrupt can be countered by the fact that defendants nowadays tend to be insurance companies (which, in theory, are less likely to go bankrupt than ordinary individuals). The risk can further be diminished by the courts' power to order defendants to provide adequate security to ensure the continued payment of the award. § 843 II BGB expressly gives this discretionary power to the court, though it is generally taken not to confer upon the plaintiff a right to demand that he be provided with such a security. (By contrast, the Swiss Code of Obligations makes the provision of security mandatory in such cases: Article 43 II CO). Another supposed disadvantage of the annuity system is that it requires defendants to set up complicated and time consuming mechanisms for the continued payments of awards. This, too, may be less convincing when one, again, realises that in most of these cases the typical defendants are insurers who are equipped to deal with the problems of periodical payments. The finality of the award is also widely regarded as the real virtue of the lump-sum method of compensation. In reality, however, it is also its great drawback, since it does not allow the court (or any other body) to correct errors in the forecasts that the judge has to make when fixing the lump sum. Thus, the medical condition of the plaintiff may get better or worse and thus prove the award too generous or inadequate. The same can happen with the plaintiff's employment prospects. In German law, courts view capital awards as settlements that cannot be revised because of subsequent change in circumstances. See, BGH 8 January 1981, BGHZ 79, 187 even though academic writers seem to dislike this view. But awards involving periodic payments can and are revisable. (See, for instance, BGH 20 December 1960, BGHZ 34, 110.)

These imponderables affect the English Common law method of calculation of future pecuniary losses. The multiplier and multiplicand method of compensation (described in detail in Markesinis and Deakin, *Tort Law*, 757 *et seq.*) allows the judges to reflect all these imponderables in their "rough-and-ready" calculations (recently made more precise by the House of Lords judgment in *Wells* v. *Wells* [1999] 1 AC 345.) Moreover, the Administration of Justice Act 1982 has provided a new mechanism which is limited to certain instances of personal injuries and which allows the court to abstain from this guessing game and make an award on the basis that the feared eventuality (deterioration of health of the victim) may not be realized. But if it is (for example the plaintiff's cranial injuries caused by the defendant lead many years later to the development of epilepsy), the plaintiff will be given the chance to return to the court and seek an upward adjustment of the award.

A further difficulty is that awarding a lump sum could lead to overcompensation since part of the money can be invested and earn interest. At the same time, it is clear that money will not retain a constant value. The solution adopted by the House of Lords is this. When assessing damages for anticipated future losses and expenses the court should fix the award by assuming that the plaintiffs will invest their damages in index-linked government stocks (*Wells* v. *Wells* [1999] 1 AC 345) and make a discount accordingly. The purpose of the discount is to eliminate the element of overcompensation that results from the damages reaching the plaintiff in one large sum and then being invested for him to produce income. The difficulty was that prior to *Wells* v. *Wells* the award was "discounted" by reference to the rate of financial return which one could expect from investing in equities—i.e. something in the order of 4–5 per cent per annum—instead of the lower yield but safer investment (in such stocks as Index Linked Government Securities) which were more appropriate to plaintiffs. Their Lordships decision, which led to an increase in the multipliers used and, correspondingly an increase in awards is, undoubtedly, going to have some impact on insurance premiums. But this was something that they were prepared to accept not only because it expressed their dislike for the earlier rough and ready way of selecting the multiplier. Additionally, they also decided to act because they felt that something had to be done for the fact that in modern times money was loosing its value and these kind of claimants needed better protection.

Almost exactly the same words were used by the BGH in its seminal judgement of BGHZ 79, 187 in which it held that in assessing the lump sum awarded under § 843 III BGB the courts must also take into account future developments. This should include a rise in wages even if this is necessarily uncertain and might cause an overall increase in insurance premiums. Hence, in German law where lump sums are awarded the annual income tends to be computed with a figure (capitalisation factor) arrived at in a manner not very dissimilar to the English method.

The German method of calculating the annuity is no less complicated. German judges, too, have to indulge in all sorts of calculations before they can reach a final figure for the annuity. Useful guidelines were laid down by the BGH in its decision of 8 January 1981 (BGHZ 79, 187). In this task the judges are greatly assisted by the traditional requirement that the plaintiff itemise his losses as precisely as possible, something which has led to an almost complete neglect of § 287 ZPO and the discretion it offers judges to estimate freely the amount of damages. But at least they do have the possibility of adjusting the amounts upwards or downwards so as to take into account changes in circumstances. (Incidentally, in French law an award can only be adjusted upwards.) And in one area at least, this different method of payment has altogether avoided a problem which has caused considerable difficulties to many Common law judges. The problem we are referring to is linked with the judge's duty to evaluate the chances of remarriage of a widow when assessing the size of the lost dependency. This unsavoury exercise led to the partial abolition of this duty in English Common law by the Law Reform (Miscellaneous Provisions) Act 1971 (now § 3 II of the Fatal Accidents Act 1976). Nowadays judges are thus not obliged to take into account the remarriage of the widow or her prospect of remarriage. But the duty to indulge in this exercise remains when the courts have to evaluate the chances of remarriage of a widower (claiming loss of economic support from his deceased wife). More importantly, this exercise still has to be attempted when calculating the loss of support of orphaned children (since if their mother remarries and the new father takes them into his home he assumes a legal obligation to maintain them). The old law was, as already stated, greatly resented by judges and feminist organisations; but the new solution, partly because of the inconsistencies mentioned above, and partly because it can lead to overcompensation, is also treated as an anomaly. German law, on the other hand, with its attachment to the periodical payment system, seems to have avoided this problem altogether as it has avoided another problem that occupied English courts in the 1970s, namely that of inflation.

The final observation that one may make is, perhaps, the most intriguing of all. For despite the differences of approach that have been described, and the apparent superiority of the rent system over the lump sum award, the Germans (and the French) whenever possible seem to opt for the lump sum method of payment. Thus Professor Fleming has estimated that in Germany 99 per cent of all compensated claims take the form of a lump sum award. Practice has in his words "dwarfed [the codal orthodoxy] into statistical insignificance". (Dr McGregor in his excellent chapter 9 of vol. XI of the *International Encyclopedia of Comparative Law*, 26 states that the same figure applies to French law, as well; see also Nehl's "Kapitalisierung von Schadensersatzrenten", *VersR* 1981, 407, 412.) It thus becomes essential to enquire first why practice has bypassed the codal solution and secondly the way this evasion has been accomplished given the clear contrary wording of the Code.

The deviation from the wording of the Code is clearly due to the fact that whatever the theoretical merits of the rent system, both plaintiffs and defendants prefer the lump sum award. In many cases the plaintiff will in fact not be the victim. The plaintiff in such cases is a social security carrier (exercising its right to subrogation) and the defendant will be the tortfeasor's insurer. For obvious practical considerations, both may have an interest in the award of a lump sum. (Kötz/Wagner, no. 534.) Such defendants (in practice insurance companies perfectly able to cope with the mechanics of periodical payments) are, understandably, anxious to "close their books"—something which only lump sum awards allows them to do. But there are other reasons why the plaintiffs may also prefer lump sums. Two can be mentioned here.

The first is because they are encouraged in this by their lawyers who know that any fees they may have negotiated with their clients (*additional* to those provided by statute *and paid by the losing party*) will be met more promptly and with less resentment by their client if they are taken out of a large lump sum award rather than from periodical payments. The second is due to the attractions offered by larger awards. This is particularly true in Germany where as we have seen the bulk of medical and other pecuniary losses will be paid by a social security carrier in the form of periodical payments. With his basic needs thus being met, it becomes particularly attractive to a plaintiff to receive the top slice of the future economic loss award (along with the compensation for pain and suffering) in the form of a large lump sum. For this will enable him to indulge in purchases etc. which before the accident may have been entirely outside his financial means.

As for the method of circumventing the wording of the Code this can be found in the practice of extra-judicial settlements which are encouraged or even "suggested" by the courts. In other words, once the liability issue has been determined, the lawyers and the court may encourage the parties to agree on a lump sum award and even "suggest" its level. As a result, in Professor Fleming's words (*op. cit.*, 299) "the lump sum settlements have like termites reduced the rent system to but a hollow shell".

This then is an area of the law of torts where the use of the comparative method can be profitably employed by both legal families (Common law and Civil law) since both could benefit from the study of each other's weaknesses and strengths. For example, would it not be preferable if each system (English, German) adopted a more flexible mixed system which would allow the parties (or, in the last resort, the court) to decide which method of payment was more appropriate in their case, than opt for rigid schemes or preferences? From a didactic angle the study of this topic is also useful in so far as it reveals to the Common lawyer (and, perhaps, to the Civil lawyer) how unrealistic the treatment of the law can be in civil law textbooks. For their emphasis on what the law is according to the code rather than how it works in practice can be misleading to say the least. The subject we have just briefly discussed offers an excellent illustration.

(c) Personal injury (non-pecuniary losses)

Personal injury does not only lead to pecuniary losses of the kind described above; typically it also entails non-pecuniary losses such as pain and various forms of mental suffering. The German term *Schmerzensgeld* is wider than any equivalent found in the Common law and it should thus be made clear that it encompasses such headings of damage as pain and suffering, loss of amenity, disfigurement, loss of expectation of life etc. These distinctions and sub-divisions are not always made clear in the German books on the subject; yet they are in the judges minds when fixing the level of compensation for *Schmerzensgeld* as is seen from the actual decisions and books which contain summaries of awards. Yet, it is in a certain respect narrower than some of its common law counterparts. For an award of *Schmerzensgeld* presupposes that the victim suffered personal injury. In short, the object of an award of *Schmerzensgeld* is to compensate for all kinds of non-material harm suffered as a consequence of personal injury. (In this book, however, instead of *Schmerzensgeld* (which is quite a mouthful to pronounce) we have, for convenience's sake, used the term "pain and suffering" whilst also warning the reader not to understand it in the technical English sense.) The indemnification of the victim for such losses has caused difficulties of a similar kind both in England and in Germany. For though both systems, unlike those of the socialist and Islamic worlds, are prepared to take cognisance of such losses, both realize that they are dealing with unquantifiable items of loss where *restitutio in integrum* is not possible. Instead, the idea of "fair compensation" (*Ausgleich*) or "satisfaction" (*Genugtuung*) is introduced into the legal vocabulary, suggesting not only an inability for precise calculation, but also a desire for a certain degree of uniformity of awards. (Once again, where, as in America, juries have the last word, such uniformity is often impossible to attain and, in turn, its absence must hinder the out-of-court settlement process.) The above, however, should not be taken to suggest that money paid for pain and suffering is an insignificant part of the total award. On the contrary, there is a clear tendency to increase the size of the awards under this heading. Academic opinion in particular is, on the whole, firmly behind this trend and argues in favour of further increases (see Teplitzky, "Umwelt und Recht", *NJW* 1966, 388; Kötz in *Festschrift von Caemmerer* (1978) 389; Foerste "Schmerzensgeld bei brutalen Verbrechen", *NJW* 1999, 2951 etc.). Ott and Schäfer, "Schmerzensgeld bei Körperverletzungen", *JZ* 1991, 563, give the example of compensation for the loss of one eye which in 1952 was DM 2,000 but had risen to DM 45,000 by 1980, which represents a substantial increase even if the figures are adjusted to take account of inflation. (See also the table at p. 569 where the average "tariffs" up to 1984 are compared.) The reader should note from the outset that all examples of awards given throughout this section refer exclusively to damages for pain and suffering. So, for instance, cost of medical treatment, loss of earnings, and other pecuniary heads of damages are not included in these sums but are awarded separately over and above the damages for pain and suffering.

Since these charts were compiled, one can observe further significant increases in awards. For instance, in 1996 a court awarded to a three-year old child DM 500,000 as damages for pain and suffering for total blindness. The claim arose from a product liability incident when a bottle of sparkling lemonade exploded and injured the child. (Decision no. 1418 = OLG Frankfurt ZfS 1996, 131, confirming LG Hanau = no. 2010; the no. refer to the database IMM-DAT, and the decisions can be found for instance in *Beck'sche Schmerzensgeldtabelle* 4. ed. (2001).) Other illustrations will be given below. Ott and Schäfer approach the problem of the "right" level of awards from the angle of economic analysis and in 1991 concluded that in cases of serious injuries there should be a drastic (threefold) increase in payments. Though they accepted that this would result in a rise in insurance premiums they also thought that this hike in damage wards would provide incentives for avoiding personal injury and enhance the use of mechanisms for loss prevention. Not everyone, of course, agreed; nor have they been converted since. But it is, nonetheless, interesting to observe that a similar discussion has taken place in England.

Thus, in 1999 the Law Commission (Law Com. No. 257) proposed a large increase in damages for pain, suffering, and loss of amenity. (In the case of current awards above £3,000 by a factor between 1.5 and 2; a series of tapered increases for awards below £3,000 and above £2,000 by less than a factor of 1.5.) Rather unusually the Commission also recommended that, at least initially, legislation should be avoided and the task of adjusting the levels of awards left to the courts. The Court of Appeal and the House of Lords were thus urged to use their existing powers to lay down guidelines. (Para. 5.10 of the Report.) A specially constituted Court of Appeal considered the Commission's proposal in a conjoined appeal of eight test cases: *Heil* v. *Rankin* [2000] 2 *WLR* 1173. The Court accepted the task set by the Commission but did not follow all its recommendations as to substance. Lord Woolf MR handed down a judgment to which each member of the court had contributed. He stated (at pp. 1200 ff.) that there was no need to increase awards which were at present below £10,000. However, awards at the highest level should be increased by one third, while the extent of the adjustment of the awards in between should taper downwards (see graph at p. 1219). Illustrations are provided by the actual decisions reached in the test cases. (See, also, R Lewis (2001) 64 *MLR* 100.) So, for instance, if in the case of brain damage the award was £150,000 (which is the threshold for the "highest level") it will be increased by a third to £200,000 while in the middle of the range, for instance, an award of £80,000 is to be increased by 17 per cent to £95,000. The Court doubted some of the evidence relied upon by the Commission and, most interestingly, it stated that it would attach more importance than the Commission to the level of awards in other member states of the E.U. (at p. 1201). (The Commission had confined its comparative survey to jurisdictions closely allied to the English, mainly Irish. See, para. 3.90.) Despite these real or apparent limitations highlighted by the Court of Appeal, the Report contains invaluable information for anyone who wishes to approach the problem from a wider perspective. The following remarks can naturally provide only first and tentative guidelines as to the position in Germany.

Fair compensation for injury to body or health or for deprivation of liberty is expressly provided for by § 847 BGB. Section II of this Article, displaying its rather antiquated origins, provides the same for a woman who has been the victim of an immoral crime or has been induced by cunning or threats or abuse of a relationship into an extra-marital cohabitation. These provisions were necessary because of the general principle enunciated by § 253 BGB, which prohibits the award of monetary compensation for non-pecuniary losses except where the law expressly provides for an exception. It must be also remembered that a claim under § 847 BGB will be allowed only if the action is based on the breach of one of the tort provisions of the Civil Code. If, on the other hand, the action is based on the violation of one of the provisions of a strict liability statute, then no claim for pain and suffering will be allowed. (The only exceptions can be found in § 53 III of the Air Traffic Act and in 29 II Atomic Energy Act. For further details see Ch. 3, Section A.5.). The same is true, if the cause of action is contractual; and that is why the attempt to circumvent the unfortunate § 831 BGB through § 278 BGB has not been entirely satisfactory. One way of bypassing this drawback is to base the action on both contract and tort. Case 52 shows how this can be done in the context of medical malpractice where the hospital is sued on the basis of § 278 BGB and the doctor on the basis of § 823 I BGB, see, also, cases 53–55.

Much of the above may change if the aforementioned proposed 2. *Gesetz zur Änderung schadensrechtlicher Vorschriften* becomes law. (At the time of writing: Government proposal of 24 September 2001). Following recommendations of the *Verkehrsgerichtstag* of 1995, 1998, and 2000, the reform proposal suggests that § 847 BGB is repealed and a more general exception introduced as § 253 II BGB. (A translation is provided at p. 21.) In practical terms this will mean that damages for pain and suffering will henceforth become available also in cases of breach of contract and for liability under strict liability statutes. Personal injury remains, however, an essential condition of recovery. The main impetus for reform came from the belief that the injured person deserves fuller protection also in cases of strict and contractual liability. In the seminal case of BGHZ 18, 149 the court held that the object of an award of damages for pain and suffering is twofold. On the one hand it serves to compensate the victim for a non-pecuniary loss, while on the other it serves the purpose of *satisfying the victim for the wrong done to him*. The traditional reason for confining compensation for pain and suffering to § 823 BGB was, accordingly, the belief that the second purpose did not apply to strict—i.e. no fault—liability. This argument is no longer considered to be compelling for three reasons.

First, the BGB, itself, has provided for damages for pain and suffering in the context of strict liability, namely in the context of § 833 BGB sentence 1 ("luxury" animals). Though this is, admittedly, a minor provision of the Code, the rule it contains would seem to undermine the above-mentioned rationale of not awarding damages for pain and suffering in strict liability cases. Secondly, and more importantly, most German lawyers would nowadays accept that the compensatory function of the award has become increasingly central in the jurisprudence of the BGH. Thirdly, the underlying idea behind the notion of compensation is, itself, sufficiently strong to justify extending liability to other grounds. The absence of fault may thus, in the future, be reflected in lower awards being made whenever the harm is not the result of proven fault. (In this sense the reasons accompanying the proposal at p. 10.) However, one must also note that if courts were minded routinely to award lower amounts in the case of strict liability (compared to "simple" negligence) there will remain a lingering incentive to invoke § 823 I BGB and thus defeat one of the aims of liability without fault. Finally, the present state of the law is unsatisfactory. Since plaintiffs are forced to base their claim also on § 823 BGB, the strict liability statutes have been undermined *de facto* if not *de iure*. Their purpose to provide a simple and efficient risk allocation in their respective areas of liability becomes futile if in almost every case the court is also obliged to investigate whether the plaintiff was negligent in the sense of § 823 I BGB. Moreover, the duties of care developed by the courts in these areas approximate in many cases to the rules of strict liability. (For a recent example of this trend see ch 3 section A 5 (c) (iv) 2, BGH JZ 1998, 358, concerning the Environmental Liability Act.)

In addition, the proposed Bill also seeks to refine the conditions of recovery. It has, for instance, been argued that damages for pain and suffering should not be awarded in the case of minor or trivial injuries. The proposed reform adopts a balanced approach and seeks to avoid the consequence of a rise in insurance premiums (see Bollweg *NZV* 2000, 185, 187). The means to achieve this is to exclude minor injuries from the scope of § 253 II BGB (in which, at present, courts award amounts less than DM 1,000). However, given that the threshold will be controversial, this might diminish the effect of simplifying procedures. (In that sense, the recently retired President of the BGH, Dr Karlmann Geiß in DAR 1998, 416, 420.) Consequently, the new § 253 II BGB stipulates that if damages for pain and suffering are to be awarded the injury must not be insubstantial ("nicht unerheblich") in nature and duration. This limit, however, will not apply where the injury was caused with intent ("vorsätzlich").

Unlike § 844 II BGB which, as we have seen, expresses a clear preference for the annuity system, § 847 BGB is silent as to the form the award has to take. In the event, it provides one of the clearly exceptional cases where the lump sum is the solution both favoured by theory and adopted by practice. This, however, does not mean that annuities cannot be paid in addition to or in lieu of lump sum awards if the circumstances of a particular case make this the more appropriate form of payment (see BGH NJW 1957, 383). But annuities for pain and suffering cannot be index-linked (BGH NJW 1973, 1653).

The leading case on this topic (BGHZ 18, 149) is reproduced in full (case 140) and it deserves careful reading. In the words of the Great Senate, ". . . damages for pain and suffering have a dual function. They are meant to provide the injured party with adequate compensation for that kind of damage. At the same time, however, they are meant to indicate that the tortfeasor owes the victim 'satisfaction' for what he has done to him." This latter element, however, brings the tort award close to the realm of criminal law and since punitive damages in civil actions are, on the whole, frowned upon in the civil law systems, this heading has caused considerable discussion. (See, however, BGHZ 35, 363; von Bar, "Schmerzensgeld und gesellschaftliche Stellung des Opfers bei Verletzungen des allgemeinen Persönlichkeitsrechts", *NJW* 1980, 1742; E. Lorenz, *Immaterieller Schaden und "billige Entschädigung in Geld". Eine Untersuchung auf der Grundlage des § 847 BGB* (1981).) Apart from this doubtful situation therefore, the notion of punitive damages in a civil action, so well known to American (and less so English) law, is (in theory) ignored by the German system.

Fair compensation and satisfaction are notions so inherently vague that they inevitably allow much room for judicial discretion. The courts accept that they must undertake the task in an "equitable manner" (*billiges Ermessen*). (BGH *MDR* 1993, 847.) One of the most important elements that can be taken into account is the relative economic strength of the parties so that on occasion it may be equitable to increase the tortfeasor's liability in a way that will reflect his economically robust position. Whether the tortfeasor is insured or not is also a factor that can be taken into account and this irrespective of whether the insurance is obligatory or simply widespread (BGHZ 18, 149, 165). (*Cf.* English law where the financial means of the defendant are not taken into account, and awards are not adjusted upwards (if the defendant is properly insured—e.g. *Fletcher* v. *Autocar and Transporters Ltd.* [1968] 2 QB 322, 335, per Lord Denning MR), nor downwards (if the award will be ruinous to him—as per Lord Lloyd's statement in *Wells* v. *Wells* [1999] 1 AC 345, 373). Apart from § 829 BGB, this is the only other paragraph in the Code that allows such economic factors to be *openly* considered by the courts when determining the level of awards. However, according to § 829 BGB both the ground for holding a person liable as well as the extent of his liability are determined according to the principles of equity, while according to § 847 BGB only the extent of liability is so to be fixed. (The differences and similarities of the two sections are usefully considered in case 140.)

In fixing these awards the German courts tend to attach much importance to the pain suffered by the victim. The great intensity and duration of the pain will thus help push the awards higher (BGH VersR 1960, 401; BGHZ 18, 149; BGH 16 December 1975, NJW 1976, 1148.). It comes as no surprise, therefore, to see that the various special Tables of Cases, which collect and systematise the case law, structure their account of awards for damages for pain and suffering according to the injury suffered by the victim. For instance the *Beck'sche Schmerzensgeldtabelle* 4. edn. (2001) comprises more than 2700 judgments ordered in such a fashion. Needless to say that this kind of book ensures at a general level the uniformity of awards by providing judges with a starting guideline which they can then adjust to fit their own case. But the actual award must, nonetheless, be calculated *de nuovo* taking the circumstances of the individual case into account; and the judge must give his reasons for the sum he has reached. (BGH 8 June 1976, VersR 1976, 967.) The mere fact that a comparable award was made in a similar (or apparently similar) case is not sufficient justification. (BGH, 24 May 1988, NJW 1989, 773.)

The way the material is presented in these works is also interesting. For in almost all cases the information given about the facts of the case is confined to the type, duration, and further peculiarities of the injury suffered. For instance how many operations were necessary, how quickly the plaintiff recovered from it etc. The personal details of the plaintiff are also given—e.g. his age and health and whether the injury affected the exercise of his profession—but little if anything said about the wrong itself, the degree of the defendant's fault etc. As we noted earlier, this underlines the general observation that in most cases the purpose of compensation clearly stands in the forefront of awarding damages for pain and suffering. The aim of satisfying the plaintiff for the wrong done to him may play a role in the individual case, in particular if the defendant was grossly negligent but has generally come to weigh less in the mind of the judge. The same is true if the claim is based on an infringement of privacy carried out in order to make a profit. But the plaintiff's satisfaction is by no means the overriding consideration. It is interesting to note that the defendant's conduct after the tort may, in exceptional cases, also be a factor. For instance, where the settlement of the claim is unnecessarily delayed by the defendant's insurer, the award may be increased considerably. (E.g. OLG Frankfurt NJW 1999, 2447, doubling the regular award).

Generally speaking, this is regarded as a subjective heading of damage. So, if pain is not experienced, either because the victim was rendered unconscious by his injuries or because pain-killers have helped reduce his pain, the sum awarded was, until fairly recently, diminished or even be obliterated (see BGH NJW 1982, 2123, reproduced in the 3rd edn. of this book at p. 959). In some instances (BGH 16 December 1975, BGH NJW 1976, 1147; BGH 22 June 1982, NJW 1982, 2123) the BGH felt that the money awarded should be seen as a "symbolic atonement" "for the interference with rights and interests unconditionally protected by the legal order". Thus for these courts, the unconsciousness removed the element of "compensation" and "satisfaction" from the notion of *Schmerzensgeld*. Such phrases, however, help to confuse rather than clarify the issues, especially if one is trying to see German law from the optic of the English Common law. For the use of words such as "atonement" can again appear to be trespassing into the area of criminal law. More importantly, it could be argued that German law, which on the whole does not follow rigidly to the English headings of damages, was in some of these cases trying to compensate the victim's loss of amenity and not his pain and suffering which he clearly was not experiencing. Such an interpretation, if plausible, would bring the two systems closer together. For, once again, it would approximate the result achieved in England (*H West & Son Ltd* v. *Shephard* [1964] AC 326) where loss of amenity is compensated objectively, i.e. irrespective of whether the victim is aware of the loss. (On the above see E. Lorenz, *op. cit.*) But whatever the merits of such a "conciliatory" approach, it is now been overtaken by the important decision of the BGH of 13 October 1992, case 143, BGHZ 120, 9 (with an approving note by Gießen, *JZ* 1993, 519; followed in BGH NJW 1993, 1531), which adopts a more generous position towards plaintiffs.

First, the court felt compelled to depart from the previous case law if it were to give adequate weight to the victim's right to have his personality protected (Article 1, 2 I GG). Secondly, the purpose of an award of damages for pain and suffering was not primarily to satisfy the victim for the wrong done to him. This is necessarily subjective and was relied on by the older judgments. In the decision of 1992 the BGH stressed that the purpose of compensation provided the real basis of recovery in such a case and that accordingly damages were not to be reduced if the victim was not aware of the loss. The "objective" predicament of the victim's personality as such called for compensation. It was thus inconsequential that the plaintiff did not suffer pain. The damages that must thus be awarded to unconscious plaintiffs must be calculated by reference to all the relevant circumstances (*angemessene Entschädigung*). The court also felt that the notion of *Schmerzensgeld* does not only perform a "compensatory" function but also helps serve the notion of human dignity (*Würdefunktion*). In the light of this, it may no longer be necessary to reduce visibly the plaintiff's compensation because of his unconsciousness.

A similar approach was deployed in the controversial decision of BGH 9 November 1993, BGHZ 124, 52 (annotated by Laufs, *NJW* 1994, 775; Taupitz, *JR* 1995, 22; Rohe, *JZ* 1994, 465). In that case the plaintiff knew he would become infertile as a result of an operation. Therefore, he instructed the defendant to preserve his sperm in order to be able to have children after the operation. The sperm was negligently destroyed. It was held that the donor was entitled to damages for pain and suffering (§§ 823 I, 847 BGB). In order to arrive at this conclusion the court had to surmount another obstacle. It had to show that the destruction of the sperm amounted to physical damage to the plaintiff's "body" (§ 823 I BGB). The court affirmed that the destruction of the sperm constituted the violation of one of the protected interests in § 823 I BGB, namely bodily integrity. Yet, in the ultimate analysis, liability was based on the protection of the plaintiff's personality (Article 1 I, 2 I GG). The court argued that taking the possibilities of modern medicine into account it was necessary to define "body" in the light of the victim's right of self-determination. Thus, if part of the body is separated from it, it will be decisive whether the plaintiff intended to make use of the separated part's function (sperm) or to re-implant the severed part (blood donation) at a later stage. In assessing the amount of damages, the court stressed that the knowledge of no longer being able to ever have children was a heavy burden upon the plaintiff. On the other hand the defendant's negligence was only slight. On balancing these factors the court arrived at an amount of DM 25,000 of damages for pain and suffering.

Apart from pain, mental suffering is also compensated. English law usually tends to use a global term such as "loss of amenity" or "enjoyment of life" for all sums given to the victim to alleviate his anguish for loss of a particular enjoyment or pastime or pleasure. Clearly, a footballer who has lost his legs or a pianist who has lost his fingers will have to receive additional compensation for these very personal losses. This is certainly true in German law as it is in English law, though in the former mental suffering appears classified under different subheadings. Thus mental suffering occasioned by disfigurement (especially in the case of a woman) will be compensated; and this sum will be additional to any economic loss claimable as a result of the disfigurement (BGH NJW 1959, 1031; OLG Celle NJW 1968, 1677). Mental suffering caused by loss of marriage occasioned by disfigurement will also be compensatable (BGH NJW 1959, 1031). On the other hand, German law has not known (as English law did until the Administration of Justice Act 1982 abolished it) an independent heading for "loss of expectation of life". But anguish caused by the realization of a shorter life expectancy can be and has been taken into account when calculating the sum for satisfaction (BGH VersR 1961, 374).

Perhaps one should conclude by saying that the above are mere illustrations of some of the headings of recoverable harm. For a fuller list and the amount of damages recoverable one must consult the case law and the "Tables of Damages for Pain and Suffering" already referred to and which are customarily used by judges as the starting-point for their calculations. So here we shall only give a first impression of the current general level of awards. (The examples are taken from *Beck'sche Schmerzensgeldtabelle* 4. edn. (2001)).

Starting at the lower end one must note the great number of cases where awards are below DM 3,000. Courts can disregard only obviously trivial injuries (*Bagatellverletzungen*); but the criteria appear to be strict. (BGHZ 132, 341; BGHZ 137, 142 reproduced above, case 90; BGH VersR 2000, 372; all concerning psychiatric illness.) As was already stated, in the reform proposals very minor injuries will not, in the future, justify an award of damages for pain and suffering. Such injuries are at the moment compensated with sums that are below DM 1,000. (See, for instance, decisions no. 47, 896, 2491, 55 etc. all concerning the so-called "HWS-Syndrom" (whiplash) and in which between DM 100 and 200 were awarded.) In the overwhelming majority of cases in which the plaintiff suffers from whiplash the awards are below DM 2,000 (references in *op. cit.*, pp. 518 ff.). This syndrome is one of the typical effects of a car accident and is therefore also one of the most common claims brought under § 847 BGB. By excluding minor injuries the reform might well have a major impact in this area. In any case, one finds only 9 decisions where more than DM 10,000 were awarded for this condition and in all of them the injury was serious and had long term effects.

Awards in nervous shock cases (see above, cases 1–3) where close relatives suffered from psychiatric injury from learning of the death of the victim are also relatively small, usually in the area of DM 10,000 or less. But notable exceptions can be found. Examples of cases of "distant" shock, where the 'secondary victim" was merely informed of the death, are: no. 606 (LG Gießen ZfS 1987, 39). There the mother suffered from a severe depression when her 10 year old daughter was attacked and killed by two shepherd dogs. The award was DM 10,000. Case no. 2719 (OLG Oldenburg, 1998) concerns a father who suffered from "medium" depression after receiving the news of the death of his 17 year old (adopted) daughter. He was awarded DM 20,000. In case no. 2036 (OLG Nürnberg DAR 1995, 447), the plaintiff suffered from severe depression, his three children were killed in a traffic accident caused by the gross negligence of the defendant. DM 70,000 were awarded. This seems to be the current maximum. It is interesting to note that the awards are not significantly higher where the "secondary" victim *actually witnessed* the incident. The highest amount seems to be that of Case no. 711, LG Verden 1982, DAR 1988, 320, where the father witnessed his youngest son being run over by a drunk driver. DM 15,000 were awarded. An extreme case is no. 2467 (OLG Nürnberg, 1998) where two infants witnessed how their mother was shot. Despite the horrific nature of the incident, only DM 10,000 were awarded. Similarly, in cases where the "primary victim" suffered nervous shock as a result of the accident the awards are also not higher than in the case of "distant" shock. The highest award seems to have been DM 25,000 in no. 799, BGH VersR 1986, 241, victim in constant medical treatment, accident neurosis. Another area where the awards are small involves injuries such as bruises, contusions, or lacerations (references, *op. cit.*, pp. 588 ff.). The range is from zero to DM 25,000 (no. 2655, LG Braunschweig), while most awards are below DM 2000. In the case decided by the LG Braunschweig the victim had additionally suffered brain damage and lost the sense of smell completely. This leads us to the more serious types of injuries.

The awards in cases of brain damage are naturally among the highest (references, *op. cit.*, pp. 123 ff.). So for instance the OLG Hamm (no. 780) awarded in 1997 DM 500,000 of damages for "pain and suffering" to a 14 year old child which needed constant care and was borne with serious brain damage as a result of medical malpractice. One can find at least 14 further examples of decisions from the last decade where the awards exceeded DM 200,000 and where the injury consisted in serious brain damage with the consequence that the plaintiff could no longer take care of himself (pp. 135–138). Similar figures can be found in cases where the brain damage caused blindness (p. 138) or deafness (p. 142) etc.

Awards are also high where arms or other extremities had to be amputated. See, for instance, case no. 1881 (OLG Frankfurt) where DM 135,000 were awarded for pain and suffering (The victim had also incurred serious knee injuries). An extreme case is no. 824 (OLG Hamm) where the 17 years old victim lost all her fingers except her thumbs. She was awarded DM 30,000 (in 1988). In the case of quadriplegia (*Querschnittslähmung*), references, *op. cit.*, pp. 326 ff., the awards are regularly around DM 100,000 depending on the circumstances of the case and can go up to and above DM 300,000 (15 decisions from the last ten years or so from different regions). In two cases the plaintiff was awarded DM 500,000 (no. 2469, LG Flensburg, 1997, and no. 1067, LG Oldenburg, 1989; in both cases the plaintiff was a child when injured).

A special category form the cases of infringement of personality rights (references, *op. cit.*, pp. 685 ff.) where in the wake of the "Caroline" jurisprudence of the BGH (discussed above, notes to cases 39–49) the level of awards was drastically increased. (In the Caroline case, itself, no. 2298, OLG Hamburg, 1996, the final award was DM 180,000 (note however that three newspaper articles violated the plaintiff's rights which, in common law terms, count as three separate causes of action.) So far this seems to be also the maximum award). (For further details on privacy cases see discussion above, chapter 2, section A.2, 3(iv).) In this category one can also include unlawful restrictions of personal freedom, where the maximum award has been DM 500,000 (no. 1997, LG Marburg, 1995). In this case the plaintiff was locked up in a psychiatric hospital for 9 years and treated with 2.3 kg of anti-depressant drugs (Neuroleptika) during this period. The defendant was the doctor who had negligently diagnosed the plaintiff's condition and had led to his incarceration.

Article 3 I of the Constitution requires, in essence, that similar cases should be treated in the same way. This provision, which embodies a fundamental principle of justice, can also have indirect horizontal effect with important procedural consequences: in principle plaintiffs could seek to rely on Article 3 GG if awards in one area are unjustifiably lower than in some other area and bring the case before the BVerfG. For instance, after the Caroline jurisprudence awards in the field of personality rights are likely to increase substantially. Is it fair then if victims of nervous shock are awarded—on average—lower amounts? Recently, this question came before the BVerfG. (See, decision of 8 March 2000, NJW 2000, 2187, case 146). In that case, (already referred to above OLG Nürnberg, no. 2036) the plaintiffs suffered nervous shock upon learning that their three children died in a car accident negligently caused by the first defendant (the second defendant being the first defendant's insurer). The Court of Appeal awarded them DM 70,000 and DM 40,000 respectively and founded its decision primarily on the seriousness of the psychiatric illness. The BGH dismissed an appeal against the size of the award. The plaintiffs then referred the case to the BVerfG. The Constitutional Court thus had to decide whether the award was arbitrary in so far as the level of damages was below what can nowadays be given in cases where the right to one's personality had been violated. The court held that the different levels did not entail an unjustified discrimination between different categories of plaintiffs. (To put it more explicitly: between claimants such as Caroline of Monaco who complain about an unfair or misleading newspaper article and are awarded DM 180000, and "ordinary" parents who lose their children in horrific circumstances.) The judgment of the civil courts thus did not violate the plaintiffs' right "to equal treatment" under Article 3 I of the Constitution. The reason why the apparently "unequal" treatment was justified is this. In cases of infringements of the right to privacy (Article 1 and Article 2 I GG, discussed below) the rational of awarding substantial (by German standards) non-pecuniary damages is that without such awards, violations of one's dignity would very often not entail any legal sanctions. One of the main considerations in assessing such damages is, therefore, deterrence (and, incidentally, assume thus also a restitutionary function). This, in turn, requires one to take account of the expected profit that will have resulted from the intrusion. (Interestingly enough, the court remarked that these damages were not restitutionary in the sense that all profits were to be handed over.) On the other hand, in the case of damages for shock no such deterrent reasoning was called for. For nervous shock cases arose typically in the context of car accidents—as the present case clearly illustrated—and were not deliberately caused or motivated by commercial motives. As a result, the judgment of the civil court did not violate any rights of the plaintiffs under the Constitution. As to whether or not the assessment of damages in the instant case was accurate, this was not for the Constitutional court to determine. The decision is remarkable not only because it demonstrates once again the difficult task of the Constitutional Court to strike a balance between upholding constitutional values and respecting the jurisdiction of civil courts, but also in the way that this conflict was finally resolved. Thus the implicit invitation to treat the high awards in the "Caroline" cases (of recent vintage and approved of by the BVerfG, see case 47) as a basis for increasing the level of damages under § 847 BGB on a large scale was turned down and potentially far-reaching financial consequences were skilfully averted by the Constitutional court. An interference with the competence of the "ordinary" courts to assess damages on the merits of the individual cases was also avoided, the Constitutional court exercising self-restraint and accepting that in privacy cases there were other material factors which justified a more generous approach.

So far we have been considering the case of an accident victim who survives his injuries. If the victim dies, problems of a different nature arise. Some of them are related to the new cause of action, which is given to his dependants and will be discussed in the next section (in English law known as the Fatal Accident action). The problem that will be dealt with here, however, is different and concerns the issue of active transmissibility of the victim's action to his heirs. (Since the Law Reform (Miscellaneous Provisions) Act of 1934 English law has recognised this possibility without any restrictions, save that in the case of defamation the cause of action dies with the injured person; also penal damages cannot be claimed by the estate.)

Until recently the position of German law was opaque and unsatisfactory. This was because according to § 847 I, 2 BGB the right devolved upon the victim's heirs only if the injurer recognised this by contract before the victim's death or if a legal action had been commenced before that time. Whatever the original justification for this limitation, in practice it caused much dispute and an unsavoury scramble to institute actions as soon as possible after the accident lest the victim die too soon (see BGHZ 69, 323; BGH NJW 1984, 2348). The position was thus deemed unsatisfactory (see Deutsch, *Haftungsrecht* I (1976), 477; Kötz, *Festschrift von Caemmerer* (1978) 389, 404) and, in the end, transmissibility facilitated by the legislative abolition of § 847 I 2 on 14 March 1990. (BGBl. I, 478.) For more details on the old position see page 684 of the 2nd edition of this work. For the transmission of the deceased's *Schmerzensgeld* to his heirs see: BGH 6 December 1994, NJW 1995, 783. So the victim's heirs will obtain—through his will or the rules of intestacy—the amount awarded to the *deceased* for his pain and suffering. The amount thus awarded to the deceased (or, rather, his estate) will, of course, vary depending on how long he lived between injury and death. The above will, however, make clear that no damages are awarded to the "dependants" of the deceased victim. This is because the rules that determine their rights can be found § 844 BGB and this provision does not allow such a heading of damages. In the final result German law thus, once again, comes closer to English law (which also does not allow solatium except in the limited sense provided by the Administration of Justice Act 1982) than to French or American law which take a more liberal approach towards this matter.

Further reading

Coester-Waltjen, "Der Ersatz immaterieller Schäden im Deliktsrecht", *Jura* 2001, 133; Deutsch, "Pläne zur Reform des Schmerzensgeldes", *ZRP* 1998, 291; *idem*, "Schmerzensgeld für Vertragsver-letzungen und bei Gefährdungshaftung", *ZRP* 2001, 351; von Gerlach, "Die prozessuale Behandlung von Schmerzensgeldansprüchen", *VersR* 2000, 525; Jäger, "Schmerzensgeldbemessung bei Zer-störung der Persönlichkeit und bei alsbaldigem Tod", *MDR* 1998, 450; Scheffen, "Tendenzen bei der Bemessung des Schmerzensgeldes für Verletzungen aus Verkehrsunfällen, ärztlichen Kunstfehlern und Produzentenhaftung", *ZRP* 1999, 189

(d) Ricochet damage in the context of fatal accidents

When the victim dies from his injuries, third parties can suffer further loss. A young girl may lose her father's much needed financial support; an ageing relative the services of a younger member of the family; an employee may see his job disappear as a result of the death of his employer; a football club may be deprived of a sizeable transfer fee when one of its star players is killed (the facts of a classic French case: Colmar, 20 avril 1955, *D.* 1956, 723). The list of ricochet victims can be endless; the harm they suffer can range from emo-tional distress to severe pecuniary loss. Three main questions arise under this heading: the first is whether a *new* cause of action should be created for this type of situation, the second is to whom should it be given, and the third is what should it be for. An impor-tant supplementary issue is connected with the victim's own fault and the effect it should have on the dependant's claims. We shall look at all these points in turn.

The first question is whether a new cause of action should arise whenever there is a fatal accident. The answer given by all systems is a positive one, but the ways this result is achieved differ. In one group of systems (French, Belgian) the amorphous delict pro-visions of the Code (e.g. Article 1382 French CC) are wide enough to justify this exten-sion. Another way is to be found in the English Fatal Accident Acts and their American derivatives, (known as the Wrongful Death statutes). These opt for specific statutory enactments expressly creating such rights, which otherwise were not recognised by the Common law. Yet a third group of systems include special provisions in the delict sec-tions of their Codes. Germany belongs to this group and, incidentally, so do Austria (Article 1327 Austrian CC), Switzerland (CO Arts. 45, 47), and Greece (Article 922 Greek CC).

German law, always striving for logic and terminological precision, makes a distinction between loss of support, which is regulated in § 844 BGB, and loss of services, which is the subject of separate treatment (§ 845 BGB). The former, as we shall note below, typi-cally consists of an action brought by a wife and/or child for the loss of the breadwin-ner/father. The latter, statistically more rare in practice, is brought by an "older" person for the loss of the services of a younger member of the family. Natural and adopted children are, in certain circumstances, under a duty to provide such services to their parents (see §§ 1619 and 1754 BGB) so that if they are injured the parents can claim their loss. (BGH 25 October 1977, BGHZ 69, 380.) When the wife is injured she can claim under § 842 BGB for amongst other things her inability to continue to provide services to her family; but where she is killed a claim for loss of *support* under § 844 II BGB may be available to her husband (BGHZ 51, 109). On the other hand, her work as "housewife" does not qualify as a *service* (*Dienstleistung*) to justify an action under § 845 BGB. (BGH 20 May 1980, BGHZ 77, 157.) Since similar rules apply to both §§ 844 and 845 BGB, and cases tend to overlap as the previous illustration demonstrates, it is not entirely clear that anything is really gained by this distinction between loss of support and loss of services.

To the second question mentioned above—who will be given the new right of action—three answers are, once again, possible. The most generous, adopted both by a number of German-inspired systems (e.g. Swiss CO Article 45 III; former East German Code, § 332 II) as well as by the Romanistic legal family (France etc.), grants this action to anyone who can actually prove to have suffered a loss. This approach may, in theory, cause some uncertainty to the extent that the courts have to deal with each case on its merits, but it can also produce more equitable results in a few, deserving situations. Besides, its apparent disadvantages can be exaggerated by ignoring the fact that in practice the courts have, through a cluster of causative notions, managed to keep liability very much under control. (On this see B S Markesinis, "A Comparative Look at Certain Problems of Pure Economic Loss", published in *The Cambridge Lectures* 1981 (ed. N. Eastham and B. Krivy) 45–61.)

The exact opposite way is to leave it to the legislator to determine which persons will be classified as dependants in law and be given the right to sue. This is the Common law method as seen in the Fatal Accident legislation. Interestingly enough, however, the list of dependants in these Acts has been greatly widened over the years and in practice the results reached by English and French law are more similar than the different starting-points would suggest.

German law has opted for a third method. According to § 844 II BGB only those persons to whom the deceased owed a statutory duty to provide support will be allowed to sue. (Typically this includes spouses (§ 1360 BGB) and children, including adopted children and adopted parents: § 1766 BGB). This right of maintenance must exist at the time of the *injury*. So, if a couple gets married after one of them has been injured and then dies, the surviving spouse will not have a right of action since there existed no right to support at the time of the injury. But if the legal relationship, from which the duty to support flows, exists at the time of the injury, then the right to sue will not be affected by the fact that at that time no support was yet being provided.

This can give rise to considerable difficulties where parents claim for the loss of their child. In many cases, the parents of a young or very young child will not, at the time of issuing the writ, be in a position to make a maintenance claim from the child. On the one hand, even a future entitlement may be seen as speculative since the child might never be able to support the parents. Awarding damages in such a case could thus, in effect, be seen as amounting to a claim—and what is more a potentially substantial one—for bereavement, which is not recognised in German law. On the other hand, it would seem harsh to deny claims merely because it is difficult to assess the award. In such cases German law has thus resorted to procedural devices to reconcile these concerns. In our example, therefore, no fixed amount will be awarded until the parent actually becomes entitled to claim maintenance from the child. Nonetheless, the parents are entitled at the time of the trial to a (merely) declaratory judgment (*Feststellungsklage*) recognising such a right for the future. Even this "contingent" recognition, however, will not come easily. For the parents will be required to establish that it is not "wholly unlikely" that the deceased would have supported them in the fullness of time. Thus, in BGH, NJW 1952, 741, the parents' claim was allowed even though the child was only five years of age at the time of the trial. This result was reached because of the danger that the parents' claim would become time-barred. A right of suit was also confirmed in the case of the death of a 12-years-old daughter. (BGHZ 4, 133). Before reaching its decision, the court took account of the education planned, the "character" of the child etc. The decision is reminiscent of the English *Taff Vale* Ry Co. v. *Jenkins* [1913] AC 1; and also has American counterparts. (See, for instance, *Gary* v. *Schwartz*, 339 NYS 2d 39 (1972)—awarding to a widowed mother $98,000 (subsequently reduced on appeal to $52,000) for the loss of her sixteen-year old son who intended to become a dentist. See, also, *Hart* v. *Forchelli*, 445 F.2d 1018 (2d Cir. 1971)—a case involving the death of an eighteen-year-old boy with "tentative plans to become an attorney".) But some American courts have extended this attempt to do "justice" to borderline situations (*Haumersen* v. *Ford Motor Co.*, 257 2d 7 (Iowa 1977) awarding $100,000 for the loss of a seven-year-old child "with a talent as a cartoonist"); while a handful have literally gone overboard. (See: *Andrews* v. *Reynolds Memorial Hospital, Inc.*, 499 SE 2d 846 (W.Va. 1997) where the court awarded $1.75 million for lost of future earnings attributable to the death of a one-day-old baby! Note, however, that not all courts have been willing to depart from the original model of the Fatal Accident Acts. Thus, see, *Prather* v. *Lockwood*, 310 NE 2d 815 (1974).) Such generosity is, from a legal point of view, extremely dubious if justified under the heading of loss of future maintenance. So, if it is to be tolerated or even encouraged, it is best done under a carefully circumscribed (and, preferably, legislatively authorised) new heading of damage which, in the last thirty years or so has become known in the USA as a "loss of companionship" claim. This has, indeed, happened in some States in the USA (Fla. Stat. Ann. § 768.21; Hawaii Rev. Stat. § 663–3; W.Va. Code Ann. § 55–7–6; and in some it has been accompanied by caps. (See, Kan. Stat. Ann § 60–1903: $ 100,000; Me. Rev. Stat. Ann. Tit. 18, § 2552: $50,000.) As always, however, one concession usually leads to another. In this instance the result has been that some States now even allow claim for pure grief for the death of a loved one. (See: Ark. Stat. Ann. § 27–909; Kan Stat. Ann. § 60–1904.) The resulting dichotomy between emotional harm which is not compensated in personal injury cases involving no physical injury and grief that is compensated in cases of wrongful death claims may thus not be easy to justify.

In the light of the above, the German procedural device may, therefore, be more flexible than English law without incurring the risk of giving the green light to "gold digging" actions of the kind that we find in some American litigation. Generally speaking, therefore, courts are willing to hold *in the abstract* that the plaintiff is entitled to the payment of a rent *as soon as* he would have been entitled to maintenance from the deceased. (See, also, RG JW 1909, 314; BGH MDR 1954, 160; VersR 1966, 735.) The equitable balance thus struck between the English and American positions has not, however, addressed all the problems that arise in such cases. Thus, when calculating the award, does the court have to take into account whatever amount the parents saved by not incurring the costs of bringing up the child? This is left open by the leading case, BGHZ 4, 133. So, while in theory this approach appears to be well balanced, one must question how attractive it is and, above all, how often it is encountered in practice. For, such declaratory judgments do not have much practical value. It thus comes as little surprise then that the number of reported cases seems to be very small and it seems that none of them concern the plaintiff's actual claim for maintenance: all are *Feststellungsklagen*. (E.g. LG Braunschweig VersR 1972, 567; OLGR Hamm 1992, 44.)

An important group of potential claimants who are left without an action in German (and, very likely, English) law are fiancés (of both sexes) since before their marriage there is no obligation to provide support (KG NJW 1967, 1089). Mistresses are also treated with similar harshness and, for the same reasons, denied any right of action. Finally, to give one last example, stepsons are also denied compensation even where it can be shown that the deceased had maintained and would have continued to maintain his stepson to whom he was very attached. In the last two instances (mistresses, stepsons), English, French, and Swiss law would provide an action. In practice the right to sue under § 844 BGB will thus be given to surviving spouses, direct relatives, adopted children since in all these cases there is a statutory duty to support (see §§ 1360, 1601, 1766 BGB). The loss of a "housewife" is, like in English law, usually assessed by reference to the cost of hiring a nanny, housekeeper etc. (Kötz/Wagner, no. 536; Palandt, § 844 BGB, no. 11). To foreign eyes, German law thus appears excessively preoccupied with legal certainty even if this can lead to injustice in a number of deserving cases.

What will the "dependants" be allowed to claim? Once again there is no unanimity in the systems. For some (e.g. Common law) the action should be limited to "pounds, shillings and pence" though most recently the English Administration of Justice Act 1982 (new section 1(A) of the Fatal Accidents Act 1976) recognised a right to claim a fixed sum (at the moment £3,500) for bereavement. Rather anomalously, however, this new right is limited to a spouse claiming for the loss of the other spouse or parents claiming for the loss of a child, but not vice versa. (For details see Markesinis and Deakin, pp. 773–774.) French law, on the other hand, is again the most generous, allowing a claim for both pecuniary losses and moral damage. The German solution is very much like Common law, though where the victim has suffered nervous shock as a result of the death of a relative, he may be able to claim for it under § 823 I BGB and also recover damages for pain and suffering under § 847 BGB. Perhaps, at this stage, we should make it clear that we are always talking about the dependants claiming for their moral damage in a fatal accident action. The victim's own damages (for the period during which he was alive) will, of course, now be claimable by his estate. (For the transmission of the primary victim's *Schmerzensgeld* see BGH 6 December 1994, NJW 1995, 783.)

Two further points concerning the assessment of the award deserve mentioning. The first concerns the scope of § 844 I BGB. Under this provision "funeral expenses" can be recovered. In BGH NJW 1989, 2317 (case 2), the plaintiffs attempted to persuade the courts to adopt an extensive "interpretation" of this provision. The plaintiff parents had lost their twenty-two year old son one day before they were due on a holiday cruise. "Shocked" by his death they stayed at home. They claimed the price of the missed journey, which was roughly DM 10,000 *inter alia* as "funeral expenses". The BGH denied their claims on the ground that they did not suffer from a physiological or psychological condition in the meaning of § 823 I BGB. (Nervous shock, for which see notes to cases 1–3, above). The disappointment for a lost holiday could not be brought under the heading "funeral related costs". Some might regard this restrictive approach as a missed opportunity to extend § 844 BGB to other heads of consequential loss beyond lost maintenance and thus, in effect, award some compensation for non-material harm. But the legislative history and the wording of § 844 I BGB did not enable the court to take this step; and

English law (though not the law in the USA) would seem to share this philosophy. (On German law see, also, Deutsch and Schramm, "Schockschaden und frustrierte Aufwendungen", VersR 1990, 715).

Secondly, the dependant's claim regularly raises delicate issues of *res inter alios acta*. They concern the question whether pecuniary "benefits" that result from the death of the person who provided maintenance are to be taken into account. English law has moved from a restrictive approach (under which pecuniary advantages flowing from the death were generally taken into account to reduce the tort award) to a more plaintiff-orientated stance. This is now found in section 3(4) of the Fatal Accidents Act 1976 as amended by the Administration of Justice Act 1982 and states that benefits which may accrue as a result of the death shall be disregarded. This formula excludes from the assessment of damages all the pecuniary gains a dependant is likely to receive as a result of the death of the person killed, including insurance money, return of premiums and gratuities. (For details: Markesinis and Deakin, pp. 776–777.) In practice the most pressing question is whether benefits that accrue from the deceased's estate must be taken into account in assessing the dependant's damages. The BGH clarified early on that, generally speaking, the value of the inheritance as such is *res inter alios acta*, but that the interest earned must be taken into account and deducted from the tort award. (BGHZ 8, 325; *cf.* RGZ 130, 258.) But in this area of the law the German courts adopt a pragmatic approach. For instance, they make a full deduction where the defendant can prove that the dependant would have been excluded (disinherited) from the succession had the deceased survived.

Another issue that can give rise to difficulties is connected with the widow's remarriage, especially if, by the time of the trial, she is financially supported by her new husband. The general rule is that the provision of maintenance by a third party is not taken into account (§§ 843 IV, 844 II BGB). However, in the case of remarriage the courts have made an exception to this rule. Damages are reduced to the extent that the widow is supported by her new husband. (BGH NJW 1970, 1127.) Mere prospects of remarriage are, however, not considered as relevant in the assessment of the award so the unsavoury task of calculating the chances of re-marriage of the plaintiff have always been avoided. (Incidentally, German law has never made any distinction between man or woman, husband or wife in these cases.) It should also be noted that the widow's claim appears to be merely "suspended": if she divorces the new husband (or he dies) the right to the lost dependency under § 844 BGB revives. (For the position of English law see Markesinis and Deakin, 774 ff.).

The last point to which we must turn our attention is that of contributory negligence on the part of the deceased/victim of the tort. Once again, there is an express provision in the Code that deals with this matter in conjunction with § 254 BGB. This is § 846 BGB which, quite simply, declares that the dependants" claim will be reduced to take into account the victim's own fault in the realisation of the harm. The solution is similar to that adopted by the English Fatal Accident Act 1976 and is irreproachable. More debatable, perhaps, is the recent extension of this principle to another factual situation (see BGH NJW 1971, 1883). Thus, it will be remembered that the widow of a victim cannot claim for her mental anguish under the German fatal accident action but can claim under § 823 I BGB for the nervous shock that she may have suffered as a result of seeing or being told of her husband's death. § 846 BGB, discussed above, will not be applicable here since the widow is not suing under § 844 BGB but proceeding under § 823 I BGB. Nevertheless, the Supreme Court held that reasons of equity dictated that once again the deceased person's own contributory fault should be taken into account and reduce accordingly the widow's own claim under § 823 I BGB. This result, which is not compatible with earlier decisions (e.g. RGZ 157, 11), has been severely criticized by Professor John Fleming in 20 *American Journal of Comparative Law* 485 (1972).

(e) Interference with honour and reputation

This subsection deals briefly with indemnification for interference with the general right to one's personality. This has already been discussed in chapter 2, section A.2, 3(iv) so the comments made here must be read in conjunction with the earlier observations and the notes accompanying the translated cases reproduced in chapter 2, section B.11 and 12.

The starting-point must again be § 249 BGB which, as already stated, ordains restitution in kind. In most of these cases this will mean the publication of a correction of the statement or representation that gave rise to the dispute. The correcting statement must, normally, receive the same prominence as the offending statement and it is usually the defendant who is asked to publish the correction in his paper or journal. If he refuses to do so, the complainant may claim from him the cost of a correction inserted by him. But this cost must be reasonable, so in one case where the plaintiff tried to correct his tarnished image by inserting full-page statements in some fifteen national papers, he was not allowed to claim his enormous cost of about DM 300,000 (BGHZ 66, 182).

Monetary compensation is, therefore, treated as the ultimate remedy and is most commonly claimable where pecuniary loss results from the offending statement. This will clearly arise where, for example, the victim/plaintiff has lost a lucrative contract as a result of the statement made about him. But considerable amounts have, as we have seen, been awarded in cases where no proof of such loss was forthcoming. (See, for example, the case of the Canon Law Professor, no. 41.) Here damages are awarded to provide "satisfaction" to the plaintiff rather than compensation so they are, as the Common lawyers would put it, at large (note the Supreme Court's views in the "Gentleman rider" case (no. 40, above), to provide guidelines for the calculation of the awards). This development, of course, meant bypassing the obstacles posed by § 253 BGB; but common sense dictated this result and we have seen that the Constitutional Court gave it its blessing.

A more important limitation in the granting of monetary compensation is the court's insistence that the tortfeasor's fault be *serious* and the intrusion into the victim's private sphere *objectively* serious. The laudable purpose of these limitations is to prevent individuals making capital out of the slightest intrusion into their private lives. The ultimate decision is thus made to turn on the facts of each case. BGH NJW 1971, 698 (case 145) offers an excellent illustration. In that case, a professional actress took part in a sex education film, which involved some rather explicit sexual scenes. Provocative pictures from this film were subsequently used by the defendants without her permission in order to advertise a certain product. For this she brought an action complaining of unauthorised invasion of her privacy and she succeeded. In reaching the conclusion that the interference was both grave and unwarrantable the Supreme Court took into consideration the following factors: (i) the wide circulation of the magazine that carried the advertisements; (ii) the impression given that the actress had given her permission for the use of the photos in consideration for a fee; (iii) the desire to make a large profit from the advertisement (which contrasted sharply with the educational aims of the film-makers); and, finally, (iv) the effect that this affair could have on the plaintiff's future career as a serious actress. The case is thus typical of the careful balancing of interests that is attempted by the courts in this part of the law when deciding (*a*) the issue of liability and (*b*) the quantum of damages appropriate under this heading. Overall, one could conclude this section by saying that there are, apparently, no empirical studies available providing details of such awards, the average amount is rather low (estimated to be in the order of DM 7–8,000). A first indication was given above at the end of section c. Few awards seem to exceed DM 10,000 and there seems to be less than a dozen cases that have surpassed DM 50,000. On the other hand, the reader must be reminded that there are the sums awarded for "pain and suffering" resulting from the actionable invasion of one's privacy and that further financial losses are recoverable if properly proved. (See, for example, OLG München NJW 1988, 915.) One must also note that the Caroline cases, discussed in the privacy sections of the book, have opened the way for large awards to be made. Finally, one must note that the calculation of the damages may, in some cases, proceed on the compensatory principle of tort law but in other instances may be based on restitutionary ideas. The differences are discussed by Professor Peter Schlechtriem, among others, in *Protecting Privacy*, (Markesinis ed.) (1998) pp. 131 *et seq.* and Professor Gerhard Wagner, "Geldersatz für Persönlichkeitsverletzungen", *ZEuP* 2000, 200.

(f) Damage to property

Once again the rather inadequate and fragmented delict provisions of the Code (§§ 848, 849 BGB) must be supplemented by the general provisions found in §§ 249–52 BGB. The starting-point is, in fact, the restoration of the status quo (first sentence of § 249 BGB). Taken literally, it suggests that the defendant must through his own efforts restore or repair the damaged property. However, the second sentence of § 249 BGB enables the plaintiff in the case of physical damage to property to claim the cost of restoration instead. In practice it is the plaintiff who has his property repaired or replaced and then seeks to recoup his expenditure from the defendant. Once again, therefore, what is presented by the second sentence of § 249 BGB as the possible exception to sentence one of that provision is, in practice, the rule. Monetary compensation is, however, openly recognised to be the rule where restoration in kind is impossible (§ 251 I BGB); or requires a disproportionate economic expenditure (§ 251 II BGB).

The defendant's obligation is to make good all primary and consequential losses occasioned by the damage to the plaintiff's property, subject of course to the rules of legal cause. Normative theories of causation (such as the scope of the rule theory) can, once again, be used to impose effective legal limits on the extent of the obligation to compensate. The evaluation takes the form of a mathematical calculation, which estimates the difference between the state of the damaged property if the damaging act had not occurred and the actual state of the property after the damaging act or event. A more recent trend favours a more liberal assessment of the damage. Older codes—e.g. the Prussian Code of 1794—made the compensation of lost profits depend on other factors (e.g. a higher degree of fault: §§ 287 1, 5, 288, and §§ 7 1, 6, 10–15; see also §§ 1325, 1331 of the Austrian Civil Code of 1811). But § 252 BGB specifically authorizes the compensation of actual damage and of lost profits. According to the second sentence of § 252, "Profit is deemed to have been lost which could probably have been expected in the ordinary course of events, or according to the special circumstances, especially in the light of the preparations and arrangements made." However, even though this rule favours the injured plaintiff, it does not allow him to claim for a possible chance. Thus the BGH has ruled that a tenderer to a public contract which was unjustifiably cancelled could not claim his costs for preparing his offer so long as he could not establish that he would have been awarded the contract (BGH NJW 1981, 1673). The loss of a 10 per cent chance of receiving an X DM amount will not entitle the victim to 10 per cent of that amount. For losses that are certain to arise in the future but have not yet arisen at the trial, plaintiffs are often advised to seek declaratory judgments stating their relevant rights. This may be particularly relevant in order to prevent the action becoming statute barred by the three-year prescription period (*Festellungsklage*).

The bulk of claims for damage to property arise in the context of car accidents. The grounds of liability were discussed in chapter 3 section 5 c (iii). (There were 2.4 million traffic accidents in 1999, 84 per cent involving only material damage. The annual pay out by the insurance companies for 1999 was 27.7 billion DM, 74.5 per cent of which concerned property damage.) This then is an important topic on which we can concentrate for our illustrations. But it is also interesting from a didactic point of view to focus our attention on this topic since it reveals very clearly how the needs of practical life (quick settlements of disputes—not always achieved in practice) have helped fashion a series of detailed rules that concretise the rather abstract provisions of the Code.

(For a comprehensive account of the jurisprudence see: Greger *Haftungsrecht des Strassenverkehrs* 3rd ed. (1997) Anhang I "Schadensberechnung bei Sachschäden"; and for a more recent overview Kötz/Wagner *Deliktsrecht* 9th edn. (2001) nos. 481–505. Recent reform proposals are discussed by Bollweg "Gesetzliche Änderung im Schadensersatzrecht?", *NZV* 2000, 185. See, also, the discussion of the previous reform proposal of 27 January 1998 which then failed due to pressure from lobby groups: Geiß, *DAR* 1998, 416; Huber, *DAR* 2000, 20; Müller, *ZRP* 1998, 258.)

Clearly, one of the primary losses likely to be suffered by the owner of a damaged vehicle is the cost of repair. The cost of repair can also include what is sometimes referred to as the "commercial inferiority" of the repaired vehicle ("merkantiler Minderwert"). This occurs whenever the damaged vehicle, though fully repaired, becomes "marked" as a repaired vehicle and thereby loses some of its resale value (BGHZ 35, 396). It is not material in this context whether the plaintiff intends to sell the car or whether he intends to go on using it. In *Payton* v. *Brooks* [1974] 1 Lloyd's Rep. 241 the plaintiff alleged, but failed to prove, that the value of the damaged new car was diminished even though repairs were well done. Roskill LJ, as he then was, elegantly summarised the applicable principles in the following passage:

"There are many cases which arise, whether in the field of contract law or of tort, where the cost of repairs is a prima facie method of ascertaining the diminution in value. But it is not the only method of measuring the loss. In a case where the evidence justifies a finding that there has been, on top of the cost of repairs, some diminution in market value—or, to put the point another way, justifies the conclusion that the loss to the plaintiff has not been fully compensated by the receipt of the cost of complete and adequate repairs, because of a resultant diminution in market value—I can see no reason why the plaintiff should be deprived of recovery under that head of damage also. I would only add one word of caution. This conclusion is not a charter under which infuriated plaintiffs, who have the misfortune to have their cars damaged by careless drivers, acquire an unfettered right to recover diminution of value in every case in addition to the cost of repairs. It is essential in such a case, in my judgment, for appropriate evidence to be called to prove diminution in value."

The reverse situation arises where repairing the car has actually (and substantially) increased its value compared to the *status quo ante*. In principle it would be unfair to allow this to stand, for the defendant cannot be required to improve the plaintiff's overall financial position. The courts' approach is a pragmatic one. So if the replaced part would have normally lasted for the car's "lifetime" then damages are not reduced (KG Berlin NJW 1971, 142). On the other hand, if the part is already worn off and is replaced by a new part then the "betterment" must be taken into account (so called "Abzug neu für alt"); BGHZ 30, 29 (in tort). In this case the defendants burned down the plaintiff's house. The house was rebuilt and the defendants argued that it should be taken into account that now the plaintiff had a new house and therefore more than he would had but for the tort. The BGH accepted this in principle and made a reduction. However, it added that it must be sensible to make a reduction in the specific circumstances. So, for instance, if the plaintiff is not capable of paying for rebuilding the house himself it would be unfair to take the betterment into account and award him a lower amount of cost of repair than that which will be actually necessary to rebuild. (A similar approach was adopted in *British Westinghouse Electric and Manufacturing Co. Ltd.* v. *Underground Electric Railways Co. of London, Ltd.* [1912] AC 673, 690 (Viscount Haldane) in a contract case. The defendant supplied defective turbines. The plaintiff after having used them for a time replaced them by the other turbines which proved very efficient. Even if the original turbines had complied with the contract, it would still have been to the pecuniary advantage of the railway company at their own cost to have replaced them by other turbines. Damages were accordingly reduced. *Cf.* BGH NJW 1996, 584 (in contract). A more cautious note is struck in other cases. In *Harbutt's "Plasticine" Ltd.* v. *Wayne Tank and Pump Co. Ltd.* [1970] 1 QB 447 for instance the betterment caused by rebuilding a factory according to a new design was not deducted. It may have also been relevant that the plaintiffs apparently were not allowed to rebuild following the old design.)

Cost of repair will be borne by the defendant even if the plaintiff did not carry out the necessary repairs. The amount claimable in such cases will be equal to the sum that the garage would have charged had it carried out the repairs. In practice the plaintiff will claim damages on the basis of the estimate of an expert instructed by him (or by the defendant's insurance company) to prepare a report on the necessary repairs. But the plaintiff is then not required to use the compensation given him to carry out the necessary repairs. It is no concern of the law what the plaintiff does with the damages. He may thus use them for a holiday or for some other unrelated purpose. Indeed, a great number of plaintiffs resort to this method of assessing damages. (In 1998 the figures amounted to 12 per cent of the total of awards for damage to property, around 3 billion DM; figures from Geiß *DAR* 1998, 416, 421.) The theoretical basis of such "fictitious" damages is said to be § 249 sentence 2 BGB according to which the plaintiff may claim the cost of repair instead of having the property repaired by the defendant. However, as Professor Greger has pointed out (*op. cit.*, § 7 StVG, no. 204), the provision does not compel one to adopt such a view since it has not addressed the question expressly. Furthermore, in personal injury claims, the plaintiff must intend to spend the money on the necessary medical treatment. Otherwise, it is said, he would be awarded compensation for a non-pecuniary loss and this would be contrary to § 253 BGB. (It will be remembered that this provision excludes as a general rule compensation for non-pecuniary loss.) But this distinction between damages for personal injury and damage to property is by no means self-evident even though the BGH (as stated above, section 3(b)) has provided some plausible arguments in its defence. (BGHZ 97, 12.) Overall, therefore, the present practice of awarding "fictitious" damages in cases of property damages must be seen as an example of the (perhaps too) generous attitude of German courts towards compensation for physical damage to chattels. Further illustrations of this trend can be found throughout the rest of the section.

The "peculiarities" of German law do not cease there. The figure claimed in the case of "fictitious" damage can, rather oddly, also include the amount of VAT which the garage would have added to its bill. (BGH NJW 1973, 1647; BGH NJW 1982, 1864.) This amount clearly exceeds the plaintiff's real loss. Following the recommendations of the 20th *Verkehrsgerichtstag* of 1982 the proposals to reform the law of compensation alluded to above—2. *Gesetz zur Änderung schadensrechtlicher Vorschriften*—already envisage the abolition of the VAT claim where the repairs have not been carried out. (Recommended section § 249 II BGB).

"Fictitious" damages are also awarded where the plaintiff legally deprives himself of the chance of carrying out the repairs, for example, by selling the damaged vehicle (BGHZ 66, 239. But the issue is controversial. See: Greger, *op. cit.*, no. 67 for references). This line of cases is difficult to reconcile with BGHZ 81, 385 (confirmed by BGH NJW 1993, 1793) where the plaintiff's claim *in tort* failed because he had sold a damaged *building* to a third party. The italicised word gives a clue to the court's reasoning. For it sought to distinguish damaged buildings from damaged cars by pointing out that cost of repair of cars was standardised. But the distinction seems weak; and a different result has been reached in the Scottish case of *GUS Property Management Ltd* v. *Littlewoods Mail Order Stores Ltd* (1982) SLT 533. (Negligently damaged building transferred at book value to an associated company. See, also BGHZ 99, 81, which concerned a claim for breach of contract.) Recently, however, the BGH departed from BGHZ 81, 385 in BGH, 4 May 2001, NJW 2001, 2250. It allowed the original owner to recover the cost of repairs in tort even after the building was transferred to a third party *provided that* the original owner had assigned his claim in respect of the building to the third party. The court was obviously keen to avoid awarding to the original owner what it regarded as a windfall payment.

Where the cost of repair and replacement are approximately the same, the owner of the damaged vehicle will be free to decide what he will do. It must be remembered, however, that § 254 II BGB always obliges the plaintiff to mitigate his loss. Furthermore, according to § 251 II BGB, the cost of repair must not be disproportionate. A further and more specific principle has been developed by the courts in the context of § 249 sentence 1 BGB. According to this provision, only costs that are "necessary" can be recovered. From this the courts have inferred the requirement that the plaintiff's conduct must be reasonable from an economic point of view (*Wirtschaftlichkeitsgebot*). This means that if there are several ways of restoration within the meaning of § 249 BGB the plaintiff must choose the most cost-effective. Cost of replacement and cost of repair serve both the same purpose. So, generally speaking, if the cost of replacement is lower than the cost of repair, the owner of the vehicle will have to take the former option, however much he may wish to repair and retain his original car. If the plaintiff's estimate of the cost of repair is proved wrong and the cost of repair is actually higher than the cost of replacement then he may recover nevertheless the actual cost provided that he was not responsible for the error. (*Cf.* Greger, *op. cit.*, no. 42.)

A limited exception is made if the plaintiff has a legitimate and special interest in having the damaged car repaired. To give an example: a car that is particularly fitted for the needs of a disabled plaintiff (AG Lahr NZV 1990, 356). Somewhat surprisingly, the BGH extended this exception to used cars *in general*. Thus, the cost of repair can be claimed provided that it does not exceed by 30 per cent the cost of buying a comparable car (BGH VersR 1972, 1024. The principle and this arbitrarily fixed sum were subsequently confirmed by a decision dated 15 October 1991. BGHZ 115, 364, case 149, with an approving note by Lange, JZ 1992, 480). The BGH there argued that the interest in the integrity of the car (*Integritätsinteresse*) deserves special protection and it, therefore, justifies a higher award provided it does not exceed 130 per cent of the cost of buying an equivalent car. However, this seems questionable (Greger, *op. cit.*, no. 38) if one takes into account that used cars can nowadays be easily replaced and do not reflect any specific value (as Harman LJ remarked in *Darbyshire* v. *Warran* [1963] 1 WLR 1067: a used car is not generally speaking an irreplaceable article). It is important, however, to note that cost of repair can be recovered in all these special cases *only* if the victim actually uses the money for repairs. Similarly, in BGH JZ 1992, 481, the court sought to limit the impact of its decision in BGHZ 115, 364 by adding a limiting rider. If the cost of repair is actually 150 per cent of the replacement value, the owner can only claim 100 per cent. The attempt that he be reimbursed for 130 per cent (paying the remaining 20 per cent himself) was rejected on the grounds that the extra repair cost cannot /should not be split into two parts. The rational of this—to foreign eyes strange rule—seems to be that the BGH is getting cold feet with its previous decision and is trying to avoid inflated claims. (A similar solution—cost of replacement is awarded if cost of repair considerably exceeds cost of replacement—was reached in the Court of Appeal in *Darbishire* v. *Warran* [1963] 1 *WLR* 1067. Unique items (e.g. vintage car), however, are not covered by this rule (*cf. O'Grady* v. *Westminster Scaffolding Ltd* [1962] 2 Lloyd's Rep. 238)).

More problematical, though equally well compensated in practice, are the so-called "consequential" losses. § 252 sentence 1 BGB makes it clear that lost profits—for example resulting from the immobilisation of a van during its repairs—can be claimed from the tortfeasor. According to § 252 sentence 2 BGB, "profit is presumed to have been lost which could probably have been expected in the ordinary course of events, or according to special circumstances, especially in the light of the preparations and arrangements made". This means that for instance if the car is used for commercial purposes the owner will be able to recover the consequential loss of profit that results from the non use the car. This presumption, however, can be rebutted by showing, for example, that the owner of the damaged van had other spare vans that could be used for the same purpose. But what if the plaintiff deliberately keeps and maintains an extra vehicle precisely for this eventuality? Can he in such a case claim from the tortfeasor the monthly cost of maintenance of this spare vehicle? The point is disputed. (See for details Greger, *op. cit.*, § 7 StVG, no. 199.) From a theoretical point of view it is difficult to see how an expense incurred *before* the accident can be treated as its consequence. But the Supreme Court has on occasion sanctioned such claims. (BGHZ 32, 280; *cf.* also BGHZ 79, 199.) The cost of instructing an expert to evaluate the extent of the damage may also be recovered as consequential loss (Greger, *op. cit.*, no. 141).

It should be noted, however, that the BGH regards the cost of hiring a substitute car as part of the reparation owed by the defendant under § 249 sentence 1 BGB and does not treat it as consequential loss (§ 252 BGB). This is because these costs restore the position in which the plaintiff would have been in but for the tort. An important consequence of this is that the costs must be "necessary". Such claims can be maintained only if the plaintiff is in some way *economically affected* by the loss of use of the car. The manner in which the courts interpret these criteria have far-reaching consequences. For this head of damage is the second largest of awards for damage to property and often it exceeds the

cost claimed for repairing the car. Insurance payments covering the cost of hiring substitute cars amounted to 1.5 billion DM in 1994 (Greger, *op. cit.*, Rn. 94). In the case of
commercially used cars, this will not—in most cases—present major problems. (It will
be remembered that while the cost of a substitute car is part of the cost of restoration
(§ 249 sections 2 BGB), if the victim sustains loss of profit because he could not use the
car, this is regarded as consequential loss. (§ 252 BGB).)

That the courts are generous in allowing such claims under § 249 BGB for a substitute
car can be seen from the following example. The cost of a substitute car can sometimes
be recovered even if the lost profit that would have been incurred *if no car had been rented*
is less than the cost of hiring the car. In case 150 (BGH NJW 1993, 3321) the plaintiff
claimed the cost of hiring a substitute cab which was more than double the amount he
actually earned during the relevant period. The case raises three points.

First, although German compensation law proceeds on the basis of total reparation and
thus aims for *restitutio in integrum* (all costs are to be reimbursed which are necessary for
the complete restoration of the plaintiff's property) the rules for the compensatable harm
are subject to limitations. If monetary compensation is required for restoration, the sum
asked for by the plaintiff must be "necessary": § 249 sentence 2 BGB. The plaintiff cannot,
therefore, take as a basis for his computation of the damage the most expensive way to
restitutio in integrum if other ways exist for getting better value for money. Besides this,
§ 251 II BGB limits the applicability of the yardstick of *restitutio in integrum*. If this
requires disproportionate expenditure, the plaintiff can only ask for a—lesser—"equivalent" or, if there is no such equivalent, liability is totally excluded. (For a similar rule in
English law see: *Ruxley Electronics & Construction Ltd.* v. *Forsyth* [1996] 1 AC 344—a contract case. In a comparable case in Germany, however, no loss of amenity could have been
awarded because of § 253 BGB). In interpreting the concept of "disproportionate", the
costs of the restoration are to be compared with the plaintiff's loss that results to him
from the damage to his property. When vehicles used for business are damaged, the profit,
which the plaintiff loses, is therefore to be compared with the costs of *restitutio in integrum* by hiring of a replacement vehicle.

Secondly, it is interesting to note how the *Bundesgerichtshof* has approached the issue
of "reasonableness". In case 150 the BGH explained that only a price for the hiring of a
replacement vehicle which is "entrepreneurially unjustifiable" (in comparison with the
profit which the plaintiff would have obtained with the vehicle) will be regarded as
"disproportionate". In the case at hand the BGH regarded the proportionality requirement to be fulfilled although it was at pains to emphasise that the case was special (Christmas and New Years Eve trade was affected) and at the very end of the scale of tolerable
conduct. The BGH's plaintiff-oriented attitude ultimately derives from respecting the
victim's right to self-determination in economic terms. The court stressed that the costs
were not automatically out of proportion when the vehicle hire costs are more than 100
per cent (or some other percentage) in excess of a predictable loss of profit. This was
"because it is part of the nature of entrepreneurial organisation and the freedom to make
business arrangements to put up with short term losses, even if these are considerable,
for the sake of longer term advantages".

Finally, in this case, the rules of mitigation must arguably be interpreted in the light of
the importance of the right of self-determination in the economic sphere (Article 2 I GG)
and the right to the free exercise of one's vocation (Article 12 GG). (This would give these
provisions an indirect, horizontal effect (*mittelbare Drittwirkung*). *Cf.* Bernicke, *JuS* 1994,

1004, 1008.) Generally speaking, it is for the plaintiff to determine whether it is reasonable to try to earn a living from carrying out his profession.

The same generous attitude prevails where the owner of the damaged vehicle is a private individual rather than a commercial firm. As already stated, the BGH requires that the plaintiff must be economically affected by the loss of use of the car. This is clearly not the case for instance where the plaintiff was unable to use the car because he was injured. It seems, however, that the plaintiff need not change his lifestyle and is not required for instance to use public transport if he has not done so on a regular basis prior to the accident. The victim of a road accident is entitled to hire a replacement car provided that he can show that he has regularly used the car. However, it is not a condition that the victim used the car in a commercially relevant sense, for instance to go to work. (Against such an extensive approach is Schiemann *JZ* 1996, 1077, 1079, arguing that, in effect, it extends liability into the realm of non-pecuniary loss). All this, however, must be constantly viewed against the duty to mitigate so that, for example, a plaintiff who happens to have an extra car available, will have to use it and will not normally be allowed to claim the cost of substitute hire. Also, if it is clear in advance that the substitute car will not be regularly used, then such costs cannot be awarded. If the plaintiff establishes according to these considerations that it was reasonable to rent a car then what can be claimed is the cost of hiring an *appropriate* substitute which, quite simply, means that the owner of a damaged Volkswagen cannot go out and hire a Rolls-Royce at the defendant's expense. This is self-evident.

The problem in recent years has been however that at least most hire companies have introduced special tariffs for accident car hire. It is doubtful whether these tariffs are really justified by reason of a better, enhanced service. What is even more worrying is that there is no incentive for the victim to shop around for a better price because he will be able to recover the cost of hiring a substitute from the tortfeasor's insurer. Some lower courts had attempted to limit this relatively extensive liability for car hire costs by denying recovery of special "accident tariffs"; but the attempts have proved controversial. (See Greger, *NZV* 1994, 337 and Tschöpe, *MDR* 1996, 1091 with references.) The BGH came to a different conclusion in case 151.

If the plaintiff does not have an alternative way of achieving *restitutio in integrum* the point of departure is the principle of mitigation which the BGH usefully summarised in the present case. The victim must choose the more economical way of rectifying the loss, within the scope of what can be reasonably expected of him. The requirement that rectification of loss should be sensible from an economic point of view does not, however, call for the victim to economise for the benefit of the tortfeasor. This is because the victim will often make sacrifices or efforts which, in his relationship with the tortfeasor, are over and above his obligations and which the tortfeasor cannot, therefore, demand from him. One must thus not loose sight of the basic concern: if the tortfeasor is fully liable, the victim should receive compensation for loss which is as complete as possible. Therefore, in examining whether the victim has kept the expenditure within sensible limits, the loss must be considered in the context of the actual circumstances. Thus, account must be taken of the special situation of the victim, especially of his individual opportunities for knowledge and influence as well as the difficulties which he might have. A more recent decision (of 30 November 1999, BGHZ 143, 189) provides us with a good illustration. Where the victim has the damaged car valued by a professional surveyor and sells it at that price, this is regarded as reasonable even if the tortfeasor informed him about a more profitable opportunity to sell the car but which would have required an additional effort in selling it.

In the case at hand the issue was whether the victim of an accident who hires a replacement car can recover the costs of hire even if the hire company charges a special "accident car replacement tariff" (up to 25 per cent above the normal rate). Such practices can be contrary to fair-trading (see BGH NJW 1995, 2355); and it is questionable whether they are founded on any reasonable extra-effort by the hire company. (See Albrecht, *NZV* 1996, 49.) The rationale of the present decision seems to be that these market practices in the hiring sector, dubious though they may be, cannot work to the victim's disadvantage in the relationship between the tortfeasor and victim. The victim has no choice but to accept the market as it is and is required only to choose a reasonable tariff among the existing accident car replacement tariffs. (It should be noted that the BGH adopts a very "consumer" friendly approach also in this respect. Thus, the victim is required to compare rates only if it is foreseeable that the replacement car will be needed for a considerable period of time; see e.g. BGH VersR 1985, 1090: three weeks are sufficient; LG Freiburg Schaden-Praxis 1997, 75: two weeks). The BGH insinuated that the victim would have to lie about his motives to rent a car in order to obtain a standard tariff; this however cannot be reasonably required. Yet, the court merely assumed that the victim cannot as a matter of fact openly choose a different tariff. Whether this is really the case must remain open to doubt. (See Freyberger *MDR* 1996, 1091, 1092.) Moreover, the only way to put an end effectively to such practices is to deny the victim recovery of the increased cost. Calls for boycott by an insurer for instance were held to interfere with the car hirer's right to an established and operating business (see case 35 above).

A similar situation had to be confronted by the House of Lords in *Dimond* v. *Lovell* [2000] 2 WLR 1121. Mrs Dimond's car was negligently damaged in an accident caused by Mr Lovell. While the car was in a garage for repairs she needed a replacement vehicle to go to work. She hired a car from a car accident hire company called 1st Automotive at a rate that exceeded the usual rate of hiring an equivalent car. The only issue relevant here, namely whether the increased cost of hiring a car from an accident car hire company could be recovered (or whether the normal cost of hiring a replacement car was the maximum amount allowable) did not arise for decision. Yet Lord Hoffmann invited their Lordships to express an opinion on this point given its importance in daily life. The majority stated obiter that such damages cannot be recovered since the victim fails to mitigate his loss.

Lord Nicholls of Birkenhead dissented (pp. 1124–1125). Much of his reasoning reminds one of the line taken by the BGH even though the two cases differ in one important respect. For unlike *Dimond* v. *Lovell*, the plaintiff in the German case had actually already paid for the hire. Lord Nicholls based his argument mainly on the interests involved in the former type of situation. Normal insurance, he explained, does not provide for a replacement car; and there are a number of factors that deter victims to make arrangements for hire of a replacement car themselves. They may be required to produce the hire charge up front or may hesitate to rent a car because they are put off by the prospect of having to sue the negligent driver for the relatively small amount of hire. So accident hire companies full fill a real need. The hirer does not have to produce any money; the hire-company pursues the allegedly negligent driver's insurers. For this additional service they charge more than the usual hiring rate (in the present case double). As suggested, this consideration does not apply with equal force to the situation in case 151. But since in Germany most hire companies charge a higher "accident tariff", the victim will find it difficult to avoid the higher tariff and would be in the end burdened with the costs of the doubtful trading practice. However, there are also schemes in operation which are similar to that used by 1st Automotive: the victim does not need to pay for hiring a replacement car but merely assigns his claim against the insurance to the care hire company. (See e.g. LG Gießen, ZfSch 1997, 454.) Lord Nicholls also pointed out the Achilles' heel of such a scheme (regardless whether the hire company offers the additional service of pursuing the claim or not). It is this aspect that raises a point of general interest. Does tort law provide rules which can deal satisfactorily with situations where there is no market mechanism to control the adequacy of the bargain? Since the victim does not have to bear the cost of the hire he will, in the end, be much less critical towards the price of such hiring arrangements. It lies in the nature of such a scheme (someone else, the insurance company, is paying for the service) that there is *no market mechanism* to contain the price of the service. (See in particular Schiemann, *JZ* 1996, 1077, 1078 and also Jaffey [2000] *LMCLQ* 449, 455). Lord Nicholls sought to accommodate this fear by limiting the damages recoverable to "a reasonable charge". A similar approach was adopted in *Giles* v. *Thompson* [1994] 1 AC 142 where the question was whether the accident hire contract was champertous. Lord Mustill held that this was not so provided that the charge did not exceed the market rate for car hire companies (at p. 165). It follows also from the German case law that once such extended liability is accepted the only realistic control factor is whether the rate is a reasonable one compared to the average *accident* tariffs which will be at an inflated level already. Hence, Lord Hoffmann was justified in warning of the danger of inflated claims. (At p. 1126.) For this reason, most German commentators have strongly criticised the decision of the BGH. (See Hootz, *BB* 1996, 2215 with further references.) In their view the consequence of the decision of the BGH is that the public at large through insurance premiums pays the price for the unreasonable.

From the above it should be clear that additional expenditure incurred as a consequence of damage to vehicles can, in principle, be claimed. But what if the owner of the car has incurred no such expenditure because, for example, he has not hired a substitute vehicle? The case law is rich on the subject, and generalisations can be misleading. It is clear that cost of hiring a substitute can be awarded only if a substitute has been actually hired (as explained a different approach is adopted in relation to cost of repair). If no substitute has been hired the plaintiff is in effect seeking compensation for the mere loss of use of the car. The theoretical difficulty raised by such claims is whether loss of use does, in itself, embody a financial loss or is merely a possible source of further financial loss. In principle, however, one can say that the Supreme Court has characterised the "loss of the possibility of using a car" as property loss and thus treated it as an indemnifiable item of damage. See BGHZ 40, 345; BGHZ 45, 212. The Great Civil Senate reaffirmed its stance BGHZ 98, 212, 9 July 1986, case 148. This area of the law has nevertheless remained extremely controversial (see Greger *op. cit.* no. 127 ff. with references).

If the owner of the vehicle would not or could not have used it anyway because he, himself, was injured in the same accident, a claim will not usually be allowed because the plaintiff has not been really affected (*fühlbar beeinträchtigt*) by the loss of use of the car (BGH NJW 1968, 1778). The reason for this requirement becomes immediately clear if one considers the rationale behind awarding damages for loss of use. The cost of a substitute car can be claimed as was explained if the loss of use of the car affects the plaintiff economically. It was also suggested that the criteria applied by the courts in this respect were anything but strict. At the same time a plaintiff who does not hire a substitute car even though he was entitled to do so would get nothing. But in many cases using other means of transport rather than hiring a car is certainly more reasonable, prudent, and cost-effective. Therefore, awarding damages also where the plaintiff did not rent a substitute undeniably serves as an incentive not to hire a substitute and also as a gift to those who exercise self-restraint and save expense. (This point is emphasised by Medicus *Schuldrecht AT I* 11th edn. (1999) p. 300). It goes without saying that the amount of compensation for (simple) loss of use must be less than the cost of the substitute. In practice roughly 30% of the normal rate of hiring a comparable car are awarded and the relevant figures are published in specialised and up-to-date tables.

It will have been noticed that by calling this type of loss "property loss" the courts have bypassed once again the obstacles of § 253 BGB. However, in order to try to maintain the impression of consistency a number of theories have, finally, been developed to explain why the exception was only "apparent". According to one view the loss of use as such represents an economic value capable of sounding in damages (*Kommerzialisierungstheorie*). In this sense BGHZ 45, 212. This may be plausible at first sight, but it fails to explain why the BGH awarded no such damages in the case of objects that do not typically fulfil a *vital or central role* in everyday life. This has been accepted for cars and for the matrimonial home (BGHZ 98, 212), but claims were denied in the case of "luxury" objects such as a racing boat (BGHZ 89, 60), a swimming pool (BGHZ 76, 179), a caravan (BGHZ 86, 128) or even a garage (BGH NJW 1993, 1793). Thus, this "evasive" action is not always possible. However, all these uses have commercial significance; evidenced by the fact that there is a market for them. The restriction of "vital" use must however be seen as an attempt to keep liability under control and the floodgates shut. In the meantime the principal area of application are claims in the context of traffic accidents. To mention just one further "theory" it suffices to refer to the "frustration" approach. The plaintiff invested in being able to use an object. Being deprived of this use amounts to a frustration of his investment. The drawback of this is that it is difficult to see why it should be relevant whether the car was a gift or whether it was bought. (This highly controversial problem is thoroughly reviewed in BGH NJW 1986, 2037 = VersR 1986, 189 and, in a less clear manner, in BGHZ 98, 212 = NJW 1987, 50 = JZ 1987, 306, reproduced below as cases 147 and 148.)

A further interrelated problem arises in the context of the lost enjoyment of a holiday. Thus, a damaged car may frustrate a family's carefully planned holiday arrangements. Can the "lost holiday" be claimed as consequential loss? The answer really depends upon whether we are faced here with a claim for disappointment and frustration or something, which is capable of being equated with a pecuniary loss. Where there is no wasted expenditure incurred prior to the accident, the better view is to deny such claims (BGHZ 60, 214). But in another famous case (BGH NJW 1956, 1234) the German customs authorities were held liable under § 839 BGB to a young married couple whose luggage was delayed as a result of their negligence thereby ruining their honeymoon in the Canaries. (In BGHZ 86, 212 the Supreme Court tried to reconcile BGHZ 60, 214 with BGH NJW 1956, 1234.) Perhaps one should add that in recent times a number of decisions *pleaded on breach of contract* have allowed sums for "disappointed holidays"; and an enactment—the *Reisevertragsgesetz* of 4 May 1979, § 651 f II BGB, one of the few exceptions in the Code where damages for non-pecuniary loss are provided for—has adopted the same view in the narrow context of travel contracts. But what is particularly interesting in these judgments is a growing tendency to look at holidays as representing a pecuniary interests which can give rise to material loss if they are wholly or partially ruined (BGHZ 63, 98; in similar vein BGHZ 77, 116; 80, 366; 82, 219; 85, 50). This must suggest that the recognition of such claims in tort actions may be imminent though a recent decision (BGHZ 86, 212, case 141), *pleaded in tort,* refused to sanction such a development.

Until this happens, German law will thus differ from English law. (See *Jackson* v. *Horizon Holidays Ltd.* [1975], 1 *WLR* 1468 (in contract); *Ichard* v. *Frangoulis* [1977], 1 *WLR* 556 (in tort).) But this difference is certainly not great from a practical point of view as far as the holiday cases are concerned. The difference may be greater in relation to claims for the loss of use of a car. Thus, in *Alexander* v. *Alpe Jack Rolls Royce Motor Cars Ltd.* [1996] RTR 95 the Court of Appeal refused to apply by analogy the rule in *Jackson* v. *Horizon Holidays Ltd.* in the context of the loss of use of a car. Breach of a contract to repair a motor car, even as prestigious as a Rolls Royce, does not give rise to a liability for damages for distress and inconvenience or loss of enjoyment in the use of the car. This ruling reveals also a crucially different point of departure of the German and English courts. The English court asked whether the defendant owed a duty to the plaintiff not to cause distress by depriving him of the loss of the enjoyment of the chattel (non-pecuniary loss), while the German courts inquired whether the object is of such central importance to the plaintiff that its use acquires *economic* value. In English law, the cost of actual hire must be proved as special damage. It is not certain whether compensation for a *pecuniary* loss can be recovered by basing the claim on (simple) loss of use. (See Burrows *Remedies for Breach of Contract and Tort* 2nd edn. (1994) 164–165.) Occasionally, however, English courts appear to have allowed such claims. For instance in *The Mediana* [1900] AC 113 the plaintiff recovered damages for the loss of use of a non-profit-earning ship (and even though the plaintiff maintained a substitute ship as cover). More recently, however, Lord Mustill remarked in *Giles* v. *Thompson* [1994] 1 A.C. 142, 167 regarding claims for loss of use of a car: "In principle, if such a claim is made it will often be quantified by reference to the cost of hiring a substitute vehicle, and will be recoverable upon proof that the motorist needed a replacement car whilst his own was off the road."

From the extensive literature on these problems see: Brinker, *Die Dogmatik zum Vermögensschadensersatz* (1982); Dunz, "Schadensersatz für entgangene Sachnutzung", *JZ* 1984, 1010; Flessner, "Geldersatz für Gebrauchsentgang", *JZ* 1987, 271; Jahr, "Schadensersatz wegen deliktischer Nutzungsentziehung—zu den Grundlagen des Rechtsgüterschutzes und des Schadensersatzrechts", *AcP* 183 (1983), 725; Hagen, "Entgangene Gebrauchsvorteile als Vermögensschaden?", *JZ* 1983, 833; Kötz/Wagner, nos. 497 *et seq.*; Lange, *Schadensersatz*, § 6 VII 4b; Larenz, *Schuldrecht* I, § 29 II (p. 499); Medicus, "Nutzungsentgang als Vermögensschaden", *Jura* 1987, 240; Ott/Schäfer, "Begründung und Bemessung des Schadensersatzes wegen entgangener Sachnutzung", *ZIP* 1986, 613; Schwerdtner, "Grundzüge des Schadensersatzrechts", *Jura* 1987, 143, 304, 475; Weber, "Entschädigung für den entgangenen Gebrauch eines Kraftfahrzeuges", *VersR* 1985, 111.

SECTION B. CASES

1. § 823 II BGB

Case 129

BUNDESGERICHTSHOF (SIXTH CIVIL SENATE) 12 NOVEMBER 1957
BGHZ 26, 42

The defendant was the owner of a business running omnibuses. On 6 February 1950 he was granted a licence by the competent authority permitting him to operate two omnibuses to be employed for hire or on excursions. The licence stated expressly that the employment of the buses on regular service between specified places was prohibited.

The plaintiffs, the German Federal Railways, alleged that the defendant had regularly conveyed persons between G and L with his buses. They argued that, since most of these persons would otherwise have used the Federal Railways, they had suffered damage as a result of this unlicensed regular traffic. The plaintiffs asked for an account of the number of journeys and passengers and claimed a sum representing part of their damage. The defendant denied that he carried on regular services and contended that the Act on the Carriage of Persons is not a law serving to protect the German Federal Railways. Moreover it violated the Constitution by restricting the commercial activities of transport undertakings.

The District Court rejected the claim, the Court of Appeal of Hamm allowed it. A second appeal was unsuccessful for the following

Reasons

1. The Court of Appeal was correct in regarding as a protective law in the meaning of § 823 II BGB in favour of the plaintiffs the provisions of the Act concerning the Transport of Persons on Land which require a licence by the administrative authorities for the operation of regular traffic with land-based vehicles and provide penalties for such operations without a licence. The crucial question is whether the legislature, in providing regulations for public traffic, also wished to protect the special interest of the Federal Railways [reference]. This question must be answered in the affirmative without hesitation. The special position of the German Federal Railways within the legal framework of public passenger transport is shown by the fact that § 14 of the Act on Passenger Transport exempts them from licensing and that § 27 II only requires them to give notice of the intended establishment of a regular route. According to § 5 of the Decree for the Execution of the Act on Passenger Transport, the Federal Railways must be consulted if a dispute arises as to whether a traffic undertaking is subject to the provisions of the Act on Passenger Transport or to which type of traffic the traffic undertaking belongs. § 9 I 2 of the Decree requires the competent regional directorate of the Federal Railways to be heard if an application is submitted for a licence to operate a regular cross-country route. According to § 11 II of the Decree a licence for a regular service is not to be granted if a new enterprise constitutes inequitable competition for an existing traffic undertaking.

Together these provisions show clearly that in the proceedings of consultation the Federal Railways are granted a right to intervene as the guardian of the public interests concerning traffic but that they may *also* plead any adverse effects upon their own interests. This is the reason why the Federal Railways are accorded the right to start proceedings in the administrative courts if their objections have been overruled [references]. The fact that according to §§ 17 and 24 of the Act on Passenger Transport the administrative authorities also control the price and the conditions of travel is a safeguard against a ruinous competition by undercutting at the expense of the Federal Railways. The importance of the Act on Passenger Transport consists precisely in the fact that it restricts competition between the various transport undertakings because the legislature allots to each branch of transport those tasks which it can fulfil best within the framework of traffic as a whole and of the economy. In so doing, the legislature has attached special significance to the interest of the Federal Railways on the assumption that the maintenance of their efficiency must be assured in the public interest.

2. The appellant is wrong in asserting that the provisions of the Act on Passenger Transport which pursue this goal contravene Article 12 of the Constitution (GG). Article 12 I of the Constitution guarantees the right to choose an occupation freely but reserves the exercise of an occupation or trade for regulation or statute. It is generally recognised that the legislature is not prohibited in principle from regulating, in particular, the conditions for carrying on a profession or exercising a trade and from requiring a licence by the administrative authorities for commercial activities. It is equally recognized that in establishing the conditions for exercising a profession the legislature is not completely unfettered and that the essence of the fundamental right to carry on a trade must not be touched [reference]. Opinions are divided as to how the limits set for the legislature are to be drawn in detail and as to when, in particular, the essence of the right to carry on an occupation is being fettered. In this controversy the view of the Federal Administrative Court which grants the legislature a considerable measure of discretion is to be contrasted with the very restrictive view of the First Civil Division of the Federal Supreme Court expressed in its references to the Federal Constitutional Court, but these do not bind this Division [references].

The first opinion stresses that all fundamental rights contain their own intrinsic limits and is less concerned with the compelling reasons for these restrictions than with the problem of what remains of the fundamental right, once these restrictions have been recognized.

The restrictive opinion allows fundamental rights to be limited for reasons of urgent necessity only and requires the encroachment to be as small as possible in the light of the circumstances, guided by the desire to leave the fundamental right an extensive scope. Nevertheless, the First Division [references] acknowledges that the legislature may also enact laws in the interest of individual groups if this should be necessary in the public interest and does not arbitrarily detract from the interest deserving protection of other parties. In its decision the First Division also recognizes that the legislature enjoys a measure of discretion in the sphere of Article 12 I of the Constitution and points out that the judicial control of the legislature is limited correspondingly.

It is unnecessary here to discuss in detail the many attempts to determine and to circumscribe the extent of the prohibition expressed by Article 19 II of the Constitution. Even if a statutory restriction of occupational activities is only regarded as constitutional within narrow limits, it cannot be said that the Law on Passenger Transport has infringed illegally the essence of the fundamental right enshrined in Article 12 I of the Constitution by having made the commercial operation of a regular traffic route of land-based vehicles subject to a licence for the reason, *inter alia,* in order to save the Federal Railways from inequitable competition by motorized traffic undertakings. In this connection it is important that despite an increase in motorized traffic the Federal Railways deal with the major portion of public transport. The pre-eminent interest of the community in the efficiency of the Federal Railways is expressed in the organization of the Federal Railways by the Act of 13 December 1951 concerning the Federal Railways. The act treats the discharge of the functions of the Federal Railways as a public service and requires that in the administration of the Federal Railways the interests of the German economy are safeguarded [references]. For this reason, the operation of the Federal Railways is subject to a number of restrictions which could not be justified from a purely commercial point of view. They cannot in their discretion discontinue routes which are unprofitable and, in particular, they are not free to determine the fares. (Fares must be established, must be equal, serve social needs, and must offer free passes.) Moreover the Federal Railways are burdened with extensive maintenance obligations towards their present and past employees which private traffic operators do not have to carry. The Federal Railways would no longer be able to fulfil their function in the service of the community if private commercial motor transport operators were allowed to exploit the economically profitable routes, which alone are of interest to them, with the result that the Federal Railways would be relegated increasingly to carrying out less profitable transport services. For this reason alone, the legislature must be interested in the maintenance of the efficient operation of traffic by rail, since the service of mass traffic by the railways is indispensable in present conditions and since any interruption in the ability of the railways to function would lead to a crisis. In this connection it is relevant that any shift of public passenger traffic from the railways to motor vehicle traffic is restricted if for no other reason than because the capacity of the German road system is strictly limited. The special character of public transport makes it appear unlikely that the regulating effect alone of offer and demand can achieve a satisfactory solution to the far-reaching problems of public transport which satisfies the needs of the community. This explains why § 99 of the Act against Restrictions of Competition of 27 July 1957 [reference] does not apply to the Federal Railways and other public traffic institutions.

The Federal Administrative Court has pointed out rightly that the safeguarding of orderly operations of public traffic is one of the protected legal interests essential for the existence of the community [reference]. It is a primary task of the legislature which is concerned with maintaining and extending an efficient transport system to regulate and to plan public transport by a process of adjustment and balancing [references]. This Division cannot discern in the discharge of this task by the legislature, which must necessarily include the regulation of the competition between rail and road traffic, an act of unconstitutional interference in the freedom of commerce, all the more since public transport had already been regulated by statute at the time when the Constitution was being enacted. Moreover, it does not appear that in enacting the Constitution the intention was to question the validity of this regulation on the ground that freedom of occupation was being restricted or to restrict the legislature and the administration to measures for controlling safety and the proper conduct of trade [references]. If the public interest in an efficient system of passenger transport must be the principal object of the legislation measure for regulating traffic, the legislature was justified for this reason in regarding the protection of the Federal Railways as especially important where route transport is concerned and in fashioning its traffic regulations accordingly [reference].

The enactment of the Act on Passenger Transport does not constitute a closure of the occupation for private transport enterprises but the control of their commercial activity dictated by the overriding interests of the community. This control does not interfere with the essence of the fundamental right enshrined in Article 12 I; on the contrary, in the opinion of this Division the statutory provisions fall within the framework of the task set for the legislature by Article 12 II inasmuch as, by requiring the consent of the administration, the legislature wishes to ensure that the Federal Railways are protected against inappropriate competition and that every traffic institution is allotted that task which it can best perform in the interest of the common good.

... even if the refusal of a transport licence on the sole ground of insufficient need is regarded as illegal, the need for a licence remains justified in the opinion of this Division inasmuch as, apart from other reasons, the just interest of the Federal Railways in averting inequitable competition must be taken into consideration. Consequently there are no objections from the point of view of Article 12 of the Constitution against regarding the penal provision of § 40 I of the Act on Passenger Transport as a valid protective law in the meaning of § 823 II BGB in favour of the Federal Railways by penalising unlicensed route transport (as the dominant practice holds [references]). The view taken by this Division is in keeping with its decision of 27 March 1956 [reference] where the comparable provision of the Act concerning Milk and Fats regulating that market were found to protect by an action in tort dairies, the economic activities of which had been interfered with in the absence of a licence [reference]. Finally, the First Civil Division in its judgment [reference] allowed a claim under § 823 II BGB by chemists against drug stores which had contravened the Act on Medicaments.

3. ...

Case 130

BUNDESGERICHTSHOF (FIRST CIVIL SENATE) 30 NOVEMBER 1954
BGHZ 15, 315

The plaintiff is a registered association founded in 1946. According to § 1 of its statutes its purpose is to protect and to further the professional and economic interests of the Hamburg Bar.

The third defendant is an association founded in 1890 as a legal entity. According to § 2 of its statutes its purpose is to better the "tenancy and housing conditions" of the population and, especially, to protect the legitimate interests of its members. According to § 2(d) and (e) of its statutes this goal is to be achieved by providing free oral advice as well as written advice for a fee for all members of the association; in addition it offers to represent them for a fee in dealings with public authorities, civil and administrative courts. The fees payable to the association are the same as those charged by legal counsellors.

The first and the second defendants are the legal advisors of the third defendant who are entitled, according to § 8(6) of the statutes, to represent the members before public authorities and courts. Until 1 October 1952 they were paid their own expenses and 80 per cent of the fees after deducting the expenses incurred by the association. The parties disagree as to what fees are paid to them after 1 October 1952.

The plaintiff contends that the first and the second defendants have contravened the Act against Abuses in the Field of Legal Advice and the Unfair Competition Act (UWG) and that the third defendant had enabled them to carry on their illegal activity, and had assisted them.

The plaintiff has asked that the first and second defendants be ordered to desist from advising the members of the third defendants gratuitously or against a fee and from representing them in court and to order the third defendant to desist from according to the first and second defendants the right to give free advice or advice for a fee and to represent it in court.

The defendants have denied that the plaintiff has a legal interest calling for protection. They argue that the first and second defendants do not give legal advice on a commercial or professional basis. Nor did their conduct constitute unfair competition.

The District Court rejected the claim. On appeal, the plaintiff has asked as an alternative to prohibit the third defendant from handling legal matters professionally, especially by charging fees similar to those of procedural representatives or the like, and to prohibit the first and second defendants from collaborating with the third defendant in handling legal matters. The Court of Appeal of Hamburg rejected the entire claim. The plaintiff's appeal was successful in most respects for the following

Reasons

The plaintiff has based his claim for orders to desist primarily on § 823 II BGB in conjunction with § 1 I of the Act concerning Legal Counsellors. Since this act aims at protecting the citizen against the dangers arising from the employment of unqualified and unreliable persons, but also seeks to protect the Bar against competition by such persons who engage in legal advice who are not subject to the constraints relating to professional etiquette, fees, and the like created in the interest of the administration of justice, it cannot be doubted that it bears the character of a protective act . . .

The appellant is wrong in contending that the third defendant must not demand any "consideration", for his legal services, not even to reimburse him for his expenses.

The claims of the members of the association to receive assistance in legal matters follows from their membership. The expenses incurred by the association in satisfying this claim must naturally be covered somehow, be it by contributions by *all* members, or by special payments to those members who ask the association for assistance in legal matters. It is an internal matter to be decided as such by the association as it sees fit. The question as to whether in so doing it exceeds the limits set by § 7 I of the Act concerning Legal Counsellors is not necessarily identical with that as to whether the association may only provide "gratuitous" assistance in legal matters or whether it can do so also for "remuneration". For, as will be shown later on, even to claim actual expenses only, i.e. to provide assistance in legal proceedings gratuitously in the strict meaning of the word, may be illegal in certain circumstances; e.g. if the association grants the persons who act for it in assisting in legal proceedings a remuneration in accordance with the scale of fees for lawyers or for legal counsellors and then seeks to recover it from the members as actual expenses. The plaintiff contends, in agreement with the literature and practice, that "remuneration" in the meaning of § 7 I of the above-mentioned law consists of any money payment by a member of the association, even if it only represents a reimbursement of expenses and not a genuine remuneration. However, this Division cannot accept his view that the assistance in legal proceedings by the association must be "gratuitous" in this sense.

Contrary to the view of the appellant the wording of § 7 I of the Act concerning Legal Counsellors . . . does not indicate that this exceptional provision is to apply only if the assistance in legal matters is "gratuitous". In so far as § 1 VII of the Act concerning Legal Counsellors permits the association concerned acting within the limits of their established task to "provide" advice and assistance in legal matters for their members, the word "provide" does compel the conclusion that the legislature only wished to allow a gratuitous activity . . . The Court of Appeal was therefore correct in holding that a comparison of § 7 I and § 1 I does not lead to the conclusion that the advice and assistance must only be gratuitous. . . .

Nevertheless, the objections of the appellant must succeed in so far as they are directed against the assessment of the remuneration in accordance with the official scale of fees. The appellant is right in stating that to allow remuneration to be charged on the scale of charges fixed for legal counsellors (§ 2(e) of the statutes) is incompatible with the provision of § 7 I of the Act concerning Legal Counsellors and therefore illegal.

§ 7 I of the above-mentioned Act is based on the consideration that voluntary legal assistance is to be judged by different standards than those activities which, in looking after the legal affairs of others, serve a gainful purpose [reference]. An association is only exempt from the need to have a licence if advice and assistance is provided within the framework of its professional duties. Its activity must be strictly limited to these tasks; it becomes illegal if the association, in exceeding the limits set to it, e.g. by the way in which it regulates the remuneration payable by its members, participates in the pursuit of economic gain, which in the case of legal advice is only permitted by the law in strictly fixed circumstances.

According to § 1 I of the above-mentioned Act, not only physical persons but also legal entities and other associations which intend to act for others in legal matters require a licence. In this connection the legislature has established special protective measures for entities which appear in the form of corporations, especially private companies and similar associations of persons. The grant of the licence depends not only on the consideration that the circumstances of the individual case justify the desired legal form for the operation [reference] but it presupposes also that the exercise of the profession is limited to the persons who are designated by name in the licence [reference]. Moreover, like individuals these associations are subject to the supervision by the President of the District Court and are controlled as to the proper conduct of their operations [reference]. The intention of the legislature expressed in these provisions to protect the community against damage and to protect the Bar which is subject to extensive restrictions against competition by an immeasurable number of persons must not be evaded or frustrated. § 7 I of the Act concerning Legal Counsellors must be interpreted in accordance with this purpose of the law. The meaning and the purpose of this Act would be reversed if the associations which have a professional basis were allowed to exercise an activity which, in the main, distinguishes them no longer from the circle of persons who require a licence. If an association with a professional or similar basis looks after the legal affairs of others in a manner which comes near to the activity of an individual or association requiring a licence to such an extent that a member of the association occupies a position in relation to the association which does not differ essentially from that towards a person covered by § 1 I of the above-mentioned Act, that association can no longer claim that its activity is permitted by § 7 I. Such is the case, in particular, if the professional association which looks after the affairs of a member demands a fee which is assessed on the scale of fees for advocates and legal counsellors. Only advocates and, to a certain extent [reference], legal counsellors [reference] may claim fees on this scale. The reason is that this profession, which is required for the administration of justice, must be guaranteed an adequate remuneration for its service and thus a dignified position in life [reference]. This consideration does not apply, however, to an association formed in accordance with § 7 I of the above-mentioned Act. It is true that such an association cannot be prohibited from seeking reimbursement for those expenses and costs incurred in the course of safeguarding the legal interests of their members. The association must therefore remain entitled to bill its members—either all of them or only those requiring legal assistance— for the salaries actually paid to its employees and for the compensation paid to an agent as well as for other general office expenses by apportioning them in its discretion without undue need for restrictions. However, the association exceeds the legal limits set for its operations if it provides assistance and support for its members on the basis of a scale of fees which is only permitted in entirely different circumstances to a circle of persons to which admission is by registration or by a licence according to § 1 of the above-mentioned Act. It is irrelevant in this connection whether in the end by using this scale of fees the association *in fact* made a profit by rendering assistance in legal proceedings. It is common experience that a scale of fees of this kind at least encourages the tendency to make a business out of looking after the legal affairs of others. If so, all the dangers facing those seeking advice would be allowed to materialize which persuaded the legislature to require a licence for gainfully engaging in looking after the legal affairs of others. If the professional associations were given dispensation by § 7 I of the above-mentioned Act from the need to apply for a licence the reason was because, and to the extent that, a genuine activity of assistance appeared to exclude these dangers from the outset. This privilege is, however, no longer justified if as a result of the method of determining the remuneration for its activities the association creates the same dangerous situation which the requirement of a licence sought to meet in the case of non-privileged individuals and associations.

By providing in its statutes that its fees are to be those applicable to legal counsellors, the third defendant has therefore contravened § 1 I of the above-mentioned law in conjunction with § 823 II BGB. He is therefore obliged to refrain from doing so in so far as he allows his members to be advised or to be represented in court by the first and second defendant in consideration of fees as they are established for legal counsellors . . . Since it may be assumed without hesitation that the first and second defendants were familiar with the statutes of the third defendant, they are equally liable for having contravened § 823 II as accomplices or accessories and are therefore equally under the obligation to desist.

Case 131

BUNDESGERICHTSHOF (SIXTH CIVIL SENATE) 16 DECEMBER 1958
BGHZ 29, 100

The defendant and B, a merchant, were the sole shareholders and directors of a . . . private company [GmbH]. On 17 July 1954, on the application of the company, bankruptcy proceedings were started against it.

The plaintiff, who had supplied raw materials to the company over many years, claimed DM 26,604 as a non-privileged creditor. According to the report of the trustees in bankruptcy, the assets only sufficed to satisfy in part the claims of the privileged creditors.

Claiming only part of the sum registered in the bankruptcy proceedings, the plaintiff sued the defendant personally on the ground that he had neglected in several respects his duties as a director of the company and that the plaintiff had suffered considerable damage as a result. In particular he had failed, in contravention of § 64 of the Act relating to Private Companies [henceforth cited as GmbHG] to initiate bankruptcy proceedings in time, although the company had been insolvent and overburdened with debts for some time.

The District Court rejected the claim; the Court of Appeal of Hamburg allowed it. Upon a further appeal the judgment of the Court of Appeal was quashed and the case referred back for the following

Reasons

I. The managers of a private company are obliged under § 64 I GmbHG to apply for the start of bankruptcy proceedings as soon as the company becomes insolvent or if the annual or an interim balance sheet shows that the debts exceed the assets . . . The Court of Appeal regarded this provision as a law for the protection (§ 823 II BGB) of the creditors of a private company and held that the defendant had culpably violated his duty to initiate bankruptcy proceedings . . .

II. The appellant denies that § 64 I GmbHG is a protective law in the meaning of § 823 II BGB in favour of the creditors of a private company. He contends that this conclusion was ruled out by § 64 II GmbHG which hardly made any sense if § 64 I bore a protective character. This view cannot be accepted. § 64 II GmbHG only establishes the consequence as between the directors and the company if bankruptcy proceedings are begun too late. It provides that the directors must compensate the company in respect of payments made after the company became insolvent or overburdened with debts if these payments cannot be reconciled with the case of a merchant. It does not follow therefore that this provision determines exhaustively the responsibility of the directors for their dereliction of duty and that the creditors of the company are denied protection in their own right. The Act relating to Private Companies does not state whether the directors are liable to the creditors, and this question must therefore be determined in accordance with the general principles of private law [references].

The plaintiff may claim damages based on a violation of § 64 I GmbHG in conjunction with § 823 II BGB if this provision of the Act relating to Private Companies is also intended to protect the creditors of a private company and to afford them the type of protection which the plaintiff claims for himself [references]. Whether this is so must be determined in the light of the substance and the purpose of § 64 GmbHG.

1. § 64 I GmbHG provides that the directors must initiate bankruptcy proceedings as soon as the private company becomes insolvent or if the balance sheet discloses that the debts exceed the assets. If the directors fail to initiate these proceedings in time they are liable to imprisonment or a fine in accordance with § 84 I GmbHG. Clearly these provisions are intended to protect the creditors of the company as well. They, in particular, always suffer damage if bankruptcy proceedings are not begun or are not begun in time. It is obvious that the duty to apply to the court laid down by § 64 I GmbHG is also to

protect them. This protection of the creditors is all the more called for as the partner shareholders of a private company are not liable personally for the debts of the company. The Reichsgericht, too, has held in a constant practice that § 64 GmbHG is a law for the protection of the creditors of the company. It has held that, while this provision does not protect everyone, particularly not those persons who are extraneous to the company, it is intended to protect not only the interests of the company but also the creditors [references].

2. The appellant argues further that even if § 64 GmbHG bore the character of the protective law, it could only protect the creditors existing at the time when bankruptcy proceedings should have been begun. If, as the Court of Appeal has held, the defendant should have started bankruptcy proceedings in January 1954 at the latest, the plaintiff could not, as regards claims arising after this date, be placed in a better position than other subsequent creditors for the reason that other claims of his were of an earlier date. At best he could claim damages in respect of the loss resulting from the fact that the dividend in respect of his claims outstanding in 1954 was smaller owing to the delay in starting bankruptcy proceedings than it would have been otherwise. However, the plaintiff had not incurred such a loss for he had admitted himself that his claims arising during the period up to January 1954 had been satisfied. As regards goods supplied between 31 January and 15 July 1954, which were alone in issue, the plaintiff could not claim any damages against the defendant on the basis of § 823 II BGB, § 64 GmbHG.

The appellant is wrong in believing that § 64 GmbHG only protects those persons who were already creditors of the company when the conditions for the operation of § 64 I GmbHG materialised [reference]. The duty of the directors to start bankruptcy proceedings continues even after this date, as long as the company's debts exceed the assets or the company is insolvent. No reason exists for restricting this continuous duty to apply to the court to the claims of old creditors, that is to say, creditors whose claims already existed at the time in which the delay occurred in making the application. The duty of a director to initiate bankruptcy proceedings exists also towards a creditor who after this date supplies goods to the company on credit or who becomes its creditor otherwise. As a present creditor of the private company he is protected against subsequent infringements of § 64 I GmbHG in the same way as are old creditors. Therefore, contrary to the appellant, the protection accorded to the plaintiff extends also to claims against the private company which arose after 31 January 1954.

3. The question remains as to how far the protection extends which the plaintiff enjoys for this period by virtue of § 64 I GmbHG. The plaintiff seeks as damages the full price of the goods which he supplied after 31 January 1954, i.e. after the date when, in the plaintiff's opinion, the defendant should have started bankruptcy proceedings at the latest. The plaintiff can claim compensation for this damage on the strength of § 823 II BGB only if the entire damage falls within the range of dangers to protect against which § 64 GmbHG was enacted [reference]. If a statute serves to protect certain persons they can only claim compensation for such damage which occurred within the range of the interests protected by the statute. Therefore, before it is possible to apply § 249 BGB on which the plaintiff relies, it is necessary first to examine the range of protection afforded by § 64 I GmbHG and to determine, first of all, whether this provision is intended to provide that protection which the plaintiff claims in his favour.

In examining the question of the meaning and the purpose of this provision it appears, first of all, that the purpose of the legislature is to secure a prompt initiation of bankruptcy proceedings in the case where the debts are no longer covered by the assets. Therefore, the legislature in requiring the directors to start bankruptcy proceedings as soon as the annual balance sheet or an interim balance sheet discloses an excess of debts over the assets, clearly aims primarily at preventing that the company assets necessary for satisfying the creditors are not available for this purpose. The intention is to preserve the company assets for the benefit of the creditors so as to allow them to receive payment and to protect them against excessive losses as a result of the bankruptcy. This protection alone, which is clearly the primary purpose of the Act, cannot assist the plaintiff, however, for the plaintiff's claim for damages is not based primarily on the ground that owing to the delay in initiating bankruptcy proceedings the assets available to the creditors have been diminished and that therefore his claim lost totally or partially. Instead the plaintiff holds the defendant liable in the first place for the fact that the plaintiff still gave a credit to the private company, the debts of which exceeded the assets. According to § 823 II BGB the defendant is only liable to pay damages for loss occasioned thereby if § 64 I GmbHG protects the interests of the creditors also in this respect, i.e. if it seeks to protect them quite generally against the dangers resulting from the continuing operation of a company the debts of which exceed its assets. It is true that the community is in fact protected in this respect as well as by the existence of § 64 GmbHG. This fact alone cannot suffice, however, to attribute to § 64 GmbHG the character of a protective act having such an extensive range. For this purpose not the effect of the law but its substance and aim must be considered, more particularly whether the legislature intended to provide such a far-reaching protection or at least accepted it [references]. This cannot be assumed, however. Confidence in the solvency and the creditworthiness of another does not enjoy special protection in trade and commerce. He who makes a mistake and suffers a loss must normally prove that § 826 BGB or § 823 II BGB in conjunction with § 263 of the Criminal Code applies, unless he can rely on contractual claims. The Act does not indicate that a different rule is to apply in relations with private companies and that those dealing with private companies are to be given more extensive protection. Gadow and Weipert [reference] and Bergenroth justify the need for special protection of the public on the ground that public and private companies are legal entities whose shareholders are not liable for the debts of the company with their entire assets. It must be admitted that a need exists for this reason to protect the creditors. The legislative history of the Act concerning Private Companies [GmbHG] shows that the fact that only the assets of a private company are liable for its debts led to the provision that bankruptcy proceedings are to be begun against the company not only if the company is insolvent, but also if its debts exceed its assets [references]. No indications exist that in enacting § 64 I GmbHG the legislature also intended, in addition to the protection mentioned above, to protect the creditors against giving credit to a private company which is overburdened with debts or from entering into business relations with it at all. If they suffer damage in this way such creditors, like creditors of an individual or of a partnership, are therefore restricted to the protection offered by § 826 BGB and by other provisions such as § 823 II BGB in conjunction with § 263 of the Criminal Code, leaving aside any contractual claims.

It follows that the plaintiff can only claim damages against the defendant on the basis of § 823 II BGB in conjunction with § 64 I GmbHG if, and to the extent that, at the time when his claim for the payment of goods sold arose he would have participated in the distribution of the assets. It is not clear whether and to what extent this was the case. Certainly the plaintiff cannot, on this interpretation of the law, contrary to the view of the Court of Appeal, receive the full price of the goods sold, which he claims as damages.

Therefore, the judgment appealed against cannot be maintained, having regard to the reasons given by the Court of Appeal . . .

Notes to Cases 129–131

1. In all the systems under comparison a rich case law can be found under the heading of tort liability for breach of statute, but there is no need to give more than a few illustrations. For, as Professor Medicus has said about German law (*op. cit.*, no. 621), each case turns on its facts and the construction of the wording of the statute in question. Yet, some basic principles do exist and they have been discussed briefly in chapter 4, section A1(*a*), above. For English law see Clerk and Lindsell, *On Torts* (18th edn. chapter 11), and the older but seminal article of Glanville Williams, "The Effect of Penal Legislation in the Law of Tort," 23 *MLR* 233. For American law see Prosser, Wade, and Schwartz, 205 ff.

2. As we have already noted, German judges are spared the need of discussing whether the legislator intended to allow a civil remedy when a particular statute has been breached—§ 823 II BGB providing, subject to what we said above, a clear positive answer. But the court still has to discover the purpose of the statute: Was the mischief that occurred the one the statute wished to avoid? Was the plaintiff the person the statute wished to protect? (For an illustration see BGHZ 108, 134.) Cases 107–109 give some idea of how the German courts tackle these problems; but other decisions, reproduced elsewhere, have also discussed this problem. (See, for example, cases 9 and 54.)

3. The search for the purpose of the statute only thinly disguises the value judgements that have to be made in each case by the court. Policy thus strongly determines the result, though it is done under the guise of statutory construction. Thus, where more valuable interests are at stake (e.g. life and not just the protection of property) the courts tend to construe the statute in a way that is favourable to the plaintiff (*cf. Kornan v. American Dredger Co.* 355 US 426, 78 S. Ct. 394 (1958) with *Gorris v. Scott* LR 9 Exch. 125 (1874)). And where certain types of plaintiffs are involved (e.g. children, workmen etc.) the courts will, again, have their interests very much at heart when "construing" the relevant enactments. (See Prosser, Wade and Schwartz, 246.)

4. Courts often talk of the "purpose" of a statute, but is there any reason why a statute should not have more than one? (See, for example, *Hines v. Foreman* (Tex. Comm'n. App. 1922) 243, SW 479.) Could it be that looking for "one" aim or purpose makes it easier to limit liability, if that is what the judge wishes to achieve?

2. § 839 BGB

Case 132

BUNDESGERCHTSHOF (THIRD CIVIL SENATE) 30 APRIL 1953
LM § 839 [FG] BGB NO. 5

Reasons

The defendant asks first for a re-examination of the appeal court's opinion that the police officers were under an official duty to take action against the members of a gang of thieves, two of whom later committed a break-in at the plaintiff's residence. The appeal in law refers in this connection to the decision of 11 June 1952 [reference omitted]. There is no ground to deviate from the principles set out in this decision. Accordingly, it cannot be doubted that the police officers were under a duty to take action against those members of the gang who were known to them and who were committing crimes in their area of operation. According to the indisputable facts of the case, it was known to H [one of the police officers] that, among other things, N, who took part in the later break-in at the plaintiff's residence had committed a burglary with two other people. However, in his examination as a witness in the main proceedings before the *Schöffengericht* (lay assessors court) because of this theft, he deliberately gave false evidence in order to help N, who was in fact acquitted, as were the other perpetrators, for lack of evidence. Shortly afterwards, K as well as H found out the names of all those involved in the burglary. Both, however, still failed to bring a criminal charge. H and K therefore had definite knowledge of the serious crimes committed by the gang and in particular of the co-perpetrators of the break-in later committed at the plaintiff's. This left them no room for discretion when deciding whether measures were necessary against the perpetrators known to them. Criminal prosecution of law-breakers and preventing crimes came within the scope of the official tasks of the two officers as police officers. Non-intervention by them in the given situation could not be justified by any sort of objective or policing considerations. Remaining inactive was unambiguously outside the boundary of discretion of "harmfulness". A situation of danger was present which made action by the police officers an unconditional duty.

The question was raised in the said decision of how the establishment of the boundaries of discretion of "harmfulness" or of "excess" is to be treated in the individual case. Was it a pure issue of law and to be undertaken by the court "in accordance with relevant considerations" [reference omitted]? Or was it a question here of a "pure issue of discretion" to be decided by the appropriate authority, which the judge cannot generally re-examine [reference omitted]? No final position needs to be taken here on this question. Even if the establishment of the boundaries of discretion is in principle regarded as a "pure issue of discretion" which cannot generally be re-examined judicially, the police officers involved were still under a duty to take action. This is because we have a case here in which even a decision based on discretion (which is not in principle subject to judicial re-examination) can still be subjected to such a re-examination. The officer's failure to act was not based on a weighing-up of the arguments for and against in accordance with objective considerations but was based exclusively on irrelevant and purely personal grounds. They therefore have acted with such a high degree of impropriety that their behaviour—and this needs no further explanation in the given circumstances—is irreconcilable with the requirements of proper police administration and does not satisfy the needs of proper administration from any possible point of view [references omitted].

2. The further question of whether the official duty violated by the police officers by failing to act against the gang also existed against the plaintiff as a "third party" in the sense of § 839 of the BGB was, likewise, correctly answered in the affirmative by the appeal court.

According to the case law of the *Reichsgericht* [reference omitted], which the Senate followed in [reference omitted], the question of whether an official duty is owed by an official to a third party is to be adjudged taking into consideration the officer's official area of activity and the type of work which he is carrying out. In this connection the main emphasis is on the purpose which the official duty is to serve. If this is imposed on the officer in the interests of individual persons, everyone whose interests are, according to the special nature of the official business, affected by it will be a third party. But if the purpose of the official duty is only the maintenance of public order or the interest which the state has in officials carrying out the responsibilities of their office properly, the official owes no duty to third parties, even if there is indirect intrusion into the interests of third parties by the exercise of this duty. The task of preventing crimes is not however owed by the police in the interest of the general public alone, but, as to crimes which also intrude directly into the protected legal sphere of the individual, to the endangered individuals as well. If the police do not properly fulfil this task, this not only violates a duty owed by the police to the general public but also a duty owed by it to the endangered individuals.

The appeal in law refers in this connection to the decision of the *Reichsgericht* in [reference omitted] in which the duty imposed on the state prosecutor by § 152 (2) of the Criminal Procedure Code to prosecute for crimes is described as a task serving exclusively the interests of the general public. It then takes the view that in this respect the task of the *police* could not be regarded in any different way. But it can be left open in this case whether and, if appropriate, how the area of responsibility of the state prosecutor and of the police is to be judged differently in relation to the prosecution of crimes. This is because the issue is not the duty of criminal prosecution incumbent on both authorities but the duty to prevent crimes, which falls on the police as a task arising directly from their duty of protection from danger. For the state prosecutor a general direct responsibility to prevent crimes does not exist; at the most it arises only insofar as the purpose of prosecution for crime is to prevent further crime. In this respect therefore the reference to the decision of the *Reichsgericht* mentioned above misses the point.

The appeal in law further takes the view, having regard to [references omitted], that the general duty of protection by the police (and therefore also their duty to prevent crimes) is not a duty owed to third parties but only to the general public. This would be so at least as long as no concrete relationship to a definite third party has yet developed and the actual person harmed has not so far stood out from the mass of people who could be harmed. In the present case, no such actual relationship to a particular person harmed has yet been established. The possible crimes which lawbreakers known to police officers might commit could have been directed against simply any inhabitant of the area concerned and therefore against an entirely undetermined circle of people. The duty of the officers was owed only to the general public and not the plaintiff as a member of the general public, which should be protected. That cannot however be agreed. A person who stands out from the mass of people at risk because he was specially at risk is not the only person to be regarded as a third party to whom the police owe a duty to prevent crimes, as was the case with the facts which formed the basis of the decision [reference omitted]. The circle of third parties should be drawn much more widely. Thus the *Reichsgericht* has, among other things, regarded the fulfilment of the general protective duty of care (subject to the prerequisite that exercise of public power is in question) as among the official duties owed by an official to every third party [reference omitted] and confirmed that the official duty of a teacher supervising a ball game is owed to anyone not participating who could come into the area of the game [reference omitted]. Accordingly, the duty of an official to prevent improper use of service vehicles has also been described by the Senate in the decision [reference omitted] as an official duty which exists against every highway user with whom the vehicle could come in contact while it is being improperly used. Therefore the duty of the police to prevent crimes must also be regarded as an official duty which is owed to anyone whose legal interests are endangered by a violation of this duty.

In the present case the following additional considerations also arise in this connection. All officials entrusted with the exercise of public power have an official duty to refrain from any misuse of their office. An official can make himself guilty of an improper exercise of office by omitting to act within the framework of the public power entrusted to him. That is always the case when the official duty unambiguously requires such action but the action does not take place because of completely irrelevant, purely personal and reprehensible reasons. It needs no further discussion that the police officers H and K have made themselves guilty in this respect of a misuse of office. However, the duty to refrain from any misuse of office is owed by the officials to anyone who could be harmed by the misuse [references omitted]. It cannot therefore be doubted that the official duty of the police officers to act as police against the gang was also owed to the plaintiff.

Case 133

BUNDESGERICHTHOF (THIRD CIVIL SENATE) 10 JULY 1980
NJW 1980, 2194 = VERSR 1980, 946

Facts

The plaintiff demands compensation from the defendant city because of violation of the duty of protective care in relation to highways. On 3 June 1975 at about 9.45 pm the plaintiff's wife, who was driving the plaintiff's car, turned left at a dual carriageway (the A Ring). There was a hedge (which has since been removed) approximately 1.2 metres in height on the central reservation. The plaintiff's wife crossed the lane which led to her right, drove through a gap in the central reservation, tried to turn into the lane leading left and collided with a car approaching from the left. The plaintiff claimed that his wife edged carefully into the lane and could not see the other vehicle in time because the hedge was too high.

Reasons

I. The appeal court found no violation of the defendant's duty of protective care and in this connection stated that the central reservation did not form part of the highway. It was true that a duty to warn about limitations on visibility, which were not obvious (or to remove them), could also exist for areas outside the street. But here the restriction on visibility caused by the hedge was obvious anyway. The danger was in the end due to the conduct of the plaintiff's wife, who turned to the left without taking sufficient precautions. A reasonably experienced driver would have been able to cope with the situation in question. Besides this, a claim under § 839(1), sentence 2 of the BGB would not arise as the plaintiff has another option for compensation by claiming against his wife.

There are fundamental legal objections to this judgment.

II. 1. The appeal court's starting point, that a violation of the duty of protective care in relation to highways by the officers of the defendant is to be assessed in accordance with the provisions on official liability (§ 839 of the BGB, Article 34 of the GG), is certainly correct. According to § 10, paragraph 1 of the Highways Act of Lower Saxony of 14 December 1962 [reference omitted] the building and maintenance of public highways (inclusive of the federal trunk roads) and surveillance of their safety for traffic falls on the organs and public employees of the body dealing with them, as an official duty in exercise of state activity. This formulation contained in the public law statutes of the state (*Land*) of the duties of the office holder of a municipality (*Gemeinde*) in ensuring traffic safety on public highways is—as the Senate has explained in the judgments [references omitted]—permissible in the context of the division of legislative competence between the Federation and the states. Nor are there any other constitutional law objections to it derived from the Basic Law.

2. The Senate's judgment [reference omitted] explains in detail that a body liable for breach of official duty cannot rely on the provisions of § 839(1) sentence 2 of the BGB as they contradict the basic principle of the equal treatment of highway users in liability law. These principles also apply, as the Senate has explained in more detail in the judgment [reference omitted] (issued after the publication of the judgment in the appeal) for cases like this one involving surveillance of traffic safety on a public highway, if this duty falls on the office holder as a state responsibility. The official duty to ensure safety of road traffic is closely related to the duties owed by an official as a public highway user. Accordingly the defendant city cannot exonerate itself by reference to the possibility that the plaintiff's wife is liable for the accident.

3. The appeal court's finding that there was no violation of the duty of protective care in relation to highways cannot be endorsed either.

(a) The official duty formulated in public law to ensure the safety of road traffic corresponds in its content to the general duty of protective care [references omitted]. Its scope is determined by the type and frequency of use of the highway and its importance. It includes the necessary measures for the creation and maintenance of road conditions, which are sufficiently safe for road users. It is true that a road user must in principle adjust to the given road conditions and accept the highway in the form in which it appears to him. A party under a duty of protective care must, in an appropriate and objectively reasonable manner, remove (and if necessary warn about) all those dangers (but no others) which are not visible or not visible in time for a highway user who is exercising the necessary care and to which he cannot adjust or cannot adjust in time.

(b) In applying these principles to the present case, an official duty by the public employees of the defendant must be accepted to keep the hedge at a height which prevents serious obstruction of visibility for road users on turning into the highway from an access. The appeal court interprets the concept of the highway too narrowly when it includes in it, apart from the carriageway, only those surfaces which "also serve traffic in some way or other e.g. for escape in case of emergency . . .". According to both § 2II No. 1 Lower Saxony Highways Act and § 1IV No. 1 Federal Highways Act in 1 October 1974 version [reference omitted] separation strips, verges, and marginal and safety strips are also included in public highways [references omitted]. As federal and state law agree here, it has no significance for the outcome of the case whether the A Ring was a federal, state or municipality highway. According to these statutory rules, the duty of protective care extends to the central reservation as a part of the highway. It is therefore not necessary to fall back on the case law cited by the appeal court according to which the duty of protective care extends to things not forming part of the highway insofar as they represent a danger for the use of the highway, as for instance trees and shrubs in front gardens [references omitted]. Nor is it necessary to refer to the duties, which fall on the owner of the hedge as such.

(c) A high hedge created special dangers in a place where there was a gap in the central reservation to enable highway users to turn in and out of it. Drivers turning in could only be sure of seeing the traffic on the other side of the hedge if the hedge was at least, for an appropriate distance from the entrance, kept low enough for it not significantly to conceal moving vehicles behind it. Contrary to the view of the appeal court, this danger did not cease in whole or in part to arise just because the hedge could be seen, and because this was so even in darkness, with the help of street lighting and car headlights. The danger was not the hedge itself, but the hindrance to visibility, which it caused, and this hindrance did not cease to exist just because the hedge was visible.

(d) The defendant city claimed in its submissions that it complied with these principles. According to these submissions, hedges are cut once-yearly, and twice-yearly at traffic focal points, and kept in "shape". The end sections of a hedge before and after accesses are cut back further than the middle parts of the hedge. Actually, however, the defendant has not kept to these principles in the area of the site of the accident, according to the findings of the appeal court. The shrubs situated on the central reservation had reached a height of about 1.2 metres on the day of the accident. The appeal court has described the hindrance to visibility consequently occurring as "obvious" and in another place has spoken of a hedge height "undoubtedly hindering visibility". But it regarded this as insignificant for the outcome of the case, because every driver could escape the threat of danger which this caused, either by increased attention on turning in or out or by the choice of another driving route. This view is, it should be acknowledged in support of the appeal in law, affected by legal error.

(aa) A driver must certainly in principle accept the highway as it presents itself to him, and therefore make his own investigations as to whether he has sufficient visibility. The hedge height of about 1.2 metres could however seriously hinder the necessary visibility even for an attentive driver, and the appeal court has not paid sufficient attention to this. According to the findings of the *Landgericht*, the height of vision of the plaintiff's wife in his car used in the accident-. . .-was 1.1 metres, and that of an assessor of the *Landgericht* 1.2 metres. Cars of the usual construction, as is revealed by type surveys in the press, are without exception between 1.3 and 1.5 metres high. Cars of this type protruded, at the most, only marginally above the hedge. The extent to which they were visible depended to a large degree on their type of construction. The defendant city could in any case not act on the basis that drivers would, on turning at the site of the accident, see cars approaching behind the hedge in time in every case. This possible danger which, as the appeal court has pertinently explained, could not be removed by a warning sign, resulted in the hindrance to visibility caused by the 1.2 metre high hedge at the site of the accident being dangerous even for an attentive driver. A careful tentative entry—which the appeal court did not even consider to be necessary—into the lane situated on the other side of the hedge could not remove these dangers. This is because a sufficient view could not be obtained of this lane *before* turning into it. That follows from the finding of the appeal court about the effect which the hedge had in restricting visibility.

(bb) The duty of ensuring traffic safety did not cease to apply, as the appeal court thought it did, just because no driver *had* to turn in at the place in question. It cannot in principle be held against highway users by a party under a duty of protective care that they should have avoided dangerous places. This would enable the party to shift its responsibility to the driver in an impermissible manner. It is the task of the party under the duty of protective care either to remove or at least to defuse danger spots which it can recognise as such so far as is reasonable and as soon as possible.

(cc) The party under the duty of protective care must further protect traffic from the mistakes which, according to experience, are exactly what has to be reckoned with in heavy traffic in large cities—here, underestimating the dangers caused by restriction of visibility and possible violations of the right of way. The principle of trust, which applies to the mutual relationship of highway users, has no application in the relationship between the party under a duty of protective care and highway users. On the contrary, the duty of protective care can include in individual cases those measures which have the purpose of protecting traffic from the consequences of inappropriate conduct of individual highway users [reference omitted].

These prerequisites are present here. In the heavy traffic in inner cities, violations of rules of priority are not rare. If visibility of the road having priority is substantially impaired, and a particularly careful driving style is indicated (taking up more time than usual), one must reckon on more frequent violations of these duties. The defendant city could also have recognised this. Regular cutting of the hedge down to 70–80 centimetres in height was therefore obviously required. This relatively simple and cheap measure was to be expected of the defendant—and pertinently the appeal court accepted this.

4. The disputed judgment also cannot be based on different reasoning. It is not possible to proceed on the basis that the violation by the defendant city of the duty of protective care is completely superseded by the contribution of the plaintiff's wife to the accident. According to her statement as witness, the plaintiff's wife—in contrast to the case decided by the Kammergericht which was otherwise similar [reference omitted]—did not turn into the space behind the hedge without any regard to the restriction on visibility. Instead, she claims at first to have stopped briefly and only after starting off again to have collided with the other car, which had approached in the meantime. It may be that, as a result of carelessness, she did not pay attention or sufficient attention to the distance and speed of this vehicle, because it approached on the left lane of the carriageway (its driver wanting to turn to the left further on). Nevertheless, it cannot be assumed that there would have been a collision even without the restriction of visibility by the hedge, especially as it has to be borne in mind that the driver of the other car was also unable to see, in sufficient time, the car driven by the plaintiff's wife turning in because of the hedge.

5. The matter must be referred back to the appeal court, because the weighing-up in accordance with § 254 of the BGB of the extent of the contributions to the accident from both sides is not possible according to the findings which have been made, and must remain an issue for the judge of fact.

Case 134

BUNDESGERICHTSHOF (THIRD CIVIL SENATE) 28 MARCH 1996
NJW 1996, 2373

Facts

The A Group offered facilities for investment of capital for small investors. In October 1987, because of a fall in share prices, the group suffered heavy losses so that the whole capital investment was exhausted. This was concealed from the investors, and the group carried on advertising investment facilities. The state prosecutor took investigatory proceedings against those responsible. The group's money deposited with a bank was first of all seized, but the Amtsgericht (district court) quashed the seizure and the state prosecutor discontinued the investigatory proceedings. Five months later, the plaintiff made a financial management contract with the A Group. Over a year later the A Group suffered further heavy losses and the investigatory proceedings were recommenced against those responsible which led to their conviction for deceit. The plaintiff, who had lost about three-quarters of his capital, claimed compensation from the defendant state (Land).

Reasons

The case is not of significance on an issue of principle; and the appeal in law has no prospect of success [reference omitted].

1. The appeal court denied that the official duty of the state prosecutor to pursue crimes, to carry out investigatory proceedings against the perpetrators and, if necessary, to start a public prosecution is owed to third parties. It stated that this duty was exclusively to serve public interests, namely the fulfilment of the criminal powers of the state. The arguments raised in the appeal in law against this are unsuccessful. The introduction of investigatory proceedings in criminal law, the initiation and execution of a search order, a decision about the starting of a public prosecution and measures in proceedings for fines can represent violations of the official duty owed to the suspect if they are undertaken without justification [references omitted]. But there is no official duty on the part of the state prosecutor to intervene in the interest of a person possibly affected by a crime—in contrast to the position in relation to the police (see *Senate*, LM § 839 [Fg] BGB No. 5). The duty of the state prosecutor to pursue crimes, to arrest an accused, etc., exists only in the public interest. Failure to carry it out cannot therefore, as a rule, violate an official duty against the person harmed by the crime [references omitted]. It can be otherwise if concrete protective duties to the person harmed by a crime are acquired by the state prosecutor in current investigatory proceedings, perhaps to secure stolen property in the interests of the person from whom it has been stolen [references omitted]. The principles set out above also apply to the prevention of crimes, which is the issue in the case of plaintiff.

2. As the appeal court further states, the plaintiff did not, in May 1988, come within the category of those who had already paid their money to the A Group. They could not therefore possibly have been protected from harm by the seizure being kept in force and the proceedings against the suspects being pursued on the grounds that those steps would have deprived the suspects of access to further accounts. As the plaintiff first made his investment on 18 June 1988, he was not directly affected by the decision of the state prosecutor to order the quashing of the seizure and to discontinue the proceedings on 2 May 1988 [reference omitted]. The harm he has suffered is based on the fact that the accused persons had not been forced to give up their activity. It can however be left undecided whether, if an official duty on the part of the state prosecutor owed to third parties suffering harm could be accepted, this would stand in the way of including the plaintiff within the circle of those protected (see *Senate*, LM § 839 [Fg] BGB No. 5), as the duty is not owed to third parties.

3. The appeal court judgment does not reveal any other legal errors, which are significant in the context of the decision and are to the disadvantage of the plaintiff.

Case 135

BUNDESGERICHTSHOF (THIRD CIVIL SENATE), 16 OCTOBER 1997
NJW 1998, 751 = MDR 1998, 43 = VERSR 1998, 493

Facts

The plaintiff was until the end of 1988 a member of the board of directors of the KHG AG. On the application of the state prosecutor, the Amtsgericht (district court) ordered the arrest on the 27th February 1990 of the plaintiff and others for suspected breach of trust (Untreue) to the detriment of KHD. He was arrested on the 14th March 1990 in Italy, and brought to Germany. On the 11th May 1990 he was released from custody on conditions. The order for arrest was later revoked and the investigatory proceedings against the plaintiff discontinued. The order for arrest was based effectively on an accusation by B (who himself was in custody awaiting trial). B had claimed that he had arranged with the plaintiff at a hunting event in the Westerwald in 1983 to manipulate accounts for wood deliveries to the detriment of KHD ("the hunting hide agreement"); and that the plaintiff had received substantial sums of money for this. This accusation was substantially incorrect. At the time of his arrest the plaintiff was also managing director of the V-GmbH and had a consultancy contract with the P firm, at an annual fee of DM 50,180. This firm terminated the contract on the 11th May 1990 with immediate effect after the press had reported the arrest of the plaintiff. On the 15th May 1990, the plaintiff and the V-GmbH agreed to cancel the managing director's contract. The Amtsgericht decided that the plaintiff should be compensated for the harm resulting from the arrest from the 14th March to the 11th May 1990 in accordance with the Compensation for Measures related to Criminal Prosecution Act. The plaintiff claimed as material harm his loss of earnings with the V GmbH and the P firm and legal and other expenses. The Ministry of Justice of the defendant state (Land) accepted liability for material harm in the sum of DM 16,664.64. This sum consisted of part of the legal and other expenses.

In the present claim the plaintiff seeks amongst other things compensation for loss of earnings due to the termination of the consultancy contract with the P firm, further legal costs and a finding that any further harm resulting from the termination of the consultancy contract should be compensated.

Reasons

II. The investigating state prosecutor when examining whether an order for arrest should be made against the plaintiff, stated there was strong suspicion of breach of trust (§ 266 of the Criminal Code and § 112 (1) sentence 1 of the Criminal Procedure Code). The appeal court regarded this as a culpable violation of official duty on his part. That satisfies legal examination in the end result.

1. According to the case law of the Senate certain measures by the state prosecutor, which include application for issue of an order for an arrest are not to be examined in official liability proceedings for their "correctness" but only as to whether they are justifiable [references omitted].

Proceeding from this legal principle, the appeal court held that the assumption by the state prosecutor that there was strong suspicion at that time of breach of trust by the plaintiff was unjustifiable. It interpreted the statements of B, on which the state prosecutor principally based his assessment, as meaning that the plaintiff and B in their conversation of August / September 1983 (the hunting hide agreement) had agreed to a future manipulation of accounts. This would mean that the manipulations would only have begun after this point in time. In reality, so the appeal court found, it was already obvious at the point in time of the application for the order for the arrest (on the basis of witness statements and other documents on the investigatory proceedings) that accounting manipulations of this kind had been going on since the nineteen sixties. In these circumstances, the accusation made by B was incredible from the start, and the application for the order for arrest was unjustifiable.

This assessment can only be examined by the court hearing the appeal in law by considering whether the judge of fact misunderstood the concept of justifiability, violated rules of logic or general principles of experience and considered all the circumstances which were of significance for the judgment [references omitted]. The appeal in law does not reveal mistakes of this kind. Insofar as it complains of a violation of rules of logic it puts its own assessment of the facts in place of those of the appeal court in a manner which the rules about appeals in law do not permit. The procedural objections raised by the appeal in law in this connection have been examined by the Senate and not considered to be decisive. No ground was therefore found here either (§ 565 a of the Civil Procedure Code). It accordingly has been established in a binding manner that the assumption of strong suspicion on which the application by the state prosecutor for an order for arrest was based was unjustifiable and making the application for an order for arrest was therefore contrary to official duty.

2. The appeal court also, without any legal error, found the investigating state prosecutor to be culpable. In this connection it basically assumes that no blame as a rule attaches to an official if a collegial court with several legal experts sitting on it has regarded the official action as objectively lawful [references omitted]. According to the view of the appeal court, this general principle, from which the Senate has repeatedly permitted exceptions [references omitted], did not apply here. There are no legal grounds for objecting to this in the end result.

(a) The appeal court denied that the principle applied here, even though the civil chamber of the *Landgericht* regarded the conduct of the state prosecutor as justifiable and therefore as objectively in accordance with his official duties. It considered that the chamber basically proceeded in this assessment from a legally flawed approach. Whether this is correct does not need to be considered, because in any case there is another ground for the said principle not applying here.

The principle is based on the consideration that a better understanding of the law cannot as a rule be expected and demanded from an official than from a collegial court with several legal experts sitting on it [reference omitted]. This justifies a denial of culpability only in those cases in which the collegial court—after careful examination—has affirmed the legality of the official action. If on the other hand the collegial court has merely approved the action on the basis of a yardstick for testing—here the yardstick of justifiability—which is *reduced* in comparison with the official's own duty of testing, this does not necessarily mean that the conduct of the official should be assessed as lawful.

Whilst therefore in cases like the present one the official himself has a duty to regulate his conduct entirely by the yardstick of legality, the judicial examination in the official liability proceedings decides merely on the basis of the reduced yardstick of justifiability whether he has acted in accordance with his official duty. In such cases the principle becomes subject to a further exception over and above the group of cases decided by the Senate so far. The defendant state cannot therefore successfully rely in the present case on the first instance judgment for saying that no accusation of culpability can be levelled at the investigating state prosecutor.

(b) The appeal court was also right in not considering itself to be required to apply the general principle by the decision of the 14th great criminal chamber of the *Landgericht* in the proceedings concerning the complaint about arrest. This is because a comprehensive and careful examination of the issue of lawfulness which could justify the application of the principle did not, according to the findings of the appeal court, take place in those proceedings. The appeal court explained in this respect, in its assessment as a judge of fact of the circumstances which influenced the proceedings concerning the complaint about arrest, that the criminal chamber had "tested in an extremely summary fashion" the question of strong suspicion "and instead of this, concentrated on the question of the ... danger of flight". It concludes this from the fact that the decision by the chamber was issued on the same day as the decision by the *Amtsgericht* that there would be no review. In a "fast-track" procedure of this kind, a dependable formation of opinion by the collegial court was not possible in the light of the scope of the documentation. This assessment, the real core of which was not addressed by the appeal in law, is confirmed by the content of the decision about the complaint:

The *Amtsgericht* in the original order for arrest had suspended its execution. The state prosecution service complaint against this only disputed the exemption from arrest. The attention of the criminal chamber was therefore principally directed to the question of whether the danger of flight was to be assessed as so small that a suspension of execution should be considered. It is true that the criminal chamber was also obliged of its own motion to examine the question of strong suspicion. In this respect however it contented itself, according to the wording of its decision, with referring to the order for arrest and pointing out that this was essentially based on the testimony of the co-accused B, who severely incriminated the plaintiff. This reasoning makes it clear that the assessment of strong suspicion which influenced the order for arrest and formed the basis of the application for the order for arrest, and which the appeal court regarded without any legal error as unjustifiable, has left its mark on the decision by the *Landgericht* about the complaint.

On the basis of the findings made by the appeal court the starting point must accordingly be that the criminal chamber did not assess the established facts of the case carefully and exhaustively; or it formed its conclusion that there was strong suspicion from facts established on the basis of procedural irregularity. In such cases the general principle does not apply [references omitted].

3. The statements of the appeal court about the extent of the claim for official liability awarded to the plaintiff and about the calculation of the period covered by the declaration are not challenged by the appeal in law.

Case 136

OBERLANDESGERICHT OLDENBURG, 20 MAY 1988
VERSR 1991, 306

Facts

On the 22nd December 1982, the plaintiff was committed to the secure section of the state (Land) hospital X at the request of the defendant. On the same day the defendant applied for committal of the plaintiff in accordance with §§ 10 ff. of the PsychKG ND. The medical opinion supporting the application diagnosed "paranoia (delusions of jealousy and persecution)". It said the illness was a risk to the plaintiff and others. Dr D, the defendant's medical officer, signed the opinion after telephone conversations with the doctor in attendance, Dr F, who also signed it. Dr D did not personally examine the plaintiff.

The Amtsgericht (district court) decided on the 23 December 1982 to commit the plaintiff for a maximum of six weeks for observation. From the 29 December 1982 to 4 January 1983 the hospital gave him leave of absence. He lodged a complaint, and the Landgericht quashed the committal decision on the 13 January 1983.

By a letter of the 18 July 1983 the defendant's road traffic division asked the plaintiff to submit a medico-psychological report about his fitness to drive. He did not reply, so the defendant withdrew his driving licence on the 29 August 1983. It did not order immediate implementation of this decision. The Oberverwaltungsgericht (upper administrative court) quashed the defendant's decision, because the plaintiff had not been proved unfit to drive. No severe mental illness had been shown for the period from the end of 1982 to the beginning of 1983. The plaintiff was justified in refusing to undergo the examination demanded.

The plaintiff now claimed from the defendant payment of compensation for distress estimated at DM 100,000, and payment of loss of earnings of DM 140,626.60. He also wanted a declaration that the defendant was obliged to compensate for future material harm.

The plaintiff claimed that the medical officer, who had approved the committal without making his own investigation, and the official in the administrative office, who had ordered the committal without a previous court decision, had violated their official duties. There was no risk to either to the plaintiff himself or others. This was not the typical consequence of paranoia, and the official would have realised this if he had shown proper care. Even the withdrawal of the driving licence had been a breach of duty because it had been based on the unlawful provisional committal (or the temporary committal) without a proper investigation. The withdrawal of the driving licence had resulted in the plaintiff losing his job.

(The Bundesgerichtshof in its decision of the 29th March 1990 (III ZR 160/88) (BGH VersR 1991, 308) rejected the plaintiff's appeal in law against the judgment set out here).

Reasons

The plaintiff has a claim against the defendant for compensation for distress in the sum of DM 5,000 for unlawful deprivation of freedom. On the other hand he cannot ask for compensation for his loss of earnings because it cannot be established that the loss claimed was caused by a culpable violation by the defendant of official duty. The plaintiff's claim for a declaration in relation to his future harm is accordingly likewise unfounded.

1. The prerequisites for the granting of compensation for distress in accordance with § 847 of the BGB are present. The plaintiff has been deprived of freedom by a tort by the defendant in the sense of § 839 of the BGB in combination with Article 34 of the Basic Law. The medical officer in the service of the defendant, Dr D has violated an official duty owed by him to the plaintiff in that he signed a medical certificate for the instigation of the committal procedure, without making it sufficiently clear that the findings of Dr F which formed the basis of it had been made several days before the submission of the opinion. Therefore a provisional committal of the plaintiff on this basis in accordance with § 16 of the PsychKG ND could not be considered. The opinion which was sent to the administrative section of the defendant on 22 December 1982 contains no date. Nor can it be deduced from the text of the opinion when the plaintiff was examined and when the findings which were decisive for the opinion were ascertained.

And yet the opinion form signed by the medical officer gives the impression that it was filled up immediately after the ascertaining of the findings. This is because in the first line (which contains the word "Urgent" in bold) and in the text of the request before the signatures of the doctors (which asks for an immediate decision) it is made clear that the committal procedure could not be postponed and that the medical experts had also taken that into account.

But actually the plaintiff had last spoken with the doctor in attendance, Dr F, on 15 December 1982, as the medical officer indicated in his testimony in the investigatory proceedings. Further contacts after this point in time, for instance on 21 December 1982, indisputably broke down. The medical officer himself did not examine the plaintiff at any time.

The medical officer was under a duty to provide appropriate explanations in his area of work and therefore in particular in the content of the opinion. It was true that it was not part of the responsibility of the medical officer to arrange directly for the committal of the person affected or to apply to the court. It should however have been obvious to him that the competent official in the administrative section of the defendant would rely on the statement by the doctors and because of the urgency of the matter would very probably first of all arrange for a provisional committal in accordance with § 16 of the PsychKG ND. It was therefore a duty of the medical officer, which he owed to the person affected, to ensure that this foreseeable unlawful provisional committal did not take place.

The violation of duty by the medical officer led with adequate causality to the unlawful deprivation of the plaintiff's freedom. The responsible officer in the administrative office relied on the statements in the opinion without himself investigating at what point in time the findings were ascertained and he arranged for a provisional committal of the plaintiff in accordance with § 16 of the PsychKG ND.

It is true that the defendant has not expressly issued a formal administrative act in respect of the committal. The plaintiff was however indisputably moved to the state hospital X with the official assistance of the police before the issuing of the judicial committal decision. This amounts to conclusive conduct (*schlüssiges Handeln*) on the part of the defendant which was made known to the plaintiff when it was carried out. If the point in time when the findings were ascertained had been known to the official of the administrative office, the provisional committal would not have taken place, since it must be assumed that the authorities would act in accordance with their duties.

It can be left open whether the plaintiff, had the medical officer acted lawfully, would possibly on the 22 December 1982 have been examined again, perhaps compulsorily, whether the diagnosis would have been confirmed and whether he then would likewise have been provisionally committed. This is because the defendant cannot rely on the fact that it could have achieved the deprivation of freedom in a lawful manner which would have not formed the basis of a duty to compensate (reliance on lawful alternative action).

When a person causes harm by a breach of duty, the question of the extent to which the consequences of his conduct can rightly be assessed as attributable to him is to be answered according to the protective purpose of the violated norm involved [references omitted]. In the present case, there has been a violation of the conditions laid down in § 16 of the PsychKG ND. This provision is the expression of a constitutional guarantee according to which the state is only permitted to limit the freedom of a person on the basis of a formal statute and only if it takes into account the provisos described in it (Articles 2 and 104 of the Basic Law).

The protective purpose of the statute thus lies in permitting a deprivation of freedom only under the conditions prescribed in it. In this particular case it should also be ensured that, up to a point directly before the decision to commit, the state of health of the person concerned has not improved to such an extent that deprivation of freedom is no longer justified. The special urgency of immediate deprivation of freedom must thus be accepted in each case. Unless it is certain that the state of health will continue, the deprivation of freedom must not occur.

It is therefore a question of a fundamental protective norm to guarantee the rights of the citizen, which is not allowed to lose its significance in the context of compensation law just because some form of alternative action would have been lawful [references omitted].

On the same basis the argument of the *Landgericht* that the *Amtsgericht*, if it *had* been in a position to make a decision on the relevant day, would have ordered the committal cannot exonerate the defendant either. Here also the protective purpose of the violated norm excludes appeal to lawful alternative action.

The medical officer has also acted culpably. By using the required care, he could recognise and foresee that the official of the administrative section would see himself as compelled, on the basis of the dangerous situation for the plaintiff and other third parties as certified in the opinion, not only to arrange for a judicial committal but also to order immediately a provisional committal in accordance with § 16 of the PsychKG ND to avert the danger. (Details are given).

The defendant must therefore pay to the plaintiff compensation for distress for the non-material detriments suffered in consequence of the deprivation of freedom. In this connection, when calculating the amount of the damages for distress not only must the length of time of the provisional committal to be taken into account, but also that of the judicial committal. This is because it can be assumed that the court also would have come to another conclusion in its decision in accordance with § 15 of the PsychKG ND if it had known that the last examination of the plaintiff by the medical expert had taken place a week ago.

Taking into account all the circumstances, damages for distress of DM 5,000 seem fair but also sufficient to the Senate. The plaintiff was committed from 22 to 29 December 1982. According to his own account he was given leave of absence on 29 December 1982 so that the consequences of the deprivation of freedom did not continue beyond this point in time. At the most the possibility remained of the further detriment of revocation of the leave of absence. This however did not happen. Long term harm to the plaintiff did not therefore occur.

Even if freedom is to be regarded as a legal interest worthy of the highest protection, the plaintiff's ideas about compensation (DM 10,000) for distress seem greatly exaggerated. They bear no relationship to the compensation which is payable for unjustified criminal arrest. Admittedly the plaintiff was temporarily arrested by the police in order to implement the committal order, and these circumstances and the fact of committal in his home town have been talked about and have had a disadvantageous effect on his social relationships and his reputation. But even bearing these matters in mind compensation for distress in the approved sum is the most that should be considered.

The claim of the plaintiff is not excluded by § 839 (1) sentence 2 of the BGB. Firstly Dr D has disregarded the protective provisions of PsychKG ND not merely negligently but (at least) grossly negligently. Besides this the plaintiff has no other option for compensation available.

The issue of whether a possibility exists of obtaining compensation from the state can remain open, as this is also a public law body and the claim would therefore likewise be directed against the public sector; and it is necessary to proceed on the basis of the unity of the public sector [reference omitted]. The plaintiff can also not claim against the other medical expert, Dr F. (Details are given).

II. On the other hand the plaintiff has no claim against the defendant under § 839 of the BGB and Article 34 of the Basic Law to compensation for his loss of earnings nor to a declaration that the defendant is obliged to compensate for future harm. This is because it can neither be established that the defendant has culpably violated an official duty in taking proceedings for withdrawal of the driving licence nor that the alleged harm to the plaintiff arose as a consequence of the measures taken by the defendant.

In the present case no blame, as the *Landgericht* has already pertinently explained, attaches to the defendant in any case, since in relation to this measure, a collegial court in which three professional judges sat, namely the *Verwaltungsgericht*, has adjudged its conduct to be objectively justified. The conditions developed in this respect for justifying a denial of the culpability of the office holder are present. The *Verwaltungsgericht* in its decision used the right facts as a basis, evaluated these carefully and in its assessment of the legal situation neither misjudged clear and unambiguous rules nor blatantly falsely interpreted unambiguous rules.

With reference to the grounds of the court decision of 27 November 1984 the *Verwaltungsgericht* proceeding on the basis of the relevant provisions (§§ 4 (1) of the Implementation of Punishment Act (*StVG*) and 15b (1) of the Road Traffic Licences Order (*StVZO*)) looked carefully at the documents which were available about the plaintiff's psychological condition and came to the conclusion that they justified doubts about the fitness of the plaintiff to drive.

It accepted that this, together with the plaintiff's lack of preparedness to dispel the doubts by producing a medico-psychological opinion, justifies the conclusion that the plaintiff wanted to conceal defects which made him unfit to drive a vehicle. One must therefore, so it explained, proceed on the basis of his unsuitability to drive vehicles. These considerations of the *Verwaltungsgericht* do not violate rules of logic. The legal views referred to are at least defensible, taking into consideration the provisions cited.

Beside this it is not evident that the withdrawal of the driving licence was the cause of the harm claimed by the plaintiff. (Details are given).

Case 137

OBERLANDESGERICHT HAMM, 15 JULY 1992
NJW-RR 1994, 394 = FAMRZ 1993, 704 = VERSR 1994, 677

The plaintiff married couple and their adopted son, the former third plaintiff, sought compensation from the defendant town because of violation of official duty in connection with an adoption placement.

Reasons

The appeal of the defendant is permissible, but unsuccessful.

I.

The *Landgericht* was correct in accepting the plaintiffs' claims for official liability against the defendant on the basis of § 839 of the BGB in combination with Article 34 of the GG and allowed the demands for payment and a declaration.

1. The appropriate officials who were involved in preparing and carrying out an adoption by the plaintiffs have negligently violated their official duties owed to the plaintiffs by not informing them that there was a suspicion that the child N, who was very disturbed, was mentally retarded.

(a) It is necessary to proceed on the basis that the actions of the Youth Welfare Department in the area of adoption placement, even according to the legal situation in the years 1981 to 1983 (which is the relevant period here), are the exercise of public office in the sense of Article 34 of the GG [reference omitted]. Action in exercise of public office occurs if the real objective in the context of which the official is acting is part of the area of sovereign activity of a public body. There must also be an internal and external connection between this objective and the act (or omission) which causes the damage, so that the act (or omission) must also be regarded as belonging to this area of sovereign activity [reference omitted]. Such a connection exists for the actions of the Youth Welfare Department in the framework of adoption placement. According to § 2 (1) sentence 1 of the Adoption Placement Act in its 2nd July 1976 version [reference omitted] adoption placement is a task for the Youth Welfare Department (and for the State (Land) Youth Welfare Department). Adoption placement is bringing together children under the age of majority and persons who want to adopt a child (adoption applicants) with the object of adopting it as well as providing the evidence of adoption (§ 1 of the Adoption Placement Act). Leaving exceptions aside, the Youth Welfare Departments who have set up an Adoption Placement Office and the State Youth Welfare Departments have a placement monopoly (§§ 2 (1) sentence 2 and 5 (1) of the Adoption Placement Act). The actions of the Youth Welfare Department in the area of adoption placement are accordingly a public task, the purpose of which is to find appropriate and suitable parents who are prepared to adopt for a child who does not have the care of its natural parents. These actions are therefore to assist the young.

(b) The employees of the Youth Welfare Department of the defendant acted contrary to their official duty because they neglected to inform the plaintiffs as adoption applicants about the suspicion of mental retardation due to brain damage which was known to them and not dispelled. The content and scope of the official duties of a public employee are determined by the provisions regulating the area of his tasks and duties, whether they are statutes, regulations, administrative provisions or individual directions in the context of employment; and from the kind of tasks to be carried out [reference omitted]. The duty to inform the plaintiffs about the suspicion which existed arose in the present case from the kind of tasks to be carried out by the officials within the framework of the adoption placement.

The Adoption Placement Act itself admittedly contains no express regulations which make it a duty of the Adoption Placement Office to inform the adoption applicants about the state of health of the child to be adopted. However, according to § 7 (1) sentence 1 of the Adoption Placement Act, the Adoption Placement Office must make without delay the enquiries which are necessary for preparing for a placement, and these must also extend to the state of health of the child. Admittedly the implementation regulations provided for in § 7 (2) of the Adoption Placement Act have not so far been made. But the Working Group of the State Youth Welfare Departments has worked out guidelines which at that time applied in the version of the 3rd edition of 1966 and which provided in para. 2.22 that the physical as well as the mental and psychological state of health of the child was to be ascertained by a doctor experienced in these areas—if possible a paediatrician or a psychiatrist specialising in the young. Further, it says in para. 2.23 (1) that an investigation by a specialist, if necessary even in-patient observation, was to be arranged if inquiries revealed that the child has educational difficulties, suspicion of illness or unexplained abnormalities. Even if these guidelines (which were replaced in the meantime by the "Recommendations of the Federal Working Group of State Youth Welfare Departments and Non-local Education Committees on Adoption Placement"—Version of 28 November 1988) were merely for practical work assistance, and they therefore did not represent legal or administrative provisions, they nevertheless express what a proper individual adoption placement requires. This is that the adoption applicants should be able to decide to adopt a child in the knowledge of all important facts, so that a successful parent-child relationship which is free from anxiety can come into existence for the welfare of the child. § 9 (1) of the Adoption Placement Act which makes it a duty of the Adoption Placement Office to give detailed advice and support not only to the child and its natural parents but also to the adopters is in harmony with this. It follows from the duty of inquiry mentioned above (§ 7 (1) of the Adoption Placement Act) as well as from the duty of advice owed by the Adoption Placement Office (§ 9 (1) of the Adoption Placement Act) that the adoption applicants have a right to be notified of all the relevant circumstances affecting the child, and especially of suspicion of an illness [reference omitted]. The guidelines of the Working Group of the State Youth Welfare Departments, if and so far as they required that the state of health of the child was to be established by medical examination, therefore corresponded with these requirements. Admittedly the adoption of children with physical or mental peculiarities should also be facilitated. But that can only be considered if the adopters feel they are ready for this in the knowledge of all the circumstances and the consequences of their decision (para. 2.23 (2) of the Guidelines).

(c) The defendant's officials knew of the suspicion of mental retardation on the basis of brain damage parentally or in early childhood.

That emerges clearly from the memorandum by the witness N dated 7 October 1981, in which the possibility of mental retardation on the basis of inborn brain damage was expressly taken into consideration. Even the official doctor, Dr M, who had examined the child, regarded the mental retardation as so significant that, according to the memorandum of the witness M referred to above, she thought a "very meticulous examination" in a hospital was necessary. Arrangements were consequently made to examine the child in the children's clinic B; but this did not happen. But the doctors at the children's clinic at the St V hospital in P, according to their letter of 11 November 1981, of which the defendant's Youth Welfare Department received a copy, diagnosed not only wildness and behavioural disturbance in the child but also the suspicion of mental retardation, which could have meant that this retardation had its cause in brain damage. The appropriate officials could not regard this suspicion of mental retardation as dispelled by the interim report of the 8 December 1981 by the witness T. The only thing which emerged from this report was that a particular positive development had occurred on the basis of psychotherapeutic treatment by the witness T. No grounds for saying that N had been subjected to a detailed specialist examination were revealed by the interim report. T made no comment at all in it on the question of mental retardation based on brain damage. From the outcome of the evidence taken by the Senate, it is not possible to proceed on the basis that the witness T (who in any case was not a neurologist or a psychiatrist, but a psychologist) explained to the witness M (as it says in her memorandum of 4 December 1981) that the child had a normal intelligence and no mental handicap could be established. The witnesses T and M who were heard on this issue made contradictory statements. The witness T denied having expressed himself in this way to the witness M. But even if T had so expressed himself to the witness M, as she describes, the employees of the defendant cannot reassure themselves by saying that the suspicion of mental retardation was dispelled. This is because the statement by T did not in any case mean anything more than that he—as a psychologist—had not established any such damage.

(d) The employees of the defendant did not tell the plaintiffs about the suspicion which existed of mental retardation.

The witness M has stated that she did not speak about this with the plaintiffs. According to her testimony, the witness Ü had had nothing to do with the adoption placement. The claim by the defendant that the plaintiffs had been advised in detail by the witness T as well as by the Adoption Placement Office is unsubstantiated, as it cannot be deduced from this allegation whether the plaintiffs were also informed about the suspicion which existed of mental handicap. According to the account of the defendant's representative in the hearing before the Senate of 15 May 1992, nothing was known to the witness B who was summoned to this hearing of the suspicion of mental handicap, so she could not explain about this to the plaintiffs. As the witness M was at least informed by the defendant's Youth Welfare Department about the suspicion which existed, she would have had to take care that the plaintiffs were correctly, clearly, unequivocally and completely informed about this suspicion. That did not happen.

2. This duty to inform was also owed to the plaintiffs as third parties in the sense of § 839 (1) sentence 1 of the BGB. This follows—for the reasons given more precisely above—from the fact that the adoption applicants should have been able to make their decision to adopt in the knowledge of all the important facts and that this is not ensured if such facts—even if it is only a question of suspicion of a serious illness—are not communicated to them.

3. The employees of the defendant culpably, i.e. negligently, did not inform the plaintiffs about the suspicion which existed of the child N being mentally handicapped, although they must have realised that the knowledge of this suspicion was of fundamental importance for the plaintiffs as adoption applicants. They ought not, without arranging a detailed specialist examination to make matters clear, to have proceeded on the basis that the suspicion was dispelled by the interim report of the witness T, a qualified psychologist, or in some other way. Without satisfying themselves in this respect, they ought not to have relied on T informing the plaintiffs about a suspicion of mental retardation. It is true that the employees of the Youth Welfare Department cannot be assumed to have the knowledge of a doctor or a psychologist. But they had medical statements before them about the child N, from which it was to be inferred that there was suspicion of mental retardation. They ought to have informed the plaintiffs about this, so that they could then freely decide whether they wanted nevertheless to adopt the child.

4. The violation of official duty was also the cause of the harm which is the subject of the claim.

(a) It has to be asked here what course things would have taken if the official had acted in accordance with his duty and what the financial position of the injured parties would have been if the official had not committed the breach of official duty, but had acted in accordance with it [reference omitted]. This question is to be decided in accordance with § 287 of the Civil Procedure Code. If—as here—the violation of official duty consists in an omission, then there is only a causal connection with the harm if action according to duty would have prevented the occurrence of the harmful consequences [reference omitted].

(b) If the appropriate officials had informed the plaintiffs about the suspicion which existed, they would not have adopted the child N. This follows from the fact that the plaintiffs had stated with sufficient clarity in the application form that they did not want to adopt a mentally handicapped child. This is not changed by the fact that they had made this declaration subject to limitations which did not affect its essential content.

(c) It would certainly have been possible for the plaintiffs, after receiving information about the suspicion of mental retardation, to have made the adoption dependent on a prior detailed neurological or psychiatric examination. Such an examination could not be expected to have dispelled the suspicion which existed, in the face of the child's evident behavioural symptoms. Such an examination would either have—as in the case of the later examinations in the children's hospital O and in the University clinic—revealed the presence of childhood brain damage or would have had an outcome which was admittedly unclear, but which would not have dispelled the suspicion. But even in the latter case, the plaintiffs would have refrained from adopting the child N because of the risk of adopting a mentally handicapped child. As they did not want to adopt such a child, they would also not have taken the risk of possibly having to bear the responsibility and burdens of such a child.

5. (a) The plaintiff can claim from the defendant compensation for her loss of earnings in the undisputed sum of DM 30,610.44. The plaintiffs have, without being contradicted, argued that the plaintiff giving up her job had been a prerequisite for the adoption placement. According to the testimony of the plaintiff, which likewise remained uncontradicted, when she gave evidence at the Senate hearing of 15 July 1992, she had given up

her job on 16 December 1981, when the plaintiffs took N into their care. The plaintiff would have not have suffered loss of earnings if the defendant's officials had fulfilled the duty to inform which they owed to the plaintiffs; because then no adoption would have taken place and the plaintiff would not have needed to give up her job for the time being. The defendant, in this respect under a duty of explanation, has not substantiated that the plaintiffs, who certainly wanted to adopt a child, would have had the actual opportunity before the lapse of 19 months—reckoned from 16 December 1981—to adopt another child, and that the loss of earnings would therefore still have arisen in whole or in part.

(b) On the same grounds the court costs and notarial expenses borne by the plaintiff in the undisputed sum of DM 91.59 are to be compensated.

6. The claim for a declaration by the plaintiffs in relation to the duty of the defendant to compensate for possible future harm is also well founded. The prerequisite for the issue of a declaratory judgment is merely that there is a certain probability that claims have arisen or could arise from the legal relationship which is to be established [reference omitted]. The prerequisite is fulfilled in this case. The future harm exists predominantly in the expenditure on maintenance which the plaintiffs must provide for the handicapped child, possibly for the whole of its life. The duty to compensate for harm is not limited to the additional expenditure on maintenance which arises through the special needs of a mentally handicapped child. The defendant must instead reimburse the plaintiffs for the whole of the expenditure on maintenance. The provision of information about all the important facts and circumstances of the adoption to the adoption applicants which was due from the employees of the Youth Employment Department is not only to protect them from the additional expenditure which they incur for the maintenance of a handicapped or sick child. The fulfilment of the duty to give information is also to ensure freedom of decision by the adoption applicants, and this consists of not adopting a mentally handicapped child at all. If such a child is adopted, the risk of providing full maintenance has been realised, and fulfilment of the duty to provide information should protect the adopters from this. In this respect the legal situation is similar to the one which arises when a doctor advises a pregnant woman during early pregnancy incorrectly or incompletely about the possibilities on early recognition of damage to the foetus which would have provided legal justification for the wish of the mother to terminate the pregnancy. Even in this case, the BGH has not limited the claim of the parents to compensation for harm to the additional expenditure on maintenance, but extended it to the complete maintenance requirement for the child who has been harmed [reference omitted]. In this case, the issue cannot be decided otherwise.

II.
No contributory fault for the origination of the harm can be laid at the door of the plaintiffs in connection with the adoption of the child N (§ 254 (1) of the BGB).

III.
The appeal is accordingly rejected.

Case 138

OBERLANDESGERICHT HAMM, 20 NOVEMBER 1996
ZFJ 1997, 433

Facts

K was born in February 1976. The plaintiff was her mother and the sole person entitled to look after her.

In November 1992 K presented herself at the Youth Welfare Department of the defendant district and told them about recent domestic difficulties with the plaintiff. (K had already been accommodated for a time by the Youth Welfare Department in the children's home B in M, in early 1991). She explained to the officer in charge, Me, that she could not stand things at home any more. She refused a mediation interview with the plaintiff. But K and the plaintiff had a conversation of at least one and a half hours on the morning of 17 November 1992. Me was present for part of the time. No settlement was reached.

The Youth Welfare Department applied to the Guardianship Court C, which arranged a hearing on the afternoon of 17 November 1992. K was heard first, and she repeated to the judge her statements contained in the report of the Youth Welfare Department, and said she did not want to go back home. Then the plaintiff was heard. The Guardianship Court tried to arrange a settlement between K and the plaintiff, but failed. It made a temporary order taking away the plaintiff's right to determine K's place of residence, and transferring this to the Youth Welfare Department as guardian.

K was then accommodated by the Youth Welfare Department at first in the Youth Protection Centre in D and from 10 December 1992 in the children's home B in M. On 5 September 1993 K left the home of her own accord and returned to the plaintiff.

On 27 September 1993 the Guardianship Court transferred full custody rights back to the plaintiff. But because of a new argument, the plaintiff finally excluded K from home on 11 November 1993. The two have since lived separately from one another.

The plaintiff lodged a complaint against the decision of the Guardianship Court. This was rejected by the Landgericht M on 2 July 1993 because K's wish not to return home had to be respected.

The plaintiff claimed compensation from the defendant district including damages for distress because the Youth Welfare Department deprived her of K in a manner contrary to their official duty.

The action and the appeal were unsuccessful.

Reasons

The prerequisites for a claim for official liability under §§ 839 and 847 of the BGB in combination with Article 34 of the GG, which is the only for basis a claim to be considered here, are not present.

I. The work and tasks of youth assistance—and along with this the official duties of the Youth Welfare Department—arise from § 2 of the KJHG. This work includes amongst other things educational assistance and supplementary services (§§ 2 (2) nos. 4, 27–37, 39 and 40 KJHG), and the other tasks include amongst other things taking children and young people into care (§§ 2 (3) Nos. 1 and 42 KJHG SGB VIII).

On this basis, the Youth Welfare Department of the defendant district has not violated any official duties which could be the cause of the plaintiff's alleged harm.

1. The decision of the Youth Welfare Department to take K into care on 16 November 1992 and to seek a decision of the Guardianship Court on 17 November 1992 was in accordance with their official duty.

(a) According to § 42 (2) of the KJHG the Youth Welfare Department is under a duty to take a young person into care if he or she asks for this. It has to inform the person having custody about the taking into care without delay.

These prerequisites are fulfilled in the present case. K asked to be taken into care by the Youth Welfare Department of the defendant district on 16 November as a so-called "voluntary admission". The duty of the Youth Welfare Department to take into care applies without any limitation, regardless of the grounds on which the young person asks for care and of whether these grounds are convincing; the requirements to be placed on the content of these grounds must not be too high [references omitted].

The plaintiff as the person having custody had unquestionably been notified of the taking into care, and in this connection it does not matter for the purpose of the decision whether this notification was based on her own initiative or on that of the Youth Welfare Department.

(b) According to § 42 (2) sentence 3 of the KJHG the Youth Welfare Department must, if the person having custody challenges the taking into care, either hand the young person over to the person having custody (option 1) or obtain a decision by the Guardianship Court about the necessary measures for the welfare of the young person (option 2). These steps must take place without delay.

(aa) Unquestionably, the plaintiff challenged the taking into care in the conversation on the morning of 17 November 1992. She accuses the Youth Welfare Department of not having kept the appointment arranged at 12 o'clock for the continuation of the discussion, but it is not evident that this would have made a difference in the context of the plaintiff's challenge. On the evidence of the memorandum of the hearing before the Guardianship Court, the plaintiff still stated to the court that she did not agree with the taking into care—at any rate not unconditionally.

(bb) In this situation, the Youth Welfare Department was under a duty to make an "immediate" decision. No objection can be raised to the fact that it chose, out of the two alternatives to be considered, not to hand K over to the plaintiff, but to invoke the Guardianship Court. This was in accordance with their official duty.

In the literature [reference omitted] the view is taken that when a person having custody challenges a taking into care, the Youth Welfare Department is always obliged to bring in the Guardianship Court even if the Department considers there is no danger to the child's welfare. According to another view [reference omitted] the Youth Welfare Department only needs to obtain a decision of the Guardianship Court (and also must, without there being any discretion) if the welfare of the young person is endangered. Both opinions lead here to the same conclusion.

In making its decision, the Youth Welfare Department could (and had to) take into account that help for K's upbringing had already been necessary (in January / February

1991), that there were unquestionably school, alcohol and drug problems and that again K absolutely refused to go back home. As K was at that time already nearly 17 years old, the Youth Welfare Department could take this refusal seriously.

Assuming a danger to the child's welfare in this situation, and bringing in the Guardianship Court, were not contrary to the Youth Welfare Department's official duty. It could regard the decisions of the Guardianship Court and of the *Landgericht* based on §§ 1666 and 1666a of the BGB (endangering of child's welfare) as retrospectively confirming this assumption. The urgency of the measures to be taken by the Youth Welfare Department also did not permit—contrary to the view of the plaintiff—the making of further enquiries, in particular the hearing of the witnesses who were later heard by the Guardianship Court. The necessary elucidation of the matter was ensured because the Guardianship Court was under a duty to investigate of its own motion (§ 12 of the FGG).

2. The Youth Welfare Department would certainly have acted contrary to its official duty if it had "wangled" the right to determine K's accommodation by—as the plaintiff claims—influencing K by insinuation to make untrue statements to the Guardianship Court.

But the plaintiff has not substantiated this sweeping accusation in any greater detail, either in writing or at her examination in accordance with § 141 of the Civil Procedure Code at the Senate's hearing; so taking evidence did need to be considered here. The plaintiff has merely asserted that the Youth Welfare Department stated to K that she must only stick to her point of view and say that she did not want to return home in any circumstances. The Senate cannot see any improper influencing of K in this.

The decision of the Guardianship Court is based in substance on K's wish, as stated to it, that she did not want to go back home. This stated wish was not however inconsistent with the truth.

The plaintiff herself admitted on her personal examination before the Senate that K, at the point in time in question, did not in fact want to go back home and that even in the conversation on the morning of 17 November 1992 there were no prospects of this. Moreover, K stated this wish approximately eight months later to the Complaints Chamber of the *Landgericht*. There is no allegation that the facts of the case were presented to the Guardianship Court in some other way which was inconsistent with the truth and based on improper influence by the Youth Welfare Department.

3. The Youth Welfare Department has also not violated its official duties by accommodating K after the decision of the Guardianship Court, at first in the Youth Protection Centre Ka in D and afterwards in the children's home B in M.

(a) On the basis of the decision of the Guardianship Court, the right to determine K's place of residence was provisionally transferred to the Youth Welfare Department as guardian (§§ 1631 (1), 1666 and 1666a of the BGB). The Youth Welfare Department could therefore decide on K's place of residence without the agreement of the plaintiff [reference omitted]. The right to determine a place of residence also includes the authority to exercise care of the person concerned to the extent necessary for a parent. This includes entrusting the person to a family or—as here—the houseparents in a home. This authority is part of the right to determine the place of residence.

(b) Besides this, the plaintiff shows no alternative to accommodation in a home— which was in any case only provisional for the period of the temporary order—especially as she and K could not agree at the hearing before the Guardianship Court on accommodation with another appropriate care person. Accommodation with the plaintiff herself was out of the question as a serious alternative after the Guardianship Court had just taken this aspect of guardianship away from her.

4. Finally it cannot be established that the Youth Welfare Department violated its official duty just because it did not, following the decision of the Guardianship Court, provide any services—additionally to accommodation in the home—under § 2 (2) of the KJHG.

(a) In this connection, the Senate can leave open the question of whether the Youth Welfare Department, under the given circumstances of the plaintiff, ought to have offered such services, namely educational assistance (§ 27 of the KJHG) educational advice (§ 28 of the KJHG) or socio-pedagogical family assistance (§ 31 of the KJHG). The Senate can therefore also leave open the question of whether it was due to lack of readiness on the part of the Youth Welfare Department or on the part of the plaintiff that this did not occur; even at the Senate hearing this could not be resolved by examination of the parties on both sides.

(b) But this does not need to be resolved in order to decide the legal dispute; that is why it is not necessary to go into the question of whether the memoranda submitted by the defendant district were—as the plaintiff asserts—made out after the event or not. Because even if the Youth Welfare Department breached its duty in not offering to the plaintiff and K services in accordance with § 2 (2) of the KJHG, it cannot be established within the framework of the necessary examination of causality that matters would then have taken such a course that the harm which is the subject of the plaintiff's claim would not have arisen.

(aa) Even according to the plaintiff's own allegation, no sufficient grounds were present for saying that if services under § 2 (2) of the KJHG had been obtained the relationship between the plaintiff and K would have improved. The plaintiff herself described K as a "very egocentric girl with a very strongly demanding nature". K's behaviour, in so far as this is of importance for the resolution of the legal dispute, confirms the plaintiff's own assessment. Within the framework of § 287 of the Civil Procedure Code, which is to be applied here, success from services under § 2 (2) of the KJHG cannot in any case be established or even assumed; demonstrating this is the responsibility of the plaintiff who is under a duty of explanation and proof in respect of causality.

(bb) Even if a different view is taken, there is nothing to indicate within the framework of § 287 of the Civil Procedure Code that services under § 2 (2) of the KJHG would have succeeded so quickly that the harm which is the subject of the plaintiff's claim would thereby have been avoided or at least reduced; demonstrating this also falls to the plaintiff who is under a duty of explanation and proof in respect of it.

The harm to her reputation which the plaintiff asserts—and the sale of her house in H associated with this—is based only on the taking into care under § 42 (2) of the KJHG, the ensuing deprivation of the right to determine the place of residence by the Guardianship Court and the subsequent accommodation of K in the Youth Protection Centre Ka and in the children's home B. Even the legal costs and the costs of visits and telephone calls arose exclusively in connection with the taking into care, the deprivation of the right of determination of the place of residence and the accommodation. This harm would therefore also not have been avoided by additional services by the Youth Welfare

Department under § 2 (2) of the KJHG. The same applies to the impairment which the plaintiff claimed occurred to her health. Apart from the fact that, according to the statements of the plaintiff to the expert D, this impairment must for the most part have existed previously, there is nothing to indicate that it would have been avoided or even significantly reduced by services by the Youth Welfare Department under § 2 (2) of the KJHG.

Case 139

OBERLANDESGERICHT HAMM, 23 MARCH 1990
AZ: 11 U 108/89 (NOT PUBLISHED)

Official liability for refusing to allow a sick child to participate in special tuition.

[Headnote: Officials of the Education Office and head teachers can breach their official duties as against the mother of a child who is required to attend school but who suffers from school phobia if they do not ensure that the child can take part in special tuition in accordance with SchpflG NW § 7 (1). The mother can demand in such a case that the costs spent on private tuition are reimbursed in accordance with principles of official liability.]

On the plaintiff's appeal (*Berufung*) (in other respects rejected) the judgment of the third civil chamber of the Bochum Landgericht, delivered on 24 April 1989, is amended. The defendant Land is ordered to pay to the plaintiff DM 2,500.00 with interest at 4 per cent from 12 January 1990. The remainder of the claim is rejected. . . .

Reasons

The appeal of the plaintiff is permissible and is largely successful. It results in judgment against the defendant Land for payment of DM 2,500.00 with interest.

II.
The plaintiff is entitled in her own right to a claim for damages in the sum of 2,500.00 DM against the defendant Land under § 839 (1) of the BGB in combination with Article 34 of the Basic Law. This is because the employees of the education office for the . . . town and the head teachers of the . . . Grammar School and the . . . Secondary School did not ensure (or did not ensure in time) that the plaintiff's son was given special education in the form of home tuition.

1.
(a) It was a breach of official duty for the competent officials of the Education Office (in particular the educational supervisor, but also the head teacher of the W Grammar School and the head teacher of the . . . Secondary School) not (or not at the right time) to take steps which ensured that the plaintiff's son was given special tuition. The setting up of special tuition was unreasonably delayed as a result.

It must be assumed that a sick child has a subjective public right to schooling in a special school or to take part in special tuition, which corresponds to his or her duty to attend a special school or to take part in special tuition which is regulated in § 7 (1) of the SchpflG. But the entitlement following from this provision is limited by the educational standards of primary and secondary schools, so that no breach of official duty falls to be considered insofar as the Education Office has not enabled the plaintiff's son to take part in special tuition at grammar school level.

According to § 7 (1) sentence 2 of the SchpflG, the education authority to be designated by the Minister of Education and the Articles by statutory instrument decides on the special tuition in which children required to attend school have to take part. The competent education authority is the Education Office (§ 1 of the Education Office Competence Regulations in combination with para. 2 of the Appendix). The official duties of the Education Office officials and the head teachers arise from the Circular of the Minister for Education and the Arts of 17 July 1980, amended by the Circular of 10 and 23 October 1984 and the Circular of 16 November 1987. Until the amendment of the Circular of 17 July 1980 by the Circular of 16 November 1987 (with effect from 15 February 1988) a pupil had a claim to special tuition if he was prevented from attending school on the grounds of illness for longer than eight weeks (six weeks from 15 February 1988). If it is established from the start that a pupil will have to stay away from school lessons for more than eight weeks, special tuition can be given earlier (para. 1.1 of the said Circular). According to para. 5 of the Circular of 10 October 1984, applications for special tuition (home tuition) through the direction of the school so far attended by the pupil are to be directed or referred on to the Education Office. The Education Office then decides on the application in accordance with para. 6 of the Circular and arranges the special tuition (home tuition). Before the decision it has to be established by medical opinion—in cases of doubt by the medical officer—whether the prerequisites for special tuition are present and whether the pupil is in a position to take part in the special tuition (para. 3 of the Circular of 17 July 1980; but different provision is made in § 7 (1) sentence 3 of the SchpflG, in which the obtaining of an opinion of the Public Health Department is essential).

Until the report of the head teacher of the . . . Grammar School of 5 March 1986 [reference omitted], the plaintiff's son had been absent from lessons for about $1\frac{1}{2}$ years i.e. from 3 September 1984 to 6 March 1986. This occurred without the responsible head teacher of the Grammar School and the Education Office having arranged anything to secure the fulfilment of the duty to attend school in accordance with §§ 1 (1) and 7 (1) of the SchpflG. The pupil had been ill from the 3rd September 1984. It is revealed by the report of the head teacher to the Education Office for the town of . . . of 5 March 1986 that the plaintiff had submitted to the school a psychological certificate which stated that her son had acute attacks of school anxiety and declared that school attendance was not possible for half a year for this reason. Even at that time the head teacher of the . . . Grammar School ought, according to the legal and administrative provisions previously mentioned, to have considered the giving of special tuition and arranged for the plaintiff to make an appropriate application. Then the Education Office would also have been immediately involved in the matter. According to the psychological certificate (possibly relating to certification by the qualified psychologist . . . of 4 October 1984) it was certain from the start that the pupil would have to be absent from school lessons for more than eight weeks. When the certificate had run out and the plaintiff appeared at the school with her son on 1 March 1985, he refused to attend school of any kind. It may admittedly have been proper to refer the plaintiff to an education advice centre. But no-one at the Grammar School and the . . . Secondary School at which the plaintiff's son was enrolled then troubled any further about the educational fate of this pupil. There was no co-ordination of any kind between the two schools. The Education Office too was not brought in at first, so it became possible for the plaintiff's son to miss several years of compulsory schooling. It was true that the persons having the right of upbringing have, according to § 16 (2) of the SchpflG, to see to it that a child who is under a duty to attend school takes part regularly in lessons and in the other events of the school. But as the pupil had school phobia, which emerges from the certification of the clinics of the state capital D of 24 November 1987 and their opinions of 16 December 1987, the plaintiff could not urge her son to take part in lessons at the school.

In this situation, the Education Office had to ensure that the necessary special tuition was given to the plaintiff's son. In the same way as the persons having the right of upbringing, it has the task of encouraging pupils to fulfil the duties incumbent upon them (§ 14 (3) sentence 2 of the SchpflG). These include in particular that the pupils should comply with their duty to attend school to the required extent. For this purpose, the Education Office has to ensure that it learns of school absences of long duration in good time, so that it can if necessary take the measures needed to fulfil the duty to attend school. Substantial absences must have occurred here, because a pupil could not otherwise have received no lessons for more than three years. Even after the receipt of the report of the head teacher of the . . . Grammar School of 5 March 1986, it was more than a year until the attempt at setting up special tuition from 6 July 1987 was undertaken. As indications of the existence of school anxiety emerged from the report anyway, the Education Office ought immediately to have clarified whether the pupil had a school phobia which made the arrangement of special tuition (home tuition) necessary. It should have done this by obtaining an opinion from the Public Health Office. The lawyer's letter of 10 February 1987 in which it was announced that the pupil would attend a boarding school with immediate effect changed nothing in this respect, because it was immediately overtaken by the further lawyer's letter of 16 February 1987 in which it was stated that the best thing would be to give private tuition to the boy until his psychological condition had been overcome. It was only on the basis of the letter by the plaintiff's legal representative of 8 December 1987 that private tuition at home was set up, but admittedly only four hours a week initially.

(b) The officials of the defendant Land, in particular the employees of the Education Office, have negligently breached their duties in that they did not arrange and expedite the setting up of the special tuition in a purposeful manner. Even the head teachers involved did not take sufficient steps to ensure compulsory school attendance and thereby likewise negligently breached their official duties. They have violated unambiguous legal and administrative provisions. Every official must possess or acquire the knowledge of law and administration necessary for the conduct of his office.

(c) The defendant Land is liable in accordance with Article 34 of the Basic Law for the breaches of official duty. According to this provision, the liability applies in principle to the body which the official who acts contrary to duty serves. Here that is the Land of NW. The head teachers of the named schools are officials of the defendant Land. The same applies to the employees of the Education Office. Admittedly the Education Office in a town which is an administrative district in its own right (. . . is such a town) consists of the chief executive and the educational supervisor (§ 18 (2) sentence 1 of the SchVG). It is not however here a question of breaches of the official duty of the chief executive, who is in principle a local official. It can therefore be left undecided whether on breaches of official duty by the chief executive as a member of the Education Office, the town of . . . or the defendant Land is the body liable in the sense of Article 34 of the Basic Law. The breaches of official duty established in the case in question are to be laid at the door of the educational supervisor. According to the Circular of the Minister for Education and the Articles of 10 October 1984 (para. 7) competence for special tuition (home tuition) was to be transferred at the Education Office into the overall charge of an educational supervisor. According to the standing orders for the Education Office—§ 3 (3) sentence 2 of the Circular of the Minister for Education and the Articles of 4 December 1984—the arrangement and carrying out of the special lessons is in any case predominantly in the educational service area. The former defendant's reply to the appeal, which the defendant Land has clearly adopted, also proceeds on this basis. The educational supervisor is however an official of the defendant Land.

2.

The official duties which have been breached do not only exist as against the pupil but also as against the plaintiff as the person having the right to bring him up. Whether in the individual case the person harmed belongs to the class of third parties in the sense of § 839 (1) of the BGB is not to be judged according to whether the official duty—even if not necessarily solely—has the purpose of looking after the interest of the person harmed. It must follow from the provisions which form the basis of the official duty and which outline it, as well as from the nature of the official business, that the person harmed belongs to the group of persons whose interests are to be protected and promoted according to the goal and legal purpose of the official business. Only then will a duty to compensate exist as against him following a culpable breach of duty. On the other hand, no duty to compensate is established as against other persons, even if the breach of official duty has had a more or less disadvantageous effect for them. A special relationship must therefore exist between the official duty breached and the third party harmed (constant case law of the Bundesgerichtshof, see e.g. BGHZ 106, 323, 331 with further references). Such a special relationship exists here between the official duties breached and the plaintiff. It arises from the fact that education of her son (who is required to attend school) is incumbent on the plaintiff and she therefore has a paramount interest in his well ordered school education in the same way as the pupil. According to Article 8 (1) sentence 2 of the Constitution of the Land of NW it is the natural right of parents to determine the instruction and education of children. The defendant Land has taken over the public school system and exercises supervision over it. The competent officials are therefore breaching their official duties as against the parents as the persons having the right of upbringing, if they do not ensure (or do not ensure in time) that a pupil who has a long lasting illness receives that special tuition which is provided for and formulated in the relevant legal and administrative provisions.

3.

It cannot be in doubt that substantial deficits in the pupil's education have occurred through the lengthy delays by the responsible officials. This is also expressly emphasised in the letter of the Institute for Remedial Education and Psychotherapy of the town of . . . of 23 February 1987. These deficits could not be made up for by the special tuition which was given in the end after a long wait. The expenditure claimed by the plaintiff for the giving of private tuition is therefore adequately caused by the breaches of duty by the officials of the defendant Land. On the basis of the credible testimony of the witness . . . Sch, it is established that the plaintiff's expenditure on the private tuition amounted to at least DM 2,500.00. The witness stated that in the period from the end of September or the beginning of October 1987 to the end of June 1988—with the exception of school holidays—she gave the plaintiff's son a double hour of private tuition twice each week for a payment of DM 20.00 per hour. Altogether the plaintiff paid her almost DM 3,000.00, but at least DM 2,500.00. The last named sum is to be taken as a basis for the measurement of the harm. A higher level of harm cannot be established with certainty in the face of the testimony of the witness, especially as receipts are not available.

4.

Contributory fault by the plaintiff for the origin of the harm (§ 254 (1) of the BGB) cannot be established. Contributory fault by the plaintiff could at best be deduced from the fact that in 1987 she did not arrange earlier for the Institute for Remedial Education and Psychotherapy of the town of . . . to give an opinion about her son and then make the report available to the Education Office. This first happened with the letter of the 23rd April 1987 by the plaintiff's legal representative. But then the substantial deficits in education which were caused by the delays on the part of the officials of the defendant Land had already occurred. Also, it was not until the beginning of 1988 that the special tuition for the plaintiff's son was at last arranged.

5.

Finally, the plaintiff can also not be blamed for the fact that she omitted to avert the harm by the use of legal redress. The raising of a complaint in the administrative courts for failure to act would not have been able to change anything in relation to the onset of the harm, especially as the plaintiff might fairly have hoped that she could have achieved the arrangement of special tuition without taking legal action in the administrative courts. . . .

3. COMPENSATION AND SATISFACTION

Case 140

BUNDESGERICHTSHOF (GREAT CIVIL DIVISION) 6 JULY 1955
BGHZ 18, 149

The Great Civil Senate has answered as follows the question referred to it by the Sixth Civil Senate as to whether in assessing the amount of reasonable compensation in money in accordance with § 847 BGB all the circumstances must be taken into account, including the financial circumstances and the degree of blameworthiness of the person liable to pay damages:

In assessing equitable compensation in money in accordance with § 847 BGB all circumstances of the case can be taken into account, among them the degree of blameworthiness of the person who is liable and the financial circumstances of both parties. In this connection account must also be taken of the extent to which the person who is liable is indemnified by a liability insurance or a claim for redress.

Reasons

According to § 847 BGB "equitable compensation" in money may be claimed in case of injury to the body or to health even in respect of damage which is not pecuniary. The older view, held in particular by the Reichsgericht, was that compensation under § 847 BGB must be "equitable" in respect of *all* the circumstances which characterise the damaging event in issue; it therefore took into account not only the extent and the duration of the pain, disfigurement, suffering, and intrusion, which were always matters of primary concern, but also particularly the economic situation of the injured party and of the tortfeasor, the degree of blameworthiness, and the circumstances which led to the damage (e.g. gratuitous transportation). According to a more recent view the compensation must only be "equitable" with reference to the purpose, which is to compensate non-pecuniary damage; it therefore only takes into account the extent and the duration of the pain, disfigurement, suffering, and intrusion as well as the means necessary to compensate for non-pecuniary damage; thus it takes into account only the general circumstances of the injured party. This more recent view was adopted by the Third Civil Senate in its decision of 29 September 1952 [reference] to the extent that in assessing the amount of damages for pain and suffering it did not take into account the economic circumstances of the tortfeasor, while leaving open the question as to whether the degree of this blameworthiness should also not be considered.

I. 1. The modern practice bases its view on the ground that claims for damages for pain and suffering, too, are true claims for damages; it therefore regards as decisive the non-pecuniary damage which the injured party suffered as a result of the tort; as in all cases of claims for damages it seeks to take into account only those consequences which the act giving rise to damages has had for the injured party.

This view assumes correctly that as a result of the treatment of the Civil Code of claims in respect of torts—including those based on non-pecuniary damage—it is impossible to attribute to them a direct penal function. This applies equally to claims for non-pecuniary damage. However, by denying the penal character of claims for non-pecuniary damage no final answer has been given to the question for decision in the present case which is in respect of what circumstances damages to be awarded under § 847 BGB must be "equitable".

2. First of all the provision of § 847 BGB must be considered as part of the system of the Civil Code as a whole, which in the most diverse places determines the extent of a performance in accordance with "equitable discretion" or allows "equitable compensation". In these cases the Code intends normally that account should be taken of all the circumstances of a case which are relevant according to equitable considerations, and more particularly the situation of all the parties involved.

(*a*) If a performance is to be fixed in accordance with "equitable discretion", as §§ 315, 317 BGB require, or an act must be carried out in accordance with "equitable discretion", as §§ 1246, 2048, 2156 BGB demand, it means undoubtedly in these cases that not only the economic circumstances of the creditor, but also those of the debtor must be taken into account.

(*b*) In connection with claims for damages, too, the Civil Code refers not only in § 847 but also in §§ 829, 1300 to equitable compensation or to damages in accordance with the requirements of equity.

When § 829 BGB speaks of equitable considerations, the Code refers expressly to "the circumstances of the parties involved", and thus the economic circumstances of the parties must also be taken into account. It is true that normally § 847 BGB presupposes that the tortfeasor is to be blamed, while § 829 establishes strict liability. Moreover, according to § 829 both the ground for holding a person liable as well as the extent of his liability are determined according to the principles of equity, while according to § 847 only the extent of liability is so to be fixed. Nevertheless, it is the express intention of § 829, also in so far as it determines the extent of the claim for damages in accordance with equity, that the circumstances of those involved should be taken into account, albeit on the basis of detailed particulars. It is not possible either to refer to § 829 in order to further the argument in support of a restrictive interpretation of § 847, as adopted by the more recent practice, if only for the reason that the Civil Code by requiring that something is to be performed in accordance with the principles of equity intends not only in that case, but regularly, that all circumstances are to be taken into account which may be relevant.

(c) A closer connection than that between § 847 and § 829 BGB exists between the claims arising under § 847 and the claim for defloration under § 1300 BGB, in respect of which the law provides also that "equitable compensation" in money is to be granted. It must be admitted that the liability under § 1300 arises from the breach of an agreement which forms part of Family Law while that under § 847 is based on a tort. However, in both cases the extent of liability is to be determined in accordance with equity.

This history of § 1300 BGB shows that the legislature intended the considerations which had led it to allow "equitable compensation under § 1300" to apply equally to "equitable compensation in § 847". Thus the proposal to replace the expression "equitable compensation" in what is now § 1300 by the term "adequate compensation" was rejected together with the further proposal to grant, instead of "equitable compensation", "compensation which takes into account the financial circumstances of either party to the engagement to marry as well as the reduced expectation of another marriage". One of the reasons was that § 831 of the Bill, now § 847, which was followed by § 1283 of the Bill, now § 1300, also referred to equitable compensation and that in the case of a claim for damages under what is now § 1300, which follows closely the claim for damages under what is now § 847, no danger existed that the previous practice (opposed by the second proposal) in the case of claims for defloration would be continued.

The substantive considerations expressed in respect of § 1300 and applicable also to § 847, as appeared above, emerge from the reasons which accompany the rejection of the proposals referred to above. The first of these proposals was rejected on the ground that "the term 'equitable' had a clear established technical meaning". The second proposal was met by the argument that "it was not just in assessing the damages to take no notice at all of the financial circumstances and the situation in life of the girl, as might be feared, if the proposal were accepted; the best means of ensuring the development of a realistic practice of the Court was not in any way to restrict the judges in assessing damages". Another proposal to fix the damages under § 1300 at a minimum of fifty times the normal local daily wage was "countered by the argument that individual provisions concerning the assessment of damages were not advisable . . .".

Therefore the preparatory materials for the Civil Code permit the conclusion in respect of § 847 as well that it was the intention of the legislature not to constrain the courts to disregard certain circumstances in assessing damages for non-pecuniary losses. This means that in fixing equitable compensation the courts may, as a matter of principle, take into consideration all the circumstances which may arise.

3. Contrary to the modern view the same conclusion follows from the legal purpose of damages for pain and suffering. In law damages for pain and suffering have a dual function. They are meant to provide the injured party with adequate compensation for that kind of damage, for those handicaps which are not of a pecuniary nature. At the

same time they are meant to indicate that the tortfeasor owes the victim satisfaction for what he has done to him.

Of these two functions, that of compensation or redress is prominent. The purpose of the claim is redress for the loss suffered. The latter cannot, however, be assessed arithmetically. The underlying idea may perhaps be formulated as follows: the tortfeasor, who has not only inflicted pecuniary damage upon the injured party but also gravely affected his life, is to help the latter by his payments to alleviate his burden as far as possible. Having regard to this purpose of damages for pain and suffering it must be admitted that considerations of the seriousness, acuteness, and duration of the pain, suffering, and the disfigurement constitute the main basis for assessing equitable damages. The sum required to provide this redress, therefore, depends primarily upon the extent of this damage. It is the merit of the decision of the Third Division of this court [reference] to have shown this, with the result that damages for pain and suffering were treated more seriously than hitherto not only as to their legal significance, but also as to their factual evaluation. Since, however, the Code requires equitable compensation in the meaning set out above (I.2), the purpose of making good cannot determine alone the amount of damages, particularly since this purpose is insufficient alone to fix the amount with something approximating certainty.

Furthermore, even if claims in tort for damages, including damages for non-pecuniary losses, no longer bear any penal character directly, nevertheless something inherent in the purpose of making good is a reminder of its former function as a fine or, to use the apposite term of the corresponding Swiss institution, as satisfaction. Legal history shows that damages for pain and suffering have their origin in criminal law and that in the laws of the German States in modern times different types were fashioned according to the respective stages of development, which still reflect in some respects their antecedents in criminal law. The following is significant: wherever damages for pain and suffering were not excluded altogether, as for instance in § 112 I 6 of the Prussian Allgemeines Landrecht of 1792 in respect of the persons other than "peasants or common citizens" or in Article 14 of the Württemberg Act concerning the effects in private law of crimes and penalties of 5 September 1839 [reference], the laws provided expressly that in assessing the amount of damages also certain circumstances were to be taken into account which cannot be reconciled with a limited notion of damages restricted to making good. Such are the degrees of blameworthiness mentioned in §§ 168, 125 I 6 of the Prussian Allgemeines Landrecht, or the degree of blameworthiness and "the financial circumstances of the tortfeasor" as stated in § 15 of the Baden Act concerning the effects in private law of crimes of 6 March 1845 [reference] or if, according to the Saxon decree of 1 August 1856 [reference] damages were to be fixed "in the discretion of the judge, having regard to the pain inflicted on the victim", which latter provision was interpreted to mean that the status and the financial circumstances of the claimant were to be taken into account [reference]. Similar considerations influenced the unanimous view of the practice of the courts and writers up to the thirties of this century in dealing with § 847 BGB to the effect that in assessing damages for pain and suffering all circumstances must be taken into account which colour the individual case.

It is true that the legislature has given the claim for pain and suffering the form of a claim for damages according to private law. However, in substance it does not bear the character of a usual claim of this kind, which is for compensation in respect of pecuniary damage. Its purpose to effect restitution cannot be achieved through restitution in kind, as is the case where the damage is pecuniary. To that extent restitution is impossible. Certainly an attempt is to be made to make good, but it cannot be done arithmetically. It is impossible to concentrate on the notion of making good, because non-pecuniary damage can never be expressed in terms of money and since the possibility itself of making good by means of money payments is very limited. Contrary to a view to be encountered occasionally, non-pecuniary losses concern "assets not to be valued in money terms". The amount of money necessary to make good cannot be determined by "so to say balancing pain with those pleasures which are intended to wipe out the victim's memory of his sufferings". Even where it is to a certain extent possible to compensate physical and mental suffering by amenities and comforts, widely differing possibilities almost always exist as to how redress is to be effected and the purpose alone of the damages to make good does not provide a sufficient measuring-rod. The purpose of making good alone only provides a very rough standard for assessing damages the greater the non-pecuniary loss. This appears particularly if the non-pecuniary loss is so extensive that it is difficult to conceive of making it good, as for instance when restitution can hardly be achieved because the body of the victim has been extensively destroyed. This becomes particularly clear where the type of non-pecuniary damage cannot be made good at all, as for instance frequently in the case of psychological effects. It is generally recognized that damages for non-pecuniary losses must also be awarded if an assault, false imprisonment, or interference with physical integrity resulted in psychological and not in physical injuries. Especially in the case of psychological disturbances it will frequently be impossible to compensate the feelings of unhappiness since the injured party himself is not conscious of his damage. Nevertheless, damages for pain and suffering have been rightly awarded even in this case. The award of damages under § 847 BGB, it must be admitted, serves to make good non-pecuniary loss; it is not, however, a condition for awarding damages for non-pecuniary loss that this purpose can be achieved. The same would be the case if the injured party is so situated financially that no amount of money could raise a sense of happiness which would make good his non-pecuniary damage.

Precisely in these situations of non-pecuniary damage, the function of making good, which is intimately connected with the legal regulation of damages for non-pecuniary loss, acquires its special significance. The function of making good underlines that the injurious act has created a certain personal relationship between the tortfeasor and the victim—which, by its nature demands that in assessing how much the tortfeasor must pay the victim *all* the circumstances of the case must be taken into account. This appears also from the special provision that this claim dies with the claimant and cannot be assigned.

II. In accordance with the foregoing observations, the severity and the extent of the reduction in the enjoyment of life must be considered in the first place for the purpose of assessing damages for pain and suffering. This is the preponderant aspect. In addition, other circumstances may, however, be taken into account as well which are salient features of the injurious act.

1. One of these is the degree of blameworthiness on the part of the tortfeasor. The degree of blameworthiness is not only relevant, as the more recent interpreters of § 847 BGB would have it, with regard to its effect upon the injured party: the fact that the injury was caused by the reckless or even intentional behaviour of the defendant, may naturally have left the injured party embittered, while he may be more inclined to accept as his fate an injured caused by slight negligence. Leaving aside the reaction of the injured party, it

may accord with equity and the notion of satisfaction in assessing compensation under § 847 BGB if, in the individual case, intention and recklessness count against the tortfeasor, while especially slight negligence counts in his favour. It would be incomprehensible if the trial judge could not award higher damages for pain and suffering in the case of a crime than where the external consequences are the same, but occurred as result of an error in normal human intercourse which might be committed by anybody. For this reason many foreign legal systems, too, have taken, and still take, into account the degree of blameworthiness of the tortfeasor in assessing the amount of damages payable by him. The fact that German law does not offer this opportunity where the damage is pecuniary does not preclude its use where the Code offers it in arriving at the equitable compensation for non-pecuniary loss. On the contrary, this possibility is a great merit of the regulation of damages for non-pecuniary losses.

Apart from the degree of blameworthiness, the cause of injury or of the injurious act may be relevant in certain circumstances. Even if the degree of blameworthiness is the same, different acts may bear very different characteristics (injury in the course of the enjoyment of some pleasure on the one hand, or in connection with the exercise of a profession, the administration of help, or any other necessary activity on the other hand). This is particularly valid in those cases in which the tort was committed on the occasion of an activity which the tortfeasor carried out in order to oblige the injured party and which the latter welcomed—perhaps even gratefully—as, for instance, where the victim suffers an injury on the occasion of a journey as a gratuitous passenger in the car of the tortfeasor as a result of the latter's negligence who sought to do him a favour. In such a case it may even be inequitable if the victim claims damages for pain and suffering to an amount equal to that which a pedestrian could have claimed who had been run down by the tortfeasor.

2. Possibly the economic circumstances of the injured party may also influence the assessment of damages on grounds of equity.

The economic circumstances of the victim may, for instance, affect the notion of making good inasmuch as the function of making good is less significant if, for example, the injured party is so favourably circumstanced economically that sums of money paid by the tortfeasor can hardly make good the non-pecuniary damage suffered to him. In such cases the function of damages as satisfaction assumes primary importance. On the other hand, it is not impossible that in individual cases the higher standard of living to which the victim is accustomed may also lead to increased damages for pain and suffering.

3. Finally, the economic circumstances of the tortfeasor may also be taken into account in assessing the damages under § 847 BGB.

(a) Viewed from the angle of equity, i.e. by taking into account the circumstances of both parties, the idea of making good should not normally result in the tortfeasor's serious and lasting penury. It is true that here, too, the need to offer satisfaction and to make good the damage is preponderant. The fact that the tortfeasor is not well off must be of greater or lesser importance having regard to the cause of the damaging event, and especially to the degree of blameworthiness. Any behaviour of the tortfeasor which is especially reprehensible, such as inconsiderate recklessness or, even more so, acting intentionally, may consign into the background any concern to preserve him from economic distress. On the other hand, if the tortfeasor's economic situation is particularly favourable it may appear equitable in the exercise of the court's discretion to award higher damages. Moreover, the smaller the amount of damages required to make good non-pecuniary losses, the more it will be possible to disregard the economic circumstances, in particular those of the tortfeasor. Equally the economic circumstances of the victim may be relevant in this connection. If the victim is comfortably off, it may appear equitable in assessing the damages to exercise in favour of the tortfeasor the power of discretion inherent in the consideration of the economic circumstances. On the other hand, if the victim is in straitened circumstances it may seem equitable to exercise this discretion in favour of the tortfeasor to a lesser extent than if the victim is well situated financially. However, even if the tortfeasor is penniless considerations of his financial position can never release him from the duty to pay damages for pain and suffering, for the financial position of the tortfeasor constitutes only one aspect among many, and not even the most important, which must be taken into account.

(b) Any such consideration of the economic circumstances of the parties involved is not contrary to the intention of positive law—express or implied. It is, however, true that in the case of a debt consisting of fungibles the debtor is always liable, even if he cannot supply them and that therefore in the case of a debt of fungibles, he cannot plead his adverse economic circumstances. The significance of any considerations of the economic circumstances of the tortfeasor, is, however, completely misunderstood by those who argue that, as a result of his adverse economic circumstances damages for non-pecuniary loss which are appropriate "as such" are reduced and that therefore the victim is receiving less than is due to him "as such". This view assumes that in fixing equitable damages *only* the extent of the losses is to be taken into account. In reality the amount of damages for pain and suffering is ascertained only when *all* the circumstances of the individual case have been considered. Taking into account all the financial circumstances of the tortfeasor does not reduce in any way the damages which are appropriate "as such"; instead "equitable damages" are being assessed for the first time in accordance with § 847 BGB by taking into account all circumstances which can be evaluated, including the economic circumstances of the parties involved; without considering all the circumstances, and thus also where appropriate the economic circumstances, no assessment would be possible. For this reason it cannot be contended that such an interpretation amounts to "breaching the principle which governs the entire area of law in the matter, which is that the extent of an obligation is always independent of the ability of the debtor to perform". This principle applies to pecuniary damages. On the other hand, the Code intends the extent of the damages for non-pecuniary losses envisaged by § 847 BGB to be assessed having regard to all the circumstances of the case. For the same reason it follows that an injured party whose economic circumstances are taken into account in his favour cannot be awarded more than his damage. The decision DR 1941, 280 does not permit the conclusion that the Reichsgericht abandoned its current practice and assumed that there is something like damages for pain and suffering "which are appropriate as such". If such a complete change of practice had taken place, it would certainly have been accompanied by more detailed arguments; where the Reichsgericht employed the term "damages for pain and suffering which are appropriate as such", it clearly used an imprecise formulation.

If it is acknowledged that the economic circumstances of the parties involved may be taken into account as one of the possible bases for assessing the amount of pecuniary damages for non-pecuniary losses, this constitutes a facet of the facts before the court, as are also the extent of the non-pecuniary damages and the possibility of providing an opportunity for making good. It is therefore wrong to say that it is contrary to the principle of equality to take the economic circumstances of the parties into account; for if the same victim suffers non-pecuniary damage inflicted by two tortfeasors whose economic circumstances differ from each other, the two situations are not identical. It is not clear why, as is said occasionally, the consideration of the economic conditions of the parties involved should be regarded as unsocial. Surely the fundamental principles of a social state based on law are not violated if in assessing damages the economic circumstances of the parties involved are balanced against each other.

(c) Considerations of the economic circumstances of the parties do not lead to insoluble difficulties either.

The view that considerations of the economic conditions of a penniless tortfeasor must—in strict logic—lead to a complete denial of damages under § 847 BGB has already been refuted above.

The view is also incorrect that the principle of taking into account the economic conditions is breached in those cases where the Fiscus is the tortfeasor. It must be conceded that in these cases, and also where the tortfeasor is a "charitable institution" of public law, the practice of the courts, especially that of the Reichsgericht, does not take notice of the financial situation of the tortfeasor. The reason is that the assets of the *Fiscus* serve public purposes and are tied to this extent. The conclusion is drawn therefrom that these assets do not reflect a financial situation in the nature of private enterprise; they cannot therefore be related to the assets of the victim, representing private enterprise, so as to balance them against each other. In the light of this view of the assets of the *Fiscus*, the financial situation of the *Fiscus* and that of the injured party are so different as to preclude a comparison. In these cases the tortfeasor (i.e. the *Fiscus*) lacks a characteristic (i.e. the economic circumstances) which, if existing, would have to be taken into account where engaging in considerations of equity. In the case of the *Fiscus* "economic" circumstances defy evaluation. They mitigate neither in favour of nor against the *Fiscus* as a debtor. The *Fiscus* can never plead straitened economic circumstances, just as the victim cannot point to the particularly favourable circumstances of the *Fiscus* which is liable to pay damages for pain and suffering.

No objections can be raised against the admissibility of considerations concerning the economic circumstances of the parties on the possible ground that the assessment of damages for non-pecuniary losses, which is difficult in any event, will be "rendered unpredictable and complicated" if the economic circumstances of the parties are taken into account. Apart from the fact—stressed more than once before—that the amount of damages depends primarily on the extent of the damage, the possibility of making good, and the amount of the means necessary to achieve this, none of these conceivable difficulties rules out the admissibility of considering economic circumstances, now that the legislature has abolished the more or less fixed rates for assessing damages to be awarded for non-pecuniary losses. The view that "non-pecuniary damage can be assessed and also that certain maximum and minimum amounts can be laid down as to how objectively ascertainable non-pecuniary losses can be compensated" results of necessity in the re-adoption of the fixed tariffs which were established by the law of some German States (e.g. §§ 113, 118 I. 6 of the Prussian Allgemeines Landrecht; § 1497 of the Saxon Civil Code) which were abolished by the Civil Code. Not only does the variety of possible non-pecuniary losses preclude the adoption of such "maximum and minimum tariffs" altogether or the latter would not do justice to the individual character of non-pecuniary damage, but it restricts the opportunity created by the code of reaching a decision based on the discretion of the court.

Moreover, the fact that the adverse economic circumstances of the tortfeasor are taken into account does not make it difficult or inequitable if later on, in the course of execution (by way of a judicial adjustment, a composition with creditors, or of bankruptcy), the tortfeasor seeks to obtain a reduction of his debts and thus also of his liability to pay damages under § 847 BGB which had already been fixed as appropriate in view of his unfavourable economic situation. The conclusion derived therefrom that in these cases the adverse financial position of the tortfeasor leads twice to a reduction of the claims under § 847 BGB is influenced by the incorrect assumption that damages which are appropriate "as such" are being reduced if the economic circumstances of the tortfeasor are taken into account. Here, too, the damages awarded under § 847 BGB are "reduced" only once, i.e. in the course of execution. Moreover, regarded from the economic point of view, the same result is reached not only in § 847 BGB but wherever the amount of the performance owed depends upon the economic circumstances of the debtor, as for instance where the extent of a performance or act is to be determined "in accordance with equitable discretion under §§ 315, 317, 1246, 2048, 2156 BGB, where a contractual penalty is to be reduced in accordance with § 343 BGB, or where damages for breach of promise under § 1300 are in issue".

(*d*) Once it is realized that where the claim is for non-pecuniary losses, damages which are appropriate "as such" do not exist and cannot therefore be increased or reduced in view of the economic circumstances of the parties, the case where several tortfeasors acting together have committed a tort resulting in non-pecuniary damage—which is that before this court—can be solved without difficulty. Here, too—if necessary—damages under § 847 BGB must be assessed independently in respect of each tortfeasor. The same task is incumbent upon the courts if, as regards pecuniary damage, one tortfeasor is only liable under § 7*a* of the Haftpflichtgesetz (Strict Liability Act), § 12 of the Strassenverkehrsgesetz (Road Traffic Act), or § 23 of the Luftverkehrsgesetz (Air Traffic Act) while the other has incurred more extensive liability under § 843. The two tortfeasors are only liable as debtors in common to the extent that the amount of their liability is the same; as regards the excess, that tortfeasor is only liable who must pay higher damages.

In taking into account the economic circumstances, the question may arise as to whether in so doing the possibility of compensation between the tortfeasors should be considered. Since the fact that the economic circumstances are taken into account means that economic potential counts and since, on the other hand, economic potential is increased if enforceable claims for redress exist against the co-tortfeasor, it follows naturally that such enforceable claims for redress must be taken into account in determining economic potential. It must be admitted that if several tortfeasors who are liable in common have claims for redress against one another, each is liable in the end to pay only a portion of the total damages. The reason is that even in the presence of several tortfeasors the victim can only demand to be compensated once. This principle is not violated if the damages for non-pecuniary loss are fixed at a higher level because the value of the claims for redress against other tortfeasors is taken into account in determining the economic potential of one of the tortfeasors. In this case, too, the injured party can only recover once the sum of money which was awarded to him in respect of non-pecuniary losses. Therefore, no principle of positive law is being violated in this respect either.

(*e*) It was much disputed—especially in recent times—whether in considering the economic circumstances of the tortfeasor it is relevant that he is insured against liability.

The view was expressed in particular by the Reichsgericht at an early stage, that the claims of the tortfeasor arising out of liability insurance could not be taken into account since the purpose of liability insurance was to indemnify the insured in respect of payments which the latter was obliged to make because he was liable, and that this must be established first. However, this view concentrates exclusively on the relationship between the tortfeasor and the insurer of his liability; in reality the question must be as to whether and how the fact that the tortfeasor is insured against liability can affect the extent of his liability towards the injured party. For this purpose the following consideration applies quite generally to damages according to § 847 BGB: a tortfeasor who is entitled to be reimbursed by the insurer against liability to the extent of the amount insured is in a more favourable financial position than a tortfeasor who carries himself alone the burden of paying damages. The claim acquired by the payment of premiums to protection by the insurer is a financial asset in so far as any payment of compensation for damage caused is concerned.

Since in taking this financial approach it is only relevant whether the tortfeasor must bear the cost of the damages himself or will be reimbursed—at least in part—on the strength of his liability insurance, it can make no difference whether the insurance against liability is voluntary or compulsory.

Finally, it cannot be concluded that liability insurance must be disregarded because the assets of the insurer against liability constitute a special fund which is dedicated to a special purpose, similar to the assets of the *Fiscus*, which must be disregarded. This view overlooks that the assets of the *Fiscus* are not assets in the meaning of private law for the reason that they are not only dedicated to a special purpose, but because the special purpose is a public one. Therefore they cannot be related to the assets of the injured party, which are within the private sector, so as to balance them. The assets of a liability insurer, however, contrary to those of the Fiscus fall within the private sector. For this reason alone the reference to the treatment of Fiscal property is inappropriate. Moreover, in taking into account the existence of liability insurance no "purpose linked special fund" of the insurer is being considered, but the claims of the tortfeasor to be indemnified by the liability insurer.

Consequently it is admissible in assessing damages under § 847 BGB to take into account also that the tortfeasor can demand an indemnity from the insurer—up to the amount of the sum insured.

(*f*) In taking into account the economic circumstances of the tortfeasor it may be relevant that the damages for pain and suffering are not being awarded in the form of a lump sum but of periodic payments. Thereby the result can be achieved in some cases that the victim receives damages for pain and suffering which are largely in keeping with their purpose, namely to make good, even if the tortfeasor's financial circumstances are unfavourable, seeing that such periodic payments do not burden him that heavily for the time being. If damages for pain and suffering are assessed in the form of a right to periodic payments the question arises, however, as to whether a subsequent change in the financial circumstances of the tortfeasor must be taken into account under § 323 of the Code of Civil Procedure [ZPO]. The answer must be in the affirmative. It is true that when the amount of damages for pain and suffering is fixed by a judgment or a compromise, the claim for damages in respect of non-pecuniary loss loses its character as a claim for damages in money; thus the amount of the claim under § 847 BGB is henceforth fixed for the future, at least in principle. However, just as any consequences of the injurious act which occurred or manifested themselves subsequently, and therefore had not been taken into account in assessing damages under § 847 BGB, may give rise to a supplementary claim under § 847 BGB, so no objections exist in principle against reviewing the periodic payments if the conditions laid down by § 323 ZPO are fulfilled, especially if a fundamental change in economic circumstances has occurred, in particular on the part of the tortfeasor.

4. As stated above on several occasions, among the circumstances to be taken into account on grounds of equity, the extent, the severity, and the duration of pain and suffering must always contribute the determining criteria; the non-pecuniary damage inflicted, the adverse effect on life always occupies the first place among the circumstances to be taken into account. For the rest, it is impossible to establish a general order of priorities among the circumstances to be considered, for their extent and importance in assessing equitable compensation emerges only when they coincide in the individual case, as was shown above, especially in **II.** 3 (*a*). It is therefore necessary to consider the individual case. The extent to which the circumstances enumerated previously, or any other which may be relevant, affect the assessment of damages for pain and suffering must be determined in accordance with equity. Such an examination may also lead to the conclusion that certain circumstances, as for instance the financial situation, should be disregarded in fixing damages for pain and suffering.

In the light of the foregoing, the question had to be answered in the general terms in which it had been formulated by the Sixth Senate of the court, for only thus the substance of the question could be treated exhaustively. Nevertheless, it seemed appropriate to stress already by the manner in which the answer is formulated that not all the circumstances which have been mentioned must be taken into account in each individual case, but only that they may be considered, having regard to the facts. In order to eliminate doubts it also appeared appropriate to include at this stage the treatment of possible claims of the tortfeasor for an indemnity under a policy of liability insurance or for redress against other tortfeasors.

Case 141

BUNDESGERICHTSHOF (SIXTH CIVIL SENATE) 11 JANUARY 1983
BGHZ 86, 212 = NJW 1983, 1107 = JZ 1983, 390

The plaintiff, a general medical practitioner, was run down by a lorry on 20 September 1976 while walking in Bad Schönborn. The lorry was insured against accidents by the defendant who admitted liability in principle without reservation. The injuries of the plaintiff consisted in several abrasions, bruises, and haemorrhage; in addition he alleges that he suffered a renewed and more severe attack of tachycardia and palpitations, while the defendant denies that these are the results of the accident.

In the proceedings before the Court of First Instance the plaintiff claimed damages on the ground that between 20 September and 19 October 1976 he was not able to attend to his practice and had thus suffered a loss of income.

The District Court of Karlsruhe rejected the claim on the ground that the allegation of the plaintiff in specifying his damages had not been proved. On appeal the plaintiff pursued his claim to a reduced extent only. He pleaded now—correctly, as the defendant admits—that he had closed down his practice as early as 15 September 1976, when he started his vacation for reasons of health in Bad Schönborn. As a result of the accident he had lost twenty-one days of vacation.

The plaintiff contends that the sum of DM 10,873 represents the expenses of a resumed holiday on the basis of the hypothetical cost of a *locum tenens* and in running expenses for employers and maintenance. He argues that the lost vacation must be compensated according to these principles.

The Court of Appeal of Karlsruhe rejected the appeal to this effect. A further appeal by the plaintiff was unsuccessful for the following.

Reasons

I. The Court of Appeal has held that the plaintiff's claim for "spoilt holidays", which admittedly he did not resume, is not justified, even having regard to the practice initiated by the decision of the Federal Supreme Court [reference]. It referred to the criticism of this decision in the literature and is of the opinion that in any case these principles cannot be extended to the sphere of unjustifiable enrichment. In this context, non-economic damages are here in issue which according to § 253 BGB could only be recovered where an express provision so required.

II. The decision under review cannot be faulted, at least in the result.

1. The Court of Appeal rightly starts from the premise that the plaintiff cannot claim damages equal to the "value of the vacation" for having suffered the loss of a holiday which was not taken up later on.

(*a*) In so far as the law of tort is concerned, the damages for the economic consequences to be recovered in the case of injury to the person are mainly restricted to losses of gains and future earnings (§ 843 BGB). The practice of the courts has with good reason interpreted these notions broadly. However, this has not modified the principle that according to the intention of the legislators all loss of enjoyment can only result in damages for pain and suffering (§§ 253, 847 BGB). Thus a direct "commercialisation" assessment of the vacation is excluded.

Accordingly, the Federal Supreme Court has, for instance, denied damages if, as a result of his injuries, a person could not exercise his licence to hunt which he had acquired for payment [reference]. The Court also denied damages for the loss of use of a damaged motor car if during the period in question he was unable to use it—even if the inability of the plaintiff to use the motor car was the result of a personal injury suffered on the occasion of the same accident [references]. The temporary inability to work, too, does not constitute a recoverable head of damages, unless it results in a loss of income [reference].

Similarly, the Federal Supreme Court has disallowed damages for the "value of a vacation" resulting from damage to an object (a motor car) [reference]. This judgment shows that the Third Civil Senate also shares the opinion that generally a lost period of vacation cannot be treated as an economic loss resulting from the violation of the legal interests mentioned in § 823 I BGB. Normally the same applies in the case of violations of protective laws (§ 823 II BGB). The fact that in an earlier decision [reference] . . . the Third Civil Senate held differently in a case of liability for the violation of official duties (§ 839

BGB) may perhaps be explained by the special connection between the error committed by the customs authorities and the vacation; however, it is unnecessary in this context to discuss this question any further.

(*b*) This practice is to be maintained in the sphere of torts having regard also to the more recent pronouncements of the Seventh Civil Senate. According to the chain of authorities initiated by the decision [references], it is indeed admissible to claim damages for "lost holidays" as economic loss if breaches of contract are involved concerning the arrangement for or the performance in kind or by means of services connected with the form of the holidays. These efforts of the Seventh Civil Senate to start a new practice have been superseded by the statutory regulation of the travel contract (§ 651a–k), but its substance has been maintained in essence.

The Seventh Civil Senate clearly intended to create a solution for *this* (contractual) sphere in particular, which satisfies the interest concerned in the absence of a statutory regulation to this effect. The legislature, too, has restricted to this area the new rule, which may be said to limit to a certain extent the principle expressed in § 253 BGB, which also applies in principle to the law of contract. The Seventh Civil Senate did not regard its practice established before the legislative change as conflicting with the practice regarding the law of tort referred to in (*a*) above, of which it was aware [references]; the reason was that it did not regard itself as precluded from adhering to this practice because it was only concerned with contractual claims. Moreover, it regards its aim as mainly satisfied by the new regulation in the Civil Code which is limited to the law of contract [reference].

Consequently, the present Senate is not precluded from adhering to its practice pertaining to the law of tort. It is unnecessary to determine whether the above-mentioned decisions of the Seventh Civil Senate and the majority of writers [references] have only sought to find a solution by relying on a notion of economic damage which is devised to be of general validity. Objections might be raised against such an attempt. Less emphasis must be placed on the notion of economic damage, the details of which have given rise to theoretical disputes, and stress should be laid on the question whether, having regard to the purpose of the respective grounds of liability, any deleterious effect is still to be treated as economic damage. (For the attribution of consequential damage in the light of the purpose of liability in general, see the recent decision of this Senate—reference.) Accordingly, it seems entirely appropriate to treat the enjoyment of holidays in commercial terms *when*—and only when—the enjoyment of holidays has been made directly or indirectly the object of a contractual performance and if this obligation has been breached. To this extent such a close and clear relationship exists between the contractual duty to act and the interest in enjoying the holiday which had, so to say, been entrusted to the other contracting party that it appears justifiable to attribute to the enjoyment of vacations a commercial character based on the contractual agreement. This court finds support for its view in the observations of Stoll [reference] which are shared to a great extent by Lange [reference]; see also Steffen [reference]; Hagen [reference]. The need to relate the commercial qualifications of damages for loss of enjoyment to the purpose of the basis of liability is also underlined by the decision of the Third Civil Senate of 3 November 1980 [reference] which—contrary to the above-mentioned judgment of this Senate [reference]—envisaged the possibility of damages in respect of the loss of the pleasure of earning a licence to hunt in a case where this licence to hunt had been frustrated illegally.

If it is correct that the loss of enjoyment (in the present case as regards the period of vacation) can only be taken into consideration if another legally protected interest has been violated (e.g. in the present case by injuring health, but also where an object is damaged, such as a motor car needed for holiday travel), it remains necessary to observe the purpose of the provision of § 253 BGB in the absence of a special statutory rule. This is not only in accordance with the statute, but takes into account the undisputable consideration that otherwise an unpredictable expansion of liability in tort would have to be expected. The practice of the Seventh Civil Senate does not fail to perceive this either [references]. The reason is that the loss of the enjoyment of holidays is only one of many conceivable cases in which the loss of enjoyment, while not directly capable of being assessed in economic terms, can nevertheless be attributed a "commercial" value in certain circumstances. The fact that the area of damage may be incalculable is absent precisely in those cases where the enjoyment of a vacation is directly and clearly connected with the failure to perform contractual duties.

Consequently, this Senate does not believe that its view conflicts with the results of the decisions of the Seventh Civil Senate. The fact that in their reasoning these decisions differ in part from its own considerations is not determining in the view of this Senate, which approves the results reached by those decisions. Therefore they are not opposed to the present decision.

2. The foregoing considerations would not, however, exclude the possibility that in assessing the amount of damages for pain and suffering due to the plaintiff account may be taken of the fact that his injuries (which have proved to have been relatively light) have resulted in the loss of three weeks' vacation . . .

Case 142

BUNDESGERICHTSHOF (SIXTH CIVIL SENATE) 14 JANUARY 1986
BGHZ 97, 14 = NJW 1986, 1538

Facts

The claimant claims compensation for injuries suffered in a road traffic accident on 10 January 1981, from the first defendant as keeper and driver of the motor car involved and the second defendant as insurer of it.

The dispute is not about liability but only about whether the claimant can demand the anticipated costs for removing abdominal scars resulting from an operation to the small intestine which was required by the accident. She cannot yet decide whether to have this operation because of its uncertain outcome, but she claims its cost assessed at DM 10,668 on the basis of private report obtained by her. The defendants are prepared to pay for an operation actually undergone by her, but not merely fictitious costs.

The Landgericht and the Oberlandesgericht rejected the claim to payment of DM 10,668. The appeal in law by the claimant was unsuccessful.

Reasons

I. . . .

II. The appeal court correctly assumes in this case that the claim to compensation under § 249 sentence 2 of the BGB for accident injuries suffered also covers, in principle, expenditure on the cosmetic removal of a scar caused by an accident, even if no further disturbance of functions results or even is merely feared from the scar. As the Senate has already stated in its judgment of 3 December 1974 (reference omitted), those means are to be put at the disposal of the victim which are necessary in order, if possible, to restore his physical integrity in this respect. The appeal court is however of the view that the claimant's claim to payment is not well founded at the present time, for the following reasons. According to § 249 sentence 2 of the BGB, the victim could admittedly demand, instead of restoration, the sum of money necessary for it. In the case of a physical injury, however, this claim would assume a firm and recognisable intention on the part of the victim actually to rectify the injuries inflicted on him and / or their consequences. That was lacking here. On the harming of non-material interests—as with harm to persons—one would have to assume a commitment of the costs of restoration to their purpose if the provisions of § 253 of the BGB were not to be circumvented.

Over against this, the appeal in law takes the view that the victim is completely free in the use of the means placed at his disposal. A sum of money which is paid for a necessary operation would not have to be used by him for this purpose. He could therefore even demand compensation for the costs of a fictitious operation.

The deciding Senate—in agreement with the courts of earlier instance—cannot accept this.

1. When a motor vehicle is damaged, the Senate has admittedly approved in principle a claim to compensation for the so-called fictitious costs of repair (references omitted). Contrary to the view of the appeal in law, it has however not so far recognised in principle in the case of harm to persons a claim by the victim to compensation for fictitious costs. The decision of 3 December 1974 (reference omitted) expresses no view on this subject . . .

In the published case law of the courts of first instance, the compensatibility of fictitious costs of cure is variously dealt with . . .

In the academic literature opinions are also divided . . .

2. The provisions of § 249 sentence 2 of the BGB are the basis of the claim for compensation made by the claimant. According to this sentence, when a person is injured or a thing damaged, the victim can demand, instead of the restoration of the former state of affairs as required under § 249 sentence 1 of the BGB, "the sum of money necessary for this".

a) The deciding Senate has, since the seminal decision of the 23rd March 1976 (reference omitted), granted this claim to payment of the necessary costs of restoration to a victim when his motor vehicle is damaged in cases where right from the outset he has no intention at all of having the vehicle repaired. He intends to deal with the situation in some other way, perhaps by continuing to use the unrepaired vehicle or, as in that case, by giving it, unrepaired, in exchange on the purchase of a new vehicle. The Senate saw the justification for this awarding of "fictitious" repair costs in the victims' freedom of disposition, which it previously accepted by reference to the history of the provision's origin (references omitted). According to this, the victim is in principle free to decide whether he really wants to apply for this purpose the sum necessary for the restoration in accordance with § 249 sentence 2 of the BGB, or whether he wants to use it in some other way. Whether the person suffering harm makes the decision about use of the compensation money for some other purpose only after receipt of the money, or whether he has already acted accordingly before the payment, makes no difference in this connection.

All the cases in which the Bundesgerichtshof has accepted this freedom of disposition by the victim related to claims to compensation because of damage to objects (references omitted). In cases of this kind, the victim's decision about how he uses the sum of money (and, associated with this, his total or partial relinquishment of the right to restoration to which this sum of money relates) does not in substance amount to anything more than a disposition of property with a view to a transfer of the loss within his assets. The need for repair of the damaged object finds expression only within the assets of the victim and it remains expressed in these alone, regardless of how he decides to use the sum of money (reference omitted). If he has the object repaired, he will have to bear the necessary costs of this. If he disposes of the object while unrepaired, he will obtain appropriately lower proceeds from the sale. Even if he continues to use the object while unrepaired, his assets will remain burdened in so far as the value of the damaged object is smaller than that of the undamaged object. The state of the victim's assets is restored again by payment of the necessary repair costs (reference omitted). How the victim then actually structures his assets—whether he repairs the object, buys a new one or makes dispositions of a completely different kind—is his affair, which is, in principle, no concern of the tortfeasor.

b) This freedom of disposition on the part of the victim in relation to the sum of money due from the tortfeasor for restoration purposes cannot be transferred to personal injury. In this case, restitution in kind, for which the victim can demand a sum of money under § 249 sentence 2 of the BGB, is directed to the restoration of physical integrity and therefore to the removal of non-economic loss. To understand a victim's relinquishment here of a right to restitution as a mere disposition of assets, appropriately valued by the sum of money from § 249 sentence 2 of the BGB, is by the nature of the case out of the question. The decision of the victim not to submit himself to medical treatment—perhaps because of the risks associated with this or the doubtful outcome—and to continue to live with the untreated injury relates to a different plane to a disposition of assets with a sum of money from § 249 sentence 2 of the BGB. The decision is in principle no more commensurable with such a disposition than is the injury itself with which the victim remains burdened. The law grants him monetary compensation for this in the form of damages for pain and suffering. The victim who is relinquishing any kind of treatment can no more claim from the tortfeasor costs of treatment for a form of restitution which he simply does not want, than he can demand from the tortfeasor under § 249 sentence 2 of the BGB the costs of a (dearer) operation when he decides in favour of (cheaper) conservative treatment. If the victim demands the costs of treatment even though he does not want to have the treatment carried out, he is in reality demanding compensation for the continuing impairment of his health. The legal order only grants compensation of this kind to the victim in accordance with § 253 of the BGB subject to the prerequisites of § 847 of the BGB. If the victim were to be granted the fictitious costs of medical treatment which is not carried out, this would lead to evasion of § 253 of the BGB. In the cases in which the prerequisites of § 847 of the BGB are not present for the granting of damages for pain and suffering, the victim would receive such damages when they are not awarded to him under the law. In other cases he would be able to *increase* damages for pain and suffering awarded to him in accordance with § 847 of the BGB in a manner not provided for by the law. For the reasons explained, in personal injury cases the victim cannot in principle have any freedom of disposition in relation to the use of the costs of restoration. Instead, the costs of restoration in the personal injuries field are committed to their purpose. Therefore the victim can only demand costs of treatment under § 249 sentence 2 of the BGB if he has the intention of actually having the treatment carried out.

2. As a rule this intention will emerge simply from the need for treatment of the injury and the measures taken for its treatment.

In the present case the appeal court has, however, not been able to establish that the claimant will have the removal of the scars carried out . . .

Case 143

BUNDESGERICHTSHOF (SIXTH CIVIL SENATE) 13 OCTOBER 1992
BGHZ 120, 1 = NJW 1993, 781

Facts

The first claimant (the claimant) claims from the first defendant (the defendant), a consultant at the University women's clinic at M, damages for pain and suffering for serious damage to her health suffered on her birth on the 3rd July 1979.

The claimant's mother (then aged 40) had had medical check-ups at the clinic. She was told that her child was in the breech position and she would have to give birth by Caesarean section. She gave written consent for this.

She went to the clinic two weeks early on the 3rd July 1979 because of the onset of contractions. At around 1pm the defendant took over the treatment and carried out the procedures for a natural birth. He discovered that there was a footling presentation. Because there was no progress after appearance of the child's feet, the defendant decided to carry out an extraction. Because of complications, the claimant was, at around 1.24pm, born severely harmed.

The Landgericht ordered the defendant to pay as damages for pain and suffering a capital sum of DM 50,000 and DM 500 a month. On the defendant's appeal, the Oberlandesgericht ordered the defendant to pay as such damages a capital sum of DM 30,000 and DM 250 a month. In other respects it rejected the claimant's claim and referred the defendant's more extensive appeal back. The claimant's appeal in law led to the quashing of the judgment in so far as it had been decided against her. The defendant's cross appeal in law was unsuccessful.

Reasons

II. The claimant's appeal in law.

The claimant's appeal as to the level of damages for pain and suffering is however successful. The appeal in law correctly argues that the setting of the level of damages for pain and suffering has been influenced by legal errors.

1. The appeal court was admittedly correct in linking the assessment of damages for pain and suffering primarily to the serious damage to the claimant's health . . .

In mental and emotional respects, the claimant's state of development equates to that of a baby of a few months old. Her capacity for awareness scarcely goes beyond perception and reflex reaction. Her formation of concepts and ideas as the basis of capacity for experience is limited to the most simple categories like "pleasant / unpleasant" . . . Her capacity for experience is further limited by the administration of anti-epileptic medication . . .

2. These statements are open to serious legal objections. The Senate cannot even approve the starting point of the appeal court's decision. This was that damages for pain and suffering would largely lose their function because of the substantial limitation of the claimant's capacity for feeling; and this would have to have the effect of reducing the level of damages for pain and suffering.

It is admittedly correct that the function of damages for pain and suffering is, according to constant case law, to give to the victim compensation for the non-material harm suffered and, further, reparation for the pain inflicted on him (BGHZ 18, 149; other references omitted) . . .

On the other hand, the court treated as a determining factor the absence to a large extent of the functions of damages for pain and suffering and took this into account by reducing the level of the compensation. The appeal court is, however, even in cases in which the personality is almost completely destroyed or, as here, the basis for its development has been taken away by fault on the part of an obstetrician, attaching central significance for the assessment of the damages for pain and suffering to the sensation which the victim experiences of his fate. It is taking this very circumstance (which for the person affected constitutes the special severity of the impairment which is the subject of the compensation) as a cause for a decisive reduction of the damages for pain and suffering. This amounts to a curtailment of the function of damages for pain and suffering . . .

The appeal court can admittedly rely for its view on the case law of the Senate . . . Although the Senate in such cases considered payment of damages or pain and suffering as necessary, this derived from the consideration that at least symbolic reparation would have to be granted to the victim as a gesture of expiation.

Such a reduction of the damages for pain and suffering to merely symbolic compensation is no longer considered by the Senate, after a fresh examination, to be justified. It does not do justice to the almost complete destruction of the victim's personality in cases of severe brain damage. In this respect the Senate will no longer adhere to its past case law, as expressed in the above mentioned decisions. Impairments of such an extent, as in the claimant's case, demand, having regard to the constitutional value decision contained in Art. 1 of the Basic Law, stronger weighting, and preclude a merely symbolic assessment.

From this angle, the concept of expiation (which does not generally hold good for civil liability and compensation law) is less important. For negligent acts it can only play a minor role anyway. There is instead a link with the non-material harm which a person suffers through physical injury or harm to health, and which has to be compensated under § 847 of the BGB by a money payment. Such harm does not only consist in physical or mental suffering and thus in negative sensations and feelings of aversion as a reaction to the bodily injury or the damage to health. Instead, damage to the personality and the loss of personal quality as a consequence of severe brain damage represent in themselves non-material harm which is to be compensated for independently of whether the person affected feels the impairment. That does not mean that non-material harm is generally only manifested in physical impairment. A substantial manifestation of non-material harm can consist in the victim being conscious of his impairment and therefore suffering from it to a special degree. This point of view can therefore be very important for the assessment of damages for pain and suffering.

Accordingly the compensatory function of damages for pain and suffering is not exhausted in promoting mental well-being by compensating for emotional suffering or other negative mental sensations. The appeal court is not therefore taking the nature of damages for pain and suffering sufficiently into account when it merely considers that the claimant's life could be made to some extent easier and she could in particular be made happy by loving human attention. Over and above the mere bestowing of comforts, the loss which consists in what is more or less the virtual destruction of the personality, and which in itself represents non-material harm, has to be compensated for by a fair monetary sum. In this sense, the Great Senate for civil cases has in its decision of 6 July 1955 referred to the fact that "size, intensity and duration of pain, suffering and disfigurement" form the most significant basis for assessing the compensation (reference omitted). It thus proceeds on the basis that besides pain and suffering, physical impairment as such represents a decisive factor for the assessment of damages for pain and suffering. Anyway, as the Great Senate for civil cases further stresses in this connection, the sum of money to be granted as compensation could not be discovered by—so to speak—balancing sufferings with pleasures by which the victim is to eradicate the recollection of his sufferings. It is precisely in the case of psychological disturbance that compensation for feelings of aversion will frequently not be possible, because the victim has no subjective consciousness of the harm. In spite of this, entitlement to compensation for non-material harm has been correctly recognised even in such cases (reference omitted).

. . . Within the framework of this judgement it is primarily a question here of giving, in assessing loss, appropriate recognition to the fact that the extensive destruction of the basis for the capacity for perception and sensation, for which the tortfeasor is responsible, affects the victim in the core of her being and therefore has a significance for her which is related to her very existence. Harm of this kind constitutes an independent group of cases in which the destruction of the personality by the cessation or denial of the capacity for sensation is the central issue. It must therefore, in assessing compensation under § 847 of the BGB, be given an independent valuation which does justice to the central significance of this loss for the person. In this connection the judge can make gradations according to the extent of each impairment and the degree of capacity for experience and sensation which remains for the victim, to take account of the peculiarities of each individual case of harm. On the other hand, the judge is not allowed to take his bearings from an imaginary picture which is characterised by a undiminished capacity for sensation and suffering and then make reductions having regard to the complete or virtual ending of the capacity for sensation . . .

3. . . .

4. The appeal in law, however, is unsuccessful in objecting to the appeal court's failure, having regard to the reparation function of damages for pain and suffering, to express any view on the question of whether the fault on the defendant's part in relation to the treatment is to be assessed as gross. It is not necessary for this question to be considered, because in cases of the present kind, feelings by the victim on the subject of reparation by payment of damages for pain and suffering (for which the assessment of the fault in treatment as gross could play a role) are absent.

Case 144

BUNDESGERICHTSHOF (SIXTH CIVIL DIVISION) 11 OCTOBER 1994
BGHZ 127, 186 = NJW 1995, 452

Facts

The claimant demands from the defendants compensation for pain and suffering for injuries which she suffered in a road traffic accident on 17 July 1989. The first defendant ("the defendant") who was then 21, turned to the right in his car, which was insured with the second defendant against third party liability. As he did so, he lost control of the vehicle, veered on to the opposite side of the road and struck the claimant, who was then 18 years old, who was coming towards him on a bicycle. She suffered severe injuries in the accident to, amongst other things, her head and legs. She was treated in hospital until 16 September 1989, and was incapable of work until the middle of February 1990. As a result of her injuries she could neither squat nor kneel, her hearing was impaired and her capacity to work was reduced to 20 per cent. She receives incapacity benefit as well as state education grants. Her training course was extended by half a year as a result of the accident. She is at the moment unemployed and intends to pursue an alternative career because of the consequences of the accident. The claimant's material harm was dealt with under the Road Traffic Act and fully compensated. The defendants have refused payment of compensation for pain and suffering, claiming that the defendant was incapable of committing a tort at the time of the accident.

The lower courts rejected the claim. The claimant's appeal in law (which is admissible) led to quashing of the decision and reference back.

Reasons

I. The appeal court denies that there is a claim under §§ 823 (1) and 847 of the BGB because the defendant was, at the time of the accident, in a condition which excluded the free exercise of his will (§ 827). In the court's view, the expert Dr B had convincingly explained that the defendant had gradually developed a convulsive disorder which led for the first time to an epileptic semi-conscious state, over which the defendant had no control when it started to occur, during the journey on 17 July 1989. There were no grounds for saying there was any other cause of the accident. The defendant was also not to blame for the fact that he had not attached any special importance to headaches and disturbances of concentration which had occurred before the accident, after no indications had come to light of a disturbance of the functioning of the brain on an examination by a medical specialist.

According to the appeal court's view, liability on the grounds of fairness under § 829 of the BGB does not come into consideration. Even though the claimant's injuries caused by the accident were substantial and were not healed without adverse consequences, the claimant was not harmed by them in such a way as compellingly to require compensation, from the point of view of fairness, for the non-material consequences as well. Her training had merely been extended by half a year; she had received an annuity to compensate for the reduction in her earnings. The defendant had also been harmed in the long term by his illness which had been established on the occasion of the accident. In spite of successful medical treatment, he still had to put up with the uncertainty that cysts would form again. Because of this, the consequences of the claimant's accident were not so significant that, simply on the basis of the fate of the two parties, compensation for the non-financial harm was irrefutably necessary in addition to the compensation for the material harm.

There was just as little ground for saying that a comparison of the financial positions of both persons involved in the accident requires compensation. The defendant's monthly income of DM 3,800 gross as an office worker was not so high that a substantial commercial difference arose from this, especially as the cost of living in the region in which the claimant lived compared with that of the defendant was clearly lower and, apart from this, the claimant was seeking more highly qualified employment. The claim to reimbursement on the basis of the existing third party vehicle insurance cannot be regarded as part of the defendant's assets. In any case, the existing insurance cover alone could not justify liability from the point of view of fairness without the presence of further circumstances.

II. The appeal in law is admissible in its full extent. . . .

III. The appeal is also well founded.

1. . . .

2. However, the judgment does not stand up to the material legal challenges in the appeal in law. On the ground of the undisputed facts, the appeal court proceeded on the basis—admittedly without any more detailed explanation on this subject—that the defendant had, in an objective sense, behaved in a manner contrary to traffic regulations and had thereby committed an act which obliged him to provide compensation. There are no legal objections to this. But the Senate is not able follow the reasoning by which the appeal court denied a claim on the basis of fairness under § 829 of the BGB. In this respect, the appeal in law is correct in arguing that the appeal court's statements on the question of whether a comparison of the financial situations of both parties to the accident required the awarding of compensation for pain and suffering from the point of view of fairness are influenced by legal error.

a) The appeal court, in examining fairness, has wrongly left out of consideration the existence of third party insurance on the part of the defendant. It is necessary, at least in the case of compulsory insurance, as here, to recognise the fact that insurance protection exists for the person causing harm in the accident as an important factor in the defendant's financial position.

aa) Certainly the case law on the question of whether the existence of third party insurance can be considered in connection with the duty to compensate for damage as a factor in favour of a person injured in an accident has not been uniform. The Reichsgericht in 1944, abandoning its previous case law, considered the existence of third party insurance for the first time as capable of being taken into consideration for calculation of the level of compensation for pain and suffering in respect of the duty to indemnify for tortious fault (reference omitted). The Bundesgerichtshof followed this (references omitted). The Senate held this factor to be significant for the *level* of compensation in respect of the duty to indemnify on the ground of fairness liability under § 829 of the BGB on the basis of corresponding considerations (references omitted). On the other hand it has until this judgment rejected the existence of insurance protection as a factor worthy of consideration when it forms the *basis* of a claim ([references omitted]; likewise when considering a contribution to the harm by the victim under § 254 of the BGB, on the mirror image application of § 829 of the BGB to his disadvantage [references omitted]).

In the judgment of 18 December 1979 referred to (reference omitted), the Senate abandoned this distinction, when considering third party insurance protection, between the ground and the level of the claim under § 829 of the BGB as unusable. But at the same time it emphasised that a limit must be drawn in considering *whether* this compensation claim could be made, in order to take account of the purpose of third party insurance which was primarily to protect of the policy holder from liability claims and not to create a basis of liability. In this connection, the Senate, in view of the criticisms made in the academic literature of the case law so far, considered whether a change in the function of third party insurance which had since occurred in the socio-economic structure would in a quite general way permit insurance protection, as a component of the tortfeasor's wealth, to be included fully within the test of fairness under § 829 of the BGB. It was not able to convince itself of such a change of function, at any rate for the area of voluntary third party insurance and therefore refused to take into account the insurance protection from such a voluntary third party insurance to the extent, in appropriate cases, of the highest amount of cover available. On the other hand, it acknowledged the concept—as employed so far—of considering the insurance merely to correct the level of the sum to be paid.

bb) These limitations cannot, however, contrary to the judgment challenged, be carried over to compulsory vehicle insurance as it existed for the defendant. The purpose of this insurance is primarily related to the protection of the victim. This goal was already served by the Introduction of Compulsory Insurance for Vehicles Act of 7 November 1939. As follows from the official reasons (reference omitted) and as the Reichsgericht (reference omitted) and, following it, the Senate in the judgments of 10 April 1954 (reference omitted) of 13 June 1958 (reference omitted) and of 24 June 1969 (reference omitted) have explained, compulsory insurance should, on the basis of this statute, secure for the victims of traffic accidents the compensation for harm which was due to them. A protection which was as free as possible from gaps should be provided for the victims, and especially in those cases in which the tortfeasor is not able to pay. This is reflected above all in § 158c of the Insurance Contracts Act (VVG) (which was newly formulated at that time) according to which, amongst other things, the duty of the insurer still remains when he is wholly or partially released as against the policy holder. This protection of the traffic accident victim was further strengthened and extended by the Compulsory Insurance Act of 5 April 1965, and its subsequent amendments, with the direct claim against the insurer and the compensation fund (references omitted).

This special determination of the purpose of compulsory insurance in relation to vehicle traffic justifies letting the victim have the benefit of the tortfeasor's existing insurance protection in deciding *whether* the claim can be made within the framework of § 829 of the BGB as well. It is no obstacle to this that the separation principle, according to which the insurer's duty to indemnify follows the claim and not the other way round, is thereby broken. For the special claim under § 829 of the BGB the purpose of the third party vehicle insurance, which is protection of the victim, must prevail over this principle. The Senate has acknowledged the necessity of breaking this principle (which should as a rule be adhered to) in other cases as well (references omitted).

cc) Consideration of insurance protection under compulsory vehicle insurance by the tortfeasor admittedly does not mean that, simply because of it, the claim on the basis of fairness under § 829 of the BGB should always be allowed. In examining the question of whether fairness requires the injured party to be indemnified, it must instead be borne in mind that liability under § 829 of the BGB, which is independent of fault, forms an exception in the tortious liability system of the BGB. Therefore consequent on the wording of the provision, according to the constant case law of the Senate, a claim to compensation for harm under § 829 of the BGB is not to be granted simply when fairness permits it, but only when all the circumstances of the case really require liability on the part of a blameless tortfeasor on the grounds of fairness (references omitted). This exceptional character of § 829 of the BGB compels the prerequisites under which an indemnification of the victim is to be seen as fair to be set at a high level even in these cases.

In this connection it must further be borne in mind that, in relation to road traffic accidents, the material harm to the accident victim is already covered by strict liability under the Road Traffic Act (StVG) which is independent of fault. Thus the claimant is receiving full compensation for all her material harm, in particular the cost of cure and the loss of income. In this respect, the case in question differs quite substantially from the cases decided in [reference omitted] and in the Senate's judgments of 13 June 1958 and 24 April 1979 (references omitted), in which it was first a question of providing the victim with compensation for material harm with the help of § 829 of the BGB. But if the victim is already receiving full compensation for his material harm, as in this case, then there only remains the question of whether fairness requires him to be given compensation for pain and suffering over and above the compensation for material harm. Within the framework of § 829 of the BGB, there is only room for compensation for pain and suffering on the grounds of fairness in the case of serious injuries, in particular lasting harm. All in all, the granting of compensation for pain and suffering, considering the exceptional character of § 829 of the BGB, accordingly only comes into consideration, if, bearing in mind the fact that in traffic accidents caused without fault, compensation for pain and suffering is not forfeited as a rule, its refusal in the individual case blatantly contradicts feelings of fairness. In this respect the approach for the examination of fairness in § 829 of the BGB is a different one from that in § 847 of the BGB, to which the Senate referred in its judgment of 18 December 1979 (reference omitted).

b) The judge of fact must decide whether, under these prerequisites, awarding compensation for pain and suffering is required in the individual case on the grounds of fairness. He has to consider all the circumstances of the case in this connection. Besides the economic relationship of the parties to the accident, the intensity of the invasion of the protected legal interest can be of importance in this connection, as well as—for instance in relation to deliberate acts—the unusual character of the action giving rise to the duty to compensate for harm (references omitted).

In this respect also the remarks of the appeal court give cause for serious doubts. The appeal court compares the claimant's accident injuries, which had resulted in a lengthening of her original training "by merely half a year", with the defendant's illness established on the occasion of the accident, by which he additionally suffered long term harm and the uncertainty that the formation of cysts might be repeated in spite of the successful medical treatment. In the light of this uncertainty, the consequences of the accident, according to the view of the appeal court, did not have such weight for the claimant (who was harmed on a long term basis in relation to certain physical postures and in her hearing capacity) that, on the basis of the fate of the claimant and the defendant, compensation for non-material harm as well was irrefutably necessary.

These remarks are not free from legal errors. The burden of uncertainty about the future development of the defendant's health may admittedly be serious for him. But it cannot be regarded as equivalent to the claimant's accident injuries. The appeal court did not take into account that the impairment of the defendant's health was determined by fate and had nothing to do with the accident. The claimant's injuries were, on the other hand, caused by an objectively serious failure of the defendant in connection with the driving of his vehicle. The defendant at any rate suffered no injuries through the accident. The appeal court should have taken account of this circumstance, because there can be no doubt that, in connection with the considerations of fairness which are to be employed under § 829 of the BGB, a substantially smaller weight is due to harm to health which is not dependent on the accident than to that which is based on the accident.

c) From the above considerations, it follows that the reasoning by which the appeal court has denied a claim for a declaration cannot stand.

Case 145

BUNDESGERICHTSHOF (SIXTH CIVIL SENATE) 26 JANUARY 1971
NJW 1971, 698 = VERSR 1971, 465

The plaintiff is an actress who participated in 1968 in the production of a film for sex education. In a printed sheet advertising the film her picture appeared on the back page in a close embrace with her partner. The defendant sells aphrodisiacs. In nos. 10, 11, and 23 of the 1969 issue of the periodical *Stern* the defendant published advertisements which contained a picture measuring 12 by 50 millimetres, the price (DM 24), and the defendant's address together with the following text:

"Paris love potion. The intimate means for men and women. A modern inducement to love. Overwhelming—seductive—irresistible. A few drops suffice for an immediate reaction".

The picture included in the advertisement consisted of a partial reproduction measuring 12 by 35 millimetres of the above-mentioned picture of the plaintiff and her partner which figured in the printed sheet advertising the film. The plaintiff did not give her consent to the reproduction of her picture for the purposes of the defendant.

The plaintiff claimed DM 8,000 as damages of non-economic loss. The court awarded the plaintiff DM 4,000 in respect of non-economic loss and rejected any further claim. The Court of Appeal of Munich rejected the claim in its entirety. The Federal Supreme Court admitted a second appeal, quashed the judgment, and referred the case back to another Senate of the Court of Appeal.

Reasons

The plaintiff does not claim compensation for economic loss which she may have suffered because as a result of the unauthorized publication of her picture she failed to receive a fee. Instead, her claim is expressly for pecuniary compensation in respect of non-economic loss. This is undisputed by the parties. The Court of Appeal, too, proceeds from this assumption.

I. 1. Contrary to the Court of First Instance, the Court of Appeal has rejected the claim simply because it refuses as a matter of fundamental legal principle to award pecuniary damages in cases of violations of the right to personality as compensation for non-economic loss. The Court of Appeal acknowledges that in so holding it acts contrary to a constant and well established practice of the Federal Supreme Court.

2. As the Federal Supreme Court, and in particular this Senate, has consistently held, a person whose right to his personality has been severely violated in a culpable manner may demand pecuniary compensation for non-economic loss if it is otherwise impossible to compensate satisfactorily for the inflicted harm. The court has felt entitled and also bound in accordance with Article 1 III of the Constitution to grant this extended remedy in order to take into account in the sphere of the protection of personality of the principles expressed in Articles 1 and 2 I of the Constitution. The Federal Supreme Court has responded repeatedly to the attacks directed against this development of the law [references]. The observations in the decision appealed against which reproduce a summary of these opinions and adopt them in the result do not constitute a reason for this Senate to discuss this problem again in detail. Its practice, which has since become well established, will be maintained [references].

Other Senates of the Federal Supreme Court have also followed the same practice in principle [references], as have a considerable number of writers [references].

3. In so holding the consideration that an imperative need must exist for granting compensation of this kind is taken into account by two restrictions.

In the first place, the victim of an attack on his right of personality is not to be awarded pecuniary damages unconditionally and in all cases. Instead certain aggravating circumstances must exist if an imperative need is to be recognised for allowing the injured party at least a limited amount of compensation for his non-economic loss by awarding him pecuniary damages. This is only the case if the injury is to be regarded as severe [references].

Further, according to the practice of this Senate the victim of a severe culpable attack upon his right of personality can only demand payment of pecuniary damages by the tortfeasor if the harm which has been inflicted cannot be compensated sufficiently by other means [references]. The grant of a right to pecuniary compensation is based in essence on the idea that otherwise the right of personality would lack sufficient legal protection. In the light of this consideration, the right to pecuniary damages is to be postponed if the injury can be compensated sufficiently by other means; according to the facts of the case the right to demand an order to desist and in particular to retract—rights which have equally been developed by the courts by way of an extension of the law some time ago—may supply an adequate and suitable measure.

In this connection the Court of Appeal is of the opinion that it is sufficient if the victim can redress his injury by means of the other "remedies" (*Rechtspositionen*) provided by private law, and it refers to the (prevention) injunction. This overlooks that the possibility of applying for an order to desist is directed, according to its purpose and function, against the future infliction of harm but does not affect harm which has already been caused. Moreover—and for this very reason—this possibility fails if there is no danger of repetition. The additional possibility of asking for a retraction is also not suitable in many cases of violation of the right of personality to provide sufficient compensation [reference]. This applies also when—as in the present case—a retraction cannot be considered having regard to the nature and the manner of the injury (by violation of the right to one's own likeness).

4. In the limited circumstances mentioned above, an award of pecuniary compensation for non-pecuniary damage must also be considered in principle when the violation of the right of personality consists in an infringement of the right to one's likeness, as is the case here [references].

5. For these reasons alone the decision of the Court of Appeal, which relied on the arguments set out above, cannot be upheld. Since additional facts must be considered and ascertained, this Senate cannot pronounce itself a final judgment in this matter.

II. The Court of Appeal, correctly having regard to its point of view, did not examine whether by this conduct the defendant has culpably violated the plaintiff's right of personality (§ 823 I BGB) by violating the plaintiff's right to her own likeness (§ 22 of the Act on the Copyright in Works of Art); nor did the Court of Appeal investigate whether according to the principles established by the Federal Supreme Court the existence of non-pecuniary damage suggests a claim to pecuniary damages.

1. The Court of First Instance held that the right to one's own likeness had been violated. The defendant denied this in the proceedings before the District Court but did not argue this point before the Court of Appeal. There are indications that the defendant himself now admits that the plaintiff's right of personality has been violated at least *objectively*. At any rate, the facts before this Senate are sufficient to permit the court below so to hold, at least initially.

(*a*) The court below will have to ascertain as a fact whether the plaintiff could be identified in the advertisement complained of. The circumstance that the partial reproduction was small in size does not exclude that the plaintiff's features are visible and therefore recognisable [reference]. Even if in the present case the picture was published without appending a name, the features taken from the film and reproduced on the back of the sheet advertising it, which has a wide circulation (*Film Kurier*), can lead to the identification of the plaintiff. It suffices for a violation of the right of personality if the person represented by the picture has reasonable grounds for believing that, having regard to the manner of the picture, he can be identified [reference]. Thus this Senate has also stated [reference] that the person affected cannot be required to prove who of the many spectators—the reproduction of a picture in a cinema was in issue—had recognized him in the weekly review of events and had gained the impression that he was a murderer.

(*b*) It is undisputed that the plaintiff did not consent to the reproduction of her picture for the purposes of the defendant (§ 22 of the Act on the Copyright in Works of Art). It cannot either be disputed seriously in law that the reproduction in issue here was not included by the consent given to the producer of the film. This consent did not extend to a publication which merely served to advertise a product which is not connected with the film, moreover in a manner which violated the right of personality in a particularly harmful manner, as will be shown below. For this reason alone the plaintiff has not lost her entitlement to the rights arising out of such a violation, as the defendant has argued before the Court of First Instance, quite apart from the fact that in the present case her claim for compensation in respect of non-economic loss resulting from an invasion of the right to her personality is in issue.

The publication was also not lawful without her consent (see § 23 of the Act on the Copyright in Works of Art). Even if, as the defendant argued in addition before the Court of First Instance, the plaintiff was to be counted among the personalities of contemporary history—in the meaning of § 23 I, no. 1, of the Act on the Copyright in Works of Art, which need not be decided here, the publication by the defendant is not covered by this exceptional position. The anonymous picture of the plaintiff was not reproduced in her capacity as a personality of contemporary history, as the manner of the publication shows. The publication served exclusively the business interest of the defendant and not a justifiable need of the public to receive objective pictorial information [references].

Furthermore, § 23 II of the Act on the Copyright in Works of Art would create an obstacle. Even if he is a personality of contemporary history, the person whose picture is published can decide whether he is willing to allow his picture to be used as an advertisement for goods or for commercial services.

2. By reproducing the picture of the plaintiff her right of personality was infringed. The infringement is characterized, in particular, by the fact that the defendant used the plaintiff's picture for the purpose of advertising, particularly in a denigrating manner. The publication in the form of a pictorial supplement to the advertisement for the "Paris love potion" offered by the defendant could lead to the misleading inference that for a consideration the plaintiff had given her consent to an advertisement of this kind.

3. The Court of Appeal, correctly having regard to its point of view, has also not considered and determined whether an objective infringement of the plaintiff's right of personality can be imputed to the defendant as a culpable act in the meaning of § 823 I BGB. When considering this aspect the court below will have to take into account the following:

Having regard to the previous decisions alone, the defendant, acting in accordance with the care required in mutual dealings, could not assume that he was entitled to reproduce the picture of the plaintiff without the latter's consent [reference]. The main question is, however, whether the defendant has failed in his duty of care by omitting to ascertain that the plaintiff had given her consent before he reproduced the preview of the film. Generally speaking, a person who wishes to publish a picture of another must examine of his own motion the extent of his right to reproduce. Consequently, it can be stated with some certainty that, observing the necessary care in mutual dealings, the defendant should have enquired of the printers that supplied the matrix whether the plaintiff had given her consent [reference]. This would seem to apply even more so in the present case, where a photograph of a woman is employed to advertise an aphrodisiac potion.

However, even if the court below should come to the conclusion that the plaintiff's right of personality has been infringed culpably and that therefore liability exists according to § 823 I BGB, the plaintiff is not entitled to a pecuniary compensation in respect of non-pecuniary damage as a matter of course and in all circumstances.

4. According to the practice of the Federal Supreme Court, and in particular of this Senate, as was pointed out before, the imperative need to grant the injured party at least a certain amount of compensation for non-pecuniary loss by awarding pecuniary damages is to be admitted in special aggravating circumstances. As this Senate has stated on several occasions, it must be examined in each individual case, having regard to the

manifold possibilities of infringement of the right to personality, whether the injured party whose non-pecuniary loss cannot be compensated by other means is to be awarded pecuniary damages on equitable grounds. An affirmative answer can only be given if the violation is to be regarded as severe. The question as to whether it is to be treated as a severe invasion of personality as a separate protected interest can only be answered on the basis of *all* the facts of the individual case. For this purpose the manner and the severity of the harm inflicted and the degree of blameworthiness must be considered in particular, as well as the cause and the nature of the act. (Constant practice [references].) On this basis the results of the proceedings hitherto disclose that the following aspects may be significant for the court below in reaching a decision:

In order to assess the *severity of the infringement* it may be relevant that the plaintiff was associated with an advertisement for an aphrodisiac. The impression was created that against payment she allowed her person to be used for such an advertisement by means of her picture. This unfavourable impression was possibly increased by the fact that five additional advertisements by the defendant on p. 156 of *Stern* no. 11, where the advertisement complained of was published, make it clear to the reader that the defendant, as a mail order business also sells other sex appliances and explicit sex literature.

In this connection the contention of the plaintiff may also be relevant that she was known as a film actress and that she appears in the theatre in classical plays. The plaintiff has stated further that she had gone through an apprenticeship in classical works and that in the theatre where she had her first engagement she had played almost exclusively classical roles. In this capacity in particular she had also appeared as a guest in various theatres. The discriminatory (*sic*) publications had, above all, placed her guest engagements in jeopardy. Finally, the *objective* severity of the infringement may be gauged by the fact that the advertisement appeared in three successive issues of the magazine *Stern* which has a big circulation, and that therefore it became widely known.

As regards the *degree of blameworthiness* of the defendant—an affirmative finding in principle to this effect still remains to be made by the Court of Appeal, as was pointed out before—the Court of Appeal will have to consider whether the failure to make enquiries may not have to be regarded as negligent in the light of the special circumstances. The First Civil Senate has given an affirmative answer to this effect in [reference] and has characterised the blameworthiness of the defendant in that case as gross negligence. In this connection the statement of the plaintiff may assume additional relevance that by a letter dated 14 March 1969 written by her lawyer she had warned the defendant after the first advertisement had appeared on 9 March 1969, no. 10 of *Stern*.

The *cause and the motive* of the defendant in acting as he did were clearly egotistic commercial interest and not the satisfaction of a need deserving legal protection to provide information. It certainly does not exclude a finding that the infringement was severe in the meaning of the practice of this court.

Case 146

BUNDESVERFASSUNGSGERICHT (FIRST SENATE, FIRST CHAMBER)
8 MARCH 2000, NJW 2000, 2187 = FAMRZ 2000, 943

Facts

The original proceedings related to a road traffic accident which occurred in 1986 and in which the complainants' three children were killed. The accident was caused by the first defendant, whose vehicle was insured with the second defendant. Under the influence of alcohol, the first defendant drove on to a major road at a speed of about 100 to 110 kilometres per hour, ignoring a stop sign. He collided with a car which contained the complainants' children aged between 17 and 21. Their death had a very serious physical and psychological effect on the complainants. They claimed, amongst other things, damages for pain and suffering of between DM 120,000 and DM 150,000.

After obtaining a number of medical opinions in relation to the first complainant, the Landgericht assessed damages for pain and suffering at DM 70,000 for the first complainant, and at DM 40,000 for the second complainant. The complainants appealed against this judgment asking for an increase in the damages for pain and suffering to DM 150,000 (first complainant) and DM 120,000 (second complainant). The Oberlandesgericht rejected the appeal. An appeal in law was not accepted. In their constitutional complaint, the complainants claim violation of Article 3 para. 1 of the Basic Law, of their general right of personality under Article 2 para. 1 in combination with Article 1 para. 1 of the Basic Law, and of Article 6 para. 1 of the Basic Law. The constitutional complaint was unsuccessful.

Reasons

The constitutional complaint has no sufficient prospect of success . . .

1. The judgment of the OLG under challenge does not infringe the complainants' basic rights under Article 3 para. 1 of the Basic Law. The same applies for the decision of the Bundesgerichtshof confirming the judgment. The provisions of § 847 of the BGB on which the OLG has based its decision are not open to objection in constitutional law. For the very reason that it uses the vague legal concept "fair compensation", it permits differentiations which facilitate application in a manner corresponding to the equality principle . . .

a) Article 3 para. 1 of the Basic Law is violated when a group of people to whom the norm is addressed is treated differently in some substantial respect in comparison to other addressees of the norm, even though no differences exist between the two groups of such kind and weight as to justify the unequal treatment. Such a violation of the basic right is not only present when the legislator treats several groups of persons differently without a sufficient objective ground, but likewise when the courts by way of interpretation of statutory provisions make the kind of differentiation which is forbidden for the legislator . . .

b) The unequal treatment objected to by the complainants, which relates to physical harm to health as compared with violations of the right of personality, in particular within the framework of media related cases, does not infringe their basic rights under Article 3 para. 1 of the Basic Law. Here it must be assumed that the deciding senate of the OLG would, in violations which are of this kind but which involve the right of personality, if need be grant higher damages for pain and suffering than the DM 40,000 or DM 70,000 allowed here, or would consider circumstances to which in the present case no importance has been attached and which would raise the level of damages for pain and suffering. Only on this prerequisite is it possible to assume unequal treatment in the concrete area of the OLG's competence.

However, there are objectively based differences between these two types of case which could provide justification in constitutional law for the different treatment. In this respect it must first be considered that the claim to monetary compensation in the case of violations of the right of personality is not (any longer) directly based on an analogy with § 847 of the BGB (reference omitted). Instead granting monetary compensation is based on a right which originates in the protective function of Article 1 and Article 2 para. 1 of the Basic Law and finds its foundation in § 823 (1) of the BGB in combination with these provisions (references omitted). From a material point of view, granting monetary compensation rests on the idea that without such a claim, violations of the dignity and honour of a person would frequently remain without any sanction, with the consequence that legal protection of the personality would atrophy (reference omitted). (The difference from damages for pain and suffering shows itself, apart from the different legal basis, in divergent terminology). In addition, the determination of the level of compensation partly results from considerations which are different from those used for fixing damages for pain and suffering. Thus, according to the opinion of the BGH, the level of monetary compensation should genuinely inhibit ruthless marketing of the personality when a press undertaking has deliberately broken the law in using violation of the personality as a means of increasing its circulation and thus of pursuing of its own commercial interest. Here the compensation should, by its level as well, form a counterbalance to infringement of personality rights for the obtaining of profit. Admittedly this is not a genuine case of "creaming off the profit"; the attempt to obtain profit is (merely) an assessment factor in the decision about the level of monetary compensation (references omitted). Preventative considerations, which lead, in calculating monetary compensation in personality right cases, to a distinct increase in the compensation allowed, are thus decisive.

Such a consideration is not however operative in physical injury or nervous shock cases in connection with liability for road traffic accidents. Grounds can be cited for the difference in treatment. The violation of the right does not occur intentionally in typical road traffic accidents, nor is it motivated by the pursuit of commercial interests. Since the idea of intentionally obtaining profit plays no role here, the purpose of prevention is not a starting point for similar consideration as a calculation factor for the level of damages for pain and suffering. It is also not as a rule to be expected that a person potentially responsible for an accident will be induced by an appropriate increase in the damages for pain and suffering to observe the requirements of care in road traffic. Another reason why such an effect is scarcely to be expected is because compensation in the end result—in the present case as well—is not born by the tortfeasor himself but by the insurer.

Because of these objective differences, there is no objection in constitutional law from the point of view of the equality principle to the fact that the judgment of the OLG under challenge did not, in the case of the complainants, take into account preventative considerations as a calculation factor to *increase* the damages for pain and suffering. Whether, when, and in what form the legislator could eliminate the incongruity objected to by the complainants can remain open.

c) . . .

In constitutional law it has merely to be examined whether the damages for pain and suffering actually granted to the complainants in the sums of DM 70,000 or DM 40,000 violate the equality principle. This cannot however be established. The OLG calculated the damages for pain and suffering—not in this respect differently from the case of pure physical harm—chiefly on the basis of the injury to health which occurred according to the experts' opinions obtained at first instance, and also included in the considerations here the especially severe consequences for the complainants. Whether these consequences are, as the complainants claim, comparable with paraplegia and possibly justify the granting of higher damages for pain and suffering cannot be examined by the Federal Constitutional Court. That is a question of the application of ordinary law to the individual case, which is the obligation of the specialist courts (references omitted). It is not possible to deduce from the judgment any fundamental underestimation of the complainants' sufferings in comparison with purely physical harm, at any rate in the end result. First the OLG did not see itself as bound by the relatively low levels of damages for pain and suffering granted so far in connection with nervous shock, which were in the region of DM 3,000 to DM 10,000 at the time of the decision (reference omitted). Instead it regarded significantly higher damages for pain and suffering as appropriate in the complainants' case and expressly based this on the special situation and the severity of the pain suffered by them according to the outcome of the evidence . . .

2. The decisions under challenge also do not violate the complainants' general personality right under Article 2 para. 1 in combination with Article 1 para. 1 of the Basic Law. In the end result, the radiation effect of this basic right on the ordinary law in the calculation of damages for pain and suffering has been taken into account, at least in a manner which cannot be objected to in constitutional law. In this respect, the above statements have corresponding application. The supplementary argument of the complainants that there is a parallel with the decision of the BGH of 13 October 1992 (reference omitted) cannot be sustained. In this decision the BGH, in the light of the high value which the Basic Law in Articles 1 and 2 attaches to the personality and the dignity of the human being, abandoned its earlier case law granting merely symbolic compensation in cases of serious brain damage. There can however be no question here of such merely symbolic compensation; the OLG considered the actual harm to the complainants in the individual case and allowed it to influence the level of the damages for pain and suffering.

Case 147

BUNDESGERICHTSHOF (FIFTH CIVIL SENATE) 22 NOVEMBER 1985
NJW 1986, 2037 = JZ 1986, 387

The following questions are submitted to the Great Senate by the Fifth Civil Senate:

1. If the owner of a thing which he uses himself, such as an owner-occupied house, is temporarily unable to use it by reason of a tortious interference with his ownership, does this represent a compensatable economic loss in the absence of any extra expenditure or lost revenue?

2. If such a loss of use is compensatable, how is it to be quantified?

Facts

The plaintiff owns a plot of land on which there is a substantial and well-appointed dwelling, with a living area of about 260 square metres. On the land sloping steeply away from the plaintiff's property the defendant was building some terraced houses. The excavations were improperly executed and the plaintiff's house was rendered temporarily unstable. The city issued an evacuation order, prohibiting occupation of the house between 12 August and 16 September 1981. Repairs to the façade and interior of the house cost DM 5851.75 and DM 340 respectively. In addition to these sums and interest, the plaintiff claimed DM 3000 as compensation for the fact that during the validity of the evacuation order she and her husband had had to live in their dormobile nearby.

The Landgericht upheld the claim for repairs of DM 5998.29, but dismissed the rest of the claim. The Oberlandesgericht dismissed the plaintiff's appeal, but allowed the defendant's appeal on the ground that the plaintiff had received "new for old" and reduced the damages to DM 3334.90. With the leave of the Oberlandesgericht the plaintiff appealed only as to the claim for DM 3000 for loss of use of the house. The Fifth Civil Senate laid the matter before the Great Senate for Civil Matters.

Reasons

II. As regards the claim in issue the court below found that between 12 August and 16 September 1981 the plaintiff and her husband were unable to occupy their house by reason of the local authority's evacuation order, and had instead lived in their dormobile which was equipped with all proper conveniences. The court held that the temporary loss of use of their dwelling, though complete, did not constitute an economic loss but only a non-economic loss incapable of compensation.

III. The Fifth Civil Senate was of the same opinion but regarded the question as one of principle and sought a decision from the Great Senate for Civil Matters as being necessary to resolve divergent views in the courts (§ 137 GVG).

IV. There is indeed a divergence of views between five of the senates of the Bundesgerichtshof on the question of damages for loss of use of chattels and realty.

1. At the outset we have decisions of the Third and Sixth Civil Senates on the temporary loss of use of a motor vehicle involved in an accident [references].

(*a*) Decisions of 1964 and 1966 [references] recognize that the owner of a motor vehicle, including one for private and personal use, which he is unable to use while accident damage is being repaired can claim lump-sum damages for economic loss even when he has not hired a substitute or incurred extra expenditure or lost any income (most recently BGHZ 89, 60 (63) = NJW 1984, 722).

(*b*) In order to stem the tide of liability numerous limitations have been introduced, as to the basis and *quantum* of the claim. Money damages (§ 251 BGB) are awarded only if the loss of use is "actually felt" by the victim (*ibid.*). No compensatable harm thus arises when a purely abstract possibility of use is frustrated (BGHZ 45, 212 (219) = NJW 1966, 1260) or when a power of disposition is affected (BGHZ 55, 146 (150) = NJW 1971, 796—the hunting rights case); the courts require an ability and an intention to use (BGH NJW 1985, 2471—military ambulance). Compensation has even been refused when the reason the owner could not have used his vehicle while under repair was that he himself had been injured (BGH NJW 1968, 1778).

Exceptions to these exceptions are made where the vehicle would have been used by members of the owner's family or even his fiancée (BGH NJW 1975, 922).

Damages for loss of use were denied in a case in which the victim could reasonably be expected to use a second car which was not needed for other purposes [references]. In other cases damages for the maintenance cost of a vehicle held in reserve have been allowed (BGHZ 32, 280 (284) = NJW 1960, 1339—tram in Bremen; BGHZ 70, 199 (201) = NJW 1978, 812—bus in Bremen; see also BGH NJW 1985, 2471).

A victim who rents a smaller car cannot add to the actual hire costs a sum representing the difference in use-value of the two vehicles (BGH NJW 1967, 552) but instead of claiming the hire for the rented car he may claim a lump sum for the loss of use of his own car (BGH NJW 1970, 1120).

If purely personal reasons prevent the owner from using his vehicle, for example where his driving licence has not been properly safeguarded, the Third Civil Senate finds no compensatable harm (BGHZ 65, 170, 173 ff. = NJW 1975, 2341), but if there is an invasion affecting the thing itself, the loss of use is in principle compensatable, and the courts find such an invasion even where there is no physical damage but use is prevented by some factual or legal obstacle (see BGHZ 85, 11 (15, 16) = NJW 1982, 2304; but note that the Fleet case there mentioned (BGHZ 55, 153 (159) = NJW 1971, 886) was a case of lost profits under § 252 BGB). The Third Civil Senate has occasionally allowed cases where the car's documents were withheld (BGHZ 40, 345 (351) = NJW 1964, 542) or a garage entry blocked (BGHZ 63, 203 (206) = NJW 1975, 347).

(c) The Bundesgerichtshof has also sought to limit the amount of the lump sum payable for loss of use. In order to avoid any element of profit, the Sixth Civil Senate deducts from the gross hire charges for a comparable substitute all the elements of cost which the commercial hirer adds to the 'true use value' (BGHZ 45, 212, 220 = NJW 1966, 1260; BGHZ 56, 214, 218 ff., 222 = NJW 1971, 1692), and makes a further deduction for the plaintiff's savings, taking the notional rental cost of a similar car as merely an "indicator" (see BGH NJW 1970, 1120). Finally it regarded as sufficient a sum "well in excess of the cost of a car not in use" (BGHZ 56, 214 (215 ff.) = NJW 1971, 1692). In the end result the daily tariff amounts to 25–30 per cent of the hire cost of a comparable vehicle. The details are given in tables prepared for the use of liability-insurers and the courts, and endorsed by the Bundesgerichtshof as legally accurate [references].

2. The Eighth Civil Senate has carried these decisions over into the area of contractual liability and extended them to cases where a debtor is in delay in delivering a car or its documents (BGHZ 88, 11 = NJW 1983, 2139, where the Court of Appeal awarded DM 21.50 per day, a total of DM 1075 for 50 days' loss of use).

3. In cases involving chattels other than motor cars the Bundesgerichtshof has not yet treated loss of use as a form of economic harm.

In BGHZ 63, 393 (= NJW 1975, 733) the purchaser of a fur coat in a claim for damages for non-performance sought DM 1700 because the coat had been unusable for four years while futile alterations were constantly being made, but the Eighth Civil Senate held that this was not economic harm. The same Senate held likewise in the caravan case (BGHZ 86, 128 (130) = NJW 1983, 444) where a camping site operator who had leased space for the caravan refused access to it for 311 days under the pretext that the rent had not been paid. Here the plaintiff claimed DM 311 × 15 = DM 4665.

In the motor-boat case (BGHZ 89, 60 = NJW 1984, 722) the boat was damaged in a road accident and rendered unavailable for the owner's holiday and subsequent weekends. He claimed DM 6160 as forty days' loss of use at DM 154 per day (the daily hire cost for a similar boat being DM 280), but the Sixth Civil Senate saw in the temporary loss of use only a "diminution of the individual's pleasure" and a "non-economic harm".

4. Divergent decisions have also been rendered in cases involving temporary loss of use or deprivation of enjoyment of real property.

(a) In the case decided by the Third Civil Senate on 11 July 1963 (NJW 1963, 2020) the plaintiff property owner had been badly affected by excessive noise and small emanating from an official military clubhouse, but had remained in occupation and had not had to accept a lower price for the house. The Third Civil Senate did not award damages for economic harm, but awarded compensation for the reduction of the "monthly enjoyment-value of the property". In BGHZ 91, 20 (28) = NJW 1984, 1876 the Third Civil Senate awarded "compensation for expropriatory invasion" to the owner-occupier of a dwelling affected by smells emanating from a communal distillery, and approved the quantum awarded by the trial court with reference to the probable reduction in the monthly rent hypothetically obtainable.

(b) When an owner was temporarily unable to use his house owing to malfunction of the heating due to the fault of the outgoing tenant, the Eighth Civil Senate awarded him damages for the abstract loss of use, and said that it was immaterial if the house had been used for purposes other than occupation (NJW 1967, 1803). Whether the same result would have been reached in tort was left open.

(c) The Fifth Civil Senate has twice denied the existence of economic harm in assessing damages for delay. In BGHZ 66, 277 = NJW 1976, 1630 a person for whom a dwelling was being constructed could not move into it until seven months after the due date, owing to the contractor's fault, and had to stay in his previous smaller house during that period. The Senate denied that the loss of enjoyment, valued at a monthly rental of DM 2000, constituted economic harm. The decision was the same in BGHZ 71, 234 = NJW 1978, 1805, concerning a claim by the purchaser of an apartment yet to be constructed, where the Senate said that neither the servicing of the capital deployed during the eight month delay (for the price had been paid on time) nor the community taxes assessable during that period constituted economic loss.

(d) In the swimming-pool case (BGHZ 76, 179 = NJW 1980, 1386) the Seventh Civil Senate hesitated to adopt the view of the Fifth Civil Senate that temporary loss of the chance of using a dwelling or apartment does not constitute economic harm, but found no economic harm when a private swimming pool for a housing complex had been badly designed and was unusable for the eight months it took to put it right. By contrast in a decision on 10 October 1985 (NJW 1986, 427) the Seventh Civil Senate, applying the law relating to the contract for work and materials, held that economic harm did exist when an underground garage with six parking places to service an apartment block was unusable for twenty-two months because of inadequate corrective measures.

(e) In a tort case of blast-damage (BGHZ 75, 366 (370 ff.) = NJW 1980, 775) the Fifth Civil Senate held that there was no economic harm where the use of property had been partially obstructed rather than totally prevented. In that case the authorities had temporarily forbidden the use of a house in danger of collapse, but the owner had nevertheless established a bedroom in the cellar and had continued to occupy half of the ground floor despite the prohibition.

V. This divergence of decisions in the Bundesgerichtshof on the question of damages for loss of use is not calculated to advance legal certainty. The decisions contain no clear criterion to distinguish between economic harm and non-economic harm (§ 253 BGB) or to distinguish the different types of case; nor is it clear whether the question should be treated differently in contract and in tort. The variety and incompatibility of the reasoning offered in support of the decisions reflects itself in different tests for the *quantum* of recovery.

. . .

VI. 1. According to the decisions of the Bundesgerichtshof the question whether compensatable economic harm has occurred is to be answered with reference to the *theory of difference*: one compares the economic situation produced by the occurrence said to involve liability with the situation which would exist had it not occurred [references]
. . .

2. According to the theory of difference no economic harm exists in the present case . . .

3. There do not seem to be any plausible, let alone compelling, reasons for holding that the mere loss of the benefit of use constitutes economic harm calling for compensation . . .
[The Senate discusses invasion of 'exclusive rights' and industrial property rights.]

(*bb*) To recognise as compensatable the harm consisting of loss of use in these cases would conflict with the principle of the law of liability expressed in § 252 BGB. It is true that § 252 sentence 2 BGB modifies the burden of proof in cases of lost profit (BGH NJW 1983, 758) but it permits rebuttal. If the victim intended to profit from the use of the thing (such as a commercial vehicle) during the period it was out of commission he is entitled to the profit presumed by the law unless the defendant proves that that profit would not have been made even if the damage had not occurred. The money damages legally due are payable not for the abstract loss of a possibility of use but because in the particular circumstances the occurrence probably made an economic difference [references]. The loss of the possibility of use is a source of potential harm, not an economic harm in itself [references]. The law allows the defendant to show that the planned used would have been wasteful rather than profitable [references]. Otherwise the law of liability would be preferring consumption to production, and nothing in the positive law justifies such a paradoxical result. Only in certain exceptional cases does the law provide for computation of harm *in abstracto* in order to facilitate the disposition of certain obligational relationships, usually arising by way of contract (see § 376 II, III HGB).

(*ee*) In sum, the values implicit in the law afford no basis for saying that in cases of invasion of an absolute right of disposition, damage to use in the abstract should be recognized, let alone at the rate of a hypothetical rental. All the more recent cases avoid adopting such a wide principle which would indeed undermine the effort of all the Senates concerned to restrict the extension of liability for loss of use.

(*b*) In its decision of 11 July 1963, already cited, the Eighth Civil Senate invoked decisions of the Bundesgerichtshof relating to loss of use of motor vehicles. Even in the special area of motor accidents the reasoning is open to question, and the desirable tendency of several Senates of the Bundesgerichtshof has been not to generalize this principle but to confine it to that particular area (most hesitant, BGHZ 66, 277 (279 ff.) = NJW 1976, 1630; 'The doctrinal basis for decisions concerning the use-potential of motor cars is insufficiently insecure to justify its extension to other areas').

(*aa*) The main argument which already figures in BGHZ 45, 212 (216) = NJW 1966, 1260 was one of fairness, that it is an 'unsatisfying result' to allow the tortfeasor (and his liability insurer) to escape all liability for lost use simply by an unjustified refusal to meet the (temporary) claim for natural restitution in the form of provision of, or payment for the hire of, a substitute vehicle under § 249 sentences 1 and 2 respectively BGB. But this is to ignore the basic distinction drawn by the legislator: whereas the primary remedy of restitution *in natura* is not limited to the replacement of economic losses and provides certain other advantages, the secondary and subsidiary remedy of money damages (§§ 251, 252 BGB) expressly excludes compensation for non-economic harm. Such differences as exist between restitution *in natura* and compensation in money result from the structure deliberately adopted by the legislator.

A further argument of fairness has appeared since BGHZ 56, 214 (216) = NJW 1971, 1692, namely that it is unfair that the tortfeasor should benefit from the victim's decision to forgo the convenience of a substitute vehicle. But this is inconsistent with the legislator's decision that compensation for mere inconvenience and discomfort can be granted only in the exceptional cases of §§ 847, 1300 BGB (see now § 651 BGB). This argument loses its force where liability is strict, as in the case of the guardian of a motor vehicle under § 7 StVG, and is in any case incompatible with the attempt of the courts to grant only the cost of keeping, not using, the car rather than the full cost of a hypothetical rental: for this too confers a deplorable 'benefit' on the tortfeasor and his insurer.

(*bb*) The so-called "commercialization" idea is not convincing either (leading case: BGH NJW 1956, 1234; followed in BGHZ 40, 345 (349 ff.) = NJW 1964, 542). This holds that a pleasure or convenience, far from being uneconomic, constitutes an independent economic value if it is commonly capable of being obtained for money, that is "bought" or "commercialised"; to diminish such a pleasure is to depreciate its monetary equivalent. Writers have rightly criticised the baselessness of the premise that economic harm arises every time anything "commercialised" is affected [references]. So many pleasures today are to be had for money that this test hardly serves to distinguish economic from non-economic harm, and recent cases, rather sceptical of the 'commercialisation' idea, use it as subsidiary, if at all [references]. This Senate shares such reserve [references].

(*cc*) The prevalent view of the Bundesgerichtshof is that the only valid and decisive touchstone for discerning economic harm as regards compensation for loss of use of vehicles and other things, moveable or not, is 'public perception'. (The Fifth Civil Senate has stood aloof (BGHZ 66, 277 (279) = NJW 1976, 1630).) The Third Civil Senate [references] and even more the Sixth Civil Senate [references] find it decisive that in the public perception today, the temporary loss of use of a vehicle is seen as economic loss because the availability of a car is apt to save time and effort even outside working hours so that the advantages thereby afforded are regarded as "money" [references].

. . .

As a matter of principle it must be said that "public perception" is not a source of law
. . .

One factual objection is that this "public perception" is not usually ascertained empirically but is simply assumed by the judges in the case. Reference to "public perception" not empirically ascertained may often be a shorthand justification for a solution prompted by the value judgements of the court [references]. This can lead to an unacceptable degree of legal uncertainty, and has actually done so on this very question. Courts that actually wanted to ascertain the relevant "public perception" would be led into an unduly and impractically wide range of related sociological questions.

(*ee*) In order to limit liability for loss of use several Senates of the Bundesgerichtshof have adopted the test of whether it was "actually felt". This is inconsistent with positive law.

Thus in BGHZ 40, 345 (353) = NJW 1964, 542 the Third Civil Senate said that there were cases "in which the temporary loss of possession or potential use of a vehicle was not felt by the victim and so involved, from the economic point of view, no loss". The Sixth Civil Senate has adopted this test (BGHZ 45, 212 (219) = NJW 1966, 1260), and both Senates have drawn consequences from it, some of which limit its scope.

These limitations may have been necessary as a matter of policy in order to contain the spread of liability in cases of motor accidents, but this is only a further indication that the original decisions on loss of use of a vehicle went too far. The requirement that an economic loss be "felt" in order to be compensatable is foreign to the law of liability. A millionaire who loses a small profit can claim compensation for that loss by the clear terms and obvious intent of § 252 BGB even if the effect of his failure to increase his wealth is imperceptible to him; at the other end, a person hopelessly burdened with debt can claim compensation for a further liability even if it does not perceptibly worsen his economic plight [references]. To limit compensation for harm to such harm as is "actually felt" runs counter to the legal principle of reparation in full [references].

(*c*) Finally, it is not really a question whether any standards otherwise recognised by law can be found for the evaluation in money terms of a temporary loss of use [references]. The absence of such standards indeed suggests that loss of use is not a separate economic loss [references], but not *vice versa*. The value of the use of a thing is not a value separate from and independent of the value of the thing itself, but is indiscernibly involved in its market value. A diminution of the value of the use of a thing usually leads to a drop in its market value, and making up the market value automatically compensates for loss of use-value [references].

As a matter of accounting there is an additional loss related to the duration of the loss of use which is not compensated if the loss is subsequently made good, namely periodic costs not related to actual use, which must be incurred if the thing is to be available for use [references]; in the case of a motor vehicle these would include the vehicle licence fee and the liability insurance premium. These are independent of the individual circumstances of the owner and, unlike purchase price where there is no price control, can be compensated without practical difficulties because they are the same for all and are easily ascertained. Nevertheless, there are serious objections to giving damages even in respect of these items.

These costs are not caused by the occurrence which leads to the loss of use [references], and in principle damages are payable only for harm caused by the occurrence which entails liability [references]. To the extent that the basic cost of keeping a vehicle in reserve in order to forestall harm is treated as compensatable [references] this is because of the close connection between preventing harm and mitigating harm (as required by § 254 BGB; see BGHZ 32, 280 (295) = NJW 1960, 1339); these decisions can also be justified on causal grounds if one regards the deployment of the reserve vehicle as an effect of the tortious occurrence [references].

. . .

One can get round these causal problems by concentrating not on the expenditures themselves but on their "equivalent", namely the use of the thing so facilitated, and treating the expenditures as a measure of the monetary value of the loss of use [references]. This does not, however, get us any further forward. It is true that a rule limited to these basic costs (tax, insurance) is not open to the usual objection that a thing does not have value simply because money has been spent on procuring it, much less the value of the expenditure [references]. But it *is* open to the objection that contrary to the principles of the law of liability it leads to a preference for consumption over production (see above **VI.** 3(*a*), (*bb*)). In the case of a thing put to commercial use, such as an apartment block used for rent, these basic costs reduce the profit and so diminish the damages payable for lost profits, the only compensatable item (§ 252 BGB); thus these costs are at the risk of the owner. It would be inconsistent with this legislative apportionment of risks to make the tortfeasor pay for the "frustrated" basic costs in cases of the loss of consumer use of goods.

. . .

VII. Should the Great Senate decide, on whatever grounds, to hold that damages may be claimed in tort for loss of use of things used by their owner personally, such as an owner-occupied house, there will be the further problem of the quantification of such loss.

. . .

2. In the light of the decided cases the position of the Fifth Civil Senate is as follows:

(*a*) The Sixth Civil Senate is right to hold that the notional rental value of a substitute (or the reduction in rental value in cases where enjoyment is merely impaired) cannot be used directly as a standard of measurement. The enjoyment of a thing by its owner is not profit-orientated but constitutes consumption of investment in future enjoyment, so no loss of profit is involved in the temporary loss or impairment of enjoyment. Since tort law must not result in enrichment, the notional rental must be purged of all elements of profit. Accordingly the notional rental cannot, contrary to the view of the Seventh Civil Senate, be treated as the 'decisive' factor in the computation [references].

(*b*) The best approach is that of the Sixth Civil Senate, namely to do the sums "from the bottom up", though indeed the basic costs (tax, insurance) are non-compensatable in the light of § 252 BGB, as was shown by the comparison with loss of use of commercial property (above **VI.** 3(*a*), (*bb*)). But the idea of "modest addition" must be rejected as unsupported by any sound doctrine, despite the attempts by Dunz to support it [references]. For Dunz the "addition" is simply "a rebuttable lump-sum for typical consequential harm" [references]. In relating this "addition" to the extra time and effort spent by the victim on the widespread assumption that "time means money" even outside working hours, Dunz is being inconsistent with positive law (above **VI.** 3(*b*), (*dd*)). To the extent that he has in mind extra expenses such as tram tickets and gratuities to courtesy drivers, one would have to set against them the petrol costs, maintenance costs, wear and tear and other, probably higher, expenses, involved in using one's own vehicle. The "modest addition" is unjustified and unnecessary.

Case 148

BUNDESGERICHTSHOF (GREAT SENATE) 9 JULY 1986
BGHZ 98, 212 = NJW 1987, 50 = JZ 1987, 306

The Fifth Civil Division submitted the following questions to the Great Senate:

(1) If the owner of a thing which he uses himself, such as an owner-occupied house, is temporarily unable to use it by reason of a tortious interference with his ownership, does this represent a compensatable economic loss in the absence of any extra expenditure or lost revenue?

(2) If such a loss of use is compensatable, how is it to be quantified?
 The Great Senate gave the following answer:

The owner of property which he himself uses, such as an owner-occupied house, who is temporarily deprived of its use as a result of a tort may be able to claim damages therefore as constituting an economic loss, despite the absence of extra expense or lost revenue.

Reasons

. . .

III. The Great Senate is of the view that, leaving aside cases involving cars for personal use, a compensatable economic loss arises when the owner of a thing is temporarily deprived of its use by a tort if (1) his domestic economy depends on the constant availability of the thing, such as the house he occupies, and (2) he would actually have used it during the period of deprivation. With this limitation the award of damages is permitted by law and does not imperil legal certainty; indeed, it is necessary to give compensation for such deprivations in order to ensure the full and just compensation of economic losses.

1. The BGB does not define the concepts of "patrimony" or "economic harm", but leaves it to writers and courts to flesh them out. In order to ascertain whether the plaintiff has suffered patrimonial harm, the Bundesgerichtshof generally follows the Reichsgericht in applying the "difference method", and compares his present economic situation with what it would have been had the harmful occurrence not taken place. The Fifth Civil Division is right to say that the temporary loss of personal use is not reflected in such a computation, which apart from replacement costs discloses only the income lost if the thing would have been used to produce income or the savings made if it would have involved costs and liabilities.

(*a*) But the Bundesgerichtshof has come to realize that while this accounting opera-tion is value-neutral, the courts must still determine what items are to be included in the account in the light of the protective function of tort liability and the compensatory function of damages.

In this sense the difference method, which is not actually enjoined by the law [refer-ences], takes on a normative aspect [references]. While it is true that economic loss will always reflect itself in an increase on the debit side or a decrease on the credit side, it is for the law to decide what items are to be included on the balance sheet for the purposes of compensation.

(*b*) Such a balance-sheet must take account of the fact that wealth is significant not just in its actuality but also in its potentiality, as enabling its owner to realise his goals in life [references], a function protected by law.

If, looking only to money, the system gave compensation only for loss of the com-mercial use of property, it would be ignoring the gain that comes from domestic use also, deprivation of which, though not expressed in loss of income, can comparably affect the owner's economic sphere. Thus a motor vehicle not only often represents the major item in a private person's property but is commonly the very basis of his domestic economy and lifestyle, especially if he uses it for his profession. Even more clearly, the decision to answer one's living needs by buying a home is largely based on economic considerations.

The price reflects the market's valuation of such goods precisely as domestic goods, and recognizes their temporary loss as a devaluation of them. If it puts an evident con-straint on the owner's housekeeping, as when he would otherwise have used the thing, only an approach which dealt exclusively in monetary loss and gain, an approach not required by the notion of 'patrimony', would regard this as economically insignificant.

2. Nor is § 252 BGB compelling here. Where a thing is put to productive commercial use, loss of use is essentially shown by loss of profit, compensation for which is expressly pro-vided for by § 252 sentence 1 BGB. This provision emphasises the importance attached by the legislator to loss of productive use in goods in commerce, and there is no compara-ble provision for the domestic use of goods.

But we cannot agree with the Fifth Civil Division that the law has set its face against damages for deprivation of domestic use of goods not resulting in any loss of income. Unlike provisions in earlier codes, § 252 BGB is principally designed to make it clear that damages extend to the whole economic loss regardless of the degree or type of fault which causes it [references]; to this extent the provision follows through the mandate of full compensation implied in § 249 BGB; § 252 sentence 2 BGB fits into this scheme, though hitherto the courts have seen it only as alleviating the burden of proof so as to let the plaintiff obtain proper compensation for harm which is often difficult to prove, an aim also furthered by § 287 ZPO [references]. Though the law is geared to productive use, it can be extended so as to embrace analogous domestic use without putting such a claimant in a better position as regards proof as feared by the Fifth Civil Division provided that damages are not given *in abstracto*, which the BGB permits only exceptionally (see §§ 288, 290, 849 BGB). For this purpose the courts have added the requirement, in the case of motor vehicles, that the loss of use be 'actually felt', that the victim was willing and able to use the vehicle during the period of deprivation and would actually have used it. If this limitation is carried over to other property, the victim's position as regards proof will be comparable in cases of commercial and domestic use respectively, and it will be easy enough to relate damages for loss of domestic use to the actual harm affecting the victim's estate without setting up any tariff for different types of case.

. . .

4. Any such extension of the law must certainly be limited to property on whose continuing availability domestic arrangements typically depend. Further extension would go beyond the need to give similar treatment to commercial and domestic property and might lead to granting compensation for non-economic harm, contrary to § 253 BGB; the law might become unpredictable and damages difficult to assess.

(*a*) In permitting compensation only for economic loss, § 253 seeks to limit damages to cases where objectively measurable harm occurs: when awarding damages the judge should find not on the uncontrollably subjective valuation tendered by the victim but on the valuation generally attributed to that interest by the market. The legislator also wanted to avoid any monetisation of "ideal" interests [references]. If things one uses in private life are rendered unusable, one's mode of life is inevitably affected, but compensation cannot be given for all such inconvenience without giving damages for purely personal harm, which § 253 definitively renders non-compensatable, in cases of tort at any rate. It may be different on contract cases since the parties may contract out of § 253 just as they may agree that economic interests should have less protection. But so far as goods of vital importance to general daily living are concerned, there is no risk of an undue extension of damages in the non-economic area, for not only does their use in the domestic economy clearly relate to the economic sphere [references] but their prevalence and function make it possible to measure at least their economic core by means of objective standards, eschewing subjective factors peculiar to the victim personally. To this extent, at any rate, the fact that such anfractuosities would not show up in a commercial balance sheet is not a conclusive argument against their compensatability.

. . .

(*c*) Decisions of the Bundesgerichtshof have staked out the bounds of liability for loss of use of motor vehicles, a situation where the plethora of cases makes it necessary to ignore some of the differences between individuals as regards the importance of the thing.

We need not now determine the range of property, apart from motor cars, whose temporary loss of use calls for compensation on the principles already stated. But the temporary loss of use of a home tortiously affected, as in the case in hand, can clearly constitute an economic loss.

It hardly needs saying that one's domestic economy and mode of life centre on the home and that its continuing availability for occupation is a central item in daily life and intrinsic to one's whole wealth. This very instance shows how unfair it would be to limit damages to loss of commercial use, to regard loss of domestic use not as a loss in itself but only as a source of possible loss, and to leave uncompensated the person who forbears to rent alternative accommodation: it would be an unjustifiable preference for investment in production over investment in consumption. It may be justifiable to refuse damages in cases of temporary impairment of use which the victim can reasonably temper by alternative measures he can be expected to adopt, but where the house in which the owner would have lived is rendered wholly uninhabitable even for a time, the principle that economic harm must be paid for in full requires compensation to be made.

IV. It must be for the courts to work out on a case-by-case basis methods for quantifying loss of use which are suited to the kind of property involved and the way it is treated. The only legal constraints are that quantification must satisfy the requirements of compensation, that is, apply objective standards as indicated by § 253 BGB and treat like cases alike.

It would be wrong in principle to grant damages on the basis of what it would have cost the owner to rent a substitute article for the period of deprivation. We are concerned with compensation, not reparation, and compensation is based not on the savings effected by having a thing of one's own but on the monetary value of having one's own thing to use. Nor can the owner claim what he might have charged the tortfeasor for the use of the thing. Such a method of computation may be justified in special instances of conflicting interests, but it is inconsistent with the general principles of damages law. Compensation is for the loss of domestic use, not for the loss of profit from a rental contract with a third party which the owner never dreamed of entering.

Nevertheless the rental market may provide a basis for measuring the loss once the rental charge has been carefully purged of all elements related to profit making. So, too, may the basic post-acquisition costs related to the period of loss of use (interest in capital tied up, recurrent costs of keeping the property available, depreciation). And, contrary to the view of the Fifth Civil Division there is nothing wrong in this context with adding a modest supplement to the minimum sum at which the market would put the basic costs of having a thing to use, in order to take account of the fact that the fall-out effects on a person's economy of the unavailability of such property may be very difficult to track down in detail. The mention of these possible ways of measuring the loss is not, however, intended to exclude other appropriate methods.

Case 149

BUNDESGERICHTSHOF (SIXTH CIVIL SENATE) 15 OCTOBER 1991
BGHZ 115, 364 = NJW 1992, 302

Facts

The claimant claims compensation from the defendants in respect of an accident in which his car was seriously damaged.

The claimant had his car repaired by his car repair business at a cost (according to expert opinion) of DM 93,396.30. He claimed DM 5000 for depreciation in value. While his car was out of service he hired a Mercedes 300 E from the 4 August to 22 September 1988 at a cost of DM 20,495.70. The claimant also claimed DM 1680 for a further 12 days for loss of use; and DM 1508 for expert's costs and costs of towing away. (The claimant also made ancillary claims for the loss caused by the accident but unrelated to his car).

The Landgericht awarded DM 95,204.52 plus interest on the basis that the defendants were 80% liable. The Oberlandesgericht awarded DM 105,084.71 plus interest on the basis that the defendants were fully liable. To the extent that the appeal in law has been accepted, the claimant is pursuing by it his claims to compensation for vehicle damage, in so far as they were rejected, as well as for payment of vehicle hire costs and for loss of use. The Bundesgerichtshof allowed these claims for payment of DM 122,080 plus interest.

Reasons

1. The appeal court has incorrectly assessed the damage to the claimant's vehicle under § 287 (1) of the Civil Procedure Code, on the basis of the necessary expense for providing of a replacement, at only DM 75,000. The claimant can claim the repair costs of DM 93,396 plus the depreciation in value of DM 5000 to compensate for this damage, as this expense, measured against the costs of providing a replacement vehicle, satisfies the test of economic viability.

a) The victim who himself undertakes restoration of the former state of affairs after damage to an object is entitled under § 249 sentence 2 of the BGB to demand from the tortfeasor the necessary sum of money for this. The tortfeasor can only give him monetary compensation for the loss in value suffered if and in so far as restoration is not possible or is not sufficient for compensation (§ 251 (1) of the BGB) or requires disproportionate expenditure (§ 251 (1) sentence 1 of the BGB). Disproportionality in the case of possible restitution in kind thus forms the limit beyond which the victim's claim to compensation is no longer directed to restoration (restitution in kind) but only to recompense for the loss in value of his assets (monetary compensation). To this extent restitution in kind has priority over compensation.

b) It cannot admittedly be deduced from this scheme in the law relating to damage that, when someone's motor vehicle is damaged, he may always have it repaired at the tortfeasor's cost if the expenditure is anything less than the limit of disproportionality. The comparison between the costs of restitution and the mere value of the damaged object as an item in the victim's assets is certainly important, under § 251 (2) sentence 1 of the BGB, in ascertaining the ceiling up to which the tortfeasor has to relieve the victim of the costs of restoration (references omitted; see also now the new statutory regime for injured animals in § 251 (2) sentence 2 of the BGB). However to answer the question which matters for the decision in this case (which is whether the victim can have his vehicle repaired at the expense of the tortfeasor, and if so to what level of expenditure, if he can get himself a replacement vehicle of equal value at a lower cost) the issue is not, as will be explained in greater detail below, the boundary between restitution and compensation. Here also, therefore, disproportionality does not form the limit to repair expenditure in the comparison required by § 251 (2) sentence 1 of the BGB; its limit has already been drawn by the aim of restoration in § 249 sentence 1 of the BGB and the concept of necessity in § 249 sentence 2 of the BGB.

aa) The victim who takes the rectification of the harm to his motor vehicle into his own hands has as a rule two methods for this at his disposal: he can have his vehicle repaired or he can obtain a replacement vehicle (of equal value). Even the latter form of elimination of the harm is, as the Senate has repeatedly stated and to which view it continues to adhere, a form of restitution in kind (references omitted). This is because the goal of restitution is not limited to restoration of the damaged object; it consists, according to § 249 sentence 1 of the BGB, of something more comprehensive: restoring the state of affairs which, seen from a business point of view, corresponds to the situation which would have existed without the event causing the harm (references omitted).

bb) Where there are several possible types of restitution in kind leading to recompense for the harm, the victim must in principle chose the one which requires the least expenditure. The Senate has stressed this requirement of a businesslike approach on several occasions (references omitted). It finds its statutory expression in the characteristic of necessity in § 249 sentence 2 of the BGB, but arises in the end simply from the concept of harm itself. This is because the victim's loss is, even from the point of view of the interest which is at issue for the purposes of § 249 of the BGB (i.e. the preservation of his assets in their objective composition) not greater than what must be spent in order to transpose the assets in a reasonable manner into a condition which is equal in value in economic terms to the original one—taking into account the damaged component as well.

The requirement to eliminate harm in a manner which is sensible in business terms does not, it is true, require the victim to economise so as to benefit the tortfeasor or to behave in each case as if he would have to bear the harm himself (references omitted). Nevertheless, the latter point of view can be important for the question of whether the victim has kept the expenditure within sensible limits (references omitted). This is because he can only take from the tortfeasor under § 249 sentence 2 of the BGB those expenses which from the standpoint of a sensible business-minded person in the position of the victim appear appropriate and reasonable for elimination of the harm (references omitted). In examining whether the victim has kept within this framework, consideration must admittedly be given to his special situation, and thus in particular to his individual opportunities to know and act as well as the difficulties which may exist for him alone, because § 249 sentence 2 of the BGB, takes account of restitution being in the hands of the victim. This subject-related examination of the harm does not however mean that unreasonably incurred expenditure would have to be examined only from the point of view of a violation of the duty to mitigate harm under § 254 (2) of the BGB; the duty to compensate for harm exists from the outset only insofar as the expenses are kept within the framework of business prudence (references omitted).

cc) ...

dd) In comparing repair costs with replacement costs, it admittedly has to be borne in mind that if the victim selects, in accordance with appropriate information, the method of elimination of the harm which he presumes will involve less expenditure, the tortfeasor must bear risks associated with the workshop or with the prognosis, unless exceptionally fault (in selection) in this respect can be laid at the door of the victim (references omitted).

ee) Above all it must be considered that repair of the vehicle with which the victim is familiar may as a rule satisfy his interest in preserving the state of his assets ("integrity interest") to a greater degree than a replacement (references omitted). It is therefore in harmony with the principles of the law about damage that costs of repair which exceed the expenditure on a replacement, are, within limits, to be awarded to the victim who decides to effect a repair and demonstrably carries this out. This appears to be justified for the further reason that, even taking fully into account advantageous compensation of "new for old", in particular with older vehicles, repair, according to its costs alone, would not as a rule stand up to a comparison with the costs of obtaining a replacement.

So far as concerns the extent of this area of tolerance, the deciding Senate has repeatedly approved judges of fact in the exercise of their discretion under § 287 (1) of the Civil

Procedure Code granting an addition of 30% (references omitted). It is however disputed in the case law of the courts of first instance and in the literature how this tolerance limit is to be calculated: according to one opinion, in making the comparison, the (expected) costs of repair of the vehicle and a possible depreciation in its value are to be set against its replacement *value*, i.e. the full costs of obtaining a replacement (reference omitted); according to the other view the comparison is undertaken merely with the replacement *expenditure*, i.e. the replacement value minus the residual value of the damaged vehicle (references omitted).

The deciding Senate has not thus far needed to provide an answer to the issue in dispute, but it has now to be decided. The Senate endorses the view that in cases in which—as here—the victim actually has repairs carried out, in making the comparison with the obtaining of a replacement, the replacement value need not generally be reduced by the residual value. Admittedly it must be recognised that the requirement for business prudence will as a rule cause the victim who faces the alternatives of repair or obtaining a replacement to include the residual value of the accident vehicle in his calculations when he makes his decision. The particular financial burden is the decisive factor and this in concrete terms is principally on the one hand the costs of repair including the possible depreciation in value and on the other hand the expenditure for obtaining a replacement which appears as the difference between the replacement value and the residual value of the damaged vehicle. The consequent significance which attaches to the residual value in reducing the expenditure on replacement does not however, according to the view of the Senate, require this value to be included in the comparison as an independent item in the calculation. This is because the residual value (at any rate in so far as it can be brought into this cost comparison as the price the victim can obtain when he trades in his accident vehicle on the purchase of a replacement vehicle from a responsible used car dealer, depends on the costs of repairs. It is therefore already represented in them: the higher the repair costs are, in the case of a fixed replacement value (because this is independent of the extent of the harm), the lower is the residual value of the damaged vehicle, as a rule, and vice versa. . .

c) The Senate realises that leaving the residual value out of the cost comparison leads, if an "integrity addition" (not used up by the claimant here) is retained unaltered, to a raising of the "victim limit", up to which the victim may have his damaged vehicle repaired at the cost of the tortfeasor. But this result appears, apart from simplifying the treatment of the damage, justified in order to give better protection to the integrity interest. This is because for vehicles with slight accident damage and high residual value (which for this very reason are particularly worth repairing) deduction of the residual damage from replacement value, which is frequently not substantially higher, often leads, in spite of an addition of 30 per cent to the difference, to the repair costs exceeding the 130 per cent boundary and the victim therefore no longer being allowed to have his vehicle repaired at the cost of the tortfeasor. This would amount to a reduction of interests which is not required by the law of damages. If on the other hand the victim's vehicle no longer has significant residual value after an accident, then according to the view of the Senate, even repair costs of up to 130 per cent of the unreduced replacement value do not, as a rule, exceed the boundary of what can be demanded from the tortfeasor as compensation for the victim's "integrity interest". Besides this, it must always to be borne in mind that the "integrity limit" of 30 per cent is not a rigid limit, but a recommended value, which leads as a rule in the vast majority of cases of motor vehicle damage to a just result, but which, depending on the peculiarities of the individual case can be raised or lowered (reference omitted). In addition, it must always be considered that comparison of repair costs with the replacement value can cease to be meaningful for the victim's entitlement to repair, if the periods of non-availability of the vehicle in the cases of repair and replacement are in gross disproportion to each other. This could have the result that the costs of a hired car claimed by the victim while the repair is carried out are significantly higher than in the case of a replacement and in the comparison of the *total* costs of both methods of restitution, the 130% limit is exceeded on *this* ground to a significant extent. In cases of this kind the victim may need on grounds of economic viability to be directed to the cheaper method of obtaining redress, above all when the percentage "victim limit" has already been reached according to the basic assessment, even without the comparison of these bridging costs, because of the discrepancy with the hired car costs. But that is not the way things are here. . .

2. The statements of the appeal court on the level of the hired car costs to be refunded to the claimant are also not free from legal error.

a) As the claimant was permitted, as has been explained, to have his vehicle repaired at the cost of the defendants, the costs of hiring a replacement vehicle during the period of repair must also in principle be reimbursed to him in the light of the concept of restitution in kind (§ 249 sentence 2 of the BGB). This is because these costs were necessary to restore of a state of affairs of equal economic value to the original one. . .

Case 150

BUNDESGERICHTSHOF (SIXTH CIVIL SENATE) 19 OCTOBER 1993
NJW 1993, 3321 = VersR 1994, 64 = MDR 1994, 37

Facts

The plaintiff hires out vehicles that can be used as taxis. [In this action] he seeks compensation on the basis of an assigned right for vehicle hire costs arising from an accident that occurred on 13 December 1989 in which the taxi business proprietor L and the driver of a car insured with the defendants were involved. In this accident L's Mercedes Benz 250 D was—according to the plaintiff's assertion the only taxi used by him at the time—substantially damaged. The duty of the defendant to make good in full [the damage inflicted on the plaintiff] is, in principle, beyond dispute. The damaged vehicle was being repaired during the period 13 December 1989 until 4 January 1990. By a contract of the 14 December 1989 L hired a replacement taxi from the plaintiff in which he assigned to insurers his claim for compensation against the defendant in relation to the vehicle hire costs. Until 4 January 1990 L travelled 5,875 km with the hired taxi for business purposes. Between 14 and 31 December 1989 he thereby earned a total of DM 6,211.50. His income during the early days of January 1990 has not been supplied. The plaintiff charged L vehicle hire costs for the total hiring period in the sum of DM 13,422.19 (without VAT). In the present legal action the plaintiff at first claimed the full vehicle hire costs against the defendant.

The Landgericht rejected the claim. In the appeal proceedings the plaintiff limited its money claim to a sum of DM 11,408.86 taking into account the expenditure saved by L by the non-use of his own vehicle of an estimated 15 per cent of the vehicle hire costs.

The Court of Appeal—rejecting the remainder of the plaintiff's appeal—gave judgment against the defendant in the sum of DM 4,032.39 with interest. The plaintiff's appeal on a matter of law was successful for the following.

Reasons

1. The Court of Appeal is of the view that L's claim for compensation assigned to the plaintiff does not justify claiming from the defendant the cost of hiring the replacement taxi.

It was true that a taxi proprietor could, in principle, when his vehicle was damaged, claim for harm he suffered by asking for reimbursement of the costs of a hired replacement taxi. A claim of this kind would, however, be denied to the taxi proprietor if the boundary set by § 251 II BGB were overstepped because the expenditure were disproportionately high. This would be so if the claiming of a hired vehicle by a business-minded plaintiff, as he would have seen it at the time, were simply indefensible. That was the case here. In this respect, the vehicle hire costs (subject to deduction of his own expenditure thereby saved) were to be set against the loss of earnings, which the taxi proprietor would have suffered without the hiring of the replacement vehicle. For this expected loss of earnings, the takings actually obtained with the hired vehicle were to be taken into account. One should start with L's income between 14 and 31 December 1989 (DM 6,211.50). To this one should add the takings for the period from 1 to 4 January 1990. Because of the lack of more exact information, these could [only] be assessed from an average calculation on the basis of the months of October and November 1989 at DM 137.11 daily. Thus the gross income, resulting for the above hire period, was DM 6,759.94 altogether. Value added tax, saved overheads which could be estimated at 30 per cent of the takings for diesel vehicles, as well as expenditure which L had effected in the hiring period for assistant drivers, were to be deducted from this. There then remained a fictitious profit yield of DM 4,032.39 which was to be compared with the reckonable vehicle hire costs in the sum of DM 11,408.86. This led to a ratio of 1 : 2.83. The limit of disproportionate expenditure in the sense of § 251 II BGB was thereby exceeded.

The Court of Appeal was of the view that in general one should proceed on the basis of expenditure being disproportionate if the vehicle hire costs amounted to more than double the loss of earnings to avoid which the replacement vehicle was hired. By this limit, the interest of the taxi undertaking in the maintenance of its business was sufficiently taken into account. Otherwise there would be the threat of a violation of the principle that the plaintiff should not profit from the damage-causing event. To be sure, special circumstances could lead to an approval of proportionately higher vehicle hire costs. This could, for instance, happen where a taxi proprietor was particularly dependent in his business on a regular clientele and, as a result of a temporary loss of his vehicle (and the suspension of his activities), the existence of his business was seriously under threat. Such a state of affairs was, however, not present in this case. Instead, it had been foreseeable here that the hiring of the replacement taxi would be completely uneconomical. Thus L should not have done this and, instead, should have calculated his harm on the basis of his lost earnings. This was because he was, as a plaintiff, obliged to choose from amongst several possibilities leading to compensation for the harm the one that required the least expenditure. In these circumstances it was also not justified to allow the plaintiff a part (within the limits of § 251 II BGB) of the vehicle hire costs as compensation for the harm. On the other hand, the claim was not completely unfounded as the plaintiff had a claim to compensation on the basis of the fictional loss of earnings that was to be assumed to be 4032.39 DM.

II. The judgment appealed against does not stand up to legal scrutiny insofar as the remainder of the plaintiff's appeal has been rejected and the claim to compensation for the vehicle hire costs denied.

1. The appeal court proceeded correctly in law from the principles laid down in the judgment of the Senate of 4 December 1984 [references omitted] on restitution in kind on the loss of a motor vehicle used exclusively for business purposes by the hiring of a replacement vehicle:

§ 249 S.1 BGB requires the restoration of the status quo as it existed before the event causing the harm. In the case of damage causing the loss of a motor vehicle, whether this is used privately or for business, restoration is usually best achieved by the plaintiff hiring a replacement vehicle for which the defendant has to pay: (§ 249 S.2 BGB). In such cases the limit to which restitution in kind (through the hiring of a replacement vehicle) can be asked for, is determined by § 251 II BGB. According to this, monetary compensation (here allocating to the plaintiff compensation for the gain he did not obtain) will only take the place of restoration if the latter is possible only with disproportionate expenditure. In assessing whether to proceed on the basis of such disproportionality, it is important to compare the cost of hiring a replacement vehicle and the threatened loss of earnings if the hiring does not proceed. But this is only one of a number of aspects within the global consideration to be undertaken of the interests of the plaintiff in the undisturbed continuance of his business. This is because his other interests that are worthy of protection must also be considered. [This means] for instance [taking into account] his desire not to endanger the good reputation of his business, to have at his disposal a full fleet of vehicles, and not to have to place excessive demands on the capacity of the remaining vehicles etc. The boundary of § 251 II BGB is not overstepped simply because the costs for the obtaining of a hired vehicle exceed (even significantly) the loss of profit which is otherwise threatened. But it is [exceeded] if the hiring of the replacement taxi is simply indefensible from an entrepreneurial point of view for a business-minded plaintiff . . . [but] this will only exceptionally be the case.

2. The observations which led the Court of Appeal to find that in the instant case the proportionality boundary of § 251 II BGB had been overstepped do not meet these principles in the required manner.

a) A decision as to whether the prerequisites of § 251 II BGB are present is primarily a matter for assessment by the judge of fact when applying § 287 I ZPO. However, this appeal may examine whether the relevant circumstances and standards, especially all the essential calculation factors, have been considered in the required manner [references omitted].

b) This appeal unsuccessfully challenges the calculations of the Court of Appeal on expected lost profit in the case where no replacement vehicle is hired.

aa) The judge of fact is not prevented in this respect from putting the net vehicle hire costs (reduced by the expenditure which the taxi proprietor has saved) against the profit which he has in fact made by use of the hired vehicle [reference omitted]. The figures relating to the turnover here which L made with the replacement taxi in the greater part of the hiring period namely between 14 and 31 December 1989 were available to the Court of Appeal. An average turnover, applying § 287 ZPO, had to be estimated for only a few days (1 to 4 January 1990) on the basis of the turnover figures of the previous months. The Court of Appeal's method of proceeding here is not open to objection. Even a differently attempted calculation of the turnover, which proceeded on the basis of the total of 5,875 kilometres travelled with the hired vehicle and which charged a turnover of DM 1.20 for every kilometre travelled (which was, all along, regarded by the plaintiff as realistic), would still produce a total turnover which is not significantly higher. (DM 7,050 as against the sum reached by the Court of Appeal of DM 6,759.94).

bb) There are no legal objections to the fact that the Court of Appeal deducted from the gross turnover an estimated 30 per cent for value added tax and saved overheads. (This is not challenged by the appeal in law). Contrary to the appellants' view, the Court of Appeal correctly deducted from the net turnover a further sum of DM 390 as payment for assistant drivers. Payments to drivers of taxis only have to be left out of consideration if they are fixed costs independent of performance which would have had to be paid by the taxi proprietor even if he had not hired a vehicle [references omitted]. But such costs are not involved when paying assistant drivers who are not in a fixed employment relationship but are called upon for work from case to case at irregular intervals. The Court of Appeal could, on the basis of the party's submissions and without violating the law, come to the conclusion that the expenditure here for assistant drivers would not have arisen for the taxi proprietor L if he had not hired the replacement taxi and therefore had not used any assistant drivers.

c) The appeal, however, correctly objects to the standards on the basis of which the vehicle hire costs which have arisen were considered by the Court of Appeal to be disproportionate expenditure, in the sense of § 251 II BGB, by comparison with the threatened loss of profit. In particular the considerations on which the appeal court might always regard the boundary of disproportionality of the vehicle hire costs as exceeded if the latter amounted to more than double the loss of earnings give cause for serious doubts.

aa) By indicating that the taxi proprietor L was, as plaintiff, under a duty to choose from several possibilities leading to compensation the one which required the least expenditure—in this case the calculation of the loss of earnings—the Court of Appeal calls upon a principle of liability law which is not suited to the making of an assessment within the framework of § 251 II BGB. The plaintiff has to choose the most economical alternative from several possibilities of remedying harm only if they are equivalent in outcome (for instance between two alternatives which both lead to restitution in kind [references omitted]). But here it is not a question of choice between two equivalent alternatives. Instead, only the hiring of a replacement vehicle represents restitution in kind for the taxi proprietor, and he can ask for this up to the limit of disproportionate expenditure determined in § 251 II BGB. It is true that this provision also, like liability law in general, is subject to the postulate that the remedying of the damage be economical. But the legislator has, by drawing the limit of disproportionate expenditure, emphasised that restoration in kind has priority over monetary compensation and this does not have to be given up simply because monetary compensation requires a lesser expenditure for the defendant.

bb) The observation in the judgment appealed against, that exceeding of the loss of earnings by the vehicle hire costs by 100 per cent—which was barely acceptable—could only be justified if the taxi proprietor was to be allowed a special interest in the maintenance of his business and the retaining of a regular clientele, also shows that the Court of Appeal has not adequately satisfied the standards to be applied within the framework of § 251 II BGB. The taxi proprietor, suffering harm, has as a rule a claim to restitution in kind on the basis of § 249 S.1 and S.2 BGB. This in principle needs no special justification even if he requires expenditure which exceeds—if necessary, even substantially—a compensation interest of the plaintiff (consisting here of the lost profit if no step was taken to cover for the loss of the accident vehicle). On the other hand the denial of restitution under the prerequisites of § 251 II BGB according to the state of the law represents the exception, which the defendant needs to show and provide a basis for, to the rule in § 249 BGB. This rule-exception relationship has not been taken into account in an appropriate way in the considerations of the Court of Appeal.

cc) The Court of Appeal also seeks to justify the "200 per cent limit" which it considered to be correct because otherwise there is no longer any conformity with the principle that the plaintiff should not make a profit out of the damage-causing event. However, the taxi owner suffering damage, who has hired a replacement vehicle (and has to pay for this), does not gain from the event causing the harm, regardless of whether the vehicle hire expenditure is kept within the framework of the proportionality limit of § 251 II BGB or not. This is because the compensation by the defendant for the vehicle hire costs does not remain with the plaintiff, increasing his own assets; but passes to the person hiring out the replacement vehicle.

d) The argument of the Court of Appeal in favour of establishing a "boundary rule" of double the loss of earnings for the compensability of the vehicle hire costs of the taxi owner is not only legally inappropriate. Such a "boundary rule", also favoured by the 31st German Verkehrsgerichtstag 1993 [reference omitted], is also unjustified in this case. This is because the delimitation of the exceptional case envisaged by § 251 II BGB is a matter of fact that depends on all the surrounding circumstances of each case and should not be made to turn on the existence of a general threshold, whether this is fixed by reference to double the lost profit or on any another proportion.

aa) The assessment of the disproportionality of the expenditure in the sense which is relevant here depends on a variety of factual issues which cannot be assessed by a set figure. Importance attaches to circumstances that relate to the taxi undertaking of the person suffering harm and its place in the market as well as to those which concern the accident itself and its consequences. For instance, the following points can be relevant and therefore are to be taken into overall consideration. They include: size and development of turnover of the undertaking; period of existence so far and intensity of penetration of the market; number of taxis available and used in the undertaking; degree of utilisation of the vehicles and the drivers; personnel and cost structure of the undertaking (for instance drivers in permanent employment, assistant drivers etc), composition of its clientele (regular customers, one-off journeys); structure of the market (e.g. in a large city or in a rural area); competition situation; conditions of connection to the radio centre; possibilities of co-operation with other taxi businesses; extent of and period for repair of the accident vehicle; business prospects for taxis during the repair period ("high season" because of holidays, congresses or the like).

This wealth of individual aspects which characterise the overall picture to be obtained within the framework of § 251 II BGB, forbids the determination of the exceptional case (in which there must be a deviation from the principle of restitution in kind) in a normative way from a "rule boundary".

bb) In the face of the given price situation, the costs of a hired vehicle will as a rule exceed the predictable loss of earnings of a taxi proprietor. The hiring of a replacement taxi can however only be rated as disproportionate if it is indefensible for a business minded plaintiff and was thus from the point of view of a sensible businessman simply a question of a stupid decision. Such a judgement cannot automatically be made when the vehicle hire costs are more than 100 per cent or some other percentage in excess of a predictable loss of profit. This is because it is part of the nature of entrepreneurial organisation and the freedom to make business arrangements to put up with short term losses, even if these are considerable, for the sake of longer term advantages, at least for a foreseeable period of time. For this reason, it will seldom appear indefensible from the viewpoint of a sensible businessman to accept hire costs for several weeks that will probably substantially exceed the output to be obtained from the thing hired. This will be the case if he can thereby maintain his business undisturbed, secure the entrepreneurial "goodwill", keep his regular clientele, remain present in the market and in the organisation of the radio centre and so on. Accordingly, the compensability of the hiring costs has been accepted in the case law of the courts of first instance even in cases in which this was distinctly more than 100% in excess of the loss of earnings [references omitted].

cc) In the "normal" case, therefore, in which a replacement taxi, the full utilisation of which is within a framework consistent with business practice, is hired for an average repair period, there will be no cause, having regard to § 251 II BGB, to deny reimbursement of vehicle hire costs which are in line with the market price. The plaintiff can only be confined to monetary compensation for the amount of his loss of earnings if consideration in business terms of the circumstances of the individual case as a whole leads to the conclusion that exceptionally the business decision to hire a replacement vehicle is no longer defensible. In this framework, besides all those interests of the plaintiff worthy of protection, comparison will have to be made between the hire costs and the probable loss of profit of the taxi undertaking and also the level of the hiring charge as such can play a significant role.

3. Bearing these principles in mind, the limit to the proportionality of the hiring expenses in the sense of § 251 II BGB cannot in the present case be regarded as yet exceeded. This is so, even though the hiring charge for the replacement taxi may lie in the upper regions of what is defensible in business terms. The Senate can make this decision finally itself as no more findings need to be made by the judge of fact which are important for the decision. The Court of Appeal has not given the legally required status to the relevant circumstances here.

a) If, as the plaintiff has claimed, the taxi proprietor L had at the time of the accident only one taxi in operation—the accident vehicle—he would have been obliged, had he not hired a substitute, to shut down his taxi business for the entire period of the repair. Thus, he would neither have been able to serve his regular clientele nor would he have been available to the radio centre for the providing of occasional journeys.

If a taxi proprietor, who has several taxis, loses one as a result of an accident he has a legitimate interest to secure the undisturbed continuance of his business by hiring a replacement vehicle so as to continue working with a complete fleet of vehicles [references omitted]. The interest of the "one-taxi proprietor" in not having temporarily to shut down his business on the loss of his single vehicle must, if anything, be rated much higher. This is because the compulsion for temporary suspension of independent vocational activity means a very severe interference for the person affected even if financial harm arising from this can be compensated for in a sufficient manner. It cannot therefore, in principle, be [an economically] indefensible practice for a taxi proprietor, in order to avoid the temporary closing of the business with all the resulting loss, to hire a replacement taxi for a foreseeable repair period, . . . even if this involves expenditure which significantly exceeds the profit expected from its use.

b) But even if L had not been a "one taxi proprietor", but at the time of the accident used further vehicles, the expense of the hiring—which here certainly appears high—could, according to the principle for the "normal case" explained above, still not be assessed as disproportionate in the sense of § 251 II BGB. One must also note the fact that the enforced temporary interference with the business, even through the loss of only one of several taxis, would have affected the pre-Christmas, Christmas and New Year's Eve trade. This is a period in which—according to the findings of the Court of Appeal also—the need for taxis is especially great and the opportunities for custom and earning money are especially favourable. In this period, an undisturbed maintenance of business by means of a hired replacement taxi—even accepting a higher expenditure—could appear to a sensible business minded taxi proprietor more the obvious thing to do than at any other time. The other circumstances, as they are to be deduced from the established facts of the case and the party's submissions, give no cause to find here an exceptional case in which L would have had to give up restitution in kind.

III. The judgment of the Court of Appeal must, therefore, be quashed insofar as the appeal of the plaintiff was rejected. As further elucidation of the case is no longer needed, the plaintiff's appeal is to be allowed according to his appeal application in accordance with § 565 III no.1 ZPO.

Case 151

BUNDESGERICHTSHOF (SIXTH CVIL DIVISION) 7 MAY 1996
BGHZ 132, 373 = NJW 1996, 1958 = JZ 1996, 1075

Facts

The claimant seeks compensation in respect of a road accident. His car (a BMW 318i) was damaged when the first defendant ran into it with her car on 12 February 1993. The first defendant and the second defendant (who is liable to indemnify her) are unquestionably fully liable for the claimant's loss. After the accident, the claimant's car was towed to a garage at T, where the claimant lived. By arrangement with the garage, the claimant hired a BMW 316i on the afternoon of the day of the accident (a Friday) from the K car hire business at a daily rate of DM 330. His damaged car was looked at by an expert on 15 February 1993. As the expert calculated that the repair costs would be considerable, and the repairs were expected to last for 10–11 working days, the claimant did not carry out the repairs, and obtained another car. Before this was authorised, he gave back the hired car on 26 February 1993. The parties are only in dispute about the car hire costs. The Landgericht only allowed the claimant DM 2,122.68 of the DM 5,926.96 charged by the K firm. The Oberlandesgericht allowed him a further 1,306.62 DM. By the appeal in law the claimant sought reimbursement of the remainder of the car hire costs of DM 2,497.66. The defendants cross-appealed against the award of DM 1,306.62 by the appeal court. The appeal in law led to the quashing of the judgment and reference back. The cross appeal in law was rejected.

Reasons

I.–II. 1. The appeal court correctly proceeds on the basis that the claimant (who—as is no longer in dispute—was allowed to hire a BMW 316i for 14 days) can demand compensation from the defendant for the hire costs which were objectively necessary under § 249 sentence 2 of the BGB as restoration expenses (references omitted). According to the constant case law of the Senate, those expenses which a sensible business-minded person would make in the position of the victim are to be regarded as necessary (references omitted). If the victim can influence the level of the costs to be spent to eliminate his loss, he must, in view of the duty to mitigate loss, choose the more economical way of rectifying the loss, within the scope of what can be reasonably expected of him (references omitted). This follows from the concept of loss and purpose of compensation for it and from the legal concept in § 254 II 1 BGB, which in the end derives from § 242 BGB. The requirement that rectification of loss shall be sensible from an economic point of view does not, however, as the Senate has already explained, call for the victim to economise for the benefit of the tortfeasor or to behave in every case as if he had to bear the loss himself (references omitted). This is because in the latter case the victim will often make sacrifices or efforts which, in his relationship with the tortfeasor, are over and above his obligations and which the tortfeasor cannot therefore demand from him. In the effort to objectify the need for restitution within the framework of sentence 2 of § 249 BGB in an economically sensible way, the basic concern in this provision must not be lost sight of, i.e. that if the tortfeasor is fully liable the victim should receive compensation for loss which is complete as possible (references omitted). Therefore, in examining whether the victim has kept the expenditure on rectifying loss within sensible limits, the loss must be considered in the context of the actual circumstances i.e. account must be taken of the special situation of the victim, especially of his individual opportunities for knowledge and influence as well as the difficulties which he may possible have (references omitted). In this respect, the position for the victim who hires a replacement vehicle with a well known car hire undertaking on the conditions offered him there appears similar to the trading in of a vehicle damaged in an accident to a respected used car dealer (reference omitted). Just as with the latter type of rectification of loss, the victim only needs, when hiring of a replacement vehicle, to go to the market which is open to him in his situation.

2. The considerations on which the appeal court arrived at a reduction of the car hire costs claimed by the claimant here cannot be reconciled with this understanding of the content of the authority to compensate in § 249 sentence 2 BGB, even within the framework of the freer scope which the judge of fact has to measure the loss under § 287 I of the Civil Procedure Code.

a) The appeal court leaves undecided the question of whether the K firm's hire price list was shown to the claimant, as he asserts, before the hiring of the replacement vehicle. That is not a decisive issue. This is because this list indisputably included ten further well known hire firms, also active nationwide, who were all dearer than the K firm. The appeal court has not established that the prices given for those undertakings were possibly incorrect; instead that court itself explains in another context that the list would have correctly reproduced the accident replacement tariffs named in it. Even the reply to the appeal in law does not claim anything different. Accordingly, the claimant has, in hiring the replacement vehicle, kept to the lower margin of the prices demanded by respected hire firms with their accident replacement tariffs.

b) The appeal court's view that the claimant had violated the requirement of economy by the very hiring of the replacement vehicle at the accident replacement tariff cannot be followed by the Senate.

aa) The appeal court's accusation in this connection that the claimant did not obtain any comparative offers before hiring the replacement vehicle has no effect with reference to the accident replacement tariffs demanded by the vehicle hire firms, for the simple reason that the tariff of the K firm was, as has been explained, at the lower margin in the context of the accident car replacement business. If the claimant was therefore justified in hiring a vehicle according to such a tariff (which is yet to be discussed below), his possible violation of a duty to inquire has had no effect. Therefore it can remain open here whether the duty of the victim to obtain at least one or two competitive offers (which the Senate has stated to apply before the use of a hired car for a holiday journey of three weeks or longer (references omitted)) also exists in principle when—as in the present case—the replacement vehicle is expected to be needed for only one to two weeks.

bb) The decisive issue in the legal dispute is therefore whether the victim of an accident, like the claimant in this case, is allowed to hire a vehicle in accordance with the accident replacement tariff. This question, which is disputed in the case law of the courts of first instance, is in principle to be answered in the affirmative, according to the view of the Senate.

(a) According to the constant case law of the Bundesgerichtshof (and the appeal court also proceeded on the basis of this), the victim does not first need to conduct a kind of market investigation before hiring a replacement vehicle, in order to find the vehicle hire undertaking with the most favourable price (references omitted). If the tariff at which he hires a replacement vehicle is within the framework of what is usual, the costs expended are to be refunded to him by the tortfeasor; it is only when the victim can easily recognise that the undertaking chosen by him demands car hire charges which are outside what is usual that he will not be allowed to conclude a hire contract on such conditions at the cost of the tortfeasor (reference omitted).

(b) According to the claimant's argument, only the replacement tariff is offered by car hire undertakings to road traffic accident victims. The appeal court also proceeds on the basis that the claimant, if he answered the relevant question truthfully, would likewise only have been able to obtain a vehicle after an accident from some other hire firm at the accident replacement tariff (references omitted). In view of this market practice, the car hire charges demanded by the K firm were not outside what was usual in such cases.

(c) The fact that the claimant could, as is the view of the appeal court, have found car hire undertakings on appropriate inquiry which would have granted him a special tariff which was more favourable than the accident replacement tariff does not, contrary to the view of the appeal court, cause the hire price demanded by the K firm to fall outside the scope of "necessary expense" in the sense of § 249 sentence 2 BGB. This is because the claimant had no obligation to the defendant to make such a search for a more favourable special tariff (references omitted). As the appeal court explains, hire firms offer a number of other tariffs besides the accident replacement tariff, which they describe as, amongst other things, leisure, flat rate, basic, weekly, monthly, weekend, economy, credit card or special tariff. It is not generally possible to proceed on the basis that an accident victim knows of such tariffs and that he knows of their differences from the accident replacement tariff which is offered to him as suitable for his circumstances (reference omitted). The appeal court has not established that the claimant might have had such knowledge. The circumstances in which he would be expected to try to obtain another tariff if he had such knowledge can therefore remain undecided.

It also emerges from the tariff descriptions mentioned above that numerous distinctions exist between the individual conditions. The complex tariff network of car hire firms cannot, contrary to the view of the appeal court, easily be understood by a victim. The appeal court reaches a different view on the ground that the K firm's hire price list showed that a comparison was perfectly possible. But this argument is mistaken, because that list only cites the respective accident replacement tariffs of the car hire undertakings and says nothing about the peculiarities of the other tariffs. Besides this, the accident replacement tariffs do not at all appear to be always the dearer tariffs as the appeal court thinks they are. The judgment of the Bundesgerichtshof of 5 April 1995 (reference omitted), amongst others, shows that the opposite also occurs.

(d) The claimant, sustaining an accident at midday on Friday, was allowed, according to the principles explained at the start in relation to the authority to compensate in § 249 sentence 2 BGB, to hire a replacement car on the general market accessible to him and within reach of T, the country town where he lived, at the time of the accident (and therefore specifically from a well known undertaking in the car hire sector which was active nationwide) in accordance with the tariff mentioned to him as appropriate for his purposes. He was also allowed in this connection to answer truthfully the question by the hire firm as to whether he had had an accident. If the tariff which was thereupon offered to him was within the scope of what was usual in such cases for comparable car hire suppliers, as was the case here with the accident replacement tariff of the K firm, the costs of the hire vehicle count as necessary restoration expenses in the sense of § 249 sentence 2 BGB.

(e) The question of whether up to 25 per cent higher costs are justified in the accident replacement vehicle business in comparison with the so-called free or cash business (which the appeal court denies in spite of its reference to the higher risk of non-payment in that business) has no effect on the relationships of the parties in the law on loss calculation (reference omitted). This is because even if the hire firms, by omitting to refer to a more beneficial inclusive tariff and demanding a higher accident replacement tariff, made themselves liable to compensation to their hirers for loss, as the appeal court considers, these market practices in the hiring sector cannot work to the victim's disadvantage in the relationship between the tortfeasor and the victim (references omitted). The tortfeasor's liability insurer may in such a case take a transfer from the victim, if he reimbursed him for the car hire costs expended as being necessary in his situation, of possible claims to compensation for loss against the hire firm in application of the legal concept in § 255 BGB (references omitted).

c) In the present case, the car hire costs must therefore be reimbursed to the claimant on the basis of the agreements made by him with the K firm, as necessary expenditure. [Details are given].

Index